This Book
Donated By

Curtis Whittaker

in memory of
Perry Abe

2015

STAFF OFFICERS IN GRAY

CIVIL WAR AMERICA   *Gary W. Gallagher, editor*

STAFF OFFICERS IN GRAY

A BIOGRAPHICAL REGISTER OF THE STAFF OFFICERS IN THE ARMY OF NORTHERN VIRGINIA

ROBERT E. L. KRICK

The University of North Carolina Press CHAPEL HILL AND LONDON

© 2003 The University of North Carolina Press
All rights reserved
Manufactured in the United States of America

Designed by Kristina Kachele
Set in Minion type
by Tseng Information Systems, Inc.

The paper in this book meets the guidelines for
permanence and durability of the Committee on
Production Guidelines for Book Longevity of the
Council on Library Resources.

Frontispiece: General George E. Pickett and his
staff. Courtesy Benjamin H. Baird.

Library of Congress
Cataloging-in-Publication Data
Krick, Robert E. L.
Staff officers in gray : a biographical register of the
staff officers in the Army of Northern Virginia /
Robert E. L. Krick.
   p. cm. — (Civil War America)
ISBN 0-8078-2788-6 (alk. paper)
1. Confederate States of America. Army of
Northern Virginia — Officers — Biography.
2. United States — History — Civil War, 1861–1865 —
Biography.   3. Soldiers — Confederate States of
America — Biography.   I. Title.   II. Series.
E470.2 .K745   2003
973.7'42'0922 — dc21   2002153592

07 06 05 04 03   5 4 3 2 1

CONTENTS

*A section of photographs appears
on pp. 177–90.*

ACKNOWLEDGMENTS

Confronted with about 2,300 lives to reconstruct, I relied heavily on help provided by hundreds of descendants, librarians, and colleagues, a great many of them complete strangers to me. The intense desire to solve biographical mysteries and find new material served as our bond. The majority of those kind folks are not named in the following paragraphs, but hopefully they can take pride in having helped illuminate the lives of the many Confederate soldiers profiled in these pages.

Each of the following helped me more than a little over the past dozen years: Ted Alexander; Mr. and Mrs. Jack Anderson of Stephenville, Texas; Judy Anthis; Joan Armistead; Dana Miller Bullard at the Evans Library in Aberdeen, Mississippi; Jim Clary; Gregg Clemmer; Harriett Condon; John and Ruth Ann Coski at the Museum of the Confederacy in Richmond; the cordial ladies at the Fairfield County Historical Society in South Carolina; the late George O. Ferguson, Jr., and his wife, Cynthia Donat Ferguson, of New Orleans; Melissa Ferguson; Monika Fleming; Peggy Fox at the Confederate Research Center in Hillsboro, Texas; Loretta Frazer in South Carolina; David W. Gaddy; Michael D. Gorman; Kenneth Graves in Massachusetts; Chris Hartley; Michael A. Hogle of Okemos, Michigan; Robert C. Hudson of Culpeper, Virginia; Diane Jacob and Mary Laura Kludy at the Virginia Military Institute archives; Larry Jones at the Confederate Calendar; Whit Joyner; Christie Kennard in Missouri; Richard Latture; Kitty Grey Long of Uniontown, Alabama; Dana MacBean; Charlotte Marshall of Athens, Georgia; Greg Mast; Mike Morris of Harrisonburg, Virginia; Wayne Motts; Frank A. O'Reilly; Elmer O.

Parker; Tom Perry; Alice Phillips of Poquoson, Virginia; Don Pierce; J. Tracy Power of Columbia, South Carolina; the late Lilian Reed; David and Susan Riggs; Mark Rowe; David J. Rutledge; Christopher Stokes of Washington Memorial Library, Macon, Georgia; Steve Stubbs; William Syfrett; Frank S. Walker, Jr.; Ray Watkins; Chuck Watson; Barbara Pratt Willis of the Central Rappahannock Regional Library in Fredericksburg, Virginia; Pat Wood of Richmond; and Melvin A. Young.

Although I have visited dozens of libraries, archives, and historical societies over the years, I always have considered the Virginia Historical Society in Richmond my home court. It easily is the best place to work in the South. Frances Pollard and the staff of the library and reading room have been models of efficiency—that most desirable of all traits in a research setting—for as long as I can remember. The singular Ham Dozier, also on the staff there, is conversant with that society's Civil War resources and has produced a valuable guide on the subject. His steady assistance has improved this book. The Library of Virginia, also in Richmond, has many very helpful employees and is a fine research facility despite its unfriendly hours.

A second wave of acquaintances worked long and hard over the years on many different areas of this book. They include Dana Wooley, my ally in Texas; Jeff Stepp of the North Carolina Graves Project; the always helpful Helen Trimpi in California; genial Virginians Peggy Haile McPhillips of Norfolk and George Combs of Alexandria; and cemetery hound Scott Mauger of Richmond. My good friend John Bass of Spring Hope, North Carolina, has been sending me material on Tar Heel staff officers (mixed with salty observations on life) since I began this project in 1989. Nancy Bradley, also in North Carolina, skipped numerous lunches while on the trail of elusive Confederates in Raleigh. In the same vein, I fear South Carolinian Rosalind Tedards of Greenville may have missed a few of her beloved minor league baseball games while laboring for me in various up-country libraries. Several friends who are professional historians in my boyhood home of Fredericksburg, Virginia, consistently helped, particularly Eric Mink, Donald Pfanz, and Mac Wyckoff. Jim Ogden III, the diligent historian at Chickamauga battlefield, vectored dozens of leads to me over the years. Bill Torrens in England hunted down some dozen European Confederates. Jean von Schilling and Pat Walenista, both of Richmond, answered my annoying calls for help perhaps more often than they wished. Budge Weidman and the prolifically cited Mike Musick at the National Archives in Washington each smoothed my passage through that essential repository, saving me dozens of hours of waiting and work.

Many thanks also to Ben Ritter, the authority on all things relating to Winchester, Virginia, and to Zack Waters of Rome, Georgia, an unflinching advocate of every Confederate regiment and soldier from Florida. William J. Miller of Churchville, Virginia, has been a trusted friend and adviser in all matters, including this book. Gary W. Gallagher of the University of Virginia is editor of the series in which this book appears. Clearly no person now associated with Civil War history has a broader or more positive influence on the field than Professor Gallagher, and I am grateful for his guidance and sponsorship over the years.

In the earliest days of this project, two veteran historians who specialize in biographical research helped launch me toward my destination. Bruce Allardice in Chicago has published works on similar subjects. His handwritten list of sources and data on 304 staff officers appeared in the mail one day and generated considerable momentum. He has been supportive ever since, as has Robert J. Driver of Brownsburg, Virginia. Bob generously emptied his files for me in person, by mail, by e-mail, and over the telephone.

Ever since I was a college boy, Keith Bohannon and Peter Carmichael have been my closest friends. Happily, all three of us have managed to find careers as Civil War historians. Keith and Peter are both college professors of Civil War history, in Georgia and North Carolina, respectively, and I take great joy in their success. Keith is responsible for much of the material published here on Georgia officers, and Peter provided valuable background on the host of young men who attended southern schools in the decade before the war. Both improved the prose portion of this manuscript by their very close readings.

No section of acknowledgments would be complete without thanking one's family, and in this case, it is more than just a rote ritual. My father, Robert K. Krick, well known as a historian of the Army of Northern Virginia, has taught me just about everything I know. *Staff Officers in Gray* was his idea. Together we crafted its outline and established its goals. He likely would have at least another book to his credit by now had he not spent so much time aiding me, and I'll always be grateful. My wife Julie has been an enthusiastic ally for several years. She was genuinely helpful, the embodiment of every historian's dream. Julie compiled the statistics for this book, wrestled the computer into compliance, and helped me spin countless reels of microfilm at distant libraries.

Finally I must thank Chris Ferguson, presently of Alexandria, Virginia. Had he come along to help at the very beginning of my research, he undoubtedly would be listed as coauthor. He is very close to being one as it is. No person has done more to improve this book. He has, by now, given me several thousand pieces of information, from birth dates to cemetery information. If this book travels a road to success, it will be a path largely paved by his toil.

ABBREVIATIONS

AAAG	Acting Assistant Adjutant General
AAAIG	Acting Assistant Adjutant and Inspector General
AAG	Assistant Adjutant General
AAIG	Assistant Adjutant and Inspector General
ACS	Assistant Commissary of Subsistence
ADAH	Alabama Department of Archives and History
ADC	Aide-de-Camp
Adjt.	Adjutant
AIGO	Adjutant and Inspector General's Office
ANVa.	Army of Northern Virginia
AOO	Assistant Ordnance Officer
AOT	Army of Tennessee
apptd.	appointed
Appx.	paroled at Appomattox in April 1865
AQM	Assistant Quartermaster
Arty.	Artillery
Asst.	Assistant
att.	attended
AWOL	Absent without Leave
b.	born
Bgd.	Brigade

Bn.	Battalion
Btty.	Battery
bur.	buried
ca.	circa, or approximately
Capt.	Captain
Cavy.	Cavalry
Cem.	Cemetery
C.H.	Court House
Co.	Company or County
Col.	Colonel
Coll.	College
Cpl.	Corporal
C.S.	Confederate States
CS	Commissary of Subsistence
CSA	Confederate States of America
CSMC	Confederate States Marine Corps
CSN	Confederate States Navy
d.	died
Dept.	Department
Dist.	District
Div.	Division
EO	Engineer Officer
Episc.	Episcopal
Ft.	Fort
Gen.	General
GMI	Georgia Military Institute
IFT	Inspector of Field Transportation
Inf.	Infantry
KIA	Killed in Action
KMI	Kentucky Military Institute
LDT	Local Defense Troops
Lt.	Lieutenant
Lt. Col.	Lieutenant Colonel
m.	married
Maj.	Major

MDAH	Mississippi Department of Archives and History
MSK	Military Store Keeper
Mtd.	Mounted
MWIA	Mortally Wounded in Action
NCDAH	North Carolina Department of Archives and History
NCMA	North Carolina Military Academy
OO	Ordnance Officer
PACS	Provisional Army of the Confederate States
PAVa.	Provisional Army of Virginia
PM	Provost Marshal
POW	Prisoner of War
Presby.	Presbyterian
Pvt.	Private
QM	Quartermaster
q.v.	quod vide, meaning see entry in this book
reapptd.	reappointed
Regs.	Regulars
SCMA	South Carolina Military Academy
Sgt.	Sergeant
SO	Signal Officer
Supt.	Superintendent
Surg.	Surgeon
temp.	temporary
UAla.	University of Alabama
UGa.	University of Georgia
UMiss.	University of Mississippi
UNC	University of North Carolina
Univ.	University
UPenn.	University of Pennsylvania
U.S.	United States
USHR	U.S. House of Representatives (used for both House and Senate)
USMA	U.S. Military Academy (West Point)
USMC	U.S. Marine Corps
USN	U.S. Navy
USNA	U.S. Naval Academy (Annapolis)

UVa.	University of Virginia
VADC	Volunteer Aide-de-Camp
VMI	Virginia Military Institute
WIA	Wounded in Action
Wm. & Mary	William and Mary College
WMI	Western Military Institute

STAFF OFFICERS IN GRAY

INTRODUCTION

Confederate armies in Virginia fielded hundreds of thousands of fighting men by war's end. Historians have endeavored ever since to define different categories within that mass, striving to carve out manageable blocks that can be studied individually or compared with other, similar chunks of the army. Fairly recent scholarship has produced brief but meaningful biographical sketches of all the general officers in the Army of Northern Virginia as well as those who have been mistaken for generals. At a lower grade, the nearly 2,000 field officers in that army have been the subjects of biographical paragraphs in another work. *Staff Officers in Gray*, partly inspired by those examples, is designed to plug another gap in the reference literature regarding the men who comprised the Confederate armies in Virginia.[1]

The staff officers profiled here served either in the field with the Army of Northern Virginia or at a military post in Virginia that supported that army. Most were adjutants and aides who toted messages on the battlefield, shuffled papers in camp, and rode with their generals during campaigns. Typically they bore commissions as captains and majors, but a few were lieutenants and a handful reached the rank of colonel. In many instances—but still fewer than half the cases in this book—men of commensurate rank filled noncombatant staff positions. Those officers toiled in Richmond and elsewhere to ensure that the army had weapons, food, clothes, and other logistical necessities. Nearly every soldier profiled in the following pages fits into one of those two categories.

To better appreciate the biographical sketches of staff officers that constitute the majority of this book, it is essential that these thousands of pieces of personal information be given some context. The first portion of this introduction addresses the role of staff officers in the army by examining their development as a separate entity. The second section tracks the evolution of the different jobs within that discipline. Every staff position is treated, often with commentary on how the officers functioned and how they were viewed by those around them.

The third section provides a statistical summary of the several thousand officers whose lives are reduced to paragraphs in this book. Enough personal information on these men exists to demonstrate that as a body they were surprisingly youthful, impressively educated, and from prewar occupations as white collar as those of any segment of men in the entire army. These statistics and their broad conclusions open significant new fields for the interpretation of a class of officers whose small numbers belied the considerable influence they wielded in the Army of Northern Virginia.

The final portion of the introduction offers guidelines for using the roster and explains the process by which an enormous collection of information was transformed into an alphabetical listing.

A SHORT HISTORY OF CONFEDERATE STAFF OFFICERS

In its infancy, the Confederate nation assembled very large armies. From the day of their organization, those armies raised fundamental questions that required almost immediate answers. What rank would the senior generals have? How many brigades would form a division? Who would improve the roads and build the bridges the army would need for transportation? Such concerns occupied the attention of the Confederate Congress and president for most of the war. They devoted a sizable percentage of their work to sustaining and regulating the body of men who fed, clothed, armed, and transported the army. Before examining the role and history of each staff position, it is important to trace the evolution of the staff system through the brief life of the Confederacy.

The antebellum U.S. Army, which inevitably served as a model for nearly all Confederate military organizations, had a large yet ineffective staff system. An able historian of that army has found that one-third of all U.S. Army officers in 1860 were associated with one of the staff branches. But that army's far-flung outposts and small strength offered almost no opportunities for young officers to practice the sort of staff work that would become essential later in the decade. Lessons learned in campaigns against Indians in Texas bore little resemblance to the reality of Civil War operations.[2]

Confederate lawmakers and administrators soon realized that their unique set of circumstances required new solutions. They labored to create a staff system that could train, supply, and supervise the Confederacy's rapidly growing armies. Francis S. Bartow, soon to become the Confederacy's first prominent battlefield martyr, sponsored a bill in the Provisional Congress in February 1861 entitled "An Act for the Establishment and Organization of a General Staff for the Army of the Confederate States of America." President Jefferson Davis signed the bill into law on February 26, thus taking an important step toward creating a disciplined army.[3]

The title of Bartow's bill drew attention to the term "general staff." To legislators, the term meant one thing; to army officers, another. When Congress revised or supplanted laws on the general staff later in the war, it usually did so with an eye toward adjusting the number and rank of staff officers permitted in a specific context — on an army or corps commander's staff, for example. It treated the general staff as a shapeless entity, an ideal as much as a reality. In the army, the term often meant something more concrete. It referred to officers who were not considered part of a general's personal staff and did not have traditional battlefield duties. At army headquarters, for instance, the aides, adjutants, and inspectors typically camped with R. E. Lee, rode with him, and assisted him on the battlefield. The general staff at headquarters consisted of men more concerned with supplies and operations. Thus Lee's adjutant, Walter H. Taylor, was a personal staff officer, while commissary chief Robert G. Cole was a general staff officer. Congress never fully grasped the distinction between the general staff and a general's staff.[4]

These definitions and usages can be confusing even today, so it seems likely that Confederate lawmakers also had a cloudy view of staff work. Endless legislation accompanied by acrimonious debate became common in the halls of the Confederate Congress. Most of it had little effect on the functions and appearance of a typical staff in the Army of Northern Virginia, but there were exceptions. One very significant example was a bill that slipped through in October 1862 providing that "Adjutants appointed by the President shall be deemed officers of the General Staff, and shall be regarded as part of the companies to which they are attached, and not as belonging to the personal staff of the officers under whose orders they may be serving." This rule was intended to ensure continuity, especially at the brigade and division levels. It was designed to prevent staff officers (specifically adjutants and inspectors) from jumping with generals from one assignment to the next. In practice, many adjutants were promoted upward with their generals anyway through the proper channels. Nonetheless, this legislation was an attempt to make staff officers more professional by tying them into the army's order of battle as if they were regiments indigenous to a brigade instead of individual officers.[5]

Several months later, R. E. Lee reminded Confederate president Jefferson Davis of the importance of implementing a general staff system for the whole army. "The greatest difficulty I find is in causing orders and regulations to be obeyed," Lee wrote in March 1863. "We therefore have need of a corps of officers to teach others their duty, see to the observance of orders, and to the regularity and precision of all movements." In the space of a few sentences, he had identified a primary weakness that would plague his army in varying degrees until Appomattox. Staff officers learned on the job, if at all. Instead Lee wanted a permanent body of staff officers schooled in their duties. His evaluation had its origin in the casual inefficiency of the Seven Days battles (especially the startling ineptitude of the management of the fight at Malvern Hill) and the crippling failure of supply and discipline during the Maryland Campaign. An organization modeled on the French Army, thought Lee, would be the best plan. A general staff in his estimation was a collection of career staff officers—a permanent branch of the army. Lee immediately implemented some of his notions without waiting for executive or legislative approval.[6]

The best intentions of Lee and the army's high command still did not produce a professional body of staff officers of the sort needed to manage a real army. President Davis reacted to Lee's plea by using his annual address in December 1863 as a vehicle for bringing the problem to the country's attention. A true general staff, Davis said, "would be highly conducive to the efficiency" of staff work. His remarks galvanized Congress, and the Senate at once crafted another ambitious general staff bill (S-204). It abolished the connection between staff officers and their parent organizations (the October 1862 legislation discussed above) and permitted even those with no field experience to be eligible for staff appointments. After considerable argument, it passed both bodies of Congress but then surprisingly ran afoul of its original advocate, Jefferson Davis. This bill resembled an earlier one that also had died from a presidential veto. Although anxious to accommodate the wishes of Lee and others in the field, Davis proved unwilling to let Congress dictate the terms of the staff bill, and he refused to compromise on the matter.[7]

The Army of Northern Virginia rested in its winter quarters while staff debates raged in Richmond early in 1864. Officers in the army watched with keen interest because the bill not only portended changes in the way staff officers would operate but also promised promotions for many staff men. At Second Corps headquarters near the Rapidan River, for instance, General Richard S. Ewell plotted the course he would take if the bill became law. His primary concern, according to a bystander, was to see to it that his stepson, G. Campbell Brown, would secure the top billet on the staff, with its attendant increased rank. Ewell's suspected machinations naturally annoyed the rest of the corps staff. The failure of the executive and legislative branches of the government to reach a compromise deprived Ewell's stepson of his colonel's commission. No doubt other contemplated string pulling and patronage—all in vain—went unrecorded.[8]

As soon as Congress reconvened in May 1864, Davis urged its members to renew their efforts to produce a general staff bill. His remarkably balanced plea included several very cogent observations on the purpose of a general staff. Davis argued, "It is impracticable to organize and administer armies with efficiency without the aid of a general staff, permanent in its character, trained in its duties, aspiring to promotion in its own corps, and responsible to the head of the department." A general staff "independent of the movements of general officers" would serve to "prevent their views being narrowed to the routine" inherent in serving a single officer rather than a professional corps. Under the current system, a general had the power "to lift to higher grades the officers of his staff to whom he has become attached by companionship in the field, although these officers may be far inferior . . . to others whose duties have connected them with generals less distinguished." Davis obviously had not forgotten what Lee had written fourteen months earlier.[9]

While the Army of Northern Virginia stood in the trenches at Cold Harbor in June, Congress passed a staff bill, stimulated by Davis's plea. This one met with executive approval, and Davis signed it into law on June 14. Despite the compromise, politics confused the issue until the very end. As late as March 1865, the president continued to refuse to appoint general staff officers under the new legislation because he anticipated the passage of trifling amendments to the June bill. Congress did not oblige with the alterations, and by war's end the Confederate government had nothing but acrimony to remember of its four years of investigation into the feasibility of implementing a general staff system.[10]

While those in power wrangled over the general staff issue, the officers in the Army of Northern Virginia engaged in the age-old competition between the line and the staff. Traditionally, officers of the line have viewed their authority as paramount, reserving mild scorn for their brethren in the staff branch. That prickliness existed in the Army of Northern Virginia, too, although it clearly drew its energy from professional pride rather than social or intellectual differences. While there were noticeable differences in the personal profiles of line officers and staff officers, they hardly qualify as a chasm. Although the idea that most conflict can be traced to passionate struggle among different social or economic classes apparently is prevalent in the modern academic world, such struggle surely contributed little to the actual rivalry between Confederate line officers and staff officers. The self-confidence of combat veterans led them to regard the staff profession and its associated "red tape" with skepticism. Some undoubtedly admired the famous remark about paperwork attributed to the Duke of Wellington in an earlier war: "If I attempted to answer the mass of futile correspondence that surrounds me, I should be debarred from all serious business of campaigning. . . . I shall see that no officer under my Command is debarred, by attending to the futile drivelling of mere quill-driving in your Lordship's office, from attending to his first duty— which is, and always has been, so to train the private men that they may without question, beat any force opposed to them in the field." Many staff men rode with their generals in the midst of battles, and dozens gave their lives during the war, but traditionally staff officers had the reputation of avoiding danger. It was a case of those who viewed themselves as practitioners having little respect for those they viewed as theorists at best or shirkers at worst.[11]

Congressional meddling and internal squabbling aside, the simple question of whether or not the Army of Northern Virginia had an efficient corps of staff officers remains largely unexplored and certainly unresolved. Overwhelming evidence exists to illustrate the feebleness of the army's staff system in the war's early stages. In 1861, there were too many staff officers, most of them gaudily dressed volunteers. They clogged the headquarters entourage, confused subordinates, and retarded the development of farsighted officers who were serious about professional staff work. Perceptive artillerist Ham Chamberlayne wrote from western Virginia in August 1861: "To tell you the truth, we have vastly too many aid[e]s." He recognized that limited transportation made those temporary men cumbersome and that "every shoulder strap added is an expense equal to that of many privates." Such excess perhaps could be excused during the quiet early months of the war, but when the pace quickened in 1862, the dross fell away, leaving a preponderance of unsure or untested staff officers.[12]

The crush of constant action during the Seven Days battles in June and July 1862 exposed many weak spots in the army's staff work. Critics unanimously have assigned significant blame to the staff branch of the army for the tactical and operational disappointments of the campaign. Historian Archer Jones wrote that in the Seven Days, "Lee and his staff, in their first campaign together, showed their inexperience." Generals and their staffs had yet to perfect "the techniques of maneuvering their forces." British historian G. F. R. Henderson spoke more plainly when he concluded that Lee's staff "must have been utterly incapable of directing the intricate movements devised by Lee to ensnare McClellan." The army's staff in July 1862 was "too small," "too inexperienced," and "insufficiently trained" to be useful. Douglas Southall Freeman ignored delicacy when he wrote that the campaign "will always remain a tragic monument to defective staff work." "A detailed list of the errors of the staff would be a review of the campaign," he concluded.[13]

Henderson and others perceived improvements in the army's efficiency as the war continued. The number of officers in the supply branches increased. Surprisingly this did not produce clutter. Instead it streamlined the process and reduced "red tape" by allowing each officer to fill a well-defined role without encroaching on the responsibilities of others. In 1863, the army's second invasion of Maryland compared favorably with the first. The engineering, signaling, and discipline branches also showed improvement by midwar. The personal staffs of generals, once so bloated, had been pared down to a more manageable number. Porter Alexander, who saw duty as both a line and a staff officer, was one of the few soldier-scholars who disagreed with the notion that fewer personal staff officers was better. He argued that "scarcely any of our generals had half of what they needed to keep a *constant & close supervision on the execution of important orders*." His complaint was unusual.[14]

By 1864, the number of general staff officers reached its maximum. The engineering and ordnance departments had more commissioned men in Lee's army than ever before. Regimental supply officers had disappeared, replaced by more men performing that duty at the brigade and division levels. The lessons of 1862 and early 1863 took effect in 1864. The corps commanders and their staffs, probably in collaboration with Lee, finally had started to develop through trial and error a system that allowed them to manage the army. But the war ended before the Army of Northern Virginia could implement a true general staff of the sort envisioned by Lee and Davis.

This section surveys the different types of staff officers in the Army of Northern Virginia, arranged alphabetically. Each segment describes the activities of officers of that branch, provides a short history of the evolution of the position, and includes some general observations on the men who performed those particular duties.

Adjutant General

Generals in the Army of Northern Virginia had the option of designating one of their aides as "chief of staff." Not every general chose to do so. For those who did, no rules existed to dictate which staff officer should have the honor of that title. In most instances, a general's adjutant assumed that role, but regardless of whether or not he bore the appellation of chief of staff, the adjutant almost always was viewed as the primary staff officer. Officially this officer was called assistant adjutant general (AAG)–that is, a representative of the Adjutant and Inspector General's Office (AIGO) in Richmond. Some of the most famous staff officers in the history of the army were AAGs. Walter H. Taylor filled that position for R. E. Lee, while the famed Sandie Pendleton served as Stonewall Jackson's adjutant general. Moxley Sorrel (for James Longstreet) and Henry B. McClellan (for J. E. B. Stuart) are two other prominent examples.[15]

An adjutant general at the corps or army level could, in the course of a busy winter day, dispose of hundreds of documents pertaining to the operations of his command. Taylor and the corps adjutants routinely confronted so much paperwork that they employed clerks to assist them with the copying. An efficient adjutant tried to weed out the routine business, leaving only the most significant items for the general's attention. He also screened his chief from the legions of callers seeking an audience. In practice, the AAG often was one of the most powerful officers in any organization, even at the brigade level.

That influence existed on the battlefield as well as in camp. Officers and men considered the AAG an extension of the general and often accepted orders from him as if they came from the commander himself. Moxley Sorrel wrote that at the Battle of Chickamauga he attempted to launch an attack with some Army of Tennessee troops, explaining "that I was chief of staff to Longstreet and felt myself competent to give such an order as coming from my chief, and that this was customary in our Virginia service." Sorrel's pleas failed to convince his western comrades, who apparently were unaccustomed to the flexibility exercised in the Army of Northern Virginia. In another example from the same battle, General Joseph B. Kershaw wrote that his adjutant general, Captain Charles R. Holmes, "represented me on the right wing of my brigade." In rare instances, AAGs even filled in for absent or injured generals and commanded troops in the field. Adjutants typically confronted danger much more frequently than most of their fellow staff officers. Randolph J. Barton, a bright young adjutant, mused after the war that a brigade AAG was "more exposed than anyone else in battle. Field officers of regiments invariably dismounted in our war, and staff officers of division and corps were one degree further removed from the line of fire." Barton's four wounds supported his argument.[16]

The onerous workload surely offset whatever glamour accompanied an adjutant's career. Two weeks before the Battle of Gettysburg, as the army marched north, Second Corps AAG Sandie Pendleton groaned under the weight of his daily duties. "It has been write, write, write with pen & pencil morning noon & night for a week past & I'm tired of it," he grumbled to his fiancée. "You ought to be glad to get this letter." One can scarcely get through a single piece of Walter Taylor's private wartime correspondence without encountering his lamentations about overwork. No doubt an adjutant's labor was greater on the lofty plane occupied by men like Taylor and Pendleton, but even brigade and division adjutants had dozens of daily chores to tackle. Willis F. Jones, the late-war adjutant for Charles Field's division, renewed the familiar complaint in a letter to his mother: "I have so much to do that I cannot bear the sight of pen or paper." But pen and paper were the mandatory weapons in an AAG's arsenal. When twenty-year-old Fred Fleet's mother asked him why he had been detailed for service as AAG in Henry Wise's brigade, he guessed that it was "because I write a tolerable hand and have a moderate idea of business."[17]

In the long run, adjutants in the Confederate staff service proliferated beyond the bounds of good sense. When Adjutant General Samuel Cooper in Richmond audited the books in the summer of 1864, to his horror, he found that there were "at least 500 Asst Adjt Genl. of the different grades, holding appointments in the Provisional Army of the Confederate States." Cooper knew that all of the Union armies combined mustered only 333 AAGs, despite fielding at least twice as many men as did the Southern armies. Clearly bureaucracy had run amok in this branch of the nascent Confederate system, and Cooper announced his determination to reduce the number of AAGs to a more reasonable total. Beyond blocking future appointments, there was not much he could do, and no doubt the Confederacy ended its life with more AAGs than its Federal foes had.[18]

It seems, from the available evidence, that on the whole the army's AAGs were an able lot. Nearly all were in their twenties or thirties, probably because the position required men vigorous enough to accompany generals in the field during a campaign yet steady enough to conduct paperwork assembly lines between actions. Very few came to their labors with any military background, and many keenly felt their inexperience. As late as September 1864, a civilian observer speculated that General Lee needed more "mature and earnest men on his staff—men whose age and gravity of demeanor would facilitate investigations into many army abuses which are not revealed to young men . . . and to whom less forbearance is extended by brigade and division commanders than would be accorded men of riper years." Nearly 150 years later, however, it is those young and energetic AAGs who are the best known of the army's several thousand staff officers. Men like Taylor, McClellan, and Sorrel did much, both during and after the war, to build and preserve the reputation of the Army of Northern Virginia.[19]

Aide-de-Camp

In one sense, the men who held the position of aide-de-camp (ADC) were the purest category of staff officers. Every general, from the powerful to the pedestrian, had at least one ADC in his stable of assistants, and the men who filled that spot usually were on the closest personal terms with their generals. An aide's duty was to perform whatever chores his general assigned. There were no professional requirements associated with the job. An ADC was expected to be with the general on the battlefield and in the camp and could be used in any number of ways, depending on the aide's ability and the general's command style. Some ADCs were little more than couriers. Others assisted in processing paperwork and helped their colleagues with related tasks. In almost every case, the ADC bore the lowest rank of any officer on the staff.

The AIGO took a very narrow view of the extent of a general's authority over staff officers and decreed that "only aides-de-camp are to be considered as the personal staff of general officers." Nearly everyone familiar with the personnel of the Army of Northern Virginia would argue that such was not the case. Was Walter Taylor not part of Lee's personal staff, nor Sandie Pendleton a member of Jackson's? Clearly the letter of the law in this case had little bearing on reality, since each general had at least three or four men on his personal staff, frequently more.

The AIGO's definition did allow it to secure some control over the appointment of staff officers because according to the law, generals were not permitted to appoint any of their staff officers other than their personal staff—the ADC. When John Bratton received his commission as brigadier general in 1864, he soon discovered how limiting the rule could be when firmly enforced. After choosing his ADC, Bratton found "no other appointment at present" within his reach. "What is called the General Staff is full and belongs to the Brig. not to the Gen.," he observed. Most generals solved this problem by nominating their other staff officers and then enduring the formality of having their choices approved by the authorities. They only had to wait for vacancies to occur before they could recommend someone new.[20]

Given one chance for complete control over their appointments, generals took full advantage of the opportunity and appointed all manner of men to serve as ADCs. The nepotism that existed in nearly every corner of the army occurred with greatest frequency among the aides. Dozens of generals, from corps commanders to fresh brigadiers, found spots on their staffs for sons, cousins, business partners, and in-laws. Regulations allowed most generals no more than one paid ADC. Only the highest-ranking generals could employ extra aides. With few exceptions, ADCs bore the rank and pay of lieutenant—although they were eligible for an extra $35 monthly. Cadmus M. Wilcox, commanding a Third Corps division, argued in May 1864 that aides-de-camp were important enough to warrant higher rank. He suggested that aides for major generals be given the rank of captain and that lieutenant generals' aides be promoted to major. Wilcox's proposal did not succeed in Congress, leaving nearly every ADC in the army mired at the rank of lieutenant.[21]

When Stonewall Jackson offered his brother-in-law a position as ADC in July 1862, he described the job in one sentence: "Your duties will require early rising, boldness, industry and enterprise." It may not be unfair to suggest that for many prospective ADCs, the particulars of the employment were not relevant. The prestige of serving on a general's staff and possessing inside information about plans and operations was sufficient. Sometimes it proved difficult for generals to avoid office seekers who swarmed around headquarters, invoking old associations or citing distant family connections. As early as April 1861, R. E. Lee rebuffed an acquaintance who had advanced his nephew as a possible member of the Virginian's staff. "I am sorry your nephew has left his college and become a soldier," wrote Lee. "It is necessary that persons on my staff should have a knowledge of their duties and an experience of the wants of the service to enable me to attend to other matters." Francis H. Smith, the influential superintendent of the Virginia Military Institute (VMI), attempted to install one of his students as an aide to Robert E. Rodes (also one of Smith's protégés) in 1862. Despite the pressure from a friend and mentor, Rodes was unwilling to surrender the cherished flexibility inherent in filling the ADC spot and refused to appoint Smith's man.[22]

Many generals and applicants got around the rules by agreeing to an indefinite arrangement that made the applicants *volunteer* aides-de-camp (VADCs). Nearly every general had a few VADCs at one time or another. That solution made everyone happy since it allowed the VADCs to call themselves staff officers, perform important duties on the battlefield, and share the relatively privileged lifestyle enjoyed by a general's entourage in the field. The casual manner in which generals annexed men to their staffs as VADCs is startling. This proved especially true in the war's first year, before conscription laws greatly reduced the pool of potential VADCs. Dozens of generals accommodated footloose friends and relatives by placing them on their staffs. At First Manassas, General Milledge L. Bonham had no fewer than eight men in that position, mostly wealthy South Carolinians who wanted to hold an honorable position with the army in the war's first great battle. John Bankhead Magruder also enjoyed augmenting his personal staff with VADCs. He had at least eight men fitting that description in the fifteen months he was in Virginia. J. E. B. Stuart professed "great reluctance to having an officer on his staff who draws no pay," wrote his engineer in 1863, yet the record reveals that Stuart had more than a dozen VADCs on his staff during his three years with the army. With a few exceptions, the generals with the greatest fondness for VADCs were either politicians or men who brought pomp and parade to their duties. Inflated numbers of staff officers suited their taste for display.[23]

A few examples out of perhaps dozens illustrate the casual nature of the relationships between generals and volunteer aides. Asbury Coward, who later commanded an infantry regiment in the Army of Northern Virginia, showed up near Manassas in the summer of 1861 looking for something to do. Someone introduced him socially to General David R. Jones. "When we were about to leave," recollected Coward, "General Jones kindly invited me to act as volunteer aide-de-camp. I told him I had no horse, arms, nor suitable uniform." What had been a courteous offer from one gentleman to another blossomed into a friendship that in turn led to Coward's appointment as major and AAG on Jones's staff. General Winfield S. Featherston encountered his nephew Charles in January 1862, and although he did not recognize him, "on learning his name . . . told him he would give him any office in his staff." Young Featherston—a twenty-two-year-old lawyer—accepted his uncle's offer and served as a VADC in the brigade for the last quarter of 1862. When Arnold Elzey sought a suitable young man to act as ADC in March 1862, he was directed to Murray F. Taylor, a seventeen-year-old cadet with the 13th Virginia Infantry. Elzey "looked at me earnestly & hesitated," remembered Taylor, but Colonel James A. Walker of the 13th reassured Elzey, saying, "Try him General he will do."[24]

Although the proliferation of nepotism and favoritism in the assignment of aides-de-camp has soured their reputation, some ADCs were notably able and earnest men. Occasionally colonels took deserving men from their regiments with them when they ascended to command a brigade. The reward for those men—who often were privates in the ranks—was a lieutenant's commission and an honorable position as part of the general's retinue. Those ADCs had little experience in their duties, but others came to the position with better preparation. David T. Merrick, a young Louisianian who briefly served as ADC to General Leroy A. Stafford in 1863 at age twenty-two, had received a fortnight of intensive homemade training in the war's first months. Merrick's father had imported a French drillmaster in May 1861, "who instructs him in military science during the day, and drills him . . . every night." The elder Merrick "says he must understand the movements of a brigade, battalion and regiment, as well as that of company drill; he must know something and become qualified for everything." Others brought commitment and pride to what admittedly was the least prestigious job on the staff. Thomas G. Jones, the oft-wounded ADC of General John B. Gordon, defended the importance of his position and once counseled a friend that "a gallant staff-officer is more good to his country than a private in any command."[25]

The professional track of an aide usually mirrored that of his general. When a commander received promotion or reassignment, his aide followed. In some cases, generals suddenly had larger staffs and took advantage of the opportunity to improve the careers of their aides by recommending their elevation to a staff position of more responsibility. Thus some adjutants and inspectors spent the first years of the war as aides before sharing in the rewards given to their generals. The death or resignation of a general offers the best evidence of how the law handcuffed ADCs to their generals. When generals resigned or died, their aides fell out of commission entirely and were left to find another position or run the risk of being conscripted. General Carnot Posey, for example, had two sons on his staff. Jefferson B. Posey was the ADC, while Stanhope Posey served as the brigade's adjutant general. The day their father died, Jefferson found himself an instant civilian instead of a lieutenant in the Army of Northern Virginia. His brother's official position remained unaffected by the death of the general, and Stanhope continued for another year with the brigade under General Nathaniel H. Harris.

Chief of Artillery

In the army's earliest campaigns, many batteries marched, fought, and camped with individual infantry brigades. They came to be viewed as part of the brigade's organization. Other batteries occupied places in the army's mass of reserve artillery. A third practice, especially prevalent in 1862, paired battalions of artillery with specific infantry divisions. The battalion commander then was considered a member of the division commander's staff. Often the artillery chief played the singular role of being a line officer with staff duties. In time, the army's organization evolved, clustering artillery at the corps level instead of by division. When that system took effect, there was one chief of artillery for each corps. By war's end, the position had been classified as worthy of generalship, and men like Armistead L. Long and Reuben L. Walker graduated from being considered staff officers to being generals. Not every division commander had a discernible chief of artillery, and thus no staff billet examined in this book was more irregular.

Engineer Officer

The majority of Confederate staff officers had little practical experience before the war in their duties. Engineers formed a major exception to that general rule. Both civil and military engineers enjoyed especially high esteem in the prewar years. Some of the finest minds in the South turned toward that profession, and a large number of the Army of Northern Virginia's general officers had considered engineering their primary antebellum occupation.

The daily labors of an engineer officer (EO) in the army varied so widely and were so extensive that any prewar experience a man brought to his military engineering career proved particularly valuable. Most generals used their engineers as scouts, relying on them for reconnaissance. An eye for terrain made engineers especially useful in the days or hours just before battle. They laid out lines, supervised the construction of entrenchments, and helped to improve roads and fords. Army regulations specified these duties but added somewhat lamely that "officers of engineers may be employed on any other duty whatsoever."[26]

While the army marched into Pennsylvania in June 1863, the AIGO issued a new set of rules that more explicitly defined the responsibilities of the army's engineers. The department's officers were expected to "make reconnaissances and surveys," which included collecting "all the information that can be obtained in reference to roads, bridges, fords, topographical and military features, the character and dimension of the water-courses, the practicability of constructing fixed and floating bridges, the extent of wooded and cleared lands," and a dozen other related chores. When required, they were to "form plans, projects, and estimates for all military works," including "field forts, batteries, rifle-pits, lines of infantry cover, military trenches, parallels, saps, mines, and other works of attack and siege." The same general orders pointed out that engineer officers "will not assume nor be ordered on any duty beyond the line of their immediate profession." That passage effectively quashed the early-war caveat that engineers must do whatever was asked of them. The revision likely resulted from a too-liberal use of engineers as couriers and aides on the battlefield.[27]

The army also employed a fair number of mapmakers, usually identified as "topographical engineers." Although they focused on cartography, those men were considered engineer officers. Jedediah Hotchkiss, of the army's Second Corps, is the best-known example of that contingent. By war's end, the staffs of most high-ranking generals included someone who specialized in mapwork or who bore responsibility for overseeing that branch of the trade.

Given the importance of engineers in prewar America, the Confederate authorities may have been surprised to find that far from having a surfeit of qualified engineers in 1861, there were too few. The army stood in urgent need of skilled engineers for at least the first half of the war, and competition for their services was fierce. The shortage probably reached its peak when the government began to implement a plan for the erection of permanent defenses at key spots in Virginia in late 1861 and most of 1862.[28]

The Confederate Congress made a weak first attempt to provide its army with commissioned engineers in 1861 when it approved the appointment of fifty engineer officers, all with the rank of captain or lieutenant. That legislation proved woefully inadequate to the armies in the field, to say nothing of the many strategically important cities and rivers that needed strengthening. The shortage produced a prolonged wail for help from generals stationed all over Virginia. Army commander Joseph E. Johnston wrote to the secretary of war in November 1861, begging for relief. "We have but one engineer officer, who is sick," Johnston complained. Five months after First Manassas, the largest Confederate army in the

East still had no engineer department at army headquarters. Two months later, the problem remained unresolved. "At least half a dozen competent engineers . . . should be with this army," grumbled its chief of staff, "but there is only one officer of engineers on duty with it." Stonewall Jackson lamented the same shortage. "I much need a good engineer officer," he wrote, to assist during the dolorous winter campaign in western Virginia. Those prominent examples illustrate an army-wide problem. Virginia did its best to offset the shortages by appointing a sizable number of engineers in its own provisional army. Those men usually worked on the Peninsula defenses, around Richmond, or on sorely needed mapping projects. When the Provisional Army of Virginia essentially dissolved in February 1862, many of its engineers began to work for the Confederate government as contractors, performing the same duties.[29]

Congress doubled the size of the engineer corps in April 1862, but the army continued to find itself short of competent engineers. The new provision allowed each division in the army to have its own engineer officer. Brigade commanders did not enjoy the same privilege and had to rely on the divisional representative for support. General John B. Magruder, with the largest field staff of any officer in the history of the Army of Northern Virginia, still encountered difficulty in preparing entrenchments just east of Richmond in the face of the Union army as late as June 1862. Probably because he was a seasoned engineer himself, R. E. Lee seemed to take special interest in that department's field organization. His initial plan, hatched that same June, was to insist that all engineer officers in the army report to a single man, the army's chief engineer at Lee's headquarters. From there, the chief would farm out responsibilities as required. That system would help "to secure the prompt and energetic performance of all duties" and would ensure that the overstretched army engineers would make the best use of their time. Lee's strategy may have been in effect briefly, but soon each division commander had his own engineer, to use as he pleased.[30]

When Jeremy Gilmer assumed the title of chief of the engineer department for the Confederate armed forces in the last quarter of 1862, he looked closely at the 100 officers then under his control and disliked what he saw. The Georgian found that two dozen of the appointments "have been given to worthless men of broken down Virginia families," and another 20 were in the hands of "*South Carolinians, no better than the aforesaid Virginians.*" Sacking those men was not an option, of course, so Gilmer launched a campaign to expand the department and insert men more to his liking into the new slots. Engineering, like medicine, is not a profession to be learned in haste. General Gilmer soon found that stuffing his organization with Georgians and others more to his taste would be difficult. Not only would Gilmer have to identify competent candidates; he would need the support of Congress and President Davis before he could expand the department.[31]

Certainly a few generals abused their privileges regarding the assignment of engineers to their staffs. J. E. B. Stuart proved the truth of some of General Gilmer's bitter remarks by having a pair of engineers assigned to him who were not qualified. Thomas R. Price, the brother of Stuart's outstanding aide R. Channing Price, in the spring of 1863 received a commission to serve as an assistant engineer to the famous cavalryman. At almost the same time, twenty-two-year-old Virginian Frank Robertson joined Stuart's staff as another assistant engineer. Apparently Stuart used the appointments as a sort of patronage rather than as a way to obtain men suited for engineering duty. Perhaps he felt that he did not need any extra engineers and simply used the openings to allow agreeable officers to join his staff. "I thought from what he said," Robertson later wrote, "that he got me the position more as a means of getting me on his staff than for any assistance I might give the Engineer Corps." Thomas Price "seems to know very little more about it than myself," he continued. Young Robertson subsequently confirmed his own analysis by bungling a simple job copying a map of the battlefield of Fredericksburg. "A huge red blot" on the map made it "appear as if Gen. Lee had massed about half his army in a very safe out-of-the-way place."[32]

The evolving nature of warfare in central Virginia in 1864 elevated the daily importance of engineers. Moving dirt and arranging it in piles at the most defensible spots required the professional eye of an engineer. In response to the chronic need for more officers in that branch, Congress belatedly approved another measure to increase the number and rank of engineers in the Confederate armies. Jefferson Davis signed it into law on March 2, 1865, too late for the new legislation to bear fruit on the battlefields.[33]

Inspector General

The position of inspector frequently was, and still is, confused or combined with that of adjutant. Both positions derived their authority and titles from the Adjutant and Inspector General's Office in Richmond, yet their duties had little in common. Inspectors, called assistant adjutant and inspectors general (AAIGS), were supposed to police the military efficiency of the army and maintain regularity and discipline. Although they performed a wide variety of related tasks, those officers owed their existence to the need for regular inspections of camps, drills, equipment, and other aspects of daily military life that contribute to morale and efficiency. The 1862 army regulations defined the inspectors' duties in tedious detail: "Inspection reports will show the discipline of the troops; their instruction in all military exercises and duties; the state of their arms, clothing, equipments, and accoutrements of all kinds." More than two dozen other specifications rounded out their responsibilities, including a directive "to report if any officer is of intemperate habits." An inspector, President Davis once aptly remarked, was an officer "whose duties may not be inappropriately described as those of a detective."[34]

The Army of Northern Virginia's leaders understood the importance of inspectors early on but perhaps underestimated the degree to which the army needed them. The records show only a few inspectors in the army in the early years, mostly at the division level and above. The 1862 Maryland Campaign clearly underscored the inadequacy of the army's system up to that time. Faced with unprecedented straggling, carelessness with government arms, and more bad behavior than he cared to witness, General Lee took measures to ensure a better showing by his army in the next campaign. Writing to Jefferson Davis only five days after the Battle of Sharpsburg, Lee bitterly lamented recent "outrages . . . disgraceful to the army and injurious to our cause." His short-term solution called for the return of Lieutenant Colonel E. J. Harvie, formerly the army's chief inspector. Once Harvie had supervised immediate repairs, Lee hoped for the permanent appointment of "an officer of rank, standing, and reputation to act as inspector-general, with sufficient assistants, and some tribunal to accompany the army, with power to inflict prompt and adequate punishment." Lee also wrote to top subordinates Jackson and Longstreet demanding stricter accountability of their divisional inspectors.[35]

Harvie hastened back to the army within a matter of days but soon defected to Joseph E. Johnston's command, leaving Lee to appoint Colonel Robert H. Chilton —his chief of staff—to the permanent post of army inspector general. Chilton initially demonstrated diligence in his new duties. His inspection report for Hood's division in November 1862 is a sensible and thorough document. It is not clear how closely Chilton met his own standards in later months. His unsuitability as a staff officer on the battlefields is well chronicled, but the quality of his performance as inspector and his impact on the army are less apparent. When Chilton left for a desk job in Richmond early in 1864, he was replaced by Lieutenant Colonel Edward Murray, who shortly gave way to Lieutenant Colonel Henry E. Peyton.[36]

The new emphasis on discipline from army headquarters in the autumn of 1862 led to tighter standards and stricter accountability. Most brigade commanders appointed inspectors to their staffs over the winter of 1862–63, many of them detailed to that duty from a position in the line, pending permanent appointment from the AIGO. Before the new system could take effect, it was abolished, probably in a misguided effort to reduce the number of detailed officers. Chilton delivered the orders to the army in May 1863, announcing that brigade inspectors should return to their original positions. The remaining staff, Chilton directed, should pitch in and help each other cover for the absent inspectors. General Lee still expected trimonthly inspection reports from the brigades, sent up through the division inspectors.[37]

Lee's army invaded Pennsylvania and then recuperated from Gettysburg in the autumn of 1863 without the presence of brigade inspectors. It is not clear what prompted the restoration of the old system, but in November 1863, nearly every brigade received a fully empowered inspector with the rank of captain. Those appointments mostly occurred on November 19 and were backdated to November 2, although there does not seem to be any corresponding legislation from Congress to explain the new allowance.[38]

Even after the November 1863 return of brigade inspectors, confusion continued to surround the position. The case of John R. Cooke's North Carolina brigade provides a curious example. General Cooke detailed James A. Graham, a lieutenant in the 27th North Carolina, to act as inspector just before the spring 1864 battles commenced. Cooke then asked for Graham's full-time appointment in the summer of 1864. R. E. Lee endorsed the application, stating that the army's brigades then were "so small that they hardly need Inspectors-General, but as every brigade in the Army of Northern Virginia has an Inspector-General, except Cooke's, respectfully forwarded approved." The War Department failed to support Lee's remarks, returning the application with an inexplicable veto: "No inspectors will be allowed to brigades." Nonetheless, the AIGO appointed an inspector for Cooke's brigade within a few weeks. General Cooke's ordeal probably was an odd episode, yet the constantly shifting policy on this matter assuredly reduced the long-term authority of brigade inspectors and the staff system itself.[39]

When they had the luxury of inspectors, many generals used them as aides, a tendency that predictably undercut the effectiveness of the staff men. Misuse of staff officers was a problem not unique to inspectors, but General Lee never managed to solve it. Circulars on the subject produced few improvements, and as late as 1864, many inspectors still rode beside their generals and acted as highly ranked aides. "They have not been encouraged in the discharge of their legitimate and prescribed duties," complained the army's chief inspector. Instead, "they have been in many cases ordered to do the work of adjutants and aides-de-camp."[40]

The ever-changing policy on brigade inspectors ensured that those officers would be of lower profile than many of their brethren in the staff service. Appendix 2 illustrates that point. The appendix lists the staff officers of each general in the army, with their rank, position, and dates of service. Some brigadier generals have no inspectors listed at all, an omission explained either by the unofficial nature of the position for part of the war or by the fact that some of the adjutants listed actually served as inspectors. Officers detailed from the ranks to act as brigade inspectors often left no paper trail, which further reduces the accuracy of the general-by-general list.

The men who served the army as inspectors came from no particular background, nor were their antebellum occupations slanted toward any special field. The three division inspectors for the First Corps in the autumn of 1864 provide a typical field of study. In George Pickett's division, Walter H. Harrison served as inspector. He had been a businessman and journalist in New York City before the war. Leander Masters progressed from country lawyer in Amelia County, Virginia, to inspector of Charles Field's division. In Joseph B. Kershaw's command, Ellison L. Costin performed the duties of inspector. Costin had been a farmer in Northampton County, Virginia, until 1861. No doubt their generals deemed those three men to be good officers and thus found a place for them on the divisional staff. General James H. Lane ignored all of the traditional standards when choosing Edward A. T. Nicholson to be his inspector: "I selected him for my inspector-general on account of his face, which I thought was full of character. I was not mistaken, and I am very fond of him," Lane wrote. As in so many other sectors of the army's staff system, experience and professional suitability were not always of vital importance, nor were they consistently attainable.[41]

Some inspectors did not project the no-nonsense image their duties would seem to have required. Robert Tansill, who served as AAIG for W. H. C. Whiting's division, assumed a melodramatic tone when he wrote to Jefferson Davis in search of personal promotion. His four-sentence letter included some classic passages: "I fear you have forgotten me. . . . Is devotion to our sacred cause . . . to be counted for nothing? I cannot, I will not, believe it!" Tansill's affected style left the president nonplussed, but General Samuel Cooper (himself a tougher officer than most of the inspectors in the field) knew how to deal with Tansill. "I am not acquainted with his merits," wrote Cooper dryly, "but should conclude from the tone of his letter that his rank is about as high as it should be for the present."[42]

Judge

Congress established military courts in the autumn of 1862 that would travel with the army and hear cases promptly. Their presence expedited military justice, which was a boon to both the army and some of the defendants. Although the courts were born not long after General Lee's cry of alarm about the army's state of discipline during the Maryland Campaign and only days after the official reorganization of the army into two corps, their origin had more to do with a pressing long-term need than with anything else. Earlier that summer, President Davis had begun negotiations with Congress for legislation that would create "a commission to attend each army in the field, to be composed of men whose character and knowledge . . . would give the best assurance for the punishment of crime."[43]

Davis's plan worked its way through Congress with unusual ease. The legislators passed the bill just in time to install the courts in the army's freshly formed corps system. The new table of organization proved more accommodating to the military courts. Instead of creating courts with authority over certain divisions, it was more practical to assign one court to each corps. By war's end, the Army of Northern Virginia had five corps. Each court had four members — three colonels and a captain (the judge advocate). President Davis appointed the members of the courts, subject to the approval of the Senate. With only a few exceptions, the officers sitting on these courts were either beyond mandatory-service age or demonstrably unfit for field service. Even in the 1860s, the land teemed with lawyers, and the corps positions were highly prized appointments that stimulated much competition among applicants.[44]

The courts held jurisdiction over cases that involved violations of the published articles of war or in instances where soldiers stood accused of major crimes. The military courts improved the quality of justice in the army by ensuring uniformity of judgment. Even under this more professional system, room remained for smaller courts. Regimental and brigade courts consisting of detailed officers often convened through the rest of the war, usually during the less-active winter months, to try cases that were either too small or outside the jurisdiction of the corps courts.[45]

The secretary of war conducted a one-year review of the court system late in 1863 and found it useful in a number of ways. There were fewer occasions in which line officers had to sit on courts-martial, and in general, the military courts were "found to operate beneficially on the morale and efficiency of the Army." They continued, without significant change, until the end of the war.[46]

Ordnance Officer

As with every logistical staff position in the Army of Northern Virginia, ordnance officers (oos) faced a series of duties for which there was no precedent. Supplying musket balls for a tiny Mexican War infantry division in the 1840s bore little resemblance to keeping a 12,000-man division ready for war in 1862. The absence of any obvious comparable prewar occupation made the job of ordnance officer particularly difficult. While commissary and quartermaster officers often drew on their antebellum mercantile or business experiences, few men assigned to ordnance duty in the field could approach the position with any special qualifications.

Under the able leadership of General Josiah Gorgas, the Ordnance Bureau overcame its lack of experience and became one of the most efficient services in the Confederacy. Gorgas developed a network of arsenals, armories, and laboratories across the South to produce and store the weapons of war that kept Confederate armies in the field. In addition to the officers who managed those rear-echelon posts, the Ordnance Bureau had dozens of representatives in the Army of Northern Virginia who bore specific responsibility for the daily maintenance of the army's ordnance.[47]

An ordnance officer's job required equal familiarity with both paperwork and combat. This officer was required to deliver regular reports on the condition of supplies and was held accountable for everything issued, down to bayonets and bullets. During battles, ordnance officers often filled in as unofficial members of generals' personal staffs and frequently saw more action than their colleagues in the other staff branches devoted to supply. Ham Chamberlayne, who held an unofficial ordnance spot with A. P. Hill's divisional artillery in 1862, wrote home to clarify his battlefield role: "General Hill is in the habit of using me as a staff officer, that is he tells me to do this or that, anything that comes to hand, I have no specific duty as a member of his staff and indeed am not really on it," but "in time of battle particularly he keeps me very busy." A review of the ordnance officers profiled in these pages will show that men of that branch suffered many casualties, at least in comparison to men in most other staff positions. These injuries frequently occurred while the officers were performing their regular duties. At the Wilderness in May 1864, for example, Robert Walker Anderson was "slain while at the front with ammunition for the command." The next day, in the same vicinity, enemy fire killed the ordnance officer of the Texas brigade, Whitaker P. Randall.[48]

An 1862 announcement from the AIGO sought to codify the responsibilities of ordnance officers when battle loomed. Each officer, the instructions read, was to "station the ordnance wagons at the point selected for the division field depot of ammunition" and to "keep himself acquainted with the movements of brigades, and cause the wagons of any brigade which may be detached to follow" its parent brigade. Infantry units rarely expended all of their ammunition in a battle without exhausting themselves, but replenishing the cartridge boxes of a fought-out unit was a pressing item of business after any battle. An indolent ordnance officer easily could imperil the safety of his division.[49]

The dissimilarity of weapons in the army's many units became the ordnance officers' chief difficulty. As late as 1863, many brigades still possessed a wide array of weaponry. Some companies had Enfield rifles, while others toted smoothbore muskets. Still others had Belgian or Springfield rifles. The challenge of keeping the different calibers of ammunition readily available increased the daily labor of ordnance officers. A concentrated effort to standardize the equipment in regiments and brigades produced favorable results by the Battle of Gettysburg. The enormous captures at Chancellorsville and Second Winchester played a significant part in achieving that ideal. Officers concerned with the army's artillery faced the same problem, although the use of different types of cannon by individual batteries posed a less serious handicap.[50]

Initially the army in Virginia had only a chief of ordnance (on the staff at army headquarters) and division ordnance officers. Someone had deemed it unnecessary for brigades to include ordnance officers as part of their indigenous staffs. Division commanders initially enjoyed the privilege of appointing their own ordnance officers, provided they selected a man "on account of fitness for ordnance duties." The reign of division ordnance officers did not last long. On July 1, 1862, on the very day the army suffered through a poorly managed battle at Malvern Hill, the War Department amended the rules by issuing general orders that allowed brigades to have ordnance officers. The new staffers were to have the rank of lieutenant of artillery in the Provisional Army of the Confederate States (PACS), with an annual salary of $1,200 and forage for their horses. This decree increased the number of ordnance officers by perhaps 300 percent. Henry D. McDaniel, an officer in Robert Toombs's brigade, considered the ordnance office "a very honourable position, and perhaps the least laborious of any of equal rank in the army," but probably not the shortest road to further promotion. Although some might have viewed the change as an unwelcome layer of bureaucracy, it undoubtedly improved the efficiency of the army's ordnance system. The brigade OOs received orders from the division chief and delivered all reports to him. This allowed the more experienced officers to coordinate the activities of the brigade ordnance men.[51]

Congress demonstrated more friendliness toward the Ordnance Bureau than toward most other staff branches. It enacted legislation in September 1862 that again increased the number of ordnance officers. Two months later, the Confederate Congress produced another bill, this one authorizing the appointment of seventy new ordnance officers for duty in the field. No doubt at least half of the new OOs found their way into the Army of Northern Virginia. Plenty of openings existed for the new lieutenants. When the battalion system for artillery took effect early in 1863, each of the new formations received an ordnance officer. Likewise, once Lee achieved his preferred configuration of the army, several ordnance men were posted for duty with corps ammunition and reserve trains.[52]

It soon became apparent that some of the men working as ordnance officers were poorly qualified for their jobs. A familiarity with weapons and ammunition was essential. To address this problem, the AIGO in September 1862 ordered the creation of an examining board that would test applicants and reject anyone found to be patently inept. Potential ordnance officers had to prove that they possessed both "an ordinary English education" and "a knowledge of arithmetic, including the use of fractions." The boards also evaluated their knowledge of the Ordnance Bureau's field manual and reviewed testimonials from outside sources. Finally the board members tested applicants for physical fitness and then, quaintly, "satisf[ied] themselves of the moral character of the candidates, and especially of their habitual sobriety." Such rigorous inquiries into every corner of the applicants' lives no doubt improved the quality of the talent pool and proved highly successful at identifying the intellectual elite among the aspirants. One wonders how such a system would work today in a culture increasingly scornful of anything that requires standards.[53]

The examination process also allowed the Ordnance Bureau to weed out less serious candidates. Josiah Gorgas estimated that of the roughly 500 applicants for ordnance jobs in 1862, fewer than 100 actually showed up for the testing, and more than half that number failed the interrogation. The examinations produced an order of merit that helped guide the bureau in its placement of officers. Political considerations did taint the process when it was discovered that "far more of the successful candidates were from Virginia than from any other one State." With an eye toward promoting interstate harmony, the bureau did not base its appointments strictly on merit, although it still made its selections from among the officers who had passed the examination. In later months, the members of the examining board made forays into the field to quiz prospective ordnance officers who had surfaced since the first crop was chosen in the autumn of 1862.[54]

Although the Ordnance Bureau demonstrated unusual care in the selection of its representatives, it would be wrong to assume that every ordnance officer was a scholarly practitioner of his trade. Many men who forged successful careers in ordnance duty came from unrelated backgrounds. W. C. Duxbury is one example. His colleague, Francis Dawson of General Longstreet's staff, remembered Duxbury as "good tempered, but exceedingly conceited." In a humorous passage, Dawson wrote about his friend's efforts to prove his royal lineage, when in fact he was a native of New England and had been a prewar drugstore clerk in Alabama. Duxbury ended the war as the chief of ordnance for all the artillery in the Army of Tennessee. Dawson himself offers another case. He was an immigrant and a soldier in the ranks before joining the ordnance branch, where he served with distinction. Intelligence and desire must have offset inexperience in more than a few instances. On the whole, General Gorgas declared his crop of carefully screened ordnance officers an "excellent set" and commented, "I am sure there never were in any army a better class of such officers."[55]

During the final half of the war, General Gorgas and others occasionally tweaked the regulations that guided their officers but enacted no substantial changes. Gorgas lobbied President Davis in June 1864 for authority to add even more ordnance officers to the army's rolls but encountered dissent from Davis. The president refused to grant officers already acting as ordnance men in the field priority in the proposed appointments. Davis "ranted and scolded" Gorgas and argued "that the law is an invasion of his *prerogative* in designating persons to be preferred." He "showed more sensitiveness than seemed becoming," thought Gorgas. When Davis vetoed the bill on June 7, the Senate voted on whether or not to override the president. Surprisingly, only Senator Louis Wigfall of Texas approved of trampling Davis, the other twenty-two voters choosing to respect the president's wishes. Davis signed the same bill, reworded to accommodate his micromanaging style, into law on June 10, 1864.[56]

Morale among ordnance men probably improved as the war progressed, after a bad start stemming from inexperience and disorganization. Valuable testimony from a highly placed ordnance officer describes the condition of that branch of the army in the spring of 1862. Joseph L. Brent, a major on the staff of General Magruder, served as chief of ordnance for the three divisions under Magruder's control. Army commander Joseph E. Johnston paid little attention to the ordnance operations of his army, and his inadequacy in that regard became apparent to Brent after R. E. Lee ascended to command in June. Lee had his able staff officer E. Porter Alexander investigate the situation and reorganize the department. "I was called to give my aid to convert a paper skeleton into a living body," explained Brent, "and Major Alexander used Genl. Lee's great powers to obtain for me a large reserve train. . . . Under the new impulse from Genl. Lee's headquarters, enormous progress was made, defects were supplied [remedied], and when the seven days fights began about three weeks after, we had an Ordnance system organized in the field which functioned with reasonable efficiency." Brent's recollections speak well of Lee's organizational talents, but on another level, they indicate good staff work. Alexander was on the army commander's staff, and the Georgian's ability and diligence repaired in less than a month the damage caused by Johnston's yearlong neglect of the ordnance service.[57]

Ordnance officers in the Army of Northern Virginia seemingly escaped censure more than any other staff branch. While soldiers complained about lazy or dishonest commissaries and quartermasters, tyrannical inspectors, or weak-minded aides, few negative comments survive about the men who served as ordnance officers. A letter published in the Richmond newspapers in November 1863 serves as a rare exception. An unnamed writer connected with the Second Corps ordnance department accused his branch of the service of being "one of the most defective systems in the army." Citing "vast expense" and "total inefficiency," the correspondent demanded reorganization. His chief complaint was a minor one, although very complex, and his drastic suggestion of replacing brigade ordnance officers with regimental ordnance officers stands in contrast to most other sentiment on the subject. Unlike many other provocative letters printed in Civil War newspapers, this one did not spark a prolonged and contentious debate—possibly proving that the author's arguments enjoyed little support among readers. Certainly the available records indicate that ordnance officers as a class competently filled one of the most important staff positions in the army.[58]

Signal Officer

The business of signaling as a military profession only blossomed into an organized arm of staff service during the Civil War. Confederate authorities deemed signaling important enough to warrant its own specialized branch, and in the spring of 1862, Congress created the Signal Corps. The modest legislation provided authority to commission only ten signal officers (sos) with the rank of captain in the provisional army. The AIGO took charge of the new bureau, announcing that its own officers "may be instructed in and assigned to signal duty." Each corps and division commander was eligible to have a signal officer, but of course the armies of the Confederacy comprised many more than ten divisions and corps. Men of lesser rank, given the title of signal sergeant, helped fill the gaps, and the AIGO recommended that where possible generals should "have their assistant adjutant-generals and aides-de-camp instructed" in the mysteries of signal service. But there is almost no evidence that men filling the more traditional staff positions ever bothered much with signal work. A second wave of appointments, based on a September 1862 congressional act, increased the size and legitimacy of the Signal Corps. By 1864, most division commanders in the army had signal officers attached to their staffs.[59]

William Norris from Maryland emerged as the highest-ranking Confederate signal officer. He had served in that capacity under General Magruder during the early months of the war, before the Signal Corps even existed. Norris was one of the ten original captains in that branch, and by October 1862, he had received appointment as a major, posted as a signal officer in Richmond. His key subordinates in the Army of Northern Virginia all held their positions for long periods. Jacob H. Manning worked for James Longstreet from May 1862 to October 1864; Richard E. Wilbourn served under Stonewall Jackson and the subsequent commanders of the Second Corps from July 1862 until the end of the war; and Richard H. T. Adams rode with A. P. Hill from May 1862 to August 1864. This continuity undoubtedly improved the efficiency of the army's signal work. There is one glaring omission in the roster of the army's signalmen. R. E. Lee had no signal officer on his staff. It is unclear how much the army's signaling operations suffered for lack of a coordinating hand.

The three signal officers' fidelity and longevity earned little favor with Congress. While other corps staff officers climbed to ranks commensurate with duty under a lieutenant general, the corps signal officers stalled at captain. William N. Barker, a captain filling in for Norris in Richmond in August 1864, beseeched the AIGO to consider improving the rank of the signalmen. "All I ask is that signal officers may be placed upon an equal footing with other staff officers." Barker's superiors ignored his pleas, and the corps signal officers spent three years at the grade of captain.[60]

Supply Officers: Quartermaster and Commissary

Both civilians and soldiers generally saw little distinction between officers of the quartermaster's department and those of the subsistence department. Staff officers filling posts in both agencies did share similar backgrounds, but their responsibilities differed. The 1862 Confederate army regulations explained with some precision that the quartermaster's department "provides the quarters and transportation of the army; storage and transportation for all army supplies; army clothing; camp and garrison equipage; cavalry and artillery horses; fuel; forage; straw, and stationery." In addition, the army's paymasters bore commissions from that department.

Men from the subsistence department (generally called commissaries of subsistence, or cs) bought, stored, and issued army rations. Each brigade had a commissary who bore the official title of captain acs, the abbreviation indicating that the officer was an assistant rather than the major cs found at the division level early in the war. The same system applied for quartermasters (aqm and qm). As the conflict progressed and regulations evolved, most brigade supply officers wore a major's star.[61]

The men best suited for supply jobs were those with civilian experience in transportation, merchandising, or large business. Efficient supply work depended on organization and coordination. In one respect, this was a happy requirement because many of the officers in the supply branches were beyond the age of active service and thus often brought years of successful business experience to their army jobs. John C. Whitner of Howell Cobb's staff was one of many who capitalized on his credentials to secure a supply job. In applying for staff duty, Whitner pointed out that he was "most fitted by long experience in mercantile & banking business, for a real *business* employment, such as is required in the commissary or quartermasters departments." Nonetheless, most candidates found the transition from businessman to commissary or quartermaster awkward because it required a shift from civilian life to the army.[62]

Quartermasters (and to a lesser degree commissaries) dealt with enormous sums of money in the course of their work. As a means of self-protection, the government required that commissioned quartermasters be bonded for four-year terms. The biographical register in this book includes many examples of men who served for a time, failed to secure their bonds, and were dropped. In the majority of those cases, the officers continued in service anyway, in theory without a commission or any authority, and in due time provided the mandatory surety. The pressure of fiscal accountability hung over this set of staff officers with menacing regularity. "Quarter Masters handle all the money appropriated to carry on the War, that part of their duty being an immense responsibility," mused a Georgian contemplating that branch of the service. Captain Adolphus Elhart, an Austrian-born merchant from Lexington, Virginia, rose to chief paymaster for the Second Corps by the spring of 1863. He told a visitor to his camp one night that his payroll for an average bimonthly muster totaled more than $2.5 million. Major Edgeworth Bird, the quartermaster of Henry Benning's brigade, demonstrated considerable nonchalance about his record keeping. Finding himself at least $600 short, he had his wife send him $1,000 from home to balance his books. "At first one blundered," Bird explained, "and there are so many ways to get behind. I'm thankful to have got off so well." Major Bird's case seems to show that the army's system of accountability was flawed—a predictable consequence of so much money changing hands in the field.[63]

Beyond the rigors of juggling money, quartermasters found that an endless press of paperwork made their job consistently onerous. Major Philip H. Powers, a Virginia schoolteacher who became J. E. B. Stuart's quartermaster in March 1862, complained bitterly about the weight of his duties. "My business is such that I can never expect to leave the Brigade except on business and for very short periods," Powers grumbled. He grew increasingly shrill: "My spirits are broken, the buoyancy of my disposition gone and the incessant worry of this Quartermaster's business will, I believe, drive me to desperation." Powers resigned on June 5, 1862, citing ill health. Major John A. Harman, Stonewall Jackson's profane quartermaster, is perhaps the best-known officer of that branch. In addition to having occasional spats with Jackson, Harman often complained about the particulars of his duties. Quartermaster work "is a great bore to me and I would give anything in the world to get out of it." On June 5, 1862, the very day that the broken-spirited Powers resigned and the same week that Jackson's Valley Campaign reached its thunderous conclusion, Harman threatened to quit unless Jackson reduced the size of the wagon train. "I will not be worked so," griped the major. Robert M. McClellan, a Georgia physician and schoolteacher, offers a third example. He was detailed to act as quartermaster for Matthew C. Butler's cavalry brigade in the autumn of 1863. After having "resisted the detail wildly," McClellan found, as feared, that "the duties are heavy and cumbrous." Nine weeks later, his temporary assignment long since completed, Captain McClellan still struggled "under a load of accounts and papers accumulated while I was acting Brg. Q. M."[64]

In some respects, commissary officers traveled a harder road than their colleagues in the quartermaster branch. The daily need to feed troops made it difficult to conceal laziness or incompetence. Good commissaries enjoyed the respect of both their peers and the men they were charged with feeding. Patience more than energy proved to be a requisite trait. Few soldiers outside the department knew or cared that army regulations were so specific as to provide commissaries with a chart bearing the mournful title: "Ration Table of Desiccated Potatoes, and Desiccated and Mixed Vegetables, from 1 to 100,000." The commissary department could not have attracted many enthusiastic patriots, at least not in the war's early years.[65]

On the positive side of the comparative ledger, commissaries could devote their full attention to getting rations to their men. Quartermasters' duties stretched across a broader field and invited greater entanglements. Captain Benjamin W. Justice, the commissary of William Kirkland's North Carolina brigade, claimed during the middle of the Overland Campaign in May 1864 that he had "little to do now" and was "oppressed with laziness & idleness. I sit under my little tentfly, & read my little Bible & write letters & wait for orders to attend to some duty." Often a commissary's work in the field came in brief, frantic bursts. Captain Nicholas B. Gibbon, whose brother John was one of the most famous Southern-born Union generals, supplied Lawrence Branch's brigade during the summer battles of 1862. He recounted that on the night of August 10, his brigade held the picket line and could not have fires. So Captain Gibbon hustled to the rear and slaughtered beef at first light, having it ready to hand to his charges when they marched rearward after a hungry night at the front. No doubt the men appreciated Gibbon's efficiency, and not surprisingly, he spent the second half of the war at a more responsible post, supervising the commissary department in Wilcox's division. Although brigade commissary officers occupied a strictly noncombatant post, many of them must have been proud to fill an essential position. Major Thomas C. Elder, the commissary for the army's lone Florida brigade, is one example. Writing after the Battle of Chancellorsville, Elder reflected on his success at feeding the Floridians: "It is gratifying to me to know that, in my humble way, I have done my duty. My brigade received their rations regularly without missing a meal during the whole week of the battles. I am glad to know I am serving my country with some degree of usefulness in this, her hour of trial."[66]

Supply officers shouldered increased responsibility on the occasions when the army moved north. They faced dangerously extended lines of communication and supply as well as more immediate concerns, including how to impress supplies from hostile civilians and still keep the army adequately fed. During the Maryland Campaign, Major Alexander B. Garland, commissary for his cousin Samuel Garland's brigade, asked General Lee for permission to escort Garland's corpse home after the Battle of South Mountain. Lee "positively refused, stating that we were there just on the eve of one of the grandest battles of the war, and he would not consent to see any quartermaster or commissary absent from his post at that time."[67]

Congress directed more attention toward quartermasters and commissaries than toward any other branch of the staff service. One especially important piece of legislation in April 1863 altered the army's staff structure by dropping officers rather than adding them. C. C. Clay, a prominent senator from Alabama, pushed through a bill that abolished regimental commissaries, and President Davis signed it into law on April 21. No doubt many factors led to the reduction, including the smaller size of most midwar regiments, the desire to centralize supply gathering and transportation in the interests of efficiency, and the pressing need for able-bodied men in the ranks. Several hundred men who had been captains one day were judged "supernumerary" the next and dropped from the army. The act abolishing those positions affected the brigade staffs as well. Although the less efficient regimental officers were allowed to go home or enlist, many of the more able men were snapped up by larger organizations and became assistants to brigade and division commissary officers. In the end, the legislation redistributed the weight of the subsistence department in the army, making it heavier at the top.[68]

Nearly the same situation arose in the quartermaster's department in the middle of 1864. Congress passed legislation in June that virtually eliminated the position of regimental quartermaster. It took some time for the authorities to decide the fate of the jobless officers, although most men rightly suspected that they would land in similar positions elsewhere in the army. "Quarter Masters are still on the baiter hooks of suspense," wrote one of the victims on August 27. "I hear that the assignments will probably be made next week, but they have been delayed so long I shall be agreeably disappointed if it is done so early." The official word came on

September 15. Hundreds of the affected quartermasters found new jobs, often at corps or divisional headquarters, managing trains or gathering forage from scattered outposts. Much like the reshuffling of the commissaries in 1863, this overhaul of the quartermasters situated more officers at the various headquarters while reducing the staff apparatus at the regimental level.[69]

Both branches of the Confederate Congress closely monitored the quartermaster's and subsistence departments. From the beginning, Congress suspected the worst about the men of the two departments. As early as August 1861, a congressional committee convened to "examine into the administration" of the supply branches and to debate what regulatory measures to enact. The question arose again the following August, when Congressman Henry S. Foote of Tennessee—a bitter and sarcastic critic of the general staff services—asked his peers to "investigate thoroughly" the operating procedures of both departments. His colleague Henry C. Burnett of Kentucky spoke up to complain that "he had never yet been able to find out what were the duties of a Brigade Quartermaster." The House of Representatives in February 1863 resolved to investigate whether officers in the two departments had been illegally obtaining supplies for themselves at government prices. Two months later, the House proposed a bill "to facilitate the detection of frauds in the Commissary and Quartermaster's Departments." Although the measure failed to win approval in the Senate, that body did agree to levy heavy penalties against fraud wherever found. When the House debated whether or not to allow President Davis to appoint additional quartermasters and commissaries in May 1864, Congressman Foote erupted. He called the supply officers "a set of jackanapes" and "gobbling sons of plunder, robbers and scoundrels." His vituperation had no effect on the legislation, but surely it added to the poor public reputation of staff officers in the two branches.

That scorn became even more apparent late in the war when Congress felt compelled to discuss options for policing the two departments. Undeterred by the obvious inability of a legislative body to enact a law that could account for millions of scattered documents, the congressmen pondered the efficacy of a plan that would force every officer in the two departments to list his assets, property, and debts. No one could even resign until having complied with the edict. One critic wondered how forcing an officer to state, under oath, "the price he had to pay for cigars" and "what the barber's bill was" would help to eradicate graft. Why would a quartermaster willing to embezzle government funds blanch at lying about his own small purchases? This invasive late-war bill died somewhere along the way, but it further illustrates the degree of distrust the Confederate nation seems to have held toward the supply branches of the army.[70]

Finally, early in 1865, Congress debated a bill designed to abolish entirely all purchasing officers in both departments — that is, men who bought and forwarded supplies at a specific post rather than serving with the army in the field. The plan got through Congress, to the delight of observant Richmond war clerk John B. Jones, who predicted that it would "make a great fluttering, but the Richmond rascals will probably escape." The "Richmond rascals" were supply officers based in the city, and they did indeed "escape" when Davis vetoed the bill. The Senate wound up two votes short of the number necessary to override the president, and the bill died in March.[71]

This intermittent official meddling did not extend to the other departments of the Confederate war machine. No one proposed auditing the books of ordnance officers or examining the contracts negotiated by the Engineer Bureau. Because the subsistence and quartermaster's departments dealt with large sums of money and precious supplies, their conduct earned greater scrutiny. Negative public opinion and unfounded gossip proved even more harmful to the reputations of the officers working in those bureaus.

Many soldiers in the army took a dim view of the character and bravery of supply officers, and that attitude probably fostered the ill will of the public and politicians of the Confederacy. The derisive term "bombproof officers," frequently seen in contemporaneous sources, referred to men whose duties or inclinations kept them away from harm. In nearly every identifiable case, the detractor directed that scornful epithet toward quartermasters or commissaries. Confederate soldiers sometimes referred to shells from long-range Federal artillery as "Commissary Hunters" because they often landed in the rear. The origin of that widespread contempt is a matter that deserves further study, but undoubtedly the daily functions of the staff officers in those two departments set them up for controversy and disparagement. Nothing jangles a soldier's nerves more than inefficiency on payday or inadequate food.

In time, perhaps by word of mouth, Confederate quartermasters and commissaries across the South fell into disrepute because of a few examples of malfeasance. One inoffensive clerk employed in his brigade's quartermaster office lamented that not only were his superiors unpopular, but even "their attaches are subjects of universal disrespect." A line officer who contemplated transferring into the quartermaster's department bridled at the notion of taking a post "which is open to countless grave charges and to insinuations and innuendoes that make a true man's blood tingle in his veins." An angry correspondent in the *Richmond Sentinel* suggested in October 1864 that a typical commissary officer "knows nothing about the suffering of the brave and gallant defenders of our country. I think all such able-bodied men in the 'safety department' should be compelled to go into the ranks, and let disabled soldiers take their places." In his memoirs, General Johnson Hagood distinguished between the supply officers in the field and those on the general staff. The latters' "duties never led them into the field, and [they] were too often corrupt speculators upon the necessities of their suffering country." Their colleagues in the field, Hagood believed, had "as much high tone and devotion to the cause . . . as among any other class of officers in the service."[72]

Despite the many dark hints about fiscal impropriety, a close study of the numerous quartermasters and commissaries profiled in this book reveals no more than a handful of such cases. One of the most blatant examples is Captain Thomas S. Knox, a young man from Fredericksburg, Virginia, on commissary duty at Jackson Hospital in Richmond. Knox fled to enemy lines in September 1864, having embezzled some of the funds under his control. His case, singular as it was, doubtless reenforced the widespread prejudices against the supply branches of the staff service. War Department clerk John B. Jones, who was in a position to know such things, noted with horror that in December 1863 there were fifty-one commissioned officers in the quartermaster's department in Richmond. Jones clearly thought that figure extravagant, and his dim view of noncombatant staff officers grew still bleaker.[73]

Rebuttals from aggrieved representatives of those departments generally assumed an air of injury. Some supply officers felt as if they were "free targets for the calumnies of every one who suffers a fit of spleen." "Such sweeping denunciations could the better be borne were it not the fact that they are almost universally based either upon lamentable and profound ignorance . . . or prompted by the malignant feelings of envy," charged one enraged officer. When prominent Richmond quartermaster William S. Wood was dropped for alleged improprieties, a disinterested observer noted that the "great clamor" against quartermasters had been harmful. Wood was "a sacrifice to public wrath and official purity."[74]

Although most soldiers viewed these rearward positions as a sinecure, some officers professed indifference to the safety that came with the job. Joseph E. Ficklin, a VMI-educated Virginian, claimed after the war that he had "enjoyed fighting more than feeding, and there was ever so much more excitement about it."

Ficklin's protests ring hollow when his record shows that he abandoned the saber in favor of the quill pen, transferring from the 4th Virginia Cavalry to the commissary department. He ended the war as a twenty-four-year-old major in that branch. Nonetheless, Ficklin probably reflected the feelings of a few of his fellow commissaries, some of whom wished for more active duty. Unlike most of his peers, Ficklin was young and vigorous. A typical commissary officer was disabled or too old for service in the field.[75]

Men filling the supply positions wore uniforms and held commissions, but they clearly served in the least warlike branch of the staff corps. Some of them looked like soldiers—and indeed many were veteran campaigners with honorable reputations—yet in reality their wartime duties closely resembled those of peacetime accountants, merchants, and freight managers.

Miscellany

Some staff officers bore the commission and rank of "cadet." Not every general had a cadet—in fact, most did not—and the rank was nothing more than a congressionally approved way to give very young men commissions as staff officers. In theory, the cadets would learn skills as apprentices on the staffs of generals. The experience put them on a career track and prepared them for service in the permanent Confederate army.

A few men designated military store keepers (MSK) appear in this roster. Those men generally superintended the various armories throughout the Confederacy. They were closely aligned with their brother ordnance officers and usually were men of sufficient age to be exempt from field service. The position only received congressional sanction in April 1863.[76]

The administrative personnel of the Mining and Nitre Bureau worked from offices in Richmond during the second half of the war and thus qualify for inclusion as staff officers. Their department dated from April 1863, and fewer than a dozen men managed the bureau from the capital city.[77]

CONCLUSION

Staff officers obviously influenced every aspect of the Army of Northern Virginia's daily operations. They fed the army, clothed it, conducted its marches, disciplined its soldiers, and wrestled with the paperwork that kept the mass of volunteers in line as a potent fighting force. After the Battle of Sharpsburg, Ham Chamberlayne wrote with great relish about his staff duties: "To gallop about over hill & dale, across log, ditch or fence, seeing this or that order carried out, this or that disorder made into order is great pleasure." Lieutenant Chamberlayne enjoyed freedom and responsibility, and he portrayed the more romantic side of his job. Not every staff officer leaped over logs and barked orders. In fact, most of them spent their time measuring rations of desiccated peas, trying to find ammunition that matched their units' weapons, or writing out hundreds of clothing receipts every week. Staff duty was both glamorous and pedestrian, occasionally challenging but mostly dull. It was a service of opportunity, in which young officers had ample prospects of gaining promotion and reputation, and it attracted almost every type of man. The pages of the roster tell the stories of those men, retrieving some of them from anonymity. In the process, students of the Army of Northern Virginia will be introduced, mostly for the first time, to several thousand officers who helped keep that army in the field for four years.

STATISTICS

The total number of staff officers profiled in this register is 2,284. The statistics compiled from the biographical sketches in this book shed light on the group of officers as a separate class of the army. Often numbers do not support the popular impression of a situation, but as shown in Table 1, they confirm the traditional view of Confederate staff officers as dewy-cheeked youngsters, at least in comparison to field officers. The latest edition of the standard work on field officers, R. K. Krick, *Lee's Colonels: A Biographical Register of the Field Officers of the Army of Northern Virginia* (Dayton, Ohio: Morningside, 1992), reports the average age of the majors, lieutenant colonels, and colonels of the line as 32–significantly higher than the average age of staff officers, which was 30. Furthermore, with ages known for more than 80 percent of the staff officers and nearly 90 percent of the field officers, it is safe to presume that the numbers are unlikely to change. It probably is fair to argue that the age for staff officers who served in the field with generals was considerably lower than the average age given above—perhaps in the upper twenties or even lower. The overall average age has been elevated by the inclusion of a large number of older post officers.

Table 2 shows the places of birth of staff officers in the Army of Northern Virginia. The majority of men were from Virginia, South Carolina, and Georgia.

The mortality statistics in Table 3, while proving little else, show that there was

TABLE 1.   AGES OF STAFF OFFICERS

Age	Number	Age	Number	Age	Number
15	1	31	89	47	8
16	3	32	55	48	7
17	14	33	57	49	12
18	34	34	66	50	7
19	47	35	62	51	6
20	73	36	55	52	5
21	83	37	35	53	1
22	104	38	57	54	6
23	121	39	34	55	2
24	114	40	40	56	2
25	122	41	33	57	1
26	117	42	27	58	2
27	94	43	31	59	1
28	112	44	16	60	1
29	100	45	16	61	1
30	93	46	15	62	1

Total sample, 1,986

Average age, 29.55

Note: Ages are calculated from the date at which each man first assumed staff duties with the Army of Northern Virginia or in Virginia.

no period in which staff officers died at a higher rate. A few of the stories behind these numbers deserve mention. Philip N. Page died in 1941, while the world was at war for a second time, after a lifetime of self-imposed exile in South America. The Virginia he left in 1865 had changed significantly by 1941. Feisty Samuel A. Ashe threatened the century mark and probably achieved a greater age than any other staff officer when he died two weeks short of his ninety-ninth birthday in 1938. Modern Confederate historians and speakers would do well to remember the case of Elisha Holmes Boyd, a hard-fighting Virginia staff officer. He died in 1910 while giving a speech to the United Daughters of the Confederacy on R. E. Lee's birthday.

Not all of the deaths during the war occurred while the soldiers were serving as staff officers in Virginia, but a sizable number did. In addition to 18 deaths by

TABLE 2. PLACES OF BIRTH OF STAFF OFFICERS

Alabama	49	Louisiana	27	South Carolina	166
Arkansas	1	Maryland	75	Tennessee	43
Florida	9	Mississippi	39	Texas	3
Georgia	127	Missouri	7	Virginia	768
Kentucky	35	North Carolina	116		

Total sample, 1,615

Born in the North, 101

Born outside the United States, 50 (33 in Britain)

disease, the Army of Northern Virginia lost 101 staff officers killed or mortally wounded. The latter total highlights the primary difference between staff officers and field officers. Only 4.4 percent of the staff men fell on the battlefield, while a whopping 21.7 percent of the field officers suffered that fate. Exposure at the front also taxed the health of field officers, a much higher number dying of disease than among the staff officers.

Prewar occupation statistics are available for 1,149 men—just over half of the staff officers in this study. Hundreds of others for whom no occupation is given certainly were students at the time. In Table 4, multiple occupations have been tabulated in cases where an officer pursued more than one line of work, so the sum is higher than 1,149. Although some may argue that this diminishes the usefulness of the data, it helps to display the breadth of the antebellum experiences of these officers. It also demonstrates how many men were associated before the war with business, commerce, engineering, military pursuits, and other occupations that stood them in good stead in the first half of the 1860s.

These calculations show that the typical staff officer came from a white-collar profession. Only one man had made his living as a general laborer, and for every miner and logger, there were more than two dozen lawyers. Comparing these statistics to those for field officers reveals some interesting differences. Many more field officers had been involved in antebellum politics than staff officers (9.3% to 6%). This undoubtedly reflects the importance of local influence in the process of raising and commanding Civil War regiments. Some 8.7 percent of the staff officers had clerking experience, while only 1.5 percent of the field officers could say the same. About 11 percent of the staffers were educators, in contrast to only 5.2

TABLE 3.   YEARS OF DEATH OF STAFF OFFICERS

Year	Number	Year	Number	Year	Number
1861	9	1887	23	1912	19
1862	49	1888	24	1913	32
1863	37	1889	34	1914	28
1864	62	1890	33	1915	25
1865	26	1891	32	1916	27
1866	14	1892	28	1917	19
1867	18	1893	31	1918	23
1868	19	1894	25	1919	16
1869	13	1895	42	1920	16
1870	14	1896	40	1921	19
1871	17	1897	25	1922	16
1872	23	1898	42	1923	16
1873	20	1899	42	1924	9
1874	16	1900	45	1925	7
1875	15	1901	37	1926	9
1876	20	1902	43	1927	3
1877	21	1903	40	1928	1
1878	27	1904	41	1929	3
1879	22	1905	32	1930	3
1880	12	1906	25	1931	3
1881	22	1907	43	1932	1
1882	22	1908	41	1934	1
1883	20	1909	24	1937	1
1884	29	1910	37	1938	1
1885	18	1911	25	1941	1
1886	28				

Total sample, 1,916

percent of the line officers. Lawyers dominated both branches, but nearly twice as many staff officers as field officers practiced law before the war (24.9% to 13.6%).

Postwar occupations are known for 1,221 of the approximately 2,100 staff officers who survived the war. A comparison of the statistics in Table 5 with those in Table 4 shows a significant shift in the professional directions followed by staff officers. Men who had been soldiers, clerks, and engineers in the 1850s apparently

TABLE 4.   PREWAR OCCUPATIONS OF STAFF OFFICERS

Occupation	Number	Occupation	Number
Agent	4	Judge	8
Agriculturalist	2	Laborer	1
Architect	2	Lawman	17
Artist	1	Lawyer	286
Banker	14	Logger	5
Bartender	2	Machinst	3
Bookkeeper	10	Mason	2
Bookseller	1	Merchant	209
Broker	5	Miller	2
Butcher	1	Miner	4
Carpenter	4	Newspaperman	24
Carriage maker	3	Physician	26
Cattleman	2	Plasterer	1
Civil servant	4	Politician	69
Clerk	101	Postman	4
Comptroller	1	Preacher	9
Customs agent	3	Printer	2
Dentist	3	Publisher	2
Drayman	1	Railroader	11
Druggist	7	Revenue Service	1
Educator	125	Saddler	1
Engineer	87	Sailor	21
Factor	3	Salesman	1
Farmer	195	Shoemaker	1
Flour inspector	1	Silversmith	1
Gentleman	6	Soldier	88
Glass maker	1	Speculator	1
Gunsmith	3	Steamboater	3
Horse breeder	1	Stone cutter	1
Hotel keeper	5	Surveyor	7
Indian agent	1	Tobacconist	4
Insuranceman	1	Trader	1
Ironworker	3	Warehouseman	1

Total sample, 1,149

Note: Multiple occupations were listed for some staff officers.

TABLE 5. POSTWAR OCCUPATIONS OF STAFF OFFICERS

Occupation	Number	Occupation	Number
Agent	15	Jeweler	3
Architect	7	Judge	56
Artist	1	Lawman	15
Astronomer	1	Lawyer	285
Auctioneer	1	Librarian	2
Banker	40	Lumberman	7
Bookkeeper	32	Machinist	2
Broker	10	Mason	2
Cabinet maker	1	Merchant	214
Carriage maker	2	Miller	8
Cashier	5	Miner	5
Cattleman	4	Newspaperman	59
Chemist	2	Notary public	1
Civil servant	4	Nurseryman	1
Clerk	59	Painter	1
College president	8	Physician	31
Comptroller	4	Politician	180
Contractor	5	Postman	13
Conveyancer	2	Preacher	32
Dentist	4	Publisher	1
Developer	1	Railroadman	51
Druggist	5	Realtor	16
Educator	134	Saddler	1
Engineer	67	Salesman	9
Factor	5	Secretary	1
Farmer	276	Soldier	7
Fisherman	1	Stable keeper	1
Fruit grower	2	Street inspector	1
Gentleman	2	Surveyor	11
Geologist	1	Tax collector	5
Hotel keeper	6	Tinner	1
Indian agent	1	Tobacconist	17
Insuranceman	46	Tradesman	1
Ironworker	2	Viticulturalist	1

Total sample, 1,221

Note: Multiple occupations were listed for some staff officers.

chose different fields after the war. Large increases are evident in farming, banking, journalism, and preaching. Many others turned their attention to the expanding railroad industry. Twice as many men entered the world of politics. Most of these trends are not apparent in the available figures for field officers.

The postwar occupation numbers, like those from before the war, reflect every occupation of every officer. Once again, the sum of the various occupations is considerably higher than 1,220, many staff officers holding down three or four different jobs in the volatile postwar South.

Table 6 reveals the degree to which staff officers received prewar education. In addition to the schools listed, at least 50 others had only one known enrollee who became a staff officer. More than 950 future staff men attended colleges or military academies before the war. This represents about 42 percent of the men in this book, and the percentage will only climb as more biographical details surface on the other 1,330 men.

Not many Army of Northern Virginia staff officers brought military credentials to their positions—at least in comparison to line officers. Barely 300 of the army's several thousand staff officers could point to either a military education or some sort of wartime experience in their past. The majority had attended one of the country's military schools, usually the Virginia Military Institute or West Point. Only 51 are known to have served in the Mexican War, and fewer than 100 were professional soldiers at any time before 1861. Five had served in foreign armies, three were veteran Filibusterers from the failed expedition to Nicaragua, and a handful of others were veterans of the Seminole Wars, the Black Hawk War, the Texas Revolution, the Crimean War, and assorted other conflicts. George C. Hutter was the only staff officer who is known to have served in the War of 1812.

The staff officers who were professional soldiers before the war came from all branches of the antebellum U.S. Army. At least half were infantrymen, but quite a few served in the navy, artillery, and cavalry. It is surprising to find that only one man is known to have been an Old Army engineer, while just ten men had identifiable prewar experience as staff officers.

Enough information is available on the postwar movements of the survivors of the army's staff corps to draw some modest conclusions about how those men dealt with their altered circumstances. Most of them apparently remained in the South rather than abandon that impoverished section for greener fields. Only 66 former staff officers are known to have established residences in the North, while another 31 moved to the expanding western part of the country. At least 25 emi-

TABLE 6.   PREWAR EDUCATION OF STAFF OFFICERS

School	Number	School	Number
Baltimore City College	2	Norfolk Military Academy	3
Bethany	4	North Carolina Military	
Brown	2	Academy	3
Centenary	3	Oglethorpe	3
Centre College	2	Princeton	20
College of Charleston	10	Randolph Macon	8
Columbia	3	Richmond College	4
Columbian College	9	St. James College	4
Cumberland	4	South Carolina College	47
Davidson	5	South Carolina Military	
Dickinson	4	Academy	23
Emory	11	Stewart College	2
Emory & Henry	5	Troy Polytechnical Institute	2
European schools	8	Union Theological Seminary	2
Franklin & Marshall	2	U.S. Military Academy	93
Furman	5	U.S. Naval Academy	5
Georgetown	36	University of Alabama	16
Georgia Military Institute	14	University of Georgia	34
Hampden-Sidney	32	University of Louisiana	2
Hampton Military Academy	6	University of Mississippi	11
Harvard	30	University of Nashville	3
Hillsboro Military Academy	3	University of North Carolina	62
Hobart College	3	University of Pennsylvania	13
Howard College	2	University of Virginia	333
Jefferson College	2	Virginia Military Institute	144
Jefferson Medical College	5	Wake Forest	8
Kentucky Military Institute	5	Washington College, Mo.	3
Medical College of Virginia	2	Washington College, Va.	44
Medical School of South		William & Mary	42
Carolina	3	Williams College	2
Mercer	3	Yale	18
Mt. St. Mary's	2		

Total sample, 951

Note: Multiple places of education were listed for some staff officers.

TABLE 7.   NEPOTISM BY GENERAL

General	Number	General	Number
Alexander, Edward P.	1	Johnson, Edward	1
Anderson, Richard H.	2	Jones, John M.	1
Archer, James J.	2	Jones, John R.	1
Armistead, Lewis A.	2	Kemper, James L.	1
Barksdale, William	1	Lane, James H.	2
Barringer, Rufus	1	Law, Evander M.	1
Beale, R. L. T.	1	Lawton, Alexander R.	3
Beauregard, P. G. T.	1	Lee, Fitzhugh	1
Bonham, Milledge L.	3	Lee, William H. F.	2
Bratton, John	1	Lewis, William G.	1
Breckinridge, John C.	1	McGowan, Samuel	1
Butler, Matthew C.	1	McLaws, Lafayette	2
Chambliss, John R.	1	Magruder, John B.	1
Cobb, Howell	6	Pendleton, William N.	1
Cocke, Philip St. George	1	Perry, Edward A.	1
Colquitt, Alfred H.	2	Pickett, George E.	2
Cox, William R.	1	Posey, Carnot	2
Drayton, Thomas L.	1	Rains, Gabriel J.	1
Early, Jubal A.	3	Randolph, George W.	2
Ewell, Richard S.	2	Rodes, Robert E.	2
Featherston, Winfield S.	1	Rosser, Thomas L.	1
Field, Charles W.	5	Scales, Alfred M.	1
Finegan, Joseph	1	Semmes, Paul J.	1
Garland, Samuel	2	Simms, James P.	1
Gary, Martin W.	1	Smith, Gustavus W.	1
Gilmer, Jeremy F.	1	Smith, William	2
Gordon, John B.	1	Stafford, Leroy A.	1
Hampton, Wade	3	Starke, William E.	1
Harris, Nathaniel H.	1	Steuart, George H.	1
Heth, Henry	3	Stuart, J. E. B.	9
Hill, A. P.	5	Taliaferro, William B.	3
Hill, D. H.	1	Taylor, Richard	1
Holmes, Theophilus H.	1	Toombs, Robert A.	1
Imboden, John D.	1	Winder, Charles S.	1
Jackson, Henry R.	1	Winder, John H.	1
Jackson, Thomas J.	3	Wise, Henry A.	5
Jenkins, Albert G.	1	Wright, Ambrose R.	3
Johnson, Bradley T.	1	Young, Pierce M. B.	1

Total number of cases, 132

grated to other countries. Thus scarcely more than 100 men of this sample left the South for substantial periods, meaning that more than 90 percent of the army's surviving staff officers attempted to rebuild their lives within the former boundaries of the mangled Confederacy.

The statistics assembled from this book's biographical sketches provide a glimpse of the nepotism that existed in every segment of the army. Historians always have known that many generals packed their staffs with relatives and friends. General Lee and others recognized that nepotism loomed as one of the army's chief organizational problems, yet neither Congress nor Lee ever managed to implement effective measures to quash the practice. Table 7 shows the number of relatives each Army of Northern Virginia general had on his staff during his period of service with that army. Brothers and brothers-in-law were the two most common relatives to benefit from nepotism at about 30 cases each, with cousins, nephews, and sons grouped together at 15–20 examples each. This is the first comprehensive attempt to document the degree to which nepotism spread through the army at its highest levels. As with many other numbers in this portion of the book, the total certainly is far short of reality. Previously unrecognized family connections between generals and members of their staffs undoubtedly will surface in the coming years.

USING THE ROSTER

Historians and researchers using this roster should bear in mind several peculiarities. The definition of a staff officer perhaps is more subjective than that of any other category of men in a Civil War army. Most wartime writers considered surgeons to be staff officers, particularly physicians who practiced in the higher echelons of the army. No surgeons are profiled in this book because I do not consider them staff officers in the traditional sense. Likewise tax collectors, enrolling officers, and drillmasters are omitted, despite being commissioned officers who do not fall conveniently into any other group. I have omitted most provost marshals from the roster because they held other assignments simultaneously. A typical staff had no authority for a full-time provost marshal, and most generals never employed anyone in that capacity. Contract engineers swarmed all over wartime Virginia, yet most are not in this roster because they were civilians rather than soldiers. Postwar obituaries and biographical sketches frequently confuse enlisted men or noncommissioned officers who served as couriers with commissioned officers who occupied staff positions. Riding a horse beside a general did not automatically qualify someone as a member of the staff; hundreds of bogus claimants have been weeded out of this list for that reason.

Another decision made in the early days of the research for this book was to include men who served as temporary staff officers, without commissions. Large numbers of officers suddenly found themselves out of the army in April 1862, victims of the spring reorganization. Many of those men found places as volunteer staff officers during the Peninsula Campaign and then faded out of sight. Although they never held official rank and were not paid for their duties, they were considered part of a general's staff and thus are included in this roster.

Another important decision concerns temporary staff officers who already had other duties. Stonewall Jackson's old division after the Battle of Sharpsburg provides a good example. After lurching back into Virginia with diminished numbers and few officers, the brigades in that division nonetheless retained their general organization. Colonels often commanded brigades, and some staff positions went unoccupied. While the army reconfigured itself, junior officers frequently filled in. In some instances, infantry lieutenants served a month or two as acting adjutants for brigades commanded by virtually unknown colonels. William H. Thomas, who has a short paragraph in this roster, is a good example of someone who had that fleeting legitimacy. Men of his sort were not career staff officers, nor did they occupy their positions for long, but thoroughness demands their inclusion.

Some officers acted as staff men without abandoning their regular duties elsewhere in the army. Field or line officers who occasionally volunteered for a day of staff duty were nothing more than moonlighters taking an unofficial day off from their normal work. These officers are not included in the roster. Only officers filling vacant posts at the expense of their regular assignments have been listed.

There is no formula for identifying the physical boundaries of the study area within Virginia. Samuel Jones's operations in southwestern Virginia, for instance, are deemed so far afield as to disqualify his staff from consideration as main-theater officers. They have been relegated to Appendix 1. The men who were with General Jones during his mercifully brief stint around Manassas in the late summer of 1861 are a minor exception. The staffs of Generals Robert S. Garnett and Samuel R. Anderson, both of whom saw all their action in what now is West Virginia, are deemed legitimate. This system admittedly is somewhat artificial, but it has been implemented consistently.

The same manufactured and undefinable boundaries determined which post officers should be excluded. Men at the supply hub in Dublin Depot, Virginia, were too far away to have any direct bearing on the Army of Northern Virginia. But officers at posts in eastern Virginia, the Shenandoah Valley, or downtown Richmond have been included in the roster.

There are no biographical sketches of staff officers who went on to obtain general's rank. Victor J. B. Girardey spent much of the war as a staffer and only enjoyed a few weeks as a general before being killed. His name appears in Appendix 2. Anyone searching for a summary of his life and career — or that of any other staffer turned general — should consult one of the standard biographical works on Confederate generals.

Some generals served long stints at the regimental level in Virginia before receiving their promotion and promptly leaving for another theater. Students of the Army of Northern Virginia will recognize Laurence S. Baker and James Cantey as two cases of that sort. Both commanded troops in Virginia, but once they became generals, they went elsewhere and the staffs they assembled thus belong in Appendix 1.

James Longstreet's First Corps affords another anomaly. Two of its divisions spent half a year in eastern Tennessee. In a few cases, staff officers joined that corps while it was loaned out to the Army of Tennessee, then left it before Longstreet's men returned to Virginia. Those staff officers are included in the roster because the visit of the First Corps to Tennessee was only a hiccup in an otherwise long-term association with Lee's army. Conversely, staff officers attached to brigades that came to Virginia later in the war are not included if the officers were gone by the time of the transfer. Archibald Gracie's Alabama brigade and Thomas L. Clingman's North Carolina brigade, among others, joined the Army of Northern Virginia for the first time in 1864. All staff officers with those brigades who had come and gone by that point will be found in Appendix 1 rather than in the roster.

An ideal paragraph on a staff officer includes his full name, exact dates and places of birth and death, education, occupations, burial information, and a summary of his wartime career. The Compiled Service Records at the National Archives have provided most of the military information found in these sketches. For promotions, the date at which the new rank took effect is used.

Notes

1. The standard reference works on the various types of Confederate officers are William C. Davis, ed., *The Confederate General*, 6 vols. (Harrisburg, Penn.: National Historical Society,

1991); Bruce S. Allardice, *More Generals in Gray* (Baton Rouge: Louisiana State University Press, 1995); and Robert K. Krick, *Lee's Colonels: A Biographical Register of the Field Officers of the Army of Northern Virginia*, 4th ed., rev. (Dayton, Ohio: Morningside, 1992). The most authoritative reference on Confederate staff officers to date is Marcus J. Wright, comp., *List of Staff Officers of the Confederate States Army* (Washington, D.C.: Government Printing Office, 1891). Wright's list is useful and fairly comprehensive, but it contains no biographical information. It also is an incredibly rare book. Recent scholarship has devoted more attention to the Army of Northern Virginia's staff officers than ever before, but no definitive narrative history of that body has yet appeared. J. Boone Bartholomees's book, *Buff Facings and Gilt Buttons: Staff and Headquarters Operations in the Army of Northern Virginia, 1861–1865* (Columbia: University of South Carolina Press, 1998), is a useful introduction to the subject but suffers from inadequate research and insufficient analysis. More recently, R. Steven Jones's *The Right Hand of Command: Use and Disuse of Personal Staffs in the Civil War* (Mechanicsburg, Penn.: Stackpole, 2000) addresses only R. E. Lee's staff and his handling of it.

2. William B. Skelton, *An American Profession of Arms: The Army Officer Corps, 1784–1861* (Lawrence: University Press of Kansas, 1992), 135, 221–37; Prince François F. P. L. M. de Joinville, *The Army of the Potomac: Its Organization, Its Commander, and Its Campaign* (New York: Anson D. F. Randolph, 1862), 52. Although the French prince allied himself with the Federal army early in the war, his remarks on the antebellum staff situation judged both armies: "The American system of 'every man for himself,' individually applied by the officers and soldiers of each corps to one another, is also applied by the corps themselves to their reciprocal relations. There is no special branch of the service whose duty it is to regulate, centralize and direct the movements of the army."

3. *Journal of the Congress of the Confederate States of America, 1861–1865*, 7 vols. (Washington, D.C.: Government Printing Office, 1904–5), 1:81, 88. Bartow later adjusted his own bill to ensure that all dates of commission ranked from March 1861, even for men resigning from the U.S. Army as late as September 1861. Thus nearly everyone's relative rank in the regular Confederate army depended on their status in the Old Army. This applied to all officers, of course, not just staff men.

4. T. Harry Williams, *Americans at War* (Baton Rouge: Louisiana State University Press, 1960), 30–31, 102–3, summarizes the earliest American army uses and definition of "general staff." Bartholomees argues for an entirely different division of staff officers into general and personal staffs in *Buff Facings and Gilt Buttons*.

5. J. William Jones et al., eds., *Southern Historical Society Papers*, 52 vols. (Richmond, Va.: Southern Historical Society, 1876–1959), 47:104–5 (hereafter cited as *SHSP*); *Journal of the Congress*, 3:221–22, 5:532–34, 6:430–31. These citations are for congressional debates pertaining to October 1862 and March 1863 bills. The debates addressed specific features of the plans to create a general staff and contain lists of how many staff officers each commander could have, from army headquarters down to brigade commanders, with their ranks and duties. Both bills admonished that the staff officers, except for ADCs, were to "form a part and remain attached to the several organizations to which they are assigned or appointed." These plans foundered but

were resuscitated later in the war, with some significant changes. Despite the best intentions of Congress, the army frequently ignored or sidestepped some of the staff rules. When General Thomas L. Rosser assumed command of Fitzhugh Lee's old division in December 1864, he found himself "*entirely* without a staff. An aid[e] is all I have." His predecessor had taken the entire divisional staff with him when he moved upward, leaving the division barren of its general staff officers—in direct defiance of the intent of the general staff plan (Thomas L. Rosser letter, January 2, 1865, in Holmes Conrad file, Compiled Service Records of Confederate General and Staff Officers, M331, roll 61, National Archives, Washington, D.C. [hereafter cited as NA] [emphasis in original]). Rosser's pleas merit little sympathy. When he took over William E. Jones's brigade early in 1864, he had attempted to clean out the staff that was attached to it in favor of his own (J. E. B. Stuart to "My dear Rosser," February 10, 1864, in Adele H. Mitchell, ed., *The Letters of General J. E. B. Stuart* [n.p.: Stuart-Mosby Historical Society, 1990], 372–73).

6. U.S. War Department, *The War of the Rebellion: A Compilation of the Official Records of the Union and Confederate Armies*, 127 vols., index, and atlas (Washington, D.C.: Government Printing Office, 1880–1901), ser. 4, 2:447–48, ser. 1, 25(2):786–87 (hereafter cited as *OR*). The latter reference offers a clear example of Lee's vision for a general staff. He directed that orders promulgated by his own general staff officers, delivered to their subordinates in the various commands of the army, be considered as coming from Lee himself. A. P. Hill contested the matter, arguing that such orders should be filtered down through the corps commanders. Lee dissented and of course won his point and a victory for the principles of general staff management.

7. *Journal of the Congress*, 6:509, 3:667, 760; *SHSP*, 50:379, 420–21. A comparison between Lee's army and the Federal Army of the Potomac is very far afield from the purposes of this book, but it is interesting to read George B. McClellan's view of the American staff system, written in 1887 but sounding like Lee in 1863: "One of the greatest defects in our military system is the lack of a thoroughly instructed STAFF CORPS, from which should be furnished chief of staff of armies, army corps and divisions, adjutant-general, and aides-de-camp" (George B. McClellan, *McClellan's Own Story* [New York: Charles L. Webster & Company, 1887], 120–21).

8. Mary Conner Moffett, ed., *Letters of General James Conner, C.S.A.* (Columbia, S.C.: Presses of the R. L. Bryan Company, 1950), 114–15. Conner offers a comical account of this Ewell episode.

9. *Journal of the Congress*, 4:105–9. Davis's long explanation of his thoughts on a general staff is an outstanding summary of the subject and well worth reading. It was printed as a separate official document as well, under the title *President's Message*. See T. Michael Parrish and Robert M. Willingham, Jr., *Confederate Imprints: A Bibliography of Southern Publications from Secession to Surrender* (Austin, Tex.: Jenkins Publishing Company, n.d.), 124, entry 931.

10. *Journal of the Congress*, 4:9, 12, 246, 708.

11. Robert Debs Heinl, Jr., *Dictionary of Military and Naval Quotations* (Annapolis, Md.: U.S. Naval Institute, 1966), 1–2. Ill feeling between line and staff officers sometimes sprang up because of disputes over matters of authority and control. Many officers worked in both positions at different times during the war—in fact, the majority of adjutants, inspectors, aides, and ordnance officers came from line positions. An 1862 decree from the War Department attempted to regulate that cross-pollination by ruling that a general staff officer could not hold a higher

line rank in the provisional army at the same time (*Regulations for the Army of the Confederate States, Authorized Edition, 1862* [Richmond, Va.: West & Johnston, 1862], 75). As Henry D. McDaniel (himself a line/staff man) observed in October 1862, "Everybody in the Line wishes positions on the Staff" (Henry D. McDaniel, *With Unabated Trust: Major Henry McDaniel's Love Letters from Confederate Battlefields as Treasured in Hester McDaniel's Bonnet Box*, ed. Anita B. Sams [Monroe: Historical Society of Walton County, Georgia, 1977], 109). One example of the prickliness between staff officers and line officers is in Susan C. Blackford, *Memoirs of Life in and out of the Army in Virginia*, 2 vols. (Lynchburg, Va.: J. P. Bell Company, 1894), 1:188, in which Captain Charles M. Blackford of the 2nd Virginia Cavalry expressed amazement at being treated cordially by R. E. Lee's staff, "rather an unusual thing in staff to line officers of subordinate rank."

12. John Hampden Chamberlayne, *Ham Chamberlayne–Virginian: Letters and Papers of an Artillery Officer in the War for Southern Independence*, ed. C. G. Chamberlayne (Richmond, Va.: Dietz, 1932), 31.

13. Archer Jones, *Civil War Command and Strategy: The Process of Victory and Defeat* (New York: Free Press, 1992), 70; G. F. R. Henderson, *The Science of War* (London: Longmans, Green, 1905), 218–19; Douglas Southall Freeman, *R. E. Lee: A Biography*, 4 vols. (New York: Charles Scribner's Sons, 1934–35), 2:233–34.

14. An Old Comrade [Alexander M. Garber, Jr.], *"Stonewall Jackson's Way": A Sketch of the Life and Services of Maj. John A. Harman* (Staunton, Va.: Spectator Job Print, 1876), 25; Edward Porter Alexander, *Fighting for the Confederacy: The Personal Recollections of General Edward Porter Alexander*, ed. Gary W. Gallagher (Chapel Hill: University of North Carolina Press, 1989), 236, 273 (emphasis in original).

15. *Journal of the Congress*, 3:486. In October 1862, the Senate authorized the appointment of chiefs of staff by certain commanders. This concession made no practical difference in the field. An excellent article on the subject, albeit for the wrong army, is June I. Gow, "Chiefs of Staff in the Army of Tennessee under Braxton Bragg," *Tennessee Historical Quarterly* 27, no. 4 (Winter 1968): 341–60. A provision for a chief of staff of an army, with the rank of brigadier general, was a standard part of every staff bill proposed between October 1862 and 1865.

16. G. Moxley Sorrel, *Recollections of a Confederate Staff Officer* (New York: Neale Publishing Company, 1905), 201; *OR*, ser. 1, 30(2):506; Margaretta Barton Colt, ed., *Defend the Valley: A Shenandoah Family in the Civil War* (New York: Orion, 1994), 373.

17. Alexander S. Pendleton to Kate Corbin, June 18, 1863, William Nelson Pendleton Papers, Southern Historical Collection, University of North Carolina, Chapel Hill, N.C. (hereafter cited as SHC/UNC); R. Lockwood Tower, ed., *Lee's Adjutant: The Wartime Letters of Colonel Walter Herron Taylor* (Columbia: University of South Carolina Press, 1995); Willis F. Jones letter, August 29, 1864, Jones Family Papers, Filson Club Historical Society, Louisville, Ky.; Alexander F. Fleet letter, December 1863, in Betsy Fleet and John D. P. Fuller, eds., *Green Mount: A Virginia Plantation Family during the Civil War* (Lexington: University of Kentucky Press, 1962), 288.

18. Samuel Cooper endorsement on a letter of recommendation for T. J. Peyton, July 20, 1864, in Peyton's file, Compiled Service Records of Confederate General and Staff Officers, M331, roll 197, NA.

19. G. W. Bagby letter, in *Mobile Register and Advertiser*, September 25, 1864. Bagby's letter is dated September 15, 1864. Prominent Army of Northern Virginia staff officers produced nearly a dozen influential books after the war. Some of the most famous examples are Sorrel, *Recollections of a Confederate Staff Officer*; Henry B. McClellan, *The Life and Campaigns of Major General J. E. B. Stuart* (Boston: Houghton Mifflin, 1885); and Walter H. Taylor, *Four Years with General Lee* (New York: Appleton, 1877).

20. *General Orders from Adjutant and Inspector-General's Office, Confederate States Army, from January, 1862, to December, 1863 (both inclusive)* (Columbia, S.C.: Evans & Cogswell, 1864), 66 (1862 General Orders #53); *Regulations for the Army . . . 1862*, 4; John Bratton letter, July 2, 1864, Bratton Papers, SHC/UNC. The numerous general orders issued by the AIGO during the course of a calendar year enjoyed separate printings, but for the purposes of clarity and reference, citations will be to the end-of-year collation, with the number of the general order given in parentheses.

21. William H. Fowler, *Guide for Claimants of Deceased Soldiers* (Richmond, Va.: George P. Evans, 1864), 25; Cadmus M. Wilcox to "Gus" [Augustus H. Garland?], May 3, 1864, RG 109, E 174, Legislative and Executive Papers, Miscellaneous Letters to Members of Congress, NA.

22. Robert H. Morrison, *Biography of Joseph Graham Morrison* (n.p., 1958), 6; R. E. Lee to "My Dear ——," April 25, 1861, in Clifford Dowdey and Louis H. Manarin, eds., *The Wartime Papers of R. E. Lee* (Boston: Little, Brown, 1961), 12; R. E. Rodes to F. H. Smith, July 15, 1862, Records of the Superintendent, Incoming Correspondence, 1862, Preston Library, Virginia Military Institute, Lexington, Va. (hereafter cited as VMI).

23. W. W. Blackford to Wyndham Robertson, January 10, 1863, quoted in Frank R. Reade, *In the Saddle with Stuart: The Story of Frank Smith Robertson of Jeb Stuart's Staff*, ed. Robert J. Trout (Gettysburg, Pa.: Thomas Publications, 1998), 20. Jefferson Davis perceptively wrote in 1864 that "the experience of this war has demonstrated that the most efficient commanders . . . have avoided the large retinue of personal staff." Large crowds of aides, in his view, "impede rather than improve the service" and "encourage the love of ostentation and feed a fondness for vain display, which should rather be discouraged than fostered" (*Journal of the Congress*, 4:108).

24. Asbury Coward, *The South Carolinians*, ed. Natalie J. Bond and Osmun L. Coward (New York: Vantage Press, 1968), 13; Kate Peddy letter, February 4, 1862, in George P. Cuttino, ed., *Saddle Bag and Spinning Wheel* (Macon, Ga.: Mercer University Press, 1981), 50; Murray F. Taylor memoir, Bound Volume 18, Fredericksburg and Spotsylvania National Military Park Library, Fredericksburg, Va. (hereafter cited as FSNMP).

25. Caroline E. Merrick, *Old Times in Dixie Land: A Southern Matron's Memories* (New York: Grafton Press, 1901), 30; Thomas G. Jones to Eugene C. Gordon, October 18, 1864, Jones Papers, Alabama Department of Archives and History, Montgomery, Ala.

26. *Regulations for the Army . . . 1862*, 366.

27. *General Orders . . . January, 1862, to December, 1863*, 97 (1863 General Orders #90). This same order is published in *OR*, ser. 4, 2:609–10. The AIGO's order defining an engineer's duties must not have enjoyed a close reading since the army's chief engineer felt obliged to reissue it as a circular, with slightly different language, in May 1864 (*OR*, ser. 1, 36[1]:944).

28. Readers interested in greater detail about engineer officers should consult the best source

to date on the subject: James L. Nichols, *Confederate Engineers* (Tuscaloosa, Ala.: Confederate Publishing, 1957).

29. *OR*, ser. 1, 1:796, 821, 5:953, 989, 1027. Judah P. Benjamin apparently goaded President Davis into securing the legislation that allowed the appointment of the first fifty engineers in the PACS. Until then (December 1861), there were twelve commissioned engineers in the Confederate army, all connected with the regular Confederate army rather than with the PACS.

30. *Journal of the Congress*, 5:182, 285; *OR*, ser. 1, 11(3):586. Even without congressional authority, some brigade commanders had engineers on their staffs. Usually they were volunteers or men who had received special permission to act in that capacity because of extenuating circumstances in the general's situation — perhaps an independent command or an instance where the divisional engineer was not available.

31. Jeremy F. Gilmer to wife, October 16, 1862, Gilmer Papers, SHC/UNC (emphasis in original). *Staff Officers in Gray* provides sufficient raw data for someone to calculate just how many Georgians the general managed to appoint after his tirade.

32. Reade, *In the Saddle with Stuart*, 22–24.

33. *Journal of the Congress*, 4:415, 600, 652.

34. *Regulations for the Army . . . 1862*, 49–50; *Journal of the Congress*, 4:106.

35. *OR*, ser. 1, 19:618–19.

36. Ibid., 719. Fitzgerald Ross, a European observer with the army at Gettysburg, found Chilton "riding about seeking whom he could devour in the shape of a depredator or illegal annexer of private property" (Fitzgerald Ross, *Cities and Camps of the Confederate States* [Champaign: University of Illinois Press, 1958], 49). Joseph L. Brent performed staff duty early in the war before becoming a general in the west. He lamented that Lee "was badly crippled by the personality of a chief of staff who necessarily ought to have possessed a judgment and skill, only inferior to that of the illustrious commander himself" (Joseph L. Brent, *Memoirs of the War between the States* [New Orleans: Fontana Printing Company, 1940], 204). Brent's one sentence on this subject covers nearly 15 lines and includes 158 words — surely a textbook case of ponderous prose.

37. *OR*, ser. 1, 25(2):815. Louis T. Wigfall, the bombastic senator from Texas, was one of the two most active men in Congress on behalf of the Army of Northern Virginia and its professional element. Wigfall repeatedly submitted bills to assist the army, most of which never left the floor of the Senate. In March 1863, he labored to increase the number of inspectors available to the army, and in March 1865, he introduced a bill for the organization of a separate Bureau of Inspection (*Journal of the Congress*, 3:120, 4:617, 627–28).

38. For evidence of official attention to inspectors and their duties in November 1863, see *OR*, ser. 4, 2:945, 965.

39. Walter Clark, ed., *Histories of the Several Regiments and Battalions from North Carolina in the Great War, 1861–'65*, 5 vols. (Raleigh, N.C.: E. M. Uzzell, 1901), 4:510–11. A fascinating armywide report prepared by Inspector Peyton in September 1864 is in *OR*, ser. 1, 42(2):1270–78. The Peyton report makes it clear that the army's chief inspector interested himself in discipline even down to the brigade level. A valuable body of inspection reports from the army survives

at the National Archives as "Inspection Reports and Related Records Received by the Inspection Branch of the Confederate Adjutant and Inspector General's Office," M935, 18 rolls, NA. A thorough yet complicated indexing system requires users of those records to exercise considerable patience.

40. *OR*, ser. 1, 42(2):1277. For 1864 circulars that provide excellent details on what the AIGO expected of its inspectors in the field, see *OR*, ser. 4, 3:297, 466–71.

41. *SHSP*, 18:413. For full biographical details on Harrison, Masters, and Costin, see their sketches in the roster of this book. Admittedly, Harrison and Costin attended military schools, but both abandoned arms as a profession well before the war.

42. Robert Tansill to Jefferson Davis, January 16, 1863, in Tansill's file, Compiled Service Records of Confederate General and Staff Officers, M331, roll 241, NA.

43. *Journal of the Congress*, 5:369–70.

44. *General Orders . . . January, 1862, to December, 1863*, 127–29 (1862 General Orders #93); *Journal of the Congress*, 2:452. See also ibid., 5:489, for some of the debate over particular language and *SHSP*, 47:17–22, for the full text of the bill. Jefferson Davis signed the law creating military courts on October 8, 1862.

45. Jack A. Bunch, *Military Justice in the Confederate States Armies* (Shippensburg, Pa.: White Mane, 2000), is a handy source for learning more on how Confederate courts operated. Bunch's subsequent companion volume, *Roster of the Courts-Martial in the Confederate States Armies* (Shippensburg, Pa.: White Mane, 2001), indexes thousands of trials.

46. *OR*, ser. 4, 2:1003–4.

47. Josiah Gorgas forged a seamless record as chief of the Ordnance Bureau for nearly the entire life of the Confederacy. The Pennsylvania native was one of the very few bureau chiefs to control his department for the duration of the war. The past fifty years have shed new light on his considerable contributions. See, for example, his biography, Frank E. Vandiver, *Ploughshares into Swords: Josiah Gorgas and Confederate Ordnance* (Austin: University of Texas Press, 1952), and his wartime journal, Josiah Gorgas, *The Journals of . . . 1857–1878*, ed. Sarah W. Wiggins (Tuscaloosa: University of Alabama Press, 1995).

48. Chamberlayne, *Ham Chamberlayne–Virginian*, 120; Seaton Gales, in *Our Living and Our Dead* (New Bern, N.C.), February 4, 1874.

49. *General Orders . . . January, 1862, to December, 1863*, 46 (unnumbered 1862 order), 215 (unnumbered 1863 directive, "Instructions to Ordnance Officers in the Field"). R. E. Lee, writing in October 1862, noted that D. H. Hill's division ordnance train had twenty-two wagons, which gives a good insight into the physical responsibility of a divisional OO (*OR*, ser. 1, 19:641).

50. William Allan, "Reminiscences of Field Ordnance Service with the Army of Northern Virginia, 1863–'65," *SHSP*, 13:139–40.

51. *General Orders . . . January, 1862, to December, 1863*, 28–29, 59 (1862 General Orders #24 and #46); McDaniel, *With Unabated Trust*, 96. The new lieutenants were not considered official members of the ordnance department, which was a regular army apparatus. The records usually were strict in making the distinction, and this accounts for the typical reference in an ordnance officer's service record to acting lieutenant OO. A lieutenancy in the PACS was not the

same thing as being a lieutenant oo in the permanent army. See *General Orders . . . January, 1862, to December, 1863*, 28 (1863 General Orders #33).

52. *Journal of the Congress*, 2:262–63, 5:377; *General Orders . . . January, 1862, to December, 1863*, 119 (1862 General Orders #93).

53. *General Orders . . . January, 1862, to December, 1863*, 79–80 (1862 General Orders #68)

54. Allan, "Reminiscences," *SHSP*, 13:137–38; Josiah Gorgas, "Notes on the Ordnance Department of the Confederate Government," *SHSP*, 12:90. Gorgas claimed that the only men with enough ability to pass the test for the captain's commission were graduates of the University of Virginia's M.A. program. Allan's account is the best description of an ordnance officer's duties. The initial examining board operated in Richmond and consisted of T. S. Rhett, Smith Stansbury, Benjamin Sloan, and W. Leroy Broun.

55. Francis W. Dawson, *Reminiscences of Confederate Service, 1861–1865* (1882; reprint, Baton Rouge: Louisiana State University Press, 1980), 63; Gorgas, "Notes on the Ordnance Department," *SHSP*, 12:90. Thus far it has not been possible to confirm Dawson's description of Duxbury's antebellum career, which is itself proof of his unremarkable origins. Oddly, the ordnance department did not acquire official sanction until April 1863, when Congress finally passed a bill establishing it (*SHSP*, 49:127).

56. Robert Garlick Hill Kean, *Inside the Confederate Government*, ed. Edward Younger (New York: Oxford University Press, 1957), 154; Gorgas, *Journals*, 115.

57. Brent, *Memoirs*, 152.

58. Letter of "O. S.," in *Richmond Sentinel*, December 5, 1863. The author's initials probably stood for ordnance sergeant, leaving pessimists to wonder whether his goal of commissioning an ordnance officer in each regiment was nothing more than a gambit for promotion.

59. *Journal of the Congress*, 5:290, 350, 458; *General Orders . . . January, 1862, to December, 1863*, 53 (1862 General Orders #40). The September 1862 legislation permitted the appointment of another major and twenty new lieutenants to the corps (*SHSP*, 46:133). Despite its title, David W. Gaddy's "The Confederate Signal Corps at Gettysburg," *Gettysburg Magazine*, no. 4 (January 1991): 110–12, offers a good summary of the army's signaling history and discusses that corps' capabilities in July 1863.

60. William N. Barker to Samuel Cooper, August 27, 1864, in Barker's file, Compiled Service Records of Confederate Soldiers Who Served in Organizations Raised Directly by the Confederate Government, M258, roll 116, NA.

61. *Regulations for the Army . . . 1862*, 98, 110. Edward Hagerman, *The American Civil War and the Origins of Modern Warfare* (Bloomington: Indiana University Press, 1988), 127–31, offers a useful glimpse of how the quartermaster and commissary departments attempted in midwar to make organizational changes that would better equip them to meet the requirements of the nation.

62. John C. Whitner letter, April 11, 1862, Georgia Governor's Incoming Correspondence, box 50, Georgia Department of Archives and History, Atlanta, Ga.

63. *Regulations for the Army . . . 1862*, 90–91; McDaniel, *With Unabated Trust*, 97; Jedediah Hotchkiss, *Make Me a Map of the Valley*, ed. Archie P. McDonald (Dallas: Southern Methodist

University Press, 1973), 129–30; W. Edgeworth Bird, *The Granite Farm Letters*, ed. John Rozier (Athens: University of Georgia Press, 1988), 201. For a time, there was a movement afoot in Congress to separate the paymasters from the quartermaster's department. The powerful Committee on Military Affairs in the House recommended the bill in hopes that it might expedite the payment of men in the field, but the legislation fell apart and nothing came of it. This debate occurred in August and September 1862. See *SHSP*, 45:255, 270.

64. Philip H. Powers to wife, May 15, 1862, typescript, Bound Volume 245, FSNMP; John A. Harman letters, June 5 and July 5, 1862, Jedediah Hotchkiss Papers, reel 39, Library of Congress, Washington, D.C.; Robert M. McClellan letters, September 25 and December 2, 1863, McClellan Papers, Georgia Historical Society, Savannah, Ga. Stonewall Jackson occasionally squabbled with his supply officers, as did his successor Richard S. Ewell. One of Ewell's encounters with Major Harman occurred on the day the army disengaged at Gettysburg, when Ewell told his short-tempered quartermaster to get his train safely over the Potomac River or "he wanted to see his face no more" (Hotchkiss, *Make Me a Map*, 71, 158).

65. *Regulations for the Army . . . 1862*, 192–93, 233.

66. B. W. Justice to wife, May 20, 1864, Justice Papers, Emory University, Atlanta, Ga.; Nicholas B. Gibbon Memoir, *Mecklenburg, North Carolina, Genealogical Society Quarterly* 3, no. 1 (1985): 13; T. C. Elder to wife, May 8, 1863, Elder Papers, Virginia Historical Society, Richmond, Va. Captain Justice met an unhappy end after the war when he fell to his death through a hole in the floor of his warehouse.

67. Alexander B. Garland letter, October 4, 1862, typescript, Jones Memorial Library, Lynchburg, Va.

68. *Journal of the Congress*, 3:189, 417; *General Orders . . . January, 1862, to December, 1863*, 72–74 (1863 General Orders #70).

69. John W. McLure, *Lifeline to Home for John William McLure, CSA, Union County, S.C.*, ed. Sarah Porter Carroll (Greenville, S.C.: A Press, ca. 1990), 240; *OR*, ser. 1, 42(2):1247.

70. *SHSP*, 52:66, 69; "Unus," in *Richmond Sentinel*, January 11, 1865.

71. *Journal of the Congress*, 1:374, 3:382–83, 4:688–90, 710, 5:321; *SHSP*, 45:270, 48:44, 49:133, 51:252, 52:475; John Beauchamp Jones, *A Rebel War Clerk's Diary*, 2 vols. (Philadelphia: Lippincott, 1866), 2:406, 429. The bill abolishing post quartermasters and commissaries did not apply to tax collectors, and diarist Jones wrote that the day after the bill passed, some of the Richmond supply officers ran notices in the newspapers advertising themselves as tax collectors. See *SHSP*, 50:38–39, 386, for two more examples of outbursts directed against the quartermasters and commissaries by Congressman Foote. In one, he aptly predicted that after the war, there would be "swarms of men, called colonel this and major that," who actually had been "only quartermasters and commissaries."

72. Samuel H. Wiley letter to parents, November 26, 1864, Wiley Papers, SHC/UNC; McDaniel, *With Unabated Trust*, 112; letter of "Valley," in *Richmond Sentinel*, October 28, 1864; Johnson Hagood, *Memoirs of the War of Secession* (Columbia, S.C.: The State Company, 1910), 216. For another example of a published complaint, see letter of "Georgia," "Bread for the Soldiers," *Richmond Sentinel*, December 7, 1864.

73. *Richmond Sentinel*, September 16, 1864; Jones, *Rebel War Clerk's Diary*, 2:118.

74. Letter of "Unus," "Quartermasters and Commissaries," *Richmond Sentinel*, January 11, 1865; Kean, *Inside the Confederate Government*, 48–49. The long letter by "Unus" is one of the better rebuttals seen among the wartime newspapers.

75. Joseph E. Ficklin to Joseph R. Anderson, June 3, 1901, in Ficklin's file, VMI.

76. *SHSP*, 49:192, 259; *Journal of the Congress*, 3:336. Simultaneous legislation permitted the appointment of laboratory superintendents.

77. *Journal of the Congress*, 6:413.

ROSTER

Abrams, Jacob C. b. Charleston, South Carolina, 1832. Pvt. Louisiana Guard Arty., Apr. 28, 1861. Detached as clerk in AIGO, and then in Commissary Dept. Capt. ACS, Aug. 4, 1864. Served in Richmond. Dec. 1864 was age 32. A resident of New Orleans from about 1858 until his death. d. there Oct. 20, 1918, age 86 years and 10 months. bur. Metairie Cem.

Adams, Benjamin Carter. b. Dec. 17, 1838. att. UVa. and UAla. Pvt. Co. I and Capt. ACS, 5th Alabama, Apr. 1862. Maj. CS to D. H. Hill, Dec. 12, 1862, and May 19, 1863, but failed confirmation both times. Served in that capacity anyway until Maj. CS to Rodes, June 15, 1864. Same to Grimes. Appx. Uniontown, Alabama, cotton planter. Married twice. d. Dec. 17, 1900.

Adams, James M. b. North Carolina. Of Rockingham Co. Sgt. Co. L, 21st North Carolina. POW Jan. 1863. Capt. AAIG to Hoke, May 2, 1863. Maj. AAIG to Hoke, Aug. 31, 1864. WIA several times.

Adams, James Pickett. b. Rocky Creek, South Carolina, Sept. 2, 1828. att. South Carolina Coll. Wealthy Columbia lawyer and legislator. Capt. VADC to Perrin's Bgd. at Gettysburg. Capt. VADC to Butler, May 1864. WIA at Trevilian's Station. Maj. 10th Bn. South Carolina Cavy. Planter. d. Nov. 1,

1904, in Richland Co. bur. St. John's Episc. Cem., Congaree.

Adams, Joseph Manning. b. Charleston, South Carolina, Dec. 17, 1836. att. SCMA. Principal at Anderson Military Academy. Capt. AQM, 4th South Carolina, Apr. 1861. Maj. QM to R. H. Anderson, Apr. 7, 1862, and then to Micah Jenkins. Failed to secure bond, dropped from rolls Aug. 30, 1862, and resigned officially Dec. 18, 1862. Lt. Palmetto Sharpshooters. WIA and POW Oct. 28, 1863. Pickens Co. lawyer and Oconee Co. planter. d. Dec. 18, 1878.

Adams, Richard Henry Toler. b. Lynchburg, Virginia, Nov. 6, 1839. Richmond merchant. Pvt. Co. G, 11th Virginia, Apr. 1861. Detached on telegraph duty with E. P. Alexander, Jan. 1, 1862. Capt. SO to A. P. Hill, May 29, 1862. Capt. AAAIG to Hill, Aug. 1864. Appx. Lynchburg banker and businessman. d. Nov. 14, 1900. bur. Spring Hill Cem.

Adams, Samuel Finney. b. Bedford Co., Virginia, Jan. 1837. att. VMI. Teacher. Capt. OO at Saltville, 1862. Staff of William Preston, 1863, and with Bureau of Conscription in Abingdon. Lt. ADC to W. E. Jones, Feb. 1864. Ordered to report to Echols, Mar. 18, 1865. Engineer and teacher. Lived at Lynchburg, Danville, and Washington, D.C.

d. Bedford Springs, July 23, 1900. bur. family cemetery in Campbell Co.

Addison, William A. Acting ADC to A. W. Reynolds, Apr. 1862–Feb. 1863. Appears on a May 1865 list of POWs as VADC to Gen. Barton. No other record.

Adger, Joseph Ellison. b. Charleston, South Carolina, 1824. Merchant in Anderson Co. Capt. AQM, 25th South Carolina, May 19, 1862. Capt. AQM to Hagood, Sept. 20, 1864. Paroled May 1, 1865. m. Susan Cox Johnson. Anderson Co. farmer, and merchant at Charleston. d. there Sept. 14, 1898. bur. Second Presby. Churchyard.

Adler, Adolphus H. From Hungary and claimed to have served on the staff of Garibaldi in Italy. Col. EO (PAVa.?) to Wise, July 1861. Arrested by authorities in Oct. 1861 for suspected disloyalty and attempted to cut his own throat. Convicted of bribery in Mar. 1862. Sentenced to six months in jail and expulsion from CSA. Released and went north. Arrested Dec. 18, 1862, at Cincinnati, Ohio. Took oath and released, Apr. 1863, age 39.

Agurs, John Lafayette. b. in South Carolina, Sept. 6, 1824. Chester merchant. m. Mary Mobley. Lt. Co. A, 6th South Carolina, June 1861. Capt. AQM, Apr. 1862. Capt. AQM to Bratton, Sept. 15, 1864. Appx. d. Jan. 20, 1904. bur. Evergreen Cem., Chester.

Aiken, Augustus Milton. b. Winnsboro, South Carolina, Jan. 10, 1834. Cotton merchant at Charleston. Served in Co. C, 7th South Carolina Cavy. Lt. OO to Butler and probably Dunovant, 1864. Serving as late as Dec. 1864. Postwar farmer. d. Charlotte, North Carolina, Aug. 9, 1906. bur. Greenwood, South Carolina.

Aldrich, Alfred Proctor. b. Charleston, South Carolina, June 4, 1814. att. Coll. of Charleston. Seminole War veteran. Lawyer in Barnwell. Acting QM to Bonham, June 1861, with rank of Lt. Col., probably honorary. Maj. QM to Maxcy Gregg, Apr. 1, 1862. Resigned Oct. 25, 1862, due to right shoulder injury suffered in wartime railroad accident. South Carolina legislator and aide to Governor Bonham, 1862–1865. Postwar judge. d. Feb. 1896.

Alexander, George Washington b. Francisville, Pennsylvania, 1829. Engineer in USN, 1848–1861. Participated in early war escapades of Col. Zarvona. Escaped from Ft. McHenry, Sept. 1861, with aid of wife. Capt. AAG to J. H. Winder, June 12, 1862. Commanded all of Richmond's prisons, June–Oct. 1862. Commanded Castle Thunder Prison, Oct. 1862–Feb. 1864. At Salisbury, North Carolina, 1864. Capt. AAG to Barton, Sept. 1864. Resigned Dec. 31, 1864, because his position with Barton was not recognized: "Many are trying to get out of the field I am begging to be kept in it." Taught French in Canada, then became sanitary engineer at Baltimore, Maryland. d. Laurel, Maryland, Feb. 20, 1895. bur. Ivy Hill Cem.

Alexander, James Butler Sigourney. b. Charlottesville, Virginia, Jan. 6, 1836. att. USMA. Served in the U.S. Infantry in the Northwest. Capt. of Inf., PAVa., May 8, 1861. Capt. AQM to R. S. Garnett, but another source says Capt. AAG to Garnett. d. Allegheny Springs, Virginia, August 13, 1861, of typhoid fever. bur. Charlottesville.

Alexander, James Hillhouse. b. Washington, Georgia, June 6, 1840. att. UVA and Harvard Law School. Pvt. 9th Georgia. Capt. SO, May 29, 1862, to report to T. J. Jackson, but order revoked. VADC to Lawton at Gaines's Mill. SO to French in North Carolina, July 1862. On duty as signal officer with Beauregard in South Carolina, Mar. 1863, and with J. E. Johnston from June 1863. Resigned Sept. 14, 1863. Maj. AAG to Gilmer, Sept. 16, 1863. In Richmond into 1865. Brother of Gen. E. P. Alexander. Brother-in-law of Gen. Lawton and Gen. Gilmer. Mayor of Augusta, 1891–1894, and merchant there. d. Dec. 4, 1902.

Alexander, Sydenham Benoni. b. Mecklenburg Co., North Carolina, Dec. 8, 1840.

att. UNC. Pvt. 1st North Carolina (Bethel). Capt. Co. K, 42nd North Carolina, May 1862. Capt. AAAIG to Hoke, August and September 1864, at least. Paroled Apr. 26, 1865, as AAIG 1st Bgd. North Carolina Reserves. In state and national congress. Railroad president. d. Charlotte, June 14, 1921. bur. Elmwood Cem.

Alexander, W. T. Capt. AAG to Benning in 1863. No other record, and possibly confused with some other officer.

Alexander, William Felix. b. Washington, Georgia, May 7, 1832. att. Yale. Planter. Maj. QM to Toombs, July 19, 1861. Maj. Inspector of Arty. Field Transportation, Sept. 27, 1862, based in Richmond. Maj. QM to Lawton, July 7, 1863. Served through July 1864, at least. Married twice. Brother of Gen. E. P. Alexander. Brother-in-law of Gen. Lawton and Gen. Gilmer. Son-in-law of Gen. Toombs. d. Aug. 16, 1907.

Alexander, William Kirkwood. b. Campbell C.H., Virginia, Apr. 16, 1846. att. VMI. Present at Battle of New Market. Served as a drillmaster in southwest Virginia in 1864. Cadet on the staff of Longstreet, Dec. 1, 1864, to report Jan. 31, 1865. Paroled May 30, 1865. Clerk of Campbell Co. circuit court, and a merchant. Capt. AQM in Spanish-American War. "Dropped from sight about 1900," and family unaware of his fate.

Allan, William. b. Winchester, Virginia, Nov. 12, 1837. att. UVA. Albemarle Co. teacher. QM clerk in Stonewall Brigade early in the war. Capt. OO to T. J. Jackson, Dec. 27, 1862. Maj., Mar. 17, 1863. Lt. Col., Mar. 28, 1864. Staff of Ewell, Early, and Gordon. Ordered to report to Early, Mar. 1, 1865. Staunton bank cashier, math professor at Washington & Lee, and president of the McDonough Institute, Owings Mills, Maryland. Author of numerous fine books on Confederate history. d. Sept. 17, 1889, at Owings Mills. bur. McDonough Institute. A

colleague called Allan "the most competent man for all sorts of work I ever saw."

Allan, William Galt. b. Richmond, Virginia, October 5, 1832. att. UVA. Very wealthy Goochland Co. farmer and "Gent." Lt. Co. H, 1st Virginia, June 1861. WIA at Blackburn's Ford. Capt. AQM, 1st Virginia, 1861. Probably served as acting QM to Kemper and W. R. Terry. Capt. AQM to Moore, Aug. 20, 1864. d. Richmond, October 15, 1868, of liver disease. bur. Shockoe Cem., in an unmarked grave.

Allen, John. b. Carthage, Tennessee, Apr. 22, 1837. Lt. Co. B, 7th Tennessee. WIA at Gettysburg and in Apr. 1865. Capt. AAG to McComb, 1865. m. Marietta Cullom. d. Van Buren, Arkansas, Oct. 11, 1913.

Allen, John Douglass. b. Sumner Co., Tennessee, ca. 1835. Capt. ACS, 7th Tennessee, May 30, 1861. Maj. CS to S. R. Anderson, Mar. 11, 1862. Resigned June 5, 1862, having belatedly decided to reject that appointment. Capt. ACS, 11th Tennessee Cavy., Oct. 1, 1862–June 1, 1863. Staff of "Anderson's Bgd.," late 1864. Paroled May 3, 1865. Alive 1869.

Allen, John Frederick. b. Herford Co., Ireland, ca. 1815. Moved to Richmond, Virginia, at age 5. Never married. A tobacco merchant. Clerk in QM Dept., 1861–1863. Capt. AQM, Oct. 31, 1863. Audited transportation accounts at Richmond, 1863–1865. Postwar tobacco partner of Lewis Ginter (see below). The "first man to begin manufacture of cigarettes in the country." Hobby was painting. d. Richmond, Aug. 23, 1890. bur. Shockoe Cem.

Allen, John M. From Richmond, Virginia. Clerk in QM Dept., 1861. Capt. AQM, May 20, 1862. Served as such all the way to 1865, primarily as the assistant forage QM at ANVa. headquarters, and at Dublin, Virginia. Age 25 in May 1865.

Allen, Littleberry Woodson. b. Henrico Co., Virginia, Mar. 26, 1803. Baptist preacher in Caroline Co., Virginia, and Louisville,

Kentucky. VADC to Magruder, June–Aug. 1862. Married twice. d. Caroline Co., Virginia, December 23, 1871. bur. family cem. off Ladysmith Road.

Allen, William L. b. Lycoming, Pennsylvania, ca. 1834. Pvt. Co. G, 12th Mississippi, May 5, 1861. Lt. OO to Barksdale, July 27, 1862. Same to Humphreys, 1863–1865. Appx.

Allensworth, Andrew Jackson. b. Christian Co., Kentucky, Feb. 8, 1833. Clarksville, Tennessee, "speculator" before the war. Capt. AQM, 14th Tennessee, 1861. Detailed as tax collector, last half of 1863. Capt. AQM to Archer, Sept. 15, 1864. Maj. QM to McComb, Mar. 2, 1865. Appx. Married twice. Postwar contractor. d. San Antonio, Texas, Nov. 5, 1891.

Allyn, Joseph Tyler, Jr. b. Aug. 9, 1840. att. Norfolk Military Academy, VMI, UVa., and Washington Coll. Pvt. Norfolk Light Arty. Blues. Drillmaster, Nov.–Dec. 1861. Acting Lt. OO to Cutts's Bn. Arty., May 25, 1863. Same to Lane's Bn. Arty., through at least Dec. 1864. Probably never commissioned. Postwar lawyer. d. Norfolk, Virginia, July 19, 1904.

Alston, Thomas Pinckney. b. December 7, 1832. Capt. Co. F, 1st (Gregg's) South Carolina Inf., Aug. 7, 1861. Capt. AAAG to Col. D. H. Hamilton, commanding brigade, at Chancellorsville. To Maj., Jan. 4, 1864. WIA at the Wilderness. To Lt. Col., May 19, 1864. MWIA at North Anna, May 23, 1864. d. June 19, 1864. bur. Magnolia Cem., Charleston.

Alston, William A. Lt. ADC to Magruder, Nov. 29, 1861. Capt. AAG to Magruder, Oct. 23, 1862. Recommended as Lt. Col. by Magruder in Sept. 1864, at age 30. Instead he was dropped by Congress but continued to serve into 1865. Several men bore this name in South Carolina. Best options are William Allan Allston (June 21, 1834–Nov. 14, 1878) and William Algernon

Alston, Jr. (d. 1867). Staff officer signed name as Alston, not Allston.

Ambler, John. b. Fauquier Co., Virginia, Apr. 3, 1821. att. UVa. Lawyer at Winchester, merchant at Waterloo, and U.S. Marshal in western Virginia. Capt. AQM, June 29, 1861. Maj. QM, June 27, 1862. Pay officer for ANVa. through the war, based in Richmond. Paroled 1865 at Greensboro, North Carolina. Episc. minister in Alexandria, and in Texas. d. Moundsville, West Virginia, Mar. 3, 1891. bur. Hollywood Cem., Richmond. "A good man, deservedly liked by all."

Ames, J. L. Capt. ACS to Hunton, 1864. Ordered to Petersburg, Virginia, Mar. 19, 1864. Official records very poor on this officer.

Anderson, Archer. b. Old Point Comfort, Virginia, Oct. 15, 1838. att. UVa. and school in Berlin, Germany. A lawyer and full partner at Richmond's Tredegar Iron Works, operated by his father, Gen. J. R. Anderson. Pvt. Co. F, 21st Virginia, Apr. 1861. Capt. AAG to Trimble, Sept. 2, 1861. Maj. AAG to Holmes, Feb. 6, 1862; to French, Aug. 1862; to D. H. Hill, by Aug. 25, 1862. WIA in Maryland Campaign. Lt. Col. AAG to Hill, July 11, 1863. Later staff of Breckinridge, Hindman, Hood, and J. E. Johnston. In Richmond in 1864 briefly, on inspection duty. Paroled at Greensboro, Apr. 26, 1865. Operated Tredegar Iron Works postwar. d. Jan. 4, 1918. bur. Hollywood Cem., Richmond.

Anderson, Clifford. b. Nottoway Co., Virginia, Mar. 23, 1833. Moved to Macon, Georgia, 1849. Lawyer, judge, and legislator there prewar. Pvt. Co. C, 2nd Bn. Georgia, Apr. 1861. Lt. in Nov. 1861. Lt. Acting OO to E. D. Hall's Bgd., Sept.–Oct. 1862. Lt. AAAIG to Wright, early 1863. Resigned Oct. 31, 1863, elected to C.S. Congress. Lawyer at Macon, law professor at Mercer Univ., and Georgia state attorney general. d. Dec. 19, 1899. bur. Rose Hill Cem.,

Macon. A large collection of Anderson's letters are at UNC.

Anderson, Edward McKenzie. b. May 30, 1823. Never married. att. South Carolina Coll. VADC to his brother Gen. R. H. Anderson, Apr.–May 1862. KIA at Williamsburg, May 5, 1862. bur. Cedar Grove Cem.

Anderson, Edward Willoughby. b. St. Augustine, Florida, Nov. 11, 1841. Father killed at Battle of Churubusco. att. New York Free Academy and USMA. Lt. Drillmaster, 6th Virginia, Apr. 1861. Cadet in Corps of Engineers, Sept. 25, 1861. Lt. EO to Huger, June 4, 1862. Badly injured in Seven Days. Capt. OO, Aug. 14, 1862, to report to E. P. Alexander on Sept. 3, 1862. Capt. OO to Pender, June 2, 1863. Same to Wilcox, through Dec. 1864 at least. Norfolk, Virginia, schoolteacher and lawyer. d. Washington, D.C., Sept. 1915. bur. Arlington Cem.

Anderson, John G. b. July 10, 1836. Printer at Lynchburg, Virginia. Pvt. Co. G, 11th Virginia, Apr. 23, 1861. WIA Seven Pines. Lt. Co. K, 44th Virginia, Sept. 8, 1862. WIA at Chancellorsville. Adjt. 44th Virginia, June 16, 1863. Lt. AAAG to B. T. Johnson, Aug. 1863. POW at Spotsylvania. d. June 6, 1904. bur. Bledsoe Church, near Scottsville, Virginia.

Anderson, Robert Walker. b. Jan. 23, 1838. att. UNC, where he taught Greek before the war. Of Orange Co. Sgt. 3rd North Carolina Arty., 1862. Lt. ADC to his brother Gen. G. B. Anderson, July 11, 1862. WIA in shoulder at Sharpsburg. Acting Lt. of Arty. at Fayetteville Arsenal, Apr. 1863. Lt. OO, May 2, 1863. Lt. OO to Cooke, July 16, 1863. Capt. OO to Cooke, Feb. 25, 1864. KIA at the Wilderness, May 5, 1864. bur. Orange Co.

Anderson, Samuel Smith. b. Buckingham Co., Virginia, Sept. 20, 1819. att. USMA. Lt. 2nd U.S. Arty., 1841–1861. Mexican War veteran. Maj. of Arty., Mar. 16, 1861. Maj. AAG to Huger, July 1861. Lt. Col. AAG to Huger,

Oct. 2, 1861. Later staff of Holmes, Kirby Smith, and Taylor. Building contractor in Louisville, Kentucky. d. there Feb. 20, 1901. bur. Cave Hill Cem.

Andrews, Garnett, Jr. b. Washington, Georgia, May 15, 1837. att. UGA. A lawyer. Lt. of Inf., May 4, 1861, to report to Savannah. Lt. ADC and AAAG to H. R. Jackson, July 4, 1861. Served with Cutts's Bn. Arty., 1862. To report to R. E. Lee, Sept. 20, 1862. Capt. AAG, Oct. 29, 1862, to report to Gardner, Drayton, and Garnett, all in the course of four weeks. Likely never reported. Capt. AAG to G. W. Smith, Nov. 30, 1862, and to Elzey on May 5, 1863. Maj. AAG to Elzey, July 14, 1863. Resigned Apr. 20, 1864, to become Lt. Co. I, 15th Georgia. Slightly WIA at Spotsylvania and Cold Harbor. Lt. acting ADC to G. T. Anderson, June 1864. Maj. AAG to W. M. Gardner, June 27, 1864. Lt. Col. 2nd Foreign Bn., 1865. WIA in neck and shoulder at Salisbury, Apr. 12, 1865. Yazoo City, Mississippi, lawyer and legislator. Mayor of Chattanooga, Tennessee. d. there May 6, 1903. bur. "at his old Georgia home."

Archer, James Williamson. b. 1830. A clerk. Capt. in Virginia militia prewar. Lt. Co. B, 1st Virginia, Apr. 21, 1861. Lt. OO to his brother-in-law, Gen. J. R. Anderson, Oct. 5, 1861. Lt. OO to French, Apr. 4, 1862. Capt. OO, Oct. 14, 1862, but to rank from Oct. 23, 1861. Capt. OO to G. J. Rains, late 1862. Capt. OO to Whiting, Jan. 20, 1863. Capt. OO to Heth, Nov. 13, 1863. Appx. Lived postwar at Richmond. d. there Nov. 1, 1901. bur. Hollywood Cem.

Archer, Robert Harris. b. in Maryland, May 20, 1820. Lt. U.S. Army in Mexican War. Pvt. Co. K, 1st Virginia Cavy., Apr. 1861. Capt. PACS, Sept. 23, 1861, on recruiting service. Lt. Col. 55th Virginia, Oct. 1861–May 1862. Probably VADC to Pickett at Seven Pines. Capt. AAG to his brother Gen. Archer, June 13, 1862. POW at Gettysburg.

Exchanged Jan. 1865. m. Ellen Howe Davis. d. Richmond, Virginia, Mar. 10, 1878.

Archer, Robert Pleasants. b. Amelia Co., Virginia. A farmer. Capt. AQM, June 29, 1861, stationed at Richmond. Maj. QM, July 6, 1863. Operated wagon and ambulance factories at Richmond. Postwar tobacconist at Richmond. m. Sarah Walthall. d. Richmond, Mar. 18, 1878. bur. Hollywood Cem., in unmarked grave.

Archer, William Meade. b. December 6, 1836. Pvt. 2nd Co. Richmond Howitzers (Va.), Apr. 21, 1861. To Lt., May 25, 1861. Dropped at Apr. 1862 reorganization. Lt. OO to A. P. Hill, by June 1862. Precise date of appointment not found. With Hill through the Maryland Campaign, but assistant to Chief OO of Second Corps by Dec. 1862, apparently through 1865. m. Mary Carter Deas. Wholesale merchant at Richmond. d. there Aug. 26, 1924. bur. Hollywood Cem.

Armistead, Franck Stanly. b. Upperville, Virginia, 1835. att. USMA. Lt. in U.S. Army, 1856–1861. Lt. of Arty., CSA, Mar. 16, 1861, to report to Beauregard in June. Lt. AAAG to Longstreet, July–Oct. 1861. Lt. in Peyton's Bn. Arty., early 1862. Capt. AAG to his brother, Gen. Armistead, Apr. 28, 1862. WIA at Seven Pines. Reassigned to other ANVa. duty, July 31, 1862. Lt. EO to Bragg, Dec. 11, 1862. Lt. Col. AAIG to Holmes, and later Col. 1st North Carolina Junior Reserves. d. at Central State Lunatic Asylum, Lakeland, Kentucky, Apr. 18, 1889. bur. Cave Hill Cem., Louisville.

Armistead, Walker Keith. b. Dallas Co., Alabama, Dec. 11, 1844. Cadet CSA, 1861. Pvt. Co. A, 6th Virginia Cavy., May 1862. Courier for J. E. B. Stuart. Lt. ADC to his father, Gen. Armistead, Feb. 19, 1863. WIA June 29, 1864. Appx. m. Julia Francis Appleton, a granddaughter of Daniel Webster. Moved to New England. Court reporter and stenographer in Massachusetts. d. Newport, Rhode Island, Mar. 28, 1896. bur. Berkeley

Chapel Churchyard, Middletown, Rhode Island. R. E. Lee wrote of Armistead's "amiable disposition."

Armstrong, William J. b. in Virginia, Oct. 1837. Served in Amherst (Va.) Arty., Nov. 1861, and detailed as commissary clerk immediately. Capt. ACS, June 1, 1862. Capt. ACS to Second Corps Arty. Maj. CS to Long, Dec. 26, 1864. Appx.

Arnall, Charles Steele. b. Augusta Co., Virginia, July 18, 1839. Staunton bank clerk. Adjt. 5th Virginia, Apr. 1861. Lt. AAAG to Paxton, Dec. 1862. Acting on staff of J. A. Walker by June 1863. WIA at Port Republic and Brawner's Farm. Appx. Managed a life insurance company in Atlanta, Georgia. Committed suicide there, Feb. 23, 1905. bur. Thornrose Cem., Staunton.

Arnold, Eugenius C. b. in Georgia, Jan. 31, 1839. Lt. Co. H, 11th Georgia, July 3, 1861. Lt. AAAIG to G. T. Anderson, Apr.–July 1863. Capt. Co. H, 11th Georgia, July 17, 1863. Severely injured by a deserter in Nov. 1863, and out of the army. Capt. of Arnold's Co. Light Duty Men, Feb. 1865. Dry goods merchant at Monroe. d. Oct. 16, 1889. bur. Rest Haven Cem. Middle name probably Cicero.

Arrington, James Portis. b. in Alabama. 28-year-old merchant in Greene Co. in 1860. Pvt. Co. D, 5th Alabama. Lt. ADC to Rodes, Mar. 12, 1863. Severely WIA in knee, Aug. 25, 1864. WIA and POW at Third Winchester. Released from prison June 1865.

Arrington, Robert Opie. b. in Virginia, ca. 1843. A farmer. Cpl. in 44th Virginia, 1861–1862. Pvt. Co. A, 20th Bn. Virginia Heavy Arty., Apr. 25, 1862. Lt. ADC to Long, Nov. 16, 1863. Retired to Invalid Corps, Mar. 6, 1865. m. Frances Carwile, 1866. Postwar Appomattox Co. farmer. d. Danville, Virginia, Apr. 25, 1911. bur. Greenhill Cem., in an unmarked grave.

Ashe, John Grange. b. Wilmington, North Carolina, Mar. 11, 1839. att. USMA. Lived in Florida prewar. Lt. on engineering and QM duty at Pensacola, Florida, in 1861. Ordered to report to Robert Ransom, Mar. 22, 1862. Lt. AAAG to Ransom during Seven Days. Transferred to staff of Forney, Nov. 19, 1862. Later with Waul. Resigned Jan. 20, 1865. d. Texas in 1867. A brother of S. A. Ashe (see below).

Ashe, Samuel A'Court. b. Wrightsville Sound, North Carolina, Sept. 13, 1840. att. USNA. Prewar law student. On ordnance duty at Cape Fear, 1861. Lt. OO, Dec. 11, 1861. Capt. AAG to Pender, July 12, 1862. POW at Second Manassas. Exchanged and resigned, Nov. 1, 1862. Lt. OO to Clingman, Feb. 14, 1863. Transferred to Fayetteville Arsenal, Aug. 1863. Railroad conductor, postmaster, author, and legislator in North Carolina. Owner of the *Raleigh Observer*. d. Aug. 31, 1938. bur. Oakwood Cem., Raleigh.

Ashe, William Shepperd. b. New Hanover Co., North Carolina, Sept. 14, 1814. att. Trinity Coll. in Connecticut. Lawyer in North Carolina, served in USHR, and president of Wilmington Railroad. Maj. QM, July 17, 1861. On duty at Richmond, Virginia, in charge of railroad transportation. d. Sept. 14, 1862, in a railroad accident near Wilmington. bur. "The Neck" near Ashton, in Pender Co., North Carolina.

Atkins, Michael J. b. in South Carolina, 1833. Merchant in Randolph Co., Georgia. Lt. Co. H, 51st Georgia, Mar. 4, 1862. Capt. AQM, 51st Georgia, Mar. 22, 1864. Capt. AQM to Kershaw, autumn 1864. Commanded division's ordnance train. Appx. Dry goods merchant at Cuthbert, Georgia. d. 1901.

Atkins, Robert Going. b. in County Cork, Ireland, 1833. Served with Garibaldi in Italy. Capt. Co. E, 1st Louisiana Special Bn. ("Wheat's Tigers"), Sept. 7, 1861. Capt. ADC (VADC?) to Elzey, Dec. 12, 1862. Capt. AAG, May 2, 1863, precise duties uncertain. Visited Europe, 1863–1864. Resigned Apr. 9, 1864. Possessed "a huge black beard."

Atkinson, John Wilder. b. Lunenburg Co., Virginia, May 23, 1830. Educated in Baltimore. Richmond tobacco merchant. Capt. Co. A, 15th Virginia, Apr. 1861. Dropped at reorganization. Capt. VADC to McLaws, May–June 1862. Maj. 19th Bn. Virginia Heavy Arty., June 1862. Lt. Col., Dec. 1862. Postwar Wilmington, North Carolina, merchant. d. there Oct. 26, 1910. bur. Oakdale Cem.

Atwell, William H. A resident of DeKalb Co., Tennessee. Pvt. Co. A, 7th Tennessee, May 21, 1861, age 22. Capt. ACS, 7th Tennessee, June 15, 1862. Capt. ACS to Heth, Aug. 1, 1863. Appx.

Aubrey, William. Apptd. Capt. of Inf. from Alabama, June 23, 1864. Capt. MSK at General Supply Store in Richmond, Dec. 1864.

August, Thomas Pearson. b. Fredericksburg, Virginia, Oct. 1821. Mexican War veteran. Richmond lawyer and legislator. Brigadier gen. of state militia. Col. 15th Virginia, May 17, 1861. WIA at Malvern Hill. Col. in Conscript Bureau, stationed at Richmond, 1862. On duty as commandant at a conscript camp in North Carolina, Jan. 1863. Retired Dec. 31, 1864. d. July 31, 1869. bur. Hollywood Cem., Richmond.

Aunspaugh, Robert Tilghman. b. Bedford Co., Virginia, Sept. 3, 1838. Prewar merchant. Lt. Bedford Arty., May 1861. Lt. acting AQM, 10th Bn. Virginia Heavy Arty., July 1863 through at least Aug. 1864. d. Chase City, Virginia, Nov. 6, 1905.

Averett, John Taylor. b. in Virginia, Dec. 24, 1827. Capt. AQM 38th Virginia, July 1, 1861. Capt. AQM to Barton, Sept. 15, 1864. Same to Steuart. Appx. Postwar teacher at Danville. Cofounder of Averett College there. d. Danville, Feb. 16, 1898.

Ayer, William Franklin. b. Barnwell Dist., South Carolina, Jan. 23, 1830. Moved to Floyd Co., Georgia, ca. 1850. Maj. QM to S. Jones, Aug. 21, 1861. Maj. QM to G. T. Anderson's Bgd. until about July 1862.

Maj. QM at Dalton, Georgia, July 31, 1862. Later at LaGrange, Georgia, and then Chief QM for AOT, Sept. 1864 into 1865. Hardware dealer and mayor of Rome, Georgia. d. June 21, 1904. bur. Myrtle Hill Cem.

Babbitt, Amzi. b. in New Jersey, Feb. 11, 1825. Bank clerk at Aberdeen, Mississippi. Pvt. Co. I, 11th Mississippi, Feb. 20, 1861. Maj. CS to Law, Feb. 24, 1862. Maj. CS to W. F. Perry, 1864–1865. Appx. Married twice. d. June 30, 1883. bur. Odd Fellows' Cem., Chickasaw Co.

Bacon, Waddy Street. b. in Virginia, 1837. Said to have seen military service in Central America. Deputy sheriff in Hinds Co., Mississippi, age 23 in 1860. Lt. ADC to Wise, Aug. 18, 1861. Resigned June 20, 1862, and dropped next day for extended absence. Attempted to raise units behind the lines in Kentucky and Tennessee. May have been on the staff of R. S. Garnett in 1861. d. Dinwiddie Co., Virginia, 1905.

Badger, Richard Cogsdell. b. Raleigh, North Carolina, Aug. 8, 1839. att. UNC. Wake Co. attorney. Sgt. Maj., 14th North Carolina, June 1861. Capt. ACS, 45th North Carolina, June 2, 1862. Capt. VADC to Daniel, Seven Days. Maj. CS to Daniel, July 15, 1862. Maj. CS to Grimes, May 1864. Resigned Dec. 3, 1864, due to his election as clerk of the North Carolina state senate. Postwar lawyer and legislator. d. Raleigh, Apr. 22, 1882. bur. Oakwood Cem.

Bagwell, George H. Member of U.S. Coast Survey. On engineer duty with his kinsman Gen. Wise in North Carolina, 1862. Capt. EO, Aug. 1863. Served around Richmond. Paroled in Apr. 1865. Lived nearly all his life at Onancock, Virginia. Customs collector and surveyor there. d. Northampton Co., December 15, 1892, age about 63. bur. Onancock Cem.

Bailey, William L. Maj. QM, Sept. 21, 1861, on duty at Richmond for the entire war. In charge of finances for the department. Age 56 in December 1864.

Baird, Edward Rouzie. b. near Occupacia, Virginia, Sept. 29, 1840. att. UVA. Sgt. Co. F, 9th Virginia Cavy., June 1861. VADC to Pickett, Feb. 1862. Lt. ADC to Pickett, May 21, 1862. Capt. ADC, June 2, 1863. Occasionally acted as AAAG to Pickett in 1863–1864. Appx. Farmer and supt. of Essex Co. schools. d. at "Epping Forest," Essex Co., Sept. 22, 1931. bur. there. Baird's war letters are at Wm. & Mary, and his memoir of Gettysburg is at the Museum of the Confederacy in Richmond.

Baker, Alexander. b. Frederick Co., Virginia, May 16, 1814. Capt. AQM at Mt. Jackson, 1861. Capt. AQM at Harrisonburg, early 1863. Paroled there Apr. 27, 1865. Postwar farmer. m. Caroline M. Hite. d. Jan. 7, 1892. "A large man six feet tall."

Baker, John Algernon. Lawyer at Wilmington, North Carolina. att. Yale and Columbia (S.C.) Coll. Married six times. Lt. Wilmington Light Arty., May 16, 1861. VADC to French, June–Sept. 1862. Col. 3rd North Carolina Cavy., Sept. 3, 1862. POW at Petersburg, June 21, 1864. One of the Immortal 600. Took Oath of Allegiance Mar. 6, 1865, and supposedly left the country. d. Galveston, Texas, Mar. 15, 1903, age 71. bur. Calvary Catholic Cem., unmarked. A subordinate wrote of Baker: "He was the finest-looking man I ever saw: a perfect Antinous, very tall, and muscular, and looked as if he were about to step into the Olympic Arena. . . ."

Baker, William J. b. Gates Co., North Carolina, June 20, 1816. att. St. Mary's Coll. Merchant at Raleigh, North Carolina, and then a banker at Norfolk, Virginia, prewar. m. Sarah F. Collins, 1842. Early in the war on staff of Walter Gwynn, PAVA. Later miltary agent for North Carolina, at Norfolk. Maj. CS to Pettigrew, July 10, 1862. Same to Kirkland, 1863–1864. Transferred to Raleigh, Aug. 29, 1864, because of health and age. d. Feb. 23, 1882. bur. Elmwood

Cem., Norfolk. His war letters are at UNC. A brother of Gen. L. S. Baker.

Baldwin, Briscoe Gerard. b. Staunton, Virginia, Aug. 12, 1828. att. VMI. Capt. OO in U.S. Army, 1851–1861. A distant kinsman of J. E. B. Stuart, who called him "Buck" and wrote that "he ought to be a general." Lt. OO, Mar. 16, 1861, on duty at Ordnance Bureau in Richmond. Commander of Richmond Arsenal, Sept. 1, 1861. Capt. OO, Jan. 1, 1862. Capt. AAAG to Rodes, Apr. 16, 1862. Maj. OO, June 12, 1862. Acting Lt. Col. of 6th Alabama in Seven Days, and badly WIA in lungs at Malvern Hill. Reported to R. E. Lee, July 1862. Lt. Col. OO to Lee, Nov. 29, 1862. Appx. Richmond businessman. Moved to Texas in 1870, where he was a cattle rancher on the Brazos River and school superintendent at Bryan. d. Sept. 28, 1898. bur. Bryan City Cem. A fellow staff officer called Baldwin "a nice fellow & a thorough gentleman."

Balfour, James R. 24-year-old planter in Madison Co., Mississippi, worth $66,000 in 1860. Capt. AAIG to Cabell and Craven, 1862. Served as staff officer in J. R. Davis's Bgd., 1864, and appointed Capt. AAIG to Cooke, July 26, 1864. Never served, as Cooke didn't want him. In limbo until Capt. AAIG to W. H. Forney, Feb. 28, 1865.

Balfour, Joseph D. b. in Mississippi. att. school in Paris, France, and served under Garibaldi in Italy. Living in Harrison Co. in 1860, age 20. A nephew of Jefferson Davis. Lt. CSA, Mar. 16, 1861. On duty at Pensacola, Florida, Apr.–Aug. 1861. Maj. AAG to Van Dorn, Oct. 9, 1861. Was AAIG to Van Dorn, perhaps from the start. KIA at Corinth, Oct. 1862. A fellow staff officer called Balfour "the most excitable person I have ever encountered . . . he simply became frantic in battle . . . he was of very little real use because of his total loss of self-command."

Ball, Beaufort Watts. b. Laurens Co., South Carolina, Nov. 16, 1830. att. Erskine Coll. and South Carolina Coll. Laurens lawyer.

Pvt. Co. B, Hampton Legion, July 10, 1861. Adjt. Hampton Legion, Nov. 1, 1862. Lt. AAAG to Gary, May 1864. WIA once slightly. Appx. Postwar legislator and editor of *Laurens Advertiser.* d. Mar. 27, 1902. bur. Laurens Cem.

Ball, Dabney. b. Fairfax Co., Virginia, May 1820. Methodist preacher prewar. Chaplain, 1st Virginia Cavy., July 1861. Maj. CS to Stuart, Oct. 2, 1861. Resigned July 15, 1862, to make way for someone "less annoying to you [Stuart]." Chaplain, 5th Virginia Cavy., July 26, 1862. Resigned July 19, 1863. Postwar preacher, mostly in Baltimore. d. there, Feb. 15, 1878. bur. Mt. Olivet Cem.

Ball, Mottrom Dulany. b. Fairfax Co., Virginia, June 23, 1835. att. Wm. & Mary. Lawyer and schoolteacher. Capt. VADC to Magruder, Apr.–May 1862. Capt. Co. I, 11th Virginia Cavy., 1862. Ultimately Lt. Col. of that unit. WIA twice. U.S. District Attorney in Alaska, 1876–1887. m. Sallie Lewis Wright. d. Sitka, Alaska, Sept. 13, 1887. bur. Old Falls Church Episc. Graveyard, Virginia.

Ballard, Robert Edgar. b. Franklin Co., North Carolina, 1839. m. Sarah Agnes Branch. Pvt. 15th North Carolina Infantry, May 1861. Later to Lt. Became Lt. Co. K, 32nd North Carolina Inf., July 4, 1862. WIA at Gettysburg. Lt. acting ADC to Daniel, from about July 1863 until May 1864. Returned to regiment after Daniel's death. Paroled May 15, 1865, at Raleigh. d. 1893.

Ballard, Thomas Edwin. b. in Virginia. Farmer, merchant, and proprietor of Richmond's famous Ballard Hotel, prewar. Pvt. 4th Virginia Cavy., May 23, 1861. Capt. ACS, July 19, 1861, posted at Ashland, Virginia. Ordered to Monterey, Virginia, Nov. 25, 1861. Capt. ACS to Elzey and Trimble, 1862. Capt. ACS to Ed. Johnson, June 1863–1864. Maj. CS to John B. Gordon, June 15, 1864. Maj. CS to R. H. Anderson, Oct. 31, 1864. Appx. Staff of Breckinridge, date unknown. Resumed hotel business. d. Salem, Virginia,

Feb. 22, 1902, age 77 or 78. bur. East Hill Cem.

Ballard, Walter S. b. in Georgia, ca. 1832. Bookkeeper at Macon. Lt. Co. A, 20th Georgia, May 17, 1861. Adjt., Nov. 1, 1861. WIA at Malvern Hill. Maj. CS to Benning, Mar. 6, 1863. Appx. Alive 1878 at Macon, working in a brickyard.

Banks, Andrew Dewees. b. Hampton, Virginia, Jan. 6, 1833. att. UVA. Edited newspapers in Petersburg (with Roger A. Pryor) and Cincinnati. Maj. ADC to G. W. Smith, Dec. 1861. Maj. AAG to J. E. Johnston, Dec. 1862 to Nov. 1863. Wartime owner and editor of *Montgomery* (Ala.) *Mail*. Postwar farmer in Warren Co., Mississippi. d. July 21, 1881. bur. St. John's Cem., Hampton.

Barbour, Alfred Madison. b. Culpeper Co., Virginia, Apr. 17, 1829. att. UVA. and Harvard Law School. Prewar legislator. Supt. of Harpers Ferry Armory, 1858–1861, including during the John Brown episode. Maj. QM, July 19, 1861. Maj. QM to Bonham, Aug. 1, 1861. Maj. QM to J. E. Johnston, Dec. 4, 1861. Under investigation in Nov. 1863 for "inefficiency" in 1861. Staff of Polk, and on QM duty in Montgomery, Alabama, and Meridian, Mississippi. Paroled at Greensboro. d. Montgomery, Apr. 4, 1866. bur. Fairview Cem., Culpeper. Jubal Early called Barbour "not energetic or efficient."

Barbour, Edwin. b. 1831. att. VMI and Jefferson Medical Coll. Never married. Physician and farmer. Lt. PAVA., May 23, 1861. Duty uncertain until Lt. OO at Danville, Virginia, by Jan. 1862. Ordered to report to Longstreet, Apr. 24, 1863, but resigned Apr. 28, 1863, due to "urgent private considerations." d. Culpeper Co., Virginia, 1891. bur. Fairview Cem. Perhaps not eligible for inclusion in this compilation.

Barbour, James. b. Feb. 26, 1828. att. UVA. Lawyer and legislator in Virginia. Member of 1861 Secession Convention. VADC to Ewell, early 1862. Maj. AAG to Ewell,

Apr. 28, 1862. Had a dispute with Jubal Early and probably never served under him. Resigned Jan. 30, 1863. Editor of *Richmond Enquirer*. d. Alexandria, Virginia, Oct. 29, 1895. bur. Fairview Cem., Culpeper.

Barbour, John Strode, Jr. b. Culpeper Co., Virginia, Dec. 29, 1820. att. Wm. & Mary and UVA. Virginia lawyer, legislator, and railroad president. VADC to Cocke, Apr. 1861. Postwar U.S. Senator. d. Washington, D.C., May 14, 1892. bur. "Poplar Hill," Prince George's Co., Maryland.

Barbour, Philip Pendleton. b. Oct. 23, 1839. Of Orange Co., Virginia. att. Hampden Sidney and UVA. Pvt. Co. C, 13th Virginia, June 1861. WIA in leg at Chantilly. Capt. AQM, Aug. 6, 1863. On duty in Raleigh, Greensboro, and Richmond. Postwar Gordonsville, Virginia, lawyer. d. Jan. 26, 1914. bur. Maplewood Cem.

Barclay, Alexander Tedford. b. "Sycamore" near Lexington, Virginia, May 16, 1844. att. Washington Coll. Lt. staff of Stafford, May 1864. POW at Spotsylvania, May 10, 1864. Postwar farmer and newspaperman. d. Lexington, Nov. 27, 1915. Barclay's war letters have been published.

Barham, Theophilus Gilliam. b. Laxis, Virginia, either Aug. 10, 1833, or Jan. 1, 1834. m. Virginia Ann Prince. Lt. Co. F, 5th Bn. Virginia, 1861–1862. Lt. VADC to McLaws during Seven Days. VADC to Micah Jenkins during Suffolk campaign, and VADC to Matt. Ransom in North Carolina. Lt. Col. 24th Virginia Cavy., Dec. 3, 1864. POW at Sailor's Creek. Newspaperman at Petersburg. d. Sussex Co., Virginia, Dec. 31, 1885.

Barker, Theodore Gaillard. b. Charleston, South Carolina, Aug. 24, 1832. att. South Carolina Coll. Lawyer and rice planter around Charleston most of his life. Adjt. 1st South Carolina, 1860. Adjt. Hampton Legion, Sept. 2, 1861. Lt. AAAG to Hampton, summer 1862. Capt. AAG to Hampton, July 12, 1862, backdated to Nov. 28, 1861.

Maj. AAG to Hampton, Aug. 3, 1863. Maj. AAG to Butler, 1864. WIA in hip at Burgess's Mill. WIA Feb. 1865 at Cheraw, South Carolina. m. Louisa Preston King, 1875. In South Carolina legislature. d. Flat Rock, North Carolina, May 31, 1917. bur. St. John's in the Wilderness Episc. Churchyard.

Barker, William Nelson. b. in Pennsylvania, Aug. 1821. att. USMA. Businessman in California and Washington, D.C. Later a clerk in Comptroller's Office in Washington, D.C. Pvt. Co. E, 1st Virginia, Apr. 22, 1861. Promoted to Lt. and detached for signal duty, July 1861. Capt. SO, Apr. 29, 1862. Stationed at Richmond, Virginia, through 1865. Acting Chief of the Signal Corps for much of 1864. Paroled Apr. 26, 1865. Postwar clerk for Board of Public Works. d. Washington, D.C., July 3, 1872.

Barksdale, George Annesley. b. Jan. 3, 1835. Of Amelia Co., Virginia. Treasurer of Gallego Flour Mills in Richmond. Capt. AQM, 16th Virginia, July 19, 1861. Capt. AQM in Richmond, Sept. 6, 1861. Stationed there in pay bureau for entire war, but paroled at Appx. Postwar recording secretary of the Virginia Historical Society. d. Albemarle Co., Nov. 19, 1910. bur. Hollywood Cem., Richmond.

Barksdale, Harris. b. Yazoo Co., Mississippi, Sept. 14, 1844. Pvt. Co. K, 18th Mississippi, Aug. 1861. Sgt. Jackson Light Arty., Mar. 1862. Apptd. Cadet, Mar. 26, 1862. Cadet ADC to his uncle, Gen. Barksdale, Aug. 25, 1862. Reported to J. E. Johnston, Sept. 14, 1863, for duty at Jackson, Mississippi. Cadet ADC to Humphreys, Jan. 19, 1864. Cadet ADC and acting OO to Wirt Adams, June 16, 1864. On recruiting duty in Mississippi 1864–1865. d. Jackson, Aug. 22, 1881. bur. Greenwood Cem.

Barksdale, John Allen Job. b. Yalobusha Co., Mississippi, Feb. 5, 1836. Known as "Chock." att. UMiss. Prewar Interior Dept. employee (post office). Cpl. Co. A, 21st Mississippi. Detached with Signal Corps,

summer 1862. Lt. ADC to Barksdale, Sept. 5, 1862. Capt. AAG to Barksdale, Feb. 25, 1863. Same to Humphreys. KIA May 8, 1864, at Spotsylvania. Never married. Brother of W. R. Barksdale (see below). Thought to be a distant cousin of Gen. Barksdale.

Barksdale, William Robert. b. in Alabama, Apr. 26, 1834. att. UMiss. Prewar lawyer. Capt. AQM, 11th Mississippi, May 18, 1861. Maj. QM to Featherston, June 1, 1862. Somehow converted into Capt. AAG to Featherston, July 14, 1862. Later on staff of Hindman and Walthall. d. Grenada, Mississippi, Jan. 10, 1877. Barksdale's letters are at MDAH.

Barnes, ——. VADC to Pryor in February 1863. Possibly a civilian.

Barnes, George Badger. b. Northampton Co., North Carolina, Aug. 30, 1839. att. UNC. Prewar lawyer. Lt. Co. E, 56th North Carolina, Apr. 1862. Capt. AQM, 56th North Carolina, Aug. 1, 1862. Capt. AQM to Matt. Ransom, Oct. 1, 1864. Appx. Lived postwar in Norfolk, Virginia. d. Dec. 28, 1893.

Barnes, William Sharpe. b. Wilson Co., North Carolina, 1843. Sgt. Co. F, 4th North Carolina, June 28, 1861. To Adjt., Mar. 14, 1863. Lt. acting ADC to Grimes, June 14, 1864. WIA at Third Winchester, Sept. 19, 1864. Lt. ADC to Grimes, Feb. 4, 1865. WIA at Ft. Stedman. Alive 1901 in North Carolina.

Barnett, William H. b. Vicksburg, Mississippi. Pvt. Co. A, 21st Mississippi, May 15, 1861, a clerk. Apptd. Cadet, Oct. 7, 1863, age 19, to report to S. D. Lee. On duty with W. H. Jackson and Wirt Adams in the western theater. Cadet on staff of Butler, Dec. 22, 1864. Lt. ADC to Wirt Adams, Jan. 31, 1865.

Barnwell, Edward H. Had no middle name but adopted the initial to distinguish himself from his many cousins. b. Beaufort, South Carolina, Nov. 27, 1832. att. South Carolina Coll. and UVA. Charleston cotton merchant. Lt. Co. B, 7th South Carolina

Cavy. Capt. AAAG to W. S. Walker, May 1862. Capt. AAG to same, Feb. 3, 1863. Also AAAIG on occasion. Capt. AAG to Chesnut. Cotton merchant at Charleston and Summerville. Farmer in Yazoo City, Mississippi. m. Harriet Butler Hayne. d. Charleston, Jan. 3, 1908. bur. Magnolia Cem.

Barnwell, John Gibbes. b. June 16, 1831. att. South Carolina Coll. and UVA. Lt. OO, Mar. 18, 1861. On duty in Virginia by 1st Manassas. To report to Pendleton July 31, 1861, and apptd. Capt. OO to him Apr. 16, 1862. Maj. OO to Pendleton, Apr. 15, 1863. Appx. Beaufort lawyer and planter. Librarian at Univ. of South Carolina, 1887–1888. d. Sept. 19, 1888. bur. St. Helena's Churchyard, Columbia.

Barnwell, John Gibbes, III. b. Apr. 3, 1839. att. Harvard. Lt. Co. H, 1st (Gregg's) South Carolina, Sept. 2, 1861. WIA at Gaines's Mill. Lt. AAAG to McGowan by Feb. 1863, and apparently acted in that capacity for much of 1863. To Capt., July 2, 1863. WIA at the Wilderness and at Fussell's Mill. Appx. Married twice. Architect and engineer in Georgia and Alabama. d. Aug. 13, 1918. bur. family cemetery in Rome, Georgia.

Barnwell, Nathaniel Berners. b. Beaufort, South Carolina, Mar. 5, 1845. Pvt. Co. B, 7th South Carolina Cavy., Feb. 22, 1862. POW at Dabney's Ferry, May 27, 1864. Cadet CSA, Dec. 28, 1864. Acting ADC to H. P. Jones's Bn. Arty., Jan. 2, 1865. Postwar lawyer and secretary of Board of Trustees, Univ. of South Carolina. m. Eliza Maxwell Longstreet, 1875. d. Columbia, January 5, 1883, from effects of accidental gunshot wound suffered on a hunting trip. bur. Trinity Churchyard.

Barnwell, Stephen Elliott. b. Apr. 17, 1842. Resident of Beaufort, South Carolina. Pvt. Beaufort Arty., Apr. 1861. Lt. ADC to Elliott, June 9, 1864. d. Aug. 7, 1923.

Barraud, Thomas Lawson. b. in Virginia, May 26, 1828. att. UVA. A clerk at Portsmouth. Lt. Co. C, 16th Virginia, Apr. 20, 1861. Maj. QM to Armistead, Apr. 30, 1862. Dropped Aug. 30, 1862, and may not have served in that capacity at all. WIA at Second Manassas. MWIA at Bristoe Station. d. Oct. 15, 1863. Has a memorial stone at Cedar Grove Cem., Norfolk.

Barringer, Victor Clay. b. Cabarrus Co., North Carolina, Mar. 29, 1827. att. UNC. Lawyer in Concord, member of state legislature, and author of legal texts. Maj. 1st North Carolina Cavy., May to Sept. 1861. Capt. AAG to Robert Ransom, Apr. 5, 1862. Resigned July 5, 1862, after an episode with Ransom, who felt "the service will be benefitted by his leaving it." Professor at Davidson Coll. On International Court of Appeals in Egypt, 1874–1894. d. Washington, D.C., May 27, 1896.

Barrow, James. b. Oglethorpe Co., Georgia, Mar. 26, 1841. att. GMI and USMA. Lt. of Inf., CSA, Mar. 16, 1861, to drill troops at Ft. Pulaski. Adjt. 16th Georgia, July 19, 1861. Capt. AAG to Howell Cobb, Mar. 6, 1862. WIA at Lee's Mill, Apr. 16, 1862. Lt. Col. 64th Georgia, May 26, 1863. KIA at Olustee, Feb. 20, 1864. bur. Oconee Hill Cem., Athens. Barrow's war letters have been published.

Barrows, A. S. Lt. EO stationed in Virginia. May have been promoted to captain and serving in North Carolina by 1863. Paroled Augusta, Georgia, May 7, 1865.

Barry, William Taylor Sullivan. b. Columbus, Mississippi, Dec. 10, 1821. att. Yale. Lawyer, planter, and member of USHR. Capt. AAG to Clark, Sept. 9, 1861. Resigned Mar. 15, 1862, to become Col. of the 35th Mississippi. Later in Confederate Congress. Postwar Columbus lawyer. d. there Jan. 29, 1868. bur. Friendship Cem.

Barton, Randolph Jones. b. Apr. 24, 1844. att. VMI. Sgt. Major 33rd Virginia, July 1861. WIA in side at First Manassas. POW at Kernstown. Lt. Co. K, 2nd Virginia, Oct. 1, 1862. Lt. AAAG to Paxton, Mar. 7, 1863.

Capt. AAG to Paxton, Mar. 28, 1863. WIA in both shoulders at Chancellorsville, May 3, 1863. Capt. AAG to J. A. Walker, Sept. 5, 1863. Capt. AAIG to Walker, Feb. 15, 1864. WIA in arm at Spotsylvania, May 12, 1864. Capt. AAG to William Terry, June 1864. Capt. AAAG to York, Aug.–Sept. 1864. WIA left leg at Third Winchester. WIA left leg at Hatcher's Run, Feb. 6, 1865. Maj. AAIG to J. A. Walker, Apr. 1, 1865. Postwar Baltimore, Maryland, law partner of Skipwith Wilmer (q.v.). Author of a very rare memoir. d. Mar. 16, 1921. bur. Druid Hill Cem., Pikesville, Maryland.

Barton, Thomas Scott. b. Fredericksburg, Virginia, Aug. 8, 1833. Brother of Gen. Seth Barton. Sutler at Fort Cobb, Indian Territory, Apr. 1861. Capt. ACS, July 3, 1861, to report to Greenville, North Carolina. Capt. ACS to Holmes by June 1862. Capt. ACS to Heth, Aug. 15, 1862. Capt. ACS at Greenville again, May 29, 1863. Capt. ACS at Petersburg, Virginia, by Sept. 1864. Later at Buchanan, Virginia. Broker in New Orleans, Louisiana, postwar. d. there Feb. 2, 1894. bur. Lafayette Cem. #1.

Barton, William Stone. b. Sept. 29, 1820. att. UVA. Staff of Ruggles, May 1861. Maj. 30th Virginia, May 17, 1861, to Apr. 1862. Detailed as Judge Advocate in Fredericksburg, Mar. 1862. Maj. AAG to Holmes, Apr. 24, 1862; to G. W. Smith, Sept. 29, 1862; and to French, May 25, 1863. Duties mostly those of Judge Advocate. Maj. AAG to Cooper, Feb. 26, 1864, through 1865. Fredericksburg lawyer. Brother of Gen. Barton. d. Fredericksburg, Jan. 18, 1898. bur. there.

Baskerville, Henry Embra Coleman. b. Mecklenburg Co., Virginia, Oct. 14, 1817. att. Hampden Sidney. Prewar merchant at Petersburg, and then to Richmond in 1844. Capt. ACS, 21st Virginia, July 1861. Capt. ACS to Loring, late 1861. Capt. ACS at Culpeper, Jan. 17, 1862. Resigned May 28, 1862. Married three times. Wholesale grocer

at Richmond. d. there, Jan. 14, 1900. bur. Hollywood Cem.

Bason, George Francis. b. Orange Co., North Carolina, May 20, 1840. att. UNC. Pvt. Co. F, 6th North Carolina, Aug. 1861. Sgt. Maj., 6th North Carolina, Oct. 1862. Acting OO to Pender, Jan. 27, 1863, apparently not commissioned. Lt. OO, Feb. 25, 1864, to report to Scales, Apr. 1, 1864. "Appointment as Captain directed by the Secy. of War" on Mar. 31, 1865, but no further record. Postwar lawyer. m. Fannie Bradham. d. May 1907.

Bassett, George Washington. b. Hanover Co., Virginia, Mar. 23, 1831. att. UVA. Principal of Woodburn School at Old Church. Lt. Co. H, 9th Virginia Cavy., Aug. 1861–Apr. 1862. Lt. acting OO to B. H. Robertson, Mar. 5, 1863. Lt. OO to Barringer, May 1864. Bassett's official record is sketchy. d. Hanover Co., Aug. 25, 1886.

Battle, Dossey. b. Rocky Mount, North Carolina, July 12, 1842. att. UNC. In 12th North Carolina, Aug. 1861–Aug. 1863. WIA at Chancellorsville, May 2, 1863. Lt. in 7th North Carolina, Aug. 1863 into 1865. Lt. ADC to his cousin Gen. Lewis at Appomattox. Editor of Tarboro newspaper postwar. Lawyer and judge in Rocky Mount. d. Mar. 28, 1900. bur. Pineview Cem.

Battle, James Smith. b. Tarboro, North Carolina, May 30, 1846. att. UNC. Pvt. 3rd North Carolina Cavy., May 10, 1864. Lt. ADC to Cox, June 10, 1864. Appx. Manufacturer and North Carolina politician postwar. Cousin of Gen. Lewis and nephew of Gen. Cox's wife. d. Jan. 26, 1894. bur. Calvary Episc. Churchyard, Tarboro.

Baya, Hanaro Thomas. b. St. Augustine, Florida, Sept. 1835. Often went by Thomas H. Baya. Broker at Charleston, South Carolina. Commissary clerk in Hardeeville, South Carolina, Oct. 1861. Capt. ACS, 8th Florida, July 13, 1862. Capt. ACS at Gainesville, Florida, Aug. 1863. Capt. ACS to Finegan, June 23, 1864. Capt. ACS in Florida again by Nov. 1864. Surrendered May 18, 1865, at Lake City. Jacksonville grocer postwar. d. Jan. 18, 1912. bur. St. Mary's Cem.

Baylor, William Smith Hanger. b. Augusta Co., Virginia, Apr. 7, 1831. att. UVA. and Washington Coll. Staunton Commonwealth's attorney. m. Mary Harris Johnson. Capt. Co. L, 5th Virginia, Apr. 1861. Maj., May 28, 1861. Lt. Col. AAAIG to T. J. Jackson, Jan.–Apr. 1862. Col. 5th Virginia, Apr. 21, 1862. KIA at Second Manassas. bur. Hebron Presby. Church, Augusta Co.

Bayly, Samuel Thomas. b. Accomack Co., Virginia, Apr. 30, 1830. att. UVA. Richmond lawyer pre- and postwar. Capt. Co. A, 20th Virginia, May 25, 1861. Capt. of Bayly's Btty., Apr.–June 1862. Capt. AAG to J. H. Winder, July 7, 1862. Capt. AAG to report to Richmond, Apr. 1, 1865. Paroled May 3, 1865, at Charlotte. d. Richmond, Apr. 15, 1872. bur. Hollywood Cem.

Bayne, Thomas Levingstone. b. Clinton, Georgia, August 4, 1824. Grew up in Alabama. att. Yale. New Orleans lawyer, 1848–1891. Pvt. 5th Co. Washington Arty (La.). WIA in shoulder at Shiloh. Capt. OO to Gorgas, Aug. 16, 1862. Maj. OO, June 18, 1863. Lt. Col. OO, Feb. 19, 1864. Chief of "Bureau of Foreign Supplies," 1864–1865. m. Anna Maria Gayle, a daughter of Alabama's governor. d. New Orleans, Dec. 10, 1891. bur. Magnolia Cem., Mobile, Alabama.

Beale, Richard Channing. b. Westmoreland Co., Virginia, May 30, 1846. Pvt. Co. K, 40th Virginia, May 1861. Pvt. Co. C, 9th Virginia Cavy., Aug. 1861. Lt. ADC to his father, Gen. Beale, Feb. 1, 1865. Took Oath Mar. 20, 1865, at Stoney Creek Depot. Postwar judge in Texas. d. Corsicana, June 9, 1889.

Beall, Julius Ceasar Alford. b. in Georgia, June 7, 1841. Student in Warren Co. in 1860. Lt. Co. H, 22nd Georgia, Aug. 31, 1861. WIA in Seven Days. To Capt. May 21, 1863. Capt.

acting ADC to Wright at Chancellorsville. WIA in thigh and POW at Gettysburg, July 2, 1863. Exchanged Mar. 10, 1864. d. Feb. 12, 1905. bur. Baker-Beall Cem., Warren Co. Spelling of middle name probably Caesar, but only available source gives the odd rendering shown above.

Beall, Thomas Jeremiah. b. Thomaston, Georgia, May 12, 1836. Moved to Marshall, Texas, 1850. att. U. of Louisiana and Cumberland Univ. Lawyer at Marshall. Pvt. Co. D, 7th Texas, May 1, 1861. WIA and POW at Ft. Donelson. Lt. ADC to John Gregg, Oct. 9, 1862. WIA at Wilderness. Resigned July 29, 1864, suffering from asthma. Married twice. Lawyer at Bryan, El Paso, and Ft. Worth, Texas. d. Ft. Worth, July 29, 1921. bur. Evergreen Cem., El Paso.

Beard, W. W. Drillmaster in North Carolina in 1861. Has a brief record as AAIG to Gen. Lewis, Feb. 1865.

Beckham, Abner Camp. b. Sept. 11, 1843. Of Brandy Station, Virginia. att. VMI. VADC to Kemper, 1861–1862. After foot torn off by a shell at Sharpsburg, "borne from the field cheering," and POW. Apptd. Drillmaster in the Virginia Reserves, Aug. 1864. Lynchburg lumber merchant and then moved to Texas and became a railroad contractor. d. there in June 1883.

Beckham, Henry Clay. b. Nov. 24, 1836. att. UVA, VMI, and Jefferson Medical Coll. Pvt. Co. C, 7th Virginia, Apr. 30, 1861. Lt. Co. E, Apr. 26, 1862. Resigned Sept. 22, 1862, Gen. Kemper noting the regiment would be better off without him. VADC to Corse, Aug. to Oct. 1862. Contract surgeon at Lynchburg, Oct. 16, 1862, but declared incompetent by Oct. 31, 1862. Contract surgeon in Richmond most of 1863. Conscripted into 1st Engineer Regiment, Jan. 28, 1864, and rose to Sgt. Physician in Culpeper Co. and at Charlestown, West Virginia. d. Apr. 2, 1916.

Beckham, Robert Franklin. b. Culpeper, Virginia, May 6, 1837. att. USMA. U.S. Army engineer. Lt. of Arty., Mar. 16, 1861. Lt. ADC to G. W. Smith, Jan. 14, 1862. Maj. OO to Smith, Aug. 16, 1862. Maj. Stuart Horse Arty. Bn., Apr. 8, 1863. Maj. Chief of Arty. to Stuart. Col. Chief of Arty. to Hood, Feb. 16, 1864. MWIA at Columbia, Tenn., Nov. 29, 1864. d. Ashwood, Tennessee, Dec. 5, 1864. bur. St. John's Church.

Beggs, Thomas. b. Jefferson Co., Mississippi. WIA in right thigh at Battle of Churubusco, Aug. 1847. 41-year-old commission merchant at Columbia, South Carolina, in 1860. Capt. ACS, Hampton Legion, June 12, 1861. Maj. CS to Hampton, July 29, 1862. Failed to execute bond and dropped, Feb. 5, 1863. Restored to duty May 16, 1863. Maj. CS to Butler, Mar. 23, 1863. Paroled at Greensboro, Apr. 26, 1865. Operated a "huckster shop" at Montgomery, Alabama, postwar. Alive 1887 at Abbeville C.H., South Carolina, age 67, a saddle and harness maker.

Bell, Henderson Moffett. b. Staunton, Virginia, July 3, 1826. att. Washington Coll. Staunton lawyer, 1849–1899. Capt. AQM at Staunton, July 19, 1861. Maj. QM at Staunton, July 10, 1862. Served there through 1865. Postwar law partner of Gen. Echols and member of state legislature. Extracts of Bell's 1862 letters are in the Jedediah Hotchkiss Papers at the Library of Congress.

Bell, John Wesley. b. Culpeper Co., Virginia, 1819. Lawyer there, 1840–1861. Capt. AQM, 49th Virginia, July 17, 1861. Failed bond and dropped, Feb. 24, 1862, but continued to serve. Maj. QM to his brother-in-law, Gen. Wm. Smith, May 2, 1863, an appointment protested by Gen. Early, who complained that Bell was unfit "by reason of inefficiency, bad temper, and an insubordinate spirit. . . ." Maj. QM to Pegram, 1863–1864. Suspended Mar. 14, 1865, a board of examination having questioned his competence. Subjected to one court of inquiry and perhaps a court martial. Judge in Cul-

peper Co. Author of standard biography of Gen. "Extra Billy" Smith. d. Culpeper, Virginia, Sept. 13, 1896. bur. Masonic Cem.

Bell, Robert F. b. 1840. att. VMI. Pvt. 2nd Co. Richmond Howitzers, June 5, 1861. Served with Co. I, 4th Virginia Cavy., Oct. 1861–Jan. 1862. Back with Richmond Howitzers, Mar. 29–Aug. 1862. VADC to Wright, Aug. 16, 1862–Feb. 1864. Has a record as Capt. ADC to A. P. Hill, Dec. 1864–Apr. 1865, though no commission found. Merchant in New York City. d. sometime after 1914.

Bell, Robert S. 21-year-old overseer in Augusta Co., Virginia, in 1860. Pvt. Co. E, 1st Virginia Cavy., Apr. 19, 1861. Left company in Aug. 1862 as a Cpl. Capt. AQM, Aug. 7, 1862, to report to T. J. Jackson. Apparently served as Capt. AQM at Second Corps headquarters. Capt. AQM at Staunton and Dublin, Virginia, Sept. 15, 1864. Paroled May 1, 1865. Farmer in Augusta Co. d. Apr. 18, 1895. bur. Thornrose Cem., Staunton. Middle name possibly Sherrard.

Bell, Thomas Parker. b. in North Carolina, December 6, 1835. Moved to Kemper Co., Mississippi, in the 1840s. A lawyer, judge, and newspaper editor there. Lt. Co. F, 13th Mississippi, May 14, 1861. Dropped Apr. 26, 1862. Lt. ADC to Barksdale, June 10, 1863. Out of service with July 1863 death of Barksdale. No further military record. m. Amelia Eiland, 1865. Legislator and planter in Mississippi. d. December 8, 1907. bur. Pinecrest Cem., Kemper Co.

Bellinger, John. b. in South Carolina, Mar. 1841. att. Georgetown Coll. Clerk at Charleston, South Carolina. Pvt. Co. I, 2nd South Carolina, May 9, 1861. Discharged Dec. 29, 1862, for poor health. Lt. SO, Dec. 29, 1862. Staff of W. E. Jones by Apr. 20, 1863. Lt. SO to Ed Johnson, Nov. 7, 1863, but revoked before effective. Lt. SO to Breckinridge, Dec. 1, 1863. Lt. SO to Hindman later. WIA in 1864. Alive 1880 in Falls Co., Texas, a bank clerk.

Belton, Joseph Francis. A government employee in New York City prewar. Pvt. Hampton Legion (S.C.) Arty., June 15, 1861. To Cpl. Oct. 9, 1861. Lt. ADC to his cousin, Gen. E. K. Smith, Nov. 16, 1861. Capt. AAG to Smith, June 21, 1862. Capt. AAG to Holmes, Sept. 29, 1863. Subsequently Lt. Col. AAG to Price, Magruder, and Smith. One of Belton's relatives wrote of him: "a fine looking young man but I fear is pursuing a downward, disgraceful career owing to a want of truth & strict integrity of principle & character."

Bender, William G. A resident of Baltimore, Maryland. Lt. EO, June 6, 1862. Capt. EO, Mar. 17, 1864. Served in Virginia. In charge of railroad defenses at High Bridge by Sept. 1864. Paroled Apr. 26, 1865.

Bennett, William Henry. b. Columbus, Georgia, Aug. 7, 1836. A clerk there. Cpl. in 17th Georgia, Aug. 14, 1861. Capt. ACS, 17th Georgia, Sept. 23, 1862. Capt. ACS to Benning, July 31, 1863. POW in Jefferson Co., Tennessee, Jan. 20, 1864. Released from Ft. Delaware, June 1865. d. Dec. 22, 1868, from a disease contracted in prison. bur. Linwood Cem., Columbus.

Benning, Seaborn Jones. b. Columbus, Georgia, July 8, 1840. att. GMI. Lt. Co. C, 1st Georgia Regs., Sept. 4, 1861. WIA badly at Second Manassas and on July 2, 1863, at Gettysburg. Capt. AAG to his father, Gen. Benning, Jan. 17, 1863. Appx. Columbus law partner of his father. d. there Dec. 12, 1874, of consumption. bur. Linwood Cem. "His faults will lie in the grave in which he is placed," said his obituary.

Bentley, William G. Capt. AQM, Aug. 31, 1862. Maj. QM, Oct. 23, 1863. Served at Richmond, Virginia, where he issued clothing to the army and supervised production of tents and other camp materials.

Berkeley, Charles Fenton. b. Nov. 13, 1832. Pvt. Co. D, 8th Virginia, May 3, 1861. To Lt., Dec. 1, 1862. Lt. AAAIG to R. B. Garnett for several months between Jan. and June 1863. POW at Gettysburg. To Capt., Mar. 31, 1864. POW at Sailor's Creek. Took Oath, June 19, 1865, a resident of Aldie, Virginia. d. Oct. 22, 1877. bur. Sharon Cem., Middleburg.

Berkeley, Francis Brooke. b. Staunton, Virginia, Sept. 5, 1835. att. military school in Maryland. Paymaster's clerk in U.S. Army. Pvt. Staunton Arty., Nov. 1, 1861. Discharged Apr. 28, 1862. Adjt. 62nd Virginia, Aug. 6, 1862. Capt. AAG to Imboden, Jan. 28, 1863. m. Susan Jane Baird. Baltimore express agent and Staunton druggist. d. Oct. 12, 1898. bur. Thornrose Cem., Staunton.

Bernard, Jesse Talbot. b. Portsmouth, Virginia, Aug. 20, 1829. att. Norfolk Academy, Wm. & Mary, Randolph Macon, and Centenary Coll. Florida schoolteacher, lawyer, and newspaperman. Pvt. Gamble's (Fla.) Btty., Apr. 24, 1862. Capt. AQM, 8th Florida, July 13, 1862. Capt. AQM in charge of ANVa. ambulance train, Sept. 15, 1864. Appx. Mayor of Tallahassee. d. October 29, 1909.

Berney, John. Lt. CSA, Apr. 10, 1861, appointed from Alabama. On recruiting duty at Mt. Vernon, Alabama, May–June 1861. At Camp of Instruction, Richmond, Virginia, June–Aug. 1861. On unspecified duty with 13th Alabama, and with 6th Alabama, later in 1861. Lt. ADC to Rodes, Aug. 9, 1862. WIA in face at Sharpsburg. Reassigned to Mobile, Alabama, Feb. 2, 1863. PM of a military court for rest of war. Never married. d. St. Louis, Missouri, 1878, of yellow fever. "He is a handsome, pleasant fellow with a red head. . . ."

Berrien, John McPherson. b. Savannah, Georgia, October 27, 1841. Father was a U.S. Senator. Lt. Co. B, 8th Georgia. Lt. AAG to Col. Francis S. Bartow, May 17, 1861. Lt. OO to Barksdale, Aug. 4, 1862. Lt. OO to T. R. R. Cobb, Sept. 24, 1862. WIA in hip at Fredericksburg. "Remained a cripple for life."

Savannah Justice of the Peace. d. July 8, 1875, of typhoid fever. bur. Laurel Grove Cem.

Bessent, Ransom Powell. b. in North Carolina, May 14, 1818. Salisbury dentist, pre- and postwar. Lt. Co. B, 42nd North Carolina, Jan. 10, 1862. To Capt. AQM, Oct. 14, 1862. Capt. AQM to Martin, June 14, 1864. Capt. AQM to Kirkland, Sept. 20, 1864. Paroled at Greensboro. d. Aug. 8, 1892. bur. Jerusalem Church Cem., Cooleemee, Davie Co., North Carolina.

Best, Emory Fiske. b. in Maryland, Mar. 28, 1840. Occupation was "gentleman." Lt. Co. C, 23rd Georgia, Aug. 31, 1861. Up through the ranks to colonel by Nov. 1862. WIA at Sharpsburg. Col. AAAIG to Rodes at Chancellorsville. Dismissed by court-martial for Chancellorsville disaster. Postwar Washington, D.C., clerk. d. Apr. 23, 1912. bur. Macon, Georgia.

Bier, George Henry. b. Baltimore, Maryland, July 11, 1824. In USN, 1841–1861. Lt. CSN, Nov. 13, 1861. Maj. OO to T. J. Jackson, May 23, 1862, apparently without leaving the navy. Rejoined the navy in Jan. 1863. POW running the blockade off Wilmington in 1864, but "escaped in Boston Harbor." Lived postwar in Washington, D.C. Married three times. d. Key West, Florida, Apr. 13, 1905. bur. St. Mary's Catholic Cem., Monroe Co., Florida.

Bigger, Robert H. Resident of Washington, D.C. Maj. QM to John Gregg, Oct. 9, 1862, but never confirmed by Congress. Served in unknown position at Atlanta, Georgia, Nov. 1863–July 1864. Maj. QM to Dearing, Sept. 19, 1864. Maj. QM to Roberts, Feb. 20, 1865. Probably Robert Hamilton Bigger who att. Harvard from North Carolina, and d. Nov. 13, 1888, when he jumped from a burning hotel at Chattanooga, Tennessee.

Bird, William Edgeworth. b. July 21, 1825. att. Georgetown. m. Sarah C. J. Baxter. Capt. Co. E, 15th Georgia. WIA at Second Manassas. Capt. AQM to Benning, Mar. 30, 1863. Maj. QM to Benning, Apr. 11, 1863. Reassigned to duty with Board of Slave Claims, Sept. 23, 1864. d. Hancock Co., Georgia, Jan. 11, 1867, of pneumonia. bur. Oconee Hill Cem., Athens. Bird's wartime correspondence has been published under the title of *The Granite Farm Letters*.

Biscoe, Henry Lawson. b. Lancaster Co., Virginia, 1841. att. Columbian Coll. Lived prewar in Richmond Co. Pvt. Co. B, 40th Virginia, May 22, 1861. To Capt. ACS, May 30, 1861. Capt. ACS to Pettigrew, Mar. 30, 1862. Maj. CS to Pender, June 28, 1862. Maj. CS to Scales, 1863–1865. Appx. Lived postwar in Washington, D.C. A lumber dealer. d. Pensacola, Florida, Apr. 5, 1905, age 63. bur. Washington, D.C.

Biscoe, Thomas H. Unmarried clerk at New Orleans, Louisiana. Lt. Co. K, 5th Louisiana, May 21, 1861, age 22. To Capt. Dec. 26, 1861. WIA during Seven Days. POW at Second Manassas. VADC to Monaghan's Louisiana Brigade at Mine Run. KIA at the Wilderness, May 5, 1864.

Blackburn, John Sinclair. b. October 9, 1838. Of Clarke Co., Virginia. Pvt. Co. D, 6th Virginia Cavy., Apr. 18, 1861. Acting Lt. of Arty., Dec. 24, 1862. Lt. OO, Feb. 7, 1863, assigned to staff of Gen. Thomas, Feb. 18, 1863. Lt. OO to Lomax, Dec. 1863. Lt. OO to Payne. Paroled May 1, 1865, at Summit Point, Virginia. att. UVA. postwar. Academy principal at Alexandria. d. Dec. 1, 1911. bur. St. Paul's Episc. Churchyard.

Blackford, Benjamin Lewis. b. Fredericksburg, Virginia, Aug. 5, 1835. att. UVA. Lynchburg merchant and civil engineer on Orange & Alexandria Railroad. Sgt. Co. G, 11th Virginia, Apr. 23, 1861. Lt. EO in PAVa., on duty at Norfolk, June 1861. Contract topographer with Engineer Dept., June 1862. Lt. EO in PACS, Mar. 17, 1864. Slightly WIA at Appomattox. Washington, D.C., civil engineer, insurance agent, and broker. d. Staunton, Virginia, Sept. 26, 1908. bur.

Lynchburg. Blackford has papers at UNC and the Virginia Historical Society.

Blackford, Charles Minor. b. Fredericksburg, Virginia, October 17, 1833. att. UVA. Lawyer in Lynchburg pre- and postwar. Lt. Co. B, 2nd Virginia Cavy., May 13, 1861. Capt. of Cavy. and Judge on First Corps court, Dec. 16, 1862. On temporary duty in Richmond as AAAG to Cooper, Sept. 18, 1864. Bank president. d. Mar. 10, 1903. bur. Spring Hill Cem., Lynchburg.

Blackford, William Willis. Originally William Wilberforce, but changed middle name, reportedly to show affection for kinsmen in Willis family. b. Fredericksburg, Virginia, Mar. 23, 1831. att. UVA. Railroad engineer and businessman. Adjt. 1st Virginia Cavy. Capt. EO, May 26, 1862. Capt. EO to Stuart, June 24, 1862. WIA in leg, Nov. 3, 1862. Maj. EO, Feb. 19, 1864. Lt. Col. 1st C.S. Engineers, Apr. 1, 1864. Appx. Postwar farmer and professor at Virginia Tech. d. Norfolk, Apr. 30, 1905. bur. Sinking Spring Cem., Abingdon.

Blackwell, Reuben W. Said to have served in 10th Alabama, but has no record with that unit. Lt. ADC to Longstreet, Apr. 22, 1862. Dropped Aug. 27, 1863, for prolonged absence without leave. Pvt. Co. C, 1st Virginia Bn. Light Arty., Oct. 20, 1863. Transferred to 34th Virginia, Dec. 7, 1864. Deserted Dec. 31, 1864.

Blackwell, Thomas J. b. December 14, 1839. att. GMI. Lt. Co. I, 8th Georgia, May 16, 1861. WIA at Garnett's Farm. Lt. AAAG to G. T. Anderson, Aug. and Sept. 1862. Capt. Co. I, 8th Georgia, Dec. 16, 1862. KIA at the Wilderness, May 6, 1864. Body never recovered, although he has a memorial stone at the family cemetery in Cobb Co.

Blair, James Edwin. b. Scottsville, Virginia, Mar. 21, 1837. Pvt. Co. C, 19th Virginia, Apr. 1861. WIA at Gaines's Mill and Second Manassas. Capt. AQM, 19th Virginia, Jan. 1, 1863. Capt. AQM Stark's Bn. Arty., Aug. 5, 1864. "Agent" in Scottsville postwar.

Moved to Richmond about 1876 and was a bookkeeper. d. there Jan. 26, 1916.

Blair, William Barrett. b. in Virginia, Sept. 25, 1817. att. USMA. Capt. U.S. Army, 1838–1861, partly in artillery and partly as staff officer. Mexican War veteran. Maj. Chief Commissary of Confederate army in Virginia, Mar. 16–Dec. 9, 1861, when he was relieved due to poor health. Returned to duty briefly in May 1862. Chief Commissary in Trans-Mississippi Dept., Nov. 26, 1862. Maj. AAAG in Arkansas, May 1863. Paroled at Marshall, Texas, June 24, 1865. The Jackson Professor of Natural and Experimental Philosophy at VMI postwar. d. Mar. 23, 1883.

Blake, Frederick Rutledge. b. Jan. 24, 1838. Of Hendersonville, North Carolina. Capt. Co. H, 25th North Carolina, July 15, 1861. Failed reelection. VADC to Robert Ransom during Seven Days. VADC to Ripley. Lt. ADC to Clingman, Feb. 25, 1863. Capt. AAIG to Clingman, Jan. 17, 1864. WIA in leg at Cold Harbor, June 1, 1864. Apptd. to duty with Gen. Hebert, Dec. 1864. m. Olivia Middleton. d. Feb. 18, 1907. bur. Calvary Episc. Churchyard Cem., Hendersonville.

Blakemore, James Hamilton. Resident of Petersburg, Virginia. Pvt. Co. E, 12th Virginia, Apr. 15, 1862. Detailed as courier for Gen. R. H. Anderson, Jan. 19, 1863. Courier for Mahone, too. Served as AAAG and AAAIG to Mahone, autumn 1864, while still a private. Lt. Asst. OO to Matt. Ransom, Mar. 20, 1865. Appx. m. Catherine E. Pollard, 1869. Alive in New York, 1880. Probably died there in October 1902.

Blakemore, William Thomas. b. Clarke Co., Virginia, Aug. 21, 1835. Moved to Christian Co., Kentucky, just before the war. On staff of Gen. Tilghmann, 1861–1862. Lt. ADC to B. R. Johnson, Mar. 14, 1862. WIA at Drewry's Bluff, May 20, 1864, a gunboat shell taking off his right leg. On court-martial duty at Richmond, Sept. 1864 into 1865. Cotton broker at New Orleans, Louisiana. Spent his summers at Hopkinsville, Kentucky. d. Feb. 12, 1919. bur. Metairie Cem., New Orleans.

Blanton, Benjamin Harrison. b. Franklin Co., Kentucky, Dec. 16, 1829. A resident of Frankfort. Grew wealthy in 1849 gold rush and "owned much of the business section of down-town Denver" before the war, but sold it for Confederate bonds. VADC to Hood during Seven Days. Lt. ADC to Hood, Oct. 15, 1862, to rank from Apr. 1, 1862. Resigned Aug. 1, 1864, but seems never to have left. Capt. ADC to Hood, Apr. 1865. m. Alice Elizabeth Bacon. d. June 29, 1884. bur. Frankfort Cem.

Blocker, John Rufus. b. Edgefield Co., South Carolina, Sept. 29, 1838. att. USMA. Commanded a battery at Ft. Sumter in Apr. 1861. Adjt. 59th Virginia, Oct. 14, 1861. POW at Roanoke Island, Feb. 8, 1862. Lt. Co. H, 1st South Carolina Arty., Nov. 1862. Maj. AAIG to Butler, Jan. 1864. MWIA late May 1864. d. Richmond, Virginia, June 6, 1864. bur. family cemetery eight miles northwest of Edgefield C.H., South Carolina.

Bloom, Francis S. b. in New York. 41-year-old cotton merchant at Macon, Georgia, in 1860. Lt. ADC to H. R. Jackson, Sept. 5, 1861, but had been serving with him as early as July. d. Macon, Georgia, December 19, 1861, of pneumonia.

Bloomfield, Benjamin. b. New Orleans, Louisiana, Dec. 30, 1824. In prewar Washington Arty. company. Capt. AQM, 2nd Louisiana, Apr. 27, 1861. Capt. AQM to Magruder by June 1861. Maj. QM to Magruder, Dec. 24, 1861. Served through 1864 at least. d. Opelousas, Louisiana, Mar. 17, 1903.

Blount, Robert P. b. in Georgia, 1819. Veteran of the Texas Revolution and the Mexican War. Farmer in Sumter Co., Alabama, worth $77,000 in 1860. Capt. Co. F, 5th Alabama. Resigned Sept. 19, 1861. Lt. Col. 9th Alabama Bn., 1862. Dropped at reorganization. VADC and PM to Longstreet during

Maryland Campaign. POW Nov. 6, 1862. Still with Longstreet in June 1863. No later record.

Blount, Thomas M., Jr. b. in Florida. att. Georgetown Coll. A physician at Washington, D.C., in 1860. Sgt. Co. E, 4th North Carolina, June 15, 1861, age 28. Capt. AQM, 4th North Carolina, July 19, 1861. Capt. AAAG to G. B. Anderson during Seven Days. KIA at Gaines's Mill while carrying a flag. bur. Oakwood Cem., Richmond, Virginia.

Blount, William Augustus., Jr. b. October 6, 1823. Of Washington, North Carolina. att. UNC. Lt. ADC to his brother-in-law Gen. Branch, Mar. 20, 1862. WIA at Gaines's Mill. Resigned July 1862. North Carolina legislator and planter. d. June 30, 1901. bur. Beaufort Co.

Boarman, Alexander. b. Yazoo City, Mississippi, Dec. 10, 1839. att. KMI and Univ. of Kentucky. Lt. Co. A, 1st Louisiana, Apr. 15, 1861. Capt., Apr. 28, 1862. Capt. AAAG to Nicholls, Apr. 1863. Capt. AAAG to Iverson, Aug. 1863. Capt. VADC to Stafford, Nov. 1863. Capt. AAIG to Stafford, date uncertain. POW at Wilderness, May 5, 1864. Exchanged Oct. 1864. On recruiting and other light duty in Louisiana, due to "permanent disability." Became "a bitter Republican." Mayor of Shreveport, 1866–1867. Lawyer and judge in Louisiana. d. Franklin Co., New York, Aug. 30, 1916. bur. Oakland Cem., Shreveport.

Bolling, George Washington, Jr. b. in Virginia, Oct. 15, 1842. Brother of W. N. Bolling (q.v.). Clerk in tax-in-kind office at Petersburg. Capt. ACS, Mar. 3, 1865, to report to ANVa. headquarters. Appx. d. May 4, 1903. bur. Blandford Cem., Petersburg.

Bolling, Stith. b. Lunenburg Co., Virginia, Feb. 28, 1835. Merchant at Richmond. Served in Co. G, 9th Virginia Cavy., in ranks from Sgt. through Capt., June 1861 to 1865. Capt. AAAG to W. H. F. Lee, Feb. 1863. WIA in head at Morton's Ford, Oct. 11,

1863, and in thigh in May 1864. Postmaster at Petersburg and state legislator. d. there Nov. 1, 1916.

Bolling, William Nicholls. b. Petersburg, Virginia, Aug. 1, 1830. att. Princeton and school in Berlin, Germany. Taught at Princeton, and was a diplomat in Brazil, 1857–1861. m. Susan Meade, 1857. Pvt. Co. E, 12th Virginia, Apr. 19, 1861. Lt. EO, PAVa., May 7, 1861. Lt. EO, PACS, Nov. 21, 1863. Worked mostly between Petersburg and Weldon. Staff of Beauregard, June 1864. Appx. m. Hannah Lamb Bonham, 1870. Railroad engineer and real estate manager based at Baltimore, Maryland. d. 1898.

Bolton, Channing Moore. b. Richmond, Virginia, Jan. 24, 1843. att. UVa. Apparently a Lt. in PAVa., 1861, and worked on Richmond's defenses into 1862, partially as a volunteer engineer. Civilian engineer constructing Piedmont Railroad, spring 1862–Apr. 1863. EO to Pender at Gettysburg, and to Wilcox July 1863–1864. No commission found, but probably a Lt. EO (PACS). Lt. Co. E, 1st C.S. Engineers, Mar. 29, 1864. POW at Farmville, Apr. 1865. m. Elizabeth Calhoun Campbell, daughter of Parker Campbell (q.v.). Postwar railroad engineer. d. Charlottesville, Virginia, Dec. 6, 1922. bur. Hollywood Cem., Richmond.

Bolton, Henry. b. in England. Prewar resident of Georgia. Civil engineer on duty with Wise Legion (Va.), Aug. 1861. Lt. EO to Wise, Oct. 7, 1861. Lt. EO to Magruder, Apr. 11, 1862. Back to Wise, June 1862. On torpedo service under Gen. Whiting at Wilmington, North Carolina, Jan. 1863–June 1864. Capt. (PACS), June 1, 1863. Capt. EO to G. J. Rains, June 8, 1864. Capt. EO to Wilcox, Dec. 1864. Appx.

Bond, Frank Augustus. b. Harford Co., Maryland, Feb. 6, 1838. Captain in state guard and farmer at Bel Air. Drilled troops early in the war. Pvt. Co. K, 1st Virginia Cavy., May 14, 1861. To Lt. later, but dropped at Apr. 1862 reorganization. Lt.

Co. A, 1st Maryland Cavy., May 15, 1862. Lt. AAAG to Steuart, June 6, 1862. Lt. AAAG to B. T. Johnson by Seven Days. WIA at Second Manassas. Capt. Co. A, 1st Maryland Cavy., Nov. 12, 1862. WIA July 8, 1863. Retired to Invalid Corps, Oct. 1864. Staff of Leventhorpe in 1865. Postwar farmer in Anne Arundel Co. and supt. of state house of corrections. d. Philadelphia, Pennsylvania, Nov. 12, 1923. bur. Loudon Park Cem., Baltimore. Bond's memoir is at the Museum of the Confederacy in Richmond.

Bond, William Robert. b. Halifax Co., North Carolina, Aug. 20, 1839. att. UNC. Pvt. Co. G, 12th North Carolina, May 1861. Lt. Co. F, 43rd North Carolina, Feb. 1862. Lt. VADC to Daniel, June 1862 until Lt. ADC, Sept. 1, 1862. WIA in side and POW at Gettysburg. Released from Ft. Delaware, June 1865. Farmer and bank cashier. Wrote famous pamphlet on Gettysburg. d. June 20, 1922. bur. Halifax Co.

Booker, George. b. Elizabeth City Co., Virginia, Sept. 15, 1805. att. Wm. & Mary. Wealthy planter and legislator. Maj. QM, Oct. 24, 1861. Stationed at Williamsburg, Jan. and Feb. 1862. Maj. QM in Richmond and Petersburg until he resigned, Mar. 23, 1865, citing poor health. Father of R. M. Booker (q.v.). m. Ann Massenburg. d. Feb. 11, 1868. bur. St. John's Cem., Hampton, Virginia.

Booker, Richard Marshall. b. near Hampton, Virginia, Feb. 3, 1837. att. J. B. Cary's Military Academy and Wm. & Mary. Farmer. Pvt. Co. D, 1st (Ramsey's) Georgia, Mar. 1861. Lt. of Inf., May 24, 1861, to report to Magruder. Reported to J. H. Winder, July 1861, to help establish Richmond prison system. Detailed to QM Dept., Feb. 1, 1862. Staff of McLaws around Yorktown. Apptd. Capt., July 17, 1862. Adjt. at Ft. Caswell, North Carolina, Dec. 17, 1863. Hampton oysterman and brick manufacturer postwar. A director of the Richmond

Soldiers' Home. d. Feb. 1898. bur. St. John's Cem., Hampton.

Boone, John Baxter F. b. in South Carolina, Apr. 25, 1828. A boot and shoe dealer at Charlotte, North Carolina, in 1860. Capt. AQM, 1st North Carolina (6 months), May 13, 1861. Maj. QM to D. H. Hill, Sept. 30, 1861. Resigned Mar. 29, 1862. d. Apr. 21, 1899. bur. Oak Cliff Cem., Dallas, Texas.

Booth, George Wilson. b. in Maryland, July 29, 1844. att. Baltimore City Coll. Lived in California prewar. Pvt. and Adjt. 1st Maryland, May 1861. Lt. VADC to B. T. Johnson, Aug. 1862. WIA in thigh at Second Manassas, Aug. 30, 1862. Adjt. 1st Maryland Bn. Cavy., Jan. 1863. WIA at Greenland Gap, Apr. 23, 1863. Capt. AAG to B. T. Johnson, Sept. 25, 1863. WIA at Pollard's Farm, May 27, 1864. Resigned Mar. 25, 1865. m. Mrs. Susanna Eubank, 1866. Baltimore businessman and author. d. there Jan. 6, 1914. bur. Loudon Park Cem.

von Borcke, Johann August Heinrich Heros. b. Ehrenbreitstein, Prussia, July 23, 1835. att. school in Berlin and Halle. Prussian army prewar. Capt. VADC to Stuart, May–June 1862. Capt. AAAG to Stuart during Seven Days. Maj. AAIG to Stuart, July 25, 1862. WIA in throat at Middleburg, June 19, 1863. In Richmond on light duty, Feb. 1864. Lt. Col. AAG to Gorgas, Dec. 20, 1864. Ran blockade to Europe. Served in Austro-Prussian War. d. Berlin, May 10, 1895. Stuart called him "a noble fellow," but a close acquaintance also called von Borcke "ornamental" and "useless."

Boswell, James Keith. b. Fauquier Co., Virginia, Nov. 18, 1838. Civil engineer in Missouri and Alabama. Lt. PAVA. Lt. EO to Magruder, Nov. 1861, constructing entrenchments near Williamsburg. Lt. EO, PACS, to T. J. Jackson, Feb. 15, 1862. Capt. EO, Sept. 29, 1862. KIA at Chancellorsville, May 2, 1863. Portions of wartime diary published. bur. Fredericksburg Confederate Cem. Nicknamed "Preserves" because he loved jelly.

Boteler, Alexander Robinson. b. Shepherdstown, Virginia, May 16, 1815. att. Princeton. A great-grandson of famous painter Charles Wilson Peale. Farmer and member of USHR. Col. VADC to T. J. Jackson, May 30, 1862, into Aug. 1862. Col. VADC to Stuart, Aug. 15, 1863, through May 1864. Col. of Cavy. and Judge on military court of Anderson's corps, Nov. 1, 1864. Appx. Politician, farmer, and Dept. of Justice official. m. Helen Macomb Stockton. d. May 8, 1892. bur. Elmwood Cem., Shepherdstown.

Boteler, Alexander Robinson, Jr. b. Shepherdstown, Virginia, Aug. 18, 1842. Pvt. Co. B, 2nd Virginia, June 10–Oct. 8, 1861. Pvt. 1st Rockbridge (Va.) Arty., Mar. 1, 1862. WIA twice at First Winchester. Lt. of Inf., Oct. 1862. On ordnance duty at Lynchburg, Virginia. Lt. OO to Kemper, Mar. 5, 1863. Lt. OO to Hoke, Apr. 13, 1863. Lt. OO to Stuart's Horse Arty. Bn., May 1864. m. Mary Selden. Lived at Farmville and in Amherst Co., Virginia. d. Salem, Virginia, Sept. 22, 1893.

Boudinot, William E. b. Wilmington, North Carolina, Oct. 17, 1817. Served in USN, 1836–1858. Mexican War veteran. Capt. OO to Holmes, May 1, 1861. Maj. OO to Whiting, Nov. 8, 1862. No other military record found. m. Leonora Watters, 1863. d. Chatham Co., North Carolina, Mar. 15, 1889.

Boughan, James Herbert. b. Fredericksburg, Virginia, ca. 1832. Lt. Co. B, 13th Virginia, Apr. 17, 1861. Capt. AQM, 13th Virginia, June 19, 1861. Failed bond and dropped, Feb. 24, 1862, but served on anyway. WIA at Port Republic. Capt. VADC to Ewell at Cedar Mountain. Capt. AQM to Wm. Smith, about Jan. 1863, and hence Capt. AQM to Pegram. WIA at Spotsylvania. Served into 1865 on the staff of Peck. Postwar civil engineer and surveyor. Lived in Isle of Wight Co., Virginia, and at Norfolk.

d. Norfolk, May 24, 1910. bur. Elmwood Cem.

Bouldin, Wood, Jr. b. Charlotte C.H., Virginia, Sept. 28, 1838. att. UVA. Lawyer at Richmond and in Charlotte Co. Lt. at Camp of Instruction (Richmond?), May 12, 1861. Lt. Staunton Hill (Va.) Arty., Sept. 23, 1861. VADC to Rodes during Seven Days. Lt. Drillmaster, Oct. 20, 1862. Lt. AAIG to Echols, Apr. 10, 1863. AAIG for Col. Patton's Bgd. through war. Injured in capitol disaster at Richmond, 1870. Farmer, lawyer, and judge at Richmond, and in Halifax Co. d. Apr. 12, 1911. bur. St. John's Episc. Churchyard, Halifax Co.

Bowen, Achilles. b. Bourbon Co., Kentucky, July 1825. att. Union Seminary and Jackson Coll. att. USMA, 1850, but resigned from army same year. Engineer in Tennessee and farmer in Maury Co. Maj. EO to S. R. Anderson, Aug. 1861. Served only briefly, "feeling that too low an office had been given one of his training and well known military ability." Maury Co. farmer postwar. m. Rebecca Ophelia Helm. d. Columbia, Tennessee, June 6, 1896. bur. unmarked grave in Rose Hill Cem.

Bower, Byron Benaniel. b. Talbotton, Georgia, Sept. 26, 1839. Raised in Cuthbert. Lawyer and Justice of the Peace at Newton. 5th Georgia, 1861–1862. Later Adjt. and then Capt. Co. B, 8th Georgia Cavy. Capt. AAIG to Dearing, summer 1864. Same to Roberts. Paroled May 10, 1865, Albany, Georgia. Lawyer and judge at Bainbridge. Married three times. d. Sept. 25, 1923.

Bowie, Thomas Fielder. b. Upper Marlboro, Maryland, May 14, 1836. Classmate of Fitzhugh Lee at St. Timothy's Hall, Baltimore. att. Union Coll. and Princeton. Pvt. 1st Maryland Light Arty., June 1861. VADC to Fitz. Lee, Jan. 1863. Maj. AAIG to Fitz. Lee, Sept. 16, 1863. Took Oath Apr. 28, 1865, in Maryland. WIA four times. d. Dec. 13, 1896. bur. family cemetery at "The Valley." "Tall, of athletic build."

Bowling, Henry Aloysius. b. Prince George's Co., Maryland, Feb. 21, 1837. att. UVA and Georgetown. Planter and lawyer. Unspecified staff duty with Fitz. Lee, Mar. 1863. Capt. AAIG, Nov. 2, 1863, to report to Wickham on Dec. 7, 1863. Capt. AAIG to W. H. F. Lee, Dec. 22, 1863. Same to Chambliss. MWIA Aug. 17, 1864. Left leg amputated. d. Richmond, Virginia, Oct. 18, 1864. bur. "private burying grounds in Richmond."

Bowyer, Thomas Mickie. b. Botetourt Co., Virginia, Feb. 22, 1830. att. UVA. and UPENN. Physician at Fincastle. Capt. Co. G, 28th Virginia, May 15, 1861. Capt. OO, May 13, 1862, on duty at Liberty, Virginia. Capt. Chief OO for Dept. of Western Virginia, Sept. 8, 1862. Maj. OO, June 23, 1863. Maj. OO to Kemper, Oct. 21, 1864. Mayor of Liberty. d. Battle Creek, Michigan, Sept. 8, 1900. bur. Longwood Cem., Bedford Co., Virginia.

Boyce, Henry Archinard. b. in Louisiana, Feb. 12, 1836. att. UVA. Law student in Rapides Parish in 1860. VADC to Magruder, Dec. 1861–July 1862. In Louisiana as a "special agent" for the engineer bureau, Apr. 1863. Paroled June 6, 1865, as Lt. OO to Steele. Planter in Rapides Parish. m. Anna Gertrude Seip, 1869. d. 1922. bur. Old Rapides Cem.

Boyce, Ker. b. Charleston, South Carolina, 1833. Lived in New York City prewar. ADC to Bonham around Charleston in 1861. Capt. ACS, 12th Bn. Georgia Arty., May 1, 1862. Capt. AQM, 12th Bn. Georgia Arty., Jan. 12, 1863. Capt. AQM to C. A. Evans, Sept. 15, 1864. Postmaster and money order clerk at Augusta, Georgia. d. there Mar. 20, 1891. bur. Magnolia Cem.

Boyd, Charles Rufus. b. Wytheville, Virginia, October 3, 1841. Pvt. Co. A, 4th Virginia, Apr. 24, 1861. Lt. EO in PAVA., July 20, 1861. Worked on Richmond's defenses, 1861–1862. Worked briefly as an agent for the Nitre & Mining Bureau. Lt. Co. B, 30th Bn. Virginia Sharpshooters, May 1, 1862. Lt.

Co. E, 3rd C.S. Engineers, Apr. 30, 1864. att. uva. postwar. Mineralogist and geologist at Wytheville. d. Rockfish, Virginia, Apr. 16, 1903.

Boyd, David French. b. Wytheville, Virginia, Oct. 4, 1834. att. uva. Professor at the Louisiana Military Academy and "an intimate personal friend of Gen. W. T. Sherman." QM Sgt. and Capt. ACS, 9th Louisiana, 1861. Maj. CS to Taylor, May 24, 1862. Failed bond but was reinstated in Nov. 1862 as Maj. CS to Hays. Resigned Apr. 15, 1863. On engineer duty in Louisiana by Nov. 1863. POW Feb. 3, 1864. Left engineers Oct. 1864. Staff of Brent, Mar. 1865. President of Louisiana State Univ. Brigadier gen. in Egyptian Army and president of a military school near Cairo. Boyd's memoirs have been published. d. Baton Rouge, Louisiana, May 27, 1899. bur. Magnolia Cem.

Boyd, Elisha Holmes. b. near Martinsburg, Virginia, Apr. 3, 1840. att. uva. Pvt. Rockbridge (Va.) Arty., June 28, 1861. WIA at Malvern Hill. Detailed on ordnance duty, Sept. 26, 1862. Lt. OO to J. R. Jones, Jan. 29, 1863. Same to J. M. Jones and William Terry. Appx. Baltimore lawyer. m. Lily Dandridge. d. Winchester, Virginia, Jan. 19, 1910, while delivering a speech on R. E. Lee's birthday to a United Daughters of the Confederacy gathering. bur. Mt. Hebron Cem.

Boyd, Robert Watson. b. May 27, 1833. att. Wofford Coll. Studied law prewar. Pvt. Co. F, 15th South Carolina, Aug. 29, 1861. Ordnance Sgt., May 15, 1862. WIA June 1864. Lt. OO to Gary, Aug. 24, 1864. Appx. Darlington lawyer. d. Aug. 10, 1900.

Boyd, Thomas G. Resident of Sullivan Co., Tennessee. Pvt. Co. H, 3rd Tennessee Mtd. Inf., Sept. 18, 1861. Lt. OO to Vaughn, by 1863, though commission not found. POW at Vicksburg. Took Oath, May 26, 1865, at Chattanooga.

Boyle, Cornelius. b. Washington, D.C., 1817. att. Columbian Coll. Very wealthy physi-

cian at Washington. Maj. PAVA., Apr. 28, 1861. Served as PM around Manassas. Maj. QM, Apr. 11, 1862. Sent to Gordonsville, Virginia, where he commanded the post (with title of PM) until the end of the war. d. Mar. 11, 1878. bur. Glenwood Cem., Washington, D.C., in unmarked grave.

Boyle, John Henry, Jr. b. Anne Arundel Co., Maryland, 1843. Pvt. Co. F, 1st Virginia, June 1–Nov. 13, 1861. VADC to Steuart, June–July 1863. No other record.

Boylston, Robert Bentham. b. Charleston, South Carolina, Nov. 22, 1822. att. South Carolina Coll. Winnsboro lawyer and legislator. VADC to Beauregard at Ft. Sumter. Lt. Col. CS to Bonham, Apr. 1861–Jan. 1862. Rank probably honorary. Lt. Enrolling Officer in South Carolina, Aug. 1, 1863. Apptd. Col. of Cavy., Nov. 11, 1864. No further record. d. Winnsboro, Sept. 4, 1865.

Bradford, Edmund. b. Philadelphia, Pennsylvania, July 31, 1816. att. USMA. In U.S. Army, 1837–1849. Maj. PAVA., May 2, 1861. Maj. AAIG to Huger. Resigned May 1862. Maj. QM, June 16, 1863, on tax-in-kind duty in Virginia in North Carolina through 1865. m. Anne Elizabeth Tazewell. d. Norfolk, Virginia, Apr. 26, 1889.

Bradford, William Albert. b. Culpeper Co., Virginia, Jan. 1823. att. uva. m. Louisa Christine Smith. Physician at Winchester and chemistry professor at Winchester Coll. of Medicine. Capt. AQM, 5th Virginia Cavy., 1861. Maj. CS to H. Marshall, Sept. 24, 1862. Maj. CS to Preston, 1863. Maj. CS at Abingdon, Virginia, Jan. 14, 1864. Maj. CS to Breckinridge, May 12, 1864. Dropped Jan. 27, 1865, but reinstated Mar. 24, 1865. Clarke Co. physician, farmer, and politician. d. there Nov. 13, 1882. bur. Mt. Hebron Cem., Winchester.

Bradford, William Kell. b. in Maryland. Son of Maryland's wartime governor. Possibly a secret service agent for T. J. Jackson at Harpers Ferry, 1861. VADC to Trimble, May 1861. Lt. of Inf., CSA, July 3, 1861. Assigned to duty at Richmond's prisons, and part of J. H. Winder's staff, Oct. 14, 1861. Later on conscription and prison duty in North Carolina. Lt. AAIG, Dec. 1862–June 1863, duty uncertain. Capt. AAIG, June 29, 1863. Acting Asst. PM at Savannah, Georgia. Capt. PM at Augusta, Georgia, Apr. 13, 1864. Under arrest Aug. 1864 for "malfeasance in office." Relieved Nov. 21, 1864, and resigned Mar. 9, 1865. d. near Baltimore, Maryland, Oct. 16, 1871, age 33.

Braithwaite, Jacob R. b. in Virginia, ca. 1841. Sgt. in Harrisonburg city corporation prewar. Capt. AQM, 33rd Virginia, Apr. 5, 1861. Capt. acting AQM to R. B. Garnett, Jan.–Mar. 1862. Capt. acting AQM to C. S. Winder, Apr.–Aug. 1862. Maj. QM to Paxton, Oct. 14, 1862. Stayed with brigade until Aug. 1864, and thus staff of J. A. Walker and probably Wm. Terry. Maj. QM to Walker, Aug. 20, 1864. Paroled at Winchester, Apr. 30, 1865. Express agent at Baltimore, Maryland, and Richmond, Virginia. d. Harrisonburg, Virginia, July 18, 1867. Stonewall Jackson called Braithwaite "an excellent Q. Master."

Brame, Tignal Hoke. b. in Virginia, Apr. 28, 1831. att. Hampden Sidney. "Professor of languages" at Raleigh, North Carolina. Sgt. Co. B, 12th North Carolina. Capt. ACS, 54th North Carolina, July 1, 1862. Capt. AQM, 6th North Carolina, May 12, 1863. Capt. AQM to Godwin, Sept. 15, 1864, then to Lewis a few days later. Capt. AQM on temporary duty with Second Corps ordnance train, Mar. 20, 1865. A miller at Henderson, North Carolina. d. July 24, 1920. bur. Oakwood Cem., Raleigh.

Branch, Edward Benjamin. b. in Virginia, June 1, 1828. Petersburg clerk and Mexican War veteran. Capt. AQM at Petersburg, Nov. 6, 1861. Maj. QM, May 14, 1863. Paroled Apr. 1865 in Richmond. Newspaperman in Richmond and Petersburg. Taught classes in bookkeeping and penmanship. d. Peters-

burg, Apr. 16, 1901, of carbuncles. bur. Blandford Cem., in unmarked grave.

Branch, Thomas Plummer. b. Petersburg, Virginia, Jan. 10, 1837. att. UVA. and Randolph Macon. Brother of Col. J. R. Branch. Petersburg clerk. Pvt. Co. B, 13th Virginia Cavy., May 27, 1861. Lt. Branch's (Va.) Btty., Aug. 1862. Maj. AAIG to Robert Ransom, June 16, 1863. POW at Drewry's Bluff, May 16, 1864. Member of Immortal 600. Maj. AAG to Rosser, 1865. Appx. Married twice. Augusta, Georgia, cotton merchant and banker. d. there May 13, 1900. bur. Magnolia Cem.

Branham, James William. b. Greenbrier Co., Virginia, 1835. Clerk and superintendent of railroad hands in Alleghany Co., 1860. Pvt. Co. A, 27th Virginia (later Carpenter's Btty.), Apr. 22, 1861. WIA at First Manassas. Pvt. in 60th Virginia in 1862. Lt. ADC to Echols, Mar. 18, 1863. Paroled Apr. 26, 1865, at Greensboro.

Brannan, William Henry. b. Alto, Franklin Co., Tennessee, October 2, 1833. att. Irving Coll. Winchester schoolteacher. Pvt. Co. C, 1st Tennessee, Apr. 27, 1861. Capt. AQM, Oct. 7, 1861. Capt. AQM to Heth, Sept. 15, 1864. POW at Sailor's Creek. Took Oath, June 1865. Postwar lawyer. d. Mar. 7, 1901. bur. Winchester City Cemetery. One source says Brannan's middle name was Hood.

Braselman, Berkeley Longbothom. b. Lynchburg, Virginia, ca. 1835. Grocer at New Orleans, Louisiana. Pvt. Third Co. Washington (La.) Arty., May 26, 1861. Lt. OO of that artillery battalion, May 2, 1863. Paroled Apr. 1865. Alive 1889 at Washington, D.C.

Brashear, Dennis F. b. in Maryland, Jan. 10, 1821. Merchant at Fredericksburg, Virginia. VADC to Magruder by Apr. 1862. Capt. ACS, May 2, 1863, and served in Dept. of West Texas, Arizona, and New Mexico. Paroled June 14, 1865, at Shreveport, Louisiana. d. Alexandria, Virginia, Apr. 8, 1881. bur. Ivy Hill Cem.

Braxton, Elliott Muse. b. Mathews Co., Virginia, Oct. 8, 1823. Lawyer in Richmond Co. and Fredericksburg. Capt. Co. I, 30th Virginia, July 1, 1861. Maj. QM to J. G. Walker, Aug. 11, 1862. Maj. QM to J. R. Cooke, Nov. 1862. Postwar USHR. d. Fredericksburg, Oct. 2, 1891. bur. Fredericksburg Confederate Cemetery. "One of the most quiet and sedate gentlemen that I ever knew," remembered one of his colleagues.

Braxton, John Staige. b. in Virginia. 33-year-old farmer in Richmond Co., in 1860. Lt. Co. I, 30th Virginia, July 1, 1861. Resigned May 14, 1862. Capt. AAG to J. G. Walker, June 2, 1862. Assigned to duty with Dept. of the State, Oct. 29, 1862. On duty as Enrolling Officer in eastern Virginia, Dec. 1862–Sept. 1863. Capt. AAG to Elzey, Oct. 15, 1863. Capt. AAG to Wise, Jan. 27, 1865. Merchant at Warsaw, Virginia, and port collector at Norfolk. d. there Aug. 9, 1878. bur. Fredericksburg City Cem.

Brent, George William. b. Alexandria, Virginia, Aug. 15, 1821. att. UVA. Fauquier Co. lawyer and legislator. Member of state Secession Convention. Maj. 17th Virginia, May 2, 1861. Maj. AAIG to Beauregard, Mar. 10–June 21, 1862. Later Col. on staffs of Bragg, E. K. Smith, Hardee, and J. E. Johnston. Col. AAG to Bragg in Richmond, Feb. 26, 1864. Col. AAG to Beauregard, June 17, 1864. Paroled Apr. 26, 1865, at Greensboro. Thigh broken in 1870 Richmond capitol disaster. d. Alexandria, Jan. 2, 1872, of pneumonia. bur. St. Mary's Cem.

Brent, Henry Moon, Jr. b. Frederick Co., Virginia, 1842. att. VMI. Lt. Dixie (Va.) Arty., Aug. 26, 1861. Lt. OO, 20th Bn. Virginia Heavy Arty., Dec. 8, 1861. Lt. OO to Pemberton, autumn 1864. Paroled at Winchester, Apr. 17, 1865. Postwar banker. d. St. Louis, Missouri, Feb. 1907.

Brent, Joseph Lancaster. b. Charles Co., Maryland, Nov. 30, 1826. att. Georgetown. Lawyer in Louisiana and California. Acting OO to Magruder, Apr. 1862. Maj.

OO to Magruder, May 9, 1862. Later Col. OO to Taylor and acting Brigadier Gen. commanding Louisiana cavalry. Lawyer, planter, and politician. Lived at Baltimore and in Louisiana. His posthumously published memoir is a classic rarity. m. Rosella Kenner. d. Baltimore, Nov. 27, 1905. bur. Green Mount Cem.

Brevard, E. F. VADC to D. H. Hill at Fredericksburg. Positive identity not established, but probably either Alexander Franklin Brevard (Oct. 3, 1825–Oct. 22, 1909) or Ephraim Joseph Brevard (Sept. 26, 1828–June 8, 1885). Both possibilities are bur. at Macpleah Cem. in Lincoln Co., North Carolina.

Brewer, Richard Henry. b. Anne Arundel Co., Maryland, Sept. 22, 1834. att. USMA. Served in 1st U.S. Dragoòns. Lt. of Cavy., CSA, Mar. 16, 1861. Lt. AAAG to Polk, Oct. 8, 1861. Commanded Brewer's Bn. Cavy., Apr.–July 1862. Lt. VADC to Pender, Aug. 10, 1862. Commanded Pender's Bgd. at Harpers Ferry. Maj. AAG to Polk, Dec. 31, 1862. To report to Robert Ransom, Apr. 13, 1864. MWIA at Piedmont. d. June 25, 1864. "A very nice fellow," wrote Pender, but he "swears so much."

Brewer, Samuel Blount. b. near Covington, Georgia, Nov. 2, 1834. Farmer, newspaperman at Atlanta, and then teacher and journalist at Montgomery, Alabama. m. Marian Grant McFarland, 1861. Clerk in Commissary Dept. at Richmond. Maj. CS, June 9, 1863. Served at Richmond into 1865. Worked in real estate, insurance, and railroads postwar at Anniston, Alabama. Alive there in 1921.

Brewster, Walter Scott. b. Buxton, Maine, 1833. att. SCMA. A lawyer. Lt. Vigilant Rifles Arty. (S.C.). Capt. Co. G, 24th Georgia. Capt. AAAIG to T. R. R. Cobb. MWIA at Fredericksburg while standing beside Gen. Cobb. Leg amputated. d. Dec. 14, 1862. bur. Alta Vista Cem., Gainesville, Georgia.

Bridge, Frederick E. b. Boston, Massachusetts. Pvt. Co. H, 7th Louisiana, a clerk. Capt. ACS, 7th Louisiana, July 19, 1861. Capt. AQM, 7th Louisiana, July 31, 1863. Capt. AQM to Kemper, July 28, 1864, into 1865. d. Mar. 31, 1874, age 39 years and 7 months.

Bridgford, David Benjamin. b. in Canada, ca. 1831. Ship's broker and commission merchant at New York City and at Richmond, Virginia. Capt. Co. B, 1st Bn. Virginia, May 17, 1861. To Maj., Oct. 11, 1862. Maj. PM to T. J. Jackson, Jan. 1, 1863. Resumed business at New York City postwar. Involved in Cuban Revolution. d. New York City, Feb. 21, 1888.

Brien, Luke Tlernan. b. Urbana, Maryland, Dec. 22, 1827. att. Georgetown. A farmer. Civilian serving with 1st Virginia Cavy. at First Manassas. Capt. AAG to Stuart, Oct. 2, 1861. Lt. Col. 1st Virginia Cavy., Apr. 22, 1862, but still served with Stuart sometimes. Resigned Sept. 30, 1862. Maj. AAAG to W. H. F. Lee, from about Apr. 1864 to Appomattox. Apparently never recommissioned. Lived in New York City and Chicago. Railroad builder and businessman. d. Frederick, Maryland, Nov. 25, 1912. bur. St. Ignatius-Loyola Catholic Church, Urbana.

Briggs, Edmund B. b. in Missouri. 21-year-old bookkeeper at Columbus, Georgia, in 1860. Pvt. Co. G, 2nd Georgia, Apr. 16, 1861. Later promoted to Sgt. Maj. of regiment. Lt. ADC to Semmes, Apr. 10, 1862. WIA at Malvern Hill ("stricken senseless to the ground by a grape shot"). Relieved Apr. 1863 and resigned May 11, 1863. Maj. in Georgia State Militia, 1864.

Briggs, William Henry. b. July 22, 1836. Valdosta, Georgia, businessman. Pvt. Co. D, 50th Georgia, Mar. 4, 1862. Capt. AQM, 50th Georgia, Jan. 31, 1863. Capt. AQM to Simms, Sept. 15, 1864. Paroled May 18, 1865, Thomasville, Georgia. Valdosta hardware merchant. d. Apr. 12, 1901. bur. Sunset Hill Cem.

Briggs, William W. Maj. QM to Mahone, June 1, 1862. Served briefly, but left Mahone on July 28, 1862, either by resignation or dismissal. Collected taxes later in the war. Possibly the William W. Briggs bur. at Poplar Springs Cem., in Franklin, Virginia (Feb. 12, 1829–Nov. 16, 1886).

Bright, Robert Anderson. b. Williamsburg, Virginia, Mar. 23, 1839. att. Wm. & Mary and UVA. Lt. Cosnahan's (Va.) Battery, May 18, 1861, to Aug. 1862. Uncommissioned staff officer to Pickett, Oct. 1862 until Capt. ADC, Sept. 24, 1863. Appx. Williamsburg farmer. d. there Mar. 17, 1904. bur. Cedar Grove Cem.

Bringier, Martin Doradou. b. Aug. 3, 1842. Of New Orleans. att. UVA. Lt. ADC to his brother-in-law, Gen. Taylor, Mar. 31, 1862. Resigned Jan. 16, 1864. New Orleans merchant. Never married. d. Aug. 3, 1887.

Briscoe, Frederick A. b. Shepherdstown, Virginia, July 26, 1819. att. UVA. Farmer in Jefferson Co. Col. QM in PAVA., Apr. 1861. Capt. AQM, Oct. 24, 1861. Post QM at Charlestown, and managed transportation for Army of the Valley in early 1862. Dropped Apr. 19, 1862, as supernumerary. May have been VADC to T. J. Jackson at First Winchester. Reinstated, date not known. Capt. AQM in Valley District, Sept. 1862. Spent rest of war collecting and forwarding leather to ANVa. and supervising tanneries. Farmer at Charlestown. d. there, Apr. 9, 1882. "An enterprising and valuable officer," in Jackson's view.

Briscoe, John L. b. Jefferson Co., Virginia. Clerk at Raymond, Mississippi. Pvt. Co. A, 12th Mississippi, Apr. 30, 1861. Capt. AQM, 12th Mississippi, Dec. 15, 1861. Capt. AQM to R. H. Anderson, June 1863. Same to Mahone, May 1864. Appx. Moved to Maryland by 1894. d. Apr. 22, 1900, age 64. bur. Loudon Park Cem., Baltimore, Maryland.

Brockenbrough, John Bowyer. b. Apr. 6, 1836. att. Washington Coll. and UVA. A lawyer, known as "Beau." Lt. Rockbridge (Va.) Arty., 1861. WIA at First Manassas.

Capt. Baltimore (Md.) Light Arty., Mar. 2, 1862. Capt. Chief of Arty. to Taliaferro, Nov.–Dec. 1862. WIA at Fredericksburg. Maj., Mar. 2, 1863. Retired Mar. 23, 1864, and served on the Slaves Claim Board in Richmond. Federal land inspector in the far west, and a lawyer at Lexington, Virginia. d. Nov. 15, 1901. bur. Loudon Park Cem., Baltimore. "A very nice, gentlemanly fellow."

Brockenbrough, William Austin. b. Dec. 11, 1836. att. VMI. Adjt. 40th Virginia, 1861. WIA at Gaines's Mill. Lt. acting AOO to Third Corps, Aug. 1863. Capt. AAAG to Heth, summer 1864. Farmer and county clerk. d. Richmond Co., Virginia, Aug. 6, 1896. bur. Emmanuel Episc. Church.

Brodnax, John W. Maj. CS to Robert Ransom, Apr. 28, 1862. Dropped Feb. 5, 1863, but managed to post bond and reinstated Feb. 24, 1863. Maj. CS to Matt. Ransom, probably 1864–1865.

Brodnax, William Edward. b. Brunswick Co., Virginia, Jan. 8, 1827. att. Yale. Farmer in Rockingham Co., North Carolina. Lt. Co. G, 1st North Carolina Cavy., Oct. 1, 1861. Resigned Mar. 1, 1862. Lt. ADC to Robert Ransom, Apr. 5, 1862. Resigned Feb. 12, 1863, citing ill health. Conscription officer in Georgia and Florida, 1864. d. Sept. 2, 1907.

Brooks, H. Clay. Lt. AAAG to Wise, July 1–Sept. 30, 1861. Later a Drillmaster in Tennessee. No further record after summer 1862. Gave his residence as Nashville, Tennessee, and education as VMI, but there is no record of Brooks at VMI. Possibly Hiram Clay Brooks (Dec. 8, 1817–Apr. 17, 1876), bur. Ramble Creek Cem., Benton Co., Tennessee. Another option is the H. Clay Brooks who died at Brooklyn, Alabama, Oct. 29, 1874.

Brooks, John David. b. Augusta Co., Virginia. att. Washington Coll. Pvt. and QM Sgt., 5th Virginia, 1861. Capt. AQM, 5th Virginia, Sept. 16, 1863. Capt. AQM to John B.

Gordon, Sept. 16, 1864. Appx. Farmer at Fishersville, Virginia. Later lived in Saline Co., Missouri, in New York, and in New Mexico. Became a lawyer. d. Canon City, Colorado, Apr. 3, 1899. bur. Confederate Veterans' Home Cem.

Broun, William. b. Heathsville, Virginia, Dec. 20, 1842. att. UVA. Pvt. Co. F, 47th Virginia, July 1, 1861. Lt., Jan. 10, 1862. Capt. AAAIG to Brockenbrough's Bgd., July 1863. Capt. AAIG to H. H. Walker, Nov. 2, 1863. Same to Fry. WIA at Cold Harbor, June 3, 1864. POW at Sailor's Creek. Released June 18, 1865. Postwar farmer. d. Washington, D.C., May 15, 1908. bur. family cem. in Northumberland Co., Virginia.

Broun, William LeRoy. b. Loudoun Co., Virginia, Oct. 1, 1827. att. UVA. Teacher at Charlottesville. Lt. Albemarle (Va.) Arty., July 3, 1861. Lt. Col. and Supt. Richmond Arsenal by Sept. 30, 1862. Served there into 1865. Simultaneously Lt. Col. 5th Bn. Virginia LDT. Professor at Vanderbilt, UGA., Univ. of Texas, and Auburn. d. Auburn, Alabama, Jan. 23, 1902. bur. Pine Hill Cem.

Brown, A. J. Supposedly served in 4th Tennessee, but has no official record there. Capt. AQM to Donelson, Nov. 12, 1861. Resigned May 14, 1862, citing health and advanced age.

Brown, Charles D. Of Mobile, Alabama. Maj. CS to Gracie, Dec. 14, 1862. AWOL Sept. 27, 1864–Feb. 1865.

Brown, George Campbell. b. Davidson Co., Tennessee, Nov. 27, 1840. att. Univ. of Nashville and Georgetown. Lt. 3rd Tennessee, Apr. 1861. Lt. ADC to Ewell, July 1, 1861. WIA in shoulder at Cross Keys. Capt. AAG to Ewell, May 4, 1862. Served with J. E. Johnston during Ewell's 1862–1863 absence from the army. Maj. AAG to Ewell, June 1, 1863. Maj. AAIG to Ewell, July 5, 1864. POW at Sailor's Creek. Released July 19, 1865. Farmer, stock breeder, and legislator in Tennessee. Shot himself in the head at Grand Rapids, Michigan, Aug. 30, 1893. bur.

St. John's Church, Ashwood, Tennessee. His estate reportedly valued at $1 million. Brown was a son-in-law of Gen. Ewell, and also was his cousin, once removed. Brown's wife, Susan, was a daughter of Gen. Leonidas Polk. Brown wrote extensively after the war, some of it still unpublished.

Brown, J. J. Lt. Co. B, 2nd South Carolina Arty., Oct. 23, 1862. Capt. AQM, 15th South Carolina, July 11, 1864. Capt. AQM to Barton, Oct. 26, 1864. Capt. AQM to G. W. C. Lee, Feb. 8, 1865.

Brown, John Badger. Capt. Co. B, 3rd North Carolina, May 23, 1861. WIA at Malvern Hill and Spotsylvania. Capt. AAG to Cox, 1865. Appx. Lived postwar at Wilmington, North Carolina, at New York City, and at Baltimore, Maryland. Alive 1898 at Baltimore.

Brown, John T. Very likely the John T. Brown, age 45, a planter at Macon, Georgia, in 1860 census. Capt. AQM, 45th Georgia, June 6, 1862. Capt. AQM at Macon, Georgia, July 15, 1864. Capt. AQM to Thomas, Sept. 15, 1864. POW at Macon, Apr. 1865.

Brown, John Thompson. b. Petersburg, Virginia, Feb. 6, 1835. att. UVA. Lawyer. Lt. Richmond Howitzers, Apr. 21, 1861. Capt., May 1861. Maj., Sept. 1861. Lt. Col., spring 1862. Col., June 2, 1862. Col. Chief of Arty. for Second Corps, May 2, 1863, through Sept. 1863. Chief of Second Corps Reserve Arty., Oct. 1863. KIA at Wilderness. A large collection of Brown's official wartime papers can be found at the Museum of the Confederacy in Richmond.

Brown, John Wesley. A resident of Atlanta, Georgia. Pvt. Co. A, 9th Bn. Georgia Arty., Feb. 27, 1862, age 31. Capt. AQM, 9th Bn. Georgia Arty., Apr. 25, 1862. Served in 1864 as AQM at Lynchburg and Staunton, Virginia. Surrendered Apr. 14, 1865, at Farmville.

Brown, John Willcox. b. Petersburg, Virginia, July 17, 1833. att. UVA. Petersburg lawyer and gentleman. Lt. Co. E, 12th Virginia. Lt. OO at Richmond, 1863. Capt. OO, May 2, 1863, on inspection duty at Richmond. Maj. OO, Nov. 1, 1864. Banker at Baltimore, Maryland. d. Albemarle Co., Virginia, Feb. 21, 1914.

Brown, Robert W. Lt. ADC to J. H. Winder, June 10, 1862. POW May 13, 1863. Aug. 1864 reported himself "partially paralyzed."

Brown, Victor Moreau. b. Dec. 18, 1834. att. UVA. Front Royal lawyer. Lt. Co. B, 17th Virginia, Apr. 18, 1861. Capt. ACS, 17th Virginia, Sept. 23, 1861. Maj. CS to Corse, Dec. 3, 1862. Appx. m. Mary Jacobs. d. Front Royal, Aug. 21, 1868. bur. Prospect Hill Cem.

Browne, James T. Lt. ADC to Robert Ransom, June 8, 1863. Capt. AAIG to Ransom, Feb. 17, 1864. Capt. AAIG to Lomax, Dec. 1864. Paroled May 1, 1865, at Greensboro.

Brownfield, Robert James. b. ca. 1840. Clerk at Stateburg, South Carolina. Pvt. Co. I, 2nd South Carolina, May 27, 1862. Detached at McLaws's headquarters by June 1862. Lt. SO to McLaws, Dec. 19, 1862. Ordered to report to W. S. Walker, July 27, 1863. Sumter Co. farmer postwar. d. Jan. 14, 1913. bur. Thomas Sumter's Memorial Park.

Bruce, James William. b. Albemarle Co., Virginia, Feb. 9, 1834. A merchant. Capt. AQM, May 30, 1862, to report to the Valley Army. Capt. AQM to C. S. Winder, July 1, 1862. Maj. QM to J. R. Jones, Oct. 14, 1862. Subsequent duty uncertain until Maj. QM to C. A. Evans, Sept. 15, 1864. Maj. QM to William Terry, Nov. 14, 1864. Appx. In state legislature. Richmond merchant until 1880, and then at Danville. d. there Apr. 14, 1907. bur. Greenhill Cem.

Bryan, B. S. Maj. QM to N. G. Evans, Mar. 1, 1862. Court-martialed Dec. 11, 1863, for "drunkeness and disobedience of orders." Suspended, and then dropped effective Aug. 8, 1864.

Bryan, Edward Pliny. b. Prince George's Co., Maryland. Wealthy planter, militia officer, and member of state legislature.

Volunteer signal officer, July 1861. Arrested at Mason's Neck, Virginia, Feb. 21, 1862. Capt. AAG, June 10, 1862. On duty as SO "in Longstreet's command," Aug.–Oct. 1862. Performed spy duty for R. E. Lee along the Potomac River. Capt. AAG to Beauregard, Jan. 1863. Capt. AAG to Sam. Jones, Apr. 1864. Returned to Beauregard, May 23, 1864, and engaged in torpedo work along James River. d. Charleston, South Carolina, Sept. 30, 1864, of yellow fever, age 33. bur. Magnolia Cem.

Bryan, Henry. b. Savannah, Georgia, Oct. 31, 1835. VADC to Magruder, July–Aug. 1861. Lt. ADC (CSA) to Magruder, Sept. 4, 1861. Capt. AAG to Magruder, Jan. 14, 1862. Served briefly on staff of D. R. Jones, May 1862. Maj. AAG to Magruder, May 26, 1862. WIA at Malvern Hill, leaving his left arm "helpless." Maj. AAIG to Beauregard, late in 1862. Served in that capacity at Charleston, South Carolina, under a succession of commanders. Paroled Apr. 26, 1865. Banker and broker. d. Lookout Mountain, Tennessee, July 25, 1879. bur. Bonaventure Cem., Savannah.

Bryan, James Augustus Washington. b. New Bern, North Carolina, Sept. 13, 1839. att. Princeton. Lt. of Arty., CSA, Sept. 13, 1861. On ordnance duty at New Bern, fall 1861. Lt. OO to Branch, June 1862. Same to Lane. Capt. OO, Sept. 20, 1864. Paroled Apr. 26, 1865, at Greensboro. Banker, farmer, railroad man, lumberman, and legislator in New Bern. d. there Jan. 30, 1923. bur. Craven Co.

Bryan, James C. Lt. Co. K, 6th Alabama. Capt. ACS, 6th Alabama, Sept. 28, 1861. Maj. QM to Rodes, June 11, 1862. Maj. QM to Battle, Aug. 1863. Maj. QM to Rodes, Feb.–Sept. 1864, and then back to Battle for rest of war.

Bryan, John Randolph, Jr. b. Gloucester Co., Virginia, Jan. 9, 1841. att. VMI. Clerk at Magruder's headquarters, Dec. 1861. VADC to Magruder, Apr. 1862. Ordnance

Sgt. with McLaws's Reserve Train, Dec. 25, 1862. Clerk at Dublin Depot, Virginia, June 1, 1863. Capt. AQM there, Nov. 14, 1863. Planter, broker, and real estate agent. Lived in Louisiana, and at Charlottesville, Virginia, and Birmingham, Alabama. d. Richmond, Virginia, Dec. 27, 1917. bur. Hollywood Cem.

Bryant, John Carlyle Herbert. b. Lexington, Virginia, May 19, 1843. att. Catonsville Military Academy and UVA. Apptd. to USMA, Feb. 1861, but never matriculated. Pvt. Co. A, 17th Virginia, Apr. 17–June 5, 1861. Lt. PACS, June 17, 1861. Apptd. Cadet, Oct. 18, 1861. Adjt. 17th Virginia, Apr. 27, 1862. Lt. AAAG to A. P. Hill, May 1862. Lt. VADC to Corse at Second Manassas. WIA and POW in Maryland, 1862. Lt. ADC to Corse, Nov. 14, 1862. Capt. AAG to Corse, Nov. 2, 1863. Same to William R. Terry, Oct. 1864. WIA in left foot and POW at Sailor's Creek. Released June 6, 1865. Fertilizer merchant at Alexandria. d. Apr. 11, 1914. bur. Ivy Hill Cem.

Buchanan, George B. b. ca. 1833 in Georgia. Grocer at Zebulon. Lt. Co. G, 27th Georgia, Oct. 14, 1861. Capt. AQM, 27th Georgia, May 1, 1862. Capt. AQM to Colquitt, Sept. 20, 1864. Paroled Apr. 26, 1865. Alive 1870 in Spalding Co., deputy clerk of supreme court.

von Buckholtz, Louis. Officer in the Austrian army. Capt. OO, PAVa., June 7, 1861. Capt. OO to Wise, Aug. 1, 1861. Left Wise, Jan. 20, 1862. Capt. OO in charge of gas and water works at Richmond, Virginia, remainder of war. Wrote a two-volume work on fortifications (1860) and a book on tactics (1861).

Buckner, James. b. Louisville, Kentucky, Oct. 13, 1837. A New Orleans clerk. Lt. Co. B, 10th Louisiana, July 22, 1861. To Capt. July 1, 1862. Capt. AQM, 10th Louisiana, Oct. 13, 1862. Capt. AQM to York, Sept. 15, 1864. Same to Peck, late war. New

Orleans commission merchant. d. there Oct. 16, 1917. bur. Metairie Cem.

Burgwyn, William Hyslop Sumner. b. Boston, Massachusetts, July 23, 1845. att. Hillsboro Military Academy and UNC. Lt. Drillmaster in 1861. Lt. Co. H, 35th North Carolina. Lt. ADC to Clingman, Jan. 1864. Capt. AAIG to Clingman, 1864. WIA in hand at Cold Harbor, June 1, 1864. POW at Fort Harrison. Tried to raise a unit of black troops in 1865. Postwar att. Harvard Law School and Washington Medical University, Baltimore. Baltimore lawyer and Henderson, North Carolina, banker and tobacconist. Col. 2nd North Carolina in Spanish-American War. d. Jan. 3, 1913. bur. Raleigh. Burgwyn's wartime diary has been published.

Burke, Edmund. b. in Alabama. Served in Co. B, 1st U.S. Mounted Rifles, 1857–1861. Killed a Navajo Indian in 1860 skirmish. Pvt. Meckling's (Tex.) Btty., July 4, 1861. Later a Cpl. Lt. SO, Oct. 10, 1862. Ordered to ANVa., June 19, 1863. Lt. SO to Heth, July 8, 1863. Resigned Aug. 1, 1864, to join Co. D, 2nd Alabama Cavy. Heth wrote that "Burke's habits are such as to disqualify him for the position of a comm'd officer."

Burke, Redmond. b. ca. 1816 in Ireland. A stonecutter at Harpers Ferry, Virginia. Pvt. Co. B, 1st Virginia Cavy., July 2, 1861. Scout for Stuart, 1861. Lt. of Cavy., Apr. 3, 1862, assigned to Stuart. Apparently served as ADC. WIA twice in Aug. 1862. KIA at Shepherdstown, Nov. 24, 1862. bur. Elmwood Cem.

Burks, Richard Horseley. b. Botetourt Co., Virginia, Nov. 1826. att. VMI. Mexican War veteran and Lt. Col. of Militia prewar. Adjt. 2nd Virginia Cavy. Lt. Col. 12th Virginia Cavy., June 20, 1862. Resigned Mar. 2, 1863. Lt. ADC to McCausland, June 15, 1864. Postwar farmer. d. Washington, D.C., Nov. 24, 1899.

Burnett, Eugene Paul. Sgt. Co. A, 6th Georgia, Apr. 22, 1861. WIA at Seven Pines. To

Lt., July 4, 1862. Lt. acting PM to Colquitt, Nov. 19, 1862. Capt. AAIG to Colquitt, July 1, 1864. Maj. AAIG, Jan. 1865. m. Delia D. Jordan, 1867. d. either Dec. 1909 or Jan. 1910, age 72. bur. Linwood Cem., Columbus, Georgia.

Burns, Robert. b. in Kentucky, 1834. Moved to Houston, Texas, prewar. Pvt. Co. A, 5th Texas, July 19, 1861. Capt. ACS, 5th Texas, May 7, 1862. Capt. ACS to J. B. Robertson, Aug. 1863. Same to John Gregg, Apr.–Oct. 1864. Maj. CS to Texas Bgd., Mar. 1, 1865. Appx. m. Lucy Marion Munson, 1866. Bookkeeper and postmaster at Houston. Also a lumber and cotton merchant, and an auctioneer. d. Houston, June 29, 1895. bur. Glenwood Cem., in unmarked grave.

Burrows, Howard Lansing. b. Philadelphia, Pennsylvania, Apr. 10, 1843. Son of a prominent Baptist preacher. att. Wake Forest. Sgt. Richmond (Va.) Fayette Arty., Apr. 25, 1861. Artillery instructor during the 1861 western Virginia campaign. Detailed for special duty with the Naval Ordnance Bureau. Pvt. Co. E, 6th Alabama, Feb. 21, 1864. Probably also on duty as a topographical engineer with the Second Corps, summer 1864. POW Sept. 20, 1864, and exchanged Oct. 31, 1864. Paroled Apr. 17, 1865, at Richmond. Dropped his first name after the war. Postwar Baptist minister in Kentucky, Missouri, New Jersey, Georgia, and Tennessee. d. Augusta, Georgia, Oct. 17, 1919. The confusion in this soldier's record makes some of the above uncertain.

Burton, James Henry. b. Jefferson Co., Virginia, Aug. 17, 1823. att. Westchester Academy in Pennsylvania. Baltimore machine shop apprentice. Worked at Harpers Ferry Armory, 1844–1855, and as Chief Engineer at Royal Small Arms factory near London, 1855–1861. Lt. Col. PAVa., June 1861, in charge of state armory. Apptd. Supt. of Armories, CSA, Sept. 2, 1861. Served in Richmond until mid-1862. Supt. of Armory at Macon, Georgia, for most of the war. Bore the rank of Col. in correspondence. Lived postwar in England and in Loudoun Co., Virginia, where he farmed. d. Winchester, Virginia, Oct. 18, 1894. bur. Mt. Hebron Cem.

Burton, John B. Pvt. Co. A, 1st Arkansas, May 2, 1861, age 25, a farmer. Capt. AQM, 1st Arkansas, June 4, 1861. Capt. acting AQM to Holmes, late in 1861 or early in 1862. Maj. QM to J. G. Walker, Feb. 1862. Maj. QM to Holmes, July 29, 1862. Maj. QM at Little Rock, Arkansas, Aug. 1862. Later chief QM in District of Arkansas.

Burton, Watkins Leigh. b. Henrico Co., Virginia, Feb. 12, 1830. A clerk. Capt. AQM (PAVa.), 1861. Stationed at Fredericksburg. Out of service, 1862–1864. Conscripted in 1864, but detailed immediately for dental work in Richmond's hospitals. Postwar dentist. Invented the Burton Electrical Heater. Married twice. d. Dec. 17, 1892. bur. Hollywood Cem., Richmond.

Burwell, John Bott. b. Chesterfield Co., Virginia, Oct. 3, 1834. att. Hampden Sidney. Teacher at a girls' school. QM Sgt., 53rd North Carolina, June 4, 1862. Capt. AQM, 53rd North Carolina, Dec. 15, 1862. Capt. AQM to Rodes, Sept. 15, 1864. Same to Ramseur and then Grimes. Appx. Married twice. Teacher and insurance man. d. Statesville, North Carolina, Jan. 26, 1904. bur. Oakwood Cem., Raleigh.

Burwell, Philip Lewis Carter, Jr. b. Nov. 19, 1838. att. UVa. A physician. Pvt. 1st Rockbridge (Va.) Arty., Sept. 1861. Lt. CSA, Sept. 23, 1861. Served with Gatlin in North Carolina, Nov. 1861. VADC to Branch, Mar. 1862. Capt. PM at Goldsboro, Apr. 1862. Capt. Co. E, 50th North Carolina, Oct. 1863 to Mar. 1864. Reported to Ewell and Second Corps, Apr. 20, 1864, and served remainder of war in some staff position, as a Lt. Paroled Apr. 27, 1865, at Winchester. att. a medical school in Baltimore. Physician at Millwood, Va. d. May 30, 1909. bur. Old Chapel.

Butler, Andrew Pickens. b. Columbia, South Carolina, Mar. 7, 1839. Son of a state governor. att. South Carolina Coll. Lt. 1st S.C. Regs., Mar. 1861. Lt. 1st South Carolina Inf., PACS, 1862. Staff of Butler in 1864, and Lt. VADC to Dunovant, Sept. 1864. POW Sept. 30, 1864. Released June 17, 1865. m. Maria Burt. d. Benton, Louisiana, Oct. 18, 1899. Known as "Pick" Butler.

Butler, Henry Alexander. b. Henderson Co., North Carolina, Sept. 18, 1836. Merchant at Tulip, Arkansas. Lt. Co. I, 3rd Arkansas, Nov. 8, 1861. Lt. AAAG to Cooke, Sept. 1, 1862. Capt. AAG to Cooke, Nov. 11, 1862. Appx. m. Mary E. Coulter. d. Malvern, Arkansas, June 29, 1907. Butler's war letters have been published.

Butler, Oliver Nathaniel. b. near Greenville, South Carolina, Sept. 4, 1843. att. Furman. Pvt. 1st South Carolina Regs. Lt. ADC to his brother, Gen. Butler, Sept. 11, 1863. POW Sept. 30, 1864. WIA Mar. 10, 1865. m. Mary Spence. Lawyer at Augusta, Georgia. d. Apr. 12, 1877. bur. Magnolia Cem. "One of the handsomest boys in the Army."

Butler, William Pulaski. b. 1816. Merchant at Edgefield, C.H., South Carolina. m. Laura A. Nance. VADC and PM to Bonham, July 1861. Later served in local defense troops in South Carolina. Postwar planter. d. 1893. bur. Willowbrook Cem., Edgefield Co.

Butts, Edward Scott. b. Greene Co., Alabama, Mar. 1838. Merchant at Vicksburg, Mississippi. Cpl. Co. A, 21st Mississippi, 1861. Ultimately became Capt. Co. A. Capt. AAIG to Humphreys, May 1864. Appx. m. Lucy McCutchen. Vicksburg banker. d. May 31, 1907.

Byrd, Abraham Samuels. b. June 7, 1824. Capt. AQM, 10th Virginia, Sept. 9, 1861. Capt. AQM to Battle, Sept. 27, 1864. Commanding Second Corps ambulance train at Appomattox. d. July 31, 1903.

Byrd, Richard Willing. b. Aug. 3, 1832. Served in Letcher (Va.) Arty., 1863. Acting

Lt. oo to Pegram's Bn. Arty., by July 31, 1863. Probably possessed a PACS appointment. Paroled as Lt. oo, Apr. 29, 1865, occupation "gentleman." Of Caroline Co., Virginia. m. Jane Broadnax Dejarnette. d. June 21, 1879.

Byrd, Samuel Masters Hankins. b. DeKalb Co., Georgia, Mar. 11, 1830. att. Emory. Planter and civil engineer near Cedartown. Capt. AQM, Phillips Legion, July 19, 1861. Capt. acting QM to Wofford, July 1863 until apptd. Maj. QM to Wofford, Feb. 19, 1864. Not confirmed until Jan. 28, 1865, to rank from June 15, 1864. Appx. In Georgia senate. m. Anne Wingfield Potts. d. near Cedartown, Mar. 28, 1895. bur. Greenwood Cem.

Cabaniss, Thomas Banks. b. Forsyth, Georgia, Aug. 31, 1835. att. UGA. and Penfield Coll. (now Mercer Univ.). A lawyer. Capt. Co. H, 1st Georgia, Apr. 22, 1861. Later Pvt. and Sgt. Maj., 11th Bn. Georgia Arty., 1862. Lt. oo to Doles, Oct. 6, 1862, though commission probably came at a later date. Same to Cook. Appx. In Georgia state legislature and USHR. Mayor of Forsyth. d. there Aug. 14, 1915. bur. Oakland Cem.

Cabell, Henry Coalter. b. Feb. 14, 1820. att. UVA. Lawyer at Richmond. Capt. Richmond Fayette Arty., Apr. 25, 1861. Lt. Col., Sept. 12, 1861. Col., July 4, 1862. Chief of Arty. to Magruder, Apr. 1862, and to McLaws, Oct.–Dec. 1862. Commanded an artillery battalion for most of the war. d. Jan. 31, 1889. bur. Hollywood Cem., Richmond.

Caddall, Samuel S. Sgt. Co. C, 4th Virginia, Apr. 17, 1861, a 25-year-old constable. POW at Kernstown. Exchanged Aug. 5, 1862. WIA in right foot at Fredericksburg. Lt. ADC to J. A. Walker, June 1, 1863. Appx. d. "shortly after the surrender" from exposure.

Cage, John F. Pvt. Co. E, 7th Tennessee, May 26, 1861, age 26. Often detailed as clerk at brigade headquarters. Bgd. and Div.

wagon master, 1862–1863. Capt. AQM to Heth, Oct. 26, 1863. Appx.

Cage, William Clinton. b. in Mississippi, Oct. 16, 1840. Pvt. Co. K, 16th Mississippi, Apr. 21, 1861. Courier for Longstreet from Feb. 1863. Lt. ADC to Hays, July 19, 1863. Paroled June 6, 1865. d. Apr. 17, 1914. bur. Collier Cem., Lenaly, Mississippi.

Caldwell, James Fitz James. b. Newberry, South Carolina, Sept. 19, 1837. att. South Carolina Coll. Charleston lawyer. Pvt. 3rd South Carolina State Troops. Pvt. Co. B, 1st (Gregg's) South Carolina, Apr. 1862. To Lt., Jan. 1863. Lt. acting oo to McGowan, Feb.–Mar. 1863. WIA at Gettysburg and Fussell's Mill. Lt. acting ADC to McGowan, Nov. 1864–Apr. 1865. Newberry lawyer. Author of brigade history and some fiction. d. Columbia, South Carolina, Feb. 3, 1925.

Call, Wilkinson. b. Russellville, Kentucky, Jan. 9, 1834. Lawyer at Jacksonville, Florida. Capt. AAG to Finegan, May 1, 1862. Detached on duty with Patton Anderson, spring 1864. Back to Finegan by May 1864. Capt. AAG in District of Florida, June 1864. Serving with Florida reserves at war's end. U.S. Senator from Florida, 1879–1897. d. Washington, D.C., Aug. 24, 1910. bur. Oak Hill Cem.

Callahan, Dennis. b. Ireland. Sgt. Co. E, 1st Louisiana, Apr. 28, 1861, age 31, a clerk. Lt. CSA, Nov. 1, 1861. Served around Norfolk, Virginia, and on drillmaster duty at Richmond. Lt. Asst. PM in Richmond, Mar. 1863. Appointed Capt. PACS, June 30, 1863, and served at Richmond's prisons. Adjt. at Castle Thunder Prison. Paroled from Libby Prison, Apr. 1865.

Callaway, William Giles. b. Franklin Co., Virginia, July 21, 1841. Sgt. Co. B, 24th Virginia, May 23, 1861. WIA at Second Manassas, Aug. 30, 1862. Lt. ADC to Early, Jan. 21, 1863. POW at Waynesboro, Mar. 2, 1865. Released June 7, 1865. d. May 24, 1877.

Cameron, William Evelyn. b. Petersburg, Virginia, Nov. 29, 1842. att. Hillsboro

Military Academy and Washington Coll. (St. Louis). Clerk on Mississippi River steamboat. Drillmaster with Missouri state troops. Pvt. Co. A, 12th Virginia, June 4, 1861. Adjt., 12th Virginia, May 1862. WIA at Second Manassas, Aug. 30, 1862. Lt. AAAIG to Mahone, Jan. 1863. Capt. AAIG to Mahone, Nov. 2, 1863. Same to Weisiger. Appx. Newspaper editor at Petersburg and Norfolk. Mayor of Petersburg three terms. Elected state governor, 1881. d. Jan. 25, 1927. bur. Blandford Cem., Petersburg.

Campbell, ——. Lt. OO to McLaughlin's Bn. Arty., by Dec. 1864. Precise identity unknown. Possibly Lt. John Campbell of Lowry's (Va.) Btty.

Campbell, Albert Henry. b. Charleston, Virginia, Oct. 28, 1826. att. Brown. Member of several boundary surveying parties. Railroad engineer in Virginia and in far west. Appointed to C.S. Post Office Dept., May 15, 1861. Capt. EO, June 6, 1862, to report to Walter Stevens. In charge of ANVa. topographic department by Dec. 1862. Maj. EO, Oct. 19, 1864. Appx. m. Mary P. Stebbins. d. Ravenswood, West Virginia, Feb. 23, 1899. bur. Hollywood Cem., Richmond, in an unmarked grave.

Campbell, Duncan Green. b. Mobile, Alabama, Nov. 7, 1835. Studied engineering in Austria. Son of Asst. Secretary of War John A. Campbell. Volunteer EO to G. W. Smith, Sept. 1861. Lt. EO to Smith, Feb. 15, 1862. Lt. EO to D. R. Jones, Mar. 1862. Lt. EO to Kershaw, Oct.–Dec. 1862. Lt. EO to McLaws at Fredericksburg and early in 1863. Lt. EO at Charleston, South Carolina, Sept. 1863. Capt. EO, Mar. 17, 1864. Paroled Apr. 28, 1865. m. Ella Calvert. Law partner of his father postwar. d. "several years prior" to 1889.

Campbell, John G. b. in Scotland. Prewar resident of New Orleans, Louisiana. Sgt. Co. E, 6th Louisiana, June 4, 1861, age 25. Capt. ACS, 6th Louisiana, Dec. 24, 1861. Failed to secure bond and dropped, Aug. 2,

1862. Reinstated Oct. 17, 1862. Dropped again, for same cause, Feb. 5, 1863. Capt. AQM to Hays, Feb. 1863. Maj. CS to Hays, June 3, 1863. Maj. CS to York, and probably to Peck. Appx.

Campbell, Parker. b. Washington, Pennsylvania, 1815. att. Washington (Pa.) Coll. Glass maker at Wheeling, Virginia, and sugar planter in Louisiana. m. Isabell Sprigg. Capt. ACS, June 12, 1861. Capt. ACS to Taliaferro, Sept. 5, 1861. Capt. ACS at Monterey, Virginia, Oct. 1861–June 1862. Capt. ACS at Knoxville, Tennessee, June 26, 1862. Maj. CS, July 31, 1863, and served in Georgia, Tennessee, and Alabama. Banker, broker, and insurance man at Richmond, Virginia. d. Jacksonville, Florida, Mar. 28, 1882. bur. Hollywood Cem., Richmond. "Always frail."

Cannady, William Erastus. b. June 26, 1838. att. Wake Forest and USMA. Of Granville Co., North Carolina. VADC to Branch, Nov. 16, 1861. Lt. ADC to Branch, Jan. 30, 1862. Capt. AAG to Branch, Apr. 28, 1862. d. July 7, 1862, of typhoid fever. bur. family cem., Creedmor, North Carolina.

Cannon, Henry Gibbons. b. Richmond, Virginia, Nov. 17, 1830. att. UVA. Richmond law partner of A. R. Courtney. Lt. Co. B, 60th Virginia, Aug. 6, 1861. Lt. AAIG to Thomas Smith's Bgd., Apr. 20, 1863. Also served as AAAG and Judge Advocate when needed. Same to McCausland. m. Margaret Blair. d. Richmond, June 7, 1900.

Canova, Antonio A. b. ca. 1825. Merchant at Jacksonville, Florida. Pvt. Co. A, 3rd Florida, May 8, 1861. Member of Florida legislature during the war. Maj. CS to Trapier, Mar. 3, 1862. Maj. CS to Finegan in Virginia, 1864–1865. Ordered to report to Commissary Gen., Mar. 11, 1865, for post duty. Alive 1870 in St. John's Co., Florida.

Capers, William Henry. b. 1844. Of Charleston, South Carolina. VADC to Donelson, spring–winter 1862. VADC to J. H. Winder, Sept. 1863. Lt. ADC to Gartrell, Nov. 2, 1864.

Episcopal vicar in Mississippi. m. Anna Margaret Missroon. d. Crystal Springs, Mississippi, June 25, 1896. bur. Crystal Springs Cem., Copiah Co.

Carey, James. b. Baltimore, Maryland, Oct. 2, 1832. Bank cashier pre- and postwar. Lt. SO, Oct. 10, 1862. POW in King George Co., Virginia, Dec. 8, 1862. Lt. SO at Richmond, by July 1863. Acting Chief of Signal Corps, July–Sept. 1863. Lt. SO to Whiting, Nov. 13, 1863. Lt. SO to J. E. Johnston, June 1864. Resigned Jan. 14, 1865. Pvt. Co. E, 43rd Bn. Virginia Cavy., dates unclear. m. Martha Ward, 1869. d. Baltimore, Oct. 17, 1875. bur. Loudon Park Cem.

Carr, Charles Edward. b. Natchitoches, Louisiana. An AQM in the Mexican War. Maj. QM to Huger, May 25, 1861. Relieved June 12, 1862. Maj. QM and Chief Paymaster for Trans-Mississippi Dept., July 10, 1862. On staff of Holmes and E. K. Smith. Served into 1865. Lived postwar at New Orleans, Louisiana. d. there Dec. 25, 1882, age 66, of gout.

Carr, George Watson. b. Albemarle Co., Virginia, June 1823. att. UVA. Lt. U.S. Army in Mexican War and 1855–1861. Spectator in Crimean War. Kanawha Co. lawyer. Capt. of Inf., CSA, Mar. 16, 1861. Capt. and Mustering Officer, Wise Legion, June 1861. Judge Advocate around Manassas, Aug.–Sept. 1861. Lt. Col., 57th Virginia, Sept. 25, 1861. Dropped, May 1862. Later in Richmond defenses. Capt. AAIG Army of Southwest Virginia, Nov. 1862–Mar. 1863. Capt. AAIG to Bragg. Maj. AAIG to Breckinridge, Mar. 5, 1864. POW Sept. 27, 1864, at Fisher's Gap. Exchanged Feb. 27, 1865. Roanoke farmer. d. Apr. 19, 1899. bur. Watts Farm, near Roanoke. "Rather too fond of gunpowder," according to Gen. A. G. Jenkins.

Carr, Wilson Cary Nicholas. b. Feb. 18, 1827. Capt. AQM, 15th Virginia. Capt. AAQM to Corse, May 1, 1863, and Capt. AQM, Sept. 15, 1864. Appx. Suffered from deafness. m. Susan Henderson. d. Apr. 17, 1886. bur. Hollywood Cem., Richmond.

Carraway, Daniel Tolson. b. Feb. 7, 1833. Capt. ACS, Sept. 11, 1861, to report to Gatlin. On QM duty at New Bern. Capt. ACS to Branch, Jan. 1, 1862. Capt. acting ACS to A. P. Hill, Aug.–Dec. 1862. Maj. CS to Lane, Apr. 11, 1863, to rank from Jan. 1, 1862. Maj. CS to Pender, June 30, 1863. Maj. CS to Wilcox, Sept. 1, 1863. Appx. d. Nov. 26, 1898. bur. Cedar Grove Cem., New Bern. "I consider him one of the best staff officers in service," wrote A. P. Hill.

Carrere, William. b. in Maryland. Of Baltimore, but lived at Boston, Massachusetts, and at Richmond, Virginia, prewar. VADC to Trimble, Sept. 1861. Capt. AQM to Trimble, Nov. 22, 1861, but dropped Feb. 24, 1862, for bond failure. Maj. QM to Trimble, May 19, 1862. Maj. acting Adjt. to Maj. Snodgrass, division QM for Ewell, July 1862. Resigned Dec. 20, 1862, under cloud of charges pressed by Trimble, supported by Early. POW Jan. 12, 1864, at Warsaw, Virginia, while on a private beef-buying expedition. Brother-in-law of fellow staffer William Carvel Hall.

Carrington, Charles Scott. b. Halifax Co., Virginia, Aug. 26, 1820. att. Hampden Sidney. A lawyer. Pvt. Co. B, 6th Virginia Cavy., Aug. 19, 1861. Capt. AQM, Oct. 18, 1861. Forage agent at West Point, Virginia. Maj. QM, June 6, 1862. Served as forage purchaser for ANVa., based in Richmond and elsewhere. Paroled at Greensboro. President of James River & Kanawha Canal, lawyer, and farmer. d. Dec. 24, 1891.

Carrington, Clement. Sgt. Co. C, 3rd Virginia Cavy., May 20, 1861, age 24. To Lt. later. Lt. acting ADC to Col. T. H. Owen, commanding Wickham's brigade, Oct. 1863. WIA at Wilson's Wharf. Capt. Co. H, 3rd Virginia Cavy., Dec. 1864.

Carrington, Eugene. b. Richmond, Virginia, Mar. 1, 1840. m. Cora Carrington Dimmock, 1859. Capt. AQM, May 19, 1862.

Paymaster for transportation and forwarder of stores, based at Richmond, 1862–1865. Moved to Baltimore, Maryland, postwar. d. Richmond, Nov. 28, 1897. bur. Hollywood Cem.

Carrington, Isaac Howell. b. Richmond, Virginia, Mar. 7, 1827. att. UNC and UVA. Pittsylvania Co. lawyer. Maj. 38th Virginia, 1861–1862. Maj. chief of staff to Floyd, 1862–1863 (without a commission, apparently). Apptd. commissioner to examine prisoners in Richmond, July 14, 1863. Maj. PM in Richmond, Mar. 3, 1864. Apptd. supt. for raising black troops, late war. Richmond lawyer. d. there Jan. 30, 1887. bur. Hollywood Cem. Carrington's war letters are at Duke Univ. "He had a rough exterior and a brusque manner, but with all he had a kind heart."

Carrington, John W. MSK at Wytheville, Virginia, late 1862. Acting Lt. OO to J. S. Williams, Mar. 27, 1863. Later to Giltner and Cosby. Lt. OO, June 14, 1864.

Carroll, Robert Goodloe Harper. b. Howard Co., Maryland, Jan. 1, 1839. Usually just known as "Harper" Carroll. att. Mt. St. Mary's College and Georgetown. Pvt. Co. M, 1st Virginia Cavy. Lt. VADC to Ewell at Spotsylvania. Lt. ADC to Ewell, June 30, 1864. Resigned Nov. 18, 1864. Brother of a postwar governor of Maryland. d. Howard Co., June 20, 1915. bur. New Cathedral Cem., Baltimore. Carroll's war letters are at the Maryland Historical Society.

Carson, John Charles. b. Natchez, Mississippi, July 9, 1840. Pvt. Co. A, Jeff Davis Legion, Aug. 12, 1861. Courier for Stuart, May–Aug. 1862 and Apr. 1864. Lt. ADC to Young, 1864. POW at Trevilian's Station, June 11, 1864. Immortal 600. Released June 16, 1865. Life insurance agent at Natchez. d. May 19, 1923. bur. Natchez City Cem.

Carter, Charles D. ADC to Cosby in the Shenandoah Valley, Oct.–Nov. 1864. No commission or other record found.

Carter, David Miller. b. Hyde Co., North Carolina, Jan. 12, 1830. att. Wake Forest and UNC. State legislator before and after the war. Capt. Co. E, 4th North Carolina, May 16, 1861. WIA at Seven Pines. Lt. Col., June 19, 1862. Resigned Dec. 23, 1862. Col. of Cavy., Dec. 16, 1862, to sit on the military court of the Second Corps. Resigned Sept. 25, 1863, to accept similar position with Third Corps. Resigned again, Aug. 10, 1864. Lawyer and planter. Married twice. d. Baltimore, Maryland, Jan. 7, 1877.

Carter, Francis. b. St. Louis, Missouri, July 25, 1838. att. UVA. and St. Peter's College. St. Louis clerk. Lost arm in May 1862, particulars unknown. Lt. ADC to Bowen, July 9, 1862, to take effect May 26, 1862. POW at Vicksburg. Lt. VADC to Rodes, Oct. 1863 until at least Aug. 1864. St. Louis merchant and steamboat agent. d. Apr. 28, 1896. bur. Bellefontaine Cem.

Carter, Johnston B. Of Caswell Co., North Carolina. Served in USN during Mexican War. Capt. OO, 1861, on duty at Richmond, Virginia. Lt. Col. of Arty., Feb. 25, 1862. Lt. Col. OO at Richmond, 1862–1865. Thus marginally on staff of Gen. Gorgas.

Carter, Richard Henry. b. Apr. 21, 1817. Capt. Co. B, 8th Virginia. Maj. QM to Armistead, Aug. 25, 1862. WIA at Gettysburg. Relieved Oct. 27, 1863, to serve in Richmond. Maj. Chief IFT for ANVa., Mar. 5, 1864. Appx. m. Mary Welby DeButts. d. Apr. 7, 1880. bur. Warrenton City Cem.

Carter, Richard Welby. b. Fauquier Co., Virginia, Mar. 11, 1837. att. VMI. Loudoun Co. farmer. Capt. Co. H, 1st Virginia Cavy., Apr. 27, 1861. Capt. acting ADC to G. W. Smith at Seven Pines. Later Col., 1st Virginia Cavy. d. Loudoun Co., December 18, 1888. m. Sophia DeButts Carter. Carter "was always fat and looked greasy" according to a member of his regiment.

Carter, Robert. Lt. Co. A, 6th Virginia Cavy., July 24, 1861. Capt. AQM, 6th Virginia Cavy., Nov. 16, 1861. Capt. acting brigade QM several times in 1863–1864, and thus staff of Lomax.

Carter, Thomas Henry. b. King William Co., Virginia, June 13, 1831. att. VMI and UVA. Medical School. Of Millwood, Virginia. Capt. King William (Va.) Arty., June 1, 1861. Maj. of Arty., Nov. 1, 1862. Chief of Arty. to D. H. Hill, Oct. 1862. Later Col. of Arty., Feb. 27, 1864. Acting Chief of Arty. Second Corps, Oct. 1864–Jan. 1865. Appx. Farmer and physician in King William Co. d. there June 2, 1908.

Carwile, John Richard. b. in South Carolina, ca. 1840. Resident of Edgefield C.H. Lt. Co. A, 7th South Carolina, May 14, 1862. Adjt. 7th South Carolina, 1863–1864. Lt. ADC to Kershaw, Oct. 17, 1864. POW at Sailor's Creek. Schoolteacher in Anderson Co. Alive 1894 in Bradley, Greenwood Co., South Carolina. There were several men of this name in South Carolina, and some of this data deserves fuller scrutiny.

Cary, John Baytop. b. Hampton, Virginia, Oct. 18, 1819. att. Wm. & Mary. Established the Hampton Military Academy. Maj. of Arty., PAVa., May 24, 1861. Lt. Col. 32nd Virginia, Dec. 1861–May 21, 1862. Lt. Col. acting PM to Rains, Jan.–Feb. 1862. Lt. Col. AAAIG to Magruder, Apr.–May 1862. Maj. AAG to Magruder, June 3, 1862. Maj. QM, Aug. 16, 1862. Served in Richmond as paymaster to hospitalized troops, into 1865. New York City insurance agent and superintendent of Richmond schools. d. Richmond, Jan. 13, 1898. bur. Hollywood Cem.

Cary, Richard Milton. b. ca. 1824. att. Wm. & Mary. Lawyer at Richmond, Virginia. Author of early war drill manual. Married twice. Capt. Co. F, 1st Virginia. Col. 30th Virginia, June 13, 1861. Declined reelection Apr. 1862. Lt. OO to J. G. Walker, June 4, 1862. Lt. OO at Macon (Ga.) Arsenal, Nov. 1862 to ca. June 1863. Capt. OO, May 26, 1863. Commanded Bellona Arsenal near Richmond, June 1863 to at least Mar. 1864.

Maj. OO, Sept. 10, 1863. Maj. OO at Salisbury, North Carolina, Nov. 17, 1864, into 1865. Cotton and tobacco merchant in England. d. County of Cornwall, England, Mar. 15, 1886.

Cary, Wilson Miles. b. Baltimore Co., Maryland, Dec. 12, 1838. att. Univ. of Maryland and UVA. A brother of the famous Cary sisters, Hetty and Jenny. Baltimore lawyer and teacher. Capt. AQM, Mar. 1, 1862. To report to J. E. Johnston, Nov. 26, 1862. Capt. AQM at Montgomery, Alabama, Apr. 1863–Apr. 1864. Capt. AQM, assistant to issuing QM at ANVa. headquarters, Apr. 28, 1864. Appx. Chief clerk of Baltimore criminal court. d. Aug. 28, 1914. Often confused with another Wilson Miles Cary, from Virginia.

Cassell, Charles Emmet. b. Portsmouth, Virginia, Apr. 26, 1838. Civil engineer at Norfolk. Contract topographical engineer in Virginia and North Carolina, 1861–1862. Lt. EO, about Mar. 1864. On duty all around Virginia. Served two years in the Chilean Navy. Prominent architect at Baltimore. d. Aug. 1916. bur. Cedar Grove Cem., Portsmouth.

Catlett, Richard Henry. b. Warren Co., Virginia, Apr. 19, 1828. Rockbridge Co. lawyer. ADC to Gov. Letcher, 1861. Capt. AAG to Echols, June 11, 1862. Capt. AAG to Kemper, June 4, 1864, through 1865. Staunton law partner of Gen. Echols. d. Mar. 1898.

Caulfield, Ignatius. b. in New York. m. Mrs. Amelia Arundel, 1855. 28-year-old produce merchant at New Orleans in 1860. Maj. CS to Tracy's brigade, Louisiana state troops, 1862. Capt. ACS, 10th Louisiana, Dec. 10, 1862. Dropped May 29, 1863. Capt. ACS to Steuart, about July 1863. Capt. ACS to William Terry, May–Oct. 1864. Capt. ACS to Patton Anderson, 1864–1865. d. New Orleans, Jan. 7, 1871. bur. Lafayette Cem. #1.

Cave, William Jones. b. June 21, 1833. att. UVA. Madison Co. merchant. Lt. Co. A, 7th Virginia, Apr. 23, 1861, into 1862. Acting OO to Kemper, Nov. 1862. Served in 3rd

Virginia LDTS. Lt. ADC to Kemper, May 16, 1864. Madison Co. merchant and farmer. Brother-in-law of Gen. Kemper. d. Apr. 11, 1895. bur. City Cem. at Madison C.H.

Cavendish, Charles. Served in 18th Hussars, British Army. A volunteer EO to Fitz. Lee, from May 13, 1864. Served into Nov. 1864 at least, but no commission available for him. Killed a Yankee and had his own horse slain in a charge within minutes of reporting to Lee on May 13. Cavendish thought to be an assumed name, and true surname possibly Short.

Cawood, Charles H. From Prince George's Co., Maryland. Pvt. Co. A, 17th Virginia, Aug. 29, 1861. Detailed as scout and signalman under E. P. Alexander, Oct. 1861. Sgt. in Signal Corps, June 1862. Lt. SO, June 26, 1863. Mostly on duty in King George Co., Virginia. Paroled at Ashland, Virginia, Apr. 20, 1865. m. Mrs. Lucy Jane Johnson Macon, 1865. Probably died prior to 1869.

Cazaux, Anthony D. b. in North Carolina, 1828. Merchant at Wilmington. Capt. AQM, 18th North Carolina, June 21, 1861. Capt. AQM to Lane, Sept. 15, 1864. Served into 1865. Clerk in shipping office at Wilmington, 1870. d. Jan. 21, 1910. bur. Oakdale Cem.

Chalaron, Stephen. b. New Orleans, Louisiana, October 8, 1839. Pvt. Second Co. Washington (La.) Arty., May 26, 1861, a 22-year-old clerk from New Orleans. Later a Cpl. WIA at Gettysburg. Lt. in Nitre & Mining Bureau, May 2, 1864. Capt. Nitre & Mining Bureau, June 15, 1864. Stationed at Richmond, Virginia. d. Dec. 27, 1915. bur. New Orleans.

Chamberlaine, William Wilson. b. Norfolk, Virginia, Oct. 16, 1836. att. Norfolk Military Academy and Hampden Sidney. Lt. Co. G, 6th Virginia, Apr. 1861. WIA at Sharpsburg. Lt. AAG to Second Corps artillery, Feb. 24, 1863. Lt. AAG to Third Corps artillery, May 1863. Capt. AAG to Third Corps artillery, Oct. 23, 1863, thence to R. L. Walker in 1865.

Norfolk banker and treasurer. Moved to Washington, D.C., 1910. d. there Oct. 19, 1923. Chamberlaine's excellent memoirs have been published.

Chamberlayne, Francis West. b. Apr. 16, 1833. Richmond merchant pre- and postwar. Capt. Co. I, 4th Virginia Cavy., May 1861 to Jan. 1863. WIA at Malvern Hill, June 14, 1862. Lt. Drillmaster, Mar. 18, 1863. Lt. AAAG to W. E. Jones, Nov. 28, 1863. POW at Moorefield, Aug. 7, 1864. Lt. staff of Lomax, 1865. d. Richmond, Oct. 20, 1904. bur. Emmanuel Episc. Churchyard.

Chamberlayne, John Hampden. b. Richmond, Virginia, June 2, 1838. att. UVA. Taught briefly in Hanover Co., and then Richmond lawyer. Pvt. Co. F, 21st Virginia, 1861. Sgt. Purcell (Va.) Arty., 1862. Lt. AAG to R. L. Walker, June 1862–1864. Lt. acting ADC to A. P. Hill during the Seven Days. Commanded a battery in the 13th Bn. Virginia Arty., July 28, 1864–Apr. 1865. Louisa Co. farmer, clerk at Radford, Virginia, and newspaperman in Richmond and Petersburg. Member of state legislature. His wartime letters were published in 1932. d. Feb. 1882. bur. Hollywood Cem., Richmond.

Chambers, Thomas Jefferson. b. Orange Co., Virginia, Apr. 13, 1802. Lawyer in Kentucky and Alabama. Studied at Mexico City, 1826–1828. Judge in Texas in the 1830s and general of reserves in the Texas Revolution. Delegate to Texas Secession Convention. VADC to Hood at Gaines's Mill. Four times unsuccessful candidate for governor. Murdered Mar. 15, 1865, at Anahuac, Texas. bur. Episc. Cem. at Galveston.

Chambliss, Walter Blow. b. Hicksford, Virginia, Jan. 21, 1846. att. VMI and UNC. Pvt. Co. H, 13th Virginia Cavy., Oct. 1, 1863. Lt. ADC to his brother Gen. Chambliss, Feb. 19, 1864. Appx. m. Jenny C. Spratley. Greensville Co. farmer and lawyer. d. Mar. 23, 1886. bur. family cem. at "Woodview" in Emporia, Virginia.

Chandler, Daniel Thomas. b. Washington, D.C., 1820. Lt. U.S. Inf., 1838–Feb. 1862. WIA at Monterey in Mexican War. POW on Potomac River trying to go south, Feb. 1863. Lt. Col. AAG, Feb. 16, 1864, to report to R. E. Lee. Ordered to operate facility at Gordonsville, Virginia. Sent to command post at Staunton, Virginia, June 1864, but orders revoked. Lt. Col. AAIG, July 23, 1864, on varied inspection assignments. Resigned Feb. 28, 1865. Librarian of Baltimore, Maryland, city law library. d. there Oct. 14, 1877, age 56.

Chapman, Kena King. b. 1839. Pvt. Co. A, 19th Bn. Virginia Heavy Arty., Apr. 29, 1861. To Lt., May 20, 1862. Adjt. 19th Bn. Virginia Heavy Arty., Sept. 11, 1862. Lt. acting OO to Crutchfield's Arty. Bgd., Feb. 1865. Bookkeeper in Isle of Wight Co. d. 1892 or 1895.

Cherry, Edward B. b. in Georgia. 21-year-old merchant at Demopolis, Alabama, in 1860. m. Helen A. Quinn, 1860. Pvt. Co. A, 43rd Alabama, Apr. 7, 1862. Detached on service with Army of Kentucky, July 1862. Lt. ADC to Gracie, Nov. 4, 1862. Requested to stay with brigade after Gracie's death. Permission not granted, but nonetheless was paroled at Appx. as Lt. [V]ADC to Moody.

Chestney, Theodore Oscar. b. Nov. 21, 1837. Lived at Washington, D.C., 1848–1860. Lt. of Inf., CSA, May 20, 1861. Lt. AAG to Elzey, June 30, 1861. WIA at First Manassas. Capt. AAG to Elzey, Dec. 11, 1861. WIA in shoulder at Gaines's Mill. Possibly staff of Early in summer and fall 1862. Maj. AAG to Elzey, Dec. 20, 1862. Maj. AAG to Robert Ransom, Ewell, and G. W. C. Lee in Dept. of Richmond. POW at Sailor's Creek. Banker at Macon, Georgia. d. there Nov. 2, 1925.

Cheves, Edward Richardson. Cadet and VADC to Lawton by early 1862. KIA at Gaines's Mill, June 27, 1862, age 18. bur. Magnolia Cem., Charleston, South Carolina.

Chew, Roger Preston. b. Loudoun Co., Virginia, Apr. 9, 1843. att. VMI. Lt. Ashby (Va.) Btty. Maj. Chief of Arty. to Stuart, Feb. 27, 1864. Same to Hampton. Lt. Col., Feb. 18, 1865. Farmer, realtor, and legislator after the war. m. Louisa Fontaine Washington. d. Charlestown, West Virginia, Mar. 16, 1921. bur. Zion Episc. Church Cem.

Chichester, Arthur Mason. b. Leesburg, Virginia, Apr. 6, 1831. A civil engineer. Acting Engineer on the staff of D. H. Hill by Sept. 1862. Same to Rodes by June 1863. POW at Leesburg, July 13, 1863. Exchanged May 3, 1864. Appx. Received pay as acting Capt. EO, but apparently never commissioned. War record is very sketchy. Leesburg farmer. m. Mary Beverley. d. near Leesburg, Apr. 11, 1916. bur. Union Cem.

Chichester, John Henry. b. in Virginia, 1823. A farmer in Fairfax Co. m. Sarah Ellen Dulany. VADC to Longstreet at First Manassas. Maj. CS to Longstreet, Sept. 17, 1861. Relieved Nov. 4, 1862, and ordered to report to Maj. Cole at ANVa. headquarters. Maj. CS at Gordonsville, Virginia, by July 1863. Paroled there June 3, 1865. Fairfax Co. treasurer. d. there June 27, 1889. bur. Falls Church Episc. Church Cem.

Chisholm, J. M. ADC to Butler. Present at Appx., capacity uncertain. Incarcerated at Libby Prison in mid-Apr. 1865. Documentation very thin on this soldier. Probably either John Maxwell Chisholm (Sept. 18, 1839–Jan. 22, 1898) or James Misroon Chisholm (d. Sept. 25, 1871).

Chisman, Samuel Reade. b. 1838. m. Martha Kennon Whiting, 1861. Lt. Co. A, 32nd Virginia, May 13, 1861, a 24-year-old druggist. Resigned to become Capt. AQM at Jamestown Island, Sept. 1861. Capt. AQM at Richmond, Virginia, May 1862–Apr. 1863. Capt. AQM at Greensboro, North Carolina, Apr. 15, 1863. Later promoted to Maj. QM. d. June 14, 1885. bur. St. John's Cem., Hampton, Virginia.

Chisolm, Alexander Robert. b. Beaufort, South Carolina, Nov. 19, 1834. att. Columbia Univ. ADC to Beauregard, Mar. 12, 1861. Lt. ADC to Beauregard, Nov. 6, 1861, and served as such into 1865. New York City publisher postwar. d. there Mar. 1910.

Christian, Bolivar. b. Augusta Co., Virginia, Apr. 26, 1825. att. Washington Coll. Lawyer and legislator pre- and postwar. Capt. ACS, 52nd Virginia, Sept. 10, 1861. Capt. acting CS to Col. James A. Walker's Bgd., Dec. 1862. Capt. ACS at Saltville, Virginia, Aug. 1, 1863. Capt. ACS at Farmville, Virginia, late in the war. Served in the Virginia state legislature during the war. d. Staunton, July 17, 1900. bur. Bethel Presby. Church Cem., Augusta Co.

Christian, Charles M. Lt. of Arty., PACS, Sept. 17, 1862, to report to Maj. A. R. Courtney. Lt. acting AQM to D. B. Bridgford, Second Corps PM, 1863. May have held that post into 1865. Particulars of his service are unknown.

Christian, Isaac Hill. b. May 25, 1831. Said to be "a northern man" but practiced law in Charles City Co., Virginia, prewar. VADC to Stuart, July–Aug. 1862. Scout for Wise in southern Virginia, early 1863. Pvt. Co. D, 3rd Virginia Cavy., Oct. 17, 1863. WIA at Todd's Tavern, May 7, 1864. d. Charles City Co., Aug. 31, 1904.

Christian, Jones Rivers. b. New Kent Co., Virginia, ca. 1834. A farmer there prewar. Capt. Co. F, 3rd Virginia Cavy., June 28, 1861. Capt. acting ADC to Stuart, June–July 1862. POW at Spotsylvania, May 8, 1864. Post office clerk at Richmond. Entered R. E. Lee Camp Soldiers' Home, 1893. d. there May 20, 1895. bur. Hollywood Cem.

Christian, Richmond Lacy. b. Charles City Co., Virginia, Dec. 27, 1829. Richmond grocer pre- and postwar. Pvt. 2nd Co. Richmond Howitzers, July 20, 1861. Capt. AQM, 1st Virginia Arty., Oct. 22, 1861, and served into 1865. Never married. d. Richmond, Apr. 13, 1909. bur. Hollywood Cem.

Christian, Thomas Llewellyn. b. Charles

City Co., Virginia, Jan. 4, 1837. Farmer there pre- and postwar. Lt. Co. D, 4th Alabama, Apr. 25, 1861. Lt. AAAIG to Law, 1862. POW at Gettysburg, July 2, 1863. Capt. AAIG to Law, Nov. 2, 1863. Same to Perry, 1864–1865. Appx. m. Louisa Christian, his cousin. d. Charles City Co., Jan. 17, 1915.

Christy, George William. b. New Orleans, Louisiana, Nov. 22, 1818. att. Harvard. New Orleans lawyer. Lt. Co. G, 6th Louisiana, May 9, 1861. Maj., Nov. 22, 1861. Failed re-election. Capt. OO to Ewell, May 15, 1862. WIA in leg and POW at Cedar Mountain. Capt. OO to Early. Maj. OO to J. A. Walker, Jan. 17, 1865. POW at Sailor's Creek. Released July 25, 1865. d. New Orleans, Feb. 7, 1891.

Church, William Lee. b. Apr. 21, 1843. att. UGA. and UNC. Sgt. Co. C, Cobb's Legion Cavy., Aug. 1, 1861. To Adjt., Dec. 4, 1862. Capt. AAG to Young, Sept. 28, 1863. Commanded 9th Georgia Cavy. periodically in last year of the war. m. Laura Randolph. Professor at UGA. and a planter. Moved to Washington, D.C., and was a physician there. d. Mar. 31, 1871. bur. Oconee Hill Cem., Athens, Georgia.

Clagett, Henry Oden. b. Apr. 5, 1833. Capt. AQM, Nov. 16, 1861, to report to the QM Gen. To report to J. E. Johnston, Dec. 12, 1861. Capt. AQM to Holmes, Apr. 29, 1862. Capt. AQM to Pemberton, May 27, 1862. Capt. AQM stationed at Richmond, Aug. 1862 into 1865. On duty as paymaster for artillery defenses and some of the city's hospitals. Leesburg newspaperman. d. Baltimore, Maryland, July 3, 1904. bur. Union Cem., Leesburg.

Claiborne, Herbert Augustine. b. Richmond, Virginia, July 11, 1819. att. Wm. & Mary. Richmond lawyer. Capt. ACS, June 29, 1861. On duty at Richmond until he resigned, Apr. 23, 1862. Married three times, including the daughter of Col. H. C. Cabell, who later married Gen. W. R. Cox after Claiborne's death. Insurance company president at Richmond. d. there Feb. 15, 1902. bur. Hollywood Cem.

Claiborne, John. Maj. QM to Ruggles, Jan. 28, 1862. At various posts in Alabama, Mississippi, and Georgia, 1862–1863. Maj. QM to Bryan, Mar. 16, 1864. Relieved Apr. 20, 1864. Maj. QM in Bureau of Conscription at Richmond, May–Nov. 1864. Maj. QM in Pay Dept. at Richmond, Mar. 1865. To Dept. of Alabama, Mar. 24, 1865.

Claiborne, John Hayes. b. Richmond, Virginia, Feb. 4, 1823. A grocer there. Capt. ACS, June 29, 1861. Maj. CS, Sept. 2, 1861. Worked at Richmond into 1865. Richmond chief of police and insurance agent. Married twice. Claiborne's daughter married Gen. S. B. Buckner. d. Richmond, Dec. 18, 1890. bur. Shockoe Cem.

Clark, Frank Peyton. b. Winchester, Virginia, Mar. 27, 1838. att. UVA. Pvt. Co. F, 2nd Virginia. Capt. AQM at Winchester, June 14, 1861. Worked as claims adjuster throughout the Shenandoah Valley, 1861–1863. Capt. AQM and IFT in the valley, Nov. 13, 1863, into 1865. Said to have volunteered on T. J. Jackson's staff at First Winchester, and on Jubal Early's staff at Second Winchester. Lawyer at New York City and Baltimore. d. Baltimore, Jan. 13, 1912. bur. Green Mount Cem.

Clark, George Washington. b. Eutaw, Alabama, July 18, 1841. att. UAla. Lt. Co. B, 11th Alabama, 1861. To Capt. June 30, 1862. Capt. AAAG to Sanders, July–Aug. 1864, at least. WIA at Gaines's Mill, Gettysburg, and Reams's Station. Alabama lawyer, and then attorney general of Texas. Lived at Waco. d. there Mar. 28, 1918. Clark's memoirs are published but very scarce.

Clark, James Louis. b. Savannah, Georgia, Dec. 12, 1840. Baltimore lawyer. Capt. AQM, 1st Maryland, Nov. 20, 1861. Resigned June 13, 1862. POW at Baltimore, July 21, 1862. Exchanged Aug. 11, 1862. Capt. VADC and possibly OO to Stuart, May 22, 1863, until only June 1863. Capt. Co. F,

12th Virginia Cavy., June 16, 1863. POW at Moorefield, Aug. 7, 1864. Appx. Lawyer at Columbine, Colorado. d. Baltimore, Sept. 6, 1910. bur. Loudon Park Cem. Clark's uniform is at the Museum of the Confederacy in Richmond.

Clark, Meriwether Lewis. b. St. Louis, Missouri, Jan. 10, 1809. Son of William Clark, from Lewis and Clark fame. att. USMA. Left U.S. Army in 1833. Veteran of Black Hawk War and Mexican War. Prewar architect. Capt. CSA, Mar. 19, 1861. Major, Apr. 1861. Brigadier Gen. Missouri State Guard, Oct. 1861. Maj. of Arty., Nov. 11, 1861, and sent to Ft. Smith, Arkansas. Served under Van Dorn and Price. Col. Chief of Arty. to Van Dorn. VADC to Bragg at Murfreesboro. Ordered to inspection duty at Richmond, Aug. 15, 1864. Col. OO, temporarily commanding Barton's Bgd., Nov. 1864. POW at Amelia C.H., Apr. 5, 1865. Math professor at KMI. d. Frankfort, Kentucky, Oct. 28, 1881. bur. Bellefontaine Cem., St. Louis.

Clarke, Colin Douglas. b. Mar. 22, 1832. m. Bettie Berkley Cooke. Capt. AQM in Virginia by Sept. 1861, probably in PAVA. Capt. AQM, Feb. 4, 1862, to report to Magruder. On duty as Capt. AQM at Gloucester, Virginia, 1862. d. there Apr. 10, 1862, of jaundice. bur. Hollywood Cem., Richmond.

Clarke, John J. Graham. b. in Virginia, ca. 1832. A civil engineer. On duty at Yorktown, Virginia, Apr. 1861. Capt. EO, Feb. 15, 1862. In charge of defenses at Mulberry Island, Virginia. At Drewry's Bluff by May 13, 1862, and supervised work there. Maj. EO, May 4, 1863, and reported to Longstreet, May 15. Maj. EO at Richmond, Nov. 1863. Maj. EO at Savannah, Georgia, Dec. 1863. Lt. Col. EO, Mar. 17, 1864. Col. EO, Oct. 19, 1864. Chief EO, AOT, 1865. Supt. of Georgia Central Railroad and bridge builder in South. Run over by a train at Paterson, New Jersey, Sept. 15, 1880. bur. Hollywood Cem., Richmond, in an unmarked grave. All of Clarke's wartime signatures are as John J., but nearly all post-war sources call him John G., suggesting he may have changed his middle name, or adopted the third middle name later in life.

Clarke, John W. Capt. AQM, 34th North Carolina, May 1, 1862. Capt. acting QM to Scales, Sept.–Dec. 1863, at least. Capt. AQM to Scales, Sept. 15, 1864, through 1865.

Clarke, William E. Capt. AQM to Marshall, Aug. 19, 1862. Later to Preston and to J. S. Williams. Maj. QM to Williams, Oct. 1, 1863. Same for Cosby. Served into 1865 with that brigade.

Clarke, William H. ADC to Ewell, 1865. Appx. No other record.

Clarke, William Henry. b. Richmond, Virginia, Jan. 21, 1839. att. VMI. Teacher at the Norfolk Academy, pre- and postwar. Contract engineer in central Virginia, Dec. 1861–1862. Lt. OO to E. A. Perry, Mar. 20, 1863. Same to Finegan. Appx. Henrico Co. farmer. Interred, Hollywood Cem., Richmond, Dec. 31, 1895, and probably died two days earlier.

Clarke, William J. Capt. AQM, 8th Virginia Cavy., Oct. 18, 1861. Capt. acting QM to B. T. Johnson, Nov. 1864. Appx.

Clarkson, John Nicholas. b. Albemarle Co., Virginia, Oct. 24, 1816. Salt maker and deputy sheriff in Kanawha Co. m. Anna Early, sister of Jubal Early. Apparently was the Lt. Col. of the 10th Virginia Cavy. very briefly in 1861. VADC to Wise in western Virginia in 1861, engaged in partisan operations. Commanded state line cavalry under Floyd. Col. 3rd Virginia State Line Cavy., 1862–1863. Operated Saltville works for Confederacy, 1863–1865. Contractor in Washington, D.C. d. Charleston, West Virginia, Oct. 12, 1906.

Clay, Hugh Lawson. b. Alabama, Jan. 24, 1823. att. UAla. and UVa. Capt. of U.S. Inf. in Mexican War. Huntsville lawyer, pre- and postwar. Maj. AAG, Mar. 16, 1861. Commanded post at Lynchburg, Virginia, June–Oct. 1861. Maj. AAG to E. K. Smith, Mar. 21,

1862, but was serving with Smith as early as Nov. 1861. Maj. AAG to Heth, Dec. 6, 1862. Assigned to duty in Richmond, Jan. 26, 1863. Lt. Col. AAG, Apr. 30, 1863, backdated to rank from Oct. 14, 1862. In Richmond through 1865, in Samuel Cooper's office. Brother of Confederate Sen. C. C. Clay. d. Huntsville, Dec. 28, 1890.

Clayton, James. b. Murfreesboro, Tennessee, Mar. 7, 1833. Clerk and merchant there pre- and postwar. QM Sgt., 23rd Tennessee, Oct. 1, 1861. Capt. AQM, 23rd Tennessee, May 2, 1863. Capt. AQM to McComb, Mar. 4, 1865. Appx. m. Hadassah Cowan. d. Murfreesboro, Jan. 3, 1913. bur. Evergreen Cem.

Cleary, Frank D. Capt. AQM to Wise, June 24, 1861. Maj. QM to Wise, Aug. 27, 1861. Maj. QM at Charlottesville, Virginia, Mar. 1863. Probably never reported. Dropped from rolls, Apr. 8, 1863. POW at Baltimore, Maryland, June 16, 1863. Said he was going north to be married. Released from Ft. Delaware prison, Aug. 10, 1863, and expected to go to Europe until the end of the war.

Cleary, Reuben. b. Alexandria, Virginia, Apr. 29, 1835. Physician at Washington, D.C. Capt. Co. H, 7th Virginia. Lost his commission in May 1862. On recruiting duty at Jackson, Mississippi, 1863. AAAG to J. M. Jones, May 26, 1863. Capt. AAAG to B. T. Johnson, July 1863 into early autumn. Capt. AAG to Jones, Nov. 2, 1863. Later staff of Wm. Terry. Capt. AAIG to Wharton. Capt. AAG to M. L. Clark's reserve Bgd., Dec. 10, 1864. Capt. AAAG to G. W. C. Lee, Feb. 1865. Capt. AAG to Alexander, Mar. 8, 1865.

Clemons, Welcom G. b. Pennsylvania. Manufacturer of cotton gins at Columbus, Georgia. Lt. Co. G, 2nd Georgia, Apr. 16, 1861. Capt. AAG to Semmes, Mar. 11, 1862. Maj. QM, Nov. 18, 1862, and assigned to duty in Georgia. Staff of Cumming later in war. Relieved Feb. 9, 1865. Resumed cotton gin business at Columbus. Later lived at

Richmond, and then near Baltimore, Maryland. d. Reisterstown, Maryland, Jan. 31, 1896, of diabetes, age 72.

Cobb, John Addison. b. October 20, 1838. att. UGA. Planter. Pvt. Co. D, 2nd Bn. Georgia. QM Sgt., 16th Georgia. Lt. ADC to his father, Howell Cobb, Mar. 8, 1862. Resigned Sept. 27, 1862. Farmer and legislator in Georgia. d. Dec. 8, 1925. bur. Oak Grove Cem., Americus, Georgia.

Cobb, John Boswell. b. Jefferson Co., Georgia, Feb. 3, 1826. att. UGA. Merchant in New York, and Athens, Georgia, bank president. Youngest brother of Howell and T. R. R. Cobb. Lt. Co. D, Cobb's Legion, Sept. 1861. Maj. CS to Howell Cobb, June 6, 1862. Same to Finegan and Gardner in Florida, late in 1863. With Howell Cobb in Georgia through 1865. Macon insurance agent. d. there Nov. 21, 1893.

Cobb, Lamar. b. July 15, 1840. att. UGA. Pvt. Co. B, 2nd Bn. Georgia, Apr. 20, 1861. Sgt. Maj., 16th Georgia, July 31, 1861. Lt. ADC to his father, Howell Cobb, Sept. 27, 1862. Capt. AAG to Cobb, June 25, 1863. Maj. AAG to Cobb, Dec. 14, 1863. Athens lawyer. d. Mar. 17, 1907. bur. Oconee Hill Cem., Athens.

Cochran, George Moffett, Jr. b. Stribling Springs, Virginia, Feb. 26, 1832. att. UVA. Staunton lawyer pre- and postwar. On ordnance duty at Harpers Ferry, May 1861. Capt. AQM, 52nd Virginia, Sept. 2, 1861. Capt. AQM to Pegram, Sept. 15, 1864. Stayed with that brigade until Appx. Unfit for front-line duty because of extreme nearsightedness. In state legislature. d. Apr. 7, 1900.

Cochran, Howe Peyton. b. Augusta Co., Virginia, Sept. 18, 1834. att. UVA. and VMI. Sgt. Albemarle Arty. Lt. OO in Staunton by Feb. 1863. Probably staff of Pegram in 1864, and certainly OO to Pickett, 1864–1865, though rank is unclear. Appx. Charlottesville teacher. m. Jane Kent. d. Staunton, Sept. 28, 1892.

Cochran, John Lewis. b. Staunton, Virginia, Aug. 22, 1827. att. UVA. Lawyer at Charlottesville. Pvt. Co. B, 19th Virginia, May 8, 1861. To Lt., July 1, 1861, and then Capt., Apr. 28, 1862. Transferred to First Corps as PM, Jan. 30, 1863. Capt. on military court of the corps, spring 1863–1865. Charlottesville judge, lawyer, and newspaperman. m. Mary James Massie, 1868. d. Mar. 6, 1900. bur. UVA. Cem.

Cochran, William Lynn Lewis. b. May 27, 1838. att. UVA. and VMI. Brother of H. P. Cochran (above). Charlottesville lawyer. Capt. AQM, Oct. 18, 1861. Served in Virginia, possibly on Gen. Floyd's staff. Resigned Dec. 12, 1861, one leg being shorter than the other. Mayor of Charlottesville and lawyer. Never married. d. Sept. 22, 1875.

Cochrane, Robert Elam. b. Cabarrus Co., North Carolina, Jan. 26, 1836. Merchant there. Pvt. Co. F, 5th North Carolina Cavy., July 7, 1862. Capt. AQM, 5th North Carolina Cavy., Oct. 18, 1862. Probably Capt. AQM to Barringer, autumn 1864. Paroled May 24, 1865, Albany, Georgia. m. Elizabeth Orr. d. June 2, 1917. bur. Elmwood Cem., Charlotte.

Cocke, Daniel Fenton. b. Fauquier Co., Virginia, Aug. 1, 1816. Farmer at Chattanooga, Tennessee. Maj. CS to S. R. Anderson, July 19, 1861. Resigned June 5, 1862. Commissary agent in Tennessee later in the war. m. Margaret Augusta Roberson. d. Mar. 15, 1885. bur. Rest Haven Cem., Williamson Co., Tennessee.

Cocke, John Bowdoin. b. Richmond, Virginia, Oct. 2, 1836. att. VMI and UVA. Powhatan Co. farmer and officer in the state militia. VADC and AAAG to his father, Gen. Cocke, at First Manassas. On detail at Beauregard's headquarters, Sept.–Oct. 1861. Pvt. Co. E, 4th Virginia Cavy., Jan. 15, 1864. Resumed farming postwar. d. at "Belmead" in Powhatan Co., Apr. 2, 1889.

Cody, Bailey Hardeman. b. Franklin Co., Tennessee, Jan. 25, 1829. m. Elizabeth A.

Cunningham, 1851. VADC to Semmes during Seven Days, and up through Chancellorsville, at least. No other military service found. Farmer in Williamson Co., Tennessee. d. Franklin, Mar. 17, 1909. bur. Mt. Hope Cem.

Cody, David C. b. Nov. 22, 1831. Pvt. Co. G, 31st Georgia, Nov. 10, 1861. Capt. of that company by June 1863. WIA at Gettysburg. Capt. AAIG to C. A. Evans, around summer 1864. Appx. Farmer in Chattahoochee Co., Georgia. d. June 13, 1880.

Cody, James Adolphus. b. October 24, 1842. att. UNC. Pvt. Co. G, 2nd Georgia, Apr. 16, 1861. Present into autumn 1861. Served on staff of Semmes at Chancellorsville and Gettysburg, probably as VADC. Later AAIG to Cumming and lost a leg at Missionary Ridge.

Coghlan, Patrick G. b. Limerick, Ireland. Member of the "Young Ireland Party." Moved to Richmond, Virginia, ca. 1849. Worked at Dooley's hat store and was a newspaper reporter. Capt. OO at Richmond, by Sept. 1863, possibly affiliated with the state forces rather than CSA. Served to end of war. Clerk and newspaperman at Richmond. d. there Apr. 27, 1881, age 67. bur. Oakwood Cem.

Coke, George Hankins. b. Williamsburg, Virginia. att. Wm. & Mary. Capt. ACS at Taylorsville, Virginia, Apr.–July 1863. Commission "expired" July 31, 1863. Thought to be the man who was Asst. Surg., 12th North Carolina, in 1861, and Capt. ACS, 52nd North Carolina, 1862–1863.

Coker, James Lide. b. Darlington Dist., South Carolina, Jan. 3, 1837. att. SCMA and Harvard. Capt. Co. G, 9th South Carolina, 1861. Capt. Co. E, 6th South Carolina, 1862–1864. Capt. AAAG to Micah Jenkins's Bgd., Oct. 1863. WIA severely at Wauhatchie, with "little hope of recovery." Maj. 6th South Carolina. In state legislature, 1864 and postwar. Banker and merchant in Darlington. Author of a good book on the regiments

in which he served. d. June 25, 1918. bur. Hartsville Baptist Church.

Cole, Archibald H. VADC to J. E. Johnston at First Manassas. Maj. QM to Johnston, Jan. 20, 1862. Inspector of transportation for army. Chief IFT for CSA, Oct. 17, 1862. Based at Richmond, Virginia. Lt. Col. QM, Nov. 30, 1863, but failed confirmation and commission revoked. Lt. Col. QM, Mar. 31, 1865, assigned to Dept. of Florida.

Cole, Hugh Laign. b. May 20, 1838. att. UNC and Princeton. Of Craven Co. Capt. Co. F, 2nd North Carolina, May 16, 1861–Oct. 21, 1862. Capt. acting QM to G. B. Anderson, July–Sept. 1862. Capt. AAG on conscription duty in North Carolina, 1863. EO to Bragg, 1865. Lawyer in New York City. d. Nov. 5, 1898.

Cole, Robert Granderson. b. Manchester, Virginia, Sept. 29, 1830. att. USMA from Palatka, Florida. Lt. U.S. Inf., 1850–1861. Capt. of Inf., CSA, Mar. 16, 1861. Capt. on staff of R. S. Garnett, June 18, 1861. Maj. CS (PACS) to Garnett, July 1, 1861. Maj. CS to J. E. Johnston, Dec. 24, 1861. Lt. Col. (PACS), July 5, 1862, to rank from Dec. 9, 1861. Chief Commissary, ANVa., until Appx. Thus staff of R. E. Lee, June 1862–Apr. 1865. Planter in Florida and businessman at Savannah, Georgia. d. Savannah, Nov. 7, 1887. bur. Bonaventure Cem.

Coleman, Henry Eaton. b. Halifax Co., Virginia, Jan. 5, 1837. att. VMI and Wm. & Mary. Granville Co., North Carolina, farmer. Capt. Co. B, 12th North Carolina, Apr. 26, 1861, to May 1862. Col. 12th North Carolina, May 4, 1863. VADC to Iverson, July 1863. WIA at Spotsylvania and Staunton River Bridge. Civil engineer. d. June 25, 1890.

Coleman, Samuel Henry. b. Petersburg, Virginia, Feb. 5, 1830. att. UVa. Staunton teacher. Pvt. Staunton Arty., Apr. 17, 1861. Lost eye and most of hearing in June 1861 explosion. Lt. OO to Ramseur, Feb. 7, 1863. Later same to Cox. Appx. Roanoke teacher.

d. June 5, 1900. bur. Thornrose Cem., Staunton.

Coleman, W. M. Capt. OO to Cox, no date. Records too thin to make any deductions about this officer's identity.

Coleman, William F. b. Oct. 1, 1835. att. UVA. Pvt. Co. G, 23rd Virginia Inf., Dec. 23, 1861. Lt. AAAG to A. G. Taliaferro's Bgd. at Cedar Mountain. To Adjt., Sept. 21, 1862. Capt. Co. G, 23rd Virginia, about Apr. 1863. Alive 1878 at Trevilian's Station, Louisa Co., Virginia, a farmer.

Collier, Thomas James. b. Hawkinsville, Georgia, May 21, 1841. Pvt. Co. D, 6th Georgia, May 1861. Capt. ACS, 6th Georgia, Dec. 24, 1861. Capt. ACS to Colquitt, June 23, 1863. Paroled at Greensboro, May 1, 1865. Physician at Griffin, Georgia. d. Atlanta, Dec. 12, 1910. bur. Oak Hill Cem., Griffin.

Collins, Charles Read. b. in Pennsylvania, Dec. 7, 1836. att. Georgetown and USMA. Lt. of Engineers, U.S. Army, 1859–1861. m. Augusta Mason, making him a brother-in-law of Gen. Alexander and Gen. Field. Lt. of Arty., July 23, 1861. Capt. EO, Oct. 7, 1861. Capt. EO to French, by Dec. 1861. Capt. EO to G. W. Smith, June 1862. VADC to Field, Seven Days. Possibly staff of Kershaw, too. Maj. 15th Virginia Cavy., Apr. 29, 1863. Col., Feb. 28, 1864. KIA at Todd's Tavern, May 7, 1864. bur. St. John's Episc. Church, King George C.H., Virginia.

Collins, George Pumpelly. b. New York City, Dec. 26, 1835. Of Washington Co., North Carolina. att. UVA. Lt. Co. G, 17th North Carolina, Apr. 1862. Capt. acting QM to Pettigrew, Aug. 28, 1862. Maj. QM to Pettigrew, Oct. 14, 1862. Same to Kirkland and then to MacRae. Farmer in North Carolina and Mississippi. d. Hillsborough, North Carolina, Aug. 30, 1903. bur. St. Matthew's Episc. Church.

Colquitt, Hugh Haralson. b. LaGrange, Georgia, Apr. 29, 1845. att. Emory. Pvt. Co. A, 2nd Bn. Georgia and Co. H, 6th Geor-

gia. VADC to his half-brother, Gen. Colquitt, from early 1863. Lt. ADC to Colquitt, Sept. 22, 1863. Paroled May 24, 1865. Served in Spanish-American War. d. Atlanta, Nov. 2, 1922. bur. Marietta Confederate Cem.

Colquitt, John H. ADC to Thomas in 1865. Paroled at Burkeville, Virginia, Apr. 21, 1865. No other record.

Colston, Frederick Morgan. b. near Leesburg, Virginia, Oct. 1, 1835. att. Georgetown and Columbian Coll. Baltimore banker pre- and postwar. Acting OO to Andrews's Bn. Arty., Feb. 1863, and to Alexander's Bn. Arty., Mar. 23, 1863. Lt. OO to Alexander's Bn. Arty., Nov. 18, 1863. Same to Huger's Bn. Arty. Capt. OO to Huger's Bn. Arty., Sept. 10, 1864. Capt. OO in charge of ANVa. reserve ordnance train, Oct. 1864 until Appx. d. Baltimore, Maryland, Apr. 19, 1922. Some sources give Colston's middle name as Mason.

Colston, Raleigh. b. Richmond, Virginia, Mar. 13, 1821. Grand-nephew of Chief Justice John Marshall. Farmer in Fauquier and Albemarle Co. m. Gertrude Powell. Capt. AQM at Charlottesville, Oct. 14, 1862. Served into 1864, at least. Treasury Dept. clerk in Richmond postwar. d. there Nov. 25, 1893. bur. Hollywood Cem.

Compton, James. b. 1835. Capt. AQM, 9th Virginia, Nov. 14, 1861. Capt. AQM to Barton, Sept. 15, 1864. Capt. Asst. IFT, ANVa., Oct. 7, 1864. Appx. d. May 5, 1902. bur. Lexington (Ky.) Cem.

Cone, Aurelius Franklin. b. in Georgia, Aug. 1836. att. USMA. In U.S. Army, 1857–1861. Lt. CSA, Mar. 16, 1861. Lt. ADC to Holmes, May 10, 1861. Maj. QM to Holmes, July 19, 1861. Maj. QM to G. W. Smith, Aug. 20, 1862. Lt. Col. acting AQM of the Confederacy, Apr. 21, 1863, into 1865. d. Mar. 24, 1894.

Connell, William C. b. in Mississippi, 1821. Wilkinson Co. planter. m. Eveline Posey, 1842. Pvt. Co. K, 16th Mississippi, Mar. 15, 1862. Capt. ACS, 16th Mississippi, July 9,

1862. Capt. ACS to Posey, Feb. 1863. Capt. ACS to Harris, Jan. 1864. Appx. d. 1899.

Connelly, William C. Lawyer at Albany, Georgia, age 37 in 1860. Pvt. Co. D, Cobb's Legion (Ga.) Cavy., Aug. 10, 1861. Later Ordnance Sgt. and acting QM Sgt. Lt. Asst. OO to T. R. R. Cobb, at least in Dec. 1862. Lt. OO to Butler, by Nov. 1863.

Conrad, Holmes. b. Winchester, Virginia, Jan. 31, 1840. att. UVA. and VMI. School-teacher prewar. Sgt. Co. A, 1st Virginia Cavy., Apr. 19, 1861. Later Co. D, 11th Virginia Cavy., and then Adjt., Oct. 2, 1862–Oct. 31, 1863. Capt. ACS, Apr. 18, 1864, on duty in the Shenandoah Valley, but still served with 11th Cavy. Capt. ACS to Imboden, June 9, 1864. Maj. AAIG to Rosser from about Oct. 1864. Paroled Apr. 27, 1865, at Winchester. Prominent lawyer and legislator. Solicitor-General of the United States, 1895–1897. d. Winchester, Sept. 4, 1915. bur. Mt. Hebron Cem.

Contee, Richard Snowden. b. Prince George's Co., Maryland, Feb. 8, 1836. Farmer in Anne Arundel Co. m. Anna Bowling, 1858. VADC to Elzey at First Manassas. Lt. ADC to Elzey, Sept. 11, 1861. Resigned Jan. 17, 1863, but retracted. Resigned again June 3, 1863. Elzey wrote that Contee was dissatisfied "with his position, with his present rank, and thinks he is entitled to more." Postwar farmer. d. Prince George's Co., May 1, 1908.

Cooke, Augustus Buckner. b. Portsmouth, Virginia, Feb. 8, 1824. Lived in California, 1849–1852. Worked as Norfolk, Virginia, customs official. Maj. QM to Pemberton, July 17, 1861, at Norfolk. Maj. QM to J. E. Johnston, Polk, and Taylor in the West. Mayor of Norfolk, ship broker, and cotton merchant. d. there Apr. 13, 1904. bur. Elmwood Cem.

Cooke, Giles Buckner. b. Portsmouth, Virginia, May 13, 1838. att. VMI. Prewar lawyer. VADC to Cocke, May 1861. Capt. AAG to Cocke, Oct. 29, 1861. Resigned Dec. 3, 1861.

Capt. AAG to Bragg, Apr. 1, 1862. Staff of Sam Jones and W. M. Gardner. Maj. AAG to Beauregard by May 1864. Maj. AAIG to R. E. Lee, Oct. 8, 1864. WIA at Sailor's Creek. Appx. Married twice. Teacher and minister at Mathews C.H. d. Feb. 4, 1937. bur. Ware Episc. Church, Gloucester Co. Cooke's late-war diary has been published.

Cooke, John Esten. b. Winchester, Virginia, Nov. 3, 1830. Prewar Richmond lawyer. Sgt. Richmond Howitzers. VADC to Stuart, Apr. 1862. Lt. OO to Stuart, May 19, 1862. Capt. OO to Stuart, July 25, 1862. Capt. AAIG to Stuart, Oct. 27, 1863. Stuart hoped to replace Cooke with "a more efficient officer." Capt. AAIG to Pendleton, May 1864. Appx. m. Mary Francis Page. Famous novelist who also wrote popular early biographies of Lee and Jackson. d. Clarke Co., Virginia, Sept. 1886. bur. Old Chapel Cem. Cooke was a cousin of Gen. Stuart's wife.

Coontz, Charles Washington. b. Frederick Co., Virginia, Nov. 11, 1827. Winchester carpenter and iron foundryman. Civilian acting CS at Winchester, June 24, 1861. Capt. ACS there July 19, 1861. Performed similar duty up and down Shenandoah Valley, into 1865. Official title late in war was "Capt. ACS Post & Purchasing Comsy., Early's Corps." Paroled at Winchester, Apr. 19, 1865. Farmer and lumberman. d. Hagerstown, Maryland, June 26, 1907. bur. Mt. Hebron Cem., Winchester.

Cooper, John Alexander. b. Clemmonsville, North Carolina, 1839. Clerk at Salem, and then merchant and cotton factor in Iredell Co. Lt. Co. E, 21st North Carolina, 1861. Capt. Co. B, 1st Bn. North Carolina Sharpshooters, Apr. 26, 1862. Capt. AAAG to Hoke, late in 1863 all the way into 1865. WIA several times. Merchant and bank president at Statesville, North Carolina. d. Mar. 18, 1907. bur. Oakwood Cem.

Cooper, Lunsford Pitts. b. Rutherford Co., Tennessee, June 8, 1830. att. Union Univ. Teacher and planter. Pvt. Co. H, 42nd

Mississippi. Capt. AQM, 42nd Mississippi, July 16, 1862. Capt. AQM to Davis, Sept. 15, 1864. Appx. Panola lawyer and Memphis law partner of Gen. Chalmers. d. Aug. 1902. bur. Elmwood Cem., Memphis.

Cooper, Samuel Mason. b. Virginia, June 4, 1836. att. USMA. Lt. 2nd U.S. Arty., 1857–1861. Lt. of Arty., CSA, Mar. 16, 1861. Commanded an artillery camp at Richmond, July 1861. Lt. serving with Second Corps artillery in unspecified role, probably as a staff officer, Oct. 1863–June 10, 1864. Maj. of Arty., PACS, July 18, 1864. Maj. AAIG to McLaws, Sept. 16, 1864–Jan. 1865. Lingering in Richmond without duty, 1865. Son of Gen. Samuel Cooper. m. Maria Mason. d. Jan. 20, 1908. bur. Christ Church Cem., Alexandria.

Corbin, Richard Washington. b. in France, Dec. 1837. Lived in Paris much of his life. att. Trinity Coll. in England. Capt. VADC to Field, July 1864 to Appx. d. Newport, Rhode Island, Feb. 22, 1922. bur. there. Corbin's excellent late-war letters have been published.

Cordell, Eugene Fauntleroy. b. Charlestown, Virginia, June 25, 1843. att. VMI. Sgt. Maj., 60th Virginia, Jan. 27, 1862. Lt. Co. C, 60th Virginia, Sept. 1, 1862. Lt. AAAG to Forsberg's Bgd., May 1864, through at least Sept. 1864. WIA at Third Winchester. POW at Waynesboro. att. Univ. of Maryland postwar and taught there. Baltimore physician. d. Aug. 27, 1913.

Corley, James Lawrence. b. in South Carolina, Oct. 5, 1829. att. USMA. Lt. QM in U.S. Army, 1850–1861. Capt. of Inf., June 7, 1861, to report to R. S. Garnett. On QM duty by July 1861, apparently as Chief QM, PAVA. Maj. PACS, Aug. 1, 1861. Lt. Col. 60th Virginia, Oct. 12, 1861–Mar. 10, 1862. Lt. Col. PACS, June 20, 1862, and Chief QM of ANVa. Maj. QM, CSA, Dec. 27, 1864. Appx. Norfolk, Virginia, insurance agent. d. Mar. 28, 1883. bur. Elmwood Cem.

Corling, Charles Thompson, Jr. b. Peters-

burg, Virginia, Nov. 1, 1842. att. VMI. VADC to B. R. Johnson, late war. Appx. Petersburg merchant and Richmond store clerk. d. Nov. 20, 1911.

Corprew, Oliver Hazard Perry, Jr. b. Norfolk, Virginia, Oct. 25, 1827. att. UVA. and Randolph Macon. A farmer, and a professor at Randolph Macon. Pvt. Co. A, 3rd Virginia Cavy., May 16, 1861. Capt. AQM, 6th Virginia, Nov. 16, 1861. Capt. AQM to R. H. Anderson, Sept. 15, 1864. Capt. AQM to Mahone. Appx. Taught at Randolph Macon, and at Central Coll. in Missouri. d. Norfolk, Oct. 12, 1908. bur. Elmwood Cem.

Corrie, Samuel J. b. Charleston, South Carolina, 1826. Pvt. in Rutledge Mounted Rifles, 1861. VADC to N. G. Evans, Mar. 1862. Lt. ADC to Evans, Sept. 22, 1862. Paroled May 27, 1865, at Augusta, Georgia. d. Charleston, Feb. 25, 1877, of tongue cancer. bur. Magnolia Cem., in unmarked grave.

Corse, Wilmer Douglass. b. in Virginia, Mar. 10, 1826. Capt. ACS at Charlottesville, Oct. 30, 1862. Maj. CS to Corse, Nov. 14, 1862, but declined the appointment. At Charlottesville into 1865. Alexandria banker. d. Jacksonville, Florida, July 27, 1896. Has gravestones at both Ivy Hill Cem., Alexandria, and Evergreen Cem., Jacksonville. Probably buried at the former site.

Cosby, Dabney, Jr. b. Halifax Co., Virginia, Apr. 6, 1836. A lawyer there. Pvt. Co. A, 53rd Virginia, June 12, 1861. Lt. OO, Apr. 2, 1863, and assigned to duty at Staunton. Lt. OO to Wharton by Dec. 1864. d. Aug. 17, 1886. bur. St. John's Episc. Church Cem., Halifax Co.

Costin, Ellison Lewis. b. Northampton Co., Virginia, Nov. 14, 1834. att. USMA and UVA. Lawyer and farmer at Eastville, Virginia. Lt. ADC to Griffith, Nov. 16, 1861. VADC to Semmes in Seven Days. VADC to McLaws, Aug. 1862. Maj. AAIG to McLaws, Oct. 20,

1862. Maj. AAIG to Kershaw. POW at Sailor's Creek. Northampton Co. lawyer and book-keeper. Moved to Washington, D.C., late in life. d. Pittsburgh, Pennsylvania, Oct. 12, 1910. "Very fond of dress and quite a good looking fellow."

Coughenour, William Chambers. b. Mar. 3, 1836. Of Rowan Co., North Carolina. Lt. and Capt. Co. K, 4th North Carolina. Capt. AAAG to Ramseur, summer 1863. Capt. AAG to Ramseur, Nov. 2, 1863. Capt. AAIG to Cox. Capt. AAIG to Dearing, Jan. 25, 1865. Capt. AAIG to Roberts, Mar. 1, 1865. WIA Apr. 5, 1865. Paroled May 16, 1865, at Salisbury. Mayor of Salisbury. d. June 16, 1917. bur. Chestnut Hill Cem.

Courtney, Alfred Ranson. b. King and Queen Co., Virginia, Nov. 17, 1833. Capt. of Arty., July 18, 1861. Maj. of Arty., July 14, 1862. Maj. Chief of Arty. to Ewell, Aug. 1862, and to Early, Sept. 1862. Relieved Apr. 20, 1863, at own request, after being court-martialed for bad behavior during Maryland Campaign. Commanded an artillery battalion in AOT, July 1863 into 1865. Virginia legislator postwar. d. Richmond, Nov. 4, 1914. bur. Hollywood Cem.

Coward, Asbury. b. Berkeley Dist., South Carolina, Sept. 19, 1835. att. SCMA. Co-founder of King's Mountain Military Academy. VADC to D. R. Jones at First Manassas. Capt. AAG to Jones, Aug. 15, 1861. Maj. AAG to Jones, July 11, 1862. Col. 5th South Carolina, Aug. 12, 1862. WIA at the Wilderness. Appx. Supt. of the Citadel. m. Eliza Larimore Blum. d. Rock Hill, South Carolina, Apr. 28, 1925.

Cox, Friend Clay. b. Tyler Co., Virginia, Apr. 21, 1844. Pvt. and Cpl., Co. G, 27th Virginia, Aug. 29, 1861. Courier to Gen. C. S. Winder, May 1862. Lt. ADC to Paxton, Jan. 19, 1863. VADC to J. A. Walker, May 1863. Capt. AAG to Walker, Nov. 27, 1863. Capt. AAG to William Terry, May 25, 1864. Capt. AAG to Beale, Jan. 25, 1865, but may not have served in that position as he was

WIA at Hatcher's Run while still with Terry. Appx. d. New Martinsville, West Virginia, Jan. 26, 1876.

Cox, Henry Winston. b. Chesterfield Co., Virginia, Nov. 25, 1835. att. VMI. Mining engineer. Served in the Otey Btty. and the 36th Virginia. Lt. OO to McCausland, Mar. 29, 1863. Served through Dec. 1864, at least. Christiansburg farmer, and later an educator at Rolla, Missouri, and in Texas. Married twice. Brother of Kate Cox, a Confederate memoirist. d. Pyle's Prairie, Texas, Feb. 27, 1890. This death date is from the family and seems to be the best of several options.

Cox, Joseph J. b. in North Carolina. Merchant in Anson Co. Capt. AQM, 31st North Carolina, Oct. 16, 1862, age 36. Capt. AQM in charge of Hoke's Div. ordnance train, Sept. 20, 1864. Farmer in Anson Co., alive 1870.

Cox, Richard Smith. b. Jan. 18, 1825. Of Georgetown, Maryland, and Loudoun Co., Virginia. Capt. AQM, Mar. 1, 1862. Maj. QM, Sept. 10, 1862, serving as Paymaster for ANVa. Stationed at Richmond through 1865. Possibly on the staff of G. W. C. Lee, late war. Married twice. d. Oct. 12, 1889.

Cox, Richard Threlkeld. b. Loudoun Co., Virginia. A planter there. Later mayor of Georgetown, D.C., and died there. An unofficial source calls him staff of G. W. C. Lee, and there is evidence that a Richard H. Cox was Maj. ADC to Lee in 1864. The latter Cox could be the man who was a King and Queen Co. physician, but that has not been proved.

Craige, Kerr. b. Catawba Co., North Carolina, Mar. 14, 1843. att. Catawba Coll. and UNC. Lived prewar in Rowan Co. Sgt. 1st North Carolina Cavy., June 15, 1861. Later Lt. in two companies of that unit. Lt. acting ADC to James B. Gordon, Oct. 10, 1863, probably into spring 1864. Capt. Co. I, 1st North Carolina Cavy., Mar. 1, 1865. POW Namozine Church. m. Josephine Branch, daughter of the general. Salisbury lawyer, banker, and legislator. d. Sept. 1904. bur. St. Luke's Episc. Church Cem. "Of massive frame, with clear-cut features and handsome form and face, agreeable, companionable, and kind. He had a fund of wit and humor in his make-up."

Craighill, James Brown. b. Charleston, Virginia, July 28, 1838. Pvt. Co. G, 2nd Virginia, June 6, 1861. Detailed as Ordnance Sgt. with E. P. Alexander, 1862. Acting Lt. OO to Nelson's Bn. Arty., Mar. 25, 1863. Took Oath Apr. 22, 1865. att. Episc. High School and became a priest. Posted in Virginia, Maryland, Georgia, and Washington, D.C. d. Washington, Feb. 4, 1913. bur. Christ Episc. Churchyard, Northampton Co., Virginia.

Cramer, John V. R. b. in New York. A clerk at Vicksburg, Mississippi, prewar. Sgt. in 21st Mississippi. Lt. ADC to Humphreys, about 1863. Paroled May 12, 1865, at Jackson. Alive 1870 at Vicksburg, a merchant. Cramer's official military record is unusually sketchy.

Crane, Benjamin Elliott. b. Athens, Georgia, Dec. 19, 1835. att. UGA., and Troy Polytechnic Institute in New York. Civil engineer at Lexington, Georgia. Pvt. Troup (Ga.) Arty. Capt. AQM, Cobb's Legion, May 15, 1862. Capt. acting QM to T. R. R. Cobb, Sept. 1, 1862. Capt. acting QM to Wofford, 1863. Capt. AQM to H. R. Jackson, Oct. 1863. Maj. QM to Jackson, Feb. 19, 1864. Serving with Georgia reserves late war, and possibly staff of DuBose. Wealthy Atlanta wholesale merchant. d. Jan. 15, 1885. bur. Oakland Cem.

Crane, George Washington. b. in Ohio. Moved to Augusta, Georgia, ca. 1855, and was a merchant. Capt. AQM, 12th Bn. Georgia Arty., May 27, 1862. Maj. QM to Heth, Oct. 27, 1862. Collected supplies in Georgia, most of 1863. Maj. QM to Howell Cobb, Sept. 23, 1863. Maj. QM to Corse, Dec. 2, 1863. Relieved July 4, 1864, at Corse's request. No further military record. Postwar

cotton factor. d. Augusta, Feb. 5, 1895, age 67. bur. Magnolia Cem.

Creel, Henry Clay. b. Parkersburg, Virginia, Jan. 17, 1829. Member of Virginia state legislature. Pvt. Co. A, 46th Bn. Virginia Cavy., Oct. 1, 1864. Lt. ADC to W. L. Jackson, Feb. 3, 1865. d. Missouri, Jan. 13, 1907.

Crenshaw, James Richard. b. Richmond, Virginia, Apr. 15, 1830. Richmond lawyer. Maj. acting CS to R. E. Lee, Apr. 26, 1861. Lt. Col. 15th Virginia, July 1, 1861. Dropped Apr. 1862. Confederate commissary agent in the Bahamas. Cotton merchant in Brazil, New York City, and Richmond. d. Richmond, July 25, 1891. bur. Hollywood Cem.

Crisler, Nelson Weaver. b. Madison Co., Virginia, Sept. 12, 1830. Merchant at Madison C.H. Lt. Co. A, 7th Virginia, Apr. 25, 1861. Capt. AQM, 7th Virginia, Sept. 17, 1861. Dropped Feb. 24, 1862. Maj. QM to Kemper, June 13, 1862. Maj. acting QM to Pickett, Nov. 1862. Maj. QM to William R. Terry. Appx. Madison Co. farmer and judge. d. Apr. 14, 1902. bur. Madison C.H. City Cem.

Crittenden, Churchill. b. 1840, probably in May. Moved to California in 1851. att. Hanover Coll. in Indiana. VADC to Archer. Pvt. Co. C, 1st Bn. Maryland Cavy., Aug. 4, 1862. Captured and murdered by Yankees near Luray, Virginia, Oct. 4, 1864. bur. Shockoe Cem., Richmond, Virginia, in unmarked grave. A few of Crittenden's war letters are at the University of Washington.

Crittenden, James Love. b. Dec. 15, 1841. att. UVA. Brother of Churchill Crittenden (see above). Of San Francisco, California. VADC to Archer during Seven Days. WIA at Gaines's Mill. Sgt. SO for Bragg, Oct. 15, 1862. Lt. SO to Cleburne, and then with Price, Shelby, and Hood. Resigned June 25, 1864. d. 1915. A female diarist in Virginia called Crittenden "a queer fish, seems a mixture of misanthrope, universalist, and fame-worshiper."

Crittenden, Rudolphus D. A resident of

Greenville, South Carolina. Adjt. 4th South Carolina, Nov. 23, 1861. Maj. AAIG to R. H. Anderson, Aug. 1, 1862. Resigned Nov. 23, 1862, complaining of a hernia. Arrested Mar. 1863 at Brooklyn, New York. Lived in the North in 1864. Possibly the Rodolphus L. Crittenden (Feb. 21, 1808–June 6, 1868) bur. at Christ Church Cem., Greenville.

Crockett, John Newton. b. July 6, 1832. Lancaster Co., South Carolina, merchant. Lt. Co. A, 5th South Carolina, Apr. 1862. Capt. AQM, 5th South Carolina, Apr. 23, 1862. Capt. AAQM to Jenkins, Jan.–Mar. 1863. Capt. AQM to Field, Aug. 22, 1864. Lancaster Co. farmer. m. Henrietta Price. d. Mar. 16, 1914. bur. Westside Cem.

Crockford, John. b. Westbourne, England, May 8, 1814. Constructed railroads in the Northeast and at Alexandria, Virginia, prewar. Capt. AQM and IFT, Mar. 16, 1864. Stationed at Gordonsville. d. May 16, 1869. bur. Warrenton (Va.) City Cem. Crockford's military records are sporadic.

Cross, Alexander H. b. Washington, D.C. Lt. U.S. Army, 1847–1848 and 1855–1856. Capt. of Inf., Feb. 15, 1862. Served in uncertain capacity in artillery defenses at Richmond, Virginia. Relieved from that, June 4, 1862. Capt. EO to Van Dorn, June 27, 1862. Capt. IFT in Virginia, Apr. 12, 1864, through 1865. d. 1869.

Cross, James Lucius. b. Frederick Co., Virginia, Oct. 27, 1834. att. VMI. Professor of math, tactics, and geography at Virginia Coll., in Winchester. Taught at West Florida Seminary, 1860–1861. Capt. of Inf., July 5, 1861. Capt. 2nd Florida, Sept. 27, 1861. Capt. AAAG to Finegan, Apr. 18, 1862, to July 1862. Maj. AAG, July 12, 1862. Reported to G. W. Smith, Oct. 30, 1862. Maj. AAG to D. H. Hill, Mar. 4, 1863. Maj. AAG to W. M. Gardner, Jan. 8, 1864. Maj. AAG to Hoke, Aug. 24, 1864. Paroled at Greensboro. Professor at Florida Military Institute and later

at Tulane. d. Glade Spring, Virginia, July 15, 1893. bur. Mt Hebron Cem., Winchester.

Cross, William B. B. b. ca. 1823. Prewar resident of Washington, D.C. Capt. AQM, June 29, 1861. Maj. QM, Nov. 16, 1861. "In charge of orders and correspondence relating to clothing camp and garrison equipage" in the QM office at Richmond, Virginia. Back at Washington by 1867.

Croxton, Thomas. b. Tappahannock, Virginia, Mar. 15, 1822. att. UVA. Prewar lawyer. Cpl. Co. F, 9th Virginia Cavy., June 10, 1861. Working in Gen. Pickett's office, Aug. 1861. Lt. AAAG to Pickett, Nov. 18, 1861. Resigned May 12, 1862, due to poor health. Croxton's record is odd. He was appointed as a Lt. and served exclusively on Pickett's staff, yet that position should have been filled by a Capt. and AAG. There is no evidence Croxton did anything after his commission but serve with Pickett. Postwar lawyer. d. Tappahannock, July 3, 1903. bur. St. John's Episc. Churchyard.

Crump, James H. Lt. Co. C, 3rd Virginia Cavy. Capt. AQM, 26th Virginia. Capt. AQM at Gloucester Point, Virginia, Feb. 1862. Capt. AQM at Chaffin's Farm, Virginia, June 1862 into 1865. Capt. AQM to G. W. C. Lee, Mar. 11, 1865.

Crump, J. R. Lt. EO (PAVa.), May 17, 1861. Lt. EO to Magruder, Nov. 25, 1861. Civilian EO to Floyd in early 1862. No other certain record. Possibly became Lt. ADC to W. H. Jackson in 1863, and was KIA near Sharon, Mississippi, Feb. 27, 1864.

Crump, Malcolm Hart. b. in Virginia. 42-year-old clerk at Fredericksburg in 1860. Staff of Ruggles, Apr.–June 1861. Capt. AQM to Holmes, July 19, 1861. Relieved Aug. 23, 1862, and ordered to report to Lt. Col. Corley at ANVa. headquarters. Failed to report and was dropped, Aug. 29, 1862, but was reinstated in Jan. 1863. Maj. QM, July 1, 1863. Apparently worked as an IFT. d. Richmond, Virginia, Jan. 12, 1864. bur. Fredericksburg City Cem.

Crutchfield, Stapleton, Jr. b. Spotsylvania Co., Virginia, June 21, 1835. att. VMI, and prewar instructor of math and tactics there. Maj. 9th Virginia, July 1861. Later Lt. Col. 58th Virginia. Lt. Col. Chief of Arty. to T. J. Jackson, Apr. 21, 1862. Col. Chief of Arty. to Jackson, May 6, 1862. Lost leg at Chancellorsville. Col. Inspector of Ammunition and Equipment for coastal batteries, Mar. 16, 1864. Commanded Arty. Bgd., spring 1865. KIA at Sailor's Creek.

Cullingsworth, Joseph Nathaniel. b. Richmond, Virginia, Feb. 10, 1840. att. UVA. Pvt. 1st Co. Richmond Howitzers, June 3, 1861. Lt. OO, Henry's Bn. Arty., by July 1863. Lt. OO, Haskell's Bn. Arty., by Jan. 1864. Lt. Inspector of Richmond Laboratories, Apr. 1864. Appx. m. Cordelia Jones McMinn. Richmond tobacco merchant. d. there July 14, 1911. bur. Hollywood Cem.

Cunningham, Alexander Telfair. b. Augusta, Georgia, Feb. 4, 1834. Bookkeeper at Savannah. Clerk for an ordnance officer there, Jan. 1862. Lt. of Arty., May 19, 1862, to report to Lawton. Lt. OO at Savannah, Aug. 1862–Sept. 1864. Lt. OO to MacRae, Sept. 27, 1864. Paroled at Greensboro, May 1, 1865. Savannah cotton merchant. Also lived in Alabama and at Milwaukee, Wisconsin. d. Milwaukee, Dec. 10, 1905. bur. Laurel Grove Cem., Savannah.

Cunningham, Arthur Sinclair. b. Norfolk, Virginia, Apr. 1835. att. USMA. Lt. 11th U.S. Infantry, 1857–1861. Lt. of Arty., CSA, Mar. 16, 1861. Capt. AAG to Crittenden, Sept. 12, 1861. Maj. AAG to Crittenden, Nov. 16, 1861. Commanded 10th Alabama during Seven Days. Lt. Col. PACS, June 12, 1862. Mostly commanding troops in the Richmond defenses, though also with the 10th Alabama again for a time and at Charleston briefly. Lt. Col. 40th Virginia, Jan. 1864. WIA at Pegram's Farm, Sept. 30, 1864. Lt. Col. on court-martial duty under Ewell, Dec. 1, 1864. Later AAIG in ANVa.,

1865. Wells Fargo employee. d. Eureka, California, July 26, 1885.

Cunningham, Edward, Jr. b. Cumberland Co., Virginia, Aug. 21, 1841. att. VMI, and professor of tactics there. Capt. EO, PAVa., May 23, 1861. Capt. EO to E. K. Smith at First Manassas. Lt. of Arty. CSA, Oct. 29, 1861. Lt. ADC to Smith, Nov. 13, 1861. Staff of Lovell, Nov. 29, 1861. Lt. acting ADC to E. K. Smith, Mar. 28, 1862. Lt. ADC to Smith, Nov. 4, 1862. Maj. Chief of Arty. to Smith through 1865. Cofounder of Norwood Academy in Nelson Co., Virginia. Professor at Univ. of Louisiana and at Kirby Smith's school in New Castle, Kentucky. St. Louis lawyer. d. Oct. 18, 1904. bur. Bellefontaine Cem.

Cunningham, Edward Hall. b. Van Buren, Arkansas, July 7, 1835. att. Cumberland Univ. Moved to Bexar Co., Texas, in 1856. Capt. Co. F, 4th Texas, July 11, 1861. WIA at Sharpsburg (arm amputated). Resigned Nov. 1, 1862. Maj. AAIG to Hood, Nov. 5, 1862. Lt. Col. AAIG to Hood, Feb. 6, 1864. Probably staff of S. D. Lee in the West. m. Narcissa Brahan, 1882. Established a sugar refinery in Texas, became a millionaire, and was known as the "Sugar King of Texas." d. San Antonio, Texas, Aug. 27, 1912.

Curell, James R. VADC to D. R. Jones, June–Aug. 1861. Capt. Rousseau Guards of Louisiana, Dec. 1861. VADC to S. D. Lee, Feb. 1863. Lt. ADC to Lee, July 13, 1863. Resigned Nov. 14, 1863, to become assistant commissioner of prisoner exchanges. Probably stationed in Richmond, Virginia, 1863–1865. Paroled May 9, 1865, as a Maj., though date of commission not found. m. Virginia C. Dunbar, 1854.

Cussons, John, Jr. b. Horncastle, England, Apr. 6, 1838. Came to United States in 1855. Lived in far west, 1855–1859. Newspaperman at Selma, Alabama, 1859–1861. Pvt. Co. A, 4th Alabama. VADC to Law by Aug. 1862, through 1864. POW at Second Manassas. Fought a famous duel with an officer in the

55th North Carolina. POW at Gettysburg, July 2, 1863. Exchanged Mar. 17, 1864, and granted leave to visit parents in England. However, m. Mrs. Sue Allen, of Glen Allen, Virginia, May 1864. Lived at Glen Allen postwar, where he was "amusing himself by opening roadways, making artificial lakes and stocking a spacious deer park." d. there Jan. 4, 1912. bur. Hollywood Cem., Richmond. One of Gen. Law's men described Cussons as "a tall, long-haired, wild-looking, unnaturalized Englishman." "He was frequently mistaken for Buffalo Bill."

Cuthbert, James E. b. Petersburg, Virginia, Jan. 5, 1825. Railroad executive and banker there prewar. m. Mary L. Bragg, 1846. Bank cashier as late as 1863. Maj. ADC to Bragg, Oct. 17, 1864. Railroad treasurer at Petersburg, postwar. d. Brooklyn, New York, July 22, 1883. bur. Blandford Cem., Petersburg.

Cutshaw, Wilfred Emory. b. Harpers Ferry, Virginia, Jan. 25, 1838. att. VMI. Lt. CSA, Oct. 31, 1861. Capt. Jackson (Va.) Arty., Mar. 1862. Lt. AAAIG to T. J. Jackson, Feb. 27, 1862. Lt. acting Chief of Arty. to Jackson, Mar. 1–Apr. 21, 1862. WIA and POW, May 1862. Capt. AAAIG to Long, Oct.–Nov. 1863. Maj. commanding an artillery battalion, 1864–1865. Lost leg at Sailor's Creek. Professor at VMI and Richmond city engineer. Author of an important pamphlet on the Battle of Spotsylvania. d. Richmond, Dec. 19, 1907. bur. Hollywood Cem.

Dabney, Chiswell. b. Campbell Co., Virginia, July 25, 1844. Lt. ADC to Stuart, Dec. 20, 1861. Capt. AAIG to James B. Gordon, Nov. 2, 1863. Capt. AAIG to Barringer. WIA, June 1864. Lawyer and Episcopal minister in Pittsylvania Co. d. Apr. 28, 1923. bur. Chatham City Cem. A fellow staff officer described Dabney as "ornamental."

Dabney, Robert Lewis. b. Louisa Co., Virginia, Mar. 5, 1820. att. Hampden Sidney and UVA. Schoolteacher, pastor, and college professor. Chaplain, 18th Virginia, 1861. Maj. AAG to T. J. Jackson, Apr. 22, 1862. Resigned Aug. 1, 1862, citing "virulent" camp fever. Professor at Union Theological Seminary and Univ. of Texas. Author of popular Jackson biography. d. Victoria, Texas, Jan. 3, 1898. bur. Union Theological Seminary Cem. at Hampden-Sidney, Virginia.

Dabney, Virginius. b. Gloucester Co., Virginia, Feb. 15, 1835. att. UVA. Lawyer at Raymond, Mississippi. Pvt. Co. D, 1st Virginia, Apr. 21, 1861. Lt. 21st Virginia, July 1861. Lt. ADC to J. R. Jones, June 25, 1862. VADC to Col. T. S. Garnett at Cedar Mountain and to J. M. Jones at Gettysburg. Commanded 48th Virginia at Second Manassas as a Lt. WIA there. AAAG to Ed. Johnson, 1863. Capt. AAG to Johnson, Sept. 10, 1863. Capt. AAG to John B. Gordon, 1864, through Appx. Established a boys' school in New York City and wrote two novels. Married twice. d. June 2, 1894.

Dade, Albert Gallatin. b. King George Co., Virginia, Jan. 27, 1815. Westmoreland Co. farmer. Lt. Co. C, 9th Virginia Cavy., May 26, 1861. Maj. CS to W. H. F. Lee, Oct. 30, 1862. Paroled May 10, 1865. Married twice. Orange Co. farmer. d. there Apr. 1, 1890.

Dade, Lawrence Alexander. b. Orange Co., Virginia, prior to 1840. Lt. Asst. EO (PAVa.?) to Magruder, Nov. 25, 1861. Lt. Asst EO (PACS), Feb. 15, 1862. In Virginia all of the war, mostly in Richmond's defenses. m. Caroline Armstrong. d. 1896.

Dallas, William Wallace. Of Maryland. Prewar director with Western Maryland Railroad. Recommended as Lt. ADC to Trimble, Feb. 2, 1863. Approved by T. J. Jackson and R. E. Lee, but no record of further service. Probably never commissioned and may not have served at all. Alive 1873 in Carroll Co., Maryland.

Dancy, John Sessums. b. Edgecomb Co., North Carolina, May 13, 1821. att. UNC. Tarboro farmer. In North Carolina legislature. Capt. AQM, 17th North Carolina, May 17, 1862. Capt. AQM to Martin, June 10, 1864. Later to Kirkland. m. Ann E. Hyman. d. Aug. 23, 1888. bur. Calvary Episc. Churchyard, Tarboro.

Dandridge, Edmund Pendleton. b. Jan. 28, 1841. att. UVA. Jefferson Co. farmer. Pvt. Co. D, 2nd Virginia, Apr. 18, 1861. WIA in foot at First Manassas. Lt. AAG to Pendleton, Feb. 18, 1862. Lt. AAIG of Second Corps batteries, Jan. 14, 1863. Lt. AAIG to Pendleton, spring 1863 to Appx. Winchester lawyer. d. there Sept. 29, 1884. bur. Mt. Hebron Cem.

Dandridge, Philip Pendleton. b. Jefferson Co., Virginia, Nov. 5, 1843. Pvt. Co. F, 2nd Virginia, May 1, 1861. Cadet CSA, July 19, 1861, and assigned to Co. F, 9th Virginia Cavy. Cadet staff of W. H. F. Lee, June 15, 1863. Lt. CSA, Dec. 6, 1864. Lt. acting ADC to W. H. F. Lee, 1863–1865. Paroled May 7, 1865. Civil engineer. d. Baltimore, Maryland, Jan. 8, 1921. bur. Mt. Hebron Cem., Winchester.

Danforth, Henry Delaplaine. b. Richmond, Virginia, Oct. 7, 1840. Pvt. Co. F, 21st Virginia, June 21, 1861–May 19, 1862. WIA at Kernstown. Cpl. 12th Bn. Virginia Arty. Acting Lt. OO to Hunton by Nov. 1862. Lt. OO to Hunton, July 23, 1864. Appx. A clerk. m. Jennie M. Knight. d. Richmond, Aug. 19, 1878. bur. Hollywood Cem.

Daniel, Henry K. b. in Georgia. att. Oglethorpe Coll. Wealthy farmer at Americus in 1860. Pvt. Co. K, 4th Georgia, Apr. 27, 1861. Capt. AQM, 4th Georgia, July 19, 1861. Maj. QM to Doles, Dec. 1, 1862. Same to Cook, June 1864. Relieved Oct. 29, 1864, and sent to Americus where he secured forage for ANVa. d. Sept. 9, 1870, age 32. "A cultured gentleman."

Daniel, John Moncure. b. Stafford Co., Virginia, Oct. 24, 1825. Newspaper editor at Richmond. U.S. Minister to Sardinia, 1853–1860. Lt. ADC to Floyd, Sept. 11, 1861. Maj. AAG to Floyd, Sept. 23, 1861, but "out of service by non-assignment." VADC to A. P. Hill, Seven Days. WIA right arm at Gaines's Mill. Wartime editor of *Richmond Examiner*. Famous duelist. d. Richmond, Mar. 30, 1865, of typhoid pneumonia and consumption. bur. Hollywood Cem. Douglas Southall Freeman called him "half genius, half misanthrope."

Daniel, John Warwick. b. Lynchburg, Virginia, Sept. 5, 1842. att. Lynchburg Coll. Served with 27th Virginia at First Manassas and WIA three times. Lt. Co. A, 11th Virginia, Sept. 11, 1861. Adjt. 11th Virginia, June 17, 1862. Maj. AAG to Early, Mar. 24, 1863. WIA and permanently disabled at the Wilderness, May 6, 1864. USHR and lawyer. Very active in postwar Confederate things and wrote extensively. d. Lynchburg, June 29, 1910. bur. Spring Hill Cem. Daniel's papers are at UVA., Duke, and the Virginia Historical Society. "So young, so clever, so gallant and . . . so exquisitely handsome."

Daniel, Raleigh Travers, Jr. b. Stafford Co., Virginia, May 26, 1832. att. VMI. Richmond lawyer. Lt. PAVa., May 26, 1861, to report to Huger. Adjt. 5th Kentucky, Nov. 16, 1861. Staff of J. S. Williams, 1861–1862. Lt. VADC to Armistead in Seven Days. WIA twice at Malvern Hill while filling in as commander of Co. F, 38th Virginia. Capt. AAG to Pegram, Nov. 19, 1862. Same to Lilley and J. A. Walker. Washington, D.C., attorney. Asst. Secretary of Virginia Military Records, 1909. d. Richmond Soldiers' Home, Feb. 11, 1919. bur. Hollywood Cem.

Daniel, Thomas Cushing. b. ca. 1811. Employed in government offices at Washington, D.C., 1842–1861. Worked for Treasury Dept. m. Eliza Bronaugh, 1835. Capt. ACS, Nov. 14, 1863. Served in that capacity with CSA Treasury Dept. at Richmond, Virginia, in to 1865. d. Washington, D.C., Aug. 11, 1896.

Daniell, Charles. b. Hall Co., Georgia. Sgt. Co. B, 8th Georgia, May 21–Oct. 31, 1861. VADC to G. T. Anderson during Seven

Days. Pvt. 5th Co. Washington Arty., (La.), Mar. 24, 1863. Capt. Daniell's (Ga.) Btty., Dec. 12, 1863. m. Elizabeth P. Richardson, 1865. Rice planter in South Carolina. d. Savannah, Georgia, Mar. 30, 1872, age 32 or 33. bur. Laurel Grove Cem.

Darden, James Dawley. b. Smithfield, Virginia, 1828. Custom House official at San Francisco, California, and merchant at Washington, D.C. Lt. ADC to Armistead, Apr. 15, 1862. Capt. AAG to Armistead, July 31, 1862. WIA at Gettysburg and Rappahannock Bridge. Capt. AAG to Barton, by May 1864. Capt. AAG to Steuart, Nov. 4, 1864. Lived postwar in Texas, Arkansas, Tennessee, and Washington, D.C. d. May 6, 1900.

Dashiell, Charles C. b. in Virginia. Lt. Co. H, 12th Virginia, Apr. 19, 1861. WIA and POW at Crampton's Gap. Retired to Invalid Corps, Apr. 5, 1864, and assigned to provost duty at Petersburg. Lt. AAIG to J. A. Walker, by Sept. 29, 1864. Served with Walker into 1865. 34-year-old carpenter at Norfolk in 1870. A contractor in Henrico Co., age 65 in 1900. d. R. E. Lee Camp Soldiers' Home, at Richmond, Feb. 7, 1907. bur. Hollywood Cem.

Davenport, Hugh McCall. b. Savannah, Georgia. Inspector of Customs at Savannah. m. Martha A. E. Stone, 1847. Lt. acting ACS at Fort Pulaski, Apr. 1861. Capt. AQM, Sept. 11, 1861. Served at Tybee Island, at Brunswick, and at other Georgia posts. Maj. QM, July 30, 1863. Maj. QM to Benning, Sept. 23, 1864. Appx. d. Lamonia, Florida, Aug. 1, 1880, age 58. A comrade called Davenport "a very stirring man, a great blower, mighty fussy."

Daves, Graham. b. New Bern, North Carolina, July 16, 1836. Private secretary to his brother-in-law, Gov. Ellis. Adjt. 22nd North Carolina. Capt. AAG to French, Apr. 1, 1862. Maj. AAG to French, Nov. 5, 1862. Dropped Nov. 16, 1863, by General Order #48. VADC to James B. Gordon, intermittently, Dec.

1863 to May 1864. Lt. ADC to Holmes, July 7, 1864. Paroled Apr. 26, 1865. Vice president of Wilmington Railroad. d. Asheville, North Carolina, Oct. 27, 1902. bur. Cedar Grove Cem., New Bern.

Davidson, Maxwell T. Pvt. Co. D, 11th Virginia, Apr. 23, 1861, a 26-year-old clerk. Detached summer 1861, probably on signal duty, and never rejoined unit. Capt. SO, May 29, 1862. Staff of M. L. Smith. POW at Vicksburg. Capt. SO to Field, Aug. 18–Sept. 9, 1864. Capt. SO to Pemberton, Sept. 17, 1864. Capt. SO to Echols, Feb. 18, 1865.

Davies, Sydney Herbert. Of England. A Royal Navy midshipman in the Crimean War. Served in British Army at Halifax, Nova Scotia, from 1857 onward. Carried dispatches into CSA through blockade in 1863. Volunteered with 7th Tennessee, Aug. 1863–Nov. 1864, but has no official record. Lt. Drillmaster to Heth, Nov. 30, 1864, but actually seems to have been AAAIG. Appx.

Davies, Thomas J. Of Barnwell Co., South Carolina. Maj. ADC to Bonham, 1861. Present at First Manassas. Resigned Aug. 1861. ADC [VADC?] to Floyd. Served in South Carolina legislature from Aiken Co. Railroad contractor and Beech Island planter.

Davis, Aaron. b. in New York. A New Orleans, Louisiana, clerk. Lt. Co. A, 7th Louisiana, June 7, 1861, age 30. Maj. CS to W. H. T. Walker, Sept. 17, 1861. Maj. CS to Taylor by Feb. 1862. KIA at Front Royal, May 23, 1862, when "carried away by his ardor" in pursuing fleeing Yankees. bur. on the battlefield. Taylor called Davis "the very pearl of commissaries."

Davis, Alfred Ward Grayson. b. Vanceburg, Kentucky, Oct. 15, 1806. att. college at Athens, Ohio. att. USMA, and thought to be the roommate of Jefferson Davis. Attorney in Arkansas Territory, 1831–1835. Cotton planter at Bolivar, Mississippi. Mexican War veteran. Lived in Greenbrier Co., Virginia.

In legislature and state Secession Convention. Maj. QM to Floyd, Sept. 18, 1861 to Feb. 1862. Maj. QM at Greenville, South Carolina, 1862–1863. Resigned Aug. 1863. d. "The Cliffs" in Greenbrier Co., West Virginia, Jan. 20, 1865. bur. there. A shadow of uncertainty remains on this man's identification and service.

Davis, E. Hayne. b. in South Carolina, Nov. 1836. Attorney at Statesville, North Carolina. m. Mary Earson. Pvt. Co. E, 3rd North Carolina Cavy., Oct. 7, 1861. Capt. Co. H, 55th North Carolina, Oct. 10, 1862. Resigned Mar. 10, 1863. Lt. Drillmaster in Conscript Bureau. Capt. AAIG to R. D. Johnston, Feb. 15, 1865. WIA and lost right arm at Petersburg, probably at Ft. Stedman. d. Statesville, Oct. 23, 1890. bur. Oakwood Cem.

Davis, Eugene. b. Middlesex Co., Virginia, Mar. 26, 1822. att. UVA. Lawyer and farmer at Charlottesville. Capt. Co. K, 2nd Virginia Cavy., May 20, 1861. Resigned Nov. 20, 1861. VADC to Pendleton, May–July 1862, at least. Pvt. Co. D, 6th Virginia Cavy., Aug. 15, 1863. POW at Yellow Tavern. Mayor of Charlottesville. d. near there, May 19, 1894. bur. UVA. Cem.

Davis, H. J. VADC to Robert Ransom at the Battle of Fredericksburg. This is thought to be Dr. Hugh Johnston Davis of Co. G, 3rd North Carolina Cavy., who was from Warren Co., North Carolina, b. ca. 1824, a farmer. That man was MWIA and POW, June 21, 1864, near Petersburg, and died July 7, 1864, at Alexandria, Virginia.

Davis, James Moore. b. Wilmington, North Carolina, Apr. 1834. att. South Carolina Coll. Camden, South Carolina, lawyer. Lt. Co. D, 15th South Carolina, Aug. 26, 1861. WIA at Gettysburg. Lt. AAAG to Kershaw, June 1864. Lt. ADC to Kershaw, Aug. 17, 1864. POW at Sailor's Creek. m. Mary Louise DeSaussure. d. Camden, June 15, 1879.

Davis, John Eayers. b. New York City, June 10, 1811. Moved to Georgia as a young man. Columbus merchant. m. Sarah Cropp. Maj. QM to Semmes, June 1, 1862. Maj. QM to Bryan. Relieved Oct. 2, 1863, at own request. Maj. QM at Columbus, Georgia, Dec. 1, 1863. d. there Aug. 19, 1864. bur. Linwood Cem.

Davis, Matthew L., Jr. b. in North Carolina, Aug. 1829. att. USMA. Lt. U.S. Army, 1852–1861. From Rutherford Co., North Carolina, though his family was from New York City and Syracuse. Capt. of Inf., CSA. Capt. AQM, July 11, 1861, to report to J. E. Johnston. Capt. AQM to G. W. Smith by Sept. 25, 1861. Maj. QM to G. W. Smith, Oct. 9, 1861. Resigned Apr. 18, 1862, to become Col. 2nd North Carolina Cavy. d. Goldsboro, North Carolina, Apr. 23, 1862, of pneumonia.

Davis, Samuel Boyer. b. Delaware, Dec. 5, 1843. Pvt. Latimer's (Va.) Btty. Lt. ADC to his uncle, Gen. Trimble, Feb. 2, 1863. WIA in lung and POW at Gettysburg. Lt. AAIG to J. H. Winder, Oct. 22, 1863. Commanded prison at Macon, Georgia, summer 1864. Lt. ADC to Kemper, Oct. 28, 1864. Lt. in Signal Corps, Dec. 27, 1864. POW Jan. 14, 1865, at Newark, Ohio, using an alias. Nearly hanged as a spy. Released Dec. 20, 1865. m. Anna Mason. d. Washington, D.C., Feb. 24, 1914. bur. Ivy Hill Cem., Alexandria, Virginia. Davis's account of his late-war experiences was published in 1892.

Davis, Thomas Edward. b. Bedford Co., Virginia, Sept. 25, 1835. att. UVA. Tobacco merchant and civil engineer. QM Sgt., 2nd Virginia Cavy., May 13, 1861. WIA at First Manassas. Capt. EO, PAVA. Maj. AAG (PAVA.) to Floyd, 1861. Out of service in early 1862. Adjt. 21st Virginia Cavy., Sept. 14, 1864. Appx. Miner in Montana, tobacconist at Galveston, Texas, and newspaper editor at Houston. d. New Orleans, Louisiana, Feb. 20, 1917. bur. there.

Davis, William S. b. in Georgia. A 24-year-old "factory agent" in Augusta in 1860. Lt. Co. B, 10th Georgia, May 18, 1861. Lt. AAAG to McLaws, Aug. 1861, and Lt. oo, Dec. 1861–Feb. 1862. Lt. AAAIG to Semmes at Chancellorsville. WIA in face there. Capt. Co. B, 10th Georgia, May 29, 1863. Retired to Invalid Corps, Oct. 24, 1864.

Davis, Zimmerman. b. Fairfield Dist., South Carolina, Oct. 8, 1834. att. Coll. of Charleston. Cotton merchant at Charleston. Capt. Co. D, 5th South Carolina Cavy., Apr. 12, 1862. Capt. AAAIG to Dunovant, Aug. 1864, and then to Butler, Sept. and Oct. 1864. Col. 5th South Carolina Cavy., Oct. 27, 1864. Slightly WIA at Lynch's Creek, Mar. 1865. Secretary and treasurer at Charleston waterworks. d. there Mar. 30, 1910. bur. Magnolia Cem.

Dawson, Francis Warrington. b. London, England, May 20, 1840. Changed his name from Austin John Reeks. Master's Mate CSN, 1862. Volunteered with the Purcell (Va.) Arty., June 1862. WIA at Mechanicsville. Lt. oo to Longstreet, Aug. 10, 1862. Capt. oo, Apr. 2, 1864. Capt. oo to R. H. Anderson, May–Oct. 1864. Capt. oo to Rosser, Nov. 10, 1864, and then to Fitz. Lee in early 1865. WIA at Dinwiddie C.H. Paroled Apr. 18, 1865. Newspaperman at Richmond and Charleston. Second wife was Sarah Morgan. Murdered at Charleston, South Carolina, Mar. 12, 1889. Author of a famous memoir.

Dawson, Lemuel Hawkins. b. Upson Co., Georgia, Dec. 9, 1828. Farmer in Chambers Co., Alabama. Served in Co. F, 21st Georgia and Co. D, 47th Alabama, 1861–1862. Capt. AQM, 47th Alabama, June 1, 1862. Capt. AQM to G. T. Anderson, by Sept. 1, 1864. Capt. AQM to W. F. Perry, Mar. 8, 1865. Appx. Farmer in Lee Co., Alabama. d. Chambers Co., Alabama, Jan. 6, 1911.

Dawson, Pleasant. Pvt. Co. F, 28th Virginia, Apr. 26, 1861. Later to Sgt. WIA and POW at South Mountain, Sept. 14, 1862. Lt. ADC to William Terry, July 2, 1864. Appx.

Dean, Thomas W. Lt. oo to Jenkins's Cavy.

Bgd., Dec. 1864. Probably staff of McCausland. Exact identity not confirmed.

Deane, Francis Browne. b. Goochland Co., Virginia, Mar. 18, 1836. In the iron business at Lynchburg. Capt. AQM, PAVa., May 7, 1861, to report to Pendleton. Capt. AQM (PACS) to Pendleton, June 3, 1862. Capt. AQM Nelson's Bn. Arty. Resigned Aug. 20, 1863, to rejoin iron business at Lynchburg. d. there Oct. 16, 1903. bur. Lynchburg Presby. Cem.

Deas, George. b. in Pennsylvania, 1816. Capt. 5th U.S. Inf., 1838–1861. m. Mary Elizabeth Garland, 1844, making him the brother-in-law of Gen. Longstreet. Lt. Col. AAG, Mar. 16, 1861. Staff of R. E. Lee, June 15, 1861–Jan. 1862. Lt. Col. AAIG to Cooper, Jan. 27, 1862. Lt. Col. acting Asst. Secretary of War, Oct. 1862. Lt. Col. AAG to Polk, S. D. Lee, Maury, and Richard Taylor, beginning in Apr. 1864. d. Flint, Michigan, May 23, 1870. bur. Glenwood Cem.

Delaigle, Louis. b. in Georgia. 29-year-old lawyer at Augusta in 1860. Capt. AQM, 1st Georgia Regs., July 1861. Capt. AQM to G. W. Smith, Nov. 11, 1861. Capt. acting QM to D. R. Jones during Seven Days. Relieved at own request, July 25, 1862. Capt. AQM at Knoxville, Tennessee. Maj. QM to Bryan, Apr. 20, 1864. Resigned June 13, 1864.

del 'Isle, Victor Gaschet. b. Jan. 15, 1837. Lt. Co. C, 7th Bn. Louisiana, June 8, 1861. Capt. AQM, 7th Bn. Louisiana, May 1, 1862. Staff of Micah Jenkins in May 1862. Ordered to report to R. E. Lee, Aug. 23, 1862, duties not specified. Capt. AQM at Narrows, Virginia, Jan. 3, 1863. Served there into 1865. Worked in sheriff's office. d. New Orleans, Louisiana, Sept. 30, 1910. bur. St. Louis Cem., #2.

DeMill, William Edward. May have changed spelling of name to deMille postwar. b. North Carolina, Feb. 1, 1824. Ran a furniture and hardware store in Washington, North Carolina. Acting post CS at Greenville, North Carolina, Apr. 13, 1863. Maj. CS to Martin, June 1, 1863. Same to Kirkland. Maj. CS at Greenville again, Dec. 24, 1864. POW Feb. 18, 1865. Washington merchant. d. Sept. 27, 1873. bur. Episc. Churchyard. Was the grandfather of famous Hollywood figure Cecil B. deMille.

Denegre, Joseph. b. New Orleans, Louisiana, Mar. 9, 1839. att. UVA. Cotton merchant. Sgt. 5th Co. Washington (La.) Arty., Mar. 6, 1862. Capt. of Inf. and MSK, June 9, 1863. Stationed at Richmond on ordnance duty. Asst. to T. L. Bayne in Bureau of Foreign Supplies. d. Paris, France, July 21, 1868.

Dennis, George E. b. July 13, 1832. att. UVA. Lawyer at Rocky Mount, Virginia. Lived in same boarding house as Jubal Early in 1860. Pvt. Co. B, 24th Virginia, May 23, 1861. Capt. ACS, 24th Virginia, June 29, 1861. Capt. acting ADC to Early, July 1861. Capt. ACS to Kemper's Bgd., Aug. 3, 1863 through 1865. Thus on staff of William R. Terry. Lawyer and bank president in Franklin Co. d. May 24, 1894. bur. High Street Cem., Rocky Mount.

Derrick, Henry Clay. b. Jan. 13, 1832. On engineer duty at Mulberry Island, Virginia, early war. Staff of Magruder, Nov. 1861. No other record. d. May 9, 1915. Derrick's war record is very sketchy.

DeRussy, Charles A. Pvt. Co. K, 51st Virginia, June 25, 1861. Later to Sgt. Maj. Adjt. 51st Virginia, Oct. 5, 1862. Lt. AAAG to Wharton, by Sept. 1862. Capt. AAG to Wharton, Oct. 14, 1862.

DeSaussure, Louis Daniel. b. Charleston, South Carolina, May 19, 1824. Broker in that city. m. Sarah Martin DeSaussure (his cousin). Capt. Inspector of outposts in South Carolina. VADC to W. S. Walker, Jan. 1863. Capt. AAG to Walker, Feb. 19, 1864. Capt. AAIG to Elliott, Jan. 25, 1865. Capt. AAG to Hagood, Mar. 27, 1865. Paroled Apr. 26, 1865. d. June 20, 1888. bur. Magnolia Cem., Charleston, in an unmarked grave.

Deshields, Henry Clay. b. Northumberland Co., Virginia, Apr. 11, 1832. att. UVA. Lt. Co. G, 40th Virginia, May 26, 1861. Capt. AQM, 40th Virginia, Sept. 9, 1861. Capt. AQM to Field, May 1, 1862. Maj. QM to Field, May 7, 1862. Same to Heth and H. H. Walker, 1863. Maj. QM to Field again, Mar. 1, 1864. Appx. Richmond lawyer and insurance agent. d. Heathsville, Virginia, Oct. 16, 1884. bur. St. Stephens Episc. Church, Northumberland Co.

Deslonde, Edmond Antoine. b. June 14, 1828. att. Georgetown Coll. Of New Orleans, Louisiana. Capt. AQM, 1st Louisiana, Apr. 27, 1861. Capt. AQM to his brother-in-law, Gen. Beauregard, July 19, 1861. Capt. AQM and acting Engineer at Richmond, Oct.–Dec. 1861. Capt. AQM to Beauregard at Shiloh. Maj. QM, Sept. 25, 1862. Later staff of Sam. Jones and Hardee. d. Apr. 5, 1886. bur. Metairie Cem., New Orleans.

Des Portes, Richard Smallwood. b. Charleston, South Carolina, Sept. 21, 1841. Lt. Co. G, 3rd Bn. South Carolina, May 1, 1862. Lt. acting OO to French, Apr. 1862. Clerk at Petersburg, Virginia, Oct.–Nov. 1862. Lt. OO to D. H. Hill, June 1863. Lt. OO to Hood, Hindman, Cheatham, S. D. Lee, and Stewart. Paroled Apr. 26, 1865. Merchant at Ridgeway and Columbia, South Carolina. d. Jan. 23, 1898, at Columbia. bur. Trinity Episc. Churchyard.

Dickinson, Allen C. b. Caroline Co., Virginia, Mar. 20, 1838. Lived prewar at New Orleans, Louisiana. Lt. Co. D, Wheat's (La.) Bn., Apr. 30, 1861. WIA at First Manassas. Adjt. of Bn. until resigned, Apr. 18, 1862. VADC to his cousin, Gen. Magruder, during Seven Days. Adjt. 15th Virginia Cavy., Oct. 14, 1862. WIA twice on Oct. 15, 1863. Lt. ADC to Lomax, Nov. 2, 1864. Insurance agent at San Francisco, California. Prospector in Utah, and lived in Arizona and New Mexico. Survived an Apache Indian attack near Florence, Arizona. Returned to

Caroline Co. d. Spotsylvania Co., Virginia, Apr. 22, 1900. bur. Berea Church. Brother of A. G. Dickinson (see below). May have spelled first name Allan.

Dickinson, Andrew Glassel. b. Bowling Green, Virginia, Apr. 15, 1835. Capt. Co. C, 1st Texas, May 19–Nov. 13, 1861. Capt. AAG to his cousin, Gen. Magruder, Feb. 24, 1862. Maj. AAG to Magruder, Oct. 14, 1862. Lost an eye at Galveston. Maj. AAIG to Drayton, Aug. 26, 1864. Paroled Aug. 4, 1865, at San Antonio. Life insurance agent in New York City. d. there June 5, 1906. bur. Mt. Hope Cem.

Digges, Charles Walter. b. in Virginia, Aug. 25, 1839. Cpl. Co. K, 17th Virginia. WIA at Seven Pines. Pvt. Co. H, 4th Virginia Cavy. Lt. ADC to Payne, Nov. 7, 1864. "Young Digges is very poor and needs his pay," according to Payne. POW Apr. 15, 1865, and released June 2, 1865. Missouri merchant. m. Ida Rucker. d. Jan. 26, 1907. bur. Oakland Cem., Moberly, Missouri.

Dillingham, George Washington Ticknor. b. Columbus, Georgia, July 28, 1833. Clerk at a hardware store and Columbus businessman. Pvt. Co. G, 2nd Georgia, Apr. 16, 1861. Capt. ACS, 2nd Georgia, Oct. 18, 1861. Capt. ACS First Corps staff, June 6, 1863. Appx. Hardware merchant and bank cashier at Columbus. d. Dec. 1896. bur. Linwood Cem.

Dimmock, Charles Henry. b. Baltimore, Oct. 18, 1831. Moved to Richmond, Virginia, very early. Civil engineer and surveyor. Capt. EO, PAVa., Apr. 18, 1861. Served at Norfolk, Craney Island, Roanoke Island, and Gloucester Point. Lt. EO (PACS), Feb. 15, 1862. Capt. EO, Feb. 24, 1862. Worked on Petersburg defenses, Aug. 1862 into 1864. Capt. EO to Hoke, May 1864. Capt. EO to Wise, June 1864. Capt. EO to Mahone, Aug. 1864. Capt. EO at ANVA headquarters, Jan. 1865. Appx. m. Elizabeth Lewis Selden. d. Gloucester Co., Virginia, Mar. 28, 1873, of stomach cancer. bur.

Hollywood Cem., Richmond. Dimmock's war letters are at the Virginia Historical Society.

Dinkins, Henry Herreld. b. Jan. 27, 1841. Sgt. Co. C, 18th Mississippi. Sgt. Maj. 49th North Carolina, Dec. 29, 1862. Adjt. 49th North Carolina, May 2, 1863. Lt. AAAIG to Matt Ransom, Aug. 1864. Paroled May 14, 1865, at Jackson, Mississippi. d. Oct. 25, 1874. bur. Old Madison Presby. Cem., Madison Co., Mississippi.

Dinkins, Thomas Waties. b. Sumter, South Carolina, Dec. 1837. att. South Carolina Coll. Sumter lawyer. Sgt. Co. A, Holcombe Legion. Capt. AQM, Holcombe Legion, May 26, 1863. Capt. AQM, 7th South Carolina Cavy. Capt. acting QM to Gary, Aug.–Sept. 1864. m. Sarah Ann Moise. Sumter newspaperman. d. there June 11, 1868.

Dinwiddie, James. b. Campbell Co., Virginia, June 9, 1837. att. Hampden Sidney and UVA. Lt. Co. G, 59th Virginia. Lt. AAAG to Wise, Sept.–Dec. 1861. Lt. Charlottesville Arty. Lt. OO to Gorgas, Feb. 16, 1863. Capt. OO to Gorgas. Capt. Co. C, 5th Bn. Virginia LDT. Stationed at Richmond Arsenal, Aug. 1863 into 1865. Principal at Sayre Female Institute in Kentucky and professor at schools in Tennessee, Florida, Virginia, and North Carolina. d. San Francisco, California, July 2, 1907. bur. Oakwood Cem., Raleigh, North Carolina. Dinwiddie's papers are scattered among the Virginia Historical Society, UVA., and the Library of Virginia.

Dobbin, James Cochran, Jr. b. Sept. 9, 1839. att. UNC. Son of the Secretary of the U.S. Navy. Lt. of Inf., Dec. 9, 1861. Lt. ADC to Holmes, May 6, 1862. Served in an artillery company, 1862–1863. Lt. on enrolling duty in North Carolina, Dec. 2, 1863, into 1865. Fayetteville lawyer. d. there Aug. 13, 1869, "by falling from a third story, breaking his skull and causing instant death." bur. Cross Creek Cem.

Doby, Alfred English. b. Camden, South Carolina, Oct. 20, 1840. att. South Carolina

Coll. and UVA. m. Elizabeth M. Kennedy, a sister of the general. Pvt. Co. E, 2nd South Carolina, Apr. 24, 1861. Orderly to Kershaw, 1861. Lt. ADC to Kershaw, Mar. 22, 1862. KIA at Wilderness, May 6, 1864. bur. Quaker Cem., Camden. The Museum of the Confederacy in Richmond has eight of Doby's war letters.

Doherty, Patrick M. b. in Massachusetts. A 22-year-old clerk and farmer at Yazoo City, Mississippi, in 1860. Capt. AQM, 18th Mississippi, Apr. 17, 1861. Capt. acting AQM to Barksdale, Aug. 1862. Maj. QM to Barksdale, Feb. 10, 1863. Subsequently to Humphreys, and served into 1865. m. Mary Ann O'Reilly. Alive 1871 at Yazoo City.

Donnellan, George. A land office clerk in Nebraska and railroad engineer in Iowa prewar. Attempted to raise a company of sappers and miners in Richmond, 1861. Spy for Gen. Beauregard in Washington, D.C., 1861–1862. Lt. EO, Mar. 3, 1862. Ordered to report to Magruder, Apr. 6, 1862, and to Beauregard, May 21, 1862. Lt. EO to Van Dorn, M. L. Smith, Stevenson, Pemberton, Polk, S. D. Lee, Maury, and Richard Taylor. Paroled May 1, 1865.

Dorsey, John Thomas Beale. b. in Maryland, June 4, 1821. Carroll Co. lawyer and farmer in Howard Co. Married three times before the war. Capt. AQM, Mar. 29, 1862. On duty at Richmond as a paymaster. Paroled Apr. 19, 1865. State's attorney for Howard Co., and in Maryland legislature. d. Pikesville, Maryland, June 30, 1898. bur. Loudon Park Cem., Baltimore.

Doswell, Richard M. A resident of Richmond, Virginia. Lt. ADC to Barton. POW at Sailor's Creek. Took the Oath June 18, 1865, age 20. Almost certainly the man who was born at Galveston, Texas, Dec. 2, 1844, and died Jan. 15, 1926, at Norfolk, Virginia. That man is buried in the city cemetery at Fredericksburg, Virginia.

Doswell, Thomas Walker. b. Nov. 20, 1823. att. Washington Coll. Sheriff of Hanover Co., Virginia. Well-known horse breeder at Hanover Junction. Battle of North Anna fought, in part, on his farm. VADC to Starke in Maryland Campaign. Commandant of Richmond City Police, 1863–1864. m. Frances Anne Sutton. d. July 17, 1890. bur. Hollywood Cem., Richmond.

Douglas, Henry Kyd. b. Shepherdstown, Virginia, Sept. 29, 1838. att. Franklin & Marshall Coll. and Washington Coll. St. Louis lawyer. Sgt. Co. B, 2nd Virginia, Apr. 18, 1861. Later Capt. same company. Lt. AAAIG to T. J. Jackson, Apr.–Nov. 11, 1862. Capt. AAAIG to Paxton, Dec. 1862. Maj. AAAG to Ed Johnson, May 18, 1863. WIA at POW at Gettysburg. Exchanged Mar. 20, 1864. Maj. AAAG to Pegram. Appx. Lawyer at Hagerstown, Maryland. d. there Dec. 18, 1903. bur. Elmwood Cem., Shepherdstown. There is some confusion about Douglas's various ranks. He seems to have been in an acting capacity for all these staff positions. "A handsome, offhand, jaunty fellow."

Douglas, Henry Thompson. b. James City Co., Virginia,, Sept. 15, 1838. att. Wm. & Mary. A civil engineer. Lt. PAVA., 1861, on duty on lower peninsula and at Chaffin's Farm. Lt. EO, Feb. 17, 1862. Serving as EO and AADC to Magruder by Apr. 1862. Capt. EO to A. P. Hill, June 9, 1862. Maj. EO, May 27, 1863. With Longstreet at Gettysburg. Lt. Col. Apr. 1, 1864. Lt. Col. Chief Engineer of Trans-Mississippi Dept., Mar. 1865. Also staff of E. K. Smith. Helped design Intermediate Defense line around Richmond. Railroad engineer in Mexico and Baltimore, postwar. Staff of Fitz. Lee during the Spanish-American War. d. near Providence Forge, Virginia, July 20, 1926.

Downer, William S. MSK at Harpers Ferry, Virginia, early in the war. Working at C.S. Armory at Richmond by Sept. 1861, and Supt. of that facility, Dec. 1862. Maj. 1st Bn. Virginia LDT, 1863. Resigned Mar. 1864. Probably William Spiller Downer, born ca. 1820, a newspaperman in Mecklenburg Co., Virginia, postwar, and later at Huntington, West Virginia, where he died May 1877.

Downman, John Joseph. b. in Virginia, Dec. 5, 1835. Farmer at Upperville, Fauquier Co., pre- and postwar. Pvt. Co. H, 4th Virginia Cavy., Apr. 25, 1861. To Ordnance Sgt. in Nov. 1862. Lt. oo to Munford's Bgd., Oct. 23, 1864, into 1865. d. Apr. 8, 1873. bur. Fredericksburg City Cem.

Downman, Robert Henry. b. Fauquier Co., Virginia, Sept. 9, 1833. att. uva. Capt. acs, 4th Virginia Cavy., Jan. 9, 1863. Maj. cs to B. H. Robertson, Jan. 25, 1863. Maj. cs to James B. Gordon, Sept. 30, 1863. Maj. cs to Barringer, May 1864. Appx. Lawyer at Warrenton, and Fauquier Co. clerk. d. Oct. 8, 1891. bur. Warrenton City Cem.

Drake, Richard. b. Pontotoc, Mississippi, Aug. 14, 1840. Sgt. Co. G, 2nd Mississippi, Apr. 30, 1861. wia at Gaines's Mill. Sgt. acting oo to Law, Oct. 29, 1862. Lt. oo to Law, date unknown. Served there until assigned to duty as Lt. Asst. oo to Longstreet, Feb. 22, 1865. pow at Amelia C.H., Apr. 5, 1865. Took Oath June 17, 1865. Clerk at Memphis, Tennessee, before entering that state's soldiers' home. d. Nashville, July 30, 1926. bur. Soldiers' Home Cem.

Drayton, John Edward. b. in South Carolina, Mar. 27, 1839. att. uva. Planter in Beaufort Co., worth $175,000 in 1860. Lt. adc to his father, Gen. Drayton, Oct. 4, 1861. Resigned Feb. 28, 1862. Reappointed to same position, Sept. 26, 1862. Resigned again Apr. 2, 1864. Pvt. 2nd Co. Rockbridge (Va.) Arty., June 20, 1864. Served into 1865. m. Esther Parsons, 1879. Railroad official at Port Royal, South Carolina.

Drewry, Clay. b. King William Co., Virginia, Aug. 9, 1833. Richmond wholesale merchant. Present at John Brown's hanging, 1859. Lt. Co. B, 41st Virginia, May 29, 1861. To Capt., May 1, 1862. wia at Malvern Hill and Second Manassas. Capt. aqm to Robert Ransom, Oct. 22, 1862. Maj. qm to

Ransom, Dec. 31, 1862. Through 1864, at least. Farmer, 1865–1873, and then Richmond merchant. d. there Mar. 14, 1911. bur. Hollywood Cem.

Drinkard, William Francis. b. Prince Edward Co., Virginia, Nov. 23, 1825. Printer's apprentice at Lynchburg. Newspaper editor at Fairmont, Virginia, prewar. Capt. oo, July 23, 1864. On duty at Richmond as msk. Paroled Apr. 22, 1865, at Burkeville, Virginia. m. Mary Jane Ellyson. Worked at the *Richmond Dispatch*, 1865–1890s. d. Richmond, July 11, 1898. bur. Hollywood Cem.

Ducie, Daniel W. b. in England. Pvt. Co. D, 16th Mississippi, June 1, 1861, age 27, a clerk. Later to Lt., and then Capt. aqm, 16th Mississippi, Jan. 19, 1863. Capt. aqm to Harris, Sept. 15, 1864. Appx. Living at Natchez in 1870, a painter.

Duckwall, Joseph S. Lawyer in Morgan Co., Virginia. Served in 89th Virginia Militia in 1861. Capt. aqm, Oct. 6, 1862. Spent the war at Richmond, investigating claims for back pay. Paroled there Apr. 22, 1865. Possibly the Joseph Smith Duckwall who lived postwar in Maryland.

Dudley, B. W. Asst. Surg. 2nd Kentucky, Sept. 21, 1861. Lt. acting adc to Cosby, Feb.–May 1863. Lt. adc to Cosby, May 2, 1863.

Dudley, Thomas Underwood, Jr. b. Richmond, Virginia, Sept. 26, 1837. att. uva., and taught Latin there prewar. Clerk at Richmond, Mar. 1862. Capt. acs, Jan. 28, 1863. Maj. cs, Nov. 5, 1864. Stationed at Richmond entire war. Married three times. Chancellor, Univ. of the South. Episc. Bishop of Kentucky. d. Jan. 22, 1904.

Duffey, George. b. Alexandria, Virginia, Apr. 6, 1820. Lt. Col. of Alexandria City Arty. for 20 years prewar, and silversmith there. Served as "Master Armorer" under E. P. Alexander, 1861. Lt. of Arty., csa, May 19, 1862. Capt. oo, Dec. 23, 1862, but never confirmed. Reappt. Capt. oo, Dec. 8,

1864, to rank from Dec. 23, 1862. Commanded ANVa. Field Park reserve ordnance train, 1863–1865. Appx. Alexandria jeweler. d. there July 10, 1896. bur. Methodist Protestant Cem.

Duffield, Charles Bishop. b. in Maryland, May 30, 1823. Lawyer at Norfolk. Acting Maj. AAG to Wise, July 19, 1861. Maj. 8th Bn. Virginia Cavy., Aug. 13, 1861, but apparently stayed on Wise's staff despite this. Resigned Apr. 24, 1862, due to "severe chronic rheumatism." Capt. AAG, Feb. 23, 1863. Served in Bureau of Conscription at Richmond. Maj. AAG, Mar. 20, 1865, still at Richmond. d. Asheville, North Carolina, June 21, 1887. bur. Riverside Cem.

Dugan, Hammond. A civil and mechanical engineer from Baltimore, Maryland. Pvt. Co. B, 21st Virginia, May–June 1861. Cpl. in J. L. Clark's Maryland Bn., 1861. Capt. AQM, 10th Virginia Cavy., July 1, 1862. Dropped Feb. 7, 1863. Capt. AQM at Richmond, by July 1863, serving the city's hospitals. Present at Appx. Married twice.

Du Heaume, Philippe. Resided at Isle of Jersey, England. att. school in France. Capt. in Royal Jersey Militia for 17 years, and listed occupation as professor of musketry. Lt. acting oo to Clingman, Apr. 1863. Lt. Drillmaster, Apr. 4, 1864, but in fact served as Lt. oo to Clingman for remainder of war. A fellow staffer called Du Heaume "lively and ridiculous."

Duke, Thomas L. b. Fayette Co., Alabama. Pvt. Co. K, 19th Mississippi, May 26, 1861. Discharged Nov. 14, 1861, age 24, to become regimental chaplain. VADC to Posey "in several battles." Possibly the man of that name who was from Columbus, Mississippi, born Dec. 10, 1836, and died in California in 1920.

Dunbar, David B. b. in Virginia, ca. 1834. Lived prewar in Nansemond Co. Lt. of Arty., May 19, 1862. Lt. acting oo, 18th Bn. Virginia Heavy Arty., by Aug. 1862. Lt. oo at Mobile, Alabama, July 23, 1863. Lt.

AAAIG to Col. C. A. Fuller, 1864. Alive at Suffolk, Virginia, 1870.

Duncan, Henry Blanton. b. Louisville, Kentucky, July 2, 1827. Lt. Col. 1st Bn. Kentucky by June 1861. Lt. Col. VADC to J. E. Johnston at First Manassas. Left regiment soon thereafter. Head of money printing operation at Augusta, Georgia. Newspaperman at Louisville. Moved to Los Angeles in 1886. d. there Apr. 8, 1902. bur. Evergreen Cem. until removed to Cave Hill Cem. in Louisville in 1903. Apparently never used first name.

Duncan, Lawson L. b. Nov. 19, 1833. att. UVA. A resident of Jefferson Co., Kentucky. Lt. oo, July 19, 1862. On unspecified ordnance duty at Richmond, Virginia, Aug. 1863–Sept. 1864, at least. Surrendered at Augusta, Georgia, May 5, 1865. Suffers from a sparse official record.

Duncan, Robert Perry. b. Feb. 18, 1838. att. UVA. and Furman. Of Greenville, South Carolina. Lt. Co. F, 4th South Carolina, May 5, 1861. Lt. ADC to R. H. Anderson, July 11, 1862. Maj. AAIG to Anderson, Dec. 4, 1862. Maj. AAIG to Mahone, May 1864. Maj. AAIG to Anderson again, Nov. 23, 1864. Lawyer at Memphis, Tennessee. Also lived at Louisville, Kentucky. d. July 20, 1905. bur. Mt. Hope Cem., Westchester Co., New York.

Duncan, William Erastus. b. Amherst Co., Virginia, May 19, 1825. att. Columbian Coll. Professor at Hollins Coll. and Allegheny Coll. Capt. AQM, Oct. 18, 1861. Stationed at posts in southwest Virginia, including White Sulphur Springs, Giles C.H., Jackson River Depot, and Buchanan. Temporarily dropped, May 1863, for failure to submit reports in a timely fashion. Capt. AQM to Cutts's Bn. Arty., Nov. 1863–Feb. 1864. Finished the war in southwest Virginia. Farmer and educator. President Allegheny Coll. d. Feb. 15, 1912. bur. family cem. in Franklin Co., Virginia.

Dunlop, John. b. in England, Feb. 14, 1833.

att. Wadham Coll., 1851. Known as "English John." Pvt. 12th Virginia. VADC to Armistead June 1862. WIA in thigh at Second Manassas. Lt. ADC to Armistead, Oct. 29, 1862. Resigned Jan. 24, 1863, due to poor eyesight, and returned to England. Lawyer at Richmond, Virginia. d. June 14, 1901. bur. Hollywood Cem.

Dunn, Andrew. b. Londonderry, Ireland, Dec. 17, 1822. Lived at Petersburg, Virginia. Lt. Co. D, 5th Virginia Cavy., May 17, 1861. Discharged Apr. 1862. Lt. ADC to Longstreet, Aug. 24, 1863. WIA by sharpshooter, Nov. 21, 1863, and by shell fragment in the back on July 26, 1864. Appx. d. Petersburg, Jan. 1, 1893. bur. Blandford Cem.

Dunn, Archibald W. b. Chesterfield Co., Virginia, Nov. 19, 1830. Farmed there prewar. Pvt. Co. B, 13th Virginia Cavy., May 17, 1861. Capt. AQM, June 3, 1863. On duty at Petersburg, 1863–1865. m. Susanna E. Burton. Farmer and insurance agent at Petersburg. Later lived at Manchester and then at Richmond, selling insurance. d. at the "Home for the Incurables" in Richmond, Apr. 30, 1897. bur. Blandford Cem., Petersburg. Middle name probably Walthall.

Dunn, George R. R. b. in Ohio, Apr. 24, 1832. Depot agent at Abingdon, Virginia, prewar. Serving in QM Dept. of Floyd's command by July 1861. Capt. AQM to Floyd, Nov. 11, 1861. Capt. AQM at Dublin Depot, Virginia, Jan. 1862. Capt. AQM, 36th Virginia, Apr. 22, 1862. Maj. QM to McCausland, Nov. 14, 1862. Back to Dublin Depot, Nov. 1864. Banker, clerk, and "retired landlord" at Abindgon and Wytheville. d. at Wytheville, Apr. 29, 1902. bur. Sinking Spring Cem., Abingdon. Third initial possibly spurious.

Dunn, Isaac Baker. b. in Virginia, ca. 1816. A Washington Co. farmer, prewar. Capt. ACS, 50th Virginia, July 10, 1861. Maj. QM to Floyd, July 16, 1861. Resigned Oct. 6, 1861. Capt. AQM in southwest Virginia and in Tennessee, 1862–1864. Also served in 6th

Bn. Virginia Reserves, 1864. Merchant and farmer in Washington Co., alive 1870.

Dunn, Thomas Robert. b. "Dunn's Hill," Chesterfield Co., Virginia, Mar. 8, 1841. att. VMI. Schoolteacher. Lt. and acting Adjt., Co. D, 1st Bn. Virginia Arty., Nov. 1861. Lt. AAAG to J. R. Jones's Bgd., Aug. 10–Oct. 25, 1862. Capt. Co. A, 1st Bn. Virginia Inf., July 27, 1863. Appx. Chesterfield Co. farmer. Chief engineer for Richmond & Petersburg Railroad. d. Petersburg, July 18, 1904.

Du Val, Harvie Sheffield. b. Hardin Co., Kentucky, June 30, 1833. att. UNC. A Florida-based mathematician and scientific engineer. Member of U.S. Coast Survey, 1853–1861. Lt. of Inf., July 19, 1861. Worked as engineer in northern Virginia, 1861–62. Probably Lt. EO to Griffith, early 1862. Lt. acting Chief EO to D. H. Hill, Apr. 1862. Lt. OO in Florida from July 1862. Paroled May 16, 1865, at Madison, Florida. m. Olivia Harrison. d. Sante Fe, New Mexico, Dec. 12, 1910.

Duvall, Eli., Jr. b. in Maryland, 1837. m. Alice Cary Ball, 1857. Treasury Dept. clerk at Washington, D.C. Lt. Co. H, 7th Virginia, Apr. 22, 1861. WIA at Blackburn's Ford. On signal duty, 1861–1862. Dropped from 7th at reorganization, Apr. 1862. Lt. SO, Oct. 13, 1862. Ordered to duty with First Corps, Nov. 24, 1862, and served with Law, Hood, and McLaws. Lt. SO to Field, July–Aug. 1864. Lt. SO to Hood, Aug. 18, 1864. Chief SO, AOT, Feb.–Apr. 1865. d. Lynchburg, Virginia, Aug. 26, 1892. bur. Oak Hill Cem., Washington, D.C.

Duvall, Henry. Capt. AAG and acting ADC to Donelson, Aug. 1861. No other record, and quite possibly an uncommissioned volunteer.

Duxbury, W. C. b. in Massachusetts. Supposedly a druggist at Montgomery, Alabama, prewar. Lt. OO to Longstreet, Apr. 22, 1862. Lt. OO, Dept. of North Carolina, by June 1863. Subsequently Lt. OO to D. H. Hill, Breckinridge, Hindman, Hood, and AOT artillery. Capt. oo, May 26, 1863. May have received promotion to Major oo before surrender. Called "good tempered, but exceedingly conceited" by Francis Dawson, whose memoirs contain comical references to Duxbury.

Dwight, Charles Stevens. b. Charleston, South Carolina, July 11, 1834. att. Coll. of Charleston. A civil engineer. Pvt. and Cpl. Co. I, 2nd South Carolina, May 22, 1861 to June 24, 1862. Detached as volunteer engineer to McLaws, early 1862. Lt. EO to McLaws, June 4, 1862. Lt. EO to Kershaw, 1864–1865. POW at Sailor's Creek. Released June 17, 1865. Surveyor in British Honduras, and then railroad engineer in Missouri and South Carolina. Brother of R. Y. and W. M. Dwight (q.v.). d. Winnsboro, South Carolina, Sept. 6, 1921. bur. St. John's Episc. Churchyard. Dwight's memoirs have been published.

Dwight, Richard Yeadon. b. South Carolina, Oct. 4, 1837. att SCMA. Walterboro physician. Pvt. Co. B, Holcombe Legion, Dec. 16, 1861. VADC to Col. P. F. Stevens (commanding Evans's Bgd.) at Second Manassas. Lt. Co. D, 3rd South Carolina Heavy Arty., Aug. 6, 1862–July 27, 1864. Asst. Surg., July 14, 1864, stationed at Macon, Georgia. Physician in Missouri and South Carolina. Brother of C. S. and W. M. Dwight (q.v.). d. Berkeley Co., South Carolina, Dec. 6, 1919. bur. Black Oak Cem., Bonneau, South Carolina.

Dwight, William Moultrie. b. Farmington, South Carolina, June 28, 1839. att. UVA. and SCMA. Teacher in South Carolina. Lt. Co. K, 2nd South Carolina, 1861. WIA in hand and thigh at First Manassas. Lt. AAAIG to Kershaw, June 1862. Injured in a fall on Maryland Heights and POW, Sept. 1862. WIA in head at Fredericksburg. Capt. AAG to Kershaw, Nov. 2, 1863. Capt. AAG to Conner, 1864. POW at Spotsylvania, May 8, 1864. Exchanged 1865. Capt. AAG to Butler, Jan. 25, 1865, but did not return from

prison in time to take that duty. Mayor of Winnsboro, South Carolina, a druggist, and principal of Mt. Zion Academy. m. his sister-in-law, Elizabeth Porcher Gaillard. Brother of C. S. and R. Y. Dwight (q.v.). d. Apr. 1877. bur. St. John's Episc. Churchyard, Winnsboro. "Of stalwart frame & great personal elegance."

Early, Robert Davies. b. Sept. 23, 1841. Lt. 11th Virginia. Dropped Apr. 1862. VADC to Garland, June–Sept. 1862. WIA at Malvern Hill. Continued as VADC to McRae and Iverson. VADC to Early from Chancellorsville through Gettysburg. Capt. AAG to J. M. Jones, Aug. 14, 1863. KIA at the Wilderness, May 5, 1864. bur. Lynchburg Presby. Cem. No known relation to Gen. Early, according to the general himself.

Early, Samuel Henry. b. Franklin Co., Virginia, Jan. 22, 1813. att. Wm. & Mary. Lawyer and postmaster in Franklin Co. Farmer in Texas. Pvt. Co. B, 2nd Virginia Cavy., May 13, 1861. Lt. ADC to his brother, Gen. Early, Sept. 11, 1861. WIA left leg at Sharpsburg. Resigned Nov. 19, 1862. VADC to Early at Gettysburg, and WIA slightly in foot there. Conscription officer at Lynchburg. Lumberman and salt maker at Charleston, West Virginia. d. there Mar. 11, 1874. bur. Spring Hill Cem., Lynchburg.

Eason, Thomas Dotterer. b. Oct. 9, 1822. Machinist at Charleston, South Carolina. Lt. Washington (N.C.) Arty. Lt. acting oo to N. G. Evans, Jan. 1862. Lt. oo to Evans, May 1, 1862. Resigned Oct. 27, 1862, to return to his business at Charleston. VADC to Ripley, July 1863. Charleston millwright and machinist. d. Dec. 27, 1872. bur. Magnolia Cem.

Echols, Robert Joseph. b. Nov. 9, 1819. Capt. AQM at Strasburg, Virginia, June 1861–May 1863. Maj. QM at Charlotte, North Carolina, May 14, 1863. Paroled there May 3, 1865. Brother of Gen. John Echols. d. July 12, 1899. bur. Lynchburg (Va.) Presby. Cem.

Ector, John T. Lt. ADC to Iverson, Dec. 18,

1862. Served there into 1865. Appointed from Georgia.

Edelin, Thomas Boyd. b. Prince George's Co., Maryland, Sept. 1833. Known almost exclusively as "Boyd." Served in 7th U.S. Inf., 1855–1861. Lt. of Inf., May 23, 1863, to report to Garnett's Bn. Arty. Lt. AAAIG to Butler, Dec. 1863. Capt. AAIG to Young, Jan. 13, 1864. VADC to Hampton, Sept. 1864. Apptd. temporary Lt. Col., 16th Bn. North Carolina Cavy., Dec. 7, 1864. POW at Dinwiddie C.H., Mar. 30, 1865. d. Culpeper Co., Virginia, Feb. 8, 1902.

Edings, John Evans. ADC to Drayton by Nov. 1861, but no evidence of commission found until appointed Capt. AAG to Drayton, Aug. 28, 1862. Capt. AAIG to Beauregard, Aug. 9, 1863. Length of service with Beauregard not known. It is not yet apparent whether this was the man born Nov. 8, 1808, or his son (John Evans Edings, Jr.). There are conflicting dates of life for both father and son.

Edmonds, William Bell, Jr. b. Albemarle Co., Virginia, Mar. 1832. Capt. ACS, 38th Virginia, Sept. 20, 1861. Failed bond, and out of duty Feb.–May 1863. Relieved Aug. 1, 1863. Capt. ACS to Pickett, Sept. 17, 1863, serving into 1865. d. Feb. 2, 1908. bur. East Mount Cem., Greeneville, Tennessee.

Edmondston, James Nicolson. b. 1831. Lived prewar in New Mexico and at Raleigh, North Carolina. On ordnance duty in North Carolina with Gen. Martin, early in the war. Maj. QM to Daniel, May 9, 1862. Relieved May 6, 1864, citing poor health. Maj. AAIG for field transportation, based at Greensboro, North Carolina, 1864–1865. d. Augusta, Georgia, Mar. 28, 1896. His sister-in-law was famous diarist Catherine Ann Devereux Edmondston.

Edwards, Alfred. b. Jefferson Co., Kentucky, Apr. or May 1837. Lawyer at Louisville. Pvt. Co. H, 1st Kentucky, June 2, 1861. To Lt., Apr. 30, 1862. Lt. OO to his aunt's husband, Gen. McLaws, July 22, 1862. Lt. OO to

Kershaw, Dec. 17, 1863 to Feb. 1865. Capt. OO, Jan. 7, 1865. Ordered to report to Chief of Ordnance, Mar. 1865. Lawyer, judge, and editor in Kentucky. Moved to Texas about 1870. Alive 1913 in Brazoria Co. A brother of John F. Edwards (see below).

Edwards, Jeremiah. Lt. Co. F, 48th Alabama, Apr. 10, 1862, age 29. Later promoted to Capt. Capt. AAAG to Law at Gettysburg. POW July 2, 1863. Exchanged in 1865.

Edwards, John Franklin. b. in Kentucky, 1832. Merchant at Louisville. Pvt. Co. B, 5th Kentucky, Oct. 2, 1861. Maj. CS to his aunt's husband, Gen. McLaws, Jan. 18, 1862. Maj. CS to Kershaw, Dec. 1863. Maj. CS to Longstreet, Oct. 6, 1864. Appx. m. Virginia Louise Magill, 1865. d. Atlanta, Georgia, Dec. 1904. bur. Oakland Cem. Brother of Alfred Edwards (see above).

Edwards, John Gibson. b. Abbeville Co., South Carolina, Feb. 14, 1832. Abbeville C.H. merchant. Capt. ACS Orr's Rifles, July 19, 1861. Capt. ACS to McGowan, Aug. 1, 1863. Capt. ACS to Wilcox, Nov. 15, 1864. Appx. Banker and railroad company treasurer. d. Aug. 23, 1904. bur. Upper Long Cane Presby. Church, Abbeville.

Edwards, O. W. Lt. of Arty., Sept. 11, 1861. MSK at Richmond, Virginia. Capt. of Arty., Feb. 2, 1863. Served at Richmond into 1865. Ran an "ordnance store" on 7th Street near the James River. Took Oath May 8, 1865, age 52, occupation "gentleman."

Edwards, William Albert. b. Norfolk, Virginia, Aug. 20, 1835. A clerk. Pvt. Co. E, 41st Virginia, Mar. 4, 1862. Pvt. Co. C, 19th Bn. Virginia Heavy Arty., Apr. 19, 1862. Clerk in Ordnance Dept. at Richmond. Lt. OO, Mar. 23, 1864, and Asst. to Chief OO of Third Corps. Relieved Sept. 27, 1864. Lt. OO, Huger's Bn. Arty., late in 1864. Relieved Feb. 7, 1865, and ordered to C.S. Arsenal at Richmond. Appx. d. Eureka, Nevada, 1882.

Effinger, John Frederick. b. Harrisonburg, Virginia, May 13, 1846. att. VMI. Ran away from VMI to briefly serve with Mosby. Pvt.

Co. F, 14th Virginia Cavy., spring 1864. Lt. ADC to Echols, probably in 1864. Paroled May 16, 1865, at Staunton. att. UVA. and Washington Coll. postwar. Lawyer and "coal operator" in West Virginia. Later lived at Washington, D.C., and New York City. d. Bronxville, New York, Mar. 9, 1932. bur. Thornrose Cem., Staunton.

Elder, Thomas Claybrook. b. Lunenburg Co., Virginia, Apr. 16, 1834. att. UVA. and Randolph Macon. Petersburg law partner of Roger A. Pryor. Maj. CS to Pryor, May 13, 1862. Maj. CS to E. A. Perry, by Dec. 1862. Maj. CS to Finegan. Appx. m. Anna Fitzhugh May. President of the Virginia State Bar Association. Augusta Co. judge. d. Staunton, Nov. 21, 1904. Elder's letters are at the Virginia Historical Society.

Elford, T. Joseph. b. in South Carolina, Feb. 6, 1821. Spartanburg merchant. m. Emma Butler Blasingame. Capt. ACS, 5th South Carolina, Apr. 13, 1861. Dropped Aug. 2, 1862. Capt. acting CS to D. R. Jones for "several months" in winter 1861–1862. Maj. CS to Micah Jenkins, Apr. 29, 1862. Maj. CS to Bratton, May 1864 into 1865. Postwar lawyer. d. Aug. 10, 1872. bur. Oakwood Cem., Spartanburg.

Elhart, Adolphus. b. in Austria, Feb. 2, 1830. Came to United States in 1847. Merchant at Lexington, Virginia. Pvt. Co. C, 1st Virginia Cavy., Apr. 18, 1861. Capt. AQM, 1st Virginia Cavy., Dec. 18, 1861. Capt. AQM 1st Div. of the Army of the Potomac [ANVa.], Mar. 1862. Capt. AQM to report to T. J. Jackson, July 15, 1862. Capt. AQM and Paymaster to Second Corps, Dec. 23, 1862 through 1865. Baltimore merchant and Rockbridge Co. farmer. d. Lexington, Dec. 1, 1913. bur. Oxford Presby. Church Cem.

Ellicott, John. b. Baltimore, Maryland, Sept. 12, 1834. Civil engineer with B & O Railroad and in Illinois. Worked on Pacific coast with the Lighthouse Board. Lt. EO, Sept. 2, 1862. Lt. EO at Richmond, Nov. 4, 1862. Capt. in Nitre & Mining Bureau, Dec.

1863. Baltimore engineer and architect. Built the grounds and clubhouse at Pimlico Racetrack. d. Baltimore, Jan. 11, 1890. bur. Green Mount Cem.

Elliott, Charles Grice. b. Elizabeth City, North Carolina, Mar. 8, 1840. Clerk there. Lt. 17th North Carolina, 1862. POW at Roanoke Island. Lt. AAAG to Martin, May 8, 1862. Lt. ADC to Martin, Aug. 2, 1862. Capt. AAG to Martin, May 16, 1863. Same to W. W. Kirkland. Paroled Greensboro. Grocer, merchant, and cotton manufacturer at Norfolk, Virginia. d. Healing Springs, Virginia, Aug. 14, 1901. bur. Elmwood Cem., Oxford, North Carolina.

Elliott, Middleton Stuart. b. in South Carolina, May 10, 1841. att. SCMA. Brother of Gen. Elliott. Capt. Beaufort (S.C.) Arty., June–Sept. 1862. Acting EO to W. S. Walker, Sept. 1862. Lt. EO at Savannah, June 1864. Lt. EO to Beauregard, July 1864. WIA in head at Petersburg. Lt. EO to R. H. Anderson, by Dec. 1864. Appx. d. Apr. 21, 1921.

Elliott, Robert Woodman Barnwell. b. Beaufort, South Carolina, Aug. 16, 1840. att. South Carolina Coll. Son of the famous Bishop Elliott. Lived Savannah, Georgia, prewar. Lt. ADC to Lawton, Sept. 23, 1861. WIA at Second Manassas, Aug. 28, 1862. VADC to Ewell at Gettysburg. Lt. AAAG to Gilmer, Sept. 1863. Capt. AAG to Gilmer, Oct. 20, 1863. Capt. AAG to McLaws, Dec. 12, 1864. Capt. AAG to Walthall, Apr. 17, 1865. Episc. bishop in Atlanta and Texas. d. Sewanee, Tennessee, Aug. 26, 1887. bur. Sewanee Cem.

Elliott, Samuel C. b. Belfast, Maine. 45-year-old steamboat agent at Norfolk, Virginia, in 1860. Capt. ACS, June 29, 1861, at Smithfield, Virginia. Capt. acting ACS to Colston, 1861. Capt. ACS, Burkeville, Virginia, May–Sept. 1862. Capt. ACS, Culpeper, Virginia, Sept. 1862. Capt. ACS at Drewry's Bluff, Dec. 1862 to at least Sept. 1864. Capt. ACS, date unknown. Appx. d. Norfolk, Virginia, Dec. 3,

1865, age 49, of diarrhea. bur. Elmwood Cem.

Ellis, Roswell. b. Georgia, Apr. 8, 1822. Mexican War veteran. Columbus publisher. Capt. Co. G, 2nd Georgia, Apr. 16, 1861. Capt. AAG to Semmes, Dec. 24, 1862. Capt. AAG to Bryan, July 1863. WIA in left shoulder at Knoxville, Nov. 29, 1863. Dropped July 1864, having failed confirmation by Senate. Capt. AAG to Field, Nov. 17, 1864. Retired to Invalid Corps, Mar. 25, 1865. Columbus auctioneer. Married twice. d. Mar. 30, 1909. bur. Hillview Cem., LaGrange, Georgia.

Ely, Robert N. b. Muscogee Co., Georgia, 1835. Dougherty Co. lawyer and legislator. Pvt. Co. E, 4th Georgia, May 2, 1861. Capt. AQM, 6th Georgia, May 21, 1861. Maj. QM to Colquitt, Nov. 11, 1862. Paroled Apr. 26, 1865. Farmer at Albany. Attorney general of Georgia. d. Jan. 14, 1895. bur. Hillview Cem., LaGrange.

Emmett, John William. b. in Louisiana, Jan. 1, 1839. New Orleans clerk. Sgt. 2nd Company Washington Arty., May 26, 1861. Adjt. 5th Virginia Cavy., May 27, 1863. Capt. AAG to Rosser, Nov. 20, 1863. WIA at the Wilderness, May 5, 1864. WIA in ankle at Tom's Brook. Appx. New Orleans bookkeeper. d. Mar. 9, 1916. bur. Greenwood Cem., New Orleans.

Emory, Frederick. b. in Maryland. Clerk in QM Dept. at Richmond, Virginia. Capt. AQM, Feb. 19, 1864, but failed confirmation. Reappt., June 15, 1864, and served as IFT and Purchasing Agent for Army of the Valley. Paroled June 14, 1865, at Baldwin, Florida. d. May 2, 1901, age 71. bur. Confederate Soldiers' Home, Higginsville, Missouri.

Engelhard, Joseph Adolphus. b. Monticello, Mississippi, Sept. 27, 1832. att. UNC and Harvard Law School. Capt. AQM, 33rd North Carolina, Sept. 20, 1861. Maj. QM to Branch, June 10, 1862. Maj. QM to Lane. Resigned Feb. 3, 1863. Capt. AAG to Pender,

to rank from Dec. 19, 1862. Maj. AAG to Pender, June 2, 1863. Maj. AAG to Wilcox. WIA slightly at Reams Station. Appx. Tarboro, North Carolina, lawyer. Editor of Wilmington newspaper. d. Raleigh, Feb. 15, 1879. bur. Oakwood Cem.

English, William O. b. Westmoreland Co., Virginia, 1833. Farmer in Albemarle Co. Pvt. Co. K, 2nd Virginia Cavy., May 11, 1861. To Sgt. autumn 1862. Lt. OO to Andrews's Bn. Arty., Feb. 27, 1863. Lt. OO to Braxton's Bn. Arty., by Dec. 1863, and into 1865. Schoolteacher at Richmond. d. there Mar. 1, 1896, age 63. bur. in unmarked grave at Hollywood Cem.

Erwin, Alfred Martin. b. Montgomery Co., North Carolina, 1829. att. Davidson Coll. Lawyer in Burke Co. Lt. Co. B, 35th North Carolina, Sept. 11, 1861. Failed reelection in Apr. 1862. Lt. ADC to Clingman, Nov. 7, 1862. Maj. QM to Clingman, Dec. 17, 1862. Paroled Apr. 26, 1865. North Carolina legislator postwar. d. Asheville, North Carolina, Dec. 2, 1888. bur. Forest Hill Cem., Morganton, North Carolina. Called "cross and good" by a wartime acquaintance.

Estes, Henry Bacon. b. Pulaski, Tennessee, Nov. 21, 1838. att. Cumberland Univ. Moved from New York City to Aberdeen, Mississippi, in 1860 and opened a law practice. Sgt. Co. I, 11th Mississippi. Lt. ADC to Davis, Nov. 25, 1862. POW in Richmond hospital, Apr. 3, 1865. d. Spring Hill, Tennessee, Feb. 2, 1898.

Estill, Charles Patrick. b. Nov. 2, 1834. att. UVA. and Washington Coll. Professor at D. H. Hill's military academy. Cpl. Charlottesville (Va.) Arty., 1862. Lt. acting OO to D. H. Hill, Dec. 1862. Lt. acting OO to Paxton, Apr. 2, 1863. Lt. OO, May 2, 1863, staff of J. A. Walker soon thereafter. Lt. acting OO to Ed. Johnson, Jan. 1864. Capt. OO to Johnson, Feb. 25, 1864. Capt. OO to Gordon, May 1864. Appx. Brother of H. M. Estill (q.v.). Professor at Texas A & M and Sam Houston State. d. Huntsville, Texas,

Aug. 9, 1882. bur. Stonewall Jackson Cem., Lexington, Virginia.

Estill, Henry Miller, Jr. b. Lexington, Virginia, Mar. 14, 1841. att. UVA. and Washington Coll. In 3rd Co. Richmond Howitzers. Cpl. Charlottesville (Va.) Arty. Acting OO to Colquitt, Feb. 1863 into Feb. 1864, at least. Possibly never commissioned. Estill's records are very poor. POW at Waynesboro, Mar. 2, 1865. Brother of C. P. Estill (q.v.). Math professor at Washington Coll. and Randolph Macon. d. May 16, 1880. bur. Stonewall Jackson Cem., Lexington.

Estill, Huston. b. ca. 1812. Capt. ACS to Wise, Aug. 18, 1861. Capt. ACS, 60th Virginia, Aug. 18, 1861. Dropped Aug. 2, 1862, for failing bond. Maj. QM to Starke, Oct. 4, 1862, to rank from Aug. 17, 1862. Never accepted because Starke was dead by time of appointment. Probably served in that capacity Aug.–Sept. Returned to 60th Virginia, but dropped Feb. 5, 1863. Capt. ACS to McCausland, Feb. 12, 1864. Capt. ACS to Wharton, by Oct. 1864. POW at Waynesboro. d. Ft. Delaware, Apr. 27, 1865, of chronic diarrhea. bur. Finn's Point Confederate Cem., New Jersey. Estill's family gives him the middle initial "Z," but there is no confirmation in his signature or anywhere else.

Etheridge, Alexander E. b. in Virginia, Dec. 19, 1837. Clerk at Portsmouth. m. Emma Jane Parker, 1858. Sgt. Co. C, 16th Virginia, Apr. 20, 1861. Capt. AQM, 61st Virginia, 1862–1864. Capt. AQM to Weisiger, Sept. 16, 1864. Appx. Commission merchant and cotton factor at Portsmouth. d. there June 16, 1909. bur. Cedar Grove Cem.

Eustis, James Biddle. b. New Orleans, Louisiana, Aug. 27, 1834. att. Harvard Law School. New Orleans lawyer. Lt. ADC to Magruder, Nov. 28, 1861. Maj. AAG to Magruder, Oct. 15, 1862. Maj. AAG to J. E. Johnston, June 1863. Judge on military court in AOT. Maj. AAIG to Beauregard, Oct. 17, 1864. Paroled May 2, 1865. Louisiana legisla-

tor and law professor at Univ. of Louisiana. In U.S. Senate, and Ambassador to France. d. Newport, Rhode Island, Sept. 9, 1899. bur. Cave Hill Cem., Louisville, Kentucky. "A man of great mental vigor, but a very indolent man," according to a fellow staff officer.

Evans, Asa Louis. b. in South Carolina, Apr. 10, 1834. Capt. AAAG to his brother, Gen. N. G. Evans, at First Manassas. Capt. AAG to Evans, Oct. 9, 1861. Capt. AAG to Elliott and Wallace. Appx. Lawyer at Marion C.H. and deputy clerk of county court. d. Mar. 11, 1905. bur. Rose Hill Cem.

Evans, Daniel James. b. in Virginia, July 25, 1838. Of Campbell Co. Lt. 44th Virginia, 1861. Lt. 20th Bn. Virginia Arty., 1862. Lt. AAQM, 20th Bn. Virginia Arty., July 1863 into 1864. POW at Amelia C.H., Apr. 6, 1865. Lynchburg schoolteacher. d. Feb. 19, 1934. bur. Franklin Cem., Campbell Co.

Evans, George W. b. in Georgia, 1842. Prewar resident of Augusta. Pvt. Co. C, 48th Georgia, Mar. 11, 1862. Capt. AQM, 48th Georgia, Mar. 22, 1862. Capt. AQM to Wright's Bgd., Sept. 15, 1864. Capt. AQM to Sorrel, Oct. 1864. Appx. A detective at Augusta, alive 1882.

Evans, James, Jr. b. ca. 1844. A resident of Greene Co., Alabama. Pvt. Co. B, 11th Alabama, May 27, 1861. Clerk at brigade headquarters, 1861–1864. Lt. ADC to W. H. Forney, Mar. 24, 1865. Appx.

Evans, John Joseph. b. Madison, Georgia, Aug. 8, 1842. att. GMI and WMI. Pvt. Co. I, 11th Mississippi, Apr. 27, 1861. Adjt. 11th Mississippi, Aug. 25, 1863. Capt. AAG to Davis, June 15, 1864. Suffered severed achilles in 1864. Appx. Planter at Aberdeen, Mississippi, and state treasurer. d. Jackson, Mississippi, Nov. 19, 1899.

Evans, Joshua K. b. Burke Co., Georgia, Jan. 1, 1838. Lt. Co. C, 48th Georgia, Feb. 28, 1862. WIA in neck at Mine Run. To Capt., June 23, 1864. Capt. AAAG to Girardey, summer 1864. Capt. AAAG to Sorrel, Oct.

1864. Never married. A cotton shipper at Augusta postwar. d. there Nov. 4, 1884. bur. Magnolia Cem.

Evans, Oliver Few. b. Macon, Georgia, Dec. 22, 1830. A brick mason at Macon. m. Amanda Wilder, 1855. Sgt. Co. H, 12th Georgia, June 9, 1861. To Lt., Jan. 21, 1862. WIA at McDowell and Sharpsburg. Capt. Co. H, 12th Georgia, Sept. 17, 1862. Capt. AAAG to Sorrel, Nov. 1864. WIA in thigh at Ft. Stedman. Returned to Macon postwar. d. Oct. 8, 1910. bur. Rose Hill Cem.

Ewell, Benjamin Stoddert. b. Washington, D.C., June 10, 1810. att. Georgetown and USMA. Professor at USMA, Hampden Sidney, Washington Coll, and Wm. & Mary. Col. 32nd Virginia, July 1, 1861. Dropped May 1862. Col. AAG to J. E. Johnston, Nov. 24, 1862. Col. AAG to his brother, Gen. Ewell, Sept. 26, 1864. Resigned Mar. 8, 1865, because of varicose veins and chronic diarrhea. President of Wm. & Mary. d. Williamsburg, Virginia, June 19, 1894. bur. there.

Eyster, George Hupp. b. Strasburg, Virginia, Mar. 4, 1840. att. VMI. Drillmaster with 44th Virginia, July 1861–Jan. 1862. Cadet AOO to Early, and then to James A. Walker and William Smith, 1862–1863. Capt. AAG to Smith, June 4, 1863. Capt. AAG to Pegram. WIA in jaw and groin, early May 1864. Capt. AAG to McCausland, Aug. 19, 1864. Paroled May 1, 1865. att. UVA. postwar. Physician at Staunton, and later at New York, Baltimore, and in West Virginia. "Acting Surgeon" in World War One. d. Augusta Co., Virginia, May 28, 1925. A female diarist noted during the war that Eyster was "possessor of the prettiest pair of eyes that I ever saw in a man's head."

Fain, Hiram, Jr. b. Sept. 9, 1835. Capt. ACS, 63rd Tennessee, July 30, 1862. Capt. ACS to Gracie, Aug. 7, 1863. AWOL Apr. 18, 1864. Apparently returned to duty by autumn 1864. Details on 1864 service are slim and available information is confusing. d. Jan. 5,

1869. bur. New Providence Cem., Hawkins Co., Tennessee.

Faircloth, William Turner. b. Edgecombe Co., North Carolina, Jan. 8, 1829. att. Wake Forest. Goldsboro lawyer. Lt. Co. C, 2nd North Carolina, May 16, 1861. Capt. AQM, 2nd North Carolina, Mar. 14, 1862. Capt. AQM to Cox, Sept. 1, 1864. Associate justice, North Carolina Supreme Court. d. Goldsboro, Dec. 29, 1900. bur. Fairview Cem., La Grange, North Carolina.

Fairfax, Archibald Blair. b. Greenbrier Co., Virginia, May 22, 1809. Served in USN, 1823–1861. Commander CSN, Mar. 26, 1861. Maj. Inspector of Ordnance at Norfolk, Sept. 1861. Performed this duty from the office of John Mercer Brooke for the entire war, and thus may fall outside the scope of this study. Paroled May 3, 1865, at Warrenton, North Carolina. Moved to Yazoo City, Mississippi, in 1865 and managed a plantation. d. there Jan. 3, 1867. bur. there, but later moved to Green Mount Cem., Baltimore.

Fairfax, Herbert Carlyle. b. in Virginia, Apr. 29, 1838. Fairfax Co. farmer. Sgt. Co. D, 17th Virginia, Apr. 25, 1861. Capt. AQM, Dec. 8, 1862. Served in Richmond, 1862–1864. Capt. AQM, 1st Confederate Engineers, May 1864. Paroled May 2, 1865. Farmer and commissioner of revenue for Fairfax Co. d. Racine, West Virginia, May 5, 1890.

Fairfax, John Walter. b. Prince William Co., Virginia, June 30, 1828. att. UPenn. Lived at James Monroe's old home outside Leesburg. VADC to Longstreet, Aug. 1861. Capt. AAG to Longstreet, Apr. 17, 1862. Maj. AAIG to Longstreet, May 5, 1862. Maj. AAIG to R. H. Anderson, 1864. Lt. Col. AAIG to Longstreet, Dec. 19, 1864. Appx. d. Prince William Co., Mar. 22, 1908. bur. Union Cem., Leesburg. "Fond of his bottle, his Bible, and baths. . . ." "Clownish and silly," thought another comrade.

Fairly, John Spencer. b. in Great Britain,

Mar. 7, 1832. Pvt. Hampton Legion Cavy., June 22, 1861. Pvt. Co. B, 2nd Carolina Cavy. Acting ADC to Whiting, Nov. 1862. Lt. ADC to Whiting, May 2, 1863. Lt. AAAG to Hebert, Nov.–Dec. 1863, then back to Whiting. Lt. ADC to Pillow and acting ADC to Hampton, 1865. On Hampton's political staff postwar. d. Fletcher, North Carolina, Aug. 8, 1898. bur. Magnolia Cem., Charleston, South Carolina.

Fallin, John H. Capt. ACS, Aug. 14, 1862. Served with artillery defenses at Richmond, Virginia, 1863–1865. Capt. ACS to Crutchfield's Arty. Bgd., 1865. Appx. A resident of Heathsville, Virginia. Possibly John Hobson Fallin, born 1828.

Farish, Thomas Laughlin. b. Albemarle Co., Virginia, Dec. 24, 1823. att. UVA. Capt. VADC to Wise, by Sept. 1861. Capt. AAG to B. H. Robertson, June 24, 1862. Relieved June 15, 1863. On Examining Board, Jan.–Aug. 1864. Capt. AAG to J. A. Walker, Aug. 27, 1864. Capt. AAG to H. H. Walker, Mar. 1865. POW at Charlottesville, Mar. 5, 1865. Farmer at Charlottesville. d. Oct. 2, 1885.

Farland, Z. S. b. Washington, D.C. A 34-year-old merchant in Essex Co., Virginia, in 1860. Capt. ACS, Oct. 11, 1863. Posted at Center Cross and Newtown, Virginia, both in the eastern section of the state. d. in Essex Co., 1868.

Farley, Henry Saxon. b. Laurensville, South Carolina, Feb. 11, 1840. att. SCMA and USMA. Lt. of Inf., CSA, Mar. 16, 1861. Capt. 1st South Carolina Arty. Capt. acting on staff of Wade Hampton, June 1862. Resigned from artillery, June 22, 1863. Staff of Stuart, July 4–Sept. 30, 1863. Maj., Nov. 6, 1863, assigned to duty with Gen. Young. Commanded troops for remainder of war, usually dismounted troopers. New York lawyer, military school professor, miner in California, and newspaperman in South Carolina. Appeared in several silent movies

late in life. Brother of W. D. Farley (q.v.). d. Flushing, New York, June 3, 1927.

Farley, Hugh Legare. b. Laurens Co., South Carolina, June 15, 1844. att. King's Mountain Military Academy. Lt. Co. G, 3rd South Carolina, Apr. 14, 1861. WIA at Savage's Station and Wilderness. Lt. acting ADC to Kershaw at Chickamauga. Lt. AAAG to Young, July 4, 1864, to 1865. Cotton grower, railroad man, lawyer, newspaper editor, and legislator, mostly in South Carolina. d. Spartanburg, Sept. 30, 1897. bur. Laurens Cem.

Farley, William Downs. b. Laurensville, South Carolina, Dec. 19, 1835. att. UVA. Brother of H. S. Farley (q.v.). Served in 1st South Carolina. Pvt. acting ADC to Bonham, Feb. 1862. VADC to Stuart, May 1862 until KIA at Brandy Station, June 9, 1863. bur. Fairview Cem., Culpeper, but remains removed to Laurens City Cem. in Apr. 2002.

Farrell, John. A resident of Halifax Co., North Carolina. Capt. AQM, 24th North Carolina, Oct. 14, 1861. Capt. acting AQM to Matt. Ransom, Sept. 1863–Sept. 1864. Capt. AQM to Ransom, Oct. 31, 1864. Appx.

Faulkner, Charles James. b. Martinsburg, Virginia, July 6, 1806. att. Georgetown. Martinsburg lawyer and legislator. Minister to France, 1859. VADC to T. J. Jackson, Dec. 28, 1861, into Jan. 1862. Lt. Col. AAG to Jackson, Nov. 15, 1862. Same to Ewell. Resigned July 23, 1863. USHR and lawyer postwar. d. near Martinsburg, Nov. 1, 1884. bur. Norbourne Cem., Berkeley Co., West Virginia. Described by one colleague as "useless but highly ornamental — suave & smooth to a painful extent."

Faulkner, Charles James, Jr. b. near Martinsburg, Virginia, Sept. 21, 1847. att. school in Switzerland and Paris. Father and brother were staff officers. att. VMI, and present at New Market, possibly as VADC to Breckinridge. VADC to Wise, Mar. 1865. Appx. Lawyer, judge, and U.S. Senator. d. near Martinsburg, Jan. 13, 1929. bur. Norbourne Cem., Berkeley Co., West Virginia.

Faulkner, Elisha Boyd. b. near Martinsburg, Virginia, July 24, 1841. att. Georgetown and UVA. Also studied in Paris, and secretary to American legation there. Pvt. Wise (Va.) Arty., 1861. WIA at First Manassas. Pvt. 1st Rockbridge (Va.) Arty., July 25, 1862. Aide to Governor Letcher. Capt. AQM at Lynchburg, Feb. 1, 1863. POW June 1864, possibly at Piedmont as staff officer to W. E. Jones. Lawyer at Hopkinsville, Kentucky, and at Martinsburg. In West Virginia legislature and "accumulated a large fortune." Son of Charles J. and brother of Charles J., Jr. (q.v.). d. Martinsburg, Sept. 18, 1920. bur. Norbourne Cem., Berkeley Co., West Virginia.

Fauntleroy, Charles Magill. b. Aug. 21, 1822. Lt. USN and Mexican War veteran. Capt. CSN. Acting ADC to J. E. Johnston, 1861. Serving with navy by Nov. 1861. AAAIG to Johnston, Sept. 30, 1862, to Jan. 1863. Sent to France for CSN, Sept. 16, 1863. Married three times. Brother of T. T. Fauntleroy (q.v.). d. July 28, 1889. bur. Leesburg (Va.) Presby. Church Cem. "A very clever man with an inveterate passion for practical joking," and "excessively ugly . . . and rather vain."

Fauntleroy, Thomas Turner, Jr. b. Winchester, Virginia, Dec. 23, 1823. att. UVA. Winchester lawyer and legislator. Lt. PAVA., May 25, 1861. Staff of T. J. Jackson, 1861, duties uncertain. State secretary and member of state supreme court. Lawyer at St. Paul, Minnesota, and St. Louis, Missouri. d. St. Louis, Oct. 2, 1906. bur. Mt. Hebron Cem., Winchester. There is a chance that the man briefly on Jackson's staff actually was Fauntleroy's father, Thomas Turner Fauntleroy, Sr.

Fayssoux, James Hunter. b. in South Carolina, 1824. m. Jemima Dover. "Agent at Depot" at Yorkville. OO to Wallace in 1864,

presumably with rank of Lt. Has no official service record, which is not unusual for an ordnance officer. d. 1887. bur. Oakwood Cem., Gastonia, North Carolina, in an unmarked grave.

Fayssoux, Templar Shubrick. b. near Philadelphia, Pennsylvania, May 8, 1829. Merchant at Chester, South Carolina. Lt. ACS, DeSaussure's South Carolina Cavy., Apr. 1861. Lt. AQM, 1st Bn. South Carolina Arty. Capt. AQM, 1st Bn. South Carolina Cavy., Nov. 16, 1861. Lt. OO to N. G. Evans, Nov. 6, 1862. Capt. OO to Evans by May 1863. Capt. OO to Elliott and Wallace. Captain an unusual rank for a brigade OO. Probably never promoted beyond Lt. Appx. Brother of J. H. Fayssoux and brother-in-law of T. S. Mills (q.v.). d. Houston, Texas, Jan. 1, 1868, of yellow fever.

Featherston, Charles Nicholas. b. Heard Co., Georgia, Oct. 25, 1839. att. Emory. Schoolteacher in Polk Co. and lawyer at Rome. Capt. Co. G, 7th Georgia, May 31, 1861. Dropped May 12, 1862. VADC to his uncle Gen. Featherston at Second Manassas. Lt. of Arty., May 2, 1863, on ordnance duty in Dept. of Gulf. Lt. OO to several brigades in western army. Paroled May 12, 1865. Teacher, lawyer, and legislator at Rome. d. Seattle, Washington, Aug. 29, 1909. bur. Myrtle Hill Cem., Rome.

Feldburg, Charles P. Lt. Co. C, 14th Ky. Cavy., Apr. 1864. Lt. acting OO to Rains at Richmond, Nov. 21, 1864, into at least Mar. 1865.

Fellers, William. b. in Virginia, 1836. Of Bedford Co. Lt. Co. I, 34th Virginia, Mar. 26, 1862. Capt. AQM, 34th Virginia, July 16, 1862. Capt. AQM to B. R. Johnson, Sept. 20, 1864.

Fennelly, John. b. in Ireland. A plasterer in New Orleans. Pvt. Co. H, 14th Louisiana, July 1, 1861. To Lt., Nov. 14, 1862. Lt. AAAG to brigade, June 1863. Adjt. 14th Louisiana, Oct. 12, 1863. MWIA and POW May 19,

1864, at Spotsylvania. d. June 1, 1864. bur. Spotsylvania CSA Cem.

Ferguson, James DuGue. b. Charleston, South Carolina, May 30, 1837. att. UVA. and South Carolina Coll. Brother of Gen. S. W. Ferguson. Charleston lawyer. Capt. AAG to Fitz. Lee, July 30, 1862. Maj. AAG to Lee, Sept. 16, 1863. POW at Namozine Church, Apr. 3, 1865. Released July 24, 1865. Lawyer and bank president at Baltimore, Maryland. d. there Nov. 26, 1917. Most of Ferguson's 1864 journal has been published.

Ferguson, William Gay. b. Augusta Co., Virginia, Sept. 11, 1822. Gunmaker in Waynesboro. Mexican War veteran. Lived in Norfolk and Richmond. m. Sarah E. Small, 1849. Capt. AQM, Sept. 13, 1862. Maj. QM, Oct. 23, 1862. Served at Richmond, 1862–1865. In charge of Clothing Depot. Naval engineer on Virginia riverboats postwar. Drowned at Richmond, Dec. 8, 1909.

Ferrell, Epaproditus Thomas. b. in Virginia, Mar. 18, 1838. Salesman at Halifax C. H. Pvt. Co. C, 38th Virginia, May 30, 1861. A wardmaster at Chimborazo Hospital, Jan. 1862–June 1863. Capt. ACS, June 15, 1863, stationed at Chimborazo. Probably there until Apr. 1865. m. Mary Frayser. d. Apr. 30, 1900. bur. Greenhill Cem., Danville.

Ferry, Albert Zenon. b. New Orleans, Louisiana, December 29, 1840. A resident of St. Joseph Parish. att. Georgetown Coll. VADC to Beauregard, Mar. 1862. Capt. AAG to Hardee, Sept. 26, 1863. Capt. AAG to Beauregard, Oct. 21, 1863, until late in 1864, when he rejoined Hardee. Back with Beauregard about Jan. 1865. Dropped Feb. 21, 1865, but paroled with AOT, Apr. 26, 1865. d. Dec. 22, 1883.

Ficklin, Joseph Edward. b. Culpeper Co., Virginia, Dec. 26, 1840. att. Richmond Coll. and VMI. Part of Pony Express Line business founded by his cousin Ben Ficklin. OO to Floyd, 1861–1862. Pvt. Co. D, 4th Virginia Cavy., Apr. 1, 1862. WIA June 1862 in Stuart's Ride. Capt. ACS, 51st Virginia,

Nov. 22, 1862. Maj. CS to Wharton, May 19, 1863, through 1865. Culpeper farmer, and then a railroad contractor in Texas. Truck grower at Corpus Christi. d. Soldiers' Home at Austin, Texas, Sept. 24, 1925. bur. Texas State Cem. Spelled his name Ficklen until midwar, when he changed it because his namesake was a Unionist.

Field, Henry S. b. Culpeper Co., Virginia, Oct. 1827. Capt. AQM to A. P. Hill, Oct. 1862. Served until Appx. m. Edmonia Wiggington. Culpeper farmer. d. there July 12, 1914, his death certificate noting that he was a traveling salesman at time of death, at age 88. bur. Fairview Cem.

Field, James Gaven. b. Culpeper Co., Virginia, Feb. 24, 1826. Went to California in 1849. Secretary of that state's first Consitutional Convention. Culpeper lawyer. Pvt. Co. B, 13th Virginia, Apr. 17, 1861. Maj. QM to A. P. Hill, Mar. 23, 1862. Lost leg at Cedar Mountain. Maj. Chief QM of Third Corps until Appx. Lawyer and farmer in Albemarle Co., Virginia. State attorney general, and 1892 Populist Party vice-presidential candidate. d. May 18, 1902. bur. Fairview Cem., Culpeper.

Figures, Henry Stokes. b. in Alabama. Salesman at Huntsville. Clerk in QM Gen.'s office, 1861. Pvt. Co. F, 4th Alabama, June 10, 1861, age 18. To Sgt., Apr. 21, 1862. Adjt. 48th Alabama, May 2, 1863. Lt. AAAG to Law, Aug. 1863, duration unknown. KIA at the Wilderness, May 6, 1864. Figures's war letters are scattered among several repositories, including ADAH and Gettysburg National Military Park.

Finegan, Joseph Rutledge. b. Nassau Co., Florida, May 2, 1843. Worked for his father, Gen. Finegan, prewar. Sgt. Co. I, 2nd Florida Cavy., Mar. 1, 1862. Lt. ADC to his father, June 9, 1862, into 1865. d. Jacksonville, Apr. 9, 1871. bur. Evergreen Cem.

Finley, Howard. Pvt. Co. H, 4th Texas, May 7, 1861. To Sgt. On duty with brigade commissary department, Dec. 1861–Mar.

1863. Acting AQM to Henry's Bn. Arty., Mar. 26, 1863. Capt. AQM, Henry's Bn. Arty., Aug. 26, 1863. Capt. AQM, Haskell's Bn. Arty. Relieved Mar. 26, 1864. Capt. AQM to Hood, D. H. Hill, and S. D. Lee, 1864–1865. Paroled Apr. 26, 1865.

Finney, Randolph Harrison. b. Powhatan Co., Virginia, 1835. Educated in England. Lost an eye from an "arrow shot" as a boy. Capt. AAG to Heth, Oct. 11, 1861. Maj. AAG to Heth, June 2, 1863. Appx. Lost other eye postwar to erysipelas attack. m. Emily Creed. Was living at Richmond, Virginia, when he hanged himself with his daughter's jumprope, Feb. 25, 1901, age 65 years and 7 months. bur. Hollywood Cem.

Fiser, John Calvin. b. Dyer Co., Tennessee, May 4, 1838. Clerk and merchant in Panola Co., Mississippi. Adjt. 17th Mississippi. Said to have been Lt. AAAG to Featherston, early 1862. Lt. Col. 17th Mississippi, Apr. 26, 1862. Later promoted to Col. WIA at Gettysburg. Lost right arm at Knoxville, and retired June 12, 1864. Col. on inspection duty in Dist. of Georgia under McLaws, June 1864. Memphis merchant. d. there June 14, 1876. bur. Elmwood Cem. Surname often spelled Fizer.

Fishburne, Clement Daniels. b. Waynesboro, Virginia, May 26, 1832. att. UVA. and Washington Coll. Math professor at Davidson Coll. Sgt. 1st Co. Rockbridge (Va.) Arty., June 21, 1861. Clerk to Second Corps Judge Advocate. Lt. OO to Cabell's Bn. Arty., Feb. 25, 1864. Married twice. Lawyer, bank cashier, and newspaper editor at Charlottesville. d. there May 16, 1907. bur. Maplewood Cem. Fishburne's memoirs are at UVA.

Fisher, Thomas Frazer. Of New Orleans, Louisiana. m. Louisa Isabella Killett, 1851. Capt. Co. H, 6th Louisiana, June 4, 1861. Resigned Aug. 20, 1861, because he had been apptd. Maj. QM to Bonham, July 19, 1861. Maj. QM at Manassas, Virginia, Oct. 1861. Maj. QM to Marshall, Feb. 2, 1862.

Maj. QM to Heth, Aug. 25, 1862. Later at Dalton, Georgia. Resigned Apr. 8, 1863. Left New Orleans shortly postwar, but is bur. there at St. Louis Cem. #2.

Fite, John Amenas. b. DeKalb Co., Tennessee, Feb. 10, 1832. att. Cumberland U. A lawyer. Capt. Co. B, 7th Tennessee, May 20, 1861. To Col. by Apr. 1863. WIA at Mechanicsville, Cedar Mountain, and Chancellorsville. POW at Smithburg, July 7, 1863, while Col. VADC to "Gen. Jones," probably W. E. Jones. Banker, legislator, and state Adjt. Gen. in Tennessee. d. Lebanon, Tennessee, Aug. 23, 1925. bur. Cedar Grove Cem.

Fitzhugh, ——. VADC to D. H. Hill at Seven Pines, and perhaps later. No other record available.

Fitzhugh, Edmund Claire. b. Stafford Co., Virginia. att. USMA and Georgetown Coll. A lawyer and farmer. Living in Fairfax Co. in 1860, age 40. Capt. AAG, Nov. 2, 1863, and assigned to duty with Gen. Daniel, Dec. 7, 1863. Capt. AAIG to Hunton, Dec. 29, 1863. WIA at Hatcher's Run. Appx. U.S. Judge in Washington Territory during President Cleveland's administration.

Fitzhugh, Edward Henry. b. Caroline Co., Virginia, autumn 1816. Deputy sheriff in Fauquier Co., lawyer at Wheeling, and legislator at Richmond. Member of Virginia Secession Convention. m. Maria Gordon. Clerk of Virginia Auditing Board, June 1861. Capt. AQM, 1863, and Maj. QM, 1864, in state service. Remained in that post until 1865, stationed at Richmond. Duties were to examine claims against Virginia, and to purchase and distribute supplies to the indigent in state's war-torn counties. Postwar law partner of Gen. Wise. Judge and legislator at Richmond. d. June 26, 1890. bur. Hollywood Cem. "Intensely Virginian."

Fitzhugh, Henry Martyn. b. Dec. 12, 1835. Lt. Purcell (Va.) Arty., Apr. 20, 1861. WIA at Mechanicsville and lost leg at Malvern Hill. Lt. Inspector of Ordnance at Richmond, 1864. m. Frances Louise Edwards, Apr. 6, 1864, and d. in Brunswick Co., Virginia, Apr. 29, 1864, when he fell, opened his stump, and bled to death.

Fitzhugh, Nicholas. b. Fauquier Co., Virginia, Jan. 4, 1823. att. Marietta Coll., Ohio. Lawyer at Charleston, Virginia. Lt. Co. H, 22nd Virginia, May 22, 1861. Capt. AAG to A. G. Jenkins, Aug. 6, 1862. Capt. AAG to McCausland, May 28, 1864. Paroled May 17, 1865. Lawyer and legislator in Charleston, West Virginia. d. there Dec. 10, 1892. bur. Spring Hill Cem.

FitzHugh, Norman Richard. b. Alexandria, Virginia, Dec. 8, 1831. Cpl. Co. E, 9th Virginia Cavy. Capt. AAG to Stuart, June 21, 1862. Maj. AAG to Stuart, July 25, 1862. POW at Verdiersville, Aug. 18, 1862. Maj. QM to Stuart, May 11, 1863. Maj. QM to Hampton, Aug. 11, 1864. POW at Stony Creek, Dec. 1, 1864. Released June 4, 1865. Florida orange grower. d. there May 13, 1915. bur. Evergreen Cem., Jacksonville.

Fitzhugh, Robert Hunter. b. May 14, 1836. att. UVA. Son of famous proslavery author George Fitzhugh. A civil engineer. Topographical engineer under Holmes, Nov. 1861, to Jan. 2, 1862. Capt. EO to Pike and Churchill. POW at Arkansas Post. Capt. EO to Lt. Col. W. P. Smith, at ANVa. headquarters, June 2, 1863. Relieved from ANVa., Apr. 26, 1864. Capt. EO to Hardee by 1865. Episc. minister in Maryland. Also lived in Lexington, Kentucky. d. Nov. 17, 1919. "Tall in stature, slender in build."

Fitzpatrick, John Archer. b. Autauga, Alabama, Dec. 14, 1836. Father was a state governor. Pvt. Co. I, 3rd Alabama, Apr. 27, 1861, to July 1862. Capt. AQM, 3rd Bn. Alabama, July 3, 1862. Capt. AQM, 23rd Bn. Alabama Sharpshooters, Nov. 25, 1863. Capt. AQM to Gracie, Sept. 20, 1864. Capt. AQM to Moody, 1865. Appx.

Fitzwilson, George H. Capt. AQM, June 16, 1863. Served at Richmond, Virginia, in office of AQM Gen. Capt. AQM at Augusta,

Georgia, July 1864. Capt. AQM at Richmond again, Sept. 3, 1864. Capt. AQM to Hoke, Dec. 30, 1864, but never reported. Age 28 at the time. Recommended to be dropped for absence without leave, Mar. 1865.

Fleet, Alexander Frederick. b. King and Queen Co., Virginia, June 6, 1843. att. UVA. Professor of languages at a boys' academy in Fredericksburg. Lt. Co. I, 26th Virginia, June 13, 1861. WIA twice, May 1864. Lt. AAAG to Wise, 1863–1865. Appx. Taught postwar at several different schools in Missouri, and founded the Missouri Military Academy. d. Atlanta, Georgia, Sept. 3, 1911. Some of Fleet's war letters have been published.

Fletcher, Thomas Jefferson. b. Sumter Co., Georgia, Mar. 12, 1830. Planter at Forsyth all his life. Lt. Co. K, 53rd Georgia. WIA in arm at Knoxville. Lt. acting QM to Simms at Appx. m. Rebecca Ellen McCowen. d. Oct. 24, 1892. bur. McCowen Fam. Cem., Monroe Co., Georgia.

Flood, Joel Walker. b. Appomattox Co., Virginia, Jan. 9, 1839. att. Emory & Henry and UVA. In state legislature. Capt. Co. H, 2nd Virginia Cavy. Dropped Apr. 1862. VADC to Kemper at Second Manassas. Lt. ADC to Kemper, Jan. 30, 1864. Resigned May 16, 1864. Farmer in Appomattox Co. m. Sallie Whiteman Delk. d. Appomattox Co., Nov. 1, 1916.

Flowers, William Blanchard. b. Oct. 30, 1824. Married twice prewar. Lt. Co. H, 1st (Hagood's) South Carolina, July 20, 1861. Capt. AQM to regiment, Apr. 12, 1862. Capt. AQM to J. A. Walker, Oct. 31, 1864, through at least Jan. 1865. Paroled Apr. 26, 1865, as Capt. AQM to Brantly's Bgd. d. ca. 1870. bur. Smyrna Church Cem., Allendale Co., South Carolina.

Floyd, Charles. Capt. AQM, Oct. 10, 1861. Served around Manassas, 1861–1862. Dropped under Special Order #44. An unofficial source says he was Capt. AQM to Pickett early in the war.

Foard, Frederick Cicero. b. Concord, North Carolina, Apr. 15, 1844. att. UNC. In Co. A, 20th North Carolina, Apr. 1861. Sgt. Co. F, 1st North Carolina Cavy., Nov. 4, 1863. Lt. ADC to Barringer, June 15, 1864. POW June 21, 1864. Escaped July 1864. POW at Namozine Church, Apr. 3, 1865. Released June 10, 1865. Lived in Roanoke, Virginia, and in Los Angeles, California. d. San Diego, Apr. 27, 1922. Foard's memoirs are at NCDAH.

Folsom, Henderson Mitchell. b. Greene Co., Tennessee, Oct. 4, 1831. An attorney. Maj. QM to A. E. Jackson, Feb. 9, 1863. Maj. QM to Col. George S. Patton's old brigade, Oct. 1864. Maj. QM Thomas's (N.C.) Legion, Jan. 1865. m. Sarah Berry Shryock. Lawyer at Elizabethton, Tennessee. d. there, Aug. 13, 1908.

Fontaine, Peter. b. Hanover Co., Virginia, Apr. 20, 1840. att. UVA. Hanover Co. lumber dealer. Pvt. Co. F, 4th Virginia Cavy., May 9, 1861. Adjt. 4th Virginia Cavy., June 3, 1862. WIA in neck at Kelly's Ford. Capt. AAG to Wickham, Sept. 11, 1863. Capt. AAG to Rosser, Jan. 1865. Lawyer and schoolteacher in Louisa Co., Virginia, and at Charleston, West Virginia. m. Mrs. Lydia Whittaker Laidley, 1879. d. at Charleston, 1908.

Fontaine, William Morris. b. Hanover Co., Virginia, Dec. 1, 1835. att. UVA. Professor at Hanover Academy. Lt. Hanover Arty. Lt. acting OO to H. P. Jones's Bn. Arty., Feb. 1863. Lt. OO to Jones's Bn., June 14, 1864. Lt. OO for Anderson's corps by Dec. 1864. Capt. OO (to Anderson?), Jan. 1865. Paroled Apr. 1865 at Richmond, listed as Chief OO of Third Corps. Studied at Freiburg Mining Academy in Heidelburg, Germany. Professor of chemistry and geology at West Virginia Univ. and UVA. Published widely in his field. d. Apr. 30, 1913. bur. Beaver Dam Church, Hanover Co.

Foote, George Pratt. b. in Mississippi. att. UMiss. A 23-year-old attorney at Panola in

1860. Capt. Co. H, 17th Mississippi. Capt. AAG to Featherston, May 1, 1862. Acting on staff of Garland at Seven Pines, in Featherston's absence. KIA at Gaines's Mill, June 27, 1862. bur. Oakwood Cem., Richmond.

Foote, Romley Erskine. A resident of Davidson Co., Tennessee. Lt. Jackson (Tenn.) Btty., by Aug. 1861. Dropped at reorganization, spring 1862. Capt. AAG to McNair, Nov. 1, 1862. Capt. AAG to B. R. Johnson, Feb. 1864. Maj. AAG to Johnson, Jan. 27, 1865. POW at Namozine Church, Apr. 3, 1865.

Footman, Robert Habersham. b. in Georgia, Oct. 17, 1836. Capt. AQM, 1st Bn. Georgia Sharpshooters, 5th Georgia Cavy., and 18th Bn. Georgia Inf. Capt. AQM to J. A. Walker, Sept. 5, 1864. Capt. AQM to Robert H. Anderson, Feb. 7, 1865. Paroled Apr. 26, 1865. Savannah life insurance agent. d. June 4, 1889. bur. Laurel Grove Cem.

Forbes, Francis Thornton. b. Falmouth, Virginia, Aug. 11, 1826. Stafford Co. merchant and Spotsylvania Co. farmer. Pvt. 30th Virginia, 1861. Capt. ACS, Sept. 23, 1862. Served in Richmond, 1862–1865. Capt. ACS to Ewell, Aug. 16, 1864. Maj. CS, Feb. 15, 1865. Paroled Apr. 23, 1865. Fredericksburg postmaster. d. Nov. 22, 1904. bur. Fredericksburg City Cem.

Forbes, Horatio W. b. Habersham Co., Georgia, Mar. 1830. Hotelkeeper at Sparta. m. Sarah F. Pinkston, 1858. Served in Co. K, 15th Georgia, before becoming Capt. AQM for regiment, Sept. 30, 1861. Capt. AQM to Benning, Sept. 15, 1864. Paroled at Augusta, Georgia, May 20, 1865. Suffered during war "from something like paralysis or rheumatism" and feet paralyzed by war's end. Planned to start a hack service at Milledgeville in 1865. d. Sparta, Georgia, Mar. 6, 1866.

Forbes, James Fitzgerald. b. Falmouth, Virginia, Sept. 1828. att. VMI. A lawyer. Pvt. and ACS 9th Virginia Cavy., possibly with later rank of Capt. VADC to A. P. Hill at

Chancellorsville. KIA May 2, 1863. bur. on Bridgewater Street in Fredericksburg. An uncle of M. F. Taylor (q.v.).

Forbes, Joseph Harris. b. St. Mary's Co., Maryland, Dec. 20, 1837. att. Princeton. Pvt. 1st Maryland Arty. Capt. AQM to Andrews's Bn. Arty., Feb. 28, 1863, and later to Braxton's Bn. Arty. Convicted in Mar. 1864 for stealing a stove from a church.

Force, Charles Fairchild. b. Washington, D.C., Feb. 9, 1827. Served in 1st Virginia Inf. in Mexican War. 5th Alabama. Maj. CS to Rodes, Nov. 6, 1861. Resigned Mar. 1, 1862. Adjt. and later Capt. 51st Ala. Partisan Cavy. Paroled May 12, 1865, as a Capt. AAG. Selma, Alabama, hardware merchant. d. there Aug. 5, 1884. bur. Live Oak Cem.

Force, Henry Clay. b. Washington, D.C., May 13, 1832. att. Harvard. Pvt. and Sgt. Co. H, 5th Alabama, Apr. 1861–Apr. 1862. Lt. EO to Rodes, Aug. 6, 1862. Lt. EO to Bragg by Jan. 1863. Capt. EO, Mar. 17, 1864. Paroled May 10, 1865, in Mississippi. m. Katharine O. Frierson. Civil engineer in Alabama. d. Carthage, Alabama, Feb. 7, 1874, of consumption.

Ford, Edwin Augustus. b. May 12, 1836. att. Harvard. Civil engineer at Canton, Mississippi. Sgt. Madison (Miss.) Arty. Lt. EO, Sept. 15, 1862. Staff of G. W. Smith, Nov. 1862, and probably to Elzey in 1863. Lt. EO to G. J. Rains, Maury, and in AOT. POW in Alabama, Apr. 8, 1865, on staff of Liddell. Canton civil engineer. d. Aug. 14, 1898. bur. Canton City Cem.

Ford, James W. VADC to D. R. Jones at First Manassas. Lt. ADC to Jones, Aug. 24, 1861. Position vacated by death of Jones, Jan. 1863. May have been on staff of Bratton subsequently.

Forrest, Douglas French. b. Aug. 17, 1837. att. Yale and UVA. A lawyer. Pvt. Co. H, 17th Virginia, Apr. 17, 1861. Lt. acting ADC to Trimble, Sept. 1861–Jan. 1862. VADC to Admiral Buchanan on the *CSS Virginia*. Resigned from 17th Virginia, May 6, 1862.

Asst. Paymaster, CSN, 1862. Lawyer at Baltimore, Maryland, and then an Episc. rector at Cincinnati. d. May 3, 1902. bur. Congressional Cem., Washington, D.C. Forrest's papers are at the Library of Virginia.

Forrest, John. b. July 13, 1838. Of Charleston, South Carolina. Pvt. Washington (S.C.) Arty., Feb. 20, 1862. Detached on signal duty. Lt. OO, May 2, 1863, and serving in ANVa. Lt. OO to Hays, Aug. 7, 1863. Lt. OO to York, late in the war. Appx. A physician. d. Feb. 28, 1916. bur. First Presby. Churchyard, Charleston. "He looks and talks like a young girl from boarding school," wrote a Confederate general during the war.

Forsberg, Ludwig August. b. Stockholm, Sweden, Jan. 13, 1832. att. Stockholm School of Engineering. Baltimore, Maryland, engineer and draughtsman. Volunteer EO to Floyd, July–Oct. 1861. Lt. of Inf., Oct. 11, 1861, still serving as EO to Floyd. Lt. EO to Wharton, Feb. 1862. Lt. Col. 51st Virginia, May 1862, and later Col. WIA at Third Winchester. d. Lynchburg, Virginia, July 15, 1910. bur. Presby. Cem.

Foster, Thomas Redman. b. Fauquier Co., Virginia, Apr. 2, 1817. Farmer and merchant at The Plains. Agent for commissary dept. Capt. ACS, Aug. 25, 1863, operating in Virginia. Paroled May 7, 1865, at Winchester. d. Jan. 22, 1896. bur. Fauquier Co.

Foster, William Edward. b. Williamsburg, Virginia, Sept. 1, 1825. Richmond gunsmith and Norfolk newspaperman. In charge of armory and laboratory at Norfolk, 1861. OO to Huger, possibly as a volunteer. Lt. OO, July 24, 1862. In charge of ordnance repair shops at Danville. Lt. OO to G. W. C. Lee, 1864–1865. WIA around Richmond in 1864. Paroled Apr. 26, 1865, at Burkeville. Norfolk plumber, gas fitter, and furniture dealer. In state legislature. d. Norfolk, Aug. 28, 1901.

Fouche, Robert T. b. Oct. 29, 1835. att. UGA. An attorney at Rome, Georgia. Lt. Co. A, 8th Georgia. Lt. acting ADC to G. T. Anderson, Jan., Sept., and Nov. 1864, at least. WIA at Second Manassas, at Dandridge, and at Fussell's Mill. Maj. 8th Confederate Inf. Postwar lawyer and legislator in Georgia. Ran Rome Military Academy. d. Mar. 1, 1908. bur. Myrtle Hill Cem.

Fowle, William Henry, Sr. b. Alexandria, Virginia, Oct. 19, 1808. att. Harvard. Disfigured in 1827 duel. Introduced water and gas to Alexandria. Commission merchant there. Capt. ACS, PAVa., May 3, 1861. Capt. ACS to Beauregard, Apr.–July 1861. Capt. ACS at Manassas Junction, July–Aug. 1861. Capt. ACS at Orange C.H., Aug. 1861–Feb. 1862. Out of service subsequently. m. Eliza Thacker Hooe. Alexandria banker. d. there Oct. 4, 1869. bur. St. Paul's Churchyard.

Fowler, William Shelton. b. Cumberland Co., Virginia, Dec. 12, 1810. Physician there until 1835. m. Martha Anderson Shelton, 1835. Louisa Co. farmer. Volunteer aide to Governor Letcher. In state legislature. VADC to Pickett at Seven Pines and Gaines's Mill. No other wartime service found. Louisa Co. farmer in 1870. Probably died around 1885.

France, Spencer L. b. in Washington, D.C. att. Georgetown Coll. A wealthy 25-year-old farmer in Talbot Co., Maryland, in 1860. Pvt. King William (Va.) Arty., Aug. 13, 1862. Acting AAG to Col. T. H. Carter, 1863–1864, as a private. Capt. AAG to Carter, 1864. WIA at Strasburg, Oct. 13, 1864. POW in Goochland Co., Apr. 3, 1865. Merchant at Baltimore, Maryland, in 1870. d. Sumter, South Carolina, Dec. 3, 1876.

Francis, James, Jr. b. in Virginia. Pvt. Co. C, 36th Virginia, June 3, 1861, age 30. To Lt., May 15, 1862. Lt. AAAG to "4th Bgd." in the Shenandoah Valley, May 1864. Lt. OO to Smith's Bgd., of Wharton's division, Dec. 1864. Farmer at Marsh Fork in Raleigh Co., West Virginia, in 1870.

Francisco, Robert LaFayette. b. in Alabama, ca. 1825. A cabinetmaker at Blacksburg, Virginia. m. Keziah Black. Pvt. Co. E, 4th Virginia, Apr. 18, 1861. Capt. AQM, 4th Virginia, June 1, 1862. Capt. AQM to William

Terry, Sept. 15, 1864. Appx. d. Blacksburg, Virginia, Aug. 9, 1886.

Frank, Samuel. b. in Wurtemberg. Merchant at Holly Springs, Mississippi, prewar. Pvt. in 17th Mississippi, May 27, 1861, age 30. Later QM Sgt. Capt. AQM, 17th Mississippi, Mar. 1, 1862. Capt. AQM to Humphreys, Sept. 15, 1864. Appx.

Franklin, Jacob Henry. b. Pittsylvania Co., Virginia, Apr. 28, 1836. Lynchburg clerk and merchant. Pvt. Co. G, 11th Virginia, June 28, 1861. Detached in Commissary Dept., 1861–1863. Capt. ACS, May 23, 1863, to serve at First Corps headquarters. Capt. ACS to Alexander by Mar. 1865. Maj. CS, Mar. 2, 1865. Appx. Lynchburg salesman and grocer. d. there Apr. 29, 1898.

Franklin, Peter A. b. Richmond, Virginia. Lt. Parker's (Va.) Btty., Mar. 14, 1862, age 23. Capt. AQM to Alexander's Bn. Arty., Oct. 14, 1862. Court-martialed over some matter concerning a horse. Cashiered, June 4, 1864. Served with Mosby's 43rd Bn. Virginia Cavy. Postwar merchant at Brooklyn, New York. d. there Nov. 28, 1914. bur. Moravian Cem., New Dorp Township, Staten Island.

Fraser, James Ladson. b. Beaufort, South Carolina, July 18, 1840. att. UVA. VADC to Sam. Jones, Aug. 9, 1861–Apr. 28, 1862. Lt. ADC to Jones, Apr. 28, 1862. Paroled May 12, 1865, at Tallahassee, Florida. Bookkeeper at Charleston in the 1870s.

Frayser, Richard Edgar. b. New Kent Co., Virginia, Oct. 1830. A merchant. Served in Co. F, 3rd Virginia Cavy. Pvt. VADC to Stuart, June 1862. POW at Fallsville, July 6, 1862. Capt. SO to Stuart, Sept. 1, 1862. POW at Spotsylvania, May 20, 1864. Immortal 600. Probably on the staff of Wise very late in the war. Richmond newspaperman and lawyer. d. there Dec. 22, 1899. bur. Hollywood Cem.

Freaner, George. b. Hagerstown, Maryland, Jan. 20, 1831. att. Dickinson Coll. Lawyer and newspaperman. Lived in California for a time before the war. In the Maryland legislature. Adjt. 1st Virginia Cavy. Lt. AAAG to Fitz. Lee, late in 1862 and into 1863. Maj. AAIG to Stuart, Nov. 2, 1863. Maj. AAIG to Fitz Lee, May–Aug. 1864. Maj. AAIG to Hampton, Aug. 11, 1864. Served briefly again with Fitz. Lee, Jan.–Feb. 1865. Lawyer and legislator in Maryland. d. Hagerstown, Nov. 10, 1878. bur. Rose Hill Cem.

Frederic, H. C. A resident of New Orleans, Louisiana. Sgt. Co. B, Crescent (La.) Regiment, Mar. 5, 1862. Later a Lt. in 18th Louisiana. Lt. SO, date unknown. Exact duty in Virginia unknown. POW at Drewry's Bluff, May 17, 1864. Escaped from Ft. Delaware, July 1, 1864. Paroled as Lt. SO, June 3, 1865, at Alexandria, Louisiana.

Freeland, John Duncan. b. New Orleans, Louisiana, May 20, 1843. att. VMI. VADC to Hays, summer 1862. WIA at Gettysburg, July 2, 1863. Lt. Drillmaster, Aug. 1, 1864, serving under Ewell. Appx. A tobacconist. d. Richmond, Virginia, May 18, 1872. bur. Hollywood Cem.

French, Samuel Bassett. b. Norfolk, Virginia, Mar. 21, 1820. att. Hampden Sidney. Lawyer at Berryville and in Chesterfield Co. Asst. clerk in state legislature. Aide and private secretary to Governors Wise, Letcher, and Smith. VADC to T. J. Jackson at Romney and Aug. 16 to Sept. 1862. Richmond newspaperman. d. Apr. 25, 1898. bur. Maury Cem., Manchester, Virginia. Known as "Chester." His memoirs have been published.

French, Seth Barton. b. Spotsylvania Co., Virginia, Oct. 1832. Merchant at Fredericksburg. Capt. ACS (PAVA.) to Ruggles, May 4–June 7, 1861. Capt. ACS (PACS), June 29, 1861. Maj. CS to Holmes, Sept. 24, 1861. Maj. CS to G. W. Smith, May 1862. Maj. CS to Stevenson, July 28, 1862. Maj. CS to Smith again, Aug. 30, 1862. Maj. CS to Northrop, and then to St. John by Feb. 1865. Asst. Commissary Gen., CSA. New York

merchant and New Orleans cotton broker. d. Palm Beach, Florida, Feb. 17, 1910. bur. Fredericksburg Confederate Cem.

Frensley, John L. b. Camden Co., North Carolina, 1838. Pvt. Co. B, 32nd North Carolina, 1861. Capt. AQM, 32nd North Carolina, Nov. 29, 1861. Capt. acting AQM to Grimes, Sept. 15, 1864. May have received official appointment as Capt. AQM to Grimes in Mar. 1865. Appx.

Friend, John Wesley. b. Boligee, Greene Co., Alabama, Mar. 20, 1842. att. UAla. and Howard Coll. Pvt. Co. B, 11th Alabama, May 27, 1861. Acting Lt. and Asst. to Chief OO of Third Corps, 1864. Lt. OO, Jan. 7, 1865, serving at Third Corps headquarters. Took Oath May 9, 1865. Practiced law at Newport News and Petersburg, Virginia. d. Richmond, Virginia, Oct. 28, 1915.

Fristoe, Mark Reid. b. Jan. 7, 1838. Pvt. Co. G, 49th Virginia, July 22, 1861. Sgt. by mid-1863. WIA at Gettysburg. To Lt., Dec. 1, 1864, but served as Lt. OO to Pegram's Bgd. (commanded by colonels) from Dec. 1864 until Appx. Postmaster at Phoenix, Maryland. d. there Dec. 30, 1919. bur. Clynmalira M.E. Church Cem.

Frobel, Bushrod Washington. b. near Alexandria, Virginia, 1826. A civil engineer in U.S. Revenue Service prewar. Served on *Harriet Lane* during trip to Paraguay, 1858–1859. In CSN early war. Lt. of Arty., Oct. 7, 1861, to command "Cockpit Battery" on Potomac River. Staff of Whiting during Seven Days. Maj. of Arty., July 22, 1862, and Chief of Arty. to Hood. Maj. Chief of Arty. to Whiting, Nov. 8, 1862. Lt. Col. of Arty., June 15, 1863. Lt. Col. on engineer duty with AOT, 1864–1865. Supt. of Public Works in Georgia. d. Monticello, Georgia, July 12, 1888. bur. Oakland Cem., Atlanta, but probably removed soon thereafter.

Frobel, David W. b. in Virginia. Brother of Bushrod W. Frobel. One of Walker's filibusters. Tried to raise a guerilla company at Richmond in June 1861. Instead served as

Master's Mate in CSN around Richmond, 1861–1862. Discharged Mar. 5, 1862. Acting Lt. on staff of Holmes, Mar. 1862. Lt 18th Bn. Virginia Heavy Arty., Mar. 8, 1862. Lt. PACS, Apr. 5, 1864, and acting OO, 18th Bn. Virginia Heavy Arty. Lt. acting OO to J. A. Walker, 1865. Living in Fairfax Co., 1870, at Fernandina, Florida, in 1874, and at Thomasville, Georgia, in 1879.

Frost, Elias Horry. b. Charleston, South Carolina, Nov. 12, 1827. att. Yale. Charleston merchant. Pvt. Marion (S.C.) Arty. Capt. ACS, 6th South Carolina Cavy., Nov. 1, 1862. Capt. ACS to Hagood, July 1, 1863. Paroled Apr. 26, 1865. m. Frances Ravenel. d. Sept. 4, 1897. bur. Magnolia Cem., Charleston.

Fry, William T. b. ca. 1838, probably at Mobile, Alabama. att. VMI. Adjt. 1st Virginia, May 3, 1862. Capt. AAG to Kemper, June 14, 1862. WIA at Gettysburg. With Kemper at Richmond in 1864. m. Emma Jones. Cotton merchant at Mobile and New Orleans postwar. Fry's mother married Samuel Lewis, whose house was on the Port Republic battlefield.

Fulton, John Hall. b. in Virginia, July 17, 1837. Lawyer at Wytheville. Lt. Co. A, 4th Virginia, Apr. 17, 1861. To Capt., Apr. 22, 1862. Capt. AAAG to Stonewall Bgd. at Cedar Mountain. WIA in two places at Brawner's Farm. Lost leg at Chancellorsville. Discharged Aug. 1, 1863. Wytheville circuit court judge. d. Jan. 7, 1907. bur. Wytheville.

Funkhouser, Milton Pifer. b. Shenandoah Co., Virginia, Mar. 17, 1836. Staunton merchant. Capt. AQM at Staunton, by June 1862. Pvt. Co. E, 19th Bn. Virginia Heavy Arty., 1862. Pvt. Co. A, 39th Bn. Virginia Cavy., Jan. 1864 through 1865. Staunton dry goods merchant. d. there June 9, 1897. bur. Thornrose Cem.

Furlow, Charles Timothy. b. Bibb Co., Georgia, Apr. 15, 1842. att. Emory and Mercer Univ. Pvt. Co. K, 4th Georgia, May 27,

1861. Orderly to Gen. Doles. WIA at Gettysburg. Lt. ADC to Doles, Nov. 2, 1863. WIA in head at Spotsylvania, May 10, 1864. Service after Doles's death in June 1864 not clear. Worked in Georgia treasury office. d. Clarkesville, Georgia, Sept. 3, 1919. bur. Americus, Georgia.

Gage, Robert S. b. Henderson Co., North Carolina, Sept. 29, 1833. Laborer, teacher, and clerk. Capt. ACS for state of North Carolina. Maj. CS to Clingman, Nov. 27, 1862. Paroled at Greensboro, Apr. 26, 1865. Lawyer in Madison Co., postwar. d. Marshall, Aug. 30, 1883. bur. County Home Cem.

Gaillard, Richard Walter. b. May 16, 1830. att. SCMA. Planter at Winnsboro, South Carolina. Capt. AQM, 12th South Carolina, May 1, 1862. Capt. AQM to Wilcox, by Sept. 15, 1864. m. Frances A. Boyce. d. Feb. 8, 1905. bur. Episc. Cem., Winnsboro.

Gaines, James Luttrell. b. Knoxville, Tennessee, Dec. 3, 1839. att. UNC. Lt. Co. G, 1st North Carolina Cavy., Aug. 15, 1861. To Adjt., Apr. 15, 1862. WIA at Willis Church, June 29, 1862. Capt. AAG to Baker, July 23, 1863. Same to James B. Gordon and Barringer. Lt. Col. 2nd North Carolina Cavy., Mar. 1, 1865. Lost arm at Chamberlain's Run. Tennessee state comptroller and railroad executive. d. Sept. 19, 1910. bur. Old Gray Cem., Knoxville.

Gales, Seaton. b. Raleigh, North Carolina, May 17, 1828. att. UNC. Wake Co. lawyer and newspaper editor. Adjt. 14th North Carolina, June 1861. Capt. AAG to G. B. Anderson, Aug. 19, 1862. Capt. AAG to Ramseur, Nov. 1862, and to Cox, May 1864. POW at Fisher's Hill. d. Washington, D.C., Nov. 29, 1878. bur. Oakwood Cem., Raleigh. *Our Living and Our Dead* magazine published Gales's war diary serially in 1874.

Gallaway, Alexander Henderson. b. Rockingham Co., North Carolina, Oct. 7, 1838. att. UNC. Capt. Co. F, 45th North Carolina,

Mar. 1862. WIA at Gettysburg, July 3, 1863. Maj. QM to Scales, Oct. 25, 1863. Appx. Lived at Reidsville, where he was a tobacco salesman, postmaster, mayor, and county sheriff. m. Sally Scales. d. Dec. 22, 1921. bur. Greenview Cem.

Galt, John Allan. b. Fluvanna Co., Virginia, Feb. 17, 1834. att. VMI and UVA. A lawyer. Pvt. Co. I, 4th Virginia Cavy., June 1861. Lt. ADC to J. G. Walker, about Feb. 1862. Capt. OO to Walker, Feb. 17, 1863. Capt. AAIG to Walker, late 1864. Paroled June 21, 1865, at Houston. Postwar farmer. d. at Lee Camp Soldiers' Home, Richmond, Virginia, Jan. 15, 1902. bur. Hollywood Cem.

Galt, John Minson. b. Williamsburg, Virginia, 1810. att. Wm. & Mary and Medical Coll. of Pennsyvania. A physician, and then served in Old Army as MSK, 1842–1861. Capt. ACS, Mar. 16, 1861. Served with Twiggs at New Orleans, 1861. Capt. ACS to Polk, July 1861. Capt. ACS at Lynchburg, Virginia, July 31, 1861. Maj. CS at Lynchburg, Aug. 10, 1863. Relieved Mar. 24, 1865. d. at Lynchburg in 1869.

Gantt, Richard Plantagenet. b. Barnwell Dist., Dec. 10, 1834. Capt. AQM, 11th South Carolina, June 9, 1862. Capt. AQM to Hagood, Sept. 20, 1864. Paroled Apr. 26, 1865. Walterboro planter. m. Ella Elliott Mackay. d. Barnwell Co., July 13, 1919. bur. Boiling Springs Presby. Church, Lyndhurst, South Carolina.

Garber, Alexander Menzies, Jr. b. Staunton, Virginia, ca. 1837. Newspaper editor and publisher at Okalona, Mississippi, prewar. Pvt. in 11th Mississippi, Mar.–Sept. 1861. Capt. AQM to T. J. Jackson, Jan. 4, 1862. Capt. AQM to Ewell, probably June 1863. Maj. QM to Ewell, Apr. 5, 1864, but failed bond. Capt. AQM to Early, summer 1864. Capt. AQM on duty with ANVa. forage dept., Sept. 15, 1864. Capt. AQM, McGregor's Bn. Horse Arty., Mar. 27, 1865. m. Aurelia Elizabeth Baldwin, 1864. Edited a Staunton newspaper and then moved to

Texas and was a newspaperman. d. Dallas, Texas, Dec. 20, 1879, on the street, in a snowstorm. bur. Greenwood Cem. Garber was "poor, very poor" late in life. His short biography of John A. Harman (see below) was published in 1876.

Gardner, Fleming. b. Montgomery Co., Virginia, Oct. 24, 1815. att. Georgetown Coll. A civil engineer and Mexican War veteran. Capt. PAVa., 1861. Capt. AAAG to Early at First Manassas. Capt. AAG to Early, Sept. 11, 1861. Resigned July 13, 1862. Capt. EO, Apr. 3, 1864, to report to ANVa. Declined, Aug. 20, 1864, and may not have served as such. Civil engineer in the Carolinas, Georgia, and Texas. Alive 1887 at Christiansburg, Virginia.

Garland, Alexander Boyd. b. Mar. 28, 1816. Lived in Mississippi, and in Montgomery Co., Missouri, prewar. m. Fanny E. Nowlin, 1840. Lived at Lynchburg, Virginia, in 1850s. Maj. CS to his cousin (once removed) Gen. Garland, June 18, 1862. Maj. CS to Iverson, late 1862. Maj. CS to R. D. Johnston, summer 1863. Relieved May 3, 1864, to report to Commissary Dept. in North Carolina. Maj. CS at Liberty, Virginia, July 30, 1864. Served until end of war. Alive 1871 at Lynchburg, Virginia. Garland's brother was Col. of the 6th Texas Inf., and his son was a staff officer in the AOT.

Garland, J. Maury. Capt. AQM, June 29, 1861. Served at Richmond and was AQM for disbursements, 1861. Dropped, date unknown. Probably the J. M. Garland living in 1870 in Prince George Co., Virginia, age 56, a railroad agent.

Garland, Maurice Hamner. b. Mecklenburg Co., Virginia, May 14, 1841. att. UAla., where his father was president. Lt. Co. I, 3rd Alabama. Served in Co. E, 2nd Virginia Cavy., Apr. 1862. Lt. ADC to his cousin Gen. Garland, June 18, 1862. Lt. EO at Mobile, May 11, 1863. Lt. Co. C, 2nd Engineers, 1864–1865. Staff of Liddell. Lynchburg city surveyor and Amherst Co. farmer.

d. Jan. 26, 1908. bur. Lynchburg Presby. Cem.

Garnett, James Mercer. b. Aldie, Virginia, Apr. 24, 1840. att. UVA. Lt. of Inf., PAVA., Nov. 9, 1861. Lt. OO to T. J. Jackson, Jan. 1862. Lt. OO to C. S. Winder, Apr. 20, 1862. Lt. OO (PACS), June 2, 1862. Stayed with Stonewall Bgd. at least through Sharpsburg. Capt. (temp.) OO, Dec. 24, 1862. Staff of Taliaferro. Lt. commanding reserve ordnance train, ANVA, by early 1863. Capt. OO to Rodes, by 1864, and to Rodes's successors. Appx. Professor at Louisiana State Univ. and president of St. John's College in Annapolis. d. Baltimore, Maryland, Feb. 18, 1916. bur. Sharon Baptist Cem., Middleburg, Virginia. A brother of T. S. Garnett (q.v.) and a cousin of the two Confederate generals named Garnett.

Garnett, John Jameson. b. Westmoreland Co., Virginia, May 1839. att. USMA. Lt. of Arty., Mar. 16, 1861. Lt. Washington (La.) Arty., June 20, 1861. Maj. Chief of Arty. to D. R. Jones, June 25, 1862. Maj. Inspector of Arty., First Corps, Nov. 14, 1862. Commanded a battalion at Fredericksburg and through Feb. 1864. Lt. Col. of Arty., Mar. 2, 1863. Chief of Arty. to R. H. Anderson at Chancellorsville. Relieved for incompetence, Apr. 1, 1864. Post commander at Hicksford, Sept. 1864. Lt. Col. Inspector of Arty. for AOT, Nov. 30, 1864. New York newspaper editor. Committed suicide at New York City, Sept. 10, 1902.

Garnett, Theodore Stanford, Jr. b. Richmond, Virginia, Oct. 28, 1844. att. UVA. Navy Dept. clerk early in the war. Pvt. Co. F, 9th Virginia Cavy., May 15, 1863. Lt. ADC to Stuart, Jan. 27, 1864. Lt. Drillmaster for W. H. F. Lee, May 30, 1864. Lt. AAAG to Roberts, by Mar. 1865. Paroled at Ashland, Apr. 21, 1865. Married twice. Norfolk lawyer. d. there Apr. 27, 1915. bur. Elmwood Cem. Garnett's memoirs were published recently.

Garrison, George Glenn. b. Bayville, Prin-cess Anne Co., Virginia, Aug. 5, 1830. att. VMI. A farmer. Capt. AAG to Colston, Jan. 4, 1862. Probably staff of Huger, early 1862. WIA at Seven Pines. Capt. AAG to French, Dec. 6, 1862. Capt. AAG to Colston again, Apr. 4, 1863. Capt. AAG to Steuart, summer 1863. On duty at Petersburg, Sept. 16, 1863. Farmer and fishery owner in Princess Anne Co. d. there Apr. 27, 1879.

Gary, Summerfield Massilon Glenn. b. in South Carolina, Oct. 10, 1826. att. South Carolina Coll. Lawyer at Ocala, Florida, and member of state secession convention. Capt. Co. G, 9th Florida. Lt. ADC to his brother, Gen. Gary, Aug. 11, 1864. Appx. Mayor of Ocala. d. there Dec. 20, 1886. bur. Evergreen Cem.

Gary, William Theodore. b. Cokesbury, South Carolina, Oct. 10, 1841. att. South Carolina Coll. Capt. ACS, Hampton (S.C.) Legion, July 29, 1862. Capt. ACS at Mount Pleasant, South Carolina, Aug. 1, 1863. Dropped June 14, 1864, for delayed non-confirmation. Maj. CS to his brother, Gen. Gary, July 19, 1864. Practiced law with his brother at Edgefield, South Carolina, 1866–1875, and then lawyer, judge, and politician at Augusta, Georgia. d. there May 5, 1904. bur. Magnolia Cem.

Gatling, John Thomas, Jr. b. Gates Co., North Carolina, Feb. 8, 1840. att. UNC. A farmer. Lt. Co. C, 52nd North Carolina, Apr. 1862, and Capt. AQM, Dec. 1, 1862. Capt. AQM to MacRae, Sept. 15, 1864. Appx. Farmer and legislator. d. May 6, 1888.

Gee, Stirling Harwell, Jr. b. 1843. A resident of Halifax Co., North Carolina. Capt. Co. K, 1st North Carolina, May 16, 1861. WIA in thigh at Chancellorsville. Capt. AAIG to Matt. Ransom, Dec. 5, 1863. m. Sarah Bridgman Austin, 1865. KIA at Five Forks, Apr. 1, 1865, when mistakenly shot by men of the 26th South Carolina. Available sources are about divided on spelling of first name, some having it as

Sterling. Gee appears to have signed his name, however, as "Stir."

George, Moses B. Pvt. Co. D, 4th Texas, July 4, 1861, age about 27. Maj. QM to Wigfall, Dec. 20, 1861. Maj. QM to Hood, 1862. Possibly staff of Archer, too. Maj. QM to S. D. Lee, 1864. Paroled with AOT, Apr. 26, 1865. Described by a soldier in the 4th as "social plain and agreeable."

Getty, G. Thomas. Lt. OO to R. S. Garnett, July 11, 1861. Lt. OO at Monterey, Virginia, Aug. 1861. Lt. OO at Lynchburg, Virginia, Mar. 1862 into 1865.

Gibbon, Nicholas Biddle. b. Nov. 28, 1837. att. Jefferson Medical Coll. Brother of Union Gen. John Gibbon. Pvt. 1st North Carolina (Bethel). Capt. ACS, 28th North Carolina, Oct. 18, 1861. Capt. acting CS to Branch, Aug. 5, 1862, to Sharpsburg, and then to Lane until Jan. 1863. Capt. ACS to Wilcox, Aug. 24, 1863. Capt. ACS, Feb. 1865, for an ANVa. detachment chasing deserters in North Carolina. d. Oct. 17, 1917. bur. Sugar Creek Presby. Churchyard, Mecklenburg Co.

Gibbons, William Heyward. b. New York City, May 1831. att. UVa. Planter at Savannah, Georgia. Capt. AQM, 2nd Bn. Georgia, Mar. 11, 1862. Maj. QM to Lawton, June 11, 1862. Maj. IFT, Dept. of South Carolina, Dec. 15, 1862. Same at Richmond, Dec. 18, 1863, through 1865. Savannah rice planter. d. Madison, New Jersey, June 9, 1887. bur. Hillside Cem. A "most gentlemanly" officer with "charming manners."

Gibson, Gustavus A. b. in Georgia. A 24-year-old teacher at Canton, Mississippi, in 1860. Lt. Co. G, 18th Mississippi, Apr. 23, 1861. Lt. AAIG to Barksdale, May 1863. KIA at Gettysburg, July 2, 1863.

Gibson, William Eyre. b. in Maryland, Aug. 25, 1841. att. VMI and USMA. Father was a Confederate surgeon. Apptd. Cadet, 1861, to report to J. E. Johnston, July 29, 1861. To report to R. E. Lee, Dec. 7, 1861. Cadet Co. C, 15th Bn. South Carolina Arty.,

until Sept. 1862. Lt. in Dept. of Texas, 1863–1865. Commanded Gibson's (Tex.) Btty. Capt. OO to Huger's Bn. Arty., Mar. 1, 1865. Bookkeeper, farmer, and miner. d. Pioche, Nevada, Feb. 25, 1877.

Gildersleeve, Basil Lanneau. b. Charleston, South Carolina, Oct. 23, 1831. att. Jefferson Coll. in Pennsylvania, Coll. of Charleston, Princeton, and school in Germany. VADC to William Gilham, Aug.–Sept. 1861. VADC to John B. Gordon in Shenandoah Valley, summer 1864. WIA near Weyer's Cave, Sept. 25, 1864. Postwar professor at UVa. and Johns Hopkins. m. Elisa Colston, 1866–she a daughter of the general. d. Baltimore, Maryland, Jan. 9, 1924. bur. UVa. Cem., Charlottesville, Virginia. Much of Gildersleeve's wartime writing recently has been published.

Gilmer, John. Capt. AQM at Charlottesville, Virginia, July 19, 1861. Resigned Dec. 15, 1861. Very likely the man with this name who was born in Bedford Co., Virginia, Jan. 13, 1826, was a lawyer and legislator from Albemarle Co., and who died Mar. 12, 1894, at Chatham, Virginia.

Giltner, Bernard W. Served as ADC to Cosby in Oct.–Nov. 1864, probably as a volunteer. No official evidence found. Alive 1890 in Kentucky.

Ginter, Lewis. b. Apr. 4, 1824. Maj. CS to J. R. Anderson, May 1, 1862. Maj. CS to Thomas, July 1862. Maj. acting CS to Wilcox, Aug.–Sept. 1862. Appx. Extremely wealthy tobacco merchant at Richmond, Virginia. d. Oct. 2, 1897. bur. Hollywood Cem.

Glaize, John. b. Frederick Co., Virginia, Oct. 9, 1822. Capt. AQM to Virginia militia in the Shenandoah Valley, Sept. 1861. Served as AQM under John A. Harman during 1862 Valley Campaign. Capt. AQM, attached to Second Corps. Capt. AQM with reserve ordnance train, Second Corps, Mar. 1864. Capt. AQM at ANVa. Forage Depot, based at Dublin Depot, 1865. Appx. Winchester lumberman, sheriff, jailer, and city politician. d. Jan. 22, 1901. bur. Mt. Hebron Cem.

Glenn, David Chalmers. b. in North Carolina, 1824. m. Patience B. Wilkerson, 1846. Attorney Gen. of Mississippi, 1849. Member of state Secession Convention. Col. of Cavy., July 18, 1863, assigned to military court of Third Corps. Resigned Dec. 3, 1864. Lived postwar at Mississippi City. d. Okalona, Mississippi, Sept. 19, 1868.

Glenn, Robert Henry. b. Norfolk, Virginia, July 10, 1820. att. USMA. Teacher and engineer living in Princess Anne Co., Virginia. In charge of constructing defenses at Norfolk, 1861–1862, possibly as a volunteer. WIA at Hampton Roads, spring 1862. Lt. on duty with the ordnance bureau at Richmond by 1863. Promoted to Capt. of Arty., Aug. 1864. Remained in Richmond into 1865. d. Richmond, Oct. 9, 1866. bur. Hollywood Cem.

Glenn, William. b. ca. 1838. Prewar civil engineer working on railroads and canals in Kentucky and Virginia. Civilian assistant to R. H. Glenn at Craney Island, May–July 1861. Employed by Gen. Blanchard on topographic surveying, July 1861–May 1862. Did the same for Engineer Dept. until Mar. 1863, probably as a contractor. Lt. Co. D, 1st C.S. Engineers by June 1863. Resigned Sept. 28, 1864. Lt. OO, Sept. 22, 1864, and reported to Gen. Young on Nov. 2, 1864. Served into 1865.

Glover, Francis Lyon. b. Alabama, Oct. 8, 1842. Greensboro student. Sgt. Co. D, 11th Alabama, June 1861. To Lt. in 1863. Lt. ADC to Wilcox, May 25, 1864. Appx. m. Martha Stewart. d. May 13, 1889. bur. Magnolia Cem., Mobile.

Glover, George Robert. b. in Georgia, Jan. 17, 1841. Pvt. Co. I, 6th Georgia, May 27, 1861. To Lt., July 12, 1862. Lt. acting ADC to Colquitt at Cold Harbor. WIA at Petersburg, June 1864. Served into 1865.

Farmer in Twiggs Co. d. Jan. 14, 1911. bur. Orange Hill Cem., Hawkinsville.

Glover, James. Maj. QM to S. R. Anderson, July 18, 1861. Maj. Chief QM for Dept. of East Tennessee, 1862–1865.

Goggin, Edmund Pendleton. b. in Virginia, ca. 1846. Lived prewar at Lynchburg, Virginia. Serving as AAG to Lomax by Sept. 1864, and into 1865, but no commission found. Postwar Lynchburg law partner of John W. Daniel (see above). m. Alice Chinn Withers, 1870. d. Bedford Co., Nov. 7, 1894, of typhoid fever. bur. Lynchburg Presby. Cem. Goggin's account of his service with Lomax is at the Chicago Historical Society.

Goldsborough, Robert Henry. b. near Easton, Maryland, Jan. 15, 1841. Served in Chapman's (Va.) Btty. and in Co. B, 39th Bn. Virginia Cavy., into 1863. Lt. ADC to Stuart, May 2, 1863. POW at Brandy Station. Exchanged Mar. 1865. Lt. ADC to G. W. C. Lee, 1865. MWIA at Sailor's Creek. bur. family cem. in Talbot Co., Maryland.

Goldsborough, William Worthington. b. Frederick Co., Maryland, Oct. 6, 1831. Capt. Co. G, 2nd Bn. Maryland, June 29, 1861. Capt. 1st Maryland. Capt. VADC to his cousin, Col. B. T. Johnson, who commanded a brigade, 1862. WIA at Second Manassas. Resigned Oct. 20, 1862. Lt. Drillmaster, Oct. 31, 1862. Maj. 1st Bn. Maryland, Jan. 26, 1863. WIA in left side and POW at Gettysburg. Released June 1865. Newspaperman at Winchester, Virginia. Also worked in Philadelphia and Washington, D.C. d. Philadelphia, Dec. 25, 1901. bur. Loudon Park Cem., Baltimore.

Goldthwaite, Thomas. b. Jan. 11, 1841. att. Princeton. A lawyer. Pvt. Co. K, 21st Alabama. Clerk for Braxton Bragg. Pvt. Forsyth's (Ala.) Bn., 1863. Lt. Enrolling Officer, Mar. 9, 1863, on duty at Richmond with Bureau of Conscription. His commander said of him in 1864: "I do not believe his equal can be found or made in a year." d. 1865, 1869, or 1871.

Good, George M. Capt. AQM at Appx.,
command not given.

Goode, John. b. Bedford Co., Virginia,
May 27, 1829. att. Emory and Henry. Law-
yer at Liberty and in state legislature. Pvt.
Co. A, 2nd Virginia Cavy., May 11, 1861.
Transferred to Early's staff as VADC, Oct. 5,
1861–Feb. 22, 1862. Also VADC to Early at
Malvern Hill and in July 1864. Elected to
C.S. Congress, Dec. 1862. Postwar USHR
and a lawyer at Norfolk and Washington,
D.C. U.S. Solicitor Gen. d. Norfolk, Vir-
ginia, July 14, 1909. bur. Longwood Cem.,
Bedford Co.

Goodloe, Lewis D. b. Warren Co., North
Carolina, 1837. Clerk and farmer at Warrenton. Pvt. Co. F, 12th North Carolina,
Apr. 18, 1861. Lt. Co. I, 35th North Carolina,
Feb. 13, 1863. To Capt., May 22, 1864. Cashiered Jan. 12, 1865, cause not stated, but
had been Lt. [?] OO to Matt. Ransom since
at least Dec. 1864. m. Ann B. Lamay, 1866.
Probably living in Texas in 1900.

Goodridge, Ferguson E. A bookkeeper and
clerk from Norfolk, Virginia. Pvt. Co. G,
6th Virginia, Apr. 19, 1861. Transferred to
CSMC, Oct. 12, 1861. Acting Ordnance Sgt.
with division trains of Huger, R. H. Anderson, and Mahone, May 1862–Mar. 1865. Lt.
OO to G. H. Steuart, Mar. 20, 1865. Appx.
m. Annie Bell Bernard, 1869. Middle name
probably Emerson.

Goodwin, Charles Ridgely. b. in Georgia.
Cpl. Chatham (Ga.) Arty., Dec. 7, 1861.
Detailed to Engineer Dept., May 27, 1863.
Lt. ADC to Gilmer, Sept. 29, 1863. VADC to
Mahone at the Crater. Lt. AAAIG to Alexan-
der, Oct–Nov. 1864. Paroled May 11, 1865. A
27-year-old commission merchant living at
Savannah in 1870. Alive 1894 at Baltimore,
Maryland.

Goodwin, Claudius L. b. in South Carolina. Capt. AQM, Hampton's (S.C.) Legion,
June 12, 1861. Maj. QM to Hampton, July 29,
1862. m. Theodosia C. Hardy, 1863. Paroled
Apr. 26, 1865. A 35-year-old cotton broker

at Catonsville, Maryland, in 1870. Alive
1905 at Baltimore, Maryland.

Gordon, ——. VADC to A. P. Hill at the
Battle of Fredericksburg. This staff officer
has defied further identification, so far.

Gordon, Adam. Capt. AAG for state of North
Carolina. Maj. QM to Martin, June 1, 1862,
through the end of the war. Alive 1900, a
planter at Hulda, Louisiana. Last name may
have been spelled Gordan.

Gordon, Archibald Madison. b. Alexandria, Louisiana, Nov. 11, 1837. Lt. Co. B, 9th
Louisiana, July 7, 1861. Lt. AAAG to Starke,
date unknown. KIA at Sharpsburg, evening
of Sept. 16, 1862, when a shell took off both
his legs. bur. Grove Farm at Sharpsburg,
but probably moved later.

Gordon, Charles Henry. b. Albemarle Co.,
Virginia, Jan. 7, 1829. Lt. Co. H, 4th Virginia
Cavy., Apr. 25, 1861. Lt. AAAG to Bonham,
Jan. 1862. Dropped Apr. 1862. Capt. AAG to
B. H. Robertson, Sept. 12, 1862. Resigned
Jan. 19, 1863, due to a hernia and "torpidity
of the liver." d. Jan. 23, 1897. bur. Grace
Episc. Church, Fauquier Co.

Gordon, Edward Clifford. b. Richmond, Vir-
ginia, Sept. 1, 1842. att. UVA. Pvt. 3rd Co.
Richmond Howitzers, Apr. 21, 1861. Sgt.
Otey (Va.) Btty., Mar. 1862. Lt. OO to J. S.
Williams, May 1, 1863. Lt. OO to Echols,
July 1863 into 1865. Possibly staff of Early,
too. att. Washington Coll. and Union Theo-
logical Seminary, postwar. Presbyterian
minister at several places, including Savan-
nah, Georgia. President Westminster Coll.,
Missouri. d. St. Louis, Jan. 26, 1922. bur.
Bellefontaine Cem.

Gordon, Eugene Cornelius. b. Walker Co.,
Georgia, June 17, 1845. Served in 6th Alabama and 61st Georgia. VADC to his brother
Gen. John B. Gordon at Gettysburg. Lt.
ADC to C. A. Evans, June 9, 1864. WIA in
right arm at Monocacy. Resigned Jan. 25,
1865. Maj. 25th Bn. Alabama Cavy., Mar. 24,
1865. Married twice. A developer in Alabama and Georgia. Also lived at Amarillo,

Texas. d. on a train, July 14, 1913. bur. Linwood Cem., Columbus, Georgia. "Stout and well built in frame."

Goree, Thomas Jewett. b. Perry Co., Alabama, Nov. 14, 1835. att. Howard Coll. and Texas Baptist Educational School (Baylor). A lawyer. VADC to Longstreet at First Manassas. Lt. ADC to Longstreet, Dec. 31, 1861, all the way to Appx. m. Eliza Thomas Nolley. Supt. of Texas State Penitentiary. d. Galveston, Mar. 4, 1905. bur. Oakwood Cem., Huntsville. Goree's war letters have been published. Grandfather of renowned artist, author, and soldier John W. Thomason.

Gorham, Willis Jackson. b. Jefferson Co., Georgia, Feb. 5, 1835. att. UGA. and Harvard Law School. Harris Co. lawyer. Lt. Co. K, 35th Georgia, Apr. 20, 1861. Lt. AAAIG to Thomas, date unknown. Capt. AAIG to Thomas, Nov. 2, 1863. POW at Spotsylvania, May 10, 1864. One of the Immortal 600. Teacher and Baptist minister. Married twice. d. Dec. 26, 1881. bur. Oak Hill Cem., Griffin, Georgia.

Grace, John. VADC to J. B. Robertson at Gettysburg. Possibly the John W. Grace who had been a Cpl. in Co. H, 5th Texas, 1861–1862.

Grady, Cuthbert Powell. b. Loudoun Co., Virginia, July 16, 1840. att. UVA. Sgt. Co. D, 6th Virginia Cavy., July 24, 1861. Capt. AAG to Lomax, Dec. 19, 1863. WIA in left arm, early in May 1864. Capt. AAG to Payne, 1865. m. Susan Gordon Armistead. Latin professor at Washington & Lee. School principal in Baltimore. d. Dec. 4, 1922. bur. Arlington National Cem.

Grady, Cyrus Wiley. b. Camden Co., North Carolina, Nov. 12, 1839. Moved to Norfolk, Virginia, 1845. Cotton merchant before and after the war. Capt. AQM, 8th North Carolina, 1861. Capt. AQM, Coit's Bn. Arty., Aug. 11, 1864. Maj. QM to Kirkland, Jan. 19, 1865. Paroled Apr. 26, 1865. m. Mary Selden. d. Norfolk, Jan. 9, 1919. bur. Elmwood Cem.

Graham, James Augustus. b. Hillsboro, North Carolina, July 7, 1841. Son of state governor. Cpl. Co. G, 27th North Carolina, Apr. 20, 1861. Later Orderly Sgt. To Lt., Aug. 17, 1861. WIA at Bristoe Station. Lt. AAAIG to Cooke, Apr.–May 1864. WIA at Wilderness, May 5, 1864. To Capt., Nov. 2, 1864. Appx. Attorney and legislator in Alamance Co. Moved to Washington, D.C., and worked for pension bureau. d. Mar. 20, 1908. bur. Hillsboro. UNC Press published his papers in 1928.

Grant, James B. Pvt. Co. B, 8th Georgia, May 21, 1861. Lt. ADC to W. M. Gardner, May 6, 1863. Paroled May 15, 1865, at Tallahassee, Florida.

Grant, John. Of England and Canada. Contract topographical engineer, 1861, with Beauregard. Same around Richmond, Virginia, in spring–summer 1862. Capt. EO, June 4, 1862. Served with ANVa. making maps, and at Goldsboro, North Carolina. Resigned Nov. 17, 1863, to become an architect at Selma Gun Foundry.

Grant, Robert. b. Savannah, Georgia, 1835. A lawyer, clerk of state senate, and bookkeeper, living at Savannah and Milledgeville. Pvt. Co. B, 8th Georgia, May 21, 1861. Lt. CSA, Sept. 18, 1861. Lt. AAAG to Toombs, Sept. 1861, and at Malvern Hill. Lt. Read's (Ga.) Btty., July 25, 1862. WIA at Sharpsburg. Lt. AAIG to Mercer, Nov. 25, 1862. Capt. AAIG to Mercer, Aug. 15, 1863. Later staff of H. R. Jackson, 1864–1865. d. Aug. 14, 1865. bur. Laurel Grove Cem., Savannah.

Grattan, Charles. b. Albemarle Co., Virginia, Dec. 8, 1833. att. UVA. Brother of G. G. Grattan (q.v.). Member of state legislature. QM Sgt. with John Harman, 1861. Acting Lt. OO to Cabell's Bn. Arty., Mar. 5, 1863. Acting Lt. OO at Second Corps headquarters, May–Oct. 1863. Capt. OO, Oct. 6, 1863, assigned to Stuart on Oct. 27, 1863. Capt. acting OO at ANVa. headquarters, summer 1864. Capt. OO to Hampton, Aug. 11, 1864. Capt. OO to Fitz. Lee, Jan. 19, 1865. With

Hampton in Mar. 1865. Lawyer, farmer, and school supt. in Augusta Co. d. June 20, 1902. bur. Thornrose Cem., Staunton.

Grattan, George Gilmer. b. Rockingham Co., Virginia, Feb. 12, 1839. att. UVA. and UGA. Brother of Charles. Lawyer and state legislator. Lt. Co. K, 6th Georgia, May 28, 1861. Lt. VADC to Colquitt at Sharpsburg. Capt. AAG to Colquitt, Dec. 19, 1862. Lost left leg at Cold Harbor, June 4, 1864. Retired to Invalid Corps, Feb. 25, 1865. Harrisonburg, Virginia, banker, lawyer, and judge. d. there Oct. 31, 1915. Author of a useful pamphlet on the Battle of South Mountain.

Grattan, James Ferguson. b. Richmond, Virginia, July 11, 1840. Pvt. Co. G, 12th Virginia, Apr. 19, 1861. Discharged as Cpl., Oct. 28, 1862. Lt. Drillmaster, Oct. 24, 1862, serving in Conscript Bureau. Lt. AAG to Huger's Bn. Arty., Mar. 3, 1864. Appx. d. Apr. 23, 1879. bur. Hollywood Cem.

Graves, Charles Wesley. b. Lee, Massachusetts, Aug. 6, 1838. A clerk in Panola Co., Mississippi. Sgt. Co. H, 17th Mississippi, Apr. 27, 1861. VADC to Featherston by June 1862, through Fredericksburg at least. Lt. AAG to Ward's Bn. Arty., May 2, 1863. Later staff of Chalmers. m. Rosa Belle Ruffin, 1869. Lived postwar at Memphis, Tennessee. d. Feb. 12, 1900.

Graves, Henry Montfort. b. Dec. 11, 1839. Engineer with Baltimore city waterworks. Lt. PAVA., June–Nov. 1861 around Norfolk. Contract engineer in central Virginia, 1862. Lt. EO, Mar. 17, 1864, on duty with ANVa. POW at Sailor's Creek. Said to have served under Trimble and with S. R. Johnston (who was at army headquarters and with Longstreet). d. Baltimore, July 14, 1926.

Graves, John T. b. in Virginia. A 26-year-old merchant in Louisa Co. in 1860. Lt. Co. D, 44th Virginia, June 8, 1861. Capt. ACS, 44th Virginia, Mar. 3, 1862. Capt. ACS to Ed Johnson, Aug. 1863. Capt. ACS to Breckinridge, May–Sept. 1864. Capt. ACS to John B.

Gordon, Sept. 1864. Capt. ACS to William Terry, 1865. POW at a Petersburg hospital, Apr. 3, 1865. Paroled Apr. 19, 1865.

Graves, Richard Freeman, Jr. b. in Virginia. Lt. Co. F, 5th Virginia Cavy. Failed reelection in Apr. 1862. VADC to French before June 1863. Possibly ADC and AAAG to Colston in May 1864. No evidence of commission or further duty. A lawyer at Petersburg, Virginia, age 33 in 1870.

Graves, Richard Morris. b. Dec. 28, 1833. A farmer. m. Susan Vaughn Kean Boston. Capt. AQM, 7th Virginia, June 16, 1862. Capt. acting QM to brigade by Oct. 1863. Staff of W. R. Terry. d. July 21, 1864, apparently of disease. bur. Hollywood Cem., Richmond.

Gray, John H. b. in Virginia. A 30-year-old coach maker in Hancock Co., Georgia, in 1860. Pvt. Co. A, 6th Georgia, May 29, 1861. QM Sgt., 6th Georgia. Capt. AQM, 6th Georgia, Nov. 11, 1862. Capt. AQM to Hoke, Sept. 20, 1864. Paroled Apr. 26, 1865.

Grayson, E. b. Maj. QM, Virginia forces. No record of official appointment is in his military record, but he was on duty from at least June 1864 until Apr. 1865. Believed to be Edward Butler Grayson, born Apr. 20, 1807, and died Jan. 14, 1882, bur. Glenwood Cem., Washington, D.C.

Green, Austin W. Adjt. 2nd Bn. North Carolina, Sept. 1, 1862. WIA May 19, 1864. Lt. AAAG to Grimes, Oct. 1864, and at Appx., possibly serving as a staff officer for that entire span.

Green, Benjamin. b. Savannah, Georgia, Sept. 1838. att. "Prussian Cavalry School" prewar. Cotton merchant at Savannah. Sgt. Co. F, Jeff Davis Legion Cavy., Sept. 17, 1861. Discharged Jan. 13, 1862. Volunteer OO to H. R. Jackson in Georgia. VADC to W. D. Smith, Apr. 1862. Adjt. 21st Bn. Georgia Partisan Rangers, Aug. 4, 1862. Lt. AAAG to Gilmer, Aug. 31, 1863. Resigned July 23, 1864. d. Feb. 14, 1865. bur. Savannah.

Green, Charles W. b. Alexandria, Virginia,

ca. 1837. A druggist there. Sgt. Co. A, 17th Virginia, Apr. 17, 1861. Later to Lt. WIA at Frayser's Farm. Capt. AQM, 17th Virginia, Dec. 17, 1862. Capt. AQM, 13th Bn. Virginia Arty., Aug. 24, 1864, through 1865. Postwar a traveling salesman in Texas, representing a Baltimore merchant. d. Waco, Texas, Feb. 29, 1916. bur. Oakwood Cem.

Green, Ellis C., Jr. b. Monroe City, Missouri. Educated in New York. A 25-year-old clerk at Charleston, South Carolina, in 1860. Lt. Co. C, 17th Bn. South Carolina Cavy. Lt. Co. B, 5th South Carolina Cavy. Capt. AQM, 5th South Carolina Cavy., May 2, 1863. Capt. acting QM to Dunovant by Apr. 1864. Capt. acting QM to Butler, May–Oct. 1864. Capt. AQM to Logan, 1865. A 33-year-old merchant in Sumter Co. in 1870. m. Louisa Blake Yeadon. Mayor of Sumter. d. Oconee Co., South Carolina.

Green, Frank Waters. b. Nashville, Tennessee, Sept. 6, 1836. att. Univ. of Nashville. A wholesale grocer there. Served in Co. B, 1st Tennessee, and as Capt. ACS, 14th Tennessee. Capt. ACS at Third Corps headquarters, July 29, 1863. WIA at Spotsylvania. Appx. Grocer, farmer, and fire insurance agent at Nashville. d. Feb. 21, 1904. bur. Mt. Olivet Cem., in an unmarked grave.

Green, James William. b. Culpeper Co., Virginia, Mar. 7, 1824. Lawyer there prewar. Lt. Co. C, 7th Virginia, Apr. 30, 1861. Capt. ACS, 7th Virginia, Oct.–Nov. 1861. Maj. CS to Kemper, June 13, 1862. Maj. CS to W. R. Terry, 1864–1865. Appx. m. Anne Sanford McDonald. Lawyer and newspaperman at Culpeper. d. there Apr. 1, 1884.

Green, John Francis. b. Darlington Co., South Carolina, Mar. 3, 1841. att. Oglethorpe Coll. Pvt. and Sgt. Maj., 11th Georgia, 1861. To Adjt. May 22, 1862. WIA three times, including Malvern Hill and Darbytown Road. Lt. AAAIG and acting ADC to G. T. Anderson, by Oct. 1864 and into 1865. Appx. Moved to Arkansas in 1870s. City

treasurer at Hope. d. there Dec. 13, 1922. bur. Rose Hill Cem.

Green, Wharton Jackson. b. St. Mark's, Florida, Feb. 28, 1831. Known as "Jack." att. Georgetown and USMA. Lawyer at Washington, D.C. Pvt. Co. F, 12th North Carolina, Apr. 1861. Lt. Col. 2nd Bn. North Carolina, Dec. 24, 1861. POW at Roanoke Island, and dropped at reorganization. VADC to Daniel, June–July 1863. WIA in head at Gettysburg, July 1, 1863, and POW July 5. Exchanged Mar. 1865. Viticulturist and USHR. Married twice. d. Fayetteville, North Carolina, Aug. 6, 1910. bur. Cross Creek Cem. Green published an autobiography.

Green, William James. b. Falmouth, Virginia, Nov. 25, 1825. att. VMI. Lt. Col. 47th Virginia, May 2, 1861. Dropped May 1862. VADC to Pender in Seven Days. KIA at Gaines's Mill—shot in the heart. bur. Stafford Co.

Greene, Benjamin H. b. Georgetown, South Carolina, Sept. 17, 1826. A civil engineer. Worked in Tennessee and Louisiana. VADC to Ewell, July 1861. Maj. CS to Ewell, Sept. 2, 1861. Maj. CS to Early, Aug. 1862. Maj. AAIG to Ewell, June 16, 1863. Maj. EO to Ewell, May 1864. Maj. EO to Early, May 28, 1864. Hit by spent bullet at Cold Harbor. POW at Moorefield, Aug. 7, 1864. Returned to Early from prison, Feb. 26, 1865. Paroled with AOT, Apr. 26, 1865. d. Jan. 4, 1890. bur. Live Oak Cem., Pass Christian, Mississippi.

Gregory, George Henry. A resident of Buncombe Co., North Carolina. Lt. Co. E, 1st North Carolina (Bethel), Apr. 1861, age 25. Served into Nov. 1861. Lt. Co. B, 12th Bn. Virginia Arty., June 1, 1862. Capt. AQM, 12th Bn. Virginia Arty., May 29, 1863. In that capacity for remainder of the war. This may be the G. H. Gregory (Dec. 24, 1835–Dec. 13, 1913) who attended UNC.

Gregory, Johnathan Munford, Jr. b. Williamsburg, Virginia, Mar. 6, 1840. Moved to Richmond, Virginia, 1841. att. UVA.

and Richmond Baptist Coll. Cpl. Rock-bridge (Va.) Arty., 1861. WIA twice at First Winchester. Lt. OO at Second Corps head-quarters, Feb. 1863. Capt. OO, May 2, 1863, staff of Gen. Long. Appx. Charles City Co. lumberman. Moved to California in 1868 and practiced law at Vallejo. m. Evlyn T. Craven. d. Nov. 8, 1907. bur. Fairfield City Cem., Solano Co.

Gregory, William Ferdinand Chamberlayne. b. Amelia Co., Virginia, June 1827. att. Yale Law School. Planter, lawyer, and state legislator in Amelia Co. Maj. CS to Wise, May 13, 1862. Served all the way to Appx. Mayor of Petersburg. Richmond lawyer and preacher. d. Henrico Co., June 10, 1887. bur. Hollywood Cem.

Grenfell, George St. Leger Ommanney. b. London, England, May 30, 1808. att. school in Holland. British army officer. m. Hortense Louise Wyatt. ADC and AAAG to J. H. Morgan, 1862. VADC to Bragg, Nov. 1862. Lt. Col. AAIG to Wheeler, May 1863. Lt. Col. AAIG to Stuart, Sept. 12, 1863. Re-signed Jan. 21, 1864. Arrested in Chicago as spy, Nov. 7, 1864, and sentenced to life in prison. Fled from his prison in the Dry Tortugas, but never seen again, Mar. 1868. Disliked by Stuart.

Grice, George Washington. b. Portsmouth, Virginia, May 16, 1824. Virginia legisla-tor and mayor of Portsmouth. Capt. AQM at Portsmouth, July 14, 1861. Maj. QM to Blanchard, Mar. 18, 1862. Maj. QM to Wright, June 1862. Maj. QM to Blanchard, Oct. 1862. On duty purchasing forage in Georgia, Sept. 1863 into 1865. Portsmouth banker and railroad man. Married twice. d. Nov. 12, 1875.

Grier, Thomas. Joined Co. H, 5th South Carolina, Apr. 13, 1861. Pvt. Palmetto (S.C.) Sharpshooters, Apr. 13, 1862. To Ordnance Sgt., July 21, 1862. Lt. acting OO to Micah Jenkins, Jan. 1863. Lt. acting OO to Hoke, Jan. 31, 1863. Paroled May 1, 1865, at Greens-boro, North Carolina. Lived Williamsburg Co., South Carolina, postwar.

Griffin, Evander McIver. b. Society Hill, South Carolina, June 26, 1827. att. South Carolina Coll. Schoolteacher at Society Hill and in Darlington. Pvt. 8th South Carolina, 1861. Later to Lt. Capt. ACS of unit, Dec. 20, 1862. Capt. ACS to Kershaw, Sept. 17, 1863. Failed confirmation in 1864, but reappointed to same brigade (Conner), July 27, 1864. Capt. ACS to Goggin and Ken-nedy. Paroled at Greensboro. Darlington Co. merchant. d. Feb. 5, 1896. bur. Welsh Neck Baptist Church, Darlington Co.

Griffis, John Chappell. b. Marietta, Georgia, July 15, 1834. att. GMI. Adjt. 18th Georgia, June 14, 1861. To Maj., Apr. 7, 1862. WIA at Second Manassas. Maj. CS to Wofford, Feb. 17, 1863. Same to DuBose, 1864. Appx. Merchant at Americus, Georgia. Moved to Texas in 1872. Hardware merchant at Dallas. d. Sept. 27, 1901. bur. Greenwood Cem.

Grinnell, Robert M. b. in New York, ca. 1826. Prewar merchant at Liverpool, En-gland. m. Miss Musgrave, one of Florence Nightengale's Crimean War nurses. Lt. Co. E, Wheat's (La.) Bn., June 26, 1861. WIA and POW at Front Royal. Capt. AAG to H. H. Walker, Aug. 17, 1863. Likely Capt. AAG to Fry, June 1864. Capt. AAAIG to Heth, by Aug. 1864. WIA in left arm at Weldon Railroad, Aug. 20, 1864. Maj. AAIG to Heth, Feb. 2, 1865. Appx.

Griswold, Elias. b. in Ohio. Lived in Geor-gia and Florida prewar. A 41-year-old lawyer in Dorchester Co., Maryland, in 1860. Capt. AQM, Nov. 15, 1861, at Tusca-loosa, Alabama. Maj. AAG to J. H. Winder, Apr. 11, 1862. Maj. AAG to Ruggles, Mar. 25, 1865. Paroled May 3, 1865, at Salisbury, North Carolina. Founded the first telegraph company in Dorchester Co., Maryland. Life insurance agent at Baltimore in 1870. Dead by 1894.

Griswold, Joseph Goodman. b. Essex Co., Virginia, June 10, 1836. att. Wm. & Mary and VMI. A teacher. Capt. Co. D, 1st Virginia, Apr. 21, 1861. Capt. AAAG to Ewell, late 1861 or early 1862. Resigned Apr. 26, 1862. Clerk at PM's office in Richmond, 1862–1864. Capt. AAG to Hunton by summer 1864. WIA in June 1864. Professor at UAla., lawyer, and steamship purser. d. Petersburg, Jan. 9, 1893. bur. Blandford Cem.

Grogan, Charles Edward. b. Clarke Co., Virginia, Mar. 3, 1841. Pvt. Co. H, 1st Maryland, July 20, 1861. Lt. VADC to Colston at Chancellorsville, and WIA in shoulder. Lt. VADC to Trimble at Gettysburg, and WIA twice. POW July 5, 1863. Escaped from prison. Later served with Mosby. Merchant at Baltimore, Maryland. d. Jan. 4, 1922. bur. Green Mount Cem.

Guerrant, Edward Owings. b. Sharpsburg, Kentucky, Feb. 28, 1838. att. Centre Coll. A teacher. Pvt. Co. E, 1st Bn. Kentucky Mtd. Rifles, Feb.–June 1862. Clerk to Gen. Marshall. Capt. AAG to Marshall, Dec. 20, 1862. Later to Preston, J. S. Williams, and Cosby. Served into 1865. att. Jefferson Medical Coll. Physician and minister in Kentucky. d. Apr. 26, 1916. Guerrant's excellent wartime journal has been published.

Guerrant, Hugh Lindsay. b. in North Carolina, ca. 1835. A merchant in Rockingham Co. Lt. Co. K, 13th North Carolina, May 22, 1861. To Capt., Jan. 15, 1863. WIA at Chancellorsville. Capt. AAAIG to Scales at Gettysburg. WIA at the Wilderness. Appx.

Guiger, George Henry. b. Staunton, Virginia, May 28, 1826. att. UVA. Albemarle Co. farmer. Lt. Co. K, 2nd Virginia Cavy. Lt. ADC to Kemper, Nov. 5, 1862. MWIA and POW at Gettysburg, July 3, 1863. d. there July 17.

Gunn, Richard Bullington. b. July 10, 1837. Pvt. Co. A, 1st Virginia, Apr. 19, 1861, then Pvt. Co. G, 12th Virginia. Lt. Otey (Va.) Btty., Apr. 14, 1862. Slightly WIA at Fayette C.H., Sept. 10, 1862. Lt. acting OO for

Gibbes's Bn. Arty., by Dec. 1864. d. Oct. 12, 1907. bur. Hollywood Cem., Richmond.

Guthrie, Josephus. b. in South Carolina, Sept. 15, 1825. A dry goods merchant in Whitfield Co., Georgia, prewar and postwar. Lt. Co. G, 11th Georgia, July 3, 1861. Capt. acting QM, 11th Georgia, Sept. 21, 1861. Maj. QM to G. T. Anderson, Aug. 2, 1862. WIA in left leg, June 1864. Appx. d. June 11, 1884. bur. Tunnel Hill Cem., Georgia.

Gwathmey, Charles Browne. b. May 19, 1830. att. UVA. Of King and Queen Co., Virginia. Lt. Co. E, 5th Virginia Cavy., June 1862. Capt. AQM, 5th Virginia Cavy., Jan. 22, 1863. Maj. QM to Rosser, Feb. 19, 1864, but not confirmed. Reappointed June 15, 1864. Served into 1865. Richmond merchant. d. Aug. 10, 1894. bur. Hollywood Cem.

Gwin, William. Capt. on the staff of Howell Cobb in Apr. 1862. Otherwise unidentified.

Habersham, John Bolton. b. Savannah, Georgia, Aug. 31, 1825. m. Frances Hazlehurst, 1858. Adjt. 3rd Georgia, May 20, 1862. Lt. ADC to his brother-in-law, Gen. A. R. Wright, June 21, 1862. No further military record after Aug. 1862. Mayor of Brunswick, Georgia. d. there Feb. 21, 1881.

Hackett, John Taylor. b. in Georgia. A resident of Clarkesville. Pvt. Co. E, 16th Georgia, July 24, 1861. To Lt., May 1862. WIA in leg and POW at Crampton's Gap. Lt. AAAIG to Wofford, by July 1863. Capt. AAIG [?] to Wofford, Nov. 2, 1863. Same to DuBose, 1864–1865. A 39-year-old retired merchant living at Clarkesville in 1870.

Hackett, T. H. Capt. AAIG to DuBose, 1864–1865. No other record. May be confused with John T. Hackett, shown above.

Hagan, William Henry. b. Braddock Heights, Maryland, Apr. 6, 1821. Cpl. Co. F, 1st Virginia Cavy., Apr. 18, 1861. Chief courier to Stuart and occasionally listed as a staff member. Called a Lt. in many sources. Lt. VADC to Hampton, too. Has a tenuous claim to staff duty. Paroled Apr. 26, 1865.

President of a cement company, and a hotel keeper. d. June 18, 1895. bur. Elmwood Cem., Shepherdstown, West Virginia.

Hagerty, William O. b. in Alabama. Pvt. Co. C, 13th Alabama. Later Sgt. Maj. of regiment, and then Capt. ACS, Dec. 24, 1861. Capt. AQM, 13th Alabama, May 12, 1863. Capt. AQM to Archer, Sept. 15, 1864. Capt. AQM to McComb, late in 1864. Appx. A 39-year-old "warehouse keeper" at Wetumpka, Alabama, in 1870. bur. Wetumpka City Cem.

Haile, Calhoun. b. Mississippi, Apr. 14, 1828. Planter in Bolivar Co., valued at $838,000 in 1860 census. Lt. ADC to French, Nov. 9, 1861. Resigned spring 1862. Capt. Co. A, 20th Mississippi, May 16, 1863, to Aug. 1864. POW at Franklin, Tennessee, Dec. 17, 1864, and discharged from Ft. Delaware, Jan. 25, 1865. d. Mar. 1, 1893. d. Old Greenville Cem., Greenville, Mississippi.

Haile, Christopher Valery. b. Plaquemine, Louisiana, Feb. 22, 1842. att. Centenary Coll. A nephew of Gen. Louis Hebert. Cpl. Co. I, 30th Louisiana, Mar. 12, 1862. Lt. ADC to Stevens, Sept. 8, 1864. Appx. New Orleans railroad employee and real estate agent. d. Jan. 6, 1899.

Hairston, James Thomas Watt. b. Lowndes Co., Mississippi, Jan. 26, 1835. att. VMI. Mississippi cotton planter. Brother of S. H. Hairston (q.v.). Capt. Co. E, 11th Mississippi, 1861. Lt. of Inf., CSA, to rank from Mar. 16, 1861. Commanded a prison in Richmond, Oct. 1861–Jan. 1862. Lt. AAAG to his cousin, Gen. Stuart, Feb. 1862. Capt. AAG to Stuart, 1862. Maj. AAG to Stuart, July 25, 1862. Resigned Mar. 5, 1863, due to rheumatism. Lt. of Cavy., CSA, Mar. 1863. Served in South Carolina until he resigned again, May 27, 1863. Farmer in Virginia and Mississippi. d. near Columbus, Mississippi, Jan. 19, 1908. bur. family cem. at "Beaver Creek" near Martinsville, Virginia.

Hairston, Peter Wilson. b. "Oak Hill" in Pittsylvania Co., Virginia, Nov. 25, 1819. att.

UNC and UVA. A farmer. VADC to Stuart, June–Oct. 1861. He was both a cousin and brother-in-law to Gen. Stuart. VADC to his cousin Gen. Early, Nov. 1863 to early 1865. Baltimore merchant postwar. d. Feb. 1886. bur. family cem. at "Berry Hill" in Pittsylvania Co. Hairston's letters are at UNC, and his diary for late 1863 was published in 1990 in the *North Carolina Historical Review*.

Hairston, Samuel Harden. b. in Mississippi, Apr. 1822. att. Wm. & Mary and Emory & Henry. Brother of J. T. W. Hairson. Lawyer and farmer in Henry Co., Virginia. Sgt. Co. E, 11th Mississippi, 1861. VADC to his cousin Gen. Stuart, Apr.–May 1862. Maj. QM to Stuart, June 17, 1862. Resigned Jan. 14, 1863. Tobacco farmer in Henry Co. Killed in Richmond Capitol disaster, Apr. 27, 1870.

Hale, Edward Joseph, Jr. b. Fayetteville, North Carolina, Dec. 25, 1839. att. UNC. Fayetteville newspaperman. Pvt. Co. H, 1st North Carolina, Apr. 17, 1861. Adjt. 56th North Carolina, Aug. 1, 1862. WIA at Gum Springs, May 2, 1863. Capt. AAG to Lane, Oct. 24, 1863. Appx. New York City publisher and diplomat in Manchester, England, and in Costa Rica. Married twice. d. Fayetteville, Feb. 1922. bur. Cross Creek Cem. Lane called him "as handsome, elegant & brave a soldier as ever drew blade."

Hale, Samuel, Jr. b. Rocky Mount, Virginia, Mar. 25, 1839. att. UVA. Capt. Co. K, 42nd Virginia, June 1861–Apr. 1862. Acting Adjt. 48th Virginia by Apr. 1862, and commanded it until WIA at First Winchester. Maj. CS to his uncle, Gen. Early, May 1, 1862. Maj. AAAG to Early, Aug.–Dec. 1862. Maj. AAIG to Early, Jan. 21, 1863. KIA at Spotsylvania, May 12, 1864. bur. Early family plot, Spring Hill Cem., Lynchburg. A soldier in the 49th Virginia lamented Hale's death: "We loved him."

Haley, Alfred Griffin. b. St. Francisville, Louisiana, Sept. 11, 1827. Claimed to have served in the Texas Rangers prewar. Listed his residence as Hines Co., Mississippi, but also was a 32-year-old clerk at Washington, D.C., in 1860. Volunteered with 2nd Virginia Cavy., 1861. Lt. of Cavy., CSA, Nov. 20, 1861. On ordnance duty until Mar. 1862. Lt. ADC to Featherston, Apr. 11, 1862. VADC to Garland at Seven Pines, during Featherston's absence, and WIA in face. On court-martial duty in North Carolina, 1865. Took Oath as a Lt. in 1st Confederate Cavy. d. Poolesville, Maryland, Mar. 27, 1874.

Hall, Carey Judson. b. Lancaster Co., Virginia. att. Wake Forest. A 24-year-old schoolteacher in Richmond Co., Virginia, in 1860. Sgt. Co. B, 40th Virginia, May 22–Oct. 28, 1861. Pvt. Co. B, 15th Bn. Virginia Cavy., Mar. 26, 1862. Capt. AQM, 15th Bn. Virginia Cavy., July 8, 1862. Capt. AQM on duty at ANVa. headquarters, Apr. 22, 1863. Dropped June 27, 1864, as inefficient. Taught school at Warsaw, Virginia. Moved to Maysville, Kentucky, postwar. Living in Covington, Kentucky, in 1894, but back in Richmond Co, Virginia, by 1900.

Hall, John T. Capt. ACS, 28th Georgia, Apr. 11, 1862. Capt. acting ACS to Colquitt, summer 1862. Resigned May 19, 1863, in anticipation of being dropped.

Hall, Roland Butler. b. Milledgeville, Georgia, Apr. 11, 1840. Druggist there. Pvt. Co. H, 4th Georgia, Apr. 26, 1861. Pvt. Co. F, 9th Georgia, Apr. 2, 1862. Detached on signal service with Hood, Mar.–Sept. 1863. Cadet, Oct. 20, 1863. Assistant to Chief of C.S. Signal Corps. Lt. SO to Hampton, Apr. 7, 1864. WIA Oct. 1864. Druggist at Brunswick and Macon, Georgia. Cemetery supt. in Macon. Also a sanitation and food inspector. d. there June 20, 1919.

Hall, Thomas William, Jr. b. Baltimore, Maryland, Sept. 25, 1833. att. UVa. Never married. Lawyer and newspaper editor at Baltimore. Arrested there in Sept. 1861 and confined at Ft. McHenry until Nov. 1862. Capt. AAG to John Gregg, Feb. 27, 1863. Capt. assigned to General Inspection Div.,

Dec. 29, 1864. Maj. AAIG, Mar. 17, 1865. Marengo Co., Alabama, cotton planter. Law professor at Univ. of Maryland. Law partner of Charles Marshall (q.v.). d. Ruxton, Maryland, July 5, 1901.

Hall, William Carvel. b. May 10, 1833. Of Baltimore, Maryland. Lt. ADC to Trimble, Oct. 9, 1861. Capt. AAG to Trimble, Mar. 31, 1862. Capt. AAAG to Hoke, May 1863. Maj. AAG to Trimble, May 27, 1863. POW at Gettysburg. Exchanged June 1864. Maj. AAG on inspection duty all over Confederacy. Maj. AAIG to Loring, 1865. Paroled at Greensboro. d. Apr. 14, 1879.

Haller, Richard J. b. in Virginia, Apr. 9, 1823. m. Susan Beattie Thompson, 1845. A mail agent at Abingdon. Capt. AQM, 48th Virginia, July 1861. Capt. acting AQM to the 48th's brigade (commanded by colonels), Dec. 24, 1861. Resigned late in 1863, complaining of varicose veins. Railroad conductor at Abingdon postwar. d. July 29, 1891. bur. Round Hill Cem., Smyth Co., Virginia.

Halsey, Don Peters. b. Lynchburg, Virginia, Sept. 15, 1836. att. UVa., Emory & Henry, and three schools in Germany. Professor of languages at Roanoke Coll. Lt. Co. G, 2nd Virginia Cavy. Lt. ADC to Garland, May 25, 1862. WIA at Seven Pines (lost vision in right eye). Capt. AAG to Garland, June 18, 1862. WIA and POW at Sharpsburg. Capt. AAG to Iverson, Nov. 1862. Capt. AAG to R. D. Johnston, Sept. 1863. WIA in bladder at Spotsylvania. Capt. AAG to Wharton, Jan. 24, 1865. POW at Waynesboro. m. Sarah Ann Warwick Daniel, a sister of John W. Daniel (q.v.). Lawyer at Lynchburg and Richmond. d. Nelson Co., Virginia, Jan. 1, 1883. bur. Spring Hill Cem., Lynchburg.

Hamilton, James. b. in South Carolina, 1841. att. USMA. Lt. of Inf., CSA, Mar. 16, 1861. On recruiting duty. Resigned June 24, 1861. Lt. ADC to Richard Taylor, by May 1862. Lt. ADC to Hood, by Second Manassas. Appointed Capt. (PACS), Nov. 5, 1862. Maj.

ADC to Hood, Mar. 1, 1864. Maj. commanding artillery attached to Gen. Wheeler, Aug. 1864. d. 1867. Gen. Taylor called him "a gay, cheery lad," and another source describes Hamilton as having a "youthful appearance and delicate constitution, with rather effeminate features."

Hamilton, James F. Maj. CS to B. R. Johnson, Apr. 1, 1862. Served all the way to Appx.

Hamilton, Paul. b. Beaufort Dist., South Carolina, Feb. 13, 1842. att. SCMA. Lt. Hampton Legion Arty. Lt. of Arty., CSA, May 23, 1862. Lt. AAAG to S. D. Lee, Seven Days. Lt. AAAG to Hampton, July–Nov. 1862. Capt. AAG to S. D. Lee, Nov. 8, 1862. KIA at Vicksburg, Dec. 29, 1862. bur. St. Helena Episc. Churchyard, Beaufort, South Carolina.

Hamilton, Samuel Prioleau. b. Washington, D.C., Jan. 1826. att. Coll. of Charleston. Father was South Carolina governor and brother was Col. of 1st South Carolina (Gregg's). Port official at Savannah, Georgia. Capt. Co. A, 1st Georgia Regs., July 24, 1861. Maj. Chief of Arty. to McLaws, July 1, 1862. Maj. Judge Advocate by Jan. 1863. Maj. in Cabell's Bn. Arty., by July 1863. Lawyer at Chester, South Carolina, and state legislator. d. there Nov. 24, 1897. bur. Evergreen Cem.

Hamilton, Tilford A. A wholesale grocer in eastern Texas. Pvt. Co. F, 1st Texas, Sept. 20, 1861. Acted as Bgd. Commissary and QM Sgt., 1862. Maj. CS to J. B. Robertson, Feb. 1, 1863. Court-martialed in 1863 for telling Gen. Robertson to "Go to Hell." WIA at Chickamauga. Maj. CS to John Gregg, Apr. 1864. KIA at Wilderness, May 6, 1864. bur. Fredericksburg (Va.) Confederate Cem. "I don't know of a better man" for the position of commissary, wrote Gen. Hood.

Hammond, Edward Spann. b. Barnwell, South Carolina, June 26, 1834. att. UGA., UPenn., and Medical Coll. of South Carolina. Maj. in state militia. Maj. VADC to Bonham at First Manassas. Provided a substitute in army and edited *Richmond Whig*, 1863–1864. Married twice. Lawyer at Aiken and Blackville, South Carolina. d. Blackville, June 11, 1921. bur. Beech Island Cem.

Hammond, James Henry. b. Columbia, South Carolina, Mar. 30, 1832. att. South Carolina Coll., Harvard, and UPenn. Professor at UGA. m. Emily Cumming, a sister of Gen. Cumming. Capt. ACS 14th South Carolina, Oct. 1861–Mar. 1862. VADC to Maxcy Gregg during Seven Days. Maj. QM to Gregg, Oct. 14, 1862. Same to McGowan. Appx. Aiken Co. planter. d. Jan. 7, 1916. Hammond's war letters have been published.

Hammond, William May. b. Aug. 25, 1837. att. UNC. From Wadesboro, North Carolina. Lt. Co. G, 14th North Carolina. Adjt. 45th North Carolina, June 2, 1862. Lt. staff of Daniel's Bgd. during Seven Days. Capt. AAG to Daniel, Oct. 2, 1862. Transferred to inspection duty in Southeast, due to poor health, Apr. 2, 1863. Capt. AAIG to Roddey, 1864–1865. Georgia legislator and lawyer. d. Aug. 8, 1908. bur. Eastview Cem., Wadesboro.

Hampton, Christopher Fitzsimons. Known as "Kit." b. Aug. 11, 1821. Lt. ADC to his brother Gen. Hampton, Sept. 30, 1862, but declined the appointment. On staff of state governor, 1864. Lt. ADC to Hampton, Dec. 18, 1864. m. Mary Elizabeth McCord. d. June 8, 1886.

Hampton, Thomas Preston. b. Nov. 26, 1843. Lt. ADC to his father, Gen. Hampton, Nov. 8, 1862. WIA in right arm at Jack's Shop. MWIA at Burgess's Mill, Oct. 27, 1864. "Handsome" and "sunny-hearted."

Hampton, Wade, Jr. b. Mar. 2, 1840. VADC to Beauregard, Apr. 1861. Pvt. Co. A, Hampton Legion Cavy. Lt. ADC to J. E. Johnston, Nov. 16, 1861. Lt. VADC to G. W. Smith, June 1862. Lt. VADC to his father, Gen. Hampton, Sept. 1864. WIA at Burgess's Mill. Maj. ADC to Johnston, Apr. 1865. m. Kate Phelan.

d. Washington Co., Mississippi, of malaria, Dec. 22, 1879.

Hanckel, Charles Francis. b. Feb. 3, 1829. att. Coll. of Charleston. Charleston merchant. Pvt. 1st South Carolina Militia. Capt. ACS to Drayton, Apr. 8, 1862. Maj. CS to Drayton, Apr. 8, 1862. Maj. CS to Semmes, Nov. 29, 1862. Resigned May 20, 1863. Supt. of treasury at Columbia, South Carolina. Charleston attorney. m. Anne Matilda Heyward. d. May 20, 1898. bur. Magnolia Cem.

Handerson, Henry Ebenezer. b. Cuyahoga Co., Ohio, Mar. 21, 1837. att. Hobart Coll. Surveyor and tutor in Rapides Parish, Louisiana. Lt. Co. B, 9th Louisiana. Later to Adjt. Capt. AAG to Stafford, Oct. 23, 1863. POW at Wilderness, May 5, 1864. Capt. AAG to Dearing, Jan. 25, 1865, but not released from prison until June 1865. Physician at New York City and Cleveland. d. Apr. 22, 1918. bur. Woodland Cem., Cleveland. Handerson's excellent reminiscences are published.

Hanger, James Marshall. b. Waynesboro, Virginia, Nov. 12, 1833. att. UVa. Never married. Staunton lawyer. Pvt. Co. E, 1st Virginia Cavy. Capt. AQM to Stuart, Sept. 23, 1862. Not confirmed by Senate, but served anyway until appointed Capt. AQM to Hampton, July 29, 1864. Capt. acting QM to W. H. F. Lee, Jan. 19, 1865. Capt. acting QM to Fitz. Lee, Jan. 25, 1865. Maj. QM to Fitz. Lee, Feb. 15, 1865. Appx. Staunton lawyer and legislator. Consul to Bermuda, 1893–1897. d. Staunton, Aug. 26, 1912. bur. Thornrose Cem.

Hankins, Dick R. b. Wilson Co., Tennessee, Jan. 16, 1831. A book dealer at Lebanon. Pvt. Co. H, 7th Tennessee, May 20, 1861. Detailed as acting ACS at various sites in Virginia mountains, Aug. 1861. Capt. ACS, 7th Tennessee, Mar. 18, 1862. Capt. ACS to Archer, June 15, 1862. Maj. CS to Archer, June 15, 1862. Presumably same to H. H. Walker, July 1863–May 1864, and to Fry in June 1864. Maj. CS to McComb, by 1865. Appx. m. Novella Virginia Clark, 1866. Farmer in Wilson Co. in 1870. Actual name could be Richard Dale Hankins.

Hannah, George Baxter. b. Charleston, Virginia, Nov. 16, 1842. att. VMI. Of Charlotte Co., Virginia. Pvt. Co. B, 14th Virginia Cavy. Lt. ADC to A. G. Jenkins, May 2, 1863. Probably staff of McCausland later. Farmer at Wylliesburg and Cub Creek, Charlotte Co. d. Randolph, Virginia, Sept. 16, 1914. bur. family cem. in Charlotte Co.

Haralson, Hugh Anderson. b. Alabama, Nov. 5, 1835. Dallas Co. teacher. Capt. AQM, 6th Alabama, May 17, 1862. Capt. AQM to Battle, Sept. 15, 1864. Appx. m. Margaret Elizabeth Reynolds. Dallas Co. lawyer. d. Nov. 24, 1903.

Hardaway, Robert Archelaus. b. Morgan Co., Georgia, Feb. 2, 1829. att. Emory. Capt. Hardaway's (Ala.) Btty., May 1, 1861. To Maj., Dec. 3, 1862. Maj. acting Chief of Arty. to R. H. Anderson at Chancellorsville. Lt. Col., Feb. 27, 1864. WIA at Spotsylvania, May 12, 1864. Appx. Professor at UAla. and Auburn. d. Columbus, Georgia, Apr. 27, 1899.

Hardee, John Lewis. b. in Georgia, 1836. att. UGA. and a school in Paris, France. m. Mary A. Stoddard. Of Savannah. ADC to H. R. Jackson in state service, 1861. MSK at Augusta, Georgia, Nov. 1861. VADC to Lawton by Apr. 1862, through Seven Days. Capt. of "Hardee Rifles," a provost unit. VADC to his uncle Gen. Hardee, 1864. d. 1891.

Harding, Charles A. Physician in Montgomery Co., Maryland. Pvt. Co. A, 1st Maryland, July 18, 1861. Capt. ACS, 1st Maryland, Oct. 22, 1861. Capt. AQM to B. T. Johnson, Mar. 1862. Maj. QM to Bryan, Oct. 2, 1863. Maj. QM to Johnson, Apr. 23, 1864. Maj. QM to Butler, Oct. 14, 1864. Paroled Apr. 26, 1865.

Harding, Richard Chaplin. b. Dec. 24, 1839. A merchant. Cpl. 40th Virginia, May 26,

1861–June 1862. Capt. ACS, 40th Virginia, June 24, 1862. Capt. ACS to H. H. Walker, Sept. 1863. Same to Fry. Capt. ACS to Heth, Jan. 30, 1865. Appx. d. Dec. 28, 1872. m. Sarah Catharine Coles. bur. Wicomico Methodist Church.

Hardwick, Charles C. b. Hancock Co., Georgia. A 22-year-old merchant and factor at Savannah in 1860. Lt. Co. B, 8th Georgia, May 21, 1861. Lt. AAAG to G. T. Anderson, June–Aug. 1862. WIA in thigh at Second Manassas. Capt. AAG to Anderson, Nov. 8, 1862. WIA in thigh at Fort Harrison. Appx. Cotton merchant and broker at Savannah. d. there Mar. 8, 1891, from inflammation of the bowels. bur. Laurel Grove Cem. "Very reticent."

Hardy, Charles Wesley. b. Norfolk, Virginia, Oct. 12, 1836. att. VMI. Uncle of Douglas MacArthur. A merchant. Capt. AQM PAVA. Capt. AQM (PACS), June 29, 1861. Posted at Richmond. Capt. AQM, Mar. 9, 1863, assigned to ANVa. Served with Second Corps reserve train and ANVa. ordnance train until July 1864. Capt. AQM at Lynchburg, July 1864–1865. m. Victoria Taliaferro. Jacksonville, Florida, businessman. d. there Mar. 31, 1871. bur. Elmwood Cem., Norfolk.

Hardy, William Thomas. b. Norfolk, Virginia, Nov. 8, 1834. att. VMI and Randolph Macon. A civil engineer. Capt. AQM, PAVA. Capt. AQM (PACS), June 29, 1861. Paymaster for engineers on the peninsula of Virginia. Capt. AQM at Winder Hospital, Richmond, Nov. 1862. Capt. AQM, Cabell's Bn. Arty., Apr. 3, 1863. Tax collector in North Carolina, Aug. 1864–1865. Married twice. A farmer. d. Feb. 20, 1911, near Henderson, North Carolina. bur. St. John's Episc. Churchyard, Williamsboro, North Carolina.

Harlee, Edward Porcher. b. Marion C.H., South Carolina, Aug. 11, 1843. att. SCMA. Never married. Co. F, 6th South Carolina Cavy. Cadet AAIG to Conner, Aug. 1864. Same to Goggin and then Kennedy. New Orleans newspaperman and a teacher at

Little Rock, South Carolina. d. Mars Bluff, South Carolina, Feb. 25, 1878.

Harman, John Alexander. b. Waynesboro, Virginia, Feb. 29, 1824. Served in Mexican War with McCulloch's Rangers. Newspaperman at Staunton and Lewisburg. Also a cattleman and butcher. QM with T. J. Jackson, Apr. 29, 1861. Capt. AQM to Jackson, June 29, 1861. Maj. QM to Jackson, Sept. 11, 1861. Maj. QM to Ewell, May 1863. Maj. QM to Early, May 1864. Occasionally served as acting Chief QM, ANVa. On forage duty at Dublin Depot, Sept. 1864–Apr. 1865. Staunton postmaster. d. July 19, 1874, of diarrhea. bur. Thornrose Cem. Had "keen grey eyes, long heavy beard." "Rough in his manners but was kind and generous toward every one in whom he took any personal interest. . . ." "An enthusiast who was either elated or depressed by whatever news reached him." Excerpts of Harman's war letters are in the Hotchkiss Papers at the Library of Congress.

Harman, Michael Garber. b. Staunton, Virginia, Aug. 22, 1823. Operated a stage and hotel at Staunton. Maj. QM (PAVA.?) at Staunton, June 1861. Resigned Jan. 8, 1862. Simultaneously Lt. Col. 52nd Virginia, Aug. 19, 1861. Lt. Col. acting QM to T. J. Jackson, Jan. 7–Feb. 2, 1862. Col. 52nd Virginia, May 1, 1862. WIA at McDowell. Resigned June 6, 1863. Post QM at Staunton. President of Valley Railroad. d. on a train, Dec. 18, 1877. bur. Thornrose Cem.

Harman, William Henry. b. Waynesboro, Virginia, Feb. 17, 1828. Mexican War veteran. m. Margaret Singleton Garver. Staunton lawyer. Lt. Col., 5th Virginia, May 7, 1861. Col., Sept. 11, 1861. Dropped Apr. 1862. VADC to Ed Johnson, May 1862. Col. commanding Valley Reserves, May 1864. Capt. AAG to Davidson, Dec. 1864. KIA at Waynesboro, Mar. 2, 1865. bur. Thornrose Cem., Staunton.

Harper, Robert T. b. ca. 1836. att. SCMA. Pvt. Jeff Davis Arty. (Ala.), Aug. 13, 1862.

To Sgt., Mar. 1, 1863. To Lt. EO, May 24, 1863, but commission probably backdated to Feb. 15, 1862. Served with ANVa. (Hood's div.?) until relieved Sept. 5, 1863. Lt. EO in Georgia and South Carolina for remainder of the war. Professor at the Citadel, and civil engineer. Alive 1892. Harper's military record has several conflicting dates that make the interpretation above far from certain.

Harper, William Paynot. b. New Orleans, Louisiana. Clerk there. Capt. Co. H, 7th Louisiana, June 7, 1861. WIA and POW at Sharpsburg. Capt. AAAG to Nicholls, Mar. 1863. POW at Rappahannock Station. Capt. in Invalid Corps, Oct. 1864, on enrolling duty in Louisiana. Merchant, clerk, and civil sheriff at New Orleans. m. Lelia Mary Montan, 1864. d. Dec. 3, 1874, age 40. bur. Metairie Cem., New Orleans.

Harris, Charles S. b. in Virginia. Of Winchester. On AQM duty, apparently volunteer, with Valley Army's reserve ordnance train, 1862. Capt. AQM, Feb. 19, 1864, assigned to Second Corps reserve ordnance train. Failed senate confirmation. Paroled Apr. 19, 1865, age 28. A tinner at Winchester, alive in 1880.

Harris, David Bullock. b. Frederick's Hall, Virginia, Sept. 28, 1814. att. USMA. In U.S. Army, 1833–1835. Goochland Co. tobacco farmer. Capt. EO, PAVa., May 2, 1861. Capt. EO to Cocke, July 1861. Capt. EO (PACS), Feb. 15, 1862, to Beauregard. Maj. EO to Beauregard, Nov. 5, 1862. Lt. Col. EO to Beauregard, May 27, 1863. Col. EO to Beauregard, Oct. 9, 1863. d. Summerville, South Carolina, Oct. 10, 1864, of yellow fever. bur. Hollywood Cem., Richmond, Virginia.

Harris, Edwin Handy. b. Pendleton Dist., South Carolina. Wealthy cotton broker at Montgomery, Alabama, and four-term city mayor. Capt. AQM, 6th Alabama, May 23, 1861. Capt. acting AQM to Rodes, Nov. 1861. Maj. QM to Rodes, Feb. 24, 1862. Maj. QM at Montgomery, summer 1862. Moved to Baltimore, Maryland, and was a cotton merchant. d. there July 15, 1878, age 57 or 58. bur. Mt. Olivet Cem.

Harris, Hilary Valentine. b. Powhatan Co., Virginia, Mar. 8, 1839. att. Hampden Sidney. A banker. Pvt. Co. G, 11th Virginia, Apr. 23, 1861. Adjt. 11th Virginia, Apr. 7, 1863. Lt. AAAIG to Kemper's Bgd. after Gettysburg, July 1863 into 1864. Lt. ADC to W. R. Terry, probably in 1864. KIA at Sailor's Creek. bur. family cem., Mill Quarter Plantation, Powhatan Co.

Harris, James D. b. Crawford Co., Georgia, Apr. or May 1833. A resident of Pulaski Co. Lt. EO, Oct. 19, 1864. Served with ANVa. Appx.

Harris, Richard Sadler. b. Jan. 4, 1835. Farmer in Cabarrus Co., North Carolina, pre- and postwar. Lt. Co. B, 20th North Carolina, Apr. 18, 1861. Capt. AQM, 20th North Carolina, May 23, 1861. Capt. AQM to R. D. Johnston, Sept. 15, 1864. Appx. d. July 6, 1911.

Harris, William Alexander. b. near Luray, Virginia, Oct. 29, 1841. att. Columbian Coll. and VMI. Drilled troops early in the war. Lt. PAVa., July 16, 1861, to report to W. N. Pendleton. Capt. AAG to Wilcox, Jan. 31, 1862. Resigned June 23, 1862. Lt. OO to D. H. Hill, July 2, 1862. Capt. OO, Apr. 11, 1863. Capt. OO to Rodes, May 19, 1863. Resigned Dec. 8, 1863, to command a cavalry company elsewhere. Moved to Kansas in 1865. Civil engineer, stockraiser, and farmer. USHR from Kansas, and unsuccessful candidate for governor. d. Chicago, Illinois, Dec. 20, 1909. bur. Oak Hill Cem., Lawrence, Kansas.

Harris, William M. b. in Mississippi. Prewar farmer at Waterproof, Louisiana. Pvt. Co. D, 6th Louisiana, June 4, 1861, age 21. Pvt. Co. C, 19th Mississippi, Jan. 6, 1864. Lt. ADC to his brother, Gen. N. H. Harris, Feb. 19, 1864. Appx. Harris compiled the diary of his brother the general, which was published in 1901 in Duncansby,

Mississippi, and now is one of the great Confederate rarities.

Harrison, Benjamin. b. Prince George Co., Virginia, Oct. 5, 1826. Distant relative of President Harrison. Petersburg merchant from 1842 onward. Pvt. Co. E, 12th Virginia, Apr. 19, 1861. Capt. ACS, 12th Virginia, Oct. 7, 1861. Capt. acting ACS to Huger, June 1862. Dropped May 29, 1863, but continued to serve. Capt. acting ACS to Third Corps Arty., July 1863. Capt. acting ACS to Mahone, Feb. 1864. Appx. Petersburg asst. postmaster and bank cashier. d. there Mar. 16, 1898. bur. Blandford Cem.

Harrison, George Fisher. b. Richmond, Virginia, Sept. 24, 1821. Cousin of Secy. of War Randolph. Capt. Co. F, 4th Virginia Cavy., May 10, 1861. Resigned Aug. 31, 1861. Capt. AAG to Field, Apr. 17, 1862. Resigned Oct. 24, 1862, citing poor health. d. Feb. 20, 1896. bur. Longwood Cem., Goochland Co.

Harrison, Henry Heth. b. Fluvanna Co., Virginia, Feb. 15, 1820. Midshipman in USN, 1837–1845. Later a civil engineer. VADC to his cousin, Gen. Heth, spring 1862. Capt. AAG to Heth, July 6, 1862. Maj. AAIG to Heth, June 2, 1863. Retired to Invalid Corps, Dec. 9, 1864. Maj. commanding post at Buchanan, Virginia, Jan. 1865. d. Lewisburg, West Virginia, Aug. 21, 1893.

Harrison, Powell. b. Dec. 26, 1833. att. UVA. Lawyer at Leesburg, Virginia. Orderly Sgt., Staunton Arty., Apr. 17, 1861. Capt. ACS, 18th Virginia Cavy., Jan. 10, 1863. Capt. ACS to Imboden, June 22, 1863, into 1865. Paroled May 8, 1865, at Winchester. Lived Leesburg postwar. m. Janet Knox. d. Loudoun Co., Apr. 12, 1878. bur. Union Cem., Leesburg.

Harrison, Randolph. b. near Richmond, Virginia, Jan. 16, 1828. att. UPenn. m. Rosalie Freeland. Capt. Co. B, 1st Virginia, Aug. 5, 1861. Resigned Aug. 26, 1861. Adjt. 15th Virginia, May 27, 1862. Lt. AAAIG to Corse, Dec. 7, 1862. d. at Richmond Sept. 22, 1863. bur. Hollywood Cem.

Harrison, Samuel R. b. 1819. Served in Mexican War with 1st Mississippi Rifles. Prewar resident of New Orleans, Louisiana. Maj. CS to J. R. Davis, Nov. 1, 1862. Served there into 1865. m. Jennie McChinn, 1867. Postwar farmer. Committed suicide in Plaquemine Parish, Louisiana, Apr. 21, 1867. bur. "Springfield" Plantation, West Feliciana Parish.

Harrison, Thomas Randolph. b. Jan. 11, 1842. Pvt. 2nd Co. Richmond (Va.) Howitzers, July 14, 1861. Pvt. Co. F, 18th Virginia, Oct. 3, 1862. Courier to Gen. Pickett, Oct. 1862 into spring 1863. Lt. acting ADC to Garnett, July 1863. WIA and POW at Gettysburg. d. Newport News, Virginia, Aug. 12, 1920.

Harrison, Thompson. Capt. AQM, New Orleans Zouave Bn., Mar. 29, 1861. Capt. AQM to Magruder, June 20, 1861. Served with Magurder until promoted to Maj. QM to P. O. Hebert, Aug. 1864. d. Sept. 4, 1867, when he fell overboard from a steamer. Body never recovered.

Harrison, Walter Hamilton. b. Fredericksburg, Virginia, May 29, 1826. att. VMI. Journalist in New York. Lt. Col. 1st Virginia Militia, prewar. VADC to Pickett, May to Nov. 1862. Maj. AAIG to Pickett, Oct. 14, 1862, into 1865. Paroled Apr. 18, 1865. Postwar lawyer. d. Richmond, Jan. 5, 1871. bur. Hollywood Cem. Author of a book on Pickett's division.

Harrison, William Ellzey. b. Leesburg, Virginia, Feb. 17, 1832. att. VMI. Civil engineer in northern Virginia. Served with N. G. Evans and D. H. Hill in 1861. Lt. EO (PAVa.), early 1862 at Yorktown. Lt. EO, June 1, 1862. Spent most of the war working on the defenses at Chaffin's Bluff. Ft. Harrison, just below Richmond, named for him. Leesburg farmer. d. there Mar. 22, 1873. bur. Union Cem. Harrison's letters are at the Virginia Historical Society.

Hart, Camillus Sluman. b. Marietta, Ohio, July 10, 1823. Mexican War veteran and member of Cuba filibustering expedition. Cotton merchant, steamboater, and government purchasing agent. Lived in Texas, Mexico, Memphis, and Lexington, Kentucky. Lt. Co. I, 20th Georgia, May 23, 1861. Capt. AQM, 3rd Bn. Georgia, July 19, 1861. Capt. acting AQM to Garland, Mar. 1862. Capt. acting AQM to Early, May–Aug. 1862, at least. Capt. AQM to Carter's Bn. Arty., Nov. 1863. Capt. acting AQM to Pegram, Aug. 1864. Capt. AQM to Lomax, Jan. 1865. Maj. QM to Lomax, backdated to Dec. 26, 1864. New Orleans tobacco and cotton merchant. Martinsburg, West Virginia, hotel manager. Also lived at Baltimore; Washington, D.C.; and Winchester, Virginia. d. at his home in Mercersburg, Pennsylvania, Feb. 24, 1889. bur. Mt. Hebron Cem., Winchester.

Harvie, Charles Irving. b. June 9, 1842. att. UVA. Pvt. Co. G, 1st Virginia Cavy., May 9, 1861. Lt. Drillmaster to A. G. Jenkins, Dec. 9, 1862. Capt. AAG to Jenkins, Jan. 8, 1864. Capt. AAIG to McCausland, May 1864. MWIA near Front Royal, Nov. 12, 1864. d. as a prisoner in Winchester, Virginia, Nov. 14, 1864. bur. Hollywood Cem., Richmond.

Harvie, Edwin James. b. Amelia Co., Virginia, Feb. 1, 1835. att. VMI. Lt. 9th U.S. Inf., 1855–1861. Capt. of Inf., CSA, Mar. 16, 1861. Stationed at Camp of Instruction for PAVa., May 1861. Capt. AAG to Wise, June 6, 1861. Capt. AAIG to J. E. Johnston, Oct. 5, 1861. Lt. Col. AAIG to Johnston, May 20, 1862. Same to R. E. Lee, June 1862. Rejoined Johnston Nov. 1862. Col. AAIG, Mar. 31, 1863. Col. AAG to Hood, and then back to Johnston. Paroled at Greensboro. Worked as government clerk organizing Confederate records postwar. d. Washington, D.C., July 11, 1911. bur. Hollywood Cem., Richmond.

Harvie, John Blair. b. Apr. 24, 1836. Chief engineer for Richmond-Danville Railroad. Lt. EO (PAVa.), 1861, serving with Wise. Maj. QM to Early, Oct. 1, 1861. Maj. QM to Loring, May 29, 1862. Maj. QM to J. S. Williams, Apr. 12, 1863. Maj. QM at Richmond, Oct. 7, 1863, into 1865. In charge of river and canal transport. m. Mary Bell Anderson. d. Richmond, May 22, 1913. bur. Hollywood Cem.

Harvie, Lewis Edwin. b. near Frankfort, Kentucky, Oct. 8, 1825. att. Centre Coll. and Harvard. Capt. ACS, Dec. 13, 1862. Served at camps of instruction in Kentucky and at Athens, Georgia. Post commissary at Athens, in southwest Virginia, and in Tennessee, 1863. Capt. ACS and acting AQM to Robert Ransom, Oct. 10, 1863. Capt. ACS to G. W. C. Lee, June 9, 1864. Capt. ACS at Petersburg, Virginia, July 5, 1864. Back to Tennessee and Georgia, Sept. 1864. Capt. ACS to Lyon, Feb. 17, 1865. Capt. 1st C.S. Engineers, Mar. 2, 1865. Appx. d. Frankfort, Apr. 30, 1895. bur. there.

Harvie, William Old. b. Amelia Co., Virginia, Dec. 21, 1839. In 1st Virginia prewar. Capt. ACS, Oct. 19, 1861. Maj. CS, May 22, 1863. Apparently stationed in Gordonsville most of the war. Appx. Lived in Amelia Co. postwar. d. Mattoax, Virginia, Oct. 12, 1921. bur. Amelia Presby. Church.

Harvie, William Wallace. b. Nov. 6, 1827. att. UVA. Never married. Maj. CS to B. H. Robertson, June 18, 1862. Maj. CS to W. E. Jones and Rosser, 1863. Maj. CS to Robertson in South Carolina, Jan. 1864. Paroled May 13, 1865, at Charlotte. d. in Arkansas, May 29, 1868.

Haskell, Alexander Cheves. b. Abbeville Dist., South Carolina, Sept. 22, 1839. att. South Carolina Coll. Pvt. Co. D, 1st South Carolina, Jan. 1861. Later Adjt. Lt. ADC to Maxcy Gregg, Dec. 14, 1861. Capt. AAG to Gregg, Jan. 18, 1862. Later to McGowan, into mid-1863 at least. Lt. Col. 7th South Carolina Cavy., Apr. 20, 1864. Col., June 1864. WIA at Fredericksburg, Chancellorsville, Cold Harbor, and Darbytown Road. Appx. Brother-in-law of Gen. Alexander.

d. Columbia, South Carolina, Apr. 13, 1910. bur. Elmwood Cem.

Haskell, John Cheves. b. Oct. 21, 1841. Lt. Co. A, 1st South Carolina Arty., May 18, 1861. Maj. cs to G. W. Smith, Dec. 21, 1861. Maj. cs to D. R. Jones, Mar. 1862. Lost right arm at Gaines's Mill while vadc to Long-street. Maj. cs to Smith again, Nov. 1862. Maj. vadc to Longstreet at Fredericksburg. Maj. of Arty., Apr. 13, 1863, commanding a battalion. Lt. Col. of Arty., Feb. 18, 1865. Appx. m. Sally Preston Hampton, and later her cousin Lucy Hampton, both related to Gen. Hampton. In South Carolina legislature. Planter in Mississippi and lawyer at Columbia, South Carolina. d. Columbia, June 26, 1906.

Haskell, Joseph Cheves. b. Abbeville, South Carolina, Dec. 1, 1843. att. South Carolina Coll. Pvt. Co. C, 1st (Gregg's) South Carolina. Acting Cadet, csa, on staff of J. E. Johnston at Seven Pines. vadc to Alexander at Fredericksburg. Lt. of Arty., Feb. 9, 1863. Adjt. to artillery battalions of Alexander, Haskell, and McIntosh. Cadet csa, Oct. 20, 1863. Capt. aag to Alexander, Feb. 29, 1864. Appx. Postwar engineer, mine supt., planter, and railroad officer. Lived at Atlanta, Georgia. d. July 1, 1922. bur. Magnolia Cem., Charleston, South Carolina. Brother of A. C., John C., and Langdon C. Haskell (see above and below). An alternate source gives birthdate as Oct. 21, 1841.

Haskell, Langdon Cheves. b. Abbeville, South Carolina, Oct. 2, 1831. att. South Carolina Coll. Planter at Pine Bluff, Arkansas. Lt. adc to Maxcy Gregg, Jan. 18, 1862. Lt. adc to McGowan, Dec. 15, 1862. Capt. aag to McGowan, Nov. 2, 1863. Capt. aag to R. H. Anderson, Dec. 5, 1864. d. in Arkansas, Nov. 11, 1882. bur. Bellwood Cem., Jefferson Co. Eldest brother of all the Haskells shown above.

Hassell, Theodore M. b. Martin Co., North Carolina, Nov. 5, 1839. Farmed there. Sgt. Co. F, 17th North Carolina, May 1, 1861.

pow at Fort Hatteras, Aug. 29, 1861. Lt. Co. A, 17th North Carolina, Mar. 20, 1862. Lt. acting oo to Martin, Feb. 1864, and continued in that capacity with the brigade after Kirkland took command. kia near Goldsboro, North Carolina, Mar. 6 or 7, 1865. The middle initial may be bogus.

Hatch, Lewis Melvin. b. Salem, New Hampshire, Nov. 28, 1815. Moved to South Carolina in 1833. Charleston area farmer. Seminole War veteran. vadc and acting aqm to Beauregard at First Manassas. Col. 23rd South Carolina, Nov. 11, 1861. Served most of war in state troops. d. Asheville, North Carolina, Jan. 12, 1897. bur. Magnolia Cem., Charleston.

Hatch, William Henry. b. Georgetown, Kentucky, Sept. 11, 1833. Lawyer in Marion Co., Missouri. Capt. aag to G. W. Smith, Dec. 12, 1862. Cancelled by the president, but rank retained. Capt. aag at Richmond, serving as assistant to Col. Ould in the prisoner exchange bureau. ushr from Missouri, and farmer. d. near Hannibal, Missouri, Dec. 23, 1896. bur. Riverside Cem.

Hatcher, Charles. Pvt. Co. I, 4th Virginia Cavy., May 8, 1861. Detached for service with Pendleton, June 1862. Apparently served as vadc to Pendleton, 1862–1865. Believed to be the Charles Hatcher who was born Apr. 3, 1843, died at Richmond, Aug. 19, 1878, and is buried at Hollywood Cem.

Hatton, Clarence Riddick. b. Portsmouth, Virginia, July 7, 1848. att. Chuckatuck Military Academy and vmi. Lt. aaag to Godwin, June 1864. wia slightly at Third Winchester, and in throat at Cedar Creek. m. Sallie Colley Cocke. Nansemond Co. farmer. Grange agent in New York City, and later an engineer for that city. d. there Jan. 15, 1927. bur. Mount Hope Cem., Hastings-on-Hudson, New York.

Havis, James Judge. b. in Alabama, 1821. A millwright at Opelika, Alabama. Also a surveyor and machinist. m. Mary Ellen

Oslin. Lt. Co. A, 14th Alabama. Capt. AQM, 14th Alabama, May 13, 1862. Capt. AQM to Sanders's Bgd., Sept. 15, 1864, and thus staff of W. H. Forney in 1865. Appx. d. 1889.

Hawken, A. Milton. Capt. ACS, 12th Mississippi, May 1, 1861. Capt. acting ACS to Griffith, Nov. 1861. Maj. CS to Griffith, Mar. 11, 1862. Maj. CS to Barksdale, July 1862. Maj. CS to Humphreys, July 1863. Took Oath May 29, 1865. A resident of Hinds Co., Mississippi. "Indomitable."

Hawkins, Elijah. b. Hannibal, Missouri, Jan. 26, 1842. In Missouri State Guard early war. Pvt. Co. I, 18th Louisiana, Mar. 5, 1862. Lt. ADC to his uncle Gen. G. W. Smith, Aug. 30, 1862, until Feb. 1863. Capt. ADC to Smith in Georgia militia, Nov. 1864. m. Mrs. Isabelle J. Coffin. Businessman at San Francisco and in St. Louis. d. Riverside, California, Mar. 9, 1917. bur. Evergreen Cem.

Hawkins, Eugene A. b. 1842. att. UGA. Of Milledgeville, Georgia. Pvt. Co. H, 4th Georgia. Later to Lt. Resigned Dec. 28, 1862, citing "unpleasant relations with my captain." Lt. ADC to Doles, Dec. 28, 1862. Capt. AAIG to Doles, Nov. 2, 1863. KIA at the Wilderness, May 5, 1864. There was "no better nor more popular officer in the brigade" according to its published postwar history.

Hawkins, Thomas T. b. in Kentucky. Lt. 16th U.S. Inf. in Mexican War. Lt. ADC to Breckinridge, Nov. 11, 1861. WIA at Shiloh. Served with Breckinridge, 1861–1865. d. Frankfort, Kentucky, Sept. 6, 1879. bur. Frankfort Cem.

Hawks, Francis T. A civil engineer from Craven Co., North Carolina. Engineer of "the City Park in New York" in 1861. VADC to Branch, Mar. 1862. Served as EO to Branch during Seven Days. Capt. AAG to Branch, July 7, 1862. Capt. AAG to Lane, Sept. 1862. Resigned Jan. 1863 due to "unpleasant relations" with Lane. Lt. Co. A,

2nd Confederate Engineers, Aug. 6, 1863. Took Oath May 22, 1865.

Hawks, Wells Joseph. b. Deerfield, Massachusetts, Oct. 29, 1813. In Virginia legislature. Superintendent of schools, carriagemaker, and mayor of Charlestown. Married three times before the war. On commissary duty with T. J. Jackson, Apr. 29, 1861. Maj. CS to Jackson, Nov. 16, 1861. Maj. CS to Ewell, June 1863. Maj. CS to Early, May 1864. Maj. CS to John B. Gordon, Mar. 1865. Acting Chief Commissary ANVa. on occasion. Paroled at Winchester, Apr. 17, 1865. d. Charlestown, West Virginia, May 28, 1873. bur. Edge Hill Cem.

Hawn, William. Capt. MSK in Richmond, Virginia, Dec. 1864. Records are worse than skimpy on Hawn. Possibly the man of that name who served in the 7th Louisiana in 1861, and who lived postwar in New York City and wrote *All Around the Civil War*, published in 1908.

Haxall, Philip. b. Richmond, Virginia, Jan. 1, 1840. att. UVA. Part of Richmond milling family. Pvt. Co. I, 4th Virginia Cavy. VADC to J. R. Anderson, Dec. 1861–July 1862. Lt. Drillmaster to B. H. Robertson, Sept. 12, 1862. Capt. AAG to Robertson, Jan. 25, 1863. Relieved Dec. 31, 1864, and ordered to report to Kemper, but no evidence of duty with him. Capt. AAG to Stevenson, 1865. Paroled Greensboro. m. Mary Jenifer Triplett. Haxall's sister married R. E. Lee, Jr. Richmond miller. d. Feb. 11, 1897. bur. Hollywood Cem.

Hay, Richard Gantt. b. Barnwell Dist., South Carolina, Oct. 20, 1827. m. Martha Hutson Hay (his first cousin). Wealthy farmer in Colleton Co. prewar. Capt. Co. K, 11th South Carolina. Deputy PM at Charleston, 1862. Maj. CS to Hagood, Aug. 28, 1862. WIA at Bentonville. Paroled Apr. 26, 1865. Postwar insurance agent and legislator. d. Mar. 27, 1887. bur. Boiling Springs Presby. Cem., Lyndhurst, South Carolina.

Hayes, George Everard. b. in Georgia,

Mar. 28, 1835. att. UGa. and Philadelphia Coll. of Pharmacy. A druggist. Lt. Co. K, 3rd Georgia, Apr. 25, 1861. Lt. AAAG to Wright at Gettysburg. Maj. 3rd Georgia, Aug. 15, 1864. KIA at Weldon Railroad, Aug. 21, 1864. bur. Blandford Church Cem., Petersburg, Virginia.

Hayes, John Somerville. b. Fredericksburg, Virginia, Apr. 21, 1835. m. Susan McKim Gordon. Capt. ACS to Holmes, Sept. 24, 1861. Maj. CS to Cooke, Nov. 9, 1862. Served through the war. In flour and grain business at Baltimore, Maryland. d. there Dec. 21, 1913. Derisively called a "bombproof" officer by a colleague on Cooke's staff.

Haymond. Alpheus Franklin. b. near Fairmount, Virginia, Dec. 15, 1823. att. Wm. & Mary. State legislator, and lawyer in Marion Co. m. Maria F. Boggess, 1847. Capt. ACS, 31st Virginia, Dec. 24, 1861. Capt. acting ACS to William Smith, Mar.–July 1863. Maj. CS to Pegram, Sept. 12, 1863. Maj. CS to J. A. Walker, 1865. Appx. Postwar legislator in West Virginia, and member of state supreme court of appeals. Alive in 1894.

Haynes, William Decater. b. McMinn Co., Tennessee, Nov. 15, 1833. att. Hiawassee Coll. Logger near Tunnel Hill, Georgia, and a schoolteacher. Capt. AQM, Sept. 26, 1862, serving as post QM at various east Tennessee locations. Capt. acting QM to W. E. Jones, by Nov. 1863. Capt. AQM, 16th Virginia Cavy., Jan. 28, 1864. POW Dec. 14, 1864, in Sullivan Co., Tennessee. Released June 17, 1865. Blountville lawyer and railroad president. d. Bristol, Tennessee, Dec. 1890.

Hays, James. b. Mississippi, Sept. 27, 1839. Lt. Co. I, 12th Mississippi. Lt. AAAIG to Posey, Feb.–Oct. 1863. Capt. AAIG to Harris, Nov. 2, 1863. Paroled May 1865. Life insurance agent at Durant, Mississippi. d. Mar. 27, 1888. bur. Lexington Cem., Holmes Co. Hays's war letters are at the Virginia Historical Society.

Hays, Thomas N. Orderly Sgt. Co. G, 11th Alabama, 1861. Capt. ACS, 11th Alabama, May 29, 1862. Dropped in 1863 under Special Order #70. Apparently made Capt. AQM for Wilcox's Bgd., summer 1863, although evidence is thin. POW Dec. 16, 1863. Exchanged Mar. 1865. Dry goods merchant at Tuscaloosa in 1870, age 35.

Hays, Thomas S. Capt. AQM, Feb. 21, 1863, on duty at Bristol and Strawberry Plains, Tennessee. Capt. AQM to Braxton's Bn. Arty., May 1864. Forced out of army in autumn 1864 by bronchitis and apparently never returned.

Haywood, Fabius Julius, Jr. b. Oct. 1, 1840. att. UNC. Lt. 5th North Carolina, 1861. Lt. acting ADC to Garland in Seven Days. Adjt. 5th North Carolina, Jan. 26, 1863. WIA and POW at Gettysburg. Exchanged Mar. 1865. Raleigh physician. d. Dec. 14, 1911.

Hazlehurst, William. b. Apr. 13, 1836. Lt. ADC to his brother-in-law, Gen. Wright, Aug. 6, 1862. No further military record after Aug. 1863. m. Rosalie Crockford, 1865.

Head, John J. Capt. on the staff of Harris at Appx. No other record found.

Heard, Thomas Randall. b. Morgan Co., Georgia, July 12, 1812. Merchant at New Orleans, Louisiana. Capt. AQM, 6th Louisiana, July 12, 1861. Maj. QM to W. H. T. Walker, Sept. 17, 1861. Maj. QM to Taylor and Hays, 1862. Maj. QM at Shreveport by Jan. 1863. Paroled there June 8, 1865. m. Ann Brantley. d. Woodville, Mississippi, Mar. 3, 1867. bur. there.

Hearsey, Henry James. b. West Feliciana Parish, Louisiana, late in 1840. Law partner of future Gen. Carnot Posey, prewar. Pvt. Co. K, 16th Mississippi, Apr. 21, 1861. Later to Sgt. Capt. AQM, 16th Mississippi, Oct. 18, 1861. Capt. acting AQM to Trimble, Apr. 1862. Capt. acting AQM to Posey for some time before being apptd. Maj. QM, Jan. 19, 1863. Maj. QM to Harris, Jan. 1864. Appx. Postwar newspaper editor. Spent last 25 years of life in New Orleans. d. Oct. 30, 1900. bur. Metairie Cem.

Heath, Jesse Hartwell. b. Feb. 1, 1832. att. UVA. Farmer at Petersburg, Virginia. Capt. AQM, 4th Virginia Cavy., Nov. 16, 1861. Capt. acting QM to Fitz. Lee, Aug. 1863, perhaps even into 1865. d. Goochland Co., Virginia, Aug. 12, 1866. bur. Blandford Cem., Petersburg.

Heath, Roscoe Briggs. b. Dec. 19, 1827. att. UVA. and Harvard Law School. Lawyer at Petersburg, Virginia. Lt. Courtney's (Va.) Btty. Capt. AAG to J. R. Anderson, Sept. 12, 1861. Resigned Oct. 2, 1862, after a long absence due to intestinal disorder. d. Rockbridge Alum Springs, Virginia, Aug. 21, 1863. bur. Hollywood Cem., Richmond.

Heaton, Henry. b. Loudoun Co., Virginia, Mar. 18, 1834. att. UVA. Of Purcellville, Virginia. Lt. Loudoun Arty., Apr. 21, 1861. VADC to Early, Dec. 1862. Pvt. Co. B, 43rd Bn. Virginia Cavy., 1864–1865. Leesburg lawyer and legislator. d. there May 15, 1890. bur. Catoctin Church Cem., near Round Hill, Va.

Heck, John. Staff of Rosser in January 1864 and wounded at Moorefield. Very likely Jonathan McGee Heck, born May 5, 1831, in Monongalia Co., Virginia. A lawyer there. Lt. Col. 25th Virginia, July 1861. Dropped at reorganization. Postwar mining magnate at Raleigh, North Carolina. d. there Feb. 10, 1894. bur. Oakwood Cem.

Heggie, Evans Archibald. b. Mar. 10, 1840. Pvt. Co. E, 14th Georgia, July 6, 1861. Later QM Sgt. and then Capt. AQM, 14th Georgia, Nov. 14, 1861. Capt. AQM to Thomas, Oct. 22, 1864. Appx. A stable keeper at Augusta, Georgia. d. there Nov. 12, 1900. bur. Magnolia Cem.

Henagan, James Madison. b. in South Carolina, July 30, 1843. 8th South Carolina, 1861–1862. Capt. AQM, 8th South Carolina, Sept. 20, 1862. Capt. AQM to Conner, Sept. 15, 1864, and later to Goggin and Kennedy. Night clerk at a Mobile, Alabama, hotel. d. there May 21, 1903. bur. Livingston, Alabama.

Henderson, David English. b. Jefferson Co., Virginia, June 23, 1832. An artist. Pvt. Co. G, 2nd Virginia, Apr. 18, 1861. Detailed as a draftsman at army headquarters, 1861–1862. Lt. EO, July 11, 1862. Topographic engineer all through Virginia, 1862–1865. m. Anne Orfia Yates Beall, 1870. d. Nov. 16, 1887. bur. Zion Episc. Cem., Charlestown, West Virginia.

Henderson, Fenton Mercer. b. Loudoun Co., Virginia, 1818. att. Princeton. Commissioner in chancery at Leesburg, Virginia. m. Maria E. Thomas. Cpl. Co. C, 17th Virginia, Apr. 1861. Later Ordnance Sgt. for regiment. Lt. OO to Corse, Nov. 1862. Appx. Author of an 1868 book on Loudoun Co. d. Oct. 19, 1886. bur. Union Cem., Leesburg.

Henderson, Finley Houston. b. Greene Co., Tennessee. Pvt. Co. B, 2nd Tennessee Cavy., Mar. 1, 1862, age 30. Maj. CS to A. E. Jackson, Feb. 9, 1863. VADC to John B. Gordon at Third Winchester. Maj. CS to Wharton, Sept. 21, 1864. Maj. CS to Thomas's (N.C.) Legion, Jan. 1865. Maj. CS to S. R. Anderson, Mar. 1865. New York businessman postwar, and then hotel man at Knoxville, Tennessee. Alive there 1899. Rarely (if ever) used middle initial.

Henderson, Francis William. b. Prince William Co., Virginia, July 1, 1821. att. VMI. Teacher at Staunton Academy. Navy Dept. employee, and lived in California for a time. Capt. ACS, July 19, 1861. Stationed at Staunton, 1861–1863, and at Lexington, Virginia, from Mar. 18, 1863, into 1865. Rockbridge Co., Virginia, lawyer. d. Lexington, Oct. 27, 1887. bur. Stonewall Jackson Cem.

Henderson, James L. b. Warrenton, Virginia, Nov. 12, 1813. Joined USN in 1828, and worked through ranks. m. Sarah Lewis Williamson, 1839. Mexican War veteran. Held rank of Commander when he resigned in 1861. Commander CSN, Mar. 26, 1861. Capt. OO to Sam Jones, Apr. 1862. On ordnance duty in Alabama, early 1862, before returning to CSN. Col. (PACS), Dec. 12, 1862. Served at Richmond, Virginia, on court-martial duty, through June 1864, at least. Lived postwar in Princess Anne Co., Virginia. d. Charlestown, West Virginia, Dec. 20, 1875.

Henderson, Richard B. Capt. AAIG to Scales, Aug. 13, 1863. Served with Scales into 1865. This could be Richard Bullock Henderson, att. UNC, from Granville Co.

Henderson, Robert. b. May 17, 1835. Of Danville, Mississippi, a clerk and merchant. Cpl. Co. A, 2nd Mississippi, May 1861. Capt. ACS, 2nd Mississippi, Oct. 7, 1861. Dropped July 31, 1863, with bond difficulties, but reinstated Sept. 1863. Capt. ACS to Davis, by Oct. 1864 and perhaps as early as Sept. 1863. Appx. d. Mar. 9, 1903. bur. Henry Cem., near Corinth, Mississippi.

Henley, Richardson Leonard. b. James City Co., Virginia, July 27, 1836. att. Washington Coll. Lawyer at Williamsburg. Sgt. Co. C, 32nd Virginia, Apr. 28, 1861. Capt. ACS, 32nd Virginia, Oct. 7, 1861. VADC to McLaws, May 1862. Capt. acting ACS and VADC to Semmes at Sharpsburg. WIA three times there. Assigned to conscription duty, July 1863. m. Ida Dudley Spencer. Williamsburg lawyer and novelist. d. there May 23, 1897. bur. Cedar Grove Cem.

Henry, James Love. b. Buncombe Co., North Carolina, Dec. 24, 1835. Newspaper editor at Asheville by age 19. Lt. Co. G, 1st North Carolina Cavy., May 16, 1861. To Adjt., Aug. 28, 1861. Lt. OO to Robert Ransom, May 1862 through Seven Days. Staff of Hampton, Mar.–Apr. 1863. Resigned Sept. 28, 1863. Lt. Col. 14th Bn. North Carolina Cavy. Buncombe Co. judge. d. Oct. 6, 1884. bur. Riverside Cem., Asheville.

Henry, Mathis Winston. b. Bowling Green, Kentucky, Nov. 28, 1838. Of Logan Co. att. USMA. Lt. C. S. Cavy., Mar. 16, 1861. Lt. staff of Stuart, Mar. 1862. Maj. of Arty., Feb. 21, 1863. Chief of Arty. to Hood, 1863, and followed him to AOT. POW at Salisbury,

North Carolina, Apr. 12, 1865. m. Susie R. Burwell, 1875. Mining engineer in Nevada. d. Brooklyn, New York, Nov. 28, 1877. bur. Old Chapel, Clarke Co., Virginia.

Hepburn, Samuel Chew. b. Georgetown, D.C. att. Georgetown Coll. A resident of Louisiana from 1850s until death. Served in Co. B, Jefferson Mtd. Guards (La.). Lt. ADC to Nicholls, Jan. 17, 1863. Paroled June 15, 1865, at Shreveport. Civil engineer. d. New Orleans, Sept. 25, 1888, age 66. bur. Metairie Cem.

Herbert, William W. b. Dec. 25, 1826. Dry goods merchant at Alexandria, Virginia. m. Susan M. Scott. Capt. ACS, 57th Virginia, Oct. 4, 1861. Maj. CS to Armistead, Apr. 30, 1862. Maj. CS to Barton, 1863. Maj. CS to Steuart, 1864–1865. Commission merchant and postmaster at Alexandria. d. there, Mar. 10, 1901. bur. Ivy Hill Cem. Herbert's brother was the Col. of the 17th Virginia. Middle name thought to be Wirt.

Herbst, Francis Theodore. b. ca. 1819. Educated in Prussia. m. Caroline Christiana Arney, 1851. Worked as map man on U.S.–Mexico Boundary Survey, and then in Washington, D.C., 1848–1856. Lt. EO, Feb. 15, 1862. In charge of topographic records for the Engineer Bureau at Richmond, Virginia. Served there into 1865. Made surveys of Virginia battlefields for U.S. government immediately postwar.

Herndon, Edward W. b. Campbell Co., Virginia, Apr. 21, 1839. Moved to Asheville, North Carolina, 1857. Occupation there was "ambrotype artist." m. Hanna Moore Vance, sister of North Carolina's wartime governor. Pvt. Co. F, 14th North Carolina, May 3, 1861. Later Lt. Failed reelection. Capt. AQM, 29th North Carolina, June 12, 1862. Maj. QM to R. B. Vance, July 8, 1863. Maj. QM, Western Dist. of North Carolina, Apr. 1864. Maj. QM to Lane, Aug. 27, 1864, but only reported that winter. Appx. Postwar clerk. d. Jan. 16, 1886. bur. Riverside Cem., Asheville. His brother-in-law, Gov.

Vance, unkindly wrote of Herndon, "the truth is he is a low bred fellow."

Heth, Stockton. b. Richmond, Virginia, Apr. 5, 1839. att. VMI. A farmer. Capt. Co. E, 13th Virginia, Apr. 17, 1861 until dropped, Mar. 15, 1862. Lt. ADC to his brother, Gen. Heth, Jan. 23, 1862. WIA at Reams's Station. Appx. m. Isabella Norwood Hammet. Cotton planter in Mississippi. d. Roanoke, Virginia, Mar. 15, 1917.

Hewetson, Ralph Edward Babington. b. Rossgarrow, Ireland, Feb. 28, 1826. Son of a British Army officer. Coffee planter at Ceylon. Came to United States in 1852. Civil engineer in North Carolina, and architect at Columbia, South Carolina. Lt. Co. C, 1st South Carolina, July 29, 1861. To Capt. AQM, Jan. 13, 1863. Capt. AQM to McGowan, Sept. 15, 1864. Appx. Architect at Columbia and Charleston. d. Charleston, May 24, 1881. bur. Magnolia Cem. Two sources say Hewetson was born Feb. 28, 1827, instead of 1826.

Hewitt, Thomas Marshall. b. 1834. Lt. Co. A, 12th Bn. Virginia Arty., Feb. 17, 1862. Capt. AQM, Garnett's Bn. Arty., Apr. 23, 1863. Dropped Aug. 7, 1864, as "ignorant, disabled [or] incompetent." Postwar farmer in Charles City Co., Virginia. d. Sept. 3, 1902. bur. Hollywood Cem., Richmond.

Heyward, Joseph Manigault. b. Sept. 13, 1830. m. Maria Henrietta Magruder. VADC to Beauregard, Apr.–July 1861. Lt. ADC to Trapier, Nov. 16, 1861. Capt. AAG to Trapier, Apr. 14, 1862. d. Greenville, South Carolina, Nov. 7, 1862, of disease.

Higgason, Albert E. b. Sept. 15, 1836. att. Bethany Coll. Living at Negrofoot, Virginia, in 1860. Pvt. 1st Co. Richmond Howitzers, Aug. 8, 1861. Lt. Woolfolk's (Va.) Btty., Apr. 12, 1862. Lt. OO to Wilcox, Mar. 1863. Lt. OO to Perrin, Sept. 1863. Lt. OO to Sanders, May–Aug. 1864. Lt. OO to W. H. Forney, 1865. Appx. Teacher and preacher at Independence, Missouri, 1869–1911. d. there Mar. 29, 1911. bur. Woodlawn Cem.

Higgins, William H. Capt. ACS, 2nd Louisiana, Apr. 27, 1861. Capt. acting ACS to Magruder, Sept. 1861–Mar. 1862. No further record found.

Higham, Thomas. From South Carolina. Maj. QM to Ripley, July 24, 1862. Maj. QM to Doles, Nov. 1862. Transferred to Grahamville, South Carolina, Jan. 17, 1863, as post QM. On leave in Europe, Nov. 1863–Nov. 1864. POW in a Richmond, Virginia, hospital, Apr. 3, 1865.

Hill, Albert Potts. b. York Dist., South Carolina, Feb. 15, 1819. att. South Carolina Coll. Mexican War veteran of Jeff. Davis's regiment. Wealthy lawyer at Canton, Mississippi. Brother of Gen. D. H. Hill. Member of state secession convention. Capt. Co. G, 18th Mississippi, July 26, 1861. WIA twice at Ball's Bluff. Capt. in Mississippi Cavy., 1862. Col. of Cavy. and Judge on military court of First Corps, Dec. 16, 1862. Paroled May 10, 1865. m. Margaret A. Love. d. Canton, Oct. 15, 1868. bur. Canton City Cemetery.

Hill, Alonzo Alexander Franklin. b. Oglethorpe Co., Georgia, Dec. 4, 1826. att. UGA. and Jefferson Medical Coll. Surg. USN and a lawyer. Capt. Troup (Ga.) Arty., Apr. 26, 1861. Capt. Co. A, 1st Georgia Regs., June 18, 1861. Capt. acting ADC to Toombs, Oct. 1862. To Maj., 1st Georgia Regs., Sept. 3, 1864. d. Jan. 9, 1872. bur. Oconee Hill Cem., Athens.

Hill, Charles D. b. Leaksville, North Carolina, Oct. 20, 1837. Clerk at Richmond, Virginia, and a merchant at Milton, North Carolina. Pvt. Co. C, 13th North Carolina, Apr. 24, 1861. Later to QM Sgt. Capt. AQM, 13th North Carolina, Sept. 20, 1861. Capt. AQM to Wilcox, Sept. 15, 1864. Paroled with AOT. Tobacco merchant at Richmond. Also lived at Baltimore, Maryland. d. Waynesboro, Virginia, Feb. 7, 1898. bur. Hollywood Cem., Richmond.

Hill, Clement Digges. b. Aug. 3, 1828. From Prince George's Co., Maryland. A half-brother of N. S. Hill (q.v.). Maj. QM to

Trimble, Sept. 18, 1861. Maj. acting CS to J. G. Walker, Oct. 1861. Maj. QM at Manassas, Dec. 1861 to Mar. 1862. Maj. QM at Richmond, Mar. 1862–Oct. 1863. Maj. Chief IFT in Trans-Mississippi Dept., Feb. 20, 1864, into 1865. d. Jan. 8, 1897.

Hill, Edward Baptist. b. Mar. 22, 1821. Hotel keeper and merchant at Culpeper, Virginia. m. Mildred Anna Turner. Maj. CS to his brother, Gen. A. P. Hill, May 1, 1862. Appx. Postwar Culpeper merchant. d. Feb. 6, 1890. bur. Culpeper City Cem.

Hill, Francis Travis. b. Culpeper Co., Virginia, July 8, 1840. att. VMI and Harvard Law School. Son of Henry Hill and cousin of J. B. Hill. Capt. Co. G, 13th Virginia, July 12, 1861. Resigned Apr. 9, 1862. Lt. ADC to his uncle, Gen. A. P. Hill, Mar. 23, 1862. WIA at Cedar Mountain. Served into 1865. m. Marietta Byrd Miller. Culpeper lawyer. d. there Aug. 3, 1870.

Hill, Gabriel Holmes. b. Guilford Co., North Carolina, Jan. 7, 1837. Served in U.S. Army, 1857–1861. Lt. of Arty., CSA, Mar. 16, 1861. Lt. ADC to his distant cousin, Gen. Holmes, June 17, 1861. Maj. (PACS), Dec. 2, 1861. Commanded 17th North Carolina. POW at Roanoke Island. Exchanged Aug. 1862. Maj. commanding an artillery battalion in Arkansas, 1862. Maj. Chief of Arty., and then AAAIG to Holmes. Lt. Col. (PACS), May 19, 1863. Staff of Price and E. K. Smith.

Hill, George A. Lt. Co. C, 28th Georgia, Sept. 10, 1861. Capt. AQM, 28th Georgia, June 14, 1862. Relieved Aug. 13, 1864, and ordered to report to Dept. of North Carolina and Southern Virginia. Capt. AQM to R. H. Anderson by Mar. 1865. Appx., where he signed as Capt. AQM in Second Corps (Gordon).

Hill, Henry. b. Culpeper Co., Virginia, Feb. 1816. Father of F. T. Hill (q.v.). Mexican War veteran. Paymaster in U.S. Army, 1847–1861. Maj. QM, Paymaster Gen. of PAVA., from about June 5, 1861. Maj. QM (PACS), Nov. 11, 1861, but never made the transition,

and stayed in Virginia service into at least 1864. A cousin of Gen. A. P. Hill. Merchant at Baltimore, Maryland. d. Orkney Springs, Shenandoah Co., Virginia, Aug. 10, 1866.

Hill, Jacob Isaac. b. Rockbridge Co., Virginia, Feb. 1828. att. Washington Coll. Capt. AQM, 31st Virginia, Aug. 20, 1861. Capt. AQM to Ramseur, Sept. 19, 1864. Detached collecting forage for ANVa., Jan. 1865. Paroled May 1, 1865. Married twice. School principal in Missouri. d. Pomona, California, by 1913.

Hill, James Hoffman. b. in Maine, Oct. 26, 1834. att. USMA. Lt. U.S. Army, 1855–1861. Lt. of Arty., Mar. 16, 1861. Lt. AAG to Bee, 1861. WIA at First Manassas. Maj. AAG to Whiting, Oct. 2, 1861. WIA at Gaines's Mill. With Whiting into 1865. POW at Fort Fisher. m. Mary McRee Walker, who was sister-in-law of Gen. Whiting. Railroad clerk at Wilmington, North Carolina, postwar. d. there June 6, 1890. bur. Oakdale Cem.

Hill, John Booton. b. Madison Co., Virginia, Mar. 18, 1841. Clerk in U.S. Army for his uncle, Henry Hill (q.v.). Capt. AQM, Oct. 4, 1861. Maj. QM, Dec. 20, 1862. Served as a paymaster in Richmond until 1864, when he voluntarily entered the field to make room for his kinsman J. B. Cary. Maj. QM to N. G. Evans, Feb. 19, 1864. Failed confirmation and reappointed June 15, 1864. Maj. QM to Elliott. Maj. QM to Dept. of North Carolina and Southern Virginia, Sept. 20, 1864. Maj. QM to R. H. Anderson, Oct. 12, 1864. Appx. An accountant at Richmond. d. there Nov. 27, 1913. bur. Hollywood Cem. Hill's war letters are at the Virginia Historical Society.

Hill, Nicholas Snowden. b. Prince George's Co., Maryland, July 7, 1839. att. Georgetown Coll. Lawyer at Little Rock, Arkansas, in 1861. Pvt. 1st Maryland Arty., July 9–Aug. 13, 1861. Capt. ACS to J. G. Walker, Sept. 10, 1861. Maj. CS, Mar. 31, 1862, on duty as purchasing agent in Texas. Also established CSA packinghouses in Georgia and Tennessee. Maj. cs to Holmes, Price, and Magruder. Relieved Jan. 14, 1865. Took Oath, June 16, 1865. Baltimore railroadman. d. 1912. Half-brother of Clement D. Hill (above).

Hill, Robert Clinton. b. Iredell Co., North Carolina, Aug. 1833. att. usma. Lt. U.S. Army, 1855–1861. Lt. of Arty., Mar. 16, 1861. Maj. aag to Toombs, Aug. 1861. Maj. aag to Branch, Nov. 1861. Col. 48th North Carolina, Apr. 9, 1862. Capt. aag to Benning in 1863. d. in North Carolina of disease, Dec. 4, 1863. Known as "Crazy Hill."

Hill, Thomas Theopolis. b. Culpeper Co., Virginia, Mar. 28, 1818. att. uva. Lawyer at Charlottesville and Alexandria. Brother-in-law of Gen. J. M. Jones and brother of Gen. A. P. Hill. Capt. of Cavy., July 18, 1863. Judge on the Third Corps court. Culpeper lawyer. d. there June 22, 1873. bur. Maplewood Cem., Charlottesville.

Hill, Thomas T., Jr. Nephew of Gen. A. P. Hill and almost certainly the son of the Thomas T. Hill listed above. Of Alexandria, Virginia. Sgt. 4th Virginia Heavy Arty., June 1, 1861. May 1862, age 18. Pvt. Co. D, 34th Virginia, July 14, 1862. Detailed to ordnance duty early in 1863. Lt. oo to Poague's Bn. Arty., about June 1863. Stayed with that organization for remainder of the war.

Hill, William Ezekiel. b. Roanoke Co., Virginia, May 27, 1837. att. Hollins Institute and vmi. Lt. csa, July 16, 1861. Adjt. 19th Alabama, Sept. 1861. Actg. Adjt. 2nd Bn. Alabama, Oct. 1861. wia and pow at Shiloh. Lt. adc to Wheeler, Dec. 1862. Capt. on staff of Wheeler, Aug. 9, 1863. Capt. on staff of A. G. Jenkins, Feb. 1, 1864. Capt. acting aaig to W. L. Jackson, May 1864. Later on staff of Davidson. att. uva. and Hampden Sidney postwar. Presbyterian preacher in at least four states. d. DeKalb, Mississippi, Dec. 21, 1900.

Hill, William P. b. in North Carolina. Tailor at Charlotte prewar. Lt. Co. B, 1st North Carolina (Bethel). Capt. acs, 53rd North Carolina, Oct. 4, 1862. Capt. acs to Daniel, Sept. 1863. Capt. acs to Godwin, July 25, 1864. Capt. acs to Lewis, late war. Express agent at Charlotte. d. Jan. 31, 1873, age 40. bur. Elmwood Cem., Charlotte. Known as "Billy."

Hilton, Joseph. b. Preston, England, Oct. 30, 1842. Moved to Darien, Georgia, 1855. Lt. Co. M, 26th Georgia, Aug. 13, 1861. To Capt., Aug. 12, 1863. wia twice. Capt. aaag to C. A. Evans, date uncertain, until Appx. Lumber merchant at Darien. d. 1920. "Unexcelled on the field of battle," said Gen. Evans. Five of Hilton's war letters are at the Georgia Historical Society.

Hinkle, David W. On duty with U.S. Army in 1850s as topographic engineer. Lived in New Mexico, but from Montgomery, Alabama. Capt. aqm, 14th Alabama, July 19, 1861. Maj. qm to Pryor, May 13, 1862. Maj. qm to E. A. Perry, Sept. 1862. Charged with embezzlement in 1863. Maj. qm to Finegan, Sept. 1864. Appx. Possibly the man farming in Winston Co., Alabama, in 1870.

Hinrichs, Oscar. b. on Baltic coast, Feb. 1835. Father was an officer in the Swedish Guard, and a diplomat in the United States from Saxe Coburg. Worked on U.S. Coast Survey, 1855–1861. Left New York for Richmond, Jan. 1862. Lt. eo, Feb. 15, 1862, to report to J. E. Johnston. Lt. eo to Ewell, June 1862. Lt. Asst. oo to T. J. Jackson, mid-June 1862. Lt. eo to Taliaferro, Dec. 20, 1862. Lt. eo to Trimble, and then to Colston. Lt. eo to Edward Johnson, June 1863. wia at Mine Run. Lt. eo to John B. Gordon, May 1864. Lt. acting Chief eo to Early, Sept. 1864. Capt. eo, Oct. 19, 1864. Capt. eo to J. A. Walker, by 1865. wia at Farmville, Apr. 7, 1865. Appx. Engineer and architect in Washington, D.C. Committed suicide in 1893. Hinrichs was the great-grandfather of "Muppets" creator Jim Henson.

Hinsdale, John Wetmore. b. Buffalo, New York, Feb. 4, 1843. att. unc. Lt. adc to Holmes, July 27, 1861. Lt. aaag to Pender during Seven Days. Went west with Holmes. Col. 3rd North Carolina Junior Reserves, Feb. 9, 1865. President of North Carolina Bar Association. d. Sept. 15, 1921. Hinsdale's excellent memoir is at Duke.

Hinton, Drury Andrew. b. May 4, 1839. att. UVA. Of Petersburg, Virginia. Lt. Co. G, 41st Virginia, June 20, 1861. Dropped May 1, 1862. Pvt. Co. A, 44th Bn. Virginia. To Adjt., Dec. 15, 1863. VADC to Weisiger, June 1864. Lt. ADC to Weisiger, July 30, 1864. Appx. Lawyer at Petersburg. d. Oct. 19, 1909. bur. Blandford Cem.

Hobart, John Henry. b. in New York. A clerk at Vicksburg, Mississippi. Lt. Co. A, 21st Mississippi, May 15, 1861. Lt. AAAIG to Humphreys, July–Aug. 1863. Capt. AAIG to Humphreys, Nov. 2, 1863. WIA at the Wilderness. Retired Dec. 17, 1864. Vicksburg commission merchant postwar. bur. Cedar Hill Cem., in unmarked grave.

Hobday, Albert. b. Feb. 26, 1832. Resident of Gloucester Co., Virginia. Capt. ACS, Apr. 11, 1863, stationed in King and Queen Co., Virginia. Capt. AQM at Hicksford, Virginia, June 24, 1863, into 1865. d. July 2, 1901. bur. Abingdon Episc. Church Cem., Gloucester Co.

Hockenhull, John. b. in England, Mar. 7, 1811. Came to the United States in 1840. Discovered gold in Forsyth Co., Georgia, about 1842. Became wealthy planter in Lumpkin Co. and Dawson Co. Gold miner in California. Capt. ACS, 11th Georgia, July 4, 1861. Capt. acting ACS to G. T. Anderson, much of 1862. Maj. CS to Anderson, Oct. 14, 1862, through 1865. Served in state legislature. Married twice. d. Mar. 6, 1880. bur. Salem Methodist Church, Forsyth Co. Described by a soldier in the 11th Georgia as "our gentlemanly, attentive, and energetic commissary."

Hodges, John F. Lt. Co. F, Holcombe (S.C.) Legion, Dec. 28, 1861. Capt. AQM, Holcombe Legion, Oct. 16, 1862. Capt. AQM to B. R. Johnson, Jan. 10, 1865.

Hoenniger, Theodore William. b. in Germany, May 29, 1840. New York City hotelman. Later managed the famous Spotswood Hotel in Richmond, Virginia, during the war. VADC to G. W. Smith at Seven Pines. Subsequently served in the Prisoner Exchange Bureau. Postwar caterer at the Greenbrier White Sulphur Springs in West Virginia, and proprietor of the St. James Hotel in Richmond. Also a farmer and legislator. d. in Henrico Co., Nov. 4, 1882. bur. Oakwood Cem.

Hofflin, Marcus. b. in Bavaria. A 25-year-old merchant at Salisbury, North Carolina, in 1860. Lt. Co. K, 4th North Carolina, May 16, 1861. VADC to G. B. Anderson, Sept. 1862. Capt. acting ACS to regiment and brigade, dates unknown. Capt. Co. K, 4th North Carolina. Commanded regiment in Aug. 1864. Resigned Jan. 4, 1865. Capt. ACS, Jan. 26, 1865, post not given. Took Oath, May 30, 1865. Probably the Marcus Hofflin who was a travel agent at Milwaukee, Wisconsin, in 1890.

Hoffman, Alfred. b. in Maryland. Living in Baltimore in 1860, age 27. VADC to Trimble, Sept. 1862. Volunteer OO to Hoke at Fredericksburg. VADC and volunteer OO to Trimble at other times. Maj. AAG to Trimble, Feb. 2, 1863. Maj. AAG to Colston, spring 1863. MWIA at Chancellorsville, May 3, 1863. Taken to Mrs. Allan's house in Richmond, at 4th and Main Streets. d. Aug. 9, 1863, age 30. bur. Hollywood Cem.

Hoge, John Blair. b. Richmond, Virginia, Feb. 2, 1825. In Virginia House of Delegates, 1855–1859. Martinsburg lawyer. Capt. AQM, Sept. 14, 1861. Maj. QM, Mar. 5, 1862. Served in Richmond until May 6, 1862, when "services dispensed with, being supernumerary." Maj. AAG, Apr. 22, 1864, on duty in AIGO in Richmond. Lt. Col. AAG, Mar. 20, 1865, but appointment possibly not effected. USHR and Washington, D.C., lawyer. d. Martinsburg, West Virginia, Mar. 1, 1896. bur. Norbourne Cem.

Hoge, Peter Byron. b. Augusta Co., Virginia, Nov. 14, 1835. Pvt. Co. L, 5th Virginia, Apr. 17, 1861. Capt. AQM, Oct. 8, 1861. Post QM at Monterey, Virginia. Dropped May 5, 1862, "being supernumerary." m. Mary Jordan. Staunton railroad developer and grocer. Moved to Baltimore, Maryland, in the 1870s and sold fertilizer. d. there Apr. 2, 1904. bur. Thornrose Cem., Staunton.

Holcombe, William James, Jr. b. Oct. 4, 1842. att. UVA. Pvt. and Sgt. Maj., 2nd Virginia Cavy., 1861. Lt. Drillmaster, Feb. 25, 1863, to report to B. H. Robertson. Lt. Drillmaster at Camp Holmes, North Carolina, Aug. 1863. Lt. Drillmaster, to report to J. S. Williams, Sept. 3, 1863. Back to Robertson, Dec. 1863. Lt. Drillmaster with Valley Army under Early, Aug. 1864. Lt. ADC to Roberts, 1865. Paroled May 1865. Farmer at Roanoke, Virginia. Never married. d. Richmond, Jan. 31, 1901. bur. Lynchburg.

Holladay, Waller. b. in Persia, Apr. 7, 1840. Pvt. 59th Virginia, 1861. Sgt. Charlottesville (Va.) Arty., Mar. 1862. Lt. OO to Iverson, Feb. 7, 1863. Lt. OO to R. D. Johnston, Sept. 1863. Served with Toon during Johnston's absence in mid-1864. Appx. att. UVA postwar. m. Kate Emerson. Teacher in Nelson Co., Virginia, and in New York City. d. Fredericksburg, Virginia, Oct. 1, 1907. bur. UVA. Cemetery at Charlottesville.

Holliday, Robert Kennedy. b. in South Carolina, Apr. 6, 1829. Moved to Georgia as an infant. Merchant at Jonesboro. Capt. AQM, 7th Georgia, May 31, 1861. VADC to G. T. Anderson, Aug. 1862. Capt. AQM to Anderson, Sept. 15, 1864. m. Mary Anne Fitzgerald. Worked as railroad baggage clerk and died impoverished at Jonesboro, Dec. 24, 1872. Uncle of famous gunfighter "Doc" Holliday, and very distantly related to author Margaret Mitchell through his wife.

Holliday, Thomas C. b. in Mississippi,

June 13, 1840. att. UNC and GMI. A resident of Aberdeen. Lt. Co. I, 11th Mississippi, Feb. 20, 1861. Adjt. 11th Mississippi, Apr. 21, 1862. WIA at Sharpsburg. Lt. AAAIG to Davis, June–Aug. 1863. WIA at Gettysburg, July 3. Capt. AAG to Davis, Aug. 25, 1863. KIA at Wilderness, May 6, 1864. bur. at farm of James Clark, nine miles from Orange C.H., Virginia, now unmarked. Six of Holliday's war letters are at the Evans Library in Aberdeen.

Holmes, Charles Rutledge. b. July 9, 1835. Lt. Co. I, 2nd South Carolina, May 1861. Lt. AAAG to Bonham, Jan. 1862. Capt. AAG to Kershaw, Mar. 22, 1862. Capt. AAG to Conner, June 1864. WIA June 16, 1864. WIA in thigh at Gravel Hill Church, July 28, 1864. Capt. AAG to Kennedy, 1864–1865. Merchant at Charleston. d. Sept. 17, 1891. bur. Magnolia Cem.

Holmes, John Lyon. b. in North Carolina, Nov. 2, 1827. att. UNC. Lawyer at Wilmington pre- and postwar. Maj. CS to Daniel, June 17, 1862. Resigned July 15, 1862, without ever reporting to Daniel. Capt. ACS at Fayetteville (N.C.) Arsenal, Mar. 29, 1864. Served until Jan. 1865. d. Sept. 18, 1888. bur. Oakdale Cem., Wilmington.

Holmes, Theophilus Hunter, Jr. b. in Louisiana, Dec. 17, 1844. att. UNC. VADC to his father, Gen. Holmes, during Seven Days. Lt. ADC to Holmes, July 20, 1862. Serving with 5th North Carolina Cavy. as a volunteer when KIA near Ashland, June 3, 1864.

Holt, Joseph H. b. in Virginia, ca. 1829. A planter in Bedford Co. Sgt. Co. C, 28th Virginia, May 15, 1861. Capt. AQM, 28th Virginia, May 28, 1861. Capt. AQM to Pickett, Sept. 15, 1864. Served into 1865. Kept a hotel at Lynchburg postwar. d. Yellow Sulphur Springs, Virginia, Feb. 13, 1910. bur. family cem. in Bedford Co.

Hooe, Philip Beverley. b. Alexandria, Virginia, Sept. 15, 1833. Worked on U.S. Coast Survey, 1849–1853, and then Alexandria businessman. Lt. Co. A, 17th Virginia,

1861–1862. Capt. AAG to Corse, Nov. 14, 1862. WIA in leg at Drewry's Bluff, May 1864. Alexandria merchant. m. Mary Helen Daingerfield. Hooe's niece married Gen. Fitz. Lee. d. July 4, 1895. bur. Christ Church Episc. Churchyard.

Hooe, Roy Dalveen Mason. b. Sept. 10, 1840. att. USNA. Lt. PAVA., May 8, 1861. Lt. OO to Holmes, July 1861. Lt. AAAG to Ruggles, July 1861. Lt. PACS, Sept. 24, 1861. Capt. AAG to Ruggles, Dec. 20, 1861. Capt. AAG to Chalmers, Dec. 24, 1864. Back to Ruggles, Mar. 1865. d. Baltimore, Maryland, Sept. 27, 1866.

Hooff, James Lawrence. b. Jefferson Co., Virginia, Oct. 2, 1825. Merchant at Charlestown. Served in Co. G, 2nd Virginia, and later Capt. Co. E, 11th Virginia Cavy. Capt. AQM, 11th Virginia Cavy., Oct. 1, 1863. Capt. acting Bgd. QM, Oct. 22, 1863. Relieved from his regiment, Apr. 29, 1864, but reinstated Mar. 1865. Paroled at Winchester, Apr. 19, 1865, as Capt. AQM under Rosser. May have been on Rosser's staff for whole period. Charlestown farmer, merchant, and legislator. d. there Sept. 24, 1887. bur. Edge Hill Cem.

Hooff, John G. Johnston. b. Alexandria, Virginia, Sept. 1844. Married three times. Served in 4th Chesapeake (Md.) Arty., 1864. VADC to Pendleton at Appx. May have been commissioned, and may have served with Pendleton some time previous to Apr. 1865. Records are weak. Postwar Baltimore grocer and hardware merchant. Also lived at Pittsburgh, Pennsylvania, and was a broker and agent at Washington, D.C. d. Bedford, Virginia, Apr. 20, 1921. bur. St. Paul's Cem., Alexandria.

Hopkins, David Lawrence. b. Lexington, Virginia, Dec. 1827 or Jan. 1828. Listed prewar occupation as "gentleman," worth $47,000. Served in 27th Virginia, but hired a substitute. Clerk in QM Dept., Mar. 1862. Capt. AQM, Oct. 2, 1863, stationed at Lynchburg. Paroled Apr. 26, 1865. Merchant at Lexington. d. there Sept. 29, 1865. bur. Stonewall Jackson Cem. "He is determined it seems to keep out of the fight," wrote an officer in the 27th Virginia in 1862.

Hopkins, Warren Montgomery. b. Powhatan Co., Virginia, June 1, 1839. att. Abingdon Male Academy. A farmer. Lt. Co. D, 1st Virginia Cavy. Lt. ADC to W. E. Jones, Nov. 10, 1862. Maj. CS to Jones, Dec. 22, 1863. Maj. CS to B. T. Johnson, 1864. Col. 25th Virginia Cavy., Dec. 31, 1864. m. Mary H. Baltzell. d. Dec. 9, 1875. bur. Sinking Spring Cem., Abingdon.

Hopson, Virgil L. b. in Georgia, ca. 1828. Merchant at LaGrange pre- and postwar. Capt. ACS, 4th Bn. Georgia, Oct. 14, 1861. Capt. ACS, 35th Georgia. Capt. ACS to Wilcox, July 29, 1863. Capt. AQM, Oct. 26, 1863. Served with Richardson's Bn. Arty. Absent without leave, Feb. 1865. No other military record. Alive 1870.

Hord, Edward Livingston. b. Mason Co., Kentucky, Mar. 18, 1834. att. Bethany Coll. Settled in Lafayette Co., Missouri, 1853, as a farmer. Later a merchant at Covington, Kentucky. Capt. AQM, 12th Bn. Tennessee Cavy., Oct. 14, 1862. Capt. acting AQM to Gracie, Jan. 1863. Maj. QM to Gracie, Apr. 6, 1863. Dropped Apr. 11, 1864, for failed bond, but reinstated May 9, 1864. Maj. QM to Wallace, Sept. 20, 1864. Appx. Hotel keeper at Mexico, Missouri. d. St. Louis, July 1892. bur. Elmwood Cem., Mexico.

Hotchkiss, Jedediah. b. Windsor, New York, Nov. 30, 1828. Augusta Co., Virginia, schoolteacher. Topographical engineer in western Virginia campaigns, 1861. Served with H. R. Jackson at Monterey. Adjt. 25th Virginia. Joined T. J. Jackson as a topographic engineer, Mar. 28, 1862. Same to Ewell, June 1863. Same to Early, May 1864–Apr. 1865. Usually called Capt. and Maj., but in fact never commissioned. Very important postwar author, historian, and cartographer based in Augusta Co. Especially active in promoting development of

Virginia. d. Jan. 17, 1899. bur. Thornrose Cem., Staunton.

Houston, Adlie O. Pvt. Co. E, 43rd Alabama, Apr. 5, 1862. Capt. AQM, 43rd Alabama, June 2, 1862. Capt. acting AQM to Gracie, Dec. 1862. Capt. AQM to B. R. Johnson, Aug. 23, 1864. Appx.

Houston, James. Capt. AQM, 2nd Georgia, Aug. 15, 1861. Capt. acting AQM to Toombs and Benning, intermittently, 1862–1864. Relieved Sept. 13, 1864, and sent to forage duty in Georgia. Paroled at Tallahassee, Florida, May 18, 1865.

Houston, Mathew Hale, Jr. b. Wheeling, Virginia, Jan. 19, 1841. att. Washington Coll. Pvt. 3rd Company Richmond Howitzers, May 5, 1861. Pvt. Carrington's (Va.) Btty., July 20, 1862. To Cpl., Feb. 13, 1863. Lt. OO McIntosh's Bn. Arty., Feb. 27, 1863. att. Union Theological Seminary. Missionary in China, and minister in Kentucky and Virginia. d. Augusta, Virginia, Jan. 12, 1905. bur. Riverview Cem., Waynesboro.

Houston, Robert Emmett. b. Madisonville, Tennessee, May 27, 1839. Lawyer at Aberdeen, Mississippi, prewar and postwar. Pvt. Co. I, 11th Mississippi, June 1, 1861. Discharged by Apr. 1862. Capt. AAIG to Vaughn, Oct. 22, 1862. POW at Vicksburg. Took Oath, July 9, 1865. m. Mary Weaver, 1871. Lawyer at Memphis. d. 1909.

Howard, Charles. b. in Maryland, Feb. 6, 1830. Maj. CS to Elzey, May 8, 1862. Maj. CS to Lomax, Aug. 16, 1864. Postwar insurance agent. Brother of James and McHenry Howard (q.v.). d. Richmond, Virginia, Apr. 28, 1895. bur. St. Thomas Episc. Churchyard, Garrison, Maryland. A small collection of Howard's papers are at the Maryland Historical Society in Baltimore.

Howard, Conway Robinson. b. Richmond, Virginia, Jan. 31, 1832. att. Washington Coll. A civil engineer. Part of Capt. Pope's "Artisian well boring expedition" through Texas in 1857–1858. Also worked on a military road in Washington Territory, 1859–

1860. Capt. EO (PAVa.), May 2, 1861. Served at Norfolk and on the Rappahannock River. Lt. EO (PACS), Feb. 15, 1862, serving on staff of A. P. Hill by July 1862. Capt. EO to Hill, Oct. 3, 1862. Maj. EO to Hill, Mar. 17, 1864. Appx. Railroad engineer postwar. Moved to Baltimore, Maryland, 1893. d. there Aug. 2, 1895. bur. Hollywood Cem., Richmond.

Howard, George. VADC to Archer, date unknown. Probably George A. Howard, Adjt. of the 7th Tennessee, who att. USNA and Cumberland Univ., and died Jan. 3, 1900, at Dixon Springs, Tennessee.

Howard, James. b. Baltimore, Maryland, Oct. 23, 1832. Served in 3rd U.S. Arty., 1857–1861. Lt. of Arty., Apr. 16, 1861, on instruction duty. Lt. ADC to G. W. Smith, Sept. 30, 1861. Relieved Sept. 20, 1862. Lt. Col. of Arty., Aug. 30, 1862. Commanded 18th and 20th Bns. Virginia Arty. POW at Sailor's Creek. Brother of Charles and McHenry Howard (q.v.). Adjt. Gen. of Maryland. d. Baltimore, Nov. 1, 1910.

Howard, James McHenry. b. Baltimore, Maryland, Mar. 26, 1839. att. St. James Coll. and UVA. Pvt. Co. C, 1st Maryland. Lt. of Arty., June 24, 1862. Lt. AAAG to T. S. Rhett and the artillery defenses of Richmond, 1862–1863. Lt. OO to Elzey, May–July 1864. Lt. OO and AAAG to Stevens, Aug. 1864. Appx. An unofficial source says he served on the staffs of Nicholls, Hays, and B. T. Johnson in 1864. Emigrated to Canada, 1865. Later a Baltimore physician. d. Jan. 31, 1916. "Devoted to games and all kinds of sports, from cards to cricket." Howard's short autobiography was published in 1922. He also is the subject of a small biography.

Howard, McHenry. b. Baltimore, Maryland, Dec. 26, 1838. att. Princeton. Grandson of Francis Scott Key. Studied law prewar. Sgt. 1st Maryland Inf. Lt. ADC to distant cousin Gen. C. S. Winder, Mar. 31, 1862. Lt. acting OO to Maryland Line, Sept.–Dec. 1862. Lt. ADC to Trimble, Feb. 1, 1863. VADC to Steuart at Gettysburg. Lt. AAG to Steuart, by Nov. 1863. POW at Spotsylvania, May 12, 1864. Exchanged Oct. 31, 1864. Lt. AAG to G. W. C. Lee, Jan. 1865. POW at Sailor's Creek. Baltimore lawyer. d. Oakland, Maryland, Sept. 11, 1923. bur. St. Thomas's Church Cem., Owings Mills, Maryland. Howard's papers are at the Maryland Historical Society, and his memoir of the war is one of the classics.

Howard, Richard Austin. b. in Maine, 1824. Moved to Brandon, Mississippi, 1832, and to Texas in 1844. att. USMA. Served in artillery and with mounted rifles in Mexican War. Surveyor and scout with U.S. Army on frontier. Realtor and merchant at San Antonio, Texas. VADC to Van Dorn, May 1861. VADC to Barnard Bee at First Manassas. WIA there. Capt. ACS, Mar. 18, 1862, in Texas. Maj. CS in Texas, Dec. 9, 1862. Failed confirmation and reapptd. Oct. 26, 1864. POW on Red River in 1863. d. at Beauregard Station, Louisiana, of cholera, Dec. 4, 1866. In 1861 Gen. J. E. Johnston called him "the fittest Texan living for military service."

Howell, Robert Philip. b. near Goldsboro, North Carolina, Jan. 18, 1840. att. UNC. Bank cashier at Goldsboro. Pvt. Co. A, 27th North Carolina, 1861–1862. Capt. AQM, 62nd Georgia, July 21, 1862. Capt. acting QM to Dearing, July 1864. In North Carolina, 1865. Farmer in Mississippi and at Goldsboro. d. Goldsboro, May 8, 1916.

Hoyl, John Barrett. b. McMinn Co., Tennessee, May 27, 1827. att. Holston Coll. Lawyer in Polk Co. and Bradley Co. Pvt. Co. D, 5th Tennessee Cavy., Dec. 15, 1862. Maj. CS to Vaughn, Jan. 30, 1863. POW at Vicksburg. Lawyer and judge at Cleveland, Tennessee. "Accumulated a small fortune." d. there Feb. 9, 1900. bur. Fort Hill Cem., Bradley Co.

Hubard, James Lenaeus. b. Feb. 27, 1835. att. VMI and UVA. Planter in Buckingham Co., Virginia. Lt. Col. 44th Virginia, June 14, 1861. Dropped May 1862. VADC to Winder (probably John H.), summer 1862. Maj.

QM to B. H. Robertson, Nov. 22, 1862. Resigned Jan. 15, 1863, because of poor health. Lawyer, author, and farmer in Nelson Co. d. Dec. 4, 1913.

Hudgins, Benjamin Franklin. b. King William Co., Virginia, Nov. 12, 1831. att. VMI. Capt. Co. E, 32nd Virginia. Failed reelection. Lt. ADC to Pryor, May 20, 1862. Resigned Oct. 20, 1862. Lt. Drillmaster to B. H. Robertson, Feb. 3, 1863. Resigned May 22, 1863. Farmer and merchant. m. Rebecca Bland Worsham. d. Hampton, Virginia, Mar. 25, 1894.

Hudgins, James Madison. b. Mathews Co., Virginia, Aug. 30, 1835. Sgt. Co. K, 9th Virginia. Capt. ACS, Feb. 19, 1864, to report to Commissary Gen. Failed confirmation, and reappointed Sept. 15, 1864. Served in unspecified capacity with ANVa. Appx. m. Mollie S. Schofield. d. Norfolk, May 18, 1895.

Hudgins, Robert King. b. Mathews Co., Virginia, Jan. 4, 1812. Capt. of Arty., 1861. Commanded one of the Yorktown water batteries, 1861–1862. Capt. OO at Richmond Arsenal, 1862–1865. Paroled at Richmond, Apr. 26, 1865. m. Sarah J. White. d. Norfolk, Virginia, Sept. 7, 1903.

Hudson, Edward Macon. b. Lunenburg Co., Virginia, July 10, 1837. att. Randolph Macon and UVA. Diplomat at Berlin, Germany, and graduated from a school at Heidelburg. Wrote several books while in Europe (two in German language). Ran blockade into Confederacy, Feb. 1862. Lt. ADC to Elzey, June 23, 1863. Transferred with Elzey to AOT. Lawyer at New Orleans, Louisiana. d. Sept. 5, 1916. bur. Metairie Cem.

Hudson, Joseph Warren. b. in Virginia. Pvt. Co. D, 4th Alabama, Apr. 25, 1861, a 29-year-old merchant from Uniontown. QM Sgt., 4th Alabama, Oct. 19, 1861. Capt. AQM, 4th Alabama, May 1, 1862. Capt. AQM to Law's Bgd. (under Col. Perry), Sept. 15, 1864. Sent to Alabama as a tax collector, Jan. 17, 1865.

Huger, Benjamin, Jr. b. Nov. 3, 1831. att. Princeton and Harvard. Lt. of Inf., May 20, 1861, and reported as ADC to his father, Gen. Huger. Capt. AAG to Huger, Jan. 6, 1862. Capt. OO to Huger, 1862–1865. Paroled at Shreveport, June 13, 1865. d. of liver ailment, at Baltimore, Maryland, Sept. 27, 1867. bur. Green Mount Cem.

Huger, Frank. b. Fort Monroe, Virginia, Sept. 29, 1837. att. USMA. Lt. U.S. Army, 1860–1861. Served in PAVA., June 1861, commanding a battery. Lt. of Inf., Mar. 16, 1861. Capt. PACS, 1862. Commanded a battery and served on the staff of his father (Gen. Huger) simultaneously. Maj. of Arty., Mar. 2, 1863. Lt. Col. of Arty., Feb. 27, 1864. Col. of Arty., Feb. 18, 1865. Railroad president. m. Julia Trible. d. Roanoke, Virginia, June 11, 1897.

Hughes, Hampden Sidney. b. in Georgia, 1834. Prewar resident of Athens. Pvt. Co. K, 3rd Georgia, Apr. 25, 1861. Capt. ACS, 3rd Georgia, Apr. 27, 1861. Maj. CS to Wright, June 21, 1862. Maj. CS to Girardey, summer 1864. Maj. CS to Sorrel, Oct. 1864. Appx. m. Mary Atwood Norton, 1869. d. Athens, Georgia, July 30, 1883. bur. Oconee Hill Cem.

Hughes, John. b. New Bern, North Carolina, Mar. 30, 1830. att. UPENN. Lived prewar at Pottsville, Pennsylvania, where he was a lawyer. Unsuccessful candidate for Congress there in 1860. Capt. AQM, 7th North Carolina, May 1, 1862. Maj. QM to Hoke, Nov. 21, 1863. New Bern lawyer and politician. d. Beaufort, North Carolina, Sept. 9, 1889. bur. Cedar Grove Cem.

Hughes, Nicholas Collin. b. Mar. 10, 1840. att. UNC. Adjt. 2nd North Carolina, 1861. Capt. AAG to Pettigrew, Sept. 13, 1862. MWIA at Gettysburg, July 1, 1863. d. Martinsburg, Virginia, July 15, 1863. bur. Cedar Grove Cem., New Bern, North Carolina.

Hughes, William Josiah. b. in South Carolina, Aug. 29, 1837. Farmer at Rocky Mount,

Louisiana. Pvt. Co. D, 9th Louisiana, July 7, 1861. Capt. AQM, June 13, 1862. Capt. AQM to York, Sept. 15, 1864. d. Apr. 14, 1921. bur. Rocky Mount Cem., Bossier Parish.

Hull, Edward Ware. b. Athens, Georgia, Nov. 13, 1833. att. UGA. Planter at Athens. Lt. Co. E, 8th Georgia, May 14, 1861. WIA at First Manassas. Capt. AAG to Lawton, Feb. 3, 1862. Worked at Camp of Instruction in Calhoun, Georgia, Oct. 1862. Capt. AAG to Tyler, Dec. 1863. WIA at Pine Mountain, June 12, 1864. Capt. AAG to Gist's Bgd., Dec. 21, 1864. Planter and railroad agent. m. Cornelia Allen. d. Gainesville, Georgia, Sept. 16, 1887.

Hull, Felix H. b. Highland Co., Virginia. A 37-year-old farmer in 1860. Capt. AQM to H. R. Jackson in western Virginia, 1861. d. Oct. 30, 1861.

Hull, William I. Staff of Imboden, 1864–1865. Listed as Capt. ADC, which cannot have been correct. More likely VADC, or a Lt. ADC whose commission has been lost.

Hullihen, Walter Quarrier. b. Wheeling, Virginia, June 14, 1841. att. UVA. and VMI. Pvt. 2nd Co. Richmond Howitzers, May 27, 1861. Cadet with Madison Light Arty., July 24, 1862. Acting ADC to Stuart, Aug. 29, 1862. WIA at Chancellorsville. Capt. AAG to Lomax, Nov. 2, 1863. Lt. of Cavy. CSA, Dec. 10, 1863. WIA in leg at Tom's Brook. Capt. AAG to Payne, Nov. 1864. Appx. att. Virginia Theological Seminary. Episc. rector at Staunton, Virginia, 1872–1918. d. there Apr. 8, 1923.

Hume, Francis Charles. b. Walker Co., Texas, Feb. 17, 1843. att. UVA. and Austin Coll. Pvt. Co. D, 5th Texas, Aug. 1861. WIA in leg at Seven Pines and Second Manassas (bearing flag). Adjt. 32nd Bn. Virginia Cavy., Dec. 7, 1862. VADC to Gary, June 1864. WIA at Gravel Hill Church, July 27, 1864. Lawyer at Galveston and Houston. Married twice. In Texas legislature. d. Houston, Texas, Feb. 9, 1920. bur. Glenwood Cem.

Humphries, Samuel J. A resident of Columbus, Mississippi. VADC to French, Nov. 1861. Capt. ACS to French, Apr. 1, 1862. Capt. ACS at Franklin, Virginia, Dec. 1862–Sept. 1863. Capt. ACS in Alabama, Sept. 1863–Mar. 1864. Took Oath May 10, 1865, at Montgomery, Alabama.

Humphries, William D. b. Columbus, Mississippi, 1835. att. KMI and UGA. Lt. of Inf., CSA, Mar. 16, 1861. A drill officer in 1861. Lt. ADC to R. S. Garnett, June–July 1861. Lt. ADC to H. R. Jackson, Aug. 13, 1861. Lt. OO, Apr. 1862, in charge of ordnance depot at Chattanooga, Tennessee. Capt. of Arty. (PACS), May 19, 1863. In ordnance dept. at Corinth, Mississippi, Dec. 1864. Postwar planter and mayor of Columbus. d. Feb. 20, 1922. bur. Friendship Cem.

Hungerford, Philip Contee. b. Apr. 18, 1829. Farmer at Montross, Virginia. Lt. Co. C, 47th Virginia, May 16, 1861. Capt. ACS, 47th Virginia, Oct. 21, 1861. Dropped under G.O. #70, 1863. Maj. CS to Heth, by Mar. 1863. POW at Sailor's Creek. Treasurer of Democratic Association of Virginia. Lived at Washington, D.C. d. there Apr. 11, 1890. bur. Congressional Cem. One source gives his middle name as Carter.

Hunt, Leonard Henderson. b. Granville Co., North Carolina, June 23, 1837. A druggist. Lt. Co. C, 13th North Carolina, Apr. 24, 1861. Capt. Co. C, 13th North Carolina, May 1, 1862. WIA at Gaines's Mill. Capt. AAAIG to Pender, autumn 1862. Maj. AAIG to Pender, June 2, 1863. Maj. AAIG to Wilcox, 1863–1865. Mayor of Milton, North Carolina, 1882–1911. d. there Jan. 13, 1918.

Hunt, William F. A 26-year-old "collector" at Hicksford, Virginia, in 1860. Lt. Co. F, 5th Bn. Virginia, May 4, 1861. Lt. acting AQM and acting ACS at Mulberry Point, Virginia, Jan.–Apr. 1862. Later served in Co. H, 13th Virginia Cavy., 1864–1865.

Hunter, Henry Woodis. b. Norfolk, Virginia, Feb. 7, 1842. att. VMI and Georgetown. Tactics professor at VMI. Apptd. Cadet,

Nov. 16, 1861. On ordnance duty at Richmond Arsenal. d. Richmond, Jan. 15, 1862, of "congestion of the brain." bur. Elmwood Cem., Norfolk.

Hunter, James. b. Nov. 16, 1843. Of Caroline Co., Virginia. Pvt. Co. F, 9th Virginia Cavy., Mar. 22, 1862. Courier for "Col. Mallory" Apr.–Sept. 1862. Detached in QM dept., Sept. 1862–Oct. 1863. POW at Thompson's Crossroads, May 4, 1863. Lt. ADC to Lomax, Sept. 10, 1863. Paroled at Ashland, Apr. 27, 1865. d. Dec. 11, 1906. bur. St. Margaret's Episc. Church Cem., Caroline Co.

Hunter, James Dandridge. b. Mar. 3, 1844. att. VMI. Of Essex Co., Virginia. Pvt. Co. F, 9th Virginia Cavy., Mar. 18, 1862. Apptd. Cadet, July 25, 1862. On enrolling duty at Camp Lee, Oct. 1862. Cadet EO to W. H. F. Lee, Nov. 26, 1862. Cadet EO assigned to duty at ANVa. headquarters, Nov. 1863. Cadet EO with railroad bridge defenses in Virginia, June 1864–1865. Civil and mining engineer. m. Emma Lee Parker. d. Anniston, Alabama, Dec. 12, 1915.

Hunter, James Thomas. b. Shelby Co., Tennessee, Aug. 25, 1835. Deputy sheriff at Huntsville, Texas. Lt. Co. H, 4th Texas. Acting ADC to Hood, May–July 1862. Capt. Co. H, 4th Texas, July 1862. WIA at Second Manassas. Huntsville farmer. d. there Apr. 5, 1921. bur. Oakwood Cem.

Hunter, John H. b. Williamson Co., Tennessee, Aug. 15, 1828. m. Martha Bennett, 1859. Lt. Co. G, 44th Tennessee, Dec. 21, 1861. Capt. AQM, 44th Tennessee, Feb. 19, 1864. Failed confirmation. On duty as forage QM at Salem, Virginia, Sept. 1864. Capt. AQM to B. R. Johnson, Jan. 19, 1865. Capt. AQM to McComb, Mar. 1865. Appx. Farmer at Franklin, Tennessee. d. there Feb. 8, 1906. bur. Mt. Hope Cem.

Hunter, Robert Waterman. b. Martinsburg, Virginia, July 12, 1837. att. UVA. Teacher at Martinsburg and in Prince George Co. Lt. Co. D, 2nd Virginia, Apr. 18, 1861. Adjt. 2nd Virginia, Nov. 5, 1861. Staff of J. A. Walker by June 1863. Maj. AAG to Ed Johnson, July 3, 1863. Maj. AAG to John B. Gordon, May 1864. Appx. Secretary of Virginia Military Records, postwar. Lawyer, legislator, and newspaper editor. d. Washington, D.C., Apr. 4, 1916. bur. Mt. Hebron Cem., Winchester, Virginia.

Hunter, Tallaferro, Sr. b. Fredericksburg, Virginia, Jan. 25, 1811. att. UVA. Capt. AQM, Jan. 2, 1862, to report to Magruder. Capt. AQM to report to J. G. Walker, Feb. 7, 1862. Capt. AQM at Hanover Junction, Virginia, by Sept. 1862. Resigned Sept. 1, 1863, and replaced by his son. Westmoreland Co. farmer. d. Jan. 2, 1886. bur. family cem. (since destroyed) at "Pomona."

Hunter, Taliaferro, Jr. b. Fredericksburg, Virginia, Aug. 3, 1841. Pvt. Fredericksburg Arty., July 10, 1861. Capt. AQM, Sept. 4, 1863. Replaced his father at Hanover Junction. Served into 1865. att. UVA. Lawyer and cotton planter at Uniontown, Alabama. School supt. in Westmoreland Co., Virginia. d. Apr. 26, 1900. bur. family cem. (now obliterated) at "Pomona" in Westmoreland Co.

Hutcheson, Jesse Thomas. b. Amherst Co., Virginia, Sept. 4, 1826. Moved to Richmond when young and inspected tobacco. Exempt from military service. Employed at Richmond Clothing Depot. Lt. acting AQM and acting ACS for 2nd Bn. Virginia LDT, Aug. 1863. Capt. ACS to G. W. C. Lee, Feb. 27, 1865. Richmond tobacconist postwar. d. Dec. 24, 1878. bur. Hollywood Cem., in an unmarked grave.

Hutchinson, James J. Lawyer at Livingston, Alabama. Capt. ACS, 5th Alabama, Jan. 1, 1863. Resigned May 19, 1863. Lt. ADC to Rodes, May 12, 1863. KIA at Spotsylvania, May 12, 1864.

Hutchinson, Robert Randolph. b. in Virginia, Aug. 28, 1837. att. UVA., and studied in Berlin, Germany. Lawyer at St. Louis, Missouri. Lt. Co. F, 1st Missouri, Aug. 24, 1861. Lt. AAG to Bowen, Sept. 30, 1861. Capt.

AAG to Bowen, June 6, 1862. Capt. AAAG to Pemberton, 1863. Maj. AAG to Bowen, May 2, 1863. POW at Vicksburg. Maj. AAG to Rodes, Oct. 6, 1863. Maj. AAG to Ramseur, Sept. 1864. POW at Cedar Creek. Released from Ft. Delaware, May 1865. St. Louis banker. d. Nov. 21, 1910. bur. Bellefontaine Cem., St. Louis. "A small light complected man and as nice as can be."

Hutchison, John Rust. b. Oct. 24, 1829. Lived prewar at Arcola, in Loudoun Co., Virginia. Father "murdered by the vilanous Yankeys" in Fauquier Co. Lt. Co. D, 8th Virginia, May 13, 1861. Capt. ACS, 8th Virginia, Oct. 24, 1862. Capt. ACS to Hunton, Sept. 5, 1863. Capt. ACS to B. R. Johnson. Appx. d. May 3, 1895. bur. Sharon Cem., Middleburg.

Hutchison, Thomas Benton. b. in Virginia, Jan. 31, 1835. Merchant at Rectortown, Fauquier Co. Sgt. Co. B, 8th Virginia. Adjt. 8th Virginia, Feb. 1862. POW in Fauquier Co., Feb. 11, 1863. Maj. CS to Hunton, Dec. 3, 1863. Appx. d. Aldie, Virginia, July 5, 1890. bur. Sharon Cem., Middleburg.

Hutter, Edward Sixtus, Jr. b. Lynchburg, Virginia, Sept. 18, 1839. Brother of F. C. and son of G. C. (q.v.). att. VMI, UVA., and Washington Coll. A civil engineer. Capt. of Hutter's Co. Virginia Inf., Apr.–May 1861. Lt. of Cavy., Oct. 9, 1861. Capt. of Cavy., Sept. 13, 1862. Maj. of Cavy., Dec. 29, 1864. On ordnance duty in Virginia for entire war, mostly at Danville. Commanded the arsenal there late in the war. Lynchburg engineer and insurance agent. d. Pittsville, Virginia, June 22, 1904. bur. Lynchburg Presby. Cem.

Hutter, Ferdinand Charles. b. May 16, 1831. Brother of E. S. and son of G. C. (q.v.). att. USMA. Clerk in U.S. Army. Lt. Shoemaker's (Va.) Btty., Apr. 25, 1861. Capt. AQM, Sept. 11, 1861. Served 1861–1865 at Lynchburg, Virginia, as Paymaster and AQM. m. (1) Belle Goggin. m. (2) Mary Powell Lyons. d. Sept. 1885.

Hutter, George Christian. b. Bethlehem, Pennsylvania, Nov. 11, 1793. Officer in the War of 1812, the Seminole War, the Black Hawk War, and the Mexican War. In U.S. Army, 1820–1841 and 1847–1861. Father of E. S. and F. C. Hutter (q.v.). Maj. QM, Mar.–Apr. 1862, at Lynchburg. "Lived in retirement" during the war. m. Harriet James Risque. d. July 31, 1879. bur. Spring Hill Cem., Lynchburg.

Hyer, Louis. b. Feb. 4, 1830. Resident of Montgomery, Alabama. Pvt., 1st Florida, May 31, 1861. Capt. AQM, 1st Florida, Oct. 14, 1862. Capt. AQM to Finley, 1864. Capt. AQM to Finegan, Feb. 18, 1865. Appx. d. Sept. 22, 1867. bur. St. Michael's Cem., Pensacola, Florida.

Hyllested, Waldemar Valdemar. b. Copenhagen, Denmark, ca. 1822. Served in French Foreign Legion, 1839–1845. Fought in Mexican War with Palmetto Regiment. In the Danish Army, 1848–1859. m. Marie Therese Celina Bouny, 1856. Maj. 1st Bn. Louisana Zouaves, Apr. 4, 1861. Maj. VADC to Magruder during Seven Days. POW at Second Manassas. Maj. PM in Texas, 1863–1864. Postwar wine merchant and cotton inspector at New Orleans. d. on Bourbon Street in New Orleans, Jan. 21, 1892, age 70. bur. St. Louis Cem. #2, in unmarked grave.

Inge, William Murphy. b. Greene Co., Alabama, Mar. 9, 1832. Lawyer at Corinth, Mississippi. Adjt. 12th Mississippi. Capt. AAG to Griffith, Dec. 10, 1861. VADC to Clark at Shiloh, while on furlough. Capt. AAG to Barksdale, June 1862. Maj. 12th Bn. Mississippi Partisan Rangers, Feb. 1863. Col. 12th Mississippi Cavy. m. Augusta Evans. Speaker of the House in Mississippi legislature. d. Corinth, Nov. 26, 1900. bur. Henry Cem., Alcorn Co.

Ingraham, Henry Laurens. b. Charleston, South Carolina, May 1837. att. USNA. Lt. USMC, 1858–1861. Lt. CSMC, Mar. 29, 1861. Lt. of Arty., Nov. 16, 1861. On ordnance duty at Savannah, Georgia, Jan. 1862. Lt.

OO to Lawton, June 1862. Capt. OO in South Carolina, Oct. 1862 into 1864. Capt. OO to Kirkland, Dec. 30, 1864. Paroled at Greensboro. m. Sarah Moultrie. Farmer in South Carolina. d. there July 9, 1878. bur. Strawberry Chapel Churchyard at Cooper River, South Carolina.

Ireland, John C. Lt. Co. H, 4th Kentucky Cavy., Sept. 10, 1862, age 25. Lt. AAIG to Cosby, Sept. 25, 1864. Present into 1865.

Ironmonger, Francis McCready. b. Portsmouth, Virginia, Dec. 3, 1829. Kept a billiard saloon at Eastville, Virginia. Capt. Co. B, 39th Virginia, June 10, 1861. Capt. Co. H, 16th Virginia, Feb. 14, 1862. Capt. AQM, 16th Virginia, Nov. 6, 1862. Maj. QM to Mahone, Dec. 3, 1863. Appointment revoked by Congress, Aug. 1864. Capt. acting QM to Weisiger, Aug. 1864 until Appx. m. Mary Augusta Sibley. Railroad agent at Norfolk, Baltimore, and New York City. d. Brooklyn, New York, Oct. 20, 1907. bur. Greenwood Cem.

Irwin, Henry. b. June 19, 1820. Lt. ADC to his brother-in-law Gen. Elzey, Jan. 12, 1863, through late 1864, at least. d. by 1869, probably in 1868. bur. Elmwood Cem., Norfolk, Virginia.

Irwin, William H. Capt. AQM, PAVa., May 3, 1861. Capt. AQM (PACS), June 29, 1861, assigned to duty at Culpeper C.H., Virginia. Capt. AQM at Charlottesville, Apr. 1862. Found incompetent by board of examiners and relieved, Feb. 1865.

Izard, Walter. b. Landsford, South Carolina, Sept. 28, 1828. att. South Carolina Coll. A civil engineer. Lt. Co. A, 2nd Virginia Cavy., May 11, 1861. Lt. EO, June 20, 1862. On topographic engineer duty in central Virginia, 1862–1864. d. Stafford Co., Virginia, Jan. 13, 1912. bur. Bedford Co., Virginia.

Jackson, Alfred Henry. b. McConnelsville, Ohio, Jan. 1, 1836. att. Washington Coll. Lawyer and deputy U.S. Marshal in Lewis Co., Virginia. m. Mary Blair Paxton. Capt.

Co. I, 31st Virginia, 1861. Maj. AAG to T. J. Jackson, Dec. 10, 1861. Resigned Feb. 21, 1862. Lt. Col., 31st Virginia, May 1, 1862. WIA at Cedar Mountain. d. Lexington, Virginia, Aug. 1, 1863. bur. Stonewall Jackson Cem. Jackson's papers are at West Virginia Univ.

Jackson, Asbury Hull. b. Apr. 25, 1836. Pvt. Co. C, 44th Georgia. To Lt., July 15, 1862. Capt. ACS, 44th Georgia, Dec. 2, 1862. Capt. acting ACS to Doles, July 1863–June 1864. Capt. acting ACS to Cook, June–Oct. 1864. Capt. ACS to Cook, Oct. 1864. Postwar merchant at Athens, Georgia. d. there, Mar. 31, 1895. bur. Jackson family cem., Oconee Co. The brigade history said of Jackson: "not very good looking so far as beauty is concerned, but he had a big heart and a good conscience." Jackson's war letters are at Duke.

Jackson, C. F. From Mississippi. Lt. ADC to Gen. Jones—probably D. R. Jones. VADC to Stuart at Dranesville. d. of disease in Mississippi in 1862. This man's initials are not positive, and all parts of his record, except his service with Stuart, are open to question.

Jackson, Henry. b. in Georgia, July 15, 1845. att. UGA. Lived in Europe for five years. Cadet (CSA), July 12, 1861. Cadet to his father, H. R. Jackson, Oct. 1861. Cadet to Lawton, Nov. 1861–Sept. 1862. Lt. OO to W. H. T. Walker, Apr. 7, 1863. Lt. Co. B, 15th Bn. South Carolina Arty., Aug. 30–Sept. 25, 1863. Lt. ADC to Jackson, Sept. 27, 1863. Capt. AAG to Jackson, Nov. 17, 1863. Capt. AAG to Colquitt, Aug. 1, 1864. Paroled Apr. 26, 1865. Lived at Atlanta postwar, where he was a reporter for the state supreme court, a lawyer, and a legislator. m. Sallie A. Cobb, daughter of Gen. T. R. R. Cobb. d. at Atlanta, Dec. 13, 1895. bur. Oconee Hill Cem., Athens, Georgia.

Jackson, James. b. Jefferson Co., Georgia, Oct. 18, 1819. att. UGA. Lawyer and judge at Atlanta. USHR. Col. of Cavy. on military

court of Second Corps, Dec. 16, 1862. Resigned Oct. 5, 1863. Chief Justice of Georgia Supreme Court, 1879–1887. Lived at Macon and Atlanta. Married twice. d. Atlanta, Jan. 13, 1887. bur. Rose Hill Cem., Macon.

Jackson, T. J. Lt. ADC to Kemper, Mar. 1865. No other record found.

Jackson, Thomas G. Lt. Peyton (Va.) Arty., May 3, 1861. Later commanded the battery as a Capt. Dropped May 1862. VADC and acting OO to G. T. Anderson during the Seven Days until appointed Lt. ADC to Anderson, Nov. 8, 1862. WIA and POW at Gettysburg. Appx. A Virginian.

James, Joseph Shepherd. b. in New York, June 1826. att. Washington Coll. m. Martha T. Curtis, 1850. Businessman at Richmond, Virginia. Ordnance Sgt., 24th Virginia Cavy. To Capt. of Co. G, Apr. 18, 1864. Capt. ACS, 24th Virginia Cavy., Aug. 20, 1864. Capt. acting ACS to Gary, 1865. Appx. Farmer and merchant in Gloucester Co. d. there Sept. 6, 1899. bur. Abingdon Episc. Church Cem.

Jamison, David Rumph. b. Orangeburg, South Carolina, Oct. 31, 1834. att. SCMA. Lawyer and planter. Sgt. 1st South Carolina (Hagood's). Lt. OO to his brother-in-law, Gen. Micah Jenkins, July 22, 1862. Lt. OO to Bratton, May 1864. Appx. Orangeburg Co. planter. Grew oranges in Florida. d. Jan. 1908. bur. Old Presby. Churchyard, Orangeburg, in an unmarked grave. Jamison was the great-uncle of Francis Wilshin, longtime supt. of Manassas National Battlefield Park.

Jamison, John Wilson. b. Orangeburg, South Carolina, Aug. 14, 1839. Studied in Paris and at SCMA. French professor at King's Mountain Military Academy. Lt. ADC to his brother-in-law, Gen. Micah Jenkins, July 22, 1862. WIA in both lungs at Frayser's Farm, official capacity uncertain. Out of service on Jenkins's death, but exempt from further duty. Brother of D. R. Jamison (q.v.). Lived at Summerville, South Carolina. d. there Feb. 24, 1886.

Janney, Eli Hamilton. b. Loudoun Co., Virginia, Nov. 12, 1831. Capt. AQM, Jan. 30, 1862, to report to R. E. Lee. Maj. QM, Feb. 19, 1864, but failed confirmation. Reappointed June 15, 1864. Issuing QM at ANVa. headquarters. Paroled at Winchester, Apr. 22, 1865. m. Cornelia Hamilton. Invented the "automatic coupler for cars, which revolutionized railroading." d. Alexandria, Virginia, June 16, 1912. bur. Ivy Hill Cem.

Jeffords, Theodore Alexander. b. Charleston, South Carolina, Apr. 9, 1836. Clerk and merchant there. Adjt. 5th South Carolina Cavy. Lt. AAAG to Dunovant, 1864. Lt. AAAG to Butler and Logan, 1865. Paroled May 1, 1865. m. Mary E. Albergotti. Charleston grocer. Salesman at Orangeburg. d. there Jan. 9, 1923. bur. Sunny Side Cem.

Jenifer, Walter Hanson. b. St. Mary's Co., Maryland, Aug. 1823. att. USMA. Officer in U.S. Cavy., 1847–1848 and 1855–1861. Merchant on Pacific coast. Inventor of Jenifer Saddle. Capt. CSA, Mar. 16, 1861. Lt. Col. commanding Maryland Cavy., June 1861. Col. 8th Virginia Cavy., Sept. 24, 1861. Failed reelection. Staff of Stuart during the October 1862 Chambersburg Raid. Served in unknown capacity, 1862–1863, Dept. of Western Virginia. Cavy. Inspector at Richmond and Mobile. Lived postwar at Baltimore. Cavy. Inspector for Khedive of Egypt. d. Richmond, Virginia, Apr. 9, 1878. bur. Shockoe Cem.

Jenkins, Thomas Jefferson. b. Cabell Co., Virginia, Nov. 22, 1828. att. Jefferson Coll. Cabell Co. farmer all his life. Pvt. Co. E, 8th Virginia Cavy., May 29, 1861. Maj. QM to his brother, Gen. A. G. Jenkins, Oct. 25, 1863. Maj. QM to McCausland, May 1864. Paroled May 1, 1865. m. (1) Arianna Buffington. m. (2) Susan L. Holderby. d. Cabell

Co., Aug. 1, 1872. bur. Spring Hill Cem., Huntington, West Virginia.

Jett, Frederick William. b. in Virginia, ca. 1818. Civil engineer at Portsmouth. Listed as "master carpenter" at Ft. Monroe in 1860 census. Civil engineer in the Norfolk area, 1861–1862, probably as a contractor. Lt. EO to R. H. Anderson, July 1862. Acting Capt. EO to Anderson, by Nov. 1863. Acting Maj. EO to Mahone, June 1864. WIA July 20, 1864. Right arm amputated. May never have received a commission, and instead operated as a civilian contractor with a military title. Lived postwar at Portsmouth, associated with a ferry company. d. at Richmond in R. E. Lee Camp Soldiers' Home, Aug. 25, 1899. bur. St. John's Cem., Hampton, Virginia.

Jett, Jeremiah Bailey. b. Westmoreland Co., Virginia, Sept. 3, 1832. att. Wm. & Mary. Capt. Co. E, 55th Virginia, July 24, 1861. Capt. AQM, 55th Virginia, Dec. 26, 1862. Capt. AQM to Cutts's Bn. Arty., July 26, 1864. Capt. AQM to R. L. Walker, Sept. 23, 1864. Detailed on duty with IFT in Richmond, Mar. 1865. Stafford Co. lawyer. Judge in King George Co. and at St. Paul, Minnesota. d. at St. Paul, Sept. 1913.

Johns, John. b. 1831. Son of famous Episcopalian bishop John Johns. m. Mary Mercer McGuire, 1861. Lt. of Infantry, CSA, Apr. 27, 1861. IFT based at Richmond, Virginia. No other military record found. Lived postwar in Richmond. d. 1894.

Johns, Kensey. b. Sept. 1, 1825. Brother of John Johns (above). Capt. AQM, July 19, 1861. To Maj., May 2, 1863. IFT based in Richmond, Virginia, in charge of river and canal transportation. Paroled Apr. 26, 1865. Postwar resident of Norfolk, Virginia. d. Jan. 3, 1909. bur. "Sudley," West River, Maryland.

Johnson, A. H. Maj. CS, Sept. 2, 1861. Duties not clear until appointed post Commissary at Harrisonburg, Virginia, May 18, 1862. Paroled there Apr. 20, 1865, age 30.

Johnson, J. W. VADC to Robert Ransom. VADC to Matt. Ransom, summer 1863, apparently for a long period. Lt. Drillmaster to Matt. Ransom, Jan. 25, 1864. WIA at Drewry's Bluff, May 1864. Appx. Of Petersburg, Virginia. Believed to be James Waverly Johnson (June 1845–Dec. 23, 1875).

Johnson, James Barbour. b. ca. 1838. Sgt. Co. I, 2nd Fla. Cavy., Mar. 8, 1862. Adjt. 5th Florida, Apr. 15, 1863. Lt. AAAIG to Florida Bgd. at Gettysburg, and may have filled that post for the remainder of the war on the staff of Perry and then Finegan. Paroled May 19, 1865, at Madison, Florida.

Johnson, James H. b. Due West, South Carolina, Nov. 2, 1828. att. South Carolina Coll. Lawyer in South Carolina, and at Ocala, Florida. Married three times. Pvt. Co. E, 2nd Florida, July 5, 1861. Later to Lt. Capt. AQM, 2nd Florida, Sept. 12, 1863. Capt. AQM to Finegan, Sept. 15, 1864. Appx. Postwar farmer at Ocala. d. there July 30, 1902. bur. Evergreen Cem.

Johnson, John Evans. b. in Virginia, Sept. 16, 1815. att. USMA. Lived in Chesterfield Co. Maj. PAVA., May 2, 1861. Served as AAG to Virginia troops organizing in Richmond, July 1861. Col. 9th Virginia Cavy., Jan. 1862. Dropped Apr. 1862. Lt. ADC to Ewell, May 25, 1863. Apparently served only through Gettysburg, and Gen. Ewell consistently referred to him as a VADC, despite evidence of a regular commission. d. New York City, May 31, 1870. bur. Greenwood Cem., Brooklyn.

Johnson, Madison Conyers, Jr. b. in Kentucky, Aug. 16, 1842. VADC to Buckner, autumn 1862. WIA in hand at Perryville. Cadet CSA, Nov. 9, 1862. Acting OO to Cosby, Jan. 28, 1863. Served into 1865 and may have been promoted to Capt. by 1865. There is a chance that his father, Madison Conyers Johnson, Sr., also performed ordnance duty in Cosby's Bgd.

Johnson, Polk Grundy. b. Montgomery Co., Tennessee, Nov. 2, 1844. Born the same day James K. Polk was elected, hence the name. att. school in Montreal and at Stewart Coll. Pvt. Co. A, 49th Tennessee. POW at Ft. Donelson. VADC to Quarles, 1863–1864. Lt. ADC to Quarles, Sept. 4, 1864. WIA July 28, 1864, around Atlanta. Lt. ADC to McComb, late war. Appx. att. Lebanon Law School. Law partner of Gen. Quarles. Married twice. d. New York City, July 28, 1889. bur. Greenwood Cem., Clarksville, Tennessee.

Johnson, Powell Cocke. b. in Virginia. 18-year-old engineer at Covington, Virginia, in 1860. Asst. EO around Richmond and at Mulberry Island, Virginia, May 1861–June 1862. Lt. EO, June 23, 1862. Served on staff of D. H. Hill and Robert Ransom in 1863. Lt. EO at Charleston, South Carolina, Sept. 1863–May 1864. Lt. EO to Beauregard, June–Sept. 1864. Lt. EO with ANVa., Oct. 1864. Appx. d. Bath Co., Virginia, May 18, 1875.

Johnson, Richard Potts. b. Frederick Co., Maryland, Nov. 15, 1827. Pvt. Co. C, 1st Maryland, May 17, 1861. Asst. Surg., 1st Maryland, Sept. 13, 1861–Aug. 17, 1862. VADC to his cousin, Brad. T. Johnson, at Second Manassas. Surg. 2nd Maryland, autumn 1862. Later with the 8th North Carolina. Chief Surg. of the Valley District under W. E. Jones, May 1863. Medical director of the Maryland Line, 1863–1864. WIA near Petersburg, June 25, 1864. Surg. at Lynchburg, Virginia, 1865. d. Charlottesville, May 19, 1894. bur. Riverview Cem.

Johnson, William H. b. Otsego Co., New York, ca. 1834. A civil engineer at Demopolis, Alabama. Pvt. Co. D, 11th Alabama, June 11, 1861. WIA at Gettysburg. Lt. EO, Oct. 19, 1864. Staff of Heth by 1865. Appx.

Johnson, William J. b. Louisa Co., Virginia, Feb. 3, 1828. Clerk at Lexington, Virginia. Pvt. Co. C, 1st Virginia Cavy., Apr. 18, 1861. Later QM Sgt. Capt. ACS, 1st Virginia Cavy., Oct. 8, 1861. Maj. CS to Stuart, July 17, 1862. POW in Louisa Co., May 4, 1863. Maj. CS to Hampton, Aug. 11, 1864. Paroled Apr. 26,

1865. Grocer and banker at Richmond postwar. d. there Oct. 4, 1895. bur. Hollywood Cem.

Johnston, Elliott. b. May 2, 1826. Served in USN prewar. Imprisoned in Delaware early in the war for his southern sympathies. VADC to R. B. Garnett, Dec. 1861. Lt. ADC to Garnett, Mar. 24, 1862. VADC to Ewell at Cedar Mountain. Lost left leg and POW at Sharpsburg. VADC to Ewell in Pennsylvania Campaign. Capt. AAG to Stafford, Dec. 7, 1863. Probably never served, as he declared himself unfit for field duty, Nov. 1863. Retired to Invalid Corps, Dec. 14, 1864. Visited Europe in 1865 to find a new artificial leg. d. Jan. 31, 1901. bur. Green Mount Cem., Baltimore.

Johnston, George. b. Fairfax Co., Virginia. Farmer there. Brother of S. R. Johnston (q.v.). Capt. AQM, Jan. 2, 1862. Maj. QM, June 17, 1862. IFT, 1862–1865. From October 1863 he was Chief Inspector for all field transportation in Virginia and North Carolina. Married twice. d. June 17, 1897. bur. First Presby. Church Cem., Alexandria, Virginia.

Johnston, George Burgwyn. b. Edenton, North Carolina, Aug. 17, 1840. att. UNC. A cousin of Gen. G. B. Anderson. m. Ann Taylor Johnson. Pvt. Co. D, 1st North Carolina (Bethel). Capt. Co. G, 28th North Carolina, Sept. 1861. POW at Slash Church. Exchanged Nov. 10, 1862. Capt. AAG to Lane, Jan. 19, 1863. Resigned Aug. 8, 1863. d. Chapel Hill, North Carolina, Apr. 1864, of consumption. bur. Oakwood Cem., Raleigh, in unmarked grave. "Frail and delicate." Johnston's 1862 diary is at NCDAH. Family sources are split on the spelling of his middle name, some rendering it Burgwin.

Johnston, James Andrew. b. Feb. 6, 1837. att. UVA. Physician from Botetourt Co., Virginia. Pvt. Co. A, 28th Virginia, May 15, 1861. Capt. ACS, 28th Virginia, Oct. 4, 1861. Maj. CS to R. B. Garnett, Dec. 1, 1862.

Resigned Oct. 31, 1863, to enter medical service. Commissioned as Asst. Surg. On duty at Raleigh and Lynchburg. d. Mar. 7, 1882. bur. Mill Creek Cem., Botetourt Co.

Johnston, James Arthur. b. Norfolk, Virginia. Capt. AQM at Norfolk, Virginia, June 29, 1861. Maj. QM to Huger, Sept. 11, 1861. Maj. QM to R. H. Anderson, by Oct. 1862. Maj. QM to Mahone, May 1864. Appx. Merchant at Petersburg, Virginia.

Johnston, James Franklin. b. Lincoln Co., North Carolina, May 26, 1828. att. UNC. Iron manufacturer, 1846–1861. Capt. ACS, 23rd North Carolina, July 19, 1861. Capt. acting ACS to Early, Aug. 1861. Capt. acting ACS to R. D. Johnston, 1863. Relieved July 1863. Pvt. Co. C, 1st North Carolina Cavy., Apr. 7, 1864. Pvt. acting ADC to Barringer, July 1864. Lt. Co. C, 1st North Carolina Cavy., Nov. 15, 1864. To Capt., Mar. 1, 1865. WIA at Chamberlain's Run.

Johnston, Joseph Forney. b. Lincoln Co., North Carolina, Mar. 23, 1843. Moved to Alabama in 1860. Apptd. Cadet, Nov. 15, 1861. Lt. Co. I, 18th Alabama. WIA in arm at Chickamauga. Lt. ADC to his brother, Gen. R. D. Johnston, Nov. 17, 1863. Apptd. Lt. CSA, June 15, 1864. Served on Toon's staff during Gen. Johnston's absence. WIA in head at Spotsylvania. WIA in ribs Sept. 1864. WIA around Petersburg. Lawyer at Selma and banker at Birmingham. Governor of Alabama, 1896–1900. U.S. Senator, 1907–1913. d. Washington, D.C., Aug. 8, 1913.

Johnston, Josiah Stoddard. b. New Orleans, Louisiana, Feb. 10, 1833. Moved to Kentucky in 1838. att. Yale and Louisville Law School. Nephew of Gen. A. S. Johnston. VADC to Bragg by Sept. 1862. Maj. AAG to Bragg, Sept. 1, 1862. Maj. AAG to Buckner, Aug. 1863. Maj. AAG to his cousin, Gen. Breckinridge, Dec. 15, 1863. Maj. AAG to Echols, Feb. 1865. Lt. Col. AAG to Echols, Apr. 24, 1865. Lawyer in Arkansas, 1865–1867. Newspaper editor at Frankfort, Kentucky, and

Secretary of State. Wrote a two-volume history of Louisville, and the Kentucky volume of *Confederate Military History*. d. St. Louis, Missouri, Oct. 6, 1913. bur. Cave Hill Cem., Louisville.

Johnston, Robert. b. Richmond, Virginia, July 3, 1830. att. USMA. Lt. U.S. Cavy., 1850–1861. Capt. CSA, Mar. 16, 1861. Maj. PACS, staff of R. E. Lee, by Apr. 30, 1861. Col. 3rd Virginia Cavy., June 20, 1861. Dropped May 1862. Col. AAAIG to Magruder, Aug. 1861. Col. AAAG to his cousin, Gen. Pickett, 1861–1862. Volunteer AAAG to Pickett, Sept. 1862–May 1863. Postwar educator in New York. d. Geneva, New York, July 8, 1902. bur. Albany Rural Cem., Albany, New York.

Johnston, Samuel Richards. b. Fairfax Co., Virginia, Mar. 16, 1833. A civil engineer. Lt. Co. F, 6th Virginia Cavy., Apr. 20, 1861. Lt. VADC to Stuart at Dranesville, and Lt. "acting Inspector of Outposts of Gen. J. E. B. Stuart's staff," Feb.–Mar. 1862. Dropped from 6th Cavy., Apr. 20, 1862. Contract Engineer around Richmond, May–June 1862. Lt. EO to Longstreet, June 4, 1862. Capt. EO to R. E. Lee, Aug. 12, 1862. Maj. EO, Mar. 17, 1864. Lt. Col. EO, Sept. 15, 1864. Appx. Chief Engineer Walter Stevens wrote that Johnston "has no superior as constructing & locating engineer." Lived in 13 different states postwar, as an engineer. Married twice. Tastefully named one son R. E. Lee Johnston. d. East Orange, New Jersey, Dec. 24, 1899. bur. Alexandria, Virginia.

Johnston, Thomas Henry. b. Botetourt Co., Virginia, Oct. 4, 1836. att. Washington Coll. and UVA. m. Sarah Watson Holladay, 1860. Pvt. Co. A, 28th Virginia, May 15, 1861. To Capt., Apr. 21, 1862. Resigned, July 12, 1862. Lt. ADC to B. H. Robertson, May 4, 1863. Paroled May 6, 1865. Postwar farmer in Botetourt Co. d. Buchanan, Virginia, Dec. 16, 1866. bur. Allen Cem., Botetourt Co.

Johnston, Thomas Henry. A resident of

Albany, Georgia. Capt. AQM of 11th Bn. Georgia Arty., May 23, 1862. Relieved Nov. 14, 1863, to report to Col. A. H. Cole. No further military record. A 40-year-old cotton factor at Albany in 1870.

Johnston, William Preston. b. Louisville, Kentucky, Jan. 5, 1831. Son of Gen. A. S. Johnston. Staff of President Davis, Apr. 1862. Capt. Judge Advocate with G. W. Smith's command, Dec. 20, 1862. Field officer with several Kentucky infantry regiments. Taught at Washington Coll. under R. E. Lee, was president of Louisiana State Univ., and was the first president of Tulane. Wrote a large biography of his father. d. Lexington, Virginia, July 1899. bur. Louisville, Kentucky.

Jonas, Sidney Alroy. b. Williamston, Kentucky. An engineer at Aberdeen, Mississippi. Pvt. Co. I, 11th Mississippi. Acting as ACS to Whiting in July 1861. Maj. CS to Whiting, Oct. 21, 1861. Maj. CS to Hood, 1862–1864. Maj. CS to S. D. Lee, 1864. Later with Hood again, and with D. H. Hill. Newspaperman and printer at Aberdeen. d. there Sept. 13, 1915. bur. there. Jonas's postwar papers are at MDAH.

Jones, Alexander Caldwell. b. Marshall Co., Virginia, 1830. att. VMI. Judge in Minnesota prewar, and state Adjt. Gen. Lt. Col. 44th Virginia. WIA at Gaines's Mill. Lt. Col. AAG to G. J. Rains, on conscription duty at Richmond, Jan.–May 1863. Resigned June 16, 1863. Col. AAIG to Magruder, Jan. 1864. Later staff of J. G. Walker. Commanded troops in the field late in the war. Lawyer at Wheeling, West Virginia, and at Washington, D.C. U.S. Consul in China and Japan. d. Chungking, China, Jan. 13, 1898.

Jones, B. P. Capt. AQM to J. C. Haskell's Bn. Arty., spring 1864. Failed confirmation, June 14, 1864. No other details in his terrible official record. Possibly never served, though likely did.

Jones, Charles Scott Dodge. b. Sinsinewa Mound, Wisconsin, Sept. 23, 1832. Father was minister to Colombia and governor of Iowa. A lawyer prewar. Co. C, 3rd Bn. Virginia LDT. Capt. AAIG to B. R. Johnson, Sept. 7, 1863. POW at Drewry's Bluff, May 17, 1864. Exchanged Mar. 4, 1865, but found his staff position filled. m. Annie Wallace Miller. d. Dubuque, Iowa, Jan. 1899.

Jones, Crawford Haaston. att. Hampden Sidney. 31-year-old lawyer and legislator at Appomattox C.H., Virginia, in 1860. Capt. Co. I, 3rd Virginia Arty. LDT, Feb.–May 1862. Capt. AQM, Aug. 4, 1862. Chief forage master for First Corps. Maj. QM, Dec. 23, 1862. Resigned Apr. 30, 1863, complaining of consumption. d. in 1863, sometime after June 30.

Jones, David Andrew. b. Harrisonburg, Virginia, Sept. 13, 1837. Lt. Co. B, 10th Virginia, Apr. 18, 1861. Maj. CS to his brother, Gen. J. R. Jones, Oct. 14, 1862. Maj. CS to J. M. Jones, 1863. POW in a hospital at Spotsylvania, June 10, 1864. One of the Immortal 600. Released July 24, 1865. m. Nancy Montgomery. A tradesman at Abingdon postwar. d. Oct. 7, 1918. bur. Sinking Springs Cem.

Jones, Francis Buckner. b. Frederick Co., Virginia, June 14, 1828. att. VMI. A farmer. Lt. Col. (PAVa.) AAAG to T. J. Jackson, June 1861. Capt. AAG (PACS) to Jackson, Aug. 15, 1861. Maj. 2nd Virginia, Aug. 26, 1861, but still AAAG to Jackson, into 1862. MWIA at Gaines's Mill. d. Richmond, July 9, 1862. bur. Stonewall Cem., Winchester. Much of Jones's war diary is published in *Defend the Valley*.

Jones, Francis Pendleton. b. Louisa C.H., Virginia, Dec. 27, 1841. att. UVA. Co. D, 13th Virginia. Lt. ADC to his uncle, Gen. J. M. Jones, May 15, 1863. MWIA at Gettysburg, July 2, 1863. d. Louisa C.H., Sept. 2, 1863. bur. there.

Jones, Frank Freeman. b. ca. 1832. A civil engineer at Baltimore, Maryland. m. Marian Stuart Powell, 1859. Lt. of Inf., CSA, Nov. 16, 1861. Lt. (PACS), May 19, 1862. Lt. OO at Richmond Arsenal, summer 1862.

Capt. OO (PACS), Sept. 26, 1862. Maj. OO (PACS), Sept. 8, 1863. Inspector of small arms at Richmond for most of the war. Apparently commanded Richmond Armory in late 1864.

Jones, George T. b. in Virginia. A 34-year-old merchant at Charlottesville in 1860. Pvt. Co. B, 19th Virginia, May 8, 1861. Capt. AQM, 19th Virginia, July 19, 1861. Maj. QM to R. B. Garnett, Oct. 24, 1862. Hence to Hunton. Appx.

Jones, George Washington. b. 1822. Pvt. in 4th Alabama. Capt. AQM, 4th Alabama, Apr. 27, 1861. Maj. QM to Whiting, Sept. 14, 1861. Probably Maj. QM to Hood, 1862–1863. Maj. QM collecting taxes in Alabama by June 1863. d. Apr. 9, 1866. bur. Huntsville City Cem.

Jones, Harvey Ellis. b. Tuscaloosa, Alabama, Apr. 28, 1842. att. UAla., GMI, and St. James Coll. Sgt. Co. E, 3rd Alabama, Apr. 28, 1861. Later to Lt. Capt. AAG to Gracie, Nov. 4, 1862. Same to Moody, Dec. 1864. WIA in thigh at White Oak Road, Mar. 31, 1865, and leg amputated. m. Marion Wilmer, 1869. Railroad and tax commissioner in Alabama, and recording secretary to governor. Alive 1907 at Spring Hill, Alabama.

Jones, Hilary Pollard. b. Fluvanna Co., Virginia, July 13, 1833. att. UVA. Taught at Hanover Academy, near Taylorsville, pre- and postwar. Lt. Morris (Va.) Arty., Aug. 1861. To Capt., Feb. 1862. Maj. of Arty., May 28, 1862. Lt. Col. of Arty., Mar. 2, 1863. Lt. Col., acting Chief of Arty. to Ewell, 1863. Col., Feb. 27, 1864. Col. Chief of Arty. to Beauregard, May 7, 1864. Chief of Arty. to R. H. Anderson by Nov. 1864. Appx. d. Washington, D.C., Jan. 1, 1913. bur. Leeds Episc. Church Cem., Markham, Virginia.

Jones, Horace Walker. b. Fluvanna Co., Virginia, July 29, 1835. att. UVA. Charlottesville farmer and teacher. Brother of Hilary P. (q.v.). Pvt. Co. B, 19th Virginia, May 8, 1861. Later Sgt. Major. Capt. ACS, 19th Virginia, Oct. 22, 1861. Often acting CS to Pickett.

Maj. CS to Pickett, Oct. 10, 1862. Failed confirmation, May 2, 1863. Continued to serve with Pickett until reappointed, Aug. 20, 1864. Appx. Principal at various state schools. d. Charlottesville, June 1, 1904. bur. Maplewood Cem.

Jones, J. Capt. AAG to Cox at Appx. No other record found. A possible identification is Joseph Jones, Capt. in Co. K, 14th North Carolina. That officer was WIA at Sharpsburg and in May 1864, but was present with his company in Sept. 1864 and possibly promoted to Cox's staff thereafter.

Jones, J. N. Lt. VADC to W. E. Jones, Feb. 1863. No other record. This very likely is Jasper Nathaniel Jones, a cousin of the general. Jasper was a Sgt. in Co. D, 1st Virginia Cavy., and was alive in July 1892.

Jones, J. R. Lt. ADC to J. R. Jones, June 9, 1862. No further record.

Jones, James Martin. b. Salisbury, North Carolina, Aug. 26, 1833. Lt. Co. K, 5th North Carolina, May 16, 1861. Capt. AQM, 5th North Carolina, Mar. 25, 1862. Capt. AQM assigned to Third Corps, Sept. 27, 1864. On duty collecting hides for that corps. Appx. d. Asheville, North Carolina, July 26, 1886. bur. Riverside Cem.

Jones, John H. Capt. AQM, 19th South Carolina, Oct. 14, 1862. Dismissed by court martial, Dec. 23, 1862. Capt. AQM in Nelson Co., Virginia, Feb.–July 1864, at a horse infirmary. Capt. AQM at Rockfish Depot, Virginia, July 2, 1864. Capt. AQM to Beauregard, Nov. 1864.

Jones, John Mills. b. Dec. 29, 1821. Of Greenville, South Carolina. Pvt. Co. A, Cobb's Legion (Ga.) Cavy., 1861. Lt. ADC to his nephew Gen. Young, Sept. 28, 1863. POW Oct. 1, 1864, "on account of his own negligence," according to Young. Said to have lost $50,000 in the war. d. July 10, 1895. bur. Christ Churchyard, Greenville.

Jones, John Simpkins. Pvt. Co. D, 8th Virginia, July 1, 1861. Clerk to Gen. R. B. Garnett, Jan. 1863. Lt. acting ADC to Garnett

at Gettysburg. Lt. ADC to Hunton, Aug. 9, 1863. WIA in leg at Cold Harbor, June 3, 1864. Served into 1865.

Jones, John W. Capt. AQM, June 16, 1863, at Orange C.H., Virginia. Served through end of the war.

Jones, John Winston. b. in Virginia, Nov. 23, 1843. Lived in Chesterfield Co. Lt. ADC to Robert Ransom, Feb. 19, 1864. Served into 1865. d. Manchester, Virginia, May 4, 1916. bur. Maury Cem.

Jones, Junius B. b. in Virginia. A resident of Surry Co. Married twice. Pvt. Co. E, 5th Virginia Cavy., Apr. 20, 1861. Lt. Co. G, 13th Virginia Cavy., Feb. 1862. Lt. OO to Chambliss, May 2, 1864. Same to Beale, 1865. Living at Surry C.H. in 1870, age 32, a farmer.

Jones, Philip Bickerton, Jr. b. Richmond, Virginia, May 17, 1839. att. UVA and Hampden Sidney. Moved to Orange Co. in 1845. Pvt. Co. F, 21st Virginia, Apr.–Oct. 1861. VADC to D. R. Jones, possibly by Oct. 1861, certainly by Apr. 1862. Served until Jan. 1863. Clerk with Ewell's Div. Capt. AQM to Haskell's Bn. Arty., Mar. 15, 1864, but failed confirmation. Reappointed June 15, 1864. Appx. m. Bettie Morris. Orange Co. planter. d. there, Aug. 3, 1903. bur. Hollywood Cem., Richmond.

Jones, R. R. A VADC to William Nelson's Bn. Arty. during the Seven Days. "Young."

Jones, Richard Channing. b. Brunswick Co., Virginia, Apr. 12, 1841. att. UAla. Lt. Co. C, 44th Alabama. Lt. ADC to Col. P. D. Bowles (commanding brigade), Apr. 1865. Lawyer at Camden, Alabama. Brigadier Gen. in state militia. In state senate, and later president of UAla. d. Camden, Sept. 12, 1903.

Jones, Richard V. b. in South Carolina. Moved to Milledgeville, Georgia, ca. 1855. Cpl. Co. H, 4th Georgia, Apr. 26, 1861. Lt. AAAIG to Doles by May 1863. Lt. AAIG to Doles, May 5, 1864. Lt. AAIG to Cook, June 1864. Appx. m. Rebecca L. Davies,

Charles M. Blackford
Author's collection

Frank P. Clark
Courtesy Ben Ritter

John Glaize
Courtesy Ben Ritter

Charles W. Hardy
Courtesy Virginia Military Institute Archives

Philip B. Stanard
Courtesy Virginia Military Institute Archives

Thomas H. Williamson
Courtesy Virginia Military Institute Archives

Edward R. Baird and wife after their
1865 wedding
Courtesy Edward R. Baird, Jr.

Richard M. Booker
Courtesy Emily Martin

Daniel T. Carraway
Courtesy Joseph Carraway

Edward S. Hutter, Jr.
Courtesy Rusty Hicks

Murray F. Taylor (left) and Richard H. T. Adams
Courtesy Rusty Hicks

Previously unpublished view of General James Dearing (left) with David B. Bridgford of
Stonewall Jackson's staff
Courtesy Rusty Hicks

Frederick M. Colston

John Taliaferro
Courtesy Orange County (Va.)
Historical Society

Henry A. Bowling
Courtesy A. Clarke Magruder

John J. Evans
Courtesy Evans Memorial Library,
Aberdeen, Mississippi

William W. Lester and wife on their
wedding day
Courtesy Dean Simonds

Frederick W. Smith and wife

Alfred E. Doby
Courtesy Jay Brabham

George Booker and wife
Courtesy Hampton History Museum

Walter E. Winn
Courtesy National Archives

Osmun Latrobe
Author's collection

Alfred L. Scott
Courtesy Danny Lee

Henry Bryan
Courtesy Ben Ritter

Josephine Scott holding a photograph of her
husband, John G. Scott
Courtesy Lawrence T. Jones III

Kerr Craige
Courtesy David Craige

Joseph C. Haskell

Richard K. Meade, Jr.
Courtesy Julia Ferguson

James L. Meem
Courtesy J. Lawrence Meem

Richard E. Wilbourn
Courtesy Richard E. Wilbourn II

John B. Cobb
Courtesy Dr. Goodloe Y. Erwin

William M. Dwight

Thomas G. Jones

Eugene A. Hawkins, William H. Willis, and
Howard Tinsley, all officers in the 4th Georgia
Infantry. Hawkins and Tinsley became staff
officers in the Doles-Cook brigade.
Courtesy Steve Mullinax

Henry C. Lee

James K. Boswell

James H. Burton
Courtesy Eugenia M. Scheffel

A rare collage of General George E. Pickett and nine members of his staff. Six of the officers have not been identified. Charles Pickett is at the upper right, and William Symington (with the curly hair) is next on the right. Edward Baird (with hair parted in the center) is above General Pickett's shoulder on the left side.
Courtesy Benjamin H. Baird

General "Stonewall" Jackson and his staff
Courtesy U.S. Army Military History Institute

Evander Law (center, seated) and his staff. Law commanded a brigade as a colonel in 1862, and this image may date from then.
Courtesy Valentine Richmond History Center

1866. d. at Milledgeville, Dec. 6, 1866, of consumption, age 27. bur. Memory Hill Cem.

Jones, Robert Kennon. Served in Nelson's (Va.) Btty. until Oct. 1862. Sgt. Maj. 3rd Bn. Virginia Reserve Arty., and 31st Bn. Virginia Arty. Adjt. of 31st Bn. Virginia Arty., Oct. 22, 1862. Lt. acting ADC to "Artillery Corps" at Appx.

Jones, Samuel P. Lt. ADC to D. R. Jones, Oct. 27, 1862. No further record. This was just when Gen. Jones left the army permanently, so perhaps the commission never took hold.

Jones, Thomas Goode. b. Macon, Georgia, Nov. 26, 1844. att. VMI. Sgt. Co. K, 53rd Alabama Partisan Rangers. Lt. ADC to John B. Gordon, Jan. 2, 1863. WIA four times. Appx. Planter, lawyer, judge, and newspaper editor. Governor of Alabama, 1890–1894. d. Montgomery, Apr. 28, 1914. bur. Oakwood Cem.

Jones, Walter. Capt. CSA, Mar. 16, 1861. Capt. ACS at Lynchburg, Virginia, May 11, 1861–July 1861. Maj. (PACS), Aug. 16, 1861. Maj. CS to L. P. Walker, Oct. 1861–Mar. 1862. Later on QM duty in Mississippi. Maj. AAIG to Buckner, Dec. 20, 1862. Maj. CS at Montgomery, Alabama, 1863–1865.

Jones, Walter. b. in Alabama, Apr. 14, 1839. att. UAla. and GMI. Civil engineer with a railroad in Virginia. Served in Provisional Army of Alabama, Mar. 1861. Lt. Co. F, 1st Bn. Ala. Arty. Lt. acting OO to Sam. Jones, May 8, 1862. d. Bladon Springs, Alabama, July 7 or 12, 1862.

Jones, Willis Field. b. Richmond, Kentucky, Feb. 7, 1827. Farmer at Versailles. m. Martha M. Buford, 1848. Served with Gen. Buford as QM. Capt. AAG to his uncle, Gen. Field, July 3, 1863. Maj. AAG to Field, Feb. 19, 1864. KIA at Second Darbytown Road, October 13, 1864. bur. Hollywood Cem., Richmond, Virginia. Reinterred 1866 at Lexington Cem., in Kentucky. Jones's war letters are at the Filson Club Historical Society in Louisville.

Jordan, Robert Pierpont. A 23-year-old clerk in Hancock Co., Georgia. Lt. Co. A, 6th Georgia, Apr. 22, 1861. Lt. AAAG to Colquitt, May 1862. KIA at Sharpsburg–"shot through the eye and fell from his horse." bur. on the battlefield. Colquitt wrote in October 1862: "He was a noble and gallant fellow. I can't fill his place."

Jordan, William Churchill. b. July 21, 1843. att. UNC. From Greenville, North Carolina. Capt. AQM, 66th North Carolina, May 27, 1863. Capt. AQM to Hoke, Sept. 20, 1864. Paroled Apr. 26, 1865.

Joyner, James E. b. in Virginia, ca. 1808. A preacher in Henry Co., in 1860. Chaplain 57th Virginia, Oct. 2, 1861. VADC to Armistead during Seven Days. Chaplain through the end of the war. m. Mrs. Lucy Talbot Cosby Bucktrout.

Judge, Hilliard M. b. in Alabama. A 16-year-old student at Havana, Alabama, in 1860. Pvt. Co. G, 6th South Carolina, Dec. 3, 1862. Lt. ADC to his uncle, Gen. Bratton, July 13, 1864. Appx. Middle name probably Means.

Junkin, George Garrett. b. Hollidaysburg, Pennsylvania, Nov. 19, 1837. att. Washington Coll. Teacher at Christiansburg, Virginia. Sgt. Co. G, 4th Virginia, 1861. Lt. ADC to T. J. Jackson, Nov. 7, 1861. Lt. AAAG to Jackson, Feb.–Mar. 1862. POW at Kernstown. Tricked by his father into taking the Oath and forced to resign, Sept. 12, 1862, effective Apr. 4. Broke oath to become Capt. Co. E, 25th Virginia Cavy. WIA at Third Winchester and in 1865. m. Elizabeth Montague. Lawyer and judge in Montgomery Co., Virginia. d. Christiansburg, Feb. 23, 1895. Junkin was a cousin of Gen. Jackson's first wife. "A most gallant fellow, devoted to the South, and enthusiastic in support of our cause. He was full of wit & mirth. . . ."

Justice, Benjamin Wesley. b. Wake Co., North Carolina, June 10, 1827. att. Wake

Forest. Teacher at Tuscaloosa, Alabama, and a farmer in Wake Co. Lt. and later Adjt., 47th North Carolina. Capt. ACS to Kirkland, Aug. 10, 1863. Same to MacRae. Appx. Raleigh businessman. d. Sept. 22, 1871, when he fell through an open hatchway on the third floor of his office, while loading cotton bales. Justice's war letters are at Emory Univ.

Justice, John Guion. b. in North Carolina, Oct. 8, 1844. Lt. Co. H, 33rd North Carolina, July 31, 1862. Lt. ADC to Hoke, Mar. 20, 1863. Lost right leg at Fussell's Mill, Aug. 16, 1864. Retired to Invalid Corps, Mar. 29, 1865. Lincolnton retail merchant. d. Dec. 22, 1876. bur. St. Luke's Episc. Churchyard.

Kaigler, John James, Jr. b. Orangeburg, South Carolina, Dec. 8, 1827. Dry goods merchant at Eufaula, Alabama, pre- and postwar. Capt. AQM, 4th Bn. Alabama Arty., July 1, 1862. Capt. AQM, 59th Alabama, Nov. 25, 1863. Capt. AQM to Gracie, Sept. 20, 1864, and probably to Moody in 1865. d. Eufaula, May 23, 1893. bur. Fairview Cem.

Kean, Robert Garlick Hill. b. Caroline Co., Virginia, Oct. 7, 1828. att. UVA. m. Jane Nicholas Randolph. Lawyer at Lynchburg. Pvt. Co. G, 11th Virginia, Apr. 23, 1861. Later QM Sgt. Capt. AAG to Randolph (his wife's uncle), Feb. 28–Mar. 22, 1862. Resigned Apr. 14, 1862. Head of Bureau of War in Richmond, Apr. 1862–Apr. 1865. Postwar rector of UVA. and Lynchburg lawyer. d. June 13, 1898.

Kearsley, George Washington Tate. b. Jan. 15, 1819. Dry goods merchant at Charlestown, Virginia. Capt. ACS to J. E. Johnston, June 29, 1861. Replaced as army's acting Chief CS, Dec. 24, 1861. Maj. CS to Johnston, Sept. 9, 1861. Maj. CS at Gordonsville by May 1862, and at Hanover Junction by Dec. 1862. Maj. CS to Dearing, Dec. 1, 1864. Resumed dry goods business at Charlestown. m. Rebecca Brown. d. Mar. 4, 1901. bur. Zion Episc. Church Cem.

Keiley, John Denis, Jr. b. 1839. A clerk. Pvt. Co. C, 1st Virginia, Apr. 21, 1861. Maj. QM, Dec. 30, 1862, to report to Pryor. Maj. QM to Longstreet, Apr. 25, 1863. Maj. QM to H. H. Walker, Mar. 17, 1864. Probably Maj. QM to Fry, June 1864. Maj. QM to Barton, Feb. 1, 1865. Maj. QM to G. W. C. Lee, Feb. 3, 1865. Moved to New York. Brooklyn city treasurer and a newspaper writer. d. there Nov. 26, 1901.

Keith, Jasper Lay. b. Montezuma, Georgia, Apr. 2, 1828. Clerk of Cherokee Co., Georgia, Superior Court, 1852–1861. Capt. ACS, 22nd Georgia, Sept. 2, 1861. Capt. AQM, 22nd Georgia, June 24, 1863. Capt. AQM to Wright's Bgd., Sept. 15, 1864, and thus staff of Sorrel by Oct. 1864. Appx. A bookkeeper at Atlanta postwar. d. Apr. 4, 1885. bur. Oakland Cem.

Keller, Benjamin F., Jr. From Effingham Co., Georgia. att. GMI. Lt. Co. F, 60th Georgia, Apr. 21, 1862. Adjt. 60th Georgia, July 15, 1862. WIA at Fredericksburg. Capt. Co. F, 60th Georgia. Capt. AAAIG to John B. Gordon, June 1863. Commanded brigade sharpshooter battalion, May 1864. POW at Third Winchester. Released from prison, June 17, 1865.

Kellogg, Timothy H. b. Spotsylvania Co., Virginia, Dec. 23, 1830. A merchant at Richmond in 1860, living in the home of Gov. Letcher. Pvt. Co. F, 21st Virginia, Apr. 21, 1861. Lt. Co. H, 21st Virginia. Capt. ACS, 21st Virginia, Jan. 2, 1862. Capt. ACS to J. M. Jones, by Aug. 1863. POW at Clover Green, Virginia, May 1864. Maj. CS to H. P. Jones's Bn. Arty., Mar. 2, 1865. A china merchant at Richmond postwar. d. there Sept. 30, 1872, of dysentery. bur. Hollywood Cem.

Kemper, William S. Capt. AQM, Nov. 6, 1862. Paymaster for hospitals at Richmond, Virginia, 1862–1865. This probably was William Stephen Kemper (July 18, 1805–Aug. 17, 1870), the father of Confederate artillerist Lt. Col. Delaware Kemper.

Kennedy, Joseph. Commanded a company

in the Palmetto Regiment in the Mexican War. Also a veteran of "the Florida Campaign." Maj. cs to Maxcy Gregg, by June 1861, age about 50. Maj. acting cs to Bonham, July 1861. Maj. cs to Bonham, Oct. 21, 1861. Maj. cs to Kershaw, Feb. 1862. Dropped Aug. 2, 1862, for failing bond, but continued to serve. Maj. cs to Conner, June 1864, to Goggin in Oct. 1864, and to Kennedy, Dec. 1864. d. Fairfield Co., South Carolina, by 1883. This may be the man born in 1814 who is buried at Lebanon Church Cem. in Fairfield Co., under the name Joseph H. Kennedy. No other source gives a middle initial.

Kennon, Richard Byrd. b. Norfolk, Virginia, Nov. 10, 1835. Studied medicine. Lt. Co. I, 4th Virginia Cavy., 1861. Adjt. 8th Virginia Cavy., Nov. 25, 1861. Lt. AAAIG to Stuart, Apr. 26, 1863. Capt. AAAIG to Rosser, Nov. 2, 1863. Capt. AAG to Dearing, late in the war. Appx. m. Louisiana Barraud Cocke, a daughter of Gen. Cocke. Farmer in Brunswick Co., Virginia. d. there Dec. 14, 1892. bur. St. Luke's Episc. Church Cem., Northampton Co., North Carolina.

Kent, George Madison. b. Wytheville, Virginia, Dec. 6, 1840. att. VMI. A prewar clerk. Sgt. Maj., 4th Virginia, Apr. 17, 1861–Apr. 17, 1862. Lt. Drillmaster, Apr. 1863. Lt. ADC to Wharton, no date known. POW at Waynesboro. Released June 1865. m. Annie E. Radford. Merchant at Baltimore. d. Bedford Co., Virginia, Mar. 25, 1873.

Ker, Hugh. b. Northampton Co., Virginia, Feb. 28, 1831. att. VMI. m. Anne Upshur Yerby, 1852. Adjt. 39th Virginia, Oct. 7, 1861. Later a military storekeeper in Staunton. Lt. ADC to Davidson, Sept. 8, 1863. Lt. ADC (probably acting) to W. L. Jackson, Nov. 1864. Back with Davidson by Apr. 1865. "Clerk of Wharf" at Eastville, Virginia, and a steamboat purser. d. Baltimore, Maryland, Dec. 6, 1902. Name frequently spelled as Kerr, and it is thought the family added

that fourth letter during or shortly after the war.

Ker, James. b. Eastville, Virginia, Sept. 4, 1836. att. VMI. A merchant at Eastville. Brother of Hugh Ker (q.v.). Apptd. temporary Lt. of Arty., Nov. 5, 1861, on ordnance duty at Richmond. Lt. of Arty., May 19, 1862. Temporary Capt. of Arty., Sept. 24, 1862. Stationed at Richmond Arsenal. At Macon (Ga.) Arsenal, May 1863–June 1864. Capt. OO to Ewell, June 18, 1864. Served into 1865. Insurance agent and bookkeeper at Staunton, Virginia. d. there Oct. 15, 1896.

Ker, William H. b. in Virginia. Lt. 1st U.S. Inf., 1817. To Capt. 1820. Resigned 1829. Lived prewar in Louisiana and Texas. Maj. AAIG and AAAG to Holmes, May 1861. Maj. AAIG to D. H. Hill, July 29, 1862. Maj. AAG to French, Sept. 1862. Commanded post at Petersburg, Virginia, Feb. 1863–1865. d. Nansemond Co., Virginia, May 21, 1867, age 68.

Kerr, John. Capt. OO to Ewell, July 25, 1864. Present Sept. 1864. No other record.

Kerr, John William. b. Greensville Co., Virginia, Apr. 3, 1839. att. VMI. Lt. Co. I, 5th Texas, Aug. 3, 1861. To Adjt., Aug. 1, 1862. Lt. AAAIG to J. B. Robertson, Oct. 22, 1862. Capt. AAIG to Robertson, Nov. 2, 1863. Same to John Gregg, 1864. Appx. New York City merchant. d. Brooklyn, Nov. 22, 1903. bur. Greenwood Cem.

Key, John Ross, Jr. b. Hagerstown, Maryland, July 16, 1832. A grandson of Francis Scott Key. Studied in Munich and Paris. Member of U.S. Coast Survey prewar. Probably the J. R. Key who served in Co. D, 1st Maryland. That Key was WIA Apr. 21 and June 6, 1862. Draughtsman in Engineer Dept., Mar. 24, 1862. Lt. EO, Sept. 6, 1862, stationed at Richmond. Lt. EO at Charleston, Sept. 20, 1863. Back to Richmond, Dec. 1864 into Apr. 1865. Successful artist in New England. Won top prize in art at the Centennial Exhibition. d. Baltimore,

Maryland, Mar. 24, 1920. bur. Mt. Olivet Cem., Frederick.

Kibbee, Charles Carroll. b. Macon, Georgia, Aug. 20, 1839. att. Princeton. Capt. 10th Georgia, 1861–1862. Capt. AAAG to Bryan, May 1864, and to Simms, June 1864 into 1865. Lt. Col. 10th Georgia, Feb. 20, 1865. In Georgia legislature and a judge. d. Morrow's Station, Oct. 17, 1905.

Killmartin, John. A resident of Orleans Parish, Louisiana. Sgt. Co. G, 7th Louisiana, June 7, 1861. Later to Lt. Lt. acting ADC to Taylor, June 1862. WIA at Second Manassas. POW at Spotsylvania. One of the Immortal 600. Took Oath, June 10, 1865.

Kindred, John Julius. b. Southampton Co., Virginia, Aug. 1824. att. UVA. and UNC. Lawyer at Jerusalem. Member of state's secession convention. Lt. ADC to Mahone, Nov. 16, 1861. Resigned July 17, 1862. Resumed law practice in Southampton Co. d. 1887.

King, Henry Lord Page. b. Apr. 25, 1831. att. Harvard Law School and Yale. Planter at St. Simons Island, Georgia, and read law prewar. Lt. CSA, Mar. 16, 1861. Served in 10th Georgia and in Read's (Ga.) Btty. Lt. OO to McLaws, by Aug. 1861. Lt. acting ADC to McLaws, by May 1862. Lt. ADC to McLaws, July 7, 1862. KIA at Fredericksburg. A brother-in-law of Gen. W. D. Smith. Described as "dainty but knightly." King's diary for the Maryland Campaign has been published.

King, Horace Watson. b. Jan. 25, 1829. A resident of Chattanooga, Tennessee. Capt. AQM, 61st Tennessee, Oct. 10, 1862. Maj. CS to Sam Jones, Sept. 3, 1862. Maj. CS to Breckinridge, by Apr. 1864. "Commission vacated June 14, 1864." Paroled at Lynchburg, Virginia, May 22, 1865. d. Feb. 15, 1884.

King, John Barry. b. Norfolk, Virginia. A clerk there. Pvt. Co. G, 6th Virginia, Apr. 19, 1861. Later to Sgt. Maj. Capt. AQM, Lightfoot's Bn. Arty., June 2, 1863. Newspaperman at Norfolk postwar, and in the cotton weighing business. d. in a hotel at Norfolk, July 8, 1893, age 53. bur. Elmwood Cem., in an unmarked grave.

Kinney, Archibald. b. Staunton, Virginia, Feb. 12, 1838. Capt. ACS, 46th Virginia, Aug. 7, 1861. Resigned July 24, 1862, but apparently returned to duty. Capt. ACS to Wise, June 25, 1863. Appx. Augusta Co. farmer and lawyer. Listed his occupation in a 1906 questionnaire as "waiting to cross over." d. Staunton, May 24, 1913.

Kinney, Richard Stevenson. b. near Staunton, Virginia, Feb. 28, 1841. att. VMI and USMA. Teacher in Augusta Co., Virginia. Cadet CSA, Aug. 28, 1861. Cadet acting OO to Van Dorn, July 1862. Lt. Co. A, 52nd Virginia, Dec. 20, 1862, into July 1863. Lt. acting ADC and AAAIG to Pegram's Bgd., date uncertain. Probably also OO to that brigade. Capt. (temp.), Dec. 17, 1864, to Dearing. Paroled at Richmond, May 12, 1865. Postwar clerk in QM Dept. at Fort Sam Houston, Texas. d. at Staunton, Jan. 31, 1923. bur. San Antonio, Texas.

Kinney, Thomas Colston. b. Apr. 27, 1841. att. VMI from Staunton, Virginia. On duty as Drillmaster under Magruder, John Pegram, and Wise early in the war. Lt. 59th Virginia. POW at Roanoke Island. Lt. EO, Feb. 15, 1862. Lt. EO to T. J. Jackson, Aug. 18, 1862–Mar. 20, 1863. Lt. EO to Ed Johnson, May–July 1863. Caught "typhoid pneumonia" in recrossing the Potomac after Gettysburg. d. Staunton, Virginia, July 28, 1863.

Kirker, William H. b. in Ohio, Feb. 5, 1831. A clerk in Brooke Co., Virginia. Maj. PAVa., May 28, 1861. Maj. QM to R. E. Lee, apparently, Aug. 6, 1861. Maj. QM to Loring, date unknown. Maj. OO, Feb. 1862, duty unknown. Capt. AQM (PACS), Nov. 5, 1862. Duty again unclear. Capt. AQM to report to Stuart, Mar. 26, 1864. Capt. AQM to Hampton by 1865. Paroled May 1865 at Staunton, Virginia. Druggist at Charlottesville postwar. d. May 5, 1884. bur. Maplewood Cem. Victim of a fuzzy official military record.

Kirkland, John Murray. b. Sept. 11, 1834. Planter at Winnsboro, South Carolina. Capt. ACS, 15th South Carolina, Sept. 23, 1861. Failed bond and dropped, Aug. 2, 1862, but stayed on anyway. Capt. ACS to Kershaw, Mar. 10, 1863, but may not have served much longer. POW July 30, 1864. Planter at Monticello, South Carolina. d. Apr. 28, 1897. bur. Monticello Methodist Church.

Kirkland, Samuel S. b. in North Carolina, 1831. att. Wm. & Mary. A civil engineer from Hillsborough. Lt. Co. A, 6th North Carolina, May 16, 1861. Later to Capt. Resigned July 29, 1862. Lt. OO and AAAG to Pender, July 29, 1862. Lt. ADC to Pender, Dec. 13, 1862. Resigned June 1, 1863, but immediately reinstated to rank from June 6. Capt. AAG to Kirkland, Sept. 12, 1863, but declined it. Capt. AQM in North Carolina, Oct. 1863–1865. Capt. VADC to Kirkland, Apr. 1865. Engineer at Asheville, North Carolina. d. Edgefield, South Carolina, Dec. 24, 1905. bur. St. Matthews Episc. Cem., Hillsborough.

Kirkman, Thomas J. b. in Alabama. att. SCMA. Clerk at Florence. Pvt. Co. H, 4th Alabama, Apr. 28, 1861, age 28. Severely WIA in thigh at First Manassas, and discharged Jan. 26, 1862. Apparently returned on a volunteer basis as he saw service as "Capt." on staff of Law at Sharpsburg, probably as VADC.

Knox, John Somerville, Jr. b. Fauquier Co., Virginia, 1827. m. Elizabeth Welsh Horner. A merchant at Fredericksburg and Alexandria. Capt. ACS, 4th Bn. Virginia, Dec. 24, 1861. Capt. ACS at Camp Winder in Richmond, by Dec. 1862. Served until retired Nov. 28, 1864. Worked in state auditor's office at Richmond, and then resumed merchant business at Alexandria. d. at Richmond, Sept. 6, 1906. bur. Ivy Hill Cem., Alexandria.

Knox, Thomas S. b. in Virginia. A 21-year-old resident of Fredericksburg in 1860. Pvt. Co. B, 30th Virginia. Lt. Co. A, 30th Virginia, May–Oct. 1861. Capt. ACS, 30th Virginia, Oct. 10, 1861. Capt. ACS at Danville, Virginia, Feb. 1862. Served at other posts in Virginia, 1863. Capt. ACS to Hunton, Mar. 19, 1864, but never joined. Capt. ACS at Jackson Hospital in Richmond, Apr. 13, 1864. Deserted in Sept. 1864, having embezzled funds and been discovered. Possible middle names are Stuart and Soutter.

Koerner, Peter W. Oscar. b. in Prussia, ca. 1831. In 1860 census living at Cedar Key Island, in Gulf of Mexico, off Levy Co., Florida. Also listed residence as Waldo, Florida. Pvt. Co. K, 2nd Florida, July 8, 1861. Detached on engineer duty by Dec. 1861. Lt. EO, Feb. 15, 1862. Worked at Richmond and Staunton, Virginia, 1862–1864, and at Greenville and Tarboro, North Carolina. Lt. topographical EO assigned to ANVa., 1864. Lt. EO to Ewell by Jan. 1865. POW at Sailor's Creek. Surveyor in Nassau Co., Florida, in 1875.

Kyle, George H. b. in Maryland. A resident of Baltimore. Slightly wounded in 1859 election violence. A grocer before and after the war. Maj. CS to Steuart, Apr. 2, 1862. VADC to Maryland Line at Gaines's Mill. Maj. CS to Ed Johnson, July 5, 1863. Maj. CS to Col. B. T. Johnson, Nov. 18, 1863. Was absent without leave for prolonged period in 1864. POW at Cedar Creek, apparently as Maj. AAIG to John B. Gordon. May have served on staff of Dearing in early 1865. Paroled Apr. 21, 1865, in western Virginia as Maj. AAIG to Gordon, age 32. d. at Baltimore, Feb. 23, 1875, age 44. bur. Green Mount Cem.

Lacy, Drury, Jr. b. Nov. 24, 1839. att. Davidson Coll. Pvt. Co. B, 1st North Carolina. Pvt. Co. B, 43rd North Carolina, Mar. 31, 1862. Adjt. 43rd North Carolina, May 20, 1862. Lt. AAAG to Godwin, summer 1862.

Lt. AAAG to Lewis, 1864–1865. d. Oct. 22, 1869.

Lacy, James Horace. b. St. Charles, Missouri, June 10, 1823. Grew up at Summerville, Tennessee. VADC to G. W. Smith, Apr.–June 1862. POW June 10, 1862. Lt. ADC to Smith, Aug. 30, 1862. Vacated the position Feb. 17, 1863. Maj. QM, IFT, Apr. 16, 1863. In Trans-Mississippi Dept., summer 1863. Dept. of Western Virginia and Eastern Tennnessee, Nov. 1863, then back to Trans-Mississippi in Jan. 1864. Maj. QM at Dublin Depot, May–Oct. 1864. Failed confirmation but reappointed Maj. QM, Feb. 23, 1865. d. Fredericksburg, Virginia, Jan. 27, 1906. bur. Fredericksburg Confederate Cem.

Lafferty, John James. b. Greensville Co., Virginia, Apr. 20, 1837. att. UVA. Harrisonburg, Virginia, clergyman. Chaplain, 18th Virginia Cavy., Dec. 15, 1862. Maj. CS to Imboden, 1864–1865, although official appointment not found. Methodist minister and editor at Richmond. Wrote several religious books and an autobiographical pamphlet. d. July 20, 1909. bur. Mt. Moriah Methodist Church, Albemarle Co.

Lake, ——. From Maryland. VADC to Early at Second Winchester. No other record.

Lake, James Bushrod, Jr. b. Oct. 4, 1837. Resident of Cambridge, Maryland. Pvt. Warren (Miss.) Light Arty., Aug. 17, 1861. Lt. OO to B. R. Johnson, Aug. 23, 1862. POW at Sailor's Creek. Released June 19, 1865. Married twice. d. Sept. 30, 1896.

Lamar, Gazaway Bugg, Jr. b. Richmond Co., Georgia, ca. 1838. Lt. 2nd Georgia Militia. Lt. Co. B, 1st Georgia Regs., Feb. 1, 1861. Lt. ADC to McLaws, Dec. 25, 1862. Served into 1865. Postwar businessman at Savannah. Alive 1901 at Thomaston, Georgia. Spelling of first name possibly Gasaway.

Lamar, Gazaway DeRosset. b. Jan. 7, 1842. att. UVA., from Augusta, Georgia. Pvt. Co. I, 11th Mississippi, 1861. VADC to Bartow at First Manassas. Cadet to Toombs, Aug. 3, 1861. Resigned Nov. 14, 1862. Lt. ADC to

W. H. T. Walker, July 18, 1863. Lt. VADC to his brother-in-law, Gen. Cumming, July–Aug. 1864. Resigned summer 1864. Planter and lawyer at Augusta. Later lived in New York. d. Augusta, Jan. 12, 1886. bur. Summerville Cem. Known as "Derry."

Lamar, John Basil. b. Milledgeville, Georgia, Nov. 5, 1812. att. UGA. Mexican War veteran. USHR, author, member of state secession convention, and a planter with 89 slaves and a total prewar value of $425,000. Known as "White John." VADC to his brother-in-law, Howell Cobb. MWIA at Crampton's Gap. d. Sept. 15, 1862. bur. temporarily at Edge Hill Cem., Charlestown, Virginia. Later removed to Rose Hill Cem., Macon, Georgia.

Lamar, W. T. Staff of Toombs, Oct. 1862. No other record found.

Land, Albert Lewis. b. Sussex Co., Virginia, 1830. Farmer at Sussex C.H. Lt. Co. A, 41st Virginia, Aug. 12, 1861. Capt. AQM, 41st Virginia, Oct. 14, 1861. Capt. acting QM to Mahone, Aug. 1, 1862. Maj. QM to Mahone, Nov. 25, 1862. Maj. QM to Corley, at ANVA. headquarters, Nov. 30, 1863. The churlish Mahone complained about Land's competence, but Land served at ANVa. headquarters into 1865. m. Mary Louisa Urquhart, 1863. Postwar farmer in Surry Co. d. there Jan. 16, 1873.

Lane, Edward Haden. b. Dec. 28, 1827. att. UVA. Lawyer in Louisa Co., Virginia. Cpl. Louisa Arty., Apr. 1, 1862. Capt. AQM to H. P. Jones's Bn. Arty., Feb. 21, 1863. Served into 1865. County court judge and lawyer in Louisa. d. there June 3, 1879, of consumption. bur. Oakwood Cem. Known as "the Chancellor" among his Louisa friends.

Lane, Hardy B. A resident of Craven Co., North Carolina. m. Julia G. Simmons, 1851. Sgt. Co. H, 1st North Carolina Cavy., June 20, 1861, age 32. POW at Willis Church. Capt. ACS, 31st North Carolina, Jan. 8, 1863. Capt. ACS to Clingman, Aug. 20, 1863.

Paroled Apr. 26, 1865. bur. Cedar Grove Cem., New Bern.

Lane, John. b. Evansville, Indiana, May 17, 1837. att. USMA. Lt. Co. L, 1st Georgia Regs., June 11, 1861. Lt. Hamilton's (Ga.) Btty., Aug. 16, 1861. Lt. ADC (VADC?) to G. W. Smith, Sept. 25, 1861. Capt. Irwin (Ga.) Arty., Dec. 13, 1861. Maj. Cutts's Bn. Arty., March 2, 1863. To Lt. Col., Feb. 18, 1865. Lived postwar in Idaho. d. Lapwai, Idaho, Dec. 24, 1914, bur. Lewiston.

Lane, Julius Rooker. b. Apr. 2, 1842. Pvt. 61st Virginia Militia, 1861–1862. Co. E, 5th Virginia Cavy. Acting ADC to his brother, Gen. J. H. Lane, 1863. KIA by shell fragment at Chancellorsville, May 3, 1863. bur. Hollywood Cem., Richmond.

Lane, Oscar. b. June 12, 1835. Pvt. 61st Virginia Militia, 1861–1862. Lt. ADC to his brother, Gen. J. H. Lane, Sept. 17, 1862. MWIA at Spotsylvania, May 12, 1864. d. July 17, 1864. bur. Hollywood Cem., Richmond.

Langdon, Paul H. b. in North Carolina. Railroad clerk at Wilmington in 1860. Capt. AQM, Oct. 25, 1861. Served at Richmond, Virginia, first half of war. Duties included administering burials and issuing stationery. Capt. AQM at Weldon, North Carolina, by Dec. 1863.

Langdon, Richard F. b. Wilmington, North Carolina, May 1828. Lived in California, 1849–1860. Clerk to Admiral Farragut at Mare Island in 1860. Lt. Co. E, 1st North Carolina, May 16, 1861. Capt. AQM, 3rd North Carolina, Jan. 29, 1863. Capt. AQM to Rodes, Sept. 15, 1864. Presumably same to Ramseur for a month, and then to Grimes. Served into 1865. Never married. Postwar employee of Wilmington and Weldon Railroad. d. at Wilmington, Dec. 26, 1895. bur. Oakdale Cem.

Lanneau, John Francis. b. Charleston, South Carolina, Feb. 7, 1836. att. SCMA. Professor of physics and chemistry at Furman. Capt. Co. B, Hampton Legion Cavy. Lt. EO to Whiting, June 4, 1862. On duty at Drewry's Bluff and Chaffin's Bluff, 1862–1863. Lt. EO to report to M. F. Maury, Feb. 27, 1864. Serving with Col. Walter Stevens in 1864. Lt. EO to report to ANVa. July 11, 1864. Lt. EO to Hampton by Sept. 1864. Capt. EO to Hampton, Oct. 19, 1864. att. Baylor Univ. postwar. Famous astronomer. President at several small southern colleges and then professor at Wake Forest, 1890–1921. d. Mar. 5, 1921. bur. Wake Forest Cem.

Lapsley, Robert. b. Caldwell Co., Kentucky, Feb. 2, 1833. Lived prewar in Selma, Alabama. Pvt. Co. D, 8th Alabama, May 10, 1861. Discharged June 1, 1862. Capt. AQM, 44th Alabama, July 8, 1862, to rank from May 31, 1862. Capt. AQM to W. F. Perry, Sept. 15, 1864. Appx. Hardware merchant at Selma. d. 1895.

Largen, W. J. Worked for QM Dept. in Mississippi and Tennessee in 1862. Pvt. 28th Bn. Georgia Arty., July 3, 1863. To Lt. of Co. A, Dec. 5, 1863. Lt. acting OO to Finegan, July–Aug. 1864. Lt. OO to Shelley. Paroled Apr. 26, 1865. Very possibly William James Largen of Carroll Co., Virginia.

Lartigue, Gerard Bull. b. Barnwell Co., South Carolina, Apr. 10, 1829. att. SCMA and South Carolina Medical Coll. Physician at Columbia and in Barnwell Co. Capt. AQM, 1st South Carolina, July 21, 1861. Capt. Asst. PM at Charleston, May–June 1862. Maj. QM to Hagood, Aug. 28, 1862. Paroled Aug. 26, 1865. In South Carolina senate. d. Blackville, South Carolina, May 9, 1898. bur. family cem.

Latane, Samuel Peachy. b. Essex Co., Virginia, Aug. 23, 1835. att. UVA. Essex Co. teacher. Lt. Co. I, 26th Virginia, July 1, 1861. Lt. AAAIG to Wise's Bgd. (under Col. Goode), Apr.–Dec. 1864. POW at Hatcher's Run, Mar. 30, 1865. Alive 1878 in King and Queen Co., a teacher.

Latham, Frederick Graham. b. Perthshire, Scotland, 1833. Father was a British Army officer. Moved to South Carolina in 1854.

Lt. Co. G, 5th South Carolina, Apr. 13, 1861. Lt. AAAG to D. R. Jones, July 1861. WIA at Frayser's Farm and Second Manassas. Capt. Co. M, Palmetto Sharpshooters. Capt. AAAG to brigade at Wauhatchie (under Col. Bratton). On furlough in Europe, and resigned Feb. 24, 1865. Lived in Union Co., South Carolina, and superintended an ironworks. Also a planter. Alive 1899 at Charleston, managing a phosphate mine. d. 1903 in Scotland.

Latham, George Woodville. b. Lynchburg, Virginia, Dec. 16, 1833. att. UVa. Lynchburg lawyer all his life. Capt. Co. A, 11th Virginia, 1861–1862. Acting Judge Advocate and Asst. to the army's inspector gen., 1861. Capt. AAIG to J. E. Johnston, Apr. 11, 1862. Judge Advocate for ANVa., by Sept. 1862. Relieved from that duty Mar. 9, 1863. Capt. AAG at Lynchburg, Feb. 8, 1864. d. there Aug. 15, 1870. bur. Lynchburg Presby. Cem. Called "Woodie."

Latimer, Joseph White. b. Prince William Co., Virginia, Aug. 27, 1843. att. VMI. Lt. and Capt. Courtney (Va.) Arty., Sept. 1861–Mar. 1863. Capt. Chief of Arty. to Early at Fredericksburg. Maj. of Arty., Mar. 2, 1863. MWIA at Gettysburg. d. Harrisonburg, Virginia, Aug. 1, 1863. bur. Woodbine Cem.

Latrobe, Osmun. b. Natchez, Mississippi, Apr. 1835. att. Maryland Military Academy. VADC to D. R. Jones, Sept. 1861–Mar. 1862. Capt. AAIG to Jones, Mar. 11, 1862. Capt. AAIG to Longstreet, Oct. 3, 1862. Maj. AAG to Longstreet, Feb. 16, 1863. WIA in right hand and thigh at Wilderness. Maj. AAG to R. H. Anderson, June 29–Sept. 25, 1864. Lt. Col. AAG to Longstreet, Dec. 19, 1864. Appx. Lived postwar in Baltimore, New York City, and St. Petersburg, Russia. d. New York City, Oct. 8, 1915. bur. Green Mount Cem., Baltimore. Latrobe's diary is at the Virginia Historical Society.

Law, Charles H. b. in Georgia. Pvt. Co. B, 4th Georgia, Apr. 26, 1861. Appointed regimental marker, June 27, 1861. To Sgt. Maj.,

Nov. 1, 1862. Lt. ADC to Cook, Aug. 5, 1864. Appx. d. at Savannah, 1879.

Law, John Kolb. b. in South Carolina, Jan. 19, 1841. att. SCMA. Resident of Darlington. VADC to his brother, Gen. Law, summer 1862. WIA in left ankle at Sharpsburg. Lt. Enrolling Officer in South Carolina, Oct. 1, 1863. m. Mary Lavinia James. Involved in a Reconstruction episode and moved to Solano Co., California, in 1869. Taught school there, and later in Mariposa Co. Merced Co. lawyer and district attorney. d. Dec. 14, 1913. bur. Merced City Cem.

Lawrence, Alexander W. b. Raleigh, North Carolina, Oct. 14, 1834. att. UNC. A brilliant mathematician, on staff at Naval Observatory at Washington, D.C. Capt. Provisional Army of North Carolina, 1861. Capt. OO, May 20, 1862. On duty at Richmond, Virginia. One source says staff of Longstreet in 1863. Capt. OO to Holmes with North Carolina Reserves, Sept. 1, 1864. Postwar insurance agent. d. at Raleigh, Aug. 10, 1880. bur. Oakwood Cem.

Lawton, Edward Payson. b. Apr. 23, 1832. att. Brown and UVa. A commission merchant from Robertville, South Carolina. m. Evalina Loyer Davant. Capt. AAG to his brother, Gen. Lawton, Aug. 15, 1861. Bruised in leg at Gaines's Mill. MWIA in spine and POW at Fredericksburg. d. "Mansion House Hospital" at Alexandria, Virginia, Dec. 26, 1862. bur. Robertville Baptist Church.

Lawton, John W. Capt. AQM and disbursing officer for Virginia forces, 1864–1865. Based at Richmond, Virginia.

Lay, George William. b. in Virginia, Nov. 26, 1821. att. USMA. Mexican War veteran. Served in Old Army, 1842–1861. Prewar aide to Gen. Winfield Scott. Supt. Louisiana Military Academy, 1861. Capt. CSA, Mar. 16, 1861, and Lt. Col. AAG in PACS. On commissary duty at Lynchburg, Virginia, June 1861. Lt. Col. AAG to Bonham, July 1861. Lt. Col. AAIG to J. E. Johnston, Oct. 1861.

Relieved July 12, 1862, and assigned to duty as roving AAIG. Lt. Col. in Bureau of Conscription, Jan. 1863 into 1865. m. Henrietta Campbell, daughter of Asst. Secretary of War, making Lay a brother-in-law of A. P. Mason and Fred Colston, both staff officers. d. New Orleans, Louisiana, May 8, 1867. bur. Magnolia Cem., Mobile, Alabama.

Leake, Andrew Kean. b. Apr. 1842. att. Hampden Sidney. Lt. Turner's (Va.) Btty., 1862. Lt. Enrolling Officer in Goochland Co., Virginia, Oct. 1862–Apr. 1864. Lt. OO to Garnett's Bn. Arty., Apr. 7, 1864. Paroled May 1, 1865. Lawyer and judge in Goochland Co., and at Richmond. m. Julianna Elizabeth Harris. d. Goochland Co., Nov. 2, 1907.

Leake, Thaddeus Constantine. b. Aug. 17, 1829. Lt. Co. C, 12th Bn. Virginia Arty. Capt. AQM, 12th Bn. Virginia Arty., May 15, 1862. No other record, and may not have served. Henrico Co. farmer. Married twice. d. Richmond, Virginia, Jan. 18, 1904. "Somewhat bald."

Lee, Charles Henry. b. Alexandria, Virginia, 1818. Employed in U.S. Adjt. Gen.'s office. A lawyer. m. Elizabeth Dunbar. Maj. AAG to Sam. Cooper, Oct. 27, 1862. Ran Judge Advocate's Dept. for CSA. Author of the standard wartime title *The Judge Advocate's Vade Mecum*. Resigned May 31, 1864, due to prostate problems. Lawyer in Loudoun Co. and at Washington, D.C. d. Round Hill, Virginia, Mar. 25, 1900. bur. Union Cem., Leesburg.

Lee, George. Lt. ADC to Moore, 1865. No other record found.

Lee, George. b. Leesburg, Virginia, May 3, 1831. Merchant at Nashville, Tennessee, and Brooklyn, New York. Pvt. 1st Co. Richmond Howitzers, June 23, 1863–Apr. 26, 1864. Capt. ACS, Apr. 7, 1864. Stationed at Farmville, Virginia, 1864–1865. Present at Appomattox, possibly as Capt. ACS to Gen. Grimes. m. his cousin Laura Frances Orr

Rogers. d. Brooklyn, New York, Apr. 14, 1892.

Lee, Henry Carter. b. Fairfax Co., Virginia, Jan. 7, 1842. att. UVA. Cpl. Richmond Howitzers. Lt. ADC to his brother, Gen. Fitz. Lee, July 30, 1862. Lt. AAAIG to Wickham, May 4, 1864. Capt. AAIG to Wickham subsequently. Contemplated writing a brigade history in the 1870s. Insurance agent and farmer at Abingdon. d. June 6, 1889. Lee's diary is at the Museum of the Confederacy.

Lee, Hugh Holmes, Jr. b. Clarksburg, Virginia, Aug. 26, 1836. att. VMI and UVA. A lawyer. Pvt. Co. C, 31st Virginia, May 21, 1861. Lt. OO to Loring, spring 1861. "Discontinued" Sept. 1, 1861. Lt. OO to T. J. Jackson, Apr. 22, 1862. WIA and POW at McDowell. Relieved Dec. 29, 1862. Served later in the Auditor's Office at Richmond. Salem lawyer and legislator postwar. d. there July 12, 1869. bur. East Hill Cem.

Lee, John Mason. b. Clermont, Fairfax Co., Virginia, Jan. 4, 1839. Lt. of Inf., CSA, May 18, 1861. Lt. ADC to Trimble, Oct. 7, 1861. Lt. AAIG to Trimble by Apr. 1862. WIA slightly at Gaines's Mill. Capt. (temp.) AAIG to W. H. F. Lee, Nov. 1, 1862. Capt. (temp.) AAG to Wickham, Nov. 2, 1863, though he had been serving there since August. Maj. AAIG to W. H. F. Lee, June 1864. A brother of Gen. Fitz. Lee. Lived in Stafford Co. postwar. d. there Mar. 11, 1924. bur. Aquia Episc. Church Cem.

Lee, Nathaniel Ware. b. Jan. 8, 1843. Of Greenville, Mississippi. att. VMI. Cadet VADC to T. J. Jackson, July 1861. Pvt. Co. D, 28th Mississippi Cavy., Mar. 9, 1862. MWIA at Coldwater, Mississippi, Dec. 1862, and died on Christmas at Panola.

Lee, Richard Bland, Jr. b. Fairfax Co., Virginia, July 20, 1797. att. USMA. Served as an artillerist and staff officer in the Old Army, 1817–1861. WIA twice in Seminole War. A cousin of R. E. Lee. Lt. Col. CS to Beauregard, Mar. 16, 1861. Relieved Aug. 1861–Mar. 1862, due to sickness. Lt. Col. CS to A. S. Johnston, Mar. 30, 1862. Lt. Col. cs to Beauregard, Apr. 7–June 25, 1862. Seems not to have served beyond summer 1862. d. Alexandria, Virginia, Aug. 2, 1875. bur. Ivy Hill Cem.

Lee, Richard Henry. b. Alexandria, Virginia, Oct. 24, 1821. A grandson of R. H. Lee, signer of Declaration of Independence. Lawyer in Jefferson Co. Lt. Co. G, 2nd Virginia, Apr. 18, 1861. wia at Kernstown. Col. of Cavy. and Judge on Second Corps court, Dec. 16, 1862. pow at Orange C.H., Sept. 22, 1863. Exchanged Jan. 29, 1864. No further military record. Lawyer and judge in Clarke Co. d. there June 18, 1902. bur. Old Chapel Cem.

Lee, Robert Edward, Jr. b. Arlington, Virginia, Oct. 27, 1843. att. uva. Pvt. Rockbridge (Va.) Arty., Mar. 28, 1862. Lt. adc to his brother, W. H. F. Lee, Oct. 30, 1862, but rejected by President Davis due to tender age. Lt. acting adc to W. H. F. Lee, Oct. 1862–June 1863. Lt. acting oo to Lee, June 1863. Apptd. Cadet, June 10, 1863. wia at Spotsylvania and in autumn 1864. Lt. aaag to W. H. F. Lee, 1865. Appx. Farmer in King William and Fairfax Counties. m. (1) Charlotte Haxall. m. (2) Juliet Carter. d. Upperville, Virginia, Oct. 19, 1914. bur. Lee Crypt, Lexington, Virginia.

Lee, Thomas Broome. b. Camden, South Carolina, Feb. 28, 1835. att. scma. A civil engineer. Capt. aqm, 1st South Carolina Rifles, Oct. 11, 1861. Capt. aqm to Maxcy Gregg, June 1862. Capt. eo to Pemberton, Aug. 6, 1862. Served at Charleston in 1863. Capt. eo to Patton Anderson, Mar. 1864. Postwar architect and engineer. d. Charlotte, North Carolina, Mar. 13, 1922. bur. Greenwood, South Carolina.

Lee, William Franklin. b. Charleston, South Carolina, 1832. Moved to Asheville, North Carolina, in mid-1840s. Lt. Co. A, 2nd Florida, May 25, 1861. Lt. eo (volunteer?) to D. H. Hill, by Apr. 1862, and through Sharpsburg, at least. Lt. aaaig to E. A.

Perry at Fredericksburg. wia at Chancellorsville; left arm amputated. On miscellaneous engineering and ordnance duty in Alabama late in the war. Postwar city engineer at Pensacola, Florida. d. there Sept. 7, 1906. bur. St. John's Cem. Brother was Col. of the 33rd North Carolina.

Leigh, Benjamin Watkins. b. Jan. 18, 1831. vadc to A. P. Hill at Chancellorsville. Maj. aag to Edward Johnson, June 3, 1863. kia at Gettysburg, July 3, 1863. bur. Shockoe Cem., Richmond, Virginia.

Leigh, Chapman Johnson. b. in Virginia, ca. 1826. m. Anne Carter of "Shirley" Plantation. Capt. aqm, Nov. 4, 1862. Served at Richmond as a Paymaster. d. New York City, Apr. 2, 1911.

Leigh, James Young. b. Norfolk, Virginia, March 27, 1824. A merchant there. m. Fannie Johnson. Pvt. Co. G, 6th Virginia, Aug. 14–Sept. 25, 1861. Served in qm Dept. at Norfolk. Capt. aqm to Loring, Apr. 10, 1862. Capt. aqm, 30th Bn. Virginia Sharpshooters, Sept. 1862. Capt. aqm to Breckinridge, Aug. 1864. Capt. aqm to Wharton, Oct. 1864. Realtor and estate auctioneer at Norfolk. d. there Aug. 9, 1904. bur. Elmwood Cem.

Leitch, Samuel Gooch. b. in Virginia, Mar. 11, 1840. att. uva. Lt. Co. F, 19th Virginia, May 25, 1861. Lt. acting oo to Longstreet, May 1862. Lt. acting oo to Pickett, Sept. 1862–Nov. 1864. pow at Williamsport, Sept. 15, 1862. Lt. aaag to G. J. Rains, Dec. 14, 1864. In charge of self-anchoring torpedoes (mines) in James River. Physician and lawyer at Chicago, Illinois. Alive there 1882. "Very quiet and unassuming."

Lemmon, George. b. Baltimore, Maryland, Aug. 25, 1835. Wealthy merchant there prewar. Co. H, 1st Maryland, July 1861–July 1862. vadc and aaag to Archer during Seven Days. Lt. oo to Archer, July 1, 1862. Tried to resign, Feb. 1863, but failed. pow at Cashtown, July 5, 1863. Lt. oo at Richmond Arsenal, Jan. 1865. Lt. oo to Wickham's

Bgd., Mar. 6, 1865. Paroled at Greensboro, May 5, 1865. Postwar merchant. d. Fairfax, Virginia, Aug. 29, 1905, while aboard a train. bur. Green Mount Cem., Baltimore.

Lemmons, Perry O. b. in South Carolina. m. Emily Jane Camp, 1856. Served in Co. K, 18th South Carolina. Capt. AQM, 18th South Carolina, Jan. 14, 1862. Failed bond and dropped effective Aug. 30, 1862, but served on and presumably met bond. Capt. acting AQM to N. G. Evans, 1863. Capt. acting AQM to Elliott, 1864. Capt. AQM to Elliott, Sept. 20, 1864. Same to Wallace. Appx. A 42-year-old farmer in Spartanburg Co., South Carolina, in 1870. Alive 1883.

Leonard, Thomas F. b. in Georgia. A 34-year-old traveling agent at Canton, Mississippi, in 1860. Capt. ACS, 18th Mississippi, Dec. 24, 1861. Capt. ACS to Barksdale, date not certain. Capt. ACS to Humphreys, July 1863. Through Nov. 1864, at least. An acquaintance in the 18th Mississippi wrote scathingly of Leonard during the war: "He is drunk more than half the time and does not attend to his duty. He is as big a liar as ever. . . ." Another source calls him "eccentric."

Lester, William Wharton. b. Pulaski, Tennessee, Feb. 6, 1828. Moved to Mississippi in 1838 and then to Washington, D.C. in 1856. Employee of U.S. Patent Office. m. Elizabeth Jane Walker, 1858. Worked in the South as a civilian, 1861–1863. Capt. AQM, July 6, 1863, appointed from Mississippi. In charge of correspondence relating to QM Dept. assignments. Based at Richmond. Lived in Maryland, just outside Washington after the war. Worked at the Library of Congress. d. Apr. 11, 1903. bur. Glenwood Cem., Washington.

Levering, Thomas Henry. b. Baltimore, Maryland, Jan. 3, 1837. A clerk there. Pvt. Co. H, 1st Maryland, June 18, 1861–June 18, 1862. VADC to Archer at Fredericksburg. Pvt. Ward's (Ala.) Btty., June 23, 1863–June 11, 1864. Pvt. Co. L, 1st Maryland

Cavy., June 11, 1864, into 1865. Commission merchant at Baltimore in 1870.

Lewis, Edward Lloyd. b. Greene Co., Georgia, Aug. 7, 1843. Lt. ADC to Thomas, Dec. 1, 1862. Through Appx.

Lewis, Edward Parke Custis. b. Clarke Co., Virginia, Feb. 7, 1837. att. UVA. Farmer in Clarke Co. Pvt. 122nd Virginia Militia. Lt. ADC to W. H. F. Lee, July 1863. POW at Snickersville, Nov. 28, 1863. Later on the staffs of Chambliss, J. R. Cooke, and again to W. H. F. Lee. Records are very uncertain and vague. Married twice. Lawyer and politician at Hoboken, New Jersey, and Minister to Portugal. Had "a fortune of many millions" when he died at Hoboken, Sept. 3, 1892. bur. Princeton Cemetery.

Lewis, John S. Maj. CS to John B. Gordon, Dec. 13, 1862. Not confirmed by Senate, but served anyway, perhaps as late as June 1864. No further record.

Lewis, Samuel Longworth. Capt. AQM, Sept. 20, 1861. Maj. QM to Pickett, Oct. 19, 1861. Relieved Oct. 8, 1862, and made Maj. QM on paymaster duty at Staunton, Virginia. Served there through Nov. 1864, at least.

Lewis, Warner. From Brunswick Co., Virginia. VADC to J. H. Winder, late in 1861 or early in 1862. Served in that capacity through Dec. 1863, at least.

Lightfoot, John. b. Jan. 15, 1836. A farmer. Cpl. Co. A, 7th Virginia, Apr. 23, 1861. Capt. AQM, 7th Virginia, June 16, 1862. Dropped July 31, 1863. Capt. AQM in reserve medical and ordnance trains for Third Corps, Nov. 19, 1863. Appx. d. Sept. 23, 1880.

Lilly, Robert. A medical student in Anson Co., North Carolina. Pvt. Co. C, 14th North Carolina, Apr. 22, 1861, age 21. Later to Sgt., and then Capt. ACS, 14th North Carolina, Aug. 9, 1862. POW at Frederick, Maryland, Sept. 17, 1862. Dropped Feb. 5, 1863, for prolonged absence and failed bond. Reinstated Apr. 4, 1863. Capt. ACS to Ramseur,

Sept. 17, 1863. Capt. ACS to Cox and Grimes, subsequently.

Lindsay, Albert Loftus. b. Old Point Comfort, Virginia. Moved to Richmond as a boy. Lt. Co. H, 15th Virginia, Apr. 27, 1861. Detached on signal duty, Aug. 26, 1861. Served with Magruder on Peninsula. Dropped from 15th Virginia, Apr. 1862. Lt. SO, Oct. 10, 1862, assigned to Magruder. Lt. SO to Scurry for a time, and then with Magruder, mid-1863 into 1865. Lived postwar at Norfolk, Virginia. d. Portsmouth, Nov. 24, 1907, age 76. bur. Hollywood Cem., Richmond, in an unmarked grave.

Lindsay, Mellish Motte. b. Limestone Co., Alabama, Dec. 11, 1833. Raised in Boston, and in Mississippi. Served one year with Walker Expedition in Nicaragua. Alabama civil engineer. Lt. Co. A, 19th Mississippi, May 18, 1861. WIA in Seven Days. Lt. ADC to Wilcox, Aug. 19, 1862. Appx. Cotton planter in Noxubee Co. Later a farmer and businessman in Fulton Co., Tennessee. d. Dec. 20, 1891. bur. Lauderdale Co., Tennessee.

Linebaugh, John H. b. in Kentucky. Prewar resident of Alabama. Lt. ADC to Armistead, July 31, 1862. Resigned Nov. 1, 1862, due to "failing health and domestic affliction."

Linthicum, Charles Frederick. b. Frederick Co., Maryland, Dec. 17, 1838. A teacher. Chaplain 8th Virginia, Oct. 31, 1861. VADC to Eppa Hunton at Second Manassas. Resigned Nov. 24, 1862. Capt. AAG to R. B. Garnett, Nov. 24, 1862. Slightly WIA in hand at Gettysburg. KIA at Cold Harbor, June 3, 1864. bur. Hollywood Cem., Richmond.

Lipscomb, James Nathan. b. Abbeville Co., South Carolina, Apr. 11, 1827. att. South Carolina Coll. In state legislature pre- and postwar. Lt. Col. South Carolina state troops. Lt. CSA, July 3, 1861, staff of Bonham. Resigned Aug. 6, 1861. Capt. AQM, 2nd South Carolina Cavy., Oct. 14, 1862. Resigned Oct. 12, 1863. Capt. AAG to Butler,

Sept. 1, 1863. Paroled Apr. 26, 1865. Married three times, including daughter of Gov. Pickens. d. Bryson City, North Carolina, June 1891.

Lipscomb, Milledge Bonham. b. Anderson District, South Carolina, Oct. 6, 1836. att. South Carolina Coll. Farmer at Ninety Six. VADC to his uncle, Gen. Bonham, July 1861. Later Co. G, 2nd South Carolina Cavy. A brother of James N. Lipscomb (q.v.). d. Ninety Six, June 5, 1904. bur. Elmwood Cem.

Lipscomb, Thomas Jefferson. b. Abbeville Dist., South Carolina, Mar. 27, 1833. att. UVa., South Carolina Medical Coll., and Jefferson Medical Coll. Planter at Newberry. Lt. Co. B, 3rd South Carolina, 1861. VADC to his uncle, Gen. Bonham, July 1861. Capt. Co. G, 2nd South Carolina Cavy., June 20, 1862. Eventually Col. 2nd South Carolina Cavy. In state legislature postwar. Newberry physician and cotton merchant. Mayor of Columbia, 1898–1900. d. Nov. 4, 1908.

Little, John Chapman. b. Feb. 7, 1837. att. UVa. From Fauquier Co., Virginia. Capt. of Arty., Dec. 27, 1862. Served at Richmond Arsenal, Dec. 1862–Jan. 1863. Capt. OO to Whiting, Jan. 20, 1863. Reappointed as Capt. OO, May 2, 1863, cause not found. At Wilmington in Dec. 1864. Paroled Apr. 26, 1865. Ran schools in Fauquier Co. and at Norfolk. Insurance agent at Raleigh, North Carolina, and employee at Norfolk Navy Yard. d. 1907. bur. Leeds Episc. Church Cem., Fauquier Co.

Littlefield, James Harvey. b. in Indiana, Aug. 25, 1832. Moved to Texas at a young age. A merchant at Washington, Texas. m. Mary E. McCown. Sgt. Co. E, 5th Texas. Capt. AQM, 5th Texas, Oct. 31, 1861. Maj. QM to J. B. Robertson, Nov. 1, 1862. Same to John Gregg, Apr. 1864. Appx. Banker at Houston and merchant at Hillsboro. Retired in 1900 and moved to New York City.

d. there June 7, 1901. bur. Old Hillsboro Cem.

Livingston, John. b. New Orleans, Louisiana. A clerk. Cpl. Co. A, 7th Louisiana, June 7, 1861, age 40. Capt. AQM, 7th Louisiana, Oct. 28, 1861. Resigned May 6, 1862, but reinstated May 19. Capt. AQM at Farmville, Virginia, spring 1862 to June 1863. Maj. QM at Athens, Georgia, June 2, 1863. Maj. QM to Henderson's Bgd., AOT, Feb. 1865.

Lloyd, Edmund Jennings. b. in Virginia, Aug. 27, 1822. att. USMA. A merchant. Capt. ACS, July 17, 1861. Served in Army of Northwest Virginia, Oct. 1861. Capt. ACS at Gordonsville by Apr. 5, 1862. Capt. ACS with ANVa., July 1862. Capt. ACS at Danville, Virginia, Dec. 24, 1862, onward. d. Alexandria, Virginia, Oct. 1, 1889. bur. Christ Church Cem.

Lock, John J. b. in Virginia. A 35-year-old merchant at Charlestown, Virginia, in 1860. Associated with T. J. Jackson's troops from summer 1861, exact duty not clear. Probably acting ACS. Capt. ACS to T. J. Jackson, Nov. 7, 1862. Vacated by nonconfirmation. Reappointed Apr. 17, 1863. Ordered to report to R. E. Lee, Sept. 17, 1863. Capt. ACS with Second Corps, Sept. 1863. Reappointed yet again, to same post, to rank from June 15, 1864. Paroled Apr. 19, 1865, at Winchester, age given as 42.

Lock, William M. b. Charlestown, Virginia, Sept. 17, 1837. att. UVA. A farmer at Charlestown. Pvt. Co. G, 2nd Virginia, June 2, 1861. Capt. ACS, 62nd Virginia, Oct. 9, 1862. POW Nov. 9, 1862. Maj. CS to Imboden, Jan. 28, 1863. Paroled at Winchester, May 8, 1865. Postwar lawyer at Canon City, Colorado. d. May 16, 1892. bur. Edge Hill Cem., Charlestown.

Lockhart, Robert B. A resident of Columbus, Georgia. Capt. Co. D, 60th Alabama, June 25, 1862. Capt. AAIG to Moody at Appx. Probably should be AAAIG.

Lofton, Bedford H. A 22-year-old lawyer at Elberton, Georgia, in 1860. Sgt. Co. C,

15th Georgia, July 15, 1861. Ordnance Sgt., May 17, 1862. Adjt. 15th Georgia, Jan. 13, 1863, but eventually declined the appointment, probably because he was Lt. OO to Toombs by autumn 1862. Lt. OO to Benning. Appx. d. 1865. bur. Elmhurst Cem., Elberton.

London, William Lord. b. Pittsboro, North Carolina, Apr. 3, 1838. Lt. 15th North Carolina. Capt. Co. I, 32nd North Carolina. WIA at Malvern Hill and Gettysburg. Acting on staff of Gen. Daniel by late 1863. Capt. AAG to Daniel, Jan. 6, 1864. Capt. AAG to Grimes, May 1864. WIA in chest at Third Winchester. Appx. Pittsboro merchant. d. there Nov. 30, 1916. bur. St. Bartholomew Episc. Churchyard.

Long, I. J., Jr. A man with a name like this served as VADC to Daniel in 1864.

Long, Melchoir Mason. Lived in California prewar. Pvt. Co. F, 1st Virginia, May 27, 1861. Later to Sgt. Sgt. Co. C, 1st Virginia Arty. Discharged Jan. 17, 1862. Capt. of Inf., Jan. 22, 1862. Duties and tenure unspecified. Lt. 3rd C.S. Engineers, Apr. 20, 1864. Lt. VADC to Wharton. KIA at Cedar Creek, Oct. 19, 1864, age 26. bur. Union Cem., Leesburg, Virginia.

Love, S. Lucien. Pvt. Co. H, 6th South Carolina, June 22, 1861. To Lt., Dec. 21, 1861. Capt. ACS, 6th South Carolina, Apr. 27, 1862. Capt. VADC to Jenkins at Seven Pines. Capt. ACS to Bratton by Aug. 1864.

Lovelace, Benjamin Franklin. b. Edgefield Dist., South Carolina, June 11, 1833. Teacher at Edgefield C.H. Capt. AQM, 7th South Carolina, June 26, 1861. Capt. acting AQM to Kershaw, intermittently from Nov. 1861. Capt. acting AQM for Kershaw's Bgd., continuously from Oct. 1863–1865. No evidence he ever was officially assigned. Paroled May 1, 1865. m. Susan Chapman, 1867. Fruit grower and teacher at Crescent City, Florida. d. Dec. 6, 1891. bur. Palmetto Cem., Crescent City.

Lovell, Joseph. VADC to Clark, May 24,

1861. Lt. ADC to G. W. Smith, Sept. 28, 1861. Lt. ADC to Lovell, Oct. 10, 1861. Paroled May 10, 1865. Probably the Joseph Lovell (June 11, 1824–Nov. 28, 1869) who lived after the war in Natchez, Mississippi.

Lowndes, James. b. Charleston, South Carolina, Jan. 6, 1835. att. South Carolina Coll. Studied in Bonn and Gottingen, Germany. Charleston lawyer. Lt. Co. A, Hampton Legion, June 12, 1861. Dropped Apr. 1862. Capt. Co. C, 2nd Bn. South Carolina Sharpshooters, June 23, 1862. Capt. AAAG to W. S. Walker, Feb. 12, 1863. Capt. AAIG to Wallace in Virginia. Appx. Lawyer at Charleston and Washington, D.C. d. Jan. 15, 1910.

Lowndes, Rawlins. b. Charleston, South Carolina, July 23, 1838. att. South Carolina Coll. A planter. VADC to Ripley, Nov. 1861. VADC to Hampton, by Seven Days. Capt. AAIG to Hampton, July 21, 1863. Through 1865. d. Charleston, Dec. 31, 1919.

Lowrance, Rufus Newton. b. Rowan Co., North Carolina, Dec. 18, 1830. A clerk at Laurens C.H., South Carolina. Pvt. Co. B, 3rd South Carolina, June 6, 1861. Capt. ACS, 3rd South Carolina, June 1, 1862. Capt. acting ACS to Kershaw, by Mar. 1863. Capt. acting CS to McLaws, winter 1863–1864. Capt. acting CS to Kershaw, spring 1864. Maj. CS to Kershaw, Mar. 4, 1865. Appx. Farmer at Winnsboro, South Carolina. Alive 1870.

Lowry, Samuel M. b. Nov. 23, 1838. att. UVA. Of Crawfordsville, Mississippi. Listed as Capt. ADC to J. R. Davis, summer 1863, which is the wrong rank for that position. Probably VADC. Admitted to hospital at Charlottesville, Virginia, July 27, 1863, with gunshot wound. Left hospital Aug. 8, 1863. Probably the man who served as Capt. Co. K, 12th Mississippi Cavy., from Apr. 1, 1864.

Lubbock, Thomas Saltus. b. Charleston, South Carolina, Nov. 29, 1817. Cotton factor at New Orleans in 1830s and later a merchant at Houston. Veteran of the Texas Revolution. 1860 occupation was "Gentleman of Leisure," with total worth valued at $40,000. Went to Virginia in 1861 with a large contingent, including James Longstreet. VADC to Longstreet at First Manassas. Lt. Col. 8th Texas Cavy. d. Nashville, Tennessee, Jan. 9, 1862, of typhoid fever. bur. Glenwood Cem., Houston.

Lucado, Leonard Fretwell. b. Bedford Co., Virginia, Aug. 28, 1832. A merchant. Pvt. Co. G, 11th Virginia. Capt. ACS, 11th Virginia, July 19, 1861. Dropped from regiment, Aug. 1, 1863. Capt. ACS in Nelson Co., Oct. 19, 1863. Capt. ACS to R. D. Johnston, Apr. 7, 1864. Failed confirmation, but served with Gen. Toon until reappointed in August, to rank from June 15, 1864. Appx. Grocer at Lynchburg. d. July 5, 1901.

Lumpkin, Frank. b. Lexington, Georgia, Oct. 14, 1842. att. UGA. Brother-in-law of Gen. T. R. R. Cobb. Pvt. Troup (Ga.) Arty. Capt. AQM, Cobb's Legion (Ga.) Inf., Apr. 30, 1864. Capt. AQM commanding Kershaw's division commissary train. Capt. AQM to Wofford by Oct. 31, 1864. Paroled at Greensboro, May 1, 1865. A lawyer. m. Katharine Dewitt Willcox. d. Athens, Oct. 5, 1876. bur. in Tom Cobb's plot at Oconee Hill Cem.

Lumsden, ——. Staff of Rodes, June 1862. Possibly Charles Linnius Lumsden, of VMI.

Lyle, Joseph Banks. b. near Old Yonguesville, South Carolina, Dec. 6, 1829. att. So. Carolina Coll. Taught at Limestone Male Academy. Capt. Co. C, 5th South Carolina. Capt. AAAIG to Bratton, June 1864, through October at least. WIA nine times. Postwar educator in South Carolina, at Paris, Texas, and at Caddo, Oklahoma. d. at Caddo, Aug. 16, 1913. bur. Gethsemane Cemetery.

Lynes, Thomas B. A resident of Mobile, Alabama. Pvt. Co. A, 43rd Alabama, May 24, 1864. On extra duty at brigade headquarters, July–Aug. 1864. "Capt." ADC to Moody at Appx. Possibly the Thomas B. Lyons who died at Mobile, June 8, 1877.

Lynham, John Andrew. b. Henrico Co., Virginia, Nov. 5, 1840. Reading law at Richmond in 1861. Pvt. 3rd Co. Richmond Howitzers, Apr. 21, 1861 until Aug. 1862. Clerk at Conscript Bureau. Lt. Drillmaster, Jan. 27, 1864. Served in Richmond as Lt. AAAG at Conscript Bureau. Richmond lawyer. m. Bettie Cameron Hardwick. d. Richmond, Oct. 13, 1885. bur. Hollywood Cem.

Lyon, James William. b. Jan. 10, 1837. A resident of Baltimore Co., Maryland. Pvt. to Sgt., Co. H, 1st Maryland. Maj. CS to Trimble, Jan. 28, 1862. Maj. CS to Hoke, 1863–1865. Paroled at Greensboro. Lived postwar at New Orleans and Baltimore. d. Pikesville, Maryland, Mar. 1, 1907. bur. St. Thomas's Church Cem., Owings Mills, Maryland.

Lyon, William Dunn. Lt. 1st Bn. Alabama Inf. Lt. CSA, Oct. 2, 1861, to report to J. E. Johnston. Served under Holmes in North Carolina, Mar. 1862. Lt. OO with T. J. Jackson's headquarters, Sept. 22, 1862. Lt. OO to report to Gorgas, Jan. 31, 1863. Lt. OO to John B. Gordon, May 10, 1863. Same to C. A. Evans, May 1864. Capt. (PACS), to rank from Sept. 18, 1864, but MWIA same day at Martinsburg. d. Sept. 27, 1864. bur. Winchester. Evans called him "the jovial, the 'queer case,' the man of good yarns well spun." A staff officer cryptically wrote: "It would be terrible to be killed as Lyon was in a drunken spree."

Lyons, Thomas Barton. b. Nov. 17, 1838. att. UVA. Studied law in Paris. A resident of Clinton, Louisiana. Lt. ADC to Barton, Apr. 4, 1862. POW at Vicksburg and Sailor's Creek. Judge and lawyer at Clinton. m. Mary Norwood. d. Charlottesville, Louisiana, June 1, 1909.

McAfee, John J. b. in Kentucky. Capt. AAG to Hodge, Nov. 20, 1863. Capt. AAG to Cosby, Aug. 1864. Took Oath Apr. 30, 1865, at Mt. Sterling, Kentucky. Served in state legislature until 1873. m. Nelly Nichol Marshall, 1871. Probably the McAfee who published books on Kentucky history in 1886.

McCabe, William Gordon. b. Richmond, Virginia, Aug. 4, 1841. att. Hampton Military Institute and UVA. Pvt. Third Co. Richmond Howitzers, May 12, 1861–May 19, 1862. Lt. of Arty., May 19, 1862. Adjt. 19th Bn. Virginia Heavy Arty., Aug. 2, 1862. Lt. AAG to Ripley, Aug. 19, 1863. Lt. OO in Richmond, Nov. 6, 1863. Lt. OO to report to Briscoe Baldwin at ANVa. headquarters. Lt. OO to Pegram's Bn. Arty., July 20, 1864. Principal of school at Petersburg, 1865–1895. Prolific writer. Married twice. d. June 1, 1920. bur. Blandford Cem.

McCandlish, Thomas P. b. Williamsburg, Virginia, Nov. 30, 1837. att. UVA. Professor at Wm. & Mary. Pvt. Peninsula (Va.) Arty., June 4, 1861. Capt. AQM, 32nd Virginia, July 19, 1861. Capt. acting AQM to his brigade, intermittently. Capt. AQM to Corse, Sept. 15, 1864. Paroled May 4, 1865. Professor and lawyer at Williamsburg. Alive 1878.

McCann, Charles. b. County Tyrone, Ireland, 1834. Carpenter at Petersburg, Virginia. Lt. Co. E, 3rd Virginia, Apr. 19, 1861. WIA twice at Frayser's Farm. Lt. ADC to Pryor, Sept. 21, 1862. Vacated Aug. 1863. Lt. on duty as Inspector of Arty., Dept. of North Carolina, Aug. 1863–Apr. 1864. Possibly staff of Micah Jenkins during this period. WIA at Plymouth. WIA at Peeble's Farm, duty unknown. Lt. Drillmaster to Gary, Dec. 16, 1864. Paroled May 11, 1865. m. Mary Dominica Pizzini. Lived postwar at Baltimore, Maryland. d. Oct. 1905. bur. New Cathedral Cem., Baltimore.

McCardle, William Henry. b. Maysville, Kentucky, June 1, 1815. Edited newspaper at New Orleans, and lived in Mississippi for more than 25 years prewar. Vicksburg "gentleman" in 1860. Staff of Charles Clark with state troops, Jan.–May 1861. Lt. ADC to Clark, Sept. 9, 1861. Capt. AAG to Clark, Apr. 11, 1862. Capt. AAG to Pemberton.

Col. and Adjt. Gen. of Mississippi, late 1863. Paroled May 11, 1865. Married twice. A veteran duelist. d. Jackson, Mississippi, Apr. 28, 1893. bur. there.

McCarty, William Page. b. Fairfax Co., Virginia, Nov. 9, 1839. att. UVA. A great-grandson of George Mason. Adjt. 13th Bn. Virginia Heavy Arty., Oct. 26, 1863. Lt. AAAIG to Wharton by Jan. 1864. Back with battalion by Sept. 1864. A "good for nothing officer" in the judgment of one of his superiors. Newspaperman in New York, Richmond, and Washington, D.C. Victor in one of Richmond's most famous duels. d. there May 25, 1900. bur. Hollywood Cem., unmarked.

McCaslan, William Edward. b. Abbeville Dist., South Carolina, Jan. 19, 1833. att. UVA. Member of Marion Co., Florida, secession convention. Pvt. Co. E, 2nd Florida, July 5, 1861. To Capt., May 11, 1862. WIA at Seven Pines. Capt. AAAG to E. A. Perry at Chancellorsville. Capt. AAAG to the Florida Bgd. at Gettysburg, where he was KIA by a shell on July 3.

McCaughrin, Robert Lusk. b. Sept. 2, 1834. Merchant at Newberry Co., South Carolina. Pvt. Co. E, 14th South Carolina. Capt. AQM, 14th South Carolina, Mar. 23, 1863. Capt. AQM to McGowan, Sept. 15, 1864. Resigned Nov. 30, 1864. Adjt. 14th South Carolina, Dec. 26, 1864. Appx. m. Anna Parks. d. Jan. 27, 1882. bur. Rosemont Cem., Newberry Co.

McCausland, George. b. 1837. VADC to N. G. Evans, July 1861. Killed in 1861 in a duel with Capt. Alex. White of Wheat's (La.) Bn., precipitated by McCausland's insulting remarks about Wheat's "Tigers." Shot through both hips by a rifle and died "in great agony." bur. family cem. in West Feliciana Parish, Louisiana. "A strikingly handsome man."

McClain, Rufus Peter. b. Lebanon, Tennessee, Feb. 28, 1838. att. Cumberland Univ. Pvt. Co. H, 7th Tennessee. Capt. AQM, 7th Tennessee, Feb. 20, 1862. Capt. acting QM to Archer, Jan. 1863–June 1864. Capt. AQM to Heth, on paymaster duty, by Sept. 1864. Wilson Co. lawyer for 40 years (partner of A. W. Vick) and state legislator. d. Lebanon, Dec. 5, 1914. bur. Cedar Grove Cem.

McClellan, Henry Brainerd. b. Philadelphia, Pennsylvania, Oct. 17, 1840. A first cousin of Union Gen. George B. McClellan. att. Williams Coll. Schoolteacher in Cumberland Co., Virginia. Pvt. Co. G, 3rd Virginia Cavy., June 14, 1861. Adjt. 3rd Virginia Cavy., May 18, 1862. Maj. AAG to Stuart, May 2, 1863. Maj. AAG to Hampton, Aug. 11, 1864. Paroled Apr. 26, 1865. Professor at Sayre Female Institute in Lexington, Kentucky, 1869–1904. d. Oct. 1, 1904. bur. Lexington Cem.

McClellan, Robert Miller. b. Parkesburg, Pennsylvania, Sept. 5, 1833. att. Yale and Jefferson Medical Coll. Tutor in Georgia. QM Sgt. in Jeff Davis Legion Cavy. Capt. AQM and ACS, Jeff Davis Legion Cavy., Nov. 1, 1862. Capt. acting QM to Butler, Sept.–Oct. 1863. Capt. acting QM to Young, Sept. 1864. Ran schools in Macon, Georgia, and at West Chester, Pennsylvania. Physician at Philadelphia. d. there Feb. 16, 1887. McClellan's war letters are at the Georgia Historical Society.

McClelland, James Bruce. b. June 25, 1827. att. Washington Coll. Farmer and merchant in Nelson Co., Virginia. Capt. AQM, June 29, 1861. Maj. QM, Dec. 21, 1861. Served exclusively at Richmond until he died Aug. 31, 1862, of typhoid fever.

McClure, Ewing Graham. b. Washington Co., Tennessee, Sept. 15, 1837. att. Princeton. Capt. Co. F, 37th Tennessee, May 2, 1861. Dropped May 10, 1862. Capt. ACS, 37th Tennessee, June 1862 into 1863. Commanded supply train for Buckner's corps, late in 1863. Staff of Bate. Capt. ACS to Gracie, date unknown. Capt. ACS to B. R. Johnson's Bgd., June 30, 1864. m. Emma Clara Letford, 1872. d. Jonesboro, Tennessee, Nov. 7, 1908. bur. Washington Co.

McComb, Samuel. b. May 14, 1828. A resident of Baldwin Co., Georgia. Lt. Co. H, 4th Georgia, Apr. 26, 1861. Capt. ACS, 4th Georgia, June 13, 1862. Capt. ACS to Doles, July 1, 1863. Capt. ACS to Cook, June 1864. POW Nov. 23, 1864, while on sick leave in Georgia. In state legislature postwar. Killed at Milledgeville, Feb. 1872 "by a pair of runaway horses" in a buggy accident. bur. Memory Hill Cem.

McConnico, Garner M. b. Greene Co., Alabama, Feb. 2, 1819. Served with Alabama regiment in Mexican War. A clerk at Selma. m. Jane H. Weir, 1847. Pvt. 44th Alabama, Apr. 18, 1862. Capt. ACS, 44th Alabama, May 16, 1862. Dropped with other regimental commissaries in 1863. Capt. ACS to Law, 1864. Tried to resign in summer 1864, citing age. Probably did resign, though date unknown. Coal dealer at Selma. d. 1891. bur. Old Live Oak Cem.

McCormick, Edward. b. Clarke Co., Virginia, Oct. 26, 1824. att. Princeton. Clarke Co. farmer. Pvt. Co. D, 1st Virginia Cavy., May 25, 1861. Capt. AQM, Sept. 11, 1861. Post QM at Lynchburg for entire war. d. Mar. 18, 1870. bur. Grace Episc. Church Cem., Berryville, Virginia.

McCreery, William Westwood, Jr. b. in Virginia, Sept. 1836. att. USMA. Lt. of Arty., CSA, Mar. 16, 1861. To report to Floyd, Aug. 1861. Lt. OO to R. E. Lee, Nov. 30, 1861. Temporary Capt. OO to Lee, Jan. 29, 1862. Capt. Asst. OO to Pemberton, Mar. 19, 1862. Capt. OO in Dept. of Eastern Tennessee, June 30, 1862. Capt. AAAIG to Pettigrew, Jan. 8, 1863. KIA at Gettysburg, July 1, 1863, while carrying flag of 26th North Carolina. bur. Oakwood Cem., Raleigh, North Carolina.

McCue, John Howard. b. Augusta Co., Virginia, Mar. 17, 1824. att. UVA. and Washington Coll. Prewar law partner of John D. Imboden. Capt. ACS, 51st Virginia, July 19, 1861. Resigned Nov. 20, 1862. Lt. ADC to Imboden, Jan. 28, 1863. Resigned May 28, 1863. Pvt. McClanahan's (Va.) Btty. Lt. Drillmaster, Dec. 18, 1863. Capt. AAG to Lilley, date of service unclear. POW at Waynesboro. Lawyer at Staunton and member of state legislature. d. Augusta Co., July 15, 1890.

McCulloch, Robert Emmet. b. Brownsville, Tennessee, Sept. 7, 1839. att. Stewart Coll. Bookkeeper and merchant at Clarksville. Pvt. Co. H, 14th Tennessee, May 23, 1861. POW at Fredericksburg. Lt. ADC to McComb, Feb. 23, 1865. POW at Petersburg, Apr. 2, 1865. Clothing and tobacco merchant at Clarksville. d. Nashville, Tennessee, Dec. 12, 1924. bur. Greenwood Cem., Clarksville.

McDaniel, Henry Dickerson. b. Monroe, Georgia, Sept. 4, 1836. att. Mercer Univ. Member of state secession convention. Lt. Co. H, 11th Georgia, July 3, 1861. Lt. AAAG to G. T. Anderson, Apr. 1862, briefly, and from late July until Aug. 29, 1862. Capt. AQM, 11th Georgia, Aug. 29, 1862. Maj. 11th Georgia, Nov. 1862. WIA at Funkstown, and POW two days later (July 12, 1863) at Hagerstown. Governor of Georgia, 1883–1886. d. July 25, 1926.

McDonald, Angus William, Jr. b. Romney, Virginia, May 16, 1829. att. UVA. Lawyer and legislator from Hampshire Co. Lt. Co. F, 7th Virginia Cavy., June 1, 1861. Adjt. 7th Virginia Cavy., July 1861. Capt. ACS with W. E. Jones's Bgd., and at Harrisonburg. No dates for either, but probably in 1863. In Virginia legislature, Jan. 1862–May 1863. POW in Hardy Co., May 5, 1863. Mayor of Berryville postwar. In West Virginia legislature. d. Charlestown, West Virginia, Oct. 24, 1914. bur. there.

McDonald, Charles. b. Philadelphia, Pennsylvania, 1838. A manufacturer of cotton at Concord, North Carolina, prewar. Pvt. Co. A, 20th North Carolina, Apr. 19, 1861. Capt. ACS, 20th North Carolina, Oct. 4,

1861. Capt. ACS to R. D. Johnston, 1863. On Toon's staff briefly in 1864. Served into 1865. Postwar legislator and farmer in North Carolina. Mayor of Concord. Alive there 1897.

McDonald, Craig Woodrow. b. May 28, 1837. att. VMI and UVA. A schoolteacher from Winchester, Virginia. Pvt. Co. E, 13th Virginia, Apr. 17, 1861. Lt. PAVa., and ADC to Elzey, June 1861. Staff of T. J. Jackson after First Manassas, very briefly. Lt. acting ADC to Elzey, Apr.–June 1862. Lt. AAIG to Elzey, June 1862. WIA in ear at Cross Keys. KIA at Gaines's Mill. bur. Hollywood Cem., Richmond.

McDonald, John C. b. in Virginia. A merchant at Tazewell C.H. prewar. Maj. CS to Floyd, Sept. 4, 1861. Maj. CS to Echols. Resigned May 19, 1863. A 45-year-old merchant in Hampshire Co., West Virginia, in 1870.

McDonald, Marshall. b. Oct. 18, 1835. att. UVA. and VMI. "The most gifted member of the class that graduated [at VMI] in 1860," wrote Stonewall Jackson. Professor at VMI, 1860–1861. Lt. EO, PAVa., Apr. 27, 1861. Lt. of Arty., Oct. 9, 1861. Lt. EO to Lovell. Temp. Capt. OO to M. L. Smith, Apr. 1862. POW at Vicksburg. Capt. Chief EO to First Corps, June 14, 1864. Capt. EO at Weldon, North Carolina, Nov. 1864. Professor at VMI, and U. S. Fish Commissioner. Brother of C. W. McDonald. d. Sept. 1, 1895. McDonald's papers are at VMI and Duke.

McDonald, William Naylor. b. Hampshire Co., Virginia, Feb. 3, 1834. att. UVA. Teacher at Louisville, Kentucky, and lawyer at Charlestown, Virginia. Pvt. Co. G, 2nd Virginia Inf. and Co. D, 11th Virginia Cavy. Lt. OO to W. E. Jones by Feb. 1863. Capt. OO to Rosser, May 2, 1863. WIA at Wilderness, May 6, 1864. Capt. OO to Mahone, Nov. 13, 1864. Appx. Editor of *Southern Bivouac* and author of the history of the Laurel Bgd. Educator in Louisville and at Berryville,

Virginia. d. Berryville, Jan. 4, 1898. bur. Green Hill Cem.

MacDuffie, Neil Carmichael. b. South Carolina, Apr. 4, 1825. Marion Co. sheriff, 1857–1861 and 1865–1867. Capt. Co. L, 21st South Carolina. Capt. AQM, 21st South Carolina, Mar. 21, 1863. Capt. AQM to Hampton, Dec. 6, 1864. Paroled at Greensboro. Marion Co. farmer. d. Mar. 31, 1882. bur. Cedardale Cem., Mullins, South Carolina.

McElroy, James Greenlee. b. in North Carolina. A store clerk in Buncombe Co., prewar. Pvt. Co. H, 29th North Carolina, Sept. 11, 1861. Later to Sgt. Maj. Capt. ACS, 16th North Carolina, Dec. 13, 1862. Capt. AQM, 16th North Carolina, Sept. 17, 1863. Capt. AQM to Scales, Sept. 15, 1864. Served into 1865. m. Annie M. V. Bencine, 1867. Lived at Lenoir, North Carolina.

McGehee, George Thomas. b. Sept. 25, 1833. att. Yale. m. Elizabeth B. McNair. Capt. AQM, 1st Bn. Mississippi, 1861. Capt. AQM, 21st Mississippi, by 1863. Capt. AQM to Kershaw, Sept. 15, 1864. d. Feb. 5, 1906. bur. Bowling Green Cem., Wilkinson Co.

McGivern, Claudius. Capt. AQM to J. E. Johnston, Sept. 10, 1861. Capt. AQM to Van Dorn, Jan. 27, 1862. Maj. QM to Van Dorn, June 26, 1862. Later served at posts in Mississippi and Alabama, and on the staffs of Franklin Gardner and Maury, into 1865.

McHenry, James. Served on U.S. Coast Survey prewar. A civil engineer at Washington, D.C. Cpl. Co. F, 1st Virginia, May 1–Sept. 1861. Lt. of Arty., May 19, 1862. Capt. of Arty., Oct. 27, 1864. Served at Richmond Arsenal as OO, 1862–1865. Postwar railroad employee in Maryland. d. at Baltimore, Apr. 13, 1881, age 51.

McIlhany, Hugh Milton. b. Loudoun Co., Virginia, Nov. 25, 1840. A clerk. Pvt. Co. K, 17th Virginia, Apr. 22, 1861. Clerk and courier at Div. HQ, Sept. 1861–Feb. 1864. Capt. AQM to Longstreet, Feb. 19, 1864. Capt. AQM commanding ordnance train for Pickett's Div., summer 1864. Failed confirmation and dropped July 26, 1864. Served with Mosby, and POW Dec. 21, 1864. Merchant at Staunton postwar. d. Mar. 31, 1920. bur. Thornrose Cem.

McIntire, David Murdoch. b. New Hanover Co., North Carolina, Dec. 18, 1831. Duplin Co. merchant. Sgt. Co. A, 38th North Carolina, Oct. 1, 1861. Sgt. Maj., Feb. 15, 1862. Adjt. 38th North Carolina, July 9, 1862, to Appx. Lt. AAAG to Scales, July–Aug. 1863. Retail liquor dealer at Kenansville. d. June 11, 1901. bur. Myrtle Grove Cem., Wayne Co.

McIntire, James Davis. b. Charlottesville, Virginia, Oct. 23, 1840. att. UVa. A clerk. Lt. Co. F, 19th Virginia, May 25, 1861. Lt. AAAG to Garnett, by Sept. 1862. WIA at Gettysburg and Hatcher's Run. Capt. 19th Virginia, Jan. 21, 1865. Richmond insurance agent. d. there Feb. 5, 1910. bur. Hollywood Cem.

McIntosh, Edward. b. Society Hill, South Carolina, Apr. 1840. att. South Carolina Coll. In Co. B, 1st South Carolina. Lt. Pee Dee Arty. Capt. AQM to McIntosh's Bn. Arty., Aug. 26, 1863. m. Dora Evans. d. Society Hill, July 1872.

McIntosh, Thomas Spalding. b. McIntosh Co., Georgia, 1837. att. GMI. m. Maria B. Morris, 1861. Lawyer at Savannah. Lt. CSA, May 18, 1861. Lt. Co. F, 1st Georgia Regs., but resigned by July 1861. Lt. Cobb's (Ga.) Legion, July 1861. Capt. AAG to McLaws, Oct. 19, 1861. Maj. AAG to McLaws, May 23, 1862. KIA at Sharpsburg, Sept. 17, 1862. bur. on the battlefield, and later at Charlestown, Virginia, but removed to Laurel Grove Cem. at Savannah in 1867.

McKendree, George. b. Cabell Co., Virginia. A 26-year-old railroad contractor at Covington, Virginia, in 1860. Lt. Alleghany (Va.) Arty., Apr. 22, 1861. Resigned May 25, 1863. Maj. QM to Echols, May 19, 1863. POW at White Sulphur Springs, Aug. 1863. Served through 1864, at least. Alive 1911, and prob-

ably dead by 1915. Possibly carried a middle initial of "B."

McKim, Randolph Harrison. b. Baltimore, Maryland, Apr. 15, 1842. att. UVa. Cpl. Co. H, 1st Maryland. Lt. ADC to Steuart, Apr. 1, 1862, but didn't join until June 8. Resigned Sept. 1, 1863, to attend Episc. Seminary. Chaplain 2nd Virginia Cavy., Aug. 16, 1864. Prolific author postwar. Episc. rector in New York City, New Orleans, Washington, and all over Virginia. d. Bedford Springs, Pennsylvania, July 15, 1920. bur. Green Mount Cem., Baltimore.

McKim, William Duncan. b. Baltimore, Maryland, June 27, 1832. att. Harvard. Cousin of R. H. McKim (q.v.). A banker. Pvt. Co. H, 1st Maryland. Lt. ADC to Trimble, Mar. 31, 1862. WIA at Sharpsburg. Maj. AAG to Trimble, Feb. 2, 1863. WIA at Chancellorsville, May 2, 1863, and KIA next day. bur. Green Mount Cem., Baltimore.

McKinne, Barna. b. in North Carolina, 1833. att. UGa. A lawyer. m. Mary Patterson. Capt. AQM, 4th Alabama, Sept. 11, 1861. Maj. QM to G. W. Smith, May 1, 1862. Maj. QM to Mercer, Mar. 24, 1863. Maj. QM at Macon, Georgia, 1865. Of San Francisco, California.

McKinney, Charles S. b. Campbell Co., Virginia, ca. 1826. m. Ellen C. Blair, 1861. Capt. ACS, PAVa., May 21, 1861. Capt. ACS (PACS), July 19, 1861. Staff of Beauregard by Aug. 10, 1861. Capt. ACS to J. E. Johnston, 1861–Apr. 1862, at least. Capt. ACS to Whiting, Jan. 12, 1863.

McKinney, Robert Caldwell. Of Cherokee Co., Georgia. Pvt. Co. G, 23rd Georgia, Aug. 31, 1861. Capt. AQM, 23rd Georgia, Mar. 15, 1862. Relieved Sept. 20, 1864, and assigned to duty with Col. Corley at ANVa. headquarters, with reserve ordnance train. Through 1865. d. Milledgeville, Georgia, Feb. 1878.

McKoy, Thomas Hall. b. Clinton, North Carolina, Apr. 27, 1837. Lt. Co. C, 7th North Carolina. Capt. ACS, 7th North Carolina.

Capt. acting CS to Lane, May 27 to Aug. 1863. Capt. ACS to Lane, Aug. 18, 1863. Maj. CS to Lane, Feb. 15, 1865. Appx. Merchant before and after the war. d. Wilmington, North Carolina, May 10, 1902. bur. Oakdale Cemetery.

McLaws, Abram Huguenin. b. Augusta, Georgia, Apr. 13, 1824. att. Georgetown and Wm. & Mary. A nephew of Zachary Taylor. Mexican War veteran. Lived at Augusta, Georgia, and in Macon Co., Alabama. Maj. QM to his brother, Gen. McLaws, Apr. 23, 1861. Resigned July 29, 1863, due to double hernia which "frequently endangers his life by threatened strangulation." Maj. Enrolling Officer and Commandant at Camp of Instruction in Georgia, Sept. 2, 1863. Maj. QM agent at Savannah, Aug. 24, 1864. A lawyer. d. Augusta, Georgia, Oct. 12, 1901.

McLean, Eugene Eckel. b. Mar. 6, 1821. att. USMA. Staff officer in U.S. Army, 1842–1861. Maj. QM (PAVa.), Apr. 25, 1861. Maj. QM (PACS), Mar. 16, 1861. Chief QM to J. E. Johnston. Maj. QM at Memphis, Tennessee, Oct. 1861–Feb. 1862. Maj. QM to Bragg, A. S. Johnston, and Beauregard. Lt. Col. QM to Bragg, Feb. 15, 1862. On inspection duty, June 1863 onward. d. Syracuse, New York, Jan. 5, 1906. bur. Oakwood Cem.

McLemore, Owen Kenan. b. in Alabama, Oct. 21, 1835. att. USMA. Lt. in U.S. Inf., 1856–1861. Lt. C.S. Inf., no date. Lt. AAG to D. R. Jones at First Manassas. Maj. 14th Alabama, Sept. 9, 1861. Lt. Col. 4th Alabama, May 21, 1862. WIA at Seven Days. MWIA at South Mountain. d. Winchester, Virginia, Sept. 30, 1862.

McLendon, Charles Guyton. b. Monroe Co., Georgia, 1830. A trader at Albany. Pvt. Co. K, 51st Georgia, Mar. 4, 1862. To Lt., Jan. 7, 1863. Lt. acting ADC to Bryan at Cold Harbor. KIA at Cold Harbor, June 3, 1864. bur. Hollywood Cem., grave unmarked.

McLure, John William. b. Chester, South Carolina, Mar. 14, 1831. att. UVA. Farmer at Pacolet Mills, South Carolina. Lt. Co. G, 5th South Carolina, Apr. 1861. Capt. AQM, Palmetto Sharpshooters, June 1, 1862. Capt. AQM to Field, Sept. 15, 1864, acting from Aug. 1864. Capt. AQM ordered to duty with IFT, Mar. 17, 1865. Merchant at Union, South Carolina. d. June 28, 1916. bur. Episc. Cem. McLure's letters have been published.

McMahon, Edward. b. Dublin, Ireland, May 21, 1821. Stonecutter and mason in Ireland. To United States in 1847. Worked at Brooklyn Navy Yard and then moved to Richmond, Virginia. Maj. QM, Oct. 18, 1861. Serving with Wise Legion, Nov. 1861. Maj. QM to Heth, Jan. 28, 1862. Maj. QM to Loring, June 2, 1862. Resigned May 30, 1863. Maj. QM to Sam. Jones, July 20, 1863. Maj. QM to Breckinridge, 1864–1865. Postmaster and railroad conductor at Staunton, Virginia. "A thoroughly committed Republican." d. July 23, 1892. bur. Thornrose Cem., Staunton.

McMillan, Garnett. b. Elbert Co., Georgia, May 8, 1842. att. UGA. and Emory & Henry. Of Clarkesville, Georgia. Capt. Co. K, 24th Georgia. Capt. Co. B, 3rd Bn. Georgia Sharpshooters. Capt. AAAG to G. J. Rains, Aug. 6, 1864. Capt. AAAG to Hampton, Feb. 12, 1865, "in charge of subterra defenses." Clarkesville lawyer and legislator. d. Jan. 14, 1876. bur. Old Clarkesville Cem.

McMullen, ——. VADC to Pryor in February 1863.

MacMurphy, Andrew M. b. in Georgia, May 9, 1831. A clerk at Augusta. Lt. Co. B, 12th Bn. Georgia Arty., May 1, 1862. Lt. OO to Gracie by Aug. 1862. Lt. OO to Moody, 1865. Appx. Postwar builder and manufacturer of carpenter's supplies at Augusta. d. there July 13, 1918.

McNamee, John Vivian. b. Aug. 23, 1835. Merchant at Charleston, South Carolina. Pvt. Co. G, 22nd South Carolina, May 14, 1862. Capt. AQM, 22nd South Carolina, May 13, 1863. Capt. AQM to Wallace, Sept. 20, 1864. Appx. d. June 30, 1903. bur. Magnolia Cem., Charleston.

McNeely, William Gaither. b. in North Carolina 1832. m. Mrs. Mildred Ann MaCay, 1861. Capt. AQM, 57th North Carolina, Aug. 1, 1862. Capt. acting AQM to Godwin's Bgd., summer 1863 into late 1864, though briefly Capt. acting QM to Hoke, Apr.–June 1864. Capt. AQM to Ramseur, Sept. 15, 1864, but apparently stayed with Godwin's Bgd. until Dec. 1864. Capt. AQM to Pegram, Dec. 1864. Paroled May 2, 1865, at Salisbury, North Carolina. Farmer at Salisbury. d. 1899. bur. Old English Cem.

McPhail, Clement Carrington. b. Aug. 17, 1831. att. UVA. and Hampden Sidney. Halifax Co. planter. Acting Capt. OO to J. E. Johnston, June 1861–May 1862. Acting MSK assigned to E. P. Alexander, early war. Lt. of Arty., CSA, May 19, 1862. Capt. OO, to report to Alexander. On various duties of ordnance and inspection, ANVa., until Sept. 22, 1863. Capt. commanding arsenal at Asheville, North Carolina, and then at Columbia, South Carolina. Railroad and steamboat agent at Richmond, Virginia. d. there Nov. 1, 1896. bur. Hollywood Cem.

McPhail, George Wilson. b. Halifax Co., Virginia, June 25, 1841. att. Hampden Sidney. Pvt. Co. G, 20th Virginia, May 23, 1861. POW at Rich Mountain. Ordnance Sgt. 62nd Virginia, Sept. 9, 1862. Acting OO to Imboden, Mar. 1863. Lt. ADC to Imboden, May 28, 1863, through 1865. Brakeman on a North Carolina railroad. d. May 28, 1881, when he fell off a boxcar and was crushed in front of a guano warehouse at Salem, North Carolina. "Quiet, unassuming and gentlemanly in his deportment."

McWhorter, Robert Ligon, Sr. b. in Georgia, June 19, 1819. Planter, merchant, and legislator at Penfield. Capt. Co. C, 3rd Georgia, Apr. 24, 1861. Maj. QM to Wright, Aug. 6, 1862. Maj. QM to Girardey and Sorrel. Appx. Postwar legislator and Greene Co. farmer. d. Athens, Georgia, May 20, 1908. bur. Penfield Memorial Cem.

McWillie, William, Jr. b. in South Carolina, May 7, 1842. Lived at Canton, Mississippi, prewar. Pvt. Co. G, 18th Mississippi, Nov. 4, 1861. Lt. ADC to R. H. Anderson, Mar. 11, 1862. Paroled May 19, 1865, in Mississippi. Canton farmer postwar. m. Sallie Tucker. d. Sept. 2, 1922. bur. Greenwood Cem., Jackson. McWillie's journal for 1864 is at MDAH.

Maben, John Campbell. b. Petersburg, Virginia, Dec. 31, 1839. A clerk at Richmond, Virginia. Pvt. Co. G, 12th Virginia, Apr. 19, 1861. Later to Sgt., and then back to Pvt. Clerk in First Corps medical dept. (probably for his brother-in-law Dr. J. S. D. Cullen). Capt. AQM to Longstreet, Feb. 19, 1864. Failed confirmation, July 1, 1864. Reappointed, July 29, 1864. Appx. Lawyer in New York City and railroad builder in Georgia and North Carolina. Alive 1914 in New York City.

Macmurdo, Charles C. Pvt. Orleans Guard Btty. (La.), Nov. 1861. Acted as OO to his kinsman Gen. Heth, Feb.–Mar. 1863. Capt. AQM at Richmond, Virginia, May 14, 1863. Capt. AQM to Barton, Nov. 30, 1864. Capt. AQM paying paroled POWs at Richmond, Mar. 1865.

Macmurdo, Meriwether A. A resident of Ashland, Virginia. Pvt. Co. I, 4th Virginia Cavy., May 8, 1861. Discharged Nov. 14, 1861. Master's Mate, CSN. Lt. acting OO at Chaffin's Bluff, May 21, 1863–1865. Lt. on staff of Stiles's Bn. Arty., early 1865. POW at Sailor's Creek. Paroled June 19, 1865, age 21. Probably born Oct. 22, 1843.

Macmurdo, Richard Channing. b. Richmond, Virginia, 1834. A bank clerk. Pvt. Co. F, 21st Virginia, May 18, 1861. Sgt. Letcher (Va.) Arty., Mar. 29, 1862. Later to Lt. WIA at Chancellorsville. Capt. AQM, July 1, 1863. On duty at ambulance shops in Richmond. Capt. AQM to G. W. C. Lee, May 16, 1864–1865, in addition to regular duties. Paroled Apr. 24, 1865, at Richmond. Brother-in-law of A. L. Rives (see below).

Moved postwar to New Jersey. d. Arlington, New Jersey, Sept. 1914.

Macon, John. Capt. AQM at Richmond, Virginia, Dec. 1863, an assistant to Maj. J. Booton Hill. No other record found. Perhaps a garbled name, or confused with some other officer.

Macon, Thomas Littleton. b. New Kent Co., Virginia, Aug. 19, 1828. att. UVA. Lawyer at Lynchburg, 1849–1852. Cotton businessman at New Orleans, Louisiana, 1852–1861. Maj. of New Orleans LDTS. VADC to Wright during Maryland Campaign. Lt. ADC to Hays, Sept. 18, 1862. Capt. AQM, June 16, 1863, on duty collecting taxes in Georgia. Mayor of New Orleans, and real estate agent postwar. d. there Mar. 6, 1910. bur. Riverview Cem., Charlottesville, Virginia. Some evidence suggests middle name spelled Lyttleton.

Magrath, Andrew Gordon, Jr. b. Aug. 21, 1845. att. SCMA. Pvt. in the South Carolina state cadets. Lt. ADC to Conner, Aug. 5, 1864. No further record after Oct. 1864. m. E. Daisy Walker. Charleston attorney and judge. d. Sept. 28, 1894. bur. Magnolia Cem.

Magruder, Allan Bowie. b. in Virginia, Sept. 7, 1811. Washington, D.C., lawyer and author. Wrote a biography of Justice John Marshall, and published an 1861 interview with Abraham Lincoln. Envoy from U.S. authorities to Virginia during secession crisis. Maj. CS to G. J. Rains, Jan. 4, 1862. Dropped but assigned as Maj. CS to his brother, Gen. Magruder, Jan. 20, 1862. Maj. CS to Rains, July 9, 1862. Maj. CS to Whiting, by Dec. 1862. Relieved Jan. 10, 1863, and awaited new orders in vain until Dec. 26, 1863, when he resigned. Lived postwar in Frederick Co., Virginia. d. Aug. 24, 1885. bur. Mt. Hebron Cem., Winchester.

Magruder, George Allan, Jr. b. Philadelphia, Pennsylvania, Aug. 20, 1842. att. VMI and school in Europe. VADC to his uncle, Gen. Magruder, June 1861. Cadet CSA, July 19, 1861, on staff of Magruder. Lt.

Magruder Light Arty., Mar.–Oct. 1862. Lt. ADC to Magruder, Nov. 29, 1862. Maj. of Arty., Sept. 1, 1863. Sent to Paris, France, with dispatches, Oct. 1863. Chief of Arty. to Magruder. Married a wealthy English widow and immediately abandoned her. Postwar resident of Paris. Alive there in 1909.

Magruder, William Thomas. b. Upper Marlboro, Maryland, Jan. 16, 1825. att. USMA. Served in 1st Dragoons in Old Army and seen by a fellow officer as "a most rigid martinet." Served in 1st U.S. Cavy. at First Manassas and on the peninsula in 1862. Resigned Oct. 1, 1862, and joined Confederate forces. Capt. AAG to J. R. Davis, Nov. 1, 1862, but failed confirmation and reapptd. in May 1863, to rank from Nov. 1, 1862. Capt. of Cavy. CSA, to rank from Oct. 17, 1862. KIA at Gettysburg, July 3, 1863.

Mahool, Thomas. Pvt. Co. K, 3rd Georgia, Apr. 25, 1861. Capt. ACS, 3rd Georgia, July 16, 1862. Failed to execute bond, but served anyway. Capt. ACS to Wright, Oct. 1863. Capt. ACS to Sorrel, Oct. 1864–Jan. 1865. Capt. ACS to Cook, Mar. 15, 1865. Lived postwar at Baltimore, Maryland. Dead by 1894.

Mallet, John William. b. Dublin, Ireland, Oct. 10, 1832. att. Trinity Coll. at Dublin and Univ. of Gottingen. Professor at UAla. and at Amherst Coll. Lt. ADC to Rodes, Nov. 16, 1861. Resigned May 22, 1862. Later a Lt. Col. in the Ordnance Dept., and Supt. at Macon laboratory. Postwar professor at schools in Texas, Louisiana, Pennsylvania, and Virginia. Married twice. An internationally famous chemist. d. Nov. 6, 1912. bur. UVA. Cemetery, Charlottesville, Virginia. Mallet's extensive papers are at the Museum of the Confederacy.

Mallory, Charles King. b. Norfolk, Virginia, Feb. 20, 1820. att. Wm. & Mary. Judge and lawyer at Oxford, Mississippi, and in Virginia. Member of Virginia Secession Convention. Col. 115th Virginia Militia,

1861. Col. AAAIG to G. J. Rains, Jan. 1862. Maj. QM to Rains, Apr. 29, 1862. Dropped Aug. 30, 1862. Capt. AQM, Oct. 14, 1862, at Liberty, Virginia. Served there into 1865. Planter at Hampton, Virginia. d. there May 7, 1875.

Mallory, Charles O'Connor. b. Norfolk, Virginia, Feb. 28, 1842. A farmer. Pvt. Co. G, 6th Virginia, Apr. 19, 1861. Sgt. Maj., 55th Virginia, Dec. 1861. Lt. ADC to Mahone, Mar. 25, 1865. Appx. m. Ann Brooke Baylor. Essex Co. farmer. d. there Nov. 16, 1877. bur. St. John's Episc. Churchyard, Tappahannock.

Malone, William James. b. Brunswick Co., Virginia, ca. 1832. Sgt. Co. K, 16th Virginia, May 11, 1861–Mar. 18, 1862. Pvt. Branch's (Va.) Btty. Capt. AQM, Branch's Bn. Arty., June 24, 1863. Court-martialed for embezzlement, June 1864. Dropped July 8, 1864. In the cattle business, 1870–1895. A resident of Petersburg, Virginia, most of his life. Married four times. An "ardent Republican" after the war. d. there Nov. 1, 1895. bur. Blandford Cem., in unmarked grave.

Manard, Birdwell G. b. Alpha, Tennessee, Dec. 10, 1837. Pvt. Co. I, 2nd Tennessee Cavy., June 24, 1861. Later to Lt. Capt. AAG to Vaughn, Nov. 7, 1863, through at least 1864. att. UVA. m. Mary Louise Evans, 1870. Professor at King Coll., a Baptist minister, and president of a female college at Lynchburg, Tennessee. d. Warrensburg, Missouri, Jan. 27, 1899. Another source gives Manard's date of birth as Dec. 11, 1841.

Mangham, John H. b. in Georgia. A 33-year-old ordinary in Pike Co. in 1860. Pvt. Co. A, 13th Georgia, July 8, 1861. Capt. ACS, 13th Georgia, July 17, 1861. Capt. acting ACS to John B. Gordon, Jan. 1863. Capt. ACS to Early, July 31, 1863. Resigned Mar. 9, 1864, to resume duty as Pike Co. ordinary.

Manico, John Pulling. Baptised Aug. 1833 at Berry Pomeroy, Devonshire, England. Living in New Orleans, Louisiana, by 1856, a merchant. Pvt. 1st Co. Washington (La.)

Arty., May 26, 1861. Discharged Jan. 12, 1862. Disbursing clerk at Ordnance Bureau. Capt. Co. A, 3rd Va. LDT, June 29, 1863. Probably promoted to Capt. OO at about the same time. Eventually rose to Maj. OO, and then to Lt. Col. OO by Feb. 1865. Worked at Ordnance Bureau for Gen. Gorgas. Has no official record anywhere other than with the LDTs. d. Magnolia, Mississippi, July 29, 1869. bur. New Orleans.

Manning, Jacob Hite. b. Loudoun Co., Virginia, 1828. A farmer at Leesburg, prewar. Pvt. Co. C, 17th Virginia, Apr. 22, 1861. Detached on signal service, Oct. 1861. Capt. SO to Longstreet, May 29, 1862, and presumably to R. H. Anderson in 1864. Relieved Oct. 20, 1864, to report to John S. Mosby. WIA severely at Hamilton, Virginia, in service with Mosby. Paroled May 8, 1865. Resumed farming. Age 37 in Sept. 1865. d. Mar. 13, 1891. bur. Union Cem., Leesburg.

Manning, John Laurence. b. Clarendon Co., South Carolina, Jan. 29, 1816. att. Princeton and South Carolina Coll. South Carolina legislator prewar, and governor, 1852–1854. 1860 census recorded his real property at $1,256,000 and his personal property at $800,000. Married twice. VADC to Beauregard, Apr. 1861 through First Manassas, and again in Dec. 1862. d. Camden, South Carolina, Oct. 29, 1889. bur. Trinity Episc. Churchyard, Columbia.

Manning, Peyton Thompson. b. in Alabama, 1837. Raised at Aberdeen, Mississippi. att. GMI. Civil engineer with New Orleans and Jackson Railroad. Sgt. Co. I, 11th Mississippi, Feb. 20, 1861. Lt. CSA, Mar. 16, 1861. Maj. (PACS) same date. Lt. ADC to Longstreet, June 26, 1861. Maj. (PACS) OO to Longstreet, May 5, 1862, and Lt. Col. (PACS) OO, Aug. 12, 1862. Slightly WIA at Chickamauga. Appx. m. Julia Watson. d. Aberdeen, Mississippi, in 1868. Interred at Odd Fellows' Rest Cem., Feb. 3, 1868. Manning was famous for inserting himself into the front lines during battles. John C.

Haskell described him as "a little man, weighing not over 100 pounds."

Marchbanks, George. b. 1839. att. USMA, from McMinnville, Tennessee. Lt. Co. D, 16th Tennessee, May 21, 1861. Dropped at May 1862 reorganization. Lt. CSA, Dec. 4, 1862. Lt. AAIG at AOT headquarters. Lt. Co. K, 25th Tennessee, 1863. Lt. acting ADC to B. R. Johnson at Chickamauga. Lt. AAIG to Johnson, by Jan. 1864. Transferred to Gen. Wheeler, Sept. 1864.

Markoe, Frank, Jr. b. Maryland, Aug. 9, 1840. att. City Coll. of New York. Pvt. Co. H, 1st Maryland, June 18, 1861. WIA at Shepherdstown and at Battery Wagner. Lt. SO to Beauregard, Nov. 12, 1862. Lt. SO to Mercer, Feb. 11, 1863. Lt. SO to Ripley, June 1863. Lt. SO to Beauregard, Nov. 23, 1863. Lt. SO to S. D. Lee, Feb. 23, 1864. Lt. SO and VADC to John B. Gordon, Oct. 1864. Appx. Col. in Maryland National Guard, 1880s and 1890s. d. Monkton, Maryland, June 4, 1914. bur. St. Mary's Cem., Baltimore.

Marrow, William Chamberlayne, Jr. b. Warwick Co., Virginia, ca. 1832. Shoe and boot merchant at Norfolk before and after the war. Lt. Co. B, 18th Bn. Virginia Heavy Arty., Mar. 9, 1862. To Capt. AQM of Bn., Aug. 5, 1862. Capt. AQM at ANVa. headquarters, Apr. 28, 1863. Chief Paymaster for army. Maj. QM to Conner, Mar. 8, 1865. Relieved Mar. 23, 1865, and resumed paymaster duties. Appx. d. Norfolk, May 8, 1880. bur. Elmwood Cem.

Marshall, Charles. b. Warrenton, Virginia, Oct. 3, 1830. att. UVa. Professor at Univ. of Indiana, 1849–1852. Lawyer at Baltimore, Maryland, pre- and postwar. Lt. ADC to R. E. Lee, Mar. 22, 1862. Maj. ADC to Lee, Apr. 21, 1862. Lt. Col. AAG to Lee, Feb. 25, 1864. Very slightly WIA, May 18, 1864, by shell fragment. Appx. Married twice. d. Baltimore, Apr. 19, 1902. bur. Green Mount Cem.

Marshall, Fielding Lewis. b. Weyanoke, Charles City Co., Virginia, Mar. 29, 1819.

att. UVa. Fauquier Co. farmer. Sgt. Co. H, 6th Virginia Cavy., Apr. 24, 1861. Lt. OO, May 17, 1862. On ordnance duty at Lynchburg, May 1862 into 1865. In Virginia legislature postwar. Farmer and teacher at Atlanta, Georgia. Published his memoirs in 1911. d. Orange, Virginia, June 30, 1902. bur. Graham Cem.

Marshall, James Edward. b. Fauquier Co., Virginia, Oct. 17, 1830. att. UVa. Fauquier Co. farmer. Lt. Co. A, 7th Virginia Cavy., Apr. 19, 1861. To Adjt., Mar. 6, 1862. Lt. AAG to Ashby, May 23, 1862. No record until he joined Co. D, 43rd Bn. Virginia Cavy., late 1864. d. Fauquier Co., Oct. 21, 1872.

Marshall, John Prevost. b. Jan. 7, 1840. att. Georgetown Coll. Resided in Prince George's Co., Maryland. Lt. Co. C, 1st Maryland, 1861–1862. Lt. OO to Steuart, summer 1863. Lt. OO in South Carolina, Sept. 1863–Feb. 1864. Lt. Invalid Corps, Mar. 9, 1865, assigned to light duty with Gen. Kemper in Richmond, but is believed to have died Feb. 5, 1865.

Marshall, Thomas. b. Fauquier Co., Virginia, Jan. 17, 1836. att. UVa. Farmer in Fauquier Co. VADC to T. J. Jackson after First Manassas. Capt. 7th Virginia Cavy., Mar. 11, 1862. To Maj., June 20, 1862. Lt. Col., Oct. 30, 1862. KIA Nov. 12, 1864. bur. Stonewall Cem., Winchester.

Martin, Albion. b. Portland, Maine, June 10, 1822. Graduated from dentistry school in 1849. Dentist in Virginia's Shenandoah Valley. Pvt. Co. I, 33rd Virginia, June 22, 1861. Capt. ACS, 33rd Virginia, Sept. 21, 1861. Capt. AQM, 33rd Virginia, Aug. 1, 1863. Capt. AQM with 2nd Corps, Sept. 15, 1864. Dentist at Edinburg and Woodstock. d. Woodstock, Aug. 26, 1894. Five of Martin's war letters were published in 1977.

Martin, Andrew Bennett. b. Smith Co., Tennessee, Dec. 9, 1836. Drugstore clerk and lawyer at Lebanon. att. Cumberland Univ. Lt. Co. H, 7th Tennessee, May 20, 1861. Relieved Apr. 26, 1862. Lt. AAAG to

Hatton, May 1862. Lt. AAAG to Dibrell in 1864. Probably also on the staff of Wheeler. Lawyer and legislator postwar. Married three times. Professor of law at Cumberland Univ., 1878–1920. d. Lebanon, May 19, 1920.

Martin, Benjamin. Of Barnwell Co., South Carolina. Sgt. Co. H, 1st South Carolina, July 20, 1861. Reduced to Pvt. Aug. 21, 1861. Lt. ADC to Hagood, Aug. 28, 1862. WIA in knee at Weldon Railroad, Aug. 21, 1864. Alive 1884 in Hampton Co., and at Washington, D.C., in 1897. Dead by 1922. Possibly the Benjamin Martin (Apr. 29, 1842–Mar. 3, 1920) who is bur. at Black Swamp Church in Garnett, South Carolina.

Martin, Bowling J. Prewar lawyer at Panola, Mississippi. Pvt. Co. H, 17th Mississippi, Aug. 26, 1861, age 22. Capt. ACS, 17th Mississippi, May 1, 1862. Capt. ACS to McLaws, Oct.–Dec. 1862. Capt. ACS at Okalona, Mississippi, June 1863. Later in AOT. Resigned Mar. 30, 1865. Lawyer and railroad president in Bolivar Co. Alive 1892.

Martin, Dwight. b. ca. 1833. Lawyer at New Orleans, Louisiana. Pvt. Louisiana Guard Arty., Apr. 26, 1861. Lt. ADC to Hays, July 28, 1862. MWIA and POW at Sharpsburg. d. about Sept. 24, 1862, after "the most acute suffering." bur. Girod Street Cem., New Orleans, but that site dismantled in 1970s. Now bur. Hope Mausoleum, New Orleans. Martin's uniform is at the Museum of the Confederacy in Richmond.

Martin, Egbert J. Lived prewar in Kentucky, Mississippi, and probably Tennessee. VADC to his uncle Gen. Ed. Johnson, May 1863. Lt. ADC to Johnson, July 1, 1863. WIA in thigh at Wilderness. With Johnson into Apr. 1865, at which time he was age 29. Killed a man at Brunswick, Georgia, in 1868, and on trial for murder in 1870.

Martin, James G. A resident of Hill Co., Texas. Lt. ADC to Donelson, Nov. 16, 1861. Capt. AAG to Donelson, late in 1862. Later staff of Maury and Preston. Capt. AAG

commanding post at Abingdon, Virginia, July 1863–1865. Alive 1912 at Brooklyn, New York.

Martin, Walter Kevan. b. Petersburg, Virginia, Mar. 4, 1835. Adjt. 4th Virginia Cavy., Sept. 12, 1861. Capt. AAG to B. H. Robertson, June 12, 1862. Capt. AAG to W. E. Jones, autumn 1862. Capt. AAG to Rosser, Oct.–Nov. 1863, but forced out by Rosser and returned to Jones. Capt. AAG to Robert Ransom, June 14, 1864, but may never have joined. Capt. AAG to Lomax by late summer 1864. d. May 1, 1886.

Marye, Lawrence Slaughter. b. Fredericksburg, Virginia, October 1834. att. UVA. and Hampden Sidney. Lawyer at Richmond. Capt. Hampden (Va.) Arty. Capt. OO to Loring, May 26, 1862. Ordered to report to Ordnance Bureau, Nov. 18, 1862. VADC to Early at Fredericksburg. Capt. OO to Taliaferro, Dec. 30, 1862. Same to Trimble, Colston, and Ed. Johnson. Capt. OO to Elzey, Nov. 13, 1863. Capt. OO to Pemberton, May 1864. Capt. AAIG to Pemberton, Jan. 7, 1865. Lawyer at Richmond, Lynchburg, Memphis, and Chattanooga. Editor of the *Lynchburg Virginian.* d. Apr. 25, 1921.

Marye, Robert Burton. b. Madison Co., Virginia, 1819. Lawyer and farmer in Orange Co. Managed a turnpike company. Said to have given William Mahone his first job. Married twice. Lt. PAVA., May 21, 1861. On recruiting duty at Charlottesville. Commanded posts at Orange C.H. and at Charlottesville, also acting as AQM and ACS. Capt. AQM, Apr. 25, 1862, on duty at Farmville. Maj. QM at Farmville, Jan. 17, 1864. Paroled Apr. 26, 1865, with AOT. Traveling agent for a Chattanooga newspaper. d. there May 25, 1881. bur. Confederate Cem.

Mason, Alexander Hamilton, Jr. b. ca. 1837. Merchant at Fredericksburg, Virginia. m. Anne Evans Shelby, 1860. Lt. Co. C, 30th Virginia, July 6, 1861. Capt. ACS to J. G. Walker, Feb. 3, 1862. Maj. CS to Walker, May 15, 1862. Maj. acting CS to Richard

Taylor, Apr. 1864. Later Maj. cs to Taylor. d. near Aberdeen, Mississippi, Feb. 1, 1891.

Mason, Arthur Pendleton. b. Alexandria, Virginia, Dec. 11, 1835. att. uva. Lawyer in Arkansas Co., Arkansas. Lt. Co. E, 6th Arkansas. Lt. aaag to J. E. Johnston by Feb. 1, 1862. Capt. aag to Johnston, Mar. 1, 1862. Capt. aag to R. E. Lee, June 1, 1862. Back to Johnston, Nov. 21, 1862. Maj. aag to Johnston, Dec. 2, 1862. Same to Polk. Lt. Col. aag to Hood, Nov. 12, 1864. To Johnston again, Feb. 24, 1865. New Orleans merchant. m. Mary Ellen Campbell, making him a brother-in-law of G. W. Lay and Fred. Colston, both staff officers. d. Apr. 22, 1893. bur. Green Mount Cem., Baltimore, Maryland.

Mason, Beverly Randolph. b. Fairfax, Virginia, Sept. 1, 1834. Great-grandson of George Mason. Pvt. Co. H, 4th Virginia Cavy., Sept. 9, 1861. Acting acs for regiment, Mar.–July 1863. Capt. acs to Wickham, Aug. 19, 1863. Paroled May 16, 1865, at Richmond. Professor at a military academy in New York, and founded the Gunston Hall Girls School. d. Washington, D.C., Apr. 22, 1910. bur. Ivy Hill Cem., Alexandria. First name may have been spelled Beverley, or perhaps he used both versions.

Mason, Charles Taylor. b. Fredericksburg, Virginia, May 7, 1832. att. vmi. Engineer on Covington and Ohio Railroad. Lt. eo in pava., 1861. Served at Hardy's Bluff. Lt. eo, Feb. 15, 1862, at Drewry's Bluff. Helped build Ft. Drewry. Capt. eo, Oct. 1, 1862. Served mostly on the James River defenses, into 1865. Postwar realtor. d. Chillicothe, Ohio, Dec. 11, 1918. Mason's excellent wartime papers are at the Virginia Historical Society.

Mason, Claiborne Rice. b. Troy, New York, Nov. 28, 1800. Moved to Chesterfield Co., Virginia, in 1803. Coal miner and extremely successful railroad builder and engineer. Said to be a millionaire by 1861. Capt. aqm, July 19, 1861, but also has record as

Capt. Co. H, 52nd Virginia, July 23, 1861. Capt. aqm, 52nd Virginia, Sept. 4, 1861. Lt. Col. eo (probably in pava.), Oct. 1861. Worked at repairing and maintaining roads in western Virginia. Staff of T. J. Jackson, intermittently, May–July 1862. Railroad contractor postwar. Reportedly illiterate, but "possessed a wonderful mathematical talent." "Broad of shoulder, with long, sinewy, powerful arms." d. Swoope's, Virginia, Jan. 12, 1885. bur. Thornrose Cem., Staunton.

Mason, E. E. A resident of Fairfax Co., Virginia. Civilian engineer serving with csa forces at Norfolk, early in the war. Lt. eo, Feb. 15, 1862, mostly on duty at Richmond. Capt. eo, Oct. 19, 1864, assigned to defenses at Lynchburg. Paroled Apr. 26, 1865, with aot. Believed to be Edgar Eilbeck Mason (1828–July 15, 1907), bur. Ivy Hill Cem. in Alexandria.

Mason, James Murray, Jr. b. Winchester, Virginia, Aug. 25, 1839. Great-grandson of George Mason, son of Confederate politician James M. Mason, and nephew of Joel B. Mason (see below). att. uva. Lt. csa, July 19, 1861. Ordered to report to J. R. Anderson in North Carolina, Oct. 1861. Lt. acting oo to Griffith, May 1–June 29, 1862. Lt. acting oo to C. S. Winder, July 19–Aug. 9, 1862. Served at Richmond Arsenal, Aug. 1862–Jan. 1863. Capt. (temp.) oo, Aug. 26, 1862. Executive officer at Columbus Arsenal, Jan. 1863. Capt. oo at Ft. Caswell, June 1863. Capt. oo to Butler, July 25, 1864. Capt. oo, District of the Shenandoah Valley, Sept. 1864–Feb. 4, 1865. To report to R. E. Lee, Mar. 29, 1865. West Virginia legislator, lawyer, tax commissioner, and newspaper editor. d. Charlottesville, Virginia, Jan. 9, 1923. bur. Charlestown, West Virginia.

Mason, Joel Barlow. b. Fairfax Co., Virginia, June 9, 1813. Grandson of George Mason. Never married. Cotton planter in Tensas Parish, Louisiana, from the early

1840s. VADC to J. E. Johnston, July 1861. MWIA in ankle at First Manassas. Foot amputated three weeks later. d. Warrenton, Virginia, Oct. 1, 1861. bur. Mt. Hebron Cem., Winchester.

Mason, John. b. near Winchester, Virginia, Nov. 17, 1841. Pvt. Co. F, 2nd Virginia. Capt. AQM, Oct. 21, 1861. To report to T. J. Jackson, Dec. 1861, but failed bond. Reinstated Mar. 24, 1862. Service with Jackson unclear. Ordered to Richmond, Apr. 15, 1862. Paymaster for Richmond's hospitals by October 1862. Capt. AQM to Ed. Johnson, Jan. 12, 1864. Capt. AQM, McLaughlin's Bn. Arty., June 1864. Capt. AQM to Army of the Valley, Sept. 23, 1864. Capt. AQM to Cutshaw's Bn. Arty., Nov. 14, 1864. Capt. acting AQM to A. L. Long, 1865. Appx. Lived in Fairfax Co., Virginia, postwar. d. Leesburg, Virginia, June 6, 1925.

Mason, Julien Jaquelin. b. Dec. 22, 1841. att. UVA. Of King George Co., Virginia. Pvt. Co. C, 9th Virginia Cavy., Aug. 6, 1861–Oct. 25, 1861. Volunteer ACS to his brother-in-law, Gen. Field, spring 1862. Maj. CS to Field, May 1, 1862. Relieved Sept. 27, 1862, to report to Richmond. Worked at Chimborazo Hospital there. Maj. CS to H. H. Walker, July 25, 1863. Under arrest in November 1863. Maj. CS to Field, Jan. 2, 1864. Lawyer in King George Co. d. Feb. 24, 1904. bur. St. John's Episc. Church.

Mason, Robert French. b. Fairfax Co., Virginia. VADC to Ewell at First Manassas. Capt. AQM to Ewell, Sept. 1, 1861. Maj. QM to Ewell, Oct. 2, 1861. Possibly held some position on staff of A. P. Hill later. Maj. QM to his cousin, Gen. Fitz. Lee, by Feb. 1863. Maj. QM to Wickham. Briefly commanded 15th Virginia Cavy. in 1864. Maj. AAIG to Lee, Nov. 3, 1864. Appx. m. Margaret Cooke, a famous beauty. Farmed in Prince William Co. postwar. d. near Charlottesville, Virginia, June 26, 1902, age 68. Another of Ewell's staff called Mason "ener-getic & efficient," but "not useful except on the field."

Mason, Thomas Williams. b. Jan. 3, 1839. att. UVA. and UNC. Of Northampton Co., North Carolina. m. Bettie Gray, 1860. VADC to Robert Ransom at Sharpsburg. Lawyer and farmer at Garysburg, North Carolina, and in state legislature. d. Apr. 15, 1921.

Mason, Wiley Roy, Jr. b. Mar. 27, 1833. Lived at Fredericksburg, Virginia. Married twice. Lt. ADC to his brother-in-law, Gen. Field, Apr. 12, 1862. Attached to Conscript Bureau in 1863. Lt. ADC to Field again, 1864. Slightly WIA twice at Cold Harbor. WIA in liver and POW at Fussell's Mill. Exchanged Oct. 3, 1864. Fredericksburg grocer. d. Richmond, Virginia, Oct. 23, 1909. bur. Fredericksburg City Cem.

Mason, William Taylor. b. Falmouth, Virginia, August 1845. att. VMI from King George Co. Served in Breathed's (Va.) Btty., Mar. 1863. Lt. ADC to his brother-in-law, Gen. Alexander, Mar. 19, 1864. Appx. d. New Orleans, Louisiana, September 1867, of yellow fever. bur. there. "A first rate little aid + a fine fellow in every respect," wrote Alexander. Was "very young-looking, even for his age."

Massie, Robert Thomas. b. Waynesboro, Virginia, Feb. 16, 1834. att. UVA. and Washington Coll. On faculty at UVA. and Randolph Macon. A cousin of Gen. Rodes. Capt. of an artillery company from Virginia that the Confederate government refused to accept. Lt. EO, May 8, 1863. Served at Richmond under Col. A. L. Rives. d. Richmond, July 2, 1863.

Masters, Leander. b. in Virginia, 1823. An attorney at Amelia C.H. m. Jane Eggleston Irving. Capt. Feb. 26, 1862, to report to R. L. Walker. Capt. commanding heavy artillery during Seven Days. Capt. staff of Field, July–Aug. 1862. On inspection duty with Third Corps artillery later. Maj. AAIG to Field, Feb. 19, 1864. KIA Apr. 1865. bur. Grubb Hill Church Cem., Amelia Co.

Mathews, Henry Mason. b. Greenbrier Co., Virginia, Mar. 29, 1834. att. UVA. Lawyer at Lewisburg and professor at Alleghany Coll. Lt. PAVA., May 1, 1861. Capt. PAVA., May 30, 1861. Capt. EO to Loring, July 1861. Lt. ADC to Loring, Mar. 3, 1862. Lt. (acting?) ADC to Stevenson, by July 1862. Acting Maj. OO to Stevenson, Oct. 10, 1862. Maj. OO to Stevenson, May 2, 1863. Acting Chief OO to Pemberton, July 1863. Relieved from Stevenson, Jan. 14, 1865. Attorney general of West Virginia, and governor, 1876–1880. Described thusly: "blue eyes, cheerful expression, slightly bald." d. Lewisburg, West Virginia, Apr. 26, 1884. bur. City Cem.

Mauldin, William Harrison. b. Williamston, Pendleton Dist., South Carolina, Jan. 15, 1839. att. Furman Coll. Merchant in Anderson Co. Lt. Co. D, Hampton Legion. Capt. AQM, Hampton Legion, Oct. 14, 1862. Maj. QM to Gary, July 19, 1864. Appx. South Carolina legislator, lumber dealer, and railroad man. d. Hampton, South Carolina, Dec. 26, 1900. bur. Hampton Cem.

Maynard, George Fletcher. b. Richmond, Virginia, 1829. Coal merchant at Richmond. Moved to San Francisco about 1850. m. Sarah Virginia Parker, 1853. Capt. AQM, Mar. 28, 1862. Paymaster at Camp Lee in Richmond. Maj. QM, Dec. 8, 1863. Served at Richmond through the war. Paroled Apr. 26, 1865, with AOT. Returned to California in 1870s. San Francisco city auditor. d. there May 10, 1879.

Maynard, John Cringan. b. Richmond, Virginia, July 26, 1837. Married twice. Lived in San Francisco before the war. Capt. AQM, July 19, 1861. Served at Camp Lee in Richmond, with his brother George F. (see above). Maj. QM, Dec. 12, 1862. Based at Richmond, where he purchased and forwarded forage, fuel, and lumber to the army. Farmer and editor in California. Worked for Treasury Dept. at San Francisco. Alive 1887. "A most excellent man and kind to everyone," wrote one of his wartime assistants.

Mayo, Peter Helms. b. Henrico Co., Virginia, May 7, 1836. Cpl. Co. I, 4th Virginia Cavy., May 8–Oct. 3, 1861. Clerk and special agent in QM Dept. at Richmond. Capt. AQM, Mar. 12, 1864. Failed confirmation, but reappointed June 15, 1864. Worked at transportation office in Richmond. Capt. AQM, Third Corps, 1865. Appx. d. Aug. 5, 1920. bur. Hollywood Cem., Richmond.

Mayo, William Swan Plumer. b. Henrico Co., Virginia, Apr. 9, 1838. att. Hampden Sidney. Tobacco manufacturer. Pvt. to Sgt. Co. I, 4th Virginia Cavy., May 8, 1861. Capt. AQM, 19th Bn. Virginia Heavy Arty., Aug. 7, 1862. Capt. AQM and Paymaster to Third Corps, June 1863. Appx. d. Richmond, Virginia, Mar. 16, 1873. bur. Hollywood Cem.

Mays, Thomas Sumter. b. in South Carolina. A resident of Florida. Volunteered at Ft. Pickens, very early on. VADC to Bonham, Aug.–Sept. 1861. VADC to Whiting. POW at Seven Pines, age 19 or 20. Exchanged Aug. 27, 1862. No further record.

Mazyck, Edmund. b. Charleston, South Carolina, Jan. 11, 1840. att. South Carolina Coll. Sgt. Marion (S.C.) Arty. Acting Lt. OO at Morris Island, July–Oct. 1863. Acting Lt. OO to Hagood, Oct. 29, 1863. Possibly staff of Beauregard and Taliaferro in July 1863. Lt. OO, Jan. 7, 1865. Paroled Apr. 26, 1865. att. Medical Coll. of South Carolina postwar, and taught there. Physician and Santee River rice planter. d. Charleston, May 28, 1893. bur. St. Philip's Churchyard.

Meade, D. G. Capt. ACS in Richmond by Oct. 1861, probably in PAVA. Capt. ACS, Dec. 13, 1861. Served entire war at Camp Lee in Richmond. Possibly Drayton Grimke Meade, from Alexandria, Virginia.

Meade, David. b. Jan. 21, 1833. A farmer. Lt. Co. C, 2nd Virginia, Apr. 18, 1861. Capt. AQM, 11th Virginia Cavy., June 17, 1862. Failed bond and dropped, Oct. 25, 1862.

Capt. AQM to Pickett, June 15, 1863. Appx. d. June 6, 1906. bur. Meade Memorial Episc. Church, White Post, Virginia.

Meade, Everard Benjamin. b. Apr. 15, 1839. Pvt. Co. F, 21st Virginia, Apr. 21–Nov. 2, 1861. Clerk and treasurer for Piedmont Railroad, midwar. Lt. 1st C.S. Engineers, Apr. 6, 1864. Lt. ADC to Lane, Aug. 17, 1864. Appx. m. Lucy Gilmer. Richmond insurance man. d. there Apr. 19, 1896. bur. Hollywood Cem.

Meade, Hodijah Lincoln. b. in Virginia, May 30, 1842. att. UVA. Pvt. 1st Co. Richmond Howitzers, Apr. 21, 1861. Lt. OO, Mar. 1, 1863, perhaps serving with the Howitzers. Lt. OO to Read's Bn. Arty. by Dec. 1864. Lawyer and teacher at Amelia C.H. d. 1902.

Meade, Richard Kidder. b. Clarke Co., Virginia, Oct. 4, 1841. att. Washington Coll. Pvt. Co. F, 2nd Virginia, Apr. 18, 1861. WIA at First Manassas, right arm amputated. Lt. of Inf., CSA, Dec. 17, 1861. Lt. Asst. OO to Jackson, Mar. 7, 1862. Lt. AAIG to T. J. Jackson, Mar. 31, 1862. Lt. ADC to Taliaferro, July 28, 1862. Lt. AAIG to Ewell, Aug. 25, 1864. Relieved Dec. 6, 1864, to report to Kemper Dec. 7. Postwar teacher. d. Clarke Co., Jan. 20, 1903. bur. Old Chapel Cem.

Meade, Richard Kidder, Jr. b. Brunswick Co., Virginia, Aug. 1835. att. USMA, from Petersburg. Lt. of Engineers, 1857–1861. Present inside Ft. Sumter with Union forces in Apr. 1861. Maj. of Arty. PACS, to rank from Mar. 16, 1861. Maj. EO to Magruder, May 1861. Worked in Cape Fear Dist., North Carolina, early 1862. Maj. EO to Longstreet, June 9, 1862. d. at Petersburg, July 31, 1862, of disease. bur. Blandford Cem. Not a son of the Richard Kidder Meade listed above.

Meade, William T. b. Clarke Co., Virginia, Mar. 28, 1841. att. Washington Coll. Cpl. Co. I, 4th Virginia, June 2–Sept. 13, 1861. QM Sgt. at Gen. Pendleton's office by Nov. 1861. Capt. AQM to his mother's distant re-lation, Gen. Pendleton, June 3, 1862. Mostly served with First Corps ordnance train, which he commanded by Sept. 1864. Appx. Farmer at Trevilian's Station. d. in Louisa Co., July 4, 1917. bur. Clark Family Cem.

Means, Edward John. b. Feb. 10, 1831. Capt. Co. C, 6th South Carolina. Acting ADC to R. H. Anderson at Williamsburg and in September 1863. Later in CSN. m. Martha J. McPheeters, 1860. d. Mar. 28, 1877.

Meares, Oliver Pendleton. b. Wilmington, North Carolina, Feb. 24, 1828. att. UNC. Wilmington lawyer. Capt. Co. I, 18th North Carolina, Apr. 15, 1861. Lt. Col. 18th North Carolina, but failed reelection in 1862 "because I am a strict disciplinarian and moreover refused to electioneer." Capt. ACS, 61st North Carolina, Sept. 9, 1862. Capt. AQM to Clingman, Sept. 20, 1864. Paroled Apr. 26, 1865. Wilmington judge. d. there Nov. 22, 1906. bur. Oakdale Cem.

Meares, William Belvidere. b. Jan. 22, 1826. att. UNC. A physician. Asst. Surg. 20th North Carolina. Lt. ADC to Matt. Ransom, July 1, 1863. Served through late 1864, at least. d. Apr. 7, 1896.

Mebane, William Nelson, Jr. b. Greensboro, North Carolina, Apr. 14, 1843. Pvt. Co. H, 13th North Carolina, Oct. 4, 1861. To Ordnance Sgt., June 15, 1862. Lt. OO to Cooke, May 1864 through at least Dec. 1864. Lawyer in Rockingham Co. d. 1895.

Meem, James Lawrence. b. Lynchburg, Virginia, Apr. 2, 1836. att. VMI and UVA. Lynchburg merchant and engineer. Sgt. Co. G, 11th Virginia, Apr. 23, 1861. Later Adjt. Lt. AAAG to his brother-in-law, Gen. Garland, by May 25, 1862. May have received commission as Capt.–was called that by Garland. KIA at Seven Pines, May 31, 1862. Two good war letters written by Meem are at the Virginia Historical Society.

Meem, John Gaw, Jr. b. Lynchburg, Virginia, Feb. 10, 1833. att. VMI. Brother of J. L. Meem. A merchant and engineer. Lt. Co. G, 11th Virginia, Apr. 23, 1861. Dropped

Apr. 26, 1862. Lt. ADC to Kirby Smith, Feb. 3, 1862. Capt. SO to Smith, July 7, 1862. Served into 1865. Brother-in-law of Gen. Garland. Married twice. In U.S. Civil Service postwar. d. Lynchburg, Jan. 2, 1908. bur. Spring Hill Cem.

Melton, George Washington. b. York Co., South Carolina, July 6, 1834. Lt. Co. B, Holcombe Legion Cavy. Lt. AAIG to G. W. Smith, Sept. 20, 1862. Maj. QM to B. H. Robertson, Feb. 21, 1863. Relieved May 25, 1864. Maj. QM to Butler, July 4, 1864. Maj. QM to Hampton by Apr. 1865. Merchant at Chester. d. Columbia, July 9, 1876, of gastric fever. bur. Evergreen Cem., Chester.

Melton, Samuel Wickliffe. b. Yorkville, South Carolina, Feb. 7, 1830. att. South Carolina Coll. Yorkville lawyer and newspaper editor. VADC to Bonham at First Manassas. Maj. AAG to G. W. Smith, by Sept. 25, 1861. Maj. AAG to Samuel Cooper, Feb. 23, 1863. Lt. Col. AAG, Apr. 30, 1864. Judge at Columbia, and state attorney general. d. Charleston, South Carolina, Mar. 25, 1899. bur. Elmwood Cem., Columbia. Stammered when he spoke. Melton's war letters are at the Univ. of South Carolina.

Memminger, Christopher Gustavus, Jr. b. Charleston, South Carolina, Nov. 17, 1840. att. Harvard and South Carolina Coll. Lt. SO, Oct. 10, 1862. Assigned to Beauregard, Nov. 29, 1862. Lt. SO to Ripley, Mar. 18, 1863. Court-martialed by Ripley for contesting orders. Lt. SO to R. H. Anderson, June 16, 1863. Relieved Apr. 23, 1864. Lt. SO to Sam. Jones, Apr. 23, 1864. Lt. SO to Hardee by Nov. 1864. Paroled Apr. 26, 1865. Railroad contractor in New York City. Growing fruit in Florida by 1892. d. Mar. 30, 1905. bur. St. John's Episc. Church, Flat Rock, North Carolina. Son of Confederate cabinet member.

Mercer, George Douglas. b. Anne Arundel Co., Maryland, Sept. 18, 1831. Maj. QM to R. B. Garnett, Nov. 13, 1861. Maj. QM to C. S. Winder, Apr. 1862. Maj. QM to

Trimble. Later same to Ed. Johnson and to John B. Gordon. At Appx. as Chief QM of Second Corps. d. 1915. bur. St. Mary's Episc. Church, Prince George's Co., Maryland.

Mercer, Thomas Hugh. b. Williamsburg, Virginia, ca. 1843. att. Wm. & Mary. Greatgrandson of Gen. Hugh Mercer. Pvt. Co. C, 32nd Virginia, Apr. 28, 1861. Cadet CSA, Oct. 25, 1861. Served with 1st Virginia in early 1862. WIA at Williamsburg. Cadet OO to McLaws, Sept. 21, 1862. Lt. Woolfolk's (Va.) Btty., Aug. 1863. Lt. Madison (Miss.) Arty., Oct. 1864. Appx. d. at Williamsburg, Sept. 7, 1865, of pneumonia. bur. Benjamin Waller Cem.

Merchant, Anderson. b. in Virginia. Served in U.S. Army, 1847–1861. Capt. of Arty., CSA, Mar. 16, 1861. Capt. Chief of Arty. and OO to Floyd, Aug. 26, 1861. Relieved Jan. 7, 1862. Capt. Chief of Arty. and OO to Sam. Jones, Jan. 29, 1862. Relieved Apr. 16, 1862. Maj. (Lt. Col. PACS), by 1863, on staff of Pemberton. POW at Port Hudson, July 9, 1863. In prison into 1865.

Meredith, William Bernard. b. Port Royal, Virginia, October 8, 1839. att. UVA. Lt. Ashland (Va.) Arty. Drillmaster at Camp Lee in Richmond, May 1862. Adjt. Richardson's Bn. Arty., June 20, 1862. d. Aug. 22, 1862, of typhoid fever.

Merrick, David Thomas. b. Clinton, Louisiana, June 17, 1841. att. Centenary Coll. Lt. and Capt. Co. A, 15th Louisiana, 1861–1865. Capt. AAAIG or acting ADC to Stafford at Mine Run, Nov. 1863. WIA in head there. Planter in Pointe Coupee Parish. d. Merrick, Louisiana, Mar. 14, 1907. bur. St. Stephen's Episc. Church Cem. "A hairbrained youth, brave to a fault and caring for little save the fun of life."

Merritt, Christian Garber. b. Augusta Co., Virginia, Dec. 24, 1822. Mexican War veteran, a '49er, and a farmer. Lt. Co. D, 25th Virginia, May 27, 1861. Capt. AQM, 25th Virginia, Jan. 18, 1862. Capt. AQM to William Terry, 1864. Capt. AQM to J. B. Gordon,

1864–1865. Augusta Co. farmer. d. Augusta Co., Nov. 15, 1907. bur. Bethel Presby. Church Cem.

Micou, Augustin. b. New Orleans, Louisiana, Nov. 7, 1841. att. UNC. Pvt. First Co. Washington (La.) Arty., 1862. POW at Second Fredericksburg, May 1863. Lt. ADC to Fry, June 15, 1864. d. Feb. 18, 1883. bur. Pass Christian, Mississippi.

Middleton, John Izard, Jr. b. Charleston, South Carolina, Feb. 16, 1834. att. South Carolina Coll. Lawyer at Georgetown. Lt. ADC to Drayton, Mar. 20, 1862. Resigned Sept. 26, 1862, to become Capt. AQM, 15th South Carolina. Capt. acting QM to McLaws, Nov. 1862. Acting as Maj. QM to Alexander, May 10, 1864, but appointment not effective until Dec. 31, 1864. Appx. Moved in 1865 to Baltimore, Maryland. A merchant. d. there Mar. 20, 1907.

Miles, William Porcher. b. Walterboro, South Carolina, July 4, 1822. att. College of Charleston and taught mathematics there. Mayor of Charleston, 1855, and USHR. VADC to Beauregard at First Manassas, in December 1862 and in August 1863, at least. Member of C.S. Congress. Lived in Nelson Co., Virginia, 1865–1880. President, Univ. of South Carolina, 1880–1882. Grew sugar in Louisiana. d. Burnside, Louisiana, May 11, 1899. bur. Union, West Virginia.

Miller, Andrew J. Lt. Co. E, 25th North Carolina, June 15, 1861, age 31. Declined reelection in 1862. Capt. AQM, 25th North Carolina, May 30, 1862. Failed bond and out of commission by Nov. 1862. Capt. AQM to B. R. Johnson, Sept. 20, 1864. Paroled Apr. 26, 1865.

Miller, Henry Massie. b. Raleigh, North Carolina, July 12, 1839. Pvt. Co. I, 4th North Carolina. Maj. CS to Clingman, Aug. 8, 1862. Maj. CS to Ramseur, date unknown. Maj. CS to Cox. Appx. d. Norfolk, Virginia, June 28, 1898.

Miller, William. Capt. AQM, Nov. 16, 1861. Served in the Shenandoah Valley during the entire war, at posts up and down its length. Seems to have spent more time at Mt. Jackson than elsewhere.

Miller, William Henry. b. Botetourt Co., Virginia, July 13, 1833. att. Roanoke Coll. and Hampden Sidney. Sgt. Co. G, 20th Virginia. POW at Rich Mountain. Capt. AQM, 27th Bn. Virginia Cavy., Dec. 2, 1862. Capt. acting QM to Hodge. Maj. QM to Hodge, Nov. 20, 1863. Maj. QM to Gracie, Oct. 7, 1864. Maj. QM to Moody, Dec. 1864. Appx. Teacher and pension official. d. Baker, West Virginia, Jan. 8, 1926. bur. U.B. Church Cem.

Milligan, James Fisher. b. Philadelphia, Pennsylvania, Mar. 15, 1829. Lived in Missouri prewar, where he was a deputy sheriff, a clerk, and a St. Louis mail carrier. Member of John C. Fremont's fifth expedition. A trader at Bent's Old Fort, briefly. USN midshipman in Mexican War. Officer in U.S. Revenue Service, 1855–1861. Lt. Provisional Navy of Virginia, Apr. 1861. Lt. of Arty., CSA, Oct. 7, 1861, and Capt. (temp), same day. Capt. SO to Huger, Oct. 1861. Maj. (temp.) of Cavy., July 17, 1863. Commanded "Independent Signal Corps" at Petersburg, 1862–1865, serving under D. H. Hill, French, and Pickett. Paroled at Richmond, Apr. 22, 1865. "Profane to an alarming extent." Newspaperman and real estate agent in Norfolk, Virginia. d. there Mar. 22, 1899. bur. Elmwood Cem. Milligan is the subject of a good biography published in 1988.

Mills, Charles Stiles. b. in Georgia, 1826. Pvt. Co. E, 1st Texas, May 28, 1861. Capt. AQM, 1st Texas, Apr. 14, 1862. Capt. acting AQM to Hood, Mar.–Apr. 1862. Capt. acting ADC to Hood in the Maryland Campaign. Also served with Hood's Div. QM trains in autumn 1862. Resigned Aug. 13, 1864. m. Georgia Ann McCoy, 1864. d. Harrison Co., Texas, Jan. 29, 1870. bur. Woodlawn Cem.

Mills, John Columbus. b. Tryon, North Carolina, Sept. 23, 1839. att. South Carolina Coll. A resident of Spartanburg, South Carolina. Lt. Co. K, 16th North Carolina, June 5, 1861. Failed reelection. Lt. Drillmaster and Enrolling Officer in South Carolina, Jan. 1863. Lt. AAAIG to Gary, 1865. Lawyer at Charlotte, North Carolina, and at Yorkville and Union, South Carolina. d. Tryon, Jan. 17, 1878. bur. Church of the Advent Episc. Cem., Spartanburg Co., South Carolina.

Mills, Thomas Lilley. b. Lafourche Parish, Louisiana, May 6, 1835. Port Hudson farmer. m. Louise Young, 1859. Lt. 10th Louisiana. VADC to Edmund Pendleton, commanding Starke's Bgd., Dec. 1862. Farmer and physician at Port Hudson. d. Jan. 2, 1918. bur. Young Family Cem., Plains, Louisiana.

Mills, Thomas Sumter. b. Fishing Creek, South Carolina, Oct. 18, 1830. att. SCMA. Lt. Co. G, 3rd South Carolina Arty. Lt. AAAG to R. H. Anderson, May 1861. Capt. AAG to Anderson, Aug. 15, 1861. WIA Oct. 1861 at Santa Rosa Island, and May 31, 1862, at Seven Pines. Maj. AAG to Anderson, July 14, 1862. POW June 21, 1864, at Petersburg. Maj. AAG to Mahone, Nov. 4, 1864, while still a POW. Exchanged Feb. 27, 1865. May not have served with Mahone at all. Paroled May 9, 1865, at Meridian, Mississippi. Cotton buyer at Chester, South Carolina. d. there Sept. 2, 1897. bur. Evergreen Cem. Known as "the kid-gloved Major."

Minnigerode, Charles, Jr. b. Williamsburg, Virginia, June 23, 1845. Son of Richmond's famous wartime Episc. rector. Clerk to army's Chief of Ordnance, 1862. VADC to Fitz. Lee, July 1862. Lt. ADC to Fitz. Lee, Sept. 16, 1863. WIA at Appomattox, Apr. 9, 1865. Bookkeeper at Tredegar Ironworks in Richmond, and Alexandria merchant. Committed suicide at Alexandria, Jan. 25, 1888. bur. "Oatlands" Plantation, Loudoun Co., but later moved to Sharon Cem. in Middleburg.

Minor, Charles Landon Carter. b. Han-

over Co., Virginia, Dec. 3, 1835. att. UVA. A teacher. Pvt. 2nd Virginia Cavy. Volunteer rodman with CSA engineers, 1862. Lt. OO, King's Bn. Arty., Feb. 5, 1863. Capt. OO, May 2, 1863, duty uncertain. Capt. OO to A. G. Jenkins, May 1864. Capt. OO to Sam. Jones, May 1864. Resigned Sept. 19, 1864, but probably never implemented. Capt. OO at Richmond Arsenal, Sept. 1864 into 1865. President of the Univ. of the South and Maryland Agricultural College. d. Albemarle Co., Virginia, July 13, 1903.

Mitchel, James. b. Newry, Ireland, Feb. 1840. Came to New York in 1853 with his father, John Mitchel, the famous Irish agitator. Lived at Knoxville, Tennessee, and was an insurance agent at Richmond, Virginia. Pvt. Co. C, 1st Virginia, Apr. 21, 1862. WIA at Second Manassas. Capt. AAG to John B. Gordon, Dec. 20, 1862. Same to C. A. Evans, 1864. Capt. AAG to Kemper, Oct. 6, 1864. WIA three times total and lost some fingers on right hand. Had "light curling hair, blue eyes, delicate features, and possesses a slight and trimly built figure." d. October 5, 1908.

Mitchell, John White. b. Wheeling, Virginia, Dec. 31, 1838. att. Brockenbrough Law School and became a lawyer. Lt. Co. G, 27th Virginia, May 14, 1861. Failed reelection. Maj. CS to Echols, July 28, 1862. Maj. CS to Sam. Jones, spring 1863. Maj. CS to Patton's Bgd. Maj. CS to Wharton, Mar. 3, 1865. Paroled at Charleston, West Virginia, May 2, 1865. Moved to St. Louis in 1865 and practiced law. Deputy sheriff of Wheeling, 1876–1883. d. July 30, 1896.

Mitchell, Julian. b. Edisto Island, South Carolina, Apr. 24, 1836. att. Coll. of Charleston. Diplomat in Russia, and Charleston lawyer. Maj. CS to Ripley, June 2, 1862. Maj. CS to Doles, Nov. 1862. Maj. acting CS to Rodes, June–July 1863. POW at Smithburg, Pennsylvania, July 4, 1863. Exchanged Oct. 3, 1864. Maj. CS to Cook, Jan. 9, 1865. Relieved Jan. 23, 1865. Maj. Chief Commissary of South Carolina,

Jan. 24, 1865. d. Jan. 30, 1907. bur. Magnolia Cem., Charleston.

Mitchell, Samuel DeMilt. b. Oct. 26, 1842. Of Richmond, Virginia. Pvt. Co. F, 21st Virginia, Apr. 21, 1861. Discharged May 9, 1862. Served as clerk in QM office of Stonewall Brigade. VADC to Winder during Seven Days. KIA at Gaines's Mill, June 27, 1862. bur. Hollywood Cem.

Mitchell, Samuel Phillips. b. in Virginia. A 30-year-old merchant at Richmond in 1860. Pvt. Co. C, 1st Virginia, Apr. 21, 1861. Capt. AQM to Longstreet, Sept. 9, 1861. Maj. QM to Longstreet, May 5, 1862. d. near Chickamauga, Georgia, Oct. 5, 1863, of diphtheria. bur. Hollywood Cem., Richmond, in an unmarked grave.

Moffett, George Hall. b. in South Carolina, Feb. 12, 1829. Merchant at Charleston. m. Elizabeth Henry Simonton, 1854. Pvt. Co. A, 25th South Carolina, Feb. 24, 1862. To Adjt., July 30, 1862. Lt. AAAIG to Simonton's Bgd., 1863–1864. Lt. AAAIG to Hagood, July 23, 1864. Capt. AAG to Hagood, Aug. 21, 1864. d. Charleston, June 27, 1875. An extract of Moffett's wartime diary is in Gen. Hagood's published memoirs.

Moffett, John Guthrie. b. Augusta Co., Virginia, May 14, 1832. A cattle broker in Richmond in 1862. Capt. ACS, Nov. 1, 1863, to report to Chief Commissary of Virginia. m. Virginia Austin. Postwar cattle broker at Richmond. d. there May 24, 1884, of hepatitis. bur. Hollywood Cem.

Molloy, Ferdinand. b. Apr. 4, 1834. att. UVA. Of Holly Springs, Mississippi. Capt. ACS, June 26, 1861, stationed at Memphis, Tennessee. Maj. CS to Bragg, Apr. 2, 1862. Maj. post CS at Charleston, South Carolina, July 1862–Apr. 1864. Resumed service with Bragg, Apr. 23, 1864. Maj. CS to Beauregard, May 19, 1864. Paroled Apr. 26, 1865.

Molony, Patrick Kilbride. b. in South Carolina. att. St. John's Coll., in New York. A 26-year-old merchant and law student at Barnwell, South Carolina, in 1860. Pvt. Co. G, 1st (Hagood) South Carolina. Later Adjt. Capt. AAG to Hagood, Aug. 28, 1862. KIA at Weldon Railroad, Aug. 21, 1864. "Rather above the medium height, of slight but active frame, and of an intellectual and refined countenance."

Moncure, Thomas Jefferson. b. Caroline Co., Virginia, Nov. 12, 1832. att. VMI. Married twice. Engineer in Iowa, Minnesota, and Virginia. Capt. 179th Virginia Militia. To Maj. by 1862. Commanded militia at Camp Lee, Mar. 1862. Later Richmond city enrolling officer. Contract engineer on topographic duty, Dec. 1862–June 1863. Lt. EO to McLaws, by July 1863. Lt. Co. H, 1st C.S. Engineers, Mar. 29, 1864. Appx. Engineer for a railroad at Portsmouth postwar. d. Stafford Co., Aug. 28, 1912.

Montgomery, Alvis David. b. Caswell Co., North Carolina, Sept. 28, 1835. Pvt. Co. H, 13th North Carolina, July 5, 1861. Lt. ADC to his brother-in-law, Gen. Scales, June 13, 1863. Appx. m. Annie Elizabeth Scales Lawson. Merchant and salesman at Reidsville, North Carolina. d. Dec. 10, 1880. bur. Greenview Cem.

Montgomery, Charles R. b. in Virginia. A 35-year-old farmer in Hanover Co., in 1860. Pvt. Page's (Va.) Btty., Mar. 28, 1862. To Lt., May 14, 1862. Lt. acting AQM, Carter's Bn. Arty., Nov.–Dec. 1863. Capt. AQM, Cutshaw's Bn. Arty., Feb. 1864. Resumed Hanover Co. farming postwar. d. 1883.

Montgomery, John Henry. b. Spartanburg Co., South Carolina, Dec. 8, 1833. A clerk and merchant. Pvt. Co. E, 18th South Carolina. Capt. ACS, 18th South Carolina, Jan. 14, 1862. Capt. ACS to Elliott. Capt. ACS to Wallace. Capt. acting CS to B. R. Johnson, by Nov. 1864 through at least Mar. 1865. Appx. Fertilizer merchant and cotton factor. d. Oct. 31, 1902.

Moon, Ransom B. b. in Virginia. A store clerk at Halifax C. H. Lt. Co. A, 53rd Virginia, July 4, 1861. Acted as regimental

QM. Capt. AQM, 53rd Virginia, Dec. 1, 1862. Capt. AQM commanding First Corps medical and ambulance trains, Sept. 1864. Postwar merchant at Halifax C.H. d. May 3, 1876, age 40. bur. Moon Grove Cem., Halifax Co.

Moore, Edwin Lyttleton. b. Charlestown, Virginia, Feb. 14, 1831. Served in Virginia senate. Lt. and Capt. Co. G, 2nd Virginia, 1861. Capt. AAAIG to Taliaferro, Nov.–Dec. 1862. Same to Trimble and Colston, early 1863. Maj. 2nd Virginia, Apr. 29, 1863, but backdated to Sept. 16, 1862. Maj. AAAIG to Ed. Johnson, June 1863. Maj. AAIG to Johnson, Jan. 6, 1864. Maj. AAIG to Gordon, 1864. Maj. AAIG to Early, Oct. 3, 1864. Paroled Apr. 21, 1865. d. Charlestown, Dec. 11, 1881. bur. Zion Episc. Churchyard, Shepherdstown, West Virginia.

Moore, J. Blue. Capt. AQM, Oct. 24, 1861, Asst. to army's Chief QM. Dropped Feb. 24, 1862, for failed bond, but reinstated Mar. 3. Maj. QM to J. E. Johnston, Nov. 26, 1862. Maj. QM to Hood, Sept. 1864, and back to Johnston in Mar. 1865. d. Columbus, Georgia, Nov. 7, 1867. bur. Linwood Cem., in unmarked grave.

Moore, James W. b. Feb. 2, 1827. Pvt. Co. I, 49th Georgia. Capt. ACS, 49th Georgia, Mar. 22, 1862. Capt. ACS to Thomas by 1864. Dates of service unclear.

Moore, Rittenhouse. b. Greensboro, Alabama, June 27, 1844. att. Southern Univ. and UAla. Served in 5th Alabama. VADC to O'Neal's Bgd. at Chancellorsville. Cadet, June 6, 1863, at Selma Arsenal. Cadet and Asst. OO to Taylor, Jan. 17, 1865. Took Oath at Citronelle, Alabama, May 4, 1865. m. Hattie Beverly Randolph, 1866. Businessman at Mobile. Alive 1911. Son of Sydenham Moore, Col. of the 11th Alabama.

Moore, Samuel H. b. in Alabama. att. Yorkville (S.C.) Military Academy. Student at Huntsville, Alabama. Pvt. Co. I, 4th Alabama, Apr. 26, 1861. Volunteered on staff of Col. Evander Law, June 1862. Adjt. 26th

Alabama, June 3, 1862. Lt. AAAIG to O'Neal's Bgd., Apr.–July 1863. Went west with the 26th. POW near Atlanta, July 20, 1864. Paroled Meridian, Mississippi, May 12, 1865.

Moore, Samuel Johnston Cramer. b. Charlestown, Virginia, June 26, 1826. Lt. and Capt. Co. I, 2nd Virginia, 1861. WIA at Kernstown and Brawner's Farm. Capt. AAG to J. R. Jones, Oct. 14, 1862. Capt. AAG to J. M. Jones, about May 1863. Capt. AAG to B. T. Johnson, July 1863. Back with J. M. Jones in autumn 1863. Capt. AAG to Early, date unknown. WIA May 5, 1864, at the Wilderness. Lawyer and judge in Clarke Co., Virginia. Mayor of Berryville. d. there Dec. 19, 1908. bur. Greenhill Cem. Moore's extensive papers are in the Southern Historical Collection, UNC.

Moore, Thomas. b. in Virginia, July 8, 1819. Lawyer in Fairfax Co. Capt. AQM, Dec. 12, 1862. Became army's Chief IFT, date uncertain. Appx. Served in Virginia legislature postwar. d. June 17, 1899. bur. Fairfax Cem.

Moore, Thomas Jefferson. b. Apr. 30, 1840. att. UVA. From Mecklenburg Co., North Carolina. Pvt. Co. B, 1st North Carolina (Bethel), July 1, 1861. VADC to D. H. Hill, May–June 1862. Lt. OO to Hill, June 12, 1862. Resigned Sept. 9, 1862. Lt. Co. C, 33rd North Carolina, 1862–1863. Adjt. 4th North Carolina Cavy. att. Univ. of New York for medical instruction. Physician in New York, at Charlotte, North Carolina, and at Richmond, Virginia. d. Feb. 24, 1898. bur. Hollywood Cem., Richmond.

Moore, W. G. Capt. AAIG to McComb. No other record. Possibly confused with some other officer.

Moore, William F. Capt. AQM, 51st Virginia, Nov. 1, 1862. Capt. AQM in Eastern Tennessee, Dec. 10, 1863. Capt. AQM to Wharton, autumn 1864.

Moragne, William Caine. b. Mar. 15, 1818. m. Emma Butler, 1856. Lawyer at Edgefield C.H., South Carolina. Col. AAG to Bonham in 1861. Rank probably in South Carolina forces, rather than Confederate. Resigned before First Manassas, but was with Bonham in Virginia before that. Col. 19th South Carolina. d. October 5, 1862. bur. Willowbrook Cem., Edgefield Co.

Morey, John Blatchford. b. Jan. 21, 1823. Merchant at Jackson, Mississippi. Maj. QM to French, Nov. 9, 1861. Served with French into 1865. Paroled May 14, 1865, at Jackson. d. New Orleans, Louisiana, Apr. 3, 1872, of congestive chill. bur. Canton Cem., in Mississippi.

Morfit, Clarence. b. Washington, D.C., May 16, 1828. m. Annie Elise Laverty, 1860. A resident of Baltimore, Maryland. Capt. AQM to J. H. Winder, Apr. 29, 1862. Specific duties were to keep charge of the effects of dead soldiers and the money of POWs. Paroled May 24, 1865, at Raleigh, North Carolina. Brother of Mason Morfit (see below).

Morfit, Mason. b. Washington, D.C., May 2, 1836. A Baltimore, Maryland, lawyer. Capt. AQM, Jan. 5, 1862, at Richmond, Virginia. Maj. QM, Nov. 26, 1862. Managed railroad transportation from Richmond, Petersburg, and Wilmington. Maj. QM at Danville prisons, Mar. 6, 1864. Maj. QM at Salisbury prisons, Oct. 12, 1864. Paroled Apr. 26, 1865, on staff of B. T. Johnson. Lived postwar at Baltimore. d. Webster Groves, Missouri, Feb. 22, 1921, while visiting his son. bur. St. Louis.

Morgan, Charles Stephen, Jr. b. Richmond, Virginia, Dec. 6, 1834. att. USMA. Morgan's father ran the Virginia state penitentiary. Adjt. 25th Virginia. Lt. AAAIG to Imboden, Apr. 20, 1863. Capt. AAG to Imboden, Feb. 19, 1864. Capt. AAG to Lomax, Dec. 21, 1864. Capt. AAG to Wickham's Bgd., Jan. 27, 1865. Paroled May 16, 1865. d. Baltimore, Maryland, Nov. 25, 1907. bur. Hollywood Cem., Richmond.

Morgan, Jeremiah Brown. b. Nov. 8, 1835. Lawyer in Troup Co., Georgia. Lt. Co. B, 4th Georgia, Apr. 27, 1861. Capt. ACS, 4th

Georgia, Oct. 4, 1861. Resigned June 13, 1862. Maj. CS to Colquitt, Nov. 11, 1862. Paroled Apr. 26, 1865. Morgan's wife was captain of the "Nancy Harts," a wartime company of women organized at LaGrange, Georgia. Store clerk and insurance agent there. d. near Atlanta, June 24, 1884. bur. Hillview Cem., LaGrange. Always used "Jerry" instead of Jeremiah.

Morgan, John L. A resident of Fulton Co., Georgia. Adjt. 2nd Virginia, Apr. 17, 1861. Capt. AQM, 2nd Virginia, May 1, 1861. Capt. AQM to E. K. Smith, Oct. 1, 1861. Maj. QM to Howell Cobb, Oct. 1863. Paroled June 8, 1865, at Macon, Georgia. d. soon after the war.

Morgan, Lewis Allen. b. near Marion, Alabama. Merchant at Uniontown. Pvt. Co. D, 4th Alabama, Apr. 25, 1861. To Lt., Mar. 24, 1863. Lt. AAAIG or acting ADC (probably both) for the brigade, ca. Apr. 1864 to Appx. So staff of W. F. Perry. Merchant and cotton buyer in Alabama. Mayor of Uniontown. d. there Mar. 24, 1915, age 77.

Morgan, Richard Curd. b. Fayette Co., Kentucky, Sept. 13, 1836. att. KMI. VADC to Breckinridge, early 1862. Capt. AAG to his brother-in-law Gen. A. P. Hill, Mar. 23, 1862. Maj. AAG to Hill, May 26, 1862. Relieved Mar. 28, 1863. Col. 2nd Special Bn. Kentucky Cavy. Maj. AAG to his brother Gen. J. H. Morgan, Aug. 20, 1864. POW Dec. 12, 1864, while commanding Duke's Bgd. Hemp manufacturer at Lexington. d. September 28, 1918. bur. Lexington Cem. Gen. Pender called Morgan "weak," and Gen. Hill was glad to be rid of him in 1863.

Morril, William H. Capt. Co. E, 27th North Carolina, Apr. 20, 1861. Capt. ACS, 27th North Carolina, Nov. 2, 1861. Capt. ACS to Cooke, July 16, 1863. d. ca. 1887 in Pitt Co.

Morris, Charles. b. Hanover Co., Virginia, Apr. 27, 1826. att. UVA. Commonwealth's attorney in Hanover Co., and law professor at Wm. & Mary Coll. Capt. AQM, July 19, 1861. Probably staff of Magruder temporarily in

1862. Maj. QM, Feb. 15, 1865. Stationed in Richmond, where he paid damage claims against CSA government. Professor of Greek at Randolph Macon Coll., and taught English at UGA. d. Athens, Georgia, May 3, 1893.

Morris, Isaac E. A resident of Sugar Hill, North Carolina. Lt. Co. K, 22nd North Carolina, June 5, 1861. Lt. acting AQM to Pettigrew, spring 1862. Maj. QM to Pettigrew, Apr. 17, 1862. Resigned June 19, 1862, to take care of his family, and because he was more than 35 years old.

Morris, John. b. in Ireland. A 34-year-old grocer at Dalton, Georgia, in 1860. Lt. Co. B, Phillips Legion, June 11, 1861. Lt. AAIG to Wofford, date unknown. MWIA at Chancellorsville. d. Richmond, Virginia, May 25, 1863.

Morris, John, Jr. b. Goochland Co., Virginia, Nov. 1837. att. Hampden Sidney and UVA. Sgt. Goochland Arty. POW at Ft. Donelson. Lt. OO, Feb. 10, 1863, to report to Richmond. Lt. OO to R. L. Walker's Bn. Arty., Mar. 5, 1863. Lt. OO to Pegram's Bn. Arty., summer 1863. KIA at Gettysburg, July 1, 1863.

Morris, Walter Hampden Pleasants. b. in Virginia. Pvt. Co. F, 21st Virginia, Apr. 21–May 11, 1861. Sgt. Hampden (Va.) Arty., May 11, 1861. Pvt. 2nd Co. Richmond (Va.) Howitzers, May 10, 1862. Lt. acting OO to W. E. Jones, Jan.–Feb. 1863. No further record until paroled at Appx. as Lt. ADC to R. L. Walker. Date of commission unclear. Merchant, secretary, and treasurer at Richmond postwar. d. there Mar. 9, 1910, age 70. bur. Hollywood Cem.

Morris, William. b. Apr. 1, 1837. att. UVA. Served in Shield's Co. Virginia Arty. VADC to J. R. Anderson, Dec. 1861 until MWIA at Gaines's Mill, June 27, 1862. d. October 16, 1862.

Morrison, James Horace. b. Mar. 25, 1839. From Lawrenceville, Virginia. att. VMI. Later Asst. professor of tactics at UALA.

Drillmaster with heavy artillery at Pensacola, Florida, 1861. Lt. PAVA., May 1, 1861, and AAAG to Pemberton. Lt. ADC to Pemberton, Oct. 24, 1861. POW at Vicksburg. Out of commission May 18, 1864, upon Pemberton's resignation. Acting Adjt. at VMI, 1864. Taught there 1866–1889, and later taught at Luray, Virginia. d. there Mar. 20, 1910.

Morrison, Joseph Graham. b. Lincoln Co., North Carolina, June 1, 1842. att. VMI. Lt. ADC to his brother-in-law, T. J. Jackson, July 23, 1862. Lt. VADC to Ramseur, July 1863. Adjt. 57th North Carolina, Sept. 1863. WIA at Second Drewry's Bluff. Capt. Co. F, 57th North Carolina, by 1865. Lost leg around Petersburg. Cotton mill operator and member of North Carolina state legislature, postwar. d. at the home of Mrs. T. J. Jackson in Charlotte, Apr. 11, 1906. bur. Macpleah Presby. Church Cem., Lincoln Co.

Morrison, Robert Hall, Jr. b. Lincoln Co., North Carolina, Nov. 27, 1843. Brother of J. G. Morrison (see above). Brother-in-law of Gens. T. J. Jackson, D. H. Hill, and Rufus Barringer. Lt. ADC to Hill, Oct. 20, 1862. Acting ADC to Barringer, 1864. POW at Fussell's Mill, Aug. 15, 1864. Released from prison June 14, 1865. A physician. d. Aug. 7, 1922.

Morrison, Robert John. b. Brunswick Co., Virginia, Nov. 17, 1825. att. UVA. Professor at Wm. & Mary and an inventor. m. Catharine Heth Harrison, 1854. Capt. AQM, June 29, 1861, at Williamsburg, Virginia. Capt. OO at Williamsburg, July 23, 1861. d. there Oct. 31, 1861, of typhoid fever.

Morriss, Robert Fielding. b. Feb. 15, 1831. att. VMI. From Amherst Co. and Richmond, Virginia. VADC to Longstreet. Accidentally shot in the knee "in a military row" in Richmond. VADC to G. W. Smith, 1863, performing engineer duty. Postwar civil and mining engineer. d. Richmond, Mar. 25, 1904. bur. Hollywood Cem.

Morrow, James. Maj. QM to Ripley, June 2, 1862. Resigned July 25, 1862. A resident of Charleston, South Carolina. Possibly the James Morrow who was a prominent South Carolina physician and whose dates of life were 1820–1865.

Morrow, John. VADC to Jubal Early at the Battle of Williamsburg. "Young." Probably confounded with John S. Morson.

Morson, John Scott. b. Fredericksburg, Virginia, Jan. 17, 1842. att. VMI. VADC to Early, 1861–1862. QM clerk in summer 1863. Pvt. Co. E, 3rd Virginia LDT, June 16–Sept. 18, 1863. Lt. Asst. EO to Pickett, Sept. 1863–Jan. 1864. Lt. Co. F, 1st C.S. Engineers, Mar. 29, 1864. Retired to Invalid Corps, Oct. 31, 1864, with poor health. Paroled Fairfax Co., May 19, 1865. d. in Kentucky, May 27, 1886. bur. Hollywood Cem., Richmond.

Morton, Alexander C. A Mexican War veteran. Pvt. Co. G, 20th Georgia, July 15, 1861. Capt. AQM, 20th Georgia, June 24, 1862. Capt. AQM to Benning, Sept. 20, 1864. Appx.

Morton, George C. Capt. ACS, First Corps, Mar. 1865. No other record.

Morton, Richard. b. near Fredericksburg, Virginia, 1834. att. Hampden Sidney Coll. m. Mary Green. Civil engineer in Brazil and in Virginia. Lt. EO on peninsula, 1861. Was Asst. Supt. of Yorktown fortifications. Capt. EO to Magruder, Nov. 1861. Record fuzzy until appointed Maj. with Nitre & Mining Bureau, Dec. 1863. Later promoted to Lt. Col., and became chief of that bureau, Feb. 1865. Moved to Baltimore, Maryland, in 1869. Sold engineering and railroad supplies. d. there June 25, 1898. bur. St. Thomas's Church Cem., Owings Mills, Maryland.

Morton, Tazewell S. b. Richmond, Virginia, Oct. 14, 1843. Pvt. Co. D, 1st Virginia, Apr. 21, 1861, age 17, a clerk. WIA at Fredericksburg. WIA and POW at Gettysburg. Lt. Drillmaster, Feb. 1, 1864. Lt. ADC to Moore, by Jan. 1865. Paroled May 1865.

m. Maggie S. Bridges, 1868. A nurseryman in Prince Edward Co. in 1870. Later a civil engineer. Moved to Birmingham, Alabama, 1887. Supt. of city's streetcar lines. d. there Oct. 16, 1895. bur. Elmwood Cem.

Moses, Raphael Jacob. b. Charleston, South Carolina, Jan. 20, 1812. Merchant in South Carolina and Florida. Moved to Columbus, Georgia, in 1849, and pioneered Georgia peaches. Maj. CS to Toombs, July 19, 1861. Maj. acting CS to D. R. Jones, autumn 1862. Maj. CS to Longstreet, Oct. 12, 1862. Maj. Chief Commissary for Georgia, Sept. 7, 1864. Postwar Georgia legislator. d. Brussels, Belgium, Oct. 13, 1893. bur. Columbus, Georgia. A "cordial, jolly old soul," wrote one female diarist. Another called him "a waggish sort of fellow" and "so comical looking that anything he said sounded ridiculous."

Moss, Alfred. b. in Virginia, ca. 1816. Clerk of Fairfax Co. court in 1860. Member of state legislature and delegate to Virginia's Secession Convention. VADC to Bonham at First Manassas. VADC to Ewell, 1862. POW in summer 1862. Sent to Old Capitol Prison and contracted jaundice. d. Richmond, Virginia, Oct. 5, 1862.

Moss, Charles. A resident of Tensas Parish, Louisiana. Pvt. Co. A, 14th Louisiana, June 27, 1861. Detailed as clerk at regimental QM office, July 1862–Oct. 1863. QM Sgt. 14th Louisiana, Aug. 1, 1863. Lt. ADC to York, date not found. Paroled June 6, 1865, at Monroe, Louisiana.

Motley, John. b. in Virginia. A 33-year-old farmer in King and Queen Co., in 1860. Pvt. Co. K, 34th Virginia, Mar. 17, 1862. Capt. AQM, Oct. 14, 1862. On duty at Gordonsville, Virginia, through 1865. Lawyer at Williamsburg, Virginia, in 1870.

Mott, John R. b. Macon, Georgia, Sept. 2, 1841. att. GMI. Lived at Columbus prewar. Lt. Co. C, 17th Georgia, Aug. 14, 1861. Adjt. 17th Georgia, Aug. 19, 1861. Lt. AAAG to Benning, Sept. 1862 until appointed Lt. ADC to Benning, Jan. 17, 1863. Postwar book-keeper. d. Columbus, Georgia, Jan. 19, 1873. bur. Linwood Cem.

Munford, Robert Beverly. b. Hanover Co., Virginia, July 25, 1841. Served in Co. G, 12th Virginia, and as QM Sgt. of the Letcher (Va.) Arty. Capt. AQM, Pegram's Bn. Arty., June 5, 1863. Served into 1865. A grocer after the war. d. October 1, 1900. bur. Hollywood Cem., Richmond.

Munford, William. b. Richmond, Virginia, Aug. 16, 1829. att. UVA. Officer in Richmond Light Infantry Blues and 1st Virginia pre-war. Brother of Col. Thomas T. Munford. Asst. Secretary of the Commonwealth. Lt. Col. 17th Virginia, June 13, 1861. Lt. Col. 24th Virginia, 1861. Dropped Apr. 1862. VADC to Longstreet at Gaines's Mill. Pvt. Otey (Va.) Btty., late in the war. Episc. minister in Texas, Tennessee, and Louisiana. d. Annapolis, Maryland, Mar. 8, 1904. bur. Hollywood Cem., Richmond.

Murchison, David Reid. b. Cumberland Co., North Carolina, Dec. 5, 1837. Brother of Col. Kenneth Murchison, 54th North Carolina. Lt. and Capt. Co. C, 7th North Carolina, 1861. Capt. AQM, 54th North Carolina, Jan. 24, 1863. Tax collector in North Carolina, Aug. 1864. Capt. AQM to Lewis, Feb. 27, 1865. Appx. d. Feb. 28, 1882. bur. Oakdale Cem., Wilmington.

Murkland, John McGregor. b. in Santo Domingo, Dec. 1, 1838. att. Hampden Sidney. Pvt. Co. E, 12th Virginia, June–Nov. 1861. Capt. ACS, Sept. 28, 1863. Served as commissary for Jackson Hospital in Richmond. d. Apr. 8, 1864, of tuberculosis. bur. Farmville, Virginia.

Murphy, James P. b. in Ireland. A 24-year-old carpenter at New Orleans in 1860. Pvt. Co. C, 2nd Louisiana, May 11, 1861. De-tached as acting regimental commissary, Nov. 1861–1863. Capt. ACS, 2nd Louisiana, Jan. 19, 1863. Capt. ACS to Stafford, July 13, 1863. Possibly staff of York, 1864. Capt. ACS

to John B. Gordon, by Oct. 1864. Capt. ACS to R. H. Anderson, by Nov. 1864. Appx.

Murray, Edward. b. in Maryland, Aug. 12, 1819. att. USMA. Capt. U.S. Inf., 1841–1855. Farmer in Fauquier Co., Virginia, 1855–1861. Capt. Co. H, 49th Virginia. To Lt. Col., July 17, 1861. Dropped May 1, 1862. Lt. Col. AAIG to R. E. Lee, Dec. 30, 1862. Relieved Dec. 3, 1864. Lt. Col. AAIG at Lynchburg, Virginia, Jan. 1865. d. West River, Maryland, July 3, 1874. bur. Anne Arundel Co., Maryland.

Murray, J. H. VADC to Hood during Seven Days Campaign.

Muse, James H. b. Westmoreland Co., Virginia, 1833. A hotel keeper in Essex Co. Pvt. Co. F, 55th Virginia, May 21, 1861. Capt. ACS, 55th Virginia, Sept. 19, 1861. Capt. ACS to Heth, July 31, 1863. Held that post through late 1864, at least. Married twice. d. Essex Co., Sept. 18, 1895. bur. family cem. near Cedar Fork.

Myer, F. F. Capt. ACS, Aug. 15, 1863. Served at Jackson Hospital in Richmond, Virginia. Paroled at Burkeville, Apr. 28, 1865.

Myers, Abraham Charles. b. Georgetown, South Carolina, May 1811. att. USMA. Held a staff position in U.S. Army, 1833–1861. Veteran of Mexican War and Seminole War. m. Marian Twiggs, daughter of famous gen-eral. Lt. Col. QM, CS, Mar. 16, 1861. Acting QM Gen. of the CSA by Mar. 25, 1861. Apptd. QM Gen., Dec. 1861. Col. QM, Feb. 15, 1862. Replaced Aug. 7, 1863. Lived remainder of war in retirement in Georgia. Lived postwar at Lake Roland, Maryland. d. Washington, D.C., June 20, 1889.

Myers, Charles Dominicy. b. New York City, Nov. 10, 1834. Merchant at Wilming-ton, North Carolina. m. Lossie DeRosset. Adjt. 18th North Carolina, 1861. Lt. ADC to French, May 12, 1862. Capt. AAG to French, Nov. 5, 1862. Resigned Mar. 16, 1864. d. Oct. 11, 1892. bur. Oakdale Cem., Wilmington.

Myers, Edmund Trowbridge Dana. b. Petersburg, Virginia, July 13, 1830. Civil engineer for various railroads, mostly in Virginia and around Washington, D.C. Lt. EO, PAVa., May 17, 1861. Worked on defenses at Jamestown Island. Capt. EO, PAVa., May 23, 1861. Capt. EO to Magruder. Capt. EO, PACS, Feb. 15, 1862. Capt. Chief Engineer for Piedmont Railroad, at Danville, by Jan. 1863. Maj. EO, Oct. 19, 1864, on same duty. Postwar president of Richmond, Fredericksburg, and Potomac Railroad. d. Richmond, May 12, 1905. bur. Hollywood Cem. "A very big, a very brainy and a very practical man."

Myers, John Austin. b. in South Carolina, Oct. 5, 1833. att. USMA and Harvard. Sgt. Co. C, 2nd South Carolina, Apr. 8, 1861. Later a Pvt. in Co. A, 2nd South Carolina. Detached for duty with Kershaw, Dec. 31, 1861. Lt. OO to Kershaw, Aug. 1, 1862. Lt. OO to Conner and Goggin, 1864. Probably continued as Lt. OO to Kennedy, late in 1864. Alive in Richland Co., South Carolina, in 1908.

Myers, William Barksdale. b. Dec. 4, 1839. Lt. EO in PAVa., 1861. Lt. VADC to Randolph, Feb. 16–Mar. 18, 1862. Capt. AAG to Loring, May 15, 1862. Maj. AAG to Loring, Oct. 14, 1862. Maj. AAIG to Sam. Jones, Dec. 10, 1862. Maj. AAG to John B. Gordon, Apr. 8, 1863. Appx. m. Martha W. Paul, 1864. d. Nov. 5, 1873. bur. Hollywood Cem. ". . . was more than ordinarily neat in his personal appearance."

Nance, William Frederick. b. in South Carolina, Jan. 7, 1836. att. SCMA. Druggist in Newberry Co. and editor of local newspaper. Maj. AAG to Bonham, Sept. 23, 1861. Resigned Nov. 28, 1861. Apptd. to staff of Maxcy Gregg, but declined. VADC with ANVa. in summer 1862. Capt. AAG to Gist, Aug. 8, 1862. Later staff of N. G. Evans, and Ripley. Newberry insurance agent, alive 1880. bur. Rosemont Cem.

Nash, Benjamin Hatcher. b. Powhatan Co., Virginia, Apr. 7, 1835. att. UVa. Manchester lawyer and member of state senate. Capt. Co. B, 41st Virginia, May 29, 1861. Dropped at reorganization, May 1862. Adjt. 41st Virginia, Apr. 8, 1863. Lt. AAAG to Weisiger, May 1864. Resigned Jan. 14, 1865. Chesterfield Co. Commonwealth's attorney and insurance company president. d. Feb. 14, 1895. bur. Hollywood Cem.

Nash, Frederick Kollock. b. Hillsborough, North Carolina, July 22, 1839. att. UNC. A lawyer. Pvt. Co. G, 27th North Carolina, Feb. 8, 1863. Acting AAIG to Kirkland, Oct. 1863 until apptd. Capt. AAIG to Kirkland, Feb. 20, 1864. Capt. AAIG to MacRae. WIA at Reams's Station. Capt. AAG to Barton, Nov. 15, 1864. WIA Apr. 6, 1865, and right leg amputated. City treasurer of Charlotte, North Carolina, 1872–1901. d. Feb. 16, 1915.

Nash, Joseph van Holt. b. in Virginia, July 8, 1834. att. UVA. A Surry Co. farmer. Pvt. Co. B, 13th Virginia Cavy. Detached on engineer duty, 1862. Pvt. acting OO to Colston, Apr. 1862. Adjt. 13th Virginia Cavy., Aug. 16, 1862. Capt. AAG to W. H. F. Lee, Nov. 2, 1863. Same to Chambliss, probably in Dec. 1863, and to Beale in 1865. Possibly served in Custer's 7th U.S. Cavy. in the West, under an assumed name. Said to have been the closest friend of Capt. Frederick Benteen of Little Big Horn notoriety. Published the standard register of UVa. alumni. d. Augusta, Georgia, Nov. 17, 1900.

Nash, Thomas, Jr. b. Norfolk, Virginia, Mar. 2, 1836. Lt. Norfolk Light Arty. Blues, June 5, 1861. Lt. of Arty., May 19, 1862, to report to Col. Gorgas. Lt. OO to report to G. W. Smith, Sept. 17, 1862. Lt. AAAG to Davidson, Oct. 10, 1862. On duty at Staunton, Virginia, July 1863. Lt. of Arty., to report to Beauregard in South Carolina, Sept. 10, 1863. Joined Beauregard in Virginia, May 1864, as Lt. OO. Lt. OO at Cape Fear defenses, Dec. 1864. Paroled Apr. 26, 1865. d. in Colorado, Oct. 16, 1893. bur. Elmwood Cem., Norfolk.

Neal, John B. B. A resident of Gates Co.,

North Carolina. Lt. Co. I, 1st North Caro-
lina Cavy., Aug. 12, 1861, age 21. Capt. AQM,
1st North Carolina Cavy., Apr. 15, 1862.
Dropped Apr. 16, 1863, for failing bond.
Maj. QM to Baker, July 25, 1863. Maj. QM to
James B. Gordon, Sept. 1863. Maj. QM to
Barringer, May 1864, through end of war.
Probably John Burges Baker Neal, 1839–
1912, bur. Old Trinity Cem., Scotland Neck,
North Carolina.

Neal, Samuel T. Lt. Co. F, 10th Georgia,
May 1, 1861. Capt. AQM, 10th Georgia,
Oct. 2, 1861. Capt. acting AQM to Simms,
Oct. 9, 1864, into 1865.

Neale, ——. VADC to T. J. Jackson, from
about Sept. 4 until Sept. 23, 1862. This was
one of Jackson's cousins and could be one
of several men. The top candidates are
C. A. Neale (killed Mar. 30, 1863, in service
with the 8th Virginia Cavy.); George N.
Neale (also of the 8th Virginia Cavy.); and
Thomas Neale (Co. G, 20th Virginia Cavy.).

Neary, William Joshua. A 28-year-old mer-
chant in Green Co., Georgia, in 1860. Sgt.
Co. K, 44th Georgia, Mar. 4, 1862. Capt.
AQM, 44th Georgia, May 12, 1862. Capt.
AQM to Rodes, Sept. 15, 1864. Subsequently
staff of Ramseur, and then Grimes. Capt.
AQM to Cook, Mar. 22, 1865. Appx. Farmer
at Penfield, Georgia, in 1870. bur. Mount
Gilead Cem., Hancock Co.

Nelson, George Washington, Jr. b. Hanover
Co., Virginia, May 27, 1840. att. UVA. Lived
in Clarke Co., and in Caroline Co., where
he taught school. Sgt. and Capt., Hanover
Arty., 1861–1862. Capt. AAIG to Pendleton,
Jan. 14, 1863. Inspector of Bttys. in First
Corps and Reserve Arty. POW at Millwood,
Oct. 26, 1863. Episc. clergyman in Chatham,
Lexington, Wytheville, and Warrenton, Vir-
ginia. d. May 30, 1903. bur. Warrenton City
Cem.

Nelson, Hugh Mortimer. b. Hanover Co.,
Virginia, Oct. 20, 1811. att. UVA. Ran a
school in Charles City Co., was a lawyer at
Baltimore, Maryland, and spent part of the
1840s in Paris. m. Maria Adelaide Holker.
Capt. Co. D, 6th Virginia Cavy. Dropped
Apr. 20, 1862. Lt. ADC to Ewell, May 4, 1862.
WIA slightly at Gaines's Mill. d. Albemarle
Co., Aug. 6, 1862, of typhoid fever. bur. Old
Chapel, Clarke Co., Virginia. "As fine, brave
an old fellow as ever lived."

Nelson, Kinloch. b. Clarke Co., Virginia,
Nov. 2, 1839. att. UVA. Pvt. Co. D, 2nd Virginia Cavy. Pvt. 1st Co. Rockbridge (Va.)
Arty. WIA in foot at Kernstown, Mar. 23,
1862. Served in Kemper's (Va.) Btty., June
1862. Pvt. Co. D, 6th Virginia Cavy., Feb. 27,
1863. Lt. OO, Mar. 20, 1863, serving as such
with Kemper by June 1863. Lt. OO to W. R.
Terry. Appx. Episc. rector in Fauquier Co.
and Richmond. Professor at Episc. Theological Seminary, 1876–1894. d. Alexandria,
Virginia, Oct. 25, 1894.

Nelson, Samuel Warren. b. in South Caro-
lina, Nov. 6, 1831. att. South Carolina Coll.
Wealthy prewar farmer in Clarendon Co.
Served in state legislature and on the staff
of Governor Manning. VADC to Bonham at
First Manassas. Adjt. 7th Bn. South Caro-
lina, Oct. 2, 1862. Retired Dec. 12, 1864.
Resumed farming in Clarendon Co. d. near
Summerton, Mar. 18, 1908. bur. there.

Nelson, William Cowper. b. Holly Springs,
Mississippi, July 7, 1841. Lowndes Co.
farmer prewar and postwar. Pvt. Co. D,
9th Mississippi, Mar. 27, 1861. Pvt. Co. G,
17th Mississippi, Dec. 20, 1861. Acting
OO to Posey, Jan. 1863. Lt. OO to Posey,
May 2, 1863. Lt. OO to Harris, Jan. 1864.
Appx. m. Mary Louise Armistead, 1867.
d. Louisville, Kentucky, July 2, 1904.

New, John Pollard Harrison. b. Louisville,
Kentucky, July 5, 1831. att. UMiss. and Har-
vard. Lawyer at Baton Rouge, Louisiana.
Lt. Co. B, 7th Louisiana, June 7, 1861. Adjt.
7th Louisiana. Capt. AAG to Hays, July 29,
1862. Maj. AAIG to Hays, Nov. 2, 1863. Maj.
AAIG to Early, May 15, 1864. Maj. AAIG to
Ramseur, late May 1864. Sent west to Kirby
Smith, Mar. 1865. Paroled May 4, 1865. New

Orleans law partner of Gen. Hays. d. there Jan. 17, 1879. bur. Metairie Cem. Almost never used the name Pollard, which he disliked.

Newman, Howard Walker. b. Knoxville, Tennessee, 1840. Cpl. Co. C, 1st Tennessee, Apr. 29, 1861. To Sgt., Aug. 1, 1861. Later Sgt. Maj. Capt. ACS, 1st Tennessee, July 24, 1862. Dropped in 1863 during staff purges. Capt. ACS to McComb, by Jan. 1865, likely earlier. Appx. Lawyer in Franklin Co. Moved to Georgia in 1877. d. about 1904 at Atlanta, Georgia.

Newman, John G. Capt. Co. F, 36th Virginia, June 10, 1861. Maj. CS to A. G. Jenkins, Aug. 7, 1862. Maj. CS to Wharton's Bgd., late summer 1864. Served in that role into 1865.

Newman, Reuben Manning. b. Orange Co., Virginia, Mar. 20, 1843. Pvt. Co. C, 13th Virginia, Apr. 17, 1861. Sgt. Co. A, 13th Virginia, May 1862. WIA at First Winchester and Gaines's Mill. Lt. ADC to Steuart, Oct. 27, 1864. Appx. m. Kate Randolph Taylor, 1871. d. Orange Co., Apr. 17, 1916. bur. Maplewood Cem.

Newman, Wilson Scott. b. Orange Co, Virginia, May 7, 1831. att. UVA. Lawyer in Orange Co. Pvt. Co. A, 13th Virginia, Apr. 17, 1861. To Lt., Apr. 23, 1862. WIA Aug. 27, 1862. Lt. AAAG to J. A. Walker, commanding brigade, Dec. 19, 1862, to about Mar. 1863. MWIA at Third Winchester. d. Sept. 27, 1864.

Nicholas, Robert Carter, IV. b. Buckingham Co., Virginia, Nov. 21, 1838. att. VMI and Hampden Sidney. Never married. Lt. Co. D, 56th Virginia, July 8, 1861. Capt. ACS, 56th Virginia, Oct. 2, 1861. Capt. acting ACS to R. B. Garnett, Jan.–Feb. 1863. Dropped in 1863. Capt. ACS in Buckingham Co., 1864. Paroled Apr. 18, 1865, in Richmond. Wholesale merchant at Richmond. d. White Sulphur Springs, West Virginia, July 7, 1881, in a railroad accident. bur. Hollywood Cem., Richmond.

Nicholas, Wilson Cary. b. Brooklyn Navy Yard, New York, Sept. 3, 1836. att. Oxford Coll. Farmer near Baltimore, Maryland. Worked for B&O Railroad. Capt. Co. G, 1st Maryland, May 22, 1861. Later a Drillmaster at Camp Lee, with rank of Lt., until Oct. 4, 1862. Capt. AAIG to Steuart, by Mar. 25, 1863. Capt. AAIG to Col. B. T. Johnson by June 1863. Lt. 1st Maryland Cavy. late in the war. WIA and POW at Rockville, July 13, 1864. Farmer at Owings Mills. d. 1908. bur. St. Thomas's Church Cem.

Nicholson, Edward Alston Thorne. b. May 6, 1843. att. UNC. Of Halifax Co., North Carolina. Lt. Co. E, 37th North Carolina. Lt. AAAIG to Lane, May 1863. Capt. AAIG to Lane, Nov. 2, 1863. Capt. AAIG to R. D. Johnston, Jan. 27, 1865. KIA at Fort Stedman, Mar. 23, 1865, "with the colors of one of his regiments far in advance of the line."

Nicolson, James Monroe. b. Middlesex Co., Virginia, 1820. Farmer and merchant there. Pvt. Co. E, 26th Virginia, May 28, 1861. Later to Lt., and then Capt. AQM, 26th Virginia, Nov. 8, 1863. Capt. AQM to Wise, Sept. 20, 1864. Appx. Resumed farming in Gloucester Co. and conducted business at Baltimore, Maryland. d. Gloucester Co., Feb. 9, 1901. bur. Abingdon Church.

Nisbet, Adam Ross. b. Lancaster Dist., South Carolina, ca. 1835. Merchant in Lincoln Co., North Carolina. Sgt. Co. E, 34th North Carolina, Sept. 11, 1861. Sgt. Maj. 34th North Carolina, Jan. 18, 1862. Capt. ACS, 34th North Carolina, May 31, 1862. Capt. ACS to Lane, July 30, 1863. Capt. ACS to Thomas, Mar. 6, 1865. Appx. Grocer and confectioner at Charlotte. d. Mar. 1888. bur. Elmwood Cem. Some sources spell his name Nesbet, but his tombstone is Nisbet.

Noble, Thomas Jefferson. b. Prince Edward Co., Virginia, Apr. 8, 1833. Lived in Powhatan Co. prewar. Pvt. Co. E, 4th Virginia Cavy., 1861. Courier for Gen. Sam. Jones. Lt. ADC to Jones, Nov. 2, 1861. Capt. AQM to Jones, Apr. 29, 1862. Failed bond and dropped, Oct. 25, 1862, but Maj. QM to

Jones, Nov. 4, 1862. Maj. QM to Howell Cobb, Sept. 23, 1863. Served with Longstreet in East Tennessee, Feb. 1864, duties uncertain. Maj. QM at Montgomery, Alabama, May 1864–1865. Commission merchant at Richmond. d. Jan. 20, 1892. bur. Hollywood Cem.

Noland, Burr Powell. b. Loudoun Co., Virginia, Oct. 20, 1818. m. Susan Chaplain Wilson, 1845. Capt. ACS, July 19, 1861. Maj. CS, Dec. 24, 1861. Chief Commissary for Virginia, stationed in Richmond, 1861–1865. Paroled Apr. 24, 1865, at Fairfax C.H. Lawyer at Middleburg. d. there Oct. 22, 1889. bur. Sharon Cem.

Noland, Callendar St. George. b. Loudoun Co., Virginia, Mar. 1816. Served in USN for about 20 years. Joined CSN during war. Lt. commanding river batteries on lower James River. Commanded two batteries in Richmond's defenses. Lt. Col. PACS in 1862. Sat on court-martial duty in Richmond, 1862–1865. "He makes the best President of a Court Martial I ever saw," wrote Col. Robert Ould. Farmer in Hanover Co. d. Ashland, Virginia, Sept. 24, 1878. bur. Airwell Cem. near Fork Church, in Hanover Co.

Noland, Richard William Noble. b. in Virginia, Feb. 24, 1822. att. UVA. Brother of B. P. Noland. Albemarle Co. farmer. Agent for Ordnance Dept. in 1861 and for Commissary Dept. in 1862. "On a mission to the South to buy up all the double-barreled shot-guns" in July 1861. Capt. ACS, Apr. 15, 1862. Maj. CS, Feb. 19, 1864, but failed confirmation. Reapptd. Mar. 4, 1865. Served entire time at Charlottesville. Farmer in Loudoun Co. d. Richmond, Nov. 30, 1886. bur. Sharon Cem., Middleburg.

Norris, Andrew M., Jr. b. in Georgia, ca. 1834. Lived prewar at Dalton. att. GMI. Pvt. Co. B, Phillips (Ga.) Legion, June 11, 1861. Later Commissary Sgt. Capt. ACS, Phillips Legion, Oct. 10, 1862. Capt. acting ACS to Wofford, Mar. 1863. Capt. ACS to Wofford, July 31, 1863. Admitted to hospital at Richmond, May 24, 1864, with gunshot wound. Dropped Aug. 1, 1864.

Norris, William. b. Dec. 6, 1820. att. Yale. From Baltimore, Maryland. On signal duty on peninsula in early 1862. VADC to Magruder, Dec. 1861–May 1862. Capt. SO to Magruder, May 29, 1862. Stationed in Richmond from July 31, 1862. Maj. SO, Oct. 8, 1862. Maj. and Chief of Signal Corps, Apr. 16, 1863. Lived at Reisterstown, Maryland. d. Dec. 29, 1896. An observer found Norris to be "a real crafty fellow with a horrid squint," while someone else reported Norris to be "somewhat deaf."

Northington, John Stuart. b. Mecklenburg Co., Virginia, 1836. Lived in Halifax Co., North Carolina, where he was mayor. Lt. Co. G, 12th North Carolina, Apr. 25, 1861. Possibly Lt. AAAIG to Iverson, winter of 1862–1863. Capt. AQM, 12th North Carolina, Nov. 14, 1863. Capt. AQM to R. D. Johnston, Sept. 15, 1864. Appx. Dry goods clerk and merchant at Petersburg, Virginia, postwar. d. Littleton, North Carolina, Feb. 1, 1908. bur. St. Mark's Episc. Churchyard, Halifax Co.

Norton, George Chester. b. Lawrenceville, Georgia, Sept. 15, 1836. Clerk and student at Rome, Georgia. Pvt. Co. A, 8th Georgia, May 18, 1861. Capt. ACS, 8th Georgia, July 3, 1861. Capt. ACS to G. T. Anderson, July 1, 1863. Capt. ACS to Young, Dec. 9, 1864, but order revoked in favor of "more important duty" never specified. Paroled May 10, 1865, at Albany, Georgia. Living at Louisville, Kentucky, in 1900. d. Dec. 22, 1915. bur. Cave Hill Cem.

Norwood, Thomas Hill. b. Richmond, Virginia, Aug. 18, 1842. att. UVA. Sgt. Co. G, 44th North Carolina, Apr. 3, 1862. Capt. Co. H, 44th North Carolina. Capt. AAAG to Kirkland, Aug. and Oct. 1863. WIA in left foot at Cold Harbor, June 2, 1864. Appx. Conducted a school at Richmond postwar.

d. in Botetourt Co., Virginia, Nov. 23, 1917. bur. Hollywood Cem., Richmond.

Norwood, Walter Nathaniel. b. in Alabama, Aug. 20, 1838. Moved to Texas in 1839. att. Baylor and Soule Univ. Sgt. Co. E, 5th Texas, July 19, 1861. WIA at Gaines's Mill. To Lt., July 24, 1862. WIA at Sharpsburg. Capt. AQM, 5th Texas, Jan. 1, 1863. Capt. AQM to Gregg, Sept. 15, 1864. Served with brigade into 1865. Cotton planter and fire chief. d. Jan. 8, 1902.

Norwood, William. b. Nov. 5, 1836. att. UVa. Lawyer at Richmond. Pvt. Co. F, 21st Virginia, Apr. 26–Sept. 11, 1861. Lt. ADC to J. R. Anderson, Sept. 11, 1861. Capt. AAG to Thomas, July 26, 1862. POW at North Anna, but escaped same day. Commission vacated July 14, 1864, by nonconfirmation. Reappt. July 18, 1864, to rank from June 16, 1864. POW Apr. 2, 1865. WIA three times. Teacher in Monroe Co., West Virginia. d. Richmond, Feb. 6, 1914. bur. Hollywood Cem.

Oates, Robert Marcus. b. Cleveland Co., North Carolina, Jan. 15, 1829. Grocer at Charlotte. Lt. Co. I, 37th North Carolina, Oct. 22, 1861. Capt. AQM, 37th North Carolina, Jan. 1, 1862. Resigned Sept. 25, 1862. Reapptd. to same position, Oct. 7, 1862. Capt. AQM to Pender, June 1, 1863. Capt. AQM to Wilcox, July 1863. Appx. Cotton merchant and grocer at Charlotte. d. there Dec. 22, 1897, of stomach cancer. bur. Elmwood Cem. His obituary said of Oates: "outspoken to the point of brusqueness, but he meant no offense and the public took none."

Oattis, Henry J. Pvt. Co. F, 61st Georgia, Sept. 23, 1861. To Sgt, and later Capt. AQM (Oct. 27, 1861) and ACS, 61st Georgia. Capt. AQM to C. A. Evans, Oct. 5, 1864. Served through 1864, at least. Dead by 1898.

Obenchain, William Alexander. b. Buchanan, Virginia, Apr. 27, 1841. att. VMI. Cadet CSA, July 19, 1861. On engineer duty in North Carolina, Sept. 1861–Sept.

1864. Lt. of Arty., CSA, Aug. 28, 1863. Lt. EO to Stevens, Sept. 1864. Capt. of Arty., PACS, Jan. 11, 1865. Paroled May 1, 1865, at Greensboro. Businessman at Dallas, Texas. Professor in Tennessee, and president of Ogden Coll. in Bowling Green, Kentucky. d. there Aug. 17, 1916.

O'Brien, Henry. An Englishman. Resigned his commission in the British Indian Army to join CSA. Lt. Drillmaster, Dec. 19, 1864. Lt. AAIG to Crutchfield's Arty. Bgd., Mar. 21, 1865. WIA and POW at Burkeville, Apr. 6, 1865.

O'Brien, John Francis. b. Philadelphia, Pennsylvania, Feb. 1841. Father commanded a battery at the Battle of Buena Vista. Lived at New Orleans and at Indianola, Texas. att. USMA. Lt. of Arty., CSA, on duty at Charleston Arsenal in 1861. Capt. AAG to C. S. Winder, Mar. 28, 1862. Capt. AAG to Beauregard, Nov. 12, 1862 (had been acting in that capacity for some weeks). Maj. AAG to Beauregard, May 27, 1863. Later Maj. AAG to J. H. Forney, Magruder, and E. K. Smith. Paroled June 1865 at Shreveport. Lived immediately postwar in West Indies. A Louisville, Kentucky, civil engineer. d. there Oct. 12, 1902.

Ochiltree, Thomas Peck. b. San Augustine, Texas, Oct. 25, 1839. A lawyer, with red hair and gray eyes. Lt. ADC to Sibley, July 9, 1861. Capt. AAG to Sibley, Feb. 21, 1862. VADC to Longstreet at Seven Pines and during Seven Days. VADC to Taylor at Battle of Berwick Bay. Capt. AAG to E. K. Smith, Nov. 19, 1863. Capt. AAG to Maxey, Jan. 25, 1864. Capt. AAG to G. J. Rains, Sept. 27, 1864, on torpedo service. POW at Sailor's Creek. USHR. d. at a hotel, Nov. 25, 1902. bur. Mt. Hope Cem., Hastings-on-Hudson, New York.

Oden, James Skinner. b. in Virginia, July 2, 1820. m. Julia A. Hood, 1856. Farmer in Loudoun Co. Pvt. Co. K, 6th Virginia Cavy., July 15, 1861. POW at Front Royal, May 30, 1862. Served as OO (volunteer?) to

R. B. Garnett, 1862. Also said to be staff of Hunton and of Micah Jenkins. Capt. AQM, Stuart Horse Arty., June 5, 1863. Land surveyor at Aldie, Virginia, postwar. Laid out the town of Waterford. Went blind postwar. d. near Aldie, between 1870 and 1898.

Old, George D. Capt. ACS, 61st Virginia, May 22, 1862. Capt. ACS to R. H. Anderson, Sept. 17, 1863. Capt. ACS to Mahone. Served into 1865.

Old, William Whitehurst. b. Princess Anne Co., Virginia, Nov. 17, 1840. att. J. B. Strange's military academy and UVA. Lt. Co. G, 59th Virginia. Lt. AAAG to Wise, Nov. 1861. Pvt. in 14th Virginia. WIA in shoulder, June 1, 1862, at Seven Pines. Capt. AQM, 20th Bn. Virginia Heavy Arty., Aug. 7, 1862. To report to ANVa., Apr. 28, 1863. Resigned Jan. 16, 1864. Lt. ADC to Ed. Johnson, Jan. 19, 1864. Lt. VADC to Early, May–Aug. 1864. Probably returned to duty with Johnson in AOT, Sept. 1864. WIA October 1864. Paroled Apr. 26, 1865. Lawyer at Norfolk, Virginia. d. there July 19, 1911.

Oliver, Saunders Day. b. Fleming Co., Kentucky, Aug. 6, 1826. Mexican War veteran. Capt. AQM to Magruder, Apr. 14, 1862. Maj. QM to Magruder, Sept. 30, 1862. Later a tax collector in Louisiana. Notary public at New Orleans, Louisiana, postwar. d. July 24, 1889.

Oliver, Thomas Parks. b. Elbert Co., Georgia, June 14, 1840. Raised at Banks, Georgia. Sgt. Co. A, 24th Georgia, Aug. 24, 1861. Later became Adjt. of regiment. Lt. AAAG to DuBose. Appx. Married twice. Lived in Gainesville and Athens postwar, a farmer. d. Dec. 7, 1907. bur. Oconee Hill Cem., Athens.

O'Neal, Edward Asbury, Jr. b. Florence, Alabama, Aug. 21, 1845. Son of the general. Lt. 4th Alabama Cavy. VADC to Rodes at Chancellorsville. Cadet CSA, Feb. 5, 1864. Military record is sketchy. Lawyer at Florence postwar. m. Mary Coffee, 1875. d. Feb. 13, 1876. bur. Florence Cem. "Pleas-

ant, handsome, and considered very bright by every one." O'Neal's wartime diary is at the Library of Congress.

Orgain, George Craig. b. Lunenburg Co., Virginia, Nov. 6, 1838. att. VMI and UVA. A lawyer. Capt. Co. B, 20th Virginia, May 21, 1861. Capt. AQM, Oct. 2, 1862, assigned to duty at Danville. Capt. AQM in Richmond, Oct. 22, 1863. Capt. AQM to Crutchfield's Arty. Bgd., Mar. 21, 1865. Paroled Apr. 22, 1865, at Burkeville. Judge and commonwealth's attorney for Lunenburg Co. d. there June 28, 1906.

Orme, Richard McAllister, Jr. b. Harrisburg, Pennsylvania, Sept. 19, 1829. Newspaperman at Milledgeville, Georgia, pre- and postwar. Capt. AQM, 3rd Bn. Georgia, July 1, 1862. Maj. QM to Stevenson, Nov. 7, 1862. POW at Vicksburg. Maj. QM to Grimes, June 15, 1864. Maj. QM for hospitals at Albany and Americus, Georgia, by Dec. 1864. d. Birmingham, Alabama, Apr. 1873. There is a slight chance that the staff officer was simply Richard Orme, with different biographical details, but this is believed to be a correct identification.

Orr, John Mercer. b. Feb. 8, 1820. att. UPenn. Capt. ACS, 8th Virginia. Capt. ACS to N. G. Evans, Oct. 1861. Capt. ACS at Leesburg, and at Millborough Depot, early 1862. Capt. ACS to Heth, Aug. 1862–Mar. 1863. Capt. ACS at Greeneville, Tennessee, Apr. 1863. Served in Tennessee into 1865. Mayor of Leesburg postwar. d. there Jan. 11, 1905. bur. Union Cem.

Osborne, Nathaniel M., Jr. b. ca. 1842. Student at Petersburg, Virginia. Pvt. Co. E, 12th Virginia, May 1, 1861. Discharged Feb. 27, 1863. Lt. OO to Carter's Bn. Arty., ca. Mar. 1863. WIA at Chancellorsville. Lt. OO with Cutshaw's Bn. Arty. by Dec. 1864. Lived postwar at Norfolk. Alive 1889.

Osborne, Robert Cryer. b. Petersburg, Virginia, Sept. 30, 1838. att. UVA. and Hampden Sidney. A clerk at Petersburg. Pvt. Co. E, 12th Virginia, May 20, 1861. Later QM

Sgt., and then Capt. AQM for regiment, from Aug. 6, 1863. Capt. AQM to Mahone, Sept. 15, 1864. Paroled Apr. 1865, at Richmond. Tobacco merchant at Petersburg. d. there June 30, 1903. bur. Blandford Cem.

Otey, George Gaston. b. May 25, 1834. att. VMI and UVA. Merchant at Richmond, and prewar Adjt. of 1st Virginia. Lt. OO to Magruder, June 20, 1861. Capt. Otey (Va.) Btty., Mar. 14, 1862. MWIA at Lewisburg, May 23, 1862. d. Lynchburg, Virginia, Oct. 21, 1862. bur. Spring Hill Cem. Brother of Col. Kirkwood Otey and several other CSA officers.

Otey, John Marshall Warwick. b. Lynchburg, Virginia, Aug. 5, 1839. Brother of Capt. G. G. Otey. A broker. Possibly staff of Cocke, 1861. Lt. PAVa., May 3, 1861. Lt. AAG to Beauregard, June 1861. Capt. AAG to Beauregard, May 1, 1862. Capt. AAG to Bragg, July 17, 1862, before returning to Beauregard in October. Lt. Col. AAG to Beauregard, June 4, 1864. Paroled Apr. 26, 1865. Insurance agent postwar. d. Richmond, Mar. 14, 1883. bur. Hollywood Cem.

Overton, Thomas. b. Mar. 20, 1835. att. UVA. Lawyer at Opelousas, Louisiana. Capt. Louisiana state troops. Lt. of Inf., Apr. 27, 1861. Lt. on engineer and QM duty at Pensacola, Florida. Lt. ADC to his kinsman Gen. Holmes, Apr. 9, 1862. Capt. OO to Holmes, date unknown. Capt. OO to French, July 1862. Capt. OO to D. H. Hill, Sept. 1862. WIA at Sharpsburg. Back to French, Oct. 3, 1862. Rank of Capt. may have been temporary, as he is shown as a Lt. OO at Alexandria, Louisiana, by Jan. 1863, and Lt. AAIG to Maxey in Apr. 1865. Attorney at Marksville, Louisiana. d. Aug. 14, 1913.

Owens, Andrew T. b. in Virginia, Sept. 25, 1837. Merchant in Lafayette Co., Mississippi. Lt. Co. F, 19th Mississippi, May 15, 1861. Capt. ACS, 19th Mississippi, Oct. 15, 1862. Dropped July 28, 1863. Capt. AQM, 19th Mississippi, Nov. 11, 1863. Capt. AQM to Harris, Sept. 15, 1864. Appx. Retail grocer

at Oxford. d. July 14, 1897. bur. St. Peter's Cem.

Owens, Silas, Jr. b. in Virginia, May 7, 1838. Merchant in Lafayette Co., Mississippi. Capt. AQM, 11th Mississippi, Aug. 2, 1862. Capt. AQM to Davis, Sept. 15, 1864, into 1865. Grocer at Oxford, Mississippi. d. Aug. 30, 1889. bur. St. Peter's Cem., Oxford.

Pace, James McAllen. b. Troup Co., Georgia, Aug. 2, 1835. att. Emory Univ. and UGA. m. Lenora Haralson, whose sister married Gen. John B. Gordon. Adjt. 6th Alabama. Capt. AAG to Gordon, Nov. 27, 1862. Reapptd. Nov. 2, 1863. Capt. AAG to C. A. Evans, spring 1864. Capt. AAG to R. D. Johnston, and to B. R. Johnson, 1864, but both assignments revoked, probably before implementation. Capt. AAAIG to Gordon, 1865. Appx. In Georgia legislature. Law professor at Emory. Mayor of Covington, Georgia. d. there Sept. 7, 1912. bur. Westview Cem.

Packard, Joseph, Jr. b. Alexandria, Virginia, Apr. 10, 1842. att. Kenyon Coll. Pvt. and Cpl. First Rockbridge (Va.) Arty., 1861–1863. Acting Lt. OO, Aug. 1863, assigned to ANVa. reserve ordnance train. Lt. OO, June 14, 1864, still serving with train. Appx. att. UVA. postwar. Married twice. Lawyer and school board president at Baltimore, Maryland. d. there Nov. 24, 1923. bur. Green Mount Cem.

Pagan, James. b. in South Carolina, Apr. 22, 1809. Maj. ACS to Gen. R. G. M. Dunovant, Provisional Army of South Carolina, Jan. 1861. Capt. ACS, 6th South Carolina, June 20, 1861. Maj. CS to N. G. Evans, Mar. 1, 1862. Injured in railroad accident, summer 1863. Maj. CS to Elliott, and then to Wallace, 1864. Appx. d. Nov. 25, 1898. bur. Episc. Cem., Winnsboro, South Carolina.

Page, John. b. Hanover Co., Virginia, Apr. 26, 1821. att. UVA., Bristol Coll, and Newark Coll. m. Elizabeth Burwell Nelson, 1846. A lawyer. Sgt. Co. C, 15th Virginia,

Apr. 23, 1861. Capt. AQM to his brother-in-law, Gen. Pendleton, Oct. 12, 1861. Maj. QM to Pendleton, Apr. 29, 1862. Appx. Lawyer at Beaver Dam, Virginia. d. Hanover Co., Oct. 30, 1901. bur. Fork Church.

Page, Legh Richmond. b. Amherst Co., Virginia, Mar. 10, 1835. Raised in Kentucky. Lawyer at Lexington, Mississippi. Capt. AAG to J. H. Winder, Oct. 8, 1861. Maj. AAG to Winder, May 20, 1862. On special duty at AIGO, Mar. 1863 into 1864. Maj. AAIG to Ewell, June 16, 1864. Maj. AAIG to Kemper, Oct. 14, 1864. Richmond lawyer. m. Page Waller (making her married name Page Page). d. Chicago, Illinois, June 8, 1893. bur. Hollywood Cem., Richmond.

Page, Mann. b. Apr. 21, 1835. Clerk and merchant at Richmond, Virginia. Pvt. Co. F, 21st Virginia. To Adjt., May 10, 1862. WIA at Cedar Mountain. Lt. AAAG to J. R. Jones, Oct.–Nov. 1862. Lt. AAAIG to J. M. Jones, July 1863. Lt. ADC to Early, by Sept. 1864. Took oath May 26, 1865, at Richmond. Farmer at Upper Brandon and member of state legislature. d. Richmond, May 28, 1904. bur. Hollywood Cem.

Page, Peyton Nelson. b. Gloucester Co., Virginia, Aug. 10, 1840. Commonwealth's attorney there. Acting ADC to G. J. Rains, Jan.–Feb. 1862. Lt. ADC to Rains, Apr. 17, 1862, to rank from Oct. 25, 1861. Capt. AAG to Rains, Oct. 14, 1862. Capt. AAG to Taliaferro, Nov. 16, 1863. WIA Mar. 1865. Paroled Apr. 26, 1865. Gloucester Co. lawyer. d. Jan. 7, 1891, of pneumonia. bur. Abingdon Episc. Church Cem., Gloucester Co.

Page, Philip Nelson. b. Washington, D.C., May 2, 1847. att. VMI and Georgetown. Cadet CSA, Apr. 2, 1863. One of the VMI Cadets at the Battle of New Market. Cadet ADC to Corse, Aug. 1, 1864. POW at Sailor's Creek. Took Oath, June 19, 1865. Cattle dealer in Argentina, 1865–1933. Returned to Virginia in 1930s for first time since the war. d. Jan. 4, 1941.

Page, Thomas Jefferson, Jr. b. in New Jersey, Feb. 15, 1839. Lt. PAVa., May 23, 1861. Lt. acting OO and acting ADC to Magruder, by Sept. 1861. Capt. Magruder (Va.) Arty., Mar. 1862. Maj. of Arty., Nov. 8, 1862, on duty with Nelson's Bn. Arty. Granted leave Aug. 27, 1863. Went to Europe and d. at Florence, Italy, June 16, 1864.

Painter, Sidney Crockett. b. Jan. 6, 1837. A farmer. Sgt. Co. F, 4th Virginia, 1861–1862. WIA at First Manassas. Pvt. Co. B, 29th Virginia, May 20, 1862. Later Lt. in same company. Capt. AQM, 29th Virginia, May 19, 1863. Capt. AQM to Cabell's Bn. Arty., by Oct. 1864. Served into 1865. Merchant in Tazewell Co. d. July 30, 1890. bur. Round Hill Cem., Smyth Co., Virginia.

Palfrey, Edward Augustus. b. Aug. 1830. att. USMA. Lt. 7th U.S. Inf., 1851–1857. Lived prewar at New Orleans. Capt. ACS to Twiggs, July 19, 1861. Maj. AAG to Lovell, Nov. 17, 1861. Assigned to duty with Gen. Cooper at AIGO in Richmond, July 18, 1862. Capt. AAG (CSA), Oct. 4, 1862. Maj. AAG (CSA), Oct. 14, 1862. Lt. Col. AAG (CSA), by mid-1864. Paroled May 31, 1865, at Montgomery, Alabama. d. Mar. 19, 1901.

Palmer, John A. Pvt. Co. C, 3rd Virginia Cavy., May 20, 1861, a 27-year-old farmer. Later to Sgt. Maj. Capt. AQM, 3rd Virginia Cavy., June 10, 1862. Capt. acting AQM to Wickham, Aug. 1863–Apr. 1865.

Palmer, William Henry. b. Richmond, Virginia, Oct. 9, 1835. A merchant. m. Sarah Elizabeth Amiss, 1856. Adjt. 1st Virginia, 1861. Maj. 1st Virginia, Apr. 27, 1862. WIA in right arm at Williamsburg. Maj. VADC to Kemper, Aug.–Sept. 1862. Maj. AAAG to A. P. Hill, Oct. 1862–May 1863. WIA at Chancellorsville ("my right arm was torn from the socket"). Maj. AAG to Hill, May 2, 1863. Lt. Col. AAG to Hill, Feb. 19, 1864. Lt. Col. AAG to Longstreet, Apr. 3–9, 1865. Appx. Richmond banker and insurance company president. d. July 14, 1926. bur. Hollywood Cem.

Pannill, James Bruce. b. Halifax Co., Virginia, Mar. 8, 1834. att. UVa., Hampden Sidney, Washington Coll., and Wm. & Mary. Lawyer in Pittsylvania Co. Pvt. Co. K, 26th Virginia, Oct. 23, 1861. Moved to Co. A, Aug. 8, 1862. Capt. AQM at Petersburg, Virginia, Oct. 30, 1862. Resigned Apr. 25, 1863. Practiced law in Virginia and North Carolina. Member of Virginia legislature. d. 1908. bur. Chatham Cem., Pittsylvania Co. Pannill was a first cousin of Gen. J. E. B. Stuart.

Parker, Arthur. b. in South Carolina, ca. 1834. Lived at Abbeville. Pvt. Co. K, 3rd Alabama, Apr. 24, 1861. Capt. ACS, 1st South Carolina (Gregg's), June 11, 1862. Capt. acting ACS to Gregg, Aug.–Dec. 1862. Capt. ACS to R. L. Walker, date not known. Maj. CS to Walker, Mar. 2, 1865. Lost arm at Farmville or Appomattox, about Apr. 9, 1865. Merchant at New York City. Alive 1888.

Parker, Augustus Neal. b. Franklin, Tennessee, Nov. 7, 1842. Moved to Mississippi at age 5. att. college in Ohio. A clerk. Pvt. Co. C, 18th Miss., May 28, 1861. VADC to G. B. Anderson at Seven Pines. Clerk at D. H. Hill's headquarters. VADC to Featherston during Seven Days. Lt. ADC to Featherston, July 18, 1862. Served into 1865. Bookkeeper, banker, and broker at Canton, Mississippi. Married twice. d. Sept. 13, 1913. bur. Canton Cem.

Parker, Francis Simons, Jr. b. Charleston, South Carolina, Apr. 11, 1842. att. South Carolina Coll. Present at Ft. Sumter. Lt. ADC to Bragg, Oct. 15, 1861. Lt. AAAG to Richard H. Anderson in Florida, Dec. 1861. Maj. ADC to Bragg, Feb. 25, 1864. Served into 1865. Moved to Mobile, Alabama, 1869. Merchant and city councilman. d. there Sept. 11, 1906. bur. Magnolia Cem.

Parkhill, John H. b. Nov. 8, 1819. att. UVa. Lawyer at Tallahassee, Florida. Translated a book from French that was published as a Confederate imprint in 1861. Clerk

in QM Dept. Capt. AQM to J. H. Winder, Mar. 11, 1862. Maj. AAG to Winder, Aug. 28, 1862. Maj. AAG to Robert Ransom, W. M. Gardner, and Ewell, in order. Paroled at Richmond, Apr. 18, 1865. d. Baltimore, Maryland, 1870.

Parmelee, Charles H. Pvt. Co. K, 51st Georgia, Mar. 4, 1862. Capt. ACS, 51st Georgia, June 12, 1862. Capt. ACS to Bryan, Aug. 1, 1863. Maj. CS to Simms, Nov. 2, 1864. Appx. Probably Charles Harris Parmelee, born June 12, 1830, at Atlanta.

Parramore, James Buchanan. b. Thomasville, Georgia, Jan. 20, 1840. Known as "Buck." Pvt. Co. C, 4th Florida, Aug. 12, 1861. Eventually Capt. of company. Capt. AAIG to Patton Anderson, May 1864. Capt. AAIG to Finegan, June 8, 1864. Paroled May 10, 1865, at Madison, Florida. Partner of Gen. Finegan in Savannah, Georgia, cotton business. Married twice, including Agnes Finegan. Florida's asst. state chemist. Mayor of Orlando. d. there Feb. 6, 1902. bur. Greenwood Cem. The family genealogy gives date of birth as Jan. 20, 1839.

Parrish, John G. b. Fredericksburg, Virginia, Dec. 23, 1817. Clerk and merchant there. Moved to Bowling Green and became a minister. Preacher and state legislator in California, 1849–1852 and 1856–1857. Edited a religious newspaper. Capt. Co. G, 47th Virginia, July 20, 1861. Failed reelection. Apparently Capt. AQM to McIntosh's Bn. Arty. and to 49th Virginia. Maj. CS to W. L. Jackson, May 2, 1863. Served into 1865. Resumed work in Caroline Co. as minister and newspaperman. d. Bowling Green, July 30, 1871. Son was named John George Parrish, Jr., making it virtually certain that this man's middle name was George.

Parrish, Robert Lewis. b. in Virginia, Sept. 1, 1840. Son of John G. Parrish (see above). att. Bethany Coll. Lt. 47th Virginia. Pvt. Co. B, 9th Virginia Cavy., Nov. 14, 1862–Apr. 1864. Adjt. 46th Bn. Virginia Cavy., Apr. 1, 1864. Lt. AAAG to W. L. Jackson, 1864–1865. Teacher, lawyer, and rail-roadman at Covington, Virginia. d. Clifton Forge, Virginia, July 11, 1904. bur. Cedar Hill Cem., Covington. Of "Roman face and figure."

Parrott, Josiah Rhoten. b. Cocke Co., Tennessee, Feb. 1826. Moved to Georgia in 1848. Lawyer at Cartersville. Maj. QM to Wofford, Feb. 17, 1863. Resigned Nov. 16, 1863, to become solicitor gen. of the Cherokee Judicial Dist., Georgia. Postwar Republican. President of 1868 state constitutional convention. d. June 10, 1872.

Partridge, Daniel, Jr. b. Montgomery, Alabama. Lt. Co. B, 3rd Alabama. Lt. AAAIG to O'Neal's Bgd., Apr. 1863–Apr. 1864. Lt. OO to Battle, Apr. 1864 into 1865. Lived at Mobile. m. Lucy Green Harrie.

Patridge, Isaac Mitchell. b. in North Carolina, Nov. 12, 1833. Editor of *Vicksburg Whig* in Mississippi, 1857–1861. Slightly wounded in 1858 duel with W. H. McCardle (q.v.). Pvt. Co. A, 21st Mississippi, May 15, 1861. Capt. ACS, 21st Mississippi, July 19, 1861. Resigned Jan. 28, 1862. Maj. CS to Featherston, May 1, 1862. Maj. CS to G. B. Anderson at Seven Pines, in Featherston's absence. Maj. CS to Posey, 1863. Maj. CS to Harris, Nov. 1863. Appx. d. Nov. 10, 1911. bur. Little Rock National Cem., Arkansas.

Patterson, John Rice. b. Lunenburg Co., Virginia, July 12, 1834. Grocer at Petersburg. Lt. Co. E, 12th Virginia. WIA at Crampton's Gap. Lt. acting ACS to Mahone, Sept. 1863–May 1864. Lt. (Capt.?) AQM to Mahone, July 21, 1864. Capt. AAIG to Mahone, Oct. 5, 1864. Appx. m. Bettie M. Osborne, 1867. Merchant, postmaster, and insurance agent at Petersburg. d. there, Jan. 31, 1918. bur. Blandford Cem.

Pattison, Holmes A. Civil engineer at Memphis, Tennessee, Navy Yard and in Washington, D.C. Lt. Asst. EO at Jackson and Vicksburg, Mississippi. Lt. Asst. EO to Beauregard, May 1864. Capt. EO, Oct. 19,

1864. Duties uncertain for last year of the war. Appx.

Patton, A. H. Lt. Co. E, 18th Georgia, June 11, 1861. Adjt. 18th Georgia, Apr. 7, 1862. Lt. AAAG to Wofford in the Maryland Campaign. Capt. AAG to Wofford, Feb. 17, 1863. KIA at Chancellorsville, May 3, 1863. bur. on the battlefield.

Patton, Hugh Mercer. b. Richmond, Virginia, Apr. 6, 1841. Served in Co. B, 13th Virginia and in Charlottesville (Va.) Arty., 1861–1862. Adjt. 7th Virginia, 1862. WIA in right shoulder at Second Manassas. Lt. ADC to Cooke, Nov. 9, 1862. Appx. Culpeper Co. farmer. m. Fannie Dade Bull, 1870, a second cousin of Gen. Cooke's wife. d. Lynchburg, Virginia, Dec. 28, 1917. Brothers George S. and Waller T. Patton were field officers. Another brother is listed below.

Patton, John Mercer, Jr. b. Culpeper Co., Virginia, May 9, 1826. att. VMI. A Richmond lawyer. Maj. PAVA., Apr. 1861. Commanded at Jamestown Island, 1861. Lt. Col., 21st Virginia, summer 1861. Later promoted to Col. Resigned Aug. 8, 1862. Col. of Cavy., Dec. 16, 1862, and on military court of G. W. Smith's command. Later joined military court of Second Corps by 1863. Appx. Wrote several legal books. Married twice. d. Oct. 9, 1898. Patton's papers are at the Virginia Historical Society.

Paul, Samuel Buckner. b. Oct. 1826. att. UVA. m. Sophronia W. Pickerell. Flour inspector at Richmond, Virginia. Visiting Rio de Janeiro when the war broke out. Lt. Col. 28th Virginia, Sept. 6, 1861. Dropped Apr. 1862. VADC to Whiting, May 1864. VADC to Beauregard, 1864–1865. Lawyer and insurance agent at Petersburg, Virginia. d. Sept. 26, 1908. bur. Blandford Cem.

Paxton, James Gardiner. b. Nov. 4, 1821. att VMI, Washington Coll., and Harvard. Brother of Gen. E. F. Paxton. m. Ann Maria White, 1846. A lawyer. Lt. Co. E, 1st Virginia Bn., 1861. Capt. AQM at Jackson's River, Virginia, Sept. 17, 1861. Capt. AQM at

Salem, Virginia, July 14, 1862. Maj. QM to A. G. Jenkins, Aug. 16, 1862. Failed bond and dropped, Apr. 16, 1863, but reinstated Apr. 30, 1863. Maj. QM at Lynchburg, Oct. 1, 1863, through 1865. Supt. of C & O Railroad. Member of state legislature. Killed Aug. 6, 1870, in a railroad wreck near White Sulphur Springs, West Virginia. bur. Lexington, Virginia.

Payne, Rice Winfield Hooe. b. Fauquier Co., Virginia, Oct. 7, 1818. att. UVA. Lawyer at Warrenton, 1838–1884. A Catholic. Married twice, both times to a daughter of Raphael Semmes. Capt. AQM at Warrenton, Sept. 28, 1861. Maj. QM at Danville, July 28, 1862. Served at Petersburg, Oct. 1862. POW at Warrenton, Sept. 29, 1862. Resigned Dec. 29, 1862, citing poor health. Pvt. Co. A, 3rd Virginia Cavy., late in the war. Paroled May 6, 1865. d. at Warrenton, Sept. 25, 1884. bur. Warrenton Cem.

Payne, William Michel. b. Goochland Co., Virginia, Feb. 15, 1828. m. Frances Mitchell, 1852. Capt. AQM, 11th Virginia, Mar. 7, 1862. Maj. QM to Garland, June 18, 1862. Maj. QM to Iverson, Nov. 1862. Maj. QM to R. D. Johnston, Sept. 1863. Maj. QM to Toon, May–Aug. 1864, and then back with Johnston. Maj. QM to Pegram, Nov. 28, 1864. Maj. QM to J. A. Walker, Feb. 1865. Appx. d. Kinston, North Carolina, Oct. 31, 1898.

Peabody, Edward Rossiter. b. Bridgeport, Connecticut, Sept. 28, 1834. Moved to Georgia in 1837. Decatur Co. druggist. Cpl. Co. G, 1st (Ramsey's) Georgia, Mar. 18, 1861. Capt. AQM, 64th Georgia, June 19, 1863. Capt. AQM to W. H. Forney, Sept. 15, 1864. Appx. Bainbridge alderman and city treasurer. d. Jan. 8, 1892. bur. Oak City Cem.

Peacocke, Thomas Goodricke. Capt. in the 30th (Cambridgeshire) Regiment of Foot, British Army, 1848. Later in 94th Regiment of Foot. Served as VADC to Pickett, June 1864. Sporadic records show that he served with Heth in 1864 and was with Field's Div. in 1865, presumably as a VADC.

Pearce, James H. b. in England. Adjt. 60th Virginia, by Oct. 1861. Lt. Co. E, 59th Virginia, by Jan. 1862. Lt. OO (acting?) to Wise, Jan. 1862. Later Adjt. of 60th Virginia. Capt. AAG to Wise, July 24, 1862. Court-martialed for drunkenness in 1863 and acquitted. Capt. AAG to Robert H. Anderson, Jan. 12, 1865. Paroled with AOT.

Peck, William Drummond. b. Columbia, South Carolina, Apr. 4, 1833. Drayman at Columbia. Lt. Co. C, 2nd South Carolina, 1861. Capt. AQM, 2nd South Carolina, July 20, 1861. Capt. AQM to Bonham, Jan. 1, 1862. Capt. AQM to Kershaw. Maj. QM to Kershaw, May 28, 1863, to rank from Jan. 1, 1862. Maj. QM to McLaws, Nov. 1863. Failed bond and dropped, Apr. 11, 1864, but reinstated Apr. 25. Probably staff of Kershaw for remainder of war. Appx. d. Columbia, Apr. 25, 1870. bur. Elmwood Cem.

Peden, David Dantzler. b. Spartanburg Co., South Carolina, Nov. 2, 1835. att. GMI. Capt. Co. D, 12th Georgia. WIA at Malvern Hill. Capt. AAAIG to Rodes, 1863, including Gettysburg. Farmer and bank cashier in Georgia. Moved to Houston, Texas, in 1890. Operated one of the largest hardware stores in the Southwest. d. Houston, Oct. 25, 1912.

Peebles, Robert Bruce. b. Northampton Co., North Carolina, July 21, 1840. att. UNC. m. Maggie Cameron. Adjt. 35th North Carolina, May 2, 1863. Lt. AAAG to Matt. Ransom until appointed Capt. AAG to Ransom, date unknown. Appx. Legislator and judge in North Carolina. d. at Hillsborough, June 29, 1916. bur. St. Matthew's Churchyard.

Peek, Julius Algernon. b. Taliaferro Co., Georgia, Apr. 4, 1838. att. Emory Univ. Polk Co. farmer. Lt. Co. D, Phillips Legion, June 14, 1861. WIA at Fredericksburg. Lt. AAAG to Wofford, about Apr. 1863, until Appx. Farmer at Cedartown. d. July 12, 1924. bur. Greenwood Cem.

Peeler, Anderson Jones. b. Harris Co., Georgia, Apr. 22, 1838. m. Elizabeth Frances Walker Byrd, 1857. Lawyer at Tallahassee, Florida. Clerk of state legislature in 1861. Pvt. Co. I, 5th Florida, Apr. 23, 1862. To Lt., May 23, 1862. Lt. acting ADC to Bgd. Commander David Lang at Gettysburg. WIA in head and POW there. Exchanged Mar. 1865. Resumed profession at Tallahassee. Moved to Texas. d. 1886. bur. Oakwood Cem., Austin.

Pegram, James West, Jr. b. Feb. 14, 1839. m. Elizabeth Randolph Daniel. Adjt. 57th Virginia. Capt. AAG to Armistead, June 12, 1862. Capt. AAG to J. H. Winder, July 29, 1862. Maj. AAG to Winder, July 30, 1863. Maj. AAG to Robert Ransom, 1864. Maj. AAG to Ewell, 1864. Prominent in organizing black troops in Richmond, Mar. 1865. POW at Sailor's Creek. Businessman at Richmond, Virginia, and at New York City. d. Atlanta, Georgia, Mar. 31, 1881. bur. Hollywood Cem., Richmond. "Clever and comic." Brother of Gen. John Pegram and Col. William R. J. Pegram.

Pegram, John Cargill. b. Sussex Co., Virginia, Oct. 3, 1838. att. Norfolk Military Academy and VMI. A civil engineer. Adjt. 12th North Carolina, May 14, 1861. Resigned May 1, 1862. Adjt. 2nd North Carolina Cavy., June 6, 1862. Capt. AAG to Matt. Ransom, July 1, 1863. KIA at Petersburg, June 16, 1864. bur. Blandford Cem., Petersburg.

Pelham, John. b. near Alexandria, Alabama, Sept. 7, 1838. att. USMA. Lt. of Arty., Mar. 16, 1861. Lt. Drillmaster, June 1861. Lt. Wise (Va.) Arty., by July 1861. Capt. Mar. 23, 1862. Maj. Chief of Horse Arty., staff of Stuart, Aug. 9, 1862. KIA at Kelly's Ford, Mar. 17, 1863.

Pendleton, Alexander Swift. b. near Alexandria, Virginia, Sept. 28, 1840. att. Washington Coll. and UVA. Son of Gen. W. N. Pendleton. m. Catherine Carter Corbin, 1863. Lt. acting OO to T. J. Jackson, Apr. 29,

1861. Lt. ADC to Jackson, Nov. 4, 1861. Capt. AAG to Jackson, June 18, 1862. Maj. AAG to Jackson, Dec. 4, 1862. WIA slightly in thigh at Fredericksburg. Maj. AAG to Ewell, June 1863. Lt. Col. AAG to Ewell, July 23, 1863. Lt. Col. AAG to Early, May 1864. MWIA at Fisher's Hill, Sept. 22, 1864. d. Woodstock, Virginia, Sept. 23. bur. Stonewall Jackson Cem., Lexington, Virginia. A fellow staff officer called Pendleton "the most brilliant staff officer in the Army of Northern Virginia."

Pendleton, Dudley Digges. b. Louisa Co., Virginia, Mar. 2, 1840. att. Washington Coll. Pvt. Rockbridge (Va.) Arty., June 19, 1861. Pvt. Co. D, 1st Virginia Cavy., Sept. 24, 1861. Capt. AAG to his uncle, Gen. Pendleton, May 22, 1862. Appx. m. Helen Boteler, a daughter of A. R. Boteler (see above). Principal of Shepherd Coll., in West Virginia. d. Aug. 24, 1886, when he was "accidentally caught in the machinery threshing wheat — and so crushed that he died a few hours afterwards." bur. Elmwood Cem., Shepherdstown, West Virginia.

Pendleton, Henry. b. in Virginia. Capt. AQM to Magruder, Sept. 10, 1861. Followed Magruder to Texas in 1862. Maj. QM to Bankhead, July 9, 1863. Also staff of H. E. McCulloch. Dropped Apr. 11, 1864, for failed bond. Reinstated as post QM at Houston, Texas, Oct. 7, 1864. A 32-year-old commission merchant at Galveston, Texas, in 1870. d. there July 21, 1879. bur. Galveston City Cem.

Pendleton, J. S. Capt. ACS, Nov. 2, 1861. On duty at the post of Lynchburg, Virginia, 1861–1865. Several men of this name lived in Virginia, but the leading candidate is James Shepherd Pendleton, Jr., Oct. 3, 1823–Mar. 15, 1877.

Pendleton, Joseph Henry. b. Louisa Co., Virginia, Jan. 16, 1827. att. Bethany Coll. A lawyer. m. Margaret Campbell Ewing, 1848. Maj. 23rd Virginia, May 1861. WIA in head during Laurel Hill campaign. Resigned Sept. 14, 1861. Maj. QM to Taliaferro, Mar. 22, 1862. Maj. QM to Colston, early 1863. Maj. QM at Ivor Station, Virginia, Apr. 29, 1863. In Virginia legislature during the war. Lawyer at Wheeling, West Virginia. d. there Feb. 2, 1881.

Pendleton, Thornton Presley Cooke. b. in Virginia, Apr. 18, 1810. Farmer at Berryville. m. Emily Jane Richardson, 1836. Acting AQM, 7th Virginia Cavy., June 1861. Capt. AQM, 7th Virginia Cavy., June 29, 1861, but declined the appointment. Worked for most of 1862 as AQM at Winchester and as an Asst. to Maj. John A. Harman. Lived postwar in Prince George's Co., Maryland, and at Culpeper, Virginia. d. Oct. 3, 1884.

Pendleton, William Barret. b. Louisa Co., Virginia, Jan. 12, 1838. att. Hampden Sidney and VMI. Lt. Co. G, 23rd Virginia, Apr. 24, 1861. Adjt. 23rd Virginia, May 17, 1861. Lt. AAAG to Taliaferro, Aug. 1861, until appointed Capt. AAG to Taliaferro, Mar. 22, 1862. Capt. AAG to brigade until he lost left leg at Cedar Mountain. Capt. AAG on enrolling duty in Virginia, Jan. 1863. Retired Aug. 1864. Farmer and legislator. d. Cuckoo, Virginia, Jan. 17, 1914. bur. Gilboa Church.

Percy, William Alexander. b. May 10, 1834. att. Princeton and UVA. Planter and lawyer at Greenville, Mississippi. Capt. Co. I, 22nd Mississippi. Col. 1st Mississippi State Troops. Capt. AAIG to Bowen, Oct. 14, 1862. POW at Vicksburg, July 1863. Capt. AAG to Long, Oct. 8, 1863. Capt. AAG to Carter's Bn. Arty., June 1864. Returned to Long in Nov. 1864, briefly. Capt. AAG to Hodge, Dec. 3, 1864. Lt. Col. 24th Mississippi Bn. Cavy., Feb. 8, 1865. In state legislature postwar. d. Jan. 1888. bur. Old Greenville Cem. Known as "the Gray Eagle." Grandfather of famous Mississippi poet.

Perry, Heman Humphreys. b. Burke Co., Georgia, Apr. 13, 1835. att. Georgetown and UVA. A lawyer. Sgt. Co. D, 2nd Georgia. Lt. AAAIG and VADC to Benning, July 1863.

Capt. AAIG to Benning, Nov. 2, 1863. Capt. AAG to Wright's Bgd., Oct. 18, 1864. Capt. AAIG to Sorrel. Appx. Lawyer, judge, and newspaper editor at Waynesboro, Georgia. d. Feb. 14, 1908. bur. Waynesboro Cem. The odd spelling of Perry's first name is correct.

Perry, John M. Lt. Leecraft's (N.C.) Btty., Oct. 1861. Lt. Latham's (N.C.) Btty., Apr. 1862. Lt. Potts's (N.C.) Btty., Nov. 1863. Capt. of Arty., Feb. 25, 1864. Capt. OO to Kirkland, Apr. 1, 1864. Capt. OO to MacRae, June 1864. Capt. OO to Hoke, Nov. 13, 1864. Paroled Apr. 26, 1865. Probably John Merritt Perry, born Oct. 11, 1837, died in 1878.

Persinger, George Payne. A resident of Alleghany Co., Virginia. Lt. Co. C, 27th Virginia, May 10, 1861, age 31, a farmer. Capt. AQM, 27th Virginia, Nov. 23, 1861. Failed bond and dropped, Feb. 24, 1862, but reinstated Dec. 19, 1863. Probably served with the unit in the interim. Capt. AQM to William Terry, Sept. 15, 1864. Appx. Known as "Doc" Persinger.

Peterkin, George William. b. in Maryland, Mar. 21, 1841. att. UVA. Lt. Co. F, 21st Virginia, Apr. 21, 1861. Lt. ADC to Pendleton, May 22, 1862. Appx. Episc. minister at Baltimore, in Culpeper Co., Virginia, and in West Virginia. Missionary in Brazil and Puerto Rico. Married twice. d. Parkersburg, West Virginia, Sept. 22, 1916. bur. Hollywood Cem., Richmond. Subject of a 1929 biography.

Peters, Stephen Theophilus. b. Nelson Co., Virginia, 1821. Merchant and newspaperman at Lynchburg. Maj. QM to Echols, Dec. 24, 1861. Maj. QM to Wharton, Apr. 1863. Maj. QM of Forsberg's Bgd. Paroled at Lynchburg, Apr. 15, 1865. Farmer in Bedford Co. d. Mar. 7, 1903. bur. Spring Hill Cem., Lynchburg, in an unmarked grave.

Peters, William Elisha. b. Bedford Co., Virginia, Aug. 18, 1829. att. Emory & Henry and UVA. Also studied in Berlin. Capt. AAG (PAVa.?) to Floyd, Aug. 19, 1861. Appointed Lt. Col. 45th Virginia, Nov. 14, 1861. Dropped spring 1862. Col. 2nd Virginia State Line, 1862. Col. 21st Virginia Cavy., Aug. 23, 1863. WIA at Moorefield. On faculty at UVA. and Emory & Henry. d. Charlottesville, Virginia, Mar. 22, 1906.

Peterson, Batte O. Pvt. Co. B, 4th Alabama, Apr. 28, 1861, age 20, a student from Tuskegee. Later to Sgt. and then Lt. Lt. AAAG to Law during Gettysburg campaign and thereafter. KIA at Dandridge, Tennessee, Jan. 16, 1864.

Peyton, Henry E. From Cooper Co., Missouri. att. Randolph Macon Coll., 1852–1853. Maj. PAVA., July 21, 1861. VADC to Beauregard at First Manassas and onward until appointed Maj. AAG to Beauregard, May 10, 1862. Ordered to Gen. Sam. Jones, Aug. 25, 1862, but may not have served there. Maj. AAIG to R. E. Lee, Oct. 6, 1862. Lt. Col. AAIG to Lee, Sept. 20, 1864. Appx. Emigrated westward in 1865. Secretary of Texas State Democratic Committee. Also lived at Baltimore and probably in northern Virginia. Went to St. Louis, Missouri, 1900, homeless and penniless. Died on the street, there, Sept. 14, 1900. bur. in unmarked pauper's grave.

Peyton, Moses Green. b. Culpeper Co., Virginia, Jan. 6, 1826. att. UVA. Brother of T. G. Peyton (see below). A civil engineer. m. Martha Champe Carter. Lt. Everett (Va.) Arty. Lt. VADC to Rodes at Seven Pines and Seven Days. Capt. AAG to Rodes, Aug. 12, 1862. Maj. AAG to Rodes, May 12, 1863. Maj. AAG to Ramseur, Sept.–Oct. 1864. Maj. AAG to Grimes, Oct. 1864. Appx. Proctor at UVA. postwar. d. Apr. 16, 1897.

Peyton, Thomas Green. b. Richmond, Virginia, Oct. 3, 1832. att. UVA. A Richmond merchant pre- and postwar. Lt. Col. 15th Virginia, July 1861–Aug. 1862. Maj. AAAG to Ewell, Jan. 1862. Maj. AAG at Camp Lee, Aug. 21, 1862. In Richmond into 1865. d. there Sept. 18, 1900. bur. Hollywood Cem.

Peyton, Thomas Jefferson. Capt. Peyton (Va.) Arty., Apr. 17, 1861. Resigned Apr. 3, 1862. Capt. AAIG to G. W. Smith, Nov. 6, 1862. Capt. AAIG to Pemberton. Capt. OO to Pemberton, May–June 1864. Dropped for nonconfirmation. Briefly reinstated, June 20–July 1864. Farmed in Orange Co. during last year of the war. Paroled May 16, 1865.

Peyton, William H. Capt. AQM, Oct. 21, 1861. On duty at Staunton, Virginia, until "services dispensed with, S.O. #104, 1862." Almost certainly William Henry Peyton, born Apr. 22, 1827, a Staunton businessman.

Phifer, George Lowndes. b. Feb. 10, 1841. Bugler Co. A, 1st North Carolina Arty., May 8, 1861. Sgt. Maj., 49th North Carolina, Apr. 21, 1862. Capt. Co. K, 49th North Carolina. Lt. ADC to Hoke, May 31, 1864. WIA at Bermuda Hundred, June 2, 1864. Paroled May 4, 1865. Treasurer of the North Carolina School for the Deaf. d. Dec. 13, 1908. bur. Forest Hill Cem., Morganton, North Carolina.

Philips, Frederick. b. near Battleboro, North Carolina, June 14, 1838. att. St. James Coll. and UNC. Tarboro lawyer. Lt. Co. I, 15th North Carolina, May 22, 1861. Adjt. 30th North Carolina, June 5, 1862. WIA in head at Sharpsburg. WIA in thigh at Kelly's Ford, Nov. 7, 1863. Capt. AQM, 30th North Carolina, Jan. 22, 1864. Capt. AQM to Cox, Mar. 8, 1865. Mayor of Tarboro, judge, and insurance agent. Helped mark CSA positions at Sharpsburg battlefield. d. at Tarboro, Jan. 14, 1905. bur. Calvary Episc. Churchyard.

Phillips, J. C. Lt. ADC to Magruder, Jan.–June 1862, at least. This may be Jefferson Curle Phillips, Maj. of the 3rd Virginia Cavy. Records for the staff officer are painfully thin.

Phillips, James Patton. b. in North Carolina, May 17, 1826. Moved to Georgia in 1832. Habersham Co. physician and farmer. Lt. Co. C, Phillips Legion, June 11, 1861.

WIA in right leg at Fredericksburg. Capt. AQM, 3rd Georgia Bn. Sharpshooters, Jan. 25, 1863. Capt. AQM to Wofford. Capt. AQM to Longstreet, Sept. 15, 1864. Went to Georgia with Wofford, Mar. 4, 1865. d. May 24, 1918. bur. Farm Hill Community Cem., Habersham Co.

Phillips, Joseph. b. Elizabeth City Co., Virginia, Oct. 10, 1831. m. Mary Marrow, 1858. Farmer, steam sawmill operator, and livery stable owner at Hampton, Virginia. Pvt. Co. D, 3rd Virginia Cavy., May 14, 1861. Lt. of Cavy., CSA, Oct. 12, 1861. Lt. acting ADC to Magruder, Dec. 1861–Feb. 1862 and during the Seven Days. Lt. acting ADC to Hood, Sept. 1862. Capt. (temp.) of Cavy., CSA, Oct. 14, 1862, and assigned again to Magruder. Col. 3rd Texas Cavy. (Arizona Bgd.), Feb. 21, 1863. KIA at Donaldsonville, June 28, 1863.

Phillips, Richard Henry. b. Spotsylvania Co., Virginia, Nov. 19, 1810. Schoolteacher at Staunton. Chaplain, 52nd Virginia, Aug. 19, 1861. Capt. AQM, Oct. 8, 1861. Ran an army clothing factory at Staunton. POW near Lexington, June 11, 1864. Resigned Mar. 15, 1865. President of the Staunton Female Academy. d. Norfolk, Virginia, Apr. 7, 1890. bur. Thornrose Cem., Staunton.

Pickett, Alexander Hamilton. b. Macon Co., Alabama, Dec. 8, 1836. att. UAla. A planter. Pvt. Co. D, 3rd Alabama. To Adjt., Jan. 10, 1863. Lt. acting ADC to Col. E. A. O'Neal at Chancellorsville and Gettysburg. Capt. AAG to Battle, Aug. 15, 1863. Served into 1865. m. Virginia Eliza Powell, 1864. Circuit court clerk and railroad man. d. Union Springs, Alabama, Jan. 11, 1900.

Pickett, Charles Francis. b. Richmond, Virginia, June 1, 1840. att. UVa. Clerk at Richmond. m. Elizabeth H. Smith, 1863. Served in Co. F, 1st Virginia. Lt. ADC to his brother, Gen. Pickett, Mar. 1, 1862. Capt. AAG to Pickett, May 21, 1862. WIA at Frayser's Farm while carrying a flag.

Maj. AAG to Pickett, Oct. 14, 1862. Appx. Henrico Co. farmer and then businessman at Norfolk. d. there Mar. 25, 1899. bur. Elmwood Cem. The family is the source for the middle name, which Pickett seemingly never used.

Pickett, John Thomas. b. Maysville, Kentucky, Oct. 9, 1823. att. USMA. Fought in prewar expedition in Cuba, and was U.S. Consul at Vera Cruz, Mexico. Said to have been a general in Kossuth's Hungarian army. Confederate Commissioner to Mexico in 1861 and Secretary of CSA Peace Commission. Maj. AAG to Breckinridge, May 10, 1862. Relieved July 30, 1862. On special QM duty for rest of war. VADC to Breckinridge at Cold Harbor. Sold CSA State Dept. archives to U.S. government postwar. m. Katherine Keyworth. A lawyer at Washington, D.C. d. there in 1884.

Pickett, Joseph G. Maj. AAG to S. R. Anderson, Aug. 15, 1861. Maj. AAG to Lovell, Jan. 3, 1862. Maj. AAG at a camp of instruction in Louisiana, June 1862. Back with Lovell later that year. Appointment terminated, Nov. 16, 1863.

Pickett, Steptoe. b. Fauquier Co., Virginia, Nov. 17, 1816. m. (1) Mary Frances Ward, 1849. m. (2) Eugenia Sale, 1855. Moved to Alabama in 1850s. Farmer in Limestone Co., pre- and postwar. Capt. AQM, 9th Alabama, Sept. 11, 1861. Capt. AQM to Wilcox. Resigned May 23, 1862. d. Madison, Alabama, Aug. 29, 1882.

Pierce, George Foster, Jr. b. Muscogee Co., Georgia, Feb. 28, 1843. att. Emory Univ. Pvt. Co. D, 1st (Ramsey's) Georgia, Apr. 16, 1861–Mar. 18, 1862. Sgt. Co. G, Cobb's Legion Inf., 1862. To Lt., Sept. 25, 1862. WIA at Crampton's Gap, Chancellorsville, and the Wilderness. Capt. AAAG to DuBose, 1864–1865. Hancock Co. lawyer. d. Feb. 24, 1884. bur. Sparta City Cem.

Pierce, John G. Capt. AQM, 11th Alabama, July 8, 1861. Maj. QM to Wilcox, Apr. 23, 1862. Failed bond and dropped, Oct. 25,

1862, but reinstated Nov. 28, 1862. Probably continued with brigade after Wilcox left, and thus staff of Perrin, Sanders, and Forney. Paroled May 13, 1865, at Meridian, Mississippi. Middle name believed to be Gideon.

Pierce, Lovick, Jr. b. Mar. 5, 1839. att. Emory. Pvt. Co. E, 15th Georgia, July 15, 1861. WIA at Dam #1. Adjt. 15th Georgia, Aug. 1, 1862. WIA in calf at Gettysburg. Lt. AAAG to DuBose, autumn 1864. WIA in hand at Fort Harrison. d. Aug. 7, 1930. bur. Sparta City Cem. Known as "Doc."

Pierce, Thomas W. b. in Virginia. A resident of Portsmouth. Served as AAAG to Reynolds in June 1862 (as a civilian?). Capt. oo to E. K. Smith, Feb. 1863. Capt. Asst. oo to A. P. Hill, Apr. 19, 1864. Capt. oo to W. H. F. Lee, May 4, 1864. Appx.

Pierson, Scipio Francis. From France. Lt. Co. E, 1st Bn. Louisiana Zouaves. Later in DeGournay's Btty. Maj. of Arty., Mar. 27, 1862. Chief of Arty. for D. H. Hill. Detached on ordnance duty in Europe, 1863–1864. To report to E. K. Smith, July 25, 1864. Alive 1870 in Louisiana. Hill called Pierson "a splendid artillerist & a gallant soldier."

Pinckard, Thomas C. b. in Georgia. A 31-year-old teacher in Macon Co., Alabama, in 1860. Pvt. Co. A, 14th Alabama, Mar. 14, 1863. To Ordnance Sgt., Apr. 26, 1863. Lt. oo, June 14, 1864, assignment not given. Lt. oo to W. F. Perry, Feb. 22, 1865. Appx. A teacher in Butler Co., Alabama, in 1870, age 43. Probably Thomas Cicero Pinckard.

Pinckney, Thomas. b. ca. 1840. VADC to Huger, Oct. 1861–Jan. 1863. Lt. Drillmaster, Nov. 26, 1862. Post Adjt. at Columbia, South Carolina, Jan.–July 1863. Lt. AAAG in Conscript Bureau, July 1863–Mar. 1865, stationed at Richmond. Lt. AAIG to Alexander, Mar. 1865. Appx.

Pitzer, Andrew Lewis. b. near Salem, Virginia, May 29, 1827. att. VMI. A farmer. Capt. Co. C, 2nd Virginia Cavy., May 17, 1861. Accidentally wounded in leg, June

1861. Failed reelection, Apr. 1862. VADC to Early, Aug. 1862. Lt. ADC to Early, Jan. 21, 1863. Postwar farmer. d. Roanoke, Virginia, Apr. 11, 1896. An "active and zealous" Methodist, known as "Wink" Pitzer.

Pleasants, James. b. Richmond, Virginia, Apr. 29, 1831. att. UVA. A lawyer. Lt. Hampden (Va.) Arty., 1861. Lt. of Arty., May 15, 1862, assigned briefly to Fayetteville Arsenal. Lt. oo to B. H. Robertson, June 13, 1862. Lt. oo in Richmond, Sept. 5, 1862. Capt. of Arty., Nov. 12, 1862, stationed at Charlottesville and Staunton. Capt. oo to Hood, Feb. 28, 1863. Capt. oo to Field, Feb. 1864. Appx. Richmond lawyer. d. July 16, 1898. bur. Hollywood Cem.

Points, Leonidas. b. Nov. 26, 1833. att. UVA. Teacher at Staunton. Pvt. Hanover (Va.) Arty., May 21, 1861–Oct. 8, 1862. Pvt. Ashland (Va.) Arty., Oct. 8, 1862–Feb. 1863. Lt. oo, Feb. 28, 1863, with Garnett's Bn. Arty. Capt. oo, Oct. 6, 1863, to report to Josiah Gorgas. Capt. oo to R. L. Walker, by late 1863. Appx. Principal of Staunton Deaf, Dumb, and Blind Asylum. d. Staunton, May 28, 1898. bur. Thornrose Cem.

Poitiaux, Michael Benoit. b. ca. 1820. Capt. AQM, 27th Bn. Virginia Cavy., Nov. 16, 1861. Capt. AQM to A. G. Jenkins, 1863. Capt. AQM at Salem, Virginia, Apr. 1863. Later on conscript duty in Florida. Civil engineer at Richmond, Virginia. d. R. E. Lee Camp Soldiers' Home, Richmond, Mar. 4, 1895. bur. Hollywood Cem.

Pollock, Thomas Gordon. b. Richmond, Virginia, Sept. 27, 1838. att. UVA. and Yale. A lawyer, lived at Warrenton, Virginia, and Shreveport, Louisiana. Capt. Co. F, 60th Virginia. Dropped Apr. 27, 1862. Adjt. 60th Virginia, May 1, 1862. Lt. VADC to Starke at Second Manassas. Capt. AQM to Kemper, Oct. 14, 1862. Rejected by senate, so recommissioned as Capt. AAG to Kemper, June 6, 1863. KIA at Gettysburg, July 3, 1863. Shot in head. Body not recovered. Pollock's war letters are at UNC.

Ponder, James Madison. b. in Georgia. Merchant at Forsyth. Sgt. Co. K, 1st (Ramsay's) Georgia, Mar. 18, 1861. Resigned Jan. 20, 1862. Pvt. Co. D, 35th Georgia, Feb. 28, 1862. Capt Co. K, 53rd Georgia, May 6, 1862. Capt. AQM, 53rd Georgia, July 9, 1863. Capt. AQM to Simms by Sept. 15, 1864.

Poor, Richard Lowndes. b. Oct. 2, 1838. Lt. PAVa., Oct. 1861, on engineer duty. Lt. of Arty., Nov. 6, 1861, EO to McLaws. Capt. (temp.), Feb. 18, 1862, EO to Huger. Capt. EO to Loring, May 21, 1861. Later EO to J. S. Williams and Sam. Jones. Maj. (temp.) EO, Nov. 9, 1863. Chief Engineer, Dept. of Western Virginia and Tennessee, 1864–1865. Baltimore businessman. d. Mar. 20, 1908.

Pope, Young John. b. Newberry, South Carolina, Apr. 10, 1841. att. Furman. Sgt. Co. E, 3rd South Carolina, Apr. 14, 1861. Adjt. 3rd South Carolina. Lt. AAAG to Conner, Aug. 1864. Lt. AAAG to Goggin, Oct. 1864. WIA seven times, including Cedar Creek. d. Mar. 29, 1911. bur. Rosemont Cem., Newberry Co.

Porteous, John Fuller. b. Beaufort, South Carolina, ca. 1825. att. South Carolina Coll. U.S. Consul to Portugal. Cpl. Beaufort Arty., 1861. Acting Ordnance Sgt. at McPhersonville, South Carolina, 1862–1863. Lt. OO, May 2, 1863. Lt. OO to H. H. Walker, Aug. 18, 1863. Later staff of Fry and Archer, in 1864. Lt. OO to Barton, 1865. POW at Sailor's Creek. d. New Orleans, Louisiana, Sept. 16, 1878, while volunteering as a nurse during a yellow fever epidemic.

Porter, Joseph Ely. b. in North Carolina, Sept. 11, 1843. Cpl. Co. I, 15th North Carolina, June 19, 1861. Sgt. Maj., 15th North Carolina, Jan. 1, 1863. Lt. ADC to MacRae, Nov. 4, 1864. Appx. Farmer in Edgecombe Co. d. July 24, 1888. bur. Primitive Baptist Cem., Tarboro.

Porterfield, George Alexander. b. Berkeley Co., Virginia, Nov. 24, 1822. att. VMI. Mexican War veteran. m. Emily Terrill. Col. AAIG (PAVa.) at Harper's Ferry, Apr. 1861. Col. 25th Virginia, July 1861. Col. Chief OO to Loring, Aug. 1861. Banker in Jefferson Co., West Virginia. d. Charlestown, Feb. 27, 1919.

Posey, Jefferson Bryant. b. Nov. 6, 1843. att. UMiss. Resident of Woodville, Mississippi. Pvt. 9th Mississippi. Lt. ADC to his father, Gen. Posey, Jan. 19, 1863. Probably out of service after Oct. 1863. No other record until paroled May 13, 1865. d. Aug. 9, 1880.

Posey, Stanhope. b. Sept. 6, 1841. att. Spring Hill Coll. Capt. AAG to his father, Gen. Posey, Jan. 23, 1863. Slightly WIA at Chancellorsville. Capt. AAG to Harris, Nov. 1863. Capt. AAG to Wirt Adams, Dec. 24, 1864. Paroled May 12, 1865. m. Elise Whyte. d. Sept. 10, 1893.

Potts, Frank. b. in Ireland, Jan. 14, 1835. Moved to Virginia, 1851. Merchant at Richmond. m. Virginia Finley. Sgt. Co. C, 1st Virginia. Asst. to Longstreet's QM in Sept. 1861, apparently as a civilian. Capt. AQM, 38th Virginia Bn. Arty., but may not have served. Capt. AQM, Aug. 1, 1863, and Chief Paymaster to Longstreet's corps. Appx. Petersburg grocer. d. Richmond, Mar. 6, 1890. bur. Hollywood Cem. Potts's 1861 diary is at the Library of Virginia, and his memoir of the Apr. 1865 retreat is at the Museum of the Confederacy.

Powell, Hugh Lee. b. Leesburg, Virginia, July 1839. Clerk in Richmond. Pvt. 1st Co. Richmond Howitzers, 1861. Lt. OO to Cabell's Bn. Arty., by July 1863. WIA at Gettysburg. Bank employee at Leesburg. d. Feb. 6, 1910.

Powell, John Burwell. b. Warren Co., North Carolina. A farmer. Sgt. Co. G, 43rd North Carolina, Feb. 26, 1862, age 37. To Lt., July 19, 1862. Lt. OO to Grimes's Bgd., by Dec. 1864. Appx., as Lt. Co. G. Probably the J. B. Powell living at Nashville, North Carolina, in 1896.

Powell, John Simms. b. Jan. 11, 1818. Tobacco merchant at Shepherdstown, Virginia. Capt. AQM, July 19, 1861. Served around Virginia, including posts at Manassas and Lynchburg. Resigned Nov. 17, 1862. d. July 4, 1899.

Powell, William Levin. b. Loudoun Co., Virginia, May 3, 1830. att. VMI. Civil engineer and planter. Capt. AQM, 21st Virginia, July 18, 1861. Capt. acting ADC to J. M. Jones at the Wilderness. Capt. acting ADC to John B. Gordon at Spotsylvania. Capt. AQM to Lomax, Jan. 20, 1865. U.S. Indian agent. d. Neah Bay, Washington, May 12, 1894. bur. there.

Powers, James L. Capt. AQM, 22nd Bn. Virginia, Mar. 1, 1862. Capt. AQM to H. H. Walker's old brigade by Sept. 15, 1864. On staff of Barton (same brigade) in Mar. 1865, but had been absent for several months at Goldsboro, North Carolina.

Powers, Philip Henry. b. Apr. 10, 1828. A teacher. m. Roberta Macky Smith, 1852. Pvt. Co. D, 1st Virginia Cavy., Apr. 18, 1861. Sgt. Maj. 1st Virginia Cavy. Maj. QM to Stuart, Mar. 6, 1862. Resigned June 5, 1862, blaming ill health. Postwar teacher and farmer in Clarke Co. d. there Sept. 18, 1887. bur. Green Hill Cem., Berryville.

Preston, A. T. Pvt. Co. G, 12th Alabama, Aug. 15, 1861. Capt. ACS, 12th Alabama, May 27, 1862. Capt. ACS to Battle, Aug. 1863. Served through 1864, at least.

Preston, John. b. Sept. 28, 1834. Pvt. Co. F, 37th Virginia, July 24, 1861. Capt. AQM, 37th Virginia, Jan. 15, 1863. Capt. AQM to Early, Aug. 1864. Capt. AQM to John B. Gordon. d. Apr. 3, 1911.

Preston, John, Jr. b. New Hanover, Connecticut, July 13, 1836. att. South Carolina Coll. Studied in Germany. A lawyer. Son of Gen. J. S. Preston. Lt. PAVA., 1861. Lt. acting ADC to Huger, May–Oct. 1861. Lt. ADC to Huger, Oct. 29, 1861. Ordered to report to Hampton, May 1863. WIA at Upperville, June 21, 1863. Maj. AAIG to Hampton, Sept. 22, 1863. Maj. AAG to Butler, Nov. 4, 1864. Paroled Apr. 26, 1865. Professor in Kentucky and Louisiana. d. Oct. 20, 1880.

bur. Trinity Episc. Churchyard, Columbia, South Carolina.

Preston, John Thomas Lewis. b. Lexington, Virginia, Apr. 25, 1811. att. UVA., Yale, and Washington Coll. A cofounder of VMI. Second wife was prominent author Margaret Junkin, whose sister was Stonewall Jackson's first wife. Lt. Col. 9th Virginia, July 7, 1861. Lt. Col. AAG to T. J. Jackson, Oct. 22, 1861. Relieved Dec. 27, 1861, and ordered to VMI, but still serving with Jackson as late as Jan. 1862. Author of several books. d. July 15, 1890. bur. Stonewall Jackson Cem., Lexington.

Preston, Thomas Lewis. b. Nov. 20, 1812. att. UVA. Lawyer in Smyth Co., Virginia, and member of state legislature. A brother of Gen. J. S. Preston. Capt. (PAVA.) May 1861. Possibly served with Magruder briefly before joining J. E. Johnston as AAAG about June 30, 1861. Dropped spring 1862 because his commission in PAVA. was obsolete. Maj. QM to Johnston, June 10, 1862, but declined. A farmer. d. Mar. 20, 1903.

Preston, Waller Redd. b. Montgomery Co., Virginia, Apr. 27, 1841. att. UVA. Pvt. Co. G, 4th Virginia, Apr. 17, 1861. Capt. Co. G, 14th Virginia Cavy., Apr. 15, 1862. Resigned Nov. 28, 1862. Capt. AAG to Echols, Aug. 11, 1863, through 1865. Murdered in Texas, Aug. 1, 1872.

Price, Francis Lewis. b. Ceylon, East Indies, Sept. 6, 1837. Son of a British Indian Army officer. att. Sandhurst. Sgt. Co. B, 4th Texas, 1861. Adjt. 4th Texas, July 24, 1862. Capt. AAG to J. B. Robertson, Nov. 12, 1862. POW at Gettysburg. Exchanged Feb. 24, 1865. Merchant at Georgetown, Texas. m. Caroline Beall, 1870. d. July 31, 1884, of paralysis. bur. Georgetown IOOF Cem.

Price, George E. b. Frederick Co., Virginia, ca. 1820. Hardware merchant at Staunton, prewar and postwar. Served in QM office in Virginia, 1861–1863, without a commission. Capt. AQM, June 21, 1863. On duty at Staunton, 1863–1865.

Price, Richard Channing. b. Richmond, Virginia, Feb. 24, 1843. Pvt. 3rd Co. Richmond Howitzers, Oct. 10, 1861. Lt. ADC to his cousin, Gen. Stuart, July 25, 1862. Maj. AAG to Stuart, Mar. 1, 1863. KIA at Chancellorsville, May 1, 1863. bur. Hollywood Cem.

Price, Samuel Compton. b. Nov. 28, 1829. A clerk. Cpl. Co. F, 18th Virginia, Apr. 23, 1861. Later to Sgt. Maj., and then Capt. AQM, Sept. 13, 1862. WIA at Williamsburg, May 5, 1862. WIA in thigh at Second Manassas. Capt. AQM to Hunton, Sept. 15, 1864. Appx. Dry goods salesman in Prince Edward Co., Virginia. d. 1887.

Price, Thomas Randolph, Jr. b. Richmond, Virginia, Mar. 18, 1839. att. UVA. Studied in Paris and Berlin. Lt. Asst. EO to his cousin, Gen. Stuart, Mar. 17, 1863. Relieved June 7, 1863. Performed engineer duty around Richmond for rest of war. Paroled May 11, 1865. Professor at Univ. of Richmond, Randolph Macon, UVA., and Columbia. d. New York City, May 7, 1903. Brother of R. C. Price (see above).

Price, William A. Capt. AAG to A. P. Hill. POW at Frederick, Maryland, Sept. 11, 1862. Nothing further found except POW records. A strange case. Quite possibly bogus.

Price, William R. Capt. AQM, Sept. 29, 1862. Vacated by nonconfirmation, 1864. Reappointed June 15, 1864. Served entire time as Capt. AQM at Lynchburg, Virginia.

Priest, Robert L. b. Eddyville, Kentucky. A 21-year-old schoolteacher in Tishomingo Co., Mississippi, in 1860. Pvt. Co. K, 19th Mississippi. Capt. ACS, 26th Alabama, May 9, 1862. Capt. acting ACS to Rodes, July–Aug. 1862. Capt. ACS to Rodes, Sept. 1863. Capt. ACS to Wharton, Sept. 1864. Absent sick all of 1865.

Prince, Joseph Brown. b. Southampton Co., Virginia, Aug. 18, 1844. att. VMI. Lt. of Arty., June 14, 1864. Lt. OO to Hampton, Feb. 8, 1865. Lt. OO to Beale, Mar. 27, 1865. Paroled Apr. 26, 1865. att. UVA. postwar.

m. Martha Frances Drewry, 1877. Commonwealth's attorney for Southampton Co. d. Courtland, Virginia, Mar. 25, 1903.

Privett, William Girard. b. Lincolnton, North Carolina, Dec. 24, 1833. Pvt. Co. D, 8th Alabama. Capt. ACS, 8th Alabama, Mar. 28, 1862. Capt. ACS to R. H. Anderson, about Sept. 1863. Capt. ACS to Mahone, May 1864. Appx. Railroad contractor at Selma, Alabama. m. Lenora A. Phillips, 1870. d. Selma, Sept. 7, 1900. bur. Phillips Fam. Cem., Dallas Co.

Proctor, James Toutant. att. Georgetown Coll. A resident of New Orleans, Louisiana, and a nephew of Gen. Beauregard. Said to have run away from school to join army. VADC to Maxcy Gregg, autumn 1862. Lt. Co. C, 1st (Gregg's) South Carolina, Jan. 13, 1863. WIA at Chancellorsville, May 3, 1863, and lost leg. Smoked a cigar during the amputation. Lt. OO at Charleston, South Carolina, 1864. Paroled May 1, 1865, possibly on his uncle's staff.

Puryear, Henry Shepard. b. Apr. 11, 1841. att. UNC. Pvt. Co. B, 27th North Carolina, May 1, 1861. Lt. ADC to Clingman, Jan. 17, 1864. WIA at Petersburg, Aug. 19, 1864. A lawyer. d. Oct. 15, 1923.

Putney, Stephen. b. Melrose, Massachusetts, ca. 1823. Moved to Richmond, Virginia, at a very young age. Became a prominent boot and shoe merchant there. Capt. AQM, June 25, 1863. In charge of Richmond shoe factory. Paroled Apr. 18, 1865. Wrote in 1865 that he had been opposed to the war, "but engaged on local duty from necessity." Married twice. d. at Richmond, Nov. 23, 1905. bur. Hollywood Cem.

Quattlebaum, Paul Jones. b. near Leesville, South Carolina, May 19, 1836. att. USMA. Lt. 9th U.S. Inf., 1857–1861. Lt. of Inf., Mar. 16, 1861. On duty with Huger, Aug.–Sept. 1861. Maj. 5th Texas, Oct. 2, 1861. Maj. AAG to Wigfall, Oct. 30, 1861. Spent rest of war as temporary Maj. and Lt. Col., on duty commanding batteries at Mobile, Alabama. Paroled May 10, 1865. d. Columbus, Georgia, Jan. 4, 1883.

Quincy, William H. b. in Florida, ca. 1840. Clerk at Charleston, South Carolina. Capt. AAG to Micah Jenkins, Nov. 4, 1862. Maj. QM to Jenkins, Jan. 1, 1863. Maj. QM to Bratton, May 1864. Appx. Clerk at Charleston grocery, 1870.

Quintard, Charles Todd. b. Stamford, Connecticut, Dec. 22, 1824. att. Trinity School, Columbia, and Univ. of City of New York. Physician at New York City and at Athens, Georgia. Episc. rector at Memphis, Tennessee. Chaplain, 1st Tennessee, July 19, 1861. "Satan tempted me to accept a position," which was as Lt. ADC to Loring, Jan. 10, 1862. Resigned June 14, 1862. Reapptd. Chaplain same day. VADC in AOT later in the war. Postwar Episc. Bishop of Tennessee. d. Meridian, Georgia, Feb. 15, 1898. Quintard's memoirs were published posthumously.

Radford, Richard Carlton Walker. b. Bedford Co., Virginia, July 8, 1822. att. VMI and USMA. Served in U.S. Cavy., 1845–1856. Col. 2nd Virginia Cavy., May 8, 1861. Dropped Apr. 1862. Capt. AAIG to W. E. Jones, Feb. 19, 1864. Capt. AAG to B. T. Johnson, Nov. 4, 1864. Capt. AAG to Rosser, Mar. 29, 1865. Bedford Co. planter. d. there Nov. 2, 1886.

Ragan, Abraham B. b. in Georgia. Served as a paymaster in the Mexican War. Left the army but rejoined it in the same capacity in Mar. 1857. Had been a merchant at Columbus. Maj. QM, CSA, July 19, 1861. Maj. QM to J. E. Johnston, Aug. 22, 1861. Maj. QM to E. K. Smith, June 23, 1862. Maj. QM at Atlanta, Feb. 4, 1863. d. there Sept. 17, 1875.

Rains, Henry J. b. in New York, ca. 1846. Lt. ADC to his father, Gen. G. J. Rains, June 15, 1864. Served into 1865. Teacher at Augusta, Georgia, in 1870.

Ramsaur, James O. b. Lincoln Co., North Carolina, Aug. 5, 1832. A farmer at Lincolnton. Sgt. in 17th Mississippi, May 27, 1861.

To Ordnance Sgt., Jan. 4, 1862, and to Lt. in Apr. 1863. WIA at Gettysburg and the Wilderness. To Capt. in 17th Mississippi, Dec. 2, 1864. Paroled at Appx. as Capt. ACS to Humphreys. m. Sallie A. Murray, 1866, in Arkansas.

Ramsey, John Crozier. b. Knox Co., Tennessee, June 7, 1824. Maury Co. farmer. Lt. ADC to Vaughn, date uncertain. POW at Vicksburg. POW in Sullivan Co., Tennessee, Dec. 14, 1864. d. Knoxville, Tennessee, Jan. 1, 1869. bur. Lebanon Presby. Church.

Rand, Isaac Noyes. b. Charleston, Virginia, Apr. 23, 1840. att. Washington Coll. Charleston clerk. Adjt. 22nd Virginia, May 8, 1861. Lt. acting ADC to McCausland, May 1862. POW at Lewisburg, May 23, 1862. Lt. acting ADC to Col. Patton, commanding brigade, Aug. and Nov. 1863. WIA twice. Paroled Apr. 26, 1865. Bookkeeper at Kanawha C.H. Moved to El Paso, Texas, 1882. d. there Mar. 19, 1911. bur. Spring Hill Cem., Charleston. Known as "Plus" Rand.

Randal, Horace. b. McNair Co., Tennessee, Jan. 4, 1833. att. USMA. Lt. 2nd U.S. Dragoons. Lt. of Cavy., CSA, Mar. 26, 1861. Capt. AQM, mid-1861, on duty at Pensacola, Florida. Lt. ADC to G. W. Smith, Nov. 16, 1861. Col. 28th Texas Cavy., Feb. 12, 1862. MWIA at Jenkins's Ferry, Apr. 30, 1864. d. May 2, 1864. bur. Old Marshall Cem., Marshall, Texas.

Randall, Whitaker P. Cpl. Co. L, 1st Texas, Aug. 1, 1861, age 21. To Sgt., June 5, 1862. WIA at Second Manassas. To Lt., May 20, 1863. POW at Chickamauga. Lt. acting OO to John Gregg, Mar. 1864. KIA at the Wilderness, May 6, 1864. bur. Fredericksburg Confederate Cem.

Randle, James Colquitt. b. 1823. Of Sparta, Georgia. Sgt. Co. D, 3rd Alabama, Apr. 26, 1861. Lt. ADC to his kinsman (uncle or cousin) Gen. Colquitt, Dec. 19, 1862. MWIA at Battery Wagner. d. Macon, Georgia, Sept. 21, 1863.

Randolph, Benton. b. Apr. 11, 1832. Lawyer

at Huntsville, Texas, pre- and postwar. Lt. Co. H, 4th Texas, Oct. 25, 1861. WIA in heel at Gaines's Mill. Judge Advocate to Hardee, Dec. 16, 1862. Resigned Dec. 1, 1863, to assume position of Judge Advocate to Elzey's command at Richmond, same day. Served there into mid-1864, at least. Married twice. d. July 21, 1894.

Randolph, Beverley. b. Cumberland Co., Virginia, June 26, 1823. att. Hampden Sidney. Served in USN, 1839–1851. Mexican War veteran. Farmer in Clarke Co. Lt. CSN, commanding a battery on Virginia's lower peninsula, 1861. Lt. AOO to J. E. Johnston, July 1861. Lt. OO to Whiting, July–Oct. 1861. Capt. OO and AAAIG to Whiting, Oct. 7, 1861. Maj. OO to Whiting, Apr. 17, 1862. Maj. OO to Hood, 1862. Maj. OO at Staunton, Feb. 28, 1863, into 1865. d. Millwood, Virginia, Nov. 19, 1903. bur. Old Chapel Cem.

Randolph, Coleman LaFayette. b. Marshall Co., Tennessee, Dec. 21, 1830. Teacher and farmer at Belfast. Pvt. Co. E, 41st Tennessee, Nov. 28, 1861. Capt. AQM, 35th Tennessee, May 15, 1862. Capt. AQM to Buckner and Cleburne. Maj. QM to B. R. Johnson, May 2, 1863. Appx. Married twice. Alive 1879.

Randolph, James Innes. b. Winchester, Virginia, Oct. 25, 1837. att. Hobart Coll. Washington, D.C., lawyer. m. Ann Clare King. Lt. EO, PAVA., Apr. 1861. Lt. EO on topographical duty, loosely associated with staff of Ewell, May 25–July 2, 1862. Lt. EO, PACS, June 24, 1862. Assigned to duty at Petersburg, Aug. 18, 1862. May have been with the army at Gettysburg. Lt. EO at Richmond, June 1864 into 1865. Author of "I'm a Good Old Rebel." Lawyer, author, and journalist at Richmond and Baltimore. d. Baltimore, Apr. 28, 1887. "A more cranky and irritable fellow is rarely met with."

Randolph, Meriwether Lewis. b. Albemarle Co., Virginia, July 17, 1837. att. UVA. A nephew of Secretary of War G. W. Randolph. Pvt. Co. F, 21st Virginia, Apr. 21,

1861. Lt. Co. C, 1st Bn. Virginia, May 1, 1861. Capt. SO, Oct. 8, 1862, to report to T. J. Jackson. Capt. SO to D. H. Hill, Dec. 1862. Capt. SO to Rodes, by spring 1863, through Sept. 1864. Capt. SO to Ramseur, Sept.–Oct. 1864. Capt. SO to Grimes, 1864–1865. Resigned Mar. 2, 1865, to join the cavalry. d. Feb. 1, 1871, of consumption. bur. "Monticello" at Charlottesville.

Randolph, Peyton Kidder. b. Frederick Co., Virginia, Sept. 23, 1833. att. Columbian Coll. Brother of James I. Randolph (above). Engineer with railroad lines in Virginia, Indiana, and Alabama. Lt. 5th Alabama, 1861. Lt. staff of Rodes, late in 1861. Lt. of Inf., CSA, Jan. 7, 1862. Lt. EO and PM to Armistead, Sept. 1862–July 1863. Maj. 1st C.S. Engineers, Apr. 1, 1864. Appx. Railroad man postwar. d. Washington, D.C., Apr. 22, 1891. Used his middle initial before the war only.

Randolph, Thomas Hugh Burwell. b. Clarke Co., Virginia, Apr. 5, 1843. Brother of Col. W. W. Randolph, 2nd Virginia. Cpl. Co. C, 2nd Virginia, Apr. 18, 1861. To Lt. WIA at First Manassas. Probably did not rejoin his unit. VADC to Pendleton, May 1, 1862. POW along Rappahannock River, Dec. 5, 1862. Exchanged Mar. 29, 1863, and possibly out of service. POW in Clarke Co., Oct. 26, 1863. Paroled June 12, 1865, from Johnson's Island prison. Clarke Co. farmer. d. Apr. 23, 1900. bur. Old Chapel Cem., Millwood.

Randolph, Thomas Jefferson, Jr. b. Albemarle Co., Virginia, Aug. 29, 1829. att. UVA. A great-grandson of Thomas Jefferson. Married twice. Lt. Co. K, 2nd Virginia Cavy., May 11, 1861. Maj. QM to Randolph, his uncle, Feb. 24, 1862. Maj. QM to Armistead, by June 1862. Maj. QM at Richmond, July 1863 into 1865. Chief purchaser of forage for Virginia. A farmer. Killed in a railroad accident in Albemarle Co., Aug. 8, 1872. bur. Grace Episc. Church Cem.

Randolph, Tucker St. Joseph. b. Richmond, Virginia, Sept. 19, 1843. Pvt. Co. F, 21st Virginia, Apr. 21, 1861. To Cpl. and then Sgt. by Mar. 1862. WIA twice at Kernstown. VADC to John Pegram by June 1862, continuously until death. KIA May 30, 1864, at Bethesda Church—cut in half by an artillery shell. Body recovered and buried at the Mosby farm on the Mechanicsville Turnpike, west of Bethesda Church. Randolph's early-war diary is at the Museum of the Confederacy.

Randolph, William Lewis. b. Dec. 20, 1841. att. VMI and UVA. A nephew of Secretary of War Randolph. Married twice. Lt. Co. H, 57th Virginia, July 22, 1861. Lt. OO to Armistead, May 1, 1862. Lt. OO to Barton, 1864. Lt. OO to Steuart, 1864–1865. Capt. OO to G. W. C. Lee, Mar. 20, 1865. POW at Sailor's Creek. Postwar farmer. d. Albemarle Co., June 7, 1892, of "apoplexy." bur. "Monticello" at Charlottesville.

Ranson, Ambrose Robert Hite. b. Jefferson Co., Virginia, Apr. 12, 1831. att. VMI. A farmer. Lt. CSA, June 8, 1861, on duty at a camp of instruction. Adjt. 20th Virginia. POW at Rich Mountain. Exchanged. Lt. OO, Sept. 21, 1862, to report to Briscoe Baldwin at ANVa. headquarters. Assigned to Columbus, Mississippi, arsenal, Oct. 24, 1862. Maj. CS to Pegram, Nov. 19, 1862. Resigned Dec. 12, 1863, but retained rank in regular army. Lt. OO, Dec. 28, 1863, to report to Baldwin. Capt. OO at ANVa. headquarters, Oct. 28, 1864. Appx. Baltimore merchant. d. there May 12, 1919.

Ranson, James Francis Madison. b. Jefferson Co., Virginia, May 14, 1833. att. VMI. A brother of A. R. H. Ranson (see above). Lived at San Francisco, prewar. Lt. ADC to Pegram, Nov. 20, 1862. WIA in head at Fisher's Hill, and his brother testified that Ranson "never was entirely himself afterward . . . and never engaged in any business." Paroled Apr. 19, 1865, at Winchester. Drowned at Richmond, Virginia, Mar. 6, 1889. bur. Hollywood Cem.

Raoul, William Greene. b. Livingston Parish, Louisiana, July 4, 1843. Pvt. 2nd Co.

Washington (La.) Arty., Mar. 10, 1862. Discharged Mar. 21, 1864. Capt. AQM, June 15, 1864. Served at Richmond, Virginia, in connection with the railroad bureau, on construction projects. m. Mary Millen Wadley, 1868. Postwar railroadman in Georgia and Alabama. President of Mexican National Railroad in 1880s. Alive 1909 at Atlanta, Georgia. Eighteen of Raoul's war letters are at Louisiana State Univ.

Ratchford, James Wylie. b. York District, South Carolina, Feb. 24, 1840. att. NCMA and Davidson Coll. WIA in forehead at Big Bethel. Lt. ADC to D. H. Hill, Sept. 11, 1861. Maj. AAG to Hill, Sept. 30, 1861. WIA at Seven Pines. Later Maj. AAG to Hindman, Hood, and S. D. Lee. WIA in leg near Nashville. Moved to Texas in 1867. County clerk, surveyor, and schoolteacher. d. Concho Co., Texas, Dec. 3, 1910. bur. Paint Rock Memorial Cem. Hill called him "a brave & efficient officer." Ratchford's memoirs have been published.

Ravenel, Francis Gualdo. b. June 28, 1825. att. Coll. of Charleston. Lt. Marion (S.C.) Arty., 1861. Lt. ADC to Ripley, Mar. 11, 1862. KIA at Malvern Hill, July 1, 1862.

Rawle, Francis. b. New Orleans, Louisiana, July 26, 1835. A clerk. Capt. Co. C, 1st Louisiana, Apr. 28, 1861. Capt. AQM, 10th Louisiana, June 27, 1862. Maj. QM to Nicholls, Oct. 6, 1862. Later staff of Stafford and York. Maj. QM to C. A. Evans by 1865. Appx. d. New Orleans, Aug. 31, 1913.

Read, Benjamin Huger. b. in South Carolina. att. Harvard Law School. A very wealthy planter at Monck's Corner, age 50 in 1860. Capt. AAG to Ripley, Sept. 2, 1862. Served with Ripley through late 1864, at least. d. Henderson Co., North Carolina, Oct. 12, 1887.

Read, Frederick Nash. b. in Virginia, Mar. 23, 1835. att. UVA. Lawyer at Charleston. Pvt. Co. H, 22nd Virginia, May 8, 1861. Later to Sgt. Capt. AQM, 26th Bn. Virginia, Nov. 12, 1862. Capt. AQM to Patton's Bgd.,

Sept. 1864. Paroled Lewisburg, West Virginia, Apr. 26, 1865. Moved to Corsicana, Texas, and practiced law. Moved to Dallas about 1900. d. there Apr. 14, 1915. bur. Oak Cliff Cem. Read's tombstone gives Mar. 23, 1836, as his date of birth, but his application to UVa., probably in his own hand, has the 1835 date.

Read, James B. Capt. ACS, Jan. 14, 1862. On duty at Petersburg, Virginia, 1862–1865. Very probably the man who died Nov. 13, 1884, age 71, and is buried at Blandford Cem., Petersburg.

Read, John Postell Williamson. b. Savannah, Georgia, Apr. 21, 1829. Chief of Savannah police and planter. Capt. Co. K, 10th Georgia, 1861, which became Fraser's (Ga.) Btty. Capt. Chief of Arty. to McLaws, May 1862. Maj. of Arty., Mar. 2, 1864. Lt. Col. Nov. 5, 1864. d. Lynchburg, Virginia, Sept. 28, 1884.

Reading, Thomas R. b. in Mississippi, Sept. 18, 1840. att. UVa. Merchant at Vicksburg. Lt. Co. C, 19th Mississippi, May 14, 1861. Lt. VADC to Wilcox, May–June 1862. Lt. VADC to Featherston, June 1862. Capt. Co. C, 19th Mississippi, Jan. 1863. To Maj., July 14, 1863. Resigned Oct. 8, 1863. d. at Vicksburg, Oct. 25, 1876.

Reardon, Henry F. b. Norfolk, Virginia, ca. 1836. A merchant. Lt. of Arty., May 2, 1862. Duty not evident until appointed Lt. in the Nitre & Mining Bureau, May 30, 1863. Capt. Nitre & Mining, June 15, 1864. Stationed at Richmond. Paroled at Greensboro, North Carolina, as Capt. and Disbursing Officer.

Redd, John K., Jr. b. in Georgia. att. Oglethorpe Coll. Merchant at Columbus, age 32 in 1860. Pvt. Co. G, 2nd Georgia, Apr. 16, 1861. To Sgt., July 15, 1861. No later record with unit. VADC to Semmes during Seven Days and at Sharpsburg. WIA slightly at Sharpsburg. Capt. Co. F, 64th Georgia, Apr. 11, 1863. Slightly WIA in head at

Olustee. KIA at the Crater, July 30, 1864. bur. Linwood Cem., Columbus.

Reed, George F. Lt. OO to Hays, July 30, 1862. Dropped in 1863 for failing competency examination.

Reid, Alexander Sidney. b. Nov. 8, 1834. Lived in Putnam Co., Georgia, prewar and postwar. Lt. Co. G, 12th Georgia, June 15, 1861. To Capt., May 22, 1862. Capt. AQM, 12th Georgia, Nov. 16, 1863. Capt. AQM to Cook, Sept. 15, 1864. Capt. AQM to Grimes, Mar. 22, 1865. Appx. Postwar farmer and legislator. m. Mary Elizabeth Grimes, 1865. d. Eatonton, Georgia, December 2, 1909. bur. Pine Grove Cem.

Reid, Francis Welman. b. Aug. 31, 1830. A commission merchant at Savannah, Georgia, before and after the war. Capt. ACS to Lawton, Oct. 24, 1861. Maj. CS to Lawton, June 11, 1862. Maj. CS to Gordon, Nov. 1862. Maj. CS to C. A. Evans, May 1864. Charged with drunkenness in 1865. Appx. d. Aug. 15, 1898. bur. Bonaventure Cem.

Reid, George Cornelius. b. Norfolk, Virginia, Sept. 18, 1839. Merchant at Norfolk. Clerk at headquarters of Colston's Bgd., 1862. Capt. AQM, Jan. 31, 1863. Post QM at Petersburg. Probably Capt. AQM, 8th Ga. Cavy., 1864–1865. Norfolk banker and merchant. d. there July 4, 1910. bur. Elmwood Cem.

Reid, James A. Drillmaster and Cadet, 1st North Carolina. Lt. ADC to D. H. Hill, June 12, 1862. WIA at Sharpsburg. Paroled Apr. 26, 1865, apparently having served with Hill the entire time.

Reid, James Sims. b. in South Carolina. Wealthy planter and legislator at Canton, Mississippi. m. Louisa D. Ross. Lt. Madison (Miss.) Arty., Apr. 28, 1862. Maj. QM to J. R. Davis, Nov. 1, 1862. Appx. Alive 1886 at Canton.

Reid, Joseph Davis. b. in Mississippi. A resident of Sharon. Pvt. Madison (Miss.) Arty., July 1, 1862, age 16. Appointed Cadet,

Aug. 16, 1862. Staff of J. R. Davis. KIA at Gettysburg.

Reid, P. N. Capt. AQM to Wharton, Sept. 1864. No other record found.

Reid, Richard W. b. in Florida. m. Emma Turnball, 1861. Pvt. Co. A, 5th Florida, Jan. 28, 1862. Later to Sgt., and then Capt. ACS, 5th Florida, May 24, 1862. Dropped in 1863, but became Capt. ACS to Finegan. Probably also Capt. ACS to E. A. Perry, before Finegan. Appx. A 33-year-old farmer at Monticello in 1870.

Reid, Samuel Venable. b. Lynchburg, Virginia, July 19, 1833. att. UVA. and Washington Coll. Moved to Covington, Kentucky, in 1858. Capt. Co. H, 3rd Arkansas. WIA at Seven Pines. Resigned Feb. 12, 1863. Later on special duty with Commissary Dept. Capt. ACS, Feb. 1, 1863, at Atlanta. Capt. ACS to Robert Ransom, Jan. 16, 1864. Maj. CS to Ransom, Feb. 19, 1864. Maj. CS at Wilmington, North Carolina, June 4, 1864, through the end of the war. Postwar merchant at Cincinnati, Ohio. Alive 1887. "Not much bigger than a lump of chalk."

Reid, William Lysander Jackson. b. Cabarrus Co., North Carolina, Sept. 13, 1816. m. Anne Crossland Horne, 1841. Capt. AQM, 26th South Carolina, July 1, 1862. Capt. AQM to Beauregard, Sept. 20, 1864. Capt. AQM to R. H. Anderson. Appx. Cheraw businessman and planter. d. Sept. 30, 1876.

Rendet, P. C. Lt. ADC to Battle, Nov. 1863. No other record found.

Renshaw, Robert Aloysius Henry. b. Apr. 26, 1834, at either Caracas, Venezuela, or at Bristol, Pennsylvania. Son of a British diplomat and a Spanish mother. att. Harvard. Studied law at Baltimore, Maryland. Hospital steward early in the war. Capt. AQM, Mar. 8, 1864, but not confirmed. Reappt., Nov. 4, 1864, on duty with ANVa. reserve ambulance train. Appx. Lived in Clarke Co., Virginia, and farmed at Al-

toona, Pennsylvania. d. Charlottesville, Aug. 17, 1910.

Reynolds, Frank A. b. in Virginia, 1841. att. USMA. Son of Gen. A. W. Reynolds. Maj. of Cavy. (PAVa.?) under Floyd in 1861. Capt. AAG to French, Nov. 9, 1861. Maj. 39th North Carolina, May 19, 1862, and later Lt. Col. Street inspector in New York, postwar. Served as Arty. Col. on staff of Gen. Loring in Egypt, 1870. d. Ilion, New York, July 19, 1875.

Reynolds, George Norton, Jr. b. in South Carolina, 1840. att. SCMA and USMA. Lt. Co. B, 1st Bn. South Carolina Arty. Lt. of Arty., CSA, Mar. 16, 1861. Lt. OO to Magruder, Sept. 17, 1861. Maj. OO to Magruder, Mar. 27, 1862. Absent sick most of 1862 and d. 1863. Interred Mar. 25, 1863, at Magnolia Cem., Charleston, in an unmarked grave.

Reynolds, Henry S. b. Nansemond Co., Virginia, ca. 1838. att. Hampden Sidney. Merchant at Norfolk. Pvt. Co. G, 6th Virginia, June 18, 1861. Lt. Co. H, 6th Virginia, May 1, 1862. Detailed as clerk in commissary office, Nov. 1862. Capt. ACS, Mar. 9, 1864, but failed confirmation. Reappointed Mar. 13, 1865, to rank from Mar. 2, 1864. On duty at Richmond. Paroled May 4, 1865. Merchant at Norfolk. d. Staunton, Virginia, Apr. 13, 1895. bur. in unmarked grave at Elmwood Cem., Norfolk.

Reynolds, Pryor. b. in Alabama, Feb. 17, 1824. A merchant in Rockingham Co., North Carolina. Capt. AQM, 45th North Carolina, Feb. 28, 1863. Capt. AQM to Grimes, Sept. 15, 1864. Appx. d. Dec. 12, 1896. bur. Lawson Cem., Eden, North Carolina.

Rhett, Albert Moore. b. Nov. 28, 1834. Capt. AQM, July 1, 1862, assigned to duty with T. S. Rhett's artillery defenses at Richmond. Transferred to Columbia, South Carolina, Sept. 26, 1863. Collected forage there for ANVa., rest of war. d. Dec. 13, 1911.

Rhett, Thomas Grimke. b. in South Carolina, Aug. 2, 1821. att. USMA. Served in U.S.

Army, 1845–1861. Mexican War veteran. Brigadier Gen. of militia. Maj. of Arty., CSA, Mar. 16, 1861. Maj. AAG to G. H. Terrett's Virginia Bgd., May 16, 1861. Maj. AAG to J. E. Johnston, July 20, 1861–June 1862. Maj. OO to Holmes, Oct. 22, 1862. Maj. OO to E. K. Smith, Apr. 30, 1863, through 1865. Col. OO in Egyptian army. d. Baltimore, Maryland, July 28, 1878. bur. Green Mount Cem., but later moved to Loudon Park Cem.

Rhett, Thomas Smith. b. in South Carolina, Feb. 25, 1827. att. USMA. Lt. U.S. Arty., 1848–1855. Bank clerk at Baltimore, Maryland, 1855–1861. Capt. of Arty., CSA, Nov. 15, 1861, to report to Charleston, South Carolina, for ordnance duty. Col. of Arty., PACS, May 10, 1862. Inspector of ordnance based at Richmond. On ordnance examining board. Commander of city artillery defenses, Aug. 30, 1862, through most of 1863. Recommended by Elzey for promotion to Brigadier Gen. in July 1863. Ordered abroad to purchase arms, Oct. 28, 1863. Insurance agent at Baltimore. d. Dec. 26, 1893.

Rhodes, Charles Holden. b. in Vermont, Oct. 30, 1828. Lived in Virginia from 1837 onward. att. UVA. Chesterfield Co. farmer. Lt. Co. B, 4th Virginia Cavy., 1861. Capt. AQM to Ewell, June 26, 1861. Resigned Sept. 3, 1861. Probably the Charles Rhodes who served as VADC to Pickett in October 1863, and who signed as AAAG to Pickett in Mar. 1864. Postwar farmer. d. near Richmond, by 1868.

Rice, Alexander Glenn. b. Union Co., South Carolina, Oct. 24, 1822. att. Harvard. VADC to Beauregard, Apr. 1861. Present at First Manassas, and from Oct. 1862–May 1863, at least. Paroled at Greensboro. Farmer in Union Co. d. there Feb. 24, 1899. His estate valued at $300,000 when he died.

Richards, Adolphus Edward. b. Loudoun Co., Virginia, May 26, 1844. att. UVA., Randolph Macon, and Univ. of Louisville. Lt. 7th Virginia Cavy. VADC to W. E. Jones,

Feb.–May 1863. Pvt. Co. B, 43rd Virginia Bn. Cavy., Oct. 1, 1863. Later a Capt. in same regiment, and promoted to Maj. Dec. 7, 1864. Judge and lawyer at Louisville, Kentucky. d. there Jan. 20, 1920. bur. Cave Hill Cem.

Richards, William Burton, Jr. b. in Virginia. A 38-year-old "Fancy Store" merchant at Alexandria, Virginia, 1860. Capt. AQM 17th Virginia, Apr. 17, 1861. Capt. AQM at Gordonsville, Virginia, Jan. 7, 1862. Maj. QM at Gordonsville, Jan. 5, 1863. Maj. QM to Conner, Mar. 23, 1865. Still living at Gordonsville in Aug. 1865.

Richardson, Henry Brown. b. Winthrop, Maine, Aug. 23, 1837. A civil engineer in Tensas Parish, Louisiana, in 1860. Pvt. Co. D, 6th Louisiana, June 4, 1861. Orderly for Gen. Ewell at First Winchester. Lt. EO to Ewell, Aug. 6, 1862. WIA at Sharpsburg. Capt. EO, Oct. 4, 1862, to report to Gen. Gilmer for assignment. Capt. EO to Early, Dec. 11, 1862. Capt. EO to Ewell, June 1863. WIA in back at Gettysburg, July 2, 1863, and POW July 5. Paroled May 26, 1865. Chief engineer of Louisiana, 1885–1909. d. Aug. 21, 1909. bur. in an unmarked grave at Metairie Cem., New Orleans.

Richardson, James Gunn. b. in Alabama, 1830. Pvt. Co. C, 2nd Louisiana, May 11, 1861. Capt. ACS, 2nd Louisiana, Sept. 2, 1861. Capt. acting ACS to Howell Cobb, May 6, 1862. Capt. acting ACS to Pendleton's Louisiana Bgd., Aug. 1, 1862. Probably staff of Starke, Aug.–Sept. 1862. Maj. CS to Nicholls, Oct. 14, 1862. Maj. CS to Stafford, Oct. 1863. Court-martialed and cashiered, Feb. 12, 1864. Specific charges not found. m. Julia Ray, 1876. d. New Orleans, Louisiana, Apr. 10, 1911, age 80 years and 6 months.

Richardson, John Dunn. Of Clarke Co., Virginia. Capt. ACS, 7th Virginia Cavy., Oct. 18, 1861. Probably Bgd. Commissary for Gen. Ashby in the few days after that general's promotion before his death. Maj.

QM to Funsten's Bgd., Sept. 28, 1863. Maj.
QM to Rosser, Oct. 25, 1863. Maj. QM to
W. E. Jones, Jan. 29, 1864. WIA at Medley,
West Virginia, Jan. 30, 1864. POW in Aug.
1864, by own account. Paroled Apr. 20,
1865, age 49. Farmer at Berryville in 1870.
Possibly born Sept. 5, 1817, in Charlotte Co.

Richardson, John Manly. b. Sumter Dist.,
South Carolina, Mar. 13, 1831. att. SCMA,
UVA., and Harvard. Taught at Hillsboro
Military Academy, prewar. Maj. 21st North
Carolina, July 3, 1861–Jan. 28, 1862. Supt.
GMI, 1862–1863. Capt. AAIG to Hoke,
Nov. 2, 1863. Capt. AAIG to Godwin, sum-
mer 1864. WIA at Third Winchester and
lost left leg. Lawyer at Carrollton, Georgia,
before moving to Texas. d. Daingerfield,
Texas, Feb. 4, 1898. bur. Daingerfield Cem.

Richardson, Lucian W. Lt. James City (Va.)
Arty., May 16, 1861. To Capt., Jan. 7, 1862.
Left battery due to ill health, Jan. 1863, and
never returned. On miscellaneous staff duty
in Richmond. Commanded Castle Thunder
for several months in spring 1864.

Richardson, William Harvie. b. Richmond,
Virginia, Dec. 18, 1795. Lawyer and agri-
culturist. m. Mary Carter Randolph, 1816.
Capt. in War of 1812. Secretary of the
Commonwealth and patron of the state
militia system in Virginia. Adjt. Gen. of
Virginia, 1841–1876. In that role served
as AAG on staff of R. E. Lee, May 1861,
and in Richmond supporting state troops,
1861–1863, at least. d. Sept. 1, 1876. bur.
Hollywood Cem.

Richmond, Caleb Hazzard. b. Jan. 17, 1843.
att. UNC. Managed his mother's iron
foundry prewar. Cpl. Co. I, 45th North
Carolina. Lt. ADC to his brother-in-law,
Gen. Ramseur, Nov. 1, 1862. Out of commission Oct. 1864. No further military record.
m. Phereba Ellen Lewis, 1866. Farmer and
tobacco dealer in North Carolina, postwar.
d. Apr. 4, 1923. bur. Cedars Cem., Milton,
North Carolina.

Riddick, James Wilson. b. Nansemond Co.,

Virginia, 1843. Pvt. Co. K, 9th Virginia,
July 22–Oct. 8, 1861. Adjt. 34th North Caro-
lina, June 1, 1862. WIA at Gaines's Mill. Lt.
AAAG to Scales at Gettysburg. WIA July 1,
1863. Capt. AAG to Scales, Nov. 2, 1863.
Capt. AAIG to McGowan, Dec. 5, 1864.
Appx. Postwar merchant. d. Portsmouth,
Virginia, Sept. 20, 1869.

Riddick, John Thompson. b. Aug. 1, 1845.
att. VMI. Resident of Nansemond Co., Virginia. Lt. Drillmaster, Mar. 9, 1864, on duty
with Chambliss. Lt. AAAIG to Chambliss,
and subsequently to Col. Beale. No further
military record after late 1864. A merchant.
d. Suffolk, Virginia, July 18, 1884.

Riddick, Richard H. b. in North Carolina.
Lt. U.S. Cavalry, 1855–1861. Lt. Col. AAG
for State of North Carolina, 1861. Col. 34th
North Carolina, Apr. 2, 1862. MWIA at
Chantilly, Sept. 1, 1862. d. Sept. 11, 1862.

Riddick, Washington Lafayette. b. Aug. 15,
1825. att. Wm. & Mary. m. Frances Marion
Blount, 1844. Resident of Suffolk, Virginia.
Lt. Co. G, 5th Virginia Cavy., June 4, 1861.
Lt. acting ADC and AAAG to Blanchard,
Aug. 1861. Capt. AAG to Blanchard, Oct. 2,
1861. WIA at Seven Pines, June 1, 1862.
Capt. AAG to Camp Lee, Virginia, Aug.
1863. Capt. AAG to Kemper, by Jan. 1865.
Capt. AAIG to R. H. Anderson's corps arty.,
Jan. 28, 1865. Paroled May 2, 1865, at Rich-
mond. d. New Orleans, Louisiana, Feb. 3,
1871.

Ridgely, Randolph. b. Fort McHenry, Mary-
land, Nov. 21, 1844. att. St. Mary's Coll. Pvt.
Co. B, 39th Virginia Bn. Cavy. Lt. ADC to
J. M. Jones, Sept. 3, 1863. Lt. acting ADC
to Early, May 5–June 1, 1864. Lt. acting
ADC to Ramseur, June 1, 1864. WIA (frac-
tured thigh) and POW at Rutherford's Farm,
July 20, 1864. Recaptured in Winchester.
Lt. Drillmaster, Jan. 27, 1865, to report to
Kemper. Lived postwar at Waynesboro,
Georgia. d. Dec. 9, 1918. "Of rather spare
build, about five feet six or seven inches
tall."

Riely, John William. b. Jefferson Co., Virginia, Feb. 26, 1839. att. Washington Coll. Pvt. Co. I, 4th Virginia, June 2, 1861. Later promoted to QM Sgt. Clerk at G. W. Smith's headquarters, Oct. 31, 1861–Apr. 30, 1862. Capt. AAG to Smith, Sept. 5, 1862. Capt. AAG to Elzey, Dec. 12, 1862–Jan. 1863. Capt. AAG to Longstreet, Mar. 14, 1863. Moved to AIGO at Richmond, Sept. 12, 1863, and served rest of war there. Maj. AAG, Feb. 18, 1864. Lt. Col. AAG, Apr. 24, 1865. Paroled Apr. 26, 1865. Lawyer in Halifax Co. d. there Aug. 20, 1900.

Riley, Henry F. b. ca. 1837. Sgt. Co. A, 2nd Florida, May 25, 1861. WIA at Seven Pines. Lt. Co. A, 2nd Florida, Oct. 8, 1862. Lt. AAAIG to E. A. Perry at Chancellorsville. KIA at Gettysburg, July 3, 1863.

Ritter, William Bailey. b. Richmond, Virginia, Oct. 20, 1834. att. VMI and school in Germany. Lt. Sands's Co. (Va.) Arty., May 13, 1861. Capt. Henrico Arty., Apr. 30, 1862–Oct. 1862. On training duty at Richmond. Capt. OO to Daniel, Mar. 18, 1864. Capt. OO to Grimes until July 1864. Detailed on court-martial duty, Dec. 1864. Took Oath at Wilmington, North Carolina, July 24, 1865. d. July 1, 1867. bur. Hollywood Cem., Richmond, in an unmarked grave.

Rives, Alfred Landon. b. Paris, France, Mar. 25, 1830. att. UVa., VMI, and Ecole Polytechnique. m. Sarah Catherine Macmurdo, 1859. Designed Cabin John Bridge in Maryland. Capt. PAVa., May 2, 1861. Served as EO to Magruder. Capt. acting Chief of Engineer Bureau, by Dec. 1861. Capt. EO (PACS), Feb. 15, 1862. Served in Richmond remainder of war, mostly as second ranking officer in bureau. Maj. EO, Sept. 23, 1862. Lt. Col. EO, May 4, 1863. Col. EO, Mar. 17, 1864. Supt. Panama Railroad. Railroad engineer at Mobile, Alabama. d. Albemarle Co., Virginia, Feb. 26, 1903. bur. Grace Episc. Church Cem., Cobham, Virginia.

Robb, Robert Lightfoot. b. Port Royal, Virginia, Sept. 27, 1835. att. UVA. A physician. Sgt. Co. F, 9th Virginia Cavy., Oct. 7, 1861–summer 1862. VADC to Field, June 1862. Lt. ADC to Field, Feb. 19, 1864. Resigned July 8, 1864, citing "Panama Fever," never having been in the field with his general. King George Co. farmer. d. there July 5, 1897. bur. "Stuart Burying Ground" in King George Co., grave unmarked.

Roberts, Thomas Algernon. b. Kanawha Co., Virginia, Nov. 7, 1837. Sgt. Co. A, 22nd Virginia, May 22, 1861. Capt. AQM, 22nd Virginia, Nov. 1, 1862. Capt. AQM to Patton's Bgd., Sept. 17, 1864. Paroled May 29, 1865. m. Elizabeth Payne, 1865. Moved to Salem, Virginia. d. there Oct. 30, 1931. bur. East Hill Cem.

Robertson, Francis Smith. b. Richmond, Virginia, Jan. 3, 1841. att. UVA. Lt. PAVa., May 23, 1861. Lt. 48th Virginia. Lt. EO to Stuart, Apr. 1863. Lt. EO to W. H. F. Lee, May 29, 1864. Detached at army headquarters, Oct. 1864, but still staff of W. H. F. Lee into 1865. A farmer. m. Stella Wheeler. d. Aug. 10, 1926. bur. Sinking Spring Cem., Abingdon.

Robertson, Richard M. b. in Virginia. Pvt. Co. D, 11th Alabama, June 11, 1861. Capt. ACS, 11th Alabama, July 8, 1861. Capt. acting ACS to Wilcox, Aug. 1, 1861–Apr. 24, 1862. Maj. CS to Wilcox, Apr. 29, 1862. Stayed with the brigade, and thus staff of Perrin, Sanders, and Forney. 1870 census shows him as a 36-year-old farmer at Demopolis, worth $95,000. Wilcox called Robertson "the best in the army" among commissaries.

Robertson, Walter Henderson. b. Amelia Co., Virginia, Jan. 7, 1841. att. UVA. Sgt. Fayette (Va.) Arty., Apr. 25, 1861. Lt. Henrico (Va.) Arty. Lt. of Arty., date uncertain, to report to Gen. French. Lt. OO to Pettigrew. WIA in left leg at Gettysburg, July 1, 1863. Lt. OO to Kirkland. Joined 43rd Virginia Bn. Cavy., date unknown. Episc. minister in Gloucester and Warrenton. m. Georgia Ripley. d. Warrenton, July 2, 1903.

Robins, William Todd. b. Gloucester Co., Virginia, Nov. 22, 1835. att. VMI and Washington Coll. A planter. Adjt. 9th Virginia Cavy., Apr. 15, 1862. Capt. AAG to W. H. F. Lee, Oct. 30, 1862. Capt. AAG on duty in Conscript Bureau, June 12, 1863. Lt. Col. 40th Virginia Bn. Cavy., July 16, 1863. Lt. Col. 24th Virginia Cavy., June 14, 1864. WIA in arm below Richmond, Aug. 14, 1864. WIA in foot, Oct. 26, 1864. Appx. Gloucester Co. lawyer. d. at Richmond, Oct. 26, 1906. bur. family cem. in Gloucester.

Robinson, Henry. Lt. of Arty., June 19, 1861, to report to Loring. Capt. AAG to Loring, Oct. 14, 1862. Maj. AAG to Loring, Aug. 20, 1863. Maj. AAG to Longstreet, Mar. 18, 1865, but may never have served there. Paroled June 12, 1865, age 34. d. by 1894.

Robinson, John H. Sgt. Co. H, 1st North Carolina (6 months). Lt. Co. B, 52nd North Carolina, Mar. 15, 1862. Adjt. 52nd North Carolina, Nov. 1, 1862. Lt. AAAG to MacRae, by Mar. 1865. Appx. Alive Apr. 1901 at Fayetteville.

Robinson, Powhatan. Of Mississippi, and Petersburg, Virginia. att. Wm. & Mary, 1844, age 24. Capt. EO to J. E. Johnston, Feb. 15, 1862. Capt. EO to Ewell, May 1862. Capt. EO to Pemberton, Oct. 25, 1862. POW at Vicksburg. On engineer duty in northern Alabama for much of 1864.

Robinson, Thomas. Capt. ACS, Sept. 2, 1861. Stationed in eastern Virginia. Maj. CS, Sept. 23, 1863, on duty at Newtown, Virginia. Paroled May 1, 1865.

Roche, Thomas F. b. ca. 1836 at Baltimore, Maryland. A lawyer there. Pvt. Co. B, 21st Virginia, May 23, 1861. Clerk at Gen. Loring's headquarters in 1861. Acting ACS and acting AQM at Rockbridge Alum Springs Hospital, 1861–1862. Resumed clerk duties with Loring, Apr. 1862. Pvt. 30th Bn. Virginia Sharpshooters, Sept. 1, 1862. Later Adjt. Lt. AAAIG to Forsberg's Bgd., by Sept.

1864. POW at Waynesboro. Railroad employee, and then Baltimore lawyer again. d. there Oct. 3, 1876, age 40.

Rockwell, Henry Clay. b. Columbus Co., North Carolina, July 2, 1834. Merchant at Whiteville. Lt. Co. H, 51st North Carolina, Mar. 17, 1862. Capt. AQM, 51st North Carolina, May 1, 1862. May have served on Whiting's staff late in 1862. Capt. AQM to Clingman, Sept. 20, 1864. WIA Oct. 1864. Paroled Apr. 26, 1865. d. Feb. 24, 1914. bur. Whiteville Cem.

Rodes, Virginius Hudson. b. in Virginia, Jan. 5, 1824. att. VMI. VADC to his brother, Gen. Rodes, during Seven Days, and probably thereafter. Lt. ADC to Rodes, July 4, 1864. Presumably out of service in Sept. 1864, after the general's death. A merchant and planter. d. Carroll Co., Mississippi, Jan. 13, 1879. bur. Lynchburg Presby. Cem.

Rodman, William Blount. b. Washington, North Carolina, Jan. 29, 1817. att. UNC. Lawyer at Washington. Capt. Bridger's (N.C.) Arty. Maj. QM to Branch, Mar. 13, 1862. Resigned May 21, 1862. Col. of Cavy., Dec. 16, 1862, and assigned to military court of G. W. Smith's command. Subsequently judge on staff of R. H. Anderson's corps. Paroled Apr. 26, 1865. A postwar judge. d. Mar. 7, 1893. bur. Oakdale Cem., Washington.

Rogers, Alexander Hamilton. b. Loudoun Co., Virginia, Apr. 15, 1830. m. Julia Hawkins Clagett, 1858. VADC to N. G. Evans, July 1861. Lt. ADC to D. H. Hill, Apr. 12, 1862. Resigned on account of rheumatism, Oct. 28, 1862. Loudoun Co. farmer. d. Nov. 2, 1905. bur. Union Cem., Leesburg.

Rogers, George Jones. b. Aug. 30, 1841. Farmer and merchant in Sussex Co., Virginia. Sgt. Maj. 41st Virginia, May 24, 1861. To Adjt., May 19, 1862. WIA in neck at Malvern Hill, resulting in partial voice loss. Capt. AQM, 41st Virginia, Feb. 1, 1863. Capt. AQM to Weisiger, Sept. 15, 1864. Capt. AQM at army headquarters, Mar. 7, 1865. Capt.

AQM to Kirkland, Apr. 1865. Richmond bookkeeper and secretary. d. Petersburg, Virginia, Oct. 19, 1912. bur. Blandford Cem.

Rogers, Henry Judson. b. Loudoun Co., Virginia, Apr. 9, 1836. Civil engineer and surveyor at Hastings, Minnesota, 1857–1861. Lt. EO to J. E. Johnston, Mar. 1, 1862. Lt. EO to A. P. Hill, Aug. 2, 1862. Lt. EO to French, Nov. 25, 1862. POW at Suffolk, Apr. 17, 1863. Lt. EO on duty in Richmond's defenses by Aug. 1863. Capt. EO, May 17, 1864, to report to ANVa. On duty there and at Richmond, into 1865. m. Lucia Bayne, 1865. d. New York City, ca. 1890.

Rogers, Hugh Hamilton. b. Middleburg, Virginia, Nov. 8, 1839. att. UVa. Lt. ADC to Ripley, Aug. 30, 1862. WIA at Sharpsburg. Resigned Dec. 30, 1863. Lived postwar in New York City. d. on a train near Anderson, South Carolina, Feb. 9, 1896.

Rogers, John Dalrymple. b. Middleburg, Virginia, Feb. 24, 1830. A farmer there. Married twice. Maj. QM to N. G. Evans, Oct. 4, 1861. Maj. QM to D. H. Hill, Feb. 1862. Maj. QM to Rodes, May 19, 1863. Maj. QM for Second Corps, May 4, 1864, and thus on staff of Ewell, Early, and Gordon. Late in life a traveling solicitor for the Richmond and Alleghany Railroad. d. Lexington, Virginia, Nov. 30, 1889. bur. Stonewall Jackson Cem.

Rogers, Mortimer McIlhany. b. near Middleburg, Virginia, Feb. 2, 1839. A clerk there. Pvt. Co. H, 1st Virginia Cavy., May 15, 1862. WIA at Trevilian's Station. Lt. Drillmaster, July 19, 1864, to report to Wickham. Lt. acting PM for Wickham's Bgd., 1864–1865. Lt. OO for Munford's Div., Apr. 1865. Paroled Apr. 1865 at Charlottesville. A miller in Berkeley Co., West Virginia. Merchant and real estate agent at Roanoke, Virginia. d. Mar. 28, 1926. bur. in unmarked grave at Fair View Cem., Roanoke.

Rogers, William Hawling. b. near Middleburg, Virginia, Aug. 22, 1824. Indian agent in Kansas and Utah before the war. VADC to N. G. Evans, Oct. 1861. Lt. ADC to Evans, Nov. 16, 1861. Left the staff, reported AWOL, and resigned Sept. 23, 1862. Did not get along with Evans. Capt. AQM to Alexander's Bn. Arty., Sept. 16, 1863. Capt. AQM to Huger's Bn. Arty. Arrested for disobedience, Aug. 1864. Capt. AQM, Stuart Horse Arty., by 1865. Businessman in South America, 1869–1880. Farmer at Middleburg. d. Leesburg, Virginia, Jan. 13, 1907. bur. Sharon Cem., Middleburg.

Roman, Alfred. b. May 24, 1824. Son of Louisiana governor. Col. in Louisiana militia. Lt. Col. AAG to Beauregard, Oct. 4, 1862. Later AAIG. Lt. Col. AAIG to Hardee, Nov. 12, 1864. Lt. Col. AAIG to Beauregard again, about Jan. 1, 1865. m. Sarah Taylor Rhett, 1863. Judge in St. James Parish. Wrote biography of Beauregard. d. Sept. 20, 1892. bur. Metairie Cem., New Orleans.

Rondot, St. Jules. From France. Capt. AAG, Feb. 19, 1863. Served with Briscoe Baldwin at ANVa. headquarters. Relieved from there May 13, 1863. Later staff of E. K. Smith.

Rosborough, James Thomas. b. Ridgeway, South Carolina, July 31, 1842. att. Hillsborough Military Academy. Lt. Co. G, 6th North Carolina, May 16, 1861. WIA at Malvern Hill and Sharpsburg. Lt. ADC to Pender, June 2, 1863. Post-Gettysburg duty unknown. Lived postwar in Bowie Co. and Marion Co., Texas. A lumberman. d. Texarkana, Texas, May 28, 1918.

Rose, Hugh. VADC to Drayton, Nov. 24, 1861. VADC to D. R. Jones, by Sept. 1862, through at least Dec. 1862. No other record, and apparently never served as a commissioned officer. It is not even clear that he served continuously with Drayton through 1862. Most likely this is the Hugh Rose born May 15, 1820, from Charleston, South Carolina.

Rowland, Alexander M. b. Mar. 12, 1837. Lt. of Inf., CSA, Mar. 16, 1861. Lt. Co. I, 4th Alabama. Also in the 6th Georgia. Lt. AAAG to

G. J. Rains, Nov. 1861. Capt. AAIG to Tracy, Feb. 9, 1863. Later commanded a camp of instruction in Georgia, as a Maj. d. Feb. 27, 1871.

Rowland, Thomas. b. Detroit, Michigan, Mar. 25, 1842. Raised in Fairfax Co., Virginia. att. UVa., USMA, and RPI. Cadet, July 12, 1861, assigned to unspecified engineer duty. Capt. AAG to Robert Ransom, July 22, 1862. Maj. AAG to Ransom, June 8, 1863. Maj. AAG to Lomax, by Nov. 1864. Lawyer at Baltimore, Maryland. d. there Apr. 25, 1874. Rowland's letters have been published in the *William & Mary Quarterly*.

Ruby, John Christopher. b. Gallia Co., Ohio, Apr. 12, 1829. Clerk and grocer at Charleston, Virginia. Pvt. Co. H, 22nd Virginia, May 8, 1861. Capt. ACS, 22nd Virginia, Sept. 11, 1861. Capt. acting ADC to Col. McCausland, May 1862. Capt. ACS to Echols, July 1, 1863. Served into 1865. Grocer at Charleston, and city mayor. d. June 9, 1882. bur. Spring Hill Cem.

Rudd, John Speed. b. Lynchburg, Virginia, Aug. 1832. att. VMI, Wm. & Mary, Washington Coll., and USMA. Served with Walker in Nicaragua. Living in Texas in 1861. Lt. CSA, Sept. 21, 1861. Ordered to report to R. E. Lee in South Carolina, Dec. 7, 1861. To report to A. S. Johnston in Kentucky, Dec. 18, 1861. On ordnance duty. Lt. OO to report to T. J. Jackson, May 13, 1862. Duty unclear, but relieved from ANVa., Oct. 26, 1862, and sent to Mobile, Alabama. Court-martialed and cashiered, May 23, 1863, for fraud and bad conduct. Pvt. Lurty's (Va.) Btty., June 28, 1863. Transferred to Co. A, 46th Virginia Bn. Cavy., Mar. 1, 1864. POW at Martinsburg, Sept. 18, 1864. Public school principal in Monroe Co., West Virginia. d. Coal Valley, West Virginia, Apr. 14, 1888.

Ruffin, Francis Gildart. b. Dec. 1, 1816. Planter in Albemarle and Chesterfield Cos. Capt. ACS, June 29, 1861. Maj. CS, Sept. 2, 1861. Lt. Col. CS, Oct. 5, 1863. Resigned Feb. 26, 1865. Served entire war in Richmond as Asst. to chief commissary Gen. Northrop. Court-martialed for conflict of interest. Second state auditor of Virginia. Married twice. d. June 5, 1892. bur. Hollywood Cem., Richmond.

Rundell, Charles Henry. b. in New York, 1832. att. USMA. Served in 3rd and 4th U.S. Inf. Lt. ADC to G. J. Rains, Oct. 11, 1862. Dropped June 20, 1863, after prolonged absence. Worked for Gen. Magruder in Texas, using torpedoes. Called himself Maj. PACS through the end of the war, though officially he was out of service. Took Oath at Salisbury, North Carolina, May 29, 1865.

Rushin, Alonzo M. b. ca. 1835. Cpl. Co. H, 26th Georgia, Oct. 17, 1861. To Lt., May 8, 1862. Lt. acting OO to C. A. Evans by Dec. 1864, through Appx.

Rust, James Aristides. b. in Virginia, June 21, 1829. Farmer at Saline, Arkansas, prewar. Pvt. Co. C, 3rd Arkansas, June 10, 1861. Capt. AQM, 3rd Arkansas, Nov. 11, 1861. Capt. AQM to John Gregg, Sept. 15, 1864. Appx. d. Jan. 1, 1924.

Rutherfoord, James Clarke. b. June 17, 1840. From Amelia Co., Virginia. m. Pattie Hinton. Served in Co. M, 7th C.S. Cavy. Capt. AAIG to Dearing, by Jan. 1865. KIA at Amelia Springs, Apr. 5, 1865. bur. Hollywood Cem., Richmond.

Rutherford, John Cobb. b. Crawford Co., Georgia, Apr. 13, 1842. A nephew of the two Cobb generals. att. UGa., a lawyer. Sgt. Cobb's Legion Cavy. VADC to his uncle T. R. R. Cobb at Fredericksburg. Capt. AAIG to his uncle Howell Cobb, Jan. 10, 1863. Capt. AAIG to Finegan, Sept.–Oct. 1863. Capt. AAIG to Gardner, Oct. 1863. Paroled May 15, 1865, in Florida. d. in Florida, Mar. 10, 1891. bur. Oconee Hill Cem., Athens, Georgia.

Ryals, Garland Mitchell. b. Cumberland Co., Virginia, May 27, 1839. Sgt. Co. G, 3rd Virginia Cavy., May–Dec. 1861. Lt. of Cavy., Nov. 22, 1861. Lt. acting OO to Fitz. Lee,

Aug. 1862 until appointed Lt. oo to Lee, Apr. 4, 1863. Lt. pm to Stuart, June 1863. Capt. pm to Stuart, Dec. 8, 1863. Maj. pm to Stuart, Jan. 5, 1864. To Hampton from May 1864. Maj. pm to Fitz. Lee by Apr. 1865. Appx. Farmer, merchant, and legislator in Georgia. Married twice. d. Sept. 13, 1904. bur. Bonaventure Cem., Savannah.

Ryan, J. R. Acting adc to Magruder, June 1862. No other record.

Ryan, John S. b. in New York, Sept. 1805. Real estate broker at Charleston, South Carolina. Capt. acs, 1st South Carolina (Gregg's), Sept. 11, 1861. Capt. acting post commissary at Suffolk, Virginia, Oct. 1861. Capt. acting acs to J. R. Anderson, Apr. 1862. Capt. acting acs to Maxcy Gregg, 1862. Relieved from 1st South Carolina, June 21, 1862, and assigned as Capt. acs at James Island, South Carolina. Later Capt. acting acs to Ripley, and with Engineer Dept. in South Carolina. Postwar broker and railroadman. d. Charleston, June 16, 1871. bur. Magnolia Cem., in an unmarked grave.

Sadler, James A. b. in South Carolina. A 50-year-old "depot agent" at Charlotte, North Carolina, in 1860. Maj. cs to D. H. Hill, Dec. 25, 1861. Resigned Nov. 6, 1862.

St. Clair, George B. Lt. of Cavy., csa, Nov. 18, 1861. To report to the qm Gen., Feb. 1, 1862. Lt. aaag to A. G. Jenkins most of 1862 into 1864, at least. Apparently staff of Echols briefly in 1862. No further record after Jenkins's death.

St. Martin, Victor Joseph. b. Donaldsonville, Louisiana, Aug. 2, 1828. Ascension Parish clerk. m. Azema Mollere, 1847. Lt. Co. K, 8th Louisiana, 1861. Later Capt. wia and pow at Sharpsburg. Capt. aaag to Nicholls, Jan.–Mar. 1863. kia at Gettysburg, July 2, 1863. bur. Hollywood Cem., Richmond, Virginia.

Sale, John Burruss. b. Amherst Co., Virginia, June 7, 1818. att. LaGrange Coll. Moved to Lawrence Co., Alabama, 1821.

Lawyer at Aberdeen, Mississippi, 1848–1876. Married four times. Capt. Co. K, 27th Mississippi. Col. of Cavy., June 16, 1863, assigned to military court of Gen. Hardee. Resigned Mar. 18, 1864. Military secretary and aag to Bragg (probably as civilian), Mar. 30, 1864. Col. aag to Bragg, Jan. 23, 1865. Sale "was much given to punning," and "his intellect was massive." d. Memphis, Tennessee, Jan. 24, 1876.

Samuels, Green Berry, Jr. b. Woodstock, Virginia, Nov. 2, 1839. att. uva. A lawyer. Staff of Virginia militia Gen. Gilbert Meem, Apr. 1861. Pvt. Co. F, 10th Virginia, Apr. 18, 1861. To Lt., Apr. 3, 1862. pow at Front Royal, May 30, 1862. Lt. aaaig to his brigade, Feb. through June 1863, so on staff of Col. Warren and Gen. Steuart before returning to his company. pow at Third Winchester. Took Oath June 12, 1865. d. Lee Camp Soldiers' Home, Richmond, Feb. 21, 1901. bur. Woodstock Lutheran Church Cem.

Samuels, Thomas L. b. in Mississippi. Clerk at Chubula, Alabama. Cpl. Co. A, 4th Alabama, Apr. 26, 1861, age 19. To Sgt., Oct. 26, 1861. pow at Second Manassas. To Lt., May 19, 1863. Lt. acting adc to Law by Apr. 1864, into June. Retired to Invalid Corps, Dec. 20, 1864. Apparently worked with pm at Gordonsville, Virginia, in 1865.

Sanders, David Ward. b. Franklin, Mississippi, Oct. 14, 1836. att. unc. Lawyer and legislator from Yazoo City. m. Anne Stephens. vadc to French, by Aug. 1862. Lt. adc to French, Nov. 5, 1862. Maj. aag to French, Oct. 24, 1863. vadc to Walthall, Dec. 1864. Lawyer at Louisville, Kentucky. d. Nov. 1, 1909.

Sandy, Philip Augustus. A farmer in Essex Co., Virginia, in 1860, age 34. Pvt. Co. F, 55th Virginia, May 21, 1861. Capt. aqm, 55th Virginia, Sept. 3, 1861–May 10, 1862. Spent remainder of war on aqm duty in Essex Co., Middlesex Co., and other eastern Virginia locations. m. Louisa Croxton.

Lived postwar in Essex Co. d. Mar. 25, 1895, age 70.

Sanford, Thomas V. Pvt. Co. C, 47th Virginia, May 16, 1861. Lt. Co. D, 47th Virginia, Sept. 23, 1862. Capt. AQM, 47th Virginia, Sept. 15, 1863. Capt. AQM to Field, Sept. 15, 1864. Appx. "A very agreeable young man, quiet and steady," wrote a colleague.

Saunders, John E. b. in Tennessee. att. Nashville Military Academy. A grandson of Gen. Gideon Pillow. Lt. Rucker's (Tenn.) Btty. Dropped May 10, 1862. AAAIG to Pillow in 1863. Lt. ADC to B. R. Johnson, June 17, 1864. Appx. Planter at Nashville in 1870, age 27. d. at Nashville, Sept. 16, 1908. bur. Mt. Olivet Cem.

Saunders, John Selden. b. Norfolk, Virginia, Feb. 1836. att. USMA. Lt. OO in U.S. Army, 1858–1861. Capt. of Arty., PAVa., May 8, 1861. Lt. of Arty., CSA, backdated to Mar. 16, 1861. Assigned to Richmond Arsenal. Maj. PACS, on duty as Judge Advocate in Richmond, Jan. 1862. Commanded an artillery battalion at Sharpsburg. Lt. Col. PACS, Nov. 14, 1862, to report to G. W. Smith. On ordnance duty, Dec. 1862–Feb. 1863. Lt. Col. Chief of Arty. to Pemberton, Feb. 1863. POW at Vicksburg. Lt. Col. AAIG to Gilmer, Mar. 24, 1864. Lt. Col. to Col. Chilton in AIGO, July 25, 1864. Appx. Brother-in-law of Col. Walter H. Taylor. Lived postwar at Baltimore, Maryland. d. Jan. 19, 1904.

Saunders, Robert Chancellor. b. Franklin Co., Virginia, May 26, 1827. att. UVA. A farmer. m. Caryette Davis, 1851. Capt. Co. B, 11th Virginia, Apr. 23, 1861. Dropped Apr. 1862. In wartime state legislature. Maj. QM, June 16, 1863. Based at Lynchburg, 1863–1865. Campbell Co. farmer. d. Sept. 22, 1902.

Saunders, William Johnson. att. UNC. A planter from Darlington Co., South Carolina. Lt. of Arty and AAAIG to Colston, July 1861. Same to Pryor, Dec. 1861. Capt. and Asst. Chief of Arty. to Beauregard, Sept. 17,

1862. Maj. AAG to Beauregard, Nov. 11, 1862. Maj. Chief of Arty. to D. H. Hill, May 30, 1863. Later same to Whiting and L. Hebert. Maj. OO to Hampton, 1865. Paroled Apr. 26, 1865. Age 30 in June 1865.

Saunderson, Llewellyn Traherne Bassett. b. Sept. 4, 1841. Lived at Dromkeen House, County Cavan, Ireland. Lt. in 11th Hussars (Prince Albert's Own), Dec. 1860. VADC to Fitz. Lee, about Apr. 1, 1865. High sheriff of County Cavan, 1868. d. Mar. 30, 1913.

Scales, Erasmus Decatur. b. Dec. 21, 1839. att. UNC. Of Rockingham Co., North Carolina. Capt. ACS to Scales, July 20, 1863. Lived postwar at Paris, Texas. d. Jan. 1901.

Scales, James L. Lt. OO to Lomax, 1864. Skimpy records lead to the suspicion that this may be a garbled entry or a nonstaff officer.

Scales, Nathaniel Eldridge. b. Dec. 24, 1833. att. UNC. Of Salisbury, North Carolina. m. Minnie Lord, 1861. Capt. AQM, 6th North Carolina, May 16, 1861. Maj. QM to Pender, June 13, 1862. Maj. QM to Wilcox, Sept. 1863. Appx. Civil engineer and railroad contractor. d. Greensboro, North Carolina, Dec. 27, 1921.

Schley, William Cadwalader. b. Baltimore, Maryland, Apr. 30, 1840. att. Harvard. Lawyer at Baltimore prewar and postwar. Sgt. in Signal Corps, Oct. 18, 1862. On duty with First Corps, and later with Cavy. Acted on staff of Fitz. Lee at Gettysburg, as a Sgt. WIA and POW there, July 3, 1863. Lt. SO, Nov. 3, 1863. On duty at Richmond. Lt. SO to Breckinridge, Mar. 10, 1864. To J. H. Morgan, June 22, 1864. Back to Breckinridge, Aug. 1864. Lt. SO to W. M. Gardner, Nov. 15, 1864. Post Adjt. at Danville prison and ended war back at Richmond. d. Dec. 14, 1888.

Schooler, Samuel. b. Caroline Co., Virginia, Oct. 16, 1827. att. UVA. Teacher in Clarke, Hanover, and Caroline Cos. Author of *A Descriptive Geometry* prewar. Possessed "one of the best and most extensive engineering libraries in the South." Lt. of Arty., June 6, 1862, assigned to Fayetteville Arsenal. Capt. oo, Dec. 8, 1862. On duty at Richmond. Capt. oo to G. J. Rains, June 3–Sept. 21, 1863. Capt. oo at Charleston. Capt. oo with ANVa. reserve ordnance train, Feb. 8, 1864. Capt. oo back at Richmond Arsenal, Oct. 6, 1864. His appointment as Capt. oo not confirmed, so reapptd. Nov. 12, 1864. Resigned Mar. 29, 1865. Postwar teacher. d. Richmond, Virginia, Aug. 8, 1873. bur. "Locust Hill" near Guinea Station, Virginia.

Scott, Alfred Lewis. b. Spotsylvania Co., Virginia, Feb. 12, 1838. att. UVa. and Hampden Sidney. Cotton planter in Alabama. m. Fanny Herbert Taylor, 1862. Served in Co. G, 9th Alabama, and Co. F, 10th Virginia Cavy. Lt. acting oo to his brother-in-law, Gen. E. A. Perry, Nov. 29, 1862, to late 1863. Lt. AAAG to Perry and Finegan, May–June 1864. POW at Hatcher's Run, Feb. 6, 1865. Lived postwar in Alabama and at San Antonio, Texas. d. Bexar Co., Texas, June 28, 1915. Scott's memoir is at the Virginia Historical Society.

Scott, Frederic Robert. b. County Donegal, Ireland, Oct. 22, 1830. Emigrated to New York City, 1850, and then to Petersburg, Virginia, in 1852. A clerk. m. Sarah Frances Branch, 1857. Pvt. Co. E, 12th Virginia, June 8, 1861. Maj. cs to Colston, May 29, 1862. Maj. cs at ANVa. headquarters, June 2, 1863. Appx. President of the Richmond-Petersburg Railroad. Merchant and banker at Richmond. d. May 15, 1898. bur. Hollywood Cem.

Scott, John Graham. b. in Kentucky, 1826. Schoolteacher at Palestine, Texas, prewar. m. Josephine Tully, 1861. Pvt. Co. G, 1st Texas, June 23, 1861. Later Commissary Sgt., Apr. 1862. Lt. ADC to J. B. Robertson, Nov. 12, 1862. A Col. in Texas state service later in the war. Postwar lawyer at Palestine. d. Austin, Texas, Aug. 24, 1873. bur. Oakwood Cem., unmarked.

Scott, Robert Taylor. b. Warrenton, Virginia, Mar. 10, 1834. att. UVa. A lawyer. Capt. Co. K, 8th Virginia. Declined reelection. Maj. QM to Pickett, Oct. 28, 1862. Failed confirmation, but served until reapptd., June 15, 1864. Took Oath, Apr. 21, 1865. Postwar Warrenton lawyer. Attorney general of Virginia and state legislator. d. Aug. 5, 1897. bur. Warrenton Cem.

Scott, William Cowherd. b. Orange Co., Virginia, Aug. 13, 1825. A farmer there all his life. Capt. Co. C, 13th Virginia, Apr. 17, 1861. Resigned Jan. 27, 1862. Sgt. Crenshaw's (Va.) Btty., Mar. 14, 1862. Capt. AQM to R. L. Walker's Bn. Arty., Oct. 14, 1862. Apparently failed confirmation, because he was reapptd. to same position, Jan. 23, 1863. Maj. QM to Walker, Feb. 19, 1864. Once again reapptd., Nov. 4, 1864. d. Gordonsville, Virginia, Dec. 15, 1909. bur. Maplewood Cem.

Scott, William James. b. in Florida, July 21, 1830. att. UVa. Of Monticello, Florida. Lt. Co. I, 1st Florida. Adjt. 5th Florida, May 24, 1862. Resigned Feb. 3, 1863, citing bad lungs. VADC to E. A. Perry at Chancellorsville. Lt. Co. D, 9th Florida, Oct. 13, 1863. WIA and absent for last six months of the war. m. Kate Dilworth Bird, 1865. Lawyer at Monticello and instructor at the Monticello Academy. Alive 1870.

Scruggs, Louis S. b. Florence, Alabama. A resident of Holly Springs, Mississippi. m. Priscilla Shelby Hammond. Capt. Co. B, 17th Mississippi. Capt. ACS, 17th Mississippi. Resigned Aug. 8, 1861. Capt. AQM, 19th Mississippi, Sept. 19, 1861. Maj. QM to Featherston, July 14, 1862. Paroled Apr. 26, 1865. Merchant at Holly Springs. d. ca. 1913 in Harrison Co., Mississippi.

Scruggs, William H. Pvt. Co. I, 4th Alabama, Apr. 26, 1861. Detached on QM duty, Oct. 2, 1862. Maj. QM to Law, Nov. 1, 1862. Appx.

Seabrook, Cato Ashe. b. Edisto Island, South Carolina, 1831. att. South Carolina Coll. Instructor of Greek and Latin at King's Mountain Military Academy. Capt. Co. G, Palmetto Sharpshooters. Adjt. 5th South Carolina, Apr. 23, 1862. VADC to Micah Jenkins, May–June 1862. Capt. AAG to Jenkins, July 22, 1862. KIA at Second Manassas, Aug. 30, 1862. One source uses Becket as a third given name for Seabrook.

Seawell, Joseph Henderson. b. Aug. 8, 1839. Enrolling officer at Mobile, Alabama. Lt. Co. D, 24th Alabama. Capt. AQM, 61st Alabama, Feb. 19, 1864, but failed confirmation. Served on post duty at Greenwood Depot, Virginia, Aug. 1864–Jan. 1865. Capt. AQM to Battle, Jan. 7, 1865. d. Feb. 8, 1902. bur. Magnolia Cem., Mobile.

Seddon, John. b. in Virginia, Oct. 8, 1826. att. UVA. Mexican War veteran. m. Mary Alexander Little, 1848. Capt. Co. D, 1st Bn. Virginia, May 14, 1861. Brother of Secretary of War. Capt. AAAG to Ruggles, May–June 1861. Relieved June 7, 1861. Maj. 1st Bn. Virginia, May 20, 1862. Resigned Oct. 11, 1862. Served in state legislature. d. Dec. 5, 1863. bur. Fredericksburg Confederate Cem.

Seibels, Emmett. b. Lexington Dist., South Carolina, Oct. 3, 1821. att. South Carolina Coll. Lawyer and schoolteacher at Edgefield C.H. Pvt. Co. H, 7th South Carolina. Later to Maj. Maj. VADC to Butler by August 1864, into 1865. Settled at Montgomery, Alabama, Sept. 1865. m. Ann Goldthwaite, 1868. d. Montgomery, Dec. 1899.

Selden, Harry Heth. b. Goochland Co., Virginia, June 9, 1833. Merchant at Richmond. Capt. AQM, PAVa., Apr. 26, 1861. Capt. AQM, CSA, June 29, 1861, on duty at Richmond. Maj. QM to B. H. Robertson, June 18, 1862. Maj. QM to W. E. Jones. Failed bond and dropped, Apr. 16, 1863. Reinstated Sept. 26, 1863, as Maj. QM at Richmond. Maj. QM to Ewell, July 25, 1864. POW at Sailor's Creek. d. at Richmond, Oct. 20, 1891. bur. Hollywood Cem.

Selden, John. b. Washington, D.C. A farmer. Cpl. Albemarle (Va.) Arty., July 3, 1861, age

18. To Sgt. before discharged, July 3, 1862. Pvt. 2nd Co. Richmond Howitzers, Oct. 21, 1862. Lt. OO, 1st Virginia Arty., Feb. 1, 1863. Later OO to Hardaway's Bn. Arty. Lt. OO, Cutshaw's Bn. Arty., Mar. 27, 1865. Appx. Postwar resident of Washington and living there in 1910. Probably the John Selden who died Apr. 29, 1923.

Selden, John Allen. b. Charles City Co., Virginia, Apr. 18, 1827. m. Louisa Benberry, 1853. Cpl. Co. D, 3rd Virginia Cavy., May 18, 1861. Capt. ACS, 3rd Virginia Cavy., Oct. 11, 1861. Capt. ACS to Magruder, June 10, 1862. Capt. ACS at ANVa. headquarters, July 21, 1862. Appx. Farmer and merchant near Richmond and in Alabama. d. Richmond, Aug. 24, 1889. bur. Hollywood Cem.

Selden, Miles. b. July 4, 1824. m. Elizabeth Roberta Earl Taylor, 1853. Merchant at Richmond, Virginia. Capt. AQM, July 19, 1861, to report to J. E. Johnston. Resigned Aug. 28, 1861. Capt. AQM 10th Bn. Virginia Heavy Arty., Apr. 5, 1862. Dropped Aug. 30, 1862, but continued in service. Capt. AQM on duty at First Corps headquarters, Apr. 28, 1863. Capt. AQM, 5th Virginia Cavy., Mar. 23, 1864. Appx. Farmer in Princess Anne Co. d. Aug. 6, 1889. bur. Elmwood Cem., Norfolk.

Selden, Miles Cary, Jr. b. Henrico Co., Virginia, Jan. 9, 1836. att. VMI. Lived in West prewar. Never married. Lt. ADC to his brother-in-law, Gen. Heth, Jan. 22, 1862. Served into 1865. Clerk in California State Dept. d. near Richmond, Jan. 8, 1899.

Sellers, William Harvey. b. Gibson Co., Tennessee, Sept. 20, 1827. Moved to Brazos, Texas, 1835. Member of Mier Expedition into Mexico and held prisoner for 21 months. Lt. in Mexican War. Merchant at Houston and in New York City. Lt. Co. A, 5th Texas, July 19, 1861. Adjt. 5th Texas, Nov. 8, 1861. Capt. AAG to Hood, Mar. 19, 1862. Recommended by Hood in Oct. 1862 for a brigadier generalship. Maj. AAG to Hood, Nov. 5, 1862. Lt. Col. AAG to Hood,

Feb. 16, 1864. Paroled May 10, 1865. Cotton merchant at New York City, and in Galveston, Texas. d. Apr. 10, 1874. bur. Stonewall Jackson Cem., Lexington, Virginia. A Texas Bgd. veteran called Sellers "the bravest man I saw or ever expect to see."

Selph, Colin McRae. b. Mississippi City, Mississippi, Dec. 1839. att. Staunton Military Academy and UVA. m. Elizabeth Dimitry. Lt. CSA, Mar. 16, 1861. On duty with A. H. Gladden, Apr. 1861. Lt. AQM, May 3, 1861, at Richmond, Virginia. Lt. AQM at Manassas, July 27, 1861. Lt. AQM, Washington (La.) Arty., Feb. 15, 1862. Capt. AAG to T. H. Taylor's Bgd., July 15, 1862, but stayed with Washington Arty. at least through 1862. Staff of J. H. Forney at Vicksburg, and POW. Capt. AAIG to J. H. Winder, Nov. 20, 1863. Capt. AAIG to R. H. Chilton, May 27, 1864. Paroled Apr. 1865 at Greensboro. Lawyer at New Orleans, Louisiana. d. there Jan. 6, 1926.

Semmes, Abner Grigsby. b. Washington, Georgia, Apr. 22, 1833. Lt. OO to his brother, Gen. Semmes, Sept. 6, 1862. Lt. OO to Bryan, 1863–1864. Lt. OO to Simms into Dec. 1864, at least. d. before 1900.

Semmes, Benedict Joseph. b. Prince George's Co., Maryland, May 15, 1833. att. Georgetown Coll. Married twice. Lawyer at Chicago, Illinois, and at Canton, Mississippi. Pvt. Smythe's Co. Mississippi Partisan Rangers, Jan. 5, 1863. Lt. ADC to M. L. Smith, Mar. 15, 1863. POW May 8, 1865, at Athens, Georgia. d. May 29, 1879.

Semple, Charles. b. Kilkenny, Ireland, Mar. 27, 1833. Merchant at Louisville, Kentucky, from 1853. Lt. Co. K, 2nd Kentucky, July 6, 1861. Capt. Co. D, 9th Kentucky. Lt. OO to Preston, July 1862. WIA at Baton Rouge and Ft. Donelson. Capt. OO to Breckinridge, Nov. 11, 1862. Capt. AAIG to Breckinridge, Dec. 7, 1863. Back to ordnance duty, Apr. 25, 1864. Capt. OO to Echols, Feb. 1865. Louisville merchant and manufacturer. d. May 10, 1903. bur. Cave Hill Cem.

Sengstak, Henry Herman. b. Dec. 6, 1830. Pvt. Co. A, 3rd Alabama, Apr. 23, 1861. Discharged Aug. 2, 1861. Capt. Co. D, 2nd Bn. Alabama Arty., Nov. 8, 1861. VADC to Withers, Dec. 1861. Capt. AAIG to Gracie, Feb. 16, 1864. Same to Moody, Dec. 1864. MWIA in left lung, about Mar. 31, 1865. d. Petersburg hospital, Apr. 8, 1865. bur. Blandford Cem.

Sexton, Joseph Campbell. b. Wytheville, Virginia, Nov. 26, 1833. Saddle and harness maker there for many years. Pvt. Co. A, 4th Virginia. Capt. ACS, 4th Virginia, Sept. 11, 1861. Maj. CS to C. S. Winder, Apr. 1, 1862. Subsequently same to Paxton, J. A. Walker, and William Terry. Maj. CS to John B. Gordon, Oct. 31, 1864. Maj. CS to C. A. Evans, Mar. 23, 1865. Appx. d. at Wytheville, Dec. 17, 1907. bur. Old Town Cem.

Seymour, William Johnson. b. Macon, Georgia, May 12, 1832. Son of Col. Isaac Seymour, 6th Louisiana. att. Hobart Coll. m. Elizabeth Berthoud Grimshaw. New Orleans newspaperman most of his life. Imprisoned by "Beast" Butler, 1862. VADC to Duncan, Apr. 1862. POW at Ft. Jackson. VADC to Hays, by spring 1863. Capt. AAG to Hays, May 26, 1863. Capt. AAG to York. Absent sick most of late 1864 and early 1865. d. New Orleans, Nov. 14, 1886.

Shannon, Samuel Davis. b. in South Carolina, May 5, 1833. att. UVA. Wealthy planter in Kershaw Co. prewar. Lt. ADC to R. H. Anderson, Dec. 4, 1862. Served with Anderson for the remainder of the war. m. Elizabeth Peyton Giles, 1864, but she divorced him for nonsupport. Planter and railroad clerk at Camden. Secretary of State for Utah in late 1800s. d. 1900. bur. Quaker Cem., Camden. "Without means, he had a sublime contempt for toil."

Sharp, Thomas Robinson. b. Mount Carbon, Pennsylvania, Feb. 22, 1834. Railroadman in Tennessee, Alabama, Florida, and Virginia. Agent for QM Dept. in 1861. Responsible for famous transfer of locomotive from Martinsburg to Strasburg, on Valley Pike. Capt. AQM, Oct. 15, 1861. Capt. acting AQM to T. J. Jackson, Dec. 31, 1861–Jan. 7, 1862. Operated CSA locomotive shops at Raleigh, Weldon, Charlotte, Columbia, and Salisbury. Postwar troubleshooter for B & O Railroad. Alive 1885 in New York City.

Sharpe, William S. b. in North Carolina, Jan. 23, 1833. Anderson Co., South Carolina, dry goods merchant, 1855–1874. Sgt. Co. D, Orr's (S.C.) Rifles, 1861. Capt. AQM, 2nd South Carolina Rifles, Sept. 30, 1862. Capt. AQM to Bratton, Sept. 15, 1864. Served into 1865. m. Laura A. East. d. at Anderson, Nov. 4, 1896. bur. First Presbyterian Church Cem.

Shay, C. Shown unofficially as ADC to Whiting, May 1862. No other record found. Probably a mistake.

Sheats, Samuel V. b. 1829. State legislator from Cass Co., Georgia. Called "Little Sammy." Capt. AQM, 19th Georgia, Sept. 11, 1861. Capt. AQM, Coit's Bn. Arty., July 27, 1864. Capt. AQM to Colquitt, Sept. 20, 1864. Served into 1865. d. Mar. 16, 1878. bur. Kingston Cem., Bartow Co.

Sheild, William Francis. b. Princess Anne Co., Virginia, Mar. 24, 1830. Pvt. Co. A, 12th Virginia, Sept. 13, 1861. Capt. AQM, May 26, 1862, assigned to duty at Drewry's Bluff. Served there nearly the entire war. Appx. Merchant at Norfolk. d. there May 2, 1891. bur. Cedar Grove Cem.

Shell, George Washington. b. Laurens Co., South Carolina, Nov. 13, 1831. Farmer, merchant, and railroad man. Married twice. Lt. Co. A, 3rd South Carolina. Capt. AQM, 3rd South Carolina, May 27, 1862. Capt. AQM assigned to duty with ANVa. supply train, Sept. 15, 1864. Appx. Farmer and county clerk postwar. d. Laurens, Dec. 12, 1899.

Shepard, William Arthur. b. June 25, 1833. Maj. CS to Pryor, Dec. 30, 1862. Maj. CS at

Weldon, North Carolina, for most of the war. d. Ashland, Virginia, June 3, 1885. bur. Blandford Cem., Petersburg, Virginia.

Shepard, William Blount. b. Elizabeth City, North Carolina, Nov. 28, 1844. att. UVA. Married three times. VADC to Pettigrew, from 1862 up through Gettysburg. Later in Selden's (Tenn.) Btty. Farmer and legislator at Edenton, North Carolina. Merchant at Norfolk, Virginia. d. while at sea near Jamaica, Feb. 1913. bur. Orange Co., North Carolina.

Shepard, William M. A resident of Alabama. Pvt. Co. B, Murphy's Bn. (Ala.) Cavy., Mar. 10, 1862. Lt. ADC to Martin, June 23, 1863. Served through the war. Age 22 in May 1863.

Shepperd, Hamilton. A resident of Forsyth Co., North Carolina. Capt. ACS, 21st North Carolina, Sept. 5, 1861. Capt. ACS to Hoke by Sept. 1863. Paroled with AOT, Apr. 26, 1865.

Shepperd, Jacob. b. Oct. 11, 1841. Pvt. Co. F, 6th North Carolina, May 10, 1862. Lt. ADC to his brother-in-law Gen. Pender, Aug. 16, 1862. KIA at Fredericksburg. bur. Salem Cem., Winston-Salem, North Carolina.

Sherwood, William. b. Princess Anne Co., Virginia, ca. 1824. Grocer at Norfolk, prewar and postwar. m. Georgianna Day. Pvt. Co. C, 6th Virginia, Apr. 18, 1861. Capt. ACS, 6th Virginia, July 19, 1861. Capt. ACS to Mahone, July 1, 1863. Capt. ACS to Weisiger, May 1864. Appx. d. Richmond Soldiers' Home, Jan. 22, 1908. bur. Cedar Grove Cem., Portsmouth.

Shields, John Camden. b. Rockbridge Co., Virginia, Aug. 10, 1820. Capt. 1st Co. Richmond Howitzers, 1861. Capt. OO at Camp of Instruction, Nov. 1861. Lt. Col. PACS, June 20, 1862, on duty at Camp of Instruction, Richmond. Col. Nov. 13, 1862. In charge of conscription for state of Virginia. Commanded at Camp Lee into 1865. Also Lt. Col. 3rd Virginia Arty., LDT. Supposedly promoted to Brigadier Gen. late in the war and declined "on account of his inherent modesty." Newspaper editor at Richmond and Lynchburg. Farmer in Rockbridge Co. d. there June 30, 1904. bur. Stonewall Jackson Cem., Lexington.

Shingleur, James Augustus. b. South Carolina, 1839. Lawyer at Columbus, Georgia. Lt. Co. A, 2nd Bn. Georgia. Failed reelection in spring 1862. VADC to French, May–Dec. 1862. Lt. ADC to French, Dec. 8, 1862. Resigned July 1, 1863, to raise a regiment. Failing at that, he rejoined French as VADC, Oct.–Nov. 1863. Maj. AAG to French, Nov. 2, 1863. Later staff of Cockrell. Columbus cotton buyer. Moved to Jackson, Mississippi, 1885, and resumed cotton business. d. there Mar. 7, 1895. Some of Shingleur's war letters are at MDAH.

Shipp, Samuel Bray. b. Louisville, Kentucky, Sept. 7, 1832. A physician at Louisville. Capt. Co. C, 1st Kentucky Cavy., Apr. 1, 1862. Capt. probably acting ADC to Helm, Feb. 16, 1863. Capt. AAIG to Cosby, Apr. 1863 through at least Dec. 1864. Lived postwar at Louisville, occupation "gentleman."

Shook, James H. Pvt. Co. D, 1st Bn. Kentucky Mounted Rifles, June 2, 1862. Later Commissary Sgt., 3rd Bn. Kentucky Mtd. Rifles. Maj. CS to Hodge, Nov. 20, 1863. Maj. CS at Abingdon, Virginia, summer 1864, and to John H. Morgan and Echols. Maj. CS to Cosby by Nov. 1864.

Shorter, Charles S. A resident of Columbus, Georgia. Lt. Co. A, 31st Georgia, Aug. 29, 1861. Later to Capt. Capt. EO to Early, Oct. 14, 1864. POW Apr. 2, 1865, probably while on Second Corps staff. Took Oath, June 20, 1865, age 23.

Shorter, Henry Russell. b. Monticello, Alabama, Feb. 28, 1833. att. UNC and UAla. Lawyer at Eufaula. Capt. ACS, 1st Alabama, Sept. 26, 1861. Staff of Gladden, early 1862. Employed by state of Alabama, Apr. 1862–Oct. 1863. Lt. ADC to Battle, Sept. 15, 1863. WIA in chest at Wilderness. Cotton

planter and lawyer. State railroad commissioner. Shot twice in 1874 during a political street brawl. d. Eufaula, Nov. 27, 1898. bur. Fairview Cem.

Shorter, Reuben C. b. in Georgia. Merchant at Columbus, Georgia. Capt. AQM, 17th Georgia, Sept. 2, 1861. Dropped Feb. 2, 1862. Reinstated Mar. 3, 1863. Capt. AQM with First Corps Arty., Oct. 1864 onward. Was older than 45 in summer 1864.

Shortt, Stuart James. b. Oct. 15, 1833. From Heavitree, England. Lt. in the North Devonshire Regiment, England, 1858. Came to the CSA in 1861. Maj. AAG to Drayton, Nov. 11, 1861. Served there until late 1862. Maj. AAG to Martin, July 30, 1864. Resigned Feb. 12, 1865. d. Heidelburg, Germany, Aug. 26, 1908.

Shotwell, John I. Lt. Co. B, 1st Texas, Apr. 29, 1861. WIA at Sharpsburg. To Capt., Jan. 5, 1864. Capt. AAAIG to John Gregg, spring 1864 until October 1864. Transferred to Garnett Andrews's "Foreign Battalion" in December 1864. Killed after the surrender, details unknown.

Shumaker, Lindsay Mayo. b. Lynchburg, Virginia. A 36-year-old lawyer at Danville in 1860. Capt. Danville (Va.) Arty., Apr. 1861. WIA Oct. 3, 1861, at Greenbriar River. Failed reelection. Maj. of Arty., July 5, 1862. Maj. Chief of Arty. to Taliaferro, Aug. 2, 1862. Maj. Chief of Arty. to French, Nov. 5, 1862. Apparently out of service by late 1863, suffering from neuralgia and "intercostal Rheumatism." Lawyer, judge, architect, and newspaper editor at Danville. d. Lynchburg, Oct. 26, 1884. bur. Greenhill Cem., Danville.

Shumate, Thomas. b. ca. 1838. Pvt. Staunton (Va.) Arty., Apr. 17, 1861. Capt. AQM, 1st Virginia Partisan Rangers, Aug. 1, 1862. Capt. acting ACS to Imboden, Aug. 1862. Maj. QM to Imboden, Jan. 28, 1863, through 1864 at least. d. near Fishersville, Virginia, Dec. 11, 1877.

Sibert, Christian H. Capt. AQM, 14th South

Carolina, July 17, 1861. Capt. AQM to McGowan, Feb. 9, 1863. No later record.

Sides, Benjamin F. Pvt. Co. E, 10th Alabama, June 4, 1861. WIA at Dranesville. POW at Second Fredericksburg. To Lt., Aug. 1, 1863. Lt. AAAIG to W. H. Forney by Oct. 1864, for remainder of the war. Appx.

Sill, Edward Elijah, Jr. b. Liberty Hill, South Carolina, June 21, 1831. Sheriff of Kershaw Co. pre- and postwar. Lt. Co. E, 2nd South Carolina. Adjt., May 16, 1861. WIA in Maryland Campaign and at Gettysburg. Lt. acting ADC to Kennedy, 1865. Married twice. d. May 11, 1905. bur. Quaker Cem., Camden, South Carolina. Other sources, including Sill's obituary, give his date of birth as June 22, 1830.

Simmons, Benjamin Franklin. b. Mar. 5, 1830. Staff of Gen. Floyd, Florida State Troops. Adjt. 8th Florida, July 13, 1862. Lt. AAAG to E. A. Perry, mid-1863. Lt. AAAG to Finegan, Jan. 1865. Appx. President of railroad at Pensacola. d. Escambia Co., July 29, 1904.

Simmons, J. Fred. Prewar lawyer. Maj. QM to Robert Ransom, Apr. 28, 1862. Left the staff in autumn 1862, due to attack of typhoid fever. Maj. post QM at Grenada, Mississippi. Maj. QM to W. H. Jackson, Feb. 1864. Later at Panola, Mississippi. Editor of newspaper at Sardis, Mississippi. Alive in 1897.

Simms, Arthur Benjamin. b. Oxford, Georgia, Mar. 15, 1842. att. UGA. and Emory. In Co. A, Cobb's Legion (Ga.) Inf., and in 53rd Georgia. Lt. ADC to his brother, Gen. Simms, 1864. POW at Sailor's Creek. Mayor, lawyer, and legislator at Covington, Georgia. m. Sarah S. T. Jackson, 1878. d. Covington, June 6, 1887. 100 of Simms's war letters are at the Atlanta Historical Society.

Simpson, John Wistar. b. Laurens, South Carolina, June 11, 1821. att. South Carolina Coll. and Harvard. Lawyer at Laurens. VADC to Bonham in Apr. 1861, in Virginia. Pvt. in 9th South Carolina Reserves, 1862–

1863. m. Anne Patillo Farrow. Postwar lawyer. d. Spartanburg Co., South Carolina, May 7, 1893.

Simpson, William Dunlap. b. Laurens Dist., South Carolina, Oct. 27, 1823. att. South Carolina Coll. and Harvard. In state legislature. Present at Ft. Sumter affair. Lt. Col. AAIG to Bonham, 1861. Present at First Manassas. Resigned. Maj. 14th South Carolina, Sept. 9, 1861. Later Lt. Col., and then in CSA Congress. Governor of South Carolina and chief justice of state supreme court. d. Columbia, Dec. 26, 1890. bur. Laurens Cem.

Sims, Frederick William. b. Jones Co., Georgia, Oct. 18, 1823. Accountant for railroads at Macon and Savannah. Business manager of *Savannah Republican*. Capt. Co. H, 1st Georgia, Sept. 3, 1861. POW at Ft. Pulaski. Capt. AAG and Inspector of Railroad Transportation, June 4, 1863. Maj. QM to Lawton, July 7, 1863. Lt. Col. QM to Lawton, Dec. 19, 1863. Chief of Confederate Railroad Bureau, based at Richmond. Paroled May 12, 1865. Married twice. Savannah businessman postwar. Committed suicide at San Francisco, California, May 25, 1875.

Sims, Robert Gill. b. Aug. 11, 1838. att. Yale. Sgt. Co. D, 21st Mississippi. Adjt. 21st Mississippi, May 15, 1862. WIA at Gettysburg. Lt. AAAG to Humphreys, May 1864 into 1865. POW at Sailor's Creek. d. in the 1890s.

Sims, Robert Moorman. b. Fairfield Dist., South Carolina, Dec. 25, 1836. att. SCMA. Farmer at Craigsville. Sgt. Co. A, 9th South Carolina, and Lt. Co. B, 6th South Carolina. WIA at Sharpsburg. Capt. AAG to Micah Jenkins, Jan. 1, 1863. Slightly WIA at Wauhatchie. Capt. AAG to Bratton, May 1864. Capt. AAG to Gary, Aug. 9, 1864. Capt. AAIG to Longstreet, Dec. 14, 1864. Appx. Insurance agent, legislator, and secretary of state in South Carolina. Married twice. d. Columbia, Dec. 9, 1898. bur. Elmwood Cem.

Sisson, Vardy Pritchard. b. Lumpkin Co.,

Georgia, Sept. 23, 1838. Lt. Co. F, 8th Georgia, May 22, 1861. Lt. oo to G. T. Anderson, Mar. 1864. Appx. Newspaperman at Atlanta, and state legislator. d. DeKalb Co., Jan. 19, 1908. bur. Westview Cem., Atlanta.

Skinner, T. H. vadc to B. R. Johnson, July 29, 1864. Served there for remainder of the war.

Slade, William O., Jr. att. Columbian Coll. Pvt., Sgt. Maj., and acting Asst. Surg., 45th Virginia. Acting Engineer in Dept. of East Tennessee, Sept.–Nov. 1862. Lt. acting eo to Heth, Feb. 1863. wia spring 1864. Appx.

Slaughter, Philip Madison. b. Culpeper Co., Virginia, 1834. Prewar resident of Louisiana, a lawyer and civil engineer. Brother of Gen. J. E. Slaughter. Pvt. Louisiana Guard Arty., Apr. 25, 1861. Discharged Oct. 1861. Maj. cs to Mahone, Jan. 28, 1862. Served with Mahone into 1865. m. Mary Clementine Luzenburg. Civil engineer on rivers and harbors in Georgia, Alabama, and Florida. d. 1894.

Sloan, Benjamin F., Jr. b. near Old Pendleton, South Carolina, Apr. 15, 1836. att. scma and usma. Served in U.S. Dragoons, 1860–1861. Lt. of Arty., csa, Mar. 16, 1861. Adjt. Orr's (S.C.) Rifles, July 27, 1861. Lt. adc to Huger, Feb. 21, 1862. Maj. aag to Huger, June 12, 1862. Relieved Sept. 5, 1862, to command Richmond Armory. Later commanded ordnance shops at Clarksville, Virginia, and Asheville, North Carolina. Maj. oo and Chief of Arty. to Whiting, Sept. 19, 1863. Paroled Apr. 26, 1865. m. Annie Moore Maxwell, 1862. Railroad supt., farmer, cotton mill manager, and math professor. President of South Carolina Coll., 1902–1908. d. Biltmore, North Carolina, Feb. 19, 1923. bur. First Baptist Church Cem, Pendleton. Never used his middle initial after about 1860. Probably named for his uncle, Benjamin Franklin Sloan. The staff officer wrote an autobiographical sketch that makes no mention of a middle initial.

Smead, Abner. b. in Georgia, Apr. 4, 1833. att. uva. and usma. Lt. U.S. Army, 1854–1861. Lt. of Arty., Mar. 16, 1861. Maj. 19th Mississippi, June 10, 1861. Lt. Col. 12th Georgia, Dec. 13, 1861. Lt. Col. aag to Ed. Johnson, May 1862. Recommended that month by T. J. Jackson for Brigadier Gen. Lt. Col. aaig to Jackson, May 10, 1862. Col. aaig to Jackson, Aug. 11, 1862. Col. aaig to Ewell, June 1863, and later to Early. Charged with neglect of duty by R. H. Chilton in Oct. 1864. Relieved Nov. 12, 1864, and sent to duty with heavy artillery at Wilmington, North Carolina. Taught at uva. and in Benicia, California. Physician in Oregon and at Harrisonburg, Virginia. d. Salem, Virginia, July 24, 1904. bur. East Hill Cem.

Smith, Albert Justice. b. Norfolk, Virginia, 1821. Maj. Paymaster in U.S. Army, 1849–1861. Maj. qm, June 22, 1861, on paymaster duty at Richmond. Maj. qm to A. S. Johnston, Sept. 12, 1861. Later Maj. qm to Beauregard, Bragg, Hardee, and J. E. Johnston. Paroled as Lt. Col. qm to Johnston. Railroad agent at Nashville, Tennessee. d. there Mar. 28, 1871.

Smith, Anthony Austin. b. Fredericksburg, Virginia, Sept. 19, 1828. att. uva. Lawyer at Washington, D.C. Pvt. Co. B, 21st Virginia, May 23, 1861. Lt. of Arty., May 19, 1862, assigned to duty as aaag in Richmond defenses. Ordered to report to Chief of Ordnance, Oct. 30, 1863. Lt. Asst. oo to Beauregard, May 14, 1864. Lt. oo at Richmond Arsenal, Oct. 11, 1864. Lt. oo to Moore, Nov. 10, 1864. pow at Sailor's Creek. Lawyer at Richmond. d. there July 24, 1890. bur. Fredericksburg Confederate Cem. A brother-in-law of two other staff officers: Walter H. Harrison and Charles Pickett.

Smith, Augustine Meade. b. Dec. 21, 1835. att. uva. Of Norfolk, Virginia. Capt. acs, pava., May 30, 1861. Capt. acs (pacs), June 29, 1861, for duty at Suffolk. Sent to Wytheville, Sept. 6, 1861. Capt. acs at Danville, Oct. 4, 1862. Capt. acs at Richmond,

Feb. 10, 1863. Returned to Danville, May 1863. Capt. ACS to Rosser, Jan. 15, 1864. Maj. CS to Rosser, June 14, 1864. Appx. Lawyer at Norfolk. d. June 13, 1890. bur. Elmwood Cem.

Smith, Austin E. b. Culpeper Co., Virginia, 1829. Lawyer in Fauquier Co. until 1853, and then naval agent at San Francisco. Son of Gen. William Smith. Political POW at Ft. Warren, 1861–1862. VADC to Whiting at Seven Pines and Seven Days. MWIA at Gaines's Mill, June 27, 1862. d. June 28. bur. Hollywood Cem., Richmond.

Smith, Benjamin Hodges. b. Salem, Massachusetts, July 5, 1807. Bookkeeper at Richmond, Virginia. m. Grace Fenton Brook. Clerk in office of Asst. QM Gen., June 1861. Capt. AQM, Feb. 19, 1864, to work at same office. Must have failed confirmation, because reapptd. June 15, 1864. Served into 1865. d. Jan. 20, 1881. bur. Hollywood Cem., Richmond.

Smith, Benjamin Waldo. b. South Carolina, Oct. 31, 1841. att. UVa. Edgefield Co. farmer. Sgt. Co. A, 7th South Carolina, June 11, 1861. WIA at Savage's Station and Chickamauga. Discharged because of poor health. Capt. ACS, Jan. 24, 1865. Asst. to Lt. Col. Cole at ANVa. headquarters.

Smith, Charles Henry. b. Lawrenceville, Georgia, June 26, 1826. att. UGa. Lawyer at Lawrenceville until 1856, then moved to Rome. m. Mary Octavia Hutchins, 1849. On staff of Col. Bartow, July 1861. Maj. CS, Sept. 11, 1861, to report to Sam. Jones, but served on staff of G. T. Anderson instead. Resigned July 15, 1862, citing family responsibilities. Mayor of Rome and state senator postwar. Smith was the famous humorist "Bill Arp" and settled into writing at Cartersville, Georgia. d. there Aug. 24, 1903.

Smith, Charles Maurice. b. Lynchburg, Virginia, 1817. Land office clerk and newspaperman at Richmond. Lawyer in Utah, 1853–1857. Capt. AQM, Sept. 28, 1861. Maj.

QM, July 6, 1863. Auditor of transportation accounts, based at Richmond, into 1865. Newspaperman at Richmond postwar, and then commissioner of deeds at Washington, D.C. d. Port Royal, Virginia, Apr. 1, 1881, when he was thrown from a buggy.

Smith, Clifton Hewitt. b. Alexandria, Virginia, Aug. 19, 1841. att. VMI. Capt. AAG to Beauregard, by July 1861. Dropped. Reapptd. to same position, Feb. 15, 1862. Capt. AAG to Higgins, Nov. 19, 1863. Later Capt. AAG to Maury and to Page. POW at Ft. Morgan. Merchant at New Orleans and then stockbroker in New York City. d. there Jan. 27, 1902.

Smith, Edward Buckey. b. Oct. 14, 1833. att. UVa. Of Loudoun Co., Virginia. Capt. OO to Gorgas, July 4, 1862. Maj. OO to Gorgas, June 18, 1863. Lt. Col. OO to Gorgas, Jan. 17, 1865. Paroled Apr. 25, 1865, at Burkeville, Virginia. Math professor at Richmond Coll. for 24 years, and life insurance agent. d. July 31, 1890. bur. Hollywood Cem., Richmond.

Smith, Eugene Robinett. b. Nashville, Tennessee, Dec. 9, 1843. att. Tennessee Military Academy. Cpl. Co. C, 2nd Tennessee. Pvt. Co. I, 44th Tennessee, Dec. 3, 1862. Clerk at Bgd. Adjt.'s office. Lt. Co. B, 25th Tennessee, June 20, 1863. Lt. AAAIG to B. R. Johnson at Chickamauga. Capt. Co. B, 25th Tennessee, May 15, 1864. Capt. acting ADC to Johnson at the Crater. Resigned Aug. 29, 1864. Lt. CSMC, Sept. 13, 1864. POW at Sailor's Creek. att. Univ. of Nashville Medical School. Physician in Jackson Co., Alabama, for nearly 50 years. d. Section, Alabama, Mar. 28, 1929. bur. Section Methodist Cem.

Smith, Francis Williamson. b. Norfolk, Virginia, Nov. 12, 1838. att. UVa., VMI, and L'Ecole Imperiale des Ponte et Chausee, France. Supt. of Louisiana State Seminary of Learning. m. Ann Maria Dandridge. Capt. PAVa., and military secretary to R. E. Lee, May 27–July 11, 1861. Maj. 41st Virginia, 1861. Maj. (PACS), May 21, 1862.

VADC to Mahone at Seven Pines. Commanded post at Drewry's Bluff, late 1862. Commanded an artillery battalion much of war. MWIA at Amelia Springs, Apr. 5, 1865. d. Apr. 6. Smith's war letters are at the Virginia Historical Society.

Smith, Frederick L. b. ca. 1830. Carriage maker in Edgefield Co., South Carolina. Pvt. Co. A, 7th South Carolina, June 11, 1861. Capt. ACS, 7th South Carolina, May 16, 1862. Capt. acting ACS to Kershaw at Chancellorsville. Capt. ACS to Kershaw, July 31, 1863. Capt. ACS to Butler, July 6, 1864. Same to Dunovant. Maj. CS to Logan, Jan. 6, 1865. Paroled May 1, 1865. d. May 1885.

Smith, Frederick Waugh. b. Warrenton, Virginia, Jan. 19, 1843. att. VMI. Sgt. Maj., 49th Virginia. WIA at Fredericksburg. Lt. ADC to his father, Gen. Wm. Smith, May 2, 1863. Cadet CSA, Oct. 20, 1863, and stayed with father as ADC. To report to R. E. Lee, May 27, 1864, duty unspecified. Cadet AAAG and acting ADC to Wharton, June 30, 1864. To report to Col. Mosby, Mar. 13, 1865, "for duty as a supernumerary company officer, not to be allowed to perform staff duty." m. Emily Adshode, 1900. d. Cape Town, South Africa, July 8, 1928. bur. Woltemade Cem. #1.

Smith, Granville Physic. b. in Virginia, July 6, 1818. att. UVa. Merchant at Nashville, Tennessee. Acting ADC to S. R. Anderson, June 1861. Lt. ADC to Anderson, Sept. 9, 1861. Later Lt. ADC to McCown. Davidson Co. real estate agent. m. Leonora Cheney. d. at Nashville, June 6, 1890. bur. Mt. Olivet Cem.

Smith, Isaac Williams. b. Fredericksburg, Virginia, Feb. 15, 1826. att. VMI. Lt. in the Mexican War. Worked on boundary survey parties in Midwest. Lt. EO, Oct. 14, 1863. Capt. EO, Apr. 5, 1864. On duty at Richmond entire time, into 1865. Engineer on Imperial Mexican Railway, 1866. Built canals, lighthouses, and city facilities in the Northwest. Settled at Portland, Oregon. d. there Jan. 1, 1897.

Smith, J. N. Lt. of Cavy., 1861. Stationed at Smithfield, Virginia. Apparently acted on staff of Colston in Apr. 1862 (and perhaps at other times) as ADC. Stationed at Winston, North Carolina, in 1864. No other record. This officer's official records are sadly incomplete and perhaps garbled.

Smith, James Power. b. New Athens, Ohio, July 4, 1837. att. Jefferson Coll. and Hampden Sidney. Cpl. Rockbridge (Va.) Arty. Lt. ADC to T. J. Jackson, Sept. 2, 1862. Lt. ADC to Ewell, June 8, 1863. Capt. AAIG to Battle, Dec. 7, 1863. Capt. AAIG to Wharton, Dec. 23, 1864, though he had been acting in that capacity since July 1864. Capt. AAIG to Echols, 1865. Preacher at Roanoke, Fredericksburg, and Richmond, Virginia. d. Greensboro, North Carolina, Aug. 6, 1923. bur. Hollywood Cem., Richmond.

Smith, James W. Capt. ACS, 36th Virginia, Apr. 17, 1862. Dropped Feb. 5, 1863. Capt. ACS to McCausland. Paroled May 13, 1865, at Charleston, West Virginia, age 31. Signed as Maj. CS, probably to McCausland, though his promotion to that rank is not of record.

Smith, John Donnell. b. Baltimore, Maryland, June 5, 1829. att. Yale and Georgetown. Baltimore lawyer, but may not have practiced. VADC to Magruder, Feb.–Mar. 1862. Lt. Page's (Va.) Btty., Mar.–Oct. 1862. Lt. Jordan's (Va.) Btty., Oct. 7, 1862. WIA at Chancellorsville. To Capt., Feb. 1864. Paroled Apr. 10, 1865. Alabama planter, supt. of steam brick machine at Baltimore, and treasurer for a railroad company in Cincinnati. Prominent Baltimore botanist. d. there Dec. 2, 1928. bur. Green Mount Cem.

Smith, John Louis. Lt. Co. F, 1st Maryland, May 22, 1861. PM at Winchester, Virginia. Capt. AAG to Elzey, Dec. 2, 1862. Possibly attached to staff of Breckinridge in May 1864. Capt. AAG at "Maryland Camp" near

Richmond, July 1864. Capt. AAG to Gardner, Oct. 4, 1864. Capt. AAIG, Mar. 11, 1865, duty unspecified.

Smith, John S. Pvt. Co. E, 4th Texas, July 13, 1861. Lt. ADC to Hood, Dec. 27, 1862. Capt. Enrolling Officer at Columbus, Georgia, Aug. 1863. Capt. ADC to Hood, May 1864.

Smith, John Thomas. Pvt. Co. E, 26th Georgia, Sept. 25, 1861. Later to QM Sgt. Capt. AQM, 26th Georgia, June 16, 1862. Capt. AQM to Wharton, Sept. 16, 1864. Capt. AQM to R. H. Anderson, Sept. 27, 1864. Served into 1865.

Smith, Joseph Howard. b. Leesburg, Virginia, Sept. 1838. att. UVA. Pvt. Rockbridge (Va.) Arty., Sept. 2, 1861–Dec. 24, 1862. Transferred to Mining & Nitre Bureau. Acting Lt. OO to Taliaferro's Bgd., Mar. 26, 1863, and later staff of Steuart. Lt. OO to Lewis, June 14, 1864. Farmer at Charlottesville, and state legislator. d. Albemarle Co., Virginia, Mar. 1888. bur. UVA. Cem.

Smith, Larkin. b. Fredericksburg, Virginia, Apr. 9, 1814. att. USMA. Capt. in U.S. Army, 1835–1861. Mexican War veteran. Lt. Col. Asst. QM Gen., Mar. 16, 1861. Based at Richmond, 1861–1865. Also served as chief tax collector last half of war. Paroled Apr. 26, 1865, in North Carolina. Merchant and engineer at San Antonio, Texas. d. there Dec. 3, 1884. bur. San Antonio National Cem.

Smith, Orlando. b. Lunenburg Co., Virginia, Apr. 2, 1835. att. UVA. A lawyer. Capt. Co. G, 9th Virginia Cavy., June 7, 1861–Jan. 17, 1863. Capt. AQM, June 16, 1863. Stationed in Staunton, mostly collecting taxes. Paroled Apr. 30, 1865, at Winchester. Staunton lawyer. d. there July 17, 1874. bur. Thornrose Cem.

Smith, Thomas Henderson. b. Lexington, Virginia, Aug. 21, 1842. att. VMI. Son of VMI Supt. Francis H. Smith. Adjt. 9th Virginia, Sept. 11, 1861. Lt. Madison (La.) Light Arty., July 8, 1862. Lt. AAAG to E. P. Alexander's Bn. Arty., Nov. 1862. Lt. AAAG to

Ripley, July 30, 1863. Lt. OO to W. E. Jones, Dec. 2, 1863. Lt. OO to B. T. Johnson, summer 1864. Charged with cowardice, Apr. 1865. Appx. Professor at VMI and merchant. Worked for Treasury Dept. in Washington. d. Richmond, Virginia, July 1, 1909. bur. Lexington.

Smith, Thomas Towson. b. Mar. 8, 1841. att. Hampden Sidney. Resident of Fauquier Co., Virginia. Capt. Co. K, 8th Virginia, Apr. 26, 1862. Capt. AQM, 8th Virginia, Dec. 2, 1862. Capt. AQM to Crutchfield's Arty. Bgd., Feb. 1865. m. Anna Miller, 1868. Washington, D.C., capitalist. d. June 21, 1918. bur. Warrenton Cem.

Smith, William Augustine. b. King George Co., Virginia, Sept. 17, 1840. att. VMI. Lt. PAVa., May 1, 1861, on drillmaster duty. Lt. AAAG to J. G. Walker, by Oct. 1861. Capt. AAG to Walker, Apr. 23, 1862. Served in that capacity into 1865. Farmer at Port Conway, Virginia, and a Fredericksburg excelsior manufacturer. Also lived in New Orleans and Baltimore. m. Harriett Field Robb, 1869. d. Fredericksburg, Mar. 8, 1905. bur City Cem.

Smith, William Brooke. b. Feb. 10, 1834. Pvt. Co. C, 57th Virginia. Capt. AQM, 57th Virginia, Oct. 2, 1861. Capt. AQM assigned to Second Corps Arty. train, July 23, 1864. Capt. AQM, IFT with ANVa., Sept. 2, 1864. Capt. AQM to Steuart, Oct. 21, 1864. Appx. d. Confederate Soldiers' Home, Richmond, Virginia, July 18, 1896. bur. Hollywood Cem.

Smith, William H. Maj. CS to Huger, June 29, 1861. Served with Huger at least into May 1862. Spent remainder of the war on purchasing duty in Georgia and the Carolinas. Middle name possibly Henry.

Smith, William N. b. Prince George's Co., Maryland. Served prewar on ordnance duty for both the army and navy. Lt. of Arty., June 26, 1861, MSK. Capt. of Arty., June 17, 1862, MSK. Managed the ordnance laboratory on Brown's Island at Richmond,

Virginia. Resigned July 16, 1864, and became the civilian supt. of the Richmond Arsenal.

Smith, William Proctor. b. in Virginia, Apr. 10, 1833. att. USMA. Lt. topographical engineer in U.S. Army, 1857–1861. Capt. PAVa., May 8, 1861. Lt. of Arty., CSA, July 17, 1861, to rank from Mar. 16, 1861. Capt. EO (PACS), Oct. 11, 1862, to rank from Feb. 13, 1862, to report to Gen. Gatlin. Reported to ANVa., June 10, 1862, and on duty at Richmond. Maj. EO (PACS), Nov. 3, 1862, to rank from June 10. Reported to Gen. Holmes, Nov. 1862, and then to Walter H. Stevens, Jan. 3, 1863. Lt. Col. EO (PACS), Apr. 2, 1863, and Chief Engineer to R. E. Lee. Col. EO (PACS), Mar. 28, 1864, but no longer with ANVa. Back on duty with that army, but not as Chief Engineer, June–Oct. 1864. Col. EO to Early, Nov. 1864. Lived postwar at Hinton, West Virginia. d. Alderson, West Virginia, Aug. 27, 1895. bur. Greenbrier Baptist Church.

Smith, Willoughby Newton. b. Northumberland Co., Virginia, Mar. 20, 1836. att. UVA. A lawyer. Sgt. Co. C, 40th Virginia, 1861. Capt. AQM, 40th Virginia, Oct. 1, 1862. Capt. AQM for Nelson's Bn. Arty., 1864. POW at Fisher's Hill, Sept. 22, 1864. d. Northumberland Co., Mar. 4, 1866. bur. Coan Wharf.

Smoot, Luther Rice. b. Washington, D.C., Sept. 24, 1824. Mexican War veteran. Married twice. Banker in Washington, and at Kansas City, Missouri. Maj. QM, PAVa., and Capt. of a company of Virginia Partisan Rangers. QM Gen. of Virginia. No further military record after mid-1863. Moved to Baltimore, Maryland, postwar, and engaged in iron and gas businesses. d. there Apr. 28, 1892. bur. Loudon Park Cem.

Snead, Fletcher Tillman. b. Milledgeville, Georgia, July 28, 1829. Lawyer at Oglethorpe, Georgia, most of his life. Sgt. Co. I, 4th Georgia, Apr. 29, 1862. Adjt. 4th Georgia, Aug. 1862. Lt. AAAG to Doles, Sept.–

Nov. 1862. Capt. AAG to Doles, Nov. 1, 1862. Capt. AAG to Cook, June 1864. Appx. Mayor of Oglethorpe. d. there May 8, 1891. bur. Oglethorpe Cem. Snead possessed "an inexhaustible vein of good humor, wit and sarcasm."

Snead, Thomas Tully Lynch. b. Onancock, Virginia, Mar. 20, 1832. att. Wm. & Mary. Professor of math there, 1856–1861. Helped survey Williamsburg's defenses, May–June 1861. Lt of Inf., Oct. 9, 1861, and continued engineer duty. Lt. EO to T. J. Jackson, June 18, 1862. Ordered to report to Col. Gilmer, Oct. 16, 1862. Lt. EO to R. H. Anderson, Mar. 27, 1863. Lt. EO to Col. W. H. Stevens, Oct. 26, 1863. Capt. EO to Stevens, Nov. 19, 1863. Served with Stevens at Richmond. Resumed teaching at Wm. & Mary, postwar. d. July 3, 1872. bur. Wm. & Mary Coll. graveyard. Jedediah Hotchkiss called Snead "one of the worst rattle brains the world ever saw . . . a redhaired mischief."

Snodgrass, Charles Edward. b. Botetourt Co., Virginia, Oct. 8, 1830. Clerk in QM Dept. Maj. QM to Ewell, Mar. 6, 1862. Failed bond and dropped, Aug. 30, 1862, but soon restored without break in service. Maj. QM to Early, Aug. 1862. Maj. QM to Ramseur, May 1864, and probably to Pegram thereafter. Maj. QM to R. H. Anderson, Nov. 9, 1864. Maj. acting Chief QM for ANVa., at Appx. d. Richmond, Virginia, Dec. 23, 1900. bur. Hollywood Cem.

Snowden, Charles Alexander. b. Montpelier, Maryland. att. Georgetown Coll. m. Elizabeth Warfield. Lived prewar in Texas. Capt. ACS, 1st Maryland, July 4, 1861. Maj. QM to Elzey, Sept. 11, 1861. Maj. QM to Robert Ransom, Aug. 6, 1864. Maj. QM to Lomax, Aug. 1864, but probably stayed with Ransom instead. Maj. QM to Cosby, Dec. 1864. Present at Appx., duties not clear. Civil engineer at Baltimore, Maryland. d. there Feb. 15, 1899, age 68.

Snowden, Richard Nicholas. b. July 19, 1815.

att. Georgetown Coll. Of Prince George's Co., Maryland. m. Elizabeth Ridgely, 1835. "Lt. Col." on special duty with army at Manassas, July 1861. Agent for military railroad. Maj. AAG to Elzey, Sept. 23, 1861. Maj. AAG to Polk, Jan. 7, 1862. Relieved July 20, 1863. d. Sept. 16, 1863.

Snowden, Samuel Hazard. b. Mar. 12, 1836. Lt. Co. F, 1st Louisiana, Apr. 25, 1861. WIA at Second Manassas. Capt. AQM, 1st Louisiana, Jan. 12, 1864. Capt. AQM to Rodes, May–Sept. 1864. Capt. AQM to Ramseur, Sept. 1864. Failed confirmation and dropped, Oct. 1, 1864, but probably continued in service. Capt. AQM to Early, Feb. 21, 1865. Paroled Apr. 1865. m. Mary Louise McGehee, 1867. Lived postwar at New Orleans, Louisiana. d. Mar. 12, 1888.

Sollee, Francis Carrera. b. Charleston, South Carolina, Sept. 20, 1834. Moved to Florida in 1853. Served in Co. C, 10th Florida, and in the Chatham (Ga.) Arty. Capt. AQM, 1st Florida Bn., Feb. 18, 1863. Capt. AQM to Finegan, Sept. 15, 1864. Asst. postmaster of Jacksonville after the war, and customs collector. d. there June 3, 1907. bur. Evergreen Cem. A comrade called Sollee "a good military man, and the gentleman at all times."

Sommers, Samuel Mathews. b. Shenandoah Co., Virginia, Dec. 27, 1831. att. UVa. and Washington Coll. Lawyer at Clarksburg. Capt. AQM, Dec. 24, 1861, to report to T. J. Jackson. Left behind in jail at Front Royal, Virginia, May 30, 1862, accused of rape. Dropped June 5, 1862, for "conduct unbecoming an officer & a gentleman." Exchanged Sept. 21, 1862, and dismissal revoked. Ordered to report to ANVa. headquarters, Oct. 30, 1862. Capt. AQM with army's reserve ordnance train, 1862–1865. Appx. Resumed law practice. d. Parkersburg, West Virginia, Nov. 22, 1872.

Sorrel, Alexander Claxton. Pvt. Troup (Ga.) Arty. Lt. ADC to his brother-in-law, Gen. Mackall, Mar. 18, 1862. Lt. Co. I, 1st Georgia Regs., June 24, 1862. Lt. acting ADC to R. B. Garnett at South Mountain. Capt. AAG to Mackall, Oct. 3, 1863. Shown in Aug. 1864 as never having reported to AOT. Capt. AAG to Bratton, Sept. 7, 1864. Appx. Resident of Griffin, Georgia. d. Jan. 10, 1908, age 67. bur. Laurel Grove Cem., Savannah. Brother of Gen. Moxley Sorrel.

Southall, Stephen Valentine. b. Apr. 27, 1830. att. UVa. Lawyer at Charlottesville most of his life. Adjt. 1st Virginia Arty., June 24, 1862. Lt. AAAG to Col. J. Thompson Brown's artillery, May–Aug. 1863. Lt. AAAG to Long, Sept. 1863 until Appx. m. Emily Gordon Voss, 1869. Southall was a brother-in-law of Col. C. S. Venable of R. E. Lee's staff. d. Mar. 20, 1913. bur. Maplewood Cem., Charlottesville.

Spann, James G. b. South Carolina. Planter at Stateburg. m. Elizabeth Eveleigh Richardson. Capt. Co. G, Hampton (S.C.) Legion. VADC to R. H. Anderson, Nov. 20, 1862, through Gettysburg. Capt. AAIG to E. A. Perry, Nov. 2, 1863, and Capt. AAIG to Davis, Dec. 7, 1863. Did not report for those duties, however, suffering from pulmonary hemorrhage. Capt. AAIG to Finegan, July 11, 1864. KIA at Weldon Railroad, Aug. 21, 1864. bur. Church of the Holy Cross, Stateburg.

Spann, Ransom Davis. b. South Carolina. A 36-year-old planter at Stateburg in 1860. Lt. Co. D, Hampton (S.C.) Legion. VADC to R. H. Anderson, Nov. 20, 1862–Nov. 1863. Capt. AAIG to Kirkland, Nov. 2, 1863. Capt. AAIG to Perrin, Dec. 29, 1863. Capt. AAIG to Sanders, May–Aug. 1864. WIA at Weldon Railroad, Aug. 21, 1864. WIA by shell, Oct. 3, 1864. Capt. AAIG to Finegan, Jan. 27, 1865. Capt. AAIG to R. H. Anderson, Feb. 27, 1865. A 1901 source reported that Spann had died "recently." Brother of James G. Spann (see above).

Spearman, John E. Capt. ACS to Gatlin, Dec. 24, 1861. Capt. ACS at Rapidan Station, Virginia, by Oct. 1862. Capt. ACS at

Drewry's Bluff, Nov. 15, 1862. Capt. ACS at Hanover Junction, Jan. 1863. Capt. ACS with ANVa., by June 1864. Paroled Apr. 26, 1865, with AOT, as staff of Gen. Lee (Stephen D.?).

Speer, Daniel Norwood. b. Troup Co., Georgia, June 6, 1836. Lawyer at LaGrange. m. Aurelia Roberta Moreland, 1860. Capt. AQM, 4th Georgia Bn., Oct. 25, 1861. Capt. AQM, 60th Georgia, Oct. 14, 1862. Maj. QM to Lawton's Bgd., Nov. 28, 1862, and thus to John B. Gordon. Maj. IFT with ANVa., Dec. 30, 1863. Transferred to same duty in Dist. of Western Louisiana, June 1864. Paroled June 6, 1865. LaGrange lawyer and state treasurer. d. Apr. 18, 1893. bur. Westview Cem., Atlanta.

Spencer, Oliver H. b. ca. 1837. Farmer in Dale Co., Alabama. Pvt. Co. G, 4th Alabama, Apr. 24, 1861. Courier for Gen. Longstreet. Lt. ADC to Sorrel, 1864–1865, but may not have received his commission. Appx. Postwar farmer in Wilcox Co., Alabama. Alive 1870. Sorrel called Spencer "an exceedingly useful staff officer."

Sperry, A. P. Commissary for 16th Bgd. Virginia Militia. Capt. ACS at Winchester, Virginia, as late as Oct. 1862. POW. May have been in state service exclusively.

Spratt, Leonidas William. b. Fort Mill, South Carolina, Aug. 30, 1818. att. South Carolina Coll. Charleston lawyer and legislator. Also taught school at Quincy, Florida, and was a judge at Apalachicola. Loud advocate of reopening slave trade and published numerous pamphlets on the subject. Pvt. 1st South Carolina Mtd. Militia. Maj. CS to Gregg, Apr. 1, 1862. Resigned Oct. 14, 1862. Col. of Cavy., Dec. 16, 1862, appointed to military court of First Corps. Paroled May 20, 1865, in North Carolina. Postwar lawyer in South Carolina and Virginia. Moved to Jacksonville, Florida, 1875. d. Oct. 4, 1903. bur. Evergreen Cem., Jacksonville.

Spurrier, Grafton Dalrymple. b. Baltimore, Maryland, Feb. 7, 1815. Lawyer in Maryland.

Married twice. Adjt. 1st Maryland, June 1861. VADC to Trimble, 1861. Capt. AQM, Oct. 13, 1863, but to rank from June 24, 1861. Served (apparently unofficially) as Capt. AQM to Elzey from 1861 onward. Capt. AQM at Cheraw, South Carolina, Jan. 1864. Later at Charlotte, North Carolina. A Baltimore "conveyancer" postwar. d. there Sept. 21, 1879.

Stafford, George Waters. b. Cheneyville, Louisiana, June 2, 1844. att. Louisiana Seminary. Sgt. Co. I, 8th Louisiana, May 26, 1861. Later promoted to Lt. POW May 12, 1863, at Alexandria, Louisiana. Lt. ADC to his father, Gen. Stafford, Mar. 9, 1864. Absent on recruiting duty in Louisiana, Sept. 1864. Served on staff of Gen. Brent late in the war. Planter at Cheneyville. Married twice. Moved to Gainesville, Texas, and engaged in the "abstract" business. d. there Apr. 4, 1890. bur. Episc. Cem.

Stafford, Joseph B. b. Baltimore, Maryland, July 4, 1839. Educated in Europe. Capt. AQM, 43rd North Carolina, Oct. 14, 1862. WIA at Gettysburg. Capt. AQM to Grimes, Sept. 15, 1864. Paroled May 8, 1865. May have served on staff of Rodes and Daniel. Baltimore tobacco merchant. d. there May 8, 1893. bur. Green Mount Cem.

Stanard, Hugh Mercer. b. Sept. 21, 1841. Lived at Richmond, Virginia, and listed occupation as "gentleman." VADC to Magruder, May 1861–Oct. 1862. Lt. ADC to Magruder, Oct. 14, 1862. On special service in Cuba, 1863–1864. On temporary ordnance duty at Richmond, Sept. 1864. d. Philadelphia, Pennsylvania, Jan. 15, 1876, after being scalded a few days earlier. bur. Shockoe Cem., Richmond.

Stanard, John Beverly. b. Fredericksburg, Virginia, Sept. 1820. att. Wm. & Mary. A civil engineer and lawyer. Lt. PAVa., July 1861, assigned to work on Richmond's defenses. Worked there as a contract engineer until summer 1862. Lt. EO (PACS), Aug. 1, 1862, and assigned to duty as disbursing officer for Engineer Bureau. Capt. EO, Oct. 12, 1863. Served in Richmond entire war. d. Berryville, Virginia, Jan. 25, 1898. Middle name possibly spelled Beverley.

Stanard, Philip Beverley. b. Spotsylvania Co., Virginia, Feb. 2, 1835. att. VMI, and taught there prewar. Capt. Thomas (Va.) Arty., May 10, 1861. Capt. OO to A. P. Hill, July 29, 1862. Maj. OO to Hill, June 18, 1863. Appx. Farmer and teacher. m. Rose Christian. d. Goshen Depot, Rockbridge Co., Virginia, Mar. 6, 1878.

Stanard, William Beverley. b. Mar. 15, 1819. att. UVA. Goochland Co. farmer. VADC to Wise by Oct 1, 1861. Maj. CS to Taliaferro, Mar. 22, 1862. Maj. CS to Colston, 1863. Maj. CS to Steuart. Maj. CS to Wm. Terry, May 1864. Maj. CS to Taliaferro again, Oct. 1864. Paroled Apr. 17, 1865, at Richmond. Resumed farming, but later moved to Richmond and became a merchant, 1873. d. there Mar. 4, 1875. bur. Hollywood Cem.

Standley, James S. b. Mississippi, ca. 1841. Resident of Carrollton, Mississippi. Lt. Co. K, 11th Mississippi, Apr. 29, 1861. Lt. AAAG to Whiting by June 1861. Duration of staff duty not known. WIA at Seven Pines. Capt. Co. K, 11th Mississippi, July 14, 1862. Resigned Aug. 3, 1863. Farmer in Carroll Co., 1870.

Stansbury, Smith. b. Louisiana, 1820. att. USMA, from Kingsbury, Maryland. Ordnance officer in Old Army, 1841–1844. Baltimore bank clerk. Maj. of Arty., CSA, May 18, 1861. Asst. to Josiah Gorgas at Richmond, and commanded Richmond Arsenal. Often referred to as Lt. Col., officially, but promotion not found. d. Halifax, Nova Scotia, Apr. 25, 1864. "His mind was of the highest order," wrote Gorgas.

Staples, Samuel Granville. b. Patrick Co., Virginia, Nov. 29, 1821. att. UVA., Wm. & Mary, and Randolph Macon. Lawyer and legislator. VADC to his brother-in-law, Gen. Stuart, May 1862. Postwar judge in Patrick

Co. d. Roanoke, Aug. 6, 1895. bur. Fairview Cem.

Starke, Lucien Douglas. b. Cold Harbor, Virginia, Feb. 9, 1826. Newspaperman at Richmond and Norfolk, and at Elizabeth City, North Carolina. Also practiced law. Married twice. Col. in North Carolina militia, 1861. Capt. ACS, 17th North Carolina, May 17, 1862. Capt. AAAG to Pettigrew, Sept. 1862, briefly. Capt. ACS to Martin, July 29, 1863. Paroled Apr. 26, 1865. Returned to Virginia and was a lawyer and newspaperman at Norfolk. In state legislature. d. Feb. 21, 1902.

Starke, Thaddeus Burwell. b. Nov. 19, 1824. Capt. AQM, 25th Bn. Virginia, Aug. 23, 1862. Capt. acting QM to Barton, Dec. 1864 until Appx. d. Apr. 25, 1873. bur. Hollywood Cem., Richmond.

Starke, William Norborne. b. Nov. 8, 1835. att. UVA. and Univ. of Louisiana. Lt. Co. E, 1st Louisiana, Apr. 9, 1861. Lt. Judge Advocate to Loring, Aug. 29, 1861. Adjt. 60th Virginia. Capt. AAG to his father, Gen. Starke, Aug. 9, 1862. Capt. AAG to J. H. Winder, Oct. 17, 1862. Capt. AAG to A. P. Hill, June 8, 1863. Maj. AAG to Hill, Feb. 19, 1864. Appx. Salesman and clerk at St. Louis, Missouri, 1870–1878. d. at New Orleans, of yellow fever, Sept. 5, 1878. bur. there.

Starr, Silas Henry, Jr. b. Newton Co., Georgia, Aug. 25, 1838. att. Emory. Pvt. Co. H, 3rd Georgia, Apr. 25, 1861. Promoted to Lt. Lt. acting OO to Wright, Jan.–Feb. 1864. Lt. OO to Wright, Feb. 25, 1864. Capt. OO to Sorrel, Jan. 7, 1865. Appx. Farmer and merchant. "One of the most prominent and wealthy citizens of the county" at the time of his death. d. Mar. 28, 1904. bur. at a family cemetery near Starrsville, in Newton Co., Georgia.

Steele, John Frederick. b. July 7, 1826. att. UVA. and UALA. Lawyer and civil engineer at Huntsville, Alabama. Pvt. Co. I, 4th Alabama, Apr. 26, 1861. Periodically detached for engineer jobs. Lt. EO to Whiting, about

May–June 1862. Lt. EO on staff of Chief Engineer, AOT, by 1863. Lt. EO at Savannah defenses, and in Florida, 1864–1865. Huntsville civil engineer. d. July 26, 1913. bur. Maple Hill Cem.

Steger, Roger Williams. b. Amelia Co., Virginia, June 28, 1834. att. VMI. Farmer and Amelia Co. school principal. Pvt. and Sgt. Co. G, 1st Virginia Cavy., 1861. Capt. AQM to Stuart, Oct. 2, 1861. Maj. QM to Stuart, also to rank from Oct. 2, 1861. Resigned Nov. 11, 1861, and returned to his company. Postwar farmer and teacher. d. Richmond, Virginia, Nov. 24, 1877. bur. Hollywood Cem.

Stephens, Michael H. Capt. AQM, 3rd Tennessee Mtd. Inf., Mar. 11, 1862. Dropped. Capt. acting AQM to Leadbetter, Apr. 1862. Maj. QM to Vaughn, Nov. 5, 1862. POW at Vicksburg. Served with Vaughn into 1865.

Stephenson, John. b. Stephenson's Depot, Virginia, Feb. 22, 1832. m. Cornelia Mason. Pvt. Co. I, 15th Virginia Cavy., Mar. 29, 1864. WIA in leg, May 11, 1864. Lt. ADC to his brother-in-law, Gen. Field, Aug. 5, 1864. Appx. An acquaintance wrote in 1864 that Stephenson "has been too complaining to appear in some of the fights, & I think that Field don't appreciate him very much." d. Winchester, Virginia, Jan. 22, 1911. bur. Mt. Hebron Cem.

Steuart, William James. b. Baltimore, Maryland, July 21, 1832. att. Harvard. Pvt. 1st Maryland. Lt. ADC to his brother, Gen. Steuart, Apr. 7, 1864. MWIA at Spotsylvania, May 12, 1864. d. General Hospital #4 at Richmond, May 21, 1864. bur. Hollywood Cem., but removed to Green Mount Cem., Baltimore, in the 1870s.

Stevens, Harrison Harris. b. Harrisonburg, Virginia, Mar. 23, 1836. att. UVa. and Dickinson Coll. Lawyer in Rockingham Co. Lt. Co. F, 2nd Louisiana, May 9, 1861. Dropped Apr. 30, 1862. Lt. OO to A. G. Jenkins, May 2, 1863. POW at Lewisburg, Dec. 9, 1863. Exchanged by Mar. 1865.

Postwar legislator, teacher, and lawyer in Louisiana. Also practiced law at Dallas, Texas. d. New Orleans Soldiers' Home, Jan. 1, 1885, of tuberculosis.

Stevens, Henry LeNoble. b. Nov. 19, 1827. Very wealthy planter near Charleston, South Carolina. Civilian VADC to Col. P. F. Stevens, commanding Evans's Bgd. in August 1862. MWIA Aug. 23, 1862, along Rappahannock River. Hit five times.

Stevens, Joseph M. Capt. of Inf., June 23, 1864. MSK at Richmond Arsenal. Paroled Apr. 20, 1865.

Stevens, Samuel. b. Apr. 14, 1823. Glass and china merchant at Petersburg, Virginia. Lt. Co. E, 12th Virginia, Apr. 19, 1861. Capt. AQM, 12th Virginia, Sept. 11, 1861. Capt. AQM, tax collector in Bedford Co., July 1863 into Nov. 1864, at least. Paroled Appx. as Capt. AQM on duty at army headquarters. Sheriff of Petersburg. d. Mar. 1, 1894. bur. Blandford Cem.

Stewart, ——. Lt. Col. SO to Magruder, Aug. 20, 1861. Probably Lt. Col. William Dabney Stuart of the 56th Virginia.

Stewart, Benjamin Franklin. b. Westmoreland Co., Virginia, 1836. att. VMI. On VMI faculty, 1858–1859. Lt. Co. K, 40th Virginia, May 25, 1861. WIA at Gaines's Mill. Lt. AAAG to Col. J. M. Brockenbrough's Bgd., May 1863, but probably not beyond. MWIA at Spotsylvania, May 12, 1864. d. May 20, 1864. bur. Spotsylvania Confederate Cem.

Stewart, William Henry. b. Cambridge, Maryland, May 8, 1818. att. Dickinson Coll. Moved to Iowa in 1844, and then to Texas the same year. Judge at Gonzales and member of state legislature. City mayor, 1848. Pvt. Co. A, 4th Texas. QM Sgt. 4th Texas, Oct. 1, 1861. Maj. CS to Wigfall, Nov. 18, 1861. Maj. CS to Hood, Mar. 12, 1862. Resigned because of poor health, Nov. 12, 1862. Lawyer and judge at Gonzales and Galveston. Married four times. d. Galveston, Mar. 26, 1903. bur. Cahill Cem.

Stiles, William Henry, Jr. b. Oct. 22,

1834. Capt. Co. H, 60th Georgia. WIA at Brawner's Farm and Fredericksburg. Capt. AQM, 60th Georgia, Aug. 17, 1863. Capt. AQM to C. A. Evans, Sept. 15, 1864. Farmer in Bartow Co., Georgia. d. Dec. 19, 1878. Stiles's father was Col. of the 60th Georgia.

Stith, Donald Chester. b. Smyrna, Turkey, July 21, 1829. att. USMA. Capt. of Inf., U.S. Army, 1850–1861. Capt. of Inf., CSA, Sept. 24, 1861, to rank from Mar. 16, 1861. Capt. AAG to H. E. McCulloch, Sept. 4, 1861. Maj. AAG to Van Dorn, and Col. (PACS) AAIG to S. D. Lee. Capt. staff of Elzey, Apr. 2, 1864. Capt. staff of Barton, Oct. 7, 1864. Paroled Appx. as Capt. on duty at army headquarters. Insurance agent at St. Louis, Missouri, and schoolteacher in Texas. d. Austin, Texas, Mar. 18, 1920.

Stitt, William Edward. b. Sept. 1, 1833. Dry goods merchant at Charlotte, North Carolina. Pvt. Co. B, 1st (Bethel) North Carolina. Lt. Co. B, 43rd North Carolina, Feb. 12, 1862. Lt. acting ADC to Daniel, July 1863–Jan. 1864. Capt. commanding divisional sharpshooters, Jan. 1864 to Appx. WIA at Third Winchester while acting on the staff of Gen. Grimes. d. July 21, 1907. bur. Elmwood Cem., Charlotte. Some of Stitt's wartime letters are at UNC.

Stockton, John Noble Cummings. b. 1838. att. VMI. Of Charlottesville, Virginia. Pvt. Co. A, 19th Virginia, Apr. 16, 1861. To Lt. May 20, 1861. Lt. acting ADC to Cocke by Nov. 1861, into Feb. 1862 at least. May have been on Pickett's staff, too. Dropped from unit Mar. 27, 1862. Adjt. 1st Virginia, Aug. 8, 1862. Court-martialed Apr. 1863, but sentence remitted. Probably present with regiment into 1865. d. Staunton, Virginia, Apr. 4, 1884.

Stoddard, Albert Henry. b. Savannah, Georgia, Feb. 1838. Married twice. Was abroad at outbreak of war. VADC to Kirkland at Bristoe Station. Lt. ADC to Kirkland, Oct. 21, 1863. POW at Kingston, North Carolina, Mar. 10, 1865. Planter on Daufuskie Island, South Carolina. d. Sept. 21, 1918. bur. Bonaventure Cem., Savannah.

Stone, Hamilton J. b. in Virginia, ca. 1826. Grocer at Petersburg prewar. Capt. AQM, 3rd Virginia, Sept. 10, 1861. Capt. AQM to Huger, Oct. 28, 1861. Capt. AQM to R. H. Anderson, date unknown. Capt. AQM to Mahone. Appx. A farmer and miller in Mecklenburg Co., Virginia, alive in 1870.

Stone, Thomas Henry Clay. b. in Mississippi, 1842. Clerk in Desha Co., Arkansas. Pvt. Co. D, 3rd Arkansas, June 20, 1861. Capt. ACS, 3rd Arkansas, Dec. 5, 1862. Capt. ACS to Hood, July 31, 1863. Failed confirmation and thrown out of service, June 14, 1864, meanwhile having served either with the Texas Bgd. or with Hood's Div. Capt. ACS to Field, Feb. 8, 1865, to rank from June 14, 1864. Appx.

Stone, William R. Lt. Co. B, 21st Mississippi, May 1, 1861, age 21. Adjt. 2nd Bn. Mississippi, Mar. 28, 1862. Capt. Co. G, 48th Mississippi, Nov. 3, 1862. WIA at Fredericksburg, Chancellorsville, and Deep Run. Capt. AAAIG to Harris, intermittently in 1864. Capt. AAIG to Harris, by Dec. 1864. Appx. d. Madison Parish, Louisiana, Feb. 4, 1877.

Stonebraker, Abraham S. b. in Maryland, ca. 1832. m. Catherine E. Pearre, 1856. Physician at Shepherdstown, Virginia. Capt. AQM, 2nd Virginia, June 19, 1861. Capt. AQM to John B. Gordon, May 1864. Capt. AQM to C. A. Evans, probably also May 1864. Appx. Druggist at Baltimore, Maryland. Moved to Waco, Texas, 1876. d. there May 18, 1885. bur. Oakwood Cem., in an unmarked grave.

Stoney, William Edmund. b. in South Carolina, May 21, 1839. att. SCMA. Lt. CSA, Mar. 16, 1861. Lt. OO to Bonham, July 1861. Ordered to Fernandina, Florida, Oct. 28, 1861. Lt. AAG to Col. C. H. Stevens, Sept. 1862–May 1863. Capt. (PACS), Apr. 1, 1863. Capt. ADC to Taliaferro. WIA July 18, 1863, at Morris Island. Capt. AAIG to Hagood, Nov. 2, 1863. WIA in lung at Port Walthall Junction, May 7, 1864. Paroled Apr. 26, 1865. m. Ann Tallulah Allen, 1874. Comptroller general of South Carolina. Also farmer and engineer. d. Charleston, May 24, 1896. bur. Magnolia Cem.

Storke, William Day. b. July 19, 1836. att. UVA. Member of U.S. Coast Survey team. State engineer of Arkansas in 1861. Asst. EO in Arkansas, Aug. 1861–Mar. 1862. Lt. EO, Mar. 6, 1862. On duty in Arkansas, at Vicksburg, and with Franklin Gardner. POW at Port Hudson, July 9, 1863. Lt. EO at Chaffin's Bluff, Virginia, 1864.

Storrs, George Strong. b. Wetumpka, Alabama, Jan. 21, 1840. att. USNA. Sgt. Maj., 13th Alabama. Lt. of Arty., Oct. 4, 1861. On drill duty in North Carolina, early 1862. Lt. OO to French, by July 1862. Capt. OO (PACS) to French, Aug. 22, 1862. Maj. OO (PACS) to French, Nov. 24, 1863. Served into 1865. Lived postwar in Brazil, California, and Oregon. Surveyor and teacher at Dallas, Texas. d. there July 5, 1930.

Stover, William Wallace. Paroled Apr. 18, 1865, as Capt. acting ADC to Robert Ransom. Middle name may have been Walter, and possibly the man who died Jan. 15, 1888, in Richmond, Virginia, and who is buried at Hollywood Cem. A victim of incomplete official records.

Strange, Robert. b. in North Carolina, July 27, 1823. att. UNC. Paymaster during the Mexican War. A Wilmington lawyer. Member of North Carolina Secession Convention. Maj. ADC to Bragg, May 4, 1864. Reappointed to same position for some reason, Mar. 28, 1865. State solicitor and member of legislature. d. Jan. 24, 1877.

Stringfellow, Benjamin Franklin. b. in Virginia, June 18, 1840. Tutor in Noxubee Co., Mississippi, 1860–1861. Pvt. Co. E, 4th Virginia Cavy., May 28, 1861. Detailed as a scout shortly thereafter, and stayed detached from his company for most of the war. POW at Middleburg, June 12, 1863. Lt. SO, Dec. 20, 1864. m. Emma Frances Green, 1867. Farmer in Fairfax Co., and then Episc. minister. Served as a chaplain in the Spanish-American War. d. Lindsay, Virginia, June 8, 1913. bur. Ivy Hill Cem., Alexandria. "A young man of extraordinary merit," in the estimation of J. E. B. Stuart.

Stringfellow, Charles Simeon. b. Clarke Co., Virginia, Mar. 3, 1837. att. UVA. and Wm. & Mary. Lived prewar in Washington, D.C., and at Richmond and Petersburg, Virginia. A lawyer and teacher. Pvt. Co. E, 12th Virginia. Capt. AAG to Sam. Jones, Aug. 20, 1861. Maj. AAG to Jones, Mar. 10, 1862. Maj. AAG to Breckinridge, Mar.–May 1864. Returned to duty with Jones, May 27, 1864. Maj. AAG to Holmes, Feb. 1, 1865. m. Margaret W. Burwell, 1862. Petersburg lawyer. d. Aug. 11, 1912. bur. Hollywood Cem., Richmond.

Strong, William Chase. b. Mississippi. m. Mary Byrd Willis Dallas, 1860. Lt. ADC to Whiting, Nov. 16, 1861. WIA at Fort Fisher, Dec. 25, 1864. Staff of Holmes, 1865. Paroled Apr. 26, 1865. A 32-year-old farmer at Pensacola, Florida, in 1870.

Strother, John Meredith. b. Richmond, Virginia, Mar. 29, 1838. att. UVA., and taught mathematics there prewar. Of Middleburg, Virginia. Chief clerk in CSA Treasury Dept. Capt. ACS, July 9, 1864. Served in Richmond through the war. Conducted "the University School" at Richmond postwar. d. Oct. 1, 1871. bur. Hollywood Cem.

Stuart, James Hardeman. b. in Tennessee, Oct. 8, 1838. att. UMISS. Lawyer in Arkansas and Mississippi. Pvt. Co. K, 18th Mississippi, May 24, 1861. Detached to signal corps duty by Sept. 1861. Capt. SO to his cousin, Gen. Stuart, May 29, 1862. Served as VADC at Gaines's Mill. KIA at Second Manassas, Aug. 30, 1862, while serving as a volunteer in the ranks of the Texas Bgd. Buried on the battlefield.

Stuart, S. T. Agent for Commissary Dept.

Capt. ACS, June 1, 1862. Maj. CS, Feb. 19, 1864. Failed confirmation and returned to rank of Capt. Controlled purchase and distribution of all cattle for ANVa. Praised by R. E. Lee for efficiency. Served into mid-1864, at least.

Stuart, William Douglass. b. Alexandria, Virginia, Jan. 4, 1832. att. UVa. A teacher. Lt. Alexandria Arty., Apr. 17, 1861. Dropped Apr. 1862. Served as a contract engineer in Richmond's defenses, June–Sept. 1862. Lt. EO, Oct. 10, 1862. Stayed at Richmond, in charge of a portion of Intermediate Line, until May 1864. Capt. EO, Mar. 17, 1864. On duty as Capt. EO with Pickett, by Sept. 1864. Appx. Builder and civil engineer at Alexandria. d. Mar. 25, 1879. bur. Christ Church Episc. Cem.

Sublett, David Lackland. b. Powhatan Co., Virginia, June 22, 1837. att. VMI. Capt. in Texas State Guard, prewar. Lt. Co. E, 4th Texas. Lt. acting ADC and acting OO to Hood, May–July 1862. Lt. OO to Hood, July 15, 1862. Lt. OO to Robertson, about Nov. 1862. Capt. Asst. OO to Hood, Mar. 1, 1864. Capt. OO to S. D. Lee, D. H. Hill, and A. P. Stewart in AOT. m. Mary Frances Owens, 1871. A mining engineer at Richmond, Kentucky, and then a real estate agent at Chattanooga, Tennessee. d. there Mar. 24, 1896.

Sudderth, John R. b. North Carolina. Capt. AQM, 33rd North Carolina, Apr. 3, 1863. Capt. AQM to Lane, Sept. 15, 1864. Paroled Apr. 26, 1865. A 43-year-old farmer at Morganton, North Carolina, in 1870.

Sulivane, Clement. b. Port Gibson, Mississippi, Aug. 20, 1838. att. UVa. and Princeton. A lawyer at Cambridge, Maryland, prewar. Pvt. Co. A, 10th Mississippi. Pvt. Co. B, 21st Virginia, July 13, 1861. Lt. ADC to his uncle, Gen. Van Dorn, Oct. 29, 1861. POW at Dan's Bridge. Lt. AAIG to G. W. C. Lee, June 29, 1863. Recommended by Lee to command a brigade of local defense troops. Capt. AAG to Lee, July 6, 1864, through Apr. 1865. Served in Maryland senate. Lawyer and newspaperman at Cambridge. d. there Nov. 9, 1920. Gen. Van Dorn called Sulivane "my favourite nephew."

Surget, Eustace. b. in Mississippi, July 22, 1832. Planter at Natchez valued at $400,000 in 1860. Capt. AAG to W. H. T. Walker, 1861. Capt. AAG to Richard Taylor, by Nov. 1861. Maj. AAG to Taylor, July 31, 1862. Lt. Col. AAG to Taylor, Sept. 20, 1864. Paroled May 11, 1865. m. (1) "the widow Flower, but very properly divorced her immediately." m. (2) Mary Linton. Moved postwar to Bordeaux, France. d. there Feb. 1, 1882. bur. there. Taylor called Surget "an accomplished staff officer."

Sutlive, John Wesley, Jr. b. Ft. Gaines, Georgia, Oct. 26, 1839. Pvt. Co. D, 9th Georgia, June 11, 1861. Capt. AQM, 9th Georgia, Oct. 1861. Capt. AQM to G. T. Anderson, Sept. 15, 1864. Appx. m. Andrewetta Jackson Kirkland, 1865. Clerk at Savannah. d. of yellow fever, Sept. 18, 1876. bur. Laurel Grove Cem., Savannah.

Sutton, Philip Taylor. b. June 24, 1833. Of Hanover Co., Virginia. att. Wm. & Mary. Lt. ADC to Rodes, May 27, 1862. WIA and lost arm at Seven Pines. Resigned Dec. 27, 1862, with R. E. Lee's approval, "though I do not see how he is incapacitated for duty." Richmond tobacco merchant. d. there Mar. 27, 1902. bur. Hollywood Cem.

Swan, Robert. b. Allegany Co., Maryland, Nov. 24, 1827. Distinguished at Battle of Chapultepec in Mexican War. m. Ellen Macgill, 1855. Maj. 1st Virginia Cavy., July 16, 1861. Failed reelection, Apr. 1862. Served in some volunteer role at Seven Pines. VADC to Archer at Fredericksburg. Arrested by Federals in Maryland, 1864. Lived postwar in Allegany Co. d. Selma, Alabama, July 2, 1872. bur. Hollywood Cem., Richmond, Virginia.

Sydnor, Thomas White. b. Hanover Co., Virginia, Mar. 11, 1837. A farmer there. Pvt. Co. G, 4th Virginia Cavy., May 17, 1861. To

QM Sgt., Sept. 21, 1861, and to Lt. Apr. 25, 1862. WIA at Front Royal, Williamsburg, and Trevilian's Station. Lt. VADC to D. H. Hill during Seven Days. Farmer in New Kent Co., and later in Lafayette Co., Missouri. Merchant and traveling salesman at Richmond, Virginia. d. Jan. 21, 1901, on a train near White Sulphur Springs, Virginia. bur. Hollywood Cem. Sydnor's boyhood home in Hanover Co. barely stands in 2002 and soon will be gone.

Sykes, Lawson White. b. Decatur, Alabama, Jan. 5, 1841. att. UNC. Pvt. Co. A, 43rd Mississippi, July 31, 1862. Detailed as VADC to his kinsman Gen. John Gregg, Jan. 1863, and never rejoined the regiment. MWIA at Fussell's Mill, Aug. 16, 1864. d. Richmond, Virginia, Aug. 31, 1864. bur. Hollywood Cem., but likely moved to Odd Fellows' Rest Cem., Aberdeen, Mississippi.

Sykes, S. Turner. b. Oct. 31, 1838. att. UNC and UMISS. m. Mary Bynum. A minister. Pvt. Co. I, 11th Mississippi, Feb. 20, 1861. Lt. OO to Featherston, Aug. 4, 1862. Resigned Nov. 25, 1862. Pvt. Co. C, 12th Mississippi Cavy., Jan. 1, 1864. Paroled May 1865 as AAIG to Armistead's Bgd. of cavalry. Deputy clerk of U.S. Courts at Aberdeen, Mississippi. d. Oct. 16, 1917.

Sykes, William Granville. b. Monroe Co., Mississippi, Aug. 23, 1845. Sgt. Co. F, 43rd Mississippi, Mar. 29, 1862. VADC to Featherston, Seven Days Campaign through 1865. m. Eliza Brandon Clopton, 1872. d. Jan. 18, 1931. bur. Odd Fellows' Rest Cem., Aberdeen.

Symington, Thomas Alexander. b. Baltimore, Maryland, Jan. 18, 1842. Pvt. Latham's (Va.) Btty., May 24, 1861. Pvt. Blount's (Va.) Btty. Detached on ordnance duty with Pickett's Div., Jan.–Oct. 1863. Pvt. Co. E, 10th Virginia Cavy. Acting ADC to Dearing, May 1, 1864. Served in that capacity to Appx., possibly without ever being commissioned. Lived in Europe, 1865–1866. Operated a Baltimore fertilizer and chemical company and sold insurance. d. there Jan. 19, 1900.

Symington, William Stuart. b. Jan. 6, 1839. Lt. Co. B, 21st Virginia, May 23, 1861. Resigned Apr. 5, 1862. VADC to Pickett's Bgd. at Frayser's Farm. Lt. OO to Pickett, July 1, 1862. Lt. ADC to Pickett, Oct. 10, 1862. Capt. ADC to Pickett, Sept. 24, 1863, but this probably was unofficial. Appx. Baltimore chemist and insurance salesman. d. June 9, 1912.

Tabb, Thomas. b. Hampton, Virginia, Oct. 7, 1835. att. Princeton. Hampton lawyer pre- and postwar. Lt. Hampton (Va.) Arty., May 13, 1861. Refused reelection. Served as acting OO to Pryor, spring 1862. Capt. AQM, 3rd Virginia, June 20, 1862. Capt. AQM to Kemper, Aug. 25, 1864. m. Virginia Jones, 1867. d. Philadelphia, Pennsylvania, Oct. 16, 1902.

Tabb, William Barksdale. b. Amelia Co., Virginia, Sept. 11, 1840. att. UVA. and VMI. Amelia Co. lawyer. Lt. PAVA., May 1, 1861, to report to Gen. Wise. Lt. AAG to Wise. Capt. AAG to Wise, Aug. 6, 1861. Resigned July 24, 1862. Maj. 28th Bn. Virginia Heavy Arty., Sept. 9, 1862. Col. 59th Virginia, Nov. 1, 1862. WIA at Petersburg. Appx. Postwar lawyer. d. Amelia Co., Dec. 4, 1874. bur. Grub Hill Episc. Church.

Talcott, Thomas Mann Randolph. b. Philadelphia, Pennsylvania, Mar. 27, 1838. Engineer on Ohio & Mississippi Railroad. Lt. PAVA., May 17, 1861. Capt. PAVA., May 23, 1861. Lt. of Arty., CSA, Oct. 7, 1861. Lt. EO to Huger, by Jan. 1862. Capt. EO to Huger, Mar. 12, 1862. Maj. ADC to R. E. Lee, Apr. 21, 1862. Lt. Col. EO to Lee, July 23, 1863. Col. 1st C.S. Engineers, Apr. 1, 1864. Appx. m. Nannie Carrington McPhail (a sister-in-law of Gen. Imboden), 1864. Railroad engineer at Richmond, Virginia. d. there May 7, 1920. bur. Hollywood Cem.

Taliaferro, Edwin. b. Apr. 15, 1835. From Gloucester Co., Virginia. att. UVA. Professor at Wm. & Mary. Adjt. 32nd Virginia,

Sept. 2, 1861. Lt. of Inf., CSA, Nov. 11, 1861. On ordnance duty at Williamsburg Arsenal. Capt. OO (PACS), July 18, 1862. Capt. OO to McLaws, Sept.–Dec. 1862. Capt. OO at Macon, Georgia, Sept. 1863. Maj. OO (PACS), Jan. 20, 1864. Served at Macon into 1865. m. Frances Bland Beverley Tucker, 1861. Resumed teaching at Wm. & Mary. d. Gloucester Co., Sept. 1, 1867. bur. Ware Episc. Church. A brother of Gen. W. B. Taliaferro.

Taliaferro, Hay Buckner. b. in Virginia, ca. 1834. A merchant. Pvt. Co. A, 17th Virginia, May 27, 1861. Capt. ACS, 17th Virginia, Dec. 12, 1862. Capt. ACS to Corse, Aug. 11, 1863. Appx. d. Richmond, Virginia, Oct. 17, 1892. bur. Hollywood Cem., in an unmarked grave.

Taliaferro, John. b. Apr. 12, 1843. att. USMA. Lt. PAVa., May 7, 1861. Lt. VADC to Ewell, 1861. Also served in the Fluvanna (Va.) Arty. Cadet July 12, 1861, on drillmaster duty. Cadet AAAG and acting ADC to Pendleton, spring–fall 1862. Cadet acting ADC to Ewell, May 1864. WIA in elbow at Spotsylvania. Lt. CSA, June 15, 1864. Ordered to report to Kemper, Oct. 20, 1864, and then to John S. Mosby, Nov. 16, 1864. Paroled June 7, 1865, at Gordonsville, Virginia. It is not always clear where Taliaferro served during the war. Lived postwar at Savannah, Georgia. d. 1917. bur. Graham Cem., Orange Co., Virginia. "Artillery is not his forte," wrote Gen. Pendleton. Campbell Brown of Ewell's staff wrote of Taliaferro: "brave & willing but young & stupid," and "with the heart of a lion had the brains of a sheep."

Taliaferro, Philip Alexander. b. June 11, 1827. att. UVa. Physician in Gloucester Co., Virginia. m. Susan Lewis McCandlish. Surg. 21st Virginia Militia. Lt. ADC to his half-brother, Gen. Taliaferro, Mar. 29, 1862. Resigned Nov. 11, 1862, to resume medical practice. d. June 27, 1901.

Taliaferro, Thomas Seddon. b. Gloucester Co., Virginia, Oct. 17, 1831. att. UVa. A lawyer. m. Harriotte Hopkins Lee, a cousin of Gen. R. E. Lee. Maj. 21st Virginia Militia, Dec. 1861–May 1862. VADC to his brother, Gen. Taliaferro, Dec. 1862. PM and acting Judge Advocate, Second Corps, Oct. 1863, until appointed Capt. Judge Advocate, Nov. 4, 1864. Gloucester Co. lawyer and legislator. d. Richmond, Virginia, Jan. 10, 1918. bur. Ware Episc. Church, Gloucester Co. An officer in the Second Corps called Taliaferro "a very weak brother, but good, amiable, and very gentlemanly. He is a shockingly poor officer. . . ."

Taliaferro, Warner Throckmorton. b. Gloucester Co., Virginia, Oct. 30, 1833. Served in state legislature. m. (1) Martha Paul. m. (2) Frances Hardy. Maj. 40th Virginia, July 1, 1861. Dropped Apr. 1862. VADC to his half-brother, Gen. Taliaferro, Apr. and Aug. 1862, at least. Capt. AAG to Taliaferro, Sept. 10, 1862. On the staff of Trimble in 1863, briefly. Capt. AAG to Colston, Nov. 17, 1863. Capt. acting ADC to D. H. Hill, Mar. 1865. Real estate and railroad man at Norfolk, Virginia. d. there Jan. 12, 1881. bur. Elmwood Cem.

Tannahill, Edmund Duncan. b. Franklin Co., North Carolina, July 28, 1841. Prewar clerk at Petersburg, Virginia. Pvt. Co. E, 12th Virginia, Apr. 19, 1861. Detached in Commissary Dept., Apr. 1862–Feb. 1864. Capt. ACS, Feb. 19, 1864, stationed at Petersburg. Failed official confirmation, but apparently reappointed. Appx. Businessman at New York City. d. at Petersburg, Apr. 7, 1874. bur. Blandford Cem.

Tannahill, Robert. b. Nov. 12, 1832. A merchant, and brother of E. D. Tannahill (see above). Worked for QM Dept. at Norfolk, 1861–1862. Maj. CS to Loring, Mar. 19, 1862. Maj. CS at Petersburg, Virginia, June 1862. Probably on the staff of Gen. French. Served at Petersburg into 1865. d. Nov. 27, 1883. bur. Blandford Cem., Petersburg.

Tanner, William Elam. b. Buckingham Co.,

Virginia, Mar. 13, 1836. att. Richmond College. Bookkeeper at Tredegar Ironworks, Richmond. Lt. Letcher (Va.) Arty., by Feb. 1862. Lt. oo to Thomas, July 25, 1862. Resigned Sept. 23, 1862, to return to Tredegar duties. Maj. 6th Bn. Virginia LDTS. Railroad engine manufacturer at Richmond, and at Duluth, Minnesota. In Virginia legislature. d. Richmond, Aug. 6, 1898. bur. Hollywood Cem.

Tannor, Nathaniel Mitchell. b. Dinwiddie Co., Virginia, Aug. 30, 1827. Merchant at Petersburg, Virginia. m. Mary E. Rowlett. Pvt. Co. D, 5th Virginia Cavy., May 17, 1861. Maj. QM to Colston, May 25, 1862. Maj. QM to Steuart, by Oct. 1863. Maj. QM to Rodes, Aug. 16, 1864. Maj. QM to Ramseur, Sept. 1864. Maj. QM to Grimes, Oct. 1864. Appx. Resumed mercantile business at Petersburg. d. there Apr. 8, 1881. bur. Blandford Cem.

Tansill, Robert. b. Occoquan, Virginia, June 12, 1812. Served in Seminole and Mexican Wars. m. (1) Frances Weems. m. (2) Anna Lucinda Bender, 1849. Served in USMC, 1833–1861. Detained at New York City, 1861. Capt. CSA, Feb. 13, 1862. Col. 2nd Virginia Arty., Feb. 14, 1862. Unit disbanded May 23, 1862. Capt. AAIG to Whiting, June 26, 1862. Col. (PACS) AAIG to Whiting, May 27, 1863. Col. AAIG to S. D. Lee, 1865. Wrote an interesting pamphlet on causes of the Confederacy's defeat, published in 1865. d. Feb. 5, 1890. bur. family cem. northwest of Dumfries, Virginia.

Tansill, Thomas W. b. Dumfries, Virginia, ca. 1819. A clerk there. Sgt. Co. F, 49th Virginia. Capt. ACS, 3rd Virginia Arty., Mar. 11, 1862. Resigned Sept. 4, 1862, supposedly to reenter the ranks. Living in Washington, D.C., by 1864, and alive there in May 1868.

Tapscott, John B. b. Jefferson Co., Virginia. City engineer at Clarksville, Tennessee, nearly his entire adult life. Lt. EO, Mar. 3, 1862. On duty at Richmond and in central Virginia. Lt. EO at Goldsboro, North Carolina, Oct. 1863–Nov. 1864. Lt. EO with

ANVa., Dec. 1864. Married twice. d. Clarksville, Mar. 24, 1905. bur. Riverview Cem.

Tate, John M. b. North Carolina. A merchant. Lt. Co. D, 11th North Carolina, Feb. 14, 1862, age 32. Capt. AQM, 11th North Carolina, Apr. 22, 1862. Capt. AQM at Charlotte, North Carolina, July 8, 1864. Capt. AQM to Wilcox, Sept. 15, 1864. Appx. A salesman at Hillsborough postwar. d. Winston, North Carolina, Oct. 1883. Some of Tate's war letters are at UNC.

Tate, William M. b. Augusta Co., Virginia, Mar. 3, 1814. att. UVA. and Washington Coll. Augusta Co. farmer, justice of the peace, and legislator. Served as a commissary agent in the Shenandoah Valley until appointed Maj. CS, July 1, 1863. Subsequently on duty around Staunton. Paroled May 1, 1865, at Winchester. Resumed farming. d. May 5, 1889. bur. Thornrose Cem., Staunton.

Tayloe, John William. b. Buena Vista, Virginia, Nov. 30, 1831. Moved to Hale Co., Alabama, 1853. att. VMI. Capt. Co. E, Jeff. Davis (Miss.) Legion. Resigned in controversy over drunkenness. Seemingly served as Maj. AAIG to D. H. Hill, from Apr. 14, 1862. Resigned Nov. 15, 1862. Adjt. 2nd Virginia Cavy., May 28, 1864. Lt. AAAG to Wickham's Bgd., Aug. 1864 into 1865. Hale Co. farmer. Lived in Birmingham, Alabama, latter part of life. d. there Dec. 2, 1904. Tayloe's brother was Col. of the 11th Alabama, and Col. T. T. Munford was his brother-in-law.

Taylor, Benjamin F. Pvt. Semple's (Ala.) Btty., Mar. 7, 1862, age 26. Lt. ADC to Robert Ransom, Mar. 5, 1863. Paroled May 11, 1865, at Montgomery, Alabama.

Taylor, D. B. b. Alabama. Sgt. 2nd Florida. Discharged Mar. 31, 1862. Lt. ADC to E. A. Perry, Nov. 22, 1862. Paroled June 1, 1865, at Montgomery, Alabama.

Taylor, Erasmus. b. Orange Co., Virginia, July 29, 1830. att. UVA. m. Roberta Stuart Ashby (a cousin of Gen. Ashby), 1851.

VADC to D. R. Jones, July 1861 into winter 1861. Maj. QM to Longstreet, Nov. 14, 1863. Appx. Farmer and lawyer in Orange Co. d. Henderson, North Carolina, May 20, 1907. Taylor's fairly bland memoir of 1864–1865 is at the Virginia Historical Society.

Taylor, George E. Capt. AQM, Mar. 6, 1862. Dropped Aug. 30, 1862, for failed bond. Reapptd. Oct. 19, 1863. On duty at Richmond, Virginia, as IFT, assisting R. P. Archer. Served into 1865.

Taylor, Henry. Capt. acting ADC to McLaws, 1861. VADC to Loring in May 1863. Paroled at Richmond, Virginia, Apr. 26, 1865, as "Capt. ADC."

Taylor, James Marshall. b. Taylorsville, Virginia, Apr. 27, 1822. Hanover Co. farmer. Also operated a steam sawmill and was a railroad conductor in vicinity of Richmond. Capt. AQM, Oct. 25, 1861. Dropped, but restored on Jan. 31, 1863. In charge of ANVa. ambulance train. Paroled at Richmond, Apr. 23, 1865. Clerk in state treasurer's office. Lived postwar at Ashland. d. at Richmond, Sept. 9, 1901. bur. Hollywood Cem.

Taylor, James Matchett. att. Wake Forest. A resident of Gates Co., North Carolina. Pvt. Co. B, 5th North Carolina, June 12, 1861, age 22. To Sgt. Maj., Feb. 7, 1862. Later Lt. Co. G, 5th North Carolina. Lt. AAAG to McRae's Bgd., Oct. 1862. Duration of staff duty uncertain, but likely not long. Later Capt. Co. G, 5th North Carolina. WIA in groin at Gettysburg. Appx. d. Oct. 3, 1867.

Taylor, John. b. in Virginia, either Aug. 7 or Sept. 7, 1832. att. UVA. Pvt. Fredericksburg (Va.) Arty., July 15, 1861. Lt. ADC to Wickham, Sept. 11, 1863. Paroled Apr. 28, 1865, at Ashland. m. Isabella N. Locke, 1867. Farmer in Westmoreland Co. Found to be insane in spring 1911. d. Westmoreland Co., Nov. 5, 1913. bur. "Oak Grove," Westmoreland Co.

Taylor, John Cowdery. b. Norfolk, Virginia, Sept. 7, 1842. att. UVA. m. Harriet Rouzee. Lt. PAVa., May 14, 1861. Lt. AAG to Pember-

ton, May 23, 1861. VADC to Mahone, 1861–Mar. 1862. Pvt. Co. I, 5th Virginia Cavy. Lt. ADC to Pemberton, May 10, 1862. POW at Vicksburg. Lt. ADC to R. L. Page, Apr. 1, 1864. POW at Ft. Morgan. Bank cashier at Norfolk postwar. A brother of Walter H., Robertson, and Richard C. Taylor. d. Willoughby Beach, Virginia, Aug. 31, 1912. bur. Elmwood Cem., Norfolk.

Taylor, John L. From Norfolk, Virginia. Connected with the CSN in some way. VADC to S. D. Lee's Bn. Arty., from about Sept. 1, 1862. MWIA at Sharpsburg—shot in the neck.

Taylor, Joseph. b. New York. Clerk at New Orleans, Louisiana, prewar. Pvt. Co. I, 1st Louisiana, May 4, 1861, age 23. To Lt., Apr. 28, 1862. WIA at King's School House. Lt. AAAIG to the brigade, Jan.–Apr. 1863. On detached service in Louisiana, summer 1864. Commanded his regiment in Aug. 1864. Paroled June 6, 1865, at Natchitoches, Louisiana. Listed himself as a Capt. Possibly the Capt. Joseph Taylor, 1833 to Oct. 16, 1877, who is buried at Mandeville Cem. in St. Tammany Parish.

Taylor, Lawrence Berry. b. Alexandria, Virginia, Aug. 3, 1818. att. UVA. and Princeton. m. Virginia Powell. Mayor of Alexandria and a lawyer. Col. of Cavy., Mar. 23, 1865, assigned to military court of the cavalry corps. Paroled Apr. 25, 1865, at Fairfax C.H. Postwar lawyer. d. Alexandria, Nov. 16, 1873.

Taylor, Murray Forbes. b. Falmouth, Virginia, Dec. 24, 1843. att. VMI. Cadet, 13th Virginia. Cadet, acting ADC to Elzey, mid-May to mid-June 1862. Lt. ADC to A. P. Hill, June 14, 1862. Appx. Farmer in King George Co., Virginia, and a cotton planter in Alabama. Took up ranching at Bakersfield, California, 1877. m. Butler Brayne Thornton. d. Fredericksburg, Virginia, Nov. 20, 1909. bur. Union Cem., Bakersfield.

Taylor, Richard Cornelius. b. Norfolk, Virginia, Oct. 7, 1835. att. VMI. Teacher and railroad auditor. Capt. Co. H, 6th Virginia, Apr. 19, 1861. Maj. of Arty., CSA, Mar. 18, 1862. Maj. acting ADC to Mahone, May–Aug. 1862. Maj. Judge Advocate to Elzey's command, Feb.–Apr. 1863. Maj. commanding post at Chaffin's Bluff, June 1863–Sept. 1864. POW and twice WIA at Ft. Harrison, Sept. 29, 1864. Norfolk teacher postwar. d. there Dec. 12, 1917. bur. Elmwood Cem. Brother of fellow staff officers J. C., Robertson, and W. H. Taylor.

Taylor, Robert Temple. b. Nov. 1836. Employed by Bank of Virginia. Pvt. Co. F, 21st Virginia, Apr. 21, 1861. Maj. QM to J. R. Anderson, Apr. 23, 1862. Maj. QM to Thomas, July 1862 until Appx. Briefly worked at auditor's office at Richmond, then joined Piedmont & Arlington Life Insurance Co. in Richmond. d. there Apr. 9, 1876.

Taylor, Robertson. b. Norfolk, Virginia, 1840. A merchant there. Brother of Walter H. Taylor and others (see above and below). QM Sgt. and Adjt., 6th Virginia. Capt. AAG to Mahone, Nov. 16, 1861. WIA at the Wilderness, May 6, 1864. Capt. AAG with Conscript Bureau at Richmond, Mar. 1, 1865. Paroled at Greensboro. Moved to Baltimore, Maryland, in 1865, and imported coffee and sugar. Married twice. d. in Carroll Co., Maryland, Oct. 15, 1924.

Taylor, Thomas. b. Columbia, South Carolina, Feb. 11, 1826. att. South Carolina Coll. m. Sally Frank Elmore, 1856. Served in Hampton Legion (S.C.). Lt. ADC to Hampton, Sept. 22, 1863, into 1865. Member of state legislature postwar. d. Columbia, Dec. 22, 1903.

Taylor, Walter Herron. b. Norfolk, Virginia, June 13, 1838. att. VMI. Lt. AAG, PAVa., 1861. Lt. CSA, July 16, 1861. Capt. AAG to R. E. Lee, Dec. 10, 1861. Maj. ADC to Lee, Apr. 21, 1862. Maj. AAG to Lee, Nov. 24, 1862. Lt. Col. AAG to Lee, Dec. 21, 1863. Appx. Banker and businessman at Norfolk. d. there Mar. 1, 1916. bur. Elmwood Cem.

Taylor wrote two books on ANVa. matters, and his wartime letters were published in the 1990s.

Taylor, William. b. June 30, 1827. Capt. ACS, 17th Bn. Virginia Cavy., Oct. 24, 1862. Capt. AQM, 11th Virginia Cavy., June 1, 1863. Resigned Oct. 7, 1863. Maj. CS to Lomax, Sept. 18, 1863. Maj. CS to Payne later. d. Dec. 4, 1891. bur. Grace Episc. Church, Berryville, Virginia.

Taylor, William V. Lt. OO to Huger, early in 1862. Date of appointment not found. Promoted to Capt. and later Maj., PACS, and on duty at Richmond Arsenal. Second in command of that post, apparently for most of the war. Precise dates of service there are lacking. Maj. commanding the armory at Tallassee, Alabama, by 1865.

Tempe, Robert. Lt. ADC to Benning, 1862. Nothing further found. Likely a short-time VADC.

Temple, Charles Wellford. b. Jan. 10, 1834. Of Fredericksburg, Virginia. att. UVa. Pvt. Co. B, 9th Virginia Cavy., June 30, 1861. POW Mar. 1862. Lt. OO, Mar. 20, 1863, to report to Gen. Longstreet. Duty unclear. Lt. OO at Goldsboro, North Carolina, by Dec. 1863. Lt. OO to L. S. Baker, by June 1864. Mostly served at Goldsboro, but may have been at Richmond, too. Teacher at Rapidan, Virginia. d. Apr. 25, 1899. bur. Fredericksburg City Cem.

Tenney, Otis Seth. b. in New Hampshire, Dec. 4, 1822. att. Norwich Univ. Taught at military schools in Delaware and Kentucky. Lawyer at Mt. Sterling, Kentucky. m. Junia M. Warner, 1848. Maj. 2nd Bn. Kentucky Mtd. Rifles, 1862. Maj. QM to Cosby, 1864. Lawyer at Mt. Sterling and at Lexington. d. Mar. 31, 1916.

Tenney, Samuel Fisher. b. Athens, Georgia, Mar. 26, 1840. Pvt. Co. K, 3rd Georgia. WIA at Gettysburg. Lt. OO to Thomas by August 1863, into Dec. 1864 at least. Presby. minister postwar. d. Crockett, Texas, July 2, 1926. Tenney's serialized history of the 3rd Georgia was published in the *Athens Southern Banner* in 1864–1865. bur. Glenwood Cem., Houston.

Tennille, Alexander St. Clair. b. Washington Co., Georgia, Sept. 16, 1838. att. Univ. of Nashville. Served in Co. D, 9th Georgia, and as Capt. ACS of regiment. Capt. acting CS to Benning, Feb. 1865. Capt. ACS to G. T. Anderson at Appx. Florida physician postwar. Mayor of Troy, Alabama. m. Sarah Butler, 1872. d. Montgomery, Alabama, July 4, 1907.

Tennille, William Alexander. b. Washington Co., Georgia, July 3, 1840. att. UGA. Served in Co. D, 9th Georgia. Lt. acting ADC to G. T. Anderson at Second Manassas. Capt. AAIG to Anderson, Nov. 2, 1863. Retired to Invalid Corps, Jan. 16, 1865, probably due to hepatitis. On late-war duty with Howell Cobb at Macon. m. Clara Tuttle, 1870. Cotton merchant at New York City. Retired to East Orange, New Jersey. d. 1905.

Terrell, Leigh Richmond. b. in Virginia, 1835. Lawyer at Uniontown, Alabama. Lt. Co. D, 4th Alabama. Lt. AAAG to Law by Second Manassas, but only appointed Capt. AAG to Law, Oct. 14, 1862. Lt. Col. 47th Alabama, June 15, 1864. WIA at Petersburg, June 18, 1864. MWIA at Second Darbytown Road, Oct. 13, 1864. d. Richmond, Oct. 22, 1864. bur. Hollywood Cem. First name probably spelled as shown above, although his presumed namesake (a prominent religious figure) spelled it Legh.

Terrell, Lewis Franklin. b. Hanover Co., Virginia, Sept. 12, 1836. att. UVA. Studied law prewar. Adjt. of Hanover (Va.) Arty., Apr. 1861. Lt. of Arty., July 1, 1862, to report to Magruder. VADC to B. H. Robertson, Aug. 1862. Maj. of Arty., Sept. 11, 1862. Served as a sort of executive officer with the Stuart Horse Arty., and for six days in June 1863 as Judge Advocate to the cavalry corps. Degree of personal role with Stuart uncertain, but Terrell wrote in Mar. 1863, "I am heartily sick" of being with Stuart. VADC

to Stuart at Kelly's Ford that same month. Maj. Chief Arty. to Trimble, June 13, 1863. Relieved from ANVa., Aug. 14, 1863, because "disagreements arose." Commanded a light artillery brigade at Charleston, South Carolina, and was Maj. AAIG to Taliaferro. d. James Island, South Carolina, Apr. 14, 1864, of typhoid fever. bur. Hollywood Cem., Richmond, Virginia.

Terry, Benjamin Franklin. b. Feb. 18, 1821. Sugar planter in Ft. Bend Co., Texas. VADC to Longstreet, July 1861. Col. 8th Texas Cavy. KIA at Woodsonville, Kentucky, Dec. 17, 1861. bur. Glenwood Cem., Houston.

Thom, Allan C. b. June 30, 1825. att. UVA., from Fredericksburg, Virginia. Capt. AAIG to Barton, Mar. 31, 1862. POW at Vicksburg. Capt. AAIG assigned to duty at the passport office, under the PM at Richmond, Virginia, Aug. 25, 1864. On duty there through 1864, at least. d. Key West, Florida, Feb. 26, 1871.

Thom, Cameron Erskine. b. Culpeper Co., Virginia, June 20, 1825. att. UVA. Mexican War veteran. Moved to California in 1849. Wounded by Indians on his way west. Lawyer and legislator at Los Angeles. Married three times. Was Winfield S. Hancock's landlord in 1861. Returned to Virginia in 1863. VADC to Gen. Wm. Smith, July 1863. Served in 1864, apparently as a volunteer, with Col. J. W. Atkinson in the defenses of Richmond. Returned to California postwar and resumed law practice. Mayor of Los Angeles. d. Feb. 2, 1915. bur. Evergreen Cem.

Thomas, Charles H. b. North Carolina, ca. 1832. A clerk at Louisburg. Pvt. Co. L, 15th North Carolina, May 20, 1861. Capt. AQM, 15th North Carolina, Mar. 1, 1862. Capt. AQM to Cooke, Sept. 15, 1864. Appx. Alive 1870 at Louisburg, a farmer.

Thomas, Francis John. b. Charleston, South Carolina, Jan. 10, 1824. att. USMA. Lt. U.S. Army, 1844–1852. Mexican War veteran. Engineer in Virginia and Pennsylvania,

1852–1858. Merchant at Baltimore, Maryland, 1859–1861. Adjt. Gen. of Maryland troops, 1861. Col. PAVa., 1861. Acting Chief OO to J. E. Johnston, July 1861. KIA at First Manassas.

Thomas, James J., Jr. b. Franklin Co., North Carolina, ca. 1831. A merchant at Franklinton. Lt. Co. F, 47th North Carolina, Mar. 3, 1862. Capt. AQM, 47th North Carolina, May 16, 1862. Capt. AQM to Heth, Sept. 15, 1864. Capt. AQM to report to A. H. Cole (field transportation), Mar. 17, 1865. d. Dec. 7, 1874. bur. Fairview Cem., Franklinton.

Thomas, James Pinckney. b. in Georgia, Apr. 29, 1839. att. UVa. and Davidson Coll. Planter at Augusta, Georgia. Lt. Co. A, Cobb's Legion (Ga.) Cavy., May 1, 1862. WIA at Little Washington, Virginia, 1862. Clerk for Gen. P. M. B. Young, Nov. 1863. Lt. ADC to Young, 1864. May not have been commissioned. Postwar cotton planter and legislator at Waynesboro, Georgia. m. Mary Clanton. d. June 11, 1888. bur. Magnolia Cem., Augusta. Gen. Young called Thomas "my true and loyal friend, as dear to me as my own blood."

Thomas, N. J. Capt. AQM, 46th Virginia, Aug. 27, 1861. Capt. AQM to Wise, Sept. 15, 1864. Appx.

Thomas, Oliver H. Lawyer at San Francisco, California, prewar. Lt. ADC to Archer, June 13, 1862. On court-martial duty at Richmond while Gen. Archer absent in prison. Presumably rejoined Archer in fall 1864. No further record after Nov. 1864.

Thomas, Robert. b. Athens, Georgia, Jan. 28, 1828. att. UGA. Lifelong planter. Capt. AQM, 16th Georgia, July 19, 1861. Maj. QM to Howell Cobb, Mar. 6, 1862. POW at Macon, Georgia, Apr. 20, 1865. Never married. d. Hall Co., Georgia, Aug. 2, 1883. bur. Oconee Hill Cem., Athens.

Thomas, Robert Brenham. b. in Kentucky, Nov. 20, 1828. att. USMA. Served in U.S. Army, 1852–1856. Lt. of Arty., CSA, Mar. 16,

1861. Staff of Mercer in 1861. Adjt. 2nd Florida. Maj. (PACS), Feb. 18, 1862. Commanded Ft. Brook, Florida. Maj. AAIG to Finegan, Feb. 17, 1862. Col. (PACS), May 1, 1863, still AAIG to Finegan. Col. 9th Florida, probably in 1864, briefly. Relieved Aug. 11, 1864, and assigned to duty in prisons. d. Jan. 25, 1901. bur. Oaklawn Cem., Tampa, Florida.

Thomas, Willey F. b. Southampton Co., Virginia. Pvt. Co. A, 5th Bn. Virginia, Aug. 10, 1861. Later QM Sgt. To Capt. AQM, 5th Bn. Virginia, May 19, 1862. Capt. AQM with First Corps commissary train by Nov. 1862. Capt. AQM at ANVa. headquarters, by Aug. 1863. Served into 1865. Postwar merchant. d. Brunswick Co., Virginia, Sept. 9, 1868, age 40, of colic.

Thomas, William H. b. 1837. Of Rockbridge Co., Virginia. Cpl. Co. L, 4th Virginia, July 16, 1861. To Lt., Apr. 22, 1862. Lt. AAAG to Stonewall Bgd., Sept. 22, 1862. Had been assigned to Ordnance Bureau effective Aug. 23, 1862, but probably never served there. Resigned Oct. 9, 1862. d. 1919. bur. Blacksburg.

Thomas, William Hinton. b. Aug. 14, 1825. A resident of Washington, D.C. m. Catherine L. Pumphrey. Capt. ACS to Wise, June 5, 1861. Maj. CS to Wise, Aug. 7, 1861. Maj. CS to E. K. Smith, Feb. 27, 1862. Served with Smith into 1865. d. Louisville, Kentucky, Oct. 5, 1908. bur. Cave Hill Cem.

Thompson, Benjamin Stanton. b. Kanawha Co., Virginia, Mar. 26, 1818. att. Wm. & Mary. Capt. AQM, 36th Virginia, Oct. 3, 1861. Maj. QM to Barton, May 13, 1862. Maj. QM to Steuart, date uncertain. Paroled May 12, 1865, at Charleston, West Virginia. Farmer in Kanawha Co. and postmaster at Hinton, West Virginia. d. Dec. 29, 1907. Father of C. L. Thompson (see below).

Thompson, C. Macon. b. in Mississippi, ca. 1840. A resident of Lafayette Co. Capt. AQM, 19th Mississippi, June 11, 1861. Resigned July 10, 1861. VADC to Longstreet at First Manassas and returned home soon thereafter. His will was probated in Lafayette Co., in 1873. Moxley Sorrel described Thompson as "an extraordinary looking person. . . . His teeth and jaws were firmly set and locked, and no surgical ingenuity had yet succeeded in opening them."

Thompson, Cameron Lewis. b. Coalsmouth, Virginia, Apr. 22, 1842. Pvt. Co. H, 22nd Virginia, 1861. Acting ADC to Barton, May 1863. POW at Vicksburg. Capt. AQM, 52nd Georgia, Oct. 19, 1863. Capt. AQM to W. R. Terry, Sept. 15, 1864. Appx. Hardware salesman at Cincinnati, Ohio, 1865. Later a merchant in Kentucky, and ultimately a newspaper publisher, realtor, and postmaster at Huntington, West Virginia. Alive 1920.

Thompson, Charles Gratiot. b. Baltimore Co., Maryland, June 28, 1833. Sgt. 1st Maryland Arty., July 6, 1861. Also served in Hampton Legion (S.C.) Arty. Lt. OO to McGowan by May 1864. Appx. Moved to Canada postwar and then to Massachusetts. d. by 1894, probably in 1889.

Thompson, Daniel Bowly. b. Baltimore, Maryland. Sgt. Co. B, 21st Virginia, May 23, 1861. Later to Lt. Capt. ACS, 30th Bn. Virginia Sharpshooters, Jan. 18, 1863. Capt. ACS to Wharton, July 1863. Took Oath May 24, 1865. May have been staff of Gen. Williams, too. Baltimore merchant. d. LaGrange, Maryland, May 19, 1875, age 35.

Thompson, George Gardner. b. Louisa Co., Virginia, Mar. 15, 1824. att. Wm. & Mary. Lawyer at Richmond, and farmer in Culpeper Co. m. Eliza Barbour, 1850. Pvt. Co. E, 13th Virginia, Apr. 17, 1861. Capt. AQM, Sept. 5, 1861. Served at various posts around central Virginia. Assigned to ANVa. headquarters, Sept. 15, 1864. Appx. Culpeper Co. sheriff, and a railroad agent for 30 years. Kept a hotel at Culpeper. d. Mar. 5, 1908. bur. Fairview Cem.

Thompson, George Sidney. b. 1839. att. UNC. A resident of Chapel Hill, North Carolina. Pvt. Co. G, 28th North Carolina, Sept. 2, 1861. Capt. AQM, 28th North Carolina, Oct. 18, 1861. Resigned May 23, 1862. Maj. QM to Lane, Jan. 23, 1863. Relieved from Lane's Bgd. Aug. 27, 1864. Subsequently Maj. QM at posts in Florida. d. 1876.

Thompson, Tazewell. b. Norfolk, Virginia, Sept. 26, 1834. Pvt. Co. H, 9th Virginia Cavy., June–Dec. 1861. Pvt. in 26th Virginia, Dec. 1861–May 1862. Capt. ACS to J. S. Williams, July 29, 1862. Maj. CS to Williams, Apr. 30, 1863, backdated to July 29, 1862, again. Maj. CS to Cosby. Present into 1865. d. May 10, 1914.

Thomson, James Walton. b. Berryville, Virginia, Oct. 28, 1843. att. VMI. From Jefferson Co., Virginia. VADC to T. J. Jackson at First Manassas. Lt. Chew's (Va.) Btty., 1861. Capt., Mar. 14, 1864. Maj. of Arty., Feb. 18, 1865. KIA at High Bridge, Apr. 6, 1865. bur. Stonewall Cem., Winchester, Virginia.

Thorburn, Henry Clay. b. July 5, 1840. Clerk at Fredericksburg, Virginia. Sgt. Fredericksburg Arty., Apr. 23, 1861. To Lt., Apr. 1, 1862. Lt. acting QM, 3rd Corps ordnance train, May–Oct. 1863. Capt. AQM, Dec. 2, 1863. Continued service with ordnance train. Appx. A "conveyancer" at Baltimore, Maryland, postwar. d. there Oct. 15, 1898. bur. Fredericksburg City Cem.

Thorne, Edward Alston. b. Halifax Co., North Carolina, Dec. 27, 1828. att. UNC. m. Alice Marie Harriss, 1852. A farmer. Lt. Co. D, 24th North Carolina, May 15, 1862. Lt. acting OO to Robert Ransom, Sept. 1862–Dec. 1863. Resigned from unit Jan. 1, 1864, to be full-time OO, though date of commission is uncertain. Still signed as Lt. acting OO to Ransom in May 1864. Postwar physician. d. May 20, 1911. bur. Thorne-Clark Cem., Halifax Co. Thorne's war letters are at UNC.

Thornton, George Alfred. b. 1837. att. USMA

from Charleston, Virginia. Lt. of Arty., PAVa., Apr. 1861. Lt. AAAG to Magruder, May 1861. Lt. of Inf., CSA, June 1861, possibly never confirmed. Adjt. 19th Mississippi, June 17, 1861. Ordered to Ben McCulloch, Aug. 1861. Lt. AAAG to J. M. McIntosh, Dec. 1861. Ordered to Camp of Instruction at Richmond, Virginia, Apr. 15, 1862. Staff of Field, May 30, 1862, though may not have served with that general. Sent to Loring, Oct. 1, 1862. Capt. PACS, Dec. 12, 1862, to report to Holmes. Later served as AAAIG to J. G. Walker, Sept. 1864. Thornton has a very uneven and tortuous military record. No further military record after 1864. Postwar resident of Campbell Co., Kentucky. One family source suggests a middle name of Alexander.

Thornton, William Willis. b. Brentsville, Virginia, Aug. 24, 1825. A farmer in Prince William Co. m. Mary Susan Buckner, 1851. Capt. Co. A, 4th Virginia Cavy., Apr. 23, 1861. Dropped Apr. 28, 1862. Capt. ACS to Early, Aug. 4, 1862. Maj. CS to Early, Feb. 19, 1864. Failed confirmation, and reappointed to same position on staff of Ramseur, June 15, 1864. Maj. CS to Pegram, Oct. 1864. Maj. CS to J. A. Walker, Feb. 1865. Appx. Supt. of Prince William Co. schools, and farmer at Manassas. d. Brentsville, Oct. 26, 1884. bur. Manassas City Cem. Jubal Early called Thornton "the most faithful, efficient & useful officer in his department that I know." Thornton named one of his seven children Richard Ewell Thornton.

Throckmorton, John Ariss. b. Loudoun Co., Virginia, Mar. 3, 1815. Col. in Virginia Militia. Married twice. Pvt. Co. F, 6th Virginia Cavy., Apr. 20, 1861. Later served as Sgt. and Lt., before becoming Capt. of the company, Apr. 20, 1862. Lt. acting ADC to Stuart, December 1861. Resigned from 6th Virginia Cavy., Sept. 23, 1863, in promotion dispute. Throckmorton's son served in the Yankee army. d. May 28, 1891.

Thurston, Edward North. b. in South Caro-

lina, Aug. 5, 1831. Farmer near Charleston. Married twice. VADC and acting OO to D. R. Jones during Seven Days battles. Capt. OO to Jones, July 14, 1862. WIA four times, all slight, at Second Manassas. POW at Chantilly. Capt. OO to R. H. Anderson, Dec. 1862. Capt. OO to Mahone, May 1864. Capt. acting Chief OO to ANVa., June 15–Aug. 22, 1864. Maj. OO to Anderson, Jan. 17, 1865. Postwar rice broker at Charleston. d. Apr. 28, 1920. bur. Magnolia Cem.

Tidwell, Reuben William. b. Coweta Co., Georgia, Dec. 30, 1840. Lived prewar in Campbell Co. Lt. Co. G, 30th Georgia, Sept. 25, 1861. Failed to win reelection. Capt. ACS, Thomas's Legion (N.C.), Sept. 27, 1862. Capt. ACS to A. E. Jackson, Aug. 12, 1863. Capt. acting CS to W. E. Jones, Oct. 25, 1863. Capt. ACS to B. T. Johnson, 1864. m. Elizabeth Augusta Judson, 1868. Postwar merchant at Atlanta. d. Mar. 1915. bur. Westview Cem., Atlanta.

Tiller, Evans F. b. Logan Co., Virginia, Aug. 20, 1834. A lawyer in Kentucky and then at Wyoming C.H., Virginia. Sgt. Co. H, 48th Virginia, June 26, 1861. Pvt. Co. D, French's Virginia Bn. Inf., Apr. 1863. POW in Kentucky, Apr. 15, 1863. Capt. AAAG to Virginia Reserves, Oct. 1864, which probably means he was on the staff of Kemper. Postwar judge in Scott Co., Virginia, member of state legislature, and Commonwealth's attorney. Alive 1870.

Tinsley, Howard. b. Milledgeville, Georgia, Nov. 22, 1829. A merchant there. Capt. AQM, 4th Georgia, Dec. 26, 1862. Capt. AQM to Cook, Sept. 15, 1864. Appx. Operated a dry goods store at Milledgeville postwar. Also a traveling salesman. Alive there in 1907. bur. Memory Hill Cem., in an unmarked grave. "Of irreproachable character, and a man of superior business qualifications."

Todd, Everard Moore. b. near Smithfield, Virginia, Dec. 5, 1827. att. Harvard. One of the earliest developers of famous Smithfield hams. m. (1) Nannie R. Southall, 1854. m. (2) Mrs. Julia W. Dickson Carroll, 1887. Served as government supply agent in Engineer Dept., Oct. 1861. Maj. CS to Huger, June 10, 1862. On commissary duty in North Carolina, July 1862 into 1865. Paroled at Salisbury, North Carolina, May 12, 1865. Farmer in Isle of Wight Co., Virginia. d. Smithfield, Sept. 25, 1907. bur. Ivy Hill Cem.

Todd, Westwood Armistead. b. Smithfield, Virginia, May 30, 1831. att. Wm. & Mary. Pvt. Co. E, 12th Virginia, May 1861. WIA at Second Manassas. Detailed as acting Ordnance Sgt., July 27, 1863. Acting Lt. OO to Weisiger, Mar. 20, 1865. POW at Sailor's Creek. Lawyer at Norfolk. d. there May 28, 1886, from a head injury suffered when he fell from a window. bur. Elmwood Cem. Todd's outstanding war reminiscence is at UNC.

Toland, John. Lt. Co. A, 3rd Tennessee Mtd. Inf., 1861. Dropped May 14, 1862. Lt. ADC to Vaughn, date unknown. POW at Vicksburg. Served with Vaughn through late 1864, at least.

Tompkins, Samuel Stephen. b. Edgefield Co., South Carolina, Oct. 2, 1819. att. South Carolina Coll. Edgefield lawyer and farmer. Married twice. VADC and PM to Bonham, July 1861. Served in Co. K, 24th South Carolina, Apr. 23–Aug. 14, 1862. Tax collector at Hamburg, South Carolina, 1863–1864. Postwar "master of equity" in Edgefield Co. d. Jan. 28, 1907. bur. Willowbrook Cem.

Tosh, James Thomas. b. Roanoke Co., Virginia, May 16, 1838. att. UVA. and VMI. Lt. PAVA., May 1, 1861. Adjt. 16th Virginia, Aug. 30, 1861. Lt. ADC to Colston, Jan. 4, 1862. Paroled at Farmville, Virginia, Apr. 30, 1865. m. Ida Ragland, 1864. Tobacconist at Petersburg, and Chesterfield Co. farmer. Accidentally killed Apr. 7, 1894.

Towles, William Eskridge. b. Staunton, Virginia, Mar. 15, 1837. att. UVA. Served in 21st Mississippi and in the Washington (La.) Arty. VADC to his cousin, Gen. Stuart, early 1862 through July 1862. Returned to the artillery and killed Feb. 19, 1863, near Meridian, Mississippi, in a train accident. bur. family cem. in West Feliciana Parish, Louisiana.

Townshend, John H. Of Maryland, but a resident of Augusta, Georgia. Lt. ADC to Bryan, Sept. 9, 1863. WIA at Wilderness. Sent to Lynchburg Hospital, May 14, 1864. No further record found.

Tracy, Carlos Chandos. b. Sept. 1, 1825. Longtime lawyer at Walterboro, South Carolina, and member of state legislature. VADC to Drayton, Apr. 1861–May 1862. VADC to Gist, May–June 1862. VADC to Hagood, late 1862 until June 1864. Col. on Second Corps military court, June 24, 1864. d. Walterboro, South Carolina, Jan. 1, 1882. bur. St. Helena's Episc. Churchyard, Beaufort. Extracts from Tracy's war diary were published in Gen. Hagood's memoirs.

Trippe, Andrew Cross. b. Baltimore, Maryland, Nov. 29, 1839. att. Lafayette Coll. and Newton Univ. Entered bar at Baltimore in 1861. Pvt. Co. A, 2nd Maryland. WIA in right shoulder at Gettysburg. Lt. OO, Nov. 28, 1863. Almost certainly occupied position on staff of Gen. B. T. Johnson. Paroled at Burkeville, Virginia, May 12, 1865. Baltimore lawyer. d. there July 17, 1918.

Troup, James Robert. b. Darien, Georgia, June 3, 1835. att. UVA. and UPENN. Farmer and physician in Glynn Co. Lt. ADC to Toombs, Mar. 1, 1862. WIA at Sharpsburg. Capt. AAG to Toombs, May 2, 1863, but more likely to Toombs's old brigade, commanded by Benning. Capt. AAG to W. H. T. Walker, June 30, 1863. WIA at Chickamauga. Capt. AAG to Iverson, Dec. 1864. A rice planter. d. Darien in 1873.

Trueheart, Daniel, Jr. b. Richmond, Virginia, 1831. att. VMI and UVA. Taught math at VMI prewar. Lt. of Arty., CSA, Apr. 27, 1861. Inspector of Arty. for Bragg and Boggs in 1861. Maj. (PACS) and Chief of Arty. to

T. J. Jackson, Nov. 16, 1861. Later Chief oo to Jackson. Trueheart "got very drunk" near Hancock and left Jackson's staff by Mar. 1, 1862, though not officially relieved until Sept. 2, 1862. Maj. Chief of Arty. to Forney and Buckner. Later commanded an artillery battalion with AOT. POW near Nashville, Dec. 16, 1864. Postwar professor at the Texas Military Institute. d. Houston, Jan. 29, 1876. bur. Shockoe Cem., Richmond.

Tucker, John Southgate. b. Norfolk, Virginia, May 30, 1838. att. Dickinson College. A schoolteacher in Grundy Co., Missouri. Served in Missouri State Guard early in the war. Pvt. Co. H, 3rd Missouri, May 14, 1862. WIA at Corinth, and left arm amputated. Later to Sgt. Lt. oo, May 2, 1863. Capt. oo, Feb. 19, 1864. Worked last two years of the war at the Richmond Arsenal. Mayor of Norfolk and then a lawyer at Washington, D.C. d. May 23, 1920. bur. Oak Hill Cem., in an unmarked grave.

Tucker, Thomas Smith Beverley. b. Aug. 22, 1841. VADC to McLaws, Sept. 1861 until appointed Lt. ADC to McLaws, May 23, 1862. WIA in knee at Fredericksburg and permanently crippled. Retired to Invalid Corps, July 2, 1864. Ordered to duty with Conscript Bureau, July 7, 1864. m. Julia Clark. d. May 5, 1873.

Tulloss, Joseph D. b. Fauquier Co., Virginia, Mar. 8, 1824. Merchant and farmer. m. Mary Jane Clark, 1857. QM Sgt. Brooks's (Va.) Btty., Apr. 10, 1862. Capt. AQM, Poague's Bn. Arty., June 25, 1863. Served into 1865. Farmer at Upperville. d. Aug. 23, 1909. bur. Grove Presby. Church Cem., Goldvein, Virginia. Poague wrote of Tulloss: "an excellent man and efficient in the management of his department. . . . But . . . he was timid and easily demoralized."

Turk, Rudolph. b. Augusta Co., Virginia, Jan. 22, 1817. Sheriff of Augusta Co., and Col. in the state militia. Capt. AQM, Nov. 2, 1861. Stationed at Lynchburg, Staunton, Charlottesville, Harrisonburg, and Mt.

Jackson, at least into mid-1864. d. Apr. 17, 1890. bur. Augusta Presby. Stone Church, Ft. Defiance, Virginia.

Turner, Allen Shadrack. b. in Georgia, July 19, 1834. Farmer in Hart Co. m. Jane Eliza Jones, 1854. Lt. Co. B, 24th Georgia, June 9, 1861. To Capt., Apr. 1, 1862. Capt. AQM, 24th Georgia, May 22, 1862. Capt. AQM to Wofford, Sept. 15, 1864, and subsequently to DuBose. Appx. Surveyor in Hart Co., and served in state legislature. d. Dec. 7, 1890. bur. Royston City Cem.

Turner, Beverly Bradshaw. b. Nov. 21, 1843. Of Fauquier Co., Virginia. Served in Hanover (Va.) Arty. and in Co. H, 9th Virginia Cavy. Lt. oo to W. H. F. Lee, early in 1863. Lt. ADC to Lee, spring 1864, but no record of commission found. WIA at Fussell's Mill. POW at Warrenton, Oct. 21, 1864. Escaped on way to Ft. Delaware. POW Feb. 21, 1865, in Fauquier Co. d. near Chattanooga, Tennessee, Nov. 21, 1889, after falling off his horse.

Turner, E. Capt. AQM to Early, Sept. 15, 1864. No other record. Possibly a mistake for some other officer.

Turner, Franklin P. b. Charles Co., Maryland, Feb. 28, 1827. att. Franklin & Marshall. Lawyer at Ripley, Virginia, and member of secession convention. Capt. Co. G, 36th Virginia. Capt. AQM, June 17, 1862, to report to T. J. Jackson. Duties not given. Capt. AQM, Second Corps Arty., May 1, 1863. Maj. QM to Long, Feb. 19, 1864. Not confirmed, so reapptd. to same position June 15, 1864. Appx. Lawyer at Richmond, Virginia, and at Sharpsburg, Maryland. d. Jan. 1, 1889. bur. Mountain View Cem., Sharpsburg. Called "the Black Prince," by his fellow officers for some reason.

Turner, George. b. in Virginia, Jan. 31, 1821. Wealthy farmer in King George Co., prewar. m. Jane Charlotte Washington Fitzhugh. Served as "Extra ADC" to Gen. Ruggles at Fredericksburg, Apr. 1861. Farmer postwar at Walsingham, King George Co., and became known as "the Duke of Walsingham." d. Washington, D.C., July 26, 1916. bur. Emmanuel Church, Port Conway, Virginia.

Turner, James H. b. Mississippi. A 22-year-old physician at Columbus in 1860. Served at Pensacola, Florida, in early 1861. Capt. AQM, 13th Mississippi, May 21, 1861. Capt. AQM to Humphreys, Sept. 15, 1864. Paroled May 10, 1865, in Mississippi.

Turner, Robert H. Lawyer at Front Royal, Virginia, and member of 1861 state convention. Pvt. Co. B, 17th Virginia, May 3, 1861. Capt. AQM, 17th Virginia, May 20, 1862. Maj. QM to Corse, Dec. 17, 1862. On detached duty, Feb. 1863–July 1864, investigating and paying claims against the QM Dept. Appx. Served in state legislature, 1863–1865. Postwar judge at Front Royal. d. there Nov. 2, 1900. This man's middle name is variously given as Hite and Henry, and his date of birth as 1823, July 26, 1827, and 1833.

Turner, Thomas Baynton. b. Fauquier Co., Virginia, May 8, 1843. att. Georgetown Coll. A clerk. Pvt. 17th Virginia. Cadet VADC to Stuart, about Aug. or Sept. 1862. POW in Maryland Campaign. Left Stuart in Mar. 1863. Served with Mosby's guerilas until MWIA near Warrenton, Apr. 25, 1863. d. Apr. 29. bur. "Kinloch," Fauquier Co.

Turner, Thomas Pratt. b. King George Co., Virginia, Dec. 1841. att. VMI and USMA. Never married. Lt. 1st Bn. Virginia Inf. Lt. PAVA., May 1861, on unspecified duty with T. J. Jackson. Lt. CSA, Sept. 21, 1861. PM in charge of Richmond's military prisons. Capt. (PACS), July 16, 1862. PM at Lynchburg, Aug.–Oct. 1862. Maj. (PACS), Nov. 22, 1863. Commanded Libby Prison at Richmond, Oct. 1862 into 1865. Traveled incognito to Canada and Cuba postwar. Established a "large and lucrative" dentistry practice at Memphis, Tennessee. d. Odd Fellows' Home, Clarksville, Tennessee, Dec. 26, 1900. bur. Odd Fellows' Cem.

Turner, Thomas Theodore. b. St. Louis, Missouri, Oct. 23, 1842. att. VMI, USNA, a military school in Belgium, St. Louis Univ., and Washington Univ. Lt. ADC to Ewell, Apr. 22, 1862. Volunteered with Mosby's guerilas during Gen. Ewell's convalescence. WIA in both legs at Spotsylvania, May 10, 1864. POW at Sailor's Creek. m. Harriott Stoddert Brown (a stepdaughter of Gen. Ewell), 1865. Farmer, real estate man, and financier near St. Louis. d. New Orleans, Louisiana, Jan. 31, 1897. bur. St. Louis.

Turner, Vines Edmunds. b. Franklin Co., North Carolina, Jan. 19, 1837. att. Baltimore Coll. of Dental Surgery. Dentist and hardware merchant at Henderson, North Carolina. Lt. Co. G, 23rd North Carolina, June 11, 1861. To Adjt., Apr. 16, 1862. WIA at Gaines's Mill. Lt. AAAG to Col. McRae's Bgd., Oct. 1862. Capt. AQM, 23rd North Carolina, Jan. 26, 1863. Capt. AQM to Ramseur, Sept. 15, 1864. Same to Pegram and then J. A. Walker in 1865. Appx. Resumed dentistry at Henderson and Raleigh. Married twice. d. May 11, 1914.

Turpin, John G. b. in Virginia. m. Ann Eliza Saunders, 1842. Capt. ACS, 2nd Virginia Arty., Mar. 1, 1862. Resigned July 13, 1863, because of liver disease and hemorrhoids. Alive at Scottsville, Virginia, in 1870, age 50, a farmer.

Turpin, Walter Gwynn. b. in Virginia, Oct. 2, 1828. Engineer with James River & Kanawha Canal. Was living in Minnesota in 1861. Lt. of Inf., Oct. 7, 1861. Assigned to engineer duty at Norfolk, Virginia. Lt. EO, Mar. 22, 1862. Sent to duty in Shenandoah Valley, May 21, 1862. Capt. EO, May 4, 1863. Served around Richmond, 1863–1865. Civil engineer in Botetourt Co. d. June 21, 1874. bur. Hollywood Cem., Richmond.

Twiggs, Hansford Dade Duncan. b. Barnwell, South Carolina, Mar. 25, 1837. att. GMI, UGA., Furman, and UPENN. m. Lucie E. Wilkins, 1861. Capt. in 1st Georgia Regs. WIA and POW at Sharpsburg. Capt. AAAIG to G. W. Smith, Nov. 1862–Apr. 1863. Capt.

AAIG to Taliaferro, Apr. 1863. WIA at Morris Island. On conscription duty, 1864, and may have returned to 1st Georgia Regs. Lawyer, judge, and legislator at Augusta, Georgia, postwar. d. Savannah, Mar. 25, 1917.

Tyler, Charles Humphrey. b. in Virginia, ca. May 1826. att. USMA from Haymarket. Capt. U.S. Dragoons, 1848–1861. m. Elizabeth Wright, 1856. Lt. Col. PAVa., May 25, 1861. Capt. CSA, June 25, 1861. Lt. Col. AAAG to Ewell, June–July 1861. POW Aug. 1861 at Cincinnati, Ohio, "in an effort to recover my family." Exchanged Dec. 17, 1861. Capt. AAIG to Stuart, Oct. 6, 1862–Jan. 12, 1863. Temporarily commanded the 5th Virginia Cavy. until after Chancellorsville. Probably appointed Lt. Col. (PACS) at some point. Commanded a cavalry brigade in East Tennessee, late in 1863. POW Feb. 13, 1864, in Trans-Mississippi. No further military record after July 1864. Postwar farmer at Cross Keys, Virginia. d. there Mar. 17, 1882. "Almost always drunk," according to one of Ewell's staff. A prewar acquaintance wrote of Tyler: "a handsome, courtly Virginian, a Chesterfield in manners, with dignity which was rendered very agreeable by a large and ready sense of humor."

Tyler, John. b. Richmond, Virginia, May 13, 1836. A salesman. m. Mary Virginia Allen, 1862. Sgt. Co. F, 21st Virginia, Apr. 21, 1861–Mar. 3, 1862. Lt. Letcher (Va.) Arty., to rank from Feb. 17, 1862. Lt. VADC to Thomas at Second Manassas and Sharpsburg. Discharged May 19, 1863, with bad heart. Served as an Enrolling Officer. Postwar jeweler at Richmond. d. there Jan. 5, 1924. bur. Hollywood Cem. Tyler's 1862 diary is at UVA.

Tyler, Nathaniel. b. Dumfries, Virginia, Mar. 9, 1828. att. UVA., VMI, and Georgetown Coll. A nephew of President John Tyler. Served in USMC, and was a newspaper editor at Warrenton and Richmond. Maj. 20th Virginia, July 1861. To Lt. Col.,

autumn 1861. Maj. VADC to Wise, Sept. 1861. Out of service, spring 1862, when unit dissolved. Newspaper editor and broker at Baltimore, Maryland. d. Washington, D.C., Dec. 4, 1917. bur. Hollywood Cem., Richmond.

Tyler, William. b. in Virginia. Lt. CSA, May 21, 1861. Lt. acting ADC to Magruder, May 1861. Lt. AAAG and acting AQM to G. J. Rains, Jan. 28, 1862. Lt. AAG to Col. A. T. Rainey, Jan. 1863. Later staff of Hawes, 1864–1865.

Tyler, William W. b. in Virginia. A nephew of President John Tyler. Postmaster of Williamsburg and prewar auditor for Post Office Dept. in Washington, D.C. Clerk in C.S. Post Office. Pvt. Co. D, 20th Bn. Virginia Heavy Arty., June 1863. Later to Sgt. Lt. MSK, July 30, 1864. Posted at Bellona Arsenal, just outside Richmond. Transferred to Wytheville, Virginia, Nov. 1864. Court-martialed for embezzling $2,000 at Bellona. Resigned Feb. 21, 1865, when charges were dropped. Most likely William Wyatt Tyler, 1810–1895, though that doesn't match the staff officer's remark in 1861 that he was 45 years old.

Tynes, Achilles James. b. Montgomery Co., Virginia, Nov. 29, 1833. m. Harriet Fudge. Capt. ACS, 8th Virginia Cavy., July 25, 1861. Capt. acting ACS to A. G. Jenkins, 1863. Capt. acting ACS to McCausland, 1864. Paroled at Charleston, West Virginia, May 22, 1865. Lived postwar in Tazewell Co., Virginia. d. Nov. 11, 1914. Six of Tynes's wartime letters are at UNC.

Upson, Christopher Columbus. b. Syracuse, New York, Oct. 17, 1829. att. Williams Coll. A lawyer. Moved to Castroville, Texas, 1854, and later to San Antonio. VADC to Whiting, 1861–1862. Associate justice of territorial court of Confederate Arizona. Later a treasury agent for cotton in Trans-Mississippi Dept. Postwar lawyer and USHR. d. Feb. 8, 1902. bur. San Antonio Cem. #4.

Urquhart, Joseph Williamson. b. Jan. 15,

1835. att. uva. Lawyer in Southampton Co., Virginia, and at Memphis, Tennessee. m. Margaret Francis Ridley, 1864. Served in Co. A, 13th Virginia Cavy. Capt. acs of unit, Dec. 9, 1862. Failed confirmation, but retained by Special Order #221, 1863. Capt. acting cs to Chambliss, May 8–July 15, 1864. Dropped again, 1864. Reapptd. Maj. cs to Beale, Nov. 5, 1864. Judge at Enterprise, Virginia. d. July 12, 1908.

Van der Horst, Arnoldus. b. Jan. 11, 1835. m. Adele Allston. Served as a private at Charleston Harbor, 1861. vadc to Bee, June–July 1861. vadc to Whiting, July 1861–May 1863. Maj. aag to Whiting, May 2, 1863. Maj. aaig to Bragg, Feb. 24, 1865. d. Dec. 1, 1881. bur. Magnolia Cem., Charleston. Diarist Mary Chesnut called Van der Horst "a queer kind of old-fashioned gentleman."

Van Derveer, William P. b. prior to 1825. Maj. qm at the Alabama Clothing Depot, Richmond, Virginia, from at least spring 1862 to Sept. 1864. No official commission found, so Van Derveer possibly occupied a position in the state service.

Vaughan, Andrew J. Served as acting acs and acting aqm to Col. A. P. Hill, June 1861. Maj. cs to Elzey, July 19, 1861. Maj. cs at Liberty, Virginia, May 24, 1862, through late 1864, at least. May have served on the staff of Gen. Vaughn on occasion, too.

Vaughan, George A. Lt. acs to Alexander's Bn. Arty. at Gettysburg. No other record found. Probably a garbled identity.

Vaughan, Robert H. b. Elizabeth City Co., Virginia. A 41-year-old farmer there in 1860. Pvt. Co. B, 3rd Virginia Cavy., May 14 to July 1861. Capt. acs to Magruder, July 1, 1861. Acted mostly as Chief Commissary at the post of Yorktown. Capt. acs at Gordonsville, Virginia, about Sept. 1862. Capt. acs at Farmville, Virginia, Feb. 1863. d. there of pneumonia, Feb. 19, 1864. A brother of W. R. Vaughan (see below).

Vaughan, William Ryland. b. Elizabeth City

Co., Virginia, May 28, 1827. att. Wm. & Mary, upenn., Columbian Coll., and Virginia Medical Coll. Physician at Hampton, Virginia, and in North Carolina. Lt. Co. B, 3rd Virginia Cavy., May 14, 1861. Lt. acting qm to Magruder, June 1861. Resigned July 7, 1861. Surg. 16th Virginia, July 19, 1861, but resigned. Capt. Co. F, 3rd Virginia Cavy., Dec. 1861 until he resigned in June 1862. Surg. 3rd Virginia Cavy., July 15, 1862. Surg. Talladega, Alabama, Aug.–Sept. 1862. Later on duty at Petersburg, Hicksford, and Raleigh. Resigned a fourth time, July 25, 1864. Resumed medical practice at Hampton, postwar. d. Sept. 29, 1889. bur. family cem. on NASA property near Hampton.

Venable, Andrew Reid. b. Prince Edward Co., Virginia, Apr. 4, 1830. att. Washington Coll. Pvt. Co. K, 3rd Virginia Cavy., Mar. 17, 1862. Capt. aqm, Feb. 10, 1863. Served as aqm at Hanover Junction, Virginia. Capt. aqm at Abbeville, South Carolina, about Sept. 1863 through 1865. Farmer in Prince Edward Co. and a merchant. d. Hampden Sidney, Virginia, Sept. 12, 1913. bur. college cem. Known as "Black Andrew."

Venable, Andrew Reid, Jr. b. Prince Edward Co., Virginia, Dec. 2, 1832. att. Hampden Sidney. Businessman at St. Louis, Missouri, prewar. Served in 3rd Co. of Richmond Howitzers. Capt. acs, 1st Virginia Arty., Dec. 24, 1861. Serving on staff of Gen. Stuart by Nov. 1862. Maj. aaig to Stuart, May 11, 1863. Maj. aaag to W. H. F. Lee, May 1864. Maj. aaig to Hampton, Aug. 11, 1864. pow at Burgess's Mill, Oct. 27, 1864. Escaped on way to prison and secretly married Ariadne Hackney Stevens in Philadelphia. Apparently staff of R. E. Lee in March 1865. Maj. aaig to Echols, Mar. 16, 1865. Dairy farmer in Amelia and Prince Edward Co., Virginia. d. near Farmville, Oct. 15, 1909.

Venable, Charles Scott. b. Prince Edward Co., Virginia, Apr. 19, 1827. att. Hampden Sidney. Part of astronomical expedition to

Labrador coast. Taught at Hampden Sidney, UGA., in Europe, and at South Carolina Coll. prewar. Served in Hampton Legion Inf. and 2nd South Carolina early in the war. Lt. of Arty. (CSA), Oct. 18, 1861. Capt. EO (PACS), Mar. 18, 1862. Staff of Lovell in 1862, and Capt. AAG to M. L. Smith, May 1862. Maj. ADC to R. E. Lee, Apr. 21, 1862. Commenced duty with ANVa., June 1862. Lt. Col. AAG to Lee, Feb. 25, 1864. Appx. Married twice. Math professor at UVA. postwar. Author of about a dozen math textbooks. d. Aug. 11, 1900. bur. UVA. Chapel. Venable's papers are at the Virginia Historical Society, UNC, and the Univ. of South Carolina. His memoir and war letters are at UVA.

Venable, Paul Carrington. b. Aug. 8, 1840. att. UVA. and Hampden Sidney. Pvt. Co. F, 18th Virginia, Apr. 23, 1861. Lt. OO to Hampton, Jan. 21, 1863. Capt. OO to Hampton, Jan. 25, 1864. Capt. OO to Butler, by mid-1864. Paroled May 1, 1865. m. Agnes Gray, 1865. Farmer and tobacconist. d. Mar. 3, 1915. bur. Green Hill Cem., Danville, Virginia.

Venable, Thomas Brown. b. Dec. 9, 1824. att. Hampden Sidney. A resident of Oxford, North Carolina. Lt. Col. 24th North Carolina, July 16, 1861. Dropped at May 1862 reorganization. Maj. AAIG to French, Oct. 1, 1862. Later Maj. AAIG to Clingman, to Whiting (July 15, 1863), and to Holmes (Mar. 23, 1865). d. June 24, 1893. bur. Elmwood Cem., Oxford.

Vernoy, James. b. New York, Nov. 5, 1819. Served as civilian wagon master in the Mexican War. m. Mary E. Lawrence, 1849. Capt. ACS, 15th Alabama, July 19, 1861. Maj. QM to Trimble, Nov. 22, 1862. Maj. QM to Hoke, early in 1863. Dropped Aug. 27, 1863, for prolonged absence and "ceases to be an officer" on Apr. 11, 1864. Conscripted to light duty at Columbus, Georgia, Apr. 1864, age 45, "physically disabled." Alive 1887 at Atlanta, Georgia.

Vick, Alexander W. b. in Tennessee, Oct. 26, 1834. Lawyer at Lebanon prewar. Capt. AQM, 7th Tennessee, May 20, 1861. Capt. AQM to S. R. Anderson, Mar. 16, 1862. Maj. QM to Anderson, Apr. 2, 1862. Probably stayed with brigade as staff officer for Hatton and then Archer. Failed bond effective Aug. 30, 1862, but served on until reapptd. Jan. 16, 1864. Meanwhile Maj. acting QM to A. P. Hill, Aug. 10, 1862. Maj. acting QM to Heth, by July 1863. Maj. QM to Heth, officially, Oct. 7, 1864. Appx. d. Aug. 6, 1901. bur. Cedar Grove Cem., Lebanon.

Villepigue, James Irvin. b. Aug. 8, 1821. Capt. ACS and AQM, 2nd South Carolina, Apr. 9, 1861. Capt. AQM to Kershaw, Sept. 15, 1864. Served into 1865. Merchant at Camden, South Carolina. m. Sarah McKain. d. May 7, 1905. bur. Quaker Cem.

Vogler, Julius Rowland. b. Salem, North Carolina, Nov. 20, 1830. Of Forsyth Co., North Carolina. Lt. Co. E, 21st North Carolina, 1861. Capt. AQM, 21st North Carolina, Sept. 5, 1861. Capt. AQM to Early's Div., Sept. 15, 1864, probably meaning he was on the staff of Ramseur for five days before Gen. Pegram took command. Capt. AQM to J. A. Walker, 1865. Postwar salesman and a director of Wachovia National Bank. d. Jan. 18, 1886. bur. Moravian Cem., Winston-Salem, North Carolina.

Vowles, Daniel Washington. b. Warrenton, Virginia, Aug. 13, 1831. Lived in Virginia and in Missouri. Member of Walker's expedition to Nicaragua. A clerk before att. Missouri Medical Coll. Was living in Illinois in 1861. Lt. Col. ADC to T. A. Harris, Missouri State Guard, 1861. Capt. AAG to M. E. Green, Aug. 16, 1862. Capt. AAG to J. H. Winder, Dec. 11, 1862. Sat on a military court in Richmond for much of the war. Commanded Camp Lawton Prison in Georgia, Sept. 1864 into 1865. Physician at Washington, D.C., and later returned to Illinois. d. Quincy, Illinois, Aug. 14, 1919.

Waddy, John Robinson, Jr. b. Northampton Co., Virginia. att. VMI. Taught school, 1853–1857. Lt. 4th U.S. Arty., 1857–1861. Lt. of Arty., CSA, Mar. 16, 1861. Capt. AAG to Pemberton by Sept. 1861. Maj. AAG to Pemberton, Apr. 11, 1862. Lt. Col. AAG to Pemberton, Nov. 22, 1862. Lt. Col. OO to Beauregard, Apr. 10, 1863. Lt. Col. OO to Sam. Jones, Apr. 1864. Lt. Col. OO to Beauregard, May 10, 1864. Lt. Col. AAIG to Hardee, 1864, and later back to Beauregard. Farmer in Northampton Co., postmaster at Norfolk, and businessman in New York City. "A stanch Republican" by 1898. d. Norfolk, Feb. 16, 1903.

Wade, ——. Capt. AAIG to Col. P. D. Bowles, commanding Law's old brigade, Apr. 1865.

Wade, Ethelbert Barksdale. b. in Tennessee, Sept. 24, 1843. Lived in Rutherford Co. Pvt. Co. C, 18th Tennessee, Aug. 21, 1861. Cadet ADC to Hood, March 2, 1863. With Hood into Dec. 1864, at least. m. Dora Cochran, 1864. Alive 1871 in Davidson Co., Tennessee.

Waggoner, James J. b. Virginia. A 32-year-old merchant at Richmond in 1860. Capt. AQM, 3rd Virginia Arty., Mar. 11, 1862. Capt. AQM at Burkeville, Virginia, July 18, 1862. Served there into 1865. d. Danville, Virginia, Mar. 19, 1882. bur. Hollywood Cem., Richmond.

Waite, Charles. b. Spotsylvania Co., Virginia, ca. July 1838. A merchant at Fredericksburg. Pvt. Co. B, 9th Virginia Cavy., July 12, 1861. Capt. AQM, 9th Virginia Cavy., Dec. 23, 1861. May have served as acting AQM to French, late 1861. Maj. QM to W. H. F. Lee, Oct. 30, 1862. Served through 1864, at least. Dry goods merchant at Culpeper. d. there May 2, 1915. bur. Culpeper Masonic Cem. J. E. B. Stuart called Waite "the best forager" in the army.

Walke, Isaac Talbot, Jr. b. Norfolk, Virginia, Feb. 22, 1843. att. UVA. Pvt. Co. G, 6th Virginia, May 6, 1861. Pvt. Grandy's (Va.) Btty., Mar. 26, 1862. Lt. OO, Feb. 9, 1863, assigned to Second Corps Arty. Lt. OO to

First Corps Arty., June–Nov. 1863. Lt. OO to Fitz. Lee, Nov. 25, 1863. Lt. OO to Rosser, summer 1864. KIA at Tom's Brook, Oct. 9, 1864. bur. Elmwood Cem., Norfolk. Rosser called Walke "a modest, retiring gentleman and a brave and efficient officer."

Walke, Richard, Jr. b. Norfolk, Virginia, Dec. 9, 1840. att. UVA., Wm. & Mary, and Univ. of Berlin. Pvt. Co. G, 6th Virginia, July 6, 1861. Courier for Gen. Garnett, 1862. Acting Lt. OO, from about Dec. 1862, to Mahone. Capt. AAG, Mar. 28, 1864, to Col. R. L. Walker. Paroled Apr. 26, 1865. Norfolk lawyer. m. Annie Nivison Bradford. Committed suicide at sea off Norfolk, June 20, 1901. A brother of Lt. Isaac T. Walke (see above).

Walker, James W. b. in Virginia. Acting ADC to Mahone at Appx. U.S. attorney for Montana Territory. d. Feb. 1900. Thought to be the man from Madison C.H., Virginia, b. ca. 1825, a farmer and legislator.

Walker, James Wallace. b. Augusta, Georgia, Jan. 11, 1835. att. UGA. Commission merchant at Augusta. Married twice. Lt. Co. K, 20th Georgia, Aug. 8, 1861. Capt. AAIG to Bryan, Nov. 2, 1863. Capt. AAIG to Simms, June 1864. POW at Sailor's Creek. Augusta city treasurer for 27 years. d. Apr. 13, 1897. bur. Magnolia Cem. "A great lover of flowers."

Walker, John Absalom. b. May 9, 1827. Lived at Eufaula and Birmingham, Alabama, a merchant. Capt. ACS, 31st Georgia, Nov. 19, 1861. Capt. ACS to John B. Gordon, Aug. 17, 1863. Capt. ACS to C. A. Evans, May 1864. Charged with drunkenness in 1865. Appx. m. Eliza Jane Kendrick. d. Apr. 21, 1906.

Walker, Joseph. Col. and Commissary Gen. of South Carolina troops, Apr. 1861. VADC to Beauregard, July 24, 1861. Also acted as ACS to Beauregard.

Walker, Leonidas D. Served with Missouri troops in the Mexican War. m. Elizabeth C. Turnbull, 1851. Capt. AAG to Ripley, Sept. 26, 1861. Resigned Aug. 16, 1862, finding the position "no longer agreeable to me." d. Frankfort, Kentucky, Aug. 4, 1866.

Walker, Mims. b. Pulaski Co., Georgia, Nov. 5, 1838. Moved to Alabama about 1852. att. UNC. Pvt. Co. D, 4th Alabama, Apr. 25, 1861. Courier for Gen. Law. Lt. ADC to Law, June 15, 1864. Paroled May 9, 1865, at Meridian, Mississippi. m. Mary G. Pitts, 1864. Marengo Co., Alabama, farmer and legislator. d. Oct. 3, 1903. bur. Rosemont Cem., Uniontown.

Walker, Norman Stewart. b. Nov. 16, 1830. att. UVA. Lt. Co. B, 15th Virginia. Lt. ADC to Randolph, Mar. 1, 1862. Vacated by Randolph's almost immediate resignation. Capt. Co. B, 15th Virginia, Apr. 29, 1862. Resigned Sept. 25, 1862, grumbling about "disorganized condition" of the regiment. Commercial agent for C.S. in Bermuda, 1863–1865. d. Sept. 15, 1913.

Walker, Robert P. A clerk. Pvt. Co. G, 6th Virginia, Apr. 1861. Pvt. Grandy's (Va.) Btty., June 10, 1862, age 18. Lt. ADC to H. H. Walker, July 7, 1863. No further record after May 1864.

Wallace, Thomas L. Pvt. Co. G, 43rd Tennessee, Dec. 1, 1861, age 21. Capt. ACS, 43rd Tennessee, Dec. 14, 1861. Dropped May 29, 1863, in purge of regimental commissaries. POW at Vicksburg. Capt. ACS to Vaughn, Oct. 18, 1863. Likely never apptd. to that position and acted in it unofficially through the remainder of the war.

Wallace, Thomas Preston. b. Apr. 1, 1836. att. UVA. Pvt. Co. B, 30th Virginia, July 11, 1861. Capt. AQM, 30th Virginia, May 2, 1862. Capt. AQM to Pickett, Sept. 15, 1864. Appx. d. Jan. 31, 1910. bur. Fredericksburg Confederate Cem.

Wallach, Charles Simms. b. Washington, D.C. m. Lavenia Hewitt, 1839. A 43-year-old lawyer there in 1860. Capt. AQM, 2nd Virginia Cavy., Dec. 24, 1861. Capt. AQM to Ewell's Div. Arty., Aug. 11, 1862. Capt. AQM at Petersburg, Virginia, Dec. 1, 1862. Maj. QM at Petersburg, Aug. 27, 1863. Paroled at

Burkeville, Virginia, Apr. 19, 1865. Resumed law practice at Washington. Alive 1870.

Waller, Hugh Mercer. b. Dec. 3, 1829. att. Wm. & Mary. Lt. Co. C, 32nd Virginia, Apr. 28, 1861. Capt. AQM at Williamsburg, Oct. 7, 1861. Capt. AQM at Danville, Virginia, Oct. 1862 into 1865. d. May 31, 1906. bur. family cem. at Williamsburg.

Waller, Richard P. b. Nov. 3, 1820. Merchant at Richmond, Virginia. m. Nannie B. Bell, 1852. Capt. AQM, July 17, 1861. Maj. QM, Aug. 25, 1862. Maj. 2nd Bn. Virginia LDT, probably simultaneous to staff duties. In charge of a clothing depot at 14th and Cary Streets. Went to Bahamas and England on QM business late in the war. d. Richmond, Dec. 6, 1868. bur. Hollywood Cem.

Walters, Joseph M. Capt. AQM, 13th Virginia Cavy., Jan. 19, 1863. Capt. AQM to Beale, about Sept. 1864. Appx. Hotelman at Norfolk. m. Frederica Hunter Milhado. Committed suicide near Norfolk, Dec. 8, 1870, after forging some checks.

Walton, James Burdge. b. Newark, New Jersey, Nov. 18, 1813. att. Louisiana Coll. Mexican War veteran. m. Amelia Sack, 1836. Grocer at New Orleans. Served in Washington (La.) Arty., 1839–1861. Col. of Arty., Mar. 26, 1862. Chief of Arty. to Longstreet, 1862–1864. Col. Inspector of Field Artillery, 1864. Resigned July 8, 1864. d. Sept. 8, 1885. "Was large and imposing in appearance, looking . . . rather French."

Walton, N. T. Lt. ADC to J. R. Davis in Apr. 1865. A parole slip from 1865 is his only service record.

Walton, Thomas John. att. UMISS. A lawyer at Vicksburg and in Leflore Co., Mississippi. VADC to Clark, May 24, 1861. VADC to his kinsman Gen. Longstreet at First Manassas. Lt. ADC to Longstreet, Dec. 31, 1861, but "name withdrawn." Capt. ACS to Longstreet, May 27, 1862. WIA at Seven Pines. Maj. CS to Longstreet, July 11, 1862, backdated to May 27, 1862. WIA at Sharpsburg. Out of commission due to some technicality, July 31, 1863, but on duty at corps headquarters reviewing court-martial records. Acting Judge Advocate to First Corps in spring and summer 1864. Maj. AAG to Ewell, Nov. 4, 1864. Maj. AAG to Taylor, Mar. 14, 1865. Paroled May 4, 1865. Killed a man in Mississippi postwar. Judge, U.S. district attorney, and law professor. Distinguished himself during a yellow fever outbreak at Grenada, but d. there ca. Aug. 1878 of yellow fever. Moxley Sorrel wrote of Walton's "most uncertain, unexpected temper. . . . He could be dangerous at times."

Walworth, Ernest. b. Natchez, Mississippi, Jan. 20, 1840. VADC to E. K. Smith, Jan. 5, 1862. Served in that capacity until apptd. Lt. ADC to Smith, March 10, 1863. Capt. AAG to Smith, July 20, 1863, and also acted as AAIG occasionally. Paroled June 1865 at Shreveport. d. Memphis, Tennessee, March 31, 1905. bur. Elmwood Cem.

Wang, George W. b. Christina, Norway, 1828. Came to Louisiana by 1835. New Orleans clerk. Capt. AQM, 5th Louisiana, Apr. 1, 1862. Capt. AQM to Wharton, early 1864. Served with that brigade until apptd. Capt. AQM at the post of Canton, Mississippi, 1865. Paroled May 19, 1865. Railroad ticket agent at New Orleans. d. Jan. 9, 1876, age 38.

Ward, Francis Xavier. b. Baltimore, Maryland, July 11, 1839. att. Georgetown Coll. Secretary to minister of Central America. Shot through hips during Apr. 1861 Baltimore riots. Lt. Co. H, 1st Maryland, June 18, 1861. Adjt. 1st Maryland. VADC to Elzey, and to J. A. Walker, dates unclear. VADC to Wilcox, Mar. 1865. Appx. Married twice. Baltimore lawyer. Later lived at Germantown, Pennsylvania. d. Philadelphia, Aug. 1914.

Ward, Griffin Stith. b. in Virginia, May 24, 1836. Employee at Harper's Ferry Armory. "Ordnance Master" with 7th Virginia Cavy., Apr.–June 1862. Apparently acting OO to Imboden on regimental level in 1862. Lt. OO to Imboden, July 21, 1863. Farmer at Harrisonburg. d. Mar. 3, 1877. bur. Reformed Church Cem., Mt. Crawford.

Wardlaw, Andrew Bowie. b. Abbeville, South Carolina, Nov. 5, 1831. att. South Carolina Coll. Lawyer, schoolteacher, and planter. m. Sarah Elizabeth Thompson, 1858. Capt. ACS, 14th South Carolina, Mar. 26, 1862. Maj. CS to McGowan, Feb. 10, 1863. Appx. Planter and merchant at Abbeville. d. there Dec. 14, 1888.

Wardlaw, George Allen. b. Abbeville, South Carolina, July 12, 1837. att. South Carolina Coll. A lawyer. Lt. 1st South Carolina Regs., Mar.–Dec. 1861. Capt. AQM, 1st South Carolina Regs., Dec. 24, 1861. Lt. ADC to his brother-in-law, Gen. McGowan, Feb. 19, 1864. POW and slightly WIA at Gravel Hill Church, July 28, 1864. Exchanged Feb. 1865. d. Savannah, Georgia, July 9, 1865. bur. Upper Long Cane Presby. Church, Abbeville.

Warner, Jackson. b. in a flatboat on the Ohio River. A book publisher. Capt. ACS, Sept. 2, 1861. Served almost entirely as ACS and acting AQM for the military prisons around Richmond, Virginia. Out of commission Mar. 24, 1864, by virtue of nonassignment. Briefly incarcerated by Yankees at Libby Prison in May 1865, on charges of cruelty to prisoners. A "stout, hearty-looking fellow, with . . . immense circular beard and crisp moustache."

Warren, William Edward. b. Oct. 25, 1811, in Virginia. Richmond commission merchant. Capt. AQM, Sept. 20, 1861. On duty at Richmond, Virginia, where he furnished officers with quarters and secured buildings for hospital use. d. December 10, 1885. bur. Ivy Hill Cem., Alexandria.

Warwick, Abram Daniel. A farmer. Lt. Co. B, 2nd Virginia Cavy., May 13, 1861, age 25. Resigned Mar. 25, 1863, due to poor health. Possibly the Warwick who was conscripted into the 8th Virginia in Feb.

1864 and later bore the rank of Lt. with the 30th Bn. Virginia Sharpshooters. VADC to Munford's Bgd., Apr. 1865. d. Lynchburg, Virginia, Nov. 1, 1916. bur. Spring Hill Cem.

Warwick, Barksdale. b. June 20, 1844. att. VMI. VADC to Wise, intermittently, 1861–1865. KIA near Petersburg, Mar. 29, 1865. bur. Hollywood Cem., Richmond. A brother of Lt. Col. Bradfute Warwick, 4th Texas Inf.

Warwick, Peter Chevallie. b. Richmond, Virginia, Aug. 28, 1835. VADC to Sam. Jones, 1861–1862. Lt. ADC to Jones, May 9, 1862. Paroled May 12, 1865, at Tallahassee, Florida. Married twice. Miller and legislator. d. Chesterfield Co., Virginia, Dec. 30, 1899. bur. Shockoe Cem., Richmond.

Warwick, William Barksdale. b. Richmond, Virginia, Nov. 4, 1836. A miller. m. Phoebe Warren Douglas, 1858. Sgt. Co. I, 4th Virginia Cavy., 1861. Capt. ACS, 4th Virginia Cavy., Jan. 4, 1862. Maj. CS to Fitz. Lee, Nov. 8, 1862. Maj. CS to Rosser, temporarily, 1864–1865. Drowned in his bathtub at his Richmond home, Apr. 30, 1885.

Washington, George L. b. New York, Sept. 22, 1842. att. UNC. From Kinston, North Carolina. Pvt. Co. K, 42nd North Carolina, Sept. 1, 1862. Lt. ADC to W. S. Walker, Nov. 25, 1862. Lt. ADC to Hoke by 1865. Paroled at Greensboro, May 1, 1865.

Washington, James Barroll. b. Baltimore, Maryland, Aug. 26, 1839. att. USMA. Lt. PAVA. Lt. CSA, July 18, 1861, backdated to Mar. 16, 1861. Lt. ADC to J. E. Johnston, June 1861, officially appointed to rank from Aug. 31, 1861. POW at Seven Pines. Exchanged Sept. 21, 1862. Transferred to ordnance duty at Montgomery, Alabama, Mar. 28, 1864. m. Jane Bretney Lanier, 1864. Railroad president postwar. d. Pittsburgh, Pennsylvania, Mar. 6, 1900.

Washington, John Augustine. b. Jefferson Co., Virginia, May 3, 1821. att. UVA. A great-nephew of President George Washington. Farmed "Mt. Vernon." m. Eleanor Love Selden, 1842. Lt. Col. PAVA., May 3, 1861. Lt. Col. ADC to R. E. Lee, May 15, 1861. KIA Sept. 13, 1861, in western Virginia.

Washington, Littleton Quinton. b. Washington, D.C., Nov. 3, 1825. Educated at Bethlehem, Pennsylvania. Treasury Dept. clerk at Washington. Custom House collector at San Francisco. Never married. Lt. CSA, May 20, 1861. Lt. AQM to Bonham, June 10–Aug. 12, 1861. Resigned Aug. 23, 1861. Acting Asst. Secretary of War, CSA. Postwar newspaperman and author at Washington, D.C. d. there, Nov. 4, 1902. bur. Congressional Cem., Washington. His interesting journal, some of it from the war years, was recently published.

Washington, Thornton Augustine. b. Jefferson Co., Virginia, Jan. 22, 1826. att. USMA and Princeton. Lt. U.S. Army, 1849–1861. m. Olive Ann Jones, 1860. Capt. AAG, Mar. 16, 1861. Capt. AAG to Van Dorn, May 30, 1861. Capt. AAG to R. E. Lee, Nov. 8, 1861. Maj. AAG (PACS) to Lee, Jan. 1, 1862. Maj. QM to Lee, Apr. 17, 1862. Maj. QM to P. O. Hebert, Apr. 22, 1862. Purchasing agent for Texas, June 1862 onward. d. Washington, D.C., July 10, 1894.

Waters, Francis. Of Lexington, Kentucky. att. Georgetown Coll., class of 1855. On duty raising troops, Oct. 1862. Capt. AAG to Davidson, Feb. 14, 1863. Paroled at Greensboro. Poor service record leaves doubt about length of service with Davidson.

Waters, James Hurley. b. Sharptown, New Jersey, Aug. 1828. Lived at Philadelphia until 1848. Carriage maker at Staunton, Virginia. m. Elizabeth Carroll, 1851. Capt. Co. L, 5th Virginia. Capt. ACS, 5th Virginia, July 23, 1862. Capt. ACS to J. A. Walker, about Aug. 1863. Capt. ACS to Wm. Terry, May–Dec. 1864. Capt. ACS to C. A. Evans, Dec. 8, 1864. Appx. Chief of Staunton police postwar. d. Lynchburg, Virginia, Odd Fellows' Home. bur. Thornrose Cem, Staunton.

Watkins, Henry Carrington. b. in Virginia,

May 18, 1821. m. Virginia Carter Temple. Of "Ampthill" in Chesterfield Co. Maj. QM to Wise, Feb. 23, 1863. Appx. Chesterfield Co. miller. d. Feb. 26, 1888. bur. "Ampthill."

Watkins, Joel Brown. b. Powhatan Co., Virginia, Aug. 4, 1824. Clerk and merchant at Richmond. m. Elizabeth Sydnor Blair, 1848. VADC to G. W. C. Lee, spring 1864–1865. POW at Sailor's Creek. Richmond merchant postwar. Supt. of Arizona schools, 1887–1888. d. Rockbridge Alum Springs, Virginia, July 21, 1889. bur. Hollywood Cem., Richmond.

Watkins, Leigh. A clerk. Sgt. Co. D, 5th Louisiana. Capt. ACS, 5th Louisiana, July 3, 1861. Capt. acting ACS to Hays, July 31, 1863. Capt. ACS to Hays, Sept. 17, 1863. Capt. ACS to York, May 1864. Probably same to Peck, 1865.

Watts, George Owen. b. Richmond, Kentucky, May 17, 1840. att. KMI and USMA. Worked in Washington, D.C. as a Drillmaster, June–July 1861. Resigned from U.S. service, Aug. 10, 1861. Lt. of Arty. CSA, July 19, 1861, to rank from Mar. 16, 1861. Lt. EO and acting ADC to Buckner. Helped build Ft. Henry and Ft. Donelson. Maj. (PACS) Jan. 26, 1863, commanding Ward's Bn. Arty. Maj. AAIG to B. R. Johnson, May 17–June 13, 1864. Maj. Chief of Arty., Dept. of Arkansas and West Louisiana. WIA four times. May have served on the staff of Longstreet, Villepigue, and Van Dorn. Lived in Texas, and then in Rapides Parish, Louisiana. Supt. of schools. d. Emma, Texas, Dec. 5, 1905. bur. Opelousas, Louisiana.

Watts, James W. From Georgia. VADC to Young, June 1864. No other record found.

Watts, Nathaniel Greene. b. in Virginia, Jan. 25, 1816. Clerk and deputy U.S. Marshal at Vicksburg, Mississippi. Capt. of Inf., CSA, Mar. 16, 1861. Capt. AQM and ACS to Clark, June 1, 1861. Maj. QM to Clark, Oct. 4, 1861. Maj. QM to Griffith, about Nov. 1861. Agent for prisoner exchanges, Aug. 1862. Later tried to raise a sharpshooter battalion. d. Jan. 27, 1866. bur. Vicksburg City Cem.

Webb, James Edward. b. Greene Co., Alabama, Apr. 15, 1840. att. UAla. Lawyer at Eutaw. Pvt. 5th Alabama. Acting OO, possibly while still an enlisted man, to D. H. Hill, July 1862. Same to Rodes, Dec. 1862. Lt. OO, May 2, 1863, to O'Neal's Bgd. Hence to Battle, from Aug. 1863. Lt. acting OO to Rodes, Jan. and Feb. 1864, before returning to Battle. Lt. Asst. OO to Stuart, Apr. 4, 1864. Same to Hampton, May 1864. WIA at Bellfield. Lt. OO to Dearing, Sept. 19, 1864. Capt. OO, Jan. 7, 1865. Assigned as Capt. OO to Roberts, Mar. 1865. Lawyer at Greensboro and Birmingham. d. Hale Co., Alabama, Aug. 12, 1908.

Webb, Lewis Nutall. Merchant at Richmond, Virginia. m. Lucy Roy Mason, 1853, making him a brother-in-law of Gen. Field and Gen. Alexander, among others. Capt. AQM to Wise, Aug. 10, 1861. Capt. AQM commanding reserve ordnance train, First Corps, Nov. 1862. Maj. QM, Nov. 17, 1862. Subsequently on duty around Richmond, though paroled at Appx. as Maj. QM with First Corps artillery. Postwar Richmond merchant. Killed Apr. 27, 1870, in capitol collapse. bur. Shockoe Cem.

Webster, Daniel T. b. Nov. 21, 1837. A resident of Greensboro, Alabama. Pvt. Co. I, 5th Alabama. Capt. ACS, 5th Alabama, Sept. 28, 1861. Maj. CS to Rodes, Mar. 11, 1862. Maj. acting CS to D. H. Hill, Aug. 1862, for an indefinite period. Maj. CS to Battle, 1863. Paroled May 17, 1865. d. June 18, 1881. bur. New Prospect Church Cem., Hale Co.

Webster, William Eugene. b. Aug. 28, 1831. att. USMA and Yale. A civil engineer from Maryland. Lt. of Inf., CSA, Nov. 8, 1861, on duty at Richmond Arsenal. Lt. of Arty., May 19, 1862, to report to Josiah Gorgas. KIA at Gaines's Mill, June 27, 1862, while serving as VADC to Rodes. bur. Shockoe

Cem., Richmond, but moved to Annapolis, Maryland, in 1919.

Weddon, Jackson E. Sgt. Maj. Macon (Ga.) Light Arty., May 16, 1862, age 33. To Lt., July 24, 1863. Lt. acting OO to Moseley's Bn. Arty., June 17, 1864. Returned to battery in Jan. 1865. Jeweler and Sheriff at Sandersville, Ga. bur. City Cem.

Weir, Walter. b. in Virginia, Jan. 12, 1839. att. UVA. and Wm. & Mary. Of Prince William Co. Adjt. 49th Virginia. Lt. AAAG to H. Marshall, Dec. 1861–mid 1863. Lt. AAAIG to Hodge by Sept. 1863. Capt. AAG to B. R. Johnson, Nov. 2, 1863. May have failed confirmation, because reapptd. to rank from Dec. 27, 1864. Capt. AAG to Mahone, Mar. 8, 1865. Appx. Farmer and lawyer at Manassas. m. Elizabeth Joan Douglas, 1867. d. Rockbridge Alum Springs, Virginia, Aug. 11, 1870. bur. Weir Family Cem. at "Liberia," in Manassas. One of Hodge's staff called Weir "A very good, innocent, soft-handed fellow who means well" and a "modest, whole-souled & unsuspecting fellow. Well educated & smart."

Weisiger, Oscar Fitzallen. b. Richmond, Virginia, Apr. 28, 1820. m. Sarah Southall. Capt. AQM, Jan. 30, 1863. Served in Richmond into 1865, where he was the superintendent of the clothing depot. Richmond merchant and clothier postwar. d. there Feb. 14, 1886. bur. Hollywood Cem.

Weisiger, William W. b. Virginia. A 54-year-old warehouse manager in Chesterfield Co. in 1860. Capt. AQM, PAVA., May 22, 1861. Capt. AQM (PACS), June 29, 1861. To report to R. E. Lee, Aug. 24, 1862. On duty at QM Gen.'s office at Richmond by Dec. 1863. Spent remainder of war there, supervising the supply of fuel to hospitals and camps. Paroled Apr. 26, 1865. Almost certainly William Washington Weisiger, who died at Manchester on May 4, 1868.

Welch, Isaiah A. b. Doddridge Co., Virginia. Capt. AQM, 13th Bn. Virginia Light Arty., Dec. 12, 1862. Resigned July 16, 1864, to rep-

resent Kanawha Co. in the state legislature. Postwar coal merchant. d. St. Alban's, West Virginia, Feb. 1902, age 77.

Wellford, Philip Alexander. b. Aug. 24, 1834. A lawyer. m. Mary Belle Street. Lt. Co. F, 21st Virginia, 1861. Dropped at Apr. 1862 reorganization. VADC to Taliaferro, Apr. 1862. Capt. ACS, 23rd Virginia, June 1, 1862. Capt. ACS at Richmond from July 31, 1863. Employed in Virginia state commissary office latter part of the war. d. Dec. 11, 1909. bur. Hollywood Cem., Richmond.

Wertenbaker, Thomas Jefferson. b. Albemarle Co., Virginia, Mar. 3, 1816. att. UVA. Clothing merchant in Albemarle Co. pre- and postwar. m. Mary F. Hyde. Capt. ACS, PAVA., by June 1861. Capt. ACS (PACS), date unknown. Served at Charlottesville. Resigned Oct. 27, 1862. d. Aug. 29, 1884. bur. Maplewood Cem., Charlottesville.

West, Frederick H. b. Dallas Co., Alabama, 1826. Lawyer at Starkville, Georgia. Secretary of state Democratic Convention and briefly secretary of state senate. Pvt. Co. B, 51st Georgia, Mar. 4, 1862. VADC to G. T. Anderson, Aug. 1862. Adjt. 51st Georgia, Oct. 2, 1862, but probably stayed with Anderson. WIA slightly at Chancellorsville. WIA at Gettysburg—lost use of right arm and hand. Dropped as unserviceable, July 1864. Served in state legislature late in the war. m. Elizabeth Sullivan, 1871. d. Leesburg, Georgia, Oct. 23, 1884.

West, George. Lt. ADC to D. H. Hill, Sept. 30, 1861. Capt. OO to Hill, June 3, 1862. Resigned Sept. 30, 1862. Apparently lingered with Hill as VADC for rest of the war. Paroled May 6, 1865, at Greensboro.

West, James F. Capt. AQM, 15th Virginia, by Aug. 31, 1861. Capt. AQM on paymaster duty at Richmond, Jan. 1862 until the end of the war. Duty was to pay soldiers in the hospitals. Possibly James F. (Flood?) West who died Sept. 9, 1867, at Richmond, age 35, and was buried at Hollywood Cem.

Westcott, Gideon Granger. b. Providence

Co., Rhode Island, Aug. 24, 1836. Lived prewar in Greene Co., Alabama. Served in Co. D, 5th Alabama. Capt. AQM, Mar. 23, 1863, to Carter's Bn. Arty. POW at Jack's Mountain, July 5, 1863. Took Oath, June 12, 1865. Dry goods merchant at Greensboro, Alabama. Also lived at Mobile. d. 1907 or 1908 in Florida.

Wharton, John James. b. May 13, 1845. Lived in Culpeper Co., Virginia. Lt. ADC to his brother, Gen. Wharton, Nov. 1, 1863. Paroled June 1865 at Gordonsville. d. Mar. 26, 1919. bur. Fairfax City Cem.

Wheeler, Woodbury, Jr. att. Columbian Coll. Adjt. 16th North Carolina, June 17, 1861–Jan. 17, 1862. Lt. AAAG to Branch, Jan. 1862. Lt. Latham's (N.C.) Btty., Feb. 3, 1862. POW at New Bern, and exchanged Nov. 10, 1862. Lt. OO to Daniel, Oct. 2, 1862. Lt. OO to Clingman, Jan. 1863. Lt. OO to Whiting, Apr. 3, 1863. Capt. Co. D, 10th Bn. North Carolina Heavy Arty., Apr. 30, 1863. Paroled Apr. 29, 1865. Lawyer at Washington, D.C. d. 1900. Wheeler's war letters are at UNC.

Whitchard, John. b. in North Carolina, Aug. 28, 1823. A farmer in Macon Co., Georgia. Pvt. 10th Georgia Bn., Mar. 4, 1862. Capt. AQM of battalion, Aug. 8, 1862. Capt. AQM, Third Corps ambulance train, Sept. 15, 1864. Appx. Resumed Macon Co. farming. d. Mar. 28, 1905. bur. Cedar Hill Cem., Dawson, Georgia.

White, Benjamin Stephen. b. Montgomery Co., Maryland, Mar. 11, 1828. Merchant at Poolesville. Married twice. Lt. of Cavy., CSA, Nov. 16, 1861. Capt. of Cavy., Oct. 21, 1862, to report to Gen. Stuart. WIA in neck at Brandy Station, June 9, 1863. Commanded Stuart's "infirmary camp," Aug.–Dec. 1863. Maj. of Cavy., PACS, Jan. 5, 1864. Probably commanded the camp for rest of war. Paroled at Winchester, Virginia, Apr. 24, 1865. Staff duty with Stuart not entirely clear, but likely served as simple ADC most of the time. d. Mar. 28, 1891. bur. Monocacy Cem., Beallsville, Maryland.

White, Chastain. b. in Virginia, June 29, 1823. att. Wm. & Mary. Lifelong lawyer at Ashland and Richmond. Member of state legislature. Capt. AQM, 44th Virginia, July 11, 1861. Capt. acting Chief QM to Magruder, Apr.–May 1862. Capt. AQM to John B. Gordon, Sept. 15, 1864. Capt. AQM to J. A. Walker, Feb. 1865. Charged with stealing a box of money in 1865. Appx. Postwar lawyer in Hanover Co. d. Richmond, June 21, 1879. bur. Hollywood Cem.

White, Edward. b. Feb. 22, 1840. Schoolteacher at Harpers Ferry, Virginia, and present during the John Brown episode. Pvt. Co. C, 30th Virginia, May 1861. Pvt. Fredericksburg (Va.) Arty., May 8, 1862. Lt. ADC to Clingman, June 30, 1862. Capt. AAG to Clingman, Aug. 8, 1862. WIA in neck at Cold Harbor, May 31, 1864. Paroled Apr. 26, 1865. Lawyer and judge at St. Louis, Missouri. d. there June 2, 1888.

White, James Biggs. b. in Virginia, 1828. Farmer at Hampton. Cpl. Co. B, 3rd Virginia Cavy., May 14, 1861. Detached on QM duty. Capt. AQM to Magruder, Nov. 2, 1861. Capt. AQM at Richmond, June 12, 1862. Capt. AQM at Henderson, North Carolina, Apr. 30, 1863, into 1865. d. 1895.

White, James Lowry. b. Abingdon, Virginia, Aug. 29, 1842. att. UVA. Lt. Co. C, 37th Virginia. To Adjt. Dec. 12, 1862. Lt. AAIG to Wm. Terry, 1864. WIA in head, Apr. 1865. POW at Amelia Springs, Apr. 6, 1865. att. Washington Coll. postwar. m. Kate Robertson. Commonwealth's attorney for Washington Co., Virginia. d. Abingdon, Dec. 9, 1914.

White, John Josiah. b. Loudoun Co., Virginia, Dec. 23, 1836. att. Dickinson Coll. and UMiss. Married three times. Served in Co. C, 35th Bn. Virginia Cavy. WIA Oct. 21, 1862. Capt. AQM, 35th Bn. Virginia Cavy., Feb. 17, 1864. Capt. AQM to Dearing, Mar. 1865. Moved to Atlanta, Georgia, in 1876 and became a "commerical traveller." Tax collector, editor, and dealer in agricultural implements. d. at Atlanta, Mar. 12, 1894.

White, Joseph Harvey. b. York District, South Carolina, Dec. 21, 1824. att. Davidson Coll. Planter in Mecklenburg Co., North Carolina. Capt. Co. B, 53rd North Carolina, Apr. 30, 1862. WIA at Gettysburg. Capt. AAAG to Daniel, Dec. 23, 1863–Apr. 1864. KIA at Spotsylvania, May 12, 1864. Possibly buried at Spotsylvania Confederate Cem.

White, Joshua W. Lt. Co. F, 27th North Carolina, Sept. 5, 1861. Capt. AQM to Cooke, Sept. 15, 1864. Appx.

White, Oscar. b. Tallahassee, Florida, 1836. Lt. CSA, July 19, 1861. Lt. acting AQM to Loring, Sept.–Dec. 1861. Lt. commanding a company, and later acting Adjt., 1st Bn. Virginia, Jan. 1–June 9, 1862. Lt. acting ADC to J. R. Jones, June 1862, and later to various colonels commanding that brigade. WIA at Second Manassas. Maj. 48th Virginia, Nov. 20, 1862. To Lt. Col., May 3, 1863. WIA at Third Winchester. Appx. Wholesale grocer in San Francisco, 1865–1868. Managed a vineyard at San Bernadino, California, then engaged in mining. d. Colton, California, June 30, 1883. bur. Pioneer Cem., San Bernadino.

White, Robert. b. Romney, Virginia, Feb. 7, 1833. A lawyer there. Capt. Co. I, 13th Virginia, May 1861. Appointed MSK at Richmond, June 18, 1863. Maj. 41st Bn. Virginia Cavy., Sept. 21, 1863. Later Col. 23rd Virginia Cavy. Served in West Virginia legislature, was a lawyer at Wheeling and state attorney general. d. near Wheeling, July 1916.

Whited, John Buchanan. b. in Virginia, Aug. 30, 1840. att. Emory & Henry. Lt. Co. E, 50th Virginia, May 27, 1861. Capt. AQM, 50th Virginia, July 1, 1862. Capt. AQM with Second Corps ordnance train, May 16, 1864. POW at Germantown, North Carolina, Apr. 10, 1865. d. Sept. 26, 1906.

Whitehead, Charles Lowndes. b. Richmond Co., Georgia, June 29, 1835. Member of state secession convention. A resident of Miller Co. Sgt. Co. E, 4th Georgia, Apr. 28, 1861. To Maj., May 8, 1861. Resigned Apr. 28, 1862. VADC to Wright, June 1862. POW at King's School House, June 25, 1862. WIA at Sharpsburg. No further military record. d. Sept. 25, 1866.

Whitehead, William H. W. b. in Georgia. A 37-year-old shoe- and bootmaker in Habersham Co., Georgia, in 1860. Capt. ACS, 16th Georgia, Mar. 18, 1862. Dropped in mid-1863 as part of armywide removal of regimental commissaries. Capt. ACS to Bryan, Sept. 17, 1863. Same to Simms, June 1864. Served into 1865.

Whitfield, John F. Capt. AQM, July 13, 1861. Maj. QM, Aug. 31, 1862. Stationed mostly at Richmond, Virginia. Dropped Oct. 22, 1863, under AIGO Special Orders #251/2. Pvt. Co. C, 1st Bn. Virginia Cavy. LDT, Mar. 11, 1864. Probably the John F. Whitfield from Powhatan Co., Virginia, who died Feb. 9, 1900, at Rutherford, New Jersey. A subordinate called Whitfield "a drinking man."

Whiting, Clarence Carlyle. b. Aug. 31, 1844. Of Fauquier Co., Virginia. Pvt. Co. A, 6th Virginia Cavy., Mar. 1–Dec. 1, 1862. Detailed as courier for Gen. Stuart that entire time. POW May 31, 1862, and exchanged Aug. 5, 1862. Pvt. Co. G, 7th Virginia Cavy., Dec. 1, 1862. WIA at Brandy Station. To Sgt. Maj., early 1864. Lt. ADC to W. E. Jones, Feb. 25, 1864. Returned to 7th Virginia Cavy. when Jones was killed in June 1864. m. Marion Gordon Armistead, 1877. d. at Baltimore, Maryland.

Whiting, Henry Augustine. b. Hanover Co., Virginia, Jan. 8, 1832. att. VMI. Lt. Co. H, 5th Alabama. Capt. AAG to Rodes, Nov. 16, 1861. Resigned Dec. 14, 1861. Reapptd. to same position, Jan. 28, 1862, to resume rank from Nov. 28, 1861. Lt. Col. 41st Alabama, Aug. 5, 1862, but declined. WIA in arm at Sharpsburg. Maj. AAG to Rodes, May 12, 1863. Probably same to Ramseur, Sept.–Oct. 1864. Maj. AAIG to Grimes, Oct. 1864.

Appx. Civil engineer postwar. d. Dec. 26, 1907.

Whiting, Henry Clay. b. Hampton, Virginia, Dec. 24, 1832. Lt. Co. K, 32nd Virginia, May 14, 1861. Capt. AQM, Sept. 2, 1861. Duty uncertain until assigned to staff of McLaws, Jan.–June 1862. Capt. AQM to French, June 1862. Capt. AQM to Hagood, Feb. 24, 1865. Hampton banker postwar. d. Jan. 18, 1899. bur. St. John's Cem.

Whiting, Jasper Strong. b. Lowell, Massachusetts, July 13, 1828. att. Georgetown Coll. Engineer at a New Mexico mining camp. Probably Lt. EO to Loring in July 1861. Maj. AAG to G. W. Smith, Sept. 9, 1861. Also acting EO to Smith at Seven Pines. Maj. AAAG to T. J. Jackson during Seven Days campaign. Maj. on duty at AIGO in Richmond, from July 1862. d. Richmond, Dec. 25, 1862, from scarlet fever. bur. Hollywood Cem. A brother of Gen. Whiting. Gen. J. E. Johnston thought Whiting "a man of rare merit."

Whitlock, Adoniram J. b. in Georgia, ca. 1828. A merchant at Dawson. Lt. Co. E, 5th Georgia, May 11, 1861–May 8, 1862. Capt. AQM, 21st Georgia, Apr. 8, 1863. Capt. AQM to Grimes, Nov. 3, 1864. Appx. Postwar Terrell Co. farmer. Moved to Florida sometime after 1880.

Whitner, James Harrison. b. Nov. 3, 1832. Lawyer at Pendleton, South Carolina. Maj. 4th South Carolina, Apr. 14, 1861. Unit failed to reorganize in 1862. VADC to R. H. Anderson at the Battle of Williamsburg. Pvt. in Palmetto Sharpshooters. Capt. 22nd South Carolina. Postwar lawyer at Walhalla and Greenville. d. May 2, 1896. bur. Springwood Cem., Greenville.

Whitner, John Charles. b. Edgefield Dist., South Carolina, Sept. 23, 1831. att. Franklin Coll. and UGA. m. Sarah Martha Cobb, 1853. Banker and merchant in Georgia and Florida. Maj. CS to his brother-in-law, Gen. Howell Cobb, Mar. 6, 1862. Resigned May 6, 1862, citing prostate problems.

Planter at Quincy, Florida; merchant at West Point, Georgia; banker at Charleston, South Carolina; and insurance agent at Atlanta, Georgia. d. there Jan. 15, 1906. bur. Westview Cem.

Whitner, William Henry. b. Anderson, South Carolina, Nov. 1836. att. South Carolina Coll. Lawyer in Spartanburg Co. Lt. Co. F, 1st Florida. Capt. AAG to Pryor, Oct. 14, 1862. Capt. AAIG to Micah Jenkins, spring 1863 to May 1864. WIA and lost a finger at Wilderness, May 6, 1864. Capt. AAIG to B. R. Johnson, July 2, 1864. Appx. Unofficially shown as staff of E. A. Perry in Dec. 1862, and AAAIG to Hood, Nov.–Dec. 1863. Married twice. Lawyer and state's attorney at Madison, Florida. d. there Feb. 16, 1872.

Whitthorne, Washington Curran. b. near Farmington, Tennessee, Apr. 19, 1825. att. Univ. of Tennessee. Lawyer and state legislator from Columbia, prewar. Served as Adjt. Gen. of Tennessee's state forces, early war. Capt. AAG to S. R. Anderson, Sept. 9, 1861. Resigned Jan. 9, 1862. Resumed post as Adjt. Gen. of Tennessee. Later VADC to Hardee and Marcus Wright. Served in USHR and Senate, postwar. d. Columbia, Sept. 21, 1891. bur. Rose Hill Cem.

Widney, Charles T. Asst. Surg. 1862. POW in 1862. Lt. ADC to A. G. Jenkins, Sept. 25, 1862. Resigned Apr. 15, 1863. Acting Surg. 14th Virginia Cavy., 1863–1864. Apparently also Maj. commanding 37th Bn. Virginia Cavy., May 1863. Took Oath May 26, 1865, as both Maj. 37th Bn. and Surg. 3rd Florida. Said he was from Daviess Co., Kentucky. Possibly two different men with the same name.

Wilbourn, Richard Eggleston. b. Yalobusha Co., Mississippi, May 16, 1838. att. UVA. and UMISS. Pvt. Co. A, 21st Mississippi, 1861. Detailed to C.S. Signal Corps, by Dec. 1861. Capt. SO to G. W. Smith, May 29, 1862. Capt. SO to T. J. Jackson, July 15, 1862. WIA in arm at Second Manassas and out of action until Feb. 1863. Capt. SO to Ewell,

June 1863, and then to Early, May 1864. Merchant and farmer postwar. m. Annie Bryan Moseley, 1869. d. Torrance, Mississippi, Dec. 28, 1875. bur. family cem. in Yalobusha Co. Another source says he died Oct. 26, 1875.

Wilcox, Edward A. A 40-year-old cotton broker at Macon, Georgia, in 1860. Lt. Co. C, 8th Georgia, Apr. 15, 1861. To Capt. Sept. 12, 1861. Capt. AQM, 8th Georgia, Oct. 5, 1861. Capt. AQM to Field, Sept. 15, 1864. Appx. Resumed broker profession at Macon. d. Washington, D.C., about June 1, 1895, age 76. bur. New Haven, Connecticut.

Wilder, J. Dickson. A resident of Caswell Co., North Carolina. Sgt. Co. G, 22nd North Carolina, May 28, 1861, age 22. Capt. AQM, 22nd North Carolina, July 16, 1862. Capt. AQM, Sept. 15, 1864, at Third Corps headquarters.

Wildman, Charles Bennett. b. Loudoun Co., Virginia, Mar. 16, 1818. A merchant. Lt. in 17th Virginia, Apr. 27, 1861. Lt. acting ADC to N. G. Evans, Oct. 1861. Dropped Apr. 28, 1862. d. July 9, 1898. bur. Union Cem., Leesburg.

Wilkinson, Willis. Lt. of Arty., Apr. 20, 1861, apptd. from South Carolina. To report to R. E. Lee, Nov. 30, 1861. Capt. (PACS) OO, June 24, 1862, to report to Pemberton. Capt. OO at Franklin, Virginia, May 23, 1863. Capt. OO to Heth, Aug. 9, 1863. Capt. OO for First Corps artillery, Nov. 25, 1863. Served there through Dec. 1864, at least.

Willcox, John N. Lt. acting SO to J. A. Walker at Appx. No official record other than his parole.

Williams, Andrew W. Of Alabama. Capt. AQM, 2nd Bn., Hilliard's (Ala.) Legion, July 1, 1862. Capt. AQM, 11th Virginia. Capt. AQM to Pickett, date unknown. Appx.

Williams, Buckner Davis. b. Warren Co., North Carolina, July 18, 1833. m. Elizabeth Batte Symes, 1853. Merchant at Warrenton. Lt. Co. B, 30th North Carolina, Aug. 16, 1861. Capt. AQM, 30th North Carolina, Nov. 1,

1861. Capt. acting AQM to Ramseur, Oct. 1, 1862–Apr. 1, 1863. Maj. QM to Ramseur, Oct. 7, 1863. Maj. QM to Cox, Sept. 15, 1864. Served into 1865. Postwar mayor of Warrenton and justice of peace. d. there Sept. 10, 1884. bur. Williams Fam. Cem., Warren Co.

Williams, Charles Urquhart. b. Henrico Co., Virginia, Dec. 27, 1840. att. UVA. Pvt. 2nd Co. Richmond Howitzers, May 26, 1861. Lt. Drillmaster, June 9, 1862. VADC to D. R. Jones at Second Manassas and subsequently. Lt. ADC to Corse, Dec. 28, 1863. POW near Petersburg, May 1864. Paroled May 8, 1865. Richmond lawyer and legislator. d. San Francisco, California, May 13, 1901. bur. Hollywood Cem., Richmond.

Williams, George Archer. b. Dec. 14, 1826. VADC to his cousin, Gen. Archer, Nov. 1862–July 1863. WIA (twice) and POW at Gettysburg. VADC to Fry, May–June 1864. Stayed with that brigade until Appx. d. Baltimore, Maryland, Mar. 27, 1887. bur. Green Mount Cem.

Williams, James Harrison. b. Woodstock, Virginia, Feb. 6, 1836. att. UVA. Lawyer and legislator at Dubuque, Iowa, prewar. Lt. and Capt. in Chew's (Va.) Btty. Lt. Judge Advocate with Hampton's command by Jan. 1864. Promoted to Capt., Mar. 23, 1865. Lawyer and legislator at Woodstock and Winchester, Virginia. m. Cora Pritchartt, 1871. d. Woodstock, Dec. 7, 1903. bur. Massanutten Cem.

Williams, James Mortimer. b. in Virginia, Nov. 30, 1838. Pvt. Co. B, 53rd Virginia. Detailed in Commissary Dept., Sept. 1864. Capt. ACS, Mar. 11, 1865, on duty at ANVa. headquarters. Appx. d. Jan. 1896. Probably bur. Blandford Cem., Petersburg, Virginia.

Williams, James Seymour. b. Savannah, Georgia, Jan. 1812. att. USMA. Lt. U.S. Inf., 1831–1837. Commanded a company in the Black Hawk War. Railroad engineer, 1837–1861. Maj. of Inf., CSA, June 10, 1861. Maj. EO to R. S. Garnett, June 16, 1861. Maj. EO to H. R. Jackson, July 1861. Maj.

EO to Loring, Oct.–Nov. 1861. Maj. AAIG, Nov. 30, 1861, at Savannah. Served on staff of Lawton, Mercer, and McLaws. Railroad engineer and surveyor in Georgia. d. Staten Island, New York, Sept. 7, 1871.

Williams, John A. A construction engineer on railroads in Texas prewar. Capt. EO, Aug. 16, 1862. On duty around Richmond, Virginia. Maj. EO, May 5, 1863. Lt. Col. EO, Mar. 17, 1864. Joined ANVa. in the field, Aug. 1864, and operated at least partially as a member of A. P. Hill's staff. Appx. Confederate engineer C. H. Dimmock loathed Williams, calling him in 1864 "a boor and a booby."

Williams, John A. b. in North Carolina, Oct. 3, 1831. A merchant at Oxford prewar and postwar. Brother of Col. Sol. Williams, 2nd North Carolina Cavy. Capt. ACS, 24th North Carolina, July 19, 1861. Dropped in 1863. Capt. ACS to Matt. Ransom, mid-1863. Served with Ransom through 1864, at least. d. Dec. 1899. bur. Elmwood Cem., Oxford.

Williams, John Marshall. b. Cumberland Co., North Carolina, Aug. 18, 1838. Pvt. Co. H, 1st North Carolina (Bethel), Apr. 17, 1861. Lt. Co. C, 54th North Carolina, Mar. 22, 1862. WIA at Cedar Creek. Lt. AAAIG to Lewis, Apr. 1865. Appx. Married twice. Alive 1918 near Fayetteville, North Carolina.

Williams, John Shelby. b. Sumner Co., Tennessee, Mar. 7, 1832. Lawyer at New Orleans, Louisiana, and at Nashville, Tennessee. Lt. Co. G, 18th Tennessee, Jan. 20, 1862. Capt. AAG to S. R. Anderson, Jan. 10, 1862. Capt. of Cavy. and Judge Advocate to E. K. Smith, Dec. 16, 1862. Resigned. Later Capt. AAAG to J. S. Scott's Bgd. and then Maj. commanding a camp of instruction and on conscript duty in Alabama. m. Mattie Sevier, making Williams a brother-in-law of Gen. Churchill. d. Nashville, Tennessee, in 1878.

Williams, Samuel Coleman. b. Sept. 1839. att. USMA, from Rutledge, Tennessee. Lt. of

Arty., Mar. 16, 1861. On ordnance duty in South Carolina. Adjt. Cobb's (Ga.) Legion, Sept. 11, 1861. Lt. ADC to R. B. Garnett, Nov. 16, 1861. Dropped July 30, 1862. Lt. Chief of Arty. to Buckner, Aug. 1862. Maj. with same duties, Jan. 26, 1863. To Lt. Col., Feb. 23, 1864, commanding an artillery battalion.

Williams, Thomas Greenhow. b. Richmond, Virginia, Apr. 29, 1828. att. USMA. Lt. U.S. Inf., 1849–1861. m. Mary Curtis. Maj. CS (CSA), Mar. 16, 1861. Lt. Col. CS, July 1, 1863. Served at Richmond as Asst. Commissary Gen. of the Confederacy. Transferred to duty with Gen. Kemper, June 3, 1864, perhaps as commissary for the state of Virginia. Paroled Apr., 23, 1865. Postwar agent with Kickapoo Indians, then a merchant and gas company president at San Antonio, Texas. d. there Jan. 22, 1885. bur. City Cem. #1.

Williams, Thomas H. Pvt. Co. B, Cobb's (Ga.) Legion Cavy., Mar. 4, 1862. To Capt. AQM of unit, May 7, 1863. Maj. QM to Young, Apr. 28, 1864. Paroled at Greensboro.

Williams, William M. Lt. Co. B, Cobb's Legion (Ga.) Cavy., Aug. 14, 1861. To Capt. Co. G, May 30, 1862. Capt. acting ACS to Young, Apr. 1864 only.

Williams, William Grymes. b. Orange C.H., Virginia, Nov. 8, 1829. att. UVa. and Wm. & Mary. m. Roberta Hansbrough, 1857. Lawyer in Orange and schoolteacher at Richmond. Capt. ACS, 58th Virginia, Oct. 1861. Capt. ACS to Pegram, 1864. POW at Moorefield, Aug. 7, 1864, "while gathering cattle." Teacher, legislator, lawyer, and judge in Orange Co. Coal merchant in West Virginia. d. Dec. 17, 1901.

Williamson, George. b. Baltimore, Maryland, Feb. 1, 1835. att. Harvard and schools in Europe. Baltimore lawyer, 1860–1861. Sgt. Co. H, 1st Maryland. Capt. AAG to Steuart, May 1, 1862. Capt. AAIG to Steuart, Aug. 20, 1863. Returned to AAG duty,

Jan. 1864. WIA and POW at Spotsylvania, May 12, 1864, but escaped. Capt. AAAIG to John B. Gordon, May 1864. WIA at North Anna. POW at Lynchburg, Virginia, during recovery. KIA at Fisher's Hill, Sept. 22, 1864. bur. Staunton, Virginia, but removed to Loudon Park Cem., Baltimore, in 1874.

Williamson, Thomas Hoomes. b. Norfolk, Virginia, Aug. 30, 1813. att. USMA. Civil engineer. Professor at VMI, 1841–1887. Married twice. Maj. EO (PAVa.), Apr. 24, 1861. On duty at Fredericksburg. Lt. Col. EO (PAVa.). Served as Chief EO to Beauregard, July 1861. Lt. Col. EO to T. J. Jackson, May 3–15, 1862, but was present with Jackson on other occasions, too. Commanded a company of home guard troops in Rockbridge Co., 1863. Never commissioned in CSA or PACS service. d. Mar. 31, 1888. bur. Stonewall Jackson Cem., Lexington. Bore a striking resemblance to R. E. Lee, but his "face was more rugged and had less beauty."

Williamson, William Garnett. b. Norfolk, Virginia, Dec. 13, 1840. att. VMI and Washington Coll. A nephew of the two Garnett generals and the son of T. H. Williamson (see above). Civil engineer in Alabama, and a schoolteacher there. Pvt. 1st Co. Rockbridge (Va.) Arty., July 5, 1861. WIA in arm at First Winchester. Lt. EO, June 24, 1862, reported for duty to T. J. Jackson, Aug. 21, 1862. Served there until Apr. 1863. Lt. EO to W. E. Jones, Apr. 7, 1863. Lt. VADC to Early at Gettysburg. Stayed with Jones until May 1864. Capt. 1st Confederate Engineers, May 4, 1864. Postwar civil engineer in Mexico, and city engineer at Montgomery, Alabama. d. Pensacola, Florida, Aug. 2, 1898. bur. Stonewall Jackson Cem., Lexington, Virginia. Williamson's wartime journal is at the VMI archives.

Willis, Edward. b. in South Carolina, Aug. 15, 1836. m. Elizabeth Louise Hammond. Maj. QM to Drayton, Oct. 11, 1861. Maj. QM to Corse, Nov. 28, 1862, but

probably never served there. Maj. QM at Charleston, South Carolina, Dec. 26, 1862. Maj. QM to Beauregard, Apr. 23, 1864. Cotton merchant at Charleston postwar. d. Feb. 28, 1910. bur. Magnolia Cem.

Willis, Edward Shackelford. b. Wilkes Co., Georgia, Aug. 10, 1840. att. USMA. Lt. of Inf., CSA, Mar. 16, 1861. Adjt. 12th Georgia, July 5, 1861. Possibly VADC to Early at First Manassas. Capt. of Arty., CSA, Mar. 3, 1862. Lt. and then Capt. AAAG to Ed. Johnson, Dec. 13, 1861–Apr. 16, 1862. Capt. AAAG to T. J. Jackson, May 8, 1862, until Capt. AAG to Johnson, Oct. 1, 1862. Lt. Col. 12th Georgia, Dec. 13, 1862. Col., Jan. 22, 1863. WIA in thigh at the Wilderness. MWIA at Bethesda Church, May 30, 1864. d. May 31. bur. in Savannah, Georgia, but removed to Hollywood Cem. in Richmond, Virginia, 1879.

Wilmer, Skipwith. b. Kent Co., Maryland, Feb. 21, 1843. att. St. James Coll., UPenn., and law school in Louisiana. Sgt. in C.S. Signal Corps, Oct. 10, 1862, on duty at Savannah, Georgia. Ordered to ANVa., May 20, 1863. Sgt. acting ADC to Ed. Johnson at Mine Run. Lt. SO to Johnson, Feb. 19, 1864. Lt. SO to John B. Gordon, May 1864. WIA near Harpers Ferry, about July 6, 1864. On signal duty at Wilmington, North Carolina, Aug. 6, 1864. Lt. SO to Echols, Feb. 16, 1865. Baltimore law partner of Randolph Barton (see above). d. Nahant, Massachusetts, July 12, 1901. Wilmer's diary for 1863–1865 is at the Maryland Historical Society.

Wilson, Arthur Emmerson. b. Portsmouth, Virginia, Sept. 3, 1832. att. UVa. m. Annie Taylor Moler, 1856. Capt. ACS, 14th Virginia, July 19, 1861. Post commissary at Jamestown Island, July 1861–Jan. 1862. Dropped in 1863, but served in some similar capacity in King William and King and Queen Co., Virginia. POW in Kilpatrick's Raid. Postwar druggist at Portsmouth. d. there Sept. 1, 1896.

Wilson, Clayton. Capt. AQM, Hilliard's (Ala.) Legion, Feb. 16, 1863. Capt. AQM, 60th Alabama. Capt. AQM, Blount's Bn. Arty., by Aug. 1864. Served into 1865.

Wilson, Daniel Allen, Jr. b. Cumberland Co., Virginia, June 20, 1823. att. Washington Coll. and Hampden Sidney. Tobacco merchant and lawyer at New Orleans, Louisiana. ADC to the governor of Louisiana. Capt. Co. I, 7th Louisiana, June 7, 1861. Capt. of Cavy., Dec. 16, 1862, and Judge Advocate to Second Corps. Col. of Cavy., Nov. 1, 1863, and Second Corps Judge. Paroled Apr. 1865 at Farmville. Railroad man and "public administrator" postwar. d. New Orleans, May 22, 1893. bur. Presby. Cem., Lynchburg, Virginia. "From his immense size, everybody knows him."

Wilson, James William. b. Dec. 17, 1832. att. UNC. Of Alamance Co., North Carolina. m. Louisa Erwin. A civil engineer. Capt. Co. F, 6th North Carolina, May 16–Nov. 27, 1861. Capt. AQM, 49th North Carolina, May 18, 1862. Maj. QM to Ramseur, Feb. 28, 1863. Resigned Sept. 21, 1863, to serve as supt. of Western North Carolina Railroad. d. July 2, 1910. bur. Forest Hill Cem., Morganton, North Carolina.

Wilson, John Parke, Jr. b. Cumberland Co., Virginia, Sept. 16, 1833. att. VMI. Maj. 5th Bn. Virginia, Apr. 29, 1861. Dropped at May 1862 reorganization. VADC to Ewell at Second Manassas, and to Early at Sharpsburg and Fredericksburg. Pvt. Co. I, 13th Virginia, Feb. 1863. Pvt. and later Capt. Co. B, 9th Virginia, from Dec. 1863. WIA May 1864. Appx. Farmer and civil engineer in North Carolina. d. Black Mountain, Feb. 13, 1922.

Wilson, John T. Maj. CS to Cocke, Oct. 3, 1861. Same to Pickett, Jan. 1862. Resigned Sept. 25, 1862, citing rheumatism.

Wilson, Marcus L. b. Jefferson Co., Alabama, July 26, 1826. Mexican War veteran. Pvt. Co. E, 10th Alabama, June 4, 1861. Capt. ACS, 10th Alabama, May 1, 1862.

Capt. ACS to Perrin, Sept. 17, 1863. Capt. ACS to Sanders, May 1864. Capt. ACS to W. H. Forney. Appx. Farmer in Talladega Co. Alive Aug. 1902.

Wilson, Robert N. Pvt. Co. C, 42nd Virginia, July 29, 1861. Soon acting AQM for that regiment. Capt. AAG to the brigade, Nov. 2, 1861, commanded at different times by Cols. Burks, Campbell, Patton, and Garnett. Capt. AAG to J. R. Jones, July 1862. Capt. AAG to J. M. Jones, 1863. Capt. AAG to Pegram by Mar. 1864. WIA at Bethesda Church and Third Winchester. Alive 1894 at Baltimore, Maryland.

Wimberly, Fred. Acting ADC to Colquitt during the Seven Days. This is a confusing case. Probably Frederick Davis Wimberly (Mar. 23, 1840–July 16, 1893), but possibly Frederick Ezekiel Wimberly (b. Sept. 26, 1836, KIA at Sharpsburg). Both were in Co. I, 6th Georgia.

Winder, William Sidney. b. July 14, 1833. att. Maryland Military Academy and Columbian Coll. Never married. Lt. ADC to his father, Gen. J. H. Winder, Oct. 29, 1861. Capt. AAG to Winder, June 10, 1862. Capt. AAG to Ruggles, Mar. 1865. Postwar lawyer at Baltimore, Maryland. Committed suicide, Feb. 25, 1905.

Wingate, Robert Johnston. b. Frankfort, Kentucky, Dec. 18, 1829. att. USMA, KMI, and Masonic Coll. of Kentucky. A clerk at Louisville in 1860. Lt. Co. A, 5th Louisiana, May 10, 1861. To Adjt., Aug. 16, 1861. Capt. AAG to R. B. Garnett, Nov. 16, 1861. Maj. AAIG to A. P. Hill, May 26, 1862. Charged with drunkenness late in 1863. Court expressed disapproval of conduct but retained him. Appx. d. Aug. 28, 1893. bur. Frankfort Cem.

Wingfield, William Charles. b. Norfolk, Virginia, Mar. 18, 1825. One of the California "'49ers," and a grocer at Norfolk. Maj. CS to Blanchard, Oct. 2, 1861. Maj. CS to Wright, June 1862. Maj. CS to R. H. Anderson by May 1863. Relieved Mar. 14, 1864, and subsequently dropped at the request of A. P. Hill, who complained of Wingfield's lack of "energy and activity." Postwar merchant and employee of Seaboard and Roanoke Railroad. d. Norfolk, Oct. 24, 1896. bur. Oak Grove Cem., Portsmouth.

Winn, Walter Emmett. b. Greene Co., Alabama, Mar. 4, 1834. att. UAla. m. Willey Glover Griffin, 1857. Taught school, and practiced law in Uniontown and Demopolis, Alabama. Lt. Co. D, 11th Alabama, Mar. 2, 1862. Lt. acting ADC to Wilcox, June 1862. WIA at Frayser's Farm. Capt. AAG to Wilcox, by Second Manassas. WIA at Gettysburg. Capt. AAG to Perrin after Wilcox was promoted. WIA at Spotsylvania, May 12, 1864. MWIA at Petersburg, June 22, 1864. d. July 22, 1864. bur. Prairieville Episc. Church Cem., Marengo Co.

Winston, John H. C. b. in Virginia. Pvt. Co. D, 19th Bn. Virginia Heavy Arty., Mar. 24, 1862. To Lt., Dec. 8, 1862. Lt. acting AQM for battalion, from Oct. 1, 1863, through mid-1864, at least. A 38-year-old cabinetmaker in Pulaski Co., Virginia, in 1870.

Winston, Philip Bickerton. b. Hanover C.H., Virginia, Aug. 12, 1845. A farmer. Pvt. Co. E, 5th Virginia Cavy., 1862. Lt. ADC to his brother-in-law, Gen. Rosser, Oct. 23, 1863. Served into 1865. m. Katharine Deborah Stevens, 1876. Hanover Co. farmer, 1865–1872. Railroad engineer and contractor in North Dakota and Minnesota. Mayor of Minneapolis. d. Chicago, Illinois, July 1, 1901.

Winthrop, Stephen. b. Snitterfield, Warwickshire, England, May 5, 1839. Lt. in British Army, 1855–1862. VADC to Longstreet, Feb. 1863. Capt. AAG to Longstreet, Mar. 28, 1863. Capt. AAIG to Alexander, July 6, 1863. WIA in neck near Knoxville, Nov. 18, 1863. On leave to visit Europe, 1865. Committed suicide near Painswick, Gloucestershire, England, Mar. 13, 1879. Known as "Bull."

Wirz, Hartmann Heinrich. b. Zurich, Switzerland, Nov. 25, 1823. Emigrated to United States in 1849. Bartender and homeopathic physician in Kentucky and Louisiana. Pvt. 4th Bn. Louisiana, 1861. Clerk in PM's office, 1861. Asst. Commandant of Tuscaloosa Prison, 1861–1862. Capt. AAG to J. H. Winder, June 12, 1862, and temporarily commanded all of Richmond's prisons. Absent in Europe, 1863. Capt. AAG, commanded Andersonville Prison, 1864–1865. Hanged for alleged war crimes, Nov. 10, 1865. bur. Mt. Olivet Cem., Washington, D.C.

Wise, George Douglas. b. Sept. 17, 1831. m. Marietta Atkinson. Capt. 39th Virginia. Lt. ADC to his uncle, Gen. Wise, July 17, 1862. Capt. AAIG to Wise, Nov. 2, 1863. MWIA at Petersburg, June 17, 1864. d. July 5. bur. Hollywood Cem., Richmond.

Wise, George Douglas. b. Accomack Co., Virginia, June 4, 1831. att. Wm. & Mary and Univ. of Indiana. Lawyer at Richmond, Virginia. Lt. of Inf., CSA, May 22, 1861. Adjt. 1st Kentucky. VADC to Holmes during Seven Days. VADC to his uncle, Gen. Wise, 1862. Lt. OO, Sept. 20, 1862, assigned to T. H. Taylor's Bgd. Later Capt. OO and AAAIG under Stevenson and Cumming. POW at Vicksburg and WIA at Resaca. USHR and Richmond lawyer. d. there Feb. 4, 1908. bur. Hollywood Cem.

Wise, James Madison. b. Accomack Co., Virginia, June 6, 1834. att. Wm. & Mary. Lived prewar in Alabama and at Washington, D.C. m. Ann Dunlop. Pvt. Co. H, 46th Virginia, Mar. 20, 1862. Began acting as Lt. OO to his uncle, Gen. Wise, Nov. 1862. Lt. OO to Wise, Sept. 6, 1864. Appx. d. Nov. 28, 1890.

Wise, John James Henry. b. Jan. 11, 1830. Capt. Co. F, 39th Virginia, Aug. 26, 1861. Lt. ADC to his uncle, Gen. Wise, May 22, 1862. Resigned July 17, 1862. d. Accomack Co., Virginia, Mar. 16, 1895. bur. Wise family cem.

Wise, Richard Alsop. b. Philadelphia, Pennsylvania, Sept. 2, 1843. att. Wm. & Mary. VADC to his father, Gen. Wise, 1861–1862. Lt. Co. E, 10th Virginia Cavy., May 13, 1862. Lt. OO to Wise, Sept. 6, 1862. Resigned Dec. 26, 1862. Lt. ADC to Wise, Nov. 23, 1863, and acted as AAIG often, too. Appx. att. Medical Coll. of Virginia postwar. m. Maria Daingerfield Peachy, 1870. Physician and USHR. d. Williamsburg, Virginia, Dec. 21, 1900. bur. Hollywood Cem., Richmond.

Withers, John. b. in Tennessee, Feb. 22, 1827. att. USMA. Lt. U.S. Army (infantry and staff positions), 1849–1861. m. Anita Dwyer, 1857. Capt. AAG (CSA), Mar. 16, 1861. Maj. AAG, Oct. 11, 1862. Lt. Col. AAG, probably Jan. 1, 1863. Served into 1865 as top assistant to Adjt. Gen. Samuel Cooper. Postwar merchant and bank cashier at San Antonio, Texas. d. there Feb. 3, 1892. bur. San Fernando Catholic Cem. #1. "His leading characteristic was cheerfulness."

Witherspoon, Thomas Minto. b. in Alabama, June 22, 1837. att. UAla. and UMiss. Lt. Co. A, 11th Alabama. Lt. VADC to Col. J. H. King, Sept.–Oct. 1864. Lt. AAAG to W. H. Forney. Appx. Planter in Marengo Co., alive in 1870.

Withrow, Charles Howard. b. Waynesboro, Virginia, Feb. 6, 1838. att. UVa. Taught school at Natchez, Mississippi. Served in 2nd Co. of Richmond Howitzers. Lt. OO to Rosser, June 14, 1864. Later OO to Dearing. Military record is vague. Professor at Hampden Sidney Coll. and at the Danville Military Academy in Kentucky. Mayor of Waynesboro. d. there Jan. 15, 1921. bur. Riverview Cem.

Wofford, William LaFayette. b. Cartersville, Georgia, ca. 1834. Lt. Co. H, 18th Georgia, June 13, 1861. WIA at Second Manassas. Lt. ADC to Wofford, May 25, 1863. Lived in Etowah Co., Alabama, until 1875. Merchant in Bartow Co., Georgia. Alive 1900 in Indian Territory.

Wolff, Bernard Likens. b. Berkeley Co., Virginia, June 2, 1837. A clerk. Lived at Martinsburg and at Baltimore, Maryland. m. Eliza Preston Benton McDowell. Pvt. Co. D, 2nd Virginia, Apr. 21, 1861. Capt. ACS to Pendleton, Oct. 12, 1861. Maj. CS to Pendleton, May 19, 1862. Maj. CS to Kemper, Sept. 22, 1864. Appx. Moved to Guadalupe Co., Texas, immediately postwar. d. Prince Edward Co., Virginia, June 9, 1869, of consumption.

Womble, John E. b. Isle of Wight Co., Virginia, ca. 1822. m. Virginia C. Poindexter, 1844. m. (2) Kate E. Alfriend, 1871. A bacon merchant at Richmond. Capt. ACS, July 2, 1862. Apparently in Richmond through 1865. Secretary of a sugar refining company at Richmond postwar. Also clerk and asst. supt. of the city almshouse. d. Richmond, July 29, 1894. bur. Hollywood Cem. in an unmarked grave.

Wood, ———. Staff of Rodes during the Seven Days, exact position unknown.

Wood, Charles. b. Albemarle Co., Virginia, Feb. 3, 1836. att. VMI and UVA. Lt. ADC to J. B. Grayson, Sept. 11, 1861. Capt. AAG to Stevenson, Mar. 15, 1862. Capt. AAG to Garland, June–Sept. 1862. POW at Sharpsburg. Capt. AAG and AAAIG to Ripley, Oct. 1862. Spent remainder of war in Georgia, and on the staff of Gen. Manigault. Lawyer in Albemarle Co., Virginia. Later moved to St. Louis, Missouri. d. Charlottesville, Virginia, June 17, 1930.

Wood, D. H. Capt. AQM, June 29, 1861. Maj. QM, Oct. 14, 1862. In charge of securing transportation for soldiers at Richmond, Virginia. Paroled there May 16, 1865. Probably David Henry Wood, from Winchester.

Wood, George Mason. b. Culpeper Co., Virginia, Sept. 9, 1824. Culpeper Co. farmer most of his life. m. Annie Bell Knox. Pvt. Co. E, 13th Virginia, May 4, 1861. Capt. AQM 38th Bn. Virginia Arty., Mar. 28, 1864. Failed confirmation and dropped, July 1864. Reinstated, date unknown. Appx.

d. Culpeper, Aug. 2, 1892. bur. Fairview Cem.

Wood, Jesse S. b. in Alabama, Aug. 12, 1828. Mayor of Lake City, Florida. Capt. Co. I, 3rd Florida, July 13, 1861. Failed reelection, May 1862. Pvt. Co. D, 2nd Bn. Florida, Sept. 5, 1862. To Capt. AQM, Dec. 24, 1862. Capt. AQM, Huger's Bn. Arty., by Nov. 1864. Appx. Postwar grocer. d. Jan. 7, 1900. bur. Oak Lawn Cem., Lake City.

Wood, John. b. in Maryland, Jan. 1, 1832. Merchant at New Orleans, Louisiana. Served as AQM with Tracy's Bgd. Capt. AQM to Washington Arty. Bn., Dec. 1, 1862. Paroled May 1, 1865. d. Oct. 19, 1867, of pneumonia. bur. Lafayette Cem. #1, New Orleans.

Wood, Thomas W. Capt. AQM, Dec. 17, 1862. Served at Charlottesville, Virginia, through the end of the war. Probably Thomas William Wood from Albemarle Co.

Wood, William Basil. b. Nashville, Tennessee, Oct. 31, 1820. att. LaGrange Coll. m. Sarah B. Leftwich, 1843. Lawyer at Florence, Alabama. Col. 16th Alabama. Col. of Cavy., Apr. 24, 1863, and president of First Corps Military Court. Served through 1864 at least. Circuit court judge, lawyer, and railroadman at Florence. d. there Apr. 3, 1891.

Wood, William S. b. 1817. Served briefly in Co. C, 2nd South Carolina, before becoming Capt. AQM for the regiment, Apr. 24, 1861. Maj. QM, Oct. 4, 1862. On duty at Richmond, Virginia. Capt. Co. A, 1st Bn. Virginia Cavy. LDT. "Removed" by July 1863 and dropped Oct. 22, 1863. d. Aug. 4, 1895. bur. Trinity Methodist Churchyard, Alexandria, Virginia. There seem to have been two men of this name in the 2nd South Carolina. The other died in July 1861.

Woods, J. J. Capt. AAIG to Iverson, 1863. No other record found.

Woods, Micajah. b. Albemarle Co., Virginia, May 17, 1844. att. VMI. VADC to Floyd,

1861. Pvt. Co. K, 2nd Virginia Cavy., 1862. Lt. Jackson's (Va.) Horse Arty., 1863. att. UVA. postwar. Lawyer at Charlottesville. m. Matilda Minor Morris, 1874. d. Mar. 14, 1911. Woods's war letters are at UVA.

Woods, Robert Caleb. b. Rocky Mount, Virginia, Sept. 1830. att. UVA. and UPENN. Pvt. Co. B, 24th Virginia, May 23, 1861. Capt. AQM, 24th Virginia, June 23, 1861. Capt. AQM to W. R. Terry, Sept. 15, 1864. Appx. Physician in Obion Co., Tennessee, postwar. d. there Sept. 4, 1873. bur. Hornbeak City Cem.

Woodson, John William. b. Appomattox Co., Virginia, Mar. 8, 1824. att. UVA. m. Mary Elizabeth Christian. Tailor, teacher, and lawyer in Appomattox Co. Capt. AQM, Mar. 1, 1862. Served at Camp Winder, in Richmond, 1862. Capt. AQM at Lynchburg, Virginia, 1863–1864. d. there July 1, 1864. bur. family cem. in Appomattox Co. Woodson's law office survives on the grounds of the national park at Appomattox Court House.

Woodville, William. b. Baltimore, Maryland, Apr. 25, 1828. VADC to Hays at Mine Run. No other record.

Woodward, Peter Hanger. b. Willow Spout, Virginia, Jan. 6, 1823. m. Eliza C. Doak. Capt. AQM, Oct. 4, 1861. On duty at Staunton and Harrisonburg, Virginia. Capt. AQM, 12th Virginia Cavy. Maj. QM to Lomax, Sept. 18, 1863. Maj. QM to Payne later. Railroadman. d. Staunton, Mar. 4, 1902. bur. Thornrose Cem.

Woodward, Thomas William. b. Rockton, South Carolina, May 7, 1833. att. South Carolina Coll. and Wake Forest. Married twice. Maj. 6th South Carolina. WIA at Dranesville. Dropped at the spring 1862 reorganization. Capt. AQM, 20th South Carolina, July 17, 1862. Capt. acting AQM to Ripley, Jan. 1864. Capt. AQM to Conner, Sept. 15, 1864. Presumably same to Kennedy, 1864–1865. In South Carolina legislature postwar. Wrote a pamphlet on the

6th South Carolina. d. at Rockton, Sept. 4, 1902.

Wooldridge, Edwin Spencer. b. Chesterfield Co., Virginia, Sept. 7, 1840. att. VMI and Medical Coll. of Virginia. Pvt. Parker's (Va.) Btty., Mar. 14, 1862. Later to Sgt. Lt. Co. B, 1st Bn. Virginia, Aug. 1863. Resigned. Lt. Parker's Btty., Sept. 10, 1864. Lt. acting OO to Huger's Bn. Arty., by Dec. 1864, into at least Feb. 1865. Commanded Parker's Btty. at Appx. Physician in Chesterfield Co., and a Richmond merchant. d. Sept. 28, 1875, of consumption. bur. Hollywood Cem., Richmond.

Woolley, Andrew Feaster, Jr. b. Kingston, Georgia, Jan. 1840. A resident of Tuskegee, Alabama. Pvt. Co. F, 18th Georgia, June 13, 1861. WIA at Sharpsburg. Lt. ADC to Wofford, Feb. 17, 1863. Capt. AAG to Wofford, May 25, 1863. Admitted to hospital in Nov. 1864 with gunshot wound in leg. Arrested by Wofford about the same time, reason not known. bur. at family cem. at Kingston.

Wootton, Francis Hall. b. 1822. Politician in Utah before the war, and briefly acting governor of the territory in 1861. VADC to Archer and A. P. Hill at Fredericksburg. MWIA Dec. 13, 1862–shot in the head. d. in Richmond at General Hospital #24, Dec. 24, 1862. bur. Oakwood Cem.

Wortham, Richard C. b. Richmond, Virginia, Aug. 2, 1841. m. Sallie L. Staples. Pvt. 1st Co. Richmond Howitzers, Apr. 21, 1861. To Sgt. Detailed on ordnance duty, Dec. 12, 1862. Lt. OO, Apr. 25, 1863, to report to Longstreet. Lt. OO to J. R. Davis, Sept. 28, 1863. Appx. Postwar captain of the Richmond Howitzers, and Richmond grocer. d. there Dec. 28, 1895. bur. Hollywood Cem. Middle name believed to be Chandler.

Worthington, J. Capt. AQM to R. D. Johnston at Appx. No other evidence on pre-1865 service.

Worthington, William Nicholas. b. July 16, 1841. att. UVA. Pvt. Co. I, 4th Virginia Cavy., May 8–Dec. 1861. VADC to J. R. Ander-son, Oct. 1861. Lt. ADC to B. H. Robertson, June 13, 1862. Capt. AAG to Robertson, Feb. 18, 1863. Capt. AAG to Crutchfield's Arty. Bgd., Feb. 4, 1865. d. Toledo, Ohio, June 30, 1871. bur. Hollywood Cem., Richmond.

Wray, George. b. Elizabeth City Co., Virginia, Sept. 10, 1822. att. UVA. Farmer and sheriff in Elizabeth City Co. m. Charlotte Darah Skinner, 1844. Maj. 115th Virginia Militia, 1861–1862. Maj. acting ADC to Magruder, June 1861–June 1862. Capt. ACS to Magruder, Feb. 13, 1863. d. Galveston, Texas, Aug. 22, 1864, of yellow fever. bur. there.

Wrenn, Walter. b. Isle of Wight Co., Virginia, May 29, 1836. att. UVA. and schools in France and Germany. Taught at Hanover (Va.) Academy. Served in Co. I, 3rd Virginia. Capt. AAG to Pryor, May 1, 1862. KIA at Second Manassas, Aug. 30, 1862. bur. on the battlefield 150 yards from the famous Stone House. Has a stone, probably memorial only, at Ivy Hill Cem., Smithfield, Virginia.

Wright, William Ambrose. b. Louisville, Georgia, Jan. 19, 1844. Lt. OO to his father, Gen. A. R. Wright, Aug. 6, 1862. WIA at Second Manassas. WIA at Chancellorsville and right leg amputated. POW near Winchester, June 17, 1863. Retired Sept. 14, 1864. Served on his father's staff at Augusta, Georgia, late in the war, as member of Invalid Corps. Comptroller Gen. of Georgia. d. Sept. 13, 1929. bur. Oakland Cem., Atlanta.

Yancey, Henry Davis. b. Lynchburg, Virginia, Aug. 10, 1842. Cpl. Moorman's (Va.) Btty., May 10, 1861. Discharged Dec. 18, 1861. VADC to his cousin, Gen. Rodes, probably about Jan. 1862. Pvt. Co. E, 2nd Virginia Cavy., Mar. 10, 1863. To Cpl. in 1864. KIA at Spotsylvania, May 8, 1864, while bearing a flag. bur. Lynchburg Presby. Cem.

Yeatman, Philip Tabb. b. in Virginia, Nov. 26, 1829. Living in Gloucester Co. in

1860, a "mariner." Lt. Co. A, 4th Virginia Arty. (34th Virginia). Capt. ACS, Nov. 17, 1862. Post Commissary at Chaffin's Bluff, Virginia, through 1864 at least. m. Anna Maria Dandridge Smith. d. Mar. 18, 1897. bur. Christ Church Cem., Alexandria, Virginia.

Yost, Samuel McPherson. b. Union, Virginia, Nov. 13, 1838. Lived in New Mexico prewar and was a printer in Virginia at Harrisonburg, Staunton, and Clarksburg. Capt. AQM, June 10, 1861. Staff of either R. S. Garnett, W. W. Loring, or both. Post QM at Winchester and Staunton. Dismissed Mar. 23, 1863, by court-martial. Pvt. Co. C, 5th Virginia, Dec. 1, 1864. Operated a newspaper at Staunton postwar. d. there Feb. 21, 1915. bur. Thornrose Cem.

Young, Clement. Worked for Agriculture Dept. at Washington, D.C. Capt. AQM, July 19, 1861. Capt. AQM to Bonham, Oct. 1, 1861. Dropped Feb. 24, 1862, for failing bond. Maj. QM to Beauregard, Mar. 20, 1862. Relieved from duty with AOT, July 7, 1862. Maj. QM to Hays, by Sept. 1862. Maj. QM to Kemper, June 7, 1864. Maj. QM at Gordonsville, Virginia, Mar. 23, 1865. Paroled at Winchester, Apr. 30, 1865.

Young, Henry Edward. b. Grahamville, South Carolina, Aug. 9, 1831. att. South Carolina Coll. and schools in Germany. Charleston lawyer. Capt. AAG to Drayton, Oct. 14, 1861. Relieved at own request, Sept. 1862. Capt. VADC to D. R. Jones at Second Manassas and Sharpsburg. Staff of R. H. Anderson, briefly in Nov. 1862. VADC to Longstreet, Nov.–Dec. 1862. On court-martial duty until assigned as Capt. AAG to R. E. Lee, Feb. 28, 1863. Maj. AAG to Lee, Sept. 20, 1864. Served as Judge Advocate General. Appx. Married twice. d. at Charleston, Apr. 9, 1918. bur. Magnolia Cem. Young's Civil War writings are at Emory, Duke, and the South Carolina Dept. of Archives and History.

Young, Isaac M. b. in Georgia. A 30-year-old lawyer at Lawrenceville in 1860. Also justice of county court. Lt. Co. I, 16th Georgia, May 21, 1862. WIA September 1862. Lt. acting OO to DuBose, by Jan. 1865. Appx. d. July 28, 1868, of consumption.

Young, John. Lt. ADC to Pender, date of appointment not found. Served June–Dec. 1862. WIA in hand at Gaines's Mill. Possibly a VADC only.

Young, John D. Lt. Co. C, 34th North Carolina, Mar. 6, 1863. To Capt., July 1, 1863. Lt. acting ADC to Scales at Gettysburg. Appx.

Young, John M. Pvt. Co. I, 16th Georgia, 1861. Discharged Sept. 25, 1861. Reenlisted in same company, May 21, 1862. To Lt., Sept. 1863. Lt. OO to Wofford's Bgd., by Dec. 1864.

Young, Joseph Judson. b. Wake Co., North Carolina, Jan. 1, 1832. Sgt. Co. D, 26th North Carolina, May 29, 1861. Capt. AQM, 26th North Carolina, Mar. 1, 1862. Capt. AQM to MacRae, Sept. 15, 1864. Married twice. Schoolteacher in Wake Co. and Johnston Co. d. Oct. 3, 1904. bur. Oakland Presby. Church Cem., Smithfield, North Carolina.

Young, Louis Gourdin. b. Grahamville, South Carolina, May 14, 1833. att. Coll. of Charleston. On staff of Col. Pettigrew at Ft. Sumter, Apr. 1861. On engineer duty around Charleston. Lt. ADC to Pettigrew, Mar. 22, 1862. WIA at Seven Pines. Lt. VADC to Pender, June–Aug. 1862. VADC to Ewell at Gaines's Mill and WIA there. WIA three times at Gettysburg. Capt. AAIG to Kirkland, Jan. 13, 1864. WIA twice at Wilderness. Later to MacRae. WIA at Hatcher's Run, Feb. 5, 1865. m. Mary Stuart Waller, 1867. Cotton exporter at Savannah, Georgia. d. there May 31, 1922. bur. St. Michael's Episc. Church, Charleston. A brother of H. E. Young (see above).

Young, William Brooks. b. Marengo Co., Alabama, Sept. 22, 1842. att. UAla. and Furman. Lt. Co. A, 11th Alabama, June 11, 1861. WIA in chest at Gaines's Mill. Lt. AAAG to Sanders, July 1864. Lt. acting ADC to brigade in October 1864, and WIA on Oct. 8. May have been promoted to Capt. AAG of the brigade (Forney's), but official documentation not found. Lawyer in Hale Co., Alabama, in Florida, and in California. Alive 1898 at Jacksonville, Florida.

Zimmer, Louis. Chief of transportation for the Ordnance Dept., 1861–1862. Lt. OO, May 19, 1862, based at Richmond, Virginia. On duty at Richmond Arsenal, and served in Co. A, 5th Bn. Virginia LDT. Lt. Chief of Transportation for ANVa. ordnance, Feb. 9, 1864. On similar duty all around Virginia, beginning in Aug. 1864. Capt. OO, Jan. 7, 1865. Capt. OO to B. R. Johnson, 1865. Appx. Probably the man (a CSA veteran) with this name who died in 1903 and is buried at Mt. Hope Cem., Hastings-on-Hudson, New York.

APPENDIX 1

CONFEDERATE STAFF OFFICERS, OTHER THAN ARMY OF NORTHERN VIRGINIA

Many Confederate armies operated outside of Virginia. The following list, while not definitive, is the most complete roster yet published of staff officers in those armies. It is based on the Compiled Service Records of Confederate General and Staff Officers at the National Archives and on the data assembled by Marcus J. Wright after the war. Approximately 3,000 officers are listed here. Each entry gives the officer's name, rank, and position. Biographical details, such as middle name and years of birth and death, have been added when known, although the compiler admittedly has made no effort to aggressively research these men. The list is published more as a public service, with the hope that some historian of the western armies will convert this lifeless mass of names and dates into more elaborate biographical sketches. It would be a useful and important reference tool.

Users comparing this appendix with the system followed in the main body of the book will notice two significant differences. The appendix does not list any post officers, regardless of rank or duties, unless they served in Virginia at a location not considered part of the main sphere of operations. Thus a major in the quartermaster's department in Mobile would not appear anywhere in this book, and a major QM in Harrisonburg, Virginia, would receive full biographical treatment in the main roster section of this book. A second difference concerns staff officers who served in brigades not commanded by generals. Men whose only staff duty occurred at the brigade level, during the tenure of some senior colonel, have not been included in this appendix. The appendix covers officers who served on the staffs of generals only, outside the Army of Northern Virginia's zone of operations.

Abercrombie, Robert S., Capt. AAG to Clanton (d. 1864)

Abercrombie, Wiley, Lt. ADC to French

Abernathy, Samuel, Capt. AAIG to Shelley

Abrahams, A. D., Capt. AQM & IFT to S. D. Lee

Adams, ——, Lt. staff of Gano

Adams, C., Lt. OO to Richardson

Adams, Charles W., Col. AAIG to Hindman (1817–1878)

Adams, G. W., ADC to Forrest

Adams, John Dunning, Maj. VADC to Fagan (1827–1892)

Adams, Richard Henry, Jr., Capt. EO to Wheeler (1841–1896)

Adams, Thomas Patton, Maj. CS to John Adams (1836–1901)

Addison, ——, VADC to Breckinridge

Airey, Fred. W., Capt. AAG to Hays

Alderson, George W., Capt. ACS at Abingdon, Va.

Aldrich, Lyman G., Capt. AAG to Slaughter (b. 1839)

Alexander, J. C., Lt. acting ADC to L. M. Walker

Alexander, John W., Lt. OO to Reynolds

Alexander, Samuel J., Maj. acting CS to Richardson

Allen, Bryan H., Capt. AAG to E. K. Smith and Duke

Allen, George A., Maj. QM to Breckinridge

Allen, George Davidson, Capt. ADC to Davidson

Allen, George W., Lt. Col. ADC to Price (d. 1861)

Allen, Henry Watkins, Col. Military Court of Pemberton (1820–1866)

Allen, J. F., Capt. ACS to Ro. H. Anderson

Allen, John James, Capt. AQM at Buchanan, Va. (b. 1831)

Allen, T. J., Capt. AAIG to Colquitt; Capt. ACS to W. W. Allen

Allen, William Gaston, ADC to Drayton

Allison, Alexander, Jr., OO to Maney, Mercer, Featherston

Allison, Dixon A., Capt. AAG to Dibrell (d. 1863)

Allison, John D., Capt. OO to McCown

Allison, Thomas Fearn Perkins, Capt. AAIG to Bell (1832–1913)

Allston, Benjamin, Col. AAIG to E. K. Smith (1833–1900)

Alston, Robert A., Capt. AAG to J. H. Morgan; VADC to Cheatham (d. 1879)

Anderson, Alexander Givens, Maj. CS to Cockrell, French (1830–1900)

Anderson, C. Samuel, Lt. acting ADC to Cockrell

Anderson, Charles DeWitt, Maj. AAAG to Gladden (1827–1901)

Anderson, Charles W., Capt. ADC to Forrest (1825–1909)

Anderson, Edward Clifford, Jr., Lt. ADC to Mercer (1838–1876)

Anderson, H. M., VADC to Stevenson

Anderson, J. M., Col. VADC to Major

Anderson, James Boys, Maj. Chief Arty. to Vaughn (d. 1863)

Anderson, John H., Col. VADC to B. R. Johnson

Anderson, Joseph Washington, Maj. Chief Arty. to Stevenson (1836–1863)

Anderson, Robert Houstoun, Maj. AAG to W. H. T. Walker, Trapier (1835–1888)

Anderson, Thomas F., Capt. AAG to Watie

Anderson, Thomas Scott, Lt. Col. AAIG to Magruder (d. 1868)

Anderson, Walker, Lt. AAAG to Hindman, Tucker; Capt. OO to J. P. Anderson

Anderson, Waverly F., Capt. OO to Shelby

Anderson, William J., Maj. QM to Polk, Villepigue

Anderson, William L., Lt. ADC to Rust, Fagan

Andrews, Arthur W., Lt. AAIG to A. R. Johnson

Andrews, E. J., Lt. OO to Maxey

Andrews, E. Lewis, Lt. ADC to J. E. Harrison

Andrews, James Jackson, Lt. ADC to Roddey (1838–1896)

Andrews, John Frederick, Maj. AAG to Cobb (1830–1892)

Andrews, P. B., Lt. AAIG to B. R. Johnson

Andrews, Robert C., Lt. ADC to Maxey

Anglade, J. G., AAAG to Zollicoffer

Archer, William S., Lt. OO to Chalmers

Armant, Henry, VADC to Heth

Armistead, John M., Capt. OO to Loring, Pemberton

Armstrong, D. J., Lt. ADC to Armstrong; Capt. AAIG to Starke

Armstrong, Frank Crawford, Lt. AAG & ADC

to Ben McCulloch, McIntosh; VADC to
Van Dorn (1835–1909)

Armstrong, Henry Clay, Lt. ADC to Ross
(1840–1900)

Armstrong, James Trooper, Maj. OO to Fagan
(d. 1873)

Armstrong, William Park, VADC to Zollicoffer, Crittenden, McCown (1843–1901)

Atkins, Benjamin Franklin, Col. VADC to
Chalmers (d. 1894)

Atkins, George S., Maj. QM to Quarles

Auguste, Albert N., Maj. CS to Tappan
(ca. 1816–1864)

Augustin, Numa, Maj. VADC to Beauregard

Avent, W. F., Capt. AQM to Chalmers

Ayres, ———, Lt. staff of Rust

Bacon, E. M., Capt. AQM to Maxey

Bacon, John E., staff of Chesnut

Bacon, John P., Lt. ADC to J. T. Morgan

Bailey, T. B., Lt. OO to Palmer, Vance, J. G.
Martin

Baily, J. N., Capt. AAG & ACS to Dibrell

Bain, George C., Lt. SO to Breckinridge,
D. H. Hill, Whiting, Bragg

Bain, John, staff of Cobb

Baird, Albert C., Capt. ACS to McNair

Baker, A. N., Lt. AAAG to Gladden

Baker, J. W., Lt. AQM to Lyon

Baker, John W., Capt. ACS to Moore

Baker, Robert P., Lt. AAAG to Holtzclaw

Baker, Thomas Henry, Maj. VADC to French
(b. 1836)

Baldwin, John Milton, Capt. OO to French
(d. 1895)

Baldwin, John P., Maj. CS to Finegan

Ball, Charles Pollard, Maj. Chief Arty. to
Cleburne; OO to Forney

Ball, George Claiborne, Maj. CS to Kelly,
W. W. Allen (1841–1910)

Ballance, C. W., Capt. acting ADC to Maxey

Ballard, W. W., VADC to Reynolds

Ballentine, A. J., Maj. ADC to Gordon

Ballos, ———, Capt. AQM to Cabell

Baltzell, James Preston, Capt. AQM to Maxey;
AAIG to Bragg (1838–1868)

Bankhead, Smith Pyne, Maj. Chief Arty. to
Leo. Polk; Col. Chief Arty. to Magruder
(1823–1867)

Banks, Edwin Alexander, Maj. QM to Loring,
Lovell, Pemberton (1838–1868)

Banks, George T., Lt. ADC to Chalmers

Banks, Robert, Lt. AAG to G. D. Johnston

Banner, M. R., Lt. OO to Cumming

Barbee, Samuel E., Capt. ACS to Pillow; Maj.
CS to Cheatham

Barbour, Edgar P., Lt. ADC to Tilghman,
Hawes; AAAG to Buckner

Bard, Samuel, Capt. acting ADC to Ruggles

Barker, Thomas M., Lt. AAIG to Davidson

Barkley, James E., Maj. QM to J. E. Rains

Barlow, Milton, Lt. OO to Duke, Buford

Barlow, U. P., Capt. OO to Cockrell

Barnes, James M., Capt. OO to Dibrell

Barnewall, William, Jr., Maj. QM to Chalmers

Barnwell, John Gibbes, II, Maj. OO & AAIG to
Trapier (1816–1905)

Barnwell, Robert Hayne, Capt. EO to Gilmer,
Taliaferro, B. H. Robertson (1834–1872)

Barr, James, Jr., Capt. AAIG to Chalmers
(1830–1864)

Barr, John W., Lt. AAIG to W. H. Jackson

Barrett, Thomas G., Lt. OO to J. K. Jackson

Barrett, W. W., Maj. QM to E. K. Smith

Barrow, Bartholomew, Maj. AAG to McCown

Barrow, Middleton Pope, Lt. ADC to Cobb
(1839–1903)

Barry, F. B., Capt. OO to Ripley

Barth, William G., Capt. AAG to J. P. Anderson, Ed Johnson, W. M. Gardner, J. K.
Jackson, Tucker

Bartlett, George T., Capt. AAIG to Iverson

Bartlett, Thaddeus J., Capt. AAIG to Scott

Barton, James S., AAG to Palmer

Baskerville, Charles, VADC to John Adams
(1821–1890)

Bass, J. W., Lt. AAIG to Cumming

Bassett, W. H., Maj. QM to Maxey, Major

Bate, Aaron S., Lt. ADC to Bate (d. 1863)

Bate, James H., Capt. ADC to Bate

Bates, R. P., Capt. AQM to Richardson

Battle, James, Lt. ADC to Slaughter (d. 1880)

Battle, Nicholas Williams, Lt. Col. AAIG to
Maxey (1820–1905)

Bayley, Edmond, Capt. ACS to Davidson

Baylor, Eugene Wythe, Maj. QM to Duncan,
Strahl, Pettus (1834–1918)

Baylor, George Wythe, Lt. ADC to A. S.
Johnston (1832–1916)

Beall, John Alphonso, Lt. OO to Ector

Beall, Thomas Balch, Maj. QM to Tucker, J. P.
Anderson

Bean, Hugh H., Capt. AAG to Gibson

Beard, William Dwight, Maj. QM to Stewart,
Strahl (1838–1910)

Beard, William Kelly, Maj. QM to Strahl; Lt.
Col. AAG to Hardee, Jones; AAIG to J. K.
Jackson (1830–1882)

Bearden, John T., Capt. AAG to Hawthorne
(b. 1826)

Bearden, R. M., Lt. AAAIG to Humes

Beasley, James Edward, acting ADC to Strahl
(1839–1925)

Beatty, Henry K., Capt. OO to Vaughan

Beatty, Taylor, Col. Military Court of Hardee,
S. D. Lee (1837–1920)

Beauchamp, John J., Maj. CS to J. K. Jackson

Beauland, William G., Capt. AQM to Walthall

Beaumont, Henry, volunteer acting AQM &
acting ACS to Sibley

Beauregard, Rene Toutant, Maj. VADC to
Beauregard (1843–1910)

Beck, Francis P., Maj. QM to Ruggles, W. W.
Adams

Beck, G. M., Capt. VADC to Ruggles

Beck, Joseph Hardd, Maj. QM to T. Green,
Wharton

Bedford, Hugh L., Lt. OO to W. W. Adams
(b. 1836)

Beecher, Edward A., Maj. QM to Vaughan,
Hood (1834–1873)

Beggs, James, Capt. EO to Higgins

Behan, J. Henry, Maj. CS to Buford

Behan, Thomas W., Lt. VADC to Ruggles;
acting ACS to Buford

Behen, Dennis, Jr., Capt. AQM to Fagan

Bein, Hugh Hagert, Lt. AAAG to Gibson
(1841–1884)

Belding, Albert, Maj. ADC to Fagan

Bell, A. W., acting ADC to D. H. Reynolds

Bell, B. T., Capt. ADC to Bell

Bell, Isaac Thomas, Lt. ADC to Bell (1841–
1914)

Bell, J. S., Lt. AAG & AAIG to Bell (d. 1864)

Bell, James B., Capt. AQM to Sharp

Bell, Marcus Lafayette, Capt. AAG to Roane,
Maxey (1829–1893)

Bell, Percy, Lt. OO to Stovall

Bell, Thomas F., Capt. AQM to Drayton

Belt, Augustus W., Lt. ADC to D. H. Reynolds

Beltzhoover, Daniel, AAAG to Twiggs

Beltzhoover, Samuel G., Capt. AAAG to J. E.
Rains, Van Dorn

Benagh, James, Capt. AAG to E. K. Smith,
Winder (b. 1828)

Benedict, Joe, staff of J. H. Morgan

Benham, Calhoun, Maj. VADC to A. S. Johnston; Maj. AAIG to Breckinridge; Maj. AAG
to Cleburne (d. 1884)

Bennett, William K., Maj. QM to Bell, Beall

Benoit, James W., Capt. AAG to Baldwin,
Sears, Brantley

Benton, Benjamin E., Capt. ADC & AAG to
H. E. McCulloch (1839–1914)

Benton, Charles R., Capt. OO to Hawes

Berry, Joel H., VADC to Chalmers

Berry, Robert, Capt. acting ACS to Duke

Berry, Thomas J., acting ADC & AAAG to
Lawton (1835–1865)

Bertrand, Robert C., Lt. ADC & Capt. OO to
Rust

Bertus, William E., Lt. AAIG to Breckinridge

Bethea, Henry, Lt. ADC to D. W. Adams
(1836–1923)

Bethell, William Decatur, Capt. ADC to
Pillow (1840–1906)

Bilisoly, Antonio L., Lt. AAAG to Blanchard
(d. 1907)

Billups, John Marshall, Maj. QM to John
Adams (1824–1902)

Billups, Joseph Pierce, Capt. AQM to John
Adams, Lowry (1826–1887)

Bird, ——, Capt. VADC to Breckinridge

Bird, W. C., Col. Military Court of Beauregard

Bird, W. M., Capt. OO to Iverson

Bishop, Benjamin Franklin, Lt. AAAG & AAAIG to M. J. Wright (1839–1868)

Black, Edward J., Lt. ADC to A. Baker

Black, Marcus W., Lt. AAAIG to B. R. Johnson

Black, Samuel L., Capt. AAG to Hardee

Blackburn, Breckinridge F., Capt. AAIG & AAG to Churchill

Blackburn, Joseph Clay Stiles, Capt. AAG to W. Preston (1838–1918)

Blackburn, Luke Pryor, VADC to Price (1816–1887)

Blackmore, Thomas J., Lt. ADC to Hawthorne

Blackwood, Crawford, Lt. ADC to John Adams

Blake, Edward D., Lt. Col. AAIG to Leo. Polk, Hardee (d. 1882)

Blake, Walter, VADC to Ripley

Blakemore, Marcus Newton, VADC to B. R. Johnson (b. 1835)

Blanchard, Dawson A., VADC to Blanchard

Blanchard, James G., Lt. AAIG to Cheatham

Blanchard, Thomas E., Lt. AAAG & ADC to Bate

Blanchard, William L., Maj. staff of J. H. Morgan

Bledsoe, Oscar Fitzallen, Lt. OO to John Adams (b. 1840)

Blessing, P. J., acting Lt. EO to Hebert

Blice, B. B., Lt. OO to Marmaduke

Blount, John G., Maj. QM to L. Hebert

Blount, Thomas William, AAG to Gladden; Capt. ADC to H. W. Allen

Blucher, Felix A., Capt. EO to Bee; Maj. EO to Magruder (1819–1879)

Boatrite, A. V., Capt. ACS at Franklin, Va.

Boatwright, John L., Cadet acting ADC to Ripley

Boggess, R. O., Capt. AQM to J. B. Clark, Marmaduke

Boggs, Robert, Lt. ADC to Boggs

Bolles, Charles Patterson, Maj. EO to Whiting, Holmes (1823–1909)

Bolling, L. Summerfield, Capt. acting AQM to Hawes

Bond, Lewis, Capt. OO to W. H. Jackson (1839–1878)

Bondurant, James William, Lt. Col. Chief Arty. to D. H. Hill

Bonford, Peter E., Lt. ADC to R. Taylor

Bonner, William G., Maj. EO to Marshall

Boon, Hampton L., Capt. AQM to Van Dorn, Armstrong

Booth, Henry, Capt. ACS to Churchill, McRae

Booth, Roswell V., Lt. OO to Liddell

Borland, Harold, Lt. AAAG to Chalmers; Maj. AAIG to Slaughter (1835–1921)

Bostick, John Litton, Lt. ADC to Liddell, Govan (1826–1864)

Bostick, Joseph, Capt. AAIG to Cheatham (1832–1886)

Bostick, Thomas Hardin, Capt. ACS to Vaughn; Maj. CS to Maney (1833–1871)

Boswell, James R., Capt. AQM to L. E. Polk

Botts, Benjamin A., Maj. QM to E. K. Smith, Wharton

Botts, Henry Triplett, Lt. ADC to Stevenson (1838–1889)

Boudinot, Elias Cornelius, Col. VADC to Hindman (1835–1890)

Bourne, William T., Lt. Col. AAIG to Fagan

Boutwell, ——, Lt. acting ADC to Hardee

Bowen, Henry S., Maj. CS to Marshall (b. 1820)

Bowie, Allen Thomas, Capt. AAG to W. W. Adams (1840–1925)

Bowie, John A., Maj. CS to Gist

Boyd, Alfred, Maj. QM to Tilghman, Breckinridge

Boyd, Edward Kingston, Lt. OO to A. W. Reynolds

Boyd, James M., Lt. OO to Jones, W. L. Jackson

Boyd, Theodore B., Capt. acting ACS to J. H. Morgan

Boykin, A. H., Capt. Judge Advocate to Beauregard

Boyles, John M., Capt. ACS to Brantley

Bradford, Hiram S., Maj. AAG to McCown, Walthall, Pillow (1830–1873)

Bradford, James W., Capt. AQM to Breckinridge, S. D. Lee, D. H. Hill, Hindman, Hood

Bradford, Jefferson Davis, Capt. AAG to Gladden, D. W. Adams, F. Gardner (1838–1910)

Bradford, John, Capt. AAIG & AAAG to Donelson

Bradford, John R., Maj. AAIG to Davis

Bradford, Robert M., Maj. QM to Gholson

Bradford, S. P., Capt. ADC to Wheeler

Bradfute, William R., Capt. AAG to Ben McCulloch, Van Dorn (1821–1906)

Bradley, Benjamin Franklin, Capt. AAG to Marshall (1825–1897)

Bradley, John, Lt. AAIG to H. E. McCulloch

Bradley, William J., Maj. QM to Williams

Brand, Horace H., Col. AAG to Price; Capt. AAAG to Forrest, Chalmers

Brandon, James M., Maj. AAG to Steele

Brandon, Robert L., VADC & Capt. AAG to Brandon

Branham, Isham R., Capt. AAG to Iverson

Branland, W. G., Capt. AQM to Brantley

Bransford, John Sweezy, Maj. QM at AOT Headquarters (1836–1907)

Bransford, Thomas L., Capt. OO to Walthall, Quarles

Brazelton, William, Col. VADC to Vaughn

Breathe, Henry, Jr., Lt. OO to Vaughan

Breckinridge, Joseph Cabell, Lt. ADC to Breckinridge (b. 1844)

Bredell, Edward, Jr., Lt. ADC to Bowen

Bredow, Gustavus, Capt. AQM to A. Thomas

Breedlove, Napoleon B., Maj. CS to Cooper

Breedow, Robert R., Lt. OO to H. E. McCulloch

Bremer, W. J., Capt. AQM to Featherston

Brewer, James Fielding, Maj. VADC to Crittenden; Lt. Col. VADC to Breckinridge (1836–1864)

Brewer, Richard, Capt. ADC to Wheeler (d. 1864)

Brewster, D. F., Lt. ADC to Cumming

Brewster, H. B., Capt. AAG to Shelby

Brewster, Henry Percy, Capt. AAG to A. S. Johnston (1816–1887)

Brice, Jacob, Capt. OO to Lovell; OO to S. D. Lee

Brickell, William W., Lt. acting AAG to Wood

Bricknell, James Noaidle, Lt. OO to Gist

Bridewell, Charles A., Capt. AQM to Liddell

Bridewell, Lemuel O., Maj. QM to Hardee, Govan

Bridges, Lyman, Col. VADC to D. H. Hill

Bridges, William McKinnley, Lt. ADC to Duncan; acting ADC to Bragg (1835–1907)

Bridgewater, John C., Maj. CS to W. T. Martin (1823–1864)

Brien, J., Capt. OO to Lovell

Bright, A. D., Capt. staff of Chalmers

Brinker, Isaac, Maj. QM to Price

Broadfoot, Charles Wetmore, Lt. Col. VADC to Holmes (1842–1919)

Broadwell, W. A., Lt. Col. QM to E. K. Smith

Brodnax, Robert, Capt. ADC to Waul

Broocks, Lycurgus W., Lt. OO to Armstrong

Brooke, Walker, VADC to A. W. Reynolds (1813–1869)

Brooks, Samuel H., Maj. VADC to Cheatham (d. 1910)

Brooks, Uriah J., Capt. AAIG to L. M. Walker

Broome, John D., Lt. OO to Finley

Brother, Howard J., Lt. ADC to Armstrong

Broughton, A. Ben., Lt. AAAG to Gibson

Broun, Thomas Lee, Maj. QM to Heth & at Dublin Depot, Va. (1823–1914)

Brown, Benjamin Johnson, Col. VADC to Slack (1807–1861)

Brown, Esmenard, Capt. AQM to Tilghman

Brown, George W., Lt. ADC to Roddey

Brown, James Trim, Lt. ADC to Brown

Brown, John A., Capt. Chief Arty. to Gatlin; Lt. Col. Chief Arty. to E. K. Smith, Maury (d. 1877)

Brown, John Henry, Maj. AAG to H. E. McCulloch (1820–1895)

Brown, John Lucien, Maj. QM to Zollicoffer, Bate (1800–1884)

Brown, John W., Maj. CS to T. Green, Wharton

Brown, Manning, Lt. ADC to Cantey

Brown, N. H., Maj. AAAG to Trapier; Maj. CS to Withers

Brown, Nathan B., Capt. AQM to McLaws, Mercer, Walthall (d. 1876)

Brown, Thomas Woolrige, Judge Advocate to Leo. Polk

Browne, Richard Horace, Lt. AAIG to J. P. Anderson, Withers, Walthall (b. 1830)

Browne, W. R., acting OO to John Adams; staff of Hebert, Maury

Brownrigg, Richard Thomas, Maj. CS to Sibley (d. 1863)

Brusle, Charles A., Capt. ADC to L. Hebert

Bryan, Asbury M., Capt. AAIG & Maj. QM to J. K. Jackson

Bryan, Edward K., Lt. AAAG to Hagood

Bryan, Guy Morrison, Maj. AAG to Holmes, E. K. Smith (1821–1901)

Bryarly, Joseph L., Capt. ACS to Ross; acting ACS to Hebert

Bryce, Henry, Lt. OO to Wharton

Buchanan, Andrew Hays, Lt. EO to Bragg, J. E. Johnston, A. S. Johnston (1828–1914)

Buchanan, G. J., AAIG to Roddey

Buchanan, Samuel H., Capt. AAIG & AAG to Lewis (1838–1915)

Buchanan, Thomas Griffin, Capt. OO to Parsons

Buck, Irving A., Capt. AAG to Cleburne (d. 1912)

Buck, John C., Lt. OO to Breckinridge

Buck, John T., Lt. OO to Chalmers

Buck, Samuel H., Capt. AAG to Price, Holmes (1841–1929)

Buckingham, S. H., VADC to Lyon

Buckman, Thomas E., Lt. OO to Finegan, J. P. Anderson, J. K. Jackson

Buckner, D. P., Lt. VADC to Buckner, Beall

Buckner, Frank P., Lt. OO to Williams; Capt. OO to J. H. Morgan

Buckner, James R., Lt. OO to Davidson

Buckner, John Alexander, Capt. VADC to C. Clark; Maj. AAIG to E. K. Smith; Lt. Col. AAG to Breckinridge (1832–1903)

Buffaloe, Joseph G. M., Capt. VADC to Chalmers (d. 1898)

Buist, Henry, Capt. AAAG to Ripley (1829–1887)

Bulkley, Henry D., Maj. CS to J. P. Anderson, Hardee

Bull, Charles Pinckney, Lt. AAG to Wood (1846–1916)

Bull, William Izard, Col. staff of Beauregard (1813–1894)

Bullock, Waller Overton, Lt. AAG to Buckner (b. 1842)

Bullock, Waller R., Lt. ADC to Hodge

Bullock, William F., Jr., Capt. AAG to Cosby, Maury, R. Taylor

Burch, John Christopher, Capt. AAG to Pillow, Withers; ADC to Pillow (1827–1881)

Burford, Elisha Spruille, Maj. AAG to Wheeler, Hardee (1839–1894)

Burke, Edward A., Maj. IFT to E. K. Smith (b. 1841)

Burke, James A., Lt. OO to Sears

Burke, Malcolm Clayton, Lt. OO to Cantey (b. 1836)

Burke, Thomas A., Lt. OO to Sears

Burke, Thomas A., Maj. QM to Taliaferro

Burnet, David G., VADC to Hebert

Burnet, William Estes, Capt. Chief Arty. to Cabell; Col. Chief Arty. to Maury (d. 1865)

Burnett, W. K., Maj. QM to Buford

Burns, Henry, Lt. ACS to Drayton

Burr, Edwin Burton, Capt. AAG to Shelby (d. 1872)

Burriss, Fletcher R., Lt. acting ADC to Brown, Reynolds

Bursley, A. A., Capt. Chief Arty. to Loring

Burtell, J. R., Maj. AAIG to Bragg

Burton, William O., Capt. AQM to Brandon

Burtwell, John Robertson Bedford, Lt. acting ADC to Hardee; Capt. Chief Arty. to Withers (1835–1873)

Burwell, Armistead, Capt. AAG to Armstrong (1839–1913)

Bush, Augustus H., VADC to Pike

Bush, Louis, Maj. AAG to Mouton (b. 1820)

Butler, ——, Lt. EO to F. Gardner

Butler, Baxter J., Maj. CS to Cheatham

Butler, James, Capt. VADC to Butler

Butler, James W., Capt. AAG to Churchill

Butler, Lawrence Lewis, Lt. AAAG to Leo. Polk; Maj. AAAG to M. J. Wright (1837–1898)

Butler, Lee M., Capt. ADC to Gist

Butler, W. O., Lt. AAIG to Kelly

Buxton, Robert, Capt. ACS to Tappan, Frost

Byrd, Augustine J., Maj. CS to Parsons

Byrd, James, Lt. OO at Dublin Depot, Va.

Byrd, William M., Capt. ACS to W. T. Martin, Iverson

Byrne, Charles Hubert, Capt. VADC to Cleburne (d. 1908)

Byser, Charles, VADC to Little

Cabell, Algernon Sidney, Maj. QM to Steele, Cabell (b. 1832)

Cabell, Edward Carrington, Maj. QM to Price (1816–1896)

Cabler, L. F., Capt. AQM to Pillow

Cage, D. C., Maj. acting EO to Price

Cage, Duncan S., Col. VADC to E. K. Smith

Cahall, Terry H., Maj. AAIG to Stewart

Cain, William H., Capt. VADC to French

Callaway, Jonathan W., Maj. CS to Tappan

Cameron, John D., Capt. acting AQM to Stevens

Cameron, John Wilder, Maj. QM to Gatlin, Whiting, D. H. Hill (1828–1901)

Cammack, George, Lt. OO to Adams

Cammack, Richard Charles, Capt. ACS to S. D. Lee

Camp, Anthony S., Capt. AQM to Cheatham, Maney

Campbell, Charles C., Capt. OO to Wheeler

Campbell, Charles J., Capt. AQM to Strahl, Cheatham, Bowen (1836–1909)

Campbell, James Knox P., Maj. CS to Churchill, E. K. Smith

Campbell, John J., Lt. acting ADC to Cheatham (d. 1862)

Campbell, Josiah Adams Patterson, Col. Military Court of Leo. Polk (1830–1917)

Cantey, John, Maj. CS to Cantey

Cantwell, Edward Payne, Lt. ADC to Clingman (1825–1891)

Caperton, George Henry, Lt. ADC to Echols (1828–1895)

Cargill, William M., Maj. QM to Chalmers, Buford

Carington, Emmet, Lt. ADC to Lane

Carl-Lee, Reuben B., VADC to Deshler (b. 1841)

Carlisle, Samuel Stuart, Lt. OO to Baldwin, Bowen; Capt. AAG to Gardner (1836–1907)

Carlisle, Thomas J., Lt. OO to Moore

Carlton, Herman, Lt. ADC & Maj. AAIG to Cabell

Carmack, J. Y., Lt. AAIG to Lowry

Carothers, James S., Lt. ADC to Starke

Carr, ——, Capt. VADC to Trapier

Carr, H. W., Capt. VADC to N. G. Evans

Carr, James Lawrence, Maj. CS at Dublin Depot, Va. (1813–1875)

Carr, Joseph P., Maj. CS to Villepigue, Withers, Gardner

Carrington, John C., Capt. ADC to Dockery

Carrington, John S., Lt. ADC to Rust; Capt. AAG to Rust, Tappan

Carrington, L. F., ADC to Buckner

Carrington, Paul R., Capt. AAIG to Shelby (b. 1840)

Carrington, T. F., acting ADC to Baldwin

Carrington, Walter C., Capt. ADC to McNair

Carrington, William Thornton, Lt. acting OO to Sibley

Carroll, William H., Jr., Capt. ADC to Carroll; Capt. AAAG to Chalmers (1843–1916)

Carruth, E. B., Maj. CS to J. P. Anderson, Tucker

Carruthers, J. Slought, Capt. staff of Richardson

Carter, ——, Lt. oo to Brown, Reynolds

Carter, Benjamin Franklin, Lt. ADC to Bowen; Maj. CS to Bowen, Brown, Palmer (1828–1910)

Carter, J., Capt. AQM to Chalmers

Carter, Joseph P., Lt. acting oo to Walthall

Carter, Theodorick Todd, Lt. ADC to Tyler (1840–1864)

Caruth, Walter, Capt. AQM to Lane

Caruthers, R., Lt. ADC to Stewart

Cary, Samuel, acting ADC to N. G. Evans

Cason, A. H., Lt. oo to Cumming (1832 1894)

Casseday, Alexander, Capt. ADC & Maj. AAIG to Buckner (d. 1862)

Cavanaugh, John, Capt. EO to Higgins

Cave, Eber Worthington, Maj. VADC to Magruder (1831–1904)

Cearnal, James T., Capt. ADC to Price

Chaffie, Orestes P., Maj. QM to Wheeler, Bragg

Chalmers, Hamilton Henderson, Maj. AAG & VADC to Chalmers; Maj. CS to Withers (1835–1885)

Chalmers, W. Leigh, Capt. AAG to Major; Maj. AAG to T. Green

Chamberlain, D. C., Lt. acting ADC to McCown

Chambers, James R., Capt. AAIG to J. E. Johnston, Logan, W. W. Adams; ADC to Beall

Chambers, Robert A., Capt. AAG to Cantey, Humes

Chambliss, Nathaniel Rives, Capt. oo to Buckner, Hardee, A. S. Johnston; Maj. oo to Villepigue (1834–1897)

Chambliss, William R., Lt. AAAG to W. Preston

Champion, S. S., Lt. VADC to S. D. Lee

Champneys, John Tunno, Capt. oo to Leo. Polk (d. 1891)

Chandler, John Lawrence, Capt. AAG to Clanton (b. 1838)

Chapin, William P., Lt. AAIG to Dibrell

Chapman, Henry, Lt. AAIG to Wheeler; Lt. ADC to Major

Chapman, John S., Capt. AAAIG to Strahl

Chapman, John W., Capt. ACS to Clayton, Holtzclaw

Cheatham, Boyd Munroe, Maj. QM to McCown, Pillow, H. R. Jackson (1838–1877)

Cheatham, Ephraim Foster, Capt. AQM to Morgan

Cheatham, John Anderson, Lt. ADC & Maj. oo to Cheatham (1826–1903)

Cheatham, R. S., Lt. AAAG to J. K. Jackson

Cheney, Hampton Johnson, Capt. AAG to Brown, Bate (1836–1927)

Chesnut, James, Jr., Col. VADC to Beauregard (1815–1885)

Chesnut, Pleasant E., Lt. ADC to Parsons

Chester, William Yemans, Capt. ACS to Tappan (b. 1833)

Cheves, Langdon, Capt. VADC & volunteer EO to Drayton (1818–1863)

Chew, Morris R., Capt. acting AQM to Higgins

Childs, Frederick Lynn, Capt. oo to Ripley, Holmes (d. 1894)

Chilton, George Washington, Col. oo to Bee (1828–1883)

Chipley, Stephen F., Maj. ADC to Buckner

Christmas, Henry H., Capt. Chief Arty. to Wharton

Church, S., Lt. acting ADC to Wood

Clagett, Thomas Hawkins, Jr., Capt. so to Beauregard, Maury (1839–1881)

Claiborne, Thomas, Capt. VADC to Hardee; staff of Buckner (1823–1911)

Claiborne, Willis Herbert, AAG to A. W. Reynolds (1834–1869)

Clanton, William H., Lt. ADC to Clanton

Clare, William, Capt. VADC to Wood; Maj. AAIG to Bragg, Hardee, J. E. Johnston

Clark, A. G., Lt. ADC to Gibson

Clark, E. D., AAAG to Walthall

Clark, G. W., Capt. acting oo to Shoup

Clark, Henry M., Maj. AAIG to Price, Churchill

Clark, J. W., Capt. AAIG to Hawthorne

Clark, James G., Capt. OO to Cheatham
(b. 1837)

Clark, John, Capt. OO to S. D. Lee

Clark, John M., VADC to Baldwin

Clark, Michael R., Maj. AAG to Chesnut

Clark, O., Lt. AAIG to Palmer

Clark, Reuben Douglas, Capt. AAAG to Bell
(1834–1864)

Clark, Thomas C., Maj. QM to A. W. Reynolds

Clark, William, Capt. ACS to Chalmers

Clarke, Alfred G., Lt. staff of Gibson

Clarke, George W., Maj. QM to Ben
McCulloch

Clarke, John G., Capt. AAG to H. W. Allen,
Thomas

Clarke, John Lyle, Lt. ADC & Maj. AAG to
Loring (1833–1898)

Clarke, L. C., Capt. SO and VADC to W. S.
Walker

Clarke, Powhatan, Capt. OO to Polignac; Lt.
Col. OO to Buckner (1836–1903)

Clarke, William H., staff of Churchill

Clarkson, A. W., Capt. acting ADC to Hardee

Clay, C. C., Capt. OO to Richardson

Clay, Henry B., Capt. AAIG to Davidson,
E. K. Smith, Hodge, Pegram

Clay, James B., Lt. VADC to Breckinridge;
Cadet to E. K. Smith

Clay, Thomas J., Maj. AAG to Buckner
(d. 1863)

Clayton, Edwin M., Capt. acting CS to A. W.
Reynolds

Clayton, George Wesley, Lt. ADC to J. G.
Martin (1841–1900)

Clayton, Thomas L., EO to S. D. Lee

Clendenin, John P., Maj. AAG to Shelby

Cleveland, James W., Lt. acting ACS to A. W.
Reynolds, Palmer

Clift, Moses H., Capt. ACS to Dibrell (b. 1836)

Clinch, J. H. N., Lt. Col. staff of Hardee

Clopton, W. H., Lt. ADC to Gholson

Cloyd, Joseph, Maj. CS at Dublin Depot, Va.

Cluis, Frederick Victor, Capt. ACS to Page,
Maury

Cluskey, Michael W., Capt. AAG to P. Smith,
Vaughan, Gordon

Cobb, Howell, Jr., Lt. ADC to Cobb (1842–
1909)

Cobb, Oliver O., Lt. AAAG to Gibson

Cobb, R. L., Capt. EO to McCown

Cobb, Robert, Capt. Chief Arty. to Breckinridge

Cobbs, James, Capt. AAIG to Bate

Cochran, John, Col. ADC to Bragg

Cochran, John W., Lt. AAIG to Wheeler
(1835–1899)

Cocke, John Binion, Lt. VADC to Pettus
(d. 1893)

Cockrill, Emmet, Capt. acting OO to Maney,
Vaughan, P. Smith

Cockrill, Mark Sterling, Lt. OO to Brown,
Stevenson (1838–1919)

Cohen, D. C., Capt. staff of Smith

Cole, John B., Lt. AAIG to Duke

Coleman, Daniel, Capt. acting ADC to Wood
(1838–1906)

Coleman, James, Capt. VADC to Breckinridge

Coleman, John N., Maj. CS to Ross, Whitfield

Coleman, Robert Lowry, Maj. CS to Vance
(1835–1896)

Coleman, Thaddeus Charles, Capt. EO to
Hood, S. D. Lee, D. H. Hill, Hindman
(1837–1895)

Collier, Cowles Myles, Capt. OO to S. D. Lee
(1836–1908)

Collins, James A., Lt. staff of Wharton

Compton, Jordan Chappell, Lt. OO to
Moore

Cone, Horace, Capt. AAG to E. K. Smith;
Judge Advocate to Magruder

Conly, Middleton, Capt. ACS to Chalmers

Connelley, John G., Lt. staff of Ben McCulloch; Maj. CS to Fagan

Conner, Farar B., Lt. ADC to W. T. Martin
(1834–1904)

Conner, Jacob D., Lt. AAAIG to Marmaduke

Conner, Lemuel Parker, Maj. VADC & Capt.
AAG to Bragg (1827–1892)

Connor, George C., OO to E. K. Smith

Conrad, Lawrence Lewis, Lt. AAAG to Liddell, Buckner (1837–1887)

Cooke, William Mordecai, VADC to Price (1823–1863)

Cooper, Douglas Hancock, Jr., Lt. ADC to Cooper (b. 1839)

Cooper, James, Capt. AAAG to Hood; AAIG to J. E. Johnston

Cooper, James L., Lt. acting ADC & AAIG to Tyler

Cooper, John W., Lt. AAIG to Forney

Cope, George L., Capt. ACS to Capers

Corder, David W., Lt. ADC to Shelby

Corprew, J., Lt. ADC to Clayton

Corser, J. W., Capt. VADC to Cooper

Cosby, Charles Vincent, Maj. QM to Polignac (1838–1873)

Cosby, Dabney, Jr., Lt. OO to Wharton, Jones

Cosner, Henry, Capt. ACS to Marmaduke

Couper, James M., Capt. VADC to Pemberton

Cowles, Thomas M., Capt. AQM to Clanton

Cowles, W. J., Capt. AAG to Parsons

Cowley, Stephen A., Lt. AAIG to Quarles (d. 1864)

Cox, George Thomas, Capt. AAG to Quarles

Cox, Thomas, Capt. AQM to Deshler, J. G. Walker

Cox, William B., Capt. ACS to A. W. Reynolds

Coxe, W. H., Col. VADC to Ruggles

Craft, Addison, Lt. AAAG to Chalmers; Capt. AQM to Walthall; Maj. QM to Brantley (1835–1909)

Craft, Henry, Capt. AAG to Chalmers

Crane, William H., Lt. ADC to Liddell

Crawford, John, Capt. AQM & Maj. OO to Cabell

Crawford, Robert, Lt. OO to Clayton, Humes, W. W. Allen, Ro. H. Anderson

Crawford, Washington L., Col. VADC to Price

Creath, D. H., Capt. staff of Bee

Crews, James M., Lt. AAAIG to Forrest

Crockett, A. R., Capt. AQM to Palmer

Croft, Theodore Gaillard, Capt. acting OO to Gist (b. 1845)

Cromwell, Thaddeus A., Maj. CS to Strahl

Crooks, Samuel O., Lt. OO to Marshall

Croom, Cicero Stephens, Maj. AAG to Forney, Loring (1839–1884)

Crosby, John Frazer, Capt. AAG to Steele, Sibley, E. K. Smith

Cross, I. S., Capt. AAAG to Trapier

Cross, Joseph Douglass, Maj. CS to Stewart, Strahl

Crouch, B. T., acting ADC to W. H. Jackson

Crouch, Walter Virginius, Maj. CS to D. W. Adams, Gibson (1822–1902)

Crowder, Thomas M., Capt. AAG to Buford

Crump, Browdie Strachan, Maj. CS to Chalmers, Maury (1833–1878)

Crump, J. B., Maj. staff of Chalmers

Crump, John H., Maj. QM to Hindman

Crump, Samuel Howard, Capt. AAIG to W. H. T. Walker (1823–1883)

Crutchfield, Edward, Maj. QM to Marshall, W. Preston, Echols, J. H. Morgan

Cuculler, Ernest, Capt. VADC to E. K. Smith

Cuculler, S., Capt. ADC to Polignac

Culbertson, Jacob, Capt. Chief Arty. to Tilghman, Loring

Cumby, Robert H., Col. acting CS to Green (1824–1881)

Cumming, Joseph Bryan, Capt. AAG to J. K. Jackson, W. H. T. Walker, Hood; Maj. AAG to J. E. Johnston (1836–1922)

Cumming, Montgomery, ADC & AAAG to Lawton (1824–1870)

Cummins, Edmund Henry, Capt. EO to Beauregard; Capt. SO to McCown, Bragg; Maj. AAG to Maury; Maj. acting ADC to Featherston

Cunningham, E. J., VADC to Little, Hebert

Cunningham, Henry Cumming, Lt. OO to Taliaferro, Elliott (1842–1917)

Cunningham, Joseph L., Capt. AAG to Tracy

Cunningham, Sidney P., Capt. AAAG to J. H. Morgan

Cuny, R. H., Capt. VADC & Maj. CS to Ruggles

Currie, D. W., Lt. EO to D. H. Hill, S. D. Lee

Currie, Daniel McNeill, Lt. acting oo to Walthall (b. 1834)

Cuyler, Richard Matthei, Capt. oo to Lawton (1825–1879)

Dabney, Edward H., Capt. acs to L. Hebert

Dabney, Frederick Yeamans, Lt. eo to F. Gardner, Van Dorn; Capt. eo to R. Taylor (1835–1900)

Dale, John B., Maj. cs to Shelby

Dallam, Herbert Shackelford, Maj. cs to Tilghman (1836–1862)

Dallas, Trevanion Barlow, Lt. oo to Deas (1843–1903)

Danner, Albert Carey, Capt. aqm to French, Cockrell, Price, M. E. Green

Dantzler, Olin Miller, Lt. vadc to Trapier (1825–1864)

da Ponte, Alphonse, vadc to Van Dorn

da Ponte, Durant, Capt. aqm to Magruder

Darragh, Thomas B., Lt. vadc to Breckinridge

Dashiell, George, Capt. aqm to Forrest, Cheatham (b. 1828)

Dashiell, Thomas R., Capt. aqm to Ruggles

David, R. J., Capt. staff of Major

Davidson, Joseph S. M., Maj. qm to Finley

Davidson, Theodore Fulton, Lt. adc & aag to Vance; adc to Palmer (1845–1931)

Davidson, W. H., Lt. adc to D. H. Hill

Davidson, William M., Lt. adc to J. P. Anderson & E. Johnson

Davies, Harper, vadc to D. H. Reynolds

Davis, Bennett Hillsman, Col. oo to Wharton (1832–1897)

Davis, Charles Mills, Lt. adc to Davis (1845–1900)

Davis, Hugh L., Lt. adc to Hodge

Davis, Isaac N., staff of Forrest, Van Dorn

Davis, Samuel Boyer, staff of P. O. Hebert

Davis, Thomas Dixon, Lt. adc to E. G. Lee (d. 1925)

Davis, Thomas J., Maj. adc to Bonham

Davis, William D., Lt. oo to Tilghman

Davis, William J., Capt. aag to Duke

Davis, William Penn, Capt. aqm to Walthall

Dawson, James, Maj. cs to Hardee

Dawson, John W., Capt. acs to P. Smith (1844–1892)

Day, Job B., Lt. staff of Sharp

Day, W. C., Capt. aqm to Sears

Dean, H. Rufus, Capt. aaig to Manigault

Dearing, Alfred L., Maj. cs to W. H. T. Walker, French, Gist (1823–1877)

Dearing, St. Clair, Col. vadc to Ripley (b. 1833)

Dearing, William P., Lt. adc to Stovall

Deas, Henry A., Maj. cs to Deas (1826–1866)

Dennan, W. A., Lt. oo to Featherston

Dennis, Isaac N., Capt. vadc & aaig to P. O. Hebert

Dennis, Joseph F., Lt. adc to A. Baker

DeRussy, Lewis Gustavus, Col. eo to Leo. Polk (1796–1864)

De Saulles, Arthur B., Lt. eo to Ruggles, Stewart, Lovell

Devereux, John G., Lt. aaag to Twiggs; Maj. aag to M. L. Smith; staff of Walthall, Lovell

Dewey, Oliver S., Capt. aqm to J. G. Martin, R. Ransom

DeWolfe, Fred. S., Capt. aag to McCown, Vaughan

Dibrell, Montgomery C., Capt. aqm to Dibrell

Dickson, William, qm to Pillow

Dillon, Edward, Maj. cs to Ben McCulloch, Van Dorn; aaig to Van Dorn (1834–1897)

Dinkins, James, Lt. adc to Chalmers (b. 1845)

Dismukes, Thomas Crutcher, Lt. oo to Cooper

Divine, John F., Capt. aqm to L. S. Baker

Dixon, Joseph, Lt. eo to Leo. Polk, A. S. Johnston (d. 1862)

Dixon, Joseph Koger, Maj. aaig to Cleburne

Dobbins, Archibald S., Col. vadc to Hindman (1827–1872)

Dodge, Lem. P., Lt. oo & adc to Hindman; staff of Shoup

Dodson, Thomas A., Capt. aqm to Cantey

Doggett, John L., Lt. so to Whiting

Doigl, Lucien, Capt. staff of Bragg

Donelson, John, Capt. acting ADC to P. Smith (1832–1863)

Donelson, Samuel, Lt. ADC to Forrest, Davis; AAIG to Polk

Donnell, Robert, AAAG to D. H. Hill (b. 1842)

Donovan, A. D., Col. VADC to Hindman

Dooley, H. H., Lt. OO to Magruder

Doss, R. Parker, Capt. AQM to Chalmers (1835–1921)

Doss, Richard M., Capt. ACS to J. K. Jackson

Dotson, Josephus, Capt. ADC to Greer

Douglas, John M., Maj. CS to Forney

Douglass, Charles S., Capt. AAAG to Tyler

Douglass, Samuel Jones, Col. Military Court of Forney (d. 1874)

Douglass, W. C., Lt. OO to Withers

Downing, Jesse B., Capt. VADC to J. P. Anderson

Draine, W. M., Maj. ADC to Brown

Drake, R. B., Lt. OO to Floyd

Drane, Henry Martin, Capt. ACS to Holmes, Whiting, J. R. Anderson, Gatlin, J. E. Rains (1832–1908)

Drayton, Carlos, ADC to Drayton

Drayton, William S., Lt. ADC to Drayton

Drennan, William Augustus, Lt. OO & ADC & AAIG to Featherston (b. 1834)

Driver, W. C., Maj. AAG to R. Taylor

Drummond, Edward W., Capt. ACS to Mercer

Du Barry, Franklin Boche, Lt. acting OO to Bragg; Capt. OO to Beauregard, Ripley (d. 1864)

Du Bos, Louis, Capt. AAG to Beauregard, W. S. Walker, Jones

DuBose, Julius Jesse, Lt. acting OO to Steele; Capt. OO to Maxey (b. 1839)

Ducayet, Felix, Maj. IFT to E. K. Smith

Duffy, Robert J., Maj. AAIG to Shelby

Duggan, Joseph H., Lt. OO to Armstrong

Dugue, August Francis, Lt. ADC to Tracy

Dulin, James M., Lt. AAIG to Liddell

Dun, J. J., OO to Iverson

Duncan, J. P., Capt. AAG to Cantey

Duncan, Joseph W., Maj. AAG to Marmaduke, J. B. Clark

Duncan, William P., Maj. CS to Lovell, Duncan (1830–1862)

Dunham, Andrew, Lt. OO to Stovall

Dunlap, William Watkins, Lt. Col. OO to Wheeler, Price, Buford, Churchill, Buckner, Tilghman, Charles Clark, Holmes, Beauregard, Bragg (1841–1892)

Dunlevy, A. F., Capt. ACS in southwest Va.

Dunn, William M., Maj. CS to Marmaduke (b. 1819)

Dunnington, Frank C., VADC to Forrest

Dupre, Alcee, Capt. AAG to F. Gardner (1842–1888)

Dupuy, John James, Lt. ADC to Strahl (d. 1898)

Durand, Victor J., Capt. staff of E. K. Smith

Duval, Benjamin Taylor, Maj. QM to Fagan (1822–1903)

Duval, Burr G., Lt. ADC & AAAG to Steele

Dwyer, Joseph Ed., Capt. VADC to Sibley; AAIG to Bee, Drayton

Dyer, Gassa B., Maj. CS to S. D. Lee, Maury, R. Taylor

Dyer, J. C., Maj. CS to H. E. McCulloch

Dyer, Randolph Henry, Maj. QM to Hawes, Price

Dyer, W. M., AAIG to McNair

Dyer, William E., Maj. QM to McCown

Dyer, Wylie M., AAIG to D. H. Reynolds

Eakin, George N., Capt. AQM at Marion, Va. (1840–1920)

Eakin, James H., Capt. ACS to Wood, Hardee, Marmaduke, W. W. Allen, Hood (1840–1881)

Eakins, John J., Maj. CS to Gano

Earle, ———, Lt. EO to Beauregard

Earle, Isham H., Maj. CS to H. E. McCulloch

Echols, William Holding, Capt. EO to Lawton, Pemberton, Beauregard (1834–1909)

Ector, Wiley Benjamin, Maj. QM to Ector (b. 1829)

Edmondson, James H., Capt. AAIG to P. Smith

Edwards, James F., Capt. ADC to Parsons

Edwards, John Newman, Capt. AAG to Shelby (1839–1889)

Edwards, William Thomas, Maj. AAIG to Churchill

Eggeling, Wilhelm, Lt. ADC to Polignac

Eggleston, John Peyton, Capt. ACS to E. Johnson, D. H. Hill, J. P. Anderson

Eggleston, William, Lt. ADC to Starke

Elcan, Henry Lionel, Maj. QM to M. J. Wright, Maney

Elcan, Junius H., Lt. ADC to M. J. Wright

Elder, Charles A., Capt. AAIG to Humes

Eldridge, John Wesley, Maj. Chief Arty. to Stewart; staff of McCown, Withers

Elgee, Charles Le Doux, Capt. AAIG to R. Taylor (1836–1864)

Elgin, Gustavus A., Maj. QM to J. B. Clark, Price, Parsons

Eliason, Armistead C., Capt. acting ADC to Maxey

Ellenburg, Leonard, Maj. CS to Liddell, Govan (1829–1899)

Elliott, George Parsons, acting ADC to Pemberton; Capt. ACS to W. S. Walker (1807–1871)

Elliott, Ralph Ems, Capt. VADC to N. G. Evans

Elliott, Samuel N., Maj. ADC to Wheeler

Elliott, William, Maj. AAIG to S. D. Lee (1838–1907)

Elliott, William Power, Maj. CS to J. H. Morgan, Duke

Elliott, William Waight, Capt. OO to W. S. Walker (1831–1884)

Ellis, Leslie, Capt. AAG to Dibrell

Ellis, Powhatan, Jr., Capt. AAG to Tilghman, B. R. Johnson, Loring, S. D. Lee; Maj. AAG to Leo. Polk; staff of Cleburne, Floyd, John Adams, R. Taylor, F. Gardner, W. T. Martin, Forrest (1829–1906)

Ellis, Towson, Lt. ADC to Bragg

Ellison, George H., Capt. ADC to Gordon

Ellston, James M., Maj. QM to Tappan, Churchill

Elmore, Vincent Martin, Maj. AAIG to Wheeler (1840–1908)

Elstner, William H., Capt. AQM to McNair; Maj. QM to D. H. Reynolds

Ely, John Randolph, Capt. AAG to Finley

Ely, L. F., Capt. AAIG to Ector

Ely, Mathew S., Capt. acting ACS to B. R. Johnson

Emmerson, John, Capt. ACS at Dublin Depot, Va. (d. 1885)

English, Richard H., Lt. AAIG to J. A. Smith, Granbury

Enoch, Isaac V., Capt. AAIG to Sears

Erskine, Thomas Ferne, Lt. ADC to Bate

Erskine, W. Fred., Capt. AQM to Cheatham, Leo. Polk, Elzey, Hood

Erwin, James P., Capt. AAAG to McNair

Erwin, Robert, Capt. AQM to Lawton

Estes, W. G., Capt. ADC to Shelley

Eubank, E. N., Capt. ACS to Tilghman

Eustis, Cartright, Capt. ADC & AAAG to Gibson (1842–1900)

Evans, Alexander, Maj. CS to Breckinridge, W. Preston

Evans, Humphrey, Maj. ADC to Cumming; acting ADC to Stevenson; CS to Stovall

Evans, Lemuel R., Capt. OO to Van Dorn, Loring; Chief Arty. to Maury, Pemberton, J. E. Johnston (1838–1870)

Ewing, Andrew, VADC to Bragg; Col. Military Court of Leo. Polk, Hardee (1813–1864)

Ewing, E. H., Capt. AQM to Breckinridge, D. H. Hill, Hindman, Hood

Ewing, Henry, Lt. ADC to Zollicoffer; Maj. AAG to Marmaduke (1840–1873)

Ewing, Orville, ADC to W. Preston (d. 1863)

Ewing, William, Lt. ADC to W. H. Jackson

Ezell, E. H., Maj. QM to Leadbetter, E. K. Smith

Ezell, Franklin L., Capt. ACS to Stevenson

Fackler, Calvin M., Maj. CS to Pillow (1826–1865)

Fain, Richard Gammon, staff of Zollicoffer (1811–1878)

Fairbanks, Jason M., Lt. AAIG to D. W. Adams

Fairly, John Spencer, Lt. ADC to Whiting, Pillow, Hampton (1832–1898)

Falconer, Kinloch, Capt. AAG to Villepigue; Maj. AAG to Bragg, J. E. Johnston

Fall, Benjamin F., Maj. CS to Fagan, Rust (d. 1888)

Fancher, Richard, Capt. ACS to M. J. Wright

Farish, William Stamps, Cadet ADC to S. D. Lee (1843–1899)

Farlow, L. G., Maj. CS to Loring, Buford

Farr, Zachariah Pickney Herndon, Capt. acting ADC to Churchill

Farrow, M. M., Lt. EO to Hood, J. E. Johnston

Faulkner, A., Capt. staff of J. G. Walker

Fearn, John Williams Walker, Maj. QM to M. L. Smith; staff of Preston (1832–1899)

Fearn, Thomas C., Maj. acting QM to M. L. Smith

Feilden, Henry Wemyss, Capt. AAG to Beauregard, Hardee, Jones (1838–1921)

Felder, Edmond J., Capt. AQM to Taliaferro, Elliott

Felder, Hamblin R., Lt. acting OO to Cummings

Fellows, John R., Capt. AAIG to Beall (1832–1896)

Ferguson, William J., Capt. AQM to McNair

Ferguson, William Wallace, Lt. EO to Beauregard, Bragg, Clayton

Ferrell, William H., Lt. AAG to Shelby

Ferrin, J. J., Capt. staff of Buckner

Field, Ben. J., Maj. AAG to Cabell

Fields, J. H., Capt. AAIG to W. W. Allen

Finch, J. R., Maj. CS to Buford

Finks, Joseph Hughes, Capt. AQM to J. B. Clark, Frost; Maj. QM to Drayton; staff of Parsons (1837–1915)

Finlay, George P., Capt. AAIG to Slaughter; staff of Scurry, Magruder

Finlay, Luke William, VADC to Stewart (1831–1908)

Finney, William, Capt. VADC to J. B. Clark

Finnie, John G., Maj. QM to Leo. Polk, Pillow

Fisk, Stuart Wilkins, Col. Military Court of Forney (1820–1862)

Fitzhugh, Henry, Jr., Maj. AAG to Loring (1830–1891)

Fitzpatrick, Benjamin F., Capt. AQM to Featherston

Fitzpatrick, Elmore Joseph, Capt. Judge Advocate to Buckner, Maury (1828–1884)

Flanagan, Joseph M., Capt. AAG to Cockrell, Echols

Flanagin, Harris, VADC to Holmes (1817–1874)

Flash, Henry Lynden, Capt. VADC to Hardee; staff of Wheeler (1835–1914)

Fleming, Louis J., VADC to Finegan

Flippin, John R., Capt. acting QM to Vaughan (b. 1834)

Flournoy, Alfred, Jr., Lt. ADC to Sibley (1832–1901)

Flournoy, John J., staff of John Adams, Stewart

Flournoy, Jordan H., Maj. CS to Sears; staff of Baldwin

Flowerree, Daniel Walton, Maj. AAG to Maury (1838–1878)

Floyd, W. D. C., Maj. AAIG & OO to J. K. Jackson

Fogg, Henry Middleton Rutledge, Lt. ADC to Zollicoffer (1830–1862)

Fontaine, Sydney Thurston, Maj. Chief Arty. to Magruder (b. 1840)

Foote, Henry S., Jr., Lt. OO to Pillow; Lt. acting ADC to Buckner; Capt. ADC to McCown

Forney, Daniel P., Maj. AAIG to Forney (b. 1813)

Forrest, William Montgomery, Lt. ADC to Forrest (1846–1908)

Forsgard, J. W., Lt. OO to Gano

Forshey, Caleb Goldsmith, Maj. EO to P. O. Hebert; Lt. Col. EO to Magruder (1812–1881)

Fort, Elias Baldwin, Capt. AQM to Ferguson (1825–1901)

Fosgard, F. W., Lt. OO to Gano

Foster, Frank, Lt. acting ADC to Wood

Foster, James Monroe, Maj. CS to Ferguson (1824–1897)

Foster, Thaddeus, Capt. AQM to J. P. Anderson

Foster, Thomas J., Jr., Maj. QM to Maney

Foster, Thomas Jefferson, Col. VADC to Armstrong (1809–1887)

Foster, Wilbur Fisk, Maj. EO to E. K. Smith, Stewart, Maxey, Buckner (1834–1922)

Foster, William Keller, staff of Magruder, Scurry, Slaughter (1837–1881)

Foute, Augustus Marcellus, acting ADC to Ruggles; staff of John Adams; Lt. Col. AAAIG to Pemberton (1838–1894)

Fowler, L. A., Maj. CS to Buford, Loring, Leo. Polk

Fowlkes, Abner D., Capt. acting AQM to McNair

Fowlkes, Alpheus Monroe, Maj. CS to Wheeler, Frazer (b. 1838)

Fowlkes, John S., Capt. AQM to French

Francis, Thomas W., Maj. CS to Forney

Franklin, Edgar J., Capt. OO to Drayton

Franklin, Thomas Richard, Maj. QM to Bee

Fraser, Edward W., Lt. AAIG to W. S. Walker; Lt. AAG to Chesnut

Frazer, Charles W., Capt. AAG & AQM to Frazer (1834–1897)

Frederic, H. A., Lt. SO to R. Taylor, Buckner (b. 1834)

Freeman, Dandridge Claiborne, VADC to Pegram

Freeman, Edward T., Cadet AAAIG to French (1841–1878)

Fremaux, Leon J., Capt. EO to Beauregard, Price, Ruggles, Maury (1821–1898)

Fremont, Seawell Lawrence, Lt. Col. EO to J. R. Anderson (1816–1888)

French, James Henry, Capt. ACS to Bee (1835–1893)

French, John Compton, Lt. VADC to E. K. Smith; ADC to J. G. Walker (b. 1841)

French, Thomas Barton, Lt. Col. Chief Arty. to J. G. Walker (1830–1899)

Freret, James M., Lt. EO to F. Gardner, Pemberton

Freret, William A., Capt. EO & VADC to E. K. Smith

Frierson, J. W. S., Jr., Lt. AAAG to Armstrong

Frost, George H., Capt. ADC to M. L. Smith, Stewart, Armstrong

Fulgham, Richard Thomas, ADC to L. S. Baker (1842–1885)

Fuller, R. M., ADC to W. S. Walker

Fuqua, James O., Col. Military Court of Ruggles

Fuqua, John A., Capt. AAIG to W. M. Gardner, B. R. Johnson

Fusilier, Alfred A., Capt. ACS to R. Taylor

Fusilier, Fergus, AAG to R. Taylor

Fusilier, G. Laclaire, Capt. VADC to R. Taylor

Gailor, Frank P., Capt. AQM to Carroll; Maj. QM to Wood (d. 1862)

Gaines, Abner S., Capt. EO to M. L. Smith, Stevenson

Gaines, James J., Capt. Chief Arty. & Maj. AAAG to Churchill

Gaines, Reuben Reid, Lt. AAAG to J. T. Morgan, W. W. Allen (1836–1914)

Gaines, Richard M., Capt. AQM to Holmes (d. 1871)

Gale, D. O. Q., Capt. ACS to Marmaduke

Gale, William Dudley, Lt. Col. VADC to Leo. Polk; Capt. AAG to Polk, Stewart (1819–1888)

Gallagher, George Aiken, Maj. AAG to Holmes, Price, E. K. Smith (1826–1878)

Galleher, John Nicholas, Lt. ADC & Capt. AAG to Buckner (1839–1891)

Gallimard, Jules V., Capt. EO to Page

Galloway, Matthew C., Lt. acting ADC & Col. VADC to Forrest (b. 1820)

Gamble, Lewis M., Cadet ADC to Finegan

Gano, John A., Capt. ADC to Gano

Garden, H. G. D., Lt. ADC to Price

Gardenhire, Alexis, acting ADC to M. J. Wright

Gardiner, John A., Lt. OO to Buford

Gardner, G. Thomas, Capt. ACS to Cantey, Shelley

Gardner, Henry De Saussure, AAIG to Gist, Cobb, Hebert

Gardner, John D., Lt. OO to Buford

Gardner, Lee M., Maj. CS to Polk

Gardner, William H., Lt. AAIG to F. Gardner; Lt. OO to Deas

Gardner, William Montgomery, Maj. AAAG to Lawton (1824–1901)

Garey, John E., Lt. Col. QM to E. K. Smith (1824–1908)

Garland, William, VADC to McNair

Garner, George G., Lt. Col. AAG to Bragg; staff of Maury, Polk, Gardner

Garrard, W. W., Capt. AAAG to Pettus

Garrett, Kenneth, Capt. acting OO to Hardee

Gassett, C. W., Maj. QM to J. H. Morgan, Hardee, Duke

Gause, Samuel Sydney, Lt. VADC to Fagan (1839–1901)

Geary, Daniel, Lt. OO to Shoup

George, James H., Lt. OO to W. T. Martin

George, R. B., Lt. ADC & AQM to Buford

Gerard, Louis, Lt. on staff of Tilghman

Gervin, Noah H., Capt. AAIG & AAAG to Pettus

Gholson, Samuel Jameson, Col. Military Court of Hardee (1808–1883)

Gibbes, James S., VADC to Jordan

Gibbes, Octavius T., Capt. OO to Bragg

Gibbon, Lardner, Capt. OO to Ripley, Pemberton, Beauregard, Forney, Mackall, Buckner, Gardner, Maury

Gibboney, Albert Haller, VADC to Heth (1845–1917)

Gibboney, John H., Capt. AQM at Wytheville, Va.

Gibboney, William, Capt. AQM at Wytheville, Va.

Gibbons, Israel, Capt. AQM to Wheeler

Gibbs, Waites E., Capt. AQM to Moore, A. Baker, D. H. Hill

Gibbs, William E., Maj. QM to Tappan, Marmaduke

Gibson, Albert C., Maj. OO to Buckner

Gibson, Eustace, Capt. AQM at Montgomery Springs, Va.

Gibson, Nathaniel Hart, Capt. AAG to Buford, J. H. Morgan, Echols (1835–1904)

Gibson, J. M., Lt. ADC to Gibson

Gibson, Thad P., Maj. QM to Lyon

Gibson, Thomas, Lt. ADC to John Adams, Featherston (1836–1917)

Gibson, Tobias, Lt. ADC & Capt. AAIG to Preston (1838–1904)

Gilchrist, Robert C., Maj. AAAG to Hardee

Gill, William G., Lt. Col. OO to R. E. Lee, Lawton; Col. OO to Beauregard (d. 1862)

Gillespie, George L., Maj. CS to Stevenson (b. 1836)

Gillespie, James A., Capt. AAAG to Bowen

Gillespie, John W., Capt. OO to Maury

Gilmer, James Nicholas, Lt. AAIG to Gracie (b. 1839)

Gilmer, Jeremy Francis, Maj. EO to A. S. Johnston; Lt. Col. to Beauregard (1818–1883)

Gindrat, John Henry, Col. VADC to Forney (1817–1874)

Girard, Louis J., Capt. OO to F. Gardner

Girault, John F., Capt. AAG to M. L. Smith; Maj. AAIG to Leo. Polk

Gist, James D., Lt. ADC to Gist (d. 1863)

Gittings, John George Jackson, Lt. AAAG to W. L. Jackson (1835–1904)

Given, Dickson Augustus, Jr., Lt. acting ADC to Moore, Buford, Tilghman (b. 1842)

Glass, Presley Thornton, Maj. CS to McCown, Pillow, D. W. Adams (1824–1902)

Gloster, Arthur W., Lt. EO to Pemberton

Glover, A. P., Maj. CS to W. H. Jackson

Goldsmith, Jeremiah W., Capt. ADC to Anderson

Goldthwaite, Henry, Capt. AAG to Forney, Leadbetter; staff of Jones, J. P. Anderson; Maj. AAG to J. K. Jackson (1841–1895)

Goldthwaite, Joseph G., Lt. AAIG to Forrest

Gonzales, Ambrosio Jose, Col. Chief Arty. to Hardee, Ripley; VADC to Beauregard (1818–1893)

Good, John, VADC to Parsons

Good, John Jay, Col. Military Court of
Pemberton (1827–1882)

Good, William Spalding, Lt. acting oo to
P. Hebert; Capt. oo to Magruder, Scurry,
Slaughter

Goodloe, Jerman B., Capt. AQM at Wytheville, Va.

Goodman, Walter A., Capt. AAG to Chalmers

Goodwin, Francis H., Lt. oo to Ro. H.
Anderson

Goodwin, John Wallingford, Maj. QM to
Bragg, Withers

Gordon, William Washington, Capt. AAG
to Mercer; Capt. AAIG to Smith, Ro. H.
Anderson (1834–1912)

Gottheil, Edward, Capt. EO to Taylor

Gould, John McKee, Capt. AAIG to Pettus
(b. 1831)

Gourdin, Robert Newman, Col. VADC to
Beauregard (1812–1894)

Govan, Frank H., Lt. ADC to Govan

Govan, George Morgan, Capt. AAIG to
Walthall (b. 1840)

Govan, William H., Maj. QM to Hindman,
E. Johnson

Gowen, Thomas B., Capt. acting QM to Ro.
H. Anderson

Goza, George W., Maj. CS to W. W. Adams
(b. 1839)

Graham, Charles Montrose, Capt. AAIG to
Bragg, Holmes (1838–1869)

Graham, Hamilton Claverhouse, Capt. Judge
Advocate to Jones (1840–1900)

Graham, John Washington, Lt. ADC to Gatlin
(1838–1928)

Graham, Robert W., Capt. AQM to Carter

Graves, Rice E., Maj. Chief Arty. to Breckinridge (1838–1863)

Graves, William H., Capt. oo to Morgan,
Iverson

Gray, A. B., Capt. EO to Leo. Polk (d. 1862)

Gray, Edward Fairfax, Lt. Col. AAAG to Bee
(1829–1884)

Gray, Peter W., Col. VADC to Magruder
(1819–1874)

Green, Abram V., AAAG to Harrison

Green, J. S., Maj. QM to Gist; staff of Ripley,
R. E. Lee, Pemberton

Green, James P., VADC to Breckinridge

Green, John Alexander, oo to T. Green
(1821–1899)

Green, John W., Capt. EO to Hardee (1827–
1914)

Green, Joseph C., Maj. QM at Salem, Va.

Green, Nathan, Jr., Lt. ADC & Capt. AAG to
Stewart (1827–1919)

Green, Thomas B., Lt. ADC to M. E. Green

Greene, Charles C., Capt. oo to E. K. Smith

Greene, William, Capt. AAG to Trapier

Gregorie, John White, Lt. EO to Beauregard,
W. S. Walker, Hardee

Gregory, Edward H., Lt. ADC & Capt. AAG to
John Adams

Greigg, Alexander R., Lt. AAIG to Campbell

Griffin, B. D., Lt. AAAIG to Drayton

Griffin, W. S., Maj. CS to Polignac

Grigsby, John Warren, Col. staff of Wheeler
(1818–1887)

Grivot, Maurice, Col. Military Court of
Buckner (1814–1875)

Groce, Jared Ellison, Maj. AAG to Wharton
(d. 1872)

Gruber, John F., Capt. AQM to Hays

Guerard, Edgar L., Capt. AQM to Ripley

Guillet, Emile P., Capt. AAG to D. W. Adams
(d. 1863)

Guion, Louis, Lt. AAIG to Shoup (1838–
1920)

Gurley, Davis R., Capt. AAG to Ross

Gurley, Edwards Jeremiah, Capt. AAG to Ross
(d. 1914)

Guy, William Wallace, Maj. CS to Pillow, Polk
(1832–1879)

Guyton, Joseph J., Capt. ACS to Starke

Gwyn, Hugh Garvin, Maj. AAIG to Duke
(1840–1925)

Gwynn, Walter, Maj. EO to Beauregard
(1802–1882)

Haber, Abraham, Maj. CS to Maxey

Habersham, Joseph Clay, Lt. ADC to Mercer,
W. D. Smith, Gist (d. 1864)

Haines, William F., Maj. QM to Bowen, L. S. Baker (b. 1829)

Hairston, Marshall, Lt. ADC to Cabell; acting ADC to Walthall (b. 1840)

Hait, James H., ADC to D. H. Reynolds

Haley, James M., Capt. AQM to Liddell, Govan

Hall, A. J., Lt. ADC to Lowry

Hall, Dixon B., Lt. ADC to Granbury

Hall, T. Jeff., Maj. QM to Harrison

Hall, Theophilus, Capt. acting QM to Cosby

Hall, W. A., Capt. ACS to W. H. Jackson

Hallam, Theodore F., Cadet OO to Gibson, D. W. Adams

Hallett, Robert James, Capt. AAG to Cobb

Halliday, Edward Warner, Maj. CS to Tilghman (1836–1913)

Hallonquist, James Henry, Lt. Col. AAIG to Bragg, Withers (1836–1883)

Hamilton, Alexander L., VADC to Wood

Hamilton, J. Lynch, Capt. VADC to Bee

Hamilton, James T., Maj. CS to B. R. Johnson

Hamilton, John H., Capt. AQM to Stevenson

Hamilton, Patrick, Lt. ADC to Baldwin, Sears

Hamilton, R., Lt. ADC to Baldwin

Hamilton, William B., VADC to Breckinridge (b. 1832)

Hamilton, William P., Lt. AAAIG to W. Smith

Hamlin, W. D., Capt. OO to Walthall

Hammett, McKelvie Armstrong, Lt. ADC to Hindman, Hood

Hammock, Cicero C., Capt. acting QM to W. H. Jackson

Hampton, Henry, Maj. AAAG to Cheatham; on Military Court of Hardee

Hanckel, Thomas M., VADC to Ripley

Hanckel, Thomas Means, Jr., Lt. ADC to Hardee

Hand, Henry W., Capt. AAG to Rust

Hanks, Calvin Jones, Capt. ADC to McRae; VADC to Churchill (1834–1922)

Hanley, Michael, Maj. QM to Gibson, D. W. Adams

Hanly, Sylvanus P., Lt. ADC to Cleburne; AAG to J. A. Smith

Hanson, Asbury J., Lt. ADC to Stovall

Hanson, Gustavus Adolphus, Capt. ACS to Forrest (1843–1909)

Hanson, John C., Capt. AAIG to Walthall

Harcourt, John T., VADC to P. O. Hebert

Hardcastle, Aaron Bascom, Col. Military Court of Wheeler (1836–1915)

Hardee, Thomas Sydenham, Lt. ADC to Hardee (1832–1880)

Hardeman, William D., Capt. AAG to L. Hebert

Harden, Edward Harden, Maj. OO to W. H. T. Walker

Harden, William Dearing, Capt. OO to Mercer, Walthall, Stewart

Harding, James, Maj. QM to Price (1830–1902)

Hardy, William Harris, Lt. ADC to J. A. Smith (1837–1917)

Harleston, Francis H., ADC to Ripley (d. 1863)

Harley, J. N., Capt. AQM to Govan

Harnett, Richard M., Lt. acting ADC to Vaughan

Harper, Charles M., Lt. ADC to Leadbetter

Harper, J. E., Capt. ACS to Cumming

Harper, James, Capt. AAG to Churchill

Harper, W. A., Capt. AAG to Lowry

Harris, Albert Gallatin, Lt. AAG to Bell

Harris, Alexander W., Capt. AAG to Leadbetter

Harris, Anderson M., Lt. AAIG to Finley

Harris, Arthur H., Capt. AAIG to Higgins; AAAG to Maury

Harris, Conquest Cross, ACS to Bell (1840–1906)

Harris, Eugene T., VADC to Cheatham; Lt. ADC to M. J. Wright

Harris, George L., Capt. AQM to Quarles, Cheatham

Harris, Isham Green, VADC to A. S. Johnston, Bragg, Beauregard, Hood (1818–1897)

Harris, John W., Capt. AAIG to Vaughan (d. 1864)

Harris, Minor Barker, Lt. AAIG to M. J. Wright (1837–1900)

Harris, Samuel D., Capt. AAIG to Baldwin, Sears

Harris, Samuel Smith, Lt. AAIG to J. K. Jackson; Capt. AAG to Bragg (1841–1888)

Harris, William, VADC to Maney

Harris, William Henry, Lt. AAIG & ADC to Wheeler; Capt. AQM to Wheeler; Maj. QM to Humes (1835–1908)

Harris, William R., Lt. ADC to Campbell

Harrison, George E., Lt. SO to Taliaferro, Jones

Harrison, John C., Lt. AAAG to Walthall; Capt. AAAG to Brantley

Harrison, R. H., VADC to Maney

Harrison, Thomas, Cadet acting ADC to Baldwin; Lt. ADC to Loring, Hardee

Harrison, William H., Maj. QM to Sibley

Harrod, Benjamin Morgan, Capt. ADC to M. L. Smith (1837–1912)

Hart, James B., Capt. AAIG to Sears

Hart, John E., Maj. AAG to T. Green, Wharton, J. G. Walker

Hart, William, Capt. AAIG to Slaughter

Hartley, A. J., Lt. OO to Withers; Capt. OO to Mercer (d. 1883)

Hartmus, Thomas H., Maj. CS to Bate

Hartridge, Algernon S., Lt. ADC to Mercer

Hartstene, Henry J., VADC to Beauregard; ADC to W. S. Walker

Harwell, Richard M., Lt. AAAG & ADC to Vaughan

Haskell, Alexander McDonald, Lt. OO, AAG & AAIG to Van Dorn; Lt. AAIG to Beauregard; Maj. AAG to Withers

Haskins, James E., Capt. AQM at Clarksville, Va.

Hatch, Albert, Lt. staff of Wheeler

Hatch, Daniel B., Lt. AAAG to Marmaduke

Hatcher, John Epps, VADC to Stewart (1844–1882)

Hatcher, Robert A., Capt. ADC & Maj. AAG to Stewart

Hawes, James Morrison, Maj. AAIG to Buckner (1824–1889)

Hawes, Richard, Maj. CS to Marshall, Williams (1797–1877)

Hawes, Smith N., Lt. ADC to Hawes

Hawes, William F., Maj. QM to Hawes

Hawkins, Thomas, Maj. QM to L. E. Polk, Cleburne

Hawthorn, A. J., Capt. AQM to Fagan; Maj. QM to Hawthorne

Hay, E. B., AAG to Hardee

Hay, Joseph J., Lt. OO to Starke; acting OO to Forney

Hayden, Charles, Capt. EO to Tilghman

Hayden, D. M., Maj. VADC to A. S. Johnston

Haymakeur, George W., Capt. AAG & OO to Marmaduke

Hayne, Isaac W., Lt. OO to Hagood; Lt. AAAG to Chesnut

Haynes, Robert Walter, Lt. ADC to A. E. Jackson; Lt. AAG to Cheatham (1840–1905)

Haynes, William Henry, Maj. CS to Pillow, Breckinridge, C. Clark; Maj. QM to E. K. Smith (d. 1921)

Haynie, Hugh H., Maj. CS to Maxey, Scurry

Hays, Andrew Jackson, Lt. Col. AAIG to Bragg, J. E. Johnston (d. 1896)

Hays, Charles, Maj. AAIG to M. J. Wright (b. 1834)

Hays, James, Capt. AAIG to Bate

Hays, Samuel K., Maj. QM to Buckner

Hays, Thomas Hercules, Maj. AAIG to Helm; staff of W. Preston, Lewis (1837–1909)

Hayward, George A., Lt. ADC to Stevenson

Hazlehurst, George H., Capt. EO to E. K. Smith

Healey, Thomas M., Capt. EO to Kennedy

Heard, Samuel S., Col. VADC to Ruggles (b. 1807)

Hearne, Joseph T., Lt. AAAG to Deshler; Capt. AAG to J. A. Smith; staff of Granbury (d. 1864)

Hebert, Thomas Paul, Lt. ADC to P. O. Hebert

Heermann, Theodore, volunteer EO to Magruder

Heiston, Thornton Buckner, Lt. ADC & Capt. AAG to Cooper

Helm, Charles W., Capt. ACS to Helm; Maj. CS to Lewis (b. 1834)

Helm, George Meredith, Lt. EO to Beauregard, Breckinridge, S. D. Lee, Hindman, Hood, Hardee (1839–1930)

Hempstead, Beall, Capt. AAG to Beall (d. 1920)

Henderson, ——, Capt. VADC to Ruggles

Henderson, F., Lt. AAAG to Campbell

Henderson, George Washington, staff of Chalmers

Henderson, John, Capt. VADC to J. E. Rains, Cooper

Henderson, Thomas A., Lt. AAAG to Campbell

Henderson, Thomas H., Lt. VADC to Cheatham

Hennen, William D., Col. Military Court of Buckner

Henry, Benjamin C., Capt. AQM to Young

Henry, Frank A., Capt. AQM to Sears

Henry, Gustavus A., Jr., Maj. AAG to Pillow; Maj. AAG to McCown; Lt. Col. AAIG to J. E. Johnston; staff of Leo. Polk, Bragg, Hood, Stewart, Hardee (1838–1882)

Henry, Patrick, Lt. AAIG to John Adams (d. 1908)

Henry, Samuel H., Capt. ACS at Giles C. H., Va.

Henry, Thomas Frazier, Capt. ADC to Cheatham, J. E. Rains; Maj. AAG to Brown; staff of Bate, J. K. Jackson (1835–1886)

Henshaw, John H., Maj. QM to D. W. Adams, Gibson

Herndon, Addison Carmack, Capt. AQM to Davidson, Scott

Herndon, Thomas C., Lt. acting Chief Arty. to Maxey, Cooper

Herr, Benjamin F., Capt. AQM to Cockrell

Herr, William Wallace, Lt. ADC to Helm

Herron, Andrew S., Col. on Military Court of Maury

Hewitt, Fayette, Capt. AAG to Lewis, Pike, Granbury, Helm (d. 1909)

Hickman, W. H., Capt. AQM to Trapier

Higginbotham, Thomas Jefferson, Maj. CS at Liberty Hill, Va. (1817–1879)

Higgins, Charles M., Lt. ADC to Harrison

Higgins, Edward, Capt. ADC to Twiggs (1821–1875)

Higgins, R. G., Maj. QM to Gibson, Polk, Stewart; VADC to D. W. Adams

Higley, Horace A., Maj. CS to Bragg, Mackall

Hill, Charles S., Lt. OO to Hardee; Lt. acting ADC to Jones; Capt. OO to Cleburne, Forrest, Ripley

Hill, Eugene Francis, VADC to Shoup (b. 1845)

Hill, George R., Lt. OO to Deas

Hill, James Davidson, Capt. ADC to Hood, Shoup

Hill, John Atkinson, Maj. ADC to Liddell

Hill, John S., Capt. AQM to Pillow

Hill, Miles H., Capt. AAG to Gartrell (d. 1865)

Hill, Richard J., Maj. QM to Deas, J. P. Anderson, E. Johnson

Hill, Robert H., Maj. QM to Chesnut

Hill, Wash. L., Capt. acting QM to Bee, Slaughter; QM to Drayton

Hillyer, Giles M., Maj. CS to Crittenden, Bragg, Hardee, Polk, J. E. Johnston

Hinds, Howell, Maj. AAAG to C. Clark (d. 1864)

Hobart, Edward, Capt. VADC to M. L. Smith

Hodge, Eli, Lt. AAAG to Shelby

Hodges, H. K., Lt. EO to E. K. Smith

Hodges, Jack, Capt. AQM to Gibson

Hodgson, Telfair, Capt. VADC to Wheeler (1840–1893)

Hogane, James T., Capt. EO to M. L. Smith, Marmaduke, Van Dorn, Pemberton

Hogue, J. S., Capt. ACS to Cummings

Holcombe, Edward L., Maj. CS to Taliaferro, Chesnut (1840–1875)

Holcombe, John Theodore Hunt, Lt. ADC to Greer (1834–1907)

Holladay, Alexander Quarles, Lt. ACS & acting ADC to Bragg (b. 1839)

Holland, Dick F., Lt. acting ADC to Chalmers; Capt. ADC to Maury

Holland, Jackson C., Capt. ACS to Carroll

Holliday, John Duncan, Lt. OO to Drayton, Tappan (1838–1913)

Hollingsworth, William Perry, Maj. CS to Pettus, Tracy

Holloway, T., Lt. ADC to Brantley

Holloway, Thomas B., Lt. OO to Churchill, McRae

Holmes, Charles T., Lt. ADC to Finley

Holmes, Charles W., Maj. CS to Lewis

Holmes, Henry, Capt. AAIG to Humes

Holmes, James Gadsden, Jr., Capt. AAG to Law (1843–1926)

Holmes, Newland, Capt. ADC to Higgins

Holt, George Waller, Maj. AAG to S. D. Lee, F. Gardner, R. Taylor, Forrest (d. 1876)

Holtzclaw, John T., Lt. ADC to Holtzclaw

Hooe, John Gwynne Page, Capt. VADC to Hawes (1836–1888)

Hoole, James L., Capt. AAIG to S. D. Lee

Hooper, Benjamin S., Lt. ADC to Marmaduke, J. B. Clark

Hooper, Henry Rives, Maj. QM to Cabell, Cockrell, Rust, Holmes (1833–1894)

Hooper, John A., Maj. CS to Walthall, Brantley

Hooper, John R., Maj. QM to Bowen

Hope, James K., Capt. ACS to Strahl

Hope, John S., Maj. AAIG to Breckinridge; staff of R. Taylor, Hodge

Hopkins, Aristide, Lt. AAIG to Stewart (1839–1925)

Hopkins, Matthew H., AAIG to J. A. Smith

Horbach, James P., Maj. QM to Chalmers

Horner, John Joseph, Maj. AAIG to Tappan, Churchill (1831–1905)

Horton, Rodah, Capt. ACS to Deas, Cumming (b. 1835)

Hotchkiss, Thomas R., Capt. OO to Cleburne; Maj. OO to Hardee, J. P. Anderson

Hottel, James M., Maj. QM to Beauregard

Hough, Warwick, Capt. AAIG to S. D. Lee, Maury, R. Taylor (1836–1915)

Houghton, Lafayette, Maj. AAAIG to Gholson (1827–1883)

Houks, Calvin J., Lt. ADC to McRae

House, John Ford, VADC to Maney (1827–1904)

House, John Moore, Cadet to Stewart (1844–1865)

Houstoun, E., Jr., Lt. ADC to Finegan

Howard, ———, Capt. acting ADC to Wofford

Howard, George Thomas, Maj. CS to Bee, Van Dorn (1814–1866)

Howard, Henry Peyton, VADC to Van Dorn (b. 1829)

Howard, James Ross, Col. acting ADC to M. J. Wright (1822–1892)

Howard, T. G., Maj. VADC to Van Dorn

Howe, S. B., VADC to Withers

Howell, John B., Capt. OO to Fagan

Howell, Sylvanus, Capt. Chief Arty. to Maxey

Howes, J. F., Lt. ADC to Parsons

Hoxton, Llewellyn Griffith, Maj. Chief Arty. to Hardee (1838–1891)

Hoxton, William, Lt. AAIG to Elzey (1844–1876)

Hoyt, William B., Capt. AQM to Holtzclaw

Hudson, Marcellus G., Lt. AAAG to Withers; Lt. ADC & Maj. AAG to Wheeler; staff of Deas, J. K. Jackson

Huger, Charles Lowndes, Lt. ADC to Withers; AAAG to Gibson (b. 1844)

Huger, Daniel Elliott, Maj. AAG to Withers

Huger, Daniel Elliott, Jr., Maj. AAIG to Manigault (d. 1863)

Huger, Eustis, Lt. ADC to Huger

Huger, Francis Kinloch, SO to Ripley

Huger, John M., Maj. VADC to Bragg, Beauregard

Huger, Joseph Alston, Capt. VADC to Drayton

Huger, Thomas B., Lt. AAIG to Beauregard

Huger, William Elliott, Lt. ADC to Manigault

Huggins, James B., Capt. AQM to Whiting, Clingman (d. 1910)

Hughes, Maxcy G., Lt. OO to Magruder (1841–1863)

Huguenin, Abram, Lt. ADC to McLaws (b. 1838)

Huguenin, J. G., Lt. ADC to Pemberton

Hull, Fred M., Capt. AQM to J. A. Smith

Hull, Harvey H., AAIG to Stovall

Hull, O. P., Lt. AAAG to Gladden, J. P. Anderson

Hume, William, Jr., Lt. EO to Trapier

Humes, William Young Conn, Maj. Chief Arty. to Wheeler (1830–1882)

Humphreys, J. H., Capt. EO to J. E. Johnston, Cheatham

Humphries, W. W., ADC to Van Dorn

Hundley, Orville M., Capt. acting QM to J. T. Morgan

Hunt, George W., Lt. AAAG & OO to Duke

Hunt, J. M., Lt. OO to Gist, W. H. T. Walker

Hunt, Robert P., Lt. ADC to A. S. Johnston

Hunt, Thomas Winn, Lt. acting ADC & Capt. AAIG to Hardee; Capt. AAIG to Cheatham, W. H. Jackson (1842–1895)

Hunter, John H., Capt. acting CS to Cabell

Hunter, Philander D., Lt. OO to Frazer

Hunter, Samuel, Lt. ADC to S. D. Lee

Hunter, Thomas, Lt. ADC to R. Taylor

Huntt, Albert Lee, Capt. ACS to Hampton (1839–1907)

Hurd, William A., Maj. CS to Davidson, Hodge

Hurtley, S. P., Lt. OO to Withers

Hutchinson, S. W., Lt. ADC to Clanton

Huwald, Gustave A., Lt. OO to Roddey

Hyams, Samuel M., Jr., Lt. ADC to L. Hebert; staff of Greer, Armstrong, Ben McCulloch (1840–1882)

Hyer, Albert, Lt. ADC to Clanton (1838–1896)

I'Anson, William Harrison, Maj. QM to Grayson, Finegan, Cobb, Trapier, W. M. Gardner (1817–1875)

Ingram, John, Maj. AAG to Cheatham, Brown, J. K. Jackson

Inks, ——, Lt. acting ADC to Cabell

Irwin, Craft, Lt. ADC to Maxey

Irwin, Robert Cessne, Lt. acting ADC to Gartrell (1842–1921)

Irwin, Thomas Kilshaw, Capt. AAIG to Ferguson (1835–1911)

Isabell, Robert L., Lt. SO to Beall

Isenhour, J. E., Capt. AQM to Shoup

Isnard, Edward, Lt. OO to Stewart, Clayton, Humes, Holtzclaw

Ives, C. E., VADC to Tappan

Ives, Joseph Christmas, Capt. EO to R. E. Lee, Pemberton (1829–1868)

Ivey, Charles C., AAAG to Bate

Ivy, Edward, Capt. ADC to Tracy; Lt. Col. AAG to Lovell; staff of M. L. Smith

Jack, Thomas McKinney, Lt. ADC to A. S. Johnston; Lt. AAG to Loring, Stewart, J. G. Walker, Magruder; Lt. Col. AAG to Leo. Polk (1831–1880)

Jackson, Alex. M., Maj. AAG to Sibley; Maj. AAIG to F. Gardner

Jackson, Alfred Eugene, Maj. QM to Zollicoffer (1807–1889)

Jackson, Andrew Miller, Lt. ADC to J. K. Jackson

Jackson, Columbus L., Lt. acting ADC to Jones; Maj. AAIG to Maury

Jackson, Crawford M., Capt. AAIG to F. Gardner (d. 1897)

Jackson, Thomas K., Maj. CS to A. S. Johnston, Buckner, J. E. Johnston

Jackson, William Bulloch, Lt. ADC & AAAG to H. R. Jackson (1829–1875)

Jackson, William Hicks, Capt. acting ADC to Pillow (1835–1903)

James, John W., Lt. VADC to J. P. Anderson

James, Samuel L., Maj. VADC to Lovell (d. 1894)

Jamison, David Flavel, Col. Military Court of Beauregard (1810–1864)

Jamison, James J., Lt. ADC to Cleburne

Janes, John W., Lt. acting ADC to J. P. Anderson

Jaquess, John A., Col. VADC to Gardner

Jeffries, James, Capt. Judge Advocate to Magruder

Jenkins, Barton W., Capt. ADC to Marshall; staff of Williams (1832–1910)

Jenkins, Donelson Caffrey, Jr., Maj. AAG to

Van Dorn; Maj. AAIG to Wheeler; staff of Forrest, Davidson (b. 1841)

Jennings, Needler R., VADC to Polk; Maj. CS to Gibson (d. 1863)

Jennison, George A., Capt. AAAG to J. K. Jackson

Jeters, W. S., Capt. ADC to B. J. Hill

Jetton, J. White, Lt. ADC to A. S. Johnston, Cleburne; staff of Lowry, P. Smith

Jewell, George B., Lt. OO to J. A. Smith, Granbury, Deshler

Johns, Thomas, Maj. QM to Parsons

Johnson, A. W., Capt. staff of Forrest

Johnson, Albert W., Capt. Judge Advocate to E. K. Smith; EO to W. Preston

Johnson, Ashton, Lt. ADC to Quarles (d. 1864)

Johnson, Benjamin S., Capt. AAG to Churchill; Maj. AAIG to E. K. Smith; VADC to Ben McCulloch (b. 1841)

Johnson, Charles F., Lt. ADC to Buckner (b. 1829)

Johnson, Euclid, Capt. acting QM to Barton, Pettus, Shelley

Johnson, J. W., Capt. AQM to Maxey, Cooper

Johnson, Jilson Payne, Maj. AAG to Breckinridge (1828–1879)

Johnson, John, Maj. EO to J. E. Johnston (1829–1907)

Johnson, Joseph H., Lt. OO to Manigault

Johnson, Lemuel H., Lt. acting OO to Cabell

Johnson, N., Lt. ADC to McNair

Johnson, Richard H., VADC to Holmes

Johnson, Robert W., Col. VADC to A. S. Johnston

Johnson, Thomas Carter, VADC to Price (1820–1868)

Johnson, W. H., Capt. VADC to S. D. Lee

Johnson, W. O., Maj. CS to Armstrong

Johnson, W. T., Lt. OO to Pillow

Johnson, Wilbur F., Lt. OO to Bragg; staff of Pillow, Richard H. Anderson

Johnson, Willa V., Maj. CS to Cosby, Armstrong, Chalmers (1837–1913)

Johnson, William Warren, Lt. ADC to Pike

Johnson, Winder P., Capt. Judge Advocate to S. D. Lee

Johnston, Ben., VADC to Ben McCulloch

Johnston, E., Capt. AQM to Pettus; Maj. QM to Shelley

Johnston, G. A. W., Capt. AAIG to Stevenson

Johnston, Harris Hancock, Lt. ADC to W. Preston; staff of Buckner

Johnston, J. S., Lt. AAIG to B. H. Robertson

Johnston, James W., Capt. AAG to Strahl (d. 1864)

Johnston, John William, Maj. Chief Arty. to Stevenson (1839–1905)

Johnston, Leroy F., Capt. AQM to Bragg

Johnston, Theodore, Maj. VADC to M. E. Green; Maj. CS to E. K. Smith, Pemberton, H. E. McCulloch

Jollee, William B., Maj. QM to Ross, Stewart

Jones, Alfred W., Col. ADC to Price (1818–1913)

Jones, B. F., Maj. QM to J. K. Jackson, Leadbetter, Bragg (b. 1831)

Jones, Charles, Lt. Col. VADC to Ruggles (d. 1870)

Jones, Charles Colcock, Jr., Lt. Col. Chief Arty. to Mercer, McLaws, Hardee, J. P. Anderson (1831–1893)

Jones, Elcon, Capt. SO to Churchill, E. K. Smith

Jones, Henry L., Capt. AQM to Tilghman, Pillow

Jones, J. M., Lt. OO to Wheeler, Armstrong

Jones, J. Paul, VADC to Stewart

Jones, James Chamberlayne, Lt. ADC to W. H. Jackson (1844–1907)

Jones, James Sterling, Lt. AAIG to Tyler, T. B. Smith

Jones, John B., Lt. AAG to J. E. Harrison (1834–1881)

Jones, John Wyatt, Maj. QM to Pillow, Tilghman (d. 1903)

Jones, Joseph P., Capt. AAIG to Bragg

Jones, Joseph W., Lt. OO at Danville, Va. (1834–1888)

Jones, Matthew H., Cadet acting ADC to Clayton

Jones, Norman C., Maj. QM to Armstrong, Wheeler, Dibrell

Jones, Rufus R., AAIG to Forney

Jones, S. W., Lt. AAIG to Gholson

Jones, Thomas, Lt. VADC to Maxey

Jones, Thomas M., Lt. OO to Wheeler, Armstrong, Humes

Jones, Thomas Marshall, Capt. ACS to Bragg (1832–1913)

Jones, William G., VADC to Jones

Jones, William R., Capt. Chief Arty. to Slaughter

Jordan, Francis H., Capt. AAG to Beauregard, Bragg, W. W. Allen (b. 1821)

Jordan, Thomas, Col. AAG to Beauregard, J. E. Johnston (1819–1895)

Jordan, William McR., Lt. acting ADC to J. P. Anderson

Judge, Thomas James, Col. Military Courts of Forney and Maury (1815–1876)

Judkins, James Henry, Capt. AAG to Clanton (1839–1922)

Kearny, Edmund, Lt. ADC to Jordan, Beauregard

Kearny, William, Lt. AAIG to Hardee, Magruder, Hindman, Shoup (1833–1893)

Keeble, James M., Lt. AAIG to Maney

Keenan, J. E., Lt. OO to Roddey

Keller, Arthur Henley, Capt. AQM to Roddey (1836–1896)

Kelly, John G., Lt. EO to Price; Capt. AAIG to Little, Hebert (1834–1903)

Kelly, Joseph H., Capt. AAG & Maj. AAIG & Col. VADC to Parsons

Kemp, William Perrin, Lt. ADC to Taliaferro (1840–1884)

Kemper, Delaware, Lt. Col. Chief Arty. to Hagood, Wise, Hardee, B. H. Robertson, A. R. Wright (1833–1899)

Kemper, William H., Lt. staff of B. H. Robertson

Kenan, Thomas H., Lt. ADC to W. H. T. Walker

Kendall, George W., Capt. ACS to D. W. Adams

Kendall, J. Irvin, Lt. acting ADC to Walthall

Kendall, W. D., Lt. AAAIG to Strahl

Kennard, James M., Maj. OO to Hardee; Lt. Col. OO to S. D. Lee, Hood, J. E. Johnston; staff of Floyd (1840–1914)

Kennard, P. S., VADC to Hardee; Col. staff of Holmes

Kennedy, Beverly C., Maj. CS to Bragg, Duncan

Kennedy, C. W., Capt. AQM to McCown

Kennedy, Elisha W., Capt. AQM to Bragg, Hood, J. E. Johnston

Kennedy, McPherson, Lt. AAG to B. T. Johnson

Kennedy, Robert, Capt. staff of Wheeler

Kennerly, Lewis Hancock, Capt. staff of S. D. Lee (b. 1831)

Kennerly, William Clark, Maj. OO to Little, J. E. Johnston (1824–1912)

Kent, Adolph, Lt. AAAG to Gladden

Kent, Thomas J., Capt. acting QM to T. H. Taylor

Keon, John H., Lt. AAIG to Lyon

Ker, Severn Parker, Capt. OO to Wheeler (b. 1839)

Kern, James M., Capt. ACS to Wood, Cleburne

Kernochan, Henry P., Lt. VADC to D. W. Adams

Kernochan, M., Capt. ADC to D. W. Adams

Kerr, George W., Lt. OO to Price, J. B. Clark, Marmaduke, Frost

Kerrison, Charles, Jr., acting ADC to Kennedy (1839–1893)

Ketchum, William H., staff of Slaughter; Capt. Chief Arty. to Cantey (1821–1865)

Key, William O., Maj. QM to Chalmers

Keyes, Francis W., Capt. AAAG to W. W. Adams

Keyworth, Robert W., Maj. CS to E. K. Smith

Kidd, James R., Capt. AQM to Chalmers, Wheeler

Kidd, Joseph, Capt. AQM to Wheeler

Kidder, Charles E., Lt. OO to Tappan; Capt. OO to Churchill

Kilgore, Constantine Buckley, Capt. AAG to
Ector (1835–1897)

Killough, Samuel A., Capt. AAIG to Ross

Kimmel, Manning Marius, Lt. OO to Ben
McCulloch; Maj. AAG to Van Dorn,
Magruder (b. 1832)

King, Adolphe, Capt. AAG to Waul

King, Benjamin, Lt. AAG to Gibson; AAAG to
Ruggles (d. 1862)

King, Clifton A., Cadet ADC to Stevenson;
acting ADC to Hardee; Capt. AAAIG to
Colston; Capt. SO to Stevenson

King, J. H., Maj. CS to Vaughan

King, John, Capt. AAG to Cabell, Fagan

King, John Floyd, Lt. OO to Heth; Maj. Chief
Arty. to Loring (1842–1915)

King, Mallory Page, Capt. AAG to W. D.
Smith, Gist; Capt. AAIG to McLaws,
Walthall

King, Stanhope H., Maj. CS to P. Smith,
Vaughan (d. 1901)

King, Thomas Edward, Capt. acting ADC to
P. Smith (1829–1863)

King, William A., Capt. AAG to L. E. Polk

King, William G., Maj. QM to H. E. McCulloch

King, William Hugh Means, Capt. VADC to
Richard H. Anderson; Maj. QM to J. K.
Jackson; Col. ADC to Wheeler (1832–1914)

Kingsbury, T. D., Capt. AQM to E. K. Smith

Kinney, Chapman Johnson, Maj. CS to Armstrong, Williams (1828–1885)

Kirkland, William Whedbee, Col. AAG to
Cleburne (1833–1915)

Kirkman, Hugh, Capt. ADC to Roddey

Klumph, Joseph Eby, Maj. QM to Forney,
M. E. Green

Knight, B. G., Lt. VADC to Higgins

Knight, W. N., Lt. ADC to Clayton

Knox, R. F., ADC to Ruggles

Krumbhaar, William Butler, Maj. Chief Arty.
to Maxey, Polk; staff of Bee (1835–1898)

Labouisse, John Witherspoon, Capt. AAIG to
Gibson, Wheeler (1841–1896)

Lacy, Richard F., Lt. ADC to Wheeler

Lake, Thomas Harden, Capt. AQM to Stewart
(b. 1834)

Lamar, George W., Jr., Capt. ACS to Taliaferro, Colston (b. 1839)

Lamar, Lucius Mirabeau, Col. Military Court
of Beauregard (1834–1889)

Lamar, Thompson Bird, Lt. Col. AAG to J. E.
Johnston (1828–1864)

Lamb, Robert Wilson, Capt. AQM to Whiting
(d. 1900)

Lamb, William, Maj. QM to Gatlin, J. R.
Anderson (1835–1909)

Lancaster, R. T., Lt. ADC to Vaughan

Landis, Absalom Lowe, Maj. QM to Cleburne,
Liddell, Govan (1823–1896)

Landry, J. A., Maj. QM to L. Hebert

Lane, Henry Milton, Lt. ADC to Ector
(b. 1839)

Lane, Isaac N., Lt. OO to McNair, D. H.
Reynolds (1843–1923)

Lane, J., Lt. OO to Kennedy

Lane, J. W., acting OO to T. Harrison

Lane, John B., Lt. OO to B. R. Johnson

Lanford, James F., Capt. AAAG to Cleburne

Lanford, Robert C., Maj. CS to Cleburne,
Cheatham, Hardee (d. 1895)

Langden, R. S., Capt. AQM to B. T. Johnson

Lanier, F. E., Lt. acting OO to Stovall

Lanier, John S., Lt. acting ADC to Leo. Polk,
Gardner

Lanier, Richard H., Capt. AAIG to Vaughan

Lanier, Sampson M., Capt. AQM to J. P.
Anderson, Hindman

Lanier, William Lewis, Maj. CS to Lovell

Lanigan, Thomas, Maj. CS to Pike, Magruder

LaRue, James B., Capt. ADC to Helm

La Sere, Emile, Maj. QM to R. Taylor

Lassalle, A. E., Maj. QM to E. K. Smith,
Tappan

Lathrop, Charles A., Capt. acting CS to
Gracie

Latimer, James D., Capt. AQM to Churchill,
Holmes

LaTrobe, Charles Hazelhurst, Lt. EO to Jones

Lauderdale, John A., Capt. VADC & Maj. QM
to Stewart; staff of Clayton (b. 1834)

Law, G. Davies, Lt. VADC to B. T. Johnson

Lawrence, James H., staff of Iverson

Lawrence, Robert J., Lt. AAIG & Maj. QM to Shelby

Laws, George, Lt. OO to Drayton

Lawshe, Lewis M., Capt. AQM to Featherston, J. P. Anderson

Lawton, Richard F., Lt. AAAG to Iverson (d. 1892)

Lay, John Fitzhugh, Capt. AAG to Beauregard; Maj. AAIG to Jones; staff of Hardee, J. P. Anderson (1826–1900)

Lea, Albert Miller, Capt. ACS to Zollicoffer; Capt. AAG to Finegan; Maj. EO to Maxey, Leadbetter, Magruder, E. K. Smith; Lt. Col. EO to Bee (1808–1891)

Lea, James L., Capt. AQM to Buford, Bell

Lea, Sumter, Lt. ADC & Capt. AAG to Frazer (b. 1835)

Leath, Peter M., Maj. QM to Chalmers

Leavenworth, Frederick P., Capt. OO to Holmes, E. K. Smith (1833–1920)

Le Baron, Thomas M., Maj. QM to Villepigue, Maury, Buckner

Ledyard, Edward S., Lt. VADC to Wheeler

Lee, Edward F., Capt. AAIG to M. J. Wright, Maxey (d. 1864)

Lee, Francis D., Capt. EO to Beauregard (1828–1885)

Lee, Frank, Capt. AAG to A. W. Reynolds

Lee, Henry B., Lt. ADC to S. D. Lee

Lee, Jesse B., Capt. ACS to Whiting, Clingman

Lee, John, Maj. CS to Price

Lee, John M., Lt. acting ADC to Manigault

Lee, Pollok B., Maj. AAG to Zollicoffer, Bragg, Hood, Hardee, Leo. Polk, Crittenden; Maj. AAIG to J. E. Johnston (d. 1866)

Lee, Roswell Walter, Lt. ADC & OO to Hindman; Capt. AAAG to Lee, Cooper (1810–1873)

Lee, Stephen J., Maj. CS to Steele

Lee, T. Hutson, Maj. QM to Beauregard, Young (b. 1834)

Leeds, P. B., Maj. AAG to E. K. Smith

Leftwich, Lincoln Clarke, Capt. OO to Van Dorn, Ben McCulloch (1832–1907)

Legare, Joseph J., Lt. VADC to Beauregard; Lt. EO to Trapier

Legare, W. W., Lt. OO to Kirkland, B. H. Robertson

Lege, Charles L., Capt. AQM to P. O. Hebert

Legon, R. M., Capt. ACS to Campbell

Leigh, Arthur K., Capt. AAAG & AAIG to Moore

Leigh, Charles H., Lt. acting OO to Ector

Leigh, G. H., Capt. ACS to P. O. Hebert, Magruder

Leigh, H. K., Capt. AAIG to Hawes

Leigh, William, Maj. OO to Marshall (1814–1888)

Leman, Robert S., Capt. ACS to Hawes

Leonard, J. L., Capt. AAIG to J. A. Smith

Lester, H. F., Lt. OO to Hawes

Levy, Lionel Lincoln, Capt. Judge Advocate to Holmes

Levy, William Mallory, Maj. AAG & Lt. Col. AAIG to R. Taylor (1827–1882)

Lewellyn, David H., Maj. QM to J. H. Morgan, Duke

Lewis, George, Lt. OO to Drayton, Tappan, Parsons

Lewis, Granville, Col. VADC to Donelson

Lewis, Henry Llewellyn Daingerfield, Lt. AAAG to Higgins, Liddell (1843–1893)

Lewis, John William, Capt. AAG to Holmes, Hindman, E. K. Smith, Price, Magruder (1837–1882)

Lewis, Stephen D., Maj. QM to Churchill

Lewis, William, Cadet staff of W. W. Allen

Lewis, William H., Capt. OO to Maxey

Liddell, Moses John, Lt. staff of Liddell (d. 1888)

Liddell, St. John Richardson, Col. VADC to Hardee (1815–1870)

Liddell, William R., VADC to Liddell

Liernur, Charles T., Capt. EO to Forney

Lindsay, A. J., Capt. ADC & AAAIG to A. S. Johnston; AAIG to D. W. Adams; Capt. OO to Magruder

Lindsay, George, Lt. AAIG to Ector

Lindsay, Henry Clay, Lt. so to Marshall, W. Preston

Lindsay, Robert H., Capt. AQM to D. W. Adams

Lindsey, L. T., Capt. VADC & AAAG to Chalmers

Lindsley, Henry, VADC to Donelson

Lingan, James B., Capt. AAIG to S. D. Lee, Leo. Polk, Maury, R. Taylor

Little, Andrew J., Capt. so to Churchill

Little, George, Capt. OO to Breckinridge, Bragg, Bate, Cheatham (b. 1838)

Little, Lewis Henry, Col. AAG to Price (1817–1862)

Lloyd, William David Clinton, Maj. AAAIG & OO to J. K. Jackson

Locke, Joseph Lorenzo, Maj. CS to Lawton (d. 1864)

Lockett, Samuel Henry, Capt. EO to Bragg, Pemberton, M. L. Smith; Lt. Col. EO to J. E. Johnston, Leo. Polk, S. D. Lee, R. Taylor (1837–1891)

Lockhart, Harrison C., Maj. AAG & ACS to Pillow

Lockhart, Joseph D., Maj. CS to Cheatham, Brown, Reynolds

Lockhart, T. P., Capt. AQM to Tucker, Shoup

Lockman, John B., Maj. OO to Hindman

Logan, R. M., Capt. ACS to Campbell

Lomax, Lunsford Lindsay, Lt. AAG to Ben McCulloch; Lt. Col. AAIG to Van Dorn (1835–1913)

Long, John Osmond, Lt. Col. AAIG to Slaughter, Magruder (1832–1875)

Long, Lemuel, Lt. ADC to Pillow (1827–1906)

Long, Leroy William, Maj. QM to Stevenson (d. 1901)

Looney, Abraham McClellan, Maj. VADC to P. Smith (1820–1904)

Looscan, Michael, Maj. AAIG to Maxey (1838–1897)

Loring, W. W., Jr., VADC to Loring

Loughborough, James M., Capt. AAG to Cockrell, Price, A. Baker

Lovell, William Storrow, Lt. Col. AAAIG to Pemberton (1829–1900)

Loving, Alex. W., Capt. AAAG to Richardson

Lowe, Enoch Magruder, Capt. ACS at Milboro, Va. (1832–1879)

Lowe, Gideon Harris, Capt. AAIG to Brown, Reynolds, Palmer (d. 1865)

Lowe, Washington Eldridge, Capt. VADC to Donelson (1835–1862)

Lowery, David, Lt. ADC to Wheeler (d. 1864)

Lubbock, Francis Richard, Lt. Col. AAG to Magruder (1815–1905)

Lucas, Alexander H., Lt. ADC to Trapier

Lucas, J. M., Lt. VADC to Richardson

Lucas, S. E., Maj. CS to Manigault, J. P. Anderson

Luckett, Philip Noland, VADC to Van Dorn (1824–1869)

Lumpkin, Miller Grieve, Maj. CS to Young (b. 1837)

Lumpkin, W. D., Maj. staff of Hardee

Lyerly, E. A., Capt. ADC to L. Hebert

Lynch, E., Capt. VADC to Drayton

Lynch, Montgomery, Capt. EO to Leo. Polk

Lynch, Peter Guilfoile, Capt. ACS to Watie

Lynch, Thomas, Capt. staff of Higgins

Lyon, Collier F. J., Capt. ACS to Hoke

Lyon, Francis Glover, Lt. ADC to Deas (1842–1893)

Lyon, Thomas Temple Armstrong, Capt. ACS to Withers

Lyons, Henry L., Maj. CS to Buckner

McAfee, Edward Madison, VADC to Featherston (d. 1884)

McAnelly, Leander, Capt. VADC to T. Green

McArthur, William J., Maj. AAIG to Shelby

McBlair, Charles H., Col. Chief Arty. to Trapier

McBride, James Haggin, Col. VADC to Frost (1814–1864)

McBryde, Alfred, Lt. ADC to Buford

McCabe, William P., Lt. ADC to Tappan

McCall, James K., Maj. OO to Maury, R. Taylor

McCarthy, Maurice, Maj. QM to W. T. Martin, W. W. Allen

McCarty, William C., Lt. ADC to Moore

McCawley, George W., Capt. AAG to Helm, Bate

McCay, Thomas Scott Henderson, VADC to L. Hebert

McClarty, Clinton, Capt. ACS to Breckinridge; Maj. QM to Hawes

McCleish, A. H., Maj. CS at Danville, Va.

McClelland, ——, Lt. AAQM to Cockrell

McClenaghan, Cunningham, Maj. CS to Ripley (1828–1893)

McCloskey, James L., Capt. AQM to Beall, F. Gardner; Maj. QM to Withers, Gardner

McClung, Linus A., Capt. AAG to Wood (d. 1862)

McClure, John F., Capt. AAQM to C. Clark

McClure, Robert B., Lt. ADC to Bate; VADC to McCown

McConaughey, James W., Maj. AAG to McRae

McConnell, William Kennedy, Capt. AAG to Shelley, Cantey (1841–1891)

McConnico, Washington Lafayette, Maj. QM to A. W. Reynolds, Tilghman

McCown, George W., Maj. ADC & Col. Chief Arty. to McCown

McCoy, Arthur C., staff of Shelby (b. 1830)

McCoy, Henry, Capt. ADC to B. R. Johnson

McCrady, John, Capt. EO to Beauregard, McLaws; Maj. EO to D. H. Hill, Beauregard (1831–1881)

McCranie, George W., Maj. PM to Loring

McCraw, S. N., Maj. AAG to G. D. Johnston

McCulloch, Alexander, Capt. ADC to H. E. McCulloch

McDaniel, E. H., Lt. ADC to Kelly

McDavitt, James C., staff of Leo. Polk, Maury, Loring, J. E. Johnston

McDowell, J. H., Capt. AQM to Churchill

McElrath, Hugh McDowell, Maj. QM to E. K. Smith (1815–1863)

McElrath, John Edgar, Maj. QM to Pettus, Stevenson, Tracy (1844–1907)

McElwee, William Eblen, staff of Stevenson (1835–1929)

McFall, J. K. P., Lt. EO to Bragg, Stewart

McFarland, Baxter, Lt. acting ADC to Tucker (1839–1925)

McFarland, James Davis, Lt. acting ADC to S. D. Lee; ADC & AAAG to Moore

McFarland, Robert, Capt. ADC to Cleburne (1836–1892)

McFarland, William, VADC to Loring

McGaughy, John G., Maj. CS to Roddey

McGavock, Edward Jacob, Capt. AQM to Tyler, Palmer (1828–1880)

McGuire, J. E., VADC to Churchill

McGuire, Thomas, Maj. QM to Loring, Buford, Featherston

McGuirk, John, Lt. Col. VADC to Wheeler (1827–1871)

McIntire, Hamilton, Lt. ADC to Wheeler

McIntosh, James McQueen, Capt. AAG to Ben McCulloch (1828–1862)

McIvor, E. J., Capt. AQM to Bragg, Hood

McKay, Henry Clay, Lt. ADC to Lewis

McKay, John P., Capt. ACS to Lane

McKay, John R., Lt. AAAIG to McRae

McKenzie, Donald, Lt. OO to Chalmers

McKinney, John A., VADC to A. E. Jackson, Vaughn

McKnight, George, Maj. AAG to Loring (1833–1869)

McLaughlin, John, Capt. AAG to Tilghman, Cheatham

McLaughlin, William, Maj. QM, Chief Arty., & AAAG to Echols (1828–1898)

McLaws, Lafayette, Maj. acting QM & acting CS to Lawton (1821–1897)

McLean, Frank J., Lt. acting ADC to B. R. Johnson

McLellan, Alden, Lt. AAAG to Bowen

McMahon, W. J., Maj. CS to Vaughn

McMicken, Mathew B., Maj. QM to Bragg, Hardee, Leo. Polk, Hood, J. E. Johnston

McMillin, John P., Capt. Military Court of Pemberton (b. 1803)

McMinn, William, Maj. QM to Forney, Bragg

McNairy, Frank H., Maj. ADC to Cheatham; VADC to Polk, W. H. Jackson

McNeely, Abel C., Capt. ACS to H. E. McCulloch

McNeil, J. D., staff of Moore

McNeill, A. D., Maj. ADC to Hindman

McNeill, George W., Maj. acting ADC to Bee

McNeill, Harry, Lt. VADC to Chalmers

McNeill, Henry C., Col. AAIG to Sibley, Magruder (b. 1835)

McNeill, James F., Col. Military Court of E. K. Smith

McRady, Joseph A., Capt. ACS to Maxey, Quarles, Stewart

McRae, George R., Lt. EO to Cheatham, Hardee

McRae, James Cameron, Capt. OO to Whiting, Holmes; Capt. AAG to L. Baker (1838–1909)

McRory, James H., Capt. EO to Finegan (d. 1862)

McSwine, Hugh R., Capt. AQM to Strahl

McSwine, Thomas, Capt. AQM to Tappan, Roane

McVoy, Alexander, VADC to Jones; Capt. AQM to Forney, Maury

MacGreal, Clarence W., Capt. ADC to Drayton; VADC to Green, Magruder

Mackall, Thomas B., Lt. ADC to Mackall, Bragg

Mackall, William Whann, Lt. Col. AAG to A. S. Johnston (1817–1891)

Mackay, Alec., Lt. OO to S. D. Lee

Mackey, Thomas J., Capt. EO to Pike, Price, Holmes

Maclay, Robert Plunket, Maj. AAG to Holmes, J. G. Walker (1820–1903)

Maclay, William Duncan, Capt. AAG to E. K. Smith

Maclean, Lauchlan Allen, Maj. AAG to Price, Drayton, Parsons; Lt. Col. ADC to J. E. Rains (d. 1864)

Maclin, Sackfield, Maj. QM to Van Dorn, Magruder, P. O. Hebert (1809–1876)

Maclin, Thomas, Lt. acting ADC to H. E. McCulloch

Macon, Junius M., Lt. AAG to Clayton, Holtzclaw

Madison, George T., Col. VADC to T. Green

Magenis, Arthur John, Lt. Col. ADC to Frost (d. 1867)

Magenis, William MacRea, Lt. OO to Walthall; Capt. AAG to J. H. Morgan; staff of Polk (1839–1863)

Magoffin, Joseph, Capt. AAG & Maj. CS to Major; Capt. AQM to Sibley (d. 1923)

Magoffin, Samuel, Jr., Maj. VADC to Sibley

Magruder, Lawson W., Lt. OO to Pemberton, Bate, W. H. T. Walker, Tyler (d. 1908)

Major, James Patrick, Lt. VADC to Van Dorn; Lt. ADC to Twiggs; Lt. Col. acting EO & acting Chief Arty. to Van Dorn (1836–1877)

Major, John B., Capt. AAG to Davis

Mallard, Jefferson J., Capt. ACS to Parsons

Mallett, Peter, Maj. AAG to Holmes (1825–1907)

Mallett, R. J., Capt. AAG to Cobb

Malone, Frederick A., Capt. AQM to B. R. Johnson, Wheeler, Hardee

Malone, Thomas H., Capt. AAG to Maney (b. 1834)

Maney, James D., Maj. CS to Maney (b. 1830)

Mangum, James W., Capt. AAG to Moore, A. Baker

Mangum, Leonard Henderson, Lt. ADC to Cleburne (b. 1837)

Manigault, Arthur Middleton, Capt. staff of Beauregard (1824–1886)

Manigault, Edward, Col. OO to Beauregard; VADC to Ripley (1817–1874)

Manigault, Joseph, Lt. VADC to R. E. Lee; Lt. acting ADC to Pemberton; Capt. AAIG to Beauregard; Capt. AAG & SO to Pemberton, Beauregard, Mercer

Mann, John G., Lt. EO to Cheatham, Forrest

Manning, Brown, Lt. ADC to Cantey

Manning, George Felix, Lt. Asst. Chief Arty. to Wheeler; Lt. AAAIG to S. D. Lee

Manning, Richard J., Maj. ADC to J. E. Johnston

Manning, T. C., ADC to Twiggs

Marks, Samuel Blackburn, Maj. AAIG to Withers (b. 1820)

Marsh, John Henry, Lt. VADC to Cheatham; AAIG to Strahl (d. 1864)

Marsh, John T., Lt. AAIG to Strahl

Marshall, Charles Edward, Capt. AAG to Marshall (1821–1868)

Marshall, George, VADC to M. E. Green

Marshall, Levin R., Capt. AAIG to Loring

Marshall, Lewis Field, Maj. CS to Rust (1825–1877)

Marshall, Warren R., Capt. AAIG to Davidson, Humes

Marston, Bulon Ward, Capt. AAIG to Cooper, E. K. Smith, Maxey, (1841–1917)

Martin, Charles F., Lt. VADC to Pillow

Martin, Eugene S., Lt. acting OO to Kennedy (1840–1919)

Martin, George W., Capt. AAAG to R. Taylor

Martin, Henry Neil, Lt. acting ADC & Capt. AAG to S. D. Lee; VADC to Van Dorn (1844–1890)

Martin, Hugh Bradshaw, Capt. OO to Dibrell, Forrest, Kelly (b. 1838)

Martin, John Henry, Lt. ADC to W. H. Jackson, W. T. Martin (b. 1840)

Mason, Charles M., staff of P. O. Hebert, Scurry, Magruder

Mason, John C., Capt. ACS to Frazer

Mason, John Guerrard, Capt. ADC to Maury; AAG to F. Gardner (b. 1838)

Mason, John Stevens, Lt. SO to Breckinridge, Stewart

Mason, Joseph P., Capt. ACS to Frazer

Mason, M. J. M., Capt. AAAG & ACS to Forrest

Mason, Richard M., Maj. QM to Hardee, Leo. Polk, Cheatham, Stewart, Forrest

Mason, Thomas E., Maj. QM to Ross

Mason, Webb, Lt. staff of Echols

Masterson, William, Lt. ADC to Steele

Mastin, Charles J., Capt. VADC, AAG & AAIG to Breckinridge; Capt. AAG to Bate (d. 1895)

Mastin, Edward Irby., Lt. acting ADC & AAAG to Kelly (1841–1894)

Mastin, N. H., Maj. ADC to Wood

Mastin, William F., Maj. AAG to Wood, Buckner

Mathes, B. N., Lt. AAAG & AAIG to McCown

Mathes, George M., Capt. Chief Arty. to McCown

Mathewes, J. Fraser, Capt. EO to Taliaferro, Beauregard

Mathews, A. M., Maj. Chief Arty. & OO to Stevenson

Mathews, Charles L., Capt. ADC to Loring

Mathews, Joseph William, Capt. AAG to Stevenson, A. W. Reynolds

Matthews, Beverly, Lt. AAAIG to Van Dorn; Maj. AAIG to Ruggles

Matthews, W. G., Capt. AAIG to Gano

Mattison, J. B., Lt. OO to Chalmers, J. P. Anderson, Deas, Tucker, Sharp (1836–1910)

Maupin, Robert Lemon, Capt. AAG to Cockrell (1836–1919)

Maurice, Samuel Wesley, Lt. OO to B. H. Robertson (1833–1879)

Maury, James Fontaine, Capt. ADC to Bowen (d. 1875)

Maury, John Herndon, Lt. ADC to Maury (1842–1863)

Maxan, Nestor, Maj. VADC to Bee

Maxey, James P., Capt. ACS to Parsons

Maxwell, Augustus E., VADC to Bragg (b. 1820)

Maxwell, Thomas H., Capt. AQM to Bate

May, Augustus Hugh, Capt. AAG to R. Taylor, J. G. Walker (b. 1823)

May, Lambert, Capt. AAIG to J. P. Anderson, Tucker, Withers, Brown (d. 1888)

Mayer, Simon, AAAG to J. P. Anderson

Mayo, George Upshur, Lt. OO to Trapier, Pemberton; Lt. OO to Grayson; Maj. AAIG to Beauregard, Hardee

Mayo, John Henry Fitzhugh, Maj. CS to Cumming, Stevenson, Hindman (1828–1894)

Mayrant, Robert W., Capt. AQM to D. H. Hill

Mays, R. G., Capt. ACS to Barton

Meadors, John Calhoun, Capt. ACS to Moore, A. Baker (1838–1896)

Means, Samuel Clowney, Capt. ACS to Harrison (b. 1830)

Mebane, Samuel R., Lt. ADC to Maxey

Mechling, William Thompson, Capt. AAAG to E. K. Smith; Maj. AAG to Bee

Meek, John A., Capt. ADC to Forney

Mellard, Wesley, Capt. ACS to L. Hebert

Mellon, John J., Lt. OO & AAQM to Beauregard

Memminger, Robert Witherspoon, Capt. AAG to R. E. Lee; Maj. AAG to Pemberton; staff of Jones, R. Ransom, D. H. Hill (1839–1901)

Menees, George W., ACS to J. E. Johnston, Hood

Mercer, George Anderson, Capt. AAG to Mercer, J. A. Smith (b. 1835)

Meriwether, Minor, Maj. EO to Leo. Polk, Loring, Pemberton, Price (1827–1910)

Merrill, Henry, Maj. EO to Holmes

Merrimon, Branch H., Lt. AAG to Vance

Merrimon, James H., Lt. AAIG to Palmer (1832–1921)

Meslier, Gaston, Lt. ADC to Higgins

Metcalf, A. W., ADC to Liddell

Metcalf, T. S., VADC to Beauregard

Meyer, Adolphus, Capt. ADC & AAG to Williams (1842–1908)

Mhoon, John Bell, Lt. acting EO to Price, Marmaduke (1840–1911)

Mickle, Belton, Capt. AQM to Villepigue, Loring

Middleton, Jacob Motte, Lt. ADC to Ripley

Mikell, Thomas Waring, Lt. acting ADC to Logan (1837–1893)

Miller, ——, Capt. EO to Tilghman

Miller, Edgar, Maj. CS to Beall

Mills, Albert N., Capt. AAG to Scurry

Mills, Andrew Graham, Capt. AAIG to Chalmers (1839–1894)

Millsaps, Reuben Webster, Maj. AAIG to Loring (1833–1916)

Milner, Willis Julian, Lt. AAAG to Lowry (1842–1921)

Miltenburger, Ernest, Lt. ADC to H. W. Allen (d. 1908)

Mims, Livingston, Maj. QM to Pemberton (1833–1906)

Miner, Frederick William, Capt. VADC to Cooper (b. 1832)

Minnick, William J., Capt. ADC to Leo. Polk; Capt. AAAIG to Stewart

Minter, Joseph F., Capt. VADC & AAQM to Van Dorn; Maj. QM to E. K. Smith (d. 1885)

Minter, Thomas N., Capt. ACS to P. O. Hebert; Capt. AAQM to Scurry

Mirick, W. G., Capt. ACS to Little

Mitchel, Charles E., Lt. ADC & AAIG to Tappan; staff of McNair, Roane (b. 1846)

Mitchell, Julius Caesar Bonaparte, acting ADC to Cantey (1817–1869)

Mitchell, Lueco, Lt. VADC to B. T. Johnson

Mitchell, Martin Van Buren, Capt. AQM to Stewart

Mitchell, Thomas E., Capt. ACS to Manigault, D. H. Hill

Mitchell, Thomas R., Capt. AAAIG to L. E. Polk (d. 1864)

Mohler, Elisha Grigsby, Lt. OO to Van Dorn; Maj. QM to Moore, D. H. Hill, Cockrell, Maury (1838–1916)

Moise, T. S., Maj. QM to P. O. Hebert

Molony, Robert, staff of Tappan

Moncure, John C., Capt. AAG to Polignac (1827–1916)

Monroe, Thomas, Maj. QM to Parsons, Price

Monsarrat, George H., Capt. AAAIG to Carroll

Montgomery, Hugh B. T., Capt. AACS to J. K. Jackson (1824–1865)

Montgomery, Hugh W., AAAG to E. K. Smith

Montgomery, J. Byron, Lt. OO to Williams

Montgomery, Louis M., Lt. Col. staff of E. K. Smith; Lt. Col. acting ADC to Pemberton

Montgomery, William M., Maj. QM to Ben McCulloch, Greer, Price, Van Dorn (d. 1862)

Moore, Andrew, Lt. ADC to D. H. Hill

Moore, B. L., Capt. AAAG to Shoup

Moore, Benjamin Rush, Col. VADC to Bate (1834–1894)

Moore, C. L., Maj. QM to Tappan

Moore, Charles B., Maj. QM to McRae, Churchill, Magruder (d. 1911)

Moore, Charles F., Capt. AQM to J. E. Johnston, Gladden, Forney, Buckner

Moore, D. L., Capt. VADC to B. R. Johnson

Moore, J. B., Capt. AAIG to Brown

Moore, John Courtney, Lt. AAAG to Marmaduke, J. B. Clark (1834–1915)

Moore, John Edmund, Col. on Military Court of Hardee, Breckinridge (1815–1865)

Moore, Joseph C., Capt. ACS to Hood, Leo. Polk

Moore, Littleton Wilde, Maj. AAG to Steele (1835–1911)

Moore, M. A., Col. VADC to N. G. Evans

Moore, Patrick Theodore, Col. Military Court of Jones (1821–1883)

Moore, Virgil V., Lt. AAAG to Armstrong

Moore, W. B., Lt. Col. VADC to Cheatham

Moore, W. E., Lt. AAIG to McNair

Moore, William E., Maj. CS to Hardee, J. E. Johnston, Hood, R. Taylor (1828–1883)

Moore, William Franklin, Capt. staff of Price

Moores, William H., Capt. AQM to J. A. Smith; Maj. QM to Granbury; staff of Hardee, Churchill, J. E. Johnston

Moorhead, J. C., Lt. AAIG to Gracie

Moorman, George, Lt. ADC to Tilghman; Capt. AAG to W. H. Jackson (1841–1902)

Moorman, George Triplett, Lt. acting ADC to B. R. Johnson; Capt. acting ADC to McCown

Moorman, S. M., Maj. CS to Helm, Lewis

Mordecai, J. Randolph, Capt. AQM to Taliaferro, Elliott, Ro. H. Anderson

Moreno, Stephen A., Capt. AAG to J. K. Jackson (1839–1900)

Moreno, Theodore, Capt. EO to Cobb, Gardner

Morgan, Alexander G., Maj. CS to Duke

Morgan, Calvin Cogswell, Lt. ADC to Duke, J. H. Morgan (1827–1882)

Morgan, Charlton H., Capt. ADC to J. H. Morgan (b. 1838)

Morgan, George H., Lt. ADC to Dibrell

Morgan, J. A., Capt. AQM to Cleburne

Morgan, J. M., Capt. AQM to Dibrell

Morgan, Robert Jarrel, Col. Military Court & VADC to Leo. Polk (1826–1899)

Morgan, W. C., Col. AAG to Bonham

Morris, Isaac L., staff of M. J. Wright

Morris, John, Col. VADC to Williams

Morris, Thomas, staff of Chalmers

Morris, Walter J., Lt. EO to Tilghman, Leo. Polk, Breckinridge; Capt. EO to Gilmer, Taylor, Polk

Morris, William C., Capt. ADC to Price

Morrison, Richard T., Lt. ADC to Price

Morrison, William Wilberforce, ACS to L. Baker; staff of D. H. Hill, Gatlin (1826–1865)

Morse, Alexander Porter, Lt. ADC to Major

Morton, John Watson, Jr., Capt. acting Chief Arty. to Forrest

Moses, M. B., VADC to Clingman

Moses, William Q., Lt. AAAG to John Adams

Moss, J. A., Capt. ACS to S. D. Lee

Moss, Rufus L., Capt. ACS to Cobb (1825–1912)

Mouton, J. S., Maj. CS to Mouton

Muldon, Samuel C., Capt. acting QM to J. K. Jackson; Maj. QM to Manigault

Mulherrin, Samuel H., Maj. CS to McNair, Walthall, French, D. H. Reynolds

Mumford, F. M., Lt. OO to Scott

Munday, W. S., Maj. CS to Donelson, Maury, Buckner

Munford, Edward W., Maj. VADC to A. S. Johnston, Hardee; Col. Military Court of S. D. Lee

Munford, William B., VADC to Quarles (d. 1864)

Munson, M. S., Military Court of Wharton

Murdaugh, John W., Capt. OO to Davis

Murphy, John J., Maj. CS to Leo. Polk, Stewart (d. 1891)

Murphy, W. L., Capt. AQM to Polignac

Murray, J. Adair, Lt. ADC to Magruder

Murray, James Henry, Jr., Lt. ADC to J. P. Anderson

Murrell, T. L., Lt. staff of Cheatham

Musser, Richard H., Lt. Col. Military Court of J. B. Clark

Myers, Abraham, Capt. AQM to B. T. Johnson (d. 1910)

Myers, D. Emmett, Lt. ADC & Capt. AAIG to Buford

Myers, Henry, Lt. OO to Gladden; Maj. OO to Maury, Gardner

Myers, Simon, Maj. CS to Featherston

Mynatt, Pryor L., Capt. ACS to Humes (1829–1900)

Myrick, John Douglas, Capt. ADC & Chief Arty. to Loring

Nailer, J., Lt. ADC to Gibson

Nathan, Julius, acting ADC to Strahl

Neilson, Charles A., Capt. ACS to Moore, Sears

Neilson, Charles P., Capt. AAG to Featherston (1839–1894)

Nelson, R. M., Capt. AAG to Brandon

Newman, Henry A., Capt. acting QM to Stovall; Capt. AQM to D. H. Hill

Newnam, Samuel, Capt. ACS to Gibson

Newton, Frank McC., Capt. ACS to P. O. Hebert, Bee

Newton, Robert Crittenden, Col. AAG to Hindman, E. K. Smith; staff of Holmes (1840–1887)

Newton, Thomas W., Capt. AAIG to Marmaduke; Maj. AAG to J. B. Clark (1843–1908)

Nichol, Alexander, Lt. AAIG to Wheeler

Nichol, Benjamin Frank, Lt. OO to Churchill

Nichol, Bradford, Lt. OO to Bate, Breckinridge, Tyler, Mercer, W. H. T. Walker (1841–1893)

Nichol, Charles A., Capt. VADC to J. E. Rains; staff of McCown, Vance, Wheeler

Nichols, George W., Maj. staff of Shelby

Nichols, Ebenezer B., Lt. Col. VADC to Magruder (1814–1872)

Nichols, W. A., AAG to Twiggs

Nichols, William M., Lt. AAG & Capt. ADC to Gartrell

Nicholson, E. P., Capt. AAG to Gano

Nicholson, Hunter, Maj. AAG to Buford, Loring (1834–1901)

Nicholson, James H., Lt. AAAG to Finley

Nicholson, William, VADC to Vaughn

Nieman, Samuel H., Capt. AQM to Shelley

Nieman, T. A., Capt. AQM to D. W. Adams

Nocquet, James, Capt. EO to Buckner, Breckinridge, Leo. Polk, Bragg, J. E. Johnston

Noel, Frank S., VADC to Armstrong

Norcom, William, acting ADC to Barton

Norman, Henry H., OO to Palmer

Norman, William F., Capt. ACS to Higgins, Shoup

Norris, ——, Lt. AAG to Wheeler

Norris, John N., Maj. QM to Maxey

Norris, William Henry, Col. Military Court of Jones (1807–1890)

Norton, George, Capt. AAIG to Gibson

Norton, Samuel E., Maj. QM to Wheeler

Noyes, A. B., Capt. ACS to Finegan, Cobb; Maj. CS to J. P. Anderson, Gardner, J. K. Jackson

Nugent, Richard James, Capt. AQM to Mouton, Polignac (1834–1891)

Nugent, William Lewis, Capt. AAG to Ferguson (1832–1897)

O'Bannon, Lawrence W., Lt. Col. QM to Bragg, E. K. Smith (d. 1882)

Ogden, ——, Capt. AAG to Bee

Ogden, John, Capt. ADC to Hodge

Ogden, John R., Capt. AAAG to Loring

Oglesby, William M., AAG to J. K. Jackson

O'Hara, Theodore, Capt. AAIG to A. S. Johnston; Col. AAAG to Breckinridge (1820–1867)

O'Hea, Richard A., Lt. EO to Stewart

Ohlson, Charles M., Capt. ACS to McNair, Reynolds

O'Kane, Walter Scott, Col. ADC to Marmaduke (b. 1832)

Oladowski, Hypolite, Capt. OO to A. S. Johnston; Lt. Col. OO to Bragg, J. E. Johnston (d. 1878)

Old, William, Jr., Capt. AQM & acting OO to B. H. Robertson

Oldham, Williamson S., Capt. AAG to Maxey, E. K. Smith

Oliver, Lindsey H., Maj. cs to Maxey, Roane

Oliver, Thomas Winfrey, Maj. QM to Clanton (1827–1898)

Olivier, Jules G., VADC to Mouton; acting ADC to Polignac (1819–1869)

O'Neill, Samuel, Capt. AQM to Chalmers

O'Rorke, P. R., Lt. AAIG to E. K. Smith

Otey, William Newton Mercer, Lt. AAAG & so to Leo. Polk; Lt. AAAG to Forrest (1842–1898)

Overton, John, Jr., Capt. VADC to B. R. Johnson (1842–1901)

Owen, Lucien S., Capt. AAAG to Gholson

Owen, William Miller, Maj. Chief Arty. to W. Preston (1832–1893)

Owens, Charles D., Capt. ACS to Drayton (1834–1897)

Owens, John W., VADC to Lawton

Page, George D., Capt. AQM to Shelby; Maj. QM to Marmaduke, J. B. Clark

Paine, A. J., Capt. OO to M. J. Wright

Paine, James G., Capt. AAG to Gholson

Paine, William W., Lt. OO to Lawton (1817–1892)

Palfrey, William, Capt. AAG to Shoup, Elzey

Palmer, John Coleman, Maj. cs to Hindman, Holmes (b. 1823)

Palmer, Orlando Stotts, Capt. AAG to Wood, Lowrey (d. 1865)

Panchen, John S., Capt. AQM to Tyler

Parham, R. T. B., Capt. AAG to Tyler

Parker, Henry H., Lt. OO to Davidson

Parker, James Porter, Lt. Col. Chief Arty. to F. Gardner (1839–1918)

Parker, William Asa, Lt. OO to Wheeler, Hindman, Kelly (b. 1835)

Parrish, J. T., Capt. AAG to Roddey

Patterson, B. N., VADC to Maxey

Patterson, James, Lt. ADC to Wheeler (d. 1863)

Patterson, Robert F., Lt. acting ADC to Barton

Patteson, James, Lt. acting ADC & AAIG to Maxey

Patton, ——, Lt. ADC to Wheeler (d. 1863)

Patton, J. W., Maj. QM to S. D. Lee

Patton, Thomas F., Capt. ACS at Danville, Va.

Patton, Thomas J., Capt. AAAG to Slack

Patton, William A. M., Lt. ADC & AAAG to A. W. Reynolds; ADC to Stevenson

Patton, Yandell S., Capt. AQM to Hardee; Maj. QM to Cheatham

Pauk, J. W., AAAIG to Fagan

Paul, William P., Maj. QM to W. H. Jackson (1824–1878)

Payne, Lewis E., Lt. OO to Lewis, Helm

Pearce, Nicholas Bartlett, Maj. QM & cs to Hindman; staff of Ben McCulloch, Magruder (1828–1894)

Pearl, Isaac M., Capt. staff of Jackson

Pearre, Aubray, Lt. OO to Govan, Liddell

Pearre, Charles Baer, Maj. cs to Harrison (1834–1908)

Pearson, ——, Lt. AAIG to Granbury

Pearson, Edward F., Capt. AQM to J. B. Clark

Peay, Gordon Neill, Col. VADC to Holmes (1819–1876)

Peay, William Nicholas, Capt. AQM to E. K. Smith (1828–1900)

Peckham, A. P., Lt. OO to Jackson

Peden, Charles W., Capt. AAG to Bragg

Peek, Thomas C., Maj. cs to Van Dorn, Tappan

Pegram, John, Col. EO to Beauregard, Bragg; Col. AAG to E. K. Smith (1832–1865)

Pemberton, W. S., Capt. ACS to Ben McCulloch

Pendleton, Eugene B., Maj. cs to Magruder

Pendleton, W. J., acting ADC to Magruder; acting cs to Hawes

Perkins, Hardin, Col. VADC to Hardee

Perkins, S. H., Col. VADC to Hardee

Perkins, W. M., OO to Holmes

Perrie, Charles T., VADC to Price

Peters, Thomas, Maj. QM to Pillow, Leo. Polk, R. Taylor, D. H. Hill (1812–1883)

Peterson, H. B., Lt. acting ADC to Iverson

Pettus, Edmund W., Jr., Lt. ADC to Pettus (d. 1865)

Peyton, Alfred H., Lt. ACS & Capt. OO to Lyon (b. 1843)

Peyton, James Tate, Maj. QM to J. P. Anderson, Hood (1836–1869)

Peyton, William Madison, Capt. ADC to Williams (1839–1901)

Pflager, Harry W., Capt. AQM to Price

Phifer, Charles W., Maj. AAIG to A. W. Reynolds (1833–1896)

Philips, Joseph, Lt. AAAIG to Polk; acting Chief Arty. to R. Taylor (d. 1920)

Phillips, Benjamin F., Capt. AAIG to Cleburne

Phillips, Edward, Maj. CS to Taylor, Slaughter, Drayton

Phillips, W. S., Capt. AQM to Lewis

Phinizy, Charles H., Capt. AAG to Cumming (1835–1898)

von Phul, Francis, Capt. acting ADC to Little, Frost; Lt. ADC to J. B. Clark, Marmaduke (b. 1835)

Pickett, Edward, Jr., Col. VADC to Cheatham (1828–1876)

Pickett, George Blackwell, Capt. EO to Breckinridge; Maj. EO to Cheatham; staff of Hardee (b. 1826)

Pickett, William Douglas, Capt. AAG & Lt. Col. AAIG to Hardee (1827–1919)

Pierce, A. J., Capt. ACS to Ferguson

Pierce, William, Capt. AAIG to M. J. Wright

Pike, Hamilton, VADC to McCulloch, Breckinridge

Pike, Walter Lacey, Lt. ADC to Pike

Pilcher, Matthew B., Capt. AQM to Cheatham, Brown, Maney, Bate

Pillow, George M., Lt. ADC to Pillow (1839–1872)

Pinckney, ——, Lt. Col. VADC to Breckinridge

Pinckney, Charles C., Jr., Capt. OO to Ripley

Pinckney, R. J., Capt. AQM to J. K. Jackson

Pinckney, Robert Q., Capt. AQM to Trapier; Maj. QM to Withers, J. P. Anderson

Pinkney, B. G., Capt. staff of Trapier

Pirtle, John A., Capt. AAAG to Bate (b. 1842)

Pitman, Robert William, Capt. AAIG to Forrest (1836–1900)

Pittman, William B., Capt. AAG to M. E. Green, Maury

Pitts, William A., Capt. OO & VADC to H. E. McCulloch

Pledge, Frank L., Capt. AQM to Cheatham

Plummer, C. C., Lt. ADC to Ross

Plummer, P. B., Capt. ADC to Brown

Poellnitz, Charles Augustus, Maj. QM to G. D. Johnston (1839–1909)

Poindexter, W. R., Capt. AQM to Walthall

Poindexter, William Green, Lt. OO & Capt. ACS to Featherston (d. 1893)

Pointer, E., Lt. ADC to Wheeler (d. 1864)

Pointer, Marcellus, Lt. ADC to Wheeler (d. 1909)

Poland, Thomas, Capt. AQM to Lane

Polignac, Camille Armand Jules Marie, Lt. Col. AAIG to Bragg, Beauregard (1832–1913)

Polk, Alexander Hamilton, Lt. ADC to Leo. Polk; Capt. AAG to Polk, Palmer, J. G. Martin (1831–1873)

Polk, John Widener, VADC to Churchill (d. 1902)

Polk, Marshall Tate, Lt. Col. Chief Arty. to Leo. Polk (1831–1884)

Polk, Rufus J., Capt. ADC to L. E. Polk; staff of Roddey (b. 1843)

Polk, Thomas G., VADC to Tappan

Polk, Trusten, Col. Military Court of Holmes (1811–1876)

Polk, William Mecklenburg, Lt. Asst. Chief Arty. to Leo. Polk (1844–1918)

Pollard, ——, Capt. AAIG to Stevenson (d. 1864)

Pollard, Charles Teed, Lt. ADC to W. W. Allen (1842–1873)

Pollard, Hugh M., Capt. AAG to M. E. Green; Capt. AAIG to Moore, A. Baker

Pond, W. G., Capt. ACS to Walker, Bate, Tyler

Pool, Stephen Decatur, Col. Chief Arty. to L. S. Baker

Poole, Dennis H., Lt. AAAG to Bragg; Maj. AAG to Hardee

Poole, William G., Capt. AAIG to Hardee; AAAIG to Deas; Capt. AAAG to Miller

Pope, Alexander, Capt. AAG to Greer

Pope, Alexander Franklin, Capt. OO to Cobb (1829–1910)

Pope, John, Maj. QM to Hardee

Pope, Joseph J., Maj. OO to Beauregard, Mercer, H. R. Jackson

Porcher, Francis J., Maj. QM to W. S. Walker

Porter, Alexander J., Capt. AAG to Maney, Brown

Porter, Granville, Capt. ACS to T. Harrison

Porter, James Davis, Maj. AAG to Cheatham (1828–1912)

Porter, Josiah A., Capt. EO to Stewart

Porter, Thomas K., Maj. Chief Arty. to Stewart, Buckner

Porter, W. M., Lt. VADC to Leo. Polk

Porter, William W., Lt. ADC & Capt. AAG to Crittenden; VADC to Beauregard, Leo. Polk; ADC to J. E. Johnston

Portis, Thomas Jefferson, Capt. AAG to John Adams, Pillow, Scott (d. 1899)

Portlock, Edward Edwards, Jr., Capt. AAG to Roane; Col. AAIG to Maxey; staff of Wheeler (1840–1887)

Powell, Adolphus, Capt. AAG to Lane

Powell, Edward, Capt. AQM to Lovell

Powell, Hobson, Lt. ADC to Walthall (d. 1864)

Powell, Thomas E., Capt. AAG to Wheeler

Powell, W. D., Capt. AAIG to Lane

Powers, W. T., Capt. AAAG to Brown, Reynolds

Pratt, Bernard Anthony, Lt. OO to Holmes

Pratt, Henry P., Capt. AAG to E. K. Smith

Pratt, Joseph H., Maj. Chief Arty. to Marmaduke

Prentice, Clarence J., Maj. VADC to Wheeler (1840–1873)

Presstman, Stephen Wilson, Capt. EO to Hardee, Bragg (d. 1865)

Preston, Edward Carrington, Capt. AAIG to W. Preston (b. 1837)

Preston, Thomas White, Capt. AAG to Stewart (1816–1862)

Preston, William, Col. VADC to A. S. Johnston (1816–1887)

Preston, William C., Maj. AAIG to J. E. Johnston

Price, Celsus, Lt. ADC to Price (1841–1909)

Price, Harvey Hill, Lt. AAAIG to Ruggles

Price, Thomas Henry, Maj. OO to Price (1829–1882)

Price, William Cecil, Maj. AAG to Holmes (1818–1907)

Price, William H., Lt. ADC to Marmaduke (b. 1840)

Price, William Marmaduke, Lt. ADC to Marmaduke; Maj. CS to J. B. Clark (1843–1920)

Prince, J. L., Capt. AQM to J. K. Jackson

Pringle, Motte A., QM to Beauregard

Pritchard, Paul, Capt. ACS to Drayton

Prittle, John B., AAAG to Breckinridge

Procter, George M., Maj. CS to Cobb

Proctor, George A., Capt. AQM to Cleburne

Proctor, Stephen Richard, Col. VADC to Beauregard

Provence, David, Col. acting Chief Arty. to Hindman

Pryor, Roger Atkinson, Col. VADC to Beauregard (1828–1919)

Pugh, Robert, acting ADC to Gibson

Pulliam, John R., Capt. AAIG to Maxey, Gano

Purves, George, Maj. acting OO to L. Hebert

Purves, John T., Lt. acting QM to Shoup

Quaite, Angus Grant, Maj. QM to S. D. Lee, Moore (1828–1877)

Quaite, R., Maj. QM to Ross

Quarles, Clarence, acting ADC to Quarles

Quesenbury, William, Maj. QM to Pike (1822–1888)

Quillian, George T., Capt. ACS to Barton

Quinlan, James M., Capt. ACS to Bowen; Maj. CS to J. E. Johnston (1831–1867)

Quitman, F. Henry, Capt. AQM to Lovell

Ragan, W. B., Lt. ADC to Frazer

Ragland, Fenelon Washington, Lt. ADC & AAIG to D. H. Reynolds (1835–1869)

Railey, Charles R., Maj. CS to D. W. Adams

Raines, William Augustus, Lt. acting ADC to Chalmers

Rainwater, Charles C., Maj. VADC & OO to Marmaduke; OO to J. B. Clark (1838–1902)

Ralston, Joseph C., Lt. ADC to J. G. Walker

Rambaut, Gilbert Vincent, Maj. CS to Forrest (1837–1896)

Randall, James, Capt. ADC to Ruggles

Randolph, ——, Maj. OO to Davidson

Randolph, C. M., Capt. EO to E. K. Smith

Rankin, John Y., Capt. ACS to Churchill; Maj. CS to Granbury, J. A. Smith (b. 1833)

Rankin, Robert G., Capt. AQM to Whiting, Holmes

Ransom, John C., Capt. AQM to Slaughter

Raphael, H. J., Maj. AAIG to T. H. Taylor

Rapley, William Field, Maj. AAIG & VADC to Fagan (b. 1838)

Ravesies, Paul, Capt. AAIG to D. W. Adams

Rawle, Edward W., Capt. OO to Twiggs, Lovell; Capt. AAIG to Wheeler

Rawle, John, Lt. acting ADC & OO & acting Chief Arty. to Leo. Polk; Chief Arty. to Forrest

Raworth, D. B., AAG to Dibrell

Ray, Lavender Roy, Lt. acting OO to Iverson, P. M. B. Young (1842–1916)

Raynor, J. H., Lt. AAIG to G. D. Johnston

Reade, Julian, Capt. staff of Logan

Reardon, S. B., Lt. ADC to Hindman

Rector, Francis Armstrong, staff of Cabell (b. 1830)

Rector, John D., Lt. ADC to Cabell (d. 1864)

Redd, Oliver Frazer, Capt. ADC to Shelby (1838–1915)

Redmond, George S., Capt. VADC to Taliaferro (1836–1864)

Reed, B. F., Capt. AAQM to Cantey; AQM to Shelley

Reed, D. H., Lt. ADC to S. R. Anderson

Reed, Duff Green, Maj. AAG to Wheeler

Reed, Thomas B., Maj. CS to M. L. Smith

Reed, Wiley Martin, Capt. AAG to Stewart (1827–1864)

Reese, Carlos, Capt. AQM to D. H. Hill, S. D. Lee

Reese, John J., Capt. AAG to A. E. Jackson

Reese, Warren Stone, Capt. AAIG to Wheeler (1842–1898)

Reese, William B., Capt. AAG to A. E. Jackson; staff of Zollicoffer

Reeve, John James, Maj. AAG to Stevenson (1841–1908)

Reid, John, Maj. CS to Price

Reid, Robert R., Capt. AQM to Finegan

Reid, Robert S., Lt. staff of Slaughter

Reid, William A., Capt. AAIG to J. E. Johnston, Bragg, Hood

Reid, William P., Capt. ADC to Taliaferro

Reneau, William Edward, Capt. AAIG to Richardson

Rennick, John, Capt. VADC to Churchill

Reveley, William Wirt, Lt. acting ADC to Lawton (d. 1865)

Reynolds, Hal G., Maj. VADC to Moore

Reynolds, J. G., Capt. OO to French

Reynolds, James H., Capt. AQM to Parsons

Reynolds, N. J., Maj. QM to Iverson

Reynolds, Samuel H., Maj. OO to Echols (1827–1867)

Reynolds, Thomas Caute, Col. VADC to A. S. Johnston (1821–1887)

Rhea, Weston H., Capt. AQM to Bate

Rhett, Andrew Burnet, Maj. Chief Arty. to Beauregard, Taliaferro (1831–1879)

Rhett, Charles Haskell, Lt. AQM to Mackall (1822–1895)

Rice, Andrew Jackson, Lt. OO to Lowrey; Capt. OO to Wood

Rice, Clay, Capt. AQM to Ferguson

Rice, James E., Lt. OO to Bate; VADC to Pillow

Rice, James Love, Capt. VADC to Donelson (d. 1898)

Rice, Olin F., Lt. OO to Buckner; Maj. AAIG to Maury, Gardner (1839–1882)

Richards, Alexander Keene, ADC to Breckinridge

Richardson, F. E., staff of Ferguson

Richardson, F. H., Capt. AAIG to Lawton

Richardson, Jonathan Smythe, Jr., Capt. AQM to Winder (1828–1871)

Richardson, Thomas E., Lt. AAG to Bell

Richardson, William Priestley, Capt. OO to Gibson (1840–1909)

Richmond, Henry P., Capt. AQM to Gist

Richmond, William B., Lt. ADC to Leo. Polk (d. 1863)

Riddle, Haywood Y., Capt. AAAG to M. J. Wright, Mackall

Ridley, Bromfield Lewis, Jr., Lt. ADC to Stewart (1845–1917)

Ridley, George Crothwait, Capt. AAG to B. J. Hill (1842–1918)

Ridley, Jerome Shelton, Capt. ACS to Stevenson; Maj. CS to Polk (1832–1886)

Riley, Edward Bishop Dudley, Capt. OO to Withers; Maj. OO to Hardee; staff of Hindman, F. Gardner, W. T. Martin (1839–1918)

Riley, T. T., Lt. staff of Lowrey

Ritchey, James B., Capt. AQM to Maney

Rives, C. W., AAAG to Richard H. Anderson

Robards, Charles L., Capt. VADC to H. E. McCulloch (1827–1870)

Robards, Willis L., Maj. OO & AAG to Sibley; Maj. Chief Arty. to T. Green

Robbins, E. C., Lt. OO to Forney, Ross

Roberts, Goodson M., Capt. ACS to A. W. Reynolds

Roberts, Green, Capt. acting ADC to J. H. Morgan

Roberts, John Todd, Maj. QM to Stevenson; staff of Cumming, T. H. Taylor

Roberts, N. T., Lt. staff of Churchill

Roberts, Percy, Capt. EO to Loring, C. Clark

Roberts, Samuel Alexander, Lt. Col. AAG to H. E. McCulloch (1809–1872)

Robertson, Abbott L., Lt. acting ADC & AAIG to Cheatham

Robertson, Beverly Holcombe, Lt. AAIG to Ruggles (1827–1910)

Robertson, Elijah Sterling Clack, Capt. VADC to H. E. McCulloch (1820–1879)

Robertson, E. W., VADC to Ruggles

Robertson, F., Maj. AAG to J. B. Clark

Robertson, F. M., Capt. Chief Arty. to Withers

Robertson, Felix Huston, Capt. AAG to Gladden; AAAG to Ruggles; Capt. Chief Arty. to Withers, J. K. Jackson, Leo. Polk; Lt. Col. Chief Arty. to Wheeler (1839–1928)

Robertson, Frank Seldon, Maj. AAG to Marmaduke

Robertson, Harrison, Capt. AQM at Danville, Va. (1822–1908)

Robertson, J. Righton, Maj. CS to McLaws, W. D. Smith, J. P. Anderson

Robertson, John B., Capt. OO Virginia State Line

Robertson, Joseph L., Capt. AAG to Hawes, Breckinridge, Holmes

Robertson, S. C., VADC to H. E. McCullough

Robertson, Thomas Chinn, Capt. AQM to S. D. Lee, Maury (1842–1866)

Robins, L. D., Capt. AAG to Chalmers

Robins, Thomas, Capt. acting ADC to Forrest

Robinson, John Moncure, Capt. EO to Loring, Williams, Jones, Breckinridge (1835–1893)

Robinson, Norborne T. Nelson, Capt. AAG to Hodges (1838–1904)

Robinson, Samuel A., Maj. QM to Maxey; VADC to Cooper

Roche, Floyd G., Capt. acting QM to W. L. Jackson

Rockwell, William S., Lt. Col. AAAG to Lawton

Rodefer, William, Capt. AQM Abingdon, Va.

Rodgers, Frank B., Lt. ADC to P. Smith, Vaughan

Rogan, Charles Bernard, Capt. OO to Bate (b. 1839)

Rogers, Charles G., Maj. AAG to B. R. Johnson; Lt. Col. AAIG to Wheeler, Brown (d. 1888)

Rogers, J. T., Capt. AAAIG to J. H. Morgan

Rogers, Joseph E., Capt. AQM to Starke

Rogers, Samuel St. George, Maj. AAG to Beauregard (1832–1880)

Rose, Alexander, Lt. ADC to W. M. Gardner (d. 1863)

Rose, John M., Capt. oo to Churchill

Ross, Edward M., Lt. acting ADC & Capt. AAG to McCown

Ross, Horace C., Lt. oo to Clayton, Hardee

Ross, Isaac Allison, Capt. oo to Beall

Ross, Reuben Reddick, Lt. Col. AAIG to Davidson, Pillow, Bragg, Forrest (1830–1864)

Ross, W. B., Col. VADC to Stewart (1831–1863)

Ross, William Henry, Capt. AAAG to W. H. T. Walker; Capt. AAIG to Hardee

Ross, William Henry, Maj. CS to Withers, Bragg (b. 1819)

Roundtree, William, Capt. VADC to Cheatham

Routh, Horatio S., Maj. QM to Finegan, J. P. Anderson, J. K. Jackson

Routh, Stephen M., Lt. SO to R. Taylor

Rowland, Samuel H., Lt. acting oo to J. K. Jackson

Rowley, R. P., Maj. EO to E. K. Smith, Magruder

Roy, Benjamin P., Maj. QM to Brown

Roy, Thomas Benton, Col. AAG to Hardee (1838–1910)

Royston, Charles Edward, Lt. ADC to Churchill (1843–1910)

Royston, Martin H., Maj. AAG to Wharton

Rucker, William R., SO to Cleburne

Rudd, I., Capt. VADC to Wheeler (d. 1862)

Ruffin, Emmett F., Lt. SO to Beauregard, Ripley

Ruffin, Thomas, Jr., Col. Military Court of E. K. Smith (1824–1889)

Ruffin, William, Capt. ACS to W. W. Adams

Ruggles, Edward Seymour, Lt. SO to Ruggles; Maj. CS, VADC, & OO to Ruggles (1843–1919)

Ruggles, Mortimer Bainbridge, Capt. ADC to Ruggles (b. 1844)

Rumble, Steven E., Capt. AQM to Chalmers

Runnels, Hal G., Maj. VADC to Moore

Russell, Charles, Maj. QM to Bee

Russell, J. B., Capt. oo to Forrest

Russell, Oscar F., Capt. AAG to Pike (d. 1897)

Rust, Armistead Thomson Mason, Col. Military Court of Jones (1820–1887)

Ruthven, John B., Maj. QM to Hindman; Maj. CS to Parsons, Drayton

Rutledge, Arthur Middleton, Capt. Chief Arty. to Zollicoffer; Maj. OO & AAIG to Leo. Polk (d. 1876)

Rutledge, John, Lt. OO & AAIG to Beauregard

Ryan, John, Capt. AAG to Villepigue

Ryan, R. B., Lt. EO to Wheeler

St. Clair, Arthur, Capt. staff of Shelby

St. Paul, Henri, Capt. AQM to Higgins (1815–1886)

Sale, William F., VADC to Tappan

Sams, Horace H., Capt. ACS to W. S. Walker (d. 1865)

Sanchez, Bernardio S., Lt. ADC & Maj. CS to J. K. Jackson

Sanders, R. W., Maj. QM to Mouton, R. Taylor, Hodge, F. Gardner

Sanders, Reid, Maj. CS to Hawes

Sandford, John L., Capt. AAG to Marshall, W. Preston

Sandidge, John Milton, Col. acting ADC to Ruggles (1817–1898)

Sandidge, Lucien Duvergne, Capt. AAIG to Ruggles, D. W. Adams, Maury

Sandidge, S. S., VADC to Ruggles

Sandidge, T. L., Lt. AAIG to Ruggles

Sanford, John S., Capt. AAG to W. Preston

Sanford, Robert, Maj. CS to Cheatham

Sansy, J. R., acting oo to Stewart

Sapp, Philip A., Capt. AAIG to A. Baker

Saugrain, A. P., Lt. AAIG to Price

Saunders, James Edmonds, Col. acting ADC to Forrest (1806–1896)

Saunders, Mathew T., Lt. oo to Fagan

Saunders, Thomas, Capt. VADC to Beauregard

Saunders, William Hubbard, Col. Military Court of Bragg (1816–1895)

Sawrie, William Summerfield, Lt. AAAG to Liddell, Govan (1843–1912)

Sawyer, Samuel Tredwell, Maj. CS to Gatlin

Sayers, Edward B., Capt. EO to Leo. Polk

Sayers, Joseph Draper, Maj. AAG to R. Taylor, T. Green (1841–1929)

Sayers, William B., Lt. AAAIG to T. Harrison

Sayles, John, Col. AAG to Magruder (1825–1897)

Sayre, Calvin Lawrence, Capt. AAAG to Van Dorn; Lt. VADC to Richard H. Anderson; Maj. AAIG to Bragg, Winder, Fry (1832–1894)

Sayre, Philip D., Lt. OO to D. W. Adams

Scales, Joseph Absalom, Maj. AAG to Watie

Scales, Joseph Watkins, VADC to Beauregard; Capt. staff of Armstrong (1832–1896)

Scanlan, ——, VADC to J. P. Anderson

Schaeffer, Francis B., Capt. AAIG to Pike, Cooper

Schaumburg, Wright C., Capt. AAG to Little, Van Dorn; Lt. Col. AAG to E. K. Smith (1844–1896)

von Scheliha, Viktor Ernst Carl Rudolph, Lt. Col. EO to Buckner; staff of Leo. Polk, Mackall, Zollicoffer, Crittenden (1826–1903)

Schell, Abram B., Lt. acting ADC to L. E. Polk

Scherck, Isaac, Lt. acting ACS to Wood; Maj. CS to Breckinridge, D. H. Hill, J. E. Johnston; staff of Cleburne, Hood, Hindman (1833–1889)

Schirmer, Charles, Lt. OO to Drayton

Schleicher, Gustave, Capt. EO to Scurry, Magruder (1823–1879)

von Schmeling, Wedig Franz Alexander, Col. staff of Price (1834–1886)

Schnierle, John M., Lt. ADC to Ripley

Schoef, ——, Maj. AAIG to Bate

Schreiber, Adolphe, Capt. OO to Mouton

Schultz, Charles G., Capt. AAIG to Maxey

Schwarzman, Gus A., Capt. AAG to Pike

Scogin, John, Capt. AAIG to Elzey (1829–1864)

Scott, Andrew G., Maj. QM to Sears, Baldwin

Scott, Edward M., Lt. ADC to D. W. Adams

Scott, George Y., Lt. ADC to W. W. Adams

Scott, H. G., Maj. QM to Sears

Scott, H. T., Lt. OO to Villepigue; Capt. OO to Slaughter

Scott, John C., Capt. staff of Forrest

Scott, John J., Capt. AAG to Hawes

Scott, John T., Capt. AQM to Cheatham, Hardee

Scott, John Thompson, Capt. AQM to Parsons (1834–1869)

Scott, N., Maj. CS to L. Hebert

Scott, Spencer B., Capt. ACS to Scott

Scott, Thomas Morton, Capt. AAG to Maxey, Cooper (1824–1911)

Scott, Thomas W., Maj. CS to L. Hebert

Screven, John Henry, Maj. QM to W. S. Walker (1823–1903)

Scruggs, J. M., Capt. staff of Forrest

Scull, Benjamin F., Lt. VADC to Price

Scurry, Thomas Jefferson, Maj. QM to Scurry (d. 1895)

Seabrook, Ephraim M., Capt. VADC to Ripley

Seabrook, Henry, Lt. OO to Ripley

Seabrook, W., Capt. ADC to Evans

Searcy, Henry Clay, Lt. ADC to Whitfield

Searcy, James J., Lt. AAAG to J. B. Clark

Seay, William A., Capt. AAAG to Frost

Sebastian, George C., Maj. QM to W. W. Adams

Selden, William Boswell, Lt. EO to Wise (d. 1862)

Sellers, John S., Capt. AQM to Scurry

Semmes, Benedict Joseph, Capt. ACS to Bragg, Hood, J. E. Johnston (1823–1902)

Semple, Henry Churchill, Chief Arty. to Cleburne, Maury, D. H. Hill (1822–1894)

Seton, George S., Capt. AQM to Stovall

Severson, Charles S., Maj. QM to Forrest, Charles Clark

Sevier, Ambrose Handley, Lt. ADC to Churchill; Capt. AAG to E. K. Smith (1842–1908)

Sevier, Theodore Francis, Lt. Col. AAIG to Leo. Polk, Stewart

Shaaff, Arthur, Maj. AAIG to Bate (1832–1874)

Shaaff, John Thomas, Capt. ACS to Villepigue (1830–1877)

Shaler, James Riddle, Maj. AAIG to Frost, Price (1831–1910)

Shands, Edward, Col. VADC to Van Dorn

Shane, John, Lt. AAIG to Stevenson

Shane, Washington C., Lt. ADC to A. R. Johnson

Shannon, A. N., Lt. Col. staff of Wheeler (1839–1906)

Sharp, John M., Lt. ADC to Buckner

Sharp, Thomas I., Lt. ADC to Chalmers

Sharp, W. H., Lt. staff of Wharton

Sharpe, James B., Capt. AQM to Wharton

Shaw, G. H. C., Capt. AQM to Dockery

Shaw, Simmons J., ADC to L. Hebert

Shea, Daniel D., Capt. VADC to Van Dorn

Shearer, P. W., Capt. AQM to Lowrey

Shelby, Isaac, Jr., Capt. AQM to Buckner; Capt. ACS to Echols; Maj. CS to Breckinridge

Shelley, H. E., Lt. ADC to Shelley, Cantey

Shelly, Marmaduke M., Lt. acting ADC to Chalmers, Shoup, Withers

Sheppard, C. B., Capt. ADC to T. Green

Sheppard, Lemuel, Lt. VADC to Cabell

Shields, James W., Capt. ACS at Christiansburg, Va.

Shields, Thomas H., Capt. ACS to Shelby (1832–1900)

Shindler, Judge, Lt. ADC to Shelby

Shive, Milton N., Capt. ACS to Slaughter

Shoemaker, Rufus, Lt. ADC to Van Dorn

Shorter, George H., Capt. VADC to Wood

Shoup, Francis Asbury, Maj. Chief Arty. to Hardee; AAAG to Hindman; Maj. acting Chief Arty. & AAIG to Beauregard (1834–1896)

Shute, James D., VADC to Baldwin; Capt. AAIG to Quarles

Sibley, John T., Capt. AQM to J. P. Anderson; Maj. QM to S. D. Lee

Sibley, William C., Maj. CS to J. K. Jackson

Siebert, Ferdinand, Capt. AQM to E. K. Smith

Sigourney, Andrew, Capt. AQM to Holmes, Price

Simkins, E. C., Maj. QM to Finegan; staff of Cobb, W. M. Gardner, J. P. Anderson

Simmons, Joseph R., Capt. ACS to Barton, Stovall

Simmons, Robert H., Maj. CS to Wharton, Humes

Simmons, Robert W., Capt. ACS to W. W. Adams

Simmons, William C., Lt. ADC to Ripley

Simons, Maurice K., Maj. CS to Moore

Simons, Sedgwick, Maj. CS to Trapier, Hardee

Simpson, George, Capt. AAIG to F. Gardner

Simpson, George W., Lt. ADC & AAIG to Villepigue

Simpson, William, Lt. ADC to Wood

Simpson, William A., Capt. ADC to L. E. Polk

Simpson, William M., Lt. ADC to McCown

Sims, Milton Walker, Maj. staff of P. O. Hebert (1831–1912)

Sims, William Henry, Capt. AAIG to Tucker (1837–1920)

Skidmore, Thomas H., Capt. AQM to Ector

Skinner, Thomas, Cadet staff of Lyon

Slaughter, James Edwin, Maj. AAG to Bragg (1827–1901)

Slayback, Alonzo William, Capt. AAG to M. E. Green, Marmaduke (1838–1882)

Sledge, Joshua, Capt. acting ADC to Wood

Slocomb, Cuthbert H., Capt. Chief Arty. to Breckinridge (d. 1873)

Slover, A. P., Maj. CS to W. H. Jackson

Smallman, M. D., Lt. AAG to Dibrell

Smedes, Thomas M., Lt. ADC to M. L. Smith (1843–1909)

Smith, A. C. F., Capt. ACS to Tracy

Smith, A. D., Capt. ACS to Cabell

Smith, Alexander L., Maj. CS to Finley

Smith, Alfonzo Frederic, Lt. AAAG to Walthall

Smith, Ashbel, AAG to Maury (1805–1886)

Smith, Bart, Capt. OO to Clayton

Smith, Benjamin Burgh, Jr., Maj. AAIG to Gist (1835–1904)

Smith, D. Henley, VADC to Pegram

Smith, E. R., Capt. AAIG to Cumming, T. H. Taylor; Capt. AAG to Stevenson, R. Taylor

Smith, Felix R. R., Capt. AAIG to J. E. Rains,
Bate; Capt. AAG to Vance; Capt. EO to
Buckner

Smith, George Hampton, Lt. AAIG to B. R.
Johnson; Maj. AAG to Wheeler

Smith, H. Brownson, Maj. CS to McCown,
Jackson, Hood, Stewart, J. E. Johnston

Smith, H. C., AAG to Ripley

Smith, Henry W., SO to Cleburne

Smith, J. D., VADC to Churchill

Smith, J. K., Capt. VADC to Duncan

Smith, J. Webb, Lt. ADC to Cheatham

Smith, John Little, Lt. ADC to Forney (1824–
1890)

Smith, John M., Lt. ADC to Roane

Smith, John R., Maj. CS to Buford

Smith, John Springs, Capt. AAG to Pettus

Smith, John T., Capt. AQM to Sharp

Smith, Jones P., Capt. ACS to Buford

Smith, L. L., Lt. ADC to Magruder

Smith, LaRouche Jaquelin, Capt. OO to
Beauregard, McLaws (1837–1895)

Smith, Leon, Maj. VADC to Magruder

Smith, Leonidas W., Maj. QM to Stewart

Smith, Lewis E., VADC to Withers

Smith, Little, Lt. ADC to Forney

Smith, Lucius Heylin, Lt. AAIG to Vance

Smith, Marshall Joseph, Col. acting ADC
to Ruggles; Chief Arty. to F. Gardner
(1824–1904)

Smith, Martin Luther, Maj. EO to Twiggs
(1819–1866)

Smith, Melancthon, Lt. Col. Chief Arty. to
Cheatham; staff of Hardee, D. H. Hill
(d. 1881)

Smith, Norman Wallace, Maj. QM to Ripley,
W. D. Smith (1830–1908)

Smith, Pleasant A., Lt. AAIG to Bell

Smith, R. H., Lt. acting OO to Brantley

Smith, Richard Inge, Lt. ACS to Clayton

Smith, Richard P., Lt. ADC to D. H. Hill

Smith, Robert Davis, Capt. OO to L. E. Polk,
Walthall, Quarles; staff of Cleburne

Smith, Robert H., Capt. AQM to W. H.
Jackson

Smith, Robert H., Maj. QM to Marmaduke
(d. 1863)

Smith, Robert H., Col. staff of Maury

Smith, Rowland B., Maj. CS to Cabell, Dockery; Maj. AAAG to Gist

Smith, Samuel L., Lt. acting ADC to
Magruder

Smith, Sumner J., Maj. QM to Lawton

Smith, Thaddeus A., Capt. OO to Bragg,
E. Johnson

Smith, W. H., Capt. AAIG to Ector

Smith, William Duncan, Maj. AAAG to
Lawton (1825–1862)

Smith, William P., Maj. CS to Clanton

Smoot, ——, Lt. staff of Gano

Smoot, G. P., Lt. acting ADC to McCown;
staff of M. J. Wright

Smoot, Josiah H. D., Capt. AQM at Giles
C. H., Va.

Smythe, John W., Capt. ACS to Govan,
Cleburne, Liddell

Snead, Thomas Lowndes, Maj. AAG to Price
(1828–1890)

Snead, William E., Maj. CS to Barton

Sneed, S. G., Lt. AAAG to J. A. Smith; staff of
Granbury

Snowden, John Hudson, Lt. EO to Polk
(d. 1864)

Snowden, Robert Bogardus, Capt. AAG to
B. R. Johnson (1836–1909)

Soule, Nevill, Capt. AAIG to Beauregard; staff
of Jones, Hardee, D. H. Hill, Trapier

Sparks, Jesse Watlington, Lt. ADC to P. O.
Hebert

Sparks, William H., AAAG to J. P. Anderson;
Capt. ADC to Wheeler (d. 1864)

Spence, David H. C., Capt. VADC to Baldwin,
Palmer

Spence, Philip Brent, Lt. acting ADC & AAIG
to Leo. Polk (1836–1915)

Spencer, Frank M., Maj. CS to Ector

Spotswood, Edwin Allison, AAG to Forrest
(b. 1834)

Sprague, Sturges, VADC to Pemberton

Spratley, James Walter, Maj. QM to
F. Gardner

Sprigg, Horatio S., VADC to Magruder

Sprigg, John D., Capt. ACS to Tappan

Squires, M. T., Capt. Chief Arty. to Mouton

Stackpole, E. M., Maj. QM to Gano

Stafford, Frederick McKee, Lt. AAAG to Pemberton; Lt. AAIG to H. R. Jackson (1842–1920)

Stafford, J. C., Lt. ADC to Wheeler

Stainback, Littleberry E., Maj. QM to Davidson, Pegram

Stake, Thomas E., Capt. AAIG & AAAG to M. J. Wright

Standish, Austin M., Capt. AAG to Parsons (d. 1865)

Stanford, ——, Capt. ACS to J. K. Jackson

Stansifer, John Milton, Capt. AAIG to Marshall

Stanton, Henry Thomas, Capt. AAAG to Williams; Maj. AAG to Echols

Staples, Thomas J., Lt. ADC to Wheeler (d. 1864)

Stapleton, T. B., Capt. ACS to Strahl

Stark, T. O., Maj. QM to Liddell

Starr, Edwin P., Lt. AAAG to Ripley

Stebbins, Charles H., Capt. AAG to Finley

Stedman, Andrew Jackson, Lt. SO to Finegan, P. Anderson

Stedman, William, Maj. AAG to Green

Steele, S. W., Lt. EO to Beauregard; Capt. EO to Wheeler, Bragg

Steever, West, Lt. Col. staff of to Forney; Lt. Col. AAAIG to Leo. Polk (d. 1907)

Steiner, Frank, Lt. ADC to Cumming

Stephens, Absalom, Capt. AQM to Stewart

Steven, William, Capt. AQM to R. Taylor

Stevenson, Vernon King, Jr., Lt. acting ADC to Tyler

Stevenson, William A., Lt. ADC to Cabell

Stewart, B. F., Capt. AQM to Cockrell

Stewart, J. M., Lt. EO to Wheeler

Stewart, James Turner, Capt. AQM to Lawton; Maj. QM to Mercer, Smith, H. R. Jackson (b. 1834)

Stewart, John W., Capt. OO to Stewart

Stewart, Robert Caruthers, Lt. ADC to Stewart

Stith, Donald Chester, Capt. AAG to H. E. McCulloch; Maj. AAG to Van Dorn; Maj. AAIG to S. D. Lee (1829–1920)

Stith, Ferdinand, Capt. AAAG to Campbell

Stockdale, F. S., VADC to Holmes

Stockdale, John L., Maj. CS to Beall

Stockton, Philip, Capt. AAIG to Leo. Polk; Col. OO to Van Dorn; Col. CS to E. K. Smith (d. 1879)

Stoddard, John Iverson, Lt. ADC to Mercer (1843–1924)

Stokes, Bradley Tyler, Lt. ADC to B. T. Johnson (1843–1905)

Stone, Caleb, Col. AAG to J. B. Clark

Stone, James, Capt. VADC to McNair

Stone, William M., Maj. QM to J. G. Walker, Magruder

Storey, J. A., Capt. ACS to Pettus, Shelley; staff of Tracy

Stout, Jonathan, Lt. acting ADC to Deas

Stover, A. P., Maj. CS to W. H. Jackson

Strange, John Presley, Maj. AAG to Forrest (d. 1875)

Strawbridge, James, Capt. AAAG to P. O. Hebert; Maj. AAIG to Bragg

Street, William B., Maj. CS to Hawthorne

Strickland, W. T., Lt. AAAG & ADC to Chalmers

Strickland, William M., Capt. ACS to Chalmers; Maj. CS to Lovell, Pemberton

Stringfellow, Henry Martin, Lt. OO to Scurry, Bee (1839–1912)

Strocky, F. A., Capt. AQM to L. M. Walker

Strong, H. L., Capt. AAIG to Withers

Strong, Martin L., Maj. QM to Higgins

Stuart, Arthur Lee, Capt. AAIG to Gibson

Stuart, J. S., Capt. AAIG to Maxey

Stuart, N. A., Capt. acting AQM to Bowen

Stubbs, Henry A., Capt. AQM to Brantley (1830–1907)

Stubbs, James New, Lt. SO to Magruder, Scurry, Slaughter (1839–1919)

Styron, Christopher W., Capt. AQM to Whiting, J. G. Martin, Kirkland

Suber, Christian Henry, Maj. QM to Ripley; AAAG to Evans (1828–1890)

Sulakowski, Valery, Col. Chief EO to Magruder (1827–1873)

Sullins, David, Maj. QM to Breckinridge, Zollicoffer, Cumming (b. 1827)

Summers, W. M., Capt. AAIG to R. Taylor

Summerville, John W., Capt. AAIG to W. H. Jackson

Sutherlin, William Thomas, Maj. QM at Danville, Va. (1822–1893)

Swancourt, R. J., Capt. VADC to S. D. Lee

Swann, Thomas Belt, Capt. VADC to Heth (1825–1897)

Sweetman, Robert L., Lt. OO to Bragg

Swett, Charles, Capt. AAIG to Elzey (b. 1828)

Syberg, Arnold, Capt. EO to Maxey, E. K. Smith, Holmes

Sykes, Augustus James, Lt. AAAG to John Adams; Capt. AAIG to Ferguson (1824–1882)

Sykes, Edward Turner, Capt. AAG to Walthall, J. P. Anderson, W. H. Jackson (1838–1922)

Sykes, Joseph P., Cadet AAAIG to Ross

Sykes, Thomas Barrett, Capt. AAIG to John Adams, Tilghman, W. H. Jackson

Sykes, William, Capt. acting ADC to Loring

Sykes, William J., Maj. CS to Bate, Campbell

Szymanski, Ignatius S., Maj. AAG to Cooper; Col. AAAIG to John Adams (1806–1874)

Tabb, George Edward, Jr., Lt. SO to Polk

Taber, Theron M., Maj. OO to Price

Talbot, M. H., Capt. VADC to W. H. T. Walker

Talbott, L. S., Capt. AAIG & AAG to L. Hebert (d. 1863)

Taney, L. M., Maj. CS to L. M. Walker

Tappan, Amos, Capt. AAG to Tappan

Tappan, James Camp, VADC to Holmes (1825–1906)

Tarver, Edward R., Capt. ADC to Bee

Tate, John Frederic, Capt. AAAIG to Cantey, Shelley; Col. VADC to Van Dorn (b. 1838)

Tate, Mitchell B., Capt. AQM Abingdon, Va.

Tate, Samuel, Col. VADC to A. S. Johnston

Tate, Thomas S., Lt. AAIG to Forrest

Taylor, Armistead G., Lt. ADC & AAG to B. H. Robertson

Taylor, Ennis Ward, Capt. AQM to Magruder, E. K. Smith (b. 1839)

Taylor, George Louis, Lt. ADC to Wheeler (d. 1862)

Taylor, Hancock, Lt. acting on Military Court of Stevenson

Taylor, Henry Clay, Lt. Col. OO & Chief Arty. to Price

Taylor, Henry S., Maj. CS to Marmaduke

Taylor, J. A., Lt. AAAG to Chalmers

Taylor, J. M., Capt. VADC to Ruggles

Taylor, Richard, VADC to Bragg

Taylor, Theodore T., Capt. AAG to Frost, Drayton, J. B. Clark; AAIG to Price

Taylor, Thomas Hart, Col. staff of S. D. Lee; AAIG to Pemberton (1825–1901)

Taylor, William H., Lt. ADC to Lowry

Teasdale, Henry R., Maj. QM to Trapier, Finegan, J. P. Anderson, J. K. Jackson

Teasdale, Thomas A., Lt. OO to Lowry, Shelley

Templeman, Robert B., VADC to Cabell

Terrell, Alexander Watkins, Capt. VADC to H. E. McCulloch (1827–1912)

Terrell, R. A., Capt. AQM to Parsons

Terrett, Burdett Ashton, Lt. AAIG to Palmer; Capt. AAG to Kelly, W. W. Adams

Terry, David Sloan, Jr., Lt. ADC to Wharton (1823–1889)

Tessier, D. E., VADC to Van Dorn

Tevis, Robert M., Maj. CS to L. Hebert

Thomas, Barak G., Maj. CS to Wheeler, Buford

Thomas, Bryan Morel, Lt. OO & AAIG to Withers (1836–1905)

Thomas, Charles B., Col. Military Court of E. K. Smith

Thomas, J. D., Capt. AQM to L. M. Walker

Thomas, John Hanson, Jr., Lt. ADC to Loring (b. 1841)

Thomas, John Q., Maj. CS to Quarles; VADC to Maxey

Thomas, John Whit., AAAG to J. K. Jackson

Thomas, Joseph L., Capt. AQM & PM to Price

Thomas, Joseph V., Lt. ADC to McNair

Thomas, R. C., Lt. ADC to Starke

Thomas, Wyatt C., Capt. AAG to Fagan (d. 1874)

Thomason, William D., Capt. AQM to A. S. Johnston; Maj. QM to Roddy

Thompson, Fleming, acting ADC to Chalmers

Thompson, Jacob, Col. VADC to Beauregard; Maj. AAIG to Pemberton (1810–1885)

Thompson, John C., Maj. VADC to W. Preston; Maj. AAIG to Stewart; staff of W. H. T. Walker

Thompson, Joseph S., Capt. AQM to Loring

Thompson, R. H. Smith, Lt. Asst. Chief Arty. to Bragg, Hood, J. E. Johnston

Thompson, Thomas B., Lt. ADC to J. E. Rains (d. 1917)

Thompson, W. Alexander, Capt. ACS to M. J. Wright

Thompson, William Beverhout, Maj. acting EO to Branch, Holmes (1804–1867)

Thomson, J. M., Maj. QM to Chalmers

Thomson, J. West, Lt. OO to Ferguson

Thomson, P. H., Capt. AAIG to Bragg; Capt. AAIG to Duncan, E. K. Smith, Bragg

Thorburn, Charles Edmonston, Lt. Col. AAIG & OO to Loring (1831–1909)

Thorn, Reuben T., Jr., Capt. AAIG to Page

Thornton, Edward Quinn, Lt. ADC & AAAG to Clayton (1832–1878)

Thornton, Harry Innes, Lt. ADC to Crittenden; Capt. AAG to Bragg, Mackall (1834–1895)

Threadgill, T. S., Capt. ACS to D. H. Hill

Throckmorton, John R., Maj. QM to Preston, Breckinridge, Bragg, J. E. Johnston, Hood

Thyssens, Francis L. J., Capt. EO to Van Dorn

Tidmarsh, Theo. U., Lt. OO to McCown, Polk

Tilghman, Lloyd, Jr., Lt. VADC to Tilghman

Tilton, Nathaniel O., Maj. QM to W. H. T. Walker, H. R. Jackson (d. 1902)

Timanus, Henry, Capt. ACS to Finegan

Tiner, C. H., Lt. ADC to Cooper

Tipton, W. B., Lt. ADC to Marshall

Toby, Simeon, Jr., Capt. AAIG to D. W. Adams

Todd, Alex. H., Lt. ADC to Helm (1839–1862)

Todhunter, Ryland, Capt. VADC to Ector, Churchill; Capt. AAG to Ector (1840–1921)

Tomlinson, John A., Lt. ADC to Ferguson

Toomer, James H., Capt. EO to Maury

Toomer, Wiley G., Capt. AQM to Hoke

Topp, William H., Maj. CS to Gholson

Toutant, A. J., Lt. ADC to Lovell, Beauregard

Townsend, William Purnell, Col. Military Court of Holmes (1822–1882)

Tracy, Edward Dorr, Lt. Col. AAG to Wheeler (1833–1863)

Tracy, Henry W., VADC to Frost, Parsons; Maj. CS to Price

Tracy, Michael O., Maj. AAIG to Gibson

Trader, Henry G., Capt. AQM to Hoke

Trader, William H., Col. VADC to E. K. Smith

Tranum, F. M., Lt. AAAG to B. M. Thomas

Trapier, James Heyward, Capt. EO to Beauregard; Maj. EO to Ripley (1815–1865)

Travis, Elias F., Capt. AAG to Deas; Capt. AAIG to E. Johnson, J. P. Anderson

Tremmer, P. H., AAAG to Thomas

Trenholm, Frank H., Lt. ADC to Gist, D. H. Hill

Trezevant, James Hamilton, Capt. VADC to Maney (d. 1916)

Trezevant, James T., Jr., Capt. AAG to Dockery

Trezevant, John P., Maj. CS to M. J. Wright, Maney, Carter (d. 1878)

Trezevant, Theodore B., Lt. AAAIG to Ector, McCown; Lt. AAAG to Stewart

Triestra, Gregory, AAG to Stovall

Triplett, George W., Maj. QM to Helm, Breckinridge

Triplett, John A., Capt. AAAG to Vaughn

Trist, Nicholas P., Lt. ADC to Thomas (1843–1913)

Trousdale, Leon, Capt. AAG to M. J. Wright

Troutman, F. A., Capt. AQM to Cobb

Trudeau, James DeBerty, VADC to Beauregard (1817–1887)

Tuck, J. N., ADC to Liddell

Tucker, George, Maj. AAIG to E. K. Smith

Tucker, Henry T., Capt. AQM at Danville, Va. (d. 1890)

Tucker, James H., QM to Waul

Tucker, James Wood, VADC to Fagan

Tucker, Joseph, Lt. staff of Finegan

Tucker, Levi M., Lt. acting ADC & AAAG to G. J. Rains

Tucker, W. H., Capt. AAG to Johnson

Tully, A. J., VADC to Beauregard

Tunstall, Thomas J., Capt. AQM to Lomax

Tupper, Henry Clay, acting ADC to Pemberton (b. 1842)

Turk, James A., Lt. AAIG to Buford; AAAG to Lyon

Turnbull, Charles F., ADC to Ripley

Turnbull, Charles J., Col. AAIG to E. K. Smith

Turner, B. D., Capt. AAG to McRae; VADC & AAIG to Churchill

Turner, Edmund Pendleton, Lt. Col. AAG to Magruder (b. 1835)

Turner, George A., Maj. CS to Price, Little

Turner, John Brown, Lt. ADC & AAAG to Cooper

Turner, Sterling J., VADC to Colquitt

Turpin, W. H., Capt. VADC to Capers

Tutwiler, Eli Shores, Capt. AQM at Millboro, Va. (1826–1890)

Tutwiler, Thomas Harrison, Capt. AQM at Lexington, Va. (1818–1882)

Twyman, Horace D., Lt. staff of Trapier

Tyler, George, Capt. AAG to B. T. Johnson

Tyler, John, Jr., Maj. AAG to L. P. Walker; Maj. acting ADC to L. P. Walker, Price (1819–1896)

Tyler, Robert, Lt. acting ADC & AAIG to J. H. Morgan

Tyler, Robert Charles, Capt. AQM to Cheatham; Maj. QM to Pillow (d. 1865)

Tyree, Edward P., Maj. QM to Bate, Cheatham

Tyus, Robert B., Capt. ACS to Holmes

Tyus, William J., Maj. AAG to Cabell

Underhill, Stephen Edward Monaghan, Lt. VADC to S. D. Lee (1841–1904)

Underwood, John Cox, VADC to Buckner (b. 1840)

Upshaw, James R., Maj. CS to McRae, Churchill (d. 1878)

Upton, William A., VADC to Vaughn

Urquhart, David, Lt. Col. VADC, AAG & AAIG to Bragg

Vacaro, Philip, Capt. ACS to Bragg

Vanderford, Charles Frederick, Capt. OO to Cleburne, Leo. Polk, Stewart, J. E. Johnston, Hardee, Breckinridge (d. 1899)

Van Dyke, William Deaderick, Capt. ACS to A. W. Reynolds, Vaughan

Vanleer, Joseph H., Capt. VADC to B. R. Johnson

Vanleer, Rush, Capt. EO to Frazer

Vann, James S., VADC to McIntosh

Vardell, William G., Capt. AQM to Evans; Maj. QM to Ripley

Vasser, Elijah James, AAAG to Baldwin (1838–1871)

Vasser, William Hunt, Capt. ACS to Clayton, Maury (1821–1899)

Vaughan, William A. M., Lt. acting ADC to Shelby

Vaught, W. W., Jr., Lt. acting AQM to Lyon

Vaulx, Joseph, Jr., Capt. AAIG to Cheatham; Maj. AAIG to Brown, Cheatham, Maney (1835–1908)

Veal, Lafayette, acting ADC to Withers, Chalmers; VADC to Beauregard

Venable, C. W., Capt. ACS at Wytheville, Va.

Vernon, S. McD., Lt. EO to Walthall, Loring

Vertner, A. V., ADC to Van Dorn (d. 1862)

de Veuve, Henry, Capt. EO to Loring (d. 1898)

Vidmer, John, Capt. AAIG to Clayton

Vidor, Charles, Capt. AQM to Stevenson, Hood (1834–1904)

Viley, John R., Maj. QM to Bate, Lewis, Helm, Breckinridge

Villepigue, John Bordenave, Capt. AAAIG & Col. EO to Bragg (1830–1862)

Villere, Charles J., VADC to Beauregard (1821–1899)

Vinet, John Baptist, Capt. EO to Pemberton, Leo. Polk, French, S. D. Lee

Von Phul, William, Lt. OO to Cabell

Voorhies, Charles Howard, Lt. ADC to Buford (1839–1903)

Voorhies, Octave, Maj. AAAG to Polignac

Voorhies, Robert, Maj. AAAG to Frost

Vore, Israel Griffith, Maj. QM to Cooper

Voss, Douglass, Capt. AQM to Withers, B. M. Thomas

Waddell, Alfred, ACS to J. B. Clark

Waddell, B. B., Capt. VADC to Beauregard

Waddell, John, Maj. CS to Drayton, J. B. Clark, Marmaduke, Frost

Waddell, V. B., Lt. AAAG to Richardson

Wade, Fontaine C., Capt. staff of Wheeler

Wade, James, Capt. ACS at White Sulphur Springs & Salem, Va.

Wager, P. B., Capt. AQM to Moore

Waggener, Leslie, Lt. OO to Lewis (1841–1896)

Wagner, William Henry, Lt. ADC to Ripley (d. 1863)

Wailes, William Edwin, Lt. ADC & Maj. AAG to Wheeler (1837–1910)

Waldo, Jedediah, Lt. AAIG to Drayton, J. B. Clark, Frost

Waldrop, Henry, Capt. AAG to McNair, D. H. Reynolds

Walker, A. John, Capt. OO to Hawes

Walker, Clifton, Lt. ADC to Tracy, W. W. Allen (b. 1834)

Walker, Cornelius Irvine, Capt. AAG to Manigault; AAAG to J. P. Anderson (1842–1927)

Walker, David, Col. Military Court of Holmes

Walker, Hal T., ADC to Armstrong

Walker, John J., Maj. CS to Bragg, Withers

Walker, John Percy, Capt. AAIG to Lowrey, Wood

Walker, Joseph, Capt. AAG to Gist

Walker, Richard S., VADC to P. O. Hebert

Walker, Robert D., Capt. ACS to Mercer

Walker, Samuel Polk, Capt. ADC to L. P. Walker; Capt. AAAG to Humes (1824–1870)

Walker, Tipton, Capt. EO to Magruder

Walker, William Stephen, Col. AAIG to Pemberton (1822–1899)

Wall, Garrett S., Lt. ADC to Gano

Wallace, E. F., Capt. ACS to Davidson

Wallace, William Pope, ADC & AAAG to W. Preston (1837–1881)

Waller, William, Capt. VADC to B. H. Robertson

Waller, William Griffin, Cadet OO to L. P. Walker; Capt. OO to Lomax (1843–1894)

Walt, Martin, Maj. QM to Wood, Lowrey, Cleburne (1836–1915)

Walter, H. W., AAAG to Chalmers; Lt. Col. AAIG to Bragg (d. 1878)

Walthall, Benjamin A., Lt. ADC to Walthall

Walthall, George M., acting ADC to Walthall

Walthall, William T., Maj. AAG to E. Johnson

Walthour, William Lowndes, Capt. AAIG to Ro. H. Anderson (1828–1890)

Walworth, Douglass, Capt. AAG to W. T. Martin

Wampler, John Morris, Capt. EO to Bragg, Beauregard (1830–1863)

Ward, J. T., Col. VADC to Van Dorn

Ward, James, VADC to Higgins

Ward, John E., VADC to Lawton, Mercer

Warder, Elmore D., Capt. ADC to J. H. Morgan

Ware, S. L., Lt. ADC to Gibson, D. W. Adams

Warfield, Amos W., Maj. QM to Van Dorn

Warfield, E. R., Lt. OO to W. W. Adams

Warfield, John G., Lt. AAIG to Govan (b. 1840)

Waring, P. H., Capt. VADC to Taliaferro (d. 1863)

Warren, ——, Maj. OO to Davidson

Warren, Archibald, Maj. QM to Forrest, Campbell (b. 1829)

Warren, Edward A., Jr., Lt. AAG to Fagan

Warren, Herbert Charles, Lt. AAG to Wheeler (d. 1864)

Warren, Thomas D., VADC to Wise

Warren, William H., Lt. oo to Carroll, Zollicoffer, Crittenden; Capt. oo to Bragg

Washington, Hamilton, vadc to Magruder

Waters, David D., Capt. acting Chf. Arty. to Hindman

Waters, John B., Maj. vadc to Bee

Watie, Saladin Ridge, Lt. adc to Watie (1846–1868)

Waties, John, Capt. Chf. Arty. to W. H. Jackson (1826–1873)

Watkins, A. M., Maj. aaig to B. J. Hill

Watkins, J. C., Capt. adc to Wheeler (d. 1864)

Watkins, Oscar M., Maj. aag to Magruder

Watson, Alfred T., Capt. acting aqm to Lyon

Watson, Clement S., Capt. aaig to Gibson

Watson, William T., Capt. aag to Armstrong

Watt, Andrew J., Lt. adc to Mouton; Capt. aag to R. Taylor

Watts, Albert Byron, Capt. vadc to Baldwin; Maj. aaig to Lowry (1841–1907)

Watts, John Wade, staff of Clanton (1846–1913)

Watts, Sam., adc to Gwynn–Virginia Militia

Watts, W. Ormsby, Capt. oo & Maj. aaig to Tilghman; Maj. vadc to S. D. Lee; Maj. oo to Polk; acting oo to Loring

Watts, W. P., Capt. aqm to Stewart

Wayne, Henry Constantine, Col. staff of Lawton (1815–1883)

Wayne, Robert, Lt. aaig to C. H. Stevens, H. R. Jackson

Weakley, Samuel Davies, vadc to Pillow (1812–1897)

Weakley, Thomas Porter, Capt. acs to Bate; Maj. cs to Stovall; staff of W. Preston, Finley, Sears (1839–1910)

Weakly, Robert L., Capt. vadc to Cheatham

Weaver, W. E., Capt. aqm to Ector

Weaver, W. M., Lt. oo to Wilson, C. H. Stevens

Webb, Garland, Jr., Capt. aaig to W. Preston, Hardee, Buford

Webb, George F., Maj. cs to Featherston

Webb, H. T., Capt. acting oo to Pettus

Webb, Rober Howell, Maj. aaig to Stevenson (d. 1872)

Webb, John, Maj. qm to Stovall, Buford

Webb, Junius Young, Capt. aaig to Scott

Webb, Wilson T., Lt. oo to Pettus (b. 1833)

Wechsler, Henry, Maj. vadc to Van Dorn

Wedge, Daniel J., Capt. acs to H. W. Allen, Ruggles; Maj. cs to Allen, Thomas (1837–1893)

Weems, Benjamin Franklin, Capt. aag to Wharton (1839–1923)

Weidemeyer, John Mohler, Capt. acting oo to Cockrell (1834–1911)

Weiggs, James C., Capt. aaig to Shoup

Weissinger, Henry Yarbrough, Lt. adc to G. D. Johnston; acting adc to Quarles (b. 1842)

Welch, William H., Capt. aqm to Pettus

Welcher, ——, Maj. vadc to Van Dorn

Weller, William H., Lt. oo to Moore, A. Baker

Wells, E. R., Lt. aaag to T. Green

Wells, John W., Capt. aag to Cooper (1833–1917)

Welton, Louis A., Col. vadc to Parsons

Wermes, Charles, Lt. oo to Higgins

Wescott, George W., vadc to Trapier

West, Benjamin F., Lt. adc to Dockery

West, Charles S., Capt. aag to Magruder; Capt. aaig & Maj. aag to E. K. Smith; Military Court of P. O. Hebert

West, Douglas, Capt. aaaig to Deas; Maj. aaag to Leo. Polk; Maj. oo to Hodge, Stewart (1826–1901)

West, Gabriel J., Capt. oo to Dockery

West, James N., vadc to Breckinridge

West, John Austine Asbury, Maj. Chief Arty. to R. Taylor

West, W. E., vadc to S. D. Lee

West, William W., Capt. acs to Granbury, T. Harrison

Westcott, James D., Capt. Judge Advocate to Forney, Marshall

Westfeldt, Claes Henning, Maj. qm to Gracie (d. 1863)

Wharton, Edward Clifton, Capt. AQM to
Magruder (1827–1891)

Wharton, Rufus Watson, Maj. staff of Hoke
(1827–1915)

Wheadon, John Jennings, Maj. CS to F. Gardner (1837–1898)

Wheeler, John Calhoun, Lt. acting ADC to
Watie; VADC to Preston

Wheeler, Joseph, Lt. AAG to Wood, Ruggles

Wheeler, Walker, AAAG to Wharton, Hardeman; Lt. OO to Wheeler

White, David G., Lt. ADC & Maj. AAG to
Hardee

White, Dossey H., Capt. acting QM to Dibrell

White, Edward Brickell, Col. Chief Arty. to
Wise (1806–1882)

White, Edwin C., Maj. QM to Kelly

White, Edwin J., Lt. EO to Jones

White, George D., AAIG to L. Baker

White, Jesse E., Maj. AAAIG to Chalmers

White, Moses James, Lt. OO to Leo. Polk;
Col. Chief Arty. to Holmes (d. 1864)

White, Thomas W., Col. AAAIG to Chalmers

White, W. R., Capt. AQM to McNair

White, William H., AAG to Forrest

Whitehead, John Philpot Curren, Jr., Capt.
AAG to Stovall (1837–1906)

Whitfield, Anthony Dyer, acting ACS to
Baldwin (1843–1916)

Whitfield, Edwin, Lt. ADC & OO to W. Preston (1841–1869)

Whitfield, Francis Eugene, AAAG to Chalmers (1839–1885)

Whitfield, George, Capt. acting AQM to
Bragg; Maj. QM to Ruggles, Breckin-
ridge, J. E. Johnston, Leo. Polk, S. D. Lee,
Maury, R. Taylor

Whitfield, Henry Buchanon, Maj. CS to
Maury, Baldwin (1835–1883)

Whiting, Henry Clay, Capt. AQM to Whiting
(b. 1832)

Whitner, Benjamin Frank, Maj. ADC to
Bonham (1835–1919)

Whitney, Stephen Williams, Capt. ACS to
S. D. Lee, Maury, R. Taylor; Capt. acting
CS to M. L. Smith (1841–1931)

Wickham, W. L., Capt. AQM to A. S. Johnston, Cheatham, Hardee, Beall

Wickliffe, Nathaniel, Capt. AAG to A. S.
Johnston, W. Preston; Lt. Col. AAG to
Mackall; AAIG to Breckinridge (1832–
1870)

Wicks, John W., Maj. VADC to H. E. McCulloch

Wicks, Moses J., Maj. CS to Hardee

Wigfall, Francis Halsey, Lt. ADC to J. E.
Johnston (1845–1897)

Wigg, William Hutson, Capt. ACS to Trapier
(b. 1837)

Wiggs, James A., Capt. AQM to Pillow; Capt.
AAAIG to Shoup (1837–1911)

Wilburn, William A., Capt. AAG to D. H.
Reynolds

Wilcox, John Allen, Col. VADC to Van Dorn
(1819–1864)

Wilkens, W. G., VADC to T. Green

Wilkes, James H., acting ADC to Donelson

Wilkins, Hamilton, Lt. EO to Frazer (b. 1838)

Wilkins, William W., Lt. Asst. Judge Advocate and ADC to Hardee (b. 1834)

Wilkinson, George B., Col. Military Court of
Pemberton

Willard, Samuel Morrison, Capt. ACS to Pike

Williams, A. M., Capt. staff of Hindman

Williams, B. F., Lt. ADC to Hindman

Williams, C. E., Capt. AQM to Richardson

Williams, David R., Capt. OO & AAIG to J. H.
Morgan

Williams, Edward G., Capt. AAG to Marmaduke

Williams, George A., Capt. AAG to Liddell,
Govan, Hardee, J. E. Johnston (d. 1929)

Williams, Henry W., Maj. QM to Forney,
Maury, Polk

Williams, J. A., VADC to Bee

Williams, J. Minnick, VADC to Van Dorn;
AAAIG to Leo. Polk, Stewart

Williams, James T., Capt. AQM to Hood, J. E.
Johnston

Williams, John W., Maj. CS to Holtzclaw,
Clayton

Williams, L. C., Lt. AAAIG to Beauregard

Williams, N. L., Capt. VADC to Bee

Williams, R. W., Capt. OO to Duke

Williams, R. W., Jr., VADC to Davis

Williams, Robert A., Capt. ACS Abingdon, Va.

Williams, Robert C., Maj. CS to Davis

Williams, Rufus K., Capt. acting ADC to J. H. Morgan

Williams, Thomas J., Lt. AAAIG & acting ADC to Lowry

Williams, William Orton, Lt. ADC to Leo. Polk; Capt. Chief Arty. to Bragg (1839–1863)

Williamson, George A., Capt. AAG to Govan

Williamson, George McWillie, Maj. AAG to Bragg, Leo. Polk, Beauregard; Lt. Col. AAIG to E. K. Smith (1829–1882)

Williamson, Jacob D., Maj. QM to Meems–Virginia Militia (1813–1875)

Williamson, R. W., acting ADC to Walthall

Williamson, Walter S., Lt. AAAIG to Clingman

Williamson, William H., VADC to Withers

Willie, Asa Hoxey, Maj. CS to Gregg, Liddell (1829–1899)

Willie, James, VADC to Van Dorn (1822–1863)

Willson, Thomas Friend, Capt. AAG to F. Gardner

Wilson, George R., Lt. ADC to P. O. Hebert; acting ADC to H. E. McCullough; Maj. EO to Magruder, Slaughter

Wilson, Hugh G., Maj. CS to Cabell, Churchill

Wilson, James, Maj. AAIG & OO to Breckinridge; Maj. AAIG to Bate

Wilson, James M., Lt. acting ADC to Hardee

Wilson, Jerome P., Maj. AAG to Hindman, Hood, S. D. Lee, Holmes (d. 1866)

Wilson, W. P., Lt. ADC to J. A. Smith

Winchester, George W., Maj. QM to Donelson, Davis, Maury; Maj. AAIG to Bate (1822–1878)

Winder, Richard Bayley, Maj. QM to W. M. Gardner (b. 1827)

Wineship, E., Capt. AAG to Smith

Winkler, Frank J., Capt. ACS Montgomery White Sulphur Springs, Va.

Winnemore, Isaac T., Maj. QM to Twiggs

Winslow, Henry, Maj. AADC to Leo. Polk

Winstead, John M., Capt. staff of Ross

Winston, Arthur U., Lt. OO to Featherston

Winston, Joseph H., Capt. AAIG to Major; VADC to Slaughter

Winston, William, Lt. ADC to Lyon

Wintersmith, Richard C., Capt. ACS to Buckner, Maury, R. Taylor; Maj. VADC to Breckinridge

Wintter, D. Capt. EO to Leo. Polk

Wise, G. D., Capt. OO to Cumming

Withers, Charles A., Jr., Lt. VADC to Baldwin; Lt. ADC to T. H. Taylor; Capt. AAG to J. H. Morgan, Hodge, Cosby

Withers, Daniel Forney, Lt. ADC to Withers

Withers, Robert W., Jr., Lt. ADC to Withers

Withers, William Frederick, Lt. OO to Withers, Clanton (1832–1869)

Witherspoon, H. E., Lt. ADC to Leadbetter

Wofford, Jefferson Llewellyn, Maj. Chief Arty. to S. D. Lee (1834–1911)

Wolfe, Udolpho, Capt. AQM to E. K. Smith

Womack, D. M., Capt. ACS to Bell

Womack, John F., Maj. QM to Greer

Womack, Sidney, Lt. ADC & AAIG to M. J. Wright (1842–1869)

Wood, Carroll H., Lt. ADC to Shelby (d. 1905)

Wood, Fern Manly, Maj. QM to Clayton, Holtzclaw, J. P. Anderson (1835–1877)

Wood, Henry Clay, Lt. ADC to Wood; Maj. CS to Lowrey, Wood, Shelley, Hodge (d. 1907)

Wood, J. H., Lt. OO to Walthall

Wood, Robert, Capt. AQM to Bate

Wood, Robert C., Lt. ADC to Price

Wood, Robert Crooke, Jr., Capt. AAG to Bragg (1832–1900)

Wood, Robert Richard, Maj. QM to J. E. Rains, Bate, Holtzclaw (1834–1903)

Woodland, Edward N., Maj. QM to Dockery

Woodlief, Edward D., Capt. AAG to F. Gardner; AAAIG to Leo. Polk, W. T. Martin

Woodruff, William E., Maj. Chief Arty. to Price, Frost

Woolfolk, Edward T., Maj. CS to L. E. Polk

Woolfolk, Thomas J., Lt. AQM to Walthall; Maj. QM to Cantey

Woolley, Robert Wickliffe, Capt. AAG to W. Preston (1828–1905)

Worthington, Edward S., Col. Military Court of Leo. Polk

Worthington, William Mason, Lt. AAIG to Armstrong (1835–1917)

Worthington, W. S., Lt. OO to Chalmers

Wren, William, Capt. AAIG to Pemberton, Brandon

Wright, ——, Lt. staff of Marmaduke

Wright, Archibald, VADC to Cheatham (1809–1884)

Wright, Fulton W., Lt. ADC to Tappan

Wright, Henry T., Lt. ADC to Finley; Capt. ACS to Stovall, Breckinridge

Wright, John, Maj. ADC to Wheeler

Wright, Marcus Joseph, Lt. Col. AAAG to Cheatham (1831–1922)

Wright, Uriel, Maj. VADC to Van Dorn, Price (1802–1868)

Wright, William Fulton, Lt. acting ADC to Churchill (1843–1908)

Wurzbach, Charles Louis, acting ADC to Hawes (1835–1892)

Wyly, John McGehee, Lt. ADC to Forney (b. 1837)

Wynne, V. W., Maj. staff of Buckner

Yager, William Overall, Lt. AAAG to H. E. McCulloch, Bee (1833–1904)

Yancey, Stephen Davenport, Capt. AAG to E. K. Smith (b. 1840)

Yancey, William C., Capt. AAG to Bate, Tyler

Yandell, Patton, Capt. AQM to Cheatham

Yates, Joseph Atkinson, Capt. OO to Drayton (1829–1888)

Yeatman, Henry Clay, Lt. Col. ADC to Leo. Polk (1831–1910)

Yerger, George S., VADC to W. W. Adams, D. W. Adams (1836–1865)

Yerger, James Rucks, Lt. ADC to French

Yerger, William, Jr., Lt. ADC to Higgins, C. Clark

Yniestra, Gregory, Lt. AAIG to B. M. Thomas

Yoe, George P., Lt. OO to Pegram; Lt. ADC & OO to W. T. Martin (d. 1901)

Yonge, Philip, Lt. ADC to Ro. H. Anderson

Young, Casey, Capt. AAG to Carroll; Lt. Col. AAIG to Chalmers

Young, George Valerno, Maj. QM to Cheatham; Maj. AAIG to Stewart, Hood, J. E. Johnston

Young, John W., Maj. QM to S. D. Lee, Leo. Polk, Maury, R. Taylor

Young, Upton M., Lt. ADC to Cockrell (b. 1837)

Young, Wade Ross, Lt. OO to Liddell (b. 1841)

Youngblood, Joseph W., Capt. SO to Gardner

Yulee, Elias, Capt. ACS to Finegan, Trapier (1804–1878)

Zacharie, Francis Charles, Maj. AAIG to Ruggles

Zacharie, Howard H., Capt. AAIG to Magruder, Major

von Zinken, Leon, Col. AAIG to Breckinridge

APPENDIX 2

This appendix lists, in alphabetical order, every general who served in the Army of Northern Virginia or operated in Virginia in cooperation with the main army. Each general's name is followed by a full roster of his known staff. Beside the name of each staff officer is the highest rank he obtained and his dates of service in that position. If men performed multiple duties on the staff of a general, all positions are listed. Thomas G. Pollock, for instance, served on the staff of General James L. Kemper as a quartermaster before becoming Kemper's adjutant in 1863. For generals who also commanded troops outside Virginia during their careers, the list includes only those men known to have been on their staffs during the Virginia period. All others are incorporated into Appendix 1.

It will be evident that some generals' lists are incomplete. Turner Ashby, Thomas R. R. Cobb, and Victor J. B. Girardey all died within days of becoming brigadier generals, and the composition of their staffs — if indeed they even had full staffs — remains largely unknown. In other cases, the records are unclear or absent, leaving some generals without any known staff officers in specific fields. This is especially common with ordnance officers and engineers, whose records seem to be most deficient. No doubt many legitimate staff officers are missing from this biographical register because they simply do not exist in the official documents and thus far have escaped the roving eye of the author in unofficial sources.

A related problem concerns men in the Adjutant and Inspector General's Department. Confederate scribes were exceedingly careless in respecting the distinction between adjutants general (AAGs) and inspectors general (AAIGs). The same office in Richmond regulated both positions, and very often a general's staff list will contain too many AAGs and no AAIG. In those cases, one of the AAGs almost certainly was the AAIG, but indifference to the subject by those in the know has obscured the truth in some instances.

A large number of general staff officers who were more closely attached to an organization than to a general do not appear in this appendix, although they have biographical sketches in the main body of the book. Members of the military courts are the most prominent members of this category.

Edward P. Alexander

Cleary, Reuben, Capt. AAG, 1865
Franklin, James H., Maj. CS, 1865
Goodwin, Charles R., Lt. AAAIG, 1864–1865?
Haskell, Joseph C., Capt. AAG, 1864–1865
McPhail, Clement C., Capt. OO, 1862–1863
Mason, William T., Lt. ADC, 1864–1865
Middleton, John I., Jr., Maj. QM, 1864–1865
Pinckney, Thomas, Lt. AAIG, 1865
Smith, Thomas H., Lt. AAAG, 1862–1863
Winthrop, Stephen, Capt. AAIG, 1864–1865

George B. Anderson

Anderson, Robert W., Lt. ADC, 1862
Blount, Thomas M., Capt. AAAG, 1862
Cole, Hugh L., Capt. acting AQM, 1862
Gales, Seaton, Capt. AAG, 1862
Hofflin, Marcus, Lt. VADC, 1862
Parker, Augustus N., VADC, 1862
Patridge, Isaac M., Maj. CS, 1862

George T. Anderson

Andrews, Garnett, Lt. ADC, 1864
Arnold, Eugenius C., Lt. AAAIG, 1863
Blackwell, Thomas J., Lt. AAAG, 1862
Daniell, Charles, VADC, 1862
Dawson, Lemuel H., Capt. AQM, 1864–1865
Fouche, Robert T., Lt. acting ADC, 1864
Green, John F., Lt. AAAIG, 1865
Guthrie, Josephus, Maj. QM, 1862–1865
Hardwick, Charles C., Capt. AAG, 1862–1865
Hockenhull, John, Maj. CS, 1862–1865
Holliday, Robert K., VADC, 1862, & Capt. AQM, 1864–1865
Jackson, Thomas G., Lt. ADC, 1862–1865
McDaniel, Henry D., Capt. AAAG, 1862
Norton, George C., Capt. ACS, 1863–1864
Sisson, Vardy P., Lt. OO, 1864–1865
Smith, Charles H., Maj. CS, 1861–1862
Sutlive, John W., Jr., Capt. AQM, 1864–1865
Tennille, Alexander S., Capt. ACS, ?–1865
Tennille, William A., Lt. acting ADC, 1862, & Capt. AAIG, 1863–1865
West, Frederick H., Lt. VADC?, 1862–1863

Joseph R. Anderson

Ginter, Lewis, Maj. CS, 1862
Haxall, Philip, VADC, 1862
Heath, Roscoe B., Capt. AAG, 1862
Morris, William, VADC, 1862
Norwood, William, Lt. ADC, 1862
Ryan, John S., Capt. acting ACS, 1862
Taylor, Robert T., Maj. QM, 1862.

Richard H. Anderson

Adams, Joseph M., Maj. QM, 1862
Anderson, Edward M., VADC, 1862
Ballard, Thomas E., Maj. CS, 1864–1865
Briscoe, John L., Capt. AQM, 1863–1864
Corprew, Oliver H. P., Capt. AQM, 1864–?
Crittenden, Rudolphus D., Maj. AAIG, 1862
Dawson, Francis W., Capt. OO, 1864
Duncan, Robert P., Lt. ADC, 1862, & Maj. AAIG, 1862–1865
Elliott, Middleton S., Lt. EO, 1864–1865
Fairfax, John W., Maj. AAIG, 1864
Fontaine, William M., Capt. OO, 1864–1865
Garnett, James J., Lt. Col. Chief Arty., 1863
Girardey, Victor J. B., Capt. AAAG
Hardaway, Robert A., Maj. acting Chief Arty., 1863
Haskell, Langdon C., Capt. AAG, 1864–1865
Hill, George A., Capt. AQM, 1864
Hill, John B., Maj. QM, 1864–1865
Jett, Frederick W., Capt. EO, 1862–1864
Johnston, James A., Maj. QM, 1862–1864
Jones, Hilary P., Col. Chief Arty., 1864–1865
Latrobe, Osmun, Maj. AAG, 1864
McDonald, Marshall, Capt. EO, 1864
McWillie, William, Jr., Lt. ADC, 1862–1865
Maben, John C., Capt. AQM, 1864
Manning, Jacob H., Capt. SO, 1864
Manning, Peyton T., Lt. Col. OO, 1864
Means, Edward J., Capt. acting ADC, 1862–1863
Memminger, Chris., Jr., Lt. SO, 1863–1864
Mills, Thomas S., Maj. AAG, 1861–1864
Murphy, James P., Capt. ACS, 1864–1865
Old, George D., Capt. ACS, 1864–1865
Privett, William G., Capt. ACS, 1864–1865

Reid, William L. J., Capt. AQM, 1864?–1865
Riddick, Washington L., Capt. AAIG, 1865
Shannon, Samuel D., Lt. ADC, 1862–1865
Smith, John T., Capt. AQM, 1864–1865
Snead, Thomas T. L., Lt. EO, 1863
Snodgrass, Charles E., Maj. QM, 1864–1865
Spann, James G., VADC, 1862–1863
Stone, Hamilton J., Capt. AQM, 1862?–1864
Thurston, Edward N., Maj. OO, 1862–1865
Whitner, James H., VADC, 1862
Wingfield, William C., Maj. CS, 1863–1864
Young, Henry E., Capt. VADC?, 1862

Samuel R. Anderson

Allen, John D., Maj. CS, 1862
Bowen, Achilles, Maj. EO, 1861
Cocke, Daniel F., Maj. CS, 1861–1862
Glover, James, Maj. QM, 1861–1862?
Pickett, Joseph G., Maj. AAG, 1861–1862
Smith, Granville P., Lt. ADC, 1861–1862?
Vick, Alexander W., Maj. QM, 1862
Whitthorne, Wash. C., Capt. AAG, 1861–1862
Williams, John S., Capt. AAG, 1862

James J. Archer

Allensworth, Andrew J., Capt. AQM, 1864
Archer, Robert H., Capt. AAG, 1862–1864
Crittenden, Churchill, VADC
Crittenden, James L., VADC, 1862
Hagerty, William O., Capt. AQM, 1864
Hankins, Dick R., Maj. CS, 1862–1864
Howard, George, VADC
Lemmon, George, Lt. OO, 1862–1864
Levering, Thomas H., VADC?
McClain, Rufus P., Capt. acting AQM, 1863
Porteous, John F., Lt. OO, 1864
Swan, Robert, VADC, 1862
Thomas, Oliver H., Lt. ADC, 1862–1864
Vick, Alexander W., Maj. QM, 1862
Williams, George A., VADC, 1862–1863
Wootton, Francis H., VADC, 1862

Lewis A. Armistead

Armistead, Franck S., Capt. AAG, 1862
Armistead, Walker K., Lt. ADC, 1863

Barraud, Thomas L., Maj. QM, 1862
Carter, Richard H., Maj. QM, 1862–1863
Daniel, Raleigh T., Lt. VADC, 1862
Darden, James D., Lt. ADC, 1862, & Capt. AAG, 1862–1863
Dunlop, John, Lt. ADC, 1862–1863
Herbert, William W., Maj. CS, 1862–1863
Joyner, James E., VADC, 1862
Linebaugh, John H., Lt. ADC, 1862
Pegram, James W., Jr., Capt. AAG, 1862
Randolph, Peyton K., Lt. EO, 1862–1863
Randolph, Thos. J., Jr., Maj. QM, 1862–1863
Randolph, William L., Lt. OO, 1862–1863

Turner Ashby

Marshall, James E., Lt. AAG, 1862
Richardson, John D., Capt. ACS, 1862

William Barksdale

Allen, William L., Lt. OO, 1862–1863
Barksdale, Harris, Cadet ADC, 1862–1863
Barksdale, John A. J., Capt. AAG, 1862–1863
Bell, Thomas P., Lt. ADC, 1863
Berrien, John M., Lt. OO, 1862
Doherty, Patrick M., Maj. QM, 1862–1863
Gibson, Gustavus A., Lt. AAIG, 1863
Hawken, A. Milton, Maj. CS, 1862–1863
Inge, William M., Maj. AAG, 1862–1863
Leonard, Thomas F., Capt. ACS, 1862?–1863

Rufus Barringer

Bassett, George W., Lt. OO, 1864–1865?
Cochran, Robert E., Capt. AQM, 1864?
Dabney, Chiswell, Capt. AAIG, 1864–1865
Downman, Robert H., Maj. CS, 1864–1865
Foard, Frederick C., Lt. ADC, 1864–1865
Gaines, James L., Capt. AAG, 1864–1865
Morrison, Robert H., Jr., Lt. acting ADC, 1864
Neal, John B. B., Maj. QM, 1864–1865

Seth Barton

Addison, William A., VADC, 1865
Alexander, George W., Capt. AAG, 1864
Averett, John T., Capt. AQM, 1864
Brown, J. J., Capt. AQM, 1864–1865

Clark, Meriwether L., Col. oo, 1864–1865
Compton, James, Capt. aqm, 1864
Darden, James D., Capt. aag, 1864
Doswell, Richard M., Lt. adc, ?–1865
Herbert, William W., Maj. cs, ?–1864
Keiley, John D., Jr., Maj. qm, 1865
Lyons, Thomas B., Lt. adc, 1864–1865
Macmurdo, Charles C., Capt. aqm, 1864
Nash, Frederick K., Capt. aag, 1864–1865
Porteous, John F., Lt. oo, ?–1865
Powers, James L., Capt. aqm, ?–1865
Randolph, William L., Lt. oo, 1864
Starke, Thaddeus B., Capt. acting aqm, 1864–1865
Stith, Donald C., Capt. ?, 1864–?
Thom, Allan C., Capt. aaig, 1864
Thompson, Benjamin S., Maj. qm, 1864?

Cullen A. Battle

Bryan, James C., Maj. qm, 1863–1865
Byrd, Abraham S., Capt. aqm, 1865
Haralson, Hugh A., Capt. aqm, 1865
Partridge, Daniel, Jr., Lt. aaaig, 1863–1864, & Lt. oo, 1864–1865
Pickett, Alexander H., Capt. aag, 1863–1865
Preston, A. T., Capt. acs, 1863–1865
Rendet, P. C., Lt. adc, 1863
Seawell, Joseph H., Capt. aqm, 1865
Shorter, Henry R., Lt. adc, 1863–1865
Smith, James P., Capt. aaig, 1863–1864
Webb, James E., Lt. oo, 1863–1864
Webster, Daniel T., Maj. cs, 1863–1865

R. L. T. Beale

Beale, Richard C., Lt. adc, 1865
Jones, Junius B., Lt. oo, 1865
Nash, Joseph V., Capt. aag, 1865
Prince, Joseph B., Lt. oo, 1865
Urquhart, Joseph W., Maj. cs, 1865
Walters, Joseph M., Capt. aqm, 1865

P. G. T. Beauregard

Alexander, Edward P., Capt. eo and so, 1861
Blair, William B., Maj. cs, 1861

Bolling, William N., Lt. eo, 1864
Brent, George W., Col. aag, 1864
Bryan, Edward P., Capt. aag, 1864
Cabell, William L., Maj. qm, 1861
Chisolm, Alexander R., Lt. adc, 1861–1865
Cooke, Giles B., Maj. aag, 1864
Deslonde, Edmond A., Capt. aqm, 1861
Edings, John E., Capt. aaig, 1864?
Elliott, Middleton S., Lt. eo, 1864
Eustis, James B., Maj. aaig, 1864
Ferguson, Samuel W., Capt. adc, 1861
Ferry, Albert, Capt. aag, 1864
Fowle, William H., Sr., Capt. acs, 1861
Harris, David B., Col. eo, 1864
Harvie, Lewis E., Jr., Capt. acs, 1864
Hatch, Lewis M., vadc & acting aqm, 1861
Heyward, Joseph M., vadc, 1861
Hill, Daniel H., Maj. Gen. vadc, 1864
Johnson, Powell C., Lt. eo, 1864
Jones, Hilary P., Col. Chief Arty., 1864
Jones, Samuel, Col. oo & Chief Arty., 1861
Jordan, Thomas, Lt. Col. aag, 1861
Lee, Richard B., Jr., Lt. Col. cs, 1861
McKinney, Charles S., Capt. acs, 1861
Manning, John L., vadc, 1861
Miles, William P., vadc, 1861
Molloy, Ferdinand, Maj. cs, 1864
Nash, Thomas, Lt. oo, 1864
Otey, John M., Jr., Lt. Col. aag, 1861–1865
Pattison, Holmes A., Lt. eo, 1864
Paul, Samuel B., vadc, 1864
Peyton, Henry E., vadc, 1861
Polignac, Camillus J., Lt. Col. aaig, 1861
Preston, John S., Lt. Col. aag, 1861
Reid, William L. J., Capt. aqm, 1864
Rice, Alexander G., vadc, 1861–1865
Roman, Alfred, Lt. Col. aaig, 1864
Smith, Anthony A., Lt. oo, 1864
Smith, Clifton H., Capt. aag, 1861
Stevens, Walter H., Capt. eo, 1861
Waddy, John R., Jr., Lt. Col. oo, 1864
Williamson, Thomas H., Lt. Col. eo, 1861
Willis, Edward, Maj. qm, 1864

Barnard E. Bee

Hill, James H., Lt. aag, 1861

Howard, Richard A., VADC, 1861

Van der Horst, A., VADC, 1861

Henry L. Benning

Alexander, W. T., Capt. AAG, 1863

Ballard, Walter S., Maj. CS, 1863–1865

Bennett, William H., Capt. ACS, 1863–1865

Benning, Seaborn J., Capt. AAG, 1863–1865

Bird, William E., Maj. QM, 1863–1864

Davenport, Hugh M., Maj. QM, 1864–1865

DuBose, Dudley M., Lt. ADC & Capt. AAG, 1862

Forbes, Horatio W., Capt. AQM, 1864–?

Hill, Robert C., Capt. AAG, 1863

Houston, James, Capt. acting AQM, 1863–1864

Lofton, Bedford H., Lt. OO, 1863–1865

Morton, Alexander C., Capt. AQM, 1864–1865

Mott, John R., Lt. AAAG, 1862–1863, & Lt. ADC, 1863–1865

Perry, Heman H., Capt. AAIG, 1863–1864

Tempe, Robert, Lt. VADC?, 1862

Tennille, Alexander S., Capt. acting CS, 1865

Albert G. Blanchard

Grice, George W., Maj. QM, 1862

Riddick, Washington L., Capt. AAG, 1861–1862

Wingfield, William C., Maj. CS, 1861–1862

Milledge L. Bonham

Aldrich, Alfred P., Lt. Col. QM, 1861–1862

Barbour, Alfred M., Maj. QM, 1861

Boylston, Robert B., Lt. Col. CS, 1861–1862

Butler, William P., VADC, 1861

Davies, Thomas J., Maj. ADC, 1861

Fisher, Thomas F., Maj. QM, 1861–1862

Gordon, Charles H., Lt. AAAG, 1862

Hammond, Edward S., VADC, 1861

Holmes, Charles R., Lt. AAAG, 1862

Kennedy, Joseph, Maj. CS, 1861–1862

Lay, George W., Lt. Col. AAG, 1861

Lipscomb, James N., Lt. ——?, 1861

Lipscomb, Milledge B., VADC, 1861

Mays, Thomas S., VADC, 1861

McGowan, Samuel, VADC, 1861

Melton, Samuel W., VADC, 1861

Moragne, William C., Col. AAG, 1861

Moss, Alfred, VADC, 1861

Nance, William F., Maj. AAG, 1861

Nelson, Samuel W., VADC, 1861

Peck, William D., Capt. AQM, 1862

Simpson, John W., VADC, 1861

Simpson, William D., Lt. Col. AAIG, 1861

Stevens, Walter H., Capt. acting EO, 1861

Stoney, William E., Lt. OO, 1861

Tompkins, Samuel S., VADC, 1861

Washington, Littleton Q., Lt. acting AQM, 1861

Young, Clement, Capt. AQM, 1861–1862

Braxton Bragg

Brent, George W., Col. AAG, 1864

Cuthbert, James E., Maj. ADC, 1864

Molloy, Ferdinand, Maj. CS, 1864

Parker, Francis S., Jr., Maj. ADC, 1864

Sale, John B., Col. AAG, 1864

Strange, Robert, Maj. ADC, 1864

Lawrence O. Branch

Blount, William A., Jr., Lt. ADC, 1862

Bryan, James A. W., Lt. OO, 1862

Cannady, William E., Lt. ADC & Capt. AAG, 1862

Carraway, Daniel T., Capt. ACS, 1862

Engelhard, Joseph A., Maj. QM, 1862

Gibbon, Nicholas B., Capt. acting ACS, 1862

Hawks, Francis T., VADC & Capt. AAG, 1862

Hill, Robert C., Maj. AAG, 1862

Rodman, William B., Maj. QM, 1862

John Bratton

Agurs, John L., Capt. AQM, 1864–1865

Elford, T. Joseph, Maj. CS, 1864–1865?

Jamison, David R., Lt. OO, 1864–1865

Judge, Hilliard M., Lt. ADC, 1864–1865

Love, S. Lucien, Capt. ACS, 1864–1865?

Lyle, Joseph B., Capt. AAAIG, 1864–?

Quincy, William H., Maj. QM, 1864–1865
Sharpe, William S., Capt. AQM, 1864–1865
Sims, Robert M., Capt. AAG, 1864
Sorrel, Alexander C., Capt. AAG, 1864–1865

John C. Breckinridge
Bradford, William A., Maj. CS, 1864
Carr, George W., Maj. AAIG, 1864–1865
Faulkner, Charles J., Jr., VADC, 1864?
Graves, John T., Capt. ACS, 1864
Hawkins, Thomas T., Lt. ADC, 1864–1865
Johnston, Josiah S., Maj. AAG, 1864–1865
King, Horace W., Maj. CS, 1864
Leigh, James Y., Capt. AQM, 1864
McMahon, Edward, Maj. QM, 1864–1865
Pickett, John T., VADC, 1864
Schley, William C., Lt. SO, 1864
Semple, Charles, Capt. AAIG, 1864
Stringfellow, Charles S., Maj. AAG, 1864

Goode Bryan
Claiborne, John, Maj. QM, 1864
Davis, John E., Maj. QM, 1863
Delaigle, Louis, Maj. QM, 1864
Ellis, Roswell, Capt. AAG, 1863–1864
Harding, Charles A., Maj. QM, 1863–1864
Kibbee, Charles C., Capt. AAAG, 1864
McLendon, Charles G., Lt. acting ADC, 1864
Parmelee, Charles H., Capt. ACS, 1863–1864
Semmes, Abner G., Lt. OO, 1863
Townshend, John H., Lt. ADC, 1863–1864
Walker, James W., Capt. AAIG, 1863–1864
Whitehead, W. H. W., Capt. ACS, 1863–1864

Matthew C. Butler
Adams, James P., Capt. VADC, 1864
Aiken, Augustus M., Lt. OO, 1864
Barker, Theodore G., Maj. AAG, 1864–1865
Barnett, William H., Cadet, 1864–1865
Beggs, Thomas, Maj. CS, 1863–1865
Blocker, John R., Maj. AAIG, 1864
Butler, Andrew P., Lt. ——?, 1864
Butler, Oliver N., Lt. ADC, 1863–1865
Chisholm, J. M., VADC?
Connelly, William C., Lt. OO, 1863–?

Davis, Zimmerman, Lt. AAAIG, 1864
Edelin, T. Boyd, Lt. AAAIG, 1863
Green, Ellis C., Jr., Capt. acting QM, 1864
Harding, Charles A., Maj. QM, 1864–1865
Lipscomb, James N., Capt. AAG, 1863–1865
McClellan, Robert M., Capt. acting QM, 1863
Mason, James M., Capt. OO, 1864
Melton, George W., Maj. QM, 1864–1865
Preston, John, Jr., Maj. AAG, 1864–1865
Seibels, Emmett, Maj. VADC, 1864–1865
Smith, Frederick L., Capt. ACS, 1864–?
Venable, Paul C., Capt. OO, 1864–1865

John R. Chambliss
Bowling, Henry A., Capt. AAIG, 1864
Chambliss, Walter B., Lt. ADC, 1864
Jones, Junius B., Lt. OO, 1864
Lewis, Edward P. C., ?
Nash, Joseph V., Capt. AAG, 1863–1864
Riddick, John T., Lt. AAAIG, 1864
Urquhart, Joseph W., Capt. acting CS, 1864

Charles Clark
Barry, William T. S., Capt. AAG, 1861
Lovell, Joseph, VADC, 1861
McCardle, William H., Lt. ADC, 1861
Walton, Thomas J., VADC, 1861
Watts, Nathaniel G., Maj. QM, 1861

Thomas L. Clingman
Blake, Frederick R., Capt. AAIG, 1864
Burgwyn, W. H. S., Lt. ADC & Capt. AAIG, 1864
Du Heaume, Philippe, Lt. OO, 1864
Erwin, Alfred M., Maj. QM, 1864
Gage, Robert S., Maj. CS, 1864
Lane, Hardy B., Capt. ACS, 1864
Meares, Oliver P., Capt. AQM, 1864
Puryear, Henry S., Lt. ADC, 1864
Rockwell, Henry C., Capt. AQM, 1864
White, Edward, Capt. AAG, 1864

Howell Cobb
Barrow, James, Capt. AAG, 1862
Cobb, John A., Lt. ADC, 1862

Cobb, John B., Maj. CS, 1862
Cobb, Lamar, Lt. ADC, 1862
Gwin, William, Capt. ?, 1862
Lamar, John B., VADC, 1862
Richardson, James G., Capt. acting ACS, 1862
Thomas, Robert, Maj. QM, 1862
Whitner, John C., Maj. CS, 1862
Young, Pierce M. B., Lt. AAAG, 1862

Thomas R. R. Cobb

Berrien, John M., Lt. OO, 1862
Brewster, Walter S., Capt. AAAIG, 1862
Connelly, William C., Lt. OO, 1862
Crane, Benjamin E., Capt. acting AQM, 1862
Rutherford, John C., VADC, 1862

Philip St. George Cocke

Barbour, John S., Jr., VADC, 1861
Cocke, John B., Lt. VADC & AAAG, 1861
Cooke, Giles B., VADC & Capt. AAG, 1861
Harris, David B., Capt. EO, 1861
Stockton, John N. C., Lt. VADC, 1861
Wilson, John T., Maj. CS, 1861

Alfred H. Colquitt

Buchanan, George B., Capt. AQM, 1864–1865
Burnett, Eugene P., Maj. AAIG, 1864–1865
Collier, Thomas J., Capt. ACS, 1864–1865
Colquitt, Hugh H., Lt. ADC, 1864–1865
Ely, Robert N., Maj. QM, 1862–1865
Estill, Henry M., Lt. acting OO, 1865–1865
Glover, George R., Lt. acting ADC, 1864
Grattan, George G., VADC, 1862, & Capt. AAG, 1862–1865
Hall, John T., Capt. acting ACS, 1862
Jackson, Henry, Capt. AAG, 1864–1865
Jordan, Robert P., Lt. AAAG, 1862
Morgan, Jerry B., Maj. CS, 1862–1865
Randle, James C., Lt. ADC, 1862
Sheats, Samuel V., Capt. AQM, 1864–1865

Raleigh Colston

Elliott, Samuel C., Capt. ACS, 1861

Garrison, George G., Capt. AAG, 1862
Grogan, Charles E., Lt. VADC, 1863
Hinrichs, Oscar, Lt. EO, 1863
Hoffman, Alfred, Maj. AAG, 1863
Marye, Lawrence S., Capt. OO, 1863
Moore, Edwin L., Capt. AAAIG, 1863
Pendleton, Joseph H., Maj. QM, 1863
Saunders, William J., Lt. AAAIG, 1861
Scott, Frederic R., Maj. CS, 1862–1863
Smith, J. N., Lt. ADC?, 1862
Stanard, William B., Maj. CS, 1863
Taliaferro, Warner T., Capt. AAG, 1864–1865
Tannor, Nathaniel M., Maj. QM, 1862–1863
Tosh, James T., Lt. ADC, 1862–1865

James Conner

Dwight, William M., Capt. AAG, 1864
Griffin, Evander M., Capt. ACS, 1864
Harllee, Edward P., Cadet AAIG, 1864
Henagan, James M., Capt. AQM, 1864
Holmes, Charles R., Capt. AAG, 1864
Kennedy, Joseph, Maj. CS, 1864
Lovelace, Benjamin F., Capt. acting AQM, 1864
Magrath, Andrew G., Jr., Lt. ADC, 1864
Myers, John A., Lt. OO, 1864
Pope, Young J., Lt. AAAG, 1864
Woodward, Thomas W., Capt. AQM, 1864

Philip Cook

Cabaniss, Thomas B., Lt? OO, 1864–1865
Daniel, Henry K., Maj. QM, 1864
Jackson, Asbury H., Capt. ACS, 1864–1865
Jones, Richard V., Lt. AAIG, 1864–1865
Law, Charles H., Lt. ADC, 1864–1865
McComb, Samuel, Capt. ACS, 1864–1865
Mahool, Thomas, Capt. ACS, 1865
Mitchell, Julian, Maj. CS, 1865
Neary, William J., Capt. AQM, 1865
Reid, Alexander S., Capt. AQM, 1864–1865
Snead, Fletcher T., Capt. AAG, 1864–1865
Tinsley, Howard, Capt. AQM, 1864–1865

John R. Cooke

Anderson, Robert W., Capt. OO, 1863–1864
Braxton, Elliott M., Maj. QM, 1862–1865

Butler, Henry A., Capt. AAG, 1862–1865
Hayes, John S., Maj. CS, 1862–1865
Mebane, William N., Jr., Lt. OO, 1864–1865?
Morril, William H., Capt. ACS, 1863–?
Patton, Hugh M., Lt. ADC, 1862–1865
Thomas, Charles H., Capt. AQM, 1864–1865
White, Joshua W., Capt. AQM, 1864–1865

Samuel Cooper

Barton, William S., Maj. AAG, 1864–1865
Clay, Hugh L., Lt. Col. AAG, 1863–1865
Deas, George, Lt. Col. AAIG, 1862–1864
Hoge, John B., Maj. AAG, 1864–1865
Lee, Charles H., Maj. AAG, 1862–1864
Melton, Samuel W., Lt. Col. AAG, 1863–1865
Palfrey, Edward A., Lt. Col. AAG, 1862–1865
Riely, John W., Lt. Col. AAIG, 1863–1865
Withers, John, Lt. Col. AAIG, 1861–1865

Montgomery D. Corse

Beckham, Henry C., Lt. VADC, 1862
Brown, Victor M., Maj. CS, 1862–1865
Bryant, John C. H., Lt. ADC, 1862, & Capt. AAG, 1863–1864
Carr, Wilson C. N., Capt. AQM, 1863–1865
Crane, George W., Maj. QM, 1863–1864
Harrison, Randolph, Lt. AAAIG, 1862–1863?
Henderson, Fenton M., Lt. OO, 1862–1865
Hooe, Philip B., Capt. AAG, 1862–1865
McCandlish, Thomas P., Capt. AQM, 1864–1865
Page, Philip N., Cadet ADC, 1864–1865
Taliaferro, Hay B., Capt. ACS, 1863–1865
Turner, Robert H., Maj. QM, 1862–1865
Williams, Charles U., Lt. ADC, 1863–1865

George B. Cosby

Carrington, John W., Lt. OO, 1864
Carter, Charles D., ?, VADC?, 1864
Clarke, William E., Maj. QM, 1864
Dudley, B. W., Lt. ADC, 1864
Giltner, Bernard W., VADC?, 1864
Guerrant, Edward O., Capt. AAG, 1864
Ireland, John C., Lt. AAIG, 1864
Johnston, Madison C., Jr., Cadet OO, 1864

McAfee, John J., Capt. AAG, 1864
Shipp, Samuel B., Capt. AAIG, 1864
Shook, James H., Maj. CS, 1864
Tenney, Otis S., Maj. QM, 1864
Thompson, Tazewell, Maj. CS, 1864

William R. Cox

Battle, James S., Lt. ADC, 1864–1865
Brown, John B., Capt. AAG, 1865
Coleman, Samuel H., Lt. OO, 1864–1865
Coleman, W. M., Capt. OO, ?
Coughenour, W. C., Capt. AAIG, 1864–1865
Faircloth, William T., Capt. AQM, 1864–1865
Gales, Seaton, Capt. AAG, 1864–1865
Jones, J., Capt. AAG, ?–1865
Lilly, Robert, Capt. ACS, 1864–1865
Miller, Henry M., Maj. CS, ?–1865
Philips, Frederick, Capt. AQM, 1865
Williams, Buckner D., Maj. QM, 1864–1865

Junius Daniel

Badger, Richard C., Maj. CS, 1862–1864
Ballard, Robert E., Lt. acting ADC, 1863–1864
Bond, William R., Lt. ADC, 1862–1864
Edmondston, James N., Maj. QM, 1862–1864
Fitzhugh, Edmund C., Capt. AAG, 1863
Green, Wharton J., VADC, 1863
Hammond, William M., Capt. AAG, 1862–1863
Hill, William P., Capt. ACS, 1863–1864
Holmes, John L., Maj. CS, 1862
London, William L., Capt. AAG, 1864
Long, I. J., Jr., VADC, 1864
Ritter, William B., Capt. OO, 1864
Stitt, William E., Lt. acting ADC, 1863–1864
Wheeler, Woodbury, Lt. OO, 1862–1863
White, Joseph H., Capt. AAAG, 1863–1864

Henry B. Davidson

Harman, William H., Capt. AAG, 1864–1865
Hill, William E., Capt. ?, 1865?
Ker, Hugh, Lt. ADC, 1864–1865
Waters, Frank, Capt. AAG, 1864–1865?

Joseph R. Davis

Balfour, James R., ?, 1864
Cameron, William E., Capt. AAIG, 1864
Cooper, Lunsford P., Capt. AQM, 1864–1865
Estes, Henry B., Lt. ADC, 1862–1865
Evans, John J., Capt. AAG, 1864–1865
Harrison, Samuel R., Maj. CS, 1862–1865
Henderson, Robert, Capt. ACS, 1863?–1865
Holliday, Thomas C., Capt. AAG, 1863–1864
Lowry, Samuel M., VADC?, 1863
Magruder, William T., Capt. AAG, 1862–1863
Owens, Silas, Jr., Capt. AQM, 1864–1865
Reid, James S., Maj. QM, 1862–1865
Reid, Joseph D., Cadet ?, 1863
Walton, N. T., Lt. ADC, 1865
Wortham, Richard C., Lt. OO, 1863–1865

James Dearing

Bigger, Robert H., Maj. QM, 1864–1865
Bower, Byron B., Capt. AAIG, 1864–1865
Coughenour, William C., Capt. AAIG, 1865
Howell, Robert P., Capt. acting AQM, 1864
Kearsley, George W. T., Maj. CS, 1864–1865
Kennon, Richard B., Capt. AAG?, 1865
Rutherfoord, James C., Capt. AAIG, ?–1865
Symington, Thomas A., VADC?, 1864–1865
Webb, James E., Lt. OO, 1864–1865
White, John J., Capt. AQM, 1865
Withrow, Charles H., Lt. OO, 1865?

George P. Doles

Cabaniss, Thomas B., Lt.? OO, 1862–1864
Daniel, Henry K., Maj. QM, 1862–1864
Furlow, Charles T., Lt. ADC, 1863–1864
Hawkins, Eugene A., Lt. ADC, 1862–1863, & Capt. AAIG, 1863–1864
Higham, Thomas, Maj. QM, 1862–1863
Jones, Richard V., Lt. AAAIG, 1863, & Lt. AAIG, 1864
McComb, Samuel, Capt. ACS, 1863–1864
Mitchell, Julian, Maj. CS, 1862–1863
Snead, Francis T., Capt. AAG, 1862–1864

Daniel S. Donelson

Brown, A. J., Capt. AQM, 1861–1862

Duvall, Henry, Capt. AAG & acting ADC, 1861
Martin, James G., Lt. ADC, 1861–1862

Thomas F. Drayton

Drayton, John E., Lt. ADC, 1862
Edings, John E., Capt. AAG, 1862
Hanckel, Charles F., Maj. CS, 1862
Middleton, John I., Jr., Lt. ADC, 1862
Rose, Hugh, VADC, 1862?
Shortt, Stuart J., Maj. AAG, 1862
Willis, Edward, Maj. QM, 1862
Young, Henry E., Capt. AAG, 1862

Dudley M. DuBose

Byrd, Samuel M. H., Maj. QM, 1864–1865
Griffis, John C., Maj. CS, 1864–1865
Hackett, John T., Capt. AAIG?, 1864–1865
Hackett, T. H., Capt. AAIG, 1864–1865
Lumpkin, Frank, Capt. AQM, 1864–1865
Oliver, Thomas P., Lt. AAAG, ?–1865
Peek, Julius A., Lt. AAAG, 1864–1865
Pierce, George F., Jr., Capt. AAAG, 1864–1865
Pierce, Lovick, Jr., Lt. AAAG, 1864
Turner, Allen S., Capt. AQM, 1864–1865
Young, Isaac M., Lt. acting OO, 1865

John Dunovant

Aiken, Augustus M., Lt. OO, 1864
Butler, Andrew P., Lt. VADC, 1864
Davis, Zimmerman, Capt. AAAIG, 1864
Jeffords, Theodore A., Lt. AAAG, 1864
Smith, Frederick L., Capt. ACS, 1864

Jubal A. Early

Allan, William, Lt. Col. OO, 1864–1865
Archer, William M., Capt. OO, 1864
Callaway, William G., Lt. ADC, 1863–1865
Carrere, William, Maj. acting QM, 1862
Carter, Thomas H., Col. Chief Arty., 1864
Chestney, Theodore O., Capt. AAG, 1862
Christy, George W., Capt. OO, 1862–1865?
Courtney, Alfred R., Maj. Chief Arty., 1862
Daniel, John W., Maj. AAG, 1863–1864
Dennis, George E., Capt. acting ADC, 1861

Early, Robert D., VADC, 1863
Early, Samuel H., Lt. ADC, 1861–1863
Eyster, George H., Cadet OO, 1862
Garber, Alex. M., Jr., Capt. AQM, 1864?
Gardner, Fleming, Capt. AAG, 1861–1862
Goode, John, VADC, 1861–1862, 1864
Greene, Benjamin H., Maj. CS, 1862–1863,
   & Maj. EO, 1864–1865
Hairston, Peter W., VADC, 1863–1865
Hale, Samuel, Jr., Maj. CS, 1862, & Maj.
   AAIG, 1862–1864
Harman, John A., Maj. QM, 1864
Hart, Camillus S., Capt. AQM, 1862–1863
Harvie, John B., Maj. QM, 1861–1862
Hawks, Wells J., Maj. CS, 1864–1865
Heaton, Henry, VADC, 1862
Hinrichs, Oscar, Lt. EO, 1864
Hotchkiss, Jedediah, Contract EO, 1864–
   1865
Johnston, James F., Capt. acting ACS,
   1861–?
Jones, Hilary P., Lt. Col. Chief Arty., 1863
Jones, John M., Lt. Col. AAG & AAIG,
   1862–1863
Lake, ——, VADC, 1863
Latimer, Joseph W., Capt. Chief Arty., 1862
Mangham, John H., Capt. ACS, 1863–1864
Marye, Lawrence S., VADC, 1862
Moore, Edwin L., Maj. AAIG, 1864–1865
Moore, Samuel J. C., Capt. AAG, 1864–1865?
Morrow, John, VADC, 1862
Morson, John S., VADC, 1861–1862
New, John P. H., Maj. AAIG, 1864
Old, William W., Lt. VADC, 1864
Page, Mann, Lt. ADC, 1864–1865
Pendleton, Alexander S., Lt. Col. AAG, 1864
Pitzer, Andrew L., Lt. ADC, 1862–1865
Preston, John, Capt. AQM, 1864
Richardson, Henry B., Capt. EO, 1862–1863
Ridgely, Randolph, VADC, 1864
Rogers, John D., Maj. QM, 1864
Shorter, Charles S., Capt. EO, 1864
Smead, Abner, Col. AAIG, 1864
Smith, William P., Col. EO, 1864–1865
Snodgrass, Charles E., Maj. QM, 1862–1864
Snowden, Samuel H., Capt. AQM, 1865

Taliaferro, Thomas S., Capt. PM, 1863
Thornton, William W., Maj. CS, 1862–1864
Turner, E., Capt. AQM, 1864
Wallach, Charles S., Capt. AQM, 1862
Wilbourn, Richard E., Capt. SO, 1864–1865
Williamson, William G., Lt. VADC, 1862
Wilson, John P., VADC, 1862

John Echols

Bouldin, Wood, Lt. AAIG, 1863–1864
Branham, James W., Lt. ADC, 1863–1864
Catlett, Richard H., Capt. AAG, 1863–1864
Effinger, John F., Lt. ADC, 1864
Gordon, Edward C., Lt. OO, 1863–1864
McKendree, George, Maj. QM, 1863–1864
Mitchell, John W., Maj. CS, 1863–1864
Preston, Waller R., Capt. AAG, 1863–1864
Ruby, John C., Capt. ACS, 1863–1864

Stephen Elliott

Barnwell, Stephen E., Lt. ADC, 1864
Evans, Asa L., Capt. AAG, 1864
Fayssoux, Templar S., Capt. OO, 1864
Hill, John B., Maj. QM, 1864
Lemmons, Perry O., Capt. AQM, 1864
Montgomery, John H., Capt. ACS, 1864
Pagan, James, Maj. CS, 1864

Arnold Elzey

Andrews, Garnett, Maj. AAG, 1863–1864
Atkins, Robert G., Capt. ADC, 1862
Ballard, Thomas E., Capt. ACS, 1862
Braxton, John S., Capt. AAG, 1863–1864
Chestney, Theodore O., Maj. AAG, 1861–
   1864
Contee, Richard S., Lt. ADC, 1861–1863
Ford, Edwin A., Lt. EO?, 1863
Howard, Charles, Maj. CS, 1862–1864
Howard, James M., Lt. OO, 1864
Hudson, Edward M., Lt. ADC, 1863–1864
Irwin, Henry, Lt. ADC, 1863
McDonald, Craig W., Lt. acting ADC &
   AAIG, 1862
Marye, Lawrence S., Capt. OO, 1863–1864
Riely, John W., Capt. AAG, 1862–1863
Smith, John L., Capt. AAG, 1862–1864

Snowden, Charles A., Maj. QM, 1861–1864
Snowden, Richard N., Maj. AAG, 1861–1862
Spurrier, Grafton D., Capt. AQM, 1861–?
Stith, Donald C., Capt. ———, 1864
Taylor, Murray F., Cadet, acting ADC, 1862
Vaughan, Andrew J., Maj. CS, 1861–1862
Ward, Francis X., VADC

Clement A. Evans

Boyce, Ker, Capt. AQM, 1864–1865
Bruce, James W., Maj. QM, 1864
Cody, David C., Capt. AAIG, 1864–1865
Gordon, Eugene C., Lt. ADC, 1864–1865
Hilton, Joseph, Capt. AAAG, ?–1865
Lyon, William D., Lt. OO, 1864
Mitchel, James, Capt. AAG, 1864
Oattis, Henry J., Capt. AQM, 1864–1865?
Pace, James M., Capt. AAG, 1864
Rawle, Francis, Maj. QM, 1865
Reid, Francis W., Maj. CS, 1864
Rushin, Alonzo M., Lt. acting OO, 1864–
    1865
Sexton, Joseph C., Maj. CS, 1865
Stiles, William H., Capt. AQM, 1864–1865
Stonebraker, Abraham S., Capt. AQM,
    1864–1865
Walker, John A., Capt. ACS, 1864–1865
Waters, James H., Capt. ACS, 1864–1865

Nathan G. Evans

Bryan, B. S., Maj. QM, 1862
Corrie, Samuel J., Lt. ADC, 1862
Eason, Thomas D., Lt. OO, 1862
Evans, Asa L., Capt. AAG, 1861–1862
Fayssoux, Templar S., Capt. OO, 1862–1864
McCausland, George, VADC, 1861
Orr, John M., Capt. ACS, 1861
Pagan, James, Maj. CS, 1862
Rogers, Alexander H., VADC, 1861
Rogers, John D., Maj. QM, 1861–1862
Rogers, William H., Lt. ADC, 1861–1862
Wildman, Charles B., Lt. acting ADC, 1861

Richard S. Ewell

Allan, William, Lt. Col. OO, 1863–1864
Archer, William M., Capt. OO, 1863–1864

Barbour, James, Maj. AAG, 1862
Brown, G. Campbell, Lt. ADC, 1861–1862,
    Maj. AAG, 1862–1864, & Maj. AAIG,
    1864–1865
Brown, J. Thompson, Col. Chief Arty., 1863
Carrere, William, Maj. acting QM, 1862
Carroll, Robert G. H., Lt. ADC, 1864
Chestney, Theodore O., Maj. AAG, 1865
Christy, George W., Capt. OO, 1862
Clarke, William H., ADC, 1865
Courtney, Alfred R., Maj. Chief Arty., 1862
Cunningham, Arthur S., Lt. Col. AAIG,
    1864–1865
Elliott, Robert W. B., Lt. VADC, 1863
Ewell, Benjamin S., Col. AAG, 1864–1865
Faulkner, Charles J., Lt. Col. AAG, 1863
Forbes, Francis T., Maj. CS, 1864–1865
Garber, Alex. M., Jr., Capt. AQM, 1863–
    1864?
Greene, Benjamin H., VADC, 1861, & Maj.
    CS, 1861–1862, Maj. AAIG, 1863–1864, &
    Maj. EO, 1864
Griswold, Joseph G., Capt. AAAG, 1861?
Harman, John A., Maj. QM, 1863–1864
Hawks, Wells J., Maj. CS, 1863–1864
Hinrichs, Oscar, Lt. EO, 1862
Hotchkiss, Jedediah, Contract EO, 1863–
    1864
Johnson, John E., VADC, 1863
Johnston, Elliott, VADC, 1862–1863
Jones, Hilary P., Lt. Col. acting Chief Arty.,
    1863
Jones, John M., Lt. Col. AAG & AAAIG,
    1862
Ker, James, Capt. OO, 1864–1865
Kerr, John, Capt. OO, 1864–?
Koerner, Peter W. O., Lt. EO, 1865
Lee, Fitzhugh, Lt. AAAG, 1861
Mason, Robert F., VADC, 1861, & Maj. QM,
    1861–1862
Meade, Richard K., Lt. AAIG, 1864
Moss, Alfred, VADC, 1862
Nelson, Hugh M., Lt. ADC, 1862
Page, Legh R., Maj. AAIG, 1864
Parkhill, John H., Maj. AAG, 1864–1865
Pegram, James W., Jr., Maj. AAG, 1864–1865

Pendleton, Alex. S., Lt. Col. AAG, 1863–1864

Peyton, Thomas G., Maj. AAAG, 1862

Randolph, James I., Lt. EO, 1862

Rhodes, Charles H., Capt. AQM, 1861

Richardson, Henry B., Capt. EO, 1862–1863

Robinson, Powhatan, Capt. EO, 1862

Rogers, John D., Maj. QM, 1864

Selden, Harry H., Maj. QM, 1864–1865

Smead, Abner, Col. AAIG, 1863–1864

Smith, James P., Lt. ADC, 1863

Snodgrass, Charles E., Maj. QM, 1862

Taliaferro, John, VADC, 1861, & Cadet acting ADC, 1864

Turner, Thomas T., Lt. ADC, 1862–1865

Tyler, Charles H., Lt. Col. AAAG, 1861

Wallach, Charles S., Capt. AQM, 1862

Walton, Thomas J., Maj. AAG, 1864–1865

Wilbourn, Richard E., Capt. SO, 1863–1864

Wilson, John P., VADC, 1862

Young, Louis G., Lt. VADC, 1862

Winfield S. Featherston

Barksdale, William R., Capt. AAG, 1862, & Maj. QM, 1862–1863

Featherston, Charles N., VADC, 1862

Fiser, John C., Lt. AAAG, 1862?

Foote, George P., Capt. AAG, 1862

Graves, Charles W., VADC, 1862

Haley, Alfred G., Lt. ADC, 1862

Parker, Augustus N., Lt. ADC, 1862–1863

Patridge, Isaac M., Maj. CS, 1862–1863

Reading, Thomas R., Lt. VADC, 1862

Scruggs, Louis S., Maj. QM, 1862–1863

Sykes, S. Turner, Lt. OO, 1862

Sykes, William G., VADC, 1862–1863

Charles W. Field

Collins, Charles R., Capt. VADC, 1862

Corbin, Richard W., VADC, 1864–1865

Crockett, John N., Capt. AQM, 1864–1865

Davidson, Maxwell T., Capt. SO, 1864

Deshields, Henry C., Maj. QM, 1862, 1864–1865

Duvall, Eli, Lt. SO, 1864

Ellis, Roswell, Capt. AAG, 1864–1865

Harrison, George F., Capt. AAG, 1862

Jones, Willis F., Maj. AAG, 1863–1864

McLure, John W., Capt. AQM, 1864–1865

Mason, Julien J., Maj. CS, 1862, 1864–1865

Mason, Wiley R., Lt. ADC, 1862–1864

Masters, Leander, Capt. ?, 1862, & Maj. AAIG, 1864–1865

Peacocke, Thomas G., VADC, 1865

Pleasants, James, Capt. OO, 1864–1865

Robb, Robert L., VADC, 1862, & Lt. ADC, 1864

Sanford, Thomas V., Capt. AQM, 1864–1865

Stephenson, John, Lt. ADC, 1864–1865

Stone, Thomas H. C., Capt. ACS, 1864–1865

Wilcox, Edward A., Capt. AQM, 1864–1865

Joseph Finegan

Baya, Hanaro T., Capt. ACS, 1864

Call, Wilkinson, Capt. AAG, 1864

Canova, Antonio A., Maj. CS, 1864–1865

Clarke, William H., Lt. OO, 1864–1865

Elder, Thomas C., Maj. CS, 1864–1865

Finegan, Joseph R., Lt. ADC, 1864–1865

Hinkle, David W., Maj. QM, 1864–1865

Hyer, Louis, Capt. AQM, 1865

Johnson, James B., Lt. AAAG, 1864?–1865?

Johnson, James H., Capt. AQM, 1864–1865

Largen, W. J., Lt. acting OO, 1864

Parramore, James B., Capt. AAIG, 1864–1865

Reid, Richard W., Capt. ACS, 1864?–1865

Scott, Alfred L., Lt. AAAG, 1864

Simmons, Benjamin F., Lt. AAAG, 1865

Sollie, Francis C., Capt. AQM, 1864–1865

Spann, James G., Capt. AAIG, 1864

Spann, Ransom D., Capt. AAIG, 1865

Thomas, Robert B., Col. AAIG, 1864

John B. Floyd

Daniel, John M., Lt. ADC, 1861

Davidson, Henry B., Maj. AAAG, 1861

Davies, Thomas J., ADC, 1861

Davis, Alfred W. G., Maj. QM, 1861

Davis, Thomas E., Maj. AAG, 1861

Dunn, George R. R., Capt. AQM, 1861

Dunn, Isaac B., Maj. QM, 1861

Ficklin, Joseph E., ?, OO, 1861
Forsberg, Ludwig A., Lt. EO, 1861
Heth, Henry, Col. AAAIG, 1861
McCreery, William W., Jr., Lt. ——, 1861
McDonald, John C., Maj. CS, 1861
Merchant, Anderson, Capt. OO & Chief Arty., 1861
Peters, William E., Capt. AAG, 1861
Woods, Micajah, VADC, 1861

William H. Forney

Balfour, James R., Capt. AAIG, 1865
Evans, James, Jr., Lt. ADC, 1865
Havis, James J., Capt. AQM, 1865
Higgason, Albert E., Lt. OO, 1865
Peabody, Edward R., Capt. AQM, 1865
Pierce, John G., Maj. QM, 1865
Robertson, Richard M., Maj. CS, 1865
Sides, Benjamin F., Lt. AAAIG, 1864–1865
Wilson, Marcus L., Capt. ACS, 1865
Witherspoon, Thomas M., Lt. AAAG, 1865

Samuel G. French

Anderson, Archer, Maj. AAG, 1862
Archer, James W., Lt. OO, 1862
Baker, John A., VADC, 1862
Collins, Charles R., Capt. EO, 1861–1862?
Daves, Graham, Maj. AAG, 1862–1863
Des Portes, Richard S., Lt. OO, 1862
Garrison, George G., Capt. AAG, 1862–1863
Graves, Richard F., Jr., VADC, 1863
Haile, Calhoun, Lt. ADC, 1861–1862
Humphries, Samuel J., VADC, 1861–1862, & Capt. ACS, 1862
Ker, William H., Maj. AAG, 1862–1863
Milligan, James F., Capt. SO, 1862
Morey, John B., Maj. QM, 1861–1863
Myers, Charles D., Lt. ADC, 1862, & Capt. AAG, 1862–1863
Overton, Thomas, Capt. OO, 1862–1863
Reynolds, Frank A., Capt. AAG, 1861–1862
Robertson, Walter H., Lt. OO?
Rogers, Henry J., Lt. EO, 1862–1863
Sanders, David W., Lt. ADC, 1862, & Maj. AAG, 1862–1863
Shingleur, James A., Lt. ADC, 1862–1863

Shumaker, Lindsay M., Maj. Chief Arty., 1862–1863?
Storrs, George S., Maj. OO, 1862–1863
Tannahill, Robert, Maj. CS, 1862–1863?
Venable, Thomas B., Maj. AAIG, 1862–1863?
Whiting, Henry C., Capt. AQM, 1862–1863

Birkett D. Fry

Broun, William, Lt. AAIG, 1864
Grinnell, Robert M., Capt. AAG, 1864
Hankins, Dick R., Maj. CS, 1864
Harding, Richard C., Capt. ACS, 1864
Keiley, John D., Jr., Maj. QM, 1864
Micou, Augustin, Lt. ADC, 1864
Porteous, John F., Lt. OO, 1864
Williams, George A., VADC, 1864

William M. Gardner

Cross, J. Lucius, Maj. AAG, 1864
Grant, James B., Lt. ADC, 1864–1865
Parkhill, John H., Maj. AAG, 1864
Rutherford, John C., Capt. AAIG, 1864–1865
Schley, William C., Lt. SO, 1864
Smith, John L., Capt. AAG, 1864–1865

Samuel Garland

Early, Robert D., VADC, 1862
Foote, George P., Capt. AAAG, 1862
Garland, Alexander B., Maj. CS, 1862
Garland, Maurice H., Lt. ADC, 1862
Haley, Alfred G., Lt. VADC, 1862
Halsey, Don P., Lt. ADC, & Capt. AAG, 1862
Hart, Camillus S., Capt. acting AQM, 1862
Haywood, Fabius J., Jr., Lt. acting ADC, 1862
Meem, James L., Capt. AAG, 1862
Payne, William M., Maj. QM, 1862
Wood, Charles, Capt. AAG, 1862

Richard B. Garnett

Berkeley, Charles F., Lt. AAAIG, 1863
Braithwaite, Jacob R., Capt. acting AQM, 1862
Harrison, Thomas R., Lt. acting ADC, 1863
Johnston, Elliott, Lt. ADC, 1861–1862

Johnston, James A., Maj. cs, 1862–1863
Jones, George T., Maj. qm, 1862–1863
Linthicum, Charles F., Capt. aag, 1862–
    1863
McIntire, James D., Lt. aaag, 1862
Mercer, George D., Maj. qm, 1861–1862
Nicholas, Robert C., Capt. acting acs, 1863
Oden, James S., volunteer oo?, 1862
Sorrel, Alexander C., Lt. acting adc, 1862
Williams, Samuel C., Lt. adc, 1861–1862
Wingate, Robert J., Capt. aag, 1861–1862

Robert S. Garnett

Alexander, James B. S., Capt. ?, 1861
Bacon, Waddy S., vadc?, 1861
Cole, Robert G., Maj. cs, 1861
Harrison, Thomas R., vadc, 1863
Humphries, William D., Lt. adc, 1861
Williams, James S., Maj. eo, 1861
Yost, Samuel M., Capt. aqm, 1861

Martin W. Gary

Ball, Beaufort W., Lt. aaag, 1864–1865
Boyd, Robert W., Lt. oo, 1864–1865
Dinkins, Thomas W., Capt. acting aqm,
    1864
Gary, Summerfield M. G., Lt. adc, 1864–
    1865
Gary, William T., Maj. cs, 1864–1865?
Hume, Francis C., vadc, 1864
James, Joseph S., Capt. acting acs, ?–1865
Mauldin, William H., Maj. qm, 1864–1865
Mills, John C., Lt. aaaig, 1865
Sims, Robert M., Capt. aag, 1864

Jeremy F. Gilmer

Alexander, James H., Maj. aag, 1864–1865
Elliott, Robert W. B., Capt. aag, 1864–1864
Goodwin, Charles R., Lt. adc, 1864
Green, Benjamin, Lt. aaag, 1864
Saunders, John S., Lt. Col. aaig, 1864

Victor J. B. Girardey

Evans, Joshua K., Capt. aaag, 1864
Hughes, Hampden S., Maj. cs, 1864
McWhorter, Robert L., Maj. qm, 1864

Mahool, Thomas, Capt. acs, 1864
Starr, Silas H., Jr., Lt. oo, 1864

Archibald C. Godwin

Brame, Tignal H., Capt. aqm, 1864
Hatton, Clarence R., Lt. aag, 1864
Hill, William P., Capt. acs, 1864
Lacy, Drury, Jr., Lt. aaag, 1864
McNeely, William G., Capt. aqm, 1864
Richardson, John M., Capt. aaig, 1864

James M. Goggin

Griffin, Evander M., Capt. acs, 1864
Harllee, Edward P., Cadet aaig, 1864
Henagan, James M., Capt. aqm, 1864
Kennedy, Joseph, Maj. cs, 1864
Lovelace, Benjamin F., Capt. acting aqm,
    1864
Myers, John A., Lt. oo, 1864
Pope, Young J., Lt. aaag, 1864

James B. Gordon

Craige, Kerr, Lt. acting adc, 1863–1864?
Dabney, Chiswell, Capt. aaig, 1863–1864
Daves, Graham, vadc, 1863–1864
Downman, Robert H., Maj. cs, 1863–1864
Gaines, James L., Capt. aag, 1863–1864
Neal, John B. B., Maj. qm, 1863–1864

John B. Gordon

Allan, William, Lt. Col. oo, 1864–1865
Archer, William M., Capt. oo, 1864–1865
Ballard, Thomas E., Maj. cs, 1864
Brooks, John D., Capt. aqm, 1864–1865
Carter, Thomas H., Col. Chief Arty.,
    1864–1865
Dabney, Virginius, Capt. aag, 1864–1865
Estill, Charles P., Capt. oo, 1864–1865
Gildersleeve, Basil L., vadc, 1864
Gordon, Eugene C., Lt. vadc, 1863
Graves, John T., Capt. acs, 1864
Hawks, Wells J., Maj. cs, 1865
Henderson, Finley H., Maj. vadc, 1864
Hinrichs, Oscar, Lt. eo, 1864
Hunter, Robert W., Maj. aag, 1864–1865
Jones, Thomas G., Lt. adc, 1863–1865

Keller, Benjamin F., Capt. AAAIG, 1863

Kyle, George H., Maj. AAIG, 1864–1865

Lewis, John S., Maj. CS, 1862–1864?

Lyon, William D., Lt. OO, 1863–1864

Mangham, John H., Capt. acting AQM, 1863

Markoe, Frank, Jr., Lt. SO & VADC, 1864–1865

Mercer, George D., Maj. QM, 1864–1865

Merritt, Christian G., Capt. AQM, 1864–1865

Mitchel, James, Capt. AAG, 1862–1864

Moore, Edwin L., Maj. AAIG, 1864

Murphy, James P., Capt. ACS, 1864

Myers, William B., Maj. AAG, 1863–1865

Pace, James M., Capt. AAG, 1862–1864, & Capt. AAAIG, 1865

Powell, William L., Capt. acting ADC, 1864

Preston, John, Capt. AQM, 1864?–1865

Reid, Francis W., Maj. CS, 1862–1864

Rogers, John D., Maj. QM, 1864–1865

Sexton, Joseph C., Maj. CS, 1864–1865

Speer, Daniel N., Maj. QM, 1862–1863

Stonebraker, Abraham S., Capt. AQM, 1864

Walker, John A., Capt. ACS, 1863–1864

White, Chastain, Capt. AQM, 1864–1865

Williamson, George, Capt. AAAIG, 1864

Wilmer, Skipwith, Lt. SO, 1864

Josiah Gorgas

Bayne, Thomas L., Lt. Col. OO, 1862–1865

Carter, Johnston B., Lt. Col. OO, 1862–1865

deLagnel, Julius A., Col. OO, 1862–1865

Dinwiddie, James, Capt. OO, 1863–1865

Smith, Edward B., Lt. Col. OO, 1862–1865

Archibald Gracie

Brown, Charles D., Maj. CS, 1864?

Cherry, Edward B., Lt. ADC, 1864

Fain, Hiram, Jr., Capt. ACS, 1864

Fitzpatrick, John A., Capt. AQM, 1864

Hord, Edward L., Maj. QM, 1864

Jones, Harvey E., Capt. AAG, 1864

Kaigler, John J., Capt. AQM, 1864

MacMurphy, Andrew M., Lt. OO, 1864

Miller, William H., Maj. QM, 1864

Sengstak, Henry H., Capt. AAAIG, 1864

John Gregg

Beall, Thomas J., Lt. ADC, 1864

Burns, Robert, Capt. ACS, 1864

Hall, Thomas W., Jr., Capt. AAG, 1864

Hamilton, Tilford A., Maj. CS, 1864

Kerr, John W., Capt. AAIG, 1864

Littlefield, James H., Maj. QM, 1864

Norwood, Walter N., Capt. AQM, 1864

Randall, Whitaker P., Lt. acting OO, 1864

Rust, James A., Capt. AQM, 1864

Shotwell, John I., Capt. AAAIG, 1864

Sykes, Lawson W., VADC, 1864

Maxcy Gregg

Aldrich, Alfred P., Maj. QM, 1862

Hammond, James H., VADC & Maj. QM, 1862

Haskell, Alexander C., Lt. ADC, 1861–1862, & Capt. AAG, 1862

Haskell, Langdon C., Lt. ADC, 1862

Lee, Thomas B., Capt. AQM, 1862

Parker, Arthur, Capt. acting ACS, 1862

Proctor, James T., VADC, 1862

Randall, Whitaker P., Lt. OO, 1864

Ryan, John S., Capt. acting ACS, 1862

Spratt, Leonidas W., Maj. CS, 1862

Richard Griffith

Costin, Ellison L., Lt. ADC, 1861–1862

DuVal, Harvie S., Lt. EO, 1862?

Hawken, A. Milton, Maj. CS, 1862

Inge, William M., Maj. AAG, 1861–1862

Mason, James M., Lt. acting OO, 1862

Watts, Nathaniel G., Maj. QM, 1862

Bryan Grimes

Adams, Benjamin C, Maj. CS, 1864–1865

Badger, Richard C., Maj. CS, 1864

Barnes, William S., Lt. acting ADC, 1864, & Lt. ADC, 1865

Burwell, John B., Capt. AQM, 1864–1865

Frensley, John L., Capt. AQM, 1864–1865

Garnett, James M., Capt. OO, 1864–1865

Green, Austin W., Lt. AAAG, 1864–1865
Langdon, Richard F., Capt. AQM, 1864–1865
Lilly, Robert, Capt. ACS, 1864
London, William L., Capt. AAG, 1864–1865
Neary, William J., Capt. AQM, 1864–1865
Orme, Richard, Maj. QM, 1864
Peyton, Moses G., Maj. AAG, 1864–1865
Randolph, Meriwether L., Capt. SO, 1864–1865
Reid, Alexander S., Capt. AQM, 1865
Reynolds, Pryor, Capt. AQM, 1864–1865
Stafford, Joseph B., Capt. AQM, 1864–1865
Stitt, William E., Capt. VADC, 1864
Tannor, Nathaniel M., Maj. QM, 1864–1865
Whiting, Henry A., Maj. AAIG, 1864–1865
Whitlock, Adoniram J., Capt. AQM, 1864–1865

Johnson Hagood

Adger, Joseph E., Capt. AQM, 1864
Frost, Elias H., Capt. ACS, 1864
Gantt, Richard P., Capt. AQM, 1864
Hay, Richard G., Maj. CS, 1864
Lartigue, Gerard B., Maj. QM, 1864
Martin, Benjamin, Lt. ADC, 1864
Mazyck, Edmund, Lt. OO, 1864
Moffett, George H., Lt. AAAIG, 1864, & Capt. AAG, 1864
Molony, Patrick K., Capt. AAG, 1864
Stoney, William E., Capt. AAIG, 1865
Tracy, Carlos C., VADC, 1864

Wade Hampton

Barker, Theodore G., Maj. AAG, 1862–1864
Beggs, Thomas, Maj. CS, 1862–1863
Chew, Roger P., Lt. Col. Chief Arty., 1864–1865
Edelin, T. Boyd, VADC, 1864
Farley, Henry S., VADC, 1862
FitzHugh, Norman R., Maj. QM, 1864–1865
Freaner, George, Maj. AAIG, 1864–1865
Goodwin, Claudius L., Maj. QM, 1862–1865
Grattan, Charles, Capt. OO, 1864–1865
Hagan, William H., VADC, 1865
Hall, Roland B., Lt. SO, 1864–1865
Hamilton, Paul, Lt. AAAG, 1862

Hampton, Christopher F., Lt. ADC, 1864–1865
Hampton, Thomas P., Lt. ADC, 1862–1864
Hampton, Wade, Jr., Lt. VADC, 1864
Hanger, James M., Capt. AQM, 1864–1865
Henry, James L., Lt. ?, 1863
Johnson, William J., Maj. CS, 1864–1865
Kirker, William H., Capt. AQM, ?–1865
Lanneau, John F., Capt. EO, 1864–1865
Lowndes, Rawlins, VADC, 1862–1863, & Capt. AAIG, 1863–1865
McClellan, Henry B., Maj. AAG, 1864–1865
MacDuffie, Neil C., Capt. AQM, 1864–1865
Preston, John, Jr., Maj. AAIG, 1863–1864
Taylor, Thomas, Lt. ADC, 1863–1865
Venable, Andrew R., jr., Maj. AAIG, 1864–1865
Venable, Paul C., Capt. OO, 1863–1864
Webb, James E., Lt. OO, 1864

Nathaniel H. Harris

Connell, William C., Capt. ACS, 1864–1865
Ducie, Daniel W., Capt. AQM, 1864–1865
Harris, William M., Lt. ADC, 1864–1865
Hays, James, Capt. AAIG, 1864–1865
Head, John J., Capt. ?, 1865
Hearsey, Henry J., Maj. QM, 1864–1865
Nelson, William C., Lt. OO, 1864–1865
Owens, Andrew T., Capt. AQM, 1864–1865
Patridge, Isaac M., Maj. CS, 1864–1865
Posey, Stanhope, Capt. AAG, 1864–1865
Stone, William R., Capt. AAIG, 1864–1865

Robert Hatton

Martin, Andrew B., Lt. AAAG, 1862
Vick, Alexander W., Maj. QM, 1862

Harry T. Hays

Boyd, David F., Maj. CS, 1862–1863
Cage, William C., Lt. ADC, 1863–1864
Campbell, John G., Capt. AQM, 1863, & Maj. CS, 1863–1864
Forrest, John, Lt. OO, 1863–1864
Freeland, John D., VADC, 1862–1863
Heard, Thomas R., Maj. QM, 1862
Macon, Thomas L., Lt. ADC, 1862–1863

Martin, Dwight, Lt. ADC, 1862

New, John P. H., Capt. AAG, 1862–1863, & Maj. AAIG, 1863–1864

Reed, George F., Lt. OO, 1862–1863

Seymour, William J., Capt. AAG, 1863–1864

Watkins, Leigh, Capt. ACS, 1863–1864

Woodville, William, VADC, 1863

Young, Clement, Maj. QM, 1862–1864

Henry Heth

Archer, James W., Capt. OO, 1863–1865

Atwell, William H., Capt. ACS, 1863–1865

Barton, Thomas S., Capt. ACS, 1863

Brannan, William H., Capt. AQM, 1864–1865

Brockenbrough, William A., Capt. AAAG, 1864

Burke, Edmund, Lt. SO, 1863–1864

Cage, John F., Capt. AQM, 1863–1865

Davies, Sydney H., Lt. AAAIG, 1864–1865

Deshields, Henry C., Maj. QM, 1863

Finney, Randolph H., Maj. AAG, 1863–1865

Grinnell, Robert M., Maj. AAIG, 1865

Harding, Richard C., Capt. ACS, 1865

Harrison, Henry H., Maj. AAIG, 1863–1864

Heth, Stockton, Lt. ADC, 1863–1865

Hungerford, Philip C., Maj. CS, 1863–1865

Johnson, William H., Lt. EO, 1864?–1865

McClain, Rufus P., Capt. AQM, 1864–1865

Muse, James H., Capt. ACS, 1863–1865?

Peacocke, Thomas G., VADC, 1864

Selden, Miles C., Lt. ADC, 1863–1865

Slade, William O., Jr., Lt. acting EO, 1863–1865

Thomas, James J., Jr., Capt. AQM, 1864–1865

Vick, Alexander W., Maj. QM, 1863–1865

Wilkinson, Willis, Capt. OO, 1863

A. P. Hill

Adams, Richard H. T., Capt. SO, 1862–1865

Archer, William M., Capt. OO, 1862

Bell, Robert F., Capt. ADC, 1864–1865

Bryant, John C. H., Lt. AAAG, 1862

Carraway, Daniel T., Capt. acting ACS, 1862

Chamberlayne, John H., Lt. acting ADC, 1862

Daniel, John M., VADC, 1862

Douglas, Henry T., Capt. EO, 1862

Field, Henry S., Capt. AQM, 1862–1865

Field, James G., Maj. QM, 1862–1865

Forbes, James F., VADC, 1863

Gordon, ——, VADC, 1862

Hill, Edward B., Maj. CS, 1862–1865

Hill, Francis T., Lt. ADC, 1862–1865

Howard, Conway R., Maj. EO, 1862–1865

Leigh, Benjamin W., VADC, 1863

Morgan, Richard C., Maj. AAG, 1862–1863

Palmer, William H., Lt. Col. AAG, 1862–1865

Pierce, Thomas W., Capt. OO, 1864

Price, William A., Capt. AAG, 1862

Rogers, Henry J., Lt. EO, 1862

Stanard, Philip B., Maj. OO, 1862–1865

Starke, William N., Maj. AAG, 1863–1865

Taylor, Murray F., Lt. ADC, 1862–1865

Vick, Alexander W., Maj. acting QM, 1862–1863

Walker, Reuben L., Col. Chief Arty., 1862–1865

Williams, John A., Lt. Col. EO, 1864–1865?

Wingate, Robert J., Maj. AAIG, 1862–1865

Wootton, Francis H., VADC, 1862

Daniel H. Hill

Adams, Benjamin C., Maj. CS, 1862

Anderson, Archer, Lt. Col. AAG, 1862–1863

Boone, John B. F., Maj. QM, 1861–1862

Brevard, E. F., VADC, 1862

Carter, Thomas H., Maj. Chief Arty., 1862

Chichester, Arthur M., Capt. EO, 1862

Cross, J. Lucius, Maj. AAG, 1863

Desportes, Richard S., Lt. OO, 1863

DuVal, Harvie S., Lt. EO, 1862

Estill, Charles P., Lt. acting OO, 1862

Fitzhugh, ——, Lt. VADC, 1862

Harris, William A., Capt. OO, 1862–1863

Johnson, Powell C., Lt. EO, 1863

Ker, William H., Maj. AAIG, 1862

Lee, William F., Lt. EO, 1862

Milligan, James F., Capt. SO, 1862

Moore, Thomas J., Lt. VADC & OO, 1862

Morrison, Robert H., Jr., Lt. ADC, 1862–
1864

Overton, Thomas, Capt. OO, 1862

Pierson, Scipio F., Maj. Chief Arty., 1862–
1863?

Randolph, Meriwether L., Capt. SO, 1862–
1863

Ratchford, James W., Lt. ADC, 1861, & Maj.
AAG, 1861–1862?

Reid, James A., Lt. ADC, 1862–1864

Rogers, Alexander H., Lt. ADC, 1862

Rogers, John D., Maj. QM, 1862–1863

Sadler, James A., Maj. CS, 1861–1862

Sydnor, Thomas W., VADC, 1862

Tayloe, John W., Maj. AAIG, 1862

Webster, Daniel T., Maj. acting CS, 1862–?

West, George, Lt. ADC, 1861–1862, Capt.
OO, 1862, & VADC, 1862–1865

Robert F. Hoke

Adams, James M., Maj. AAIG, 1863–1864

Alexander, Sydenham B., Capt. AAAIG,
1864

Boteler, Alexander R., Jr., Lt. OO, 1863–
1864?

Cooper, John A., Capt. AAG, 1863–1864

Cox, Joseph J., Capt. AQM, 1864–1865

Cross, J. Lucius, Maj. AAG, 1864

Dimmock, Charles H., Capt. EO, 1864

Gray, John H., Capt. AQM, 1864

Grier, Thomas, Lt. acting OO, 1863–1864

Hall, William C., Capt. AAAG, 1863

Hoffman, Alfred, volunteer OO, 1862

Hughes, John, Maj. QM, 1863–1865

Jordan, William C., Capt. AQM, 1864

Justice, John G., Lt. ADC, 1863–1864

Lyon, James W., Maj. CS, 1863–1864

McNeely, William G., Capt. acting AQM,
1864

Perry, John M., Capt. OO, 1864

Phifer, George L., Lt. ADC, 1864

Richardson, John M., Capt. AAIG, 1863–
1864

Shepperd, Hamilton, Capt. ACS, 1863–1864

Vernoy, James, Maj. QM, 1863–1864

Theophilus H. Holmes

Anderson, Archer, Maj. AAG, 1862

Barton, Thomas S., Capt. ACS, 1862

Barton, William S., Maj. AAG, 1862

Boudinot, William E., Capt. OO, 1861–1862

Burton, John B., Capt. acting AQM, 1861–
1862

Clagett, Henry O., Capt. AQM, 1862

Cone, Aurelius F., Lt. ADC, 1861, & Maj.
QM, 1861–1862

Crump, Malcolm H., Capt. AQM, 1861–1862

Deshler, James, Col. Chief Arty., 1862

Dobbin, James C., Lt. ADC, 1862

French, Seth B., Maj. CS, 1861–1862

Hayes, John S., Capt. ACS, 1861–1862?

Hill, Gabriel H., Lt. ADC, 1861

Hinsdale, John W., Lt. ADC, 1861–1862

Holmes, Theophilus H., Jr., Lt. ADC, 1862

Hooe, Roy D. M., Lt. OO, 1861

Ker, William H., Maj. AAG & AAIG, 1861–
1862

Maury, Dabney H., Lt. Col. AAG, 1861–1862

Overton, Thomas, Lt. ADC & Capt. OO,
1862

Walker, Henry H., Lt. AAAG, 1861

Wise, George D., VADC, 1862

John B. Hood

Blanton, Benjamin H., Lt. ADC, 1862–1863

Chambers, Thomas J., VADC, 1862

Cunningham, Edward H., Maj. AAIG,
1862–1863

Duvall, Eli, Jr., Lt. SO, 1862?–1863?

Frobel, Bushrod W., Maj. Chief Arty., 1862

George, Moses B., Maj. QM, 1862–1863

Hamilton, James, Lt. ADC, 1862–1863

Henry, Mathis W., Maj. Chief Arty., 1863

Hunter, James T., Lt. acting ADC, 1862

Jonas, Sidney A., Maj. CS, 1862–1863

Jones, George W., Maj. QM, 1862?–1863?

Mills, Charles S., Capt. acting ADC & AQM,
1862

Murray, J. H., VADC, 1862

Phillips, Joseph, Lt. acting ADC, 1862

Pleasants, James, Capt. OO, 1862–1863

Randolph, Beverley, Maj. OO, 1862–1863

Sellers, William H., Lt. Col. AAG, 1862–1863

Smith, John S., Lt. ADC, 1862–1863

Stewart, William H., Maj. CS, 1862

Stone, Thomas H. C., Capt. ACS, 1863

Sublett, David L., Lt. OO, 1862

Wade, Ethelbert B., Cadet ADC, 1863

Benjamin Huger

Anderson, Edward W., Lt. EO, 1862

Anderson, Samuel S., Lt. Col. AAG, 1861–1862

Bradford, Edmund, Maj. AAIG, 1861–1862

Carr, Charles E., Maj. QM, 1861–1862

deLagnel, Julius A., Lt. Col. Chief Arty., 1862

Harrison, Benjamin, Capt. acting ACS, 1862

Huger, Benjamin, Jr., Lt. ADC, 1861–1862, & Capt. AAG, 1862

Huger, Frank, VADC, 1862

Johnston, James A., Maj. QM, 1861–1862

Milligan, James F., Capt. SO, 1861

Pinckney, Thomas, VADC, 1861–1862

Poor, Richard L., Capt. EO, 1862

Preston, John, Jr., Lt. ADC, 1861–1862

Sloan, Benjamin F., Jr., Lt. ADC & Maj. AAG, 1862

Smith, William H., Maj. CS, 1861–1862

Stone, Hamilton J., Capt. AQM, 1861–1862

Talcott, Thomas M. R., Capt. EO, 1862

Todd, Everard M., Maj. CS, 1862

Benjamin G. Humphreys

Allen, William L., Lt. OO, 1863–1864

Barksdale, Harris, Cadet ADC, 1864

Barksdale, John A. J., Capt. AAG, 1863–1864

Butts, Edward S., Capt. AAIG, 1864

Cramer, John V. R., Lt. ADC, 1863?–1864

Doherty, Patrick M., Maj. QM, 1863–1864

Frank, Samuel, Capt. AQM, 1864

Hawken, A. Milton, Maj. CS, 1863–1864

Hobart, John H., Capt. AAIG, 1863–1864

Leonard, Thomas F., Capt. ACS, 1863–?

Ramsaur, James O., Capt. ACS, ?

Sims, Robert G., Lt. AAAG, 1864

Turner, James H., Capt. AQM, 1864

Eppa Hunton

Ames, J. L., Capt. ACS, 1864

Danforth, Henry D., Lt. OO, 1864–1865

Fitzhugh, Edmund C., Capt. AAIG, 1863–1864

Griswold, Joseph G., Capt. AAG, 1864

Hutchison, John R., Capt. ACS, 1863–1864?

Hutchison, Thomas B., Maj. CS, 1863–1865

Jones, George T., Maj. QM, 1863–1865

Jones, John S., Lt. ADC, 1863–1865

Linthicum, Charles F., Capt. AAG, 1863–1864

Price, Samuel C., Capt. AQM, 1864–1865

John D. Imboden

Berkeley, Francis B., Capt. AAG, 1863–1864

Conrad, Holmes, Capt. ACS, 1864

Harrison, Powell, Capt. ACS, 1863–1864

Hull, William I., VADC, 1864–1865

Lafferty, John J., Maj. CS, 1864

Lock, William M., Maj. CS, 1863–1864

McCue, John H., Lt. ADC, 1863

McPhail, George W., Lt. ADC, 1863–1864

Morgan, Charles S., Jr., Lt. AAAIG, 1863, & Capt. AAG, 1864

Shumate, Thomas, Maj. QM, 1863–1864

Ward, Griffin S., Lt. OO, 1863–1864

Alfred Iverson

Boarman, Alexander, Capt. AAAG, 1863

Coleman, Henry E., VADC, 1863

Early, Robert D., VADC, 1862–1863?

Ector, John T., Lt. ADC, 1862–1863

Garland, Alexander B., Maj. CS, 1862–1863

Halsey, Don P., Capt. AAG, 1862–1863

Holladay, Waller, Lt. OO, 1863

Payne, William M., Maj. QM, 1862–1863

Woods, J. J., Capt. AAIG, 1863

Henry R. Jackson

Andrews, Garnett, Lt. ADC & AAAG, 1861

Barton, Seth M., Lt. Col. EO, 1861

Bloom, Francis S., Lt. ADC, 1861

Hull, Felix H., Capt. AQM, 1861

Humphries, William D., Lt. ADC, 1861

Jackson, Henry, Cadet ——, 1861
Williams, James S., Maj. EO, 1861

Thomas J. Jackson

Allan, William, Maj. OO, 1862–1863
Archer, William M., Capt. OO, 1862–1863
Barton, Seth M., Lt. Col. EO, 1862
Baylor, William S. H., Lt. Col. AAAIG, 1862
Bier, George H., Maj. OO, 1862–1863
Boswell, James K., Capt. EO, 1862–1863
Boteler, Alexander R., VADC, 1862
Bridgford, David B., Maj. PM, 1863
Briscoe, Frederick A., VADC, 1862?
Crutchfield, Stapleton, Col. Chief Arty.,
    1862–1863
Cutshaw, Wilfred E., Lt. AAAIG & acting
    Chief Arty., 1862
Dabney, Robert L., Maj. AAG, 1862
Douglas, Henry K., Lt. AAAIG, 1862
Faulkner, Charles J., VADC, 1861–1862, &
    Lt. Col. AAG, 1862–1863
Fauntleroy, Thomas T., Jr., Lt. ——, 1861
French, Samuel B., VADC, 1861–1862
Garber, Alexander M., Jr., Capt. AQM,
    1862–1863?
Garnett, James M., Lt. OO, 1862
Harman, John A., Maj. QM, 1861–1863
Hawks, Wells J., Maj. CS, 1861–1863
Hinrichs, Oscar, Lt. OO, 1862
Hotchkiss, Jedediah, Contract Engineer,
    1862–1863
Jackson, Alfred H., Maj. AAG, 1861–1862
Jackson, William L., Col. VADC, 1862–1863
Jones, Francis B., Capt. AAG, 1861, & Maj.
    AAAG, 1861–1862
Junkin, George G., Lt. ADC & AAAG,
    1861–1862
Kinney, Thomas C., Lt. EO, 1862–1863
Lee, Edwin G., Lt. VADC, 1861
Lee, Hugh H., Lt. OO, 1862
Lee, Nathaniel W., Cadet VADC, 1861
McDonald, Craig W., Lt. ——, 1861
Marshall, Thomas, VADC, 1861
Mason, Claiborne R., Capt. AQM, 1862
Meade, Richard K., Lt. OO, 1862
Morrison, Joseph G., Lt. ADC, 1862–1863

Neale, ——, VADC, 1862
Paxton, Elisha F., VADC, 1861–1862, & Maj.
    AAG, 1862
Pendleton, Alexander S., Lt. OO, 1861, Lt.
    ADC, 1861–1862, & Maj. AAG, 1862–1863
Preston, John T. L., Lt. Col. AAG, 1861–1862
Sharp, Thomas R., Capt. acting AQM,
    1861–1862
Smead, Abner, Col. AAIG, 1862–1863
Smith, James P., Lt. ADC, 1862–1863
Snead, Thomas T. L., Lt. EO, 1862
Sommers, Samuel M., Capt. AQM, 1861–
    1862
Thomson, James W., VADC, 1861
Trueheart, Daniel, Jr., Maj. OO & Chief
    Arty., 1861–1862
Wilbourn, Richard E., Capt. SO, 1862–1863
Williamson, Thomas H., Lt. Col. EO, 1862
Williamson, William G., Lt. EO, 1862–1863
Willis, Edward S., Capt. AAAG, 1862

William L. Jackson

Creel, Henry C., Lt. ADC, 1865
Hill, William E., Capt. AAAIG, 1864
Ker, Hugh, Lt. acting ADC?, 1864
Parrish, John G., Maj. CS, 1864–1865
Parrish, Robert L., Lt. AAAG, 1864–1865

Albert G. Jenkins

Fitzhugh, Nicholas, Capt. AAG, 1862–1864
Hannah, George B., Lt. ADC, 1863–1864
Harvie, Charles I., Capt. AAG, 1864
Hill, William E., Capt. ——, 1864
Jenkins, Thomas J., Maj. QM, 1863–1864
Minor, Charles L. C., Capt. OO, 1864
Newman, John G., Maj. CS, 1862–1864?
Paxton, James G., Maj. QM, 1862–1863
Poitiaux, Michael B., Capt. AQM, 1863
St. Clair, George B., Lt. AAAG, 1862–1864
Stevens, Harrison H., Lt. OO, 1863
Tynes, Achilles J., Capt. acting ACS, 1863
Widney, Charles T., Lt. ADC, 1862–1863

Micah Jenkins

Adams, Joseph M., Maj. QM, 1862
Barham, Theophilus G., VADC, 1863

Coker, James L., Capt. AAAG, 1863

Crockett, John N., Capt. acting AQM, 1863

Elford, T. Joseph, Maj. CS, 1862–1864

Grier, Thomas, Lt. acting OO, 1863

Jamison, David R., Lt. OO, 1862–1864

Jamison, John W., Lt. ADC, 1862–1864

Quincy, William H., Capt. AAG, 1862, & Maj. QM, 1863–1864

Seabrook, Cato A., Lt. VADC & Capt. AAG, 1862

Sims, Robert M., Capt. AAG, 1863–1864

Whitner, William H., Capt. AAIG, 1863–1864

Bradley T. Johnson

Anderson, John G., Lt. AAAG, 1863

Booth, George W., Capt. AAG, 1864

Clarke, William J., Capt. acting AQM, 1864

Cleary, Reuben, Capt. AAAG, 1863

Harding, Charles A., Maj. QM, 1864

Hopkins, Warren M., Maj. CS, 1864

Radford, Richard C. W., Capt. AAG, 1864

Smith, Thomas H., Lt. OO, 1864

Tidwell, Reuben W., Capt. ACS, 1864

Trippe, Andrew C., Lt. OO, 1864

Bushrod R. Johnson

Blakemore, William T., Lt. ADC, 1864

Corling, Charles T., VADC, ?–1865

Fellers, William, Capt. AQM, 1864–1865

Foote, Romley E., Maj. AAG, 1864–1865

Hamilton, James F., Maj. CS, 1864–1865

Hodges, John F., Capt. AQM, 1865

Houston, Adlie O., Capt. AQM, 1864–1865

Hunter, John H., Capt. AQM, 1865

Hutchison, John R., Capt. ACS, 1864?–1865

Jones, Charles S. D., Capt. AAIG, 1864

Lake, James B., Jr., Lt. OO, 1864–1865

Marchbanks, George, Lt. AAIG, 1864

Miller, Andrew J., Capt. AQM, 1864–1865

Montgomery, John H., Capt. acting ACS, 1864–1865

Randolph, Coleman L., Maj. QM, 1864–1865

Saunders, John E., Lt. ADC, 1864–1865

Skinner, T. H., VADC, 1864–1865

Smith, Eugene R., Capt. acting ADC, 1864

Watts, George O., Maj. AAIG, 1864

Weir, Walter, Capt. AAG, 1864–1865

Whitner, William H., Capt. AAIG, 1864–1865

Zimmer, Louis, Capt. OO, 1865

Edward Johnson

Ballard, Thomas E., Capt. ACS, 1863–1864

Dabney, Virginius, Capt. AAG, 1863–1864

Deshler, James, Capt. AAAG, 1861

Douglas, Henry K., Maj. AAAG, 1863

Estill, Charles P., Capt. OO, 1864

Graves, John T., Capt. ACS, 1863–1864

Harman, William H., VADC, 1862

Hinrichs, Oscar, Lt. EO, 1863–1864

Hunter, Robert W., Maj. AAG, 1863–1864

Kinney, Thomas C., Lt. EO, 1863

Kyle, George H., Maj. CS, 1863

Leigh, Benjamin W., Maj. AAG, 1863

Martin, Egbert J., Lt. ADC, 1863–1864

Marye, Lawrence S., Capt. OO, 1863

Mason, John, Capt. AQM, 1864

Mercer, George D., Maj. QM, 1863–1864

Moore, Edwin L., Maj. AAIG, 1863–1864

Old, William W., Lt. ADC, 1864

Smead, Abner, Lt. Col. AAG, 1862

Willis, Edward S., Capt. AAG, 1861–1862

Wilmer, Skipwith, Lt. SO, 1864

Joseph E. Johnston

Alexander, E. Porter, Maj. OO, 1861–1862

Barbour, Alfred M., Maj. QM, 1861–1862

Blair, William B., Maj. CS, 1861–1862

Cabell, William L., Maj. QM, 1861

Cole, Archibald H., VADC, 1861, & Maj. QM, 1861–1862

Cole, Robert G., Maj. CS, 1861–1862

Duncan, Henry B., VADC, 1861

Fauntleroy, Charles M., Capt. acting ADC, 1861

Hampton, Wade, Jr., Lt. ADC, 1861–1862

Harvie, Edwin J., Lt. Col. AAIG, 1861–1862

Haskell, Joseph C., VADC, 1862

Kearsley, George W. T., Maj. CS, 1861–1862?

Latham, George W., Capt. AAIG, 1862

Lay, George W., Lt. Col. AAIG, 1861–1862

Lee, Fitzhugh, ? AAAG, 1861
McGivern, Claudius, Capt. AQM, 1861–1862
McKinney, Charles S., Capt. ACS, 1861–1862
McLean, Eugene E., Maj. QM, 1861
McPhail, Clement C., Capt. OO, 1861–1862
Mason, Arthur P., Capt. AAG, 1862
Mason, Joel B., VADC, 1861
Maury, Dabney H., Lt. Col. AAG, 1861
Pemberton, John C., Lt. Col. AAG, 1861
Preston, Thomas L., Capt. AAAG, 1861–1862
Ragan, Abraham B., Maj. QM, 1861–1862
Randolph, Beverley, Lt. OO, 1861
Rhett, Thomas G., Maj. AAG, 1861–1862
Robinson, Powhatan, Capt. EO, 1862
Rogers, Henry J., Lt. EO, 1862
Stevens, Walter H., Maj. EO, 1861–1862
Thomas, Francis J., Col. OO, 1861
Washington, James B., Lt. ADC, 1861–1862
Whiting, William H. C., Maj. EO, 1861

Robert D. Johnston

Davis, E. Hayne, Capt. AAIG, 1865
Garland, Alexander B., Maj. CS, 1863–1864
Halsey, Don P., Capt. AAG, 1863–1865
Harris, Richard S., Capt. AQM, 1864–1865
Holladay, Waller, Lt. OO, 1863–1865
Johnston, James F., Capt. acting ACS, 1863
Johnston, Joseph F., Lt. ADC, 1863–1865
Lucado, Leonard F., Capt. ACS, 1864–1865
McDonald, Charles, Capt. ACS, 1863–1865
Nicholson, Edward A. T., Capt. AAIG, 1865
Northington, John S., Capt. AQM, 1864–1865
Payne, William M., Maj. QM, 1863–1864
Worthington, J., Capt. AQM, 1865

David R. Jones

Bryan, Henry, Capt. ?, 1862
Campbell, Duncan G., Lt. EO, 1862
Coward, Asbury, Maj. AAG, 1861–1862
Curell, James R., VADC, 1861
Delaigle, Louis, Capt. acting AQM, 1862
Elford, T. Joseph, Capt. acting ACS, 1861–1862
Ford, James W., Lt. ADC, 1861–1863
Garnett, John J., Maj. Chief Arty., 1862

Haskell, John C., Maj. CS, 1862
Jones, Philip B., Jr., VADC, 1861?–1863
Jones, Samuel P., Lt. ADC, 1862
Latham, Frederick G., Lt. AAAG, 1861
Latrobe, Osmun, VADC, 1861–1862, & Capt. AAIG, 1862
McLemore, Owen K., Lt. AAG, 1861
Moses, Raphael J., Maj. acting CS, 1862
Rose, Hugh, VADC, 1862
Taylor, Erasmus, VADC, 1861
Thurston, Edward N., VADC & Capt. OO, 1862
Williams, Charles U., Lt. VADC, 1862–1863
Young, Henry E., Capt. VADC, 1862

John M. Jones

Boyd, Elisha H., Lt. OO, 1863–1864
Clearly, Reuben, Capt. AAG, 1863–1864?
Dabney, Virginius, VADC, 1863
Early, Robert D., Capt. AAG, 1863–1864
Jones, David A., Maj. CS, 1863–1864
Jones, Francis P., Lt. ADC, 1863
Kellogg, Timothy H., Capt. ACS, 1863–1864
Moore, Samuel J. C., Capt. AAG, 1863
Page, Mann, Lt. AAAIG, 1863
Powell, William L., Capt. acting ADC, 1864
Ridgely, Randolph, Lt. ADC, 1863–1864
Wilson, Robert N., Capt. AAG, 1863–1864?

John R. Jones

Boyd, Elisha H., Lt. OO, 1863
Bruce, James W., Maj. QM, 1862
Dabney, Virginius, Lt. ADC, 1862
Jones, David A., Maj. CS, 1862–1863
Jones, J. R., Lt. ADC, 1862
Moore, Samuel J. C., Capt. AAG, 1862–1863
Page, Mann, Lt. AAAIG, 1862
White, Oscar, Lt. acting ADC, 1862
Wilson, Robert N., Capt. AAG, 1862–1863

Samuel Jones

Ayer, William F., Maj. QM, 1861–1862
Fraser, James L., VADC, 1861–1862
Jones, Walter, Lt. OO, 1862
Noble, Thomas J., Lt. ADC, 1861–1862

Stringfellow, Charles S., Capt. AAG, 1861–1862

Warwick, Peter C., VADC, 1861–1862

William E. Jones

Adams, Samuel F., Lt. ADC, 1864

Bellinger, John R., Lt. SO, 1863

Chamberlayne, Francis W., Lt. AAAG, 1863–1864

Faulkner, Elisha B., Capt. ——, 1864?

Fite, John A., Col. VADC, 1863

Harvie, William W., Maj. CS, 1863

Haynes, William D., Capt. acting AQM, 1863

Hopkins, Warren M., Lt. ADC, 1862–1863, & Maj. CS, 1863–1864

Jones, J. N., Lt. VADC, 1863

McDonald, Angus W., Jr., Capt. ACS, 1863?

McDonald, William N., Lt. OO, 1863

Martin, Walter K., Capt. AAG, 1862–1864

Morris, Walter H. P., Lt. acting OO, 1863

Radford, Richard C. W., Capt. AAIG, 1864

Richards, Adolphus E., VADC, 1863

Richardson, John D., Maj. QM, 1864

Selden, Harry H., Maj. QM, ?–1863

Smith, Thomas H., Lt. OO, 1863–1864

Tidwell, Reuben W., Capt. acting ACS, 1863–1864

Whiting, Clarence C., Lt. ADC, 1864

Williamson, William G., Lt. EO, 1863–1864

James L. Kemper

Allan, William G., Capt. AQM?

Beckham, Abner C., VADC, 1862

Boteler, Alexander R., Jr., Lt. OO, 1863

Bowyer, Thomas M., Maj. OO, 1864–1865

Bridge, Frederick E., Capt. AQM, 1864–1865

Catlett, Richard H., Capt. AAG, 1864–1865

Cave, William J., Lt. ADC, 1864–1865

Crisler, Nelson W., Maj. QM, 1862–1863

Davis, Samuel B., Lt. ADC, 1864

Flood, Joel W., VADC, 1862, & Lt. ADC, 1864

Fry, William T., Capt. AAG, 1862–1864?

Goggin, James M., Maj. AAG, 1864

Green, James W., Maj. CS, 1862–1863

Guiger, George H., Lt. ADC, 1862–1863

Jackson, T. J., Lt. ADC, 1865

Mitchel, James, Capt. AAG, 1864–1865

Nelson, Kinloch, Lt. OO, 1863

Page, Legh R., Maj. AAIG, 1864–1865

Palmer, William H., Maj. VADC, 1862

Pollock, Thomas G., Capt. AQM, 1862–1863, & Capt. AAG, 1863

Riddick, Washington L., Capt. AAG, ?–1865

Tabb, Thomas, Capt. AQM, 1864–1865

Tiller, Evans F., Capt. AAAG, 1864–1865?

Williams, Thomas G., Lt. Col. CS, 1864–1865

Wolff, Bernard L., Maj. CS, 1864–1865

Young, Clement, Maj. QM, 1864–1865

John D. Kennedy

Griffin, Evander M., Capt. ACS, 1864–1865

Harllee, Edward P., Cadet AAIG, 1864–1865

Henagan, James M., Capt. AQM, 1864–1865

Holmes, Charles R., Capt. AAG, 1864–1865

Kennedy, Joseph, Maj. CS, 1864–1865?

Lovelace, Benjamin F., Capt. acting AQM, 1864–1865

Myers, John A., Lt. OO?, 1864–1865

Sill, Edward E., Lt. acting ADC, 1865

Woodward, Thomas W., Capt. AQM, 1864–1865

Joseph B. Kershaw

Atkins, Michael J., Capt. AQM, 1864–1865

Campbell, Duncan G., Lt. EO, 1862

Carwile, John R., Lt. ADC, 1864–1865

Costin, Ellison L., Maj. AAIG, 1864–1865

Davis, James M., Lt. ADC, 1864–1865

Doby, Alfred E., Lt. ADC, 1862–1864

Dwight, Charles S., Lt. EO, 1864–1865

Dwight, William M., Lt. AAAIG, 1862–1863, & Capt. AAG, 1863–1864

Edwards, Alfred, Lt. OO, 1863–1865

Farley, Hugh L., Lt. acting ADC, 1863

Goggin, James M., Maj. AAG, 1864

Griffin, Evander M., Capt. ACS, 1863–1864

Holmes, Charles R., Capt. AAG, 1862–1864

Kennedy, Joseph, Maj. CS, 1862–1864

Kirkland, John M., Capt. ACS, 1863–?

Lovelace, Benjamin F., Capt. acting AQM,
    1861–1864
Lowrance, Rufus N., Maj. CS, 1863–1865
Lumpkin, Frank, Capt. AQM, 1864
McGehee, George T., Capt. AQM, 1864–1865
Myers, John A., Lt. OO, 1862–1864
Peck, William D., Maj. QM, 1862–1865
Smith, Frederick L., Capt. ACS, 1863–1864
Villepigue, James J., Capt. AQM, 1864–1865

William W. Kirkland

Baker, William J., Maj. CS, 1863–1864
Bessent, Ransom P., Capt. AQM, 1864
Collins, George P., Maj. QM, 1863–1864
Dancy, John S., Capt. AQM, 1864
DeMill, William E., Maj. CS, 1864
Elliott, Charles G., Capt. AAG, 1864
Hassell, Theodore M., Lt. OO, 1864
Justice, Benjamin W., Capt. ACS, 1863–1864
Nash, Frederick K., Capt. AAIG, 1864
Norwood, Thomas H., Capt. AAAG, 1863
Perry, John M., Capt. OO, 1864
Robertson, Walter H., Lt. OO, 1863–?
Spann, Ransom D., Capt. AAIG, 1863
Stoddard, Albert H., Lt. ADC, 1863–1864
Young, Louis G., Capt. AAIG, 1864

James H. Lane

Bryan, James A. W., Capt. OO, 1862–1865
Carraway, Daniel T., Maj. CS, 1862–1863
Cazaux, Anthony D., Capt. AQM, 1864–1865
Engelhard, Joseph A., Maj. QM, 1862–1863
Gibbon, Nicholas B., Capt. acting ACS,
    1862–1863
Hale, Edward J., Jr., Capt. AAG, 1863–1865
Hawks, Francis T., Capt. AAG, 1862–1863
Herndon, Edward W., Maj. QM, 1864–1865
Johnston, George B., Capt. AAG, 1863
Lane, Julius R., acting ADC, 1863
Lane, Oscar, Lt. ADC, 1862–1864
McKoy, Thomas H., Capt. ACS, 1863, &
    Maj. CS, 1865
Meade, Everard B., Lt. ADC, 1864–1865
Nicholson, Edward A. T., Capt. AAIG,
    1863–1865
Nisbet, Adam R., Capt. ACS, 1863–1865

Sudderth, John R., Capt. AQM, 1864–1865
Thompson, George S., Maj. QM, 1863–1864

Evander M. Law

Babbitt, Amzi, Maj. CS, 1862–1864
Christian, Thomas L., Capt. AAIG, 1862–
    1864
Cussons, John, VADC, 1862–1864
Drake, Richard, Lt. OO, 1863?–1864
Duvall, Eli, Jr., Lt. SO
Edwards, Jeremiah, Capt. AAAG, 1863
Figures, Henry S., Lt. AAAG, 1863
Kirkman, Thomas J., VADC?, 1862
Law, John K., VADC, 1862
McConnico, Garner M., Capt. ACS, 1864
Peterson, Batte O., Lt. AAAG, 1863–1864?
Samuels, Thomas L., Lt. acting ADC, 1864
Scruggs, William H., Maj. QM, 1862–1864
Terrell, Leigh R., Capt. AAG, 1862–1864
Walker, Mims, Lt. ADC, 1864

Alexander R. Lawton

Alexander, James H., VADC, 1862
Alexander, William F., Maj. QM, 1863–1864
Cheves, Edward, Cadet VADC, 1862
Elliott, Robert W. B., Lt. ADC, 1861–1862
Gibbons, William H., Maj. QM, 1862
Hardee, John L., VADC, 1862
Hull, Edward W., Capt. AAG, 1862
Ingraham, Henry L., Lt. OO, 1862
Jackson, Henry, Cadet, 1861–1862
Lawton, Edward P., Capt. AAG, 1861–1862
Reid, Francis W., Maj. CS, 1861–1862
Sims, Frederick W., Lt. Col. QM, 1863–1865

Fitzhugh Lee

Bowie, Thomas F., VADC, 1863, & Maj.
    AAIG, 1863–1865
Bowling, Henry A., VADC?, 1863
Cavendish, Charles, volunteer EO, 1864–
    1865?
Dawson, Francis W., Capt. OO, 1865
Ferguson, James D., Maj. AAG, 1862–1865
Freaner, George, Lt. AAAG, 1862–1863, &
    Maj. AAIG, 1864–1865
Grattan, Charles, Capt. OO, 1865

Hanger, James M., Maj. QM, 1865

Heath, Jesse H., Capt. acting AQM, 1863–1865

Lee, Henry C., Lt. ADC, 1862–1864

Mason, Robert F., Maj. QM, 1863, & Maj. AAIG, 1864–1865

Minnigerode, Charles, VADC, 1862, & Lt. ADC, 1863–1865

Ryals, Garland M., Lt. OO, 1862–1863

Saunderson, Llewellyn T. B., VADC, 1865

Walke, Isaac T., Lt. OO, 1863–1864

Warwick, William B., Maj. CS, 1862 1865

G. W. C. Lee

Brown, J. J., Capt. AQM, 1865

Chestney, Theodore O., Maj. AAG, 1864

Cleary, Reuben, Capt. AAAG, 1865

Cox, Richard T.?, VADC, 1864

Crump, James H., Capt. AQM, 1865

Foster, William E., Lt. OO, 1864–1865

Goldsborough, Robert H., Lt. ADC, 1865

Harvie, Lewis E., Capt. ACS, 1864

Howard, McHenry, Lt. AAG, 1865

Hutcheson, Jesse T., Capt. ACS, 1865

Keiley, John D., jr., Maj. QM, 1865

Macmurdo, Richard C., Capt. AQM, 1864–1865

Randolph, William L., Capt. OO, 1865

Sulivane, Clement, Lt. AAIG, 1863–1864, & Capt. AAG, 1864–1865

Watkins, Joel B., VADC, 1864–1865

R. E. Lee

Alexander, Edward P., Lt. Col. OO, 1862

Baldwin, Briscoe G., Lt. Col. OO, 1862–1865

Chilton, Robert H., Col. AAIG, 1862–1864

Cole, Robert G., Lt. Col. CS, 1862–1865

Cooke, Giles B., Maj. AAIG, 1864–1865

Corley, James L., Lt. Col. QM, 1861–1865

Crenshaw, James R., Maj. acting CS, 1861

Deas, George, Lt. Col. AAG, 1861–1862

Garnett, Robert S., Col. AAG, 1861

Harvie, Edwin J., Lt. Col. AAIG, 1862

Heth, Henry, Lt. Col. QM, 1861

Johnston, Robert, Maj. ——, 1861

Johnston, Samuel R., Lt. Col. EO, 1863–1865

Kirker, William H., Maj. QM, 1861?

Lay, George W., Lt. Col. AAIG, 1862

Long, Armistead L., Col. ADC, 1862–1863

Marshall, Charles, Maj. ADC, 1862–1864, & Lt. Col. AAG, 1864–1865

Mason, Arthur P., Capt. AAG, 1862

Murray, Edward, Lt. Col. AAIG, 1863–1864

Peyton, Henry E., Lt. Col. AAIG, 1862–1865

Richardson, William H., ? AAG, 1861

Smith, Francis W., Capt. Military Secretary, 1861

Smith, William P., Lt. Col. EO, 1863

Snodgrass, Charles E., Maj. QM, 1865

Stevens, Walter H., Maj. EO, 1862

Talcott, Thomas M. R., Lt. Col. EO, 1862–1864

Taylor, Walter H., Lt. Col. AAG, 1861–1865

Thurston, Edward N., Capt. OO, 1864

Venable, Andrew R., Jr., Maj. AAIG?, 1865

Venable, Charles S., Maj. ADC, 1862–1864, & Lt. Col. AAG, 1864–1865

Washington, John A., Lt. Col. ADC, 1861

Washington, Thornton A., Maj. AAG, 1861–1862, & Maj. QM, 1862

W. H. F. Lee

Bolling, Stith, Capt. AAAG, 1863

Bowling, Henry A., Capt. AAIG, 1863–1864

Brien, Luke T., Maj. AAAG, 1864–1865

Dade, Albert G., Maj. CS, 1862–1865

Dandridge, Philip P., Lt. acting ADC, 1863–1865

Hanger, James M., Capt. acting AQM, 1865

Hunter, James D., Cadet EO, 1862–1863

Lee, John M., Maj. AAIG, 1862–1865

Lee, Robert E., Jr., Lt. acting ADC, acting OO, & AAAG, 1862–1865

Lewis, Edward P. C., Lt. ADC, 1863–?

Nash, Joseph V., Capt. AAG, 1863

Pierce, Thomas W., Capt. OO, 1864–1865

Robertson, Francis S., Lt. EO, 1864–1865

Robins, William T., Capt. AAG, 1862–1863

Turner, Beverly B., Lt. OO, 1863, & Lt. ADC, 1863–1865

Venable, Andrew R., Jr., Maj. AAAG, 1864

Waite, Charles, Maj. QM, 1862–1865?

William G. Lewis

Battle, Dossey, Lt. ADC, 1865
Beard, W. W., ? AAIG, 1865
Brame, Tignal H., Capt. AQM, 1864–1865
Hatton, Clarence R., Lt. AAAG, 1864
Hill, William P., Capt. ACS, 1864?–1865
Lacy, Drury, Jr., Lt. AAAG, 1864–1865
McNeely, William G., Capt. AQM, 1864
Murchison, David R., Capt. AQM, 1865
Smith, Joseph H., Lt. OO, 1864–1865?
Williams, John M., Lt. AAAIG, 1865

Robert D. Lilley

Boughan, James H., Capt. AQM, 1864
Daniel, Raleigh T., Capt. AAG, 1864
McCue, John H., Capt. AAG, 1865

Lunsford L. Lomax

Blackburn, John S., Lt. OO, 1863–1864
Browne, James T., Capt. AAIG, 1864–1865
Carter, Robert, Capt. acting AQM, 1863–1864
Chamberlayne, Francis W., ——, 1865
Dickinson, Allen C., Lt. ADC, 1864–1865
Goggin, Edmund P., ? AAG, 1864–1865
Grady, Cuthbert P., Capt. AAG, 1863–1864
Hart, Camillus S., Maj. QM, 1864–1865
Howard, Charles, Maj. CS, 1864–1865
Hullihen, Walter Q., Capt. AAG, 1863–1864
Hunter, James, Lt. ADC, 1863–1865
Martin, Walter K., Capt. AAG, 1864–1865
Morgan, Charles S., Capt. AAG, 1864–1865
Powell, William L., Capt. AQM, 1865
Rowland, Thomas, Maj. AAG, 1864?–1865
Scales, James L., Lt. OO, 1864
Taylor, William, Maj. CS, 1863–1864?
Woodward, Peter H., Maj. QM, 1863–1864

Armistead L. Long

Armstrong, William J., Maj. CS, 1863–1865
Arrington, Robert O., Lt. ADC, 1863–1865
Cooper, Samuel M., Lt. ?, 1863–1864
Cutshaw, Wilfred E., Capt. AAAIG, 1863
Gregory, Johnathan M., Capt. OO, 1863–1865
Mason, John, Capt. acting AQM, 1865

Percy, William A., Capt. AAG, 1863–1864
Southall, Stephen V., Lt. AAAG, 1863–1865
Turner, Franklin P., Maj. QM, 1863–1865

James Longstreet

Alexander, Edward P., Col. Chief Arty., 1863–1864
Alexander, William K., Cadet, 1864–1865
Armistead, Franck S., Lt. AAAG, 1861
Blackwell, Reuben W., Lt. ADC, 1862–1863
Blount, Robert P., VADC, 1862–1863
Chichester, John H., VADC, 1861, & Maj. CS, 1861–1862
Clarke, John J. G., Maj. EO, 1863
Dawson, Francis W., Capt. OO, 1862–1864
Douglas, Henry T., Capt. EO, 1863
Drake, Richard, Lt. OO, 1865
Dunn, Andrew, Lt. ADC, 1863–1865
Duxbury, W. C., Lt. OO, 1862–1863
Edwards, John F., Maj. CS, 1864–1865
Fairfax, John W., Capt. AAG, 1862, & Lt. Col. AAIG, 1862–1865
Goree, Thomas J., Lt. ADC, 1861–1865
Haskell, John C., Maj. VADC, 1862
Johnston, Samuel R., Capt. EO, 1862
Keiley, John D., Jr., Maj. QM, 1863–1864
Latrobe, Osmun, Capt. AAIG, 1862–1863, & Lt. Col. AAG, 1863–1865
Leitch, Samuel G., Lt. acting OO, 1862
Lubbock, Thomas S., VADC, 1861
McDonald, Marshall, Capt. EO, 1864
McIlhany, Hugh M., Capt. AQM, 1864
Maben, John C., Capt. AQM, 1864–1865
Manning, Jacob H., Capt. SO, 1862–1864
Manning, Peyton H., Lt. ADC, 1861, & Lt. Col. OO, 1862–1865
Meade, Richard K., Jr., Lt. EO, 1862
Mitchell, Samuel P., Maj. QM, 1861–1863
Moore, Patrick T., Col. VADC, 1862
Morriss, Robert F., VADC
Moses, Raphael J., Maj. CS, 1862–1864
Munford, William, VADC, 1862
Ochiltree, Thomas P., VADC, 1862
Palmer, William H., Lt. Col. AAG, 1865
Phillips, James P., Capt. AQM, 1864–1865
Potts, Frank, Capt. AQM, 1863–1865

Riddick, Richard H., VADC, 1861
Riely, John W., Capt. AAG, 1863
Robinson, Henry, Maj. AAG, 1865?
Sims, Robert M., Capt. AAIG, 1864–1865
Sorrel, Gilbert M., Lt. Col. AAG, 1861–1864
Taylor, Erasmus, Maj. QM, 1863–1865
Terry, Benjamin F., VADC, 1861
Thompson, C. Macon, VADC, 1861
Walton, James B., Col. Chief Arty., 1862–1864
Walton, Thomas, Maj. CS, 1862–1863
Wigfall, Francis T., VADC, 1862
Winthrop, Stephen, Capt. AAG, 1863
Young, Henry E., Capt. VADC, 1862

William W. Loring

Barton, Seth M., Lt. Col. EO, 1862
Baskerville, Henry E. C., Capt. ACS, 1861
Deshler, James, Capt. acting Chief Arty., 1861
Kirker, William H., Maj. QM, ?–1862
Lee, Hugh H., Lt. OO, 1861
Long, Armistead L., Maj. Chief Arty., 1861
Mathews, Henry M., Capt. EO, 1861–1862
Porterfield, George A., Col. OO, 1861
Quintard, Charles T., Lt. ADC, 1862
Robinson, Henry, Maj. AAG, 1862
Starke, William E., VADC, 1861
Stevenson, Carter L., Lt. Col. AAG, 1861–1862
Whiting, Jasper S., Lt. EO, 1861
Williams, James S., Maj. EO, 1861
Yost, Samuel M., Capt. AQM, 1861

John McCausland

Burks, Richard H., Lt. ADC, 1864–1865
Cannon, Henry G., Lt. AAIG, 1864–1865
Cox, Henry W., Lt. OO, 1864–1865?
Dunn, George R. R., Maj. QM, 1864
Estill, Huston, Capt. ACS, 1864–?
Eyster, George H., Capt. AAG, 1864–1865
Fitzhugh, Nicholas, Capt. AAG, 1864–1865
Harvie, Charles I., Capt. AAIG, 1864
Jenkins, Thomas J., Maj. QM, 1864–1865
Smith, James W., Capt. ACS, ?–1865
Tynes, Achilles J., Capt. acting ACS, 1864

William McComb

Allen, John, Capt. AQM, 1865
Allensworth, Andrew J., Maj. QM, 1865
Clayton, James, Capt. AQM, 1865
Hagerty, William O., Capt. AQM, 1865
Hankins, Dick R., Maj. CS, 1865
Hunter, John H., Capt. AQM, 1865
Johnson, Polk G., Lt. ADC, 1865
McCulloch, Robert E., Lt. ADC, 1865
Moore, W. G., Capt. AAIG, 1865
Newman, Howard W., Capt. ACS, 1865

Samuel McGowan

Barnwell, John G., III, Lt. AAAG, 1863
Caldwell, James F. J., Lt. acting OO, 1863, & Lt. acting ADC, 1863–1864
Edwards, John G., Capt. ACS, 1863–1864
Hammond, James H., Maj. QM, 1863–1865
Haskell, Alexander C., Capt. AAG, 1862–1863
Haskell, Langdon C., Lt. ADC, 1863, & Capt. AAG, 1863–1864
Hewetson, Ralph E. B., Capt. AQM, 1864–1865
McCaughrin, Robert L., Capt. AQM, 1864
Riddick, James W., Capt. AAIG, 1864–1865
Sibert, Christian H., Capt. AQM, 1863–?
Thompson, Charles G., Lt. OO, 1864–1865
Wardlaw, Andrew B., Maj. CS, 1863–1865
Wardlaw, George A., Lt. ADC, 1864–1865

Lafayette McLaws

Atkinson, John W., Capt. VADC, 1862
Barham, Theophilus G., Lt. VADC, 1862
Booker, Richard M., Lt. ?, 1862
Brownfield, Robert J., Lt. SO, 1862–1863
Cabell, Henry C., Col. Chief Arty., 1862
Campbell, Duncan G., Lt. EO, 1862–1863
Costin, Ellison L., Maj. AAIG, 1862–1864
Davis, William S., Lt. AAAG, 1861, & Lt. OO, 1861–1862
Duvall, Eli, Jr., Lt. SO
Dwight, Charles S., Lt. EO, 1862–1864
Edwards, Alfred, Lt. OO, 1862–1863
Edwards, John F., Maj. CS, 1862–1863
Goggin, James M., Maj. AAIG, 1862–1863

Hamilton, Samuel P., Maj. Chief Arty., 1862

Henley, Richardson L., VADC, 1862

King, Henry L. P., Lt. OO, 1861, & Lt. ADC, 1862

Lamar, Gazaway B., Jr., Lt. ADC, 1862–1864

Lowrance, Rufus N., Capt. acting ACS, 1863–1864

McIntosh, Thomas S., Maj. AAG, 1861–1862

McLaws, Abram H., Maj. QM, 1861–1863

Martin, Bowling J., Capt. ACS, 1862

Mercer, Thomas H., Cadet OO, 1862–1863

Middleton, John I., Jr., Capt. acting AQM, 1862

Moncure, Thomas J., Lt. EO, 1863–1864

Peck, William D., Maj. acting QM, 1863–1864

Poor, Richard L., Lt. EO, 1861

Read, John P. W., Capt. Chief Arty., 1862

Taliaferro, Edwin, Capt. OO, 1862

Taylor, Henry, Capt. acting ADC, 1861

Tucker, Thomas S. B., VADC, 1861–1862, & Lt. ADC, 1862

Whiting, Henry C., Capt. AQM, 1862

William MacRae

Collins, George P., Maj. QM, 1864–1865

Cunningham, Alexander T., Lt. OO, 1864–1865

Gatling, John T., Jr., Capt. AQM, 1864–1865

Justice, Benjamin W., Capt. ACS, 1864–1865

Nash, Frederick K., Capt. AAIG, 1864

Perry, John M., Capt. OO, 1864

Porter, Joseph E., Lt. ADC, 1864–1865

Robinson, John H., Lt. AAAG, 1865

Young, Joseph J., Capt. AQM, 1864–1865

Young, Louis J., Capt. AAIG, 1864–1865

John B. Magruder

Allen, Littleberry W., VADC, 1862

Alston, William A., Lt. ADC, 1861–1862, & Capt. AAG, 1862

Ball, Mottrom D., Capt. VADC, 1862

Bloomfield, Benjamin, Maj. QM, 1861–1862

Bolton, Henry, Lt. EO, 1862

Boswell, James K., Lt. EO, 1861–1862

Boyce, Henry A., VADC, 1861–1862

Brashear, Dennis F., VADC, 1862

Brent, Joseph L., Maj. OO, 1862

Bryan, Henry, Lt. ADC, 1861–1862, & Maj. AAG, 1862

Bryan, John R., Jr., VADC, 1862

Cabell, Henry C., Lt. Col. Chief Arty., 1862

Cary, John B., Maj. AAG, 1862

Cosby, George B., Maj. AAAG, 1861

Crump, James R., Lt. EO, 1861

Dade, Lawrence A., Lt. EO, 1861–1862?

Derrick, Henry C., EO, 1861

Dickinson, Allen C., VADC, 1862

Dickinson, Andrew G., Capt. AAG, 1862

Donnellan, George, Lt. EO, 1862

Douglas, Henry T., Lt. EO, 1862

Eustis, James B., Lt. ADC, 1861–1862

Harrison, Thompson, Capt. AQM, 1861–1862

Higgins, William H., Capt. acting ACS, 1861–1862

Hyllested, Waldemar V., Maj. VADC, 1862

Johnston, Robert, Col. AAAIG, 1861

Jones, John M., Lt. Col. AAG, 1861–1862

Lee, Stephen D., Lt. Col. Chief Arty., 1862

Lindsay, Albert L., Lt. acting SO, 1861–1862

Magruder, Allan B., Maj. CS, 1862

Magruder, George A., Jr., Cadet, 1861–1862

Meade, Richard K., Jr., Maj. EO, 1861

Morris, Charles, Capt. AQM, 1862

Morton, Richard, Capt. EO, 1861–?

Norris, William, VADC, 1861–1862, & Capt. SO, 1862

Oliver, Saunders D., Capt. AQM, 1862?

Otey, George G., Lt. OO, 1861–1862

Page, Thomas J., Jr., Lt. acting OO & acting ADC, 1861–1862?

Pendleton, Henry, Capt. AQM, 1861–1862

Phillips, J. C., Lt. ADC, 1862

Phillips, Joseph, Lt. acting ADC, 1861–1862

Randolph, George W., Col. Chief Arty., 1861–1862

Reynolds, George N., Lt. OO, 1861–1862

Rives, Alfred L., Capt. EO, 1861

Ryan, J. R., acting ADC, 1862

St. John, Isaac M., volunteer EO, 1861–1862

Selden, John A., Capt. ACS, 1862
Smith, John D., VADC, 1862
Stanard, Hugh M., Lt. ADC, 1861–1865
Stewart, ——, Lt. Col. SO, 1861
Thornton, George A., Lt. AAAG, 1861
Tyler, William, Lt. acting ADC, 1861–?
Vaughan, Robert H., Capt. ACS, 1861–1862
Vaughan, William R., Lt. acting AQM, 1861
White, Chastain, Capt. acting AQM, 1862
White, James B., Capt. AQM, 1861–1862
Wray, George, Maj. acting ADC, 1861–1862

William Mahone

Briggs, William W., Maj. QM, 1862
Briscoe, John L., Capt. AQM, 1864–1865
Cameron, William E., Capt. AAIG, 1863–1864
Corprew, Oliver H. P., Capt. AQM, 1864?–1865
Dimmock, Charles H., Capt. OO, 1864
Duncan, Robert P., Maj. AAIG, 1864
Elliott, Samuel C., Capt. ACS, ?–1865
Girardey, Victor J. B., Capt. AAAG
Goodwin, Charles R., Lt. VADC, 1864
Harrison, Benjamin, Capt. acting ACS, 1864–?
Ironmonger, Francis M., Maj. QM, 1863–1864
Jett, Frederick W., Maj. EO, 1864
Johnston, James A., Maj. QM, 1864–1865
Kindred, John J., Lt. ADC, 1861–1862
Land, Albert L., Maj. QM, 1862–1863
McDonald, William N., Capt. OO, 1864–1865
Mallory, Charles O., Lt. ADC, 1865
Mills, Thomas S., Maj. AAG, 1865
Old, George D., Capt. ACS, 1864–1865
Osborne, Robert C., Capt. AQM, 1864–1865
Patterson, John R., Lt. acting ACS & AQM, 1863–1864, & Capt. AAIG, 1864–1865
Privett, William G., Capt. ACS, 1864–1865
Sherwood, William, Capt. ACS, 1863–1864
Slaughter, Philip M., Maj. CS, 1862–1865
Stone, Hamilton J., Capt. AQM, 1864–1865
Taylor, John C., VADC, 1861–1862
Taylor, Richard C., Maj. acting ADC, 1862

Taylor, Robertson, Capt. AAG, 1861–1864
Thurston, Edward N., Capt. OO, 1864–1865
Walke, Richard, Jr., Lt. OO, 1862–1864
Walker, James W., acting ADC, ?–1865
Weir, Walter, Capt. AAG, 1865

James G. Martin

Bessent, Ransom P., Capt. AQM, 1864
Dancy, John S., Capt. AQM, 1864
DeMill, William E., Maj. CS, 1864
Elliott, Charles G., Capt. AAG, 1864
Gordon, A., Maj. QM, 1864
Hassell, Theodore M., Lt. OO, 1864
Shepard, William M., Lt. ADC, 1864
Starke, Lucien D., Capt. ACS, 1864

Young M. Moody

Brown, Charles D., Maj. CS, 1865
Cherry, Edward B., VADC, 1865
Fitzpatrick, John A., Capt. AQM, 1865
Jones, Harvey E., Capt. AAG, 1865
Kaigler, John J., Capt. AQM, 1865
Lockhart, Robert B., Capt. AAIG, 1865
Lynes, Thomas B., VADC?, 1865
MacMurphy, A. M., Lt. OO, 1865
Miller, William H., Maj. QM, 1865
Sengstak, Henry H., Capt. AAAIG, 1865

Patrick T. Moore

Allan, William G., Capt. AQM, 1864
Lee, George, Lt. ADC, 1865
Morton, Tazewell S., Lt. ADC, 1865
Smith, Anthony A., Lt. OO, 1864–1865

Francis R. T. Nicholls

Boarman, Alexander, Capt. AAAG, 1863
Harper, William P., Capt. AAAG, 1863
Hepburn, Samuel C., Lt. ADC, 1863–1864
Rawle, Francis, Maj. QM, 1862–1863
Richardson, James G., Maj. CS, 1862–1863
St. Martin, Victor J., Capt. AAAG, 1863

Lucius B. Northrop

Ruffin, Francis G., Lt. Col. CS, 1861–1865
Williams, Thomas G., Lt. Col. CS, 1861–1864

Elisha F. Paxton

Arnall, Charles S., Lt. AAAG, 1862

Barton, Randolph J., Capt. AAG, 1863

Braithwaite, Jacob R., Maj. QM, 1862–1863

Bruce, James W., Maj. QM, 1862–1863

Cox, Friend C., Lt. ADC, 1863

Douglas, Henry K., Capt. AAAIG, 1862–1863

Estill, Charles P., Lt. OO, 1863

Sexton, Joseph C., Maj. CS, 1862–1863

William H. F. Payne

Blackburn, John S., Lt. OO, 1864–1865

Digges, Charles W., Lt. ADC, 1864–1865

Grady, Cuthbert P., Capt. AAG, 1865

Hullihen, Walter Q., Capt. AAG, 1864–1865

Taylor, William, Maj. CS, 1864–1865?

Woodward, Peter H., Maj. QM, 1864–1865

William R. Peck

Buckner, James, Capt. AQM, 1865

Campbell, John G., Maj. CS, 1865

Forrest, John, Lt. OO, 1865

Watkins, Leigh, Capt. ACS, 1865

John Pegram

Bell, John W., Maj. QM, 1863–1865

Boughan, James H., Capt. AQM, 1863–1864

Cochran, George M., Capt. AQM, 1864–1865

Cochran, Howe P., Lt. OO, 1864?

Daniel, Raleigh T., Capt. AAG, 1863–1864

Douglas, Henry K., Maj. AAAG, 1864–1865

Eyster, George H., Capt. AAG, 1863–1864

Hart, Camillus S., Capt. acting AQM, 1864–1865?

Haymond, Alpheus F., Maj. CS, 1863–1865

Kinney, Richard S., Lt. acting ADC & AAAIG, 1863–1864

McNeely, William G., Capt. AQM, 1864–1865

New, John P. H., Maj. AAAIG, 1864–1865

Payne, William M., Maj. QM, 1864–1865

Randolph, Tucker S., VADC, 1864

Ranson, Ambrose R. H., Maj. CS, 1862–1863

Ranson, James M., Lt. ADC, 1863–1865

Snodgrass, Charles E., Maj. QM?, 1864–1865

Thornton, William W., Maj. CS, 1864–1865

Turner, Vines E., Capt. AQM, 1864–1865

Vogler, Julius R., Capt. AQM, 1864–1865

Williams, William G., Capt. ACS, 1864

Wilson, Robert N., Capt. AAG, 1864?

John C. Pemberton

Brent, Henry M., Jr., Lt. OO, 1864

Cooke, Augustus B., Maj. QM, 1861

Morrison, James H., Lt. ADC, 1861

Taylor, John C., Lt. ADC, 1861

Waddy, John R., Jr., Capt. AAG, 1861

William D. Pender

Anderson, Edward W., Capt. OO, 1863

Ashe, Samuel A., Capt. AAG, 1862

Biscoe, Henry L., Maj. CS, 1862–1863

Bolton, Channing M., Lt.? EO, 1863

Brewer, Richard H., Lt. VADC, 1862

Carraway, Daniel T., Maj. CS, 1863

Engelhard, Joseph A., Maj. QM, 1862–1863

Green, William J., VADC, 1862

Hinsdale, John W., Lt. AAAG, 1862

Hunt, Leonard H., Capt. AAAIG, 1862–1863, & Maj. AAIG, 1863

Kirkland, Samuel S., Lt. OO, 1862, & Lt. ADC, 1862–1863

Oates, Robert M., Capt. AQM, 1863

Rosborough, James T., Lt. ADC, 1863

Scales, Nathaniel E., Maj. QM, 1862–1863

Shepperd, Jacob, Lt. ADC, 1862

Young, John, Lt. ADC, 1862

Young, Louis G., Lt. VADC, 1862

William N. Pendleton

Barnwell, John G., Maj. OO, 1862–1865

Cooke, John E., Capt. AAIG, 1864–1865

Dandridge, Edmund P., Lt. AAG, 1862, & Lt. AAIG, 1863–1865

Davis, Eugene, VADC, 1862

Hatcher, Charles, VADC, 1862–1863

Hooff, John G. J., VADC, 1865

Meade, William T., Capt. AQM, 1862–1865

Nelson, George W., Capt. AAIG, 1862–1863

Page, John, Maj. QM, 1861–1865

Pendleton, Dudley D., Capt. AAG, 1862–1865

Peterkin, George W., Lt. ADC, 1862–1865

Randolph, Thomas H. B., VADC, 1862

Taliaferro, John, Cadet AAG & acting ADC, 1862

Wolff, Bernard L., Maj. CS, 1862–1864

Abner Perrin

Higgason, Albert E., Lt. OO, 1863–1864

Pierce, John G., Maj. QM, 1863–1864

Robertson, Richard M., Maj. CS, 1863–1864

Spann, Ransom D., Capt. AAIG, 1863–1864

Wilson, Marcus L., Capt. ACS, 1863–1864

Winn, Walter E., Capt. AAG, 1863–1864

Edward A. Perry

Clarke, William H., Lt. OO, 1863–1864

Elder, Thomas C., Maj. CS, 1862–1864

Hinkle, David W., Maj. QM, 1862–1864

Johnson, James B., Lt. AAAG, 1863?–1864?

Lee, William F., Lt. AAAIG, 1862

McCaslan, William E., Capt. AAAG, 1863

Reid, Richard W., Capt. ACS, 1864?

Riley, Henry F., Lt. AAAIG, 1863

Scott, Alfred L., Lt. acting OO, 1862–1863, & Lt. AAAG, 1864

Scott, William J., VADC, 1863

Simmons, Benjamin F., Lt. AAAIG, 1863

Taylor, D. B., Lt. ADC, 1862–1865

William F. Perry

Babbitt, Amzi, Maj. CS, 1865

Christian, Thomas L., Capt. AAIG, 1865

Dawson, Lemuel H., Capt. AQM, 1865

Drake, Richard, Lt. OO, 1865

Lapsley, Robert, Capt. AQM, 1864–1865

Morgan, Lewis A., Lt. AAAIG & acting ADC, 1864–1865

Pinckard, Thomas C., Lt. OO, 1865

Scruggs, William H., Maj. QM, 1865

James J. Pettigrew

Baker, William J., Maj. CS, 1862–1863

Biscoe, Henry L., Capt. ACS, 1862

Collins, George P., Maj. QM, 1862–1863

Hughes, Nicholas C., Capt. AAG, 1862–1863

McCreery, William W., Capt. AAAIG, 1863

Morris, Isaac E., Maj. QM, 1862

Robertson, Walter H., Lt. OO, 1863

Shepard, William B., VADC, 1862–1863

Young, Louis G., Lt. ADC, 1862–1863

George E. Pickett

Baird, Edward R., Capt. ADC, 1862–1865

Bright, Robert A., Capt. ADC, 1862–1865

Cochran, Howe P., Lt.? OO, 1864–1865

Crisler, Nelson W., Maj. acting QM, 1862

Croxton, Thomas, Lt. AAAG, 1862

Edmonds, William B., Jr., Capt. ACS, 1863–1865

Fowler, William S., VADC, 1862

Harrison, Walter H., VADC, 1862, & Maj. AAIG, 1862–1865

Holt, Joseph H., Capt. AQM, 1864–1865

Johnston, Robert, AAAG, 1861–1863

Jones, Horace W., Maj. CS, 1862–1865

Leitch, Samuel G., Lt. acting OO, 1863–1864

Lewis, Samuel L., Maj. QM, 1861–1862

McIlhany, Hugh M., Capt. AQM, 1864

Meade, David, Capt. AQM, 1863–1865

Milligan, James F., Capt. SO, 1863–1864

Morson, John S., Lt. Asst. EO, 1863–1864

Peacocke, Thomas G., VADC, 1864

Pickett, Charles, Maj. AAG, 1862–1865

Rhodes, Charles H., VADC? & AAG, 1863–1864?

Scott, Robert T., Maj. QM, 1862–1865

Stuart, William D., Capt. EO, 1864–1865

Symington, William S., Lt. OO, 1862, & Lt. ADC, 1862–1865

Wallace, Thomas P., Capt. AQM, 1864–1865

Williams, Andrew W., Capt. AQM, ?–1865

Wilson, John T., Maj. CS, 1862

Carnot Posey

Connell, William C., Capt. ACS, 1863

Duke, Thomas L., VADC

Hays, James, Lt. AAAIG, 1863

Hearsey, Henry J., Maj. QM, 1863

Nelson, William C., Lt. OO, 1863

Patridge, Isaac M., Maj. CS, 1863

Posey, Jefferson B., Lt. ADC, 1863
Posey, Stanhope, Capt. AAG, 1863

Roger A. Pryor
Barnes, ——, VADC, 1863
Elder, Thomas C., Maj. CS, 1862
Hinkle, David W., Maj. QM, 1862
Hudgins, Benjamin F., Lt. ADC, 1862
Keiley, John D., Jr., Maj. QM, 1863
McCann, Charles, Lt. ADC, 1862–1863
McMullen, ——, VADC, 1863
Saunders, William J., Lt. AAAIG, 1861–1862?
Shepard, William A., Maj. CS, 1862–?
Tabb, Thomas, acting OO?, 1862
Whitner, William H., Capt. AAG, 1862–1863
Wrenn, Walter, Capt. AAG, 1862

Gabriel J. Rains
Cary, John B., Lt. Col. acting PM, 1862
Feldburg, Charles P., Lt. acting OO, 1864–1865
Jones, Alexander C., Lt. Col. AAG, 1863
Leitch, Samuel G., Lt. AAAG, 1864–1865
McMillan, Garnett, Capt. AAAG,, 1864–1865
Magruder, Allan B., Maj. CS, 1862
Mallory, Charles K., Capt. AAAIG & Maj. QM, 1862
Page, Peyton N., Lt. ADC, 1861–1862, & Capt. AAG, 1862
Rains, Henry J., Lt. ADC, 1864–1865
Rowland, Alexander M., Lt. AAAG, 1861
Rundell, Charles H., Lt. ADC, 1862–1863
Tyler, William, Lt. AAAG & acting ADC, 1862?

Stephen D. Ramseur
Burwell, John B., Capt. AQM, 1864
Coleman, Samuel H., Lt. OO, 1863–1864
Coughenour, William C., Capt. AAG, 1863–1864
Gales, Seaton, Capt. AAG, 1862–1864
Garnett, James M., Capt. OO, 1864
Hill, Jacob I., Capt. AQM, 1864
Hutchinson, Robert R., Maj. AAG, 1864
Langdon, Richard F., Capt. AQM, 1864

Lilly, Robert, Capt. ACS, 1863–1864
Miller, Henry M., Maj. CS, 1864
Morrison, Joseph G., VADC, 1863
Neary, William J., Capt. AQM, 1864
New, John P. H., Maj. AAIG, 1864
Peyton, Moses G., Maj. AAG, 1864
Randolph, Meriwether L., Capt. SO, 1864
Richmond, Caleb H., Lt. ADC, 1862–1864
Ridgely, Randolph, VADC, 1864
Snodgrass, Charles E., Maj. QM, 1864
Snowden, Samuel H., Capt. AQM, 1864
Tannor, Nathaniel M., Maj. QM, 1864
Thornton, William W., Maj. CS, 1864
Turner, Vines E., Capt. AQM, 1864
Vogler, Julius R., Capt. AQM, 1864
Whiting, Henry A., Maj. AAG, 1864
Williams, Buckner D., Maj. QM, 1862–1864
Wilson, James W., Maj. QM, 1863

George W. Randolph
Kean, Robert G. H., Capt. AAG, 1862.
Myers, William B., Lt. VADC, 1862
Randolph, Thomas J., Maj. QM, 1862
St. John, Isaac M., Capt. EO, 1862
Walker, Norman S., Lt. ADC, 1862

Matthew W. Ransom
Barnes, George B., Capt. AQM, 1864–1865
Blakemore, James H., Lt. OO, 1865
Brodnax, John W., Maj. CS, 1864?–1865
Dinkins, Henry H., Lt. AAAIG, 1864
Farrell, John, Capt. AQM, 1864–1865
Gee, Stirling H., Capt. AAIG, 1863–1865
Goodloe, Lewis D., Lt.? OO, 1865–1865
Johnson, J. W., VADC, 1863–1865
Meares, William B., Lt. ADC, 1863–1865?
Peebles, Robert B., Capt. AAG, ?–1865
Pegram, John C., Capt. AAG, 1863–1864
Williams, John A., Capt. ACS, 1863–1865?

Robert Ransom
Ashe, John G., Lt. AAAG, 1862
Barringer, Victor C., Capt. AAG, 1862
Blake, Frederick R., VADC, 1862
Branch, Thomas P., Maj. AAIG, 1863–1864
Brodnax, John W., Maj. CS, 1862–1864?

Brodnax, William E., Lt. ADC, 1862–1863

Browne, James T., Lt. ADC, 1863–1864, &
Capt. AAIG, 1864

Chestney, Theodore O., Maj. AAG, 1864

Davis, H. J., VADC, 1862

Drewry, Clay, Maj. QM, 1862–1864

Henry, James L., Lt. OO, 1862

Johnson, J. W., VADC

Johnson, Powell C., Lt. EO, 1863

Jones, John W., Lt. ADC, 1864

Lee, Edwin G., Col. VADC, 1864

Mason, Thomas W., VADC, 1862

Parkhill, John H., Maj. AAG, 1864

Pegram, James W., Jr., Maj. AAG, 1864

Reid, Samuel V., Maj. CS, 1864

Rowland, Thomas, Maj. AAG, 1862–1864

Simmons, J. Fred, Maj. QM, 1862

Snowden, Charles A., Maj. QM, 1864

Stover, William W., Capt. acting ADC,
?–1865

Taylor, Benjamin F., Lt. ADC, 1863–1864

Thorne, Edward A., Lt. acting OO, 1862–
1864?

Roswell S. Ripley

Higham, Thomas, Maj. QM, 1862

Mitchell, Julian, Maj. CS, 1862

Morrow, James, Maj. QM, 1862

Ravenel, Francis G., Lt. ADC, 1862

Read, Benjamin H., Capt. AAG, 1862

Rogers, Hugh H., Lt. ADC, 1862

Walker, Leonidas D., Capt. AAG, 1861–1862

William P. Roberts

Bigger, Robert H., Maj. QM, 1865

Bower, Byron B., Capt. AAIG, 1865

Coughenour, William C., Capt. AAIG, 1865

Garnett, Theodore S., Lt. AAAG, 1865

Holcombe, William J., Lt. ADC, 1865

Webb, James E., Capt. OO, 1865

Beverly H. Robertson

Bassett, George W., Lt. acting OO, 1863?

Downman, Robert H., Maj. CS, 1863

Farish, Thomas L., Capt. AAG, 1862–1863

Gordon, Charles H., Capt. AAG, 1862–1863

Harvie, William W., Maj. CS, 1862–1863

Haxall, Philip, Capt. AAG, 1863

Johnston, Thomas H., Lt. ADC, 1863

Martin, Walter K., Capt. AAG, 1862

Melton, George W., Maj. QM, 1863

Pleasants, James, Lt. OO, 1862

Selden, Harry H., Maj. QM, 1862–?

Terrell, Lewis F., VADC, 1862

Worthington, William N., Lt. ADC, 1862–
1863, & Capt. AAG, 1863

Jerome B. Robertson

Burns, Robert, Capt. ACS, 1863–1864

Gracc, John, VADC, 1863

Hamilton, Tilford A., Maj. CS, 1863–1864

Kerr, John W., Lt. AAAIG, 1862–1863, &
Capt. AAIG, 1863–1864

Littlefield, James H., Maj. QM, 1862–1864

Price, Francis L., Capt. AAG, 1862–1863

Scott, John G., Lt. ADC, 1862–1864

Sublett, David L., Lt. OO, 1862–1864

Robert E. Rodes

Adams, Benjamin C., Maj. CS, 1863–1864

Arrington, James P., Lt. ADC, 1863–1864

Baldwin, Briscoe G., Capt. AAAG, 1862

Berney, John, Lt. ADC, 1862–1863

Best, Emory F., Col. AAAIG, 1863

Bouldin, Wood, Jr., Lt. VADC, 1862

Bryan, James C., Maj. QM, 1862 & 1864

Burwell, John B., Capt. AQM, 1864

Carter, Francis, Lt. VADC, 1863–1864

Chichester, Arthur M., Capt. EO, 1863–1864

Force, Charles F., Maj. CS, 1861–1862

Force, Henry C., Lt. EO, 1862

Garnett, James M., Capt. OO, ?–1864

Harris, Edwin H., Maj. QM, 1861–1862

Harris, William A., Capt. OO, 1863

Hutchinson, James J., Lt. ADC, 1863–1864

Hutchinson, Robert R., Maj. AAG, 1863–
1864

Langdon, Richard F., Capt. AQM, 1864

Lumsden, ——, ?, 1862

Mallet, John W., Lt. ADC, 1861–1862

Mitchell, Julian, Maj. acting CS, 1863
Neary, William J., Capt. AQM, 1864
O'Neal, Edward A., Jr., VADC, 1863
Peden, David D., Capt. AAAIG, 1863
Peyton, Moses G., Lt. VADC, 1862, & Maj.
    AAG, 1862–1864
Priest, Robert L., Capt. acting ACS, 1862, &
    Capt. ACS, 1863–1864
Randolph, Meriwether L., Capt. SO, 1863–
    1864
Randolph, Peyton K., Lt. ?, 1861
Rodes, Virginius H., VADC, 1862, & Lt.
    ADC, 1864
Rogers, John D., Maj. QM, 1863–1864
Snowden, Samuel H., Capt. AQM, 1864
Sutton, Philip T., Lt. ADC, 1862
Tannor, Nathaniel M., Maj. QM, 1864
Webb, James E., Lt. acting OO, 1864
Webster, Daniel T., Maj. CS, 1862–1863?
Webster, William E., Lt. VADC, 1862
Whiting, Henry A., Maj. AAG, 1861–1864
Wood, ——, ?, 1862
Yancey, Henry D., VADC, 1862

Thomas L. Rosser

Branch, Thomas P., Maj. AAG, 1865
Conrad, Holmes, Maj. AAIG, 1864–1865
Dawson, Francis W., Capt. OO, 1864–1865
Emmett, John W., Capt. AAG, 1863–1865
Fontaine, Peter, Capt. AAG, 1865
Gwathmey, Charles B., Maj. QM, 1864–1865
Harvie, William W., Maj. CS, 1863
Heck, John, ?, 1864
Hooff, James L., Capt. acting QM, 1863–
    1865?
Kennon, Richard B., Capt. AAIG, 1863–?
McDonald, William N., Capt. OO, 1863–
    1864
Martin, Walter K., Capt. AAG, 1863
Radford, Richard C. W., Capt. AAG, 1865
Richardson, John D., Maj. QM, 1863–1864
Smith, Augustine M., Maj. CS, 1864–1865
Walke, Isaac T., Lt. OO, 1864
Warwick, William B., Maj. CS, 1864–1865
Winston, Philip B., Lt. ADC, 1863–1865
Withrow, Charles H., Lt. OO, 1864

Daniel Ruggles

Crump, Malcolm H., Capt. AQM?, 1861
French, Seth B., Capt. ACS, 1861
Hooe, Roy D. M., Lt. AAAG, 1861
Seddon, John, Capt. AAAG, 1861
Turner, George, VADC, 1861

Isaac M. St. John

French, Seth B., Maj. CS, 1865

John C. C. Sanders

Clark, George, Capt. AAAG, 1864
Higgason, Albert E., Lt. OO, 1864
Pierce, John G., Maj. QM, 1864
Robertson, Richard M., Maj. CS, 1864
Spann, Ransom D., Capt. AAIG, 1864
Wilson, Marcus L., Capt. ACS, 1864
Young, William B., Lt. AAAG, 1864

Alfred M. Scales

Bason, George F., Lt. OO, 1864–1865
Biscoe, Henry L., Maj. CS, 1863–1865
Clarke, John W., Capt. AQM, 1864–1865
Gallaway, Alexander H., Maj. QM, 1863–
    1865
Guerrant, Hugh L., Capt. AAAIG, 1863
Henderson, Richard B., Capt. AAIG, 1863–
    1865
McElroy, James G., Capt. AQM, 1864–1865
McIntire, David M., Lt. AAAG, 1863
Montgomery, Alvis D., Lt. ADC, 1863–1865
Riddick, James W., Capt. AAG, 1863–1864
Scales, Erasmus D., Capt. ACS, 1863–1865?
Young, John D., Lt. acting ADC, 1863

Paul J. Semmes

Briggs, Edmund B., Lt. ADC, 1862–1863
Clemons, Welcom G., Capt. AAG, 1862
Cody, Bailey H., VADC, 1862–1863
Cody, James A., VADC?, 1863
Costin, Ellison L., VADC, 1862
Davis, John E., Maj. QM, 1862–1863
Davis, William S., Lt. AAAIG, 1863
Ellis, Roswell, Capt. AAG, 1862–1863
Hanckel, Charles F., Maj. CS, 1862–1863

Henley, Richardson L., Capt. acting ACS & VADC, 1862

Redd, John, VADC, 1862

Semmes, Abner G., Lt. OO, 1862–1863

James P. Simms

Briggs, William H., Capt. AQM, 1864–1865

Fletcher, Thomas J., Lt. acting AQM, ?–1865

Kibbee, Charles C., Capt. AAAG, 1864–1865

Neal, Samuel T., Capt. acting AQM, 1864–1865

Parmelee, Charles H., Maj. CS, 1864–1865

Ponder, James M., Capt. AQM, 1864–1865?

Semmes, Abner G., Lt. OO, 1864–1865?

Simms, Arthur B., Lt. ADC, 1864–1865

Walker, James W., Capt. AAIG, 1864–1865

Whitehead, W. H. W., Capt. ACS, 1864–1865

E. Kirby Smith

Belton, Joseph F., Lt. ADC, 1861–1862

Cunningham, Edward, Lt. ADC & Capt. EO, 1861

Meem, John G., Jr., Lt. ADC, 1862

Morgan, John L., Capt. AQM, 1861–1862

Thomas, William H., Maj. CS, 1862

Walworth, Ernest, VADC, 1862

Gustavus W. Smith

Andrews, Garnett, Capt. AAG, 1862–1863

Banks, Andrew D., Maj. VADC, 1861

Barton, William S., Maj. AAG, 1862–1863

Beckham, Robert F., Lt. ADC, 1862, & Maj. OO, 1862–1863

Campbell, Duncan G., Lt. EO, 1861–1862

Carter, Richard W., Capt. acting ADC, 1862

Collins, Charles R., Capt. EO, 1862

Cone, Aurelius F., Maj. QM, 1862–1863

Cross, J. Lucius, Maj. AAG, 1862–1863

Davis, Matthew L., Maj. QM, 1861–1862

Delaigle, Louis, Capt. AQM, 1861–1862

Field, Charles W., Col. AAG, 1861

Ford, Edwin A., Lt. EO, 1862

French, Seth B., Maj. CS, 1862–1863

Hampton, Wade, Jr., Lt. VADC, 1862

Haskell, John C., Maj. CS, 1861–1863

Hawkins, Elijah, Lt. ADC, 1862–1863

Hoenniger, Theodore W., VADC, 1862

Howard, James, Lt. ADC, 1861–1862

Johnston, William P., Capt. Judge, 1862

Lacy, J. Horace, Lt. ADC, 1862–1863

Lane, John, Lt. ADC, 1861

Lovell, Joseph, Lt. ADC, 1861

McKinne, Barna, Maj. QM, 1862–1863

Melton, George W., Lt. AAIG, 1862–1863

Melton, Samuel W., Maj. AAG, 1861–1863

Morriss, Robert F., VADC, 1863

Peyton, Thomas J., Capt. AAIG, 1862–1863?

Randal, Horace, Lt. ADC, 1861–1862

Riely, John W., Capt. AAG, 1862–1863

Saunders, John S., Lt. Col. OO, 1862

Twiggs, Hansford D. D., Capt. AAAIG, 1862–1863

Whiting, Jasper S., Maj. AAG, 1861–1862

Wilbourn, Richard E., Capt. SO, 1862

Martin L. Smith

Semmes, Benedict J., Lt. ADC, 1864

William Smith

Bell, John W., Maj. QM, 1863

Boughan, James H., Capt. AQM, 1863

Eyster, George H., Cadet OO & Capt. AAG, 1863

Haymond, Alpheus F., Capt. acting ACS, 1863

Smith, Frederick W., Lt. & Cadet ADC, 1863

Thom, Cameron E., VADC, 1863

G. Moxley Sorrel

Evans, George W., Capt. AQM, 1864–1865

Evans, Joshua K., Capt. AAAG, 1864–?

Evans, Oliver F., Capt. AAAG, 1864–1865?

Hughes, Hampden S., Maj. CS, 1864–1865

Keith, Jasper L., Capt. AQM, 1864–1865

McWhorter, Robert L., Maj. QM, 1864–1865

Mahool, Thomas, Capt. ACS, 1864–1865

Perry, Heman H., Capt. AAG, ?–1865

Spencer, Oliver H., Lt. ADC, 1864–1865

Starr, Silas H., Capt. OO, 1865

Leroy A. Stafford

Barclay, Alexander T., Lt. ?, 1864

Boarman, Alexander, Capt. VADC, 1863, &
Capt. AAIG, 1864
Handerson, Henry E., Capt. AAG, 1863–
1864
Merrick, David T., Capt. AAAIG or acting
ADC, 1863
Murphy, James P., Capt. ACS, 1863–1864
Rawle, Francis, Maj. QM, 1863–1864
Richardson, James G., Maj. CS, 1863–1864
Stafford, George W., Lt. ADC, 1864

William E. Starke

Doswell, Thomas W., VADC, 1862
Estill, Huston, Maj. QM, 1862
Gordon, Archibald M., Lt. AAAG, 1862
Pollock, Thomas G., Lt. VADC, 1862
Richardson, James G., Capt. acting ACS,
1862
Starke, William N., Capt. AAG, 1862

George H. Steuart

Averett, John T., Capt. AQM, 1865
Bond, Frank A., Lt. AAAG, 1862
Boyle, John H., Jr., VADC, 1863
Caulfield, Ignatius, Capt. ACS, 1863–1864
Darden, James D., Capt. AAG, 1864–1865
Garrison, George G., Capt. AAG, 1863
Goodridge, Ferguson E., Lt. OO, 1865
Herbert, William W., Maj. CS, 1864–1865
Howard, McHenry, Lt. AAG, 1863–1864
Kyle, George H., Maj. CS, 1862–1863
McKim, Randolph H., Lt. ADC, 1862–1863
Marshall, John P., Lt. OO, 1863
Newman, Reuben M., Lt. ADC, 1864–1865
Nicholas, Wilson C., Capt. AAIG, 1863
Randolph, William L., Lt. OO, 1864–1865
Samuels, Green B., Jr., Lt. AAAIG, 1863
Smith, Joseph H., Lt. OO, 1863–1864
Smith, William B., Capt. AQM, 1864–1865
Stanard, William B., Maj. CS, 1863?–1864
Steuart, William J., Lt. ADC, 1864
Tannor, Nathaniel M., Maj. QM, 1863–1864
Thompson, Ben. S., Maj. QM, ?
Williamson, George, Capt. AAG, 1862–1863,
& Capt. AAIG, 1863–1864?

Walter H. Stevens

Haile, Christopher V., Lt. ADC, 1864–1865
Howard, James M., Lt. OO & AAAG, 1864–
1865
Obenchain, William A., Capt. EO, 1864–
1865
Snead, Thomas T. L., Capt. EO, 1864–1865

J. E. B. Stuart

Ball, Dabney, Maj. CS, 1861–1862
Beckham, Robert F., Maj. Chief Arty.,
1863–1864
Blackford, William W., Lt. Col. EO, 1862–
1864
von Borcke, Johann A. H. Heros, Maj.
AAIG, 1862–1863
Boteler, Alexander R., VADC, 1863–1864
Brien, Luke T., Capt. AAG, 1861–1862
Burke, Redmond, Lt. ADC, 1862
Chew, Roger P., Maj. Chief Arty., 1864
Christian, Isaac H., VADC, 1862
Christian, Jones R., Lt. acting ADC, 1862
Clark, James L., Capt. VADC, 1863
Cooke, John E., Capt. OO, 1862–1863, &
Capt. AAIG, 1863–1864
Dabney, Chiswell, Lt. ADC, 1861–1863
Farley, Henry S., Capt. VADC?, 1863
Farley, William D., Capt. VADC, 1862
FitzHugh, Norman R., Maj. AAG, 1861–
1863, & Maj. QM, 1863–1864
Frayser, Richard E., Capt. SO, 1862–1864
Freaner, George, Maj. AAIG, 1863–1864
Garnett, Theodore S., Lt. ADC, 1864
Goldsborough, Robert H., Lt. ADC, 1863–
1864
Grattan, Charles, Capt. OO, 1863–1864
Grenfell, George St. L., Lt. Col. AAIG, 1863
Hagan, William H., VADC
Hairston, James T. W., Maj. AAG, 1862–1863
Hairston, Peter W., VADC, 1861
Hairston, Samuel H., VADC, 1862, & Maj.
AAG, 1862–1863
Hanger, James M., Capt. AQM, 1862–1864
Henry, Mathis W., Lt. ?, 1862
Hullihen, Walter Q., Cadet acting ADC,
1862–1863

Jackson, C. F., VADC, 1861

Jenifer, Walter H., VADC, 1862

Johnson, William J., Maj. CS, 1862–1864

Johnston, Samuel R., VADC, 1861–1862

Kennon, Richard B., Lt. AAAIG, 1863

Kirker, William H., Capt. AQM, 1864

McClellan, Henry B., Maj. AAG, 1863–1864

Pelham, John, Maj. Chief Arty., 1862–1863

Powers, Philip H., Maj. QM, 1862

Price, Richard C., Lt. ADC, 1862–1863, & Maj. AAG, 1863

Price, Thomas R., Jr., Lt. EO, 1863

Robertson, Francis S., Lt. EO, 1863–1864

Ryals, Garland M., Maj. PM, 1863–1864

Staples, Samuel G., VADC, 1862

Steger, Roger W., Maj. QM, 1861

Stuart, James H., Capt. SO, 1862

Terrell, Lewis F., Maj. VADC, 1863

Throckmorton, John A., Lt. acting ADC, 1861

Towles, William E., VADC, 1862

Turner, Thomas B., Cadet VADC, 1862

Tyler, Charles H., Capt. AAIG, 1862–1863

Venable, Andrew R., Jr., Maj. AAIG, 1862–1864

Webb, James E., Lt. OO, 1864

White, Benjamin S., Maj. VADC?, 1862–1864

William B. Taliaferro

Brockenbrough, John B., Capt. Chief Arty., 1862

Campbell, Parker, Capt. ACS, 1861

Garnett, James M., Lt. OO, 1862–1863

Hinrichs, Oscar, Lt. OO, 1862

Marye, Lawrence S., Capt. OO, 1862–1863

Meade, Richard K., Lt. ADC, 1862–1864

Moore, Edwin L., Capt. AAAIG, 1862

Pendleton, Joseph H., Maj. QM, 1862

Pendleton, William B., Capt. AAG, 1861–1862

Shumaker, Lindsay M., Maj. Chief Arty., 1862

Stanard, William B., Maj. CS, 1862

Taliaferro, Philip A., Lt. ADC, 1862

Taliaferro, Thomas S., VADC, 1862

Taliaferro, Warner T., VADC, 1862, & Capt. AAG, 1862–1863

Wellford, Philip A., VADC, 1862

Richard Taylor

Boyd, David F., Maj. CS, 1862

Bringier, Martin D., Lt. ADC, 1862

Davis, Aaron, Maj. CS, 1862

Hamilton, James, Lt. ADC, 1862

Heard, Thomas R., Maj. QM, 1862

Killmartin, John, Lt. acting ADC, 1862

Surget, Eustace, Lt. Col. AAG, 1861–1862

William Terry

Barton, Randolph J., Capt. AAG, 1864

Boyd, Elisha H., Lt. OO, 1864–1865

?Braithwaite, Jacob R., Maj. QM, 1864

Bruce, James W., Maj. QM, 1864–1865

Caulfield, Ignatius, Capt. ACS, 1864

Cleary, Reuben, Capt. AAG?, 1864

Cox, Friend C., Capt. AAG, 1864–1865

Dawson, Pleasant, Lt. ADC, 1864–1865

Francisco, Robert L., Capt. AQM, 1864–1865

Graves, John T., Capt. ACS, 1865

Merritt, Christian G., Capt. AQM, 1864

Persinger, George P., Capt. AQM, 1864–1865

Sexton, Joseph C., Maj. CS, 1864

Stanard, William B., Maj. CS, 1864

Waters, James H., Capt. ACS, 1864

White, James L., Capt. AAIG, 1864–1865

William R. Terry

Bryant, John C. H., Capt. AAG, 1864–1865

Crisler, Nelson W., Maj. QM, 1864–1865

Dennis, George E., Capt. ACS, 1864–1865

Graves, Richard M., Capt. acting AQM, 1864

Green, James W., Maj. CS, 1864–1865

Harris, Hilary V., Lt. ADC, 1865

Nelson, Kinloch, Lt. OO, 1864–1865

Thompson, Cameron L., Capt. AQM, 1864–1865

Woods, Robert C., Capt. AQM, 1864–1865

Edward L. Thomas

Blackburn, John S., Lt. OO, 1863

Brown, John T., Capt. AQM, 1864–1865
Colquitt, John H., ? ADC, 1865
Ginter, Lewis, Maj. CS, 1862–1865
Gorham, Willis J., Capt. AAIG, 1863–1865
Heggie, Evans A., Capt. AQM, 1864–1865
Lewis, Edward L., Lt. ADC, 1862–1865
Moore, James W., Capt. ACS, 1864
Nisbet, Adam R., Capt. ACS, 1865
Norwood, William, Capt. AAG, 1862–1865
Tanner, William E., Lt. OO, 1862
Taylor, Robert T., Maj. QM, 1862–1865
Tenney, Samuel F., Lt. OO, 1863–1865?
Tyler, John, Lt. VADC, 1862

Robert A. Toombs

Alexander, William F., Maj. QM, 1861–1862
DuBose, Dudley M., Capt. AAG, 1862
Grant, Robert, Lt. AAAG, 1861–1862
Hill, Alonzo A. F., Capt. acting ADC, 1862
Hill, Robert C., Maj. AAG, 1861
Houston, James, Capt. acting AQM, 1862–1863
Lamar, Gazaway D., Cadet, 1861–1862
Lamar, W. T., ?, 1862
Lofton, Bedford H., Lt. OO, 1862–1863
Moses, Raphael J., Maj. CS, 1861–1862
Troup, James R., Lt. ADC, 1862–1863

Thomas F. Toon

Holladay, Waller, Lt. OO, 1864
Johnston, Joseph F., Lt. ADC, 1864
Lucado, Leonard F., Capt. ACS, 1864
McDonald, Charles, Capt. ACS, 1864
Payne, William M., Maj. QM, 1864

Isaac R. Trimble

Anderson, Archer, Capt. AAG, 1861
Ballard, Thomas E., Capt. ACS, 1862
Bradford, William K., VADC, 1861
Carrere, William, VADC, 1861, Capt. AQM, 1861–1862, & Maj. QM, 1862
Dallas, William W., Lt. ADC?, 1863?
Davis, Samuel B., Lt. ADC, 1863
Forrest, Douglas F., Lt. acting ADC, 1861–1862
Grogan, Charles E., Lt. VADC, 1863

Hall, William C., Lt. ADC, 1861–1862, & Maj. AAG, 1862–1863
Hearsey, Henry J., Capt. acting AQM, 1862
Hill, Clement D., Maj. QM, 1861
Hinrichs, Oscar, Lt. EO, 1863
Hoffman, Alfred, VADC, 1862–1863, & Maj. AAG, 1863
Howard, McHenry, Lt. ADC, 1863
Lee, John M., Lt. ADC, 1861–1862, & Lt. AAIG, 1862
Lyon, James W., Maj. CS, 1862–1863
McKim, William D., Lt. ADC, 1862–1863, & Maj. AAG, 1863
Marye, Lawrence S., Capt. OO, 1863
Mercer, George D., Maj. QM, 1863?
Moore, Edwin L., Capt. AAAIG, 1863
Spurrier, Grafton D., Lt. VADC, 1861
Taliaferro, Warner T., Capt. AAG, 1863
Terrell, Lewis F., Maj. Chief Arty., 1863
Vernoy, James, Maj. QM, 1862–1863

Earl Van Dorn

Balfour, Joseph D., Maj. AAG, 1861–1862
Washington, Thornton A., Capt. AAG, 1861

John C. Vaughn

Boyd, Thomas G., Lt. OO, 1864
Houston, Robert E., Capt. AAIG, 1864
Hoyl, John B., Maj. CS, 1864?
Manard, Birdwell G., Capt. AAG, 1864
Ramsey, John C., Lt. ADC, 1864?
Stephens, Michael H., Maj. QM, 1864
Toland, John, Lt. ADC, 1864?
Wallace, Thomas L., Capt. ACS, 1864

Henry H. Walker

Broun, William, Capt. AAIG, 1863–1864
Deshields, Henry C., Maj. QM, 1863–1864
Farish, Thomas L., Capt. AAG, 1865
Grinnell, Robert M., Capt. AAG, 1863–1864
Hankins, Dick R., Maj. CS, 1863–1864
Harding, Richard C., Capt. ACS, 1863–1864
Keiley, John D., Jr., Maj. QM, 1864
Mason, Julien J., Maj. CS, 1863–1864
Porteous, John F., Lt. OO, 1863–1864
Walker, Robert P., Lt. ADC, 1863–1864?

James A. Walker

Arnall, Charles S., Lt. ———, 1863

Barton, Randolph J., Capt. AAG, 1863–1864, & Maj. AAIG, 1865

Braithwaite, Jacob R., Maj. QM, 1863–1865

Caddall, Samuel S., Lt. ADC, 1863–1865

Christy, George W., Maj. OO, 1865

Cox, Friend C., Lt. VADC, 1863, & Capt. AAG, 1863–1864

Daniel, Raleigh T., Capt. AAG, 1865?

Dashiell, Charles, Lt. AAIG, 1864–1865

Eyster, George H., Cadet OO, 1862

Farish, Thomas L., Capt. AAG, 1864–1865

Flowers, William B., Capt. AQM, 1864–1865

Footman, Robert H., Capt. AQM, 1864–1865

Frobel, David W., Lt. acting OO, 1865

Haymond, Alpheus F., Maj. CS, 1865

Hinrichs, Oscar, Capt. EO, 1865

Hunter, Robert W., Lt. ———, 1863

Payne, William M., Maj. QM, 1865

Sexton, Joseph C., Maj. CS, 1863–1864

Thornton, William W., Maj. CS, 1865

Turner, Vines E., Capt. AQM, 1865

Vogler, Julius R., Capt. AQM, 1865

Ward, Francis X., VADC

Waters, James H., Capt. ACS, 1863–1864

White, Chastain, Capt. AQM, 1865

Willcox, John N., Lt. acting SO, ?–1865

John G. Walker

Braxton, Elliott M., Maj. QM, 1862

Braxton, John S., Capt. AAG, 1862

Burton, John B., Maj. QM, 1862

Galt, John A., Lt. ADC, 1862

Hill, Nicholas S., Capt. ACS, 1862

Mason, Alexander H., Maj. CS, 1862

Smith, William A., Capt. AAG, 1862

Reuben L. Walker

Chamberlaine, William W., Capt. AAG, 1863–1865

Drake, John C., VADC, 1865

Jett, Jeremiah B., Capt. AQM, 1864–1865

Masters, Leander, Capt. AAIG?, 1862?–1864

Morris, Walter H. P., Lt. ADC, ?–1865

Parker, Arthur, Capt. ACS, ?–1865, & Maj. CS, 1865

Points, Leonidas, Capt. OO, 1863–1865

Scott, William C., Maj. QM, 1862–1865

Walke, Richard, Capt. AAIG, 1864–1865

William H. T. Walker

Davis, Aaron, Maj. CS, 1861

Heard, Thomas R., Maj. QM, 1861

Surget, Eustace, Capt. AAG, 1861

William S. Walker

Barnwell, Edward H., Capt. AAG & AAIG, 1864

DeSaussure, Louis D., Capt. AAG, 1864

Lowndes, James, Capt. AAAG, 1864

Washington, George L., Lt. ADC, 1864

William H. Wallace

Evans, Asa L., Capt. AAG, 1864–1865

Fayssoux, James H., Lt.? OO, 1864–1865?

Fayssoux, Templar S., Capt. OO, 1864–1865

Hord, Edward L., Maj. QM, 1864–1865

Lemmons, Perry O., Capt. AQM, 1864–1865

Lowndes, James, Capt. AAIG, ?–1865

McNamee, John V., Capt. AQM, 1864–1865

Montgomery, John H., Capt. ACS, 1864

Pagan, James, Maj. CS, 1864–1865

David A. Weisiger

Cameron, William E., Capt. AAIG, 1864–1865

Etheridge, Alexander E., Capt. AQM, 1864–1865

Hinton, Drury A., Lt. ADC, 1864–1865

Ironmonger, Francis M., Capt. acting AQM, 1864–1865

Nash, Benjamin H., Lt. AAAG, 1864–?

Rogers, George J., Capt. AQM, 1864–1865

Sherwood, William, Capt. ACS, 1864–1865

Todd, Westwood A., acting Lt. OO, 1865

Gabriel C. Wharton

Cleary, Reuben, Capt. AAIG, 1864

Cosby, Dabney, Jr., Lt. OO, 1864–1865?

DeRussy, Charles A., Capt. AAG, 1864–1865?

Estill, Huston, Capt. ACS, 1864–1865

Ficklin, Joseph E., Maj. CS, 1864–1865

Halsey, Don P., Capt. AAG, 1865

Henderson, Finley H., Maj. CS, 1864–1865

Kent, George M., Lt. ADC, ?–1865

Leigh, James Y., Capt. AQM, 1864

Long, Melchoir M., Lt. VADC, 1864

McCarty, William P., Lt. AAAIG, 1864

Mitchell, John W., Maj. CS, 1865

Moore, William F., Capt. AQM, 1864

Peters, Stephen T., Maj. QM, ?

Priest, Robert L., Capt. ACS, 1864–1865

Reid, P. N., Capt. AQM, 1864

Smith, Frederick W., Capt. acting ADC & AAAG, 1864–1865

Smith, James P., Capt. AAIG, 1864–1865

Smith, John T., Capt. AQM, 1864

Thompson, D. Bowly, Capt. ACS, 1864–1865

Wang, George W., Capt. AQM, 1864–1865

Wharton, John J., Lt. ADC, 1864–1865

William H. C. Whiting

Frobel, Bushrod W., Lt. Chief Arty.?, 1862

Hill, James H., Maj. AAG, 1861–1865

Jonas, Sidney A., Maj. QM, 1861–1862

Jones, George W., Maj. QM, 1861–1862

Lanneau, John F., Lt. EO, 1862

Mays, Thomas S., VADC, 1862

Paul, Samuel B., VADC, 1864

Randolph, Beverley, Maj. OO & AAAIG, 1861–1862

Shay, C., ADC, 1862

Sloan, Benjamin F., Jr., Maj. Chief Arty. & OO, 1864

Smith, Austin E., VADC, 1862

Standley, James S., Lt. AAAG, 1861–?

Steele, John F., Lt. EO, 1862

Strong, William C., Lt. ADC, 1861–1864

Tansill, Robert, Col. AAIG, 1862–1865

Upson, Christopher C., VADC, 1861–1862

Van der Horst, Arnoldus, VADC, 1861–1862, & Capt. AAG, 1864

Venable, Thomas B., Maj. AAIG, 1864–1865

Williams C. Wickham

Bowling, Henry A., Capt. AAIG, 1863

Fontaine, Peter, Capt. AAG, 1863–1864

Lee, Henry C., Capt. AAIG, 1864

Lee, John M., Capt. AAG, 1863–1864

Mason, Beverly R., Capt. ACS, 1863–1864

Mason, Robert F., Maj. QM, 1863–1864

Palmer, John A., Capt. acting AQM, 1863–1864

Tayloe, John W., Lt. AAAG, 1864

Taylor, John, Lt. ADC, 1863–1864

Louis T. Wigfall

George, Moses B., Maj. QM, 1861–1862

Quattlebaum, Paul J., Maj. AAG, 1861–1862

Stewart, William H., Maj. CS, 1861–1862

Cadmus M. Wilcox

Anderson, Edward W., Capt. OO, 1863–1864

Bolton, Channing M., Lt.? EO, 1863–1864

Bolton, Henry, Capt. EO, 1865

Carraway, Daniel T., Maj. CS, 1863–1865

Edwards, John G., Capt. ACS, 1864–1865

Engelhard, Joseph A., Maj. QM, 1863–1865

Gaillard, Richard W., Capt. AQM, 1864–1865

Gibbon, Nicholas B., Capt. ACS, 1863–1865

Ginter, Lewis, Maj. acting CS, 1863

Glover, Francis L., Lt. ADC, 1864–1865

Harris, William A., Capt. AAG, 1862

Hays, Thomas N., Capt. AQM, 1863–1865

Higgason, Albert E., Lt. OO, 1863

Hill, Charles D., Capt. AQM, 1864–1865

Hopson, Virgil L., Capt. ACS, 1863

Hunt, Leonard H., Maj. AAIG, 1863–1865

Lindsay, Melish M., Lt. ADC, 1862–1865

Oates, Robert M., Capt. AQM, 1863–1865

Pickett, Steptoe, Capt. AQM, 1862

Pierce, John G., Maj. QM, 1862–1863

Reading, Thomas R., Lt. VADC, 1862

Robertson, Richard M., Maj. CS, 1862–1863

Scales, Nathaniel E., Maj. CS, 1863–1865

Tate, John M., Capt. AQM, 1864–1865

Ward, Francis X., VADC, 1865

Winn, Walter E., Lt. acting ADC, 1862, &
Capt. AAG, 1862–1863

Charles S. Winder

Braithwaite, Jacob R., Capt. acting AQM,
1862
Bruce, James W., Capt. AQM, 1862
Garnett, James M., Lt. OO, 1862
Howard, McHenry, Lt. ADC, 1862
Mason, James M., Lt. acting OO, 1862
Mercer, George D., Maj. QM, 1862
Mitchell, Samuel D., VADC, 1862
O'Brien, John F., Capt. AAG, 1862
Sexton, Joseph C., Maj. CS, 1862

John H. Winder

Alexander, George W., Capt. AAG, 1862–
1864
Bayly, Samuel T., Capt. AAG, 1862–1864
Bradford, William K., Lt. ?, 1861–1862
Brown, Robert W., Lt. ADC, 1862–1863
Capers, William H., VADC, 1863–?
Davis, Samuel B., Lt. AAIG, 1863–1864
Forbes, Francis T., Capt. ACS, 1862–1864
Griswold, Elias, Maj. AAG, 1862–1864
?Hubard, James L., VADC, 1862
Lewis, Warner, VADC, 1861?–1864?
Morfit, Clarence, Capt. AQM, 1862–1864
Page, Legh R., Maj. AAG, 1861–1863
Parkhill, John H., Capt. AQM, 1862, & Maj.
AAG, 1862–1864
Pegram, James W., Jr., Maj. AAG, 1862–1864
Selph, Colin M., Capt. AAIG, 1863–1864
Starke, William N., Capt. AAG, 1862–1863
Vowles, Daniel W., Capt. AAG, 1862–1864
Winder, William S., Lt. ADC, 1861–1862, &
Capt. AAG, 1862–1864
Wirz, Hartmann H., Capt. AAG, 1862–1863

Henry A. Wise

Adler, Adolphus H., Col. EO, 1861
Bacon, Waddy S., Lt. ADC, 1861–1862
Bolton, Henry, Lt. EO, 1861–1862
Braxton, John S., Capt. AAG, 1865
Brooks, H. Clay, Lt. AAAG, 1861
von Buckholtz, Louis, Capt. OO, 1862

Clarkson, John N., VADC, 1861
Cleary, Frank D., Maj. QM, 1861–1863
Dimmock, Charles H., Capt. EO, 1864
Dinwiddie, James, Lt. AAAG, 1861
Duffield, Charles B., Maj. AAG, 1861–1862
Farish, Thomas L., VADC, 1861
Faulkner, Charles J., Jr., VADC, 1865
Fleet, Alexander F., Lt. AAAG, 1863–1865
Frayser, Richard E., ?, 1865
Gregory, William F. C., Maj. CS, 1862–1865
Harvie, Edwin J., Capt. AAG, 1861
Kinney, Archibald, Capt. ACS, 1863–1865
McMahon, Edward, Maj. QM, 1861–1862
Nicolson, James M., Capt. AQM, 1864–1865
Old, William W., Lt. AAAG, 1861
Pearce, James H., Lt. OO, 1862, & Capt.
AAG, 1862–1865
Rosser, Thomas L., Lt. Col. OO, 1862
Stanard, William B., VADC, 1861
Tabb, William B., Capt. AAG, 1861–1862
Thomas, N. J., Capt. AQM, 1864–1865
Thomas, William H., Maj. CS, 1861–1862
Tyler, Nathaniel, Maj. VADC, 1861
Warwick, Barksdale, VADC, 1861–1865
Watkins, Henry C., Maj. QM, 1863–1865
Webb, Lewis N., Capt. AQM, 1861–1862
Wise, George D., VADC, 1862
Wise, George D., Lt. ADC, 1862–1863, &
Capt. AAIG, 1863–1864
Wise, James M., Lt. OO, 1862–1865
Wise, John J. H., Lt. ADC, 1862
Wise, Richard A., VADC, 1861–1862, Lt. OO,
1862, & Lt. ADC, 1863–1865

William T. Wofford

Byrd, Samuel M. H., Maj. QM, 1863–1864
Crane, Benjamin E., Capt. acting AQM,
1863
Griffis, John C., Maj. CS, 1863–1864
Hackett, John T., Capt. AAIG?, 1863–1864
Morris, John, Lt. AAIG, ?–1863
Norris, Andrew M., Capt. ACS, 1863–1864
Parrott, Josiah R., Maj. QM, 1863
Patton, A. H., Lt. AAAG, 1862, & Capt.
AAG, 1863

Peek, Julius A., Lt. AAAG, 1863–1864
Phillips, James P., Capt. AQM, 1863?–1864
Turner, Allen S., Capt. AQM, 1864
Wofford, William L., Lt. ADC, 1863–1864
Woolley, Andrew F., Lt. ADC, 1863, & Capt.
   AAG, 1863–1864

Ambrose R. Wright

Anderson, Clifford, Capt. AAAIG, 1863
Beall, Julius C. A., Capt. acting ADC, 1863
Bell, Robert F., VADC, 1862–1864
Girardey, Victor J. B., Capt. AAG, 1862
Grice, George W., Maj. QM, 1862
Habersham, John B., Lt. ADC, 1862
Hayes, George E., Lt. AAAG, 1863
Hazlehurst, William, Lt. ADC, 1862–1863?
Hughes, Hampden S., Maj. CS, 1862–1864
McWhorter, Robert L., Maj. QM, 1862–1864
Macon, Thomas L., VADC, 1862
Mahool, Thomas, Capt. ACS, 1863–1864
Starr, Silas H., Jr., Lt. OO, 1864
Whitehead, Charles L., VADC, 1862
Wingfield, William C., Maj. CS, 1862–1863
Wright, William A., Lt. OO, 1862–1863

Zebulon York

Barton, Randolph J., Capt. AAAG, 1864
Buckner, James, Capt. AQM, 1864
Campbell, John G., Maj. CS, 1864
Forrest, John, Lt. OO, 1864
Hughes, William J., Capt. AQM, 1864
Moss, Charles, Lt. ADC, 1864?
Rawle, Francis, Maj. QM, 1864
Seymour, William J., Capt. AAG, 1864
Watkins, Leigh, Capt. ACS, 1864

Pierce M. B. Young

Carson, John C., Lt. ADC, 1864
Church, William L., Capt. AAG, 1863–1864
Edelin, T. Boyd, Capt. AAIG, 1864
Farley, Henry S., Maj. ——
Farley, Hugh L., Lt. AAAG, 1864
Glenn, William, Lt. OO, 1864
Jones, John M., Lt. ADC, 1863–1864
McClellan, Robert M., Capt. acting AQM,
   1864
Thomas, James P., Lt. ADC, 1864
Watts, James W., VADC, 1864
Williams, Thomas H., Maj. QM, 1864